The Norton Introduction to

FICTION

SIXTH EDITION

The Norton Introduction to

FICTION

SIXTH EDITION

Jerome Beaty

W • W • NORTON & COMPANY • NEW YORK • LONDON

Copyright © 1996, 1991, 1985, 1981, 1973 by W. W. Norton & Company, Inc.

The text of this book is composed in Electra
with the display set in Univers
Composition by Vail-Ballou
Manufacturing by R. R. Donnelley
Cover illustration: Wayne Thiebaud, *Half Dome and Cloud*. Private collection.
Courtesy Allan Stone Gallery, New York City.

Library of Congress Cataloging-in-Publication Data
The Norton introduction to fiction / [edited by] Jerome Beaty. —6th ed.
p.   cm.
Includes index.
1. Literature—Collections.   I. Beaty, Jerome, Date.
PN6014.N67   1995
808.8—dc20   95-4814

ISBN 0-393-96821-9 (pbk.)

W. W. Norton & Company, Inc., 500 Fifth Avenue, New York, N.Y. 10110
W. W. Norton & Company Ltd., 10 Coptic Street, London WC1A 1PU

2 3 4 5 6 7 8 9 0

CONTENTS

v

Evaluating Fiction   569

Reading More Fiction   623

Writing About Fiction   735

FOREWORD TO THE
SIXTH EDITION

Reading is action. Even though it is often done quietly and alone, reading is a profoundly social activity, and a vigorous and demanding one. There is nothing passive about reading; it requires attention, energy, an act of will. Texts have the potential for meaning, implication, response, and result; but the reader must activate them, give them life, and turn them from quiet print into a lively interplay of ideas and feelings. Reading makes things happen, usually in the mind and imagination, but sometimes in the larger world as well, for the process of reading involves not just the consciousness of the self but an awareness of the other—what is beyond the self. Reading doesn't just happen to you; you have to **do** it, and doing it involves decision, reaching out, discovery, awareness. Reading is an act of power, and learning how to get the most out of its possibilities can be an invigorating activity. For all its association with quietness, solitude, and the sedentary life, reading involves—at its deepest level—action and interaction.

Through all of its editions, *The Norton Introduction to Fiction* has been committed to helping students learn to read and enjoy fiction. This edition, like those before it, offers many different ways of building and reinforcing the skills of reading; in addition to studying fiction in terms of its elements, my book emphasizes reading works in different contexts—authorial, historical, and cultural. I have strengthened my offering of texts in contextual groups in this edition with the addition of two new chapters: "Culture as Contexts: Border Stories," and "Literary Form as Context: The Short Short Story and the Novel." Also, I have strengthened the connection between reading and writing at several points throughout the book. The introductory chapter first treats the reading experience generally, then works to involve students in examining their own responses as a first step toward writing about fiction. Five student papers, two of them new to this edition, offer a variety of responses to selected writing suggestions. And as in previous editions, I have provided many new selections.

But the Sixth Edition remains more than a grab-bag of good things to read. The book offers in a single volume a complete course in reading and writing about fiction. It is both an anthology and a textbook—a teaching anthology—for the indispensable course in which college student and college teacher begin to read fiction, and to write about it, seriously together.

The works are arranged in order to introduce a reader to the study of fiction. *Fiction: Reading, Responding, Writing* treats the purpose and nature of fiction, the reading experience, and the first steps one takes to begin writing about fiction. This is followed by the seven-chapter section called *Understanding the Text*, in which stories are analyzed by questions of craft, the so-called elements of fiction; this section ends with a chapter entitled "The Whole Text," which makes use of all or most of the analytical aids offered in the previous chapters, putting them together to see the work as a whole. The third section, *Exploring Contexts*, suggests some ways of seeing a work of literature interacting with its temporal and cultural contexts and reaching out beyond the page.

The sections on reading, analyzing, and placing the work in context are followed, in each genre, by guidance in taking that final and extremely difficult step—evaluation. *Evaluating Fiction*, for example, discusses how one would go about assessing the merits of two stories, not to offer definitive judgments, a litmus test, or even a checklist or formula, but to show how one goes about bringing to consciousness, defining, modifying, articulating, and negotiating one's judgments about a work of fiction.

Reading More Fiction is a reservoir of additional examples, for independent study or a different approach. The book's arrangement seeks to facilitate the reader's movement from narrower to broader questions, mirroring the way people read—wanting to learn more as they experience more.

The Norton Introduction to Fiction offers a full section on *Writing about Fiction*. In it I deal both with the writing process as applied to literary works— choosing a topic, gathering evidence, developing an argument, and so forth— and with the varieties of a reader's written responses, from copying and para- phrasing to analysis and interpretation: I explore not merely the hows, but the whats and whys as well.

In this section I also offer a discussion of critical approaches, designed to provide the student with a basic overview of contemporary critical theory, as well as an introduction to its terminology.

The Sixth Edition includes 54 stories, 19 of which are new. I have added new stories by Rudolfo Anaya, Margaret Atwood, Toni Cade Bambara, Charles Baxter, Angela Carter, Denise Chávez, Kate Chopin, Joseph Conrad, Julio Cor- tázar, Richard Dokey, Ernest Hemingway, Ha Jin, Yasunari Kawabata, Margaret Laurence, Reginald McKnight, Guy Vanderhaeghe, Eudora Welty, Edith Wharton, and Lynna Williams.

Certain editorial procedures that proved their usefulness in earlier editions have been retained. First of all, the works are annotated, as is customary in Norton anthologies; the notes are informational and not interpretative, for the aim is to help readers understand and appreciate the work, not to dictate a meaning or a response. In order to avoid giving the impression that all fiction was written at the same time, I have noted at the right margin after each selec- tion the date of first book publication (or, when preceded by a *p*, first periodical publication or, when the date appears at the left margin, the year of composi- tion).

In all my work on this edition I have been guided by teachers in other English departments and in my own, by students who wrote me as the author of the textbook they were using, and by those who were able to approach me after class as their teacher: I hope that with such help I have been able to offer you a solid and stimulating introduction to the experience of fiction.

Acknowledgments I would like to thank my teachers, for their example in the love of literature and in the art of sharing that love; my students, for their patience as I am learning from them to be a better teacher of fiction; my wife and children, for their understanding when the work of preparing this text made me seem less than a perfectly loving husband and father.

I would also like to thank my colleagues, many of whom have taught my book and evaluated my efforts, for their constant encouragement and enlightenment. Of my colleagues at Emory University, I would like especially to thank Jim Boyle, John Bugge, Louis Corrigan, William B. Dillingham, Larry Eby, Mark Sanders, Ron Schuchard, Deborah Sitter, John Sitter, Sally Wolff King and Emily Wright. For their help in selecting papers by student writers, I would like to thank Geneva Ballard, Theresa Budniakiewicz, Rebecca S. Ries, and Avantika Rohatgi, of Indiana University—Purdue University at Indianapolis, and Thomas Miller, Tilly Warnock, Lisa-Anne Culp, Loren Goodman, Brendan McBryde, and Ruthe Thompson, at the University of Arizona. I also thank the students whose papers I include: Daniel Bronson, Geoffrey Clement, Teri Garrity, Sara Rosen, and Thaddeus Smith. For her work on the *Instructor's Guide*, I thank Gayla McGlamery, Loyola College in Baltimore.

And I thank also Elizabeth Alkagond, Columbia College; M. Allen, Bakersfield College; Marjorie Allen, LaSalle University; Preston Allen, Miami-Dade Community College; Sally Allen, North Georgia College; Bruce Anawalt, Washington State University; Anne Andrews, Mississippi State University; Charles Angel, Bridgewater State College; Booker Anthony, Fayetteville State University; Robert Arledge, Southern University at New Orleans; Michael Atkinson, University of Cincinnati; Janet Auten, American University; Sylvia Baer, Gloucester County College; Raymond Bailey, Bishop State Community College; Lee Baker, High Point College; Harold Bakst, Minneapolis Community College; Nancy Barendse, Christopher Newport College; Chris Barkley, Palomar College; Linda Barlow, Fayetteville State University; William Barnette, Prestonsburg Community College; Dr. Barney, Citrus College; E. Barnton, California State University, Bakersfield; Harry E. Batty, University of Maine; Shawn Beaty, Hokkaido University; Nancy Beers, Temple University; Linda Bensel-Meyers, University of Tennessee, Knoxville; Lawrence Berkoben, California State University; Tracey Besmark, Ashland Community College; Barbara Bird, St. Petersburg Community College; Lillian Bisson, Marymount College; Clark Blaise, University of Iowa; T. E. Blom, University of British Columbia; Roy L. Bond, University of Texas at Dallas; Steven Bouler, Tuskegee University; Veleda Boyd, Tarleton State University; Helen Bridge, Chabot College; Sandra Brim, North Georgia College; Loretta Brister, Tarleton State University; Patrick Broderick, Santa Rosa Junior College; Robert Brophy, California State University, Long Beach; Theresa Brown, Tufts University; William Brown, Philadelphia College of Textiles and Science; Virginia Brumbach, Eastfield College; C. Bryant, Colby College; Edward Burns, William Paterson College of New Jersey; Daniel Cahill, University of Northern Iowa; Martha Campbell, St. Petersburg Community College at Tarpon Springs; William Campbell, Monroe Community College; D. Cano, Santa Monica Community College; Nathan Carb, Rowan College of New Jersey; Roger Carlstrom, Yakima Valley Community College; Martha Carpentier, Seton Hall University; Anne Carr, Southeast Community College; Conrad Carroll, Northern Kentucky University; Gisela Casines, Florida International University; Ahwadhesh Chaudhary, Texas College; Dr. Clark, Citrus College; John Clower, Indiana University–Purdue University at Indianapolis; Steven Cole, Temple University; Cindy Collins, Fullerton College; Kathleen Collins, Creighton University; Marianne Conroy, McGill University; Pat Conner, Memphis State University; Martha Cook, Longwood College; Holly Cordova, Contra Costa College; Susan Cornett, St. Petersburg Community College at Tarpon Springs; Brian Corrigan, North Georgia College; Betty Corum, Owensboro Community College; Beverly Cotton, Cerritos College; Delmar Crisp, Wesleyan College; Virginia Critchlow, Monroe Community College; Carol Cunningham-Ruiz, Bakersfield College; Lennett Daigle, North Georgia College; Christopher Dark, Tarleton State University; Vivian Davis, Eastfield College; Hugh Dawson, University of San Francisco; Martha Day, Richard Bland College; George Diamond, Moravian College; Helen DiBona, North Carolina Central University; Sister Mary Colleen Dillon, Thomas More College; Marvin Diogenes, University of Arizona; Frank Dobson, Indiana University–Purdue University at Indianapolis; Minna Doskow, Rowan College of New Jersey; Donald Dowdey, Virginia Wesleyan College; Bonnie Duncan, Upper Iowa University; Timothy Dykstal, Auburn University; Wayne Eason, University of North Carolina at Charlotte; Paula Eckard, University of North Carolina at Charlotte; Mary Eiser, Kauai Community College; Marianne Eismann, Wake Forest University; Joyce Ellis, North Carolina Central University; Reed Ellis, St. John's Community College; Peggy Endel, Florida International University; James Erickson, Wichita State University; Dessagene Ewing, Delaware County Community College; Jim Ewing, North Georgia College; Sasha Feinstein, Indiana University; Charles Feldstein, Florida Community College at Jacksonville; Norman Feltes, York University; Jean Fields, Lindenwood College; Mildred Flynn, South Dakota University; Eileen Foley, University of Maine; Dolores Formicella, Delaware County Community College; Elsa Ann Gaines, North Georgia College; Dennis Gaitner, Frostburg State University; Reloy Garcia, Creighton University; Joseph Glaser, Western Kentucky University; Andrea Glebe, University of Nevada; Karen Gleeman, Normandale Community College; C. Golliher, Victor Valley College; Douglas Gordon, Christopher Newport College; Donna Gormly, Eastfield College; Kathryn Graham, Virginia Polytechnic Institute and State University; Pat Gregory, Community College of Philadelphia; Ann Grigsby, University of New Mexico; Alan Grob, Rice University; Lynda Haas, Hillsborough Community College; Florence Halle, Memphis State University; Jerry Harris, Western Oregon State College; Sydney Harrison, Manatee Community College; Joan Hartman, William Patterson College; Charles Hatten, Bellarmine College; Bruce Henderson, Fullerton College; Nancy Henry, SUNY at Binghamton; David Hernandez, Eastfield College; Robert Herzog, Monroe Community College; Laura Higgs, Clemson University; David Hill, SUNY College at Oswego; Robert Hipkiss, California State University; David Hoegberg, Indiana University–Purdue University at Indianapolis; Eartha Holley, Delaware State University; R. C. Hoover, Wenatchee Valley College; Roger Horn, Charles County Community College; L. C. Howard, Skyline College; Erlene Hubly, University of Northern Iowa;

William Hudson, Radford University; David Hufford, Iowa Western Community College; Deirdre Hughes, Fullerton College; Dr. Humphrey, Citrus College; Kathryn Montgomery Hunter, Northwestern University School of Medicine; Lisa Hunter, University of Wisconsin Medical School; P. Hunter, Los Angeles Valley College; Edelina Huntley, Appalachian State University; Robert Huntley, Washington and Lee University; Sharon Irvin, Florida Institute of Technology; Sylvia Iskander, University of Southwestern Louisiana; Eleanor James, Montgomery County Community College; Anne Johnson, Jacksonville State University; Christopher Johnson, Missouri Valley College; Craig Johnson, Hillsborough Community College; Darryl Johnson, St. Cloud State University; Dolores Johnson, Seattle University; Karen Johnson, Indiana University–Purdue University at Indianapolis; Dr. Jones, Citrus College; Grace Jones, Owensboro Community College; Walter Kalaidjian, St. Cloud State University; Frank Kastor, Wichita State University; E. Kenney, Colby College; Don King, Central Washington University; Andrew Kirk, University of California, Davis; John Klijinski, Idaho State University; William Klink, Charles County Community College; Michael Krasny, San Francisco State University; Anne Krause, Yakima Valley Community College; Harold Kuglemass, Onondaga Community College; Stuart Kurland, Muhlenberg College; Donald Lawler, East Carolina University; Lynn Lewis, Memphis State University; Vincent J. Liesenfeld, University of Oklahoma; Jun Liu, California State University, Los Angeles; Travis Livingston, Tarleton State University; Lillian Liwag-Sutcliffe, Old Dominion University; Mary Lowe-Evans, University of West Florida; Michael Lund, Longwood College; Kathleen Lyons, Bellarmine College; Thomas Mack, University of South Carolina; Patricia MacVaugh, Lehigh County Community College; Emory Maiden, Appalachian State University; Christina Malcolmson, Bates College; Dexter Marks, Jersey City State College; William Martin, Tarleton State University; Frank Mason, University of South Florida; Pam Mathis, North Arkansas Community College; Laura May, St. Petersburg Community College; Katherine Maynard, Rider College; R. McAllister, Victor Valley College; Kathleen McCloy, Shoreline Community College; Betty J. McCommas, Ouachita Baptist University; Clare McDonnell, Neumann College; Frank McLaughlin, Ramapo College; Thomas McLaughlin, Appalachian State University; William McMahon, Western Kentucky University; Terrence McNally, Northern Kentucky University; Alan McNarie, University of Hawaii; Nyan McNeill, Foothill College; Jay Meek, University of North Dakota; Ivan Melada, University of New Mexico; Donna Melancon, Xavier University; Linda Merions, LaSalle University; Darlene Mettler, Wesleyan College; R. Metzger, Los Angeles Valley College; Brian Michaels, Diane Middlebrook (Stanford University) St. John's Community College; Daniel Miller, Northern Kentucky University; George Miller, University of Delaware; Ron Miller, University of West Florida; Leslie Mittelman, California State University, Long Beach; Rosa Mizerski, West Valley College; Rosemary Moffett, Elizabethtown Community College; Warren Moore, Loyola College; Mike Moran, University of Georgia; Dean Morgan, Olympic College; William Morgan, Illinois State University; William Morris, University of South Florida; Sharon Morrow, University of Southern Indiana;

Renate Muendel, West Chester University; Gordon Mundell, University of Nebraska; David Murdoch, Rochester Institute of Technology; Carol Murphy, Roanoke College; Thomas Murray, Trenton State College; Joseph Nacca, Community College of Finger Lakes; Joseph Nasser, Rochester Institute of Technology; Mary Neil, Eastfield College; Kay Nelson, St. Cloud University; Dorothy Newman, Southern University; Lee Nicholson, Modesto Junior College; Mimi Nicholson, University of Southern Indiana; Elizabeth Nollen, West Chester University; Dale Norris, Des Moines Community College; Robert Ochsner, University of Maryland at Baltimore; Sarah Oglesby, Madisonville Community College; Francis Olley, Saint Joseph's University; Ann Olson, Central Washington University; Regina Oost, Wesleyan College; Mildred Orenstein, Drexel University; Kathleen O'Shea, Monroe Community College; Thornton Penfield, Southern University; Christopher Penna, University of Delaware; Rita Perkins, Camden County College; Donald Peterson, City College of San Francisco; Steven Phelan, Rollins College; Randall Popken, Tarleton State University; Robert Post, University of Washington; Pamela Postma, University of North Carolina at Greensboro; Linda Ray Pratt, University of Nebraska; Ross Primm, Columbia College; Richard Quaintance, Rutgers University; James Randall, Coe College; Rosemary Raynal, Davidson College; Mary Rea, Indiana University–Purdue University at Indianapolis; Thomas Redshaw, University of St. Thomas; Ron Reed, Hazard Community College; Donna Reiss, Tidewater Community College; Alan Richardson, Boston College; Ann Richey, Virginia Polytechnic Institute and State University; Joan Richmond, Tarleton State University; Harold Ridley, LeMoyne College; Leonard Roberts, Northampton Area Community College; Douglas Robinson, University of Mississippi; J. Robinson, Victor Valley College; Beate Rodewald, Palm Beach Atlantic College; Ruben Rodriguez, Tarleton State University; Owen Rogal, St. Ambrose University; Eva Rosenn, Wesleyan College; William Rossiter, Flathead Valley College; Connie Rothwell, University of North Carolina; Don Rud, Texas Tech University; Don Russ, Kennesaw State College; Charles J. Rzepka, Boston University; Christina Savage, Long Beach City College; Vicki Scannell, Pierce College; Paul Schacht, SUNY College at Geneseo; Steven Scherwatzky, Merrimack College; Marie Schiebold, Skyline College; Ronald Schleifer, University of Oklahoma; Linda Schmidt, Iowa Western Community College; Roger Schmidt, Idaho State College; Michael Schoenecke, Texas Tech University; Jane Schultz, Indiana University–Purdue University at Indianapolis; Lucille Schultz, University of Cincinnati; Carolyn Segal, Lehigh University; JoAnn Seiple, University of North Carolina; Bill Senior, Broward Community College; Pat Shalter, Reading Area Community College; Lewis Sheffler, Missouri Valley College; Richard Siciliano, Charles County Community College; Odette Sims, Modesto Junior College; Judy Jo Small, North Carolina State University; Louise Smith, University of Massachusetts; Peter Smith, Wesleyan College; Stephen Smith, LaSalle University; Thomas Sonith, Widener University; B. Spears, Victor Valley College; Dr. Spencer, California State University, Bakersfield; Rich Sprouse, North Georgia College; Ann Spurlock, Mississippi State University; David Stacey, Missouri Valley College; Nancy Stahl, Indiana University–Purdue University at

Indianapolis; Jamie Steckelberg, University of North Dakota; James Stick, Des Moines Community College; Bruce Stillians, University of Hawaii; McKay Sundwall, East Carolina University; Kathryn Swanson, Augsburg College; John Taylor, College of Marin; Judith Taylor, Northern Kentucky University; David Thibodaux, University of Southwestern Louisiana; Victor Thompson, Thomas Nelson Community College; Charles Thornbury, College of St. Benedict; Mike Thro, Tidewater Community College; Kathleen Tickner, Brevard Community College; Edna Troiano, Charles County Community College; Gail Tubbs, Washington College; Richard Turner, Indiana University–Purdue University at Indianapolis; Teresa Tweet, Augustana College; D. Unrue, University of Nevada; Margaret Vail, Xavier University; Diana Valdina, Cayuga County Community College; Kenneth Vandover, Lincoln University; Eleanor Vassal, St. Petersburg Community College; Tim Viator, North Georgia College; Richard Victor, Saddleback College; Jeanne Walker, University of Delaware; Cynthia Wall, University of Virginia; Leslie Wallace, DeAnza College; W. Wallis, Los Angeles Valley College; R. Warkentin, California State University, Dominguez Hills; David Weekes, Eastern Washington University; Edwin Weihe, Seattle University; Ronald Wendling, Saint Joseph's University; Agnes Whitsel, Mercer University; Keith Wicker, Henderson Community College; Inga Wiehl, Yakima Valley College; Waller Wigginton, Idaho State University; Arthur Williams, Louisiana School for Mathematics, Science and the Arts; Jack Williams, California State University; James Wilson, University of Southwestern Louisiana; Sharon Wilson, Fort Hays State University; Sandra Witt, University of Northern Iowa; Susan Wolstenholme, Cayuga County Community College; Strohn Woodward, University of Maine; James Wyatt, Lindsey Wilson College; Linda Yakle, St. Petersburg Community College; and Dr. Zounes, Los Angeles Valley College.

I would like to thank my friends at W. W. Norton & Company, especially the late John Benedict and the late Barry Wade, to whom I dedicate this revision, and also Allen Clawson, Carol Hollar-Zwick, Marian Johnson, Kate Lovelady, John Mardirosian, Fred McFarland, Diane O'Connor, Nancy Palmquist, David Sutter, Ann Tappert, Candace Watt, and Kurt Wildermuth.

J.B.

The Norton Introduction to

FICTION

SIXTH EDITION

Fiction: Reading, Responding, Writing

SPENCER HOLST

The Zebra Storyteller

Once upon a time there was a Siamese cat who pretended to be a lion and spoke inappropriate Zebraic.

That language is whinnied by the race of striped horses in Africa.

Here now: An innocent zebra is walking in a jungle and approaching from another direction is the little cat; they meet.

"Hello there!" says the Siamese cat in perfectly pronounced Zebraic. "It certainly is a pleasant day, isn't it? The sun is shining, the birds are singing, isn't the world a lovely place to live today!"

The zebra is so astonished at hearing a Siamese cat speaking like a zebra, why—he's just fit to be tied.   5

So the little cat quickly ties him up, kills him, and drags the better parts of the carcass back to his den.

The cat successfully hunted zebras many months in this manner, dining on filet mignon of zebra every night, and from the better hides he made bow neckties and wide belts after the fashion of the decadent princes of the Old Siamese court.

He began boasting to his friends he was a lion, and he gave them as proof the fact that he hunted zebras.

The delicate noses of the zebras told them there was really no lion in the neighborhood. The zebra deaths caused many to avoid the region. Superstitious, they decided the woods were haunted by the ghost of a lion.

One day the storyteller of the zebras was ambling, and through his mind ran plots for stories to amuse the other zebras, when suddenly his eyes brightened, and he said, "That's it! I'll tell a story about a Siamese cat who learns to speak our language! What an idea! That'll make 'em laugh!"

Just then the Siamese cat appeared before him, and said, "Hello there! Pleasant day today, isn't it!"

The zebra storyteller wasn't fit to be tied at hearing a cat speaking his language, because he'd been thinking about that very thing.

He took a good look at the cat, and he didn't know why, but there was something about his looks he didn't like, so he kicked him with a hoof and killed him.

That is the function of the storyteller.

1971

Th e Zebra Storyteller" suggests that the purpose of stories is to prepare us for the unexpected. Though the storyteller thinks he is just spinning stories out of his own imagination in order to amuse, his stories prove to be practical. When the extraordinary occurs—like a Siamese cat speaking Zebraic—the storyteller is prepared because he has already imagined it, and he alone is able to protect his tribe against the unheard-of.

Other storytellers make the function of fiction less extraordinary. According to them, fiction enables readers to avoid projecting false hopes and fears (such as the zebras' superstitious belief that they are being preyed on by the ghost of a lion) and shows them what they can actually expect in their everyday lives, so that they can prepare themselves. In George Eliot's novel *Adam Bede*, Hetty Sorrel is being paid admiring attention by the young squire, and she dreams of elopement, marriage, all sorts of vague pleasures. She does not dream that she will be seduced, made pregnant, abandoned. Her imagination has not been trained to project any "narrative" other than her dreams: "Hetty had never read a novel," George Eliot tells us, "[so] how could she find a shape for her expectations?"

We are all storytellers, then, of one stripe or another. Whenever we plan the future or ponder a decision, we are telling stories—projecting expectations through narrative. Whether we tell stories or read them, we are educating our imaginations, either extending our mental experience in the actual, as Hetty might have done by reading novels, or preparing ourselves for the extraordinary and unexpected, like the zebra storyteller.

The actual and the extraordinary suggest two different uses readers make of fiction. Sometimes we want to read about people like ourselves, or about places, experiences, and ideas that are familiar and agreeable. Most of us initially prefer American literature and twentieth-century literature to literature remote in time or place. Indeed, stories must somehow be related to our own lives before we can find them intellectually or emotionally meaningful. No matter what our literary experience and taste, most of us relate in a special way to stories about people like us, experiences like our own, and especially to a story that mentions our hometown or neighborhood or the name of the street that we used to walk along on our way to school. No one would deny that one of the many things that fiction may be "for" is learning about ourselves and the world around us.

But occasionally the last thing we want is a story about people like ourselves, experiences like those of our everyday lives, and places and times like here and now. On such occasions we want (or are accused of wanting) to escape. If fiction must be relevant enough to relate meaningfully to us, it must also be "irrelevant," different, strange—as strange, perhaps, as a Siamese cat speaking Zebraic. It must take us out of ourselves, out of the confining vision of our own eyes, which is conditioned by our own background and experience, and show us that there are ways of looking at the world other than our own. So, in addition to many stories about approximately our own time and place, this collection includes a sprinkling of stories written in the last century, a few written in vastly different cultures, and a few written about worlds that have not existed or do not (yet) exist.

What a story shows us or teaches us we may call its **message**—an objective, universal truth that we were unaware of before reading the story. We gradually learn, however, that stories tell us not so much what life means as what it's like. Rather than abstract or "objective" truths, stories deal with perceptions. These perceptions may be translated into messages, but we soon discover that the messages boil down to things like "There's good and bad in everybody," "Hurting people is wrong," and "Everything is not what it seems"—messages we do not need Western Union, much less Western literature, to deliver. Indeed, we do not have to agree with what a story says or shows so long as we are convinced that if we had *those* eyes and were *there*, this is what we might see.

Whenever we can say yes, we are convinced, then we have been able to go beyond the limitations of our own vision, our own past and conditions. We are able to see a new world, or the same old world in a new way. And by recognizing that we can see things differently, we realize that things we used to think were fixed, objective entities "out there," were fixed only in our perceptions. Or, as is too often the case, we realize that we have been accepting things at face value; we have been perceiving what habit and convention have told us is "really there." Stories, then, may awaken us to look at things for ourselves. For example, we "know" a table top is square, but in a story we may be told it is diamond-shaped. We understand that if we were to look at the table top from a certain angle it would appear diamond-shaped. But doesn't that mean that the table top is square only when we look at it from a certain angle? How often do we look at a table top from that angle? We look again, and we recognize that though we've always "known" a table top is a square, we may have never actually *seen* it as one. The story has not only allowed us to see reality from another angle, but it has helped us to sharpen our own vision, our own experience.

In the story that follows, both the eighteen-year-old narrator and Jack are storytellers: each projects a future. The story, however, remains in the present, so we cannot tell which projection is right. Like the characters, we are more or less in the middle of our own lives. Though they may not get to know the future, both Jack and the narrator learn through their storytelling that more than one scenario of the future can be projected. Even if we think the narrator as naive as George Eliot's Hetty, projecting a dream rather than a possible reality, she has now at least "read Jack's novel," so she knows there are alternative futures. And so do we.

ELIZABETH TALLENT

No One's a Mystery

For my eighteenth birthday Jack gave me a five-year diary with a latch and a little key, light as a dime. I was sitting beside him scratching at the lock, which didn't seem to want to work, when he thought he saw his wife's Cadillac in the distance, coming toward us. He pushed me down onto the dirty floor of the pickup and kept one hand on my head while I inhaled the musk of his cigarettes in the dashboard ashtray and sang along with Rosanne Cash on the tape deck. We'd been drinking tequila and the bottle was between his legs, resting up against his crotch, where the seam of his Levi's was bleached linen-white, though the Levi's were nearly new. I don't know why his Levi's always bleached like that, along the seams and at the knees. In a curve of cloth his zipper glinted, gold.

"It's her," he said. "She keeps the lights on in the daytime. I can't think of a single habit in a woman that irritates me more than that." When he saw that I was going to stay still he took his hand from my head and ran it through his own dark hair.

"Why does she?" I said.

"She thinks it's safer. Why does she need to be safer? She's driving exactly fifty-five miles an hour. She believes in those signs: 'Speed Monitored by Aircraft.' It doesn't matter that you can look up and see that the sky is empty."

"She'll see your lips move, Jack. She'll know you're talking to someone."

"She'll think I'm singing along with the radio."

He didn't lift his head, just raised the fingers in salute while the pressure of his palm steadied the wheel, and I heard the Cadillac honk twice, musically; he was driving easily eighty miles an hour. I studied his boots. The elk heads stitched into the leather were bearded with frayed thread, the toes were scuffed, and there was a compact wedge of muddy manure between the heel and the sole—the same boots he'd been wearing for the two years I'd known him. On the tape deck Rosanne Cash sang, "Nobody's into me, no one's a mystery."

"Do you think she's getting famous because of who her daddy is or for herself?" Jack said.

"There are about a hundred pop tops on the floor, did you know that? Some little kid could cut a bare foot on one of these, Jack."

"No little kids get into this truck except for you."

"How come you let it get so dirty?"

" 'How come,' " he mocked. "You even sound like a kid. You can get back into the seat now, if you want. She's not going to look over her shoulder and see you."

"How do you know?"

"I just know," he said. "Like I know I'm going to get meat loaf for supper. It's in the air. Like I know what you'll be writing in that diary."

"What will I be writing?" I knelt on my side of the seat and craned around to look at the butterfly of dust printed on my jeans. Outside the window Wyoming was dazzling in the heat. The wheat was fawn and yellow and parted smoothly by the thin dirt road. I could smell the water in the irrigation ditches hidden in the wheat.

"Tonight you'll write, 'I love Jack. This is my birthday present from him. I can't imagine anybody loving anybody more than I love Jack.' "

"I can't."

"In a year you'll write, 'I wonder what I ever really saw in Jack. I wonder why I spent so many days just riding around in his pickup. It's true he taught me something about sex. It's true there wasn't ever much else to do in Cheyenne.' "

"I won't write that."

"In two years you'll write, 'I wonder what that old guy's name was, the one with the curly hair and the filthy dirty pickup truck and time on his hands.' "

"I won't write that."

"No?"

"Tonight I'll write, 'I love Jack. This is my birthday present from him. I can't imagine anybody loving anybody more than I love Jack.' "

"No, you can't," he said. "You can't imagine it."

"In a year I'll write, 'Jack should be home any minute now. The table's set— my grandmother's linen and her old silver and the yellow candles left over from the wedding—but I don't know if I can wait until after the trout à la Navarra to make love to him.' "

"It must have been a fast divorce."

"In two years I'll write, 'Jack should be home by now. Little Jack is hungry for his supper. He said his first word today besides "Mama" and "Papa." He said "kaka." ' "

Jack laughed. "He was probably trying to finger-paint with kaka on the bathroom wall when you heard him say it."

"In three years I'll write, 'My nipples are a little sore from nursing Eliza Rosamund.' "

"Rosamund. Every little girl should have a middle name she hates."

" 'Her breath smells like vanilla and her eyes are just Jack's color of blue.' "

"That's nice," Jack said.

"So, which one do you like?"

"I like yours," he said. "But I believe mine."

"It doesn't matter. I believe mine."

"Not in your heart of hearts, you don't."

"You're wrong."

"I'm not wrong," he said. "And her breath would smell like your milk, and it's kind of a bittersweet smell, if you want to know the truth."

1985

Since Jack and the narrator are not zebras but people you may think of as real, maybe even people somewhat like yourself, you may feel in a position to take sides. One of the pleasures of reading and one of the ways of penetrating the meaning and effectiveness of stories is through your emotional responses, which often begin with your rooting for, identifying with, admiring, or despising one character or the other. Our wishes and fears, our expectations and emotions, and the kind of world we imagine that the characters inhabit make up the major register of our emotional responses to fiction. And one of the first moves from reading to writing about fiction may well involve this "partisanship."

Some of your emotional responses to a story will come from your own first- or second-hand experience. You may have been in a situation somewhat like that in "No One's a Mystery" (as the narrator, the wife, or Jack), and who you were in the triangle may have something to do with how you respond to the story. Or, if you are a cat-lover with four Siamese kittens, you may not be able fully to identify with the zebra storyteller.

There are two views emphasized in "No One's a Mystery," two main characters you might identify or side with. How do you feel about the narrator? You may think she's a fool for getting involved with a married man, or immoral, and so perhaps you feel bitter about her projections of a married life with Jack, and believe they will never come true. Or you may identify with her, and find her dreams poignant (if hopeless) or uplifting (if you think they might come true), while Jack may be viewed as either realistic or cynical. An early paper in a literature course may have you defend the projections into the future of Jack or the narrator. You may wish to argue that both are wrong, both right, or that the truth lies somewhere in between. Or you may argue for the story's third character, the wife, who, though not embodied, may nevertheless elicit your sympathy. Try writing down your view of a story like this in essay form before discussing it with others. You will then have a record of your uninfluenced, unchallenged view. Later, you may be surprised to find that some of your class- mates do not agree with you. But in discussing or arguing for your views you may discover not only that there are reasonable differences of opinion, but that what one believes about the future beyond the story reveals something about that person. A second paper may be either an argument with someone else's position or a composite or new view based on your discussion and exchange with classmates. And you may want to look at what you learned about yourself from your arguments about the story.

These ideas for papers are meant to be more than suggested writing assign- ments. They also suggest one *way* of writing about literature and are meant to show that writing about a story is not some special or arcane art but just a some- what more formal, responsible, committed way of talking about what you have read. Think of the last time you saw a movie with a friend and left the theater discussing the film. If you were to put such responses down on paper, look at them carefully, think about them a bit, and try to make your views or responses convincing, you've taken the first step toward writing about literature. You could even call it literary criticism.

Writing about the characters and events in stories as if they were real peo- ple and real happenings, and writing about your responses to and opinions about them, is only one kind of writing about literature. You can only write such a paper *after* you have read the whole story and formed an opinion, and your "argument" will involve going back to the story seeking out details to sup- port your position, and, perhaps, situating where you are coming from in terms of personal experience, moral or religious views, and so on. But reading a story is not just something to argue or even think about after you have read it. It is first of all an experience—made up of thoughts and feelings—that happens *while you are in the very act of reading.*

One of the things most of us do when we are actively engaged in reading a story is to anticipate or interpret: what will happen next? what kind of person is a given character? how is the world of the story related to the world as I know it? what kind of a story is it? will it end happily or not? You will notice two aspects to such anticipation. One involves our experience, direct or indirect, in the world, and may be thought of as referential or representational; that is, we take the nouns to refer to real things—the word *table* calls up a more or less concrete image of a table—and from the words describing characters we imagine more or less real people and their actions and choices as potentially if not actually real. We have discussed "No One's a Mystery" as if the narrator and Jack were real people living in the real world, specifically Wyoming. The other aspect is literary. We pay attention to the words themselves, to their sounds, their connotations, their relation to other words that look or sound like them, and not just to what they denote—tables or Cadillacs or jewels. Stories can even play with these referential and literary aspects of words, surprising us by shifting from one aspect to another. The zebra who did not tell stories was astonished, and the words say "he's just fit to be tied." This is a common figure of speech, and we do not expect to take the words "seriously" or referentially. We are surprised, then, when the story does: "So the little cat quickly ties him up. . . ."

We are aware that a story is a story and that telling a story involves certain conventions—for example, stories are generally written in the past tense, though we like to imagine them as happening in a kind of present, with the end not yet known. Different kinds of stories, too, have their own conventions: fairy tales and sometimes other fantasies, like "The Zebra Storyteller," begin with "Once upon a time"; in ghost stories and certain other scary stories there is almost always a beautiful young woman threatened by danger; these stories, adventure stories, and comic stories almost always end happily, and so on.

Anticipation begins at the beginning—or even earlier. As soon as we read the title of the story that follows, "The Jewelry," we start: will it be lost? stolen? inherited? Our anticipation is channeled by first- or second-hand life experience—how we think jewelry functions in "the real world." Notice that this anticipation is triggered by the title. Life experiences do not come with titles to guide us, but our reading experience tells us that titles are significant, worth paying attention to if we are to anticipate and understand. Perhaps not as early as our reading of the title, but soon, we begin to anticipate a shape or configuration of the entire story. Based on our own real experiences and what we've read, we project a vague shape early on, frequently adjusting it as we proceed through the story, but always connected to it as we read on. With the first sentence of "The Jewelry"—"Having met the girl one evening, at the house of the office-superintendent, M. Lantin became enveloped in love as in a net"—we begin casting our own net. The story will involve love. What do we know or believe about love? about different kinds of love? about the possible outcomes of falling in love? What is the connection between love and jewelry? We are not yet prepared to define that connection, but we may have tentative expectations about it. Though the first sentence may be summarized in "real" or experiential terms as "M. Lantin has fallen (deeply) in love," the precise *words* in the sentence that describe falling in love are "became enveloped in love as in a net." Does this merely emphasize how deeply he has fallen in love or is there something uncomfortable, painful, even ominous about the words—note, about the *words*—"enveloped as in a net"? How we anticipate and interpret what the story "means" or "says about life" will be conditioned throughout by our life experience, by such literary "devices" as the title, by the precise words of the story, and by our experience with kinds of stories and what usually happens and eventuates in such stories. We must remain tentative in our expectations, however, and alert to changes and modifications; for example, when the fourth paragraph of this story concludes with "and [he] married her," we must abandon the love-and-courtship story we anticipated and imagine an entirely new set of possibilities.

GUY DE MAUPASSANT

The Jewelry[1]

Having met the girl one evening, at the house of the office-superintendent, M. Lantin became enveloped in love as in a net.

She was the daughter of a country-tutor, who had been dead for several years. Afterward she had come to Paris with her mother, who made regular visits to several bourgeois families of the neighborhood, in hopes of being able to get her daughter married. They were poor and respectable, quiet and gentle. The young girl seemed to be the very ideal of that pure good woman to whom every young man dreams of entrusting his future. Her modest beauty had a charm of angelic shyness; and the slight smile that always dwelt about her lips seemed a reflection of her heart.

Everybody sang her praises; all who knew her kept saying: "The man who gets her will be lucky. No one could find a nicer girl than that."

M. Lantin, who was then chief clerk in the office of the Minister of the Interior, with a salary of 3,500 francs a year,[2] demanded her hand, and married her.

1. Translated by Lafcadio Hearn.   2. A midlevel bureaucratic wage, perhaps about $25,000–$30,000 today.

5 He was unutterably happy with her. She ruled his home with an economy so adroit that they really seemed to live in luxury. It would be impossible to conceive of any attentions, tendernesses, playful caresses which she did not lavish upon her husband; and such was the charm of her person that, six years after he married her, he loved her even more than he did the first day.

There were only two points upon which he ever found fault with her—her love of the theater, and her passion for false jewelry.

Her lady-friends (she was acquainted with the wives of several small office holders) were always bringing her tickets for the theaters; whenever there was a performance that made a sensation, she always had her *loge* secured, even for first performances; and she would drag her husband with her to all these entertainments, which used to tire him horribly after his day's work. So at last he begged her to go to the theater with some lady-acquaintances who would consent to see her home afterward. She refused for quite a while—thinking it would not look very well to go out thus unaccompanied by her husband. But finally she yielded, just to please him; and he felt infinitely grateful to her therefor.

Now this passion for the theater at last evoked in her the desire of dress. It was true that her toilette remained simple, always in good taste, but modest; and her sweet grace, her irresistible grace, ever smiling and shy, seemed to take fresh charm from the simplicity of her robes. But she got into the habit of suspending in her pretty ears two big cut pebbles, fashioned in imitation of diamonds; and she wore necklaces of false pearls, bracelets of false gold, and haircombs studded with paste-imitations of precious stones.

Her husband, who felt shocked by this love of tinsel and show, would often say—"My dear, when one has not the means to afford real jewelry, one should appear adorned with one's natural beauty and grace only—and these gifts are the rarest of jewels."

10 But she would smile sweetly and answer: "What does it matter? I like those things—that is my little whim. I know you are right; but one can't make oneself over again. I've always loved jewelry so much!"

And then she would roll the pearls of the necklaces between her fingers, and make the facets of the cut crystals flash in the light, repeating: "Now look at them—see how well the work is done. You would swear it was real jewelry."

He would then smile in his turn, and declare to her: "You have the tastes of a regular Gypsy."

Sometimes, in the evening, when they were having a chat by the fire, she would rise and fetch the morocco box in which she kept her "stock" (as M. Lantin called it)—would put it on the tea-table, and begin to examine the false jewelry with passionate delight, as if she experienced some secret and mysterious sensations of pleasure in their contemplation; and she would insist on putting one of the necklaces round her husband's neck, and laugh till she couldn't laugh any more, crying out: "Oh! how funny you look!" Then she would rush into his arms, and kiss him furiously.

One winter's night, after she had been to the Opera, she came home chilled through, and trembling. Next day she had a bad cough. Eight days after that, she died of pneumonia.

Lantin was very nearly following her into the tomb. His despair was so fright-   15
ful that in one single month his hair turned white. He wept from morning till
night, feeling his heart torn by inexpressible suffering—ever haunted by the
memory of her, by the smile, by the voice, by all the charm of the dead woman.

Time did not assuage his grief. Often during office hours his fellow-clerks
went off to a corner to chat about this or that topic of the day—his cheeks might
have been seen to swell up all of a sudden, his nose wrinkle, his eyes fill with
water—he would pull a frightful face, and begin to sob.

He had kept his dead companion's room just in the order she had left it, and
he used to lock himself up in it every evening to think about her—all the furniture, and even all her dresses, remained in the same place they had been on the
last day of her life.

But life became hard for him. His salary, which, in his wife's hands, had
amply sufficed for all household needs, now proved scarcely sufficient to supply
his own few wants. And he asked himself in astonishment how she had managed
always to furnish him with excellent wines and with delicate eating which he
could not now afford at all with his scanty means.

He got a little into debt, like men obliged to live by their wits. At last one
morning that he happened to find himself without a cent in his pocket, and a
whole week to wait before he could draw his monthly salary, he thought of
selling something; and almost immediately it occurred to him to sell his wife's
"stock"—for he had always borne a secret grudge against the flash-jewelry that
used to annoy him so much in former days. The mere sight of it, day after day,
somewhat spoiled the sad pleasure of thinking of his darling.

He tried a long time to make a choice among the heap of trinkets she had   20
left behind her—for up to the very last day of her life she had kept obstinately
buying them, bringing home some new thing almost every night—and finally
he resolved to take the big pearl necklace which she used to like the best of all,
and which he thought ought certainly to be worth six or eight francs, as it was
really very nicely mounted for an imitation necklace.

He put it in his pocket, and walked toward the office, following the boule-
vards, and looking for some jewelry-store on the way, where he could enter with
confidence.

Finally he saw a place and went in; feeling a little ashamed of thus exposing
his misery, and of trying to sell such a trifling object.

"Sir," he said to the jeweler, "please tell me what this is worth."

The jeweler took the necklace, examined it, weighed it, took up a magnifying
glass, called his clerk, talked to him in whispers, put down the necklace on the
counter, and drew back a little bit to judge of its effect at a distance.

M. Lantin, feeling very much embarrassed by all these ceremonies, opened   25
his mouth and began to declare—"Oh! I know it can't be worth much" . . .
when the jeweler interrupted him saying:

"Well, sir, that is worth between twelve and fifteen thousand francs; but I
cannot buy it unless you can let me know exactly how you came by it."

The widower's eyes opened enormously, and he stood gaping—unable to
understand. Then after a while he stammered out: "You said? . . . Are you sure?"

The jeweler, misconstruing the cause of this astonishment, replied in a dry tone—"Go elsewhere if you like, and see if you can get any more for it. The very most I would give for it is fifteen thousand. Come back and see me again, if you can't do better."

M. Lantin, feeling perfectly idiotic, took his necklace and departed; obeying a confused desire to find himself alone and to get a chance to think.

But the moment he found himself in the street again, he began to laugh, and he muttered to himself: "The fool!—oh! what a fool; If I had only taken him at his word. Well, well!—a jeweler who can't tell paste from real jewelry!"

30 And he entered another jewelry-store, at the corner of the Rue de la Paix. The moment the jeweler set eyes on the necklace, he examined—"Hello! I know that necklace well—it was sold here!"

M. Lantin, very nervous, asked:

"What's it worth?"

"Sir, I sold it for twenty-five thousand francs. I am willing to buy it back again for eighteen thousand—if you can prove to me satisfactorily, according to legal presciptions, how you came into possession of it"—This time, M. Lantin was simply paralyzed with astonishment. He said: "Well . . . but please look at it again, sir. I always thought until now that it was . . . was false."

The jeweler said:

35 "Will you give me your name, sir?"

"Certainly. My name is Lantin; I am employed at the office of the Minister of the Interior. I live at No. 16, Rue des Martyrs."

The merchant opened the register, looked, and said: "Yes; this necklace was sent to the address of Madame Lantin, 16 Rue des Martyrs, on July 20th, 1876."

And the two men looked into each other's eyes—the clerk wild with surprise; the jeweler suspecting he had a thief before him.

The jeweler resumed:

40 "Will you be kind enough to leave this article here for twenty-four hours only—I'll give you a receipt."

M. Lantin stuttered: "Yes-ah! certainly." And he went out folding up the receipt, which he put in his pocket.

Then he crossed the street, went the wrong way, found out his mistake, returned by way of the Tuileries, crossed the Seine, found out he had taken the wrong road again, and went back to the Champs-Elysées without being able to get one clear idea into his head. He tried to reason, to understand. His wife could never have bought so valuable an object as that. Certainly not. But then, it must have been a present! . . . A present from whom? What for?

He stopped and stood stock-still in the middle of the avenue.

A horrible suspicion swept across his mind. . . . She? . . . But then all those other pieces of jewelry must have been presents also! . . . Then it seemed to him that the ground was heaving under his feet; that a tree, right in front of him, was falling toward him; he thrust out his arms instinctively, and fell senseless.

45 He recovered his consciousness again in a drug-store to which some bystanders had carried him. He had them lead him home, and he locked himself into his room.

Until nightfall he cried without stopping, biting his handkerchief to keep himself from screaming out. Then, completely worn out with grief and fatigue, he went to bed, and slept a leaden sleep.

A ray of sunshine awakened him, and he rose and dressed himself slowly to go to the office. It was hard to have to work after such a shock. Then he reflected that he might be able to excuse himself to the superintendent, and he wrote to him. Then he remembered he would have to go back to the jeweler's; and shame made his face purple. He remained thinking a long time. Still he could not leave the necklace there; he put on his coat and went out.

It was a fine day; the sky extended all blue over the city, and seemed to make it smile. Strollers were walking aimlessly about, with their hands in their pockets.

Lantin thought as he watched them passing: "How lucky the men are who have fortunes! With money a man can even shake off grief—you can go where you please—travel—amuse yourself! Oh! if I were only rich!"

He suddenly discovered he was hungry—not having eaten anything since the evening before. But his pockets were empty; and he remembered the necklace. Eighteen thousand francs! Eighteen thousand francs!—that was a sum—that was!

He made his way to the Rue de la Paix and began to walk backward and forward on the sidewalk in front of the store. Eighteen thousand francs! Twenty times he started to go in; but shame always kept him back.

Still he was hungry—very hungry—and had not a cent. He made one brusque resolve, and crossed the street almost at a run, so as not to let himself have time to think over the matter; and he rushed into the jeweler's.

As soon as he saw him, the merchant hurried forward, and offered him a chair with smiling politeness. Even the clerks came forward to stare at Lantin, with gaiety in their eyes and smiles about their lips.

The jeweler said: "Sir, I made inquiries; and if you are still so disposed, I am ready to pay you down the price I offered you."

The clerk stammered: "Why, yes—sir, certainly."

The jeweler took from a drawer eighteen big bills,[3] counted them, and held them out to Lantin, who signed a little receipt, and thrust the money feverishly into his pocket.

Then, as he was on the point of leaving, he turned to the ever-smiling merchant, and said, lowering his eyes: "I have some—I have some other jewelry, which came to me in the same—from the same inheritance. Would you purchase them also from me?"

The merchant bowed, and answered: "Why, certainly, sir—certainly. ..." One of the clerks rushed out to laugh at his ease; another kept blowing his nose as hard as he could.

Lantin, impassive, flushed and serious, said: "I will bring them to you."

And he hired a cab to get the jewelry.

When he returned to the store, an hour later, he had not yet breakfasted.

3. French paper money varies in size; the larger the bill, the larger the denomination.

They examined the jewelry—piece by piece—putting a value on each. Nearly all had been purchased from that very house.

Lantin, now, disputed estimates made, got angry, insisted on seeing the books, and talked louder and louder the higher the estimates grew.

The big diamond earrings were worth 20,000 francs; the bracelets, 35,000; the brooches, rings and medallions, 16,000; a set of emeralds and sapphires, 14,000; solitaire, suspended to a gold neckchain, 40,000; the total value being estimated at 196,000 francs.

The merchant observed with mischievous good nature: "The person who owned these must have put all her savings into jewelry."

Lantin answered with gravity: "Perhaps that is as good a way of saving money as any other." And he went off, after having agreed with the merchant that an expert should make a counter-estimate for him the next day.

When he found himself in the street again, he looked at the Column Vendôme[4] with the desire to climb it, as if it were a May pole. He felt jolly enough to play leapfrog over the Emperor's head—up there in the blue sky.

He breakfasted at Voisin's[5] restaurant, and ordered wine at 20 francs a bottle.

Then he hired a cab and drove out to the Bois.[6] He looked at the carriages passing with a sort of contempt, and a wild desire to yell out to the passers-by: "I am rich, too—I am! I have 200,000 francs!"

The recollection of the office suddenly came back to him. He drove there, walked right into the superintendent's private room, and said: "Sir, I come to give you my resignation. I have just come into a fortune of *three* hundred thousand francs." Then he shook hands all round with his fellow-clerks; and told them all about his plans for a new career. Then he went to dinner at the Café Anglais.

Finding himself seated at the same table with a man who seemed to him quite genteel, he could not resist the itching desire to tell him, with a certain air of coquetry, that he had just inherited a fortune of *four* hundred thousand francs.

For the first time in his life he went to the theater without feeling bored by the performance; and he passed the night in revelry and debauch.

Six months after he married again. His second wife was the most upright of spouses, but had a terrible temper. She made his life very miserable.

1883

Stories are not always written. Ballads and even epics were sung, plays are still acted out on the stage, and most cultures have or had oral storytellers. Writing, however, makes a difference. Oral or dramatic "readings" or performances are communal, the responses tend to be uniform (though there's always the person in the audience who laughs at the wrong time), and their purpose is

4. Famous column with a statue of Napoleon at the top.   5. Like the Café Anglais below, a well-known and high-priced restaurant.   6. Large Parisian park where the rich took their outings.

more overtly to move or persuade the group or community. They have a closer relation to classical rhetoric, political speeches, or concerts than written narrative does. We read, usually, alone, most of the time silently, and if there are—and there usually are—emotions, they are deeply personal, not shared. There is a tendency, then, in literary criticism, and in reading for and discussing literature in class, to stress interpretation, the "ideas" in literary texts, or the formal structures, and to slight somewhat the emotional or affective aspect of our essentially solitary literary experience. But though it may be difficult to develop the vocabulary needed to talk about literature—we have to get beyond "I liked it" and "I didn't like it"—we must never forget the deeply stirring response that literature engenders and the differences in kinds and depths of response that different works stimulate.

▾ ▾ ▾

QUESTIONS

1. What specific words or phrases in the first two paragraphs of "The Jewelry" alert you to the possibility that all may not be as it seems? How are these expectations or fears allayed in the next few paragraphs? What new fears or expectations are aroused very soon thereafter?

2. Since the story is called "The Jewelry" and life does not come wrapped in such convenient titles, you may come to suspect the truth before M. Lantin. How does your attitude toward him change?

WRITING SUGGESTIONS

1. Copy "The Zebra Storyteller." Exchange papers with a classmate. Carefully proofread each other's papers. Can you believe you could have made errors in simple copying?

2. Stop "The Zebra Storyteller" after paragraph 5 ("... fit to be tied") and, in five to ten paragraphs, write your own ending.

3. Write a parody or imitation of "No One's a Mystery" giving it the same title as another recent song.

4. Write a two- or three-page scene of Jack (from "No One's a Mystery") and his wife at home.

5. Write an "off-stage" scene that shows how Lantin's first wife got one or more pieces of the jewelry.

∇ ∇ ∇

Understanding the Text

1 PLOT

I n "The Zebra Storyteller" you can see the skeleton of the typical short story **plot** or **plot structure.** Plot simply means the arrangement of the **action**, an imagined event or a series of such events.

Action usually involves **conflict**, a struggle between opposing forces, and it often falls into something like the same five parts that we find in a play: exposition, rising action, turning point (or climax), falling action, conclusion. The conflict in this little tale is between the Siamese cat and the zebras, especially the zebra storyteller. The first part of the action, called the **exposition**, introduces the characters, situation, and, usually, time and place. The exposition here is achieved in three sentences: the time is "once upon a," the place Africa, the characters a Siamese cat who speaks Zebraic and an innocent zebra, and the situation their meeting. We then enter the second part of the plot, the **rising action**: events that complicate the situation and intensify or complicate the conflict or introduce new ones. The first event here is the meeting between an innocent zebra and the Zebraic-speaking cat. That initial conflict of zebra and cat is over in a hurry—the zebra who is "fit to be tied" is tied up and eaten. Complications build with the cat's continuing success in killing zebras, and the zebras' growing fears and consequent superstitious belief that the ghost of a lion haunts the region preying on zebras. The **turning point** or **climax** of the action is the third part of the story, the appearance of the zebra storyteller: until now the cat has had it all his way, but his luck is about to change. From this point on the complications that grew in the first part of the story are untangled—the zebra storyteller, for example, is not surprised when he meets a Siamese cat speaking Zebraic, "because he'd been thinking about that very thing"; this is the fourth part of the story, the reverse movement or **falling action**. The story ends at the fifth part, the **conclusion**: the point at which the situation that was destablized at the beginning of the story (when the Zebraic-speaking cat appeared) becomes stable once more: Africa is once again free of cats speaking the language of zebras.

This typical arrangement of the action of a story is not just a formula for composing a narrative or for critical analysis; it also has its emotional and intellectual effect on your responses as reader. The exposition invites you to immediately begin building images of the time and place of the action, the people, the situation, and the issues involved, and even to identify with or root for one or more of the participants. You choose to be on the side of the zebras or the Siamese cat (though your choice is guided by the language and details of the story: the cat speaks "inappropriate" Zebraic, the zebra is introduced as "innocent"). As the situation becomes more complicated during the rising action, you are led to be increasingly concerned with how "your" zebras, the "good guys," are going to get out of the increasingly bad situation (the cat eating more and more zebras), or, if the complications of the rising action are positive (as in the marriage and prosperity and happiness of M. Lantin in "The Jewelry"), you become more and more concerned about what is going to happen to turn things around (for even if you do not know about turning points in narrative, you know that sometimes things in stories and even in real life—knock on wood—seem too good to be true or too good to last). Consciously or unconsciously you become involved in the story, trying to anticipate how the complications will unravel, how everything will come out.

Another aspect of structure that affects you the reader is the order in which the events are told. In life, actions occur one after the other, sequentially. Most stories grant this sequential unfolding of life's events but many do not describe events chronologically. When historical order is disturbed, a plot is created. "The king died and then the queen died," to use one critic's example, is not a plot, for it has not been "tampered with." "The queen died after the king died" includes the same historical events, but the order in which they are reported has been changed. The reader of the first sentence focuses on the king first; the reader of the second sentence focuses on the queen. While essentially the same thing has been said, the difference in focus and emphasis changes the effect and, in the broadest sense, the meaning as well. The **history** has been structured into plot.

The ordering of events, then, provides stories with structure and plot, and has its consequences in effect and meaning. The first opportunity for **structur-**

ing a story is at the beginning, and beginnings are consequently particularly sensitive and important. Why does a story begin where it does? No event (at least since the Big Bang) is a true beginning; your own life story begins before you were born and even before you were conceived. So to begin a story the author has to make a **selection,** to indicate that for the purposes of this story the beginning is a given point rather than any other. "Having met the girl one evening, at the house of the office-superintendent, M. Lantin became enveloped in love as in a net." That first sentence of "The Jewelry" seems a perfectly natural and "innocent" way to begin a story that will involve Lantin and his wife. But why not begin with a slightly modified paragraph 5: "M. Lantin was perfectly happy in his marriage"? or with paragraph 9, inserting a new first sentence: "M. Lantin was perfectly happy with his wife and smiled at her two little faults: her love of the theater, and her passion for false jewelry. He felt shocked by . . ."? After all, this last sentence would immediately introduce the jewelry that gives the story its title. Or the story could begin with the death of the girl's father, her move with her mother to Paris, and so on. (Note that she is never given a name, just "the girl" first, then "his wife.") These are the earliest events mentioned in the exposition, and so in the unstructured history they would come first. In searching for a reason for Maupassant's beginning, we might look at what we learn and what is emphasized in the beginning as it now stands: the class of Lantin and his income; the girl's beauty, modesty, respectability, poverty, and her mother's search for a husband for her; Lantin's falling in love as if into a "net." It might be useful to consider on your own or in an assigned essay how the details in these first eight paragraphs affect your reading, responding, and understanding of the people, events, and "meaning" of the story. Or you might want to explain why John Cheever's "The Country Husband," in this chapter, begins, "To begin at the beginning, the airplane from Minneapolis in which Francis Weed was traveling East ran into heavy weather," rather than with, say, paragraph 11, when the Weeds are preparing to go out on the evening on which Francis meets the baby-sitter; or even, with a few adjustments, with paragraph 15, when the baby-sitter opens the door and Francis sees her for the first time, for it is with their encounter that the story seems truly to begin.

The point at which a story ends is also a sensitive and meaningful aspect of its structure. A typical beginning—first sentence (Lantin meets the girl) or first **discriminated occasion** (the first encounter of a zebra with the Zebraic-speaking cat)—destabilizes the history; something happens that changes the ordinary life of one or more characters and sets off a new course of events, the story. A typical ending either reestablishes the old order (no more cats eating zebras, no more romantic escapades for Francis Weed) or establishes a new one (Lantin remarried). Endings, like beginnings, affect the reader and suggest meaning. And like beginnings, they are arbitrary structures that interrupt history, for all stories (or more precisely, histories) about individuals end the same way, as Margaret Atwood somewhat cynically suggests in "Happy Endings": "*John and Mary die. John and Mary die. John and Mary die.*" That is only true, of course, if you equate the story with the history, for the history not only extends backward as far as you can see but also forward to the end of the lives of those in the story. (And why not the lives of their children, grandchildren, and so on?) Not all stories end with the deaths of the characters who interest us; in fact, of the stories in this and the introductory chapters only Atwood's ends with the deaths of both its major characters, while "The Zebra Storyteller" ends with the death of the Zebraic-speaking cat. Where a story ends goes a long way to determining how it affects us and what we make of it. "The Zebra Storyteller" ends with the triumph of the zebra over the Siamese cat, leaving us with the feeling that good guys win, and with a moral that leads us to the "point" or meaning of the story. "No One's a Mystery" leaves us without an answer and pushes us back into our own experiences and beliefs to judge who is right and who is wrong about the couple's future.

All questions about the effect or meaning of beginnings and endings follow from an assumption that we must now recognize: that there are reasons for the structures of the narrative, indeed, that in a short story, in part because of its brevity, everything must "count." One writer has said that if there is a gun on the wall at the beginning of a story, it must be fired by the end. The relevance of events or details is not limited, however, merely to future action, events in the plot, for most seem to have relevance in other ways. In paragraph 9 of "The Country Husband," for example, Francis Weed listens to "the evening sounds of Shady Hill." These include a door slamming, the sound of someone cutting grass—which do not lead to events but may establish the nature of the suburban setting—and the sound of someone playing (badly) Beethoven's "Moonlight Sonata," which may on the one hand, because of the nature of the piece, reinforce Weed's thoughtful or dreamy mood or introduce "romance" into the story, and on the other hand, because of the petulant and self-pitying performance, show why Weed is dissatisfied with the shallowness of his suburban neighbors, and perhaps suburban life. Notice the "may" and the "perhaps" in the previous sentence. The relevancy of a detail to a story is not always as simple and incontrovertible as the inevitable shooting of the gun. Though you ought to be alert as to how the details function in affecting you or contributing to your visualization or understanding of the people, incidents, and issues of the story, there is not necessarily a precise answer to the question of how a detail functions. In Cheever's story, why does Mr. Nixon shout "Varmints! Rascals! . . . Avaunt and quit my sight!" at the squirrels? What does it add? What would be lost without it? You may see the effects and implications differently from your classmates; indeed you may not have chosen this detail to interrogate at all. These differences of selection and explanation may shed light on why readers respond to, understand, and judge stories differently.

Structuring a story is not just a matter of choosing where to begin or end it, or of choosing or inventing affective and meaningful details, but also of ordering all the events in between. Sometimes, as Atwood says, the plot is "just one thing after another, a what and a what and a what." Even when that is the case, sometimes the reader is forced to think back to prior events. In a detective story, for example, the crime has usually been committed before the story begins, in the history and not in the plot. At the end, when the detective explains "who done it," you must think back not only to the crime, but to all the hints or clues that you have been given. In such a story we expect the ending to explain what happened earlier; in "A Rose for Emily," however, and similar stories, there is an ending that forces us to reinterpret many of the details that went before, though while reading we did not realize reinterpretation would be necessary, so the ending is a surprise not only in what it tells us but in the fact that we did not know there was anything that we had not been told. Sometimes, however, the story moves back; that is, instead of making you think of earlier events, it actually breaks into its own order, reaches back into the history, and presents or dramatizes a scene that happened before the fictional present. In "Sonny's Blues," for example, there is such a replay or **flashback** (or rather a series of flashbacks). There is a very brief scene from the past triggered by the word "safe" (par. 79), the narrator recalling his father's words, which then leads to a specific dramatized scene—the last time the narrator talked to his mother. This is followed by another scene—the narrator's conversation with Sonny after their mother's funeral. This scene of course follows the previous one but in terms of where the story began (the fictional present) it is in the past, and therefore is in fact a flashback. Nor does the story return to the fictional present for some time—"I read about Sonny's trouble in the spring. Little Grace died in the fall . . ." (par. 177)—when Sonny has been living with the narrator for two weeks, and it proceeds from that point to the end.

One reason for structuring the history into plot is to engage the reader's attention, to make the reader read on. This can be done not only by arousing the reader's expectations of what will happen next but also by generating **curiosity**—the desire to know what is happening or has happened. It is the sheer power of curiosity, for example, that keeps us reading intensely when we know as little as Watson or Sherlock Holmes himself at the beginning of a story or "case." But it is not only the detective story that plays upon our curiosity. "Sonny's Blues" begins, "I read about it in the paper . . . ," and that "it" without antecedent is repeated seven times in the first paragraph and first two sentences of the second paragraph. Read those first two paragraphs and stop. If you try at this point to examine what is going on in your mind, you more than likely will find that you are asking yourself what "it" might refer to, and you will more than likely have framed for yourself several possible answers. It may be in part for this reason that Baldwin begins how and where he does, getting you engaged in the story, so that you will read on. Even a title, such as "The Zebra Storyteller," "A Very Old Man with Enormous Wings," or "The Rocking-Horse Winner," can make us curious enough to pick up a story; after that, it's up to the story to keep us engaged.

Perhaps stronger than curiosity is **suspense**—that particular kind of expectation involving anticipation of and doubt about what is going to happen next (as differentiated from expectations about what a character is like, what the theme is or how it will develop, and so on). Even in reading a little fable like "The Zebra Storyteller" our minds are—or should be—at work: a cat speaking Zebraic is killing zebras; the zebra storyteller thinking of plots comes up with the idea of a story in which a cat speaking Zebraic is killing zebras: "What an idea! That'll make 'em laugh!" he tells himself. Then he meets the cat—what will happen next? How many possibilities did you or can you anticipate? Even though you now know the ending, you could go back to this point in the story and, recalling your expectations, reconstruct or reinvent the rest of the story.

Sometimes the suspense is generated and defined not so much by what happens within the story as it is by what we expect from stories. In "The Jewelry," for example, when Lantin's wife dies so early in the story, we know this is not the end; something is going to happen or be revealed because there are several pages left and stories do not go on unless something is going to happen. But what? Lantin grieves so intensely, locks himself in her room . . . will her ghost return? He is going bankrupt, he looks over his wife's jewelry, and when he goes to sell a piece he finds it is not mere costume jewelry, but real. How much sooner than Lantin himself do you realize the source of the jewelry? There is a certain satisfaction in seeing the truth before he does. But *then* what do you expect to happen next? Do you anticipate his debauching? How did you expect the story to end?

If you were to pause just before reading the final paragraph of the Maupassant story and consciously explore your expectations, you would see that these are based on both fictional and actual conventions—indeed, most of us would probably assume the story could have ended with the word "debauch," without the final brief paragraph, and that the story would end with the irony of Lantin's getting pleasure out of his having been betrayed. We can accept this even within our conventional moral terms—he may get bitter pleasures for a time, but he will soon tire of such pleasures or be undone by them.

The final paragraph, however, if it does not contradict, deepens the irony: now he has a truly "upright" wife—and he is miserable. Our conventional expectations that morality brings happiness, that infidelity and debauchery lead to various kinds of ruin, are wrenched into question. He has tired of debauchery, but is he better off leading a moral life? Is the world amoral—or even immoral? Do good guys finish last? We do not have to believe this, but to read the story fully we need to call our perhaps more optimistic and conventional views into question.

In order to keep you engaged and alert, a story must make you ask questions about what will happen or what will be revealed next. To respond fully to a story you must be alert to the signals and guess along with the author. One way of seeing whether and how your mind is engaged in your reading is to pause at crucial points in the story and consciously explore what you think is coming. In "No One's a Mystery" the story does the pausing and the conscious specification of what might happen next for you—it gives two versions of what might happen and then the story ends, without resolution. (Though not without point; for to suggest that both naivete and cynicism are merely attitudes, and that neither is an infallible clue to the future, is an insight and a challenge, even if it is not, strictly speaking, a resolution.) At least in one aspect, fiction is a guessing game.

Like all guessing games, from quiz shows to philosophy, the plot game in fiction has certain guidelines. A well-structured plot will play fair with you, offering at appropriate points all the necessary indications or clues to what will happen next, not just springing new and essential information on you at the last minute ("Meanwhile, unknown to our hero, the Marines were just on the other side of the hill . . ."). It is this playing fair that makes the ending of a well-structured story satisfying or, when you look back on it, inevitable. Most stories also offer a number of reasonable but false signals (red herrings) to get you off the scent, so that in a well-structured story the ending, though inevitable, is also surprising. And though there is usually an overarching action from beginning to end, in many stories there are layers of expectation or suspense, so that as soon as one question is answered another comes forth to replace it, keeping you in doubt as to the final outcome.

Unlike most guessing games, however, the reward is not for the right guess—anticipating the outcome before the final paragraph—but for the number of guesses, right *and* wrong, that you make, the number of signals you respond to. If you are misled by none of the false signals in the early pages of a story—by Sonny's friend saying, " 'Listen. They'll let him out and then it'll just start all over again' " (par. 36), for example—you may be closer to being "right," but you have missed many of the implications of the story. But, more important, you have missed the pleasure of *learning* the "truth" a story has to offer, and you know how much less meaningful it is to be told something than to learn for yourself, through your own experience. Fiction is a way of transmitting not just perception but experience.

Though plot is the structuring of events, an event can be an outcome or consequence as well as a happening, and the expectation, surprise, and perception surrounding plot structure can involve meaning as well as action, as we have seen in the worldview suggested by the ending of "The Jewelry." Maupassant's ending upsets our conventional thinking about human conduct and morality. The ending of "The Country Husband" may upset your expectations based on the conventions of storytelling. We usually expect some kind of dramatic change, some revelation. Here we may expect Francis to run off with the baby-sitter and have a violent confrontation with Clayton Thomas. (Many students seem to be on the side of Francis and Anne—until they are asked to identify Francis not with themselves or with story heroes but, say, with their own fathers!) Cheever says, in effect, not only that life is not like that, but that stories should not be like that. Though expectations based on social, moral, or literary conventions that support the ordinary are not so consciously aroused as are those aroused by action and adventure—the kind of expectation described by the term *suspense*—their fulfillment, modification, or contradiction is a significant aim and effect of many stories. Fiction is in part a guessing game, but it is not merely a game. Many stories seek to give new insights into human perception, experience, meaning, or at least to challenge our more or less unconsciously held beliefs. They strive to tell truths—new, subjective truths, but truths—even though they "lie" about the actuality of the people and events represented. But first they have to get your attention, and one way is by arousing your curiosity and exciting your anticipation. That is one of the primary functions of plot. Alertness to signals, anticipating what is to come next, and remembering what has been said and signaled earlier are essential to fully appreciating and understanding stories and their structures. That is how you should function as a reader of plot.

▼   ▼   ▼

MARGARET ATWOOD

Happy Endings

John and Mary meet.
What happens next?
If you want a happy ending, try A.

A. John and Mary fall in love and get married. They both have worthwhile and remunerative jobs which they find stimulating and challenging. They buy a charming house. Real estate values go up. Eventually, when they can afford live-in help, they have two children, to whom they are devoted. The children turn out well. John and Mary have a stimulating and challenging sex life and worthwhile friends. They go on fun vacations together. They retire. They both have hobbies which they find stimulating and challenging. Eventually they die. This is the end of the story.

B. Mary falls in love with John but John doesn't fall in love with Mary. He merely uses her body for selfish pleasure and ego gratification of a tepid kind. He comes to her apartment twice a week and she cooks him dinner, you'll notice that he doesn't even consider her worth the price of a dinner out, and after he's eaten the dinner he fucks her and after that he falls asleep, while she does the dishes so he won't think she's untidy, having all those dirty dishes lying around, and puts on fresh lipstick so she'll look good when he wakes up, but when he wakes up he doesn't even notice, he puts on his socks and his shorts and his pants and his shirt and his tie and his shoes, the reverse order from the one in which he took them off. He doesn't take off Mary's clothes, she takes them off herself, she acts as if she's dying for it every time, not because she likes sex exactly, she doesn't, but she wants John to think she does because if they do it often enough surely he'll get used to her, he'll come to depend on her and they will get married, but John goes out the door with hardly so much as a good-night and three days later he turns up at six o'clock and they do the whole thing over again.

Mary gets run-down. Crying is bad for your face, everyone knows that and so does Mary but she can't stop. People at work notice. Her friends tell her John is a rat, a pig, a dog, he isn't good enough for her, but she can't believe it. Inside John, she thinks, is another John, who is much nicer. This other John will emerge like a butterfly from a cocoon, a Jack from a box, a pit from a prune, if the first John is only squeezed enough.

One evening John complains about the food. He has never complained about the food before. Mary is hurt.

Her friends tell her they've seen him in a restaurant with another woman, whose name is Madge. It's not even Madge that finally gets to

Mary: it's the restaurant. John has never taken Mary to a restaurant. Mary collects all the sleeping pills and aspirins she can find, and takes them and a half a bottle of sherry. You can see what kind of a woman she is by the fact that it's not even whiskey. She leaves a note for John. She hopes he'll discover her and get her to the hospital in time and repent and then they can get married, but this fails to happen and she dies.

John marries Madge and everything continues as in A.

C.   John, who is an older man, falls in love with Mary, and Mary, who is only   10 twenty-two, feels sorry for him because he's worried about his hair falling out. She sleeps with him even though she's not in love with him. She met him at work. She's in love with someone called James, who is twenty-two also and not yet ready to settle down.

John on the contrary settled down long ago: this is what is bothering him. John has a steady, respectable job and is getting ahead in his field, but Mary isn't impressed by him, she's impressed by James, who has a motorcycle and a fabulous record collection. But James is often away on his motorcycle, being free. Freedom isn't the same for girls, so in the meantime Mary spends Thursday evenings with John. Thursdays are the only days John can get away.

John is married to a woman called Madge and they have two children, a charming house which they bought just before the real estate values went up, and hobbies which they find stimulating and challenging, when they have the time. John tells Mary how important she is to him, but of course he can't leave his wife because a commitment is a commitment. He goes on about this more than is necessary and Mary finds it boring, but older men can keep it up longer so on the whole she has a fairly good time.

One day James breezes in on his motorcycle with some top-grade California hybrid and James and Mary get higher than you'd believe possible and they climb into bed. Everything becomes very underwater, but along comes John, who has a key to Mary's apartment. He finds them stoned and entwined. He's hardly in any position to be jealous, considering Madge, but nevertheless he's overcome with despair. Finally he's middle-aged, in two years he'll be bald as an egg and he can't stand it. He purchases a handgun, saying he needs it for target practice—this is the thin part of the plot, but it can be dealt with later—and shoots the two of them and himself.

Madge, after a suitable period of mourning, marries an understanding man called Fred and everything continues as in A, but under different names.

D.   Fred and Madge have no problems. They get along exceptionally well   15 and are good at working out any little difficulties that may arise. But their charming house is by the seashore and one day a giant tidal wave approaches. Real estate values go down. The rest of the story is about what caused the tidal wave and how they escape from it. They do, though thousands drown, but Fred and Madge are virtuous and lucky. Finally on high ground they clasp each other, wet and dripping and grateful, and continue as in A.

E. Yes, but Fred has a bad heart. The rest of the story is about how kind and understanding they both are until Fred dies. Then Madge devotes herself to charity work until the end of A. If you like, it can be "Madge," "cancer," "guilty and confused," and "bird watching."

F. If you think this is all too bourgeois, make John a revolutionary and Mary a counterespionage agent and see how far that gets you. Remember, this is Canada. You'll still end up with A, though in between you may get a lustful brawling saga of passionate involvement, a chronicle of our times, sort of.

You'll have to face it, the endings are the same however you slice it. Don't be deluded by any other endings, they're all fake, either deliberately fake, with malicious intent to deceive, or just motivated by excessive optimism if not by downright sentimentality.

The only authentic ending is the one provided here:

John and Mary die. John and Mary die. John and Mary die.

So much for endings. Beginnings are always more fun. True connoisseurs, however, are known to favor the stretch in between, since it's the hardest to do anything with.

That's about all that can be said for plots, which anyway are just one thing after another, a what and a what and a what.

Now try How and Why.

1983

JOHN CHEEVER

The Country Husband

To begin at the beginning, the airplane from Minneapolis in which Francis Weed was traveling East ran into heavy weather. The sky had been a hazy blue, with the clouds below the plane lying so close together that nothing could be seen of the earth. The mist began to form outside the windows, and they flew into a white cloud of such density that it reflected the exhaust fires. The color of the cloud darkened to gray, and the plane began to rock. Francis had been in heavy weather before, but he had never been shaken up so much. The man in the seat beside him pulled a flask out of his pocket and took a drink. Francis smiled at his neighbor, but the man looked away; he wasn't sharing his pain killer with anyone. The plane began to drop and flounder wildly. A child was crying. The air in the cabin was overheated and stale, and Francis' left foot went to sleep. He read a little from a paper book that he had bought at the airport, but the violence of the storm divided his attention. It was black outside the ports. The exhaust fires blazed and shed sparks in the dark, and, inside, the shaded lights, the stuffiness, and the window curtains gave the cabin an atmosphere of intense and misplaced domesticity. Then the light flickered and went out. "You know what I've always wanted to do?" the man beside Francis said suddenly. "I've always wanted to buy a farm in New Hampshire and raise beef cattle." The stewardess announced that they were going to make an emergency landing. All but the children saw in their minds the spreading wings of the Angel of Death. The pilot could be heard singing faintly, "I've got sixpence, jolly, jolly sixpence. I've got sixpence to last me all my life . . ."[1] There was no other sound.

The loud groaning of the hydraulic valves swallowed up the pilot's song, and there was a shrieking high in the air, like automobile brakes, and the plane hit flat on its belly in a cornfield and shook them so violently that an old man up forward howled, "Me kidneys! Me kidneys!" The stewardess flung open the door, and someone opened an emergency door at the back, letting in the sweet noise of their continuing mortality—the idle splash and smell of a heavy rain. Anxious for their lives, they filed out of the doors and scattered over the cornfield in all directions, praying that the thread would hold. It did. Nothing happened. When it was clear that the plane would not burn or explode, the crew and the stewardess gathered the passengers together and led them to the shelter of a barn. They were not far from Philadelphia, and in a little while a string of taxis took them into the city. "It's just like the Marne,[2]" someone said, but there was surprisingly little relaxation of that suspiciousness with which many Americans regard their fellow travelers.

In Philadelphia, Francis Weed got a train to New York. At the end of that journey, he crossed the city and caught just as it was about to pull out the commuting train that he took five nights a week to his home in Shady Hill.

He sat with Trace Bearden. "You know, I was in that plane that just crashed outside Philadelphia," he said. "We came down in a field . . ." He had traveled faster than the newspapers or the rain, and the weather in New York was sunny and mild. It was a day in late September, as fragrant and shapely as an apple. Trace listened to the story, but how could he get excited? Francis had no powers that would let him re-create a brush with death—particularly in the atmosphere of a commuting train, journeying through a sunny countryside where already, in the slum gardens, there were signs of harvest. Trace picked up his newspaper, and Francis was left alone with his thoughts. He said good night to Trace on the platform at Shady Hill and drove in his secondhand Volkswagen up to the Blenhollow neighborhood, where he lived.

The Weeds' Dutch Colonial house was larger than it appeared to be from the driveway. The living room was spacious and divided like Gaul,[3] into three parts. Around an ell to the left as one entered from the vestibule was the long

5

---

1. Song popular with Allied troops in World War II.   2. On September 8, 1914, over 1,000 Paris taxicabs were requisitioned to move troops to the Marne River to halt the encircling Germans.   3. Ancient France (Gaul) is so described by Julius Caesar in *The Gallic War.*

table, laid for six, with candles and a bowl of fruit in the center. The sounds and smells that came from the open kitchen door were appetizing, for Julia Weed was a good cook. The largest part of the living room centered on a fireplace. On the right were some bookshelves and a piano. The room was polished and tranquil, and from the windows that opened to the west there was some late-summer sunlight, brilliant and as clear as water. Nothing here was neglected; nothing had not been burnished. It was not the kind of household where, after prying open a stuck cigarette box, you would find an old shirt button and a tarnished nickel. The hearth was swept, the roses on the piano were reflected in the polish of the broad top, and there was an album of Schubert waltzes on the rack. Louisa Weed, a pretty girl of nine, was looking out the western windows. Her young brother Henry was standing beside her. Her still younger brother, Toby, was studying the figures of some tonsured monks drinking beer on the polished brass of the woodbox. Francis, taking off his hat and putting down his paper, was not consciously pleased with the scene; he was not that reflective. It was his element, his creation, and he returned to it with that sense of lightness and strength with which any creature returns to his home. "Hi, everybody," he said. "The plane from Minneapolis . . ."

Nine times out of ten, Francis would be greeted with affection, but tonight the children are absorbed in their own antagonisms. Francis had not finished his sentence about the plane crash before Henry plants a kick in Louisa's behind. Louisa swings around, saying, *"Damn you!"* Francis makes the mistake of scolding Louisa for bad language before he punishes Henry. Now Louisa turns on her father and accuses him of favoritism. Henry is always right; she is persecuted and lonely; her lot is hopeless. Francis turns to his son, but the son has justification for the kick—she hit him first; she hit him on the ear, which is dangerous. Louisa agrees with this passionately. She hit him on the ear, and she *meant* to hit him on the ear, because he messed up her china collection. Henry says that this is a lie. Little Toby turns away from the woodbox to throw in some evidence for Louisa. Henry claps his hand over little Toby's mouth. Francis separates the two boys but accidentally pushes Toby into the woodbox. Toby begins to cry. Louisa is already crying. Just then, Julia Weed comes into that part of the room where the table is laid. She is a pretty, intelligent woman, and the white in her hair is premature. She does not seem to notice the fracas. "Hello, darling," she says serenely to Francis. "Wash your hands, everyone. Dinner is ready." She strikes a match and lights the six candles in this vale of tears.[4]

This simple announcement, like the war cries of the Scottish chieftains, only refreshes the ferocity of the combatants. Louisa gives Henry a blow on the shoulder. Henry, although he seldom cries, has pitched nine innings and is tired. He bursts into tears. Little Toby discovers a splinter in his hand and begins to howl. Francis says loudly that he has been in a plane crash and that he is tired. Julia appears again from the kitchen and, still ignoring the chaos, asks Francis to go upstairs and tell Helen that everything is ready. Francis is happy to go; it is like

---

4. Common figurative reference to earthly life (vale is valley), though here the tears are literal.

getting back to headquarters company.[5] He is planning to tell his oldest daughter about the airplane crash, but Helen is lying on her bed reading a *True Romance* magazine, and the first thing Francis does is to take the magazine from her hand and remind Helen that he has forbidden her to buy it. She did not buy it, Helen replies. It was given to her by her best friend, Bessie Black. Everybody reads *True Romance*. Bessie Black's father reads *True Romance*. There isn't a girl in Helen's class who doesn't read *True Romance*. Francis expresses his detestation of the magazine and then tells her that dinner is ready—although from the sounds downstairs it doesn't seem so. Helen follows him down the stairs. Julia has seated herself in the candlelight and spread a napkin over her lap. Neither Louisa nor Henry has come to the table. Little Toby is still howling, lying face down on the floor. Francis speaks to him gently: "Daddy was in a plane crash this afternoon, Toby. Don't you want to hear about it?" Toby goes on crying. "If you don't come to the table now, Toby," Francis says, "I'll have to send you to bed without any supper." The little boy rises, gives him a cutting look, flies up the stairs to his bedroom, and slams the door. "Oh, dear," Julia says, and starts to go after him. Francis says that she will spoil him. Julia says that Toby is ten pounds underweight and has to be encouraged to eat. Winter is coming, and he will spend the cold months in bed unless he has his dinner. Julia goes upstairs. Francis sits down at the table with Helen. Helen is suffering from the dismal feeling of having read too intently on a fine day, and she gives her father and the room a jaded look. She doesn't understand about the plane crash, because there wasn't a drop of rain in Shady Hill.

Julia returns with Toby, and they all sit down and are served. "Do I have to look at that big, fat slob?" Henry says, of Louisa. Everybody but Toby enters into this skirmish, and it rages up and down the table for five minutes. Toward the end, Henry puts his napkin over his head and, trying to eat that way, spills spinach all over his shirt. Francis asks Julia if the children couldn't have their dinner earlier. Julia's guns are loaded for this. She can't cook two dinners and lay two tables. She paints with lightning strokes that panorama of drudgery in which her youth, her beauty, and her wit have been lost. Francis says that he must be understood; he was nearly killed in an airplane crash, and he doesn't like to come home every night to a battlefield. Now Julia is deeply concerned. Her voice trembles. He doesn't come home every night to a battlefield. The accusation is stupid and mean. Everything was tranquil until he arrived. She stops speaking, puts down her knife and fork, and looks into her plate as if it is a gulf. She begins to cry. "Poor Mummy!" Toby says, and when Julia gets up from the table, drying her tears with a napkin, Toby goes to her side. "Poor Mummy," he says. "Poor Mummy!" And they climb the stairs together. The other children drift away from the battlefield, and Francis goes into the back garden for a cigarette and some air.

It was a pleasant garden, with walks and flower beds and places to sit. The sunset had nearly burned out, but there was still plenty of light. Put into a

---

5. That is, like escaping from combat to relative safety behind the lines.

thoughtful mood by the crash and the battle, Francis listened to the evening sounds of Shady Hill. "Varmints! Rascals!" old Mr. Nixon shouted to the squirrels in his bird-feeding station. "Avaunt and quit my sight!" A door slammed. Someone was cutting grass. Then Donald Goslin, who lived at the corner, began to play the "Moonlight Sonata."[6] He did this nearly every night. He threw the tempo out the window and played it *rubato*[7] from beginning to end, like an outpouring of tearful petulance, lonesomeness, and self-pity—of everything it was Beethoven's greatness not to know. The music rang up and down the street beneath the trees like an appeal for love, for tenderness, aimed at some lovely housemaid—some fresh-faced, homesick girl from Galway, looking at old snapshots in her third-floor room. "Here, Jupiter, here, Jupiter," Francis called to the Mercers' retriever. Jupiter crashed through the tomato vines with the remains of a felt hat in his mouth.

10   Jupiter was an anomaly. His retrieving instincts and his high spirits were out of place in Shady Hill. He was as black as coal, with a long, alert, intelligent, rakehell face. His eyes gleamed with mischief, and he held his head high. It was the fierce, heavily collared dog's head that appears in heraldry, in tapestry, and that used to appear on umbrella handles and walking sticks. Jupiter went where he pleased, ransacking wastebaskets, clotheslines, garbage pails, and shoe bags. He broke up garden parties and tennis matches, and got mixed up in the processional at Christ Church on Sunday, barking at the men in red dresses.[8] He crashed through old Mr. Nixon's rose garden two or three times a day, cutting a wide swath through the Condesa de Sastagos,[9] and as soon as Donald Goslin lighted his barbecue fire on Thursday nights, Jupiter would get the scent. Nothing the Goslins did could drive him away. Sticks and stones and rude commands only moved him to the edge of the terrace, where he remained, with his gallant and heraldic muzzle, waiting for Donald Goslin to turn his back and reach for the salt. Then he would spring onto the terrace, lift the steak lightly off the fire, and run away with the Goslins' dinner. Jupiter's days were numbered. The Wrightsons' German gardener or the Farquarsons' cook would soon poison him. Even old Mr. Nixon might put some arsenic in the garbage that Jupiter loved. "Here, Jupiter, Jupiter!" Francis called, but the dog pranced off, shaking the hat in his white teeth. Looking at the windows of his house, Francis saw that Julia had come down and was blowing out the candles.

Julia and Francis Weed went out a great deal. Julia was well liked and gregarious, and her love of parties sprang from a most natural dread of chaos and loneliness. She went through the morning mail with real anxiety, looking for invitations, and she usually found some, but she was insatiable, and if she had gone out seven nights a week, it would not have cured her of a reflective look— the look of someone who hears distant music—for she would always suppose that there was a more brilliant party somewhere else. Francis limited her to two

---

6. Beethoven's *Sonata Quasi una Fantasia* (1802), a famous and frequently sentimentalized piano composition.   7. With intentional deviations from strict tempo.   8. Probably the choir. 9. Rather uncommon yellow and red roses difficult to grow.

week-night parties, putting a flexible interpretation on Friday, and rode through the weekend like a dory in a gale. The day after the airplane crash, the Weeds were to have dinner with the Farquarsons.

Francis got home late from town, and Julia got the sitter while he dressed, and then hurried him out of the house. The party was small and pleasant, and Francis settled down to enjoy himself. A new maid passed the drinks. Her hair was dark, and her face was round and pale and seemed familiar to Francis. He had not developed his memory as a sentimental faculty. Wood smoke, lilac, and other such perfumes did not stir him, and his memory was something like his appendix—a vestigial repository. It was not his limitation at all to be unable to escape the past; it was perhaps his limitation that he had escaped it so successfully. He might have seen the maid at other parties, he might have seen her taking a walk on Sunday afternoons, but in either case he would not be searching his memory now. Her face was, in a wonderful way, a moon face—Norman or Irish—but it was not beautiful enough to account for his feeling that he had seen her before, in circumstances that he ought to be able to remember. He asked Nellie Farquarson who she was. Nellie said that the maid had come through an agency, and that her home was Trénon, in Normandy—a small place with a church and a restaurant that Nellie had once visited. While Nellie talked on about her travels abroad, Francis realized where he had seen the woman before. It had been at the end of the war. He had left a replacement depot with some other men and taken a three-day pass in Trénon. On their second day, they had walked out to a crossroads to see the public chastisement of a young woman who had lived with the German commandant during the Occupation.

It was a cool morning in the fall. The sky was overcast, and poured down onto the dirt crossroads a very discouraging light. They were on high land and could see how like one another the shapes of the clouds and the hills were as they stretched off toward the sea. The prisoner arrived sitting on a three-legged stool in a farm cart. She stood by the cart while the Mayor read the accusation and the sentence. Her head was bent and her face was set in that empty half smile behind which the whipped soul is suspended. When the Mayor was finished, she undid her hair and let it fall across her back. A little man with a gray mustache cut off her hair with shears and dropped it on the ground. Then, with a bowl of soapy water and a straight razor, he shaved her skull clean. A woman approached and began to undo the fastenings of her clothes, but the prisoner pushed her aside and undressed herself. When she pulled her chemise over her head and threw it on the ground, she was naked. The women jeered; the men were still. There was no change in the falseness or the plaintiveness of the prisoner's smile. The cold wind made her white skin rough and hardened the nipples of her breasts. The jeering ended gradually, put down by the recognition of their common humanity. One woman spat on her, but some inviolable grandeur in her nakedness lasted through the ordeal. When the crowd was quiet, she turned—she had begun to cry—and, with nothing on but a pair of worn black shoes and stockings, walked down the dirt road alone away from the village. The round white face had aged a little, but there was no question but that the maid who passed his cocktails and later served Francis his dinner was the woman who had been punished at the crossroads.

The war seemed now so distant and that world where the cost of partisanship had been death or torture so long ago. Francis had lost track of the men who had been with him in Vésey. He could not count on Julia's discretion. He could not tell anyone. And if he had told the story now, at the dinner table, it would have been a social as well as a human error. The people in the Farquarsons' living room seemed united in their tacit claim that there had been no past, no war—that there was no danger or trouble in the world. In the recorded history of human arrangements, this extraordinary meeting would have fallen into place, but the atmosphere of Shady Hill made the memory unseemly and impolite. The prisoner withdrew after passing the coffee, but the encounter left Francis feeling languid; it had opened his memory and his senses, and left them dilated. Julia went into the house. Francis stayed in the car to take the sitter home.

15   Expecting to see Mrs. Henlein, the old lady who usually stayed with the children, he was surprised when a young girl opened the door and came out onto the lighted stoop. She stayed in the light to count her textbooks. She was frowning and beautiful. Now, the world is full of beautiful young girls, but Francis saw here the difference between beauty and perfection. All those endearing flaws, moles, birthmarks, and healed wounds were missing, and he experienced in his consciousness that moment when music breaks glass, and felt a pang of recognition as strange, deep and wonderful as anything in his life. It hung from her frown, from an impalpable darkness in her face—a look that impressed him as a direct appeal for love. When she had counted her books, she came down the steps and opened the car door. In the light, he saw that her cheeks were wet. She got in and shut the door.

"You're new," Francis said.

"Yes. Mrs. Henlein is sick. I'm Anne Murchison."

"Did the children give you any trouble?"

"Oh, no, no." She turned and smiled at him unhappily in the dim dashboard light. Her light hair caught on the collar of her jacket, and she shook her head to set it loose.

20   "You've been crying."

"Yes."

"I hope it was nothing that happened in our house."

"No, no, it was nothing that happened in your house." Her voice was bleak. "It's no secret. Everybody in the village knows. Daddy's an alcoholic, and he just called me from some saloon and gave me a piece of his mind. He thinks I'm immoral. He called just before Mrs. Weed came back."

"I'm sorry."

25   "Oh, *Lord!*" She gasped and began to cry. She turned toward Francis, and he took her in his arms and let her cry on his shoulder. She shook in his embrace, and this movement accentuated his sense of the fineness of her flesh and bone. The layers of their clothing felt thin, and when her shuddering began to diminish, it was so much like a paroxysm of love that Francis lost his head

and pulled her roughly against him. She drew away. "I live on Belleview Avenue," she said. "You go down Lansing Street to the railroad bridge."

"All right." He started the car.

"You turn left at that traffic light. . . . Now you turn right here and go straight on toward the tracks."

The road Francis took brought him out of his own neighborhood, across the tracks, and toward the river, to a street where the near-poor lived, in houses whose peaked gables and trimmings of wooden lace conveyed the purest feelings of pride and romance, although the houses themselves could not have offered much privacy or comfort, they were all so small. The street was dark, and, stirred by the grace and beauty of the troubled girl, he seemed, in turning into it, to have come into the deepest part of some submerged memory. In the distance, he saw a porch light burning. It was the only one, and she said that the house with the light was where she lived. When he stopped the car, he could see beyond the porch light into a dimly lighted hallway with an old-fashioned clothes tree. "Well, here we are," he said, conscious that a young man would have said something different.

She did not move her hands from the books, where they were folded, and she turned and faced him. There were tears of lust in his eyes. Determinedly— not sadly—he opened the door on his side and walked around to open hers. He took her free hand, letting his fingers in between hers, climbed at her side the two concrete steps, and went up a narrow walk through a front garden where dahlias, marigolds, and roses—things that had withstood the light frosts—still bloomed, and made a bittersweet smell in the night air. At the steps, she freed her hand and then turned and kissed him swiftly. Then she crossed the porch and shut the door. The porch light went out, then the light in the hall. A second later, a light went on upstairs at the side of the house, shining into a tree that was still covered with leaves. It took her only a few minutes to undress and get into bed, and then the house was dark.

Julia was asleep when Francis got home. He opened a second window and got into bed to shut his eyes on that night, but as soon as they were shut—as soon as he had dropped off to sleep—the girl entered his mind, moving with perfect freedom through its shut doors and filling chamber after chamber with her light, her perfume, and the music of her voice. He was crossing the Atlantic with her on the old *Mauretania*[1] and, later, living with her in Paris. When he woke from his dream, he got up and smoked a cigarette at the open window. Getting back into bed, he cast around in his mind for something he desired to do that would injure no one, and he thought of skiing. Up through the dimness in his mind rose the image of a mountain deep in snow. It was late in the day. Wherever his eyes looked, he saw broad and heartening things. Over his shoulder, there was a snow-filled valley, rising into wooded hills where the trees dimmed the whiteness like a sparse coat of hair. The cold deadened all sound but the loud, iron clanking of the lift machinery. The light on the trails was

30

1. The original *Mauretania* (1907–1935), sister ship of the *Lusitania*, which was sunk by the Germans in 1915, was the most famous transatlantic liner of its day.

blue, and it was harder than it had been a minute or two earlier to pick the turns, harder to judge—now that the snow was all deep blue—the crust, the ice, the bare spots, and the deep piles of dry powder. Down the mountain he swung, matching his speed against the contours of a slope that had been formed in the first ice age, seeking with ardor some simplicity of feeling and circumstance. Night fell then, and he drank a Martini with some old friend in a dirty country bar.

In the morning, Francis' snow-covered mountain was gone, and he was left with his vivid memories of Paris and the *Mauretania*. He had been bitten gravely. He washed his body, shaved his jaws, drank his coffee, and missed the seventy-thirty-one. The train pulled out just as he brought his car to the station, and the longing he felt for the coaches as they drew stubbornly away from him reminded him of the humors of love. He waited for the eight-two, on what was now an empty platform. It was a clear morning; the morning seemed thrown like a gleaming bridge of light over his mixed affairs. His spirits were feverish and high. The image of the girl seemed to put him into a relationship to the world that was mysterious and enthralling. Cars were beginning to fill up the parking lot, and he noticed that those that had driven down from the high land above Shady Hill were white with hoarfrost. This first clear sign of autumn thrilled him. An express train—a night train from Buffalo or Albany—came down the tracks between the platforms, and he saw that the roofs of the foremost cars were covered with a skin of ice. Struck by the miraculous physicalness of everything, he smiled at the passengers in the dining car, who could be seen eating eggs and wiping their mouths with napkins as they traveled. The sleeping-car compartments, with their soiled bed linen, trailed through the fresh morning like a string of rooming-house windows. Then he saw an extraordinary thing; at one of the bedroom windows sat an unclothed woman of exceptional beauty, combing her golden hair. She passed like an apparition through Shady Hill, combing and combing her hair, and Francis followed her with his eyes until she was out of sight. Then old Mrs. Wrightson joined him on the platform and began to talk.

"Well, I guess you must be surprised to see me here the third morning in a row," she said, "but because of my window curtains I'm becoming a regular commuter. The curtains I bought on Monday I returned on Tuesday, and the curtains I bought Tuesday I'm returning today. On Monday, I got exactly what I wanted—it's a wool tapestry with roses and birds—but when I got them home, I found they were the wrong length. Well, I exchanged them yesterday, and when I got them home, I found they were still the wrong length. Now I'm praying to high heaven that the decorator will have them in the right length, because you know my house, you *know* my living-room windows, and you can imagine what a problem they present. I don't know what to do with them."

"I know what to do with them," Francis said.

"What?"

"Paint them black on the inside, and shut up."

There was a gasp from Mrs. Wrightson, and Francis looked down at her to be sure that she knew he meant to be rude. She turned and walked away from

35

him, so damaged in spirit that she limped. A wonderful feeling enveloped him, as if light were being shaken about him, and he thought again of Venus combing and combing her hair as she drifted through the Bronx. The realization of how many years had passed since he had enjoyed being deliberately impolite sobered him. Among his friends and neighbors, there were brilliant and gifted people—he saw that—but many of them, also, were bores and fools, and he had made the mistake of listening to them all with equal attention. He had confused a lack of discrimination with Christian love, and the confusion seemed general and destructive. He was grateful to the girl for this bracing sensation of independence. Birds were singing—cardinals and the last of the robins. The sky shone like enamel. Even the smell of ink from his morning paper honed his appetite for life, and the world that was spread out around him was plainly a paradise.

If Francis had believed in some hierarchy of love—in spirits armed with hunting bows, in the capriciousness of Venus and Eros[2]—or even in magical potions, philters, and stews, in scapulae and quarters of the moon,[3] it might have explained his susceptibility and his feverish high spirits. The autumnal loves of middle age are well publicized, and he guessed that he was face to face with one of these, but there was not a trace of autumn in what he felt. He wanted to sport in the green woods, scratch where he itched, and drink from the same cup.

His secretary, Miss Rainey, was late that morning—she went to a psychiatrist three mornings a week—and when she came in, Francis wondered what advice a psychiatrist would have for him. But the girl promised to bring back into his life something like the sound of music. The realization that this music might lead him straight to a trial for statutory rape at the country courthouse collapsed his happiness. The photograph of his four children laughing into the camera on the beach at Gay Head reproached him. On the letterhead of his firm there was a drawing of the Laocoön,[4] and the figure of the priest and his sons in the coils of the snake appeared to him to have the deepest meaning.

He had lunch with Pinky Trabert. At a conversational level, the mores of his friends were robust and elastic, but he knew that the moral card house would come down on them all—on Julia and the children as well—if he got caught taking advantage of a baby-sitter. Looking back over the recent history of Shady Hill for some precedent, he found there was none. There was no turpitude; there had not been a divorce since he lived there; there had not even been a breath of scandal. Things seemed arranged with more propriety even than in the Kingdom of Heaven. After leaving Pinky, Francis went to a jeweler's and bought the girl a bracelet. How happy this clandestine purchase made him, how stuffy and comical the jeweler's clerks seemed, how sweet the women who passed at his back smelled! On Fifth Avenue, passing Atlas with his shoulders

---

2. The Roman name for the goddess of love (Greek *Aphrodite*) and the Greek name for her son (Roman *Cupid*). 3. Love-inducing and predictive magic. *Scapulae*: shoulderblades or bones of the back. 4. Famous Greek statue, described here, now in the Vatican museum; the "meaning" for Weed seems to reside in the physical struggle, not in the legend (in which the priest and his sons were punished for warning the Trojans about the wooden horse).

bent under the weight of the world,[5] Francis thought of the strenuousness of containing his physicalness within the patterns he had chosen.

40   He did not know when he would see the girl next. He had the bracelet in his inside pocket when he got home. Opening the door of his house, he found her in the hall. Her back was to him, and she turned when she heard the door close. Her smile was open and loving. Her perfection stunned him like a fine day—a day after a thunderstorm. He seized her and covered her lips with his, and she struggled but she did not have to struggle for long, because just then little Gertrude Flannery appeared from somewhere and said, "Oh, Mr. Weed . . ."

Gertrude was a stray. She had been born with a taste for exploration, and she did not have it in her to center her life with her affectionate parents. People who did not know the Flannerys concluded from Gertrude's behavior that she was the child of a bitterly divided family, where drunken quarrels were the rule. This was not true. The fact that little Gertrude's clothing was ragged and thin was her own triumph over her mother's struggle to dress her warmly and neatly. Garrulous, skinny, and unwashed, she drifted from house to house around the Blenhollow neighborhood, forming and breaking alliances based on an attachment to babies, animals, children her own age, adolescents, and sometimes adults. Opening your front door in the morning, you would find Gertrude sitting on your stoop. Going into the bathroom to shave, you would find Gertrude using the toilet. Looking into your son's crib, you would find it empty, and, looking further, you would find that Gertrude had pushed him in his baby carriage into the next village. She was helpful, pervasive, honest, hungry, and loyal. She never went home of her own choice. When the time to go arrived, she was indifferent to all its signs. "Go home, Gertrude," people could be heard saying in one house or another, night after night. "Go home, Gertrude. It's time for you to go home now, Gertrude." "You had better go home and get your supper, Gertrude." "I told you to go home twenty minutes ago, Gertrude." "Your mother will be worrying about you, Gertrude." "Go home, Gertrude, go home."

There are times when the lines around the human eye seem like shelves of eroded stone and when the staring eye itself strikes us with such a wilderness of animal feeling that we are at a loss. The look Francis gave the little girl was ugly and queer, and it frightened her. He reached into his pockets—his hands were shaking—and took out a quarter. "Go home, Gertrude, go home, and don't tell anyone, Gertrude. Don't—" He choked and ran into the living room as Julia called down to him from upstairs to hurry and dress.

The thought that he would drive Anne Murchison home later that night ran like a golden thread through the events of the party that Francis and Julia went to, and he laughed uproariously at dull jokes, dried a tear when Mabel Mercer told him about the death of her kitten, and stretched, yawned, sighed, and grunted like any other man with a rendezvous at the back of his mind. The bracelet was in his pocket. As he sat talking, the smell of grass was in his nose,

5. In Greek legend the Titan Atlas supported the heavens on his shoulders but has come to be depicted as bearing the globe; the statue is at Rockefeller Center.

and he was wondering where he would park the car. Nobody lived in the old Parker mansion, and the driveway was used as a lovers' lane. Townsend Street was a dead end, and he could park there, beyond the last house. The old lane that used to connect Elm Street to the riverbanks was overgrown, but he had walked there with his children, and he could drive his car deep enough into the brushwoods to be concealed.

The Weeds were the last to leave the party, and their host and hostess spoke of their own married happiness while they all four stood in the hallway saying good night. "She's my girl," their host said, squeezing his wife. "She's my blue sky. After sixteen years, I still bite her shoulders. She makes me feel like Hannibal crossing the Alps.[6]"

The Weeds drove home in silence. Francis brought the car up the driveway and sat still, with the motor running. "You can put the car in the garage," Julia said as she got out. "I told the Murchison girl she could leave at eleven. Someone drove her home." She shut the door, and Francis sat in the dark. He would be spared nothing then, it seemed, that a fool was not spared: ravening lewdness, jealousy, this hurt to his feelings that put tears in his eyes, even scorn—for he could see clearly the image he now presented, his arms spread over the steering wheel and his head buried in them for love.

Francis had been a dedicated Boy Scout when he was young, and, remembering the precepts of his youth, he left his office early the next afternoon and played some round-robin squash, but, with his body toned up by exercise and a shower, he realized that he might better have stayed at his desk. It was a frosty night when he got home. The air smelled sharply of change. When he stepped into the house, he sensed an unusual stir. The children were in their best clothes, and when Julia came down, she was wearing a lavender dress and her diamond sunburst. She explained the stir: Mr. Hubber was coming at seven to take their photograph for the Christmas card. She had put out Francis' blue suit and a tie with some color in it, because the picture was going to be in color this year. Julia was lighthearted at the thought of being photographed for Christmas. It was the kind of ceremony she enjoyed.

Francis went upstairs to change his clothes. He was tired from the day's work and tired with longing, and sitting on the edge of the bed had the effect of deepening his weariness. He thought of Anne Murchison, and the physical need to express himself, instead of being restrained by the pink lamps of Julia's dressing table, engulfed him. He went to Julia's desk, took a piece of writing paper, and began to write on it. "Dear Anne, I love you, I love you, I love you . . ." No one would see the letter, and he used no restraint. He used phrases like "heavenly bliss," and "love nest." He salivated, sighed, and trembled. When Julia called him to come down, the abyss between his fantasy and the practical world opened so wide that he felt it affected the muscles of his heart.

Julia and the children were on the stoop, and the photographer and his

45

6. The Carthaginian general (274–183 B.C.) attacked the Romans from the rear by crossing the Alps, considered impregnable, with the use of elephants.

assistant had set up a double battery of floodlights to show the family and the architectural beauty of the entrance to their house. People who had come home on a late train slowed their cars to see the Weeds being photographed for their Christmas card. A few waved and called to the family. It took half an hour of smiling and wetting their lips before Mr. Hubber was satisfied. The heat of the lights made an unfresh smell in the frosty air, and when they were turned off, they lingered on the retina of Francis' eyes.

Later that night, while Francis and Julia were drinking their coffee in the living room, the doorbell rang. Julia answered the door and let in Clayton Thomas. He had come to pay for some theatre tickets that she had given his mother some time ago, and that Helen Thomas had scrupulously insisted on paying for, though Julia had asked her not to. Julia invited him in to have a cup of coffee. "I won't have any coffee," Clayton said, "but I will come in for a minute." He followed her into the living room, said good evening to Francis, and sat awkwardly in a chair.

50   Clayton's father had been killed in the war, and the young man's father-lessness surrounded him like an element. This may have been conspicuous in Shady Hill because the Thomases were the only family that lacked a piece; all the other marriages were intact and productive. Clayton was in his second or third year of college, and he and his mother lived alone in a large house, which she hoped to sell. Clayton had once made some trouble. Years ago, he had stolen some money and run away; he had got to California before they caught up with him. He was tall and homely, wore hornrimmed glasses, and spoke in a deep voice.

"When do you go back to college, Clayton?" Francis asked.

"I'm not going back," Clayton said. "Mother doesn't have the money, and there's no sense in all this pretense. I'm going to get a job, and if we sell the house, we'll take an apartment in New York."

"Won't you miss Shady Hill?" Julia asked.

"No," Clayton said. "I don't like it."

55   "Why not?" Francis asked.

"Well, there's a lot here I don't approve of," Clayton said gravely. "Things like the club dances. Last Saturday night, I looked in toward the end and saw Mr. Granner trying to put Mrs. Minot into the trophy case. They were both drunk. I disapprove of so much drinking."

"It was Saturday night," Francis said.

"And all the dovecotes are phony," Clayton said. "And the way people clutter up their lives. I've thought about it a lot, and what seems to me to be really wrong with Shady Hill is that it doesn't have any future. So much energy is spent in perpetuating the place—in keeping out undesirables, and so forth—that the only idea of the future anyone has is just more and more commuting trains and more parties. I don't think that's healthy. I think people ought to be able to dream big dreams about the future. I think people ought to be able to dream great dreams."

"It's too bad you couldn't continue with college," Julia said.

60   "I want to go to divinity school," Clayton said.

"What's your church?" Francis asked.

"Unitarian, Theosophist, Transcendentalist, Humanist,"[7] Clayton said.

"Wasn't Emerson a transcendentalist?" Julia asked.

"I mean the English transcendentalists," Clayton said. "All the American transcendentalists were goops."

"What kind of job do you expect to get?" Francis asked.

"Well, I'd like to work for a publisher," Clayton said, "but everyone tells me there's nothing doing. But it's the kind of thing I'm interested in. I'm writing a long verse play about good and evil. Uncle Charlie might get me into a bank, and that would be good for me. I need the discipline. I have a long way to go in forming my character. I have some terrible habits. I talk too much. I think I ought to take vows of silence. I ought to try not to speak for a week, and discipline myself. I've thought of making a retreat at one of the Episcopalian monasteries, but I don't like Trinitarianism."

"Do you have any girl friends?" Francis asked.

"I'm engaged to be married," Clayton said. "Of course, I'm not old enough or rich enough to have my engagement observed or respected or anything, but I bought a simulated emerald for Anne Murchison with the money I made cutting lawns this summer. We're going to be married as soon as she finishes school."

Francis recoiled at the mention of the girl's name. Then a dingy light seemed to emanate from his spirit, showing everything—Julia, the boy, the chairs—in their true colorlessness. It was like a bitter turn of the weather.

"We're going to have a large family," Clayton said. "Her father's a terrible rummy, and I've had my hard times, and we want to have lots of children. Oh, she's wonderful, Mr. and Mrs. Weed, and we have so much in common. We like all the same things. We sent out the same Christmas card last year without planning it, and we both have an allergy to tomatoes, and our eyebrows grow together in the middle. Well, goodnight."

Julia went to the door with him. When she returned, Francis said that Clayton was lazy, irresponsible, affected, and smelly. Julia said that Francis seemed to be getting intolerant; the Thomas boy was young and should be given a chance. Julia had noticed other cases where Francis had been short-tempered. "Mrs. Wrightson has asked everyone in Shady Hill to her anniversary party but us," she said.

"I'm sorry, Julia."

"Do you know why they didn't ask us?"

"Why?"

"Because you insulted Mrs. Wrightson."

"Then you know about it?"

"June Masterson told me. She was standing behind you."

Julia walked in front of the sofa with a small step that expressed, Francis knew, a feeling of anger.

7. All are deviations from orthodox Christianity and tend to be more man- than God-oriented, though their differences hardly seem reconcilable; the American transcendentalists (see below) tended to change the emphasis from the study of thought to belief in "intuition."

"I did insult Mrs. Wrightson, Julia, and I meant to. I've never liked her parties, and I'm glad she's dropped us."

"What about Helen?"

"How does Helen come into this?"

"Mrs. Wrightson's the one who decides who goes to the assemblies."

"You mean she can keep Helen from going to the dances?"

"Yes."

"I hadn't thought of that."

"Oh. I knew you hadn't thought of it," Julia cried, thrusting hiltdeep into this chink of his armor. "And it makes me furious to see this kind of stupid thoughtlessness wreck everyone's happiness."

"I don't think I've wrecked anyone's happiness."

"Mrs. Wrightson runs Shady Hill and has run it for the last forty years. I don't know what makes you think that in a community like this you can indulge every impulse you have to be insulting, vulgar, and offensive."

"I have very good manners," Francis said, trying to give the evening a turn toward the light.

"Damn you, Francis Weed!" Julia cried, and the spit of her words struck him in the face. "I've worked hard for the social position we enjoy in this place, and I won't stand by and see you wreck it. You must have understood when you settled here that you couldn't expect to live like a bear in a cave."

"I've got to express my likes and dislikes."

"You can conceal your dislikes. You don't have to meet everything head on, like a child. Unless you're anxious to be a social leper. It's no accident that we get asked out a great deal! It's no accident that Helen has so many friends. How would you like to spend your Saturday nights at the movies? How would you like to spend your Sunday raking up dead leaves? How would you like it if your daughter spent the assembly nights sitting at her window, listening to the music from the club? How would you like it—" He did something then that was, after all, not so unaccountable, since her words seemed to raise up between them a wall so deadening that he gagged. He struck her full in the face. She staggered and then, a moment later, seemed composed. She went up the stairs to their room. She didn't slam the door. When Francis followed, a few minutes later, he found her packing a suitcase.

"Julia, I'm very sorry."

"It doesn't matter," she said. She was crying.

"Where do you think you're going?"

"I don't know. I just looked at a timetable. There's an eleven-sixteen into New York. I'll take that."

"You can't go, Julia."

"I can't stay. I know that."

"I'm sorry about Mrs. Wrightson, Julia, and I'm—"

"It doesn't matter about Mrs. Wrightson. That isn't the trouble."

"What is the trouble?"

"You don't love me."

"I do love you, Julia."

"No, you don't."

"Julia, I do love you, and I would like to be as we were—sweet and bawdy   105
and dark—but now there are so many people."

"You hate me."

"I don't hate you, Julia."

"You have no idea of how much you hate me. I think it's subconscious. You
don't realize the cruel things you've done."

"What cruel things, Julia?"

"The cruel acts your subconscious drives you to in order to express your   110
hatred of me."

"What, Julia?"

"I've never complained."

"Tell me."

"You don't know what you're doing."

"Tell me."   115

"Your clothes."

"What do you mean?"

"I mean the way you leave your dirty clothes around in order to express your
subconscious hatred of me."

"I don't understand."

"I mean your dirty socks and your dirty pajamas and your dirty underwear   120
and your dirty shirts!" She rose from kneeling by the suitcase and faced him,
her eyes blazing and her voice ringing with emotion. "I'm talking about the fact
that you've never learned to hang up anything. You just leave your clothes all
over the floor where they drop, in order to humiliate me. You do it on purpose!"
She fell on the bed, sobbing.

"Julia, darling!" he said, but when she felt his hand on her shoulder she got
up.

"Leave me alone," she said. "I have to go." She brushed past him to the
closet and came back with a dress. "I'm not taking any of the things you've given
me," she said. "I'm leaving my pearls and the fur jacket."

"Oh, Julia!" Her figure, so helpless in its self-deceptions, bent over the suitcase made him nearly sick with pity. She did not understand how desolate her
life would be without him. She didn't understand the hours that working women
have to keep. She didn't understand that most of her friendships existed within
the framework of their marriage, and that without this she would find herself
alone. She didn't understand about travel, about hotels, about money. "Julia, I
can't let you go! What you don't understand, Julia, is that you've come to be
dependent on me."

She tossed her head back and covered her face with her hands. "Did you say
that *I* was dependent on *you*?" she asked. "Is that what you said? And who is it
that tells you what time to get up in the morning and when to go to bed at
night? Who is it that prepares your meals and picks up your dirty clothes and
invites your friends to dinner? If it weren't for me, your neckties would be greasy
and your clothing would be full of moth holes. You were alone when I met you,
Francis Weed, and you'll be alone when I leave. When Mother asked you for a

list to send out invitations to our wedding, how many names did you have to give her? Fourteen!"

125

"Cleveland wasn't my home, Julia."

"And how many of your friends came to the church? Two!"

"Cleveland wasn't my home, Julia."

"Since I'm not taking the fur jacket," she said quietly, "you'd better put it back into storage. There's an insurance policy on the pearls that comes due in January. The name of the laundry and maid's telephone number—all those things are in my desk. I hope you won't drink too much, Francis. I hope that nothing bad will happen to you. If you do get into serious trouble, you can call me."

"Oh, my darling, I can't let you go!" Francis said. "I can't let you go, Julia!" He took her in his arms.

130

"I guess I'd better stay and take care of you for a little while longer," she said.

Riding to work in the morning, Francis saw the girl walk down the aisle of the coach. He was surprised; he hadn't realized that the school she went to was in the city, but she was carrying books, she seemed to be going to school. His surprise delayed his reaction, but then he got up clumsily and stepped into the aisle. Several people had come between them, but he could see her ahead of him, waiting for someone to open the car door, and then, as the train swerved, putting out her hand to support herself as she crossed the platform into the next car. He followed her through that car and halfway through another before calling her name—"Anne! Anne!"—but she didn't turn. He followed her into still another car, and she sat down in an aisle seat. Coming up to her, all his feelings warm and bent in her direction, he put his hand on the back of her seat—even this touch warmed him—and leaning down to speak to her, he saw that it was not Anne. It was an older woman wearing glasses. He went on deliberately into another car, his face red with embarrassment and the much deeper feeling of having his good sense challenged; for if he couldn't tell one person from another, what evidence was there that his life with Julia and the children had as much reality as his dreams of iniquity in Paris or the litter, the grass smell, and the cave-shaped trees in Lovers' Lane.

Late that afternoon, Julia called to remind Francis that they were going out for dinner. A few minutes later, Trace Bearden called. "Look, fellar," Trace said. "I'm calling for Mrs. Thomas. You know? Clayton, that boy of hers, doesn't seem able to get a job, and I wondered if you could help. If you'd call Charlie Bell—I know he's indebted to you—and say a good word for the kid, I think Charlie would—"

"Trace, I hate to say this," Francis said, "but I don't feel that I can do anything for that boy. The kid's worthless. I know it's a harsh thing to say, but it's a fact. Any kindness done for him would backfire in everybody's face. He's just a worthless kid, Trace, and there's nothing else to be done about it. Even if we got him a job, he wouldn't be able to keep it for a week. I know that to be a fact. It's an awful thing, Trace, and I know it is, but instead of recommending that kid, I'd feel obligated to warn people against him—people who knew his father and would naturally want to step in and do something. I'd feel obliged to warn them. He's a thief . . ."

The moment this conversation was finished, Miss Rainey came in and stood by his desk. "I'm not going to be able to work for you any more, Mr. Weed," she said. "I can stay until the seventeenth if you need me, but I've been offered a whirlwind of a job, and I'd like to leave as soon as possible."

She went out, leaving him to face alone the wickedness of what he had done to the Thomas boy. His children in their photograph laughed and laughed, glazed with all the bright colors of summer, and he remembered that they had met a bagpiper on the beach that day and he had paid the piper a dollar to play them a battle song of the Black Watch.[8] The girl would be at the house when he got home. He would spend another evening among his kind neighbors, picking and choosing dead-end streets, cart tracks, and the driveways of abandoned houses. There was nothing to mitigate his feeling—nothing that laughter or a game of softball with the children would change—and, thinking back over the plane crash, the Farquarsons' new maid, and Anne Murchison's difficulties with her drunken father, he wondered how he could have avoided arriving at just where he was. He was in trouble. He had been lost once in his life, coming back from a trout stream in the north woods, and he had now the same bleak realization that no amount of cheerfulness or hopefulness or valor or perseverance could help him find, in the gathering dark, the path that he'd lost. He smelled the forest. The feeling of bleakness was intolerable, and he saw clearly that he had reached the point where he would have to make a choice.

He could go to a psychiatrist, like Miss Rainey; he could go to church and confess his lusts; he could go to a Danish-massage parlor[9] in the West Seventies that had been recommended by a salesman; he could rape the girl or trust that he would somehow be prevented from doing this; or he could get drunk. It was his life, his boat, and, like every other man, he was made to be the father of thousands, and what harm could there be in a tryst that would make them both feel more kindly toward the world? This was the wrong train of thought, and he came back to the first, the psychiatrist. He had the telephone number of Miss Rainey's doctor, and he called and asked for an immediate appointment. He was insistent with the doctor's secretary—it was his manner in business—and when she said that the doctor's schedule was full for the next few weeks, Francis demanded an appointment that day and was told to come at five.

The psychiatrist's office was in a building that was used mostly by doctors and dentists, and the hallways were filled with the candy smell of mouthwash and memories of pain. Francis' character had been formed upon a series of private resolves—resolves about cleanliness, about going off the high diving board or repeating any other feat that challenged his courage, about punctuality, honesty, and virtue. To abdicate the perfect loneliness in which he had made his most vital decisions shattered his concept of character and left him now in a

135

8. Originally a British Highland regiment that became a line regiment and distinguished itself in battle.   9. Sometimes fronts for houses of prostitution.

condition that felt like shock. He was stupefied. The scene for his *miserere mei Deus*[1] was, like the waiting room of so many doctor's offices, a crude token gesture toward the sweets of domestic bliss: a place arranged with antiques, coffee tables, potted plants, and etchings of snow-covered bridges and geese in flight, although there were no children, no marriage bed, no stove, even, in this travesty of a house, where no one had ever spent the night and where the curtained windows looked straight onto a dark air shaft. Francis gave his name and address to a secretary and then saw, at the side of the room, a policeman moving toward him. "Hold it, hold it," the policeman said. "Don't move. Keep your hands where they are."

"I think it's all right, Officer," the secretary began. "I think it will be—"

"Let's make sure," the policeman said, and he began to slap Francis' clothes, looking for what—pistols, knives, an icepick? Finding nothing, he went off and the secretary began a nervous apology: "When you called on the telephone, Mr. Weed, you seemed very excited, and one of the doctor's patients has been threatening his life, and we have to be careful. If you want to go in now?" Francis pushed open a door connected to an electrical chime, and in the doctor's lair sat down heavily, blew his nose into a handkerchief, searched in his pockets for cigarettes, for matches, for something, and said hoarsely, with tears in his eyes, "I'm in love, Dr. Herzog."

140

It is a week or ten days later in Shady Hill. The seven-fourteen has come and gone, and here and there dinner is finished and the dishes are in the dishwashing machine. The village hangs, morally and economically, from a thread; but it hangs by its thread in the evening light. Donald Goslin has begun to worry the "Moonlight Sonata" again. *Marcato ma sempre pianissimo!*[2] He seems to be wringing out a wet bath towel, but the housemaid does not heed him. She is writing a letter to Arthur Godfrey.[3] In the cellar of his house, Francis Weed is building a coffee table. Dr. Herzog recommends woodwork as a therapy, and Francis finds some true consolation in the simple arithmetic involved and in the holy smell of new wood. Francis is happy. Upstairs, little Toby is crying, because he is tired. He puts off his cowboy hat, gloves, and fringed jacket, unbuckles the belt studded with gold and rubies, the silver bullets and holsters, slips off his suspenders, his checked shirt, and Levi's, and sits on the edge of his bed to pull off his high boots. Leaving this equipment in a heap, he goes to the closet and takes his space suit off a nail. It is a struggle for him to get into the long tights, but he succeeds. He loops the magic cape over his shoulders and, climbing onto the footboard of his bed, he spreads his arms and flies the short distance to the floor, landing with a thump that is audible to everyone in the house but himself.

"Go home, Gertrude, go home," Mrs. Masterson says. "I told you to go home an hour ago, Gertrude. It's way past your suppertime, and your mother will be

---

1. Have mercy upon me, O God; first words of 51st Psalm.   2. Stressed but always very softly.   3. At the time of the story, host of a daytime radio program especially popular with housewives.

worried. Go home!" A door on the Babcocks' terrace flies open, and out comes Mrs. Babcock without any clothes on, pursued by a naked husband. (Their children are away at boarding school, and their terrace is screened by a hedge.) Over the terrace they go and in at the kitchen door, as passionate and handsome a nymph and satyr as you will find on any wall in Venice. Cutting the last of the roses in her garden, Julia hears old Mr. Nixon shouting at the squirrels in his bird-feeding station. "Rapscallions! Varmints! Avaunt and quit my sight!" A miserable cat wanders into the garden, sunk in spiritual and physical discomfort. Tied to its head is a small straw hat—a doll's hat—and it is securely buttoned into a doll's dress, from the skirts of which protrudes its long, hairy tail. As it walks, it shakes its feet, as if it had fallen into water.

"Here, pussy, pussy, pussy!" Julia calls.

"Here, pussy, here, poor pussy!" But the cat gives her a skeptical look and stumbles away in its skirts. The last to come is Jupiter. He prances through the tomato vines, holding in his generous mouth the remains of an evening slipper. Then it is dark; it is a night where kings in golden suits ride elephants over the mountains.[4]

1958

JAMES BALDWIN

Sonny's Blues

I read about it in the paper, in the subway, on my way to work. I read it, and I couldn't believe it, and I read it again. Then perhaps I just stared at it, at the newsprint spelling out his name, spelling out the story. I stared at it in the swinging lights of the subway car, and in the faces and bodies of the people, and in my own face, trapped in the darkness which roared outside.

It was not to be believed and I kept telling myself that, as I walked from the subway station to the high school. And at the same time I couldn't doubt it. I was scared, scared for Sonny. He became real to me again. A great block of ice got settled in my belly and kept melting there slowly all day long, while I taught my classes algebra. It was a special kind of ice. It kept melting, sending trickles of ice water all up and down my veins, but it never got less. Sometimes it hardened and seemed to expand until I felt my guts were going to come spilling out or that I was going to choke or scream. This would always be at a moment when I was remembering some specific thing Sonny had once said or done.

When he was about as old as the boys in my classes his face had been bright and open, there was a lot of copper in it; and he'd had wonderfully direct brown

4. See Sinclair Lewis, *Main Street* (1920), in which the protagonist finds the small town of Gopher Prairie stifling and leaves with her son for Washington, D.C., where, she tells him, " 'We're going to find elephants with golden howdahs from which peep young maharanees with necklaces of rubies. . . .' "

eyes, and great gentleness and privacy. I wondered what he looked like now. He had been picked up, the evening before, in a raid on an apartment downtown, for peddling and using heroin.

I couldn't believe it: but what I mean by that is that I couldn't find any room for it anywhere inside me. I had kept it outside me for a long time. I hadn't wanted to know. I had had suspicions, but I didn't name them, I kept putting them away. I told myself that Sonny was wild, but he wasn't crazy. And he'd always been a good boy, he hadn't ever turned hard or evil or disrespectful, the way kids can, so quick, so quick, especially in Harlem. I didn't want to believe that I'd ever see my brother going down, coming to nothing, all that light in his face gone out, in the condition I'd already seen so many others. Yet it had happened and here I was, talking about algebra to a lot of boys who might, every one of them for all I knew, be popping off needles every time they went to the head.[1] Maybe it did more for them than algebra could.

I was sure that the first time Sonny had ever had horse,[2] he couldn't have been much older than these boys were now. These boys, now, were living as we'd been living then, they were growing up with a rush and their heads bumped abruptly against the low ceiling of their actual possibilities. They were filled with rage. All they really knew were two darknesses, the darkness of their lives, which was now closing in on them, and the darkness of the movies, which had blinded them to that other darkness, and in which they now, vindictively, dreamed, at once more together than they were at any other time, and more alone.

When the last bell rang, the last class ended, I let out my breath. It seemed I'd been holding it for all that time. My clothes were wet—I may have looked as though I'd been sitting in a steam bath, all dressed up, all afternoon. I sat alone in the classroom a long time. I listened to the boys outside, downstairs, shouting and cursing and laughing. Their laughter struck me for perhaps the first time. It was not the joyous laughter which—God knows why—one associates with children. It was mocking and insular, its intent was to denigrate. It was disenchanted, and in this, also, lay the authority of their curses. Perhaps I was listening to them because I was thinking about my brother and in them I heard my brother. And myself.

One boy was whistling a tune, at once very complicated and very simple, it seemed to be pouring out of him as though he were a bird, and it sounded very cool and moving through all that harsh, bright air, only just holding its own through all those other sounds.

I stood up and walked over to the window and looked down into the court-yard. It was the beginning of the spring and the sap was rising in the boys. A teacher passed through them every now and again, quickly, as though he or she couldn't wait to get out of that courtyard, to get those boys out of their sight and off their minds. I started collecting my stuff. I thought I'd better get home and talk to Isabel.

The courtyard was almost deserted by the time I got downstairs. I saw this

1. Lavatory.   2. Heroin.

boy standing in the shadow of a doorway, looking just like Sonny. I almost called his name. Then I saw that it wasn't Sonny, but somebody we used to know, a boy from around our block. He'd been Sonny's friend. He'd never been mine, having been too young for me, and, anyway, I'd never liked him. And now, even though he was a grown-up man, he still hung around that block, still spent hours on the street corners, was always high and raggy. I used to run into him from time to time and he'd often work around to asking me for a quarter or fifty cents. He always had some real good excuse, too, and I always gave it to him. I don't know why.

But now, abruptly, I hated him. I couldn't stand the way he looked at me, partly like a dog, partly like a cunning child. I wanted to ask him what the hell he was doing in the school courtyard.

He sort of shuffled over to me, and he said, "I see you got the papers. So you already know about it."

"You mean about Sonny? Yes, I already know about it. How come they didn't get you?"

He grinned. It made him repulsive and it also brought to mind what he'd looked like as a kid. "I wasn't there. I stay away from them people."

"Good for you." I offered him a cigarette and I watched him through the smoke. "You come all the way down here just to tell me about Sonny?"

"That's right." He was sort of shaking his head and his eyes looked strange, as though they were about to cross. The bright sun deadened his damp dark brown skin and it made his eyes look yellow and showed up the dirt in his kinked hair. He smelled funky. I moved a little away from him and I said, "Well, thanks. But I already know about it and I got to get home."

"I'll walk you a little ways," he said. We started walking. There were a couple of kids still loitering in the courtyard and one of them said goodnight to me and looked strangely at the boy beside me.

"What're you going to do?" he asked me. "I mean, about Sonny?"

"Look. I haven't seen Sonny for over a year, I'm not sure I'm going to do anything. Anyway, what the hell *can* I do?"

"That's right," he said quickly, "ain't nothing you can do. Can't much help old Sonny no more, I guess."

It was what I was thinking and so it seemed to me he had no right to say it.

"I'm surprised at Sonny, though," he went on—he had a funny way of talking, he looked straight ahead as though he were talking to himself—"I thought Sonny was a smart boy, I thought he was too smart to get hung."

"I guess he thought so too," I said sharply, "and that's how he got hung. And how about you? You're pretty goddamn smart, I bet."

Then he looked directly at me, just for a minute. "I ain't smart," he said. "If I was smart, I'd have reached for a pistol a long time ago."

"Look. Don't tell *me* your sad story, if it was up to me, I'd give you one." Then I felt guilty—guilty, probably, for never having supposed that the poor bastard *had* a story of his own, much less a sad one, and I asked, quickly, "What's going to happen to him now?"

He didn't answer this. He was off by himself some place.

"Funny thing," he said, and from his tone we might have been discussing the quickest way to get to Brooklyn, "when I saw the papers this morning, the first thing I asked myself was if I had anything to do with it. I felt sort of responsible."

I began to listen more carefully. The subway station was on the corner, just before us, and I stopped. He stopped, too. We were in front of a bar and he ducked slightly, peering in, but whoever he was looking for didn't seem to be there. The juke box was blasting away with something black and bouncy and I half watched the barmaid as she danced her way from the juke box to her place behind the bar. And I watched her face as she laughingly responded to something someone said to her, still keeping time to the music. When she smiled one saw the little girl, one sensed the doomed, still-struggling woman beneath the battered face of the semi-whore.

"I never *give* Sonny nothing," the boy said finally, "but a long time ago I come to school high and Sonny asked me how it felt." He paused, I couldn't bear to watch him, I watched the barmaid, and I listened to the music which seemed to be causing the pavement to shake. "I told him it felt great." The music stopped, the barmaid paused and watched the juke box until the music began again. "It did."

All this was carrying me some place I didn't want to go. I certainly didn't want to know how it felt. It filled everything, the people, the houses, the music, the dark, quicksilver barmaid, with menace; and this menace was their reality.

30   "What's going to happen to him now?" I asked again.

"They'll send him away some place and they'll try to cure him." He shook his head. "Maybe he'll even think he's kicked the habit. Then they'll let him loose"—he gestured, throwing his cigarette into the gutter. "That's all."

"What do you mean, that's *all*?"

But I knew what he meant.

"I *mean*, that's *all*." He turned his head and looked at me, pulling down the corners of his mouth. "Don't you know what I mean?" he asked, softly.

35   "How the hell *would* I know what you mean?" I almost whispered it, I don't know why.

"That's right," he said to the air, "how would *he* know what I mean?" He turned toward me again, patient and calm, and yet I somehow felt him shaking, shaking as though he were going to fall apart. I felt that ice in my guts again, the dread I'd felt all afternoon; and again I watched the barmaid, moving about the bar, washing glasses, and singing. "Listen. They'll let him out and then it'll just start all over again. That's what I mean."

"You mean—they'll let him out. And then he'll just start working his way back in again. You mean he'll never kick the habit. Is that what you mean?"

"That's right," he said, cheerfully. "*You* see what I mean."

"Tell me," I said at last, "why does he want to die? He must want to die, he's killing himself, why does he want to die?"

40   He looked at me in surprise. He licked his lips. "He don't want to die. He wants to live. Don't nobody want to die, ever."

Then I wanted to ask him—too many things. He could not have answered, or if he had, I could not have borne the answers. I started walking. "Well, I guess it's none of my business."

"It's going to be rough on old Sonny," he said. We reached the subway station. "This is your station?" he asked. I nodded. I took one step down. "Damn!" he said, suddenly. I looked up at him. He grinned again. "Damn it if I didn't leave all my money home. You ain't got a dollar on you, have you? Just for a couple of days, is all."

All at once something inside gave and threatened to come pouring out of me. I didn't hate him any more. I felt that in another moment I'd start crying like a child.

"Sure," I said. "Don't sweat." I looked in my wallet and didn't have a dollar, I only had a five. "Here," I said. "That hold you?"

He didn't look at it—he didn't want to look at it. A terrible, closed look came over his face, as though he were keeping the number on the bill a secret from him and me. "Thanks," he said, and now he was dying to see me go. "Don't worry about Sonny. Maybe I'll write him or something."

"Sure," I said. "You do that. So long."

"Be seeing you," he said. I went on down the steps.

And I didn't write Sonny or send him anything for a long time. When I finally did, it was just after my little girl died, and he wrote me back a letter which made me feel like a bastard.

Here's what he said:

Dear brother,

You don't know how much I needed to hear from you. I wanted to write you many a time but I dug how much I must have hurt you and so I didn't write. But now I feel like a man who's been trying to climb up out of some deep, real deep and funky hole and just saw the sun up there, outside. I got to get outside.

I can't tell you much about how I got here. I mean I don't know how to tell you. I guess I was afraid of something or I was trying to escape from something and you know I have never been very strong in the head (smile). I'm glad Mama and Daddy are dead and can't see what's happened to their son and I swear if I'd known what I was doing I would never have hurt you so, you and a lot of other fine people who were nice to me and who believed in me.

I don't want you to think it had anything to do with me being a musician. It's more than that. Or maybe less than that. I can't get anything straight in my head down here and I try not to think about what's going to happen to me when I get outside again. Sometime I think I'm going to flip and *never* get outside and sometime I think I'll come straight back. I tell you one thing, though, I'd rather blow my brains out than go through this again. But that's what they all say, so they tell me. If I tell you when I'm coming to New York and if you could meet me, I sure would appreciate it. Give my love to Isabel and the kids and I was sure sorry to hear about little Gracie. I wish I could be like Mama and say the Lord's will be done, but I don't know it seems to me that trouble is the one thing that never does get stopped and I don't know what good it does to blame it on the Lord. But maybe it does some good if you believe it.

Your brother,
Sonny

45

50

Then I kept in constant touch with him and I sent him whatever I could and I went to meet him when he came back to New York. When I saw him many things I thought I had forgotten came flooding back to me. This was because I had begun, finally, to wonder about Sonny, about the life that Sonny lived inside. This life, whatever it was, had made him older and thinner and it had deepened the distant stillness in which he had always moved. He looked very unlike my baby brother. Yet, when he smiled, when we shook hands, the baby brother I'd never known looked out from the depths of his private life, like an animal waiting to be coaxed into the light.

"How you been keeping?" he asked me.

55 "All right. And you?"

"Just fine." He was smiling all over his face. "It's good to see you again."

"It's good to see you."

The seven years' difference in our ages lay between us like a chasm: I wondered if these years would ever operate between us as a bridge. I was remembering, and it made it hard to catch my breath, that I had been there when he was born; and I had heard the first words he had ever spoken. When he started to walk, he walked from our mother straight to me. I caught him just before he fell when he took the first steps he ever took in this world.

"How's Isabel?"

60 "Just fine. She's dying to see you."

"And the boys?"

"They're fine, too. They're anxious to see their uncle."

"Oh, come on. You know they don't remember me."

"Are you kidding? Of course they remember you."

65 He grinned again. We got into a taxi. We had a lot to say to each other, far too much to know how to begin.

As the taxi began to move, I asked, "You still want to go to India?"

He laughed. "You still remember that. Hell, no. This place is Indian enough for me."

"It used to belong to them," I said.

And he laughed again. "They damn sure knew what they were doing when they got rid of it."

70 Years ago, when he was around fourteen, he'd been all hipped on the idea of going to India. He read books about people sitting on rocks, naked, in all kinds of weather, but mostly bad, naturally, and walking barefoot through hot coals and arriving at wisdom. I used to say that it sounded to me as though they were getting away from wisdom as fast as they could. I think he sort of looked down on me for that.

"Do you mind," he asked, "if we have the driver drive alongside the park? On the west side—I haven't seen the city in so long."

"Of course not," I said. I was afraid that I might sound as though I were humoring him, but I hoped he wouldn't take it that way.

So we drove along, between the green of the park and the stony, lifeless elegance of hotels and apartment buildings, toward the vivid, killing streets of our childhood. These streets hadn't changed, though housing projects jutted up out of them now like rocks in the middle of a boiling sea. Most of the houses in which we had grown up had vanished, as had the stores from which we had stolen, the basements in which we had first tried sex, the rooftops from which we had hurled tin cans and bricks. But houses exactly like the houses of our past yet dominated the landscape, boys exactly like the boys we once had been found themselves smothering in these houses, came down into the streets for light and air and found themselves encircled by disaster. Some escaped the trap, most didn't. Those who got out always left something of themselves behind, as some animals amputate a leg and leave it in the trap. It might be said, perhaps, that I had escaped, after all, I was a school teacher; or that Sonny had, he hadn't lived in Harlem for years. Yet, as the cab moved uptown through streets which seemed, with a rush, to darken with dark people, and as I covertly studied Sonny's face, it came to me that what we both were seeking through our separate cab windows was that part of ourselves which had been left behind. It's always at the hour of trouble and confrontation that the missing member aches.

We hit 110th Street and started rolling up Lenox Avenue. And I'd known this avenue all my life, but it seemed to me again, as it had seemed on the day I'd first heard about Sonny's trouble, filled with a hidden menace which was its very breath of life.

"We almost there," said Sonny.

"Almost." We were both too nervous to say anything more.

We live in a housing project. It hasn't been up long. A few days after it was up it seemed uninhabitably new, now, of course, it's already rundown. It looks like a parody of the good, clean, faceless life—God knows the people who live in it do their best to make it a parody. The beat-looking grass lying around isn't enough to make their lives green, the hedges will never hold out the streets, and they know it. The big windows fool no one, they aren't big enough to make space out of no space. They don't bother with the windows, they watch the TV screen instead. The playground is most popular with the children who don't play at jacks, or skip rope, or roller skate, or swing, and they can be found in it after dark. We moved in partly because it's not too far from where I teach, and partly for the kids; but it's really just like the houses in which Sonny and I grew up. The same things happen, they'll have the same things to remember. The moment Sonny and I started into the house I had the feeling that I was simply bringing him back into the danger he had almost died trying to escape.

Sonny has never been talkative. So I don't know why I was sure he'd be dying to talk to me when supper was over the first night. Everything went fine, the oldest boy remembered him, and the youngest boy liked him, and Sonny had remembered to bring something for each of them; and Isabel, who is really much nicer than I am, more open and giving, had gone to a lot of trouble about dinner and was genuinely glad to see him. And she's always been able to tease Sonny in a way that I haven't. It was nice to see her face so vivid again and to hear her laugh and watch her make Sonny laugh. She wasn't, or, anyway, she didn't seem to be, at all uneasy or embarrassed. She chatted as though there were no subject which had to be avoided and she got Sonny past his first, faint stiffness. And thank God she was there, for I was filled with that icy dread again.

75

Everything I did seemed awkward to me, and everything I said sounded freighted with hidden meaning. I was trying to remember everything I'd heard about dope addiction and I couldn't help watching Sonny for signs. I wasn't doing it out of malice. I was trying to find out something about my brother. I was dying to hear him tell me he was safe.

"Safe!" my father grunted, whenever Mama suggested trying to move to a neighborhood which might be safer for children. "Safe, hell! Ain't no place safe for kids, nor nobody."

80   He always went on like this, but he wasn't, ever, really as bad as he sounded, not even on weekends, when he got drunk. As a matter of fact, he was always on the lookout for "something a little better," but he died before he found it. He died suddenly, during a drunken weekend in the middle of the war, when Sonny was fifteen. He and Sonny hadn't ever got on too well. And this was partly because Sonny was the apple of his father's eye. It was because he loved Sonny so much and was frightened for him, that he was always fighting with him. It doesn't do any good to fight with Sonny. Sonny just moves back, inside himself, where he can't be reached. But the principal reason that they never hit it off is that they were so much alike. Daddy was big and rough and loud-talking, just the opposite of Sonny, but they both had—that same privacy.

Mama tried to tell me something about this, just after Daddy died. I was home on leave from the army.

This was the last time I ever saw my mother alive. Just the same, this picture gets all mixed up in my mind with pictures I had of her when she was younger. The way I always see her is the way she used to be on a Sunday afternoon, say, when the old folks were talking after the big Sunday dinner. I always see her wearing pale blue. She'd be sitting on the sofa. And my father would be sitting in the easy chair, not far from her. And the living room would be full of church folks and relatives. There they sit, in chairs all around the living room, and the night is creeping up outside, but nobody knows it yet. You can see the darkness growing against the windowpanes and you hear the street noises every now and again, or maybe the jangling beat of a tambourine from one of the churches close by, but it's real quiet in the room. For a moment nobody's talking, but every face looks darkening, like the sky outside. And my mother rocks a little from the waist, and my father's eyes are closed. Everyone is looking at something a child can't see. For a minute they've forgotten the children. Maybe a kid is lying on the rug, half asleep. Maybe somebody's got a kid in his lap and is absent-mindedly stroking the kid's head. Maybe there's a kid, quiet and big-eyed, curled up in a big chair in the corner. The silence, the darkness coming, and the darkness in the faces frighten the child obscurely. He hopes that the hand which strokes his forehead will never stop—will never die. He hopes that there will never come a time when the old folks won't be sitting around the living room, talking about where they've come from, and what they've seen, and what's happened to them and their kinfolk.

But something deep and watchful in the child knows that this is bound to end, is already ending. In a moment someone will get up and turn on the light.

Then the old folks will remember the children and they won't talk any more that day. And when light fills the room, the child is filled with darkness. He knows that every time this happens he's moved just a little closer to that darkness outside. The darkness outside is what the old folks have been talking about. It's what they've come from. It's what they endure. The child knows that they won't talk any more because if he knows too much about what's happened to *them*, he'll know too much too soon, about what's going to happen to *him*.

The last time I talked to my mother, I remember I was restless. I wanted to get out and see Isabel. We weren't married then and we had a lot to straighten out between us.

There Mama sat, in black, by the window. She was humming an old church song, *Lord, you brought me from a long ways off.* Sonny was out somewhere. Mama kept watching the streets.

"I don't know," she said, "if I'll ever see you again, after you go off from here. But I hope you'll remember the things I tried to teach you."

"Don't talk like that," I said, and smiled. "You'll be here a long time yet."

She smiled, too, but she said nothing. She was quiet for a long time. And I said, "Mama, don't you worry about nothing. I'll be writing all the time, and you be getting the checks. . . ."

"I want to talk to you about your brother," she said, suddenly. "If anything happens to me he ain't going to have nobody to look out for him."

"Mama," I said, "ain't nothing going to happen to you *or* Sonny. Sonny's all right. He's a good boy and he's got good sense."

"It ain't a question of his being a good boy," Mama said, "nor of his having good sense. It ain't only the bad ones, nor yet the dumb ones that gets sucked under." She stopped, looking at me. "Your Daddy once had a brother," she said, and she smiled in a way that made me feel she was in pain. "You didn't never know that, did you?"

"No," I said, "I never knew that," and I watched her face.

"Oh, yes," she said, "your Daddy had a brother." She looked out of the window again. "I know you never saw your Daddy cry. But *I* did—many a time, through all these years."

I asked her, "What happened to his brother? How come nobody's ever talked about him?"

This was the first time I ever saw my mother look old.

"His brother got killed," she said, "when he was just a little younger than you are now. I knew him. He was a fine boy. He was maybe a little full of the devil, but he didn't mean nobody no harm."

Then she stopped and the room was silent, exactly as it had sometimes been on those Sunday afternoons. Mama kept looking out into the streets.

"He used to have a job in the mill," she said, "and, like all young folks, he just liked to perform on Saturday nights. Saturday nights, him and your father would drift around to different places, go to dances and things like that, or just sit around with people they knew, and your father's brother would sing, he had a fine voice, and play along with himself on his guitar. Well, this particular Saturday night, him and your father was coming home from some place, and

85

90

95

they were both a little drunk and there was a moon that night, it was bright like day. Your father's brother was feeling kind of good, and he was whistling to himself, and he had his guitar slung over his shoulder. They was coming down a hill and beneath them was a road that turned off from the highway. Well, your father's brother, being always kind of frisky, decided to run down this hill, and he did, with that guitar banging and clanging behind him, and he ran across the road, and he was making water behind a tree. And your father was sort of amused at him and he was still coming down the hill, kind of slow. Then he heard a car motor and that same minute his brother stepped from behind the tree, into the road, in the moonlight. And he started to cross the road. And your father started to run down the hill, he says he don't know why. This car was full of white men. They was all drunk, and when they seen your father's brother they let out a great whoop and holler and they aimed the car straight at him. They was having fun, they just wanted to scare him, the way they do sometimes, you know. But they was drunk. And I guess the boy, being drunk, too, and scared, kind of lost his head. By the time he jumped it was too late. Your father says he heard his brother scream when the car rolled over him, and he heard the wood of that guitar when it give, and he heard them strings go flying, and he heard them white men shouting, and the car kept on a-going and it ain't stopped till this day. And, time your father got down the hill, his brother weren't nothing but blood and pulp."

Tears were gleaming on my mother's face. There wasn't anything I could say.

100   "He never mentioned it," she said, "because I never let him mention it before you children. Your Daddy was like a crazy man that night and for many a night thereafter. He says he never in his life seen anything as dark as that road after the lights of that car had gone away. Weren't nothing, weren't nobody on that road, just your Daddy and his brother and that busted guitar. Oh, yes. Your Daddy never did really get right again. Till the day he died he weren't sure but that every white man he saw was the man that killed his brother."

She stopped and took out her handkerchief and dried her eyes and looked at me.

"I ain't telling you all this," she said, "to make you scared or bitter or to make you hate nobody. I'm telling you this because you got a brother. And the world ain't changed."

I guess I didn't want to believe this. I guess she saw this in my face. She turned away from me, toward the window again, searching those streets.

"But I praise my Redeemer," she said at last, "that He called your Daddy home before me. I ain't saying it to throw no flowers at myself, but, I declare, it keeps me from feeling too cast down to know I helped your father get safely through this world. Your father always acted like he was the roughest, strongest man on earth. And everybody took him to be like that. But if he hadn't had me there—to see his tears!"

105   She was crying again. Still, I couldn't move. I said, "Lord, Lord, Mama, I didn't know it was like that."

"Oh, honey," she said, "there's a lot that you don't know. But you are going to find out." She stood up from the window and came over to me. "You got to hold on to your brother," she said, "and don't let him fall, no matter what it looks like is happening to him and no matter how evil you gets with him. You going to be evil with him many a time. But don't you forget what I told you, you hear?"

"I won't forget," I said. "Don't you worry, I won't forget. I won't let nothing happen to Sonny."

My mother smiled as though she was amused at something she saw in my face. Then, "You may not be able to stop nothing from happening. But you got to let him know you's *there*."

Two days later I was married, and then I was gone. And I had a lot of things on my mind and I pretty well forgot my promise to Mama until I got shipped home on a special furlough for her funeral.

And, after the funeral, with just Sonny and me alone in the empty kitchen, I tried to find out something about him.   110

"What do you want to do?" I asked him.

"I'm going to be a musician," he said.

For he had graduated, in the time I had been away, from dancing to the juke box to finding out who was playing what, and what they were doing with it, and he had bought himself a set of drums.

"You mean, you want to be a drummer?" I somehow had the feeling that being a drummer might be all right for other people but not for my brother Sonny.

"I don't think," he said, looking at me very gravely, "that I'll ever be a good   115
drummer. But I think I can play a piano."

I frowned. I'd never played the role of the oldest brother quite so seriously before, had scarcely ever, in fact, *asked* Sonny a damn thing. I sensed myself in the presence of something I didn't really know how to handle, didn't under-stand. So I made my frown a little deeper as I asked: "What kind of musician do you want to be?"

He grinned. "How many kinds do you think there are?"

"Be *serious*," I said.

He laughed, throwing his head back, and then looked at me. "I *am* serious."

"Well, then, for Christ's sake, stop kidding around and answer a serious ques-   120
tion. I mean, do you want to be a concert pianist, you want to play classical music and all that, or—or what?" Long before I finished he was laughing again. "For Christ's *sake*, Sonny!"

He sobered, but with difficulty. "I'm sorry. But you sound so—*scared!*" and he was off again.

"Well, you may think it's funny now, baby, but it's not going to be so funny when you have to make your living at it, let me tell you *that*." I was furious because I knew he was laughing at me and I didn't know why.

"No," he said, very sober now, and afraid, perhaps, that he'd hurt me, "I don't want to be a classical pianist. That isn't what interests me. I mean"—he paused, looking hard at me, as though his eyes would help me to understand, and then gestured helplessly, as though perhaps his hand would help — "I mean,

I'll have a lot of studying to do, and I'll have to study *everything*, but, I mean, I want to play *with*—jazz musicians." He stopped. "I want to play jazz," he said.

Well, the word had never before sounded as heavy, as real, as it sounded that afternoon in Sonny's mouth. I just looked at him and I was probably frowning a real frown by this time. I simply couldn't see why on earth he'd want to spend his time hanging around nightclubs, clowning around on bandstands, while people pushed each other around a dance floor. It seemed—beneath him, somehow. I had never thought about it before, had never been forced to, but I suppose I had always put jazz musicians in a class with what Daddy called "good-time people."

125   "Are you *serious?*"

"Hell, *yes*, I'm serious."

He looked more helpless than ever, and annoyed, and deeply hurt.

I suggested, helpfully: "You mean—like Louis Armstrong?"

His face closed as though I'd struck him. "No. I'm not talking about none of that old-time, down home crap."

130   "Well, look, Sonny, I'm sorry, don't get mad. I just don't altogether get it, that's all. Name somebody—you know, a jazz musician you admire."

"Bird."

"Who?"

"Bird! Charlie Parker![3] Don't they teach you nothing in the goddamn army?"

I lit a cigarette. I was surprised and then a little amused to discover that I was trembling. "I've been out of touch," I said. "You'll have to be patient with me. Now. Who's this Parker character?"

135   "He's just one of the greatest jazz musicians alive," said Sonny, sullenly, his hands in his pockets, his back to me. "Maybe *the* greatest," he added, bitterly, "that's probably why *you* never heard of him."

"All right," I said, "I'm ignorant. I'm sorry. I'll go out and buy all the cat's records right away, all right?"

"It don't," said Sonny, with dignity, "make any difference to me. I don't care what you listen to. Don't do me no favors."

I was beginning to realize that I'd never seen him so upset before. With another part of my mind I was thinking that this would probably turn out to be one of those things kids go through and that I shouldn't make it seem important by pushing it too hard. Still, I didn't think it would do any harm to ask: "Doesn't all this take a lot of time? Can you make a living at it?"

He turned back to me and half leaned, half sat, on the kitchen table. "Everything takes time," he said, "and—well, yes, sure, I can make a living at it. But what I don't seem to be able to make you understand is that it's the only thing I want to do."

140   "Well, Sonny," I said gently, "you know people can't always do exactly what they *want* to do—"

---

3. Charlie ("Bird") Parker (1920–1955), brilliant saxophonist and innovator of jazz; working in New York in the mid-1940s, he developed, with Dizzy Gillespie and others, the style of jazz called "bebop." He was a narcotics addict.

"No, I don't know that," said Sonny, surprising me. "I think people *ought* to do what they want to do, what else are they alive for?"

"You getting to be a big boy," I said desperately, "it's time you started thinking about your future."

"I'm thinking about my future," said Sonny, grimly. "I think about it all the time."

I gave up. I decided, if he didn't change his mind, that we could always talk about it later. "In the meantime," I said, "you got to finish school." We had already decided that he'd have to move in with Isabel and her folks. I knew this wasn't the ideal arrangement because Isabel's folks are inclined to be dicty[4] and they hadn't especially wanted Isabel to marry me. But I didn't know what else to do. "And we have to get you fixed up at Isabel's."

There was a long silence. He moved from the kitchen table to the window.   145
"That's a terrible idea. You know it yourself."

"Do you have a *better* idea?"

He just walked up and down the kitchen for a minute. He was as tall as I was. He had started to shave. I suddenly had the feeling that I didn't know him at all.

He stopped at the kitchen table and picked up my cigarettes. Looking at me with a kind of mocking, amused defiance, he put one between his lips. "You mind?"

"You smoking already?"

He lit the cigarette and nodded, watching me through the smoke. "I just   150
wanted to see if I'd have the courage to smoke in front of you." He grinned and blew a great cloud of smoke to the ceiling. "It was easy." He looked at my face. "Come on, now. I bet you was smoking at my age, tell the truth."

I didn't say anything but the truth was on my face, and he laughed. But now there was something very strained in his laugh. "Sure. And I bet that ain't all you was doing."

He was frightening me a little. "Cut the crap," I said. "We already decided that you was going to go and live at Isabel's. Now what's got into you all of a sudden?"

"*You* decided it," he pointed out. "*I* didn't decide nothing." He stopped in front of me, leaning against the stove, arms loosely folded. "Look, brother. I don't want to stay in Harlem no more, I really don't." He was very earnest. He looked at me, then over toward the kitchen window. There was something in his eyes I'd never seen before, some thoughtfulness, some worry all his own. He rubbed the muscle of one arm. "It's time I was getting out of here."

"Where do you want to go, Sonny?"

"I want to join the army. Or the navy, I don't care. If I say I'm old enough,   155
they'll believe me."

Then I got mad. It was because I was so scared. "You must be crazy. You goddamn fool, what the hell do you want to go and join the *army* for?"

"I just told you. To get out of Harlem."

4. Snobbish, bossy.

"Sonny, you haven't even finished *school*. And if you really want to be a musician, how do you expect to study if you're in the *army?*"

He looked at me, trapped, and in anguish. "There's ways. I might be able to work out some kind of deal. Anyway, I'll have the G.I. Bill when I come out."

160 "*If* you come out." We stared at each other. "Sonny, please. Be reasonable. I know the setup is far from perfect. But we got to do the best we can."

"I ain't learning nothing in school," he said. "Even when I go." He turned away from me and opened the window and threw his cigarette out into the narrow alley. I watched his back. "At least, I ain't learning nothing you'd want me to learn." He slammed the window so hard I thought the glass would fly out, and turned back to me. "And I'm sick of the stink of these garbage cans!"

"Sonny," I said, "I know how you feel. But if you don't finish school now, you're going to be sorry later that you didn't." I grabbed him by the shoulders. "And you only got another year. It ain't so bad. And I'll come back and I swear I'll help you do *whatever* you want to do. Just try to put up with it till I come back. Will you please do that? For me?"

He didn't answer and he wouldn't look at me.

"Sonny. You hear me?"

165 He pulled away. "I hear you. But you never hear anything *I* say."

I didn't know what to say to that. He looked out of the window and then back at me. "OK," he said, and sighed. "I'll try."

Then I said, trying to cheer him up a little, "They got a piano at Isabel's. You can practice on it."

And as a matter of fact, it did cheer him up for a minute. "That's right," he said to himself. "I forgot that." His face relaxed a little. But the worry, the thoughtfulness, played on it still, the way shadows play on a face which is staring into the fire.

But I thought I'd never hear the end of that piano. At first, Isabel would write me, saying how nice it was that Sonny was so serious about his music and how, as soon as he came in from school, or wherever he had been when he was supposed to be at school, he went straight to that piano and stayed there until suppertime. And, after supper, he went back to that piano and stayed there until everybody went to bed. He was at the piano all day Saturday and all day Sunday. Then he bought a record player and started playing records. He'd play one record over and over again, all day long sometimes, and he'd improvise along with it on the piano. Or he'd play one section of the record, one chord, one change, one progression, then he'd do it on the piano. Then back to the record. Then back to the piano.

170 Well, I really don't know how they stood it. Isabel finally confessed that it wasn't like living with a person at all, it was like living with sound. And the sound didn't make any sense to her, didn't make any sense to any of them — naturally. They began, in a way, to be afflicted by this presence that was living in their home. It was as though Sonny were some sort of god, or monster. He moved in an atmosphere which wasn't like theirs at all. They fed him and he ate, he washed himself, he walked in and out of their door; he certainly wasn't

nasty or unpleasant or rude, Sonny isn't any of those things; but it was as though he were all wrapped up in some cloud, some fire, some vision all his own; and there wasn't any way to reach him.

At the same time, he wasn't really a man yet, he was still a child, and they had to watch out for him in all kinds of ways. They certainly couldn't throw him out. Neither did they dare to make a great scene about that piano because even they dimly sensed, as I sensed, from so many thousands of miles away, that Sonny was at that piano playing for his life.

But he hadn't been going to school. One day a letter came from the school board and Isabel's mother got it—there had, apparently, been other letters but Sonny had torn them up. This day, when Sonny came in, Isabel's mother showed him the letter and asked where he'd been spending his time. And she finally got it out of him that he'd been down in Greenwich Village, with musicians and other characters, in a white girl's apartment. And this scared her and she started to scream at him and what came up, once she began—though she denies it to this day—was what sacrifices they were making to give Sonny a decent home and how little he appreciated it.

Sonny didn't play the piano that day. By evening, Isabel's mother had calmed down but then there was the old man to deal with, and Isabel herself. Isabel says she did her best to be calm but she broke down and started crying. She says she just watched Sonny's face. She could tell, by watching him, what was happening with him. And what was happening was that they penetrated his cloud, they had reached him. Even if their fingers had been a thousand times more gentle than human fingers ever are, he could hardly help feeling that they had stripped him naked and were spitting on that nakedness. For he also had to see that his presence, that music, which was life or death to him, had been torture for them and that they had endured it, not at all for his sake, but only for mine. And Sonny couldn't take that. He can take it a little better today than he could then but he's still not very good at it and, frankly, I don't know anybody who is.

The silence of the next few days must have been louder than the sound of all the music ever played since time began. One morning, before she went to work, Isabel was in his room for something and she suddenly realized that all of his records were gone. And she knew for certain that he was gone. And he was. He went as far as the navy would carry him. He finally sent me a postcard from some place in Greece and that was the first I knew that Sonny was still alive. I didn't see him any more until we were both back in New York and the war had long been over.

He was a man by then, of course, but I wasn't willing to see it. He came by the house from time to time, but we fought almost every time we met. I didn't like the way he carried himself, loose and dreamlike all the time, and I didn't like his friends, and his music seemed to be merely an excuse for the life he led. It sounded just that weird and disordered.

Then we had a fight, a pretty awful fight, and I didn't see him for months. By and by I looked him up, where he was living, in a furnished room in the Village, and I tried to make it up. But there were lots of other people in the room and Sonny just lay on his bed, and he wouldn't come downstairs with me,

175

and he treated these other people as though they were his family and I weren't. So I got mad and then he got mad, and then I told him that he might just as well be dead as live the way he was living. Then he stood up and he told me not to worry about him any more in life, that he *was* dead as far as I was concerned. Then he pushed me to the door and the other people looked on as though nothing were happening, and he slammed the door behind me. I stood in the hallway, staring at the door. I heard somebody laugh in the room and then the tears came to my eyes. I started down the steps, whistling to keep from crying, I kept whistling to myself, *You going to need me, baby, one of these cold, rainy days.*

I read about Sonny's trouble in the spring. Little Grace died in the fall. She was a beautiful little girl. But she only lived a little over two years. She died of polio and she suffered. She had a slight fever for a couple of days, but it didn't seem like anything and we just kept her in bed. And we would certainly have called the doctor, but the fever dropped, she seemed to be all right. So we thought it had just been a cold. Then, one day, she was up, playing, Isabel was in the kitchen fixing lunch for the two boys when they'd come in from school, and she heard Grace fall down in the living room. When you have a lot of children you don't always start running when one of them falls, unless they start screaming or something. And, this time, Gracie was quiet. Yet, Isabel says that when she heard that *thump* and then that silence, something happened to her to make her afraid. And she ran to the living room and there was little Grace on the floor, all twisted up, and the reason she hadn't screamed was that she couldn't get her breath. And when she did scream, it was the worst sound, Isabel says, that she'd ever heard in all her life, and she still hears it sometimes in her dreams. Isabel will sometimes wake me up with a low, moaning, strangling sound and I have to be quick to awaken her and hold her to me and where Isabel is weeping against me seems a mortal wound.

I think I may have written Sonny the very day that little Grace was buried. I was sitting in the living room in the dark, by myself, and I suddenly thought of Sonny. My trouble made his real.

One Saturday afternoon, when Sonny had been living with us, or anyway, been in our house, for nearly two weeks, I found myself wandering aimlessly about the living room, drinking from a can of beer, and trying to work up courage to search Sonny's room. He was out, he was usually out whenever I was home, and Isabel had taken the children to see their grandparents. Suddenly I was standing still in front of the living room window, watching Seventh Avenue. The idea of searching Sonny's room made me still. I scarcely dared to admit to myself what I'd be searching for. I didn't know what I'd do if I found it. Or if I didn't.

On the sidewalk across from me, near the entrance to a barbecue joint, some people were holding an old-fashioned revival meeting. The barbecue cook, wearing a dirty white apron, his conked[5] hair reddish and metallic in the pale sun, and a cigarette between his lips, stood in the doorway, watching them. Kids

---

5. Processed: straightened and greased.

and older people paused in their errands and stood there, along with some older men and a couple of very tough-looking women who watched everything that happened on the avenue, as though they owned it, or were maybe owned by it. Well, they were watching this, too. The revival was being carried on by three sisters in black, and a brother. All they had were their voices and their Bibles and a tambourine. The brother was testifying[6] and while he testified two of the sisters stood together, seeming to say, amen, and the third sister walked around with the tambourine outstretched and a couple of people dropped coins into it. Then the brother's testimony ended and the sister who had been taking up the collection dumped the coins into her palm and transferred them to the pocket of her long black robe. Then she raised both hands, striking the tambourine against the air, and then against one hand, and she started to sing. And the two other sisters and the brother joined in.

It was strange, suddenly, to watch, though I had been seeing these meetings all my life. So, of course, had everybody else down there. Yet, they paused and watched and listened and I stood still at the window. " *'Tis the old ship of Zion,"* they sang, and the sister with the tambourine kept a steady, jangling beat, *"it has rescued many a thousand!"* Not a soul under the sound of their voices was hearing this song for the first time, not one of them had been rescued. Nor had they seen much in the way of rescue work being done around them. Neither did they especially believe in the holiness of the three sisters and the brother, they knew too much about them, knew where they lived, and how. The woman with the tambourine, whose voice dominated the air, whose face was bright with joy, was divided by very little from the woman who stood watching her, a cigarette between her heavy, chapped lips, her hair a cuckoo's nest, her face scarred and swollen from many beatings, and her black eyes glittering like coal. Perhaps they both knew this, which was why, when, as rarely, they addressed each other, they addressed each other as Sister. As the singing filled the air the watching, listening faces underwent a change, the eyes focusing on something within; the music seemed to soothe a poison out of them; and time seemed, nearly, to fall away from the sullen, belligerent, battered faces, as though they were fleeing back to their first condition, while dreaming of their last. The barbecue cook half shook his head and smiled, and dropped his cigarette and disappeared into his joint. A man fumbled in his pockets for change and stood holding it in his hand impatiently, as though he had just remembered a pressing appointment further up the avenue. He looked furious. Then I saw Sonny, standing on the edge of the crowd. He was carrying a wide, flat notebook with a green cover, and it made him look, from where I was standing, almost like a schoolboy. The coppery sun brought out the copper in his skin, he was very faintly smiling, standing very still. Then the singing stopped, the tambourine turned into a collection plate again. The furious man dropped in his coins and vanished, so did a couple of the women, and Sonny dropped some change in the plate, looking directly at the woman with a little smile. He started across the avenue, toward the house. He has a slow, loping walk, something like the way Harlem hipsters

6. Publicly professing belief.

walk, only he's imposed on this his own half-beat. I had never really noticed it before.

I stayed at the window, both relieved and apprehensive. As Sonny disappeared from my sight, they began singing again. And they were still singing when his key turned in the lock.

"Hey," he said.

"Hey, yourself. You want some beer?"

185   "No. Well, maybe." But he came up to the window and stood beside me, looking out. "What a warm voice," he said.

They were singing *If I could only hear my mother pray again!*

"Yes," I said, "and she can sure beat that tambourine."

"But what a terrible song," he said, and laughed. He dropped his notebook on the sofa and disappeared into the kitchen. "Where's Isabel and the kids?"

"I think they went to see their grandparents. You hungry?"

190   "No." He came back into the living room with his can of beer. "You want to come some place with me tonight?"

I sensed, I don't know how, that I couldn't possibly say no. "Sure. Where?"

He sat down on the sofa and picked up his notebook and started leafing through it. "I'm going to sit in with some fellows in a joint in the Village."

"You mean, you're going to play, tonight?"

"That's right." He took a swallow of his beer and moved back to the window. He gave me a sidelong look. "If you can stand it."

195   "I'll try," I said.

He smiled to himself and we both watched as the meeting across the way broke up. The three sisters and the brother, heads bowed, were singing *God be with you till we meet again.* The faces around them were very quiet. Then the song ended. The small crowd dispersed. We watched the three women and the lone man walk slowly up the avenue.

"When she was singing before," said Sonny, abruptly, "her voice reminded me for a minute of what heroin feels like sometimes—when it's in your veins. It makes you feel sort of warm and cool at the same time. And distant. And— and sure." He sipped his beer, very deliberately not looking at me. I watched his face. "It makes you feel—in control. Sometimes you've got to have that feeling."

"Do you?" I sat down slowly in the easy chair.

"Sometimes." He went to the sofa and picked up his notebook again. "Some people do."

200   "In order," I asked, "to play?" And my voice was very ugly, full of contempt and anger.

"Well"—he looked at me with great, troubled eyes, as though, in fact, he hoped his eyes would tell me things he could never otherwise say—"they *think* so. And *if* they think so—!"

"And what do *you* think?" I asked.

He sat on the sofa and put his can of beer on the floor. "I don't know," he said, and I couldn't be sure if he were answering my question or pursuing his thoughts. His face didn't tell me. "It's not so much to *play.* It's to *stand* it, to be able to make it at all. On any level." He frowned and smiled: "In order to keep from shaking to pieces."

"But these friends of yours," I said, "they seem to shake themselves to pieces pretty goddamn fast."

"Maybe." He played with the notebook. And something told me that I should curb my tongue, that Sonny was doing his best to talk, that I should listen. "But of course you only know the ones that've gone to pieces. Some don't—or at least they haven't *yet* and that's just about all *any* of us can say." He paused. "And then there are some who just live, really, in hell, and they know it and they see what's happening and they go right on. I don't know." He sighed, dropped the notebook, folded his arms. "Some guys, you can tell from the way they play, they on something *all* the time. And you can see that, well, it makes something real for them. But of course," he picked up his beer from the floor and sipped it and put the can down again, "they *want* to, too, you've got to see that. Even some of them that say they don't—*some*, not all." 205

"And what about you?" I asked—I couldn't help it. "What about you? Do *you* want to?"

He stood up and walked to the window and I remained silent for a long time. Then he sighed. "Me," he said. Then: "While I was downstairs before, on my way here, listening to that woman sing, it struck me all of a sudden how much suffering she must have had to go through—to sing like that. It's *repulsive* to think you have to suffer that much."

I said: "But there's no way not to suffer—is there, Sonny?"

"I believe not," he said and smiled, "but that's never stopped anyone from trying." He looked at me. "Has it?" I realized, with this mocking look, that there stood between us, forever, beyond the power of time or forgiveness, the fact that I had held silence—so long!—when he had needed human speech to help him. He turned back to the window. "No, there's no way not to suffer. But you try all kinds of ways to keep from drowning in it, to keep on top of it, and to make it seem—well, like *you*. Like you did something, all right, and now you're suffering for it. You know?" I said nothing. "Well you know," he said, impatiently, "why *do* people suffer? Maybe it's better to do something to give it a reason, *any* reason."

"But we just agreed," I said, "that there's no way not to suffer. Isn't it better, then, just to—take it?" 210

"But nobody just takes it," Sonny cried, "that's what I'm telling you! *Everybody* tries not to. You're just hung up on the *way* some people try—it's not *your* way!"

The hair on my face began to itch, my face felt wet. "That's not true," I said, "that's not true. I don't give a damn what other people do, I don't even care how they suffer. I just care how *you* suffer." And he looked at me. "Please believe me," I said, "I don't want to see you—die—trying not to suffer."

"I won't," he said flatly, "die trying not to suffer. At least, not any faster than anybody else."

"But there's no need," I said, trying to laugh, "is there? in killing yourself."

I wanted to say more, but I couldn't. I wanted to talk about will power and how life could be—well, beautiful. I wanted to say that it was all within; but was it? or, rather, wasn't that exactly the trouble? And I wanted to promise that I would never fail him again. But it would all have sounded—empty words and lies.

So I made the promise to myself and prayed that I would keep it.

"It's terrible sometimes, inside," he said, "that's what's the trouble. You walk these streets, black and funky and cold, and there's not really a living ass to talk to, and there's nothing shaking, and there's no way of getting it out—that storm inside. You can't talk it and you can't make love with it, and when you finally try to get with it and play it, you realize *nobody's* listening. So *you've* got to listen. You got to find a way to listen."

And then he walked away from the window and sat on the sofa again, as though all the wind had suddenly been knocked out of him. "Sometimes you'll do *anything* to play, even cut your mother's throat." He laughed and looked at me. "Or your brother's." Then he sobered. "Or your own." Then: "Don't worry. I'm all right now and I think I'll *be* all right. But I can't forget—where I've been. I don't mean just the physical place I've been, I mean where I've *been*. And *what* I've been."

"What have you been, Sonny?" I asked.

He smiled—but sat sideways on the sofa, his elbow resting on the back, his fingers playing with his mouth and chin, not looking at me. "I've been something I didn't recognize, didn't know I could be. Didn't know anybody could be." He stopped, looking inward, looking helplessly young, looking old. "I'm not talking about it now because I feel *guilty* or anything like that—maybe it would be better if I did, I don't know. Anyway, I can't really talk about it. Not to you, not to anybody," and now he turned and faced me. "Sometimes, you know, and it was actually when I was most *out* of the world, I felt that I was in it, that I was *with* it, really, and I could play or I didn't really have to *play*, it just came out of me, it was there. And I don't know how I played, thinking about it now, but I know I did awful things, those times, sometimes, to people. Or it wasn't that I *did* anything to them—it was that they weren't real." He picked up the beer can; it was empty; he rolled it between his palms: "And other times—well, I needed a fix, I needed to find a place to lean, I needed to clear a space to *listen*—and I couldn't find it, and I—went crazy, I did terrible things to *me*, I was terrible *for* me." He began pressing the beer can between his hands, I watched the metal begin to give. It glittered, as he played with it like a knife, and I was afraid he would cut himself, but I said nothing. "Oh well. I can never tell you. I was all by myself at the bottom of something, stinking and sweating and crying and shaking, and I smelled it, you know? *my* stink, and I thought I'd die if I couldn't get away from it and yet, all the same, I knew that everything I was doing was just locking me in with it. And I didn't know," he paused, still flattening the beer can, "I didn't know, I still *don't* know, something kept telling me that maybe it was good to smell your own stink, but I didn't think that *that* was what I'd been trying to do—and—who can stand it?" and he abruptly dropped the ruined beer can, looking at me with a small, still smile, and then rose, walking to the window as though it were the lodestone rock. I watched his face, he watched the avenue. "I couldn't tell you when Mama died—but the reason I wanted to leave Harlem so bad was to get away from drugs. And then, when I ran away, that's what I was running from—really. When I came back, nothing had changed, I hadn't changed, I was just—older." And he stopped, drumming with his fingers on the windowpane. The sun had vanished, soon darkness would fall. I watched his face. "It can come again," he said, almost as though speaking to himself. Then he turned to me. "It can come again," he repeated. "I just want you to know that."

"All right," I said, at last. "So it can come again. All right."

He smiled, but the smile was sorrowful. "I had to try to tell you," he said.

"Yes," I said. "I understand that."

"You're my brother," he said, looking straight at me, and not smiling at all.

"Yes," I repeated, "yes. I understand that."   225

He turned back to the window, looking out. "All that hatred down there," he said, "all that hatred and misery and love. It's a wonder it doesn't blow the avenue apart."

We went to the only nightclub on a short, dark street, downtown. We squeezed through the narrow, chattering, jampacked bar to the entrance of the big room, where the bandstand was. And we stood there for a moment, for the lights were very dim in this room and we couldn't see. Then, "Hello, boy," said the voice and an enormous black man, much older than Sonny or myself, erupted out of all that atmospheric lighting and put an arm around Sonny's shoulder. "I been sitting right here," he said, "waiting for you."

He had a big voice, too, and heads in the darkness turned toward us.

Sonny grinned and pulled a little away, and said, "Creole, this is my brother. I told you about him."

Creole shook my hand. "I'm glad to meet you, son," he said, and it was clear   230
that he was glad to meet me *there*, for Sonny's sake. And he smiled, "You got a real musician in *your* family," and he took his arm from Sonny's shoulder and slapped him, lightly, affectionately, with the back of his hand.

"Well. Now I've heard it all," said a voice behind us. This was another musician, and a friend of Sonny's, a coal-black, cheerful-looking man, built close to the ground. He immediately began confiding to me, at the top of his lungs, the most terrible things about Sonny, his teeth gleaming like a lighthouse and his laugh coming up out of him like the beginning of an earthquake. And it turned out that everyone at the bar knew Sonny, or almost everyone; some were musicians, working there, or nearby, or not working, some were simply hangers-on, and some were there to hear Sonny play. I was introduced to all of them and they were all very polite to me. Yet, it was clear that, for them, I was only Sonny's brother. Here, I was in Sonny's world. Or, rather: his kingdom. Here, it was not even a question that his veins bore royal blood.

They were going to play soon and Creole installed me, by myself, at a table in a dark corner. Then I watched them, Creole, and the little black man, and Sonny, and the others, while they horsed around, standing just below the bandstand. The light from the bandstand spilled just a little short of them and, watching them laughing and gesturing and moving about, I had the feeling that they, nevertheless, were being most careful not to step into that circle of light too suddenly; that if they moved into the light too suddenly, without thinking, they would perish in flame. Then, while I watched, one of them, the small black man, moved into the light and crossed the bandstand and started fooling around with his drums. Then—being funny and being, also, extremely ceremonious— Creole took Sonny by the arm and led him to the piano. A woman's voice called Sonny's name and a few hands started clapping. And Sonny, also being funny and being ceremonious, and so touched, I think, that he could have cried, but neither hiding it nor showing it, riding it like a man, grinned, and put both hands to his heart and bowed from the waist.

Creole then went to the bass fiddle and a lean, very bright-skinned brown man jumped up on the bandstand and picked up his horn. So there they were, and the atmosphere on the bandstand and in the room began to change and tighten. Someone stepped up to the microphone and announced them. Then there were all kinds of murmurs. Some people at the bar shushed others. The waitress ran around, frantically getting in the last orders, guys and chicks got closer to each other, and the lights on the bandstand, on the quartet, turned to a kind of indigo. Then they all looked different there. Creole looked about him for the last time, as though he were making certain that all his chickens were in the coop, and then he—jumped and struck the fiddle. And there they were.

All I know about music is that not many people ever really hear it. And even then, on the rare occasions when something opens within, and the music enters, what we mainly hear, or hear corroborated, are personal, private, vanishing evocations. But the man who creates the music is hearing something else, is dealing with the roar rising from the void and imposing order on it as it hits the air. What is evoked in him, then, is of another order, more terrible because it has no words, and triumphant, too, for that same reason. And his triumph, when he triumphs, is ours. I just watched Sonny's face. His face was troubled, he was working hard, but he wasn't with it. And I had the feeling that, in a way, everyone on the bandstand was waiting for him, both waiting for him and pushing him along. But as I began to watch Creole, I realized that it was Creole who held them all back. He had them on a short rein. Up there, keeping the beat with his whole body, wailing on the fiddle, with his eyes half closed, he was listening to everything, but he was listening to Sonny. He was having a dialogue with Sonny. He wanted Sonny to leave the shoreline and strike out for the deep water. He was Sonny's witness that deep water and drowning were not the same thing—he had been there, and he knew. And he wanted Sonny to know. He was waiting for Sonny to do the things on the keys which would let Creole know that Sonny was in the water.

And, while Creole listened, Sonny moved, deep within, exactly like someone in torment. I had never before thought of how awful the relationship must be between the musician and his instrument. He has to fill it, this instrument, with the breath of life, his own. He has to make it do what he wants it to do. And a piano is just a piano. It's made out of so much wood and wires and little hammers and big ones, and ivory. While there's only so much you can do with it, the only way to find this out is to try; to try and make it do everything.

And Sonny hadn't been near a piano for over a year. And he wasn't on much better terms with his life, not the life that stretched before him now. He and the piano stammered, started one way, got scared, stopped; started another way, panicked, marked time, started again; then seemed to have found a direction, panicked again, got stuck. And the face I saw on Sonny I'd never seen before. Everything had been burned out of it, and, at the same time, things usually hidden were being burned in, by the fire and fury of the battle which was occurring in him up there.

Yet, watching Creole's face as they neared the end of the first set, I had the feeling that something had happened, something I hadn't heard. Then they finished, there was scattered applause, and then, without an instant's warning, Creole started into something else, it was almost sardonic, it was *Am I Blue*.[7] And, as though he commanded, Sonny began to play. Something began to happen. And Creole let out the reins. The dry, low, black man said something awful on the drums, Creole answered, and the drums talked back. Then the horn insisted, sweet and high, slightly detached perhaps, and Creole listened, commenting now and then, dry, and driving, beautiful and calm and old. Then they all came together again, and Sonny was part of the family again. I could tell this from his face. He seemed to have found, right there beneath his fingers, a damn brand-new piano. It seemed that he couldn't get over it. Then, for a while, just being happy with Sonny, they seemed to be agreeing with him that brand-new pianos certainly were a gas.

Then Creole stepped forward to remind them that what they were playing was the blues. He hit something in all of them, he hit something in me, myself, and the music tightened and deepened, apprehension began to beat the air. Creole began to tell us what the blues were all about. They were not about anything very new. He and his boys up there were keeping it new, at the risk of ruin, destruction, madness, and death, in order to find new ways to make us listen. For, while the tale of how we suffer, and how we are delighted, and how we may triumph is never new, it always must be heard. There isn't any other tale to tell, it's the only light we've got in all this darkness.

And this tale, according to that face, that body, those strong hands on those strings, has another aspect in every country, and a new depth in every generation. Listen, Creole seemed to be saying, listen. Now these are Sonny's blues. He made the little black man on the drums know it, and the bright, brown man on the horn. Creole wasn't trying any longer to get Sonny in the water. He was wishing him Godspeed. Then he stepped back, very slowly, filling the air with the immense suggestion that Sonny speak for himself.

Then they all gathered around Sonny and Sonny played. Every now and again one of them seemed to say, amen. Sonny's fingers filled the air with life, his life. But that life contained so many others. And Sonny went all the way back, he really began with the spare, flat statement of the opening phrase of the

240

7. A favorite jazz standard, brilliantly recorded by Billie Holiday.

song. Then he began to make it his. It was very beautiful because it wasn't hurried and it was no longer a lament. I seemed to hear with what burning he had made it his, and what burning we had yet to make it ours, how we could cease lamenting. Freedom lurked around us and I understood, at last, that he could help us to be free if we would listen, that he would never be free until we did. Yet, there was no battle in his face now, I heard what he had gone through, and would continue to go through until he came to rest in earth. He had made it his: that long line, of which we knew only Mama and Daddy. And he was giving it back, as everything must be given back, so that, passing through death, it can live forever. I saw my mother's face again, and felt, for the first time, how the stones of the road she had walked on must have bruised her feet. I saw the moonlit road where my father's brother died. And it brought something else back to me, and carried me past it, I saw my little girl again and felt Isabel's tears again, and I felt my own tears begin to rise. And I was yet aware that this was only a moment, that the world waited outside, as hungry as a tiger, and that trouble stretched above us, longer than the sky.

Then it was over. Creole and Sonny let out their breath, both soaking wet, and grinning. There was a lot of applause and some of it was real. In the dark, the girl came by and I asked her to take drinks to the bandstand. There was a long pause, while they talked up there in the indigo light and after awhile I saw the girl put a Scotch and milk on top of the piano for Sonny. He didn't seem to notice it, but just before they started playing again, he sipped from it and looked toward me, and nodded. Then he put it back on top of the piano. For me, then, as they began to play again, it glowed and shook above my brother's head like the very cup of trembling.[8]

1957

▾   ▾   ▾

---

8. See Isaiah 51:17, 22–23: "Awake, awake, stand up, O Jerusalem, which hast drunk at the hand of the Lord the cup of his fury; thou hast drunken the dregs of the cup of trembling, and wrung them out. . . . Behold, I have taken out of thine hand the cup of trembling, even the dregs of the cup of my fury; thou shalt no more drink it again: But I will put it into the hand of them that afflict thee; . . ."

PLOT A Glossary

action: an imagined event or series of events (an event may be verbal as well as physical, so that saying something or telling a story within the story may be an event)

climax: see *turning point*

conclusion: the fifth part of the structure, the point at which the situation that was destabilized at the beginning of the story becomes stable once more

conflict: a struggle between opposing forces, such as between two people, a person and something in nature or society, or even between two drives, impulses, or parts of the self

curiosity: the desire to know what is happening or has happened

discriminated occasion: the first specific event in a story, more usually in the form of a specific scene than in summary

expectation: the anticipation of what is to happen next (see *suspense*), what a character is like or how he or she will develop, what the theme or meaning of the story will prove to be, and so on

exposition: that part of the structure that sets the scene, introduces and identifies characters, establishes the situation at the beginning of the narrative, though additional exposition is often scattered throughout the story

falling action: the fourth part of plot structure, in which the complications of the rising action are untangled

flashback: structuring device whereby a scene from the fictional past is inserted into the fictional present or dramatized out of order

history: the imaginary people, places, chronologically arranged events that we assume exist in the world of the author's imagination, a world from which he or she chooses and arranges or rearranges the story elements

plot/plot structure: the arrangement of the action

red herring: a false lead, something that misdirects expectations

rising action: the second of the five parts of plot structure, in which events complicate the situation that existed at the beginning of a work, intensifying the conflict or introducing new conflict

selection: the process by which authors leave out some things that seem to be important to the story and include some things that do not seem very important

structuring: the arrangement or rearrangement of the elements in the history

suspense: the expectation of and doubt about what is going to happen next

turning point or **climax:** the third part of plot structure, the point at which the action stops rising and begins falling or reversing

QUESTIONS

1. We are advised by Margaret Atwood that if we want a happy ending to try her sketch A; does it have a happy ending? What does she claim is the only authentic ending for a story? What is the difference between the way Atwood uses the word "plot" and the way it is used in the introduction to this chapter?

2. Rearrange the incidents in "The Country Husband" in chronological order. The structured story begins, "To begin at the beginning . . ." and tells about the near-crash of Francis's plane. Why is that the beginning? What is it the beginning of? Describe the location, appearance, and socioeconomic make-up of Shady Hill. Why is the dog Jupiter "an anomaly" (par. 10)? Why do Clayton Thomas and Anne also not "belong"? Who wins the struggle between Francis Weed and Shady Hill?

3. The opening scene of "Sonny's Blues" is not the first incident in Sonny and his brother's relationship; why does the story begin here? Does this story have a "happy ending"? According to Atwood, Baldwin should, in all honesty, carry on with the story until both Sonny and his brother die; why does Baldwin's story end here?

4. In "Sonny's Blues," how is the first-person narrator, the person telling the story, identified or characterized in the first sentence? in the first paragraph? in the first couple pages? in the story as a whole?

WRITING SUGGESTIONS

1. Choose one of Atwood's "stories" (or conflate two or three) and write a scene or two illustrating the How or the Why.

2. Compare the treatment of marital infidelity in Cheever and Tallent's "No One's a Mystery," Maupassant's "The Jewelry," or one or more of the sketches in "Happy Endings."

3. Write a story or a sketch or outline of a story centering on the same situation in "The Country Husband" but set in the 1990s, and in a place you know.

4. Rearrange the episodes in "Sonny's Blues" as they would appear in the hypothetical history—that is, in chronological order. Pick the three or four changes that seem to you most important. Describe the difference in effect and significance that Baldwin has achieved with his structuring or rearrangement.

2 POINT OF VIEW

S tructuring involves more than plot, more than the ordering of events; selection involves more than the choosing or inventing of incidents. What would "Sonny's Blues" be like seen through the eyes of Sonny? What incidents might he choose to tell? In what order might he arrange them? And what does it do to "The Cask of Amontillado" when we realize, at the end, that it is being told by Montresor fifty years after the event and that his last—probably dying—words, referring to Fortunato, are, *"In pace requiescat"*? Why is he telling the story now? What additional resonance do his final words have?

Who is telling us the story—whose words are we reading? Where does this person stand in relation to what is going on in the story? In drama, events appear before us directly. In narrative, someone is always *between* us and the events—a viewer, a speaker, or both. Narrative, unlike drama, is always mediated. The way a story is mediated is a key element in fictional structure. This mediation involves both the angle of vision—the point from which the people, events, and other details are viewed—and also the words of the story lying between us and the history. The viewing aspect is called the **focus,** and the verbal aspect the **voice.** Both are generally lumped together in the term **point of view.**

Focus acts much as a movie camera does, choosing what we can look at and the angle at which we can view it, framing, proportioning, emphasizing— even distorting. Plot is a structure that places us in a time relationship to the history; focus places us in a spatial relationship.

We must pay careful attention to the focus at any given point in a story. Is it fixed or mobile? Does it stay at more or less the same angle to, and at the same distance from, the characters and action, or does it move around or in and out? In the first three and a half paragraphs of "An Occurrence at Owl Creek Bridge," for example, we seem to be seeing through the lens of a camera that can swing left or right, up or down, but that stays pretty much at the same angle and distance from the bridge. By the middle of the fourth paragraph, however, we're inside the mind of the man who's about to be hanged: "The arrangement commended itself to his judgment. . . . He looked a moment. . . . A piece of dancing driftwood caught his attention. . . . How slowly it appeared to move!" From now on we are inside the condemned man's head. The focus is more limited in scope—for almost all the rest of the story we can see and hear only what he sees and hears. But because the focus is internal as well as limited, we can also know what he thinks. This limited, internal focus is usually called the **centered** or **central consciousness.**

The centered consciousness has been perhaps the most popular focus in fiction for the past hundred years—through most of the history of the modern short story, in fact—and its tightly controlled range and concentration on a single individual seem particularly suited for the short form. During much of this period, fiction, both long and short, has been in one sense realistic—that is, treating the everyday and the natural. It has become increasingly clear, however, that the apparently real is not necessarily what "is" but what is *perceived by* the senses and mind of the individual. (This is sometimes called **psychological realism.**) The centered consciousness, in which things, people, and events are narrated as if perceived through the filter of an individual character's consciousness, has therefore seemed the more realistic way to tell a story. It is a comfortable focus for readers, too. On the one hand, they can identify with someone whose thoughts and perception they share, even if the character is fallible, like Lantin in "The Jewelry." We can identify with point of view in a story told in the first person ("I"), too, but we are too close at times. We cannot escape. The camera cannot pull back as it can in a third-person story.

First-person stories, like "The Cask of Amontillado," are always limited too, and almost always get inside the speaker's mind, though Montresor hides his plans from us. While they cannot withdraw spatially from the narrator, they almost always are withdrawn temporally; that is, the "I" telling the story is older than the "I" experiencing the events. The narrator of Poe's story, for example, is telling what happened fifty years earlier.

The psychological realism gained by having a limited narrator exacts a price from the reader. If we don't hold the author (or the story) responsible for the absolute truth, validity, accuracy, and opinions of the focal character—if he or she is just telling us what he or she thinks, feels, sees—we must accept the possibility that the narrator's vision may be **unreliable.** At a significant point in "Owl Creek Bridge," for example, you will find that the camera pulls back from Peyton Farquhar and we are made to recognize to what extent his consciousness is a reliable witness to what has been going on. The history here is only an occurrence; the limited point of view structures the mere occurrence into a story.

When the point of view is limited, whether to a first-person narrator or to a centered consciousness, it is tied to that individual. When he or she leaves the room, the camera must go too, and if we are to know what happens in the room when the focal character is gone, some means of bringing the information to that character must be devised, such as a letter or a report by another character. The camera may pull back out of the character's mind or even, as in "Owl Creek Bridge," above and away from the character, but it does not generally jump around. An unlimited point of view permits such freedom. In "The Zebra Storyteller" we are with the first zebra (who is killed) when he meets a cat speaking Zebraic and are told he is "astonished." We learn that the zebras can smell no lion and so "decided the woods were haunted by the ghost of a lion," and we get inside the mind of the storyteller and "hear" him speaking to himself. Throughout, the story seems free to see matter from one focus or another and even to dip inside a character's mind.

There are no laws governing point of view in fiction, but there is a general feeling that once a point of view is chosen that ought to be the law for that story. The movement of the focus at the beginning of "An Occurrence at Owl Creek Bridge" is not a jump but a narrowing down: the panorama at the beginning of the story, apparently from the point of view and in the voice of a distant observer, is adjusted and then we settle in, which is not an uncommon device (note how many movies used to begin with a panoramic shot of a town and gradually focused on a house or room). When toward the end of the story the "camera" moves back and away from Peyton Farquhar, we find there has been another reason for the panoramic shot at the beginning. There has been no jumping around and the narrowing and widening seem to be justifiable and meaningful. There are stories in this anthology—"The Most Dangerous Game," "Barn Burning," and "The Lame Shall Enter First," for example—in which the point of view does shift—or jump—from a previously established centered consciousness. Whether these are "flaws" must be judged in each case in terms of function: is the shift merely a narrative convenience or manipulation or is it consistent with or does it contribute to the significance or vision of the story?

Focus and voice often coincide; that is why they are commonly lumped together as point of view. There is no discrepancy that I can see (or hear) between the viewing and the telling in "The Cask of Amontillado," for example. But sometimes there is a discrepancy. Like the focus, the voice in "Owl Creek Bridge" at the beginning of the story is not centered in Peyton Farquhar, but even when the focus narrows on him the voice telling the story is not his; note, for example, "As these thoughts, *which have here to be set down in words*, were flashed into the doomed man's brain" (emphasis added). The discrepancy may prepare a careful reader for later developments in the story.

I have used the common term **narrator** in the usual way—to mean the person who tells the story. You will have noticed that often the narrator really is a person in the story, like Montresor, the narrator in "The Cask of Amontillado." But how about the narrator in "Owl Creek Bridge"? Who is it who sets down Farquhar's words and can say things that Farquhar is not thinking, such as, "Death is a dignitary who, when he comes announced, is to be received with formal manifestations of respect, even by those most familiar with him. In the code of military etiquette silence and fixity are forms of deference" (par. 2). Where is the speaker standing? What kind of person is this narrator?

Is Ambrose Bierce the narrator? Where the narrator plays some role in the story we are less likely to identify him or her with the author; where the narrator is an unidentified voice we often tend to do so. To say that Bierce is the narrator of "Owl Creek Bridge" is not necessarily wrong, but it can be misleading. We can dig up a few facts about the author's life and read them into the story, or, worse, read the character or detail of the story into the author's life. It is more prudent, therefore, especially on the basis of a single story, not to speak of the author but of the author's **persona,** the voice or figure of the author who tells and structures the story, who may or may not resemble in nature or values the actual person of the author. Mary Anne Evans wrote novels under the name of George Eliot; her first-person narrator speaks of "himself." That male narrator may be a good example of the persona or representative that most authors construct to "write" their stories.

We say *write* the stories. The narrator of "Owl Creek Bridge" has to "set down in words" what Farquhar is thinking. But just as poets write of singing their songs (poems), so we often speak of telling a story, and we speak of a narrator, which means a teller. There are stories, usually with first-person narrators, that make much of the convention of oral storytelling—Louise Erdrich's "Love Medicine" for example. "The Cask of Amontillado" is more subtly "oral." It even has an **auditor,** someone other than the reader—that is, a character or characters within the fiction—to whom the "speech" is addressed. The "You" in the second sentence is no more you the reader than the "I" is Poe. He is a silent character within the fiction, here one whose identity or role can, with some thought, be identified.

We are used to thinking of a story in terms of its plot, so that to summarize a story usually means giving a plot summary. But if you shift focus and voice you will often find that though the history has not changed, the story has. You might want to test this out by rewriting "The Cask of Amontillado" in the voice and focus of the auditor, or "The Country Husband" in the voice and focus of Anne, the baby sitter, or Francis Weed's wife.

Just as Margaret Atwood's "Happy Endings" is a story about plot-structure, so "Blow-Up," whose narrator, Michel/I, is appropriately a photographer, seems to be about focus as a means of structuring (and understanding) an event. Because it is a written story, Michel needs a voice, words, but they are chiefly means of describing the visual images, and these become clearer (if they do) not so much from the words as from the enhancement of the details through the enlargement (blowing up) of the photograph.

Point of view has been discussed here largely as a matter of structure, as having a role in creating the story and making it this story and no other. This structuring also engenders meaning and effect. What is the effect, for example, of having such a scoundrel as Montresor tell the story of "The Cask of Amontillado" in the first person? How do we feel about him during the story? Whose side are we on? Do we admire his cleverness or wit? Would we if the story were told from some other point of view? We can talk about how without the shift of the focus to Farquhar Bierce would not have a story, but what is the effect of the surprise ending of that story? How surprising is it? Do we feel cheated? Do we admire the cleverness of the telling? In some says there might be a story in "Blow-Up" without Michel the photographer, but not only would its structure be vastly different, but its current effect—mystery, puzzlement, curiosity, suspense—would be lost. "Sonny's Blues" should be the brother's story, for the outward action, the incidents, chiefly involve him, but the point of view is Sonny's and the meaning for us is the meaning for him. By sharing the experience with him, we must ask whether he/we has/have done the right thing. What do we learn? What do we feel? Much of what a story means, much of its effect upon us depends on the eyes through which it is seen and on the voice that tells it to us.

▼   ▼   ▼

EDGAR ALLAN POE

The Cask of Amontillado

The thousand injuries of Fortunato I had borne as I best could, but when he ventured upon insult I vowed revenge. You, who so well know the nature of my soul, will not suppose, however, that I gave utterance to a threat. *At length* I would be avenged; this was a point definitively settled—but the very definitiveness with which it was resolved precluded the idea of risk. I must not only punish but punish with impunity. A wrong is unredressed when retribution overtakes its redresser. It is equally unredressed when the avenger fails to make himself felt as such to him who has done the wrong.

It must be understood that neither by word nor deed had I given Fortunato cause to doubt my good will. I continued, as was my wont, to smile in his face, and he did not perceive that my smile *now* was at the thought of his immolation.

He had a weak point—this Fortunato—although in other regards he was a man to be respected and even feared. He prided himself upon his connoisseurship in wine. Few Italians have the true virtuoso spirit. For the most part their enthusiasm is adopted to suit the time and opportunity, to practice imposture upon the British and Austrian *millionaires.* In painting and gemmary, Fortunato, like his countrymen, was a quack, but in the matter of old wines he was sincere. In this respect I did not differ from him materially;—I was skilful in the Italian vintages myself, and bought largely whenever I could.

It was about dusk, one evening during the supreme madness of the carnival season, that I encountered my friend. He accosted me with excessive warmth, for he had been drinking much. The man wore motley. He had on a tight-fitting parti-striped dress, and his head was surmounted by the conical cap and bells. I was so pleased to see him that I should never have done wringing his hand.

5 I said to him—"My dear Fortunato, you are luckily met. How remarkably well you are looking to-day. But I have received a pipe[1] of what passes for Amontillado, and I have my doubts."

"How?" said he. "Amontillado? A pipe? Impossible! And in the middle of the carnival!"

"I have my doubts," I replied; "and I was silly enough to pay the full Amontillado price without consulting you in the matter. You were not to be found, and I was fearful of losing a bargain."

"Amontillado!"

"I have my doubts."

10 "Amontillado!"

"And I must satisfy them."

"Amontillado!"

"As you are engaged, I am on my way to Luchresi. If any one has a critical turn it is he. He will tell me——"

"Luchresi cannot tell Amontillado from Sherry."

15 "And yet some fools will have it that his taste is a match for your own."

"Come, let us go."

"Whither?"

"To your vaults."

"My friend, no; I will not impose upon your good nature. I perceive you have an engagement. Luchresi——"

20 "I have no engagement;—come."

"My friend, no. It is not the engagement, but the severe cold with which I perceive you are afflicted. The vaults are insufferably damp. They are encrusted with nitre."

"Let us go, nevertheless. The cold is merely nothing. Amontillado! You have been imposed upon. And as for Luchresi, he cannot distinguish Sherry from Amontillado."

---

1. A cask holding 126 gallons.

Thus speaking, Fortunato possessed himself of my arm; and putting on a mask of black silk and drawing a *roquelaire*[2] closely about my person, I suffered him to hurry me to my palazzo.

There were no attendants at home; they had absconded to make merry in honour of the time. I had told them that I should not return until the morning, and had given them explicit orders not to stir from the house. These orders were sufficient, I well knew, to insure their immediate disappearance, one and all, as soon as my back was turned.

I took from their sconces two flambeaux, and giving one to Fortunato, bowed him through several suites of rooms to the archway that led into the vaults. I passed down a long and winding staircase, requesting him to be cautious as he followed. We came at length to the foot of the descent, and stood together upon the damp ground of the catacombs of the Montresors.

The gait of my friend was unsteady, and the bells upon his cap jingled as he strode.

"The pipe," said he.

"It is farther on," said I; "but observe the white web-work which gleams from these cavern walls."

He turned towards me, and looked into my eyes with two filmy orbs that distilled the rheum of intoxication.

"Nitre?" he asked, at length.

"Nitre," I replied. "How long have you had that cough?"

"Ugh! ugh! ugh!—ugh! ugh! ugh!—ugh! ugh! ugh!—ugh! ugh! ugh!—ugh! ugh! ugh!"

My poor friend found it impossible to reply for many minutes.

"It is nothing," he said, at last.

"Come," I said, with decision, "we will go back; your health is precious. You are rich, respected, admired, beloved; you are happy, as once I was. You are a man to be missed. For me it is no matter. We will go back; you will be ill, and I cannot be responsible. Besides, there is Luchresi——"

"Enough," he said; "the cough is a mere nothing; it will not kill me. I shall not die of a cough."

"True—true," I replied; "and, indeed, I had no intention of alarming you unneccessarily—but you should use all proper caution. A draught of this Medoc[3] will defend us from the damps."

Here I knocked off the neck of a bottle which I drew from a long row of its fellows that lay upon the mould.

"Drink," I said, presenting him the wine.

He raised it to his lips with a leer. He paused and nodded to me familiarly, while his bells jingled.

"I drink," he said, "to the buried that repose around us."

"And I to your long life."

He again took my arm, and we proceeded.

"These vaults," he said, "are extensive."

2. Roquelaure: man's heavy, knee-length cloak.   3. Like De Grâve (below), a French wine.

45   "The Montresors," I replied, "were a great and numerous family."

"I forget your arms."

"A huge human foot d'or,[4] in a field azure; the foot crushes a serpent rampant whose fangs are imbedded in the heel."

"And the motto?"

"*Nemo me impune lacessit.*"[5]

50   "Good!" he said.

The wine sparkled in his eyes and the bells jingled. My own fancy grew warm with the Medoc. We had passed through long walls of piled skeletons, with casks and puncheons intermingling, into the inmost recesses of the catacombs. I paused again, and this time I made bold to seize Fortunato by an arm above the elbow.

"The nitre!" I said; "see, it increases. It hangs like moss upon the vaults. We are below the river's bed. The drops of moisture trickle among the bones. Come, we will go back ere it is too late. Your cough——"

"It is nothing," he said; "let us go on. But first, another draught of the Medoc."

I broke and reached him a flaçon of De Grâve. He emptied it at a breath. His eyes flashed with a fierce light. He laughed and threw the bottle upwards with a gesticulation I did not understand.

55   I looked at him in surprise. He repeated the movement—a grotesque one.

"You do not comprehend?" he said.

"Not I," I replied.

"Then you are not of the brotherhood."

"How?"

60   "You are not of the masons."[6]

"Yes, yes," I said; "yes, yes."

"You? Impossible! A mason?"

"A mason," I replied.

"A sign," he said, "a sign."

65   "It is this," I answered producing from beneath the folds of my *roquelaire* a trowel.

"You jest," he exclaimed, recoiling a few paces. "But let us proceed to the Amontillado."

"Be it so," I said, replacing the tool beneath the cloak and again offering him my arm. He leaned upon it heavily. We continued our route in search of the Amontillado. We passed through a range of low arches, descended, passed on, and descending again, arrived at a deep crypt, in which the foulness of the air caused our flambeaux rather to glow than flame.

At the most remote end of the crypt there appeared another less spacious. Its walls had been lined with human remains, piled to the vault overhead, in the fashion of the great catacombs of Paris. Three sides of this interior crypt were still ornamented in this manner. From the fourth side the bones had been

---

4. Of gold.   5. "No one provokes me with impunity."   6. Masons or Freemasons, an international secret society condemned by the Catholic Church. Montresor means by mason one who builds with stone, brick, etc.

thrown down, and lay promiscuously upon the earth, forming at one point a mound of some size. Within the wall thus exposed by the displacing of the bones, we perceived a still interior crypt or recess, in depth about four feet, in width three, in height six or seven. It seemed to have been constructed for no especial use within itself, but formed merely the interval between two of the colossal supports of the roof of the catacombs, and was backed by one of their circumscribing walls of solid granite.

It was in vain that Fortunato, uplifting his dull torch, endeavoured to pry into the depth of the recess. Its termination the feeble light did not enable us to see.

"Proceed," I said; "herein is the Amontillado. As for Luchresi——" 70

"He is an ignoramus," interrupted my friend, as he stepped unsteadily forward, while I followed immediately at his heels. In an instant he had reached the extremity of the niche, and finding his progress arrested by the rock, stood stupidly bewildered. A moment more and I had fettered him to the granite. In its surface were two iron staples, distant from each other about two feet, horizontally. From one of these depended a short chain, from the other a padlock. Throwing the links about his waist, it was but the work of a few seconds to secure it. He was too much astounded to resist. Withdrawing the key I stepped back from the recess.

"Pass your hand," I said, "over the wall; you cannot help feeling the nitre. Indeed, it is *very* damp. Once more let me *implore* you to return. No? Then I must positively leave you. But I will first render you all the little attentions in my power."

"The Amontillado!" ejaculated my friend, not yet recovered from his astonishment.

"True," I replied; "the Amontillado."

As I said these words I busied myself among the pile of bones of which I 75 have before spoken. Throwing them aside, I soon uncovered a quantity of building stone and mortar. With these materials and with the aid of my trowel, I began vigorously to wall up the entrance of the niche.

I had scarcely laid the first tier of the masonry when I discovered that the intoxication of Fortunato had in great measure worn off. The earliest indication I had of this was a low moaning cry from the depth of the recess. It was *not* the cry of a drunken man. There was then a long and obstinate silence. I laid the second tier, and the third, and the fourth; and then I heard the furious vibration of the chain. The noise lasted for several minutes, during which, that I might hearken to it with the more satisfaction, I ceased my labours and sat down upon the bones. When at last the clanking subsided, I resumed the trowel, and finished without interruption the fifth, the sixth, and the seventh tier. The wall was now nearly upon a level with my breast. I again paused, and holding the flambeaux over the mason-work, threw a few feeble rays upon the figure within.

A succession of loud and shrill screams, bursting suddenly from the throat of the chained form, seemed to thrust me violently back. For a brief moment I hesitated, I trembled. Unsheathing my rapier, I began to grope with it about the recess; but the thought of an instant reassured me. I placed my hand upon the solid fabric of the catacombs and felt satisfied. I reapproached the wall. I replied to the yells of him who clamoured. I re-echoed, I aided, I surpassed them in volume and in strength. I did this, and the clamourer grew still.

It was now midnight, and my task was drawing to a close. I had completed the eighth, the ninth and the tenth tier. I had finished a portion of the last and the eleventh; there remained but a single stone to be fitted and plastered in. I struggled with its weight; I placed it partially in its destined position. But now there came from out the niche a low laugh that erected the hairs upon my head. It was succeeded by a sad voice, which I had difficulty in recognizing as that of the noble Fortunato. The voice said—

"Ha! ha! ha!—he! he! he!—a very good joke, indeed—an excellent jest. We will have many a rich laugh about it at the palazzo—he! he! he!—over our wine—he! he! he!"

80 "The Amontillado!" I said.

"He! he! he!—he! he! he!—yes, the Amontillado. But is it not getting late? Will not they be awaiting us at the palazzo—the Lady Fortunato and the rest? Let us be gone."

"Yes," I said, "let us be gone."

"For the love of God, Montresor!"

"Yes," I said, "for the love of God!"

85 But to these words I hearkened in vain for a reply. I grew impatient. I called aloud—

"Fortunato!"

No answer. I called again—

"Fortunato!"

No answer still. I thrust a torch through the remaining aperture and let it fall within. There came forth in return only a jingling of the bells. My heart grew sick; it was the dampness of the catacombs that made it so. I hastened to make an end of my labour. I forced the last stone into its position; I plastered it up. Against the new masonry I re-erected the old rampart of bones. For the half of a century no mortal has disturbed them. *In pace requiescat!*[7]

1846

AMBROSE BIERCE

An Occurrence at Owl Creek Bridge

I

A man stood upon a railroad bridge in Northern Alabama, looking down into the swift waters twenty feet below. The man's hands were behind his back, the wrists bound with a cord. A rope loosely encircled his neck. It was attached to a

---

7. May he rest in peace!

stout cross-timber above his head, and the slack fell to the level of his knees. Some loose boards laid upon the sleepers supporting the metals of the railway supplied a footing for him and his executioners—two private soldiers of the Federal army, directed by a sergeant, who in civil life may have been a deputy sheriff. At a short remove upon the same temporary platform was an officer in the uniform of his rank, armed. He was a captain. A sentinel at each end of the bridge stood with his rifle in the position known as "support," that is to say, vertical in front of the left shoulder, the hammer resting on the forearm thrown straight across the chest—a formal and unnatural position, enforcing an erect carriage of the body. It did not appear to be the duty of these two men to know what was occurring at the centre of the bridge; they merely blockaded the two ends of the foot plank which traversed it.

Beyond one of the sentinels nobody was in sight; the railroad ran straight away into a forest for a hundred yards, then, curving, was lost to view. Doubtless there was an outpost further along. The other bank of the stream was open ground—a gentle acclivity crowned with a stockade of vertical tree trunks, loop-holed for rifles, with a single embrasure through which protruded the muzzle of a brass cannon commanding the bridge. Midway of the slope between bridge and fort were the spectators—a single company of infantry in line, at "parade rest," the butts of the rifles on the ground, the barrels inclining slightly backward against the right shoulder, the hands crossed upon the stock. A lieutenant stood at the right of the line, the point of his sword upon the ground, his left hand resting upon his right. Excepting the group of four at the centre of the bridge not a man moved. The company faced the bridge, staring stonily, motionless. The sentinels, facing the banks of the stream, might have been statues to adorn the bridge. The captain stood with folded arms, silent, observing the work of his subordinates but making no sign. Death is a dignitary who, when he comes announced, is to be received with formal manifestations of respect, even by those most familiar with him. In the code of military etiquette silence and fixity are forms of deference.

The man who was engaged in being hanged was apparently about thirty-five years of age. He was a civilian, if one might judge from his dress, which was that of a planter. His features were good—a straight nose, firm mouth, broad fore-head, from which his long, dark hair was combed straight back, falling behind his ears to the collar of his well-fitting frock coat. He wore a moustache and pointed beard, but no whiskers; his eyes were large and dark grey and had a kindly expression which one would hardly have expected in one whose neck was in the hemp. Evidently this was no vulgar assassin. The liberal military code makes provision for hanging many kinds of people, and gentlemen are not excluded.

The preparations being complete, the two private soldiers stepped aside and each drew away the plank upon which he had been standing. The sergeant turned to the captain, saluted and placed himself immediately behind that offi-cer, who in turn moved apart one pace. These movements left the condemned man and the sergeant standing on the two ends of the same plank, which spanned three of the cross-ties of the bridge. The end upon which the civilian stood almost, but not quite, reached a fourth. This plank had been held in place by the weight of the captain; it was now held by that of the sergeant. At a signal from the former, the latter would step aside, the plank would tilt and the condemned man go down between two ties. The arrangement commended itself to his judgment as simple and effective. His face had not been covered nor his eyes bandaged. He looked a moment at his "unsteadfast footing," then let his gaze wander to the swirling water of the stream racing madly beneath his feet. A piece of dancing driftwood caught his attention and his eyes followed it down the current. How slowly it appeared to move! What a sluggish stream!

He closed his eyes in order to fix his last thoughts upon his wife and children. The water, touched to gold by the early sun, the brooding mists under the banks at some distance down the stream, the fort, the soldiers, the piece of drift—all had distracted him. And now he became conscious of a new disturbance. Striking through the thought of his dear ones was a sound which he could neither ignore nor understand, a sharp, distinct, metallic percussion like the stroke of a blacksmith's hammer upon the anvil; it had the same ringing quality. He wondered what it was, and whether immeasurably distant or near by—it seemed both. Its recurrence was regular, but as slow as the tolling of a death knell. He awaited each stroke with impatience and—he knew not why—apprehension. The intervals of silence grew progressively longer, the delays became maddening. With their greater infrequency the sounds increased in strength and sharpness. They hurt his ear like the thrust of a knife; he feared he would shriek. What he heard was the ticking of his watch.

He unclosed his eyes and saw again the water below him. "If I could free my hands," he thought, "I might throw off the noose and spring into the stream. By diving I could evade the bullets, and, swimming vigorously, reach the bank, take to the woods, and get away home. My home, thank God, is as yet outside their lines; my wife and little ones are still beyond the invader's farthest advance."

As these thoughts, which have here to be set down in words, were flashed into the doomed man's brain rather than evolved from it, the captain nodded to the sergeant. The sergeant stepped aside.

II

Peyton Farquhar was a well-to-do planter, of an old and highly-respected Alabama family. Being a slave owner, and, like other slave owners, a politician, he was naturally an original secessionist and ardently devoted to the Southern cause. Circumstances of an imperious nature which it is unnecessary to relate here, had prevented him from taking service with the gallant army which had fought the disastrous campaigns ending with the fall of Corinth,[1] and he chafed under the inglorious restraint, longing for the release of his energies, the larger life of the soldier, the opportunity for distinction. That opportunity, he felt, would come, as it comes to all in war time. Meanwhile he did what he could. No service was too humble for him to perform in aid of the South, no adventure too perilous for him to undertake if consistent with the character of a civilian

---

1. Corinth, Mississippi, captured by General Ulysses S. Grant in April 1862.

who was at heart a soldier, and who in good faith and without too much qualification assented to at least a part of the frankly villainous dictum that all is fair in love and war.

One evening while Farquhar and his wife were sitting on a rustic bench near the entrance to his grounds, a grey-clad soldier rode up to the gate and asked for a drink of water. Mrs. Farquhar was only too happy to serve him with her own white hands. While she was gone to fetch the water, her husband approached the dusty horseman and inquired eagerly for news from the front.

"The Yanks are repairing the railroads," said the man, "and are getting ready for another advance. They have reached the Owl Creek bridge, put it in order, and built a stockade on the other bank. The commandant has issued an order, which is posted everywhere, declaring that any civilian caught interfering with the railroad, its bridges, tunnels, or trains, will be summarily hanged. I saw the order." 10

"How far is it to the Owl Creek bridge?" Farquhar asked.

"About thirty miles."

"Is there no force on this side the creek?"

"Only a picket post half a mile out, on the railroad, and a single sentinel at this end of the bridge."

"Suppose a man—a civilian and student of hanging—should elude the picket post and perhaps get the better of the sentinel," said Farquhar, smiling, "what could he accomplish?" 15

The soldier reflected. "I was there a month ago," he replied. "I observed that the flood of last winter had lodged a great quantity of driftwood against the wooden pier at this end of the bridge. It is now dry and would burn like tow."

The lady had now brought the water, which the soldier drank. He thanked her ceremoniously, bowed to her husband, and rode away. An hour later, after nightfall, he repassed the plantation, going northward in the direction from which he had come. He was a Federal scout.

III

As Peyton Farquhar fell straight downward through the bridge, he lost consciousness and was as one already dead. From this state he was awakened—ages later, it seemed to him—by the pain of a sharp pressure upon his throat, followed by a sense of suffocation. Keen, poignant agonies seemed to shoot from his neck downward through every fibre of his body and limbs. These pains appeared to flash along well-defined lines of ramification, and to beat with an inconceivably rapid periodicity. They seemed like streams of pulsating fire heating him to an intolerable temperature. As to his head, he was conscious of nothing but a feeling of fullness—of congestion. These sensations were unaccompanied by thought. The intellectual part of his nature was already effaced; he had power only to feel, and feeling was torment. He was conscious of motion. Encompassed in a luminous cloud, of which he was now merely the fiery heart, without material substance, he swung through unthinkable arcs of oscillation, like a vast pendulum. Then all at once, with terrible suddenness, the light about him shot upward with the noise of a loud plash; a frightful roaring was in his ears, and all was cold and dark. The power of thought was restored; he knew that the rope had broken and he had fallen into the stream. There was no additional strangulation; the noose about his neck was already suffocating him, and kept the water from his lungs. To die of hanging at the bottom of a river!—the idea seemed to him ludicrous. He opened his eyes in the blackness and saw above him a gleam of light, but how distant, how inaccessible! He was still sinking, for the light became fainter and fainter until it was a mere glimmer. Then it began to grow and brighten, and he knew that he was rising toward the surface—knew it with reluctance, for he was now very comfortable. "To be hanged and drowned," he thought, "that is not so bad; but I do not wish to be shot. No; I will not be shot; that is not fair."

He was not conscious of an effort, but a sharp pain in his wrist apprised him that he was trying to free his hands. He gave the struggle his attention, as an idler might observe the feat of a juggler, without interest in the outcome. What splendid effort!—what magnificent, what superhuman strength! Ah, that was a fine endeavour! Bravo! The cord fell away; his arms parted and floated upward, the hands dimly seen on each side in the growing light. He watched them with a new interest as first one and then the other pounced upon the noose at his neck. They tore it away and thrust it fiercely aside, its undulations resembling those of a water-snake. "Put it back, put it back!" He thought he shouted these words to his hands, for the undoing of the noose had been succeeded by the direst pang which he had yet experienced. His neck ached horribly; his brain was on fire; his heart, which had been fluttering faintly, gave a great leap, trying to force itself out at his mouth. His whole body was racked and wrenched with an insupportable anguish! But his disobedient hands gave no heed to the command. They beat the water vigorously with quick, downward strokes, forcing him to the surface. He felt his head emerge; his eyes were blinded by the sunlight; his chest expanded convulsively, and with a supreme and crowning agony his lungs engulfed a great draught of air, which instantly he expelled in a shriek!

He was now in full possession of his physical senses. They were, indeed, preternaturally keen and alert. Something in the awful disturbance of his organic system had so exalted and refined them that they made record of things never before perceived. He felt the ripples upon his face and heard their separate sounds as they struck. He looked at the forest on the bank of the stream, saw the individual trees, the leaves and the veining of each leaf—the very insects upon them, the locusts, the brilliant-bodied flies, the grey spiders stretching their webs from twig to twig. He noted the prismatic colors in all the dewdrops upon a million blades of grass. The humming of the gnats that danced above the eddies of the stream, the beating of the dragon flies' wings, the strokes of the water spiders' legs, like oars which had lifted their boat—all these made audible music. A fish slid along beneath his eyes and he heard the rush of its body parting the water.

He had come to the surface facing down the stream; in a moment the visible world seemed to wheel slowly round, himself the pivotal point, and he saw the bridge, the fort, the soldiers upon the bridge, the captain, the sergeant, the two privates, his executioners. They were in silhouette against the blue sky. They shouted and gesticulated, pointing at him; the captain had drawn his pistol, but did not fire; the others were unarmed. Their movements were grotesque and horrible, their forms gigantic.

Suddenly he heard a sharp report and something struck the water smartly within a few inches of his head, spattering his face with spray. He heard a second report, and saw one of the sentinels with his rifle at his shoulder, a light cloud of blue smoke rising from the muzzle. The man in the water saw the eye of the man on the bridge gazing into his own through the sights of the rifle. He observed that it was a grey eye, and remembered having read that grey eyes were keenest and that all famous marksmen had them. Nevertheless, this one had missed.

A counter swirl had caught Farquhar and turned him half round; he was again looking into the forest on the bank opposite the fort. The sound of a clear, high voice in a monotonous singsong now rang out behind him and came across the water with a distinctness that pierced and subdued all other sounds, even the beating of the ripples in his ears. Although no soldier, he had frequented camps enough to know the dread significance of that deliberate, drawling, aspirated chant; the lieutenant on shore was taking a part in the morning's work. How coldly and pitilessly—with what an even, calm intonation, presaging and enforcing tranquillity in the men—with what accurately-measured intervals fell those cruel words:

"Attention, company. . . . Shoulder arms. . . . Ready. . . . Aim. . . . Fire."

Farquhar dived—dived as deeply as he could. The water roared in his ears like the voice of Niagara, yet he heard the dulled thunder of the volley, and rising again toward the surface, met shining bits of metal, singularly flattened, oscillating slowly downward. Some of them touched him on the face and hands, then fell away, continuing their descent. One lodged between his collar and neck; it was uncomfortably warm, and he snatched it out.

As he rose to the surface, gasping for breath, he saw that he had been a long time under water; he was perceptibly farther down stream—nearer to safety. The soldiers had almost finished reloading; the metal ramrods flashed all at once in the sunshine as they were drawn from the barrels, turned in the air, and thrust into their sockets. The two sentinels fired again, independently and ineffectually.

The hunted man saw all this over his shoulder; he was now swimming vigorously with the current. His brain was as energetic as his arms and legs; he thought with the rapidity of lightning.

"The officer," he reasoned, "will not make that martinet's error a second time. It is as easy to dodge a volley as a single shot. He has probably already given the command to fire at will. God help me, I cannot dodge them all!"

An appalling plash within two yards of him, followed by a loud rushing sound, *diminuendo*, which seemed to travel back through the air to the fort and died in an explosion which stirred the very river to its deeps! A rising sheet of water, which curved over him, fell down upon him, blinded him, strangled him! The cannon had taken a hand in the game. As he shook his head free from the commotion of the smitten water, he heard the deflected shot humming through the air ahead, and in an instant it was cracking and smashing the branches in the forest beyond.

30   "They will not do that again," he thought; "the next time they will use a charge of grape. I must keep my eye upon the gun; the smoke will apprise me— the report arrives too late; it lags behind the missile. It is a good gun."

Suddenly he felt himself whirled round and round—spinning like a top. The water, the banks, the forest, the now distant bridge, fort and men—all were commingled and blurred. Objects were represented by their colors only; circular horizontal streaks of color—that was all he saw. He had been caught in a vortex and was being whirled on with a velocity of advance and gyration which made him giddy and sick. In a few moments he was flung upon the gravel at the foot of the left bank of the stream—the southern bank—and behind a projecting point which concealed him from his enemies. The sudden arrest of his motion, the abrasion of one of his hands on the gravel, restored him and he wept with delight. He dug his fingers into the sand, threw it over himself in handfuls and audibly blessed it. It looked like gold, like diamonds, rubies, emeralds; he could think of nothing beautiful which it did not resemble. The trees upon the bank were giant garden plants; he noted a definite order in their arrangement, inhaled the fragrance of their blooms. A strange, roseate light shone through the spaces among their trunks, and the wind made in their branches the music of æolian harps. He had no wish to perfect his escape, was content to remain in that enchanting spot until retaken.

A whizz and rattle of grapeshot among the branches high above his head roused him from his dream. The baffled cannoneer had fired him a random farewell. He sprang to his feet, rushed up the sloping bank, and plunged into the forest.

All that day he travelled, laying his course by the rounding sun. The forest seemed interminable; nowhere did he discover a break in it, not even a wood-man's road. He had not known that he lived in so wild a region. There was something uncanny in the revelation.

By nightfall he was fatigued, footsore, famishing. The thought of his wife and children urged him on. At last he found a road which led him in what he knew to be the right direction. It was as wide and straight as a city street, yet it seemed untravelled. No fields bordered it, no dwelling anywhere. Not so much as the barking of a dog suggested human habitation. The black bodies of the great trees formed a straight wall on both sides, terminating on the horizon in a point, like a diagram in a lesson in perspective. Overhead, as he looked up through this rift in the wood, shone great golden stars looking unfamiliar and grouped in strange constellations. He was sure they were arranged in some order which had a secret and malign significance. The wood on either side was full of singular noises, among which—once, twice, and again—he distinctly heard whispers in an unknown tongue.

35   His neck was in pain, and, lifting his hand to it, he found it horribly swollen. He knew that it had a circle of black where the rope had bruised it. His eyes felt congested; he could no longer close them. His tongue was swollen with thirst;

he relieved its fever by thrusting it forward from between his teeth into the cool air. How softly the turf had carpeted the untravelled avenue! He could no longer feel the roadway beneath his feet!

Doubtless, despite his suffering, he fell asleep while walking, for now he sees another scene—perhaps he has merely recovered from a delirium. He stands at the gate of his own home. All is as he left it, and all bright and beautiful in the morning sunshine. He must have travelled the entire night. As he pushes open the gate and passes up the wide white walk, he sees a flutter of female garments; his wife, looking fresh and cool and sweet, steps down from the verandah to meet him. At the bottom of the steps she stands waiting, with a smile of ineffable joy, an attitude of matchless grace and dignity. Ah, how beautiful she is! He springs forward with extended arms. As he is about to clasp her, he feels a stunning blow upon the back of the neck; a blinding white light blazes all about him, with a sound like the shock of a cannon—then all is darkness and silence!

Peyton Farquhar was dead; his body, with a broken neck, swung gently from side to side beneath the timbers of the Owl Creek bridge.

1891

JULIO CORTÁZAR

Blow-Up[1]

It'll never be known how this has to be told, in the first person or in the second, using the third person plural or continually inventing modes that will serve for nothing. If one might say: I will see the moon rose, or: we hurt me at the back of my eyes, and especially: you the blond woman was the clouds that race before my your his our yours their faces. What the hell.

Seated ready to tell it, if one might go to drink a bock over there, and the typewriter continue by itself (because I use the machine), that would be perfection. And that's not just a manner of speaking. Perfection, yes, because here is the aperture which must be counted also as a machine (of another sort, a Contax 1.1.2) and it is possible that one machine may know more about another machine than I, you, she—the blond—and the clouds. But I have the dumb luck to know that if I go this Remington will sit turned to stone on top of the table with the air of being twice as quiet that mobile things have when they are not moving. So, I have to write. One of us all has to write, if this is going to get told. Better that it be me who am dead, for I'm less compromised than the rest; I who see only the clouds and can think without being distracted, write without being distracted (there goes another, with a grey edge) and remember without being distracted, I who am dead (and I'm alive, I'm not trying to fool anybody, you'll see when we get to the moment, because I have to begin some way and I've begun with this period, the last one back, the one at the beginning, which in the end is the best of the periods when you want to tell something).

1. Translated by Paul Blackburn.

All of a sudden I wonder why I have to tell this, but if one begins to wonder why he does all he does do, if one wonders why he accepts an invitation to lunch (now a pigeon's flying by and it seems to me a sparrow), or why when someone has told us a good joke immediately there starts up something like a tickling in the stomach and we are not at peace until we've gone into the office across the hall and told the joke over again; then it feels good immediately, one is fine, happy, and can get back to work. For I imagine that no one has explained this, that really the best thing is to put aside all decorum and tell it, because, after all's done, nobody is ashamed of breathing or of putting on his shoes; they're things that you do, and when something weird happens, when you find a spider in your shoe or if you take a breath and feel like a broken window, then you have to tell what's happening, tell it to the guys at the office or to the doctor. Oh, doctor, every time I take a breath . . . Always tell it, always get rid of that tickle in the stomach that bothers you.

And now that we're finally going to tell it, let's put things a little bit in order, we'd be walking down the staircase in this house as far as Sunday, November 7, just a month back. One goes down five floors and stands then in the Sunday in the sun one would not have suspected of Paris in November, with a large appetite to walk around, to see things, to take photos (because we were photographers, I'm a photographer). I know that the most difficult thing is going to be finding a way to tell it, and I'm not afraid of repeating myself. It's going to be difficult because nobody really knows who it is telling it, if I am I or what actually occurred or what I'm seeing (clouds, and once in a while a pigeon) or if, simply, I'm telling a truth which is only my truth, and then is the truth only for my stomach, for this impulse to go running out and to finish up in some manner with, this, whatever it is.

5 We're going to tell it slowly, what happens in the middle of what I'm writing is coming already. If they replace me, if, so soon, I don't know what to say, if the clouds stop coming and something else starts (because it's impossible that this keep coming, clouds passing continually and occasionally a pigeon), if something out of all this . . . And after the "if" what am I going to put if I'm going to close the sentence structure correctly? But if I begin to ask questions, I'll never tell anything, maybe to tell would be like an answer, at least for someone who's reading it.

Roberto Michel, French-Chilean, translator and in his spare time an amateur photographer, left number 11, rue Monsieur-le-Prince Sunday November 7 of the current year (now there're two small ones passing, with silver linings). He had spent three weeks working on the French version of a treatise on challenges and appeals by José Norberto Allende, professor at the University of Santiago. It's rare that there's wind in Paris, and even less seldom a wind like this that swirled around corners and rose up to whip at old wooden venetian blinds behind which astonished ladies commented variously on how unreliable the weather had been these last few years. But the sun was out also, riding the wind and friend of the cats, so there was nothing that would keep me from taking a walk along the docks of the Seine and taking photos of the Conservatoire and Sainte-Chapelle. It was hardly ten o'clock, and I figured that by eleven the light would be good, the best you can get in the fall; to kill some time I detoured around by the Isle Saint-Louis and started to walk along the quai d'Anjou, I stared for a bit at the hôtel de Lauzun, I recited bits from Apollinaire[2] which always get into my head whenever I pass in front of the hôtel de Lauzun (and at that I ought to be remembering the other poet, but Michel is an obstinate beggar), and when the wind stopped all at once and the sun came out at least twice as hard (I mean warmer, but really it's the same thing), I sat down on the parapet and felt terribly happy in the Sunday morning.

One of the many ways of contesting level-zero, and one of the best, is to take photographs, an activity in which one should start becoming an adept very early in life, teach it to children since it requires discipline, aesthetic education, a good eye and steady fingers. I'm not talking about waylaying the lie like any old reporter, snapping the stupid silhouette of the VIP leaving number 10 Downing Street,[3] but in all ways when one is walking about with a camera, one has almost a duty to be attentive, to not lose that abrupt and happy rebound of sun's rays off an old stone, or the pigtails-flying run of a small girl going home with a loaf of bread or a bottle of milk. Michel knew that the photographer always worked as a permutation of his personal way of seeing the world as other than the camera insidiously imposed upon it (now a large cloud is going by, almost black), but he lacked no confidence in himself, knowing that he had only to go out without the Contax to recover the keynote of distraction, the sight without a frame around it, light without the diaphragm aperture or $\frac{1}{250}$ sec. Right now (what a word, *now*, what a dumb lie) I was able to sit quietly on the railing overlooking the river watching the red and black motorboats passing below without it occurring to me to think photographically of the scenes, nothing more than letting myself go in the letting go of objects, running immobile in the stream of time. And then the wind was not blowing.

After, I wandered down the quai de Bourbon until getting to the end of the isle where the intimate square was (intimate because it was small, not that it was hidden, it offered its whole breast to the river and the sky), I enjoyed it, a lot. Nothing there but a couple and, of course, pigeons; maybe even some of those which are flying past now so that I'm seeing them. A leap up and I settled on the wall, and let myself turn about and be caught and fixed by the sun, giving it my face and ears and hands (I kept my gloves in my pocket). I had no desire to shoot pictures, and lit a cigarette to be doing something; I think it was that moment when the match was about to touch the tobacco that I saw the young boy for the first time.

What I'd thought was a couple seemed much more now a boy with his mother, although at the same time I realized that it was not a kid and his mother, and that it was a couple in the sense that we always allegate to couples when we see them leaning up against the parapets or embracing on the benches in the squares. As I had nothing else to do, I had more than enough time to wonder

2. Guillaume Apollinaire (1880–1918), avant-garde French poet who experimented with typographical and calligraphic outrageousness as well as unusual verbal associations.   3. Residence of the British Prime Minister.

why the boy was so nervous, like a young colt or a hare, sticking his hands into his pockets, taking them out immediately, one after the other, running his fingers through his hair, changing his stance, and especially why was he afraid, well, you could guess that from every gesture, a fear suffocated by his shyness, an impulse to step backwards which he telegraphed, his body standing as if it were on the edge of flight, holding itself back in a final, pitiful decorum.

All this was so clear, ten feet away—and we were alone against the parapet at the tip of the island—that at the beginning the boy's fright didn't let me see the blond very well. Now, thinking back on it, I see her much better at that first second when I read her face (she'd turned around suddenly, swinging like a metal weathercock, and the eyes, the eyes were there), when I vaguely understood what might have been occurring to the boy and figured it would be worth the trouble to stay and watch (the wind was blowing their words away and they were speaking in a low murmur). I think that I know how to look, if it's something I know, and also that every looking oozes with mendacity, because it's that which expels us furthest outside ourselves, without the least guarantee, whereas to smell, or (but Michel rambles on to himself easily enough, there's no need to let him harangue on this way). In any case, if the likely inaccuracy can be seen beforehand, it becomes possible again to look; perhaps it suffices to choose between looking and the reality looked at, to strip things of all their unnecessary clothing. And surely all that is difficult besides.

As for the boy I remember the image before his actual body (that will clear itself up later), while now I am sure that I remember the woman's body much better than the image. She was thin and willowy, two unfair words to describe what she was, and was wearing an almost-black fur coat, almost long, almost handsome. All the morning's wind (now it was hardly a breeze and it wasn't cold) had blown through her blond hair which pared away her white, bleak face—two unfair words—and put the world at her feet and horribly alone in the front of her dark eyes, her eyes fell on things like two eagles, two leaps into nothingness, two puffs of green slime. I'm not describing anything, it's more a matter of trying to understand it. And I said two puffs of green slime.

Let's be fair, the boy was well enough dressed and was sporting yellow gloves which I would have sworn belonged to his older brother, a student of law or sociology; it was pleasant to see the fingers of the gloves sticking out of his jacket pocket. For a long time I didn't see his face, barely a profile, not stupid—a terrified bird, a Fra Filippo[4] angel, rice pudding with milk—and the back of an adolescent who wants to take up judo and has had a scuffle or two in defense of an idea or his sister. Turning fourteen, perhaps fifteen, one would guess that he was dressed and fed by his parents but without a nickel in his pocket, having to debate with his buddies before making up his mind to buy a coffee, a cognac, a pack of cigarettes. He'd walk through the streets thinking of the girls in his class, about how good it would be to go to the movies and see the latest film, or to buy novels or neckties or bottles of liquor with green and white labels on them. At home (it would be a respectable home, lunch at noon and romantic land-

4. Fra Filippo Lippi (1406?–1469), Florentine painter of the early Renaissance.

scapes on the walls, with a dark entryway and a mahogany umbrella stand inside the door) there'd be the slow rain of time, for studying, for being mama's hope, for looking like dad, for writing to his aunt in Avignon. So that there was a lot of walking the streets, the whole of the river for him (but without a nickel) and the mysterious city of fifteen-year-olds with its signs in doorways, its terrifying cats, a paper of fried potatoes for thirty francs, the pornographic magazine folded four ways, a solitude like the emptiness of his pockets, the eagerness for so much that was incomprehensible but illumined by a total love, by the availability analogous to the wind and the streets.

This biography was of the boy and of any boy whatsoever, but this particular one now, you could see he was insular, surrounded solely by the blond's presence as she continued talking with him. (I'm tired of insisting, but two long ragged ones just went by. That morning I don't think I looked at the sky once, because what was happening with the boy and the woman appeared so soon I could do nothing but look at them and wait, look at them and . . .) To cut it short, the boy was agitated and one could guess without too much trouble what had just occurred a few minutes before, at most half-an-hour. The boy had come onto the tip of the island, seen the woman and thought her marvelous. The woman was waiting for that because she was there waiting for that, or maybe the boy arrived before her and she saw him from one of the balconies or from a car and got out to meet him, starting the conversation with whatever, from the beginning she was sure that he was going to be afraid and want to run off, and that, naturally, he'd stay, stiff and sullen, pretending experience and the pleasure of the adventure. The rest was easy because it was happening ten feet away from me, and anyone could have gauged the stages of the game, the derisive, competitive fencing; its major attraction was not that it was happening but in foreseeing its denouement. The boy would try to end it by pretending a date, an obligation, whatever, and would go stumbling off disconcerted, wishing he were walking with some assurance, but naked under the mocking glance which would follow him until he was out of sight. Or rather, he would stay there, fascinated or simply incapable of taking the initiative, and the woman would begin to touch his face gently, muss his hair, still talking to him voicelessly, and soon would take him by the arm to lead him off, unless he, with an uneasiness beginning to tinge the edge of desire, even his stake in the adventure, would rouse himself to put his arm around her waist and to kiss her. Any of this could have happened, though it did not, and perversely Michel waited, sitting on the railing, making the settings almost without looking at the camera, ready to take a picturesque shot of a corner of the island with an uncommon couple talking and looking at one another.

Strange how the scene (almost nothing: two figures there mismatched in their youth) was taking on a disquieting aura. I thought it was I imposing it, and that my photo, if I shot it, would reconstitute things in their true stupidity. I would have liked to know what he was thinking, a man in a grey hat sitting at the wheel of a car parked on the dock which led up to the footbridge, and whether he was reading the paper or asleep. I had just discovered him because people inside a parked car have a tendency to disappear, they get lost in that wretched, private cage stripped of the beauty that motion and danger give it. And nevertheless, the car had been there the whole time, forming part (or deforming that part) of the isle. A car: like saying a lighted streetlamp, a park bench. Never like saying wind, sunlight, those elements always new to the skin and the eyes, and also the boy and the woman, unique, put there to change the island, to show it to me in another way. Finally, it may have been that the man with the newspaper also became aware of what was happening and would, like me, feel that malicious sensation of waiting for everything to happen. Now the woman had swung around smoothly, putting the young boy between herself and the wall, I saw them almost in profile, and he was taller, though not much taller, and yet she dominated him, it seemed like she was hovering over him (her laugh, all at once, a whip of feathers), crushing him just by being there, smiling, one hand taking a stroll through the air. Why wait any longer? Aperture at six-teen, a sighting which would not include the horrible black car, but yes, that tree, necessary to break up too much grey space . . .

15   I raised the camera, pretended to study a focus which did not include them, and waited and watched closely, sure that I would finally catch the revealing expression, one that would sum it all up, life that is rhythmed by movement but which a stiff image destroys, taking time in cross section, if we do not choose the essential imperceptible fraction of it. I did not have to wait long. The woman was getting on with the job of handcuffing the boy smoothly, stripping from him what was left of his freedom a hair at a time, in an incredibly slow and delicious torture. I imagined the possible endings (now a small fluffy cloud appears, almost alone in the sky), I saw their arrival at the house (a basement apartment probably, which she would have filled with large cushions and cats) and conjec-tured the boy's terror and his desperate decision to play it cool and to be led off pretending there was nothing new in it for him. Closing my eyes, if I did in fact close my eyes, I set the scene: the teasing kisses, the woman mildly repelling the hands which were trying to undress her, like in novels, on a bed that would have a lilac-colored comforter, on the other hand she taking off his clothes, plainly mother and son under a milky yellow light, and everything would end up as usual, perhaps, but maybe everything would go otherwise, and the initiation of the adolescent would not happen, she would not let it happen, after a long prologue wherein the awkwardnesses, the exasperating caresses, the running of hands over bodies would be resolved in who knows what, in a separate and solitary pleasure, in a petulant denial mixed with the art of tiring and discon-certing so much poor innocence. It might go like that, it might very well go like that; that woman was not looking for the boy as a lover, and at the same time she was dominating him toward some end impossible to understand if you do not imagine it as a cruel game, the desire to desire without satisfaction, to excite herself for someone else, someone who in no way could be that kid.

Michel is guilty of making literature, of indulging in fabricated unrealities. Nothing pleases him more than to imagine exceptions to the rule, individuals outside the species, not-always-repugnant monsters. But that woman invited speculation, perhaps giving clues enough for the fantasy to hit the bullseye.

Before she left, and now that she would fill my imaginings for several days, for I'm given to ruminating, I decided not to lose a moment more. I got it all into the view-finder (with the tree, the railing, the eleven-o'clock sun) and took the shot. In time to realize that they both had noticed and stood there looking at me, the boy surprised and as though questioning, but she was irritated, her face and body flat-footedly hostile, feeling robbed, ignominiously recorded on a small chemical image.

I might be able to tell it in much greater detail but it's not worth the trouble. The woman said that no one had the right to take a picture without permission, and demanded that I had her over the film. All this in a dry, clear voice with a good Parisian accent, which rose in color and tone with every phrase. For my part, it hardly mattered whether she got the roll of film or not, but anyone who knows me will tell you, if you want anything from me, ask nicely. With the result that I restricted myself to formulating the opinion that not only was photography in public places not prohibited, but it was looked upon with decided favor, both private and official. And while that was getting said, I noticed on the sly how the boy was falling back, sort of actively backing up though without moving, and all at once (it seemed almost incredible) he turned and broke into a run, the poor kid, thinking that he was walking off and in fact in full flight, running past the side of the car, disappearing like a gossamer filament of angel-spit in the morning air.

But filaments of angel-spittle are also called devil-spit, and Michel had to endure rather particular curses, to hear himself called meddler and imbecile, taking great pains meanwhile to smile and to abate with simple movements of his head such a hard sell. As I was beginning to get tired, I heard the car door slam. The man in the grey hat was there, looking at us. It was only at that point that I realized he was playing a part in the comedy.

He began to walk toward us, carrying in his hand the paper he had been pretending to read. What I remember best is the grimace that twisted his mouth askew, it covered his face with wrinkles, changed somewhat both in location and shape because his lips trembled and the grimace went from one side of his mouth to the other as though it were on wheels, independent and involuntary. But the rest stayed fixed, a flour-powdered clown or bloodless man, dull dry skin, eyes deepset, the nostrils black and prominently visible, blacker than the eyebrows or hair or the black necktie. Walking cautiously as though the pavement hurt his feet; I saw patent-leather shoes with such thin soles that he must have felt every roughness in the pavement. I don't know why I got down off the railing, nor very well why I decided to not give them the photo, to refuse that demand in which I guessed at their fear and cowardice. The clown and the woman consulted one another in silence: we made a perfect and unbearable triangle, something I felt compelled to break with a crack of a whip. I laughed in their faces and began to walk off, a little more slowly, I imagine, than the boy. At the level of the first houses, beside the iron footbridge, I turned around to look at them. They were not moving, but the man had dropped his newspaper; it seemed to me that the woman, her back to the parapet, ran her hands over the stone with the classical and absurd gesture of someone pursued looking for a way out.

What happened after that happened here, almost just now, in a room on the fifth floor. Several days went by before Michel developed the photos he'd taken on Sunday; his shots of the Conservatoire and of Sainte-Chapelle were all they should be. Then he found two or three proof-shots he'd forgotten, a poor attempt to catch a cat perched astonishingly on the roof of a rambling public urinal, and also the shot of the blond and the kid. The negative was so good that he made an enlargement; the enlargement was so good that he made one very much larger, almost the size of a poster. It did not occur to him (now one wonders and wonders) that only the shots of the Conservatoire were worth so much work. Of the whole series, the snapshot of the tip of the island was the only one which interested him; he tacked up the enlargement on one wall of the room, and the first day he spent some time looking at it and remembering, that gloomy operation of comparing the memory with the gone reality; a frozen memory, like any photo, where nothing is missing, not even, and especially, nothingness, the true solidifier of the scene. There was the woman, there was the boy, the tree rigid above their heads, the sky as sharp as the stone of the parapet, clouds and stones melded into a single substance and inseparable (now one with sharp edges is going by, like a thunderhead). The first two days I accepted what I had done, from the photo itself to the enlargement on the wall, and didn't even question that every once in a while I would interrupt my translation of José Norberto Allende's treatise to encounter once more the woman's face, the dark splotches on the railing. I'm such a jerk; it had never occurred to me that when we look at a photo from the front, the eyes reproduce exactly the position and the vision of the lens; it's these things that are taken for granted and it never occurs to anyone to think about them. From my chair, with the typewriter directly in front of me, I looked at the photo ten feet away, and then it occurred to me that I had hung it exactly at the point of view of the lens. It looked very good that way; no doubt, it was the best way to appreciate a photo, though the angle from the diagonal doubtless has its pleasures and might even divulge different aspects. Every few minutes, for example when I was unable to find the way to say in good French what José Norberto Allende was saying in very good Spanish, I raised my eyes and looked at the photo; sometimes the woman would catch my eye, sometimes the boy, sometimes the pavement where a dry leaf had fallen admirably situated to heighten a lateral section. Then I rested a bit from my labors, and I enclosed myself again happily in that morning in which the photo was drenched, I recalled ironically the angry picture of the woman demanding I give her the photograph, the boy's pathetic and ridiculous flight, the entrance on the scene of the man with the white face. Basically, I was satisfied with myself; my part had not been too brilliant, and since the French have been given the gift of the sharp response, I did not see very well why I'd chosen to leave without a complete demonstration of the rights, privileges and prerogatives of citizens. The important thing, the really important thing was having helped the kid to escape in time (this in case my theorizing was correct, which was not sufficiently proven, but the running away itself seemed to show it so). Out of plain meddling, I had given him the opportunity finally to take advantage of his fright to do something useful; now he would be regretting it, feeling his honor impaired, his manhood diminished. That was better than the attentions of a woman capable of looking as she had looked at him on that island. Michel is something of a puritan at times, he believes that one should not seduce someone from a position of strength. In the last analysis, taking that photo had been a good act.

Well, it wasn't because of the good act that I looked at it between paragraphs while I was working. At that moment I didn't know the reason, the reason I had tacked the enlargement onto the wall; maybe all fatal acts happen that way, and that is the condition of their fulfillment. I don't think the almost-furtive trembling of the leaves on the tree alarmed me, I was working on a sentence and rounded it out successfully. Habits are like immense herbariums, in the end an enlargement of 32×28 looks like a movie screen, where, on the tip of the island, a woman is speaking with a boy and a tree is shaking its dry leaves over their heads.

But her hands were just too much. I had just translated: "In that case, the second key resides in the intrinsic nature of difficulties which societies . . ." — when I saw the woman's hand beginning to stir slowly, finger by finger. There was nothing left of me, a phrase in French which I would never have to finish, a typewriter on the floor, a chair that squeaked and shook, fog. The kid had ducked his head like boxers do when they've done all they can and are waiting for the final blow to fall; he had turned up the collar of his overcoat and seemed more a prisoner than ever, the perfect victim helping promote the catastrophe. Now the woman was talking into his ear, and her hand opened again to lay itself against his cheekbone, to caress and caress it, burning it, taking her time. The kid was less startled than he was suspicious, once or twice he poked his head over the woman's shoulder and she continued talking, saying something that made him look back every few minutes toward that area where Michel knew the car was parked and the man in the grey hat, carefully eliminated from the photo but present in the boy's eyes (how doubt that now) in the words of the woman, in the woman's hands, in the vicarious presence of the woman. When I saw the man come up, stop near them and look at them, his hands in his pockets and a stance somewhere between disgusted and demanding, the master who is about to whistle in his dog after a frolic in the square, I understood, if that was to understand, what had to happen now, what had to have happened then, what would have to happen at that moment, among these people, just where I had poked my nose in to upset an established order, interfering inno-cently in that which had not happened, but which was now going to happen, now was going to be fulfilled. And what I had imagined earlier was much less horrible than the reality, that woman, who was not there by herself, she was not caressing or propositioning or encouraging for her own pleasure, to lead the angel away with his tousled hair and play the tease with his terror and his eager grace. The real boss was waiting there, smiling petulantly, already certain of the business; he was not the first to send a woman in the vanguard, to bring him the prisoners manacled with flowers. The rest of it would be so simple, the car, some house or another, drinks, stimulating engravings, tardy tears, the awakening in hell. And there was nothing I could do, this time I could do absolutely nothing. My strength had been a photograph, that, there, where they were taking their revenge on me, demonstrating clearly what was going to happen. The photo had been taken, the time had run out, gone; we were so far from one another, the abusive act had certainly already taken place, the tears already shed, and the rest conjecture and sorrow. All at once the order was inverted, they were alive, moving, they were deciding and had decided, they were going to their future; and I on this side, prisoner of another time, in a room on the fifth floor, to not know who they were, that woman, that man, and that boy, to be only the lens of my camera, something fixed, rigid, incapable of intervention. It was horrible, their mocking me, deciding it before my impotent eye, mocking me, for the boy again was looking at the flour-faced clown and I had to accept the fact that he was going to say yes, that the proposition carried money with it or a gimmick, and I couldn't yell for him to run, or even open the road to him again with a new photo, a small and almost meek intervention which would ruin the framework of drool and perfume. Everything was going to resolve itself right there, at that moment; there was like an immense silence which had nothing to do with physical silence. It was stretching it out, setting itself up. I think I screamed, I screamed terribly, and that at that exact second I realized that I was beginning to move toward them, four inches, a step, another step, the tree swung its branches rhythmically in the foreground, a place where the railing was tarnished emerged from the frame, the woman's face turned toward me as though surprised, was enlarging, and then I turned a bit, I mean that the camera turned a little, and without losing sight of the woman, I began to close in on the man who was looking at me with the black holes he had in place of eyes, surprised and angered both, he looked, wanting to nail me onto the air, and at that instant I happened to see something like a large bird outside the focus that was flying in a single swoop in front of the picture, and I leaned up against the wall of my room and was happy because the boy had just managed to escape, I saw him running off, in focus again, sprinting with his hair flying in the wind, learning finally to fly across the island, to arrive at the footbridge, return to the city. For the second time he'd escaped them, for the second time I was helping him to escape, returning him to his precarious paradise. Out of breath, I stood in front of them; no need to step closer, the game was played out. Of the woman you could see just maybe a shoulder and a bit of the hair, brutally cut off by the frame of the picture; but the man was directly center, his mouth half open, you could see a shaking black tongue, and he lifted his hands slowly, bringing them into the foreground, an instant still in perfect focus, and then all of him a lump that blotted out the island, the tree, and I shut my eyes, I didn't want to see any more, and I covered my face and broke into tears like an idiot.

Now there's a big white cloud, as on all these days, all this untellable time. What remains to be said is always a cloud, two clouds, or long hours of a sky perfectly clear, a very clean, clear rectangle tacked up with pins on the wall of my room. That was what I saw when I opened my eyes and dried them with my fingers: the clear sky, and then a cloud that drifted in from the left, passed gracefully and slowly across and disappeared on the right. And then another, and for a change sometimes, everything gets grey, all one enormous cloud, and suddenly the splotches of rain cracking down, for a long spell you can see it raining over the picture, like a spell of weeping reversed, and little by little, the frame becomes clear, perhaps the sun comes out, and again the clouds begin to come, two at a time, three at a time. And the pigeons once in a while, and a sparrow or two.

1956

▼   ▼   ▼

POINT OF VIEW A Glossary

auditor: someone other than the reader—a character within the fiction—to whom the story or "speech" is addressed

centered (central) consciousness: a limited point of view, one tied to a single character throughout the story, often revealing his or her inner thoughts but unable to read the thoughts of others

focus: the point from which people, events, and other details in a story are viewed. See *point of view*

limited point of view or **limited focus:** a perspective pinned to a single character, whether first-person or a third-person centered consciousness, so that we cannot know for sure what is going on in the minds of other characters; when the focal character leaves the room in a story we must go too and cannot know what is going on while our "eyes" or "camera" is gone. A variation on this, which generally has no name and is often lumped with the *omniscient point of view,* is the point of view that can wander like a camera from one character to another and close in or move back but cannot (or at least does not) get inside anyone's head, does not present from the inside any character's thoughts

narrator: the person who tells the story

omniscient point of view: see *unlimited focus*

persona: the voice or figure of the author who tells and structures the story, and who may or may not share the values of the actual person of the author

point of view: focus; the point from which people, events, and other details in a story are viewed. This term is sometimes used to include both focus and voice

psychological realism: a modification of the concept of realism, or telling it like it is, which recognizes that what is real to the individual is that which he or she perceives. It is the ground for the use of the centered consciousness, or the first-person narrator, since both of these present reality only as something perceived by the focal character

unlimited focus or **omniscient point of view:** a perspective that can be seen from one character's view, then another's, then another's, or can be moved in or out of any character at any time

unreliable narrator: a speaker or voice whose vision or version of the details of the story are consciously or unconsciously deceiving; such a narrator's version is usually subtly undermined by details in the story or the reader's general knowledge of facts outside the story; if, for example, the narrator were to tell you that Columbus was Spanish, and that he discovered America in the fourteenth century when his ship *The Golden Hind* landed on the coast of Florida near present-day Gainesville, you might not trust other things he tells you

voice: the acknowledged or unacknowledged source of the words of the story; the "speaker;" the "person" telling the story

QUESTIONS

1. Who is the auditor, the "You," addressed in the first paragraph of "The Cask of Amontillado"? (You may want to wait until you have finished the last sentence of the story before answering.) When is the story being told? Why? How does your knowledge of the auditor and the occasion influence the story's effect?

2. Looking back over "An Occurrence at Owl Creek Bridge," how many of Peyton Farquhar's sensory perceptions can you reinterpret now that you know what must have been really happening?

3. Summarize, as best you can, the problem the narrator of "Blow-Up" has in deciding how the story is to be told. Why does he say a typewriter would be the best narrator? Who is the narrator? Is Roberto Michel (par. 6) the same "one" who goes down five floors that Sunday in paragraph 4? In paragraph 6, sentence 2, Michel is "He," but after two sentences of description, there is a shift to "I"; what is the effect of such shifting on you as reader (besides impatience or puzzlement)?

4. Near the end of paragraph 11, the narrator of "Blow-Up" says, "I'm not describing anything, it's more a matter of trying to understand it." How do the two differ? In what way may they relate to both the reader's taking in of what is read and his or her attempt to understand it? How does the distinction justify Michel's imagining the boy's life and home (paragraph 12), his foreseeing what is going to happen next in paragraphs 13 and 15? To what extent is the distinction modified by Michel's revision of his understanding of the scene in paragraph 22? How is the narrator's statement about understanding in paragraph 11 related to his statement in paragraph 16 that "Michel is guilty of making literature, of indulging in fabricating realities," and why the word "guilty"?

5. Why is the word "now" in paragraph 7 of "Blow-Up" "a dumb lie"? How do you understand all the parenthetical remarks about clouds? From whose focus are the clouds seen? The final paragraph centers on the clouds and sky. What is the effect? How do you understand the significance of this attention? In what way(s) is it a suitable ending?

WRITING SUGGESTIONS

1. Write a parody of "The Cask of Amontillado" set in modern times, perhaps on a college campus ("A Barrel of Bud"?).

2. Write a "pre-text" narrating the "thousand injuries" and the insult that triggered Montresor's revenge, or sketch several possibilities for such a pre-text narrated from various points of view.

3. What would the effect be if "Blow-Up" were told "straight," from the simple first-person point of view? (Use specific details from the story in your analysis. You may want to duplicate several paragraphs and "edit," omitting all deviations from first-person narration.)

3 CHARACTERIZATION

I n a good many stories the narrator is a disembodied offstage voice, without an identity or a personal history, without influence on the action, without qualities other than those that a voice and style may suggest. So it is in some of the earlier stories in this volume—"The Zebra Storyteller," "No One's a Mystery," "The Jewelry," "An Occurrence at Owl Creek Bridge." Poe's narrator, however, not only tells us the story but has a part in the action as well; without him we not only would not know the story, but neither would there be a story. He looks back into his past; he is there in the story, speaking, listening, reacting. In addition to being the narrator, he is a **character:** someone who acts, appears, or is referred to as playing a part in a work.

The most common term for the character with the leading male role is **hero,** the "good guy" who opposes the **villain,** or "bad guy." The leading female character is the **heroine.** Heroes and heroines are usually larger than life, stronger or better than most human beings, almost godlike (and there's even a brand of heroes nowadays so close to being godlike that they are called superheroes). In most modern fiction, however, the leading character is much more ordinary, more like the rest of us. Such a character is called the **anti-hero,** not because he opposes the hero but because he is not like a hero in stature or perfection. An older and more neutral term than hero for the leading character, a term that does not imply either the presence or absence of outstanding virtue (and with the added advantage of referring equally to male and female), is **protagonist,** whose opponent is the **antagonist.** You might get into long and pointless arguments by calling Lantin or Montresor a hero, but either is his story's protagonist.

The **major characters** are those we see more of over a longer period of time; we learn more about them, and we think of them as more complex and frequently therefore more "realistic" than the **minor characters,** the figures who fill out the story. These major characters can grow and change, as Lantin does and as Judith does in Doris Lessing's "Our Friend Judith"; by the end of these stories both protagonists have acted unpredictably based on what we learned earlier in the story about them and their past actions. Characters who can thus "surprise convincingly," an influential critic says, are **round characters.** Because Tallent's and Poe's characters are not very complex and do not change in surprising ways, they are called **flat.** But we must be careful not to let terms like *flat* and *round* turn into value judgments. Because flat characters are less complex than round ones it is easy to assume they are artistically inferior; we need only to think of the characters of Charles Dickens, almost all of whom are flat, to realize that this is not always true.

The terms *flat* and *round*, like the terms *hero* and *antihero*, are not absolute or precise. They designate extremes or tendencies, not pigeonholes. Is Poe's Montresor entirely flat? Is Shakespeare's Falstaff? Charlie Chaplin's Little Tramp? Little Orphan Annie? Are all these characters equally flat? We will probably agree that Baldwin's Sonny is a round character, but what about Cortázar's Michel? Cheever's Francis Weed? Are they all equally round? Our answers are less important than our looking carefully at these characters to see what we know about each of them, to what degree they can be summed up in a phrase or a sentence; to discover how we learned what we know about them and how our judgment has been controlled by the story; to think about and perhaps judge the assumptions about human motivation, behavior, and nature that underlie the character and his or her characterization. Flat and round are useful as categories but are even more useful as tools of investigation, as ways of focusing our attention and sharpening our perception.

Though most of Dickens's flat characters are highly individualized, not to say unique, some, like Fagin, the avaricious Jewish moneylender, are **stereotypes**: characters based on conscious or unconscious cultural assumptions that sex, age, ethnic or national identification, occupation, marital status, and so on are predictably accompanied by certain character traits, actions, even values.

The stereotype may be very useful in creating a round character, one who can surprise convincingly: Judith, according to a Canadian woman, is "one of your typical English spinsters." Judith, however, acts in ways that deny the limitations of the stereotype. A stereotype is, after all, only a quick—and somewhat superficial—form of classification, and classification is a common first step in definitions. One of the chief ways we have of describing or defining is by placing the thing to be defined in a category or class and then distinguishing it from the other members of that class. A good deal of **characterization**—the art, craft, method of presentation, or creation of fictional personages—involves a similar process. Characters are almost inevitably identified by category—by sex, age, nationality, occupation, and so on. We learn that the narrator of "Why I Live at the P.O." is a woman, relatively young, who lives in a small town in Mississippi.

Paradoxically, the more groups a character is placed in, the more individual he or she becomes. Fenstad's mother, for example, is an old woman, a protective and critical mother, two separate but closely related stereotypes that categorize her, but she is also a social, political, and intellectual radical, which significantly individualizes her within the various categories into which she fits.

Not all generalizations involve cultural stereotypes, of course. Some may involve generalized character traits that the story or narrator defines for us (and that we must accept unless events in the story prove otherwise). Physical characteristics also serve as categories. As with stereotypes, when physical characteristics are multiplied, the result is more and more particularizing or individualizing. The detailed physical description of Judith makes it possible to visualize her rather fully, almost to recognize her as an individual:

> Judith is tall, small-breasted, slender. Her light brown hair is parted in the centre and cut straight around her neck. A high straight forehead, straight nose, and full grave mouth are setting for her eyes, which are green, large and prominent. Her lids are very white, fringed with gold, and moulded close over the eyeball.... (par. 7)

There are many other ways in which a character is characterized and individualized besides stereotyping and "destereotyping," and besides classifying and particularizing by physical description. In most cases we see what characters do and hear what they say; we sometimes learn what they think, and what other people think or say about them; we often know what kind of clothes they wear, what and how much they own, treasure, or covet; we may be told about their childhood, parents, or some parts of their past. We learn about Eudora Welty's "Sister" from her age, sex, and where she lives. We learn a good deal more from the way she talks to her family and they to her, how she decides what she owns, and what she chooses to take with her when she moves.

Though characterization is gradual, taking place sequentially through the story, it is not, as it may seem natural to assume, entirely cumulative. We do not begin with an empty space called Judith or Francis Weed or Sonny and fill it in gradually by adding physical traits, habitual actions, ways of speaking, and so on. Our imaginations do not work that way. Rather, just as at each point in the action we project some sort of configuration of how the story will come out or what the world of the story will be like or mean, so we project a more or less complete image of each character at the point at which the he or she is first mentioned or appears. This image is based on the initial reference in the text, our reading, and life experiences and associations (Don't you have an image of a Herb? a Maude? a spinster?). The next time the character is mentioned, or when he or she speaks or acts, we do not so much "adjust" our first impression as we project a new image (just as in the plot we project a new series of developments and a new outcome). There may be some carryover, but we do not in the course of the story put the character together like a Mr. Potato Head. Instead, we overlay one image on the other, and though the final image may be the most enduring, the early images do not all disappear: our view of the character is multidimensional, flickering, like a time-lapse photograph. Perhaps that is why it is rare that any actor in a film based on a novel or story matches the way we imagined that character if we have read the book or story first—our imagination has not one image but rather a sequence of images associated with that character. It is also why some of us feel that seeing the film before reading the book hobbles the imagination. A particular character's physical attributes, for example, may not be described in a novel until after that character has been involved in some incident; the reader may then need to adjust his earlier vision of that character, which is not an option for the viewer of a film. It is thus the reader, rather than a casting director, who finalizes a character in his or her own imagination.

For no matter how many methods of characterization are employed, at some point the definition of the individual stops. No matter how individualized the character may be, he or she remains a member of a number of groups, and we make certain assumptions about that character based on our fixed or stereotyped notions of those groups. To destroy a stereotype, a story must introduce a stereotype to destroy. And somehow the destereotyped character, no matter how particularized, remains to some degree representative. If Judith turns out to be not as prudish and prissy as the stereotype of the English spinster has led us to believe, we may well conclude that the stereotype is false and that Judith is more representative of the real English spinster than the stereotype is. Indeed, this tendency to generalize from the particulars of a story extends beyond cultural groups, sometimes to human character at large: if Sonny can change his ways after years of habitual conduct, then human character, the story might seem to say, is not permanently fixed at birth, in infancy, childhood, ever.

One of the reasons it is so difficult to discuss character is precisely that the principles of definition and evaluation of fictional characters (not of their characterizations, the way they are presented) are the same as those we use for real people, an area of violent controversy and confusion. The very term *character*, when it refers not to a fictional personage but to a combination of qualities in a human being, is somewhat ambiguous. It usually has moral overtones, often favorable (a man of character); it is sometimes neutral but evaluative (character reference). Judgment about character (not characterization, remember) usually involves moral terms like *good* and *bad* and *strong* and *weak*. **Personality** usually implies that which distinguishes or individualizes a person, and the judgment called for is not so much moral as social—*pleasing* or *displeasing*. An older term, **nature** (it is in one's nature to be so or do such), usually implies something inherent or inborn, something fixed and thus predictable. The **existential character** implies the opposite; that is, whatever our past, our conditioning, our pattern or previous behavior, we can, by choice, by free will, change all that right this minute, as Sonny does.

Fictional characters thus frequently seem to be part of the history that lies behind the story or beyond the story as part of our own world, to exist in a reality that is detachable from the words and events of the story in which they appear. We feel we might recognize Tom Jones, Jane Eyre, or Sherlock Holmes on the street, and we might be able to anticipate what they would say or do in *our* world, outside the story. Fictional characters are neither real nor detachable, of course, and they exist only in the words of the works in which they are presented. We must not forget the distinction between the character and the characterization, the method by which he or she is presented; so we must be careful to distinguish the *good character*, meaning someone whom, if real, we would consider virtuous, and the *good characterization*, meaning a fictional person who, no matter what his or her morality or behavior, is well presented.

We must recognize that characters are not finally detachable—that they have roles, functions, limitations, and their very existence in the context of the story; we must not confuse fictional characters with real people, or character with characterization. This is not to say, however, that we may not learn about real people from characters in fiction or learn to understand fictional characters in part from what we know about real people. For real people too exist in a context of other people and other elements, their history and geography and their "narrator," the one who is representing them—that is, *you*. Indeed, it may be worth paying particular attention to how stories create the images of people and what those images assume about human character precisely because this process and these assumptions are so similar to the way we get to know and understand real people. For we are all artists representing reality to ourselves. If we study the art of characterization we may become better artists, able to enrich both our reading and our lives.

The Grace Paley story that ends this chapter is here as a reminder that the elements of fiction are abstractions, useful for analysis but not truly separable. In that story, for example, the narrator's father tells her to tell a simple story, and her first attempt is pure plot or incident. But he says she's left everything out—what her protagonist looks like, what her parents were like—circumstances and character. She tries again, and this time her version is heavy on character of both the fictional woman and her son. Now the father challenges, then praises, the ending. The narrator says the end is not the end, the woman's character is not fixed, but what we have called existential—she can change. Throughout plot, or action, and character are fused. As Henry James has said,

> What is character but the determination of incident? What is incident but the illustration of character? . . . It is an incident for a woman to stand up with her hand resting on a table and look at you in a certain way; or if it is not an incident I think it will be hard to say what it is. At the same time it is an expression of character. If you say you don't see it, . . . this is exactly what the artist who has reasons of his own for thinking he *does* see it undertakes to show you.

▼   ▼   ▼

EUDORA WELTY

Why I Live at the P.O.

I was getting along fine with Mama, Papa-Daddy, and Uncle Rondo until my sister Stella-Rondo just separated from her husband and came back home again. Mr. Whitaker! Of course I went with Mr. Whitaker first, when he first appeared here in China Grove, taking "Pose Yourself" photos, and Stella-Rondo broke us up. Told him I was one-sided. Bigger on one side than the other, which is a deliberate, calculated falsehood: I'm the same. Stella-Rondo is exactly twelve months to the day younger than I am and for that reason she's spoiled.

She's always had anything in the world she wanted and then she'd throw it away. Papa-Daddy give her this gorgeous Add-a-Pearl necklace when she was eight years old and she threw it away playing baseball when she was nine, with only two pearls.

So as soon as she got married and moved away from home the first thing she did was separate! From Mr. Whitaker! This photographer with the popeyes she said she trusted. Came home from one of those towns up in Illinois and to our complete surprise brought this child of two.

Mama said she like to make her drop dead for a second. "Here you had this marvelous blonde child and never so much as wrote your mother a word about it," says Mama. "I'm thoroughly ashamed of you." But of course she wasn't.

5 Stella-Rondo just calmly takes off this *hat*, I wish you could see it. She says, "Why, Mama, Shirley-T.'s adopted, I can prove it."

"How?" says Mama, but all I says was, "H'm!" There I was over the hot stove, trying to stretch two chickens over five people and a completely unexpected child into the bargain without one moment's notice.

"What do you mean—'H'm'?" says Stella-Rondo, and Mama says, "I heard that, Sister."

I said that oh, I didn't mean a thing, only that whoever Shirley-T. was, she was the spit-image of Papa-Daddy if he'd cut off his beard, which of course he'd never do in the world. Papa-Daddy's Mama's papa and sulks.

Stella-Rondo got furious! She said, "Sister, I don't need to tell you you got a lot of nerve and always did have and I'll thank you to make no future reference to my adopted child whatsoever."

"Very well," I said. "Very well, very well. Of course I noticed at once she looks like Mr. Whitaker's side too. That frown. She looks like a cross between Mr. Whitaker and Papa-Daddy."

"Well, all I can say is she isn't."

"She looks exactly like Shirley Temple to me," says Mama, but Shirley-T. just ran away from her.

So the first thing Stella-Rondo did at the table was turn Papa-Daddy against me.

"Papa-Daddy," she says. He was trying to cut up his meat. "Papa-Daddy!" I was taken completely by surprise. Papa-Daddy is about a million years old and's got this long-long beard. "Papa-Daddy, Sister says she fails to understand why you don't cut off your beard."

So Papa-Daddy l-a-y-s down his knife and fork! He's real rich. Mama says he is, she says he isn't. So he says, "Have I heard correctly? You don't understand why I don't cut off my beard?"

"Why," I says, "Papa-Daddy, of course I understand, I did not say any such a thing, the idea!"

He says, "Hussy!"

I says, "Papa-Daddy, you know I wouldn't any more want you to cut off your beard than the man in the moon. It was the farthest thing from my mind! Stella-Rondo sat there and made that up while she was eating breast of chicken."

But he says, "So the postmistress fails to understand why I don't cut off my beard. Which job I got you through my influence with the government. 'Bird's nest'—is that what you call it?"

Not that it isn't the next to smallest P.O. in the entire state of Mississippi.

I says, "Oh, Papa-Daddy," I says, "I didn't say any such a thing, I never dreamed it was a bird's nest, I have always been grateful though this is the next to smallest P.O. in the state of Mississippi, and I do not enjoy being referred to as a hussy by my own grandfather."

But Stella-Rondo says, "Yes, you did say it too. Anybody in the world could of heard you, that had ears."

"Stop right there," says Mama, looking at *me*.

So I pulled my napkin straight back through the napkin ring and left the table.

As soon as I was out of the room Mama says, "Call her back, or she'll starve to death," but Papa-Daddy says, "This is the beard I started growing on the Coast when I was fifteen years old." He would of gone on till nightfall if Shirley-T. hadn't lost the Milky Way she ate in Cairo.

So Papa-Daddy says, "I am going out and lie in the hammock, and you can all sit here and remember my words: I'll never cut off my beard as long as I live, even one inch, and I don't appreciate it in you at all." Passed right by me in the hall and went straight out and got in the hammock.

It would be a holiday. It wasn't five minutes before Uncle Rondo suddenly appeared in the hall in one of Stella-Rondo's flesh-colored kimonos, all cut on the bias, like something Mr. Whitaker probably thought was gorgeous.

"Uncle Rondo!" I says. "I didn't know who that was! Where are you going?"

"Sister," he says, "get out of my way, I'm poisoned."

30 "If you're poisoned stay away from Papa-Daddy," I says. "Keep out of the hammock. Papa-Daddy will certainly beat you on the head if you come within forty miles of him. He thinks I deliberately said he ought to cut off his beard after he got me the P.O., and I've told him and told him and told him, and he acts like he just don't hear me. Papa-Daddy must of gone stone deaf."

"He picked a fine day to do it then," says Uncle Rondo, and before you could say "Jack Robinson" flew out in the yard.

What he'd really done, he'd drunk another bottle of that prescription. He does it every single Fourth of July as sure as shooting, and it's horribly expensive. Then he falls over in the hammock and snores. So he insisted on zigzagging right on out to the hammock, looking like a half-wit.

Papa-Daddy woke with this horrible yell and right there without moving an inch he tried to turn Uncle Rondo against me. I heard every word he said. Oh, he told Uncle Rondo I didn't learn to read till I was eight years old and he didn't see how in the world I ever got the mail put up at the P.O., much less read it all, and he said if Uncle Rondo could only fathom the lengths he had gone to get me that job! And he said on the other hand he thought Stella-Rondo had a brilliant mind and deserved credit for getting out of town. All the time he was just lying there swinging as pretty as you please and looping out his beard, and poor Uncle Rondo was *pleading* with him to slow down the hammock, it was making him as dizzy as a witch to watch it. But that's what Papa-Daddy likes about a hammock. So Uncle Rondo was too dizzy to get turned against me for the time being. He's Mama's only brother and is a good case of a one-track mind. Ask anybody. A certified pharmacist.

Just then I heard Stella-Rondo raising the upstairs window. While she was married she got this peculiar idea that it's cooler with the windows shut and locked. So she has to raise the window before she can make a soul hear her outdoors.

35 So she raises the window and says, "*Oh!*" You would have thought she was mortally wounded.

Uncle Rondo and Papa-Daddy didn't even look up, but kept right on with what they were doing. I had to laugh.

I flew up the stairs and threw the door open! I says, "What in the wide world's the matter, Stella-Rondo? You mortally wounded?"

"No," she says, "I am not mortally wounded but I wish you would do me the favor of looking out that window there and telling me what you see."

So I shade my eyes and look out the window.

40 "I see the front yard," I says.

"Don't you see any human beings?"

"I see Uncle Rondo trying to run Papa-Daddy out of the hammock," I says. "Nothing more. Naturally, it's so suffocating-hot in the house, with all the windows shut and locked, everybody who cares to stay in their right mind will have to go out and get in the hammock before the Fourth of July is over."

"Don't you notice anything different about Uncle Rondo?" asks Stella-Rondo.

"Why, no, except he's got on some terrible-looking flesh-colored contraption I wouldn't be found dead in, is all I can see," I says.

"Never mind, you won't be found dead in it, because it happens to be part of my trousseau, and Mr. Whitaker took several dozen photographs of me in it," says Stella-Rondo. "What on earth could uncle Rondo *mean* by wearing part of my trousseau out in the broad open daylight without saying so much as 'Kiss my foot,' *knowing* I only got home this morning after my separation and hung my negligee up on the bathroom door, just as nervous as I could be?"

"I'm sure I don't know, and what do you expect me to do about it?" I says. "Jump out the window?"

"No, I expect nothing of the kind. I simply declare that Uncle Rondo looks like a fool in it, that's all," she says. "It makes me sick to my stomach."

"Well, he looks as good as he can," I says. "As good as anybody in reason could." I stood up for Uncle Rondo, please remember. And I said to Stella-Rondo, "I think I would do well not to criticize so freely if I were you and came home with a two-year-old child I had never said a word about, and no explanation whatever about my separation."

"I asked you the instant I entered this house not to refer one more time to my adopted child, and you gave me your word of honor you would not," was all Stella-Rondo would say, and started pulling out every one of her eyebrows with some cheap Kress tweezers.

So I merely slammed the door behind me and went down and made some green-tomato pickle. Somebody had to do it. Of course Mama had turned both the Negroes loose; she always said no earthly power could hold one anyway on the Fourth of July, so she wouldn't even try. It turned out that Jaypan fell in the lake and came within a very narrow limit of drowning.

So Mama trots in. Lifts up the lid and says, "H'm! Not very good for your Uncle Rondo in his precarious condition, I must say. Or poor little adopted Shirley-T. Shame on you!"

That made me tired. I says, "Well, Stella-Rondo had better thank her lucky stars it was her instead of me came trotting in with that very peculiar-looking child. Now if it had been me that trotted in from Illinois and brought a peculiar-looking child or two, I shudder to think of the reception I'd of got, much less controlled the diet of an entire family."

"But you must remember, Sister, that you were never married to Mr. Whitaker in the first place and didn't go up to Illinois to live," says Mama, shaking a spoon in my face. "If you had I would of been just as overjoyed to see you and your little adopted girl as I was to see Stella-Rondo, when you wound up with your separation and came on back home."

"You would not," I says.

55   "Don't contradict me, I would," says Mama.

But I said she couldn't convince me though she talked till she was blue in the face. Then I said, "Besides, you know as well as I do that that child is not adopted."

"She most certainly is adopted," says Mama, stiff as a poker.

I says, "Why, Mama, Stella-Rondo had her just as sure as anything in this world, and just too stuck up to admit it."

"Why, Sister," said Mama. "Here I thought we were going to have a pleasant Fourth of July, and you start right out not believing a word your own baby sister tells you!"

60   "Just like Cousin Annie Flo. Went to her grave denying the facts of life," I reminded Mama.

"I told you if you ever mentioned Annie Flo's name I'd slap your face," says Mama, and slaps my face.

"All right, you wait and see," I says.

"I," says Mama, "*I* prefer to take my children's word for anything when it's humanly possible." You ought to see Mama, she weighs two hundred pounds and has real tiny feet.

Just then something perfectly horrible occurred to me.

65   "Mama," I says, "can that child talk?" I simply had to whisper! "Mama, I wonder if that child can be—you know—in any way? Do you realize?" I says, "that she hasn't spoke one single, solitary word to a human being up to this minute? This is the way she looks," I says, and I looked like this.

Well, Mama and I just stood there and stared at each other. It was horrible!

"I remember well that Joe Whitaker frequently drank like a fish," says Mama. "I believed to my soul he drank *chemicals*." And without another word she marches to the foot of the stairs and calls Stella-Rondo.

"Stella-Rondo? O-o-o-o-o! Stella-Rondo!"

"What?" says Stella-Rondo from upstairs. Not even the grace to get up off the bed.

70   "Can that child of yours talk?" asks Mama.

Stella-Rondo says, "Can she what?"

"Talk! Talk!" says Mama. "Burdyburdyburdyburdy!"

So Stella-Rondo yells back, "Who says she can't talk?"

"Sister says so," says Mama.

75   "You didn't have to tell me, I know whose word of honor don't mean a thing in this house," says Stella-Rondo.

And in a minute the loudest Yankee voice I ever heard in my life yells out, "OE'm Pop-OE the Sailor-r-r-r Ma-a-an!" and then somebody jumps up and down in the upstairs hall. In another second the house would of fallen down.

"Not only talks, she can tap-dance!" calls Stella-Rondo. "Which is more than some people I won't name can do."

"Why, the little precious darling thing!" Mama says, so surprised. "Just as smart as she can be!" Starts talking baby talk right there. Then she turns on me. "Sister, you ought to be thoroughly ashamed! Run upstairs this instant and apologize to Stella-Rondo and Shirley-T."

"Apologize for what?" I says. "I merely wondered if the child was normal, that's all. Now that she's proved she is, why, I have nothing further to say."

But Mama just turned on her heel and flew out, furious. She ran right upstairs and hugged the baby. She believed it was adopted. Stella-Rondo hadn't done a thing but turn her against me from upstairs while I stood there helpless over the hot stove. So that made Mama, Papa-Daddy, and the baby all on Stella-Rondo's side.

Next, Uncle Rondo.

I must say that Uncle Rondo has been marvelous to me at various times in the past and I was completely unprepared to be made to jump out of my skin, the way it turned out. Once Stella-Rondo did something perfectly horrible to him—broke a chain letter from Flanders Field—and he took the radio back he had given her and gave it to me. Stella-Rondo was furious! For six months we all had to call her Stella instead of Stella-Rondo, or she wouldn't answer. I always thought Uncle Rondo had all the brains of the entire family. Another time he sent me to Mammoth Cave with all expenses paid.

But this would be the day he was drinking that prescription, the Fourth of July.

So at supper Stella-Rondo speaks up and says she thinks Uncle Rondo ought to try to eat a little something. So finally Uncle Rondo said he would try a little cold biscuits and ketchup, but that was all. So *she* brought it to him.

"Do you think it wise to disport with ketchup in Stella-Rondo's flesh-colored kimono?" I says. Trying to be considerate! If Stella-Rondo couldn't watch out for her trousseau, somebody had to.

"Any objections?" asks Uncle Rondo, just about to pour out all of the ketchup.

"Don't mind what she says, Uncle Rondo," says Stella-Rondo. "Sister has been devoting this solid afternoon to sneering out my bedroom window at the way you look."

"What's that?" says Uncle Rondo. Uncle Rondo has got the most terrible temper in the world. Anything is liable to make him tear the house down if it comes at the wrong time.

So Stella-Rondo says, "Sister says, 'Uncle Rondo certainly does look like a fool in that pink kimono!'"

Do you remember who it was really said that?

Uncle Rondo spills out all the ketchup and jumps out of his chair and tears off the kimono and throws it down on the dirty floor and puts his foot on it. It had to be sent all the way to Jackson to the cleaners and re-pleated.

"So that's your opinion of your Uncle Rondo, is it?" he says. "I look like a fool, do I? Well, that's the last straw. A whole day in this house with nothing to do, and then to hear you come out with a remark like that behind my back!"

"I didn't say any such of a thing, Uncle Rondo," I says, "and I'm not saying who did, either. Why, I think you look all right. Just try to take care of yourself and not talk and eat at the same time," I says. "I think you better go lie down."

"Lie down my foot," says Uncle Rondo. I ought to of known by that he was fixing to do something perfectly horrible.

95   So he didn't do anything that night in the precarious state he was in—just played Casino with Mama and Stella-Rondo and Shirley-T. and gave Shirley-T. a nickel with a head on both sides. It tickled her nearly to death, and she called him "Papa." But at 6:30 A.M. the next morning, he threw a whole five-cent package of some unsold one-inch firecrackers from the store as hard as he could into my bedroom and they every one went off. Not one bad one in the string. Anybody else, there'd be one that wouldn't go off.

Well, I'm just terribly susceptible to noise of any kind, the doctor has always told me I was the most sensitive person he had ever seen in his whole life, and I was simply prostrated. I couldn't eat! People tell me they heard it as far as the cemetery, and old Aunt Jep Patterson, that had been holding her own so good, thought it was Judgment Day and she was going to meet her whole family. It's usually so quiet here.

And I'll tell you it didn't take me any longer than a minute to make up my mind what to do. There I was with the whole entire house on Stella-Rondo's side and turned against me. If I have anything at all I have pride.

So I just decided I'd go straight down to the P.O. There's plenty of room there in the back, I says to myself.

Well! I made no bones about letting the family catch on to what I was up to. I didn't try to conceal it.

100   The first thing they knew, I marched in where they were all playing Old Maid and pulled the electric oscillating fan out by the plug, and everything got real hot. Next I snatched the pillow I'd done the needlepoint on right off the davenport from behind Papa-Daddy. He went "Ugh!" I beat Stella-Rondo up the stairs and finally found my charm bracelet in her bureau drawer under a picture of Nelson Eddy.[1]

"So that's the way the land lies," says Uncle Rondo. There he was, piecing on the ham. "Well, Sister, I'll be glad to donate my army cot if you got any place to set it up, providing you'll leave right this minute and let me get some peace." Uncle Rondo was in France.

"Thank you kindly for the cot and 'peace' is hardly the word I would select if I had to resort to firecrackers at 6:30 A.M. in a young girl's bedroom," I says to him. "And as to where I intend to go, you seem to forget my position as postmistress of China Grove, Mississippi," I says. "I've always got the P.O."

Well, that made them all sit up and take notice.

I went out front and started digging up some four-o'clocks to plant around the P.O.

105   "Ah-ah-ah!" says Mama, raising the window. "Those happen to be my four-o'clocks. Everything planted in that star is mine. I've never known you to make anything grow in your life."

"Very well," I says. "But I take the fern. Even you, Mama, can't stand there

1. Nelson Eddy (1901–1967), opera singer who enjoyed phenomenal popularity in the 1930s and 1940s when he costarred in several film musicals with Jeanette MacDonald. The two were known as "America's Singing Sweethearts."

and deny that I'm the one watered that fern. And I happen to know where I can send in a box top and get a packet of one thousand mixed seeds, no two the same kind, free."

"Oh, where?" Mama wants to know.

But I says, "Too late. You 'tend to your house, and I'll 'tend to mine. You hear things like that all the time if you know how to listen to the radio. Perfectly marvelous offers. Get anything you want free."

So I hope to tell you I marched in and got that radio, and they could of all bit a nail in two, especially Stella-Rondo, that it used to belong to, and she well knew she couldn't get it back, I'd sue for it like a shot. And I very politely took the sewing-machine motor I helped pay the most on to give Mama for Christmas back in 1929, and a good big calendar, with the first-aid remedies on it. The thermometer and the Hawaiian ukulele certainly were rightfully mine, and I stood on the step-ladder and got all my watermelon-rind preserves and every fruit and vegetable I'd put up, every jar. Then I began to pull the tacks out of the bluebird wall vases on the archway to the dining room.

"Who told you you could have those, Miss Priss?" says Mama, fanning as hard as she could.   110

"I bought 'em and I'll keep track of 'em," I says. "I'll tack 'em up one on each side of the post-office window, and you can see 'em when you come to ask me for your mail, if you're so dead to see 'em."

"Not I! I'll never darken the door to that post office again if I live to be a hundred," Mama says. "Ungrateful child! After all the money we spent on you at the Normal.[2]"

"Me either," says Stella-Rondo. "You can just let my mail lie there and *rot*, for all I care. I'll never come and relieve you of a single, solitary piece."

"I should worry," I says. "And who you think's going to sit down and write you all those big fat letters and postcards, by the way? Mr. Whitaker? Just because he was the only man ever dropped down in China Grove and you got him—unfairly—is he going to sit down and write you a lengthy correspondence after you come home giving no rhyme nor reason whatsoever for your separation and no explanation for the presence of that child? I may not have your brilliant mind, but I fail to see it."

So Mama says, "Sister, I've told you a thousand times that Stella-Rondo sim-   115 ply got homesick, and this child is far too big to be hers," and she says, "Now, why don't you just sit down and play Casino?"

Then Shirley-T. sticks out her tongue at me in this perfectly horrible way. She has no more manners than the man in the moon. I told her she was going to cross her eyes like that some day and they'd stick.

"It's too late to stop me now," I says. "You should have tried that yesterday. I'm going to the P.O. and the only way you can possibly see me is to visit me there."

So Papa-Daddy says, "You'll never catch me setting foot in that post office,

2. I.e., normal school (teachers college).

even if I should take a notion into my head to write a letter some place." He says, "I won't have you reachin' out of that little old window with a pair of shears and cuttin' off any beard of mine. I'm too smart for you!"

"We all are," says Stella-Rondo.

But I said, "If you're so smart, where's Mr. Whitaker?"

So then Uncle Rondo says, "I'll thank you from now on to stop reading all the orders I get on postcards and telling everybody in China Grove what you think is the matter with them," but I says, "I draw my own conclusions and will continue in the future to draw them." I says, "If people want to write their inner-most secrets on penny postcards, there's nothing in the wide world you can do about it, Uncle Rondo."

"And if you think we'll ever *write* another postcard you're sadly mistaken," says Mama.

"Cutting off your nose to spite your face then," I says. "But if you're all determined to have no more to do with the U.S. mail, think of this: What will Stella-Rondo do now, if she wants to tell Mr. Whitaker to come after her?"

"Wah!" says Stella-Rondo. I knew she'd cry. She had a conniption fit right there in the kitchen.

"It will be interesting to see how long she holds out," I says. "And now—I am leaving."

"Good-bye," says Uncle Rondo.

"Oh, I declare," says Mama, "to think that a family of mine should quarrel on the Fourth of July, or the day after, over Stella-Rondo leaving old Mr. Whit-aker and having the sweetest little adopted child! It looks like we'd all be glad!"

"Wah!" says Stella-Rondo, and has a fresh conniption fit.

"He left *her*—you mark my words," I says. "That's Mr. Whitaker. I know Mr. Whitaker. After all, I knew him first. I said from the beginning he'd up and leave her. I foretold every single thing that's happened."

"Where did he go?" asks Mama.

"Probably to the North Pole, if he knows what's good for him," I says.

But Stella-Rondo just bawled and wouldn't say another word. She flew to her room and slammed the door.

"Now look what you've gone and done, Sister," says Mama. "You go apolo-gize."

"I haven't the time, I'm leaving," I says.

"Well, what are you waiting around for?" asks Uncle Rondo.

So I just picked up the kitchen clock and marched off, without saying, "Kiss my foot," or anything, and never did tell Stella-Rondo good-bye.

There was a girl going along on a little wagon right in front.

"Girl," I says, "come help me haul these things down the hill, I'm going to live in the post office."

Took her nine trips in her express wagon. Uncle Rondo came out on the porch and threw her a nickel.

And that's the last I've laid eyes on any of my family or my family laid eyes on me for five solid days and nights. Stella-Rondo may be telling the most horrible tales in the world about Mr. Whitaker, but I haven't heard them. As I tell everybody, I draw my own conclusions.

But oh, I like it here. It's ideal, as I've been saying. You see, I've got everything cater-cornered, the way I like it. Hear the radio? All the war news. Radio, sewing machine, book ends, ironing board and that great big piano lamp—peace, that's what I like. Butter-bean vines planted all along the front where the strings are.

Of course, there's not much mail. My family are naturally the main people in China Grove, and if they prefer to vanish from the face of the earth, for all the mail they get or the mail they write, why, I'm not going to open my mouth. Some of the folks here in town are taking up for me and some turned against me. I know which is which. There are always people who will quit buying stamps just to get on the right side of Papa-Daddy.

But here I am, and here I'll stay. I want the world to know I'm happy.

And if Stella-Rondo should come to me this minute, on bended knees, and *attempt* to explain the incidents of her life with Mr. Whitaker, I'd simply put my fingers in both my ears and refuse to listen.

1941

CHARLES BAXTER

Fenstad's Mother

On Sunday morning after communion Fenstad drove across town to visit his mother. Behind the wheel, he exhaled with his hand flat in front of his mouth to determine if the wine on his breath could be detected. He didn't think so. Fenstad's mother was a lifelong social progressive who was amused by her son's churchgoing, and, wine or no wine, she could guess where he had been. She had spent her life in the company of rebels and deviationists, and she recognized all their styles.

Passing a frozen pond in the city park, Fenstad slowed down to watch the skaters, many of whom he knew by name and skating style. From a distance they were dots of color ready for flight, frictionless. To express grief on skates seemed almost impossible, and Fenstad liked that. He parked his car on a residential block and took out his skates from the back seat, where he kept them all winter. With his fingertips he touched the wooden blade guards, thinking of the time. He checked his watch; he had fifteen minutes.

Out on the ice, still wearing his churchy Sunday-morning suit, tie, and overcoat, but now circling the outside edge of the pond with his bare hands in his overcoat pockets, Fenstad admired the overcast sky and luxuriated in the brittle cold. He was active and alert in winter but felt sleepy throughout the summer. He passed a little girl in a pink jacket, pushing a tiny chair over the ice. He waved to his friend Ann, an off-duty cop, practicing her twirls. He waved to other friends. Without exception they waved back. As usual, he was impressed by the way skates improved human character.

Twenty minutes later, in the doorway of her apartment, his mother said, "Your cheeks are red." She glanced down at his trousers, damp with melted snow. "You've been skating." She kissed him on the cheek and turned to walk into her living room. "Skating after church? Isn't that some sort of doctrinal error?"

5   "It's just happiness," Fenstad said. Quickly he checked her apartment for any signs of memory loss or depression. He found none and immediately felt relief. The apartment smelled of soap and Lysol, the signs of an old woman who wouldn't tolerate nonsense. Out on her coffee table, as usual, were the letters she was writing to her congressman and to political dictators around the globe. Fenstad's mother pleaded for enlightened behavior and berated the dictators for their bad political habits.

She grasped the arm of the sofa and let herself down slowly. Only then did she smile. "How's your soul, Harry?" she asked. "What's the news?"

He smiled back and smoothed his hair. Martin Luther King's eyes locked into his from the framed picture on the wall opposite him. In the picture King was shaking hands with Fenstad's mother, the two of them surrounded by smiling faces. "My soul's okay, Ma," he said. "It's a hard project. I'm always working on it." He reached down for a chocolate-chunk cookie from a box on top of the television. "Who brought you these?"

"Your daughter Sharon. She came to see me on Friday." Fenstad's mother tilted her head at him. "You *want* to be a good person, but she's the real article. Goodness comes to her without any effort at all. She says you have a new girlfriend. A pharmacist this time. Susan, is it?" Fenstad nodded. "Harry, why does your generation always have to find the right person? Why can't you learn to live with the wrong person? Sooner or later everyone's wrong. Love isn't the most important thing, Harry, far from it. Why can't you see that? I still don't comprehend why you couldn't live with Eleanor." Eleanor was Fenstad's ex-wife. They had been divorced for a decade, but Fenstad's mother hoped for a reconciliation.

"Come on, Ma," Fenstad said. "Over and done with, gone and gone." He took another cookie.

10   "You live with somebody so that you're living with *somebody*, and then you go out and do the work of the world. I don't understand all this pickiness about lovers. In a pinch anybody'll do, Harry, believe me."

On the side table was a picture of her late husband, Fenstad's mild, middle-of-the-road father. Fenstad glanced at the picture and let the silence hang between them before asking, "How are you, Ma?"

"I'm all right." She leaned back in the sofa, whose springs made a strange, almost human groan. "I want to get out. I spend too much time in this place in January. You should expand my horizons. Take me somewhere."

"Come to my composition class," Fenstad said. "I'll pick you up at dinnertime on Tuesday. Eat early."

"They'll notice me," she said, squinting. "I'm too old."

15   "I'll introduce you," her son said. "You'll fit right in."

Fenstad wrote brochures in the publicity department of a computer company during the day, and taught an extension English-composition class at the downtown campus of the state university two nights a week. He didn't need the money; he taught the class because he liked teaching strangers and because he enjoyed the sense of hope that classrooms held for him. This hopefulness and didacticism he had picked up from his mother.

On Tuesday night she was standing at the door of the retirement apartment building, dressed in a dark blue overcoat—her best. Her stylishness was belied slightly by a pair of old fuzzy red earmuffs. Inside the car Fenstad noticed that she had put on perfume, unusual for her. Leaning back, she gazed out contentedly at the nighttime lights.

"Who's in this group of students?" she asked. "Working-class people, I hope. Those are the ones you should be teaching. Anything else is just a career."

"Oh, they work, all right." He looked at his mother and saw, as they passed under a streetlight, a combination of sadness and delicacy in her face. Her usual mask of tough optimism seemed to be deserting her. He braked at a red light and said, "I have a hairdresser and a garage mechanic and a housewife, a Mrs. Nelson, and three guys who're sanitation workers. Plenty of others. One guy you'll really like is a young black man with glasses who sits in the back row and reads *Workers' Vanguard* and Bakunin[1] during class. He's brilliant. I don't know why he didn't test out of this class. His name's York Follette, and he's—"

"I want to meet him," she said quickly. She scowled at the moonlit snow. "A man with ideas. People like that have gone out of my life." She looked over at her son. "What I hate about being my age is how *nice* everyone tries to be. I was never nice, but now everybody is pelting me with sugar cubes." She opened her window an inch and let the cold air blow over her, ruffling her stiff gray hair.

When they arrived at the school, snow had started to fall, and at the other end of the parking lot a police car's flashing light beamed long crimson rays through the dense flakes. Fenstad's mother walked deliberately toward the door, shaking her head mistrustfully at the building and the police. Approaching the steps, she took her son's hand. "I liked the columns on the old buildings," she said, "the old university buildings, I mean. I liked Greek Revival better than this Modernist-bunker stuff." Inside, she blinked in the light at the smooth, waxed linoleum floors and cement-block walls. She held up her hand to shade her eyes. Fenstad took her elbow to guide her over the snow melting in puddles in the entryway. "I never asked you what you're teaching tonight."

"Logic," Fenstad said.

"Ah." She smiled and nodded. "Dialectics!"

"Not quite. Just logic."

She shrugged. She was looking at the clumps of students standing in the

1. *Workers' Vanguard* was an anarchist magazine published from 1932 to 1939 in New York. Its founders set out to "Americanize" the doctrines of Mikhail Bakunin (1814–1876), an anarchist and Russian revolutionary whose quarrel with Karl Marx split the European revolutionary movement apart, and to reform American society on the basis of industrial syndicates and decentralized communes.

glare of the hallway, drinking coffee from paper cups and smoking cigarettes in the general conversational din. She wasn't used to such noise: she stopped in the middle of the corridor underneath a wall clock and stared happily in no particular direction. With her eyes shut she breathed in the close air, smelling of wet overcoats and smoke, and Fenstad remembered how much his mother had always liked smoke-filled rooms, where ideas fought each other, and where some of those ideas died.

"Come on," he said, taking her hand again. Inside Fenstad's classroom six people sat in the angular postures of pre-boredom. York Follette was already in the back row, his copy of *Workers' Vanguard* shielding his face. Fenstad's mother headed straight for him and sat down in the desk next to his. Fenstad saw them shake hands, and in two minutes they were talking in low, rushed murmurs. He saw York Follette laugh quietly and nod. What was it that blacks saw and appreciated in his mother? They had always liked her—written to her, called her, checked up on her—and Fenstad wondered if they recognized something in his mother that he himself had never been able to see.

At seven thirty-five most of the students had arrived and were talking to each other vigorously, as if they didn't want Fenstad to start and thought they could delay him. He stared at them, and when they wouldn't quiet down, he made himself rigid and said, "Good evening. We have a guest tonight." Immediately the class grew silent. He held his arm out straight, indicating with a flick of his hand the old woman in the back row. "My mother," he said. "Clara Fenstad." For the first time all semester his students appeared to be paying attention: they turned around collectively and looked at Fenstad's mother, who smiled and waved. A few of the students began to applaud; others joined in. The applause was quiet but apparently genuine. Fenstad's mother brought herself slowly to her feet and made a suggestion of a bow. Two of the students sitting in front of her turned around and began to talk to her. At the front of the class Fenstad started his lecture on logic, but his mother wouldn't quiet down. This was a class for adults. They were free to do as they liked.

Lowering his head and facing the blackboard, Fenstad reviewed problems in logic, following point by point the outline set down by the textbook: *post hoc* fallacies, false authorities, begging the question, circular reasoning, *ad hominem* arguments, all the rest. Explaining these problems, his back turned, he heard sighs of boredom, boldly expressed. Occasionally he glanced at the back of the room. His mother was watching him carefully, and her face was expressing all the complexity of dismay. Dismay radiated from her. Her disappointment wasn't personal, because his mother didn't think that people as individuals were at fault for what they did. As usual, her disappointed hope was located in history and in the way people agreed with already existing histories.

She was angry with him for collaborating with grammar. She would call it unconsciously installed authority. Then she would find other names for it.

"All right," he said loudly, trying to make eye contact with someone in the room besides his mother, "let's try some examples. Can anyone tell me what, if anything, is wrong with the following sentence? 'I, like most people, have a unique problem.'"

The three sanitation workers, in the third row, began to laugh. Fenstad caught himself glowering and singled out the middle one.

"Yes, it is funny, isn't it?"

The man in the middle smirked and looked at the floor. "I was just thinking of my unique problem."

"Right," Fenstad said. "But what's wrong with saying, 'I, like most people, have a unique problem'?"

"Solving it?" This was Mrs. Nelson, who sat by the window so that she could gaze at the tree outside, lit by a streetlight. All through class she looked at the tree as if it were a lover.

"Solving what?"

"Solving the problem you have. What is the problem?"

"That's actually not what I'm getting at," Fenstad said. "Although it's a good *related* point. I'm asking what might be wrong logically with that sentence."

"It depends," Harold Ronson said. He worked in a service station and sometimes came to class wearing his work shirt with his name tag, HAROLD, stitched into it. "It depends on what your problem is. You haven't told us your problem."

"No," Fenstad said, "my problem is *not* the problem." He thought of Alice in Wonderland and felt, physically, as if he himself were getting small. "Let's try this again. What might be wrong with saying that most people have a unique problem?"

"You shouldn't be so critical," Timothy Melville said. "You should look on the bright side, if possible."

"What?"

"He's right," Mrs. Nelson said. "Most people have unique problems, but many people do their best to help themselves, such as taking night classes or working at meditation."

"No doubt that's true," Fenstad said. "But why can't most people have a unique problem?"

"Oh, I disagree," Mrs. Nelson said, still looking at her tree. Fenstad glanced at it and saw that it was crested with snow. It *was* beautiful. No wonder she looked at it. "I believe that most people do have unique problems. They just shouldn't talk about them all the time."

"Can anyone," Fenstad asked, looking at the back wall and hoping to see something there that was not wall, "can anyone give me an example of a unique problem?"

"Divorce," Barb Kjellerud said. She sat near the door and knitted during class. She answered questions without looking up. "Divorce is unique."

"No, it isn't!" Fenstad said, failing in the crucial moment to control his voice. He and his mother exchanged glances. In his mother's face for a split second was the history of her compassionate, ambivalent attention to him. "Divorce is not unique." He waited to calm himself. "It's everywhere. Now try again. Give me a unique problem."

Silence. "This is a trick question," Arlene Hubbly said. "I'm sure it's a trick question."

"Not necessarily. Does anyone know what *unique* means?"

"One of a kind," York Follette said, gazing at Fenstad with dry amusement. Sometimes he took pity on Fenstad and helped him out of jams. Fenstad's mother smiled and nodded.

"Right," Fenstad crowed, racing toward the blackboard as if he were about to write something. "So let's try again. Give me a unique problem."

"You give *us* a unique problem," one of the sanitation workers said. Fenstad didn't know whether he'd been given a statement or a command. He decided to treat it as a command.

"All right," he said. He stopped and looked down at his shoes. Maybe it *was* a trick question. He thought for ten seconds. Problem after problem presented itself to him. He thought of poverty, of the assaults on the earth, of the awful complexities of love. "I can't think of one," Fenstad said. His hands went into his pockets.

"That's because problems aren't personal," Fenstad's mother said from the back of the room. "They're collective." She waited while several students in the class sat up and nodded. "And people must work together on their solutions." She talked for another two minutes, taking the subject out of logic and putting it neatly in politics, where she knew it belonged.

The snow had stopped by the time the class was over. Fenstad took his mother's arm and escorted her to the car. After letting her down on the passenger side and starting the engine, he began to clear the front windshield. He didn't have a scraper and had forgotten his gloves, so he was using his bare hands. When he brushed the snow away on his mother's side, she looked out at him, surprised, a terribly aged Sleeping Beauty awakened against her will.

Once the car had warmed up, she was in a gruff mood and repositioned herself under the seat belt while making quiet but aggressive remarks. The sight of the new snow didn't seem to calm her. "Logic," she said at last. "That wasn't logic. Those are just rhetorical tactics. It's filler and drudgery."

"I don't want to discuss it now."

"All right. I'm sorry. Let's talk about something more pleasant."

They rode together in silence. Then she began to shake her head. "Don't take me home," she said. "I want to have a spot of tea somewhere before I go back. A nice place where they serve tea, all right?"

He parked outside an all-night restaurant with huge front plate-glass windows; it was called Country Bob's. He held his mother's elbow from the car to the door. At the door, looking back to make sure that he had turned off his headlights, he saw his tracks and his mother's in the snow. His were separate footprints, but hers formed two long lines.

Inside, at the table, she sipped her tea and gazed at her son for a long time. "Thanks for the adventure, Harry. I do appreciate it. What're you doing in class next week? Oh, I remember. How-to papers. That should be interesting."

"Want to come?"

"Very much. I'll keep quiet next time, if you want me to."

Fenstad shook his head. "It's okay. It's fun having you along. You can say whatever you want. The students loved you. I knew you'd be a sensation, and you were. They'd probably rather have you teaching the class than me."

He noticed that his mother was watching something going on behind him, and Fenstad turned around in the booth so that he could see what it was. At first all he saw was a woman, a young woman with long hair wet from snow and hanging in clumps, talking in the aisle to two young men, both of whom were nodding at her. Then she moved on to the next table. She spoke softly. Fenstad couldn't hear her words, but he saw the solitary customer to whom she was speaking shake his head once, keeping his eyes down. Then the woman saw Fenstad and his mother. In a moment she was standing in front of them.

She wore two green plaid flannel shirts and a thin torn jacket. Like Fenstad, she wore no gloves. Her jeans were patched, and she gave off a strong smell, something like hay, Fenstad thought, mixed with tar and sweat. He looked down at her feet and saw that she was wearing penny loafers with no socks. Coins, old pennies, were in both shoes; the leather was wet and cracked. He looked in the woman's face. Under a hat that seemed to collapse on either side of her head, the woman's face was thin and chalk-white except for the fatigue lines under her eyes. The eyes themselves were bright blue, beautiful, and crazy. To Fentad, she looked desperate, percolating slightly with insanity, and he was about to say so to his mother when the woman bent down toward him and said, "Mister, can you spare any money?"

Involuntarily, Fenstad looked toward the kitchen, hoping that the manager would spot this person and take her away. When he looked back again, his mother was taking her blue coat off, wriggling in the booth to free her arms from the sleeves. Stopping and starting again, she appeared to be stuck inside the coat; then she lifted herself up, trying to stand, and with a quick, quiet groan slipped the coat off. She reached down and folded the coat over and held it toward the woman. "Here," she said. "Here's my coat. Take it before my son stops me."

"Mother, you can't." Fenstad reached forward to grab the coat, but his mother pulled it away from him.

When Fenstad looked back at the woman, her mouth was open, showing several gray teeth. Her hands were outstretched, and he understood, after a moment, that this was a posture of refusal, a gesture saying no, and that the woman wasn't used to it and did it awkwardly. Fenstad's mother was standing and trying to push the coat toward the woman, not toward her hands but lower, at waist level, and she was saying, "Here, here, here, here." The sound, like a human birdcall, frightened Fenstad, and he stood up quickly, reached for his wallet, and removed the first two bills he could find, two twenties. He grabbed the woman's chapped, ungloved left hand.

"Take these," he said, putting the two bills in her icy palm, "for the love of God, and please go."

He was close to her face. Tonight he would pray for her. For a moment the woman's expression was vacant. His mother was still pushing the coat at her, and the woman was unsteadily bracing herself. The woman's mouth was open, and her stagnant-water breath washed over him. "I know you," she said. "You're my little baby cousin."

"Go away, please," Fenstad said. He pushed at her. She turned, clutching his money. He reached around to put his hands on his mother's shoulders. "Ma," he said, "she's gone now. Mother, sit down. I gave her money for a coat." His mother fell down on her side of the booth, and her blue coat rolled over on the bench beside her, showing the label and the shiny inner lining. When he looked up, the woman who had been begging had disappeared, though he could still smell her odor, an essence of wretchedness.

"Excuse me, Harry," his mother said. "I have to go to the bathroom."

She rose and walked toward the front of the restaurant, turned a corner, and was out of sight. Fenstad sat and tried to collect himself. When the waiter came, a boy with an earring and red hair in a flattop, Fenstad just shook his head and said, "More tea." He realized that his mother hadn't taken off her earmuffs, and the image of his mother in the ladies' room with her earmuffs on gave him a fit of uneasiness. After getting up from the booth and following the path that his mother had taken, he stood outside the ladies'-room door and, when no one came in or out, he knocked. He waited for a decent interval. Still hearing no answer, he opened the door.

75   His mother was standing with her arms down on either side of the first sink. She was holding herself there, her eyes following the hot water as it poured from the tap around the bright porcelain sink down into the drain, and she looked furious. Fenstad touched her and she snapped toward him.

"Your logic!" she said.

He opened the door for her and helped her back to the booth. The second cup of tea had been served, and Fenstad's mother sipped it in silence. They did not converse. When she had finished, she said, "All right. I do feel better now. Let's go."

At the curb in front of her apartment building he leaned forward and kissed her on the cheek. "Pick me up next Tuesday," she said. "I want to go back to that class." He nodded. He watched as she made her way past the security guard at the front desk; then he put his car into drive and started home.

That night he skated in the dark for an hour with his friend, Susan, the pharmacist. She was an excellent skater; they had met on the ice. She kept late hours and, like Fenstad, enjoyed skating at night. She listened attentively to his story about his mother and the woman in the restaurant. To his great relief she recommended no course of action. She listened. She didn't believe in giving advice, even when asked.

80   The following Tuesday, Fenstad's mother was again in the back row next to York Follette. One of the fluorescent lights overhead was flickering, which gave the room, Fenstad thought, a sinister quality, like a debtors' prison or a refuge for the homeless. He'd been thinking about such people for the entire week. For seven days now he had caught whiffs of the woman's breath in the air, and one morning, Friday, he thought he caught a touch of the rotten-celery smell on his own breath, after a particularly difficult sales meeting.

Tonight was how-to night. The students were expected to stand at the front of the class and read their papers, instructing their peers and answering questions if necessary. Starting off, and reading her paper in a frightened monotone, Mrs. Nelson told the class how to bake a cheese soufflé. Arlene Hubbly's paper was about mushroom hunting. Fenstad was put off by the introduction. "The advantage to mushrooms," Arlene Hubbly read, "is that they are delicious. The disadvantage to mushrooms is that they can make you sick, even die." But then she explained how to recognize the common shaggymane by its cylindrical cap and dark tufts; she drew a model on the board. She warned the class against the *Clitocybe illudens*, the Jack-o'-Lantern. "Never eat a mushroom like this one or *any* mushroom that glows in the dark. Take heed!" she said, fixing her gaze on the class. Fenstad saw his mother taking rapid notes. Harold Ronson, the mechanic, reading his own prose painfully and slowly, told the class how to get rust spots out of their automobiles. Again Fenstad noticed his mother taking notes. York Follette told the class about the proper procedures for laying down attic insulation and how to know when enough was enough, so that a homeowner wouldn't be robbed blind, as he put it, by the salesmen, in whose ranks he had once counted himself.

Barb Kjellerud had brought along a cassette player, and told the class that her hobby was ballroom dancing; she would instruct them in the basic waltz. She pushed the play button on the tape machine, and "Tales from the Vienna Woods" came booming out. To the accompaniment of the music she read her paper, illustrating, as she went, how the steps were to be performed. She danced alone in front of them, doing so with flair. Her blond hair swayed as she danced, Fenstad noticed. She looked a bit like a contestant in a beauty contest who had too much personality to win. She explained to the men the necessity of leading. Someone had to lead, she said, and tradition had given this responsibility to the male. Fenstad heard his mother snicker.

When Barb Kjellerud asked for volunteers, Fenstad's mother raised her hand. She said she knew how to waltz and would help out. At the front of the class she made a counterclockwise motion with her hand, and for the next minute, sitting at the back of the room, Fenstad watched his mother and one of the sanitation workers waltzing under the flickering fluorescent lights.

"What a wonderful class," Fenstad's mother said on the way home. "I hope you're paying attention to what they tell you."

Fenstad nodded. "Tea?" he asked.

She shook her head. "Where're you going after you drop me off?"

"Skating," he said. "I usually go skating. I have a date."

"With the pharmacist? In the dark?"

"We both like it, Ma." As he drove, he made an all-purpose gesture. "The moon and the stars," he said simply.

When he left her off, he felt unsettled. He considered, as a point of courtesy, staying with her a few minutes, but by the time he had this idea he was already away from the building and was headed down the street.

85

90

He and Susan were out on the ice together, skating in large circles, when Susan pointed to a solitary figure sitting on a park bench near the lake's edge. The sky had cleared; the moon gave everything a cold, fine-edged clarity. When Fenstad followed the line of Susan's finger, he saw at once that the figure on the bench was his mother. He realized it simply because of the way she sat there, drawn into herself, attentive even in the winter dark. He skated through the uncleared snow over the ice until he was standing close enough to speak to her. "Mother," he said, "what are you doing here?"

She was bundled up, a thick woolen cap drawn over her head, and two scarves covering much of her face. He could see little other than the two lenses of her glasses facing him in the dark. "I wanted to see you two," she told him. "I thought you'd look happy, and you did. I like to watch happiness. I always have."

"How can you see us? We're so far away."

"That's how I saw you."

This made no sense to him, so he asked, "How'd you get here?"

"I took a cab. That part was easy."

"Aren't you freezing?"

"I don't know. I don't know if I'm freezing or not."

He and Susan took her back to her apartment as soon as they could get their boots on. In the car Mrs. Fenstad insisted on asking Susan what kind of safety procedures were used to ensure that drugs weren't smuggled out of pharmacies and sold illegally, but she didn't appear to listen to the answer, and by the time they reached her building, she seemed to be falling asleep. They helped her up to her apartment. Susan thought that they should give her a warm bath before putting her into bed, and, together, they did. She did not protest. She didn't even seem to notice them as they guided her in and out of the bathtub.

Fenstad feared that his mother would catch some lung infection, and it turned out to be bronchitis, which kept her in her apartment for the first three weeks of February, until her cough went down. Fenstad came by every other day to see how she was, and one Tuesday, after work, he went up to her floor and heard piano music: an old recording, which sounded much-played, of the brightest and fastest jazz piano he had ever heard—music of superhuman brilliance. He swung open the door to her apartment and saw York Follette sitting near his mother's bed. On the bedside table was a small tape player, from which the music poured into the room.

Fenstad's mother was leaning back against the pillow, smiling, her eyes closed.

Follette turned toward Fenstad. He had been talking softly. He motioned toward the tape machine and said, "Art Tatum.[2] It's a cut called 'Battery Bounce.' Your mother's never heard it."

"Jazz, Harry," Fenstad's mother said, her eyes still closed, not needing to see her son. "York is explaining to me about Art Tatum and jazz. Next week he's

2. Art Tatum (1910–1956), jazz pianist renowned for his harmonic imagination and extravagant virtuosity.

going to try something more progressive on me." Now his mother opened her eyes. "Have you ever heard such music before, Harry?"

They were both looking at him. "No," he said, "I never heard anything like it."

"This is my unique problem, Harry." Fenstad's mother coughed and then waited to recover her breath. "I never heard enough jazz." She smiled. "What glimpses!" she said at last.   105

After she recovered, he often found her listening to the tape machine that York Follette had given her. She liked to hear the Oscar Peterson[3] Trio as the sun set and the lights of evening came on. She now often mentioned glimpses. Back at home, every night, Fenstad spoke about his mother in his prayers of remembrance and thanksgiving, even though he knew she would disapprove.

1990

DORIS LESSING

Our Friend Judith

I stopped inviting Judith to meet people when a Canadian woman remarked, with the satisfied fervour of one who has at last pinned a label on a rare specimen: "She is, of course, one of your typical English spinsters."

This was a few weeks after an American sociologist, having elicited from Judith the facts that she was fortyish, unmarried, and living alone, had enquired of me: "I suppose she has given up?" "Given up what?" I asked; and the subsequent discussion was unrewarding.

Judith did not easily come to parties. She would come after pressure, not so much—one felt—to do one a favour, but in order to correct what she believed to be a defect in her character. "I really ought to enjoy meeting new people more than I do," she said once. We reverted to an earlier pattern of our friendship: odd evenings together, an occasional visit to the cinema, or she would telephone to say: "I'm on my way past you to the British Museum. Would you care for a cup of coffee with me? I have twenty minutes to spare."

It is characteristic of Judith that the word "spinster," used of her, provoked fascinated speculation about other people. There are my aunts, for instance: aged seventy-odd, both unmarried, one an ex-missionary from China, one a retired matron of a famous London hospital. These two old ladies live together under the shadow of the cathedral in a country town. They devote much time to the Church, to good causes, to letter writing with friends all over the world, to the grandchildren and the great-grandchildren of relatives. It would be a mistake, however, on entering a house in which nothing has been moved for fifty years, to diagnose a condition of fossilised late-Victorian integrity. They read

---

3. Oscar Peterson (b. 1925), jazz pianist and composer, greatly influenced by Tatum.

every book review in the *Observer* or the *Times*,[1] so that I recently got a letter from Aunt Rose enquiring whether I did not think that the author of *On the Road*[2] was not—perhaps?—exaggerating his difficulties. They know a good deal about music, and write letters of encouragement to young composers they feel are being neglected—"You must understand that anything new and original takes time to be understood." Well-informed and critical Tories, they are as likely to dispatch telegrams of protest to the Home Secretary[3] as letters of support. These ladies, my aunts Emily and Rose, are surely what is meant by the phrase "English spinster." And yet, once the connection has been pointed out, there is no doubt that Judith and they are spiritual cousins, if not sisters. Therefore it follows that one's pitying admiration for women who have supported manless and uncomforted lives needs a certain modification?

5   One will, of course, never know; and I feel now that it is entirely my fault that I shall never know. I had been Judith's friend for upward of five years before the incident occurred which I involuntarily thought of—stupidly enough—as the first time Judith's mask slipped.

A mutual friend, Betty, had been given a cast-off Dior[4] dress. She was too short for it. Also she said: "It's not a dress for a married woman with three children and a talent for cooking. I don't know why not, but it isn't." Judith was the right build. Therefore one evening the three of us met by appointment in Judith's bedroom, with the dress. Neither Betty nor I was surprised at the renewed discovery that Judith was beautiful. We had both often caught each other, and ourselves, in moments of envy when Judith's calm and severe face, her undemonstratively perfect body, succeeded in making everyone else in a room or a street look cheap.

Judith is tall, small-breasted, slender. Her light brown hair is parted in the centre and cut straight around her neck. A high straight forehead, straight nose, a full grave mouth are setting for her eyes, which are green, large and prominent. Her lids are very white, fringed with gold, and moulded close over the eyeball, so that in profile she has the look of a staring gilded mask. The dress was of dark green glistening stuff, cut straight, with a sort of loose tunic. It opened simply at the throat. In it Judith could of course evoke nothing but classical images. Diana, perhaps, back from the hunt, in a relaxed moment? A rather intellectual wood nymph who had opted for an afternoon in the British Museum Reading Room? Something like that. Neither Betty nor I said a word, since Judith was examining herself in a long mirror, and must know she looked magnificent.

Slowly she drew off the dress and laid it aside. Slowly she put on the old cord skirt and woollen blouse she had taken off. She must have surprised a resigned glance between us, for she then remarked, with the smallest of mocking smiles: "One surely ought to stay in character, wouldn't you say?" She added,

---

1. Prestigious London newspapers representing roughly the younger, more liberal establishment and the Establishment proper, respectively.   **2.** Jack Kerouac (1922–1969), a leading writer of the Beat Generation, 1950s forerunners of the hippies. Kerouac heroes felt themselves completely cut off from and victimized by American society.   **3.** Head of the British government department responsible for domestic matters.   **4.** Famous French designer of high fashions.

reading the words out of some invisible book, written not by her, since it was a very vulgar book, but perhaps by one of us: "It does everything *for* me, I must admit."

"After seeing you in it," Betty cried out, defying her, "I can't bear for anyone else to have it. I shall simply put it away." Judith shrugged, rather irritated. In the shapeless skirt and blouse, and without makeup, she stood smiling at us, a woman at whom forty-nine out of fifty people would not look twice.

A second revelatory incident occurred soon after. Betty telephoned me to say that Judith had a kitten. Did I know that Judith adored cats? "No, but of course she would," I said.

Betty lived in the same street as Judith and saw more of her than I did. I was kept posted about the growth and habits of the cat and its effect on Judith's life. She remarked for instance that she felt it was good for her to have a tie and some responsibility. But no sooner was the cat out of kittenhood than all the neighbours complained. It was a tomcat, ungelded, and making every night hideous. Finally the landlord said that either the cat or Judith must go, unless she was prepared to have the cat "fixed."[5] Judith wore herself out trying to find some person, anywhere in Britain, who would be prepared to take the cat. This person would, however, have to sign a written statement not to have the cat "fixed." When Judith took the cat to the vet to be killed, Betty told me she cried for twenty-four hours.

"She didn't think of compromising? After all, perhaps the cat might have preferred to live, if given the choice?"

"Is it likely I'd have the nerve to say anything so sloppy to Judith? It's the nature of a male cat to rampage lustfully about, and therefore it would be morally wrong for Judith to have the cat fixed, simply to suit her own convenience."

"She said that?"

"She wouldn't have to *say* it, surely?"

A third incident was when she allowed a visiting young American, living in Paris, the friend of a friend and scarcely known to her, to use her flat while she visited her parents over Christmas. The young man and his friends lived it up for ten days of alcohol and sex and marijuana, and when Judith came back it took a week to get the place clean again and the furniture mended. She telephoned twice to Paris, the first time to say that he was a disgusting young thug and if he knew what was good for him he would keep out of her way in the future; the second time to apologise for losing her temper. "I had a choice either to let someone use my flat, or to leave it empty. But having chosen that you should have it, it was clearly an unwarrantable infringement of your liberty to make any conditions at all. I do most sincerely ask your pardon." The moral aspects of the matter having been made clear, she was irritated rather than not to receive letters of apology from him—fulsome, embarrassed, but above all, baffled.

It was the note of curiosity in the letters—he even suggested coming over to

5. Gelded, castrated.

get to know her better—that irritated her most. "What do you suppose he means?" she said to me. "He lived in my flat for ten days. One would have thought that should be enough, wouldn't you?"

The facts about Judith, then, are all in the open, unconcealed, and plain to anyone who cares to study them; or, as it became plain she feels, to anyone with the intelligence to interpret them.

She has lived for the last twenty years in a small two-roomed flat high over a busy West London street. The flat is shabby and badly heated. The furniture is old, was never anything but ugly, is now frankly rickety and fraying. She has an income of two hundred pounds[6] a year from a dead uncle. She lives on this and what she earns from her poetry, and from lecturing on poetry to night classes and extramural university classes.

20   She does not smoke or drink, and eats very little, from preference, not self-discipline.

She studied poetry and biology at Oxford, with distinction.

She is a Castlewell. That is, she is a member of one of the academic upper-middleclass families, which have been producing for centuries a steady supply of brilliant but sound men and women who are the backbone of the arts and sciences in Britain. She is on cool good terms with her family, who respect her and leave her alone.

She goes on long walking tours, by herself, in such places as Exmoor or West Scotland.

Every three or four years she publishes a volume of poems.

25   The walls of her flat are completely lined with books. They are scientific, classical and historical; there is a great deal of poetry and some drama. There is not one novel. When Judith says: "Of course I don't read novels," this does not mean that novels have no place, or a small place, in literature; or that people should not read novels; but that it must be obvious she can't be expected to read novels.

I had been visiting her flat for years before I noticed two long shelves of books, under a window, each shelf filled with the works of a single writer. The two writers are not, to put it at the mildest, the kind one would associate with Judith. They are mild, reminiscent, vague and whimsical. Typical English *belles-lettres*, in fact, and by definition abhorrent to her. Not one of the books in the two shelves has been read; some of the pages are still uncut. Yet each book is inscribed or dedicated to her: gratefully, admiringly, sentimentally and, more than once, amorously. In short, it is open to anyone who cares to examine these two shelves, and to work out dates, to conclude that Judith from the age of fifteen to twenty-five had been the beloved young companion of one elderly literary gentleman, and from twenty-five to thirty-five the inspiration of another.

During all that time she had produced her own poetry, and the sort of poetry, it is quite safe to deduce, not at all likely to be admired by her two admirers. Her poems are always cool and intellectual; that is their form, which is contra-

6. About one-third or even one-half of a subsistence income.

dicted or supported by a gravely sensuous texture. They are poems to read often; one has to, to understand them.

I did not ask Judith a direct question about these two eminent but rather fusty lovers. Not because she would not have answered, or because she would have found the question impertinent, but because such questions are clearly unnecessary. Having those two shelves of books where they are, and books she could not conceivably care for, for their own sake, is publicly giving credit where credit is due. I can imagine her thinking the thing over, and deciding it was only fair, or perhaps honest, to place the books there; and this despite the fact that she would not care at all for the same attention be paid to her. There is something almost contemptuous in it. For she certainly despises people who feel they need attention.

For instance, more than once a new emerging wave of "modern" young poets have discovered her as the only "modern" poet among their despised and well-credited elders. This is because, since she began writing at fifteen, her poems have been full of scientific, mechanical and chemical imagery. This is how she thinks, or feels.

More than once has a young poet hastened to her flat, to claim her as an ally, only to find her totally and by instinct unmoved by words like "modern," "new," "contemporary." He has been outraged and wounded by her principle, so deeply rooted as to be unconscious, and to need no expression but a contemptuous shrug of the shoulders, that publicity seeking or to want critical attention is despicable. It goes without saying that there is perhaps one critic in the world she has any time for. He has sulked off, leaving her on her shelf, which she takes it for granted is her proper place, to be read by an appreciative minority.

Meanwhile she gives her lectures, walks alone through London, writes her poems, and is seen sometimes at a concert or a play with a middleaged professor of Greek, who has a wife and two children.

Betty and I had speculated about this professor, with such remarks as: Surely she must sometimes be lonely? Hasn't she ever wanted to marry? What about that awful moment when one comes in from somewhere at night to an empty flat?

It happened recently that Betty's husband was on a business trip, her children visiting, and she was unable to stand the empty house. She asked Judith for a refuge until her own home filled again.

Afterwards Betty rang me up to report: "Four of the five nights Professor Adams came in about ten or so."

"Was Judith embarrassed?"

"Would you expect her to be?"

"Well, if not embarrassed, at least conscious there was a situation?"

"No, not at all. But I must say I don't think he's good enough for her. He can't possibly understand her. He calls her Judy."

"Good God."

"Yes. But I was wondering. Suppose the other two called her Judy—'little Judy'—imagine it! Isn't it awful? But it does rather throw a light on Judith?"

"It's rather touching."

"I suppose it's touching. But *I* was embarrassed—oh, not because of the situation. Because of how she was, with him. 'Judy, is there another cup of tea in that pot?' And she, rather daughterly and demure, pouring him one."

"Well yes, I can see how you felt."

"Three of the nights he went to her bedroom with her—very casual about it, because she was being. But he was not there in the mornings. So I asked her. You know how it is when you ask her a question. As if you've been having long conversations on that very subject for years and years, and she is merely continuing where you left off last. So when she says something surprising, one feels such a fool to be surprised?"

"Yes. And then?"

"I asked her if she was sorry not to have children. She said yes, but one couldn't have everything."

"One can't have everything, she said?"

"Quite clearly feeling she *has* nearly everything. She said she thought it was a pity, because she would have brought up children very well."

"When you come to think of it, she would, too."

"I asked about marriage, but she said on the whole the role of a mistress suited her better."

"She used the word 'mistress'?"

"You must admit it's the accurate word."

"I suppose so."

"And then she said that while she liked intimacy and sex and everything, she enjoyed waking up in the morning alone and *her own person.*"

"Yes, *of course.*"

"Of course. But now she's bothered because the professor would like to marry her. Or he feels he ought. At least, he's getting all guilty and obsessive about it. She says she doesn't see the point of divorce, and anyway, surely it would be very hard on his poor old wife after all these years, particularly after bringing up two children so satisfactorily. She talks about his wife as if she's a kind of nice old charwoman, and it wouldn't be *fair* to sack her, you know. Anyway. What with one thing and another. Judith's going off to Italy soon in order *to collect herself.*"

"But how's she going to pay for it?"

"Luckily the Third Programme's[7] commissioning her to do some arty programmes. They offered her a choice of The Cid—El Thid[8] you know—and the Borgias. Well, the Borghese, then. And Judith settled for the Borgias."

"The Borgias," I said, "*Judith?*"

"Yes, quite. I said that too, in that tone of voice. She saw my point. She says the epic is right up her street, whereas the Renaissance has never been on her wave length. Obviously it couldn't be, all the magnificence and cruelty and *dirt.*

---

7. British Broadcasting Corporation public radio service (and now also television channel) specializing in classical music, literature and plays, lectures, etc.   8. Castilian, standard Spanish, pronunciation of El Cid (rhymes with *steed*), the title of an 11th-century soldier-hero and hero of many works of literature.

But of course chivalry and a high moral code and all those idiotically noble goings-on are right on her wave length."

"Is the money the same?"

"Yes. But is it likely Judith would let money decide? No, she said that one should always choose something new, that isn't up one's street. Well, because it's better for her character, and so on, to get herself unsettled by the Renaissance. She didn't say *that*, of course."

"Of course not."

Judith went to Florence; and for some months postcards informed us tersely of her doings. Then Betty decided she must go by herself for a holiday. She had been appalled by the discovery that if her husband was away for a night she couldn't sleep; and when he went to Australia for three weeks, she stopped living until he came back. She had discussed this with him, and he had agreed that if she really felt the situation to be serious, he would despatch her by air, to Italy, in order to recover her self-respect. As she put it.

I got this letter from her: "It's no use, I'm coming home. I might have known. Better face it, once you're really married you're not fit for man nor beast. And if you remember what I used to be like! *Well!* I moped around Milan. I sunbathed in Venice, then I thought my tan was surely worth something, so I was on the point of starting an affair with another lonely soul, but I lost heart, and went to Florence to see Judith. She wasn't there. She'd gone to the Italian Riviera. I had nothing better to do, so I followed her. When I saw the place I wanted to laugh, it's so much not Judith, you know, all those palms and umbrellas and gaiety at all costs and ever such an ornamental blue sea. Judith is in an enormous stone room up on the hillside above the sea, with grape vines all over the place. You should see her, she's got beautiful. It seems for the last fifteen years she's been going to Soho[9] every Saturday morning to buy food at an Italian shop. I must have looked surprised, because she explained she liked Soho. I suppose because all that dreary vice and nudes and prostitutes and everything prove how right she is to be as she is? She told the people in the shop she was going to Italy, and the *signora*[1] said, what a coincidence, she was going back to Italy too, and she did hope an old friend like Miss Castlewell would visit her there. Judith said to me: 'I felt lacking, when she used the word friend. Our relations have always been formal. Can you understand it?' she said to me. 'For fifteen years,' I said to her. She said: 'I think I must feel it's a kind of imposition, don't you know, expecting people to feel friendship for one.' *Well.* I said: 'You ought to understand it, because you're like that yourself.' 'Am I?' she said. 'Well, think about it,' I said. But I could see she didn't want to think about it. Anyway, she's here, and I've spent a week with her. The widow Maria Rineiri inherited her mother's house, so she came home, from Soho. On the ground floor is a tatty little *rosticceria*[2] patronised by the neighbours. They are all working people. This isn't tourist country, up on the hill. The widow lives above the shop with her little

65

---

9. A section of London roughly equivalent to Greenwich Village in New York—foreign restaurants and groceries, haunt of writers, painters, etc.—but in recent years increasingly known for prostitutes and pornography.   1. Proprietress.   2. Grill.

boy, a nasty little brat of about ten. Say what you like, the English are the only people who know how to bring up children, I don't care if that's insular. Judith's room is at the back, with a balcony. Underneath her room is the barber's shop, and the barber is Luigi Rineiri, the widow's younger brother. Yes, I was keeping him until the last. He is about forty, tall dark handsome, a great *bull*, but rather a sweet fatherly bull. He has cut Judith's hair and made it lighter. Now it looks like a sort of gold helmet. Judith is all brown. The widow Rineiri has made her a white dress and a green dress. They fit, for a change. When Judith walks down the street to the lower town, all the Italian males take one look at the golden girl and melt in their own oil like ice cream. Judith takes all this in her stride. She sort of acknowledges the homage. Then she strolls into the sea and vanishes into the foam. She swims five miles every day. *Naturally.* I haven't asked Judith whether she has collected herself, because you can see she hasn't. The widow Rineiri is matchmaking. When I noticed this I wanted to laugh, but luckily I didn't because Judith asked me, really wanting to know: 'Can you see me married to an Italian barber?' (Not being snobbish, but stating the position, so to speak.) 'Well yes,' I said, 'you're the only women I know who I can see married to an Italian barber.' Because it wouldn't matter who she married, she'd always be her *own person.* 'At any rate, for a time,' I said. At which she said, asperously,[3] 'You can use phrases like for a time in England but not in Italy.' Did you ever see England, at least London, as the home of licence, liberty and free love? No, neither did I, but of course she's right. Married to Luigi it would be the family, the neighbours, the church and the *bambini.*[4] All the same she's thinking about it, believe it or not. Here she's quite different, all relaxed and free. She's melting in the attention she gets. The widow mothers her and makes her coffee all the time, and listens to a lot of good advice about how to bring up that nasty brat of hers. Unluckily she doesn't take it. Luigi is crazy for her. At mealtimes she goes to the *trattoria*[5] in the upper square and all the workmen treat her like a goddess. Well, a film star then. I said to her, you're mad to come home. For one thing her rent is ten bob[6] a week, and you eat *pasta* and drink red wine till you bust for about one and sixpence. No, she said, it would be nothing but self-indulgence to stay. Why? I said. She said, she's got nothing to stay for. (Ho ho.) And besides, she's done her research on the Borghese, though so far she can't see her way to an honest presentation of the facts. What made these people tick? she wants to know. And so she's only staying because of the cat. I forgot to mention the cat. This is a town of cats. The Italians here love their cats. I wanted to feed a stray cat at the table, but the waiter said no; and after lunch, all the waiters came with trays crammed with leftover food and stray cats came from everywhere to eat. And at dark when the tourists go in to feed and the beach is empty—you know how empty and forlorn a beach is at dusk?—well cats appear from everywhere. The beach seems to move, then you see it's cats. They go stalking along the thin inch of grey water at the edge of the sea, shaking their paws crossly at each step, snatching at the dead little fish, and throwing them with their mouths up on to

---

3. Sharply, harshly.   **4.** Children.   **5.** Inexpensive restaurant.   **6.** Shillings. There are 20 shillings to the pound; *one and sixpence* below is one and a half shillings.

the dry stand. Then they scamper after them. You've never seen such a snarling and fighting. At dawn when the fishing boats come in to the empty beach, the cats are there in dozens. The fisherman throw them bits of fish. The cats snarl and fight over it. Judith gets up early and goes down to watch. Sometimes Luigi goes too, being tolerant. Because what he really likes is to join the evening promenade with Judith on his arm around and around the square of the upper town. Showing her off. Can you *see* Judith? But she does it. Being tolerant. But she smiles and enjoys the attention she gets, there's no doubt about it.

"She has a cat in her room. It's a kitten really, but it's pregnant. Judith says she can't leave until the kittens are born. The cat is too young to have kittens. Imagine Judith. She sits on her bed in that great stone room, with her bare feet on the stone floor, and watches the cat, and tries to work out why a healthy uninhibited Italian cat always fed on the best from the *rosticceria* should be neurotic. Because it is. When it sees Judith watching it gets nervous and starts licking at the roots of its tail. But Judith goes on watching, and says about Italy that the reason why the English love the Italians is because the Italians make the English feel superior. They have no discipline. And that's a despicable reason for one nation to love another. Then she talks about Luigi and says he has no sense of guilt, but a sense of sin; whereas she has no sense of sin but she has guilt. I haven't asked her if this has been an insuperable barrier, because judging from how she looks, it hasn't. She says she would rather have a sense of sin, because sin can be atoned for, and if she understood sin, perhaps she would be more at home with the Renaissance. Luigi is very healthy, she says, and not neurotic. He is a Catholic of course. He doesn't mind that she's an atheist. His mother has explained to him that the English are all pagans, but good people at heart. I suppose he thinks a few smart sessions with the local priest would set Judith on the right path for good and all. Meanwhile the cat walks nervously around the room, stopping to lick, and when it can't stand Judith watching it another second, it rolls over on the floor, with its paws tucked up, and rolls up its eyes, and Judith scratches its lumpy pregnant stomach and tells it to relax. It makes *me* nervous to see her, it's not like her, I don't know why. Then Luigi shouts up from the barber's shop, then he comes up and stands at the door laughing, and Judith laughs, and the widow says: Children, enjoy yourselves. And off they go, walking down to the town eating ice cream. The cat follows them. It won't let Judith out of its sight, like a dog. When she swims miles out to sea, the cat hides under a beach hut until she comes back. Then she carries it back up the hill, because that nasty little boy chases it. *Well.* I'm coming home tomorrow thank God, to my dear old Billy, I was mad ever to leave him. There is something about Judith and Italy that has upset me, I don't know what. The point is, what on earth can Judith and Luigi *talk* about? Nothing. How can they? And of course it doesn't matter. So I turn out to be a prude as well. See you next week."

It was my turn for a dose of the sun, so I didn't see Betty. On my way back from Rome I stopped off in Judith's resort and walked up through narrow streets to the upper town, where, in the square with the vine-covered *trattoria* at the corner, was a house with ROSTICCERIA written in black paint on a cracked wooden board over a low door. There was a door curtain of red beads, and flies settled on the beads. I opened the beads with my hands and looked into a small dark room with a stone counter. Loops of salami hung from metal hooks. A glass bell covered some plates of cooked meats. There were flies on the salami and on the glass bell. A few tins on the wooden shelves, a couple of pale loaves, some wine casks and an open case of sticky pale green grapes covered with fruit flies seemed to be the only stock. A single wooden table with two chairs stood in a corner, and two workmen sat there, eating lumps of sausage and bread. Through another bead curtain at the back came a short, smoothly fat, slender-limbed woman with greying hair. I asked for Miss Castlewell, and her face changed. She said in an offended, offhand way: "Miss Castlewell left last week." She took a white cloth from under the counter, and flicked at the flies on the glass bell. "I'm a friend of hers," I said, and she said: *Si*,[7] and put her hands palm down on the counter and looked at me, expressionless. The workmen got up, gulped down the last of their wine, nodded and went. She *ciao*'d[8] them; and looked back at me. Then, since I didn't go, she called: "Luigi!" A shout came from the back room, there was a rattle of beads, and in came first a wiry sharp-faced boy, and then Luigi. He was tall, heavy-shouldered, and his black rough hair was like a cap, pulled low over his brows. He looked good-natured, but at the moment uneasy. His sister said something, and he stood beside her, an ally, and confirmed: "Miss Castlewell went away." I was on the point of giving up, when through the bead curtain that screened off a dazzling light eased a thin tabby cat. It was ugly and it walked uncomfortably, with its back quarters bunched up. The child suddenly let out a "Sssss" through his teeth, and the cat froze. Luigi said something sharp to the child, and something encouraging to the cat, which sat down, looked straight in front of it, then began frantically licking at its flanks. "Miss Castlewell was offended with us," said Mrs. Rineiri suddenly, and with dignity. "She left early one morning. We did not expect her to go." I said: "Perhaps she had to go home and finish some work."

Mrs. Rineiri shrugged, then sighed. Then she exchanged a hard look with her brother. Clearly the subject had been discussed, and closed forever.

"I've known Judith a long time," I said, trying to find the right note. "She's a remarkable woman. She's a poet." But there was no response to this at all. Meanwhile the child, with a fixed bared-teeth grin, was staring at the cat, narrowing his eyes. Suddenly he let out another "Sssssss" and added a short high yelp. The cat shot backwards, hit the wall, tried desperately to claw its way up the wall, came to its senses and again sat down and began its urgent, undirected licking at its fur. This time Luigi cuffed the child, who yelped in earnest, and then ran out into the street past the cat. Now that the way was clear the cat shot across the floor, up onto the counter, and bounded past Luigi's shoulder and straight through the bead curtain into the barber's shop, where it landed with a thud.

"Judith was sorry when she left us," said Mrs. Rineiri uncertainly. "She was crying."

"I'm sure she was."

7. "Yes."   8. Said goodbye to.

"And so," said Mrs. Rineiri, with finality, laying her hands down again, and looking past me at the bead curtain. That was the end. Luigi nodded brusquely at me, and went into the back. I said goodbye to Mrs. Rineiri and walked back to the lower town. In the square I saw the child, sitting on the running board of a lorry[9] parked outside the *trattoria*, drawing in the dust with his bare toes, and directing in front of him a blank, unhappy stare.

I had to go through Florence, so I went to the address Judith had been at. No, Miss Castlewell had not been back. Her papers and books were still here. Would I take them back with me to England? I made a great parcel and brought them back to England.

I telephoned Judith and she said she had already written for the papers to be sent, but it was kind of me to bring them. There had seemed to be no point, she said, in returning to Florence.

"Shall I bring them over?" 75

"I would be very grateful, of course."

Judith's flat was chilly, and she wore a bunchy sage-green woollen dress. Her hair was still a soft gold helmet, but she looked pale and rather pinched. She stood with her back to a single bar of electric fire—lit because I demanded it— with her legs apart and her arms folded. She contemplated me.

"I went to the Rineiris' house."

"Oh. Did you?"

"They seemed to miss you." 80

She said nothing.

"I saw the cat too."

"Oh. Oh, I suppose you and Betty discussed it?" This was with a small unfriendly smile.

"Well, Judith, you must see we were likely to?"

She gave this her consideration and said: "I don't understand why people 85 discuss other people. Oh—I'm not criticising you. But I don't see why you are so interested. I don't understand human behaviour and I'm not particularly interested."

"I think you should write to the Rineiris."

"I wrote and thanked them, of course."

"I don't mean that."

"You and Betty have worked it out?"

"Yes, we talked about it. We thought we should talk to you, so you should 90 write to the Rineiris."

"Why?"

"For one thing, they are both very fond of you."

"Fond," she said smiling.

"Judith, I've never in my life felt such an atmosphere of being let down."

Judith considered this. "When something happens that shows one there is 95 really a complete gulf in understanding, what is there to say?"

9. Truck.

"It could scarcely have been a complete gulf in understanding. I suppose you are going to say we are being interfering?"

Judith showed distaste. "That is a very stupid word. And it's a stupid idea. No one can interfere with me if I don't let them. No, it's that I don't understand people. I don't understand why you or Betty should care. Or why the Rineiris should, for that matter," she added with the small tight smile.

"Judith!"

"If you've behaved stupidly, there's no point in going on. You put an end to it."

100   "What happened? Was it the cat?"

"Yes, I suppose so. But it's not important." She looked at me, saw my ironical face, and said: "The cat was too young to have kittens. That is all there was to it."

"Have it your way. But that is obviously not all there is to it."

"What upsets me is that I don't understand at all why I was so upset then."

"What happened? Or don't you want to talk about it?"

105   "I don't give a damn whether I talk about it or not. You really do say the most extraordinary things, you and Betty. If you want to know, I'll tell you. What does it matter?"

"I would like to know, of course."

"*Of course!*" she said. "In your place I wouldn't care. Well, I think the essence of the thing was that I must have had the wrong attitude to that cat. Cats are supposed to be independent. They are supposed to go off by themselves to have their kittens. This one didn't. It was climbing up on to my bed all one night and crying for attention. I don't like cats on my bed. In the morning I saw she was in pain. I stayed with her all that day. Then Luigi—he's the brother, you know."

"Yes."

"Did Betty mention him? Luigi came up to say it was time I went for a swim. He said the cat should look after itself. I blame myself very much. That's what happens when you submerge yourself in somebody else."

110   Her look at me was now defiant; and her body showed both defensiveness and aggression. "Yes. It's true. I've always been afraid of it. And in the last few weeks I've behaved badly. It's because I let it happen."

"Well, go on."

"I left the cat and swam. It was late, so it was only for a few minutes. When I came out of the sea the cat had followed me and had had a kitten on the beach. That little beast Michele—the son, you know?—well, he always teased the poor thing, and now he had frightened her off the kitten. It was dead, though. He held it up by the tail and waved it at me as I came out of the sea. I told him to bury it. He scooped two inches of sand away and pushed the kitten in—on the beach, where people are all day. So I buried it properly. He had run off. He was chasing the poor cat. She was terrified and running up the town. I ran too. I caught Michele and I was so angry I hit him. I don't believe in hitting children. I've been feeling beastly about it ever since."

"You were angry."

"It's no excuse. I would never have believed myself capable of hitting a child. I hit him very hard. He went off, crying. The poor cat had got under a big lorry parked in the square. Then she screamed. And then a most remarkable thing happened. She screamed just once, and all at once cats just materialised. One minute there was just one cat, lying under a lorry, and the next, dozens of cats. They sat in a big circle around the lorry, all quite still, and watched my poor cat."

"Rather moving," I said.

"Why?"

"There is no evidence one way or the other," I said in inverted commas, "that the cats were there out of concern for a friend in trouble."

"No," she said energetically. "There isn't. It might have been curiosity. Or anything. How do we know? However, I crawled under the lorry. There were two paws sticking out of the cat's back end. The kitten was the wrong way round. It was stuck. I held the cat down with one hand and I pulled the kitten out with the other." She held out her long white hands. They were still covered with fading scars and scratches. "She bit and yelled, but the kitten was alive. She left the kitten and crawled across the square into the house. Then all the cats got up and walked away. It was the most extraordinary thing I've ever seen. They vanished again. One minute they were all there, and then they had vanished. I went after the cat, with the kitten. Poor little thing, it was covered with dust— being wet, don't you know. The cat was on my bed. There was another kitten coming, but it got stuck too. So when she screamed and screamed I just pulled it out. The kittens began to suck. One kitten was very big. It was a nice fat black kitten. It must have hurt her. But she suddenly bit out—snapped, don't you know, like a reflex action, at the back of the kitten's head. It died, just like that. Extraordinary, isn't it?" she said, blinking hard, her lips quivering. "She was its mother, but she killed it. Then she ran off the bed and went downstairs into the shop under the counter. I called to Luigi. You know, he's Mrs. Rineiri's brother."

"Yes, I know."

"He said she was too young, and she was badly frightened and very hurt. He took the alive kitten to her but she got up and walked away. She didn't want it. Then Luigi told me not to look. But I followed him. He held the kitten by the tail and he banged it against the wall twice. Then he dropped it into the rubbish heap. He moved aside some rubbish with his toe, and put the kitten there and pushed rubbish over it. Then Luigi said the cat should be destroyed. He said she was badly hurt and it would always hurt her to have kittens."

"He hasn't destroyed her. She's still alive. But it looks to me as if he were right."

"Yes, I expect he was."

"What upset you—that he killed the kitten?"

"Oh no, I expect the cat would if he hadn't. But that isn't the point, is it?"

"What is the point?"

"I don't think I really know." She had been speaking breathlessly, and fast. Now she said slowly: "It's not a question of right or wrong, is it? Why should it be? It's a question of what one is. That night Luigi wanted to go promenading with me. For him, that was *that*. Something had to be done, and he'd done it. But I felt ill. He was very nice to me. He's a very good person," she said, defiantly.

"Yes, he looks it."

"That night I couldn't sleep. I was blaming myself. I should never have left the cat to go swimming. Well, and then I decided to leave the next day. And I did. And that's all. The whole thing was a mistake, from start to finish."

"Going to Italy at all?"

130 "Oh, to go for a holiday would have been all right."

"You've done all that work for nothing? You mean you aren't going to make use of all that research?"

"No. It was a mistake."

"Why don't you leave it a few weeks and see how things are then?"

"Why?"

135 "You might feel differently about it."

"What an extraordinary thing to say. Why should I? Oh, you mean, time passing, healing wounds—that sort of thing? What an extraordinary idea. It's always seemed to me an extraordinary idea. No, right from the beginning I've felt ill at ease with the whole business, not myself at all."

"Rather irrationally, I should have said."

Judith considered this, very seriously. She frowned while she thought it over. Then she said: "But if one cannot rely on what one feels, what can one rely on?"

"On what one thinks, I should have expected you to say."

140 "Should you? Why? Really, you people are all very strange. I don't understand you." She turned off the electric fire, and her face closed up. She smiled, friendly and distant, and said: "I don't really see any point at all in discussing it."

1963

GRACE PALEY

A Conversation with My Father

My father is eighty-six years old and in bed. His heart, that bloody motor, is equally old and will not do certain jobs any more. It still floods his head with brainy light. But it won't let his legs carry the weight of his body around the house. Despite my metaphors, this muscle failure is not due to his old heart, he says, but to a potassium shortage. Sitting on one pillow, leaning on three, he offers last-minute advice and makes a request.

"I would like you to write a simple story just once more," he says, "the kind de Maupassant wrote, or Chekhov, the kind you used to write. Just recognizable people and then write down what happened to them next."

I say, "Yes, why not? That's possible." I want to please him, though I don't remember writing that way. I *would* like to try to tell such a story, if he means the kind that begins: "There was a woman ..." followed by plot, the absolute line between two points which I've always despised. Not for literary reasons, but because it takes all hope away. Everyone, real or invented, deserves the open destiny of life.

Finally I thought of a story that had been happening for a couple of years right across the street. I wrote it down, then read it aloud. "Pa," I said, "how about this? Do you mean something like this?"

> Once in my time there was a woman and she had a son. They lived nicely, in a small apartment in Manhattan. This boy at about fifteen became a junkie, which is not unusual in our neighborhood. In order to maintain her close friendship with him, she became a junkie too. She said it was part of the youth culture, with which she felt very much at home. After a while, for a number of reasons, the boy gave it all up and left the city and his mother in disgust. Hopeless and alone, she grieved. We all visit her. 5

"O.K., Pa, that's it," I said, "an unadorned and miserable tale."

"But that's not what I mean," my father said. "You misunderstood me on purpose. You know there's a lot more to it. You know that. You left everything out. Turgenev[1] wouldn't do that. Chekhov wouldn't do that. There are in fact Russian writers you never heard of, you don't have an inkling of, as good as anyone, who can write a plain ordinary story, who would not leave out what you have left out. I object not to facts but to people sitting in trees talking senselessly, voices from who knows where . . ."

"Forget that one, Pa, what have I left out now? In this one?"

"Her looks, for instance."

"Oh. Quite handsome, I think. Yes." 10

"Her hair?"

"Dark, with heavy braids, as though she were a girl or a foreigner."

"What were her parents like, her stock? That she became such a person. It's interesting, you know."

"From out of town. Professional people. The first to be divorced in their county. How's that? Enough?" I asked.

"With you, it's all a joke," he said. "What about the boy's father. Why didn't you mention him? Who was he? Or was the boy born out of wedlock?" 15

"Yes," I said. "He was born out of wedlock."

"For Godsakes, doesn't anyone in your stories get married? Doesn't anyone have the time to run down to City Hall before they jump into bed?"

"No," I said. "In real life, yes. But in my stories, no."

"Why do you answer me like that?"

"Oh, Pa, this is a simple story about a smart woman who came to N.Y.C. 20 full of interest love trust excitement very up to date, and about her son, what a

1. Ivan Sergeevich Turgenev (1818–1883); his best-known novel, *Fathers and Sons*, deals with the conflict between generations.

hard time she had in this world. Married or not, it's of small consequence."

"It is of great consequence," he said.

"O.K.," I said.

"O.K. O.K. yourself," he said, "but listen. I believe you that she's good-looking, but I don't think she was so smart."

"That's true," I said. "Actually that's the trouble with stories. People start out fantastic. You think they're extraordinary, but it turns out as the work goes along, they're just average with a good education. Sometimes the other way around, the person's a kind of dumb innocent, but he outwits you and you can't even think of an ending good enough."

25   "What do you do then?" he asked. He had been a doctor for a couple of decades and then an artist for a couple of decades and he's still interested in details, craft, technique.

"Well, you just have to let the story lie around till some agreement can be reached between you and the stubborn hero."

"Aren't you talking silly, now?" he asked. "Start again," he said. "It so happens I'm not going out this evening. Tell the story again. See what you can do this time."

"O.K.," I said. "But it's not a five-minute job." Second attempt:

Once, across the street from us, there was a fine handsome woman, our neighbor. She had a son whom she loved because she'd known him since birth (in helpless chubby infancy, and in the wrestling, hugging ages, seven to ten, as well as earlier and later). This boy, when he fell into the fist of adolescence, became a junkie. He was not a hopeless one. He was in fact hopeful, an ideologue and successful converter. With his busy brilliance, he wrote persuasive articles for his high-school newspaper. Seeking a wider audience, using important connections, he drummed into

Lower Manhattan newsstand distribution a periodical called *Oh! Golden Horse!*[2]

30   In order to keep him from feeling guilty (because guilt is the stony heart of nine tenths of all clinically diagnosed cancers in America today, she said), and because she had always believed in giving bad habits room at home where one could keep an eye on them, she too became a junkie. Her kitchen was famous for a while—a center for intellectual addicts who knew what they were doing. A few felt artistic like Coleridge and others were scientific and revolutionary like Leary.[3] Although she was often high herself, certain good mothering reflexes remained, and she saw to it that there was lots of orange juice around and honey and milk and vitamin pills. However, she never cooked anything but chili, and that no more than once a week. She explained, when we talked to her, seriously, with neighborly concern, that it was her part in the youth culture and she would rather be with the young, it was an honor, than with her own generation.

One week, while nodding[4] through an Antonioni[5] film, this boy was severely jabbed by the elbow of a stern and proselytizing girl, sitting beside him. She offered

2. "Horse" is a slang term for heroin.   3. Samuel Taylor Coleridge (1772–1834), English Romantic poet, wrote his allegedly unfinished poem *Kubla Khan* in an opium dream. Timothy Leary (b. 1920), American psychologist who promoted the use of psychedelic drugs.   4. A slang term referring to the narcotic effect of heroin.   5. Michelangelo Antonioni (b. 1912), Italian director (*Blow-Up*, *Zabriskie Point*).

immediate apricots and nuts for his sugar level, spoke to him sharply, and took him home.

She had heard of him and his work and she herself published, edited, and wrote a competitive journal called *Man Does Live By Bread Alone*. In the organic heat of her continuous presence he could not help but become interested once more in his muscles, his arteries, and nerve connections. In fact he began to love them, treasure them, praise them with funny little songs in *Man Does Live* . . .

the fingers of my flesh transcend
my transcendental soul
the tightness in my shoulders end
my teeth have made me whole

To the mouth of his head (that glory of will and determination) he brought hard apples, nuts, wheat germ, and soybean oil. He said to his old friends, From now on, I guess I'll keep my wits about me. I'm going on the natch. He said he was about to begin a spiritual deep-breathing journey. How about you too, Mom? he asked kindly.

His conversion was so radiant, splendid, that neighborhood kids his age began to say that he had never been a real addict at all, only a journalist along for the smell of the story. The mother tried several times to give up what had become without her son and his friends a lonely habit. This effort only brought it to supportable levels. The boy and his girl took their electronic mimeograph and moved to the bushy edge of another borough. They were very strict. They said they would not see her again until she had been off drugs for sixty days.

At home alone in the evening, weeping, the mother read and reread the seven issues of *Oh! Golden Horse!* They seemed to her as truthful as ever. We often crossed the street to visit and console. But if we mentioned any of our children who were at college or in the hospital or dropouts at home, she would cry out, My baby! My baby! and burst into terrible, face-scarring, time-consuming tears. The End.

First my father was silent, then he said, "Number One: You have a nice sense of humor. Number Two: I see you can't tell a plain story. So don't waste time." Then he said sadly, "Number Three: I suppose that means she was alone, she was left like that, his mother. Alone. Probably sick?"

I said, "Yes."

"Poor woman. Poor girl, to be born in a time of fools, to live among fools. The end. The end. You were right to put that down. The end."

I didn't want to argue, but I had to say, "Well, it is not necessarily the end, Pa."

"Yes," he said, "what a tragedy. The end of a person."

"No, Pa," I begged him. "It doesn't have to be. She's only about forty. She could be a hundred different things in this world as time goes on. A teacher or a social worker. An ex-junkie! Sometimes it's better than having a master's in education."

"Jokes," he said. "As a writer that's your main trouble. You don't want to recognize it. Tragedy! Plain tragedy! Historical tragedy! No hope. The end."

"Oh, Pa," I said. "She could change."

"In your own life, too, you have to look it in the face." He took a couple of nitroglycerin.[6] "Turn to five," he said, pointing to the dial on the oxygen tank.

35

40

6. Medicine for certain heart conditions.

He inserted the tubes into his nostrils and breathed deep. He closed his eyes and said, "No."

I had promised the family to always let him have the last word when arguing, but in this case I had a different responsibility. That woman lives across the street. She's my knowledge and my invention. I'm sorry for her. I'm not going to leave her there in that house crying. (Actually neither would Life, which unlike me has no pity.)

Therefore: She did change. Of course her son never came home again. But right now, she's the receptionist in a storefront community clinic in the East Village. Most of the customers are young people, some old friends. The head doctor said to her, "If we only had three people in this clinic with your experiences . . ."

"The doctor said that?" My father took the oxygen tubes out of his nostrils and said, "Jokes. Jokes again."

"No, Pa, it could really happen that way, it's a funny world nowadays."

"No," he said. "Truth first. She will slide back. A person must have character. She does not."

"No, Pa," I said. "That's it. She's got a job. Forget it. She's in that storefront working."

"How long will it be?" he asked. "Tragedy! You too. When will you look it in the face?"

1974

▼ ▼ ▼

CHARACTERIZATION A Glossary

antagonist: a neutral term for a character who opposes the leading male or female character; see *hero / heroine* and *antagonist*

antihero: a leading character who is not, like a "hero," perfect or even outstanding but is rather ordinary and representative of the more or less average person

character: (1) a fictional personage; (2) a combination of a person's qualities, especially moral qualities, so that such terms as "good" and "bad," "strong" and "weak," often apply. See *personality* and *nature*

characterization: the fictional or artistic presentation of a fictional personage; terms like "a good character" can, then, be ambiguous—they may mean that the personage is virtuous, or that he or she is well presented whatever his or her characteristics or moral qualities

existential character: a person real or fictional who, whatever his or her past or conditioning, can change by an act of will

flat character: fictional character, often but not always a minor character, who is relatively simple, who is presented as having rather few, though sometimes dominant, traits, and who thus does not change much in the course of a story. See *round character*

hero / heroine: the leading male / female character, usually larger than life, sometimes almost godlike. See *antihero, protagonist,* and *villain*

major characters: those characters whom we see and learn about the most

minor characters: those figures who fill out the story

nature: as it refers to a person—"it is his [or her] nature"—a rather old term suggesting something inborn, inherent, fixed, and thus predictable. See *character, personality*

personality: that which distinguishes or individualizes a person; its qualities are judged not so much in terms of their moral value, as in "character," but as to whether they are "pleasing" or "unpleasing"

protagonist: the main character in a work, who may be male or female, heroic or not heroic; thus the most neutral term. See *hero / heroine, antihero,* and *antagonist*

round character: a complex character, often a major character, who can grow and change and "surprise convincingly"—that is, act in a way that you did not expect from what had gone before but now accept as possible, even probable, and "realistic"

stereotype: a characterization based on conscious or unconscious assumptions that some one aspect, such as gender, age, ethnic or national identity, religion, occupation, marital status, determines what humans are like, and so is accompanied by certain traits, actions, and even values

villain: the one who opposes the hero and heroine, the "bad guy"; see *antagonist* and *hero*

QUESTIONS

1. What image do you have of Sister, the narrator of "Why I Live at the P.O.," after the first ten paragraphs? How do paragraphs 37–49 sharpen, confirm, modify, expand, or change your image? paragraphs 63–68, 94–95? 99 and 108–10? 128–30? 136–38? Is she reliable? Compare paragraphs 8 and 14, and paragraphs 47 and 89, but remember that all the words of the story are Sister's. What is the effect of the contradictions on your view of the characters? on your expectations? on your response to the story? When in relation to the time of the actions is Sister telling this story? When would you date actions of the story? based on what evidence?

2. How would you describe the relationship between Harry Fenstad and his mother? What signs are there that he loves her? What evidence is there that he is concerned about her aging? How would you describe her attitude toward him? What signs are there of affection, admiration? There are, in the course of the story, two specific differences of opinion between Fenstad and his mother—her views of love, marriage, and his relationship to his first wife (pars. 8–11), and the scene with the homeless woman (pars. 66–73)—as well as differences that might be described broadly as political (pars. 55 and 58). What is the effect on these differences on your view of their characters? Whose side are you on? To what extent do your own political beliefs influence your judgment of the characters? To what extent may it be said that Fenstad's mother's viewing everything politically and his viewing everything in personal or "liberal humanistic" terms (find examples of both) suggest a difference in their questions?

3. Because we are told the story of "Our Friend Judith" by a friend, we never get to know Judith from the inside and are never very close to the action. This seems to have the effect of lessening the suspense and perhaps even our interest in or feelings for Judith. What is gained by this focus and voice? How does it change the meaning of the story? The friend says she blundered and lost her opportunity to find out what Judith and her life were really like. How did she lose the opportunity? Was it really a blunder? Could she have found out what she wanted to know if she had not "blundered"? What is the friend "really" like?

WRITING SUGGESTIONS

1. In paragraph 63 of "Why I Live at the P.O.," after Mama says that she prefers to believe her children, the narrator tells us that Mama weighs two hundred pounds and has small feet. What is the effect of this peculiar shift from one sentence to the next? What does it contribute to your image of Sister? Find several more such non sequiturs and analyze their effect. Write a brief essay on the relationship between style and humor in "Why I Live at the P.O."

2. Trace your views of the character of Fenstad's mother from the first paragraph to the final scene, following both changes and consistencies.

3. Write an analysis of the character of the narrator of "Our Friend Judith." Base your interpretation solidly on specific passages, incidents, and attitudes in the story.

4. Write for or against one of these two interpretations of Judith's character. Or show why neither is satisfactory:

    a. Judith seems to be cool, intellectual, and respectable, but she's really fiery and passionate; she's hypocritical, since she lives one kind of life in the open and another in secret.

    b. Judith is her own woman. She does not need a man to lean on or depend on, but has her own full life, her profession, and does her own thing in her own way, the way men are praised for doing but women often condemned for doing.

5. Imagine a discussion / argument between Margaret Atwood and Grace Paley about writing stories, and especially about how to end them.

4 SETTING

All stories, like all individuals, are embedded in a context or setting—a time and place. The time can be contemporary ("No One's a Mystery") or historical ("The Cask of Amontillado") or even mythically vague ("The Zebra Storyteller"). It can be very limited, only a few minutes elapsing ("No One's a Mystery") or some years ("Sonny's Blues"). The place can be rather fixed and interior ("A Conversation with My Father") or varied ("Our Friend Judith"). It can be foreign ("The Cask of Amontillado") or American ("The Country Husband") or tied to a region ("A Rose for Emily" and the South) or a locale ("Sonny's Blues" and Harlem). Just as character and plot are so closely interrelated as to be ultimately indistinguishable (see Chapter 3), so too are character, plot, and setting. Paradoxically, to see this interpenetration, we must think of them first as separable elements. The individuals in the stories are embedded in the specific context, and the more we know of the setting, and of the relationship of the character to the setting, the more likely we are to understand the character and the story.

Even in a spare story like "No One's a Mystery" the interaction or interrelation of setting, character, and plot is important and revealing. The eighteen-year-old narrator and Jack, her lover, are in his dirty pickup truck on the highway. His wife approaches in her Cadillac—with the lights on even though it's daytime, a habit he hates. The vehicles they drive and their condition tell you a good deal about Jack, his wife, and their relationship. The significance of Jack's driving a pickup (and of the muddy manure on his boots) is modulated by the almost casually dropped information that they are in Wyoming, in or near Cheyenne.

Place or setting is seldom insignificant or unrelated to a larger historical context. "The Jewelry" is set in Paris in the late 1870s. Quite naturally, you might say, since it was written by a Frenchman in the early 1880s; he's just writing about his own time and place. True enough, but the cynicism, the somewhat bitter irony of the story set among the bourgeoisie and the bureaucracy, owes a good deal of its tone to the recent (1870–71) defeat of France and the siege and occupation of Paris by the Prussian Bismarck. (France paid Germany a billion dollars in reparations, an unheard-of amount in those days, and did so, to the world's astonishment, in just three years. Might this have something to do with the emphasis on money in the story?) The interaction of tone and times, setting and situation, are fused in this story in a way that would scarcely be possible in another context. Money, adultery, and high living are not unknown in our society, but try rewriting this story by setting it in New York in the 1990s.

John Cheever's "The Country Husband" is set in the early to middle 1950s, in my time and close enough to yours so that you know the important things about the period—Elvis, Marilyn, all that. World War II seems distant, but not too distant: a man in midlife crisis served in the army during that time. It is set in suburban New York, not too remote or exotic a setting, since it has many of the qualities of the suburbs of any medium-sized to large city in the 1990s. Yet the story is still somewhat of a period piece. The myth of the calm, undisturbed, comfortable good life—peace and plenty in the suburbs after the decades of Depression and war, the milieu of "Leave It to Beaver" and "Father Knows Best"—still prevailed. Airplane accidents and alcoholic fathers and memories of war were banned. And it seemed, at certain times, boring, almost unbearably so. All the excitement, all the romance of life, was gone, kept away by rows of white picket fences. Yes, we have suburbs like Shady Hill, but not many of the wives stay at home like Julia Weed and we no longer believe they are fenced off from the problems and promises of the Big City. The setting of this 1958 story makes of Francis a "weed" and though there are still crabgrass and dandelions in some of our finest neighborhoods, he and history would be difficult to transplant.

"The Country Husband" is, despite its relative modernity, an historical story. Its time, place, and historical setting interact with its narrative. Some stories are more overtly historical, and their milieu—or the stereotypes associated with it—are more obviously significant than those in Cheever's tale. The protagonist and the plot of "The Cask of Amontillado" are Machiavellian (characterized by subtle or unscrupulous cunning; after the Italian Renaissance politician and writer Niccolò Machiavelli, 1460–1527), and the story is set in Italy during the Renaissance. The Puritan goodman Brown lives in the reign of King William (1689–1702) in Salem, Massachusetts, where in 1692 the famous witch trials were held—what better place and time for a story whose subject is a witches' meeting and whose theme has to do with man's natural depravity? An *English* "spinster" seems (or seemed) much more prudish and virginal than just any old spinster, Italian lovers more sensual than Anglo-Saxon ones, and in "Our Friend Judith" testing those conventions is, virtually, the story.

In some stories setting, even when appropriate and natural, can symbolize whole ways of life or value systems. In "The Lady with the Dog," Yalta with its fruit, seashore, and semitropical climate exemplifies a more passionate, pleasurable, exciting life than the cold and cloudy, bureaucratic, intellectually rarefied air and routine of Moscow. Faulkner's "A Rose for Emily" is set in the deep South (Jefferson, Mississippi) in the years between, roughly, 1880 and the 1920s. Those are the years when the Civil War and the postwar Reconstruction were over and the resegregated South was nostalgic for the mythic antebellum values of gentility and gallantry. Emily is almost a symbol of the culture, its myths, and its reality.

Jing-Mei Woo, the narrator of "A Pair of Tickets," explores the relation of place, heritage, and ethnic identity. Living in San Francisco she had, at fifteen, "vigorously denied that I had any Chinese whatsoever below my skin" (par. 2), but at thirty-six, as she crosses the border from Hong Kong into China, she finds that she is "becoming Chinese." In Guangzhou, however, she discovers that within the vast change of place and cultures, in the modern world, at least among the privileged, there is a homogeneity: though men and women are working without safety belts or helmets on a scaffold made of bamboo held together with plastic strips, the hotel she is taken to "looks like a grander version of the Hyatt Regency." There are "shopping arcades and restaurants all encased in granite and glass," and in the rooms color television, a wet bar, Coke Classic, M & M's, Johnnie Walker Red, and so on. Her father's family circumvents her plan to have a Chinese feast and they dine on hamburgers, french fries, apple pie à la mode, delivered by room service. In the modern city of Shanghai, meeting her twin half-sisters for the first time, she finds she is Chinese not because of place or face, but because of "blood." But within this story is another story, her mother's story, with another setting in time and conditions. Fleeing from Kweilin and the advance of the Japanese army in 1944, Jing-Mei's mother was forced by overwhelming circumstances to abandon her twin babies. Jing-Mei can now explain a good deal about her own past, about her mother and their relationship, from the story of her actions and the historical circumstances of the war.

If one of the functions of literature is to engender the sympathetic understanding of others and of other subjective visions of the world, setting—the time and place in which the fictional characters and action are embedded—is an essential element.

▾ ▾ ▾

WILLIAM FAULKNER

A Rose for Emily

I

When Miss Emily Grierson died, our whole town went to her funeral: the men through a sort of respectful affection for a fallen monument, the women mostly out of curiosity to see the inside of her house, which no one save an old manservant—a combined gardener and cook—had seen in at least ten years.

It was a big, squarish frame house that had once been white, decorated with cupolas and spires and scrolled balconies in the heavily lightsome style of the seventies, set on what had once been our most select street. But garages and cotton gins had encroached and obliterated even the august names of that neighborhood; only Miss Emily's house was left, lifting its stubborn and coquettish decay above the cotton wagons and the gasoline pumps—an eyesore among eyesores. And now Miss Emily had gone to join the representatives of those august names where they lay in the cedar-bemused cemetery among the ranked and anonymous graves of Union and Confederate soldiers who fell at the battle of Jefferson.

Alive, Miss Emily had been a tradition, a duty, and a care; a sort of hereditary obligation upon the town, dating from that day in 1894 when Colonel Sartoris, the mayor—he who fathered the edict that no Negro woman should appear on the streets without an apron—remitted her taxes, the dispensation dating from the death of her father on into perpetuity. Not that Miss Emily would have accepted charity. Colonel Sartoris invented an involved tale to the effect that Miss Emily's father had loaned money to the town, which the town, as a matter of business, preferred this way of repaying. Only a man of Colonel Sartoris' generation and thought could have invented it, and only a woman could have believed it.

When the next generation, with its more modern ideas, became mayors and aldermen, this arrangement created some little dissatisfaction. On the first of the year they mailed her a tax notice. February came, and there was no reply. They wrote her a formal letter, asking her to call at the sheriff's office at her convenience. A week later the mayor wrote her himself, offering to call or to send his car for her, and received in reply a note on paper of an archaic shape, in a thin, flowing calligraphy in faded ink, to the effect that she no longer went out at all. The tax notice was also enclosed, without comment.

They called a special meeting of the Board of Aldermen. A deputation waited upon her, knocked at the door through which no visitor had passed since she ceased giving china-painting lessons eight or ten years earlier. They were admitted by the old Negro into a dim hall from which a stairway mounted into still more shadow. It smelled of dust and disuse—a close, dank smell. The Negro led them into the parlor. It was furnished in heavy, leather-covered furniture.

5

When the Negro opened the blinds of one window, a faint dust rose sluggishly about their thighs, spinning with slow motes in the single sun-ray. On a tarnished gilt easel before the fireplace stood a crayon portrait of Miss Emily's father.

They rose when she entered—a small, fat woman in black, with a thin gold chain descending to her waist and vanishing into her belt, leaning on an ebony cane with a tarnished gold head. Her skeleton was small and spare; perhaps that was why what would have been merely plumpness in another was obesity in her. She looked bloated, like a body long submerged in motionless water, and of that pallid hue. Her eyes, lost in the fatty ridges of her face, looked like two small pieces of coal pressed into a lump of dough as they moved from one face to another while the visitors stated their errand.

She did not ask them to sit. She just stood in the door and listened quietly until the spokesman came to a stumbling halt. Then they could hear the invisible watch ticking at the end of the gold chain.

Her voice was dry and cold. "I have no taxes in Jefferson. Colonel Sartoris explained it to me. Perhaps one of you can gain access to the city records and satisfy yourselves."

"But we have. We are the city authorities, Miss Emily. Didn't you get a notice from the sheriff, signed by him?"

"I received a paper, yes," Miss Emily said. "Perhaps he considers himself the sheriff. . . . I have no taxes in Jefferson."

"But there is nothing on the books to show that, you see. We must go by the—"

"See Colonel Sartoris. I have no taxes in Jefferson."

"But, Miss Emily—"

"See Colonel Sartoris." (Colonel Sartoris had been dead almost ten years.) "I have no taxes in Jefferson. Tobe!" The Negro appeared. "Show these gentlemen out."

II

So she vanquished them, horse and foot, just as she had vanquished their fathers thirty years before about the smell. That was two years after her father's death and a short time after her sweetheart—the one we believed would marry her— had deserted her. After her father's death she went out very little; after her sweetheart went away, people hardly saw her at all. A few of the ladies had the temerity to call, but were not received, and the only sign of life about the place was the Negro man—a young man then—going in and out with a market basket.

"Just as if a man—any man—could keep a kitchen properly," the ladies said; so they were not surprised when the smell developed. It was another link between the gross, teeming world and the high and mighty Griersons.

A neighbor, a woman, complained to the mayor, Judge Stevens, eighty years old.

"But what will you have me do about it, madam?" he said.

"Why, send her word to stop it," the woman said. "Isn't there a law?"

"I'm sure that won't be necessary," Judge Stevens said. "It's probably just 20
a snake or a rat that nigger of hers killed in the yard. I'll speak to him about
it."

The next day he received two more complaints, one from a man who came
in diffident deprecation. "We really must do something about it, Judge. I'd be
the last one in the world to bother Miss Emily, but we've got to do something."
That night the Board of Aldermen met—three gray-beards and one younger
man, a member of the rising generation.

"It's simple enough," he said. "Send her word to have her place cleaned up.
Give her a certain time to do it in, and if she don't . . ."

"Dammit, sir," Judge Stevens said, "will you accuse a lady to her face of
smelling bad?"

So the next night, after midnight, four men crossed Miss Emily's lawn and
slunk about the house like burglars, sniffing along the base of the brickwork and
at the cellar openings while one of them performed a regular sowing motion
with his hand out of a sack slung from his shoulder. They broke open the cellar
door and sprinkled lime there, and in all the outbuildings. As they recrossed the
lawn, a window that had been dark was lighted and Miss Emily sat in it, the
light behind her, and her upright torso motionless as that of an idol. They crept
quietly across the lawn and into the shadow of the locusts that lined the street.
After a week or two the smell went away.

That was when people had begun to feel really sorry for her. People in our 25
town, remembering how old lady Wyatt, her great-aunt, had gone completely
crazy at last, believed that the Griersons held themselves a little too high for
what they really were. None of the young men were quite good enough for Miss
Emily and such. We had long thought of them as a tableau; Miss Emily a
slender figure in white in the background, her father a spraddled silhouette in
the foreground, his back to her and clutching a horsewhip, the two of them
framed by the back-flung front door. So when she got to be thirty and was still
single, we were not pleased exactly, but vindicated; even with insanity in the
family she wouldn't have turned down all of her chances if they had really
materialized.

When her father died, it got about that the house was all that was left to her;
and in a way, people were glad. At last they could pity Miss Emily. Being left
alone, and a pauper, she had become humanized. Now she too would know the
old thrill and the old despair of a penny more or less.

The day after his death all the ladies prepared to call at the house and offer
condolence and aid, as is our custom. Miss Emily met them at the door, dressed
as usual and with no trace of grief on her face. She told them that her father
was not dead. She did that for three days, with the ministers calling on her, and
the doctors, trying to persuade her to let them dispose of the body. Just as they
were about to resort to law and force, she broke down, and they buried her father
quickly.

We did not say she was crazy then. We believed she had to do that. We
remembered all the young men her father had driven away, and we knew that

with nothing left, she would have to cling to that which had robbed her, as people will.

III

She was sick for a long time. When we saw her again, her hair was cut short, making her look like a girl, with a vague resemblance to those angels in colored church windows—sort of tragic and serene.

The town had just let the contracts for paving the sidewalks, and in the summer after her father's death they began to work. The construction company came with niggers and mules and machinery, and a foreman named Homer Barron, a Yankee—a big, dark, ready man, with a big voice and eyes lighter than his face. The little boys would follow in groups to hear him cuss the niggers, and the niggers singing in time to the rise and fall of picks. Pretty soon he knew everybody in town. Whenever you heard a lot of laughing anywhere about the square, Homer Barron would be in the center of the group. Presently we began to see him and Miss Emily on Sunday afternoons driving in the yellow-wheeled buggy and the matched team of bays from the livery stable.

At first we were glad that Miss Emily would have an interest, because the ladies all said, "Of course a Grierson would not think seriously of a Northerner, a day laborer." But there were still others, older people, who said that even grief could not cause a real lady to forget *noblesse oblige*—without calling it *noblesse oblige*. They just said, "Poor Emily. Her kinsfolk should come to her." She had some kin in Alabama; but years ago her father had fallen out with them over the estate of old lady Wyatt, the crazy woman, and there was no communication between the two families. They had not even been represented at the funeral.

And as soon as the old people said, "Poor Emily," the whispering began. "Do you suppose it's really so?" they said to one another. "Of course it is. What else could . . . " This behind their hands; rustling of craned silk and satin behind jalousies closed upon the sun of Sunday afternoon as the thin, swift clop-clop-clop of the matched team passed: "Poor Emily."

She carried her head high enough—even when we believed that she was fallen. It was as if she demanded more than ever the recognition of her dignity as the last Grierson; as if it had wanted that touch of earthiness to reaffirm her imperviousness. Like when she bought the rat poison, the arsenic. That was over a year after they had begun to say "Poor Emily," and while the two female cousins were visiting her.

"I want some poison," she said to the druggist. She was over thirty then, still a slight woman, though thinner than usual, with cold, haughty black eyes in a face the flesh of which was strained across the temples and about the eyesockets as you imagine a lighthouse-keeper's face ought to look. "I want some poison," she said.

"Yes, Miss Emily. What kind? For rats and such? I'd recom—"

"I want the best you have. I don't care what kind."

The druggist named several. "They'll kill anything up to an elephant. But what you want is—"

"Arsenic," Miss Emily said. "Is that a good one?"

"Is . . . arsenic? Yes ma'am. But what you want—"

"I want arsenic." 40

The druggist looked down at her. She looked back at him, erect, her face like a strained flag. "Why, of course," the druggist said. "If that's what you want. But the law requires you to tell what you are going to use it for."

Miss Emily just stared at him, her head tilted back in order to look him eye for eye, until he looked away and went and got the arsenic and wrapped it up. The Negro delivery boy brought her the package; the druggist didn't come back. When she opened the package at home there was written on the box, under the skull and bones: "For rats."

IV

So the next day we all said, "She will kill herself"; and we said it would be the best thing. When she had first begun to be seen with Homer Barron, we had said, "She will marry him." Then we said, "She will persuade him yet," because Homer himself had remarked—he liked men, and it was known that he drank with the younger men in the Elk's Club—that he was not a marrying man. Later we said, "Poor Emily," behind the jalousies as they passed on Sunday afternoon in the glittering buggy, Miss Emily with her head high and Homer Barron with his hat cocked and a cigar in his teeth, reins and whip in a yellow glove.

Then some of the ladies began to say that it was a disgrace to the town and a bad example to the young people. The men did not want to interfere, but at last the ladies forced the Baptist minister—Miss Emily's people were Episcopal—to call upon her. He would never divulge what happened during that interview, but he refused to go back again. The next Sunday they again drove about the streets, and the following day the minister's wife wrote to Miss Emily's relations in Alabama.

So she had blood-kin under her roof again and we sat back to watch develop- 45 ments. At first nothing happened. Then we were sure that they were to be married. We learned that Miss Emily had been to the jeweler's and ordered a man's toilet set in silver, with the letters H. B. on each piece. Two days later we learned that she had bought a complete outfit of men's clothing, including a nightshirt, and we said, "They are married." We were really glad. We were glad because the two female cousins were even more Grierson than Miss Emily had ever been.

So we were not surprised when Homer Barron—the streets had been finished some time since—was gone. We were a little disappointed that there was not a public blowing-off, but we believed that he had gone on to prepare for Miss Emily's coming, or to give her a chance to get rid of the cousins. (By that time it was a cabal, and we were all Miss Emily's allies to help circumvent the cousins.) Sure enough, after another week they departed. And, as we had expected all along, within three days Homer Barron was back in town. A neighbor saw the Negro man admit him at the kitchen door at dusk one evening.

And that was the last we saw of Homer Barron. And of Miss Emily for some time. The Negro man went in and out with the market basket, but the front door remained closed. Now and then we would see her at a window for a moment, as the men did that night when they sprinkled the lime, but for almost six months she did not appear on the streets. Then we knew that this was to be expected too; as if that quality of her father which had thwarted her woman's life so many times had been too virulent and too furious to die.

When we next saw Miss Emily, she had grown fat and her hair was turning gray. During the next few years it grew grayer and grayer until it attained an even pepper-and-salt iron-gray, when it ceased turning. Up to the day of her death at seventy-four it was still that vigorous iron-gray, like the hair of an active man.

From that time on her front door remained closed, save for a period of six or seven years, when she was about forty, during which she gave lessons in china-painting. She fitted up a studio in one of the downstairs rooms, where the daughters and grand-daughters of Colonel Sartoris' contemporaries were sent to her with the same regularity and in the same spirit that they were sent on Sundays with a twenty-five cent piece for the collection plate. Meanwhile her taxes had been remitted.

50   Then the newer generation became the backbone and the spirit of the town, and the painting pupils grew up and fell away and did not send their children to her with boxes of color and tedious brushes and pictures cut from the ladies' magazines. The front door closed upon the last one and remained closed for good. When the town got free postal delivery Miss Emily alone refused to let them fasten the metal numbers above her door and attach a mailbox to it. She would not listen to them.

Daily, monthly, yearly we watched the Negro grow grayer and more stooped, going in and out with the market basket. Each December we sent her a tax notice, which would be returned by the post office a week later, unclaimed. Now and then we would see her in one of the downstairs windows—she had evidently shut up the top floor of the house—like the carven torso of an idol in a niche, looking or not looking at us, we could never tell which. Thus she passed from generation to generation—dear, inescapable, impervious, tranquil, and perverse.

And so she died. Fell ill in the house filled with dust and shadows, with only a doddering Negro man to wait on her. We did not even know she was sick; we had long since given up trying to get any information from the Negro. He talked to no one, probably not even to her, for his voice had grown harsh and rusty, as if from disuse.

She died in one of the downstairs rooms, in a heavy walnut bed with a curtain, her gray head propped on a pillow yellow and moldy with age and lack of sunlight.

V

The Negro met the first of the ladies at the front door and let them in, with their hushed, sibilant voices and their quick, curious glances, and then he disappeared. He walked right through the house and out the back and was not seen again.

The two female cousins came at once. They held the funeral on the second day, with the town coming to look at Miss Emily beneath a mass of bought flowers, with the crayon face of her father musing profoundly above the bier and the ladies sibilant and macabre; and the very old men—some in their brushed Confederate uniforms—on the porch and the lawn, talking of Miss Emily as if she had been a contemporary of theirs, believing that they had danced with her and courted her perhaps, confusing time with its mathematical progression, as the old do, to whom all the past is not a diminishing road, but, instead, a huge meadow which no winter ever quite touches, divided from them now by the narrow bottleneck of the most recent decade of years.

Already we knew that there was one room in that region above stairs which no one had seen in forty years, and which would have to be forced. They waited until Miss Emily was decently in the ground before they opened it.

The violence of breaking down the door seemed to fill this room with pervading dust. A thin, acrid pall as of the tomb seemed to lie everywhere upon this room decked and furnished as for a bridal: upon the valance curtains of faded rose color, upon the rose-shaded lights, upon the dressing table, upon the delicate array of crystal and the man's toilet things backed with tarnished silver, silver so tarnished that the monogram was obscured. Among them lay a collar and tie, as if they had just been removed, which, lifted, left upon the surface a pale crescent in the dust. Upon a chair hung the suit, carefully folded; beneath it the two mute shoes and the discarded socks.

The man himself lay in the bed.

For a long while we just stood there, looking down at the profound and fleshless grin. The body had apparently once lain in the attitude of an embrace, but now the long sleep that outlasts love, that conquers even the grimace of love, had cuckolded him. What was left of him, rotted beneath what was left of the nightshirt, had become inextricable from the bed in which he lay; and upon him and upon the pillow beside him lay that even coating of the patient and biding dust.

Then we noticed that in the second pillow was the indentation of a head. One of us lifted something from it, and leaning forward, that faint and invisible dust dry and acrid in the nostrils, we saw a long strand of iron-gray hair.

1931

AMY TAN

A Pair of Tickets

The minute our train leaves the Hong Kong border and enters Shenzhen, China, I feel different. I can feel the skin on my forehead tingling, my blood rushing through a new course, my bones aching with a familiar old pain. And I think, My mother was right. I am becoming Chinese.

"Cannot be helped," my mother said when I was fifteen and had vigorously denied that I had any Chinese whatsoever below my skin. I was a sophomore at

Galileo High in San Francisco, and all my Caucasian friends agreed: I was about as Chinese as they were. But my mother had studied at a famous nursing school in Shanghai, and she said she knew all about genetics. So there was no doubt in her mind, whether I agreed or not: Once you are born Chinese, you cannot help but feel and think Chinese.

"Someday you will see," said my mother. "It's in your blood, waiting to be let go."

And when she said this, I saw myself transforming like a werewolf, a mutant tag of DNA suddenly triggered, replicating itself insidiously into a *syndrome*, a cluster of telltale Chinese behaviors, all those things my mother did to embarrass me—haggling with store owners, pecking her mouth with a toothpick in public, being color-blind to the fact that lemon yellow and pale pink are not good combinations for winter clothes.

5   But today I realize I've never really known what it means to be Chinese. I am thirty-six years old. My mother is dead and I am on a train, carrying with me her dreams of coming home. I am going to China.

We are going to Guangzhou, my seventy-two-year-old father, Canning Woo, and I, where we will visit his aunt, whom he has not seen since he was ten years old. And I don't know whether it's the prospect of seeing his aunt or if it's because he's back in China, but now he looks like he's a young boy, so innocent and happy I want to button his sweater and pat his head. We are sitting across from each other, separated by a little table with two cold cups of tea. For the first time I can ever remember, my father has tears in his eyes, and all he is seeing out the train window is a sectioned field of yellow, green, and brown, a narrow canal flanking the tracks, low rising hills, and three people in blue jackets riding an ox-driven cart on this early October morning. And I can't help myself. I also have misty eyes, as if I had seen this a long, long time ago, and had almost forgotten.

In less than three hours, we will be in Guangzhou, which my guidebook tells me is how one properly refers to Canton these days. It seems all the cities I have heard of, except Shanghai, have changed their spellings. I think they are saying China has changed in other ways as well. Chungking is Chongqing. And Kweilin is Guilin. I have looked these names up, because after we see my father's aunt in Guangzhou, we will catch a plane to Shanghai, where I will meet my two half-sisters for the first time.

They are my mother's twin daughters from her first marriage, little babies she was forced to abandon on a road as she was fleeing Kweilin for Chungking in 1944. That was all my mother had told me about these daughters, so they had remained babies in my mind, all these years, sitting on the side of a road, listening to bombs whistling in the distance while sucking their patient red thumbs.

And it was only this year that someone found them and wrote with this joyful news. A letter came from Shanghai, addressed to my mother. When I first heard about this, that they were alive, I imagined my identical sisters transforming from little babies into six-year-old girls. In my mind, they were seated next to each other at a table, taking turns with the fountain pen. One would write a neat row of characters: *Dearest Mama. We are alive.* She would brush back her wispy bangs and hand the other sister the pen, and she would write: *Come get us. Please hurry.*

Of course they could not know that my mother had died three months before, suddenly, when a blood vessel in her brain burst. One minute she was talking to my father, complaining about the tenants upstairs, scheming how to evict them under the pretense that relatives from China were moving in. The next minute she was holding her head, her eyes squeezed shut, groping for the sofa, and then crumpling softly to the floor with fluttering hands.

So my father had been the first one to open the letter, a long letter it turned out. And they did call her Mama. They said they always revered her as their true mother. They kept a framed picture of her. They told her about their life, from the time my mother last saw them on the road leaving Kweilin to when they were finally found.

And the letter had broken my father's heart so much—these daughters calling my mother from another life he never knew—that he gave the letter to my mother's old friend Auntie Lindo and asked her to write back and tell my sisters, in the gentlest way possible, that my mother was dead.

But instead Auntie Lindo took the letter to the Joy Luck Club and discussed with Auntie Ying and Auntie An-mei what should be done, because they had known for many years about my mother's search for her twin daughters, her endless hope. Auntie Lindo and the others cried over this double tragedy, of losing my mother three months before, and now again. And so they couldn't help but think of some miracle, some possible way of reviving her from the dead, so my mother could fulfill her dream.

So this is what they wrote to my sisters in Shanghai: "Dearest Daughters, I too have never forgotten you in my memory or in my heart. I never gave up hope that we would see each other again in a joyous reunion. I am only sorry it has been too long. I want to tell you everything about my life since I last saw you. I want to tell you this when our family comes to see you in China. . . ." They signed it with my mother's name.

It wasn't until all this had been done that they first told me about my sisters, the letter they received, the one they wrote back.

"They'll think she's coming, then," I murmured. And I had imagined my sisters now being ten or eleven, jumping up and down, holding hands, their pigtails bouncing, excited that their mother—*their* mother—was coming, whereas my mother was dead.

"How can you say she is not coming in a letter?" said Auntie Lindo. "She is their mother. She is your mother. You must be the one to tell them. All these years, they have been dreaming of her." And I thought she was right.

But then I started dreaming, too, of my mother and my sisters and how it would be if I arrived in Shanghai. All these years, while they waited to be found, I had lived with my mother and then had lost her. I imagined seeing my sisters at the airport. They would be standing on their tiptoes, looking anxiously, scanning from one dark head to another as we got off the plane. And I would recognize them instantly, their faces with the identical worried look.

"Jyejye, Jyejye. Sister, Sister. We are here," I saw myself saying in my poor version of Chinese.

"Where is Mama?" they would say, and look around, still smiling, two flushed and eager faces. "Is she hiding?" And this would have been like my mother, to stand behind just a bit, to tease a little and make people's patience pull a little on their hearts. I would shake my head and tell my sisters she was not hiding.

"Oh, that must be Mama, no?" one of my sisters would whisper excitedly, pointing to another small woman completely engulfed in a tower of presents. And that, too, would have been like my mother, to bring mountains of gifts, food, and toys for children—all bought on sale—shunning thanks, saying the gifts were nothing, and later turning the labels over to show my sisters, "Calvin Klein, 100% wool."

I imagined myself starting to say, "Sisters, I am sorry, I have come alone . . ." and before I could tell them—they could see it in my face—they were wailing, pulling their hair, their lips twisted in pain, as they ran away from me. And then I saw myself getting back on the plane and coming home.

After I had dreamed this scene many times—watching their despair turn from horror into anger—I begged Auntie Lindo to write another letter. And at first she refused.

"How can I say she is dead? I cannot write this," said Auntie Lindo with a stubborn look.

"But it's cruel to have them believe she's coming on the plane," I said. "When they see it's just me, they'll hate me."

"Hate you? Cannot be." She was scowling. "You are their own sister, their only family."

"You don't understand," I protested.

"What I don't understand?" she said.

And I whispered. "They'll think I'm responsible, that she died because I didn't appreciate her."

And Auntie Lindo looked satisfied and sad at the same time, as if this were true and I had finally realized it. She sat down for an hour, and when she stood up she handed me a two-page letter. She had tears in her eyes. I realized that the very thing I had feared, she had done. So even if she had written the news of my mother's death in English, I wouldn't have had the heart to read it.

"Thank you," I whispered.

The landscape has become gray, filled with low flat cement buildings, old factories, and then tracks and more tracks filled with trains like ours passing by in the opposite direction. I see platforms crowded with people wearing drab Western clothes, with spots of bright colors: little children wearing pink and yellow, red and peach. And there are soldiers in olive green and red, and old ladies in gray tops and pants that stop mid-calf. We are in Guangzhou.

Before the train even comes to a stop, people are bringing down their belongings from above their seats. For a moment there is a dangerous shower of heavy suitcases laden with gifts to relatives, half-broken boxes wrapped in miles of string to keep the contents from spilling out, plastic bags filled with yarn and vegetables and packages of dried mushrooms, and camera cases. And then we are caught in a stream of people rushing, shoving, pushing us along, until we find ourselves in one of a dozen lines waiting to go through customs. I feel as if I were getting on a number 30 Stockton bus in San Francisco. I am in China, I remind myself. And somehow the crowds don't bother me. It feels right. I start pushing too.

I take out the declaration forms and my passport. "Woo," it says at the top, and below that, "June May," who was born in "California, U.S.A.," in 1951. I wonder if the customs people will question whether I'm the same person as in the passport photo. In this picture, my chin-length hair is swept back and artfully styled. I am wearing false eyelashes, eye shadow, and lip liner. My cheeks are hollowed out by bronze blusher. But I had not expected the heat in October. And now my hair hangs limp with the humidity. I wear no makeup; in Hong Kong my mascara had melted into dark circles and everything else had felt like layers of grease. So today my face is plain, unadorned except for a thin mist of shiny sweat on my forehead and nose.

Even without makeup, I could never pass for true Chinese. I stand five-foot-six, and my head pokes above the crowd so that I am eye level only with other tourists. My mother once told me my height came from my grandfather, who was a northerner, and may have even had some Mongol blood. "This is what your grandmother once told me," explained my mother. "But now it is too late to ask her. They are all dead, your grandparents, your uncles, and their wives and children, all killed in the war, when a bomb fell on our house. So many generations in one instant." 35

She had said this so matter-of-factly that I thought she had long since gotten over any grief she had. And then I wondered how she knew they were all dead.

"Maybe they left the house before the bomb fell," I suggested.

"No," said my mother. "Our whole family is gone. It is just you and I."

"But how do you know? Some of them could have escaped."

"Cannot be," said my mother, this time almost angrily. And then her frown was washed over by a puzzled blank look, and she began to talk as if she were trying to remember where she had misplaced something. "I went back to that house. I kept looking up to where the house used to be. And it wasn't a house, just the sky. And below, underneath my feet, were four stories of burnt bricks and wood, all the life of our house. Then off to the side I saw things blown into the yard, nothing valuable. There was a bed someone used to sleep in, really just a metal frame twisted up at one corner. And a book, I don't know what kind, because every page had turned black. And I saw a teacup which was unbroken but filled with ashes. And then I found my doll, with her hands and legs broken, her hair burned off. . . . When I was a little girl, I had cried for that doll, seeing it all alone in the store window, and my mother had bought it for me. It was an American doll with yellow hair. It could turn its legs and arms. The eyes moved up and down. And when I married and left my family home, I gave the doll to 40 my youngest niece, because she was like me. She cried if that doll was not with her always. Do you see? If she was in the house with that doll, her parents were there, and so everybody was there, waiting together, because that's how our family was."

The woman in the customs booth stares at my documents, then glances at me briefly, and with two quick movements stamps everything and sternly nods me along. And soon my father and I find ourselves in a large area filled with thousands of people and suitcases. I feel lost and my father looks helpless.

"Excuse me," I say to a man who looks like an American. "Can you tell me where I can get a taxi?" He mumbles something that sounds Swedish or Dutch.

"Syau Yen! Syau Yen!" I hear a piercing voice shout from behind me. An old woman in a yellow knit beret is holding up a pink plastic bag filled with wrapped trinkets. I guess she is trying to sell us something. But my father is staring down at this tiny sparrow of a woman, squinting into her eyes. And then his eyes widen, his face opens up and he smiles like a pleased little boy.

"Aiyi! Aiyi!"—Auntie Auntie!—he says softly.

45   "Syau Yen!" coos my great-aunt. I think it's funny she has just called my father "Little Wild Goose." It must be his baby milk name, the name used to discourage ghosts from stealing children.

They clasp each other's hands—they do not hug—and hold on like this, taking turns saying, "Look at you! You are so old. Look how old you've become!" They are both crying openly, laughing at the same time, and I bite my lip, trying not to cry. I'm afraid to feel their joy. Because I am thinking how different our arrival in Shanghai will be tomorrow, how awkward it will feel.

Now Aiyi beams and points to a Polaroid picture of my father. My father had wisely sent pictures when he wrote and said we were coming. See how smart she was, she seems to intone as she compares the picture to my father. In the letter, my father had said we would call her from the hotel once we arrived, so this is a surprise, that they've come to meet us. I wonder if my sisters will be at the airport.

It is only then that I remember the camera. I had meant to take a picture of my father and his aunt the moment they met. It's not too late.

"Here, stand together over here," I say, holding up the Polaroid. The camera flashes and I hand them the snapshot. Aiyi and my father still stand close together, each of them holding a corner of the picture, watching as their images begin to form. They are almost reverentially quiet. Aiyi is only five years older than my father, which makes her around seventy-seven. But she looks ancient, shrunken, a mummified relic. Her thin hair is pure white, her teeth are brown with decay. So much for stories of Chinese women looking young forever, I think to myself.

50   Now Aiyi is crooning to me: "Jandale." So big already. She looks up at me, at my full height, and then peers into her pink plastic bag—her gifts to us, I have figured out—as if she is wondering what she will give to me, now that I am so old and big. And then she grabs my elbow with her sharp pincerlike grasp and turns me around. A man and a woman in their fifties are shaking hands

with my father, everybody smiling and saying, "Ah! Ah!" They are Aiyi's oldest son and his wife, and standing next to them are four other people, around my age, and a little girl who's around ten. The introductions go by so fast, all I know is that one of them is Aiyi's grandson, with his wife, and the other is her granddaughter, with her husband. And the little girl is Lili, Aiyi's great-granddaughter.

Aiyi and my father speak the Mandarin dialect from their childhood, but the rest of the family speaks only the Cantonese of their village. I understand only Mandarin but can't speak it that well. So Aiyi and my father gossip unrestrained in Mandarin, exchanging news about people from their old village. And they stop only occasionally to talk to the rest of us, sometimes in Cantonese, sometimes in English.

"Oh, it is as I suspected," says my father, turning to me. "He died last summer." And I already understood this. I just don't know who this person, Li Gong, is. I feel as if I were in the United Nations and the translators had run amok.

"Hello," I say to the little girl. "My name is Jing-mei." But the little girl squirms to look away, causing her parents to laugh with embarrassment. I try to think of Cantonese words I can say to her, stuff I learned from friends in Chinatown, but all I can think of are swear words, terms for bodily functions, and short phrases like "tastes good," "tastes like garbage," and "she's really ugly." And then I have another plan: I hold up the Polaroid camera, beckoning Lili with my finger. She immediately jumps forward, places one hand on her hip in the manner of a fashion model, juts out her chest, and flashes me a toothy smile. As soon as I take the picture she is standing next to me, jumping and giggling every few seconds as she watches herself appear on the greenish film.

By the time we hail taxis for the ride to the hotel, Lili is holding tight onto my hand, pulling me along.

In the taxi, Aiyi talks nonstop, so I have no chance to ask her about the different sights we are passing by.

"You wrote and said you would come only for one day," says Aiyi to my father in an agitated tone. "One day! How can you see your family in one day! Toishan is many hours' drive from Guangzhou. And this idea to call us when you arrive. This is nonsense. We have no telephone."

My heart races a little. I wonder if Auntie Lindo told my sisters we would call from the hotel in Shanghai?

Aiyi continues to scold my father. "I was so beside myself, ask my son, almost turned heaven and earth upside down trying to think of a way! So we decided the best was for us to take the bus from Toishan and come into Guangzhou — meet you right from the start."

And now I am holding my breath as the taxi driver dodges between trucks and buses, honking his horn constantly. We seem to be on some sort of long freeway overpass, like a bridge above the city. I can see row after row of apartments, each floor cluttered with laundry hanging out to dry on the balcony. We pass a public bus, with people jammed in so tight their faces are nearly wedged against the window. Then I see the skyline of what must be downtown Guangzhou. From a distance, it looks like a major American city, with highrises and construction going on everywhere. As we slow down in the more congested part of the city, I see scores of little shops, dark inside, lined with counters and shelves. And then there is a building, its front laced with scaffolding made of bamboo poles held together with plastic strips. Men and women are standing on narrow platforms, scraping the sides, working without safety straps or helmets. Oh, would OSHA[1] have a field day here, I think.

60   Aiyi's shrill voice rises up again: "So it is a shame you can't see our village, our house. My sons have been quite successful, selling our vegetables in the free market. We had enough these last few years to build a big house, three stories, all of new brick, big enough for our whole family and then some. And every year, the money is even better. You Americans aren't the only ones who know how to get rich!"

The taxi stops and I assume we've arrived, but then I peer out at what looks like a grander version of the Hyatt Regency. "This is communist China?" I wonder out loud. And then I shake my head toward my father. "This must be the wrong hotel." I quickly pull out our itinerary, travel tickets, and reservations. I had explicitly instructed my travel agent to choose something inexpensive, in the thirty-to-forty-dollar range. I'm sure of this. And there it says on our itinerary: Garden Hotel, Huanshi Dong Lu. Well, our travel agent had better be prepared to eat the extra, that's all I have to say.

The hotel is magnificent. A bellboy complete with uniform and sharp-creased cap jumps forward and begins to carry our bags into the lobby. Inside, the hotel looks like an orgy of shopping arcades and restaurants all encased in granite and glass. And rather than be impressed, I am worried about the expense, as well as the appearance it must give Aiyi, that we rich Americans cannot be without our luxuries even for one night.

But when I step up to the reservation desk, ready to haggle over this booking mistake, it is confirmed. Our rooms are prepaid, thirty-four dollars each. I feel sheepish, and Aiyi and the others seem delighted by our temporary surroundings. Lili is looking wide-eyed at an arcade filled with video games.

Our whole family crowds into one elevator, and the bellboy waves, saying he will meet us on the eighteenth floor. As soon as the elevator door shuts, everybody becomes very quiet, and when the door finally opens again, everybody talks at once in what sounds like relieved voices. I have the feeling Aiyi and the others have never been on such a long elevator ride.

65   Our rooms are next to each other and are identical. The rugs, drapes, bedspreads are all in shades of taupe. There's a color television with remote-control panels built into the lamp table between the two twin beds. The bathroom has marble walls and floors. I find a built-in wet bar with a small refrigerator stocked with Heineken beer, Coke Classic, and Seven-Up, mini-bottles of Johnnie Walker Red, Bacardi rum, and Smirnoff vodka, and packets of M & M's, honey-roasted cashews, and Cadbury chocolate bars. And again I say out loud, "This is communist China?"

My father comes into my room. "They decided we should just stay here and

_____

1. Occupational Safety and Health Administration.

visit," he says, shrugging his shoulders. "They say, Less trouble that way. More time to talk."

"What about dinner?" I ask. I have been envisioning my first real Chinese feast for many days already, a big banquet with one of those soups steaming out of a carved winter melon, chicken wrapped in clay, Peking duck, the works.

My father walks over and picks up a room service book next to a *Travel & Leisure* magazine. He flips through the pages quickly and then points to the menu. "This is what they want," says my father.

So it's decided. We are going to dine tonight in our rooms, with our family, sharing hamburgers, french fries, and apple pie à la mode.

Aiyi and her family are browsing the shops while we clean up. After a hot ride on the train, I'm eager for a shower and cooler clothes.

The hotel has provided little packets of shampoo which, upon opening, I discover is the consistency and color of hoisin sauce.[2] This is more like it, I think. This is China. And I rub some in my damp hair.

Standing in the shower, I realize this is the first time I've been by myself in what seems like days. But instead of feeling relieved, I feel forlorn. I think about what my mother said, about activating my genes and becoming Chinese. And I wonder what she meant.

Right after my mother died, I asked myself a lot of things, things that couldn't be answered, to force myself to grieve more. It seemed as if I wanted to sustain my grief, to assure myself that I had cared deeply enough.

But now I ask the questions mostly because I want to know the answers. What was that pork stuff she used to make that had the texture of sawdust? What were the names of the uncles who died in Shanghai? What had she dreamt all these years about her other daughters? All the times when she got mad at me, was she really thinking about them? Did she wish I were they? Did she regret that I wasn't?

• • •

At one o'clock in the morning, I awake to tapping sounds on the window. I must have dozed off and now I feel my body uncramping itself. I'm sitting on the floor, leaning against one of the twin beds. Lili is lying next to me. The others are asleep, too, sprawled out on the beds and floor. Aiyi is seated at a little table, looking very sleepy. And my father is staring out the window, tapping his fingers on the glass. The last time I listened my father was telling Aiyi about his life since he last saw her. How he had gone to Yenching University, later got a post with a newspaper in Chungking, met my mother there, a young widow. How they later fled together to Shanghai to try to find my mother's family house, but there was nothing there. And then they traveled eventually to Canton and then to Hong Kong, then Haiphong and finally to San Francisco. . . .

"Suyuan didn't tell me she was trying all these years to find her daughters," he is now saying in a quiet voice. "Naturally, I did not discuss her daughters

2. Sweet brownish-red sauce made from soybeans, flour, sugar, water, spices, garlic, and chili.

with her. I thought she was ashamed she had left them behind."

"Where did she leave them?" asks Aiyi. "How were they found?"

I am wide awake now. Although I have heard parts of this story from my mother's friends.

"It happened when the Japanese took over Kweilin," says my father.

"Japanese in Kweilin?" says Aiyi. "That was never the case. Couldn't be. The Japanese never came to Kweilin."

"Yes, that is what the newspapers reported. I know this because I was working for the news bureau at the time. The Kuomintang[3] often told us what we could say and could not say. But we knew the Japanese had come into Kwangsi Province. We had sources who told us how they had captured the Wuchang-Canton railway. How they were coming overland, making very fast progress, marching toward the provincial capital."

Aiyi looks astonished. "If people did not know this, how could Suyuan know the Japanese were coming?"

"An officer of the Kuomintang secretly warned her," explains my father. "Suyuan's husband also was an officer and everybody knew that officers and their families would be the first to be killed. So she gathered a few possessions and, in the middle of the night, she picked up her daughters and fled on foot. The babies were not even one year old."

"How could she give up those babies!" sighs Aiyi. "Twin girls. We have never had such luck in our family." And then she yawns again.

"What were they named?" she asks. I listen carefully. I had been planning on using just the familiar "Sister" to address them both. But now I want to know how to pronounce their names.

"They have their father's surname, Wang," says my father. "And their given names are Chwun Yu and Chwun Hwa."

"What do the names mean?" I ask.

"Ah." My father draws imaginary characters on the window. "One means 'Spring Rain,' the other 'Spring Flower,'" he explains in English, "because they born in the spring, and of course rain come before flower, same order these girls are born. Your mother like a poet, don't you think?"

I nod my head. I see Aiyi nod her head forward, too. But it falls forward and stays there. She is breathing deeply, noisily. She is asleep.

"And what does Ma's name mean?" I whisper.

"'Suyuan,'" he says, writing more invisible characters on the glass. "The way she write it in Chinese, it mean 'Long-Cherished Wish.' Quite a fancy name, not so ordinary like flower name. See this first character, it means something like 'Forever Never Forgotten.' But there is another way to write 'Suyuan.' Sound exactly the same, but the meaning is opposite." His finger creates the brushstrokes of another character. "The first part look the same: 'Never Forgotten.' But the last part add to first part make the whole word mean 'Long-Held Grudge.' Your mother get angry with me, I tell her her name should be Grudge."

3. National People's Party, led by Generalissimo Chiang Kai-shek (1887–1975).

My father is looking at me, moist-eyed. "See, I pretty clever, too, hah?"

I nod, wishing I could find some way to comfort him. "And what about my name," I ask, "what does 'Jing-mei' mean?"

"Your name also special," he says. I wonder if any name in Chinese is not something special. " 'Jing' like excellent *jing*. Not just good, it's something pure, essential, the best quality. *Jing* is good leftover stuff when you take impurities out of something like gold, or rice, or salt. So what is left—just pure essence. And 'Mei,' this is common *mei*, as in *meimei*, 'younger sister.' "

I think about this. My mother's long-cherished wish. Me, the younger sister who was supposed to be the essence of the others. I feed myself with the old grief, wondering how disappointed my mother must have been. Tiny Aiyi stirs suddenly, her head rolls and then falls back, her mouth opens as if to answer my question. She grunts in her sleep, tucking her body more closely into the chair.

"So why did she abandon those babies on the road?" I need to know, because now I feel abandoned too.

"Long time I wondered this myself," says my father. "But then I read that letter from her daughters in Shanghai now, and I talk to Auntie Lindo, all the others. And then I knew. No shame in what she done. None."

"What happened?"

"Your mother running away—" begins my father.

"No, tell me in Chinese," I interrupt. "Really, I can understand."

He begins to talk, still standing at the window, looking into the night.

·   ·   ·

After fleeing Kweilin, your mother walked for several days trying to find a main road. Her thought was to catch a ride on a truck or wagon, to catch enough rides until she reached Chungking, where her husband was stationed.

She had sewn money and jewelry into the lining of her dress, enough, she thought, to barter rides all the way. If I am lucky, she thought, I will not have to trade the heavy gold bracelet and jade ring. These were things from her mother, your grandmother.

By the third day, she had traded nothing. The roads were filled with people, everybody running and begging for rides from passing trucks. The trucks rushed by, afraid to stop. So your mother found no rides, only the start of dysentery pains in her stomach.

Her shoulders ached from the two babies swinging from scarf slings. Blisters grew on the palms from holding two leather suitcases. And then the blisters burst and began to bleed. After a while, she left the suitcases behind, keeping only the food and a few clothes. And later she also dropped the bags of wheat flour and rice and kept walking like this for many miles, singing songs to her little girls, until she was delirious with pain and fever.

Finally, there was not one more step left in her body. She didn't have the strength to carry those babies any further. She slumped to the ground. She knew she would die of her sickness, or perhaps from thirst, from starvation, or from the Japanese, who she was sure were marching right behind her.

She took the babies out of the slings and sat them on the side of the road, then lay down next to them. You babies are so good, she said, so quiet. They smiled back, reaching their chubby hands for her, wanting to be picked up again. And then she knew she could not bear to watch her babies die with her.

She saw a family with three young children in a cart going by. "Take my babies, I beg you," she cried to them. But they stared back with empty eyes and never stopped.

She saw another person pass and called out again. This time a man turned around, and he had such a terrible expression—your mother said it looked like death itself—she shivered and looked away.

When the road grew quiet, she tore open the lining of her dress, and stuffed jewelry under the shirt of one baby and money under the other. She reached into her pocket and drew out the photos of her family, the picture of her father and mother, the picture of herself and her husband on their wedding day. And she wrote on the back of each the names of the babies and this same message: "Please care for these babies with the money and valuables provided. When it is safe to come, if you bring them to Shanghai, 9 Weichang Lu, the Li family will be glad to give you a generous reward. Li Suyuan and Wang Fuchi."

And then she touched each baby's cheek and told her not to cry. She would go down the road to find them some food and would be back. And without looking back, she walked down the road, stumbling and crying, thinking only of this last hope, that her daughters would be found by a kindhearted person who would care for them. She would not allow herself to imagine anything else.

She did not remember how far she walked, which direction she went, when she fainted, or how she was found. When she awoke, she was in the back of a bouncing truck with several other sick people, all moaning. And she began to scream, thinking she was now on a journey to Buddhist hell. But the face of an American missionary lady bent over her and smiled, talking to her in a soothing language she did not understand. And yet she could somehow understand. She had been saved for no good reason, and it was now too late to go back and save her babies.

When she arrived in Chungking, she learned her husband had died two weeks before. She told me later she laughed when the officers told her this news, she was so delirious with madness and disease. To come so far, to lose so much and to find nothing.

I met her in a hospital. She was lying on a cot, hardly able to move, her dysentery had drained her so thin. I had come in for my foot, my missing toe, which was cut off by a piece of falling rubble. She was talking to herself, mumbling.

"Look at these clothes," she said, and I saw she had on a rather unusual dress for wartime. It was silk satin, quite dirty, but there was no doubt it was a beautiful dress.

"Look at this face," she said, and I saw her dusty face and hollow cheeks, her eyes shining black. "Do you see my foolish hope?"

"I thought I had lost everything, except these two things," she murmured. "And I wondered which I would lose next. Clothes or hope? Hope or clothes?"

"But now, see here, look what is happening," she said, laughing, as if all her prayers had been answered. And she was pulling hair out of her head as easily as one lifts new wheat from wet soil.

It was an old peasant woman who found them. "How could I resist?" the peasant woman later told your sisters when they were older. They were still sitting obediently near where your mother had left them, looking like little fairy queens waiting for their sedan to arrive.

The woman, Mei Ching, and her husband, Mei Han, lived in a stone cave. There were thousands of hidden caves like that in and around Kweilin so secret that the people remained hidden even after the war ended. The Meis would come out of their cave every few days and forage for food supplies left on the road, and sometimes they would see something that they both agreed was a tragedy to leave behind. So one day they took back to their cave a delicately painted set of rice bowls, another day a little footstool with a velvet cushion and two new wedding blankets. And once, it was your sisters.

They were pious people, Muslims, who believed the twin babies were a sign of double luck, and they were sure of this when, later in the evening, they discovered how valuable the babies were. She and her husband had never seen rings and bracelets like those. And while they admired the pictures, knowing the babies came from a good family, neither of them could read or write. It was not until many months later that Mei Ching found someone who could read the writing on the back. By then, she loved these baby girls like her own.

In 1952 Mei Han, the husband, died. The twins were already eight years old, and Mei Ching now decided it was time to find your sisters' true family.

She showed the girls the picture of their mother and told them they had been born into a great family and she would take them back to see their true mother and grandparents. Mei Ching told them about the reward, but she swore she would refuse it. She loved these girls so much, she only wanted them to have what they were entitled to—a better life, a fine house, educated ways. Maybe the family would let her stay on as the girls' amah. Yes, she was certain they would insist.

Of course, when she found the place at 9 Weichang Lu, in the old French Concession, it was something completely different. It was the site of a factory building, recently constructed, and none of the workers knew what had become of the family whose house had burned down on that spot.

Mei Ching could not have known, of course, that your mother and I, her new husband, had already returned to that same place in 1945 in hopes of finding both her family and her daughters.

Your mother and I stayed in China until 1947. We went to many different cities—back to Kweilin, to Changsha, as far south as Kunming. She was always looking out of one corner of her eye for twin babies, then little girls. Later we went to Hong Kong, and when we finally left in 1949 for the United States, I think she was even looking for them on the boat. But when we arrived, she no longer talked about them. I thought, At last, they have died in her heart.

When letters could be openly exchanged between China and the United States, she wrote immediately to old friends in Shanghai and Kweilin. I did not know she did this. Auntie Lindo told me. But of course, by then, all the street names had changed. Some people had died, others had moved away. So it took many years to find a contact. And when she did find an old schoolmate's address and wrote asking her to look for her daughters, her friend wrote back and said this was impossible, like looking for a needle on the bottom of the ocean. How did she know her daughters were in Shanghai and not somewhere else in China? The friend, of course, did not ask, How do you know your daughters are still alive?

So her schoolmate did not look. Finding babies lost during the war was a matter of foolish imagination, and she had no time for that.

But every year, your mother wrote to different people. And this last year, I think she got a big idea in her head, to go to China and find them herself. I remember she told me, "Canning, we should go, before it is too late, before we are too old." And I told her we were already too old, it was already too late.

I just thought she wanted to be a tourist! I didn't know she wanted to go and look for her daughters. So when I said it was too late, that must have put a terrible thought in her head that her daughters might be dead. And I think this possibility grew bigger and bigger in her head, until it killed her.

Maybe it was your mother's dead spirit who guided her Shanghai schoolmate to find her daughters. Because after your mother died, the schoolmate saw your sisters, by chance, while shopping for shoes at the Number One Department Store on Nanjing Dong Road. She said it was like a dream, seeing these two women who looked so much alike, moving down the stairs together. There was something about their facial expressions that reminded the schoolmate of your mother.

She quickly walked over to them and called their names, which of course, they did not recognize at first, because Mei Ching had changed their names. But your mother's friend was so sure, she persisted. "Are you not Wang Chwun Yu and Wang Chwun Hwa?" she asked them. And then these double-image women became very excited, because they remembered the names written on the back of an old photo, a photo of a young man and woman they still honored, as their much-loved first parents, who had died and become spirit ghosts still roaming the earth looking for them.

• • •

At the airport, I am exhausted. I could not sleep last night. Aiyi had followed me into my room at three in the morning, and she instantly fell asleep on one of the twin beds, snoring with the might of a lumberjack. I lay awake thinking about my mother's story, realizing how much I have never known about her, grieving that my sisters and I had both lost her.

And now at the airport, after shaking hands with everybody, waving good-bye, I think about all the different ways we leave people in this world. Cheerily waving good-bye to some at airports, knowing we'll never see each other again. Leaving others on the side of the road, hoping that we will. Finding my mother in my father's story and saying good-bye before I have a chance to know her better.

Aiyi smiles at me as we wait for our gate to be called. She is so old. I put one   135
arm around her and one arm around Lili. They are the same size, it seems. And
then it's time. As we wave good-bye one more time and enter the waiting area,
I get the sense I am going from one funeral to another. In my hand I'm clutching a pair of tickets to Shanghai. In two hours we'll be there.

The plane takes off. I close my eyes. How can I describe to them in my
broken Chinese about our mother's life? Where should I begin?

"Wake up, we're here," says my father. And I awake with my heart pounding
in my throat. I look out the window and we're already on the runway. It's gray
outside.

And now I'm walking down the steps of the plane, onto the tarmac and
toward the building. If only, I think, if only my mother had lived long enough
to be the one walking toward them. I am so nervous I cannot feel my feet. I am
just moving somehow.

Somebody shouts, "She's arrived!" And then I see her. Her short hair. Her
small body. And that same look on her face. She has the back of her hand
pressed hard against her mouth. She is crying as though she had gone through
a terrible ordeal and were happy it is over.

And I know it's not my mother, yet it is the same look she had when I was five   140
and had disappeared all afternoon, for such a long time, that she was convinced I
was dead. And when I miraculously appeared, sleepy-eyed, crawling from underneath my bed, she wept and laughed, biting the back of her hand to make sure
it was true.

And now I see her again, two of her, waving, and in one hand there is a
photo, the Polaroid I sent them. As soon as I get beyond the gate, we run toward
each other, all three of us embracing, all hesitations and expectations forgotten.

"Mama, Mama," we all murmur, as if she is among us.

My sisters look at me, proudly. "*Meimei jandale*," says one sister proudly to
the other. "Little Sister has grown up." I look at their faces again and I see no
trace of my mother in them. Yet they still look familiar. And now I also see what
part of me is Chinese. It is so obvious. It is my family. It is in our blood. After
all these years, it can finally be let go.

My sisters and I stand, arms around each other, laughing and wiping the
tears from each other's eyes. The flash of the Polaroid goes off and my father
hands me the snapshot. My sisters and I watch quietly together, eager to see
what develops.

The gray-green surface changes to the bright colors of our three images,   145
sharpening and deepening all at once. And although we don't speak, I know we
all see it: Together we look like our mother. Her same eyes, her same mouth,
open in surprise to see, at last, her long-cherished wish.

1989

ANTON CHEKHOV

The Lady with the Dog[1]

I

People were telling one another that a newcomer had been seen on the promenade—a lady with a dog. Dmitry Dmitrich Gurov had been a fortnight in Yalta,[2] and was accustomed to its ways, and he, too, had begun to take an interest in fresh arrivals. From his seat in Vernet's outdoor café, he caught sight of a young woman in a toque, passing along the promenade; she was fair and not very tall; after her trotted a white Pomeranian.

Later he encountered her in the municipal park and in the square several times a day. She was always alone, wearing the same toque, and the Pomeranian always trotted at her side. Nobody knew who she was, and people referred to her simply as "the lady with the dog."

"If she's here without her husband, and without any friends," thought Gurov, "it wouldn't be a bad idea to make her acquaintance."

He was not yet forty but had a twelve-year-old daughter and two sons in high school. He had been talked into marrying in his third year at college, and his wife now looked nearly twice as old as he did. She was a tall woman with dark eyebrows, erect, dignified, imposing, and, as she said of herself, a "thinker." She was a great reader, omitted the "hard sign"[3] at the end of words in her letters, and called her husband "Dimitry" instead of Dmitry; and though he secretly considered her shallow, narrow-minded, and dowdy, he stood in awe of her, and disliked being at home. He had first begun deceiving her long ago and he was now constantly unfaithful to her, and this was no doubt why he spoke slightingly of women, to whom he referred as *the lower race.*

He considered that the ample lessons he had received from bitter experience entitled him to call them whatever he liked, but without this "lower race" he could not have existed a single day. He was bored and ill-at-ease in the company of men, with whom he was always cold and reserved, but felt quite at home among women, and knew exactly what to say to them, and how to behave; he could even be silent in their company without feeling the slightest awkwardness. There was an elusive charm in his appearance and disposition which attracted women and caught their sympathies. He knew this and was himself attracted to them by some invisible force.

Repeated and bitter experience had taught him that every fresh intimacy, while at first introducing such pleasant variety into everyday life, and offering itself as a charming, light adventure, inevitably developed, among decent people (especially in Moscow, where they are so irresolute and slow to move), into a problem of excessive complication leading to an intolerably irksome situation.

1. Translated by Ivy Litvinov.   2. Russian city on the Black Sea; a resort for southern vacations.
3. Conventional sign that was used following consonants; to omit it was then "progressive."

But every time he encountered an attractive woman he forgot all about this experience, the desire for life surged up in him, and everything suddenly seemed simple and amusing.

One evening, then, while he was dining at the restaurant in the park, the lady in the toque came strolling up and took a seat at a neighboring table. Her expression, gait, dress, coiffure, all told him that she was from the upper classes, that she was married, that she was in Yalta for the first time, alone and bored. . . . The accounts of the laxity of morals among visitors to Yalta are greatly exaggerated, and he paid no heed to them, knowing that for the most part they were invented by people who would gladly have transgressed themselves, had they known how to set about it. But when the lady sat down at a neighboring table a few yards away from him, these stories of easy conquests, of excursions to the mountains, came back to him, and the seductive idea of a brisk transitory liaison, an affair with a woman whose very name he did not know, suddenly took possession of his mind.

He snapped his fingers at the Pomeranian and, when it trotted up to him, shook his forefinger at it. The Pomeranian growled. Gurov shook his finger again.

The lady glanced at him and instantly lowered her eyes.

"He doesn't bite," she said, and blushed.

"May I give him a bone?" he asked, and on her nod of consent added in friendly tones: "Have you been long in Yalta?"

"About five days."

"And I am dragging out my second week here."

Neither spoke for a few minutes.

"The days pass quickly, and yet one is so bored here," she said, not looking at him.

"It's the thing to say it's boring here. People never complain of boredom in godforsaken holes like Belyev or Zhizdra, but when they get here it's: 'Oh, the dullness! Oh, the dust!' You'd think they'd come from Granada[4] to say the least."

She laughed. Then they both went on eating in silence, like complete strangers. But after dinner they left the restaurant together, and embarked upon the light, jesting talk of people free and contented, for whom it is all the same where they go, or what they talk about. They strolled along, remarking on the strange light over the sea. The water was a warm, tender purple, the moonlight lay on its surface in a golden strip. They said how close it was, after the hot day. Gurov told her he was from Moscow, had a degree in literature but worked in a bank; that he had at one time trained himself to sing in a private opera company, but had given up the idea; that he owned two houses in Moscow. . . . And from her he learned that she had grown up in Petersburg, but had gotten married in the town of S., where she had been living two years, that she would stay another month in Yalta, and that perhaps her husband, who also needed a rest, would join her. She was quite unable to explain whether her husband was a member of the province council, or on the board of the *zemstvo*,[5] and was greatly

4. Romantic city in southern Spain.   5. An elective provincial council.

amused at herself for this. Further, Gurov learned that her name was Anna Sergeyevna.

Back in his own room he thought about her, and felt sure he would meet her the next day. It was inevitable. As he went to bed he reminded himself that only a very short time ago she had been a schoolgirl, like his own daughter, learning her lessons; he remembered how much there was of shyness and constraint in her laughter, in her way of conversing with a stranger—it was probably the first time in her life that she found herself alone, and in a situation in which men could follow her and watch her, and speak to her, all the time with a secret aim she could not fail to divine. He recalled her slender, delicate neck, her fine gray eyes.

"And yet there's something pathetic about her," he thought to himself as he fell asleep.

II

A week had passed since the beginning of their acquaintance. It was a holiday. Indoors it was stuffy, but the dust rose in clouds out of doors, and people's hats blew off. It was a parching day and Gurov kept going to the outdoor café for fruit drinks and ices to offer Anna Sergeyevna. The heat was overpowering.

In the evening, when the wind had dropped, they walked to the pier to see the steamer come in. There were a great many people strolling about the landing-place; some, bunches of flowers in their hands, were meeting friends. Two peculiarities of the smart Yalta crowd stood out distinctly—the elderly ladies all tried to dress very youthfully, and there seemed to be an inordinate number of generals about.

Owing to the roughness of the sea the steamer arrived late, after the sun had gone down, and it had to maneuver for some time before it could get alongside the pier. Anna Sergeyevna scanned the steamer and passengers through her lorgnette, as if looking for someone she knew, and when she turned to Gurov her eyes were glistening. She talked a great deal, firing off abrupt questions and forgetting immediately what it was she had wanted to know. Then she lost her lorgnette in the crush.

The smart crowd began dispersing, features could no longer be made out, the wind had quite dropped, and Gurov and Anna Sergeyevna stood there as if waiting for someone else to come off the steamer. Anna Sergeyevna had fallen silent, every now and then smelling her flowers, but not looking at Gurov.

"It's turning out a fine evening," he said. "What shall we do? We might go for a drive."

She made no reply.

He looked steadily at her and suddenly took her in his arms and kissed her lips, and the fragrance and dampness of the flowers closed round him, but the next moment he looked behind him in alarm—had anyone seen them?

"Let's go to your room," he murmured.

And they walked off together, very quickly.

Her room was stuffy and smelt of some scent she had bought in the Japanese shop. Gurov looked at her, thinking to himself: "How full of strange encounters life is!" He could remember carefree, good-natured women who were exhilarated by love-making and grateful to him for the happiness he gave them, however short-lived; and there had been others—his wife among them—whose caresses were insincere, affected, hysterical, mixed up with a great deal of quite unnecessary talk, and whose expression seemed to say that all this was not just love-making or passion, but something much more significant; then there had been two or three beautiful, cold women, over whose features flitted a predatory expression, betraying a determination to wring from life more than it could give, women no longer in their first youth, capricious, irrational, despotic, brainless, and when Gurov had cooled to these, their beauty aroused in him nothing but repulsion, and the lace trimming on their underclothes reminded him of fish-scales.

But here the timidity and awkwardness of youth and inexperience were still   30
apparent; and there was a feeling of embarrassment in the atmosphere, as if someone had just knocked at the door. Anna Sergeyevna, "the lady with the dog," seemed to regard the affair as something very special, very serious, as if she had become a fallen woman, an attitude he found odd and disconcerting. Her features lengthened and drooped, and her long hair hung mournfully on either side of her face. She assumed a pose of dismal meditation, like a repentant sinner in some classical painting.

"It isn't right," she said. "You will never respect me anymore."

On the table was a watermelon. Gurov cut himself a slice from it and began slowly eating it. At least half an hour passed in silence.

Anna Sergeyevna was very touching, revealing the purity of a decent, naïve woman who had seen very little of life. The solitary candle burning on the table scarcely lit up her face, but it was obvious that her heart was heavy.

"Why should I stop respecting you?" asked Gurov. "You don't know what you're saying."

"May God forgive me!" she exclaimed, and her eyes filled with tears. "It's   35
terrible."

"No need to seek to justify yourself."

"How can I justify myself? I'm a wicked, fallen woman, I despise myself and have not the least thought of self-justification. It isn't my husband I have deceived, it's myself. And not only now, I have been deceiving myself for ever so long. My husband is no doubt an honest, worthy man, but he's a flunky. I don't know what it is he does at his office, but I know he's a flunky. I was only twenty when I married him, and I was devoured by curiosity, I wanted something higher. I told myself that there must be a different kind of life I wanted to live, to live. . . . I was burning with curiosity . . . you'll never understand that, but I swear to God I could no longer control myself, nothing could hold me back, I told my husband I was ill, and I came here. . . . And I started going about like one possessed, like a madwoman . . . and now I have become an ordinary, worthless woman, and everyone has a right to despise me."

Gurov listened to her, bored to death. The naïve accents, the remorse, all was so unexpected, so out of place. But for the tears in her eyes, she might have been jesting or play-acting.

"I don't understand," he said gently. "What is it you want?"

She hid her face against his breast and pressed closer to him.

"Do believe me, I implore you to believe me," she said. "I love all that is honest and pure in life, vice is revolting to me, I don't know what I'm doing. The common people say they are snared by the Devil. And now I can say that I have been snared by the Devil, too."

"Come, come," he murmured.

He gazed into her fixed, terrified eyes, kissed her, and soothed her with gentle affectionate words, and gradually she calmed down and regained her cheerfulness. Soon they were laughing together again.

When, a little later, they went out, there was not a soul on the promenade, the town and its cypresses looked dead, but the sea was still roaring as it dashed against the beach. A solitary fishing-boat tossed on the waves, its lamp blinking sleepily.

They found a carriage and drove to Oreanda.

"I discovered your name in the hall, just now," said Gurov, "written up on the board. Von Diederitz. Is your husband a German?"

"No. His grandfather was, I think, but he belongs to the Orthodox Church himself."

When they got out of the carriage at Oreanda they sat down on a bench not far from the church, and looked down at the sea, without talking. Yalta could be dimly discerned through the morning mist, and white clouds rested motionless on the summits of the mountains. Not a leaf stirred, the grasshoppers chirruped, and the monotonous hollow roar of the sea came up to them, speaking of peace, of the eternal sleep lying in wait for us all. The sea had roared like this long before there was any Yalta or Oreanda, it was roaring now, and it would go on roaring, just as indifferently and hollowly, when we had passed away. And it may be that in this continuity, this utter indifference to the life and death of each of us lies hidden the pledge of our eternal salvation, of the continuous movement of life on earth, of the continuous movement toward perfection.

Side by side with a young woman, who looked so exquisite in the early light, soothed and enchanted by the sight of all this magical beauty—sea, mountains, clouds and the vast expanse of the sky—Gurov told himself that, when you came to think of it, everything in the world is beautiful really, everything but our own thoughts and actions, when we lose sight of the higher aims of life, and of our dignity as human beings.

Someone approached them—a watchman, probably—looked at them and went away. And there was something mysterious and beautiful even in this. The steamer from Feodosia could be seen coming towards the pier, lit up by the dawn, its lamps out.

"There's dew on the grass," said Anna Sergeyevna, breaking the silence.

"Yes. Time to go home."

They went back to the town.

After this they met every day at noon on the promenade, lunching and dining together, going for walks, and admiring the sea. She complained of sleep lessness, of palpitations, asked the same questions over and over again, alternately surrendering to jealousy and the fear that he did not really respect her. And often, when there was nobody in sight in the square or the park, he would draw her to him and kiss her passionately. The utter idleness, these kisses in broad daylight, accompanied by furtive glances and the fear of discovery, the heat, the smell of the sea, and the idle, smart, well-fed people continually crossing their field of vision, seemed to have given him a new lease on life. He told Anna Sergeyevna she was beautiful and seductive, made love to her with impetuous passion, and never left her side, while she was always pensive, always trying to force from him the admission that he did not respect her, that he did not love her a bit, and considered her just an ordinary woman. Almost every night they drove out of town, to Oreanda, the waterfall, or some other beautyspot. And these excursions were invariably a success, each contributing fresh impressions of majestic beauty.

All this time they kept expecting her husband to arrive. But a letter came in which he told his wife that he was having trouble with his eyes, and implored her to come home as soon as possible. Anna Sergeyevna made hasty preparations for leaving.

"It's a good thing I'm going," she said to Gurov. "It's the intervention of fate."

She left Yalta in a carriage, and he went with her as far as the railway station. The drive took nearly a whole day. When she got into the express train, after the second bell had been rung, she said:

"Let me have one more look at you. . . . One last look. That's right."

She did not weep, but was mournful, and seemed ill, the muscles of her cheeks twitching.

"I shall think of you . . . I shall think of you all the time," she said. "God bless you! Think kindly of me. We are parting forever, it must be so, because we ought never to have met. Good-bye—God bless you."

The train steamed rapidly out of the station, its lights soon disappearing, and a minute later even the sound it made was silenced, as if everything were conspiring to bring this sweet oblivion, this madness, to an end as quickly as possible. And Gurov, standing alone on the platform and gazing into the dark distance, listened to the shrilling of the grasshoppers and the humming of the telegraph wires, with a feeling that he had only just awakened. And he told himself that this had been just one more of the many adventures in his life, and that it, too, was over, leaving nothing but a memory. . . . He was moved and sad, and felt a slight remorse. After all, this young woman whom he would never again see had not been really happy with him. He had been friendly and affectionate with her, but in his whole behaviour, in the tones of his voice, in his very caresses, there had been a shade of irony, the insulting indulgence of the fortunate male, who was, moreover, almost twice her age. She had insisted in calling him good, remarkable, high-minded. Evidently he had appeared to her different from his real self, in a word he had involuntarily deceived her. . . .

There was an autumnal feeling in the air, and the evening was chilly.

"It's time for me to be going north, too," thought Gurov, as he walked away from the platform. "High time!"

III

When he got back to Moscow it was beginning to look like winter; the stoves were heated every day, and it was still dark when the children got up to go to school and drank their tea, so that the nurse had to light the lamp for a short time. Frost had set in. When the first snow falls, and one goes for one's first sleigh-ride, it is pleasant to see the white ground, the white roofs; one breathes freely and lightly, and remembers the days of one's youth. The ancient lime-trees and birches, white with hoarfrost, have a good-natured look, they are closer to the heart than cypresses and palms, and beneath their branches one is no longer haunted by the memory of mountains and the sea.

65   Gurov had always lived in Moscow, and he returned to Moscow on a fine frosty day, and when he put on his fur-lined overcoat and thick gloves, and sauntered down Petrovka Street, and when, on Saturday evening, he heard the church bells ringing, his recent journey and the places he had visited lost their charm for him. He became gradually immersed in Moscow life, reading with avidity three newspapers a day, while declaring he never read Moscow newspapers on principle. Once more he was caught up in a whirl of restaurants, clubs, banquets, and celebrations, once more glowed with the flattering consciousness that well-known lawyers and actors came to his house, that he played cards in the Medical Club opposite a professor. He could once again eat a whole serving of Moscow Fish Stew served in a pan.

He had believed that in a month's time Anna Sergeyevna would be nothing but a vague memory, and that hereafter, with her wistful smile, she would only occasionally appear to him in dreams, like others before her. But the month was now well over and winter was in full swing, and all was as clear in his memory as if he had parted with Anna Sergeyevna only the day before. And his recollections grew ever more insistent. When the voices of his children at their lessons reached him in his study through the evening stillness, when he heard a song, or the sounds of a music-box in a restaurant, when the wind howled in the chimney, it all came back to him: early morning on the pier, the misty mountains, the steamer from Feodosia, the kisses. He would pace up and down his room for a long time, smiling at his memories, and then memory turned into dreaming, and what had happened mingled in his imagination with what was going to happen. Anna Sergeyevna did not come to him in his dreams, she accompanied him everywhere, like his shadow, following him everywhere he went. When he closed his eyes, she seemed to stand before him in the flesh, still lovelier, younger, tenderer than she had really been, and looking back, he saw himself, too, as better than he had been in Yalta. In the evenings she looked out at him from the bookshelves, the fireplace, the corner, he could hear her breathing, the sweet rustle of her skirts. In the streets he followed women with his eyes, to see if there were any like her. . . .

He began to feel an overwhelming desire to share his memories with some-one. But he could not speak of his love at home, and outside his home who was there for him to confide in? Not the tenants living in his house, and certainly not his colleagues at the bank. And what was there to tell? Was it love that he had felt? Had there been anything exquisite, poetic, anything instructive or even amusing about his relations with Anna Sergeyevna? He had to content himself with uttering vague generalizations about love and women, and nobody guessed what he meant, though his wife's dark eyebrows twitched as she said:

"The role of a coxcomb doesn't suit you a bit, Dimitry."

One evening, leaving the Medical Club with one of his card-partners, a government official, he could not refrain from remarking:

"If you only knew what a charming woman I met in Yalta!"

The official got into his sleigh, and just before driving off, turned and called out:

"Dmitry Dmitrich!"

"Yes?"

"You were quite right, you know—the sturgeon was just a *leetle* off."

These words, in themselves so commonplace, for some reason infuriated Gurov, seemed to him humiliating, gross. What savage manners, what people! What wasted evenings, what tedious, empty days! Frantic card-playing, gluttony, drunkenness, perpetual talk always about the same thing. The greater part of one's time and energy went on business that was no use to anyone, and on discussing the same thing over and over again, and there was nothing to show for it all but a stunted wingless existence and a round of trivialities, and there was nowhere to escape to, you might as well be in a madhouse or a convict settlement.

Gurov lay awake all night, raging, and went about the whole of the next day with a headache. He slept badly on the succeeding nights, too, sitting up in bed, thinking, or pacing the floor of his room. He was sick of his children, sick of the bank, felt not the slightest desire to go anywhere or talk about anything.

When the Christmas holidays came, he packed his things, telling his wife he had to go to Petersburg in the interests of a certain young man, and set off for the town of S. To what end? He hardly knew himself. He only knew that he must see Anna Sergeyevna, must speak to her, arrange a meeting, if possible.

He arrived at S. in the morning and engaged the best suite in the hotel, which had a carpet of gray military frieze, and a dusty ink-pot on the table, surmounted by a headless rider, holding his hat in his raised hand. The hall porter told him what he wanted to know: von Diederitz had a house of his own in Staro-Goncharnaya Street. It wasn't far from the hotel, he lived on a grand scale, luxuriously, kept carriage-horses, the whole town knew him. The hall porter pronounced the name "Drideritz."

Gurov strolled over to Staro-Goncharnaya Street and discovered the house. In front of it was a long gray fence with inverted nails hammered into the tops of the palings.

"A fence like that is enough to make anyone want to run away," thought Gurov, looking at the windows of the house and the fence.

He reasoned that since it was a holiday, Anna's husband would probably be at home. In any case it would be tactless to embarrass her by calling at the house. And a note might fall into the hands of the husband, and bring about catastrophe. The best thing would be to wait about on the chance of seeing her. And he walked up and down the street, hovering in the vicinity of the fence, watching for his chance. A beggar entered the gate, only to be attacked by dogs, then, an hour later, the faint, vague sounds of a piano reached his ears. That would be Anna Sergeyevna playing. Suddenly the front door opened and an old woman came out, followed by a familiar white Pomeranian. Gurov tried to call to it, but his heart beat violently, and in his agitation he could not remember its name.

He walked on, hating the gray fence more and more, and now ready to tell himself irately that Anna Sergeyevna had forgotten him, had already, perhaps, found distraction in another—what could be more natural in a young woman who had to look at this accursed fence from morning to night? He went back to his hotel and sat on the sofa in his suite for some time, not knowing what to do, then he ordered dinner, and after dinner, had a long sleep.

"What a foolish, restless business," he thought, waking up and looking towards the dark windowpanes. It was evening by now. "Well, I've had my sleep out. And what am I to do in the night?"

He sat up in bed, covered by the cheap gray quilt, which reminded him of a hospital blanket, and in his vexation he fell to taunting himself.

85 "You and your lady with a dog . . . there's adventure for you! See what you get for your pains."

On his arrival at the station that morning he had noticed a poster announcing in enormous letters the first performance at the local theatre of *The Geisha*.[6] Remembering this, he got up and made for the theatre.

"It's highly probable that she goes to first nights," he told himself.

The theatre was full. It was a typical provincial theatre, with a mist collecting over the chandeliers, and the crowd in the gallery fidgeting noisily. In the first row of the stalls[7] the local dandies stood waiting for the curtain to go up, their hands clasped behind them. There, in the front seat of the governor's box, sat the governor's daughter, wearing a boa, the governor himself hiding modestly behind the drapes, so that only his hands were visible. The curtain stirred, the orchestra took a long time tuning up their instruments. Gurov's eyes roamed eagerly over the audience as they filed in and occupied their seats.

Anna Sergeyevna came in, too. She seated herself in the third row of the stalls, and when Gurov's glance fell on her, his heart seemed to stop, and he knew in a flash that the whole world contained no one nearer or dearer to him, no one more important to his happiness. This little woman, lost in the provincial crowd, in no way remarkable, holding a silly lorgnette in her hand, now filled his whole life, was his grief, his joy, all that he desired. Lulled by the sounds coming from the wretched orchestra, with its feeble, amateurish violinists, he thought how beautiful she was . . . thought and dreamed. . . .

---

6. Operetta by Sidney Jones (1861–1946) that toured eastern Europe in 1898–99.   7. Seats at the front of a theater, near the stage and separated from nearby seats by a railing.

Anna Sergeyevna was accompanied by a tall, round-shouldered young man   90
with small whiskers, who nodded at every step before taking the seat beside her
and seemed to be continually bowing to someone. This must be her husband,
whom, in a fit of bitterness, at Yalta, she had called a "flunky." And there really
was something of a lackey's servility in his lanky figure, his side-whiskers, and
the little bald spot on the top of his head. And he smiled sweetly, and the badge
of some scientific society gleaming in his buttonhole was like the number on a
footman's livery.

The husband went out to smoke in the first interval, and she was left alone
in her seat. Gurov, who had taken a seat in the stalls, went up to her and said in
a trembling voice, with a forced smile: "How d'you do?"

She glanced up at him and turned pale, then looked at him again in alarm,
unable to believe her eyes, squeezing her fan and lorgnette in one hand, evidently struggling to overcome a feeling of faintness. Neither of them said a word.
She sat there, and he stood beside her, disconcerted by her embarrassment, and
not daring to sit down. The violins and flutes sang out as they were tuned, and
there was a tense sensation in the atmosphere, as if they were being watched
from all the boxes. At last she got up and moved rapidly towards one of the exits.
He followed her and they wandered aimlessly along corridors, up and down
stairs; figures flashed by in the uniforms of legal officials, high-school teachers
and civil servants, all wearing badges; ladies, coats hanging from pegs flashed
by; there was a sharp draft, bringing with it an odor of cigarette butts. And Gurov,
whose heart was beating violently, thought:

"What on earth are all these people, this orchestra for? . . ."

The next minute he suddenly remembered how, after seeing Anna Sergeyevna off that evening at the station, he had told himself that all was over, and
they would never meet again. And how far away the end seemed to be now!

She stopped on a dark narrow staircase over which was a notice bearing the   95
inscription "To the upper circle."

"How you frightened me!" she said, breathing heavily, still pale and half-
stunned. "Oh, how you frightened me! I'm almost dead! Why did you come?
Oh, why?"

"But, Anna," he said, in low, hasty tones. "But, Anna. . . . Try to understand
. . . do try. . . ."

She cast him a glance of fear, entreaty, love, and then gazed at him steadily,
as if to fix his features firmly in her memory.

"I've been so unhappy," she continued, taking no notice of his words. "I
could think of nothing but you the whole time, I lived on the thoughts of you.
I tried to forget—why, oh, why did you come?"

On the landing above them were two schoolboys, smoking and looking   100
down, but Gurov did not care, and, drawing Anna Sergeyevna towards him,
began kissing her face, her lips, her hands.

"What are you doing, oh, what are you doing?" she said in horror, drawing
back. "We have both gone mad. Go away this very night, this moment. . . . By
all that is sacred, I implore you. . . . Somebody is coming."

Someone was ascending the stairs.

"You must go away," went on Anna Sergeyevna in a whisper. "D'you hear me, Dmitry Dmitrich? I'll come to you in Moscow. I have never been happy, I am unhappy now, and I shall never be happy—never! Do not make me suffer still more! I will come to you in Moscow, I swear it! And now we must part! My dear one, my kind one, my darling, we must part."

She pressed his hand and hurried down the stairs, looking back at him continually, and her eyes showed that she was in truth unhappy. Gurov stood where he was for a short time, listening, and when all was quiet, went to look for his coat, and left the theatre.

IV

And Anna Sergeyevna began going to Moscow to see him. Every two or three months she left the town of S., telling her husband that she was going to consult a specialist on female diseases, and her husband believed her and did not believe her. In Moscow she always stayed at the Slavyanski Bazaar, sending a man in a red cap to Gurov the moment she arrived. Gurov went to her, and no one in Moscow knew anything about it.

One winter morning he went to see her as usual (the messenger had been to him the evening before, but had not found him at home). His daughter was with him, for her school was on the way and he thought he might as well see her to it.

"It is forty degrees," said Gurov to his daughter, "and yet it is snowing. You see it is only above freezing close to the ground, the temperature in the upper layers of the atmosphere is quite different."

"Why doesn't it ever thunder in winter, Papa?"

He explained this, too. As he was speaking, he kept reminding himself that he was going to a rendezvous and that not a living soul knew about it, or, probably, ever would. He led a double life—one in public, in the sight of all whom it concerned, full of conventional truth and conventional deception, exactly like the lives of his friends and acquaintances, and another which flowed in secret. And, owing to some strange, possibly quite accidental chain of circumstances, everything that was important, interesting, essential, everything about which he was sincere and never deceived himself, everything that composed the kernel of his life, went on in secret, while everything that was false in him, everything that composed the husk in which he hid himself and the truth which was in him— his work at the bank, discussions at the club, his "lower race," his attendance at anniversary celebrations with his wife—was on the surface. He began to judge others by himself, no longer believing what he saw, and always assuming that the real, the only interesting life of every individual goes on as under cover of night, secretly. Every individual existence revolves around mystery, and perhaps that is the chief reason that all cultivated individuals insisted so strongly on the respect due to personal secrets.

After leaving his daughter at the door of her school Gurov set off for the Slavyanski Bazaar. Taking off his overcoat in the lobby, he went upstairs and knocked softly on the door. Anna Sergeyevna, wearing the gray dress he liked most, exhausted by her journey and by suspense, had been expecting him since the evening before. She was pale and looked at him without smiling, but was in his arms almost before he was fairly in the room. Their kiss was lingering, prolonged, as if they had not met for years.

"Well, how are you?" he asked. "Anything new?"

"Wait, I'll tell you in a minute. . . . . I can't. . . ."

She could not speak, because she was crying. Turning away, she held her handkerchief to her eyes.

"I'll wait till she's had her cry out," he thought, and sank into a chair.

He rang for tea, and a little later, while he was drinking it, she was still standing there, her face to the window. She wept from emotion, from her bitter consciousness of the sadness of their life; they could only see one another in secret, hiding from people, as if they were thieves. Was not their life a broken one?

"Don't cry," he said.

It was quite obvious to him that this love of theirs would not soon come to an end, and that no one could say when this end would be. Anna Sergeyevna loved him ever more fondly, worshipped him, and there would have been no point in telling her that one day it must end. Indeed, she would not have believed him.

He moved over and took her by the shoulders, intending to caress her, to make a joke, but suddenly he caught sight of himself in the looking-glass.

His hair was already beginning to turn gray. It struck him as strange that he should have aged so much in the last few years, have lost so much of his looks. The shoulders on which his hands lay were warm and quivering. He felt a pity for this life, still so warm and exquisite, but probably soon to fade and droop like his own. Why did she love him so? Women had always believed him different from what he really was, had loved in him not himself but the man their imagination pictured him, a man they had sought for eagerly all their lives. And afterwards when they discovered their mistake, they went on loving him just the same. And not one of them had ever been happy with him. Time had passed, he had met one woman after another, become intimate with each, parted with each, but had never loved. There had been all sorts of things between them, but never love.

And only now, when he was gray-haired, had he fallen in love properly, thoroughly, for the first time in his life.

He and Anna Sergeyevna loved one another as people who are very close and intimate, as husband and wife, as dear friends love one another. It seemed to them that fate had intended them for one another, and they could not understand why she should have a husband, and he a wife. They were like two migrating birds, the male and the female, who had been caught and put into separate cages. They forgave one another all that they were ashamed of in the past and in the present, and felt that this love of theirs had changed them both.

Formerly, in moments of melancholy, he had consoled himself by the first argument that came into his head, but now arguments were nothing to him, he felt profound pity, desired to be sincere, tender.

"Stop crying, my dearest," he said. "You've had your cry, now stop. . . . Now let us have a talk, let us try and think what we are to do."

Then they discussed their situation for a long time, trying to think how they could get rid of the necessity for hiding, deception, living in different towns, being so long without meeting. How were they to shake off these intolerable fetters?

"How? How?" he repeated, clutching his head. "How?"

And it seemed to them that they were within an inch of arriving at a decision, and that then a new, beautiful life would begin. And they both realized that the end was still far, far away, and that the hardest, the most complicated part was only just beginning.

1899

▼ ▼ ▼

QUESTIONS

1. What is there in the second paragraph of "A Rose for Emily" that suggests the speaker is not just casually spinning a yarn about a weird lady but sees some more general meaning in the tale? What might that meaning be? What might it have to do with the setting in time and place? In what ways may the manipulation of historical time relate to that more general meaning?

2. The mother of Jing-mei Woo, in "A Pair of Tickets," told her that being Chinese is a matter of genetics and she finds that that is true. What is the role of place and time (history), then, in this story?

3. Yalta, where "The Lady with the Dog" opens, is a resort on the Black Sea; Moscow, where Gurov lives, is described at the beginning of section III. To what extent do the settings relate to the events and emotions of the story? How do other details—such as the watermelon in II (Yalta) and the slightly "off" sturgeon in III (Moscow)—relate to the settings and the attitudes and feelings associated with the places? Which are conventionally assumed to be more real, the feelings we have on holiday or those in our everyday lives? How is this convention related to our expectations about the outcome of the story? to the meaning of the story?

WRITING SUGGESTIONS

1. Write an outline of "A Rose for Emily" arranging the events in chronological order and dating them as precisely as possible. Then write a three-para-

graph analysis of why the story is structured—the chronology rearranged—as it is.

2. Compare the use of episodes from World War II in "The Country Husband" and "A Pair of Tickets."

3. Write a personal narrative about a visit to a place important in your family history that you had never visited before and how you felt about your relation to that place; or about an episode that made you recognize or affirm your ethnic identity or heritage.

4. Write a fifth section of "The Lady with the Dog."

5 SYMBOLS

O ne of the chief devices for bridging the gap between the writer's vision and the reader's is the **symbol,** commonly defined as something that stands for something else: a flower, for example, may be seen as a symbol of a particular state. Symbols are generally **figurative;** that is, they compare or put together two *unlike* things. While a senator may represent a state, he represents it *literally:* the state is a governmental unit, and the senator is a member of the government. But the flower has nothing to do with government, and so represents the state only figuratively.

But why speak of anything in terms of something else? Why should snakes commonly be symbolic of evil? Sure, some snakes are poisonous, but for some people so are bees, and a lot of snakes are not only harmless but actually helpful ecologically. (In Kipling's *The Jungle Book* the python Ka, while frightening, is on the side of Law and Order.) Through repeated use over the centuries, the snake has become a traditional symbol of Evil—not just danger, sneakiness, and repulsiveness, but theological, absolute Evil. Had Peyton Farquhar, in "An Occurrence at Owl Creek Bridge," been confronted by a snake when he was thrown ashore, we would not necessarily have said, "Aha—snake, symbol of Evil," though that potential meaning might have hovered around the incident and sent us looking backward and forward in the story for supporting evidence that this snake was being used symbolically. However, when we discover that the stranger in "Young Goodman Brown" has a walking stick upon which is carved the image of a snake, we are much more likely to find it such a symbol because of other, related potential symbols or meanings in the context: the term *goodman,* used throughout the story, suggests the distinct possibility that Brown (how common a name) stands for more than a "mere" individual young man. Brown's bride is named Faith—a common name among the early Puritans, but together with *goodman* suggesting symbolic possibilities. Then, just before the stranger with the walking stick appears, Brown says, "What if the devil himself should be at my very elbow!"

A single item, even something as traditionally fraught with meaning as a snake or a rose, becomes a symbol only when its potentially symbolic meaning is confirmed by something else in the story, just as a point needs a second point to define a line. Multiple symbols, potential symbols, direct and indirect hints such as Brown's mention of the devil: these are among the ways in which details may be identified as symbols (for interpreting symbols is relatively easy once you know what is and what probably is not a symbol).

One form of what may be called an indirect hint is repetition. That an "old maid" like Judith should have a cat seems so ordinary it borders on the trite. But when she chooses to have her male cat put to death rather than neutered, it is likely to make some of us sit up and take notice. This choice may suggest something about the unconventional in her character, but we probably don't think of the cat as itself representing anything. What happens, though, when there appears another cat, a female this time, whose sex life calls forth strange behavior on Judith's part? And when the killing of a kitten interrupts Judith's affair with Luigi? It is difficult to say when or if the literal cats shade off into symbols, for they remain so solidly cats in the story. All we can say for sure is that cats become more important in reading and understanding this story than, say, the cask of Amontillado does in the Poe story. The cask remains a thing pure and simple. Repetition, then, calls attention to details and may alert us to potential symbolic overtones, but it does not necessarily turn a thing into a symbol; so long as we get the suggestions of significance, however, agreeing on exactly what—or when—something may be called a symbol is not important.

Direct hints may take the form of explicit statements. (Authors are not so anxious to hide their meanings as some readers are prone to believe.) We also may be alerted to the fact that something is standing for something else when it does not by itself seem to make literal sense. It does not take us long to realize that "Young Goodman Brown" is not entirely as realistic a story as "Sonny's Blues" or "The Lady with the Dog." When things do not seem explicable in terms of everyday reality, we often look beyond them for some meaning. Roses are real enough, but neither Faulkner's narrator nor anyone else in the story gives Emily a real rose. What, then, does the rose in the title "A Rose for Emily" suggest?

We must remember, however, that symbols do not exist solely for the transmission of a meaning we can paraphrase; they do not disappear from the story, our memory, or our response once their "meaning" has been sucked out of them, any more than Emily ceases to exist as an individual after we recognize her representative or universal nature. Faith's pink ribbons and Judith's cats are objects in their stories, whatever meanings or suggestions of meanings they give rise to.

As I have often implied and occasionally said, few symbols can be exhausted, translated into an abstract phrase or equivalent: the "something else" that the "something" stands for is ultimately elusive. After you have read

Ann Beattie's "Janus," try to paraphrase just what the bowl stands for. Or explain with certainty what Faith's pink ribbon symbolizes in "Young Goodman Brown." It is not that the bowl and the ribbon mean nothing but that they mean so many things that no single equivalence will do; even an abstract statement seems to reduce rather than fully explain the significance to the reader.

When a figure is expressed as an explicit comparison, often signaled by *like* or *as*, it is called a **simile:** "eyes as blue as the sky"; "the baby brother I'd never known looked out from the depths of his private life, like an animal waiting to be coaxed into the light" ("Sonny's Blues"). An implicit comparison or identification of one thing with another unlike itself, without a verbal signal but just seeming to say "A *is* B," is called a **metaphor:** "His heart, that bloody motor" ("A Conversation with My Father"); "What I hate about being my age is how *nice* everyone tries to be. . . . everybody is pelting me with sugar cubes" ("Fenstad's Mother"). Sometimes all figures are loosely referred to as metaphors.

An **allegory** is like a metaphor in that one thing (usually nonrational, abstract, religious) is implicitly spoken of in terms of something that is concrete and usually sensuous (perceptible by the senses), but the comparison in allegory is extended to include a whole work or a large portion of a work. *The Pilgrim's Progress* is probably the most famous prose allegory in English; its central character is named Christian; he was born in the City of Destruction and sets out for the Celestial City, passes through the Slough of Despond and Vanity Fair, meets men named Pliable and Obstinate, and so on.

When an entire story, like "Young Goodman Brown," is symbolic, it is sometimes called a **myth.** *Myth* originally meant a story of communal origin that provided an explanation or religious interpretation of man, nature, the universe, and the relation between them. When used by one culture to describe the stories of another culture, the word usually implies that the stories are false: we speak of classical myths, but Christians do not speak of Christian myth. We also apply the term *myth* now to stories by individuals, sophisticated authors, but often there is still the implication that the mythic story relates to a communal or group experience, whereas a symbolic story may be more personal or private. It is hard to draw the line firmly: "Young Goodman Brown" seems to have clearly national, American implications, and "A Rose for Emily" seems to encapsulate something about the southern culture of seventy to a hundred years ago, but is "The Loons" personally symbolic or mythic? A plot or character element that recurs in cultural or cross-cultural myths, such as images of the devil, as in "Young Goodman Brown," is now widely called an **archetype.**

A symbol can be as brief and local as a metaphor or as extended as an allegory. Like an allegory it usually speaks in concrete terms of the non- or superrational, the abstract, that which is not immediately perceived by the senses. Though some allegories can be complex, with paraphrasable equivalences, allegory usually implies one-to-one relationships (as do the names from *The Pilgrim's Progress*), and literary symbols usually have highly complex or even inexpressible equivalences, as in "Janus." "Janus" is complexly symbolic in that there are areas of meaning or implication that cannot be rendered in other terms or conveniently separated from the particulars of the story. The ultimate unparaphrasable nature of most symbolic images or stories is not vagueness but richness, not disorder but complexity.

▼   ▼   ▼

NATHANIEL HAWTHORNE

Young Goodman Brown

Young goodman Brown came forth, at sunset, into the street of Salem village,[1] but put his head back, after crossing the threshold, to exchange a parting kiss with his young wife. And Faith, as the wife was aptly named, thrust her own pretty head into the street, letting the wind play with the pink ribbons of her cap, while she called to goodman Brown.

"Dearest heart," whispered she, softly and rather sadly, when her lips were close to his ear, "pr'y thee, put off your journey until sunrise, and sleep in your own bed to-night. A lone woman is troubled with such dreams and such thoughts, that she's afeard of herself, sometimes. Pray, tarry with me this night, dear husband, of all nights in the year!"

"My love and my Faith," replied young goodman Brown, "of all nights in the year, this one night must I tarry away from thee. My journey, as thou callest it, forth and back again, must needs be done 'twixt now and sunrise. What, my sweet, pretty wife, dost thou doubt me already, and we but three months married!"

"Then, God bless you!" said Faith, with the pink ribbons, "and may you find all well, when you come back."

"Amen!" cried goodman Brown. "Say thy prayers, dear Faith, and go to bed at dusk, and no harm will come to thee."   5

So they parted; and the young man pursued his way, until, being about to turn the corner by the meeting-house, he looked back, and saw the head of Faith still peeping after him, with a melancholy air, in spite of her pink ribbons.

"Poor little Faith!" thought he, for his heart smote him. "What a wretch am I, to leave her on such an errand! She talks of dreams, too. Methought, as she spoke, there was trouble in her face, as if a dream had warned her what work is to be done to-night. But, no, no! 't would kill her to think it. Well; she's a blessed

1. Salem, Massachusetts, Hawthorne's birthplace (1804), was the scene of the famous witch trials of 1692; *goodman:* husband, master of household.

angel on earth; and after this one night, I'll cling to her skirts and follow her to Heaven."

With this excellent resolve for the future, goodman Brown felt himself justified in making more haste on his present evil purpose. He had taken a dreary road, darkened by all the gloomiest trees of the forest, which barely stood aside to let the narrow path creep through, and closed immediately behind. It was all as lonely as could be; and there is this peculiarity in such a solitude, that the traveler knows not who may be concealed by the innumerable trunks and the thick boughs overhead; so that, with lonely footsteps, he may yet be passing through an unseen multitude.

"There may be a devilish Indian behind every tree," said goodman Brown, to himself; and he glanced fearfully behind him, as he added, "What if the devil himself should be at my very elbow!"

His head being turned back, he passed a crook of the road, and looking forward again, beheld the figure of a man, in grave and decent attire, seated at the foot of an old tree. He arose, at goodman Brown's approach, and walked onward, side by side with him.

"You are late, goodman Brown," said he. "The clock of the Old South was striking as I came through Boston; and that is full fifteen minutes agone."

"Faith kept me back awhile," replied the young man, with a tremor in his voice, caused by the sudden appearance of his companion, though not wholly unexpected.

It was now deep dusk in the forest, and deepest in that part of it where these two were journeying. As nearly as could be discerned, the second traveler was about fifty years old, apparently in the same rank of life as goodman Brown, and bearing a considerable resemblance to him, though perhaps more in expression than features. Still, they might have been taken for father and son. And yet, though the elder person was as simply clad as the younger, and as simple in manner too, he had an indescribable air of one who knew the world, and would not have felt abashed at the governor's dinner-table, or in king William's[2] court, were it possible that his affairs should call him thither. But the only thing about him, that could be fixed upon as remarkable, was his staff, which bore the likeness of a great black snake, so curiously wrought, that it might almost be seen to twist and wriggle itself, like a living serpent. This, of course, must have been an ocular deception, assisted by the uncertain light.

"Come, goodman Brown!" cried his fellow-traveler, "this is a dull pace for the beginning of a journey. Take my staff, if you are so soon weary."

"Friend," said the other, exchanging his slow pace for a full stop, "having kept covenant by meeting thee here, it is my purpose now to return whence I came. I have scruples, touching the matter thou wot'st of."

"Sayest thou so?" replied he of the serpent, smiling apart. "Let us walk on, nevertheless, reasoning as we go, and if I convince thee not, thou shalt turn back. We are but a little way in the forest, yet."

---

2. William III (1650–1702), ruler of England from 1689 to 1702, until 1694 jointly with his wife, Mary II.

"Too far, too far!" exclaimed the goodman, unconsciously resuming his walk. "My father never went into the woods on such an errand, nor his father before him. We have been a race of honest men and good Christians, since the days of the martyrs. And shall I be the first of the name of Brown, that ever took this path, and kept"—

"Such company, thou wouldst say," observed the elder person, interpreting his pause. "Good, goodman Brown! I have been as well acquainted with your family as with ever a one among the Puritans; and that's no trifle to say. I helped your grandfather, the constable, when he lashed the Quaker woman so smartly through the streets of Salem. And it was I that brought your father a pitch-pine knot, kindled at my own hearth, to set fire to an Indian village, in king Philip's[3] war. They were my good friends, both; and many a pleasant walk have we had along this path, and returned merrily after midnight. I would fain be friends with you, for their sake."

"If it be as thou sayest," replied goodman Brown, "I marvel they never spoke of these matters. Or, verily, I marvel not, seeing that the least rumor of the sort would have driven them from New-England. We are a people of prayer, and good works, to boot, and abide no such wickedness."

"Wickedness or not," said the traveler with the twisted staff, "I have a very general acquaintance here in New-England. The deacons of many a church have drunk the communion wine with me; the selectmen, of divers towns, make me their chairman; and a majority of the Great and General Court are firm supporters of my interest. The governor and I, too—but these are state-secrets."

"Can this be so!" cried goodman Brown, with a stare of amazement at his undisturbed companion. "Howbeit, I have nothing to do with the governor and council; they have their own ways, and are no rule for a simple husbandman, like me. But, were I to go on with thee, how should I meet the eye of that good old man, our minister, at Salem village? Oh, his voice would make me tremble, both Sabbath-day and lecture-day[4]!"

Thus far, the elder traveler had listened with due gravity, but now burst into a fit of irrepressible mirth, shaking himself so violently, that his snake-like staff actually seemed to wriggle in sympathy.

"Ha! ha! ha!" shouted he, again and again; then composing himself, "Well, go on, goodman Brown, go on; but, pr'y thee, don't kill me with laughing!"

"Well, then, to end the matter at once," said goodman Brown, considerably nettled, "there is my wife, Faith. It would break her dear little heart; and I'd rather break my own!"

"Nay, if that be the case," answered the other, "e'en[5] go thy ways, goodman Brown. I would not, for twenty old women like the one hobbling before us, that Faith should come to any harm."

As he spoke, he pointed his staff at a female figure on the path, in whom goodman Brown recognized a very pious and exemplary dame, who had taught

3. Metacom or Metacomet, chief of the Wampanoag Indians, known as King Philip, led a war against the New England colonists in 1675–76 that devastated many frontier communities.
4. The day—in the New England colonies usually a Thursday—appointed for an informal sermon.
5. Just.

him his catechism, in youth, and was still his moral and spiritual adviser, jointly with the minister and deacon Gookin.

"A marvel, truly, that goody[6] Cloyse should be so far in the wilderness, at night-fall!" said he. "But, with your leave, friend, I shall take a cut through the woods, until we have left this Christian woman behind. Being a stranger to you, she might ask whom I was consorting with, and whither I was going."

"Be it so," said his fellow-traveler. "Betake you to the woods, and let me keep the path."

Accordingly, the young man turned aside, but took care to watch his companion, who advanced softly along the road, until he had come within a staff's length of the old dame. She, meanwhile, was making the best of her way, with singular speed for so aged a woman, and mumbling some indistinct words, a prayer, doubtless, as she went. The traveler put forth his staff, and touched her withered neck with what seemed the serpent's tail.

30   "The devil!" screamed the pious old lady.

"Then goody Cloyse knows her old friend?" observed the traveler, confronting her, and leaning on his writhing stick.

"Ah, forsooth, and is it your worship, indeed?" cried the good dame. "Yea, truly is it, and in the very image of my old gossip, goodman Brown, the grandfather of the silly fellow that now is. But, would your worship believe it? my broomstick hath strangely disappeared, stolen, as I suspect, by that unhanged witch, goody Cory, and that, too, when I was all anointed with the juice of smallage and cinque-foil and wolf's-bane[7]"—

"Mingled with fine wheat and the fat of a new-born babe," said the shape of old goodman Brown.

"Ah, your worship knows the receipt," cried the old lady, cackling aloud. "So, as I was saying, being all ready for the meeting, and no horse to ride on, I made up my mind to foot it; for they tell me, there is a nice young man to be taken into communion to-night. But now your good worship will lend me your arm, and we shall be there in a twinkling."

35   "That can hardly be," answered her friend. "I may not spare you my arm, goody Cloyse, but here is my staff, if you will."

So saying, he threw it down at her feet, where, perhaps, it assumed life, being one of the rods which its owner had formerly lent to the Egyptian Magi.[8] Of this fact, however, goodman Brown could not take cognizance. He had cast up his eyes in astonishment, and looking down again, beheld neither goody Cloyse nor the serpentine staff, but his fellow-traveler alone, who waited for him as calmly as if nothing had happened.

"That old woman taught me my catechism!" said the young man; and there was a world of meaning in this simple comment.

They continued to walk onward, while the elder traveler exhorted his companion to make good speed and persevere in the path, discoursing so aptly, that

6. Short for "goodwife" or housewife.   7. Plants traditionally associated with witchcraft.   8. Exodus 7:8–12. The Lord instructs Moses to have his prophet Aaron throw down his rod before the Pharaoh, whereupon it will be turned into a serpent. The Pharaoh has his magicians (magi) do likewise, "but Aaron's rod swallowed up their rods."

his arguments seemed rather to spring up in the bosom of his auditor, than to be suggested by himself. As they went, he plucked a branch of maple, to serve for a walking-stick, and began to strip it of the twigs and little boughs, which were wet with evening dew. The moment his fingers touched them, they became strangely withered and dried up, as with a week's sunshine. Thus the pair proceeded, at a good free pace, until suddenly, in a gloomy hollow of the road, goodman Brown sat himself down on the stump of a tree, and refused to go any farther.

"Friend," said he, stubbornly, "my mind is made up. Not another step will I budge on this errand. What if a wretched old woman do choose to go to the devil, when I thought she was going to Heaven! Is that any reason why I should quit my dear Faith, and go after her?"

"You will think better of this, by-and-by," said his acquaintance, composedly. "Sit here and rest yourself awhile; and when you feel like moving again, there is my staff to help you along."

40

Without more words, he threw his companion the maple stick, and was as speedily out of sight, as if he had vanished into the deepening gloom. The young man sat a few moments, by the roadside, applauding himself greatly, and thinking with how clear a conscience he should meet the minister, in his morning-walk, nor shrink from the eye of good old deacon Gookin. And what calm sleep would be his, that very night, which was to have been spent so wickedly, but purely and sweetly now, in the arms of Faith! Amidst these pleasant and praiseworthy meditations, goodman Brown heard the tramp of horses along the road, and deemed it advisable to conceal himself within the verge of the forest, conscious of the guilty purpose that had brought him thither, though now so happily turned from it.

On came the hoof-tramps and the voices of the riders, two grave old voices, conversing soberly as they drew near. These mingled sounds appeared to pass along the road, within a few yards of the young man's hiding-place; but owing, doubtless, to the depth of the gloom, at that particular spot, neither the travelers nor their steeds were visible. Though their figures brushed the small boughs by the way-side, it could not be seen that they intercepted, even for a moment, the faint gleam from the strip of bright sky, athwart which they must have passed. Goodman Brown alternately crouched and stood on tip-toe, pulling aside the branches, and thrusting forth his head as far as he durst, without discerning so much as a shadow. It vexed him the more, because he could have sworn, were such a thing possible, that he recognized the voices of the minister and deacon Gookin, jogging along quietly, as they were wont to do, when bound to some ordination or ecclesiastical council. While yet within hearing, one of the riders stopped to pluck a switch.

"Of the two, reverend Sir," said the voice like the deacon's, "I had rather miss an ordination-dinner than to-night's meeting. They tell me that some of our community are to be here from Falmouth[9] and beyond, and others from Connecticut and Rhode-Island; besides several of the Indian powows, who, after

9. A port in extreme southern Massachusetts; Salem is in northern Massachusetts.

their fashion, know almost as much deviltry as the best of us. Moreover, there is a goodly young woman to be taken into communion."

"Mighty well, deacon Gookin!" replied the solemn old tones of the minister. "Spur up, or we shall be late. Nothing can be done, you know, until I get on the ground."

45
The hoofs clattered again, and the voices, talking so strangely in the empty air, passed on through the forest, where no church had ever been gathered, nor solitary Christian prayed. Whither, then, could these holy men be journeying, so deep into the heathen wilderness? Young goodman Brown caught hold of a tree, for support, being ready to sink down on the ground, faint and overburthened with the heavy sickness of his heart. He looked up to the sky, doubting whether there really was a Heaven above him. Yet, there was the blue arch, and the stars brightening in it.

"With Heaven above, and Faith below, I will yet stand firm against the devil!" cried goodman Brown.

While he still gazed upward, into the deep arch of the firmament, and had lifted his hands to pray, a cloud, though no wind was stirring, hurried across the zenith, and hid the brightening stars. The blue sky was still visible, except directly overhead, where this black mass of cloud was sweeping swiftly northward. Aloft in the air, as if from the depths of the cloud, came a confused and doubtful sound of voices. Once, the listener fancied that he could distinguish the accents of town's-people of his own, men and women, both pious and ungodly, many of whom he had met at the communion-table, and had seen others rioting at the tavern. The next moment, so indistinct were the sounds, he doubted whether he had heard aught but the murmur of the old forest, whispering without a wind. Then came a stronger swell of those familiar tones, heard daily in the sunshine, at Salem village, but never, until now, from a cloud of night. There was one voice, of a young woman, uttering lamentations, yet with an uncertain sorrow, and entreating for some favor, which, perhaps, it would grieve her to obtain. And all the unseen multitude, both saints and sinners, seemed to encourage her onward.

"Faith!" shouted goodman Brown, in a voice of agony and desperation; and the echoes of the forest mocked him, crying—"Faith! Faith!" as if bewildered wretches were seeking her, all through the wilderness.

The cry of grief, rage, and terror, was yet piercing the night, when the unhappy husband held his breath for a response. There was a scream, drowned immediately in a louder murmur of voices, fading into far-off laughter, as the dark cloud swept away, leaving the clear and silent sky above goodman Brown. But something fluttered lightly down through the air, and caught on the branch of a tree. The young man seized it, and beheld a pink ribbon.

50
"My Faith is gone!" cried he, after one stupefied moment. "There is no good on earth; and sin is but a name. Come, devil! for to thee is this world given."

And maddened with despair, so that he laughed loud and long, did goodman Brown grasp his staff and set forth again, at such a rate, that he seemed to fly along the forest-path, rather than to walk or run. The road grew wilder and drearier, and more faintly traced, and vanished at length, leaving him in the heart of the dark wilderness, still rushing onward, with the instinct that guides mortal man to evil. The whole forest was peopled with frightful sounds; the creaking of the trees, the howling of wild beasts, and the yell of Indians; while, sometimes, the wind tolled like a distant church-bell, and sometimes gave a broad roar around the traveler, as if all Nature were laughing him to scorn. But he was himself the chief horror of the scene, and shrank not from its other horrors.

"Ha! ha! ha!" roared goodman Brown, when the wind laughed at him. "Let us hear which will laugh loudest! Think not to frighten me with your deviltry! Come witch, come wizard, come Indian powow, come devil himself! and here come goodman Brown. You may as well fear him as he fear you!"

In truth, all through the haunted forest, there could be nothing more frightful than the figure of goodman Brown. On he flew, among the black pines, brandishing his staff with frenzied gestures, now giving vent to an inspiration of horrid blasphemy, and now shouting forth such laughter, as set all the echoes of the forest laughing like demons around him. The fiend in his own shape is less hideous, than when he rages in the breast of man. Thus sped the demoniac on his course, until, quivering among the trees, he saw a red light before him, as when the felled trunks and branches of a clearing have been set on fire, and throw up their lurid blaze against the sky, at the hour of midnight. He paused, in a lull of the tempest that had driven him onward, and heard the swell of what seemed a hymn, rolling solemnly from a distance, with the weight of many voices. He knew the tune; it was a familiar one in the choir of the village meeting-house. The verse died heavily away, and was lengthened by a chorus, not of human voices, but of all the sounds of the benighted wilderness, pealing in awful harmony together. Goodman Brown cried out; and his cry was lost to his own ear, by its unison with the cry of the desert.

In the interval of silence, he stole forward, until the light glared full upon his eyes. At one extremity of an open space, hemmed in by the dark wall of the forest, arose a rock, bearing some rude, natural resemblance either to an altar or a pulpit, and surrounded by four blazing pines, their tops a flame, their stems untouched, like candles at an evening meeting. The mass of foliage, that had overgrown the summit of the rock, was all on fire, blazing high into the night, and fitfully illuminating the whole field. Each pendent twig and leafy festoon was in a blaze. As the red light arose and fell, a numerous congregation alternately shone forth, then disappeared in shadow, and again grew, as it were, out of the darkness, peopling the heart of the solitary woods at once.

"A grave and dark-clad company!" quoth goodman Brown.

In truth, they were such. Among them, quivering to-and-fro, between gloom and splendor, appeared faces that would be seen, next day, at the council-board of the province, and others which, Sabbath after Sabbath, looked devoutly heavenward, and benignantly over the crowded pews, from the holiest pulpits in the land. Some affirm, that the lady of the governor was there. At least, there were high dames well known to her, and wives of honored husbands, and widows, a great multitude, and ancient maidens, all of excellent repute, and fair young girls, who trembled, lest their mothers should espy them. Either the sudden gleams of light, flashing over the obscure field, bedazzled goodman Brown, or he recognized a score of the church-members of Salem village, famous for their especial sanctity. Good old deacon Gookin had arrived, and waited at the skirts of that venerable saint, his revered pastor. But, irreverently consorting with these grave, reputable, and pious people, these elders of the church, these chaste dames and dewy virgins, there were men of dissolute lives and women of spotted fame, wretches given over to all mean and filthy vice, and suspected even of horrid crimes. It was strange to see, that the good shrank not from the wicked, nor were the sinners abashed by the saints. Scattered, also, among their pale-faced enemies, were the Indian priests, or powows, who had often scared their native forest with more hideous incantations than any known to English witch-craft.

"But, where is Faith?" thought goodman Brown; and, as hope came into his heart, he trembled.

Another verse of the hymn arose, a slow and solemn strain, such as the pious love, but joined to words which expressed all that our nature can conceive of sin, and darkly hinted at far more. Unfathomable to mere mortals is the lore of fiends. Verse after verse was sung, and still the chorus of the desert swelled between, like the deepest tone of a mighty organ. And, with the final peal of that dreadful anthem, there came a sound, as if the roaring wind, the rushing streams, the howling beasts, and every other voice of the unconverted wilder-ness, were mingling and according with the voice of guilty man, in homage to the prince of all. The four blazing pines threw up a loftier flame, and obscurely discovered shapes and visages of horror on the smoke-wreaths, above the impi-ous assembly. At the same moment, the fire on the rock shot redly forth, and formed a glowing arch above its base, where now appeared a figure. With rever-ence be it spoken, the apparition bore no slight similitude, both in garb and manner, to some grave divine of the New-England churches.

"Bring forth the converts!" cried a voice, that echoed through the field and rolled into the forest.

60   At the word, goodman Brown stept forth from the shadow of the trees, and approached the congregation, with whom he felt a loathful brotherhood, by the sympathy of all that was wicked in his heart. He could have well nigh sworn, that the shape of his own dead father beckoned him to advance, looking down-ward from a smoke-wreath, while a woman, with dim features of despair, threw out her hand to warn him back. Was it his mother? But he had no power to retreat one step, nor to resist, even in thought, when the minister and good old deacon Gookin, seized his arms, and led him to the blazing rock. Thither came also the slender form of a veiled female, led between goody Cloyse, that pious teacher of the catechism, and Martha Carrier, who had received the devil's promise to be queen of hell. A rampant hag was she! And there stood the prose-lytes, beneath the canopy of fire.

"Welcome, my children," said the dark figure, "to the communion of your race! Ye have found, thus young, your nature and your destiny. My children, look behind you!"

They turned; and flashing forth, as it were, in a sheet of flame, the fiend-worshippers were seen; the smile of welcome gleamed darkly on every visage.

"There," resumed the sable form, "are all whom ye have reverenced from youth. Ye deemed them holier than yourselves, and shrank from your own sin, contrasting it with their lives of righteousness, and prayerful aspirations heavenward. Yet, here are they all, in my worshipping assembly! This night it shall be granted you to know their secret deeds; how hoary-bearded elders of the church have whispered wanton words to the young maids of their households; how many a woman, eager for widow's weeds, has given her husband a drink at bedtime, and let him sleep his last sleep in her bosom; how beardless youths have made haste to inherit their fathers' wealth; and how fair damsels—blush not, sweet ones!—have dug little graves in the garden, and bidden me, the sole guest, to an infant's funeral. By the sympathy of your human hearts for sin, ye shall scent out all the places—whether in church, bed-chamber, street, field, or forest—where crime has been committed, and shall exult to behold the whole earth one stain of guilt, one mighty blood-spot. Far more than this! It shall be yours to penetrate, in every bosom, the deep mystery of sin, the fountain of all wicked arts, and which, inexhaustibly supplies more evil impulses than human power—than my power, at its utmost!—can make manifest in deeds. And now, my children, look upon each other."

They did so; and, by the blaze of the hell-kindled torches, the wretched man beheld his Faith, and the wife her husband, trembling before that unhallowed altar.

"Lo! there ye stand, my children," said the figure, in a deep and solemn tone, almost sad, with its despairing awfulness, as if his once angelic nature could yet mourn for our miserable race. "Depending upon one another's hearts, ye had still hoped, that virtue were not all a dream. Now are ye undeceived! Evil is the nature of mankind. Evil must be your only happiness. Welcome, again, my children, to the communion of your race!"

65

"Welcome!" repeated the fiend-worshippers, in one cry of despair and triumph.

And there they stood, the only pair, as it seemed, who were yet hesitating on the verge of wickedness, in this dark world. A basin was hollowed, naturally, in the rock. Did it contain water, reddened by the lurid light? or was it blood? or, perchance, a liquid flame? Herein did the Shape of Evil dip his hand, and prepare to lay the mark of baptism upon their foreheads, that they might be partakers of the mystery of sin, more conscious of the secret guilt of others, both in deed and thought, than they could now be of their own. The husband cast one look at his pale wife, and Faith at him. What polluted wretches would the next glance shew them to each other, shuddering alike at what they disclosed and what they saw!

"Faith! Faith!" cried the husband. "Look up to Heaven, and resist the Wicked One!"

Whether Faith obeyed, he knew not. Hardly had he spoken, when he found himself amid calm night and solitude, listening to a roar of the wind, which died heavily away through the forest. He staggered against the rock and felt it chill and damp, while a hanging twig, that had been all on fire, besprinkled his cheek with the coldest dew.

70

The next morning, young goodman Brown came slowly into the street of Salem village, staring around him like a bewildered man. The good old minister was taking a walk along the graveyard, to get an appetite for breakfast and meditate his sermon, and bestowed a blessing, as he passed, on goodman Brown. He shrank from the venerable saint, as if to avoid an anathema. Old deacon Gookin was at domestic worship, and the holy words of his prayer were heard through the open window. "What God doth the wizard pray to?" quoth goodman Brown. Goody Cloyse, that excellent old Christian, stood in the early sunshine, at her own lattice, catechising a little girl, who had brought her a pint of morning's milk. Goodman Brown snatched away the child, as from the grasp of the fiend himself. Turning the corner by the meeting-house, he spied the head of Faith, with the pink ribbons, gazing anxiously forth, and bursting into such joy at sight of him, that she skipt along the street, and almost kissed her husband before the whole village. But, goodman Brown looked sternly and sadly into her face, and passed on without a greeting.

Had goodman Brown fallen asleep in the forest, and only dreamed a wild dream of a witch-meeting?

Be it so, if you will. But, alas! it was a dream of evil omen for young goodman Brown. A stern, a sad, a darkly meditative, a distrustful, if not a desperate man, did he become, from the night of that fearful dream. On the Sabbath-day, when the congregation were singing a holy psalm, he could not listen, because an anthem of sin rushed loudly upon his ear, and drowned all the blessed strain. When the minister spoke from the pulpit, with power and fervid eloquence, and, with his hand on the open bible, of the sacred truths of our religion, and of saint-like lives and triumphant deaths, and of future bliss or misery unutterable, then did goodman Brown turn pale, dreading, lest the roof should thunder down upon the gray blasphemer and his hearers. Often, awakening suddenly at midnight, he shrank from the bosom of Faith, and at morning or eventide, when the family knelt down at prayer, he scowled, and muttered to himself, and gazed sternly at his wife, and turned away. And when he had lived long, and was borne to his grave, a hoary corpse, followed by Faith, an aged woman, and children and grandchildren, a goodly procession, besides neighbors, not a few, they carved no hopeful verse upon his tomb-stone; for his dying hour was gloom.

1835

MARGARET LAURENCE

The Loons

Just below Manawaka, where the Wachakwa River ran brown and noisy over the pebbles, the scrub oak and grey-green willow and chokecherry bushes grew in a dense thicket. In a clearing at the centre of the thicket stood the Tonnerre family's shack. The basis of this dwelling was a small square cabin made of poplar poles and chinked with mud, which had been built by Jules Tonnerre some fifty years before, when he came back from Batoche[1] with a bullet in his thigh, the year that Riel was hung and the voices of the Metis entered their long silence.[2] Jules had only intended to stay the winter in the Wachakwa Valley, but the family was still there in the thirties, when I was a child. As the Tonnerres had increased, their settlement had been added to, until the clearing at the foot of the town hill was a chaos of lean-tos, wooden packing cases, warped lumber, discarded car tyres, ramshackle chicken coops, tangled strands of barbed wire and rusty tin cans.

The Tonnerres were French halfbreeds, and among themselves they spoke a *patois* that was neither Cree nor French. Their English was broken and full of obscenities. They did not belong among the Cree of the Galloping Mountain reservation, further north, and they did not belong among the Scots-Irish and Ukrainians of Manawaka, either. They were, as my Grandmother MacLeod would have put it, neither flesh, fowl, nor good salt herring. When their men were not working at odd jobs or as section hands on the C.P.R.[3] they lived on relief. In the summers, one of the Tonnerre youngsters, with a face that seemed totally unfamiliar with laughter, would knock at the doors of the town's brick houses and offer for sale a lard-pail full of bruised wild strawberries, and if he got as much as a quarter he would grab the coin and run before the customer had time to change her mind. Sometimes old Jules, or his son Lazarus, would get mixed up in a Saturday-night brawl, and would hit out at whoever was near-est or howl drunkenly among the offended shoppers on Main Street, and then the Mountie would put them for the night in the barred cell underneath the Court House, and the next morning they would be quiet again.

Piquette Tonnerre, the daughter of Lazarus, was in my class at school. She was older than I, but she had failed several grades, perhaps because her atten-dance had always been sporadic and her interest in schoolwork negligible. Part of the reason she had missed a lot of school was that she had had tuberculosis of the bone, and had once spent many months in hospital. I knew this because my father was the doctor who had looked after her. Her sickness was almost the only thing I knew about her, however. Otherwise, she existed for me only as a vaguely embarrassed presence, with her hoarse voice and her clumsy limping walk and her grimy cotton dresses that were always miles too long. I was neither friendly nor unfriendly towards her. She dwelt and moved somewhere within my scope of vision, but I did not actually notice her very much until that pecu-liar summer when I was eleven.

"I don't know what to do about that kid," my father said at dinner one eve-ning. "Piquette Tonnerre, I mean. The damn bone's flared up again. I've had her in hospital for quite a while now, and it's under control all right, but I hate like the dickens to send her home again."

---

1. In Saskatchewan, where in 1885 a battle of the Northwest Rebellion was fought.   2. Louis Riel (1844–1885), leader of the Metis, a people of mixed white and native Canadian blood.   3. Canad-ian Pacific Railway.

"Couldn't you explain to her mother that she has to rest a lot?" my mother said.

"The mother's not there," my father replied. "She took off a few years back. Can't say I blame her. Piquette cooks for them, and she says Lazarus would never do anything for himself as long as she's there. Anyway, I don't think she'd take much care of herself, once she got back. She's only thirteen, after all. Beth, I was thinking—what about taking her up to Diamond Lake with us this summer? A couple of months rest would give that bone a much better chance."

My mother looked stunned.

"But Ewen—what about Roddie and Vanessa?"

"She's not contagious," my father said. "And it would be company for Vanessa."

"Oh dear," my mother said in distress, "I'll bet anything she has nits in her hair."

"For Pete's sake," my father said crossly, "do you think Matron would let her stay in the hospital for all this time like that? Don't be silly, Beth."

Grandmother MacLeod, her delicately featured face as rigid as a cameo, now brought her mauve-veined hands together as though she were about to begin prayer.

"Ewen, if that halfbreed youngster comes along to Diamond Lake, I'm not going," she announced. "I'll go to Morag's for the summer."

I had trouble in stifling my urge to laugh, for my mother brightened visibly and quickly tried to hide it. If it came to a choice between Grandmother MacLeod and Piquette, Piquette would win hands down, nits or not.

"It might be quite nice for you, at that," she mused. "You haven't seen Morag for over a year, and you might enjoy being in the city for a while. Well, Ewen dear, you do what you think best. If you think it would do Piquette some good, then we'll be glad to have her, as long as she behaves herself."

So it happened that several weeks later, when we all piled into my father's old Nash, surrounded by suitcases and boxes of provisions and toys for my ten-month-old brother, Piquette was with us and Grandmother MacLeod, miraculously, was not. My father would only be staying at the cottage for a couple of weeks, for he had to get back to his practice, but the rest of us would stay at Diamond Lake until the end of August.

Our cottage was not named, as many were, "Dew Drop Inn" or "Bide-a-Wee," or "Bonnie Doon." The sign on the roadway bore in austere letters only our name, MacLeod. It was not a large cottage, but it was on the lakefront. You could look out the windows and see, through the filigree of the spruce trees, the water glistening greenly as the sun caught it. All around the cottage were ferns, and sharp-branched raspberry bushes, and moss that had grown over fallen tree trunks. If you looked carefully among the weeds and grass, you could find wild strawberry plants which were in white flower now and in another month would bear fruit, the fragrant globes hanging like miniature scarlet lanterns on the thin hairy stems. The two grey squirrels were still there, gossiping at us from the tall spruce beside the cottage, and by the end of the summer they would again be tame enough to take pieces of crust from my hands. The broad moose antlers that hung above the back door were a little more bleached and fissured after the winter, but otherwise everything was the same. I raced joyfully around my kingdom, greeting all the places I had not seen for a year. My brother, Roderick, who had not been born when we were here last summer, sat on the car rug in the sunshine and examined a brown spruce cone, meticulously turning it round and round in his small and curious hands. My mother and father toted the luggage from car to cottage, exclaiming over how well the place had wintered, no broken windows, thank goodness, no apparent damage from storm-felled branches or snow.

Only after I had finished looking around did I notice Piquette. She was sitting on the swing, her lame leg held stiffly out, and her other foot scuffing the ground as she swung slowly back and forth. Her long hair hung black and straight around her shoulders, and her broad coarse-featured face bore no expression—it was blank, as though she no longer dwelt within her own skull, as though she had gone elsewhere. I approached her very hesitantly.

"Want to come and play?"

Piquette looked at me with a sudden flash of scorn.

"I ain't a kid," she said.

Wounded, I stamped angrily away, swearing I would not speak to her for the rest of the summer. In the days that followed, however, Piquette began to interest me, and I began to want to interest her. My reasons did not appear bizarre to me. Unlikely as it may seem, I had only just realised that the Tonnerre family, whom I had always heard called halfbreeds, were actually Indians, or as near as made no difference. My acquaintance with Indians was not extensive. I did not remember ever having seen a real Indian, and my new awareness that Piquette sprang from the people of Big Bear and Poundmaker, of Tecumseh, of the Iroquois who had eaten Father Brébeuf's[4] heart—all this gave her an instant attraction in my eyes. I was devoted reader of Pauline Johnson[5] at this age, and sometimes would orate aloud and in an exalted voice, *West Wind, blow from your prairie nest; Blow from the mountains, blow from the west*—and so on. It seemed to me that Piquette must be in some way a daughter of the forest, a kind of junior prophetess of the wilds, who might impart to me, if I took the right approach, some of the secrets which she undoubtedly knew—where the whippoorwill made her nest, how the coyote reared her young, or whatever it was that it said in Hiawatha.[6]

I set about gaining Piquette's trust. She was not allowed to go swimming, with her bad leg, but I managed to lure her down to the beach—or rather, she came because there was nothing else to do. The water was always icy, for the lake was fed by springs, but I swam like a dog, thrashing my arms and legs around at such speed and with such an output of energy that I never grew cold.

20

4. Father Brebeuf, 17th-century Jesuit missionary. *Tecumseh:* Shawnee chief who fought on the side of the British in the War of 1812. *Big Bear, Poundmaker:* Cree chiefs and supporters of Riel. 5. Native Canadian author.   6. The eponymous hero of Henry Wadsworth Longfellow's *The Song of Hiawatha* (1854–55) learns similar—though not identical— "secrets" (III, 145–58).

Finally, when I had enough, I came out and sat beside Piquette on the sand. When she saw me approaching, her hand squashed flat the sand castle she had been building, and she looked at me sullenly, without speaking.

"Do you like this place?" I asked, after a while, intending to lead on from there into the question of forest lore.

Piquette shrugged. "It's okay. Good as anywhere."

"I love it," I said. "We come here every summer."

"So what?" Her voice was distant, and I glanced at her uncertainly, wondering what I could have said wrong.

"Do you want to come for a walk?" I asked her. "We wouldn't need to go far. If you walk just around the point there, you come to a bay where great big reeds grow in the water, and all kinds of fish hang around there. Want to? Come on."

She shook her head.

"Your dad said I ain't supposed to do no more walking than I got to." I tried another line.

"I bet you know a lot about the woods and all that, eh?" I began respectfully.

Piquette looked at me from her large dark unsmiling eyes.

"I don't know what in hell you're talkin' about," she replied. "You nuts or somethin'? If you mean where my old man, and me, and all them live, you better shut up, by Jesus, you hear?"

I was startled and my feelings were hurt, but I had a kind of dogged perseverance. I ignored her rebuff.

"You know something, Piquette? There's loons here, on this lake. You can see their nests just up the shore there, behind those logs. At night, you can hear them even from the cottage, but it's better to listen from the beach. My dad says we should listen and try to remember how they sound, because in a few years when more cottages are built at Diamond Lake and more people come in, the loons will go away."

Piquette was picking up stones and snail shells and then dropping them again.

"Who gives a good goddamn?" she said.

It became increasingly obvious that, as an Indian, Piquette was a dead loss. That evening I went out by myself, scrambling through the bushes that overhung the steep path, my feet slipping on the fallen spruce needles that covered the ground. When I reached the shore, I walked along the firm damp sand to the small pier that my father had built, and sat down there. I heard someone else crashing through the undergrowth and the bracken, and for a moment I thought Piquette had changed her mind, but it turned out to be my father. He sat beside me on the pier and we waited, without speaking.

At night the lake was like black glass with a streak of amber which was the path of the moon. All around, the spruce trees grew tall and close-set, branches blackly sharp against the sky, which was lightened by a cold flickering of stars. Then the loons began their calling. They rose like phantom birds from the nests on the shore, and flew out onto the dark still surface of the water.

No one can ever describe that ululating sound, the crying of the loons, and no one who has heard it can ever forget it. Plaintive, and yet with a quality of chilling mockery, those voices belonged to a world separated by aeons from our neat world of summer cottages and the lighted lamps of home.

"They must have sounded just like that," my father remarked, "before any person ever set foot here."

Then he laughed. "You could say the same, of course, about sparrows, or chipmunks, but somehow it only strikes you that way with the loons."

"I know," I said.

Neither of us suspected that this would be the last time we would ever sit here together on the shore, listening. We stayed for perhaps half an hour, and then we went back to the cottage. My mother was reading beside the fireplace. Piquette was looking at the burning birch log, and not doing anything.

"You should have come along," I said, although in fact I was glad she had not.   45

"Not me," Piquette said. "You wouldn' catch me walkin' way down there jus' for a bunch of squawkin' birds."

Piquette and I remained ill at ease with one another. I felt I had somehow failed my father, but I did not know what was the matter, nor why she would not or could not respond when I suggested exploring the woods or playing house. I thought it was probably her slow and difficult walking that held her back. She stayed most of the time in the cottage with my mother, helping her with the dishes or with Roddie, but hardly ever talking. Then the Duncans arrived at their cottage, and I spent my days with Mavis, who was my best friend. I could not reach Piquette at all, and I soon lost interest in trying. But all that summer she remained as both a reproach and a mystery to me.

That winter my father died of pneumonia, after less than a week's illness. For some time I saw nothing around me, being completely immersed in my own pain and my mother's. When I looked outward once more, I scarcely noticed that Piquette Tonnerre was no longer at school. I do not remember seeing her at all until four years later, one Saturday night when Mavis and I were having Cokes in the Regal Café. The jukebox was booming like tuneful thunder, and beside it, leaning lightly on its chrome and its rainbow glass, was a girl.

Piquette must have been seventeen then, although she looked about twenty. I stared at her, astounded that anyone could have changed so much. Her face, so stolid and expressionless before, was animated now with a gaiety that was almost violent. She laughed and talked very loudly with the boys around her. Her lipstick was bright carmine, and her hair was cut short and frizzily permed. She had not been pretty as a child, and she was not pretty now, for her features were still heavy and blunt. But her dark and slightly slanted eyes were beautiful, and her skin-tight skirt and orange sweater displayed to enviable advantage a soft and slender body.

She saw me, and walked over. She teetered a little, but it was not due to her once-tubercular leg, for her limp was almost gone.   50

"Hi, Vanessa." Her voice had the same hoarseness. "Long time no see, eh?"

"Hi," I said. "Where've you been keeping yourself, Piquette?"

"Oh, I been around," she said. "I been away almost two years now. Been all over the place—Winnipeg, Regina, Saskatoon. Jesus, what I could tell you! I come back this summer, but I ain't stayin'. You kids goin' to the dance?"

"No," I said abruptly, for this was a sore point with me. I was fifteen, and thought I was old enough to go to the Saturday-night dances at the Flamingo. My mother, however, thought otherwise.

55   "Y'oughta come," Piquette said. "I never miss one. It's just about the on'y thing in this jerkwater town that's any fun. Boy, you couldn' catch me stayin' here. I don' give a shit about this place. It stinks."

She sat down beside me, and I caught the harsh over-sweetness of her perfume.

"Listen, you wanna know something, Vanessa?" she confided, her voice only slightly blurred. "Your dad was the only person in Manawaka that ever done anything good to me."

I nodded speechlessly. I was certain she was speaking the truth. I knew a little more than I had that summer at Diamond Lake, but I could not reach her now any more than I had then. I was ashamed, ashamed of my own timidity, the frightened tendency to look the other way. Yet I felt no real warmth towards her—I only felt that I ought to, because of that distant summer and because my father had hoped she would be company for me, or perhaps that I would be for her, but it had not happened that way. At this moment, meeting her again, I had to admit that she repelled and embarrassed me, and I could not help despising the self-pity in her voice. I wished she would go away. I did not want to see her. I did not know what to say to her. It seemed that we had nothing to say to one another.

"I'll tell you something else," Piquette went on. "All the old bitches an' biddies in this town will sure be surprised. I'm gettin' married this fall—my boyfriend, he's an English fella, works in the stockyards in the city there, a very tall guy, got blond wavy hair. Gee, is he ever handsome. Got this real classy name. Alvin Gerald Cummings—some handle, eh? They call him Al."

60   For the merest instant, then, I saw her. I really did see her, for the first and only time in all the years we had both lived in the same town. Her defiant face, momentarily, became unguarded and unmasked, and in her eyes there was a terrifying hope.

"Gee, Piquette—" I burst out awkwardly, "that's swell. That's really wonderful. Congratulations—good luck—I hope you'll be happy—"

As I mouthed the conventional phrases, I could only guess how great her need must have been, that she had been forced to seek the very things she so bitterly rejected.

When I was eighteen, I left Manawaka and went away to college. At the end of my first year, I came back home for the summer. I spent the first few days in talking non-stop with my mother, as we exchanged all the news that somehow had not found its way into letters—what had happened in my life and what had happened here in Manawaka while I was away. My mother searched her memory for events that concerned people I knew.

"Did I ever write you about Piquette Tonnerre, Vanessa?" she asked one morning.

"No, I don't think so," I replied. "Last I heard of her, she was going to marry some guy in the city. Is she still there?"

My mother looked perturbed, and it was a moment before she spoke, as though she did not know how to express what she had to tell and wished she did not need to try.

"She's dead," she said at last. Then, as I stared at her, "Oh, Vanessa, when it happened, I couldn't help thinking of her as she was that summer—so sullen and gauche and badly dressed. I couldn't help wondering if we could have done something more at that time—but what could we do? She used to be around in the cottage there with me all day, and honestly it was all I could do to get a word out of her. She didn't even talk to your father very much, although I think she liked him in her way."

"What happened?" I asked.

"Either her husband left her, or she left him," my mother said. "I don't know which. Anyway, she came back here with two youngsters, both only babies—they must have been born very close together. She kept house, I guess, for Lazarus and her brothers, down in the valley there, in the old Tonnerre place. I used to see her on the street sometimes, but she never spoke to me. She'd put on an awful lot of weight, and she looked a mess, to tell you the truth, a real slattern, dressed any old how. She was up in court a couple of times—drunk and disorderly, of course. One Saturday night last winter, during the coldest weather, Piquette was alone in the shack with the children. The Tonnerres made home brew all the time, so I've heard, and Lazarus said later she'd been drinking most of the day when he and the boys went out that evening. They had an old wood-stove there—you know the kind, with exposed pipes. The shack caught fire. Piquette didn't get out, and neither did the children."

I did not say anything. As so often with Piquette, there did not seem to be anything to say. There was a kind of silence around the image in my mind of the fire and the snow, and I wished I could put from my memory the look that I had seen once in Piquette's eyes.

I went up to Diamond Lake for a few days that summer, with Mavis and her family. The MacLeod cottage had been sold after my father's death, and I did not even go to look at it, not wanting to witness my long-ago kingdom possessed now by strangers. But one evening I went down to the shore by myself.

The small pier which my father had built was gone, and in its place there was a large and solid pier built by the government, for Galloping Mountain was now a national park, and Diamond Lake had been re-named Lake Wapakata, for it was felt that an Indian name would have a greater appeal to tourists. The one store had become several dozen, and the settlement had all the attributes of a flourishing resort—hotels, dance-hall, cafés with neon signs, the penetrating odours of potato chips and hot dogs.

I sat on the government pier and looked out across the water. At night the lake at least was the same as it had always been, darkly shining and bearing within its black glass the streak of amber that was the path of the moon. There was no wind that evening, and everything was quiet all around me. It seemed too quiet, and then I realized that the loons were no longer here. I listened for some time, to make sure, but never once did I hear that long-drawn call, half mocking and half plaintive, spearing through the stillness across the lake.

I did not know what had happened to the birds. Perhaps they had gone away to some far place of belonging. Perhaps they had been unable to find such a place, and had simply died out, having ceased to care any longer whether they lived or not.

I remembered how Piquette had scorned to come along, when my father and I sat there and listened to the lake birds. It seemed to me now that in some unconscious and totally unrecognized way, Piquette might have been the only one, after all, who had heard the crying of the loons.

1966

ANN BEATTIE

Janus

The bowl was perfect. Perhaps it was not what you'd select if you faced a shelf of bowls, and not the sort of thing that would inevitably attract a lot of attention at a crafts fair, yet it had real presence. It was as predictably admired as a mutt who has no reason to suspect he might be funny. Just such a dog, in fact, was often brought out (and in) along with the bowl.

Andrea was a real estate agent, and when she thought that some prospective buyers might be dog lovers, she would drop off her dog at the same time she placed the bowl in the house that was up for sale. She would put a dish of water in the kitchen for Mondo, take his squeaking plastic frog out of her purse and drop it on the floor. He would pounce delightedly, just as he did every day at home, batting around his favorite toy. The bowl usually sat on a coffee table, though recently she had displayed it on top of a pine blanket chest and on a lacquered table. It was once placed on a cherry table beneath a Bonnard[1] still life, where it held its own.

Everyone who has purchased a house or who has wanted to sell a house must be familiar with some of the tricks used to convince a buyer that the house is quite special: a fire in the fireplace in early evening; jonquils in a pitcher on the kitchen counter, where no one ordinarily has space to put flowers; perhaps the slight aroma of spring, made by a single drop of scent vaporizing from a lamp bulb.

The wonderful thing about the bowl, Andrea thought, was that it was both subtle and noticeable—a paradox of a bowl. Its glaze was the color of cream and seemed to glow no matter what light it was placed in. There were a few bits of color in it—tiny geometric flashes—and some of these were tinged with flecks

1. Pierre Bonnard (1867–1947), French painter.

of silver. They were as mysterious as cells seen under a microscope; it was difficult not to study them, because they shimmered, flashing for a split second,
and then resumed their shape. Something about the colors and their random
placement suggested motion. People who liked country furniture always commented on the bowl, but then it turned out that people who felt comfortable
with Biedermeier[2] loved it just as much. But the bowl was not at all ostentatious,
or even so noticeable that anyone would suspect that it had been put in place
deliberately. They might notice the height of the ceiling on first entering a
room, and only when their eye moved down from that, or away from the refrac-
tion of sunlight on a pale wall, would they see the bowl. Then they would go
immediately to it and comment. Yet they always faltered when they tried to say
something. Perhaps it was because they were in the house for a serious reason,
not to notice some object.

Once, Andrea got a call from a woman who had not put in an offer on a   5
house she had shown her. That bowl, she said—would it be possible to find out
where the owners had bought that beautiful bowl? Andrea pretended that she
did not know what the woman was referring to. A bowl, somewhere in the
house? Oh, on a table under the window. Yes, she would ask, of course. She let
a couple of days pass, then called back to say that the bowl had been a present
and the people did not know where it had been purchased.

When the bowl was not being taken from house to house, it sat on Andrea's
coffee table at home. She didn't keep it carefully wrapped (although she transported it that way, in a box); she kept it on the table, because she liked to see it.
It was large enough so that it didn't seem fragile, or particularly vulnerable if
anyone sideswiped the table or Mondo blundered into it at play. She had asked
her husband to please not drop his house key in it. It was meant to be empty.

When her husband first noticed the bowl, he had peered into it and smiled
briefly. He always urged her to buy things she liked. In recent years, both of
them had acquired many things to make up for all the lean years when they
were graduate students, but now that they had been comfortable for quite a
while, the pleasure of new possessions dwindled. Her husband had pronounced
the bowl "pretty," and he had turned away without picking it up to examine it.
He had no more interest in the bowl than she had in his new Leica.[3]

She was sure that the bowl brought her luck. Bids were often put in on
houses where she had displayed the bowl. Sometimes the owners, who were
always asked to be away or to step outside when the house was being shown,
didn't even know that the bowl had been in their house. Once—she could not
imagine how—she left it behind, and then she was so afraid that something
might have happened to it that she rushed back to the house and sighed with
relief when the woman owner opened the door. The bowl, Andrea explained—
she had purchased a bowl and set it on the chest for safekeeping while she
toured the house with the prospective buyers, and she . . . She felt like rushing
past the frowning woman and seizing her bowl. The owner stepped aside, and
it was only when Andrea ran to the chest that the lady glanced at her a little

2. Mid-19th-century heavy, stuffed German furniture.   3. An expensive German camera.

strangely. In the few seconds before Andrea picked up the bowl, she realized that the owner must have just seen that it had been perfectly placed, that the sunlight struck the bluer part of it. Her pitcher had been moved to the far side of the chest, and the bowl predominated. All the way home, Andrea wondered how she could have left the bowl behind. It was like leaving a friend at an outing—just walking off. Sometimes there were stories in the paper about families forgetting a child somewhere and driving to the next city. Andrea had only gone a mile down the road before she remembered.

In time, she dreamed of the bowl. Twice, in a waking dream—early in the morning, between sleep and a last nap before rising—she had a clear vision of it. It came into sharp focus and startled her for a moment—the same bowl she looked at every day.

10   She had a very profitable year selling real estate. Word spread, and she had more clients than she felt comfortable with. She had the foolish thought that if only the bowl were an animate object she could thank it. There were times when she wanted to talk to her husband about the bowl. He was a stockbroker, and sometimes told people that he was fortunate to be married to a woman who had such a fine aesthetic sense and yet could also function in the real world. They were a lot alike, really—they had agreed on that. They were both quiet people—reflective, slow to make value judgments, but almost intractable once they had come to a conclusion. They both liked details, but while ironies attracted her, he was more impatient and dismissive when matters became many sided or unclear. But they both knew this; it was the kind of thing they could talk about when they were alone in the car together, coming home from a party or after a weekend with friends. But she never talked to him about the bowl. When they were at dinner, exchanging their news of the day, or while they lay in bed at night listening to the stereo and murmuring sleepy disconnections, she was often tempted to come right out and say that she thought that the bowl in the living room, the cream-colored bowl, was responsible for her success. But she didn't say it. She couldn't begin to explain it. Sometimes in the morning, she would look at him and feel guilty that she had such a constant secret.

Could it be that she had some deeper connection with the bowl—a relationship of some kind? She corrected her thinking: how could she imagine such a thing, when she was a human being and it was a bowl? It was ridiculous. Just think of how people lived together and loved each other . . . But was that always so clear, always a relationship? She was confused by these thoughts, but they remained in her mind. There was something within her now, something real, that she never talked about.

The bowl was a mystery, even to her. It was frustrating, because her involvement with the bowl contained a steady sense of unrequited good fortune; it would have been easier to respond if some sort of demand were made in return. But that only happened in fairy tales. The bowl was just a bowl. She did not believe that for one second. What she believed was that it was something she loved.

In the past, she had sometimes talked to her husband about a new property she was about to buy or sell—confiding some clever strategy she had devised to persuade owners who seemed ready to sell. Now she stopped doing that, for all her strategies involved the bowl. She became more deliberate with the bowl, and more possessive. She put it in houses only when no one was there, and removed it when she left the house. Instead of just moving a pitcher or a dish, she would remove all the other objects from a table. She had to force herself to handle them carefully, because she didn't really care about them. She just wanted them out of sight.

She wondered how the situation would end. As with a lover, there was no exact scenario of how matters would come to a close. Anxiety became the operative force. It would be irrelevant if the lover rushed into someone else's arms, or wrote her a note and departed to another city. The horror was the possibility of the disappearance. That was what mattered.

She would get up at night and look at the bowl. It never occurred to her that she might break it. She washed and dried it without anxiety, and she moved it often, from coffee table to mahogany corner table or wherever, without fearing an accident. It was clear that she would not be the one who would do anything to the bowl. The bowl was only handled by her, set safely on one surface or another; it was not very likely that anyone would break it. A bowl was a poor conductor of electricity: it would not be hit by lightning. Yet the idea of damage persisted. She did not think beyond that—to what her life would be without the bowl. She only continued to fear that some accident would happen. Why not, in a world where people set plants where they did not belong, so that visitors touring a house would be fooled into thinking that dark corners got sunlight— a world full of tricks?

She had first seen the bowl several years earlier, at a crafts fair she had visited half in secret, with her lover. He had urged her to buy the bowl. She didn't *need* any more things, she told him. But she had been drawn to the bowl, and they had lingered near it. Then she went on to the next booth, and he came up behind her, tapping the rim against her shoulder as she ran her fingers over a wood carving. "You're still insisting that I buy that?" she said. "No," he said. "I bought it for you." He had bought her other things before this—things she liked more, at first—the child's ebony-and-turquoise ring that fitted her little finger; the wooden box, long and thin, beautifully dovetailed, that she used to hold paper clips; the soft gray sweater with a pouch pocket. It was his idea that when he could not be there to hold her hand she could hold her own—clasp her hands inside the lone pocket that stretched across the front. But in time she became more attached to the bowl than to any of his other presents. She tried to talk herself out of it. She owned other things that were more striking or valuable. It wasn't an object whose beauty jumped out at you; a lot of people must have passed it by before the two of them saw it that day.

Her lover had said that she was always too slow to know what she really loved. Why continue with her life the way it was? Why be two-faced, he asked her. He had made the first move toward her. When she would not decide in his favor, would not change her life and come to him, he asked her what made her think she could have it both ways. And then he made the last move and left. It

15

was a decision meant to break her will, to shatter her intransigent ideas about honoring previous commitments.

Time passed. Alone in the living room at night, she often looked at the bowl sitting on the table, still and safe, unilluminated. In its way, it was perfect: the world cut in half, deep and smoothly empty. Near the rim, even in dim light, the eye moved toward one small flash of blue, a vanishing point on the horizon.

1986

▼   ▼   ▼

SYMBOLS A Glossary

allegory: as in *metaphor*, one thing (usually nonrational, abstract, religious) is implicitly spoken of in terms of something concrete, usually sensuous, but in an allegory the comparison is extended to include an entire work or large portion of a work

archetype: a plot or character element that recurs in cultural or cross-cultural myths

figurative: nonliteral; implicitly or explicitly representative of something in terms of some other unlike thing that seems to be similar or analogous

metaphor: an implicit comparison or identification of one thing with another unlike itself without the use of a verbal signal

myth: like allegory, myth usually is symbolic and extensive, including an entire work or story; though it no longer is necessarily specific to or pervasive in a single culture—individual authors may now be said to create myths—there is still a sense that myth is communal or cultural, while the symbolic can often be private or personal

simile: a figure that explicitly expresses the comparison, often signaled by *like* or *as*

symbol: a person, place, thing, event, or pattern in a literary work that designates itself and at the same time figuratively represents or "stands for" something else. Often the thing or idea represented is more abstract, general, non- or superrational; the symbol more concrete and particular

QUESTIONS

1. Why does goodman Brown go to a witches' meeting?

2. Why does Faith Brown, his wife, wear pink ribbons?

3. In what way are the Tonnerres stereotyped in the first two paragraphs of "The Loons"? How do you explain young Piquette's behavior toward the narrator? How has Piquette changed when Vanessa sees her at seventeen? How has Piquette changed again at eighteen? Is this a reversion to the white American stereotype of Native Americans / Canadians? How does the story of Piquette's life modify the stereotype?

4. What do the loons represent to young Vanessa and her father? What does the disappearance of the loons mean to Vanessa?

5. In reading "Janus," what impression do you get of Andrea—and her attachment to the bowl—in the first half of the story? What expectations—if any—are aroused by that first half? What does it mean to you that Andrea thought the bowl was meant to be empty (par. 6)? What other qualities of the bowl seem to suggest something about Andrea or her life? In paragraph 14, Andrea wonders how the situation would end. This probably makes some readers, perhaps most, think about how this story is going to end. How does it? Where did Andrea get the bowl? How significant is that? Why is the story called "Janus"?

WRITING SUGGESTIONS

1. Write a parody of "Young Goodman Brown" or an imitation, perhaps in the style of Stephen King or Anne Rice.

2. Write an analysis of the symbolism used in one of the stories in *Fiction: Reading, Responding, Writing* or in one of the stories in the first three chapters of this textbook.

3. Write an essay in which you define and then argue for or against the proposition that neither the narrator nor her father but only Piquette had really "heard the crying of the loons" (par. 76).

4. Paraphrase several possible meanings of the bowl in "Janus," argue for one or explain how the symbol of the bowl may be both meaningful and yet elude any possible paraphrase of its meaning.

STUDENT WRITING

Geoffrey Clement's essay on "Sonny's Blues" (from Chapter 1) responds to the second writing suggestion, above. In it, he traces the symbolism and the thematic and evaluative force of images of water in its solid (ice), liquid, and gaseous (steam, boiling) states in the story.

The Struggle to Surface
in the Water of "Sonny's Blues"

Geoffrey Clement

In "Sonny's Blues," James Baldwin employs water as a symbol that enables him to concentrate more clearly on the lack of and the crucial need for a real sense of communication among members of society. As Baldwin captures the intensity of Sonny's and his brother's struggles to understand their situation, he vividly depicts a society that seeks to swallow up the souls of its inhabitants and gradually to drown them spiritually. Thus, Baldwin illustrates quite clearly his sense of the hopelessness in man's plight. In portraying the struggle of street life in Harlem, he uses water in its opposite forms-- frozen water and boiling water--and toward the end of the story, as Sonny's and his brother's revelations help to resolve the conflict, the water becomes calm.

Initially, and as a result of Sonny's arrest, Sonny's brother gradually realizes that he has not fulfilled his promise and that his feelings of love for his brother have certainly gone unexpressed, if indeed they exist. As a result, he feels physically the coldness that has permeated his emotional life: "It was a special kind of ice. It kept melting, sending trickles of ice water all up and down my veins, but it never got less. Sometimes it hardened and seemed to expand . . ." (par. 2). So the ice represents his guilt and his fears, both of which will lessen little. Although he learns to adapt to these feelings, they occasionally resurface. Upon Sonny's return from prison, for example, his brother thinks, "and thank God she [his wife] was there, for I was filled with that icy dread again. Everything I did seemed awkward to me, and everything I said sounded freighted with hidden meaning. . . . I was dying to hear him tell me he was safe" (par. 78). In addition to this guilt, Sonny's brother experiences much of the same emotional turmoil that Sonny has endured. In this passage in particular, he is seeking reassurance that there is a way to survive their imprisonment without having to feel the pain Sonny felt. Baldwin not only uses ice to show the brother's disappointment in his failures as a brother but also to point to the brother's own struggle for security, identity, and communication.

As Sonny's brother begins to realize that
within him there has grown a heart hardened and
haunted by the cold darkness of Harlem's streets,
he also begins to recognize many of the realities
that his brother has faced and that he too must
eventually face. Sonny's brother is spiritually
walking through "the vivid, killing streets of
our childhood. These streets hadn't changed,
though housing projects jutted up out of them now
like rocks in the middle of a boiling sea" (par.
73). Here, Baldwin paints an almost hellish
picture of pain and suffering, of emotional
torment and fears, and of spiritual drowning and
isolation, all of which slowly become real in the
mind of Sonny's brother. He begins to feel for
the first time in his life the depth of his
denial of his brother. Tragically, he finds that
when he is ready to reach out to help Sonny, he
cannot, for he is even more lost and confused
than Sonny himself. Sonny's brother wants
desperately to save Sonny from the inevitable
struggle, yet he learns from Sonny that "the
storm inside" (par. 217) will pass over only with
the constant expression of love. Clearly, the
process of revelation is a very dramatic one,
since Sonny's brother comes to understand Sonny's
need for a giving, communicating, responsible
relationship, a commitment filled with careful
listening, compassion, and understanding. Sonny
does not believe he can make his brother

understand his experiences with drugs: "I can never tell you. I was all by myself at the bottom of something . . . and I thought I'd die if I couldn't get away from it and yet, all the same, I knew that everything I was doing was just locking me in with it" (par. 220). Once his brother grasps the importance of listening with love and understanding, however, Sonny is finally able to reach out.

Toward the end of the story, the ice and the boiling sea come together, and there is peace; Sonny is able to reach out, and he starts to swim in the calmer water. Now, he finds freedom in expressing his struggles through his music, while at the same time alerting his audience to the lessons he has learned. Creole "wanted Sonny to leave the shoreline and strike out for the deep water. He was Sonny's witness that deep water and drowning were not the same thing" (par. 234). As Sonny ventures further and further into his own understanding of life's struggles, he tries, his brother tells us, "to find new ways to make us listen. For, while the tale of how we suffer, and how we are delighted, and how we may triumph is never new, it always must be heard. . . . it's the only light we've got in all this darkness" (par. 238). In a powerful way, Sonny taught the audience to listen: "Freedom lurked around us and I understood, at last, that he could help us be free if we would listen, that we would never be free until we did" (par. 240). The boiling rage of the streets and the coldness within his heart are reconciled as the brother finally witnesses "Sonny's world" (par. 231). Finally, he recognizes that Sonny has found the strength of knowing that he has discovered in music the outlet through which he can express himself and warn others of his mistakes. He sends up to the bandstand not water, not ice, but Scotch and milk. Sonny sips it in a sort of communion and puts it back on top of the piano, where "it glowed and shook above [his] head like the very cup of trembling" (par. 241).

Thoughout his story, Baldwin stresses the lack of companionship to try to manipulate the reader's emotions. Playing on the contrasts between forms of water, he draws parallels to the theme of emotional conflict within the minds of Sonny and his brother. While the sea is calmer toward the end, there is still a sense of rage, because only in the expression of his struggle is Sonny able to find meaning, satisfaction, and forgiveness for his brother. The streets, society's common ground, still try to isolate its members as each person individually struggles to reach the surface. But if the struggler can find a listening helper, which Sonny finds in his brother, then he will reach the surface and breathe the fulfilling breath of love. The cup of trembling will be taken out of the struggler's

hand, the Bible tells us, and will be put "into
the hand of them that afflict thee" (p. 70n.).
Light gracefully touches and penetrates the
surface of the water, and the cup of trembling
is still.

6 THEME

If you ask what a story is "about," an author is likely to answer by telling you the **subject.** Indeed, many authors tell you the subject in their titles: "An Occurrence at Owl Creek Bridge," "Her First Ball." Though a subject is always concrete, it may be stated at somewhat greater length than the few words of a title: "a man's thoughts as he faces execution for spying during the Civil War" ("Owl Creek Bridge"); "a young girl's excitement at her first grown-up dance and an incident that temporarily depresses her" ("Her First Ball").

A friend might be more likely to tell you what a story is about by giving you a summary of the action: "This weird Southern lady is jilted by a Yankee. She kills him and sleeps with his corpse. There's a smell around the house before too long, but nobody knows about the murder until she dies." (We sometimes call this a **plot summary,** but you will notice that this summary describes the history, the events, in more or less chronological order, while the plot arranges or structures the history differently; in "A Rose for Emily," remember, we do not figure out there's been a murder and certainly don't know about Emily's sleeping with the corpse until the end of the story, though of course the jilting, murder, and so on happen in the order described in the summary of the history.)

Your teacher may well explain a story by summarizing its **theme.** Some refer to the central idea, the thesis, or even the message of the story, and that is roughly what we mean by theme: a generalization or abstraction from the story. Thus, the subject of "Young Goodman Brown" may be said to be a coven (witches' meeting) or, more fully, "a young colonial New England husband is driven mad by finding everyone he thought good and pure attending a witches' meeting." The theme may be "everyone partakes of evil," or, more succinctly, "the Fall." There are, as you can see, degrees of generalization and abstraction; subject (a young man finds that everyone is evil) shades off into theme, which itself can be more or less general and abstract.

Discussions of literature in or out of class sometimes seem to suggest that stories exist for their themes, that we read only to get the "point" or message. But most themes, you must admit, are somewhat less than earth-shattering. That all men and women are evil may be debatable, but it certainly isn't news. That not all unmarried women (even English women) of a certain age are prudish, dried up, and repressed—an apparent theme of "Our Friend Judith"—is rather widely recognized, something we scarcely need a dozen or so pages of fiction to find out. No wonder, then, that some of our more skeptical friends contend that stories are only elaborate ways of "saying something simple," that literature is a game in which authors hide their meanings under shells of words. Of course, reading a dozen or so pages of a story like "Our Friend Judith" can be enjoyable. Could it be that we really read fiction for fun, and all our talk about themes is just hiding from our Puritan natures the fact that we are goofing off?

I don't believe that articulating the theme of a story is either the purpose of or the excuse for reading fiction, or that authors hide their meanings like Easter eggs. In order to relate his or her unique vision of reality to an absent and unknown reader, a writer must find a way of communicating—some common ground on which to meet the various unique individuals who will read the story. Common experiences, common assumptions, common language, and commonplaces offer such ground. Readers reach out from their own subjective worlds toward that new and different vision of the author with the help of the common elements (the general), and especially through the commonplaces of theme, bringing back the particulars and generalizations of the story to their own reading and living experience. In "Janus," the reader sees a successful suburban real estate agent who is married to a stockbroker but who has lost her lover, a man she truly loved, because she could not or would not decide to leave her husband; a woman whose world is "perfect," but cut in half and empty, like the beloved bowl her lover picked out for her and gave her. Generalizing, the reader may conclude that what the story says (its theme) is that life, or a full or happy life, is more than convention and material success, that love is more important than comfort and "perfection." Though the reader's own situation and choices may be considerably different from those of the protagonist in Beattie's story, he or she may be led by the story to ponder what is truly important and valuable in life, what "the perfect life" consists in, thereby coming to a greater understanding of the story—and, whether he or she agrees with the conclusions of the story or not, to a fuller understanding of the issues and theme of the story.

The significance of any story is modified to some extent by the reader's experience of books and life. You should not reduce every story to the dimensions of what you already know and feel, but you should reach out to the story and bring it back to you as an addition to and modification of your own experience. To make a story yours, to make it more than a yarn about a woman who sells real estate and has been unfaithful to her stockbroker husband and was left by her lover because she would not get a divorce, requires translating it somehow into terms that, while not necessarily psychological or moral precepts, alter or broaden to some degree your own vision of yourself, others, life in general.

When I discussed symbols, I said that even while a symbol suggests the meaning beyond the particulars of the fiction, it remains a detail in the fictional world—the snakelike staff of the stranger in "Young Goodman Brown" remains a staff, Judith's cats remain cats. Some critics would say that this is true also of theme and that theme is related to the story as integrally as symbolic meaning is to detail; that is, rather than "Young Goodman Brown" telling us something we did not know before, its theme and its story modify each other. The theme as I've stated it relates to spiritual evil, the kind of evil suggested by the snake and Satan figures. But this theme is not entirely portable— it cannot be taken out of the story and used as substitute for what the story "means"—nor can it, without qualification, be used to explain all the significant details in the story. The facts that Brown is a newlywed, that Faith wears pink (coquettish?) ribbons, and that she, whom Brown thought so pure and innocent, shows up at the meeting of witches and sinners, suggest a more specific kind of evil than the spiritual or theological evil suggested by the snake and Satan: moral or, even more specifically, sexual evil. This means we must modify our definition of the theme. But how? What does the story imply about the relationship of sex and evil? Is all sex evil? Is Original Sin sexual? Some details—the snake, the Satanic guide—suggest a theme, other details modify it; still others—Brown's behavior after the night of the witches' meeting—may modify it further, so that the theme, though an approximate version of it may be abstracted from the story, remains embedded in it, ultimately inseparable from the details of plot, character, setting, and symbol.

A statement that can do justice to all the complexity and all the particulars of the story is not likely to take the simple form of a **message.** Indeed, it is the complex particularity of literature, its ultimate irreducibility, that makes critics and teachers reject message (which suggests a simple packaged statement) as a suitable term even for the paraphrasable thematic content of a story.

"Young Goodman Brown" is an allegorical story whose details do function as symbols with paraphrasable meanings, yet even its theme refuses to be reduced to a simple statement. "How Much Land Does a Man Need?" is a **parable,** a short fiction that illustrates an explicit moral lesson. That lesson, the theme, is implied by the title. (And here the devil appears not only, at times, in disguise, but also in his proper person.) Even so, Tolstoy's story is not without complexity. How do you account for the first section of the story? Does your paraphrase of the theme accommodate the conversation between the sisters there? "Her First Ball" is not allegorical and neither is it parabolic. Though realistic, however, it is a short, rather simple story that seems to have a simple theme overtly enunciated by one of the characters: Leila's elderly partner. But the scene with the elderly partner is not the end of the story. Leila goes on to dance with a young partner and seems to forget the man's "message." What is the story "saying"? Is her forgetting "bad"? Or "sad"? Or "good"? The specifics of the story modify and enrich all the generalizations we can abstract from it, while these themes and questions, if we recognize them, modify and enrich our reading, our experience of the story.

I realize I may have been talking as if a theme or themes spring out at the reader, while to some of you my inferences of themes may seem like pulling rabbits out of hats. "How Much Land Does a Man Need?" does not involve much of a trick: the title asks the question that, once answered, suggests the theme. But neither is too much conjuring needed to infer the theme of "Young Goodman Brown": I derived the theme of theological evil from the symbols (the snake-staff, Satan figure, names) and I tested physical details— like pink ribbons and the narrative situation (the three-month marriage)—that had sexual implications against the theme to see if I would have to modify my paraphrase. In "Her First Ball" a character raises a general issue that is tested by subsequent events in the story and modified by them.

There are, of course, other ways that details suggest generalizations or meaning, and other ways to abstract meaning from detail. Aided by footnotes, perhaps, you likely noticed the historical and biblical **allusions**—references to history, the Bible, sometimes literature, paintings, and so on—in "Young Goodman Brown." The scene is Salem in the time of King William—that is, about the time of the Salem witch trials—and the stranger's serpentine staff is related to those of the Pharoah's Egyptian magi, which turn to snakes. So allusion as well as symbols, plot, focus and voice, and character are elements that contribute to and must be accounted for in paraphrasing a theme. That is why theme is important, and why it comes last in a discussion of the elements of fiction.

But remember, the theme is an inadequate abstraction from the story; the story and its details do not disappear or lose significance once distilled into theme, nor could you reconstruct a story merely from its paraphrased theme. Indeed, theme and story, history and structure, do not so much interact, are not so much interrelated, as they are fused, inseparable.

▼   ▼   ▼

LEO TOLSTOY

How Much Land Does a Man Need?[1]

I

An elder sister came to visit her younger sister in the country. The elder was married to a tradesman in town, the younger to a peasant in the village. As the sisters sat over their tea talking, the elder began to boast of the advantages of town life: saying how comfortably they lived there, how well they dressed, what fine clothes her children wore, what good things they ate and drank, and how she went to the theatre, promenades, and entertainments.

The younger sister was piqued, and in turn disparaged the life of a trades-man, and stood up for that of a peasant.

"I would not change my way of life for yours," said she. "We may live roughly, but at least we are free from anxiety. You live in better style than we do, but though you often earn more than you need, you are very likely to lose all you have. You know the proverb, 'Loss and gain are brothers twain.' It often happens that people who are wealthy one day are begging their bread the next. Our way is safer. Though a peasant's life is not a fat one, it is a long one. We shall never grow rich, but we shall always have enough to eat."

The elder sister said sneeringly:

5 "Enough? Yes, if you like to share with the pigs and the calves! What do you know of elegance or manners! However much your goodman may slave, you will die as you are living—on a dung heap—and your children the same."

"Well, what of that?" replied the younger. "Of course our work is rough and coarse. But, on the other hand, it is sure, and we need not bow to anyone. But you, in your towns, are surrounded by temptations; to-day all may be right, but to-morrow the Evil One may tempt your husband with cards, wine, or women, and all will go to ruin. Don't such things happen often enough?"

Pahóm, the master of the house, was lying on the top of the stove and he listened to the women's chatter.

"It is perfectly true," thought he. "Busy as we are from childhood tilling mother earth, we peasants have no time to let any nonsense settle in our heads. Our only trouble is that we haven't land enough. If I had plenty of land, I shouldn't fear the Devil himself!"

The women finished their tea, chatted a while about dress, and then cleared away the tea-things and lay down to sleep.

10 But the Devil had been sitting behind the stove, and had heard all that was said. He was pleased that the peasant's wife had led her husband into boasting,

---

1. Translated by Louise and Aylmer Maude.

and that he had said that if he had plenty of land he would not fear the Devil himself.

"All right," thought the Devil. "We will have a tussle. I'll give you land enough; and by means of that land I will get you into my power."

II

Close to the village there lived a lady, a small landowner who had an estate of about three hundred acres. She had always lived on good terms with the peasants until she engaged as her steward an old soldier, who took to burdening the people with fines. However careful Pahóm tried to be, it happened again and again that now a horse of his got among the lady's oats, now a cow strayed into her garden, now his calves found their way into her meadows—and he always had to pay a fine.

Pahóm paid up, but grumbled and, going home in a temper, was rough with his family. All through that summer, Pahóm had much trouble because of this steward, and he was even glad when winter came and the cattle had to be stabled. Though he grudged the fodder when they could no longer graze on the pasture-land, at least he was free from anxiety about them.

In the winter the news got about that the lady was going to sell her land and that the keeper of the inn on the high road was bargaining for it. When the peasants heard this they were very much alarmed.

"Well," thought they, "if the innkeeper gets the land, he will worry us with fines worse than the lady's steward. We all depend on that estate."

So the peasants went on behalf of their Commune, and asked the lady not to sell the land to the innkeeper, offering her a better price for it themselves. The lady agreed to let them have it. Then the peasants tried to arrange for the Commune to buy the whole estate, so that it might be held by them all in common. They met twice to discuss it, but could not settle the matter; the Evil One sowed discord among them and they could not agree. So they decided to buy the land individually, each according to his means; and the lady agreed to this plan as she had to the other.

Presently Pahóm heard that a neighbor of his was buying fifty acres, and that the lady had consented to accept one half in cash and to wait a year for the other half. Pahóm felt envious.

"Look at that," thought he, "the land is all being sold, and I shall get none of it." So he spoke to his wife.

"Other people are buying," said he, "and we must also buy twenty acres or so. Life is becoming impossible. That steward is simply crushing us with his fines."

So they put their heads together and considered how they could manage to buy it. They had one hundred rúbles laid by. They sold a colt and one half of their bees, hired out one of their sons as a laborer and took his wages in advance; borrowed the rest from a brother-in-law, and so scraped together half the purchase money.

15

20

Having done this, Pahóm chose out a farm of forty acres, some of it wooded, and went to the lady to bargain for it. They came to an agreement, and he shook hands with her upon it and paid her a deposit in advance. Then they went to town and signed the deeds; he paying half the price down, and undertaking to pay the remainder within two years.

So now Pahóm had land of his own. He borrowed seed, and sowed it on the land he had bought. The harvest was a good one, and within a year he had managed to pay off his debts both to the lady and to his brother-in-law. So he became a landowner, ploughing and sowing his own land, making hay on his own land, cutting his own trees, and feeding his cattle on his own pasture. When he went out to plough his fields, or to look at his growing corn, or at his grass-meadows, his heart would fill with joy. The grass that grew and the flowers that bloomed there seemed to him unlike any that grew elsewhere. Formerly, when he had passed by that land, it had appeared the same as any other land, but now it seemed quite different.

III

So Pahóm was well-contented, and everything would have been right if the neighboring peasants would only not have trespassed on his corn-fields and meadows. He appealed to them most civilly, but they still went on: now the Communal herdsmen would let the village cows stray into his meadows, then horses from the night pasture would get among his corn. Pahóm turned them out again, and forgave their owners, and for a long time he forbore to prosecute any one. But at last he lost patience and complained to the District Court. He knew it was the peasants' want of land, and no evil intent on their part, that caused the trouble, but he thought:

"I cannot go on overlooking it or they will destroy all I have. They must be taught a lesson."

So he had them up, gave them one lesson, and then another, and two or three of the peasants were fined. After a time Pahóm's neighbors began to bear him a grudge for this, and would now and then let their cattle on to his land on purpose. One peasant even got into Pahóm's wood at night and cut down five young lime trees for their bark. Pahóm passing through the wood one day noticed something white. He came nearer and saw the stripped trunks lying on the ground, and close by stood the stumps where the trees had been. Pahóm was furious.

"If he had only cut one here and there it would have been bad enough," thought Pahóm, "but the rascal has actually cut down a whole clump. If I could only find out who did this, I would pay him out."

He racked his brain as to who it could be. Finally he decided: "It must be Simon—no one else could have done it." So he went to Simon's homestead to have a look round, but he found nothing, and only had an angry scene. However, he now felt more certain than ever that Simon had done it, and he lodged a complaint. Simon was summoned. The case was tried, and retried, and at the end of it all Simon was acquitted, there being no evidence against him. Pahóm felt still more aggrieved, and let his anger loose upon the Elder and the Judges.

"You let thieves grease your palms," said he. "If you were honest folk yourselves you would not let a thief go free."

So Pahóm quarrelled with the Judges and with his neighbors. Threats to burn his building began to be uttered. So though Pahóm had more land, his place in the Commune was much worse than before.

About this time a rumor got about that many people were moving to new parts.

"There's no need for me to leave my land," thought Pahóm. "But some of the others might leave our village and then there would be more room for us. I would take over their land myself and make my estate a bit bigger. I could then live more at ease. As it is, I am still too cramped to be comfortable."

One day Pahóm was sitting at home when a peasant, passing through the village, happened to call in. He was allowed to stay the night, and supper was given him. Pahóm had a talk with this peasant and asked him where he came from. The stranger answered that he came from beyond the Vólga, where he had been working. One word led to another, and the man went on to say that many people were settling in those parts. He told how some people from his village had settled there. They had joined the Commune, and had had twenty-five acres per man granted them. The land was so good, he said, that the rye sown on it grew as high as a horse, and so thick that five cuts of a sickle made a sheaf. One peasant, he said, had brought nothing with him but his bare hands, and now he had six horses and two cows of his own.

Pahóm's heart kindled with desire. He thought:

"Why should I suffer in this narrow hole, if one can live so well elsewhere? I will sell my land and my homestead here, and with the money I will start afresh over there and get everything new. In this crowded place one is always having trouble. But I must first go and find out all about it myself."

Towards summer he got ready and started. He went down the Vólga on a steamer to Samára, then walked another three hundred miles on foot, and at last reached the place. It was just as the stranger had said. The peasants had plenty of land: every man had twenty-five acres of Communal land given him for his use, and any one who had money could buy, besides, at a rúble an acre as much good freehold land as he wanted.

Having found out all he wished to know, Pahóm returned home as autumn came on, and began selling off his belongings. He sold his land at a profit, sold his homestead and all his cattle, and withdrew from membership in the Commune. He only waited till the spring, and then started with his family for the new settlement.

30

35

IV

As soon as Pahóm and his family reached their new abode, he applied for admission into the Commune of a large village. He stood treat to the Elders and obtained the necessary documents. Five shares of Communal land were given him for his own and his sons' use: that is to say—125 acres (not all together, but in different fields) besides the use of the Communal pasture. Pahóm put up the buildings he needed, and bought cattle. Of the Communal land alone he had three times as much as at his former home, and the land was good corn-land. He was ten times better off than he had been. He had plenty of arable land and pasturage, and could keep as many head of cattle as he liked.

At first, in the bustle of building and settling down, Pahóm was pleased with it all, but when he got used to it he began to think that even here he had not enough land. The first year, he sowed wheat on his share of the Communal land and had a good crop. He wanted to go on sowing wheat, but had not enough Communal land for the purpose, and what he had already used was not available; for in those parts wheat is only sown on virgin soil or on fallow land. It is sown for one or two years, and then the land lies fallow till it is again overgrown with prairie grass. There were many who wanted such land and there was not enough for all; so that people quarreled about it. Those who were better off wanted it for growing wheat, and those who were poor wanted it to let to dealers, so that they might raise money to pay their taxes. Pahóm wanted to sow more wheat, so he rented land from a dealer for a year. He sowed much wheat and had a fine crop, but the land was too far from the village—the wheat had to be carted more than ten miles. After a time Pahóm noticed that some peasant-dealers were living on separate farms and were growing wealthy; and he thought:

"If I were to buy some freehold land and have a homestead on it, it would be a different thing altogether. Then it would all be nice and compact."

40   The question of buying freehold land recurred to him again and again.

He went on in the same way for three years, renting land and sowing wheat. The seasons turned out well and the crops were good, so that he began to lay money by. He might have gone on living contentedly, but he grew tired of having to rent other people's land every year, and having to scramble for it. Wherever there was good land to be had, the peasants would rush for it and it was taken up at once, so that unless you were sharp about it you got none. It happened in the third year that he and a dealer together rented a piece of pasture-land from some peasants; and they had already ploughed it up, when there was some dispute and the peasants went to law about it, and things fell out so that the labor was all lost.

"If it were my own land," thought Pahóm, "I should be independent, and there would not be all this unpleasantness."

So Pahóm began looking out for land which he could buy; and he came across a peasant who had bought thirteen hundred acres, but having got into difficulties was willing to sell again cheap. Pahóm bargained and haggled with him, and at last they settled the price at 1,500 rúbles, part in cash and part to be paid later. They had all but clinched the matter when a passing dealer happened to stop at Pahóm's one day to get a feed for his horses. He drank tea with Pahóm and they had a talk. The dealer said that he was just returning from the land of the Bashkírs,[2] far away, where he had bought thirteen thousand acres of

---

2. Extreme eastern European Russia, extending southwest from the Ural Mountains; the land is chiefly steppes with fertile meadows in the valleys.

land, all for 1,000 rúbles. Pahóm questioned him further, and the tradesman said:

"All one need do is to make friends with the chiefs. I gave away one hundred rúbles' worth of silk robes and carpets, besides a case of tea, and I gave wine to those who would drink it; and I got the land for less than a penny an acre." And he showed Pahóm the title-deeds, saying:

"The land lies near a river, and the whole prairie is virgin soil."

45

Pahóm plied him with questions, and the tradesman said:

"There is more land there than you could cover if you walked a year, and it all belongs to the Bashkírs. They are as simple as sheep, and land can be got almost for nothing."

"There now," thought Pahóm, "with my one thousand rúbles, why should I get only thirteen hundred acres, and saddle myself with a debt besides? If I take it out there, I can get more than ten times as much for the money."

V

Pahóm inquired how to get to the place, and as soon as the tradesman had left him, he prepared to go there himself. He left his wife to look after the homestead, and started on his journey taking his man with him. They stopped at a town on their way and bought a case of tea, some wine, and other presents, as the tradesman had advised. On and on they went until they had gone more than three hundred miles, and on the seventh day they came to a place where the Bashkírs had pitched their tents. It was all just as the tradesman had said. The people lived on the steppes, by a river, in felt-covered tents. They neither tilled the ground, nor ate bread. Their cattle and horses grazed in herds on the steppe. The colts were tethered behind the tents, and the mares were driven to them twice a day. The mares were milked, and from the milk kumiss was made. It was the women who prepared kumiss, and they also made cheese. As far as the men were concerned, drinking kumiss and tea, eating mutton, and playing on their pipes, was all they cared about. They were all stout and merry, and all the summer long they never thought of doing any work. They were quite ignorant, and knew no Russian, but were good-natured enough.

As soon as they saw Pahóm, they came out of their tents and gathered round their visitor. An interpreter was found, and Pahóm told them he had come about some land. The Bashkírs seemed very glad; they took Pahóm and led him into one of the best tents, where they made him sit on some down cushions placed on a carpet, while they sat around him. They gave him some tea and kumiss, and had a sheep killed, and gave him mutton to eat. Pahóm took presents out of his cart and distributed them among the Bashkírs, and divided the tea amongst them. The Bashkírs were delighted. They talked a great deal among themselves, and then told the interpreter to translate.

50

"They wish to tell you," said the interpreter, "that they like you, and that it is our custom to do all we can to please a guest and to repay him for his gifts. You have given us presents, now tell us which of the things we possess please you best, that we may present them to you."

"What pleases me best here," answered Pahóm, "is your land. Our land is crowded and the soil is exhausted; but you have plenty of land and it is good land. I never saw the like of it."

The interpreter translated. The Bashkírs talked among themselves for a while. Pahóm could not understand what they were saying, but saw that they were much amused and that they shouted and laughed. Then they were silent and looked at Pahóm while the interpreter said:

"They wish me to tell you that in return for your presents they will gladly give you as much land as you want. You have only to point it out with your hand and it is yours."

55 The Bashkírs talked again for a while and began to dispute. Pahóm asked what they were disputing about, and the interpreter told him that some of them thought they ought to ask their Chief about the land and not act in his absence, while others thought there was no need to wait for his return.

VI

While the Bashkírs were disputing, a man in a large fox-fur cap appeared on the scene. They all became silent and rose to their feet. The interpreter said, "This is our Chief himself."

Pahóm immediately fetched the best dressing-gown and five pounds of tea, and offered these to the Chief. The Chief accepted them, and seated himself in the place of honor. The Bashkírs at once began telling him something. The Chief listened for a while, then made a sign with his head for them to be silent, and addressing himself to Pahóm, said in Russian:

"Well, let it be so. Choose whatever piece of land you like; we have plenty of it."

"How can I take as much as I like?" thought Pahóm. "I must get a deed to make it secure, or else they may say, 'It is yours,' and afterwards may take it away again."

60 "Thank you for your kind words," he said aloud. "You have much land, and I only want a little. But I should like to be sure which bit is mine. Could it not be measured and made over to me? Life and death are in God's hands. You good people give it to me, but your children might wish to take it away again."

"You are quite right," said the Chief. "We will make it over to you."

"I heard that a dealer had been here," continued Pahóm, "and that you gave him a little land, too, and signed title-deeds to that effect. I should like to have it done in the same way."

The Chief understood.

"Yes," replied he, "that can be done quite easily. We have a scribe, and we will go to town with you and have the deed properly sealed."

65 "And what will be the price?" asked Pahóm.

"Our price is always the same: one thousand rúbles a day."

Pahóm did not understand.

"A day? What measure is that? How many acres would that be?"

"We do not know how to reckon it out," said the Chief. "We sell it by the day. As much as you can go round on your feet in a day is yours, and the price is one thousand rúbles a day."

Pahóm was surprised.

"But in a day you can get round a large tract of land," he said.

The Chief laughed.

"It will all be yours!" said he. "But there is one condition: If you don't return on the same day to the spot whence you started, your money is lost."

"But how am I to mark the way that I have gone?"

"Why, we shall go to any spot you like, and stay there. You must start from that spot and make your round, taking a spade with you. Wherever you think necessary, make a mark. At every turning, dig a hole and pile up the turf; then afterwards we will go round with a plough from hole to hole. You may make as large a circuit as you please, but before the sun sets you must return to the place you started from. All the land you cover will be yours."

Pahóm was delighted. It was decided to start early next morning. They talked a while, and after drinking some more kumiss and eating some more mutton, they had tea again, and then the night came on. They gave Pahóm a feather-bed to sleep on, and the Bashkírs dispersed for the night, promising to assemble the next morning at daybreak and ride out before sunrise to the appointed spot.

VII

Pahóm lay on the feather-bed, but could not sleep. He kept thinking about the land.

"What a large tract I will mark off!" thought he. "I can easily do thirty-five miles in a day. The days are long now, and within a circuit of thirty-five miles what a lot of land there will be! I will sell the poorer land, or let it to peasants, but I'll pick out the best and farm it. I will buy two oxteams, and hire two more laborers. About a hundred and fifty acres shall be plough-land, and I will pasture cattle on the rest."

Pahóm lay awake all night, and dozed off only just before dawn. Hardly were his eyes closed when he had a dream. He thought he was lying in that same tent and heard somebody chuckling outside. He wondered who it could be, and rose and went out, and he saw the Bashkír Chief sitting in front of the tent holding his sides and rolling about with laughter. Going nearer to the Chief, Pahóm asked: "What are you laughing at?" But he saw that it was no longer the Chief, but the dealer who had recently stopped at his house and had told him about the land. Just as Pahóm was going to ask, "Have you been here long?" he saw that it was not the dealer, but the peasant who had come up from the Vólga, long ago, to Pahóm's old home. Then he saw that it was not the peasant either, but the Devil himself with hoofs and horns, sitting there and chuckling, and before him lay a man barefoot, prostrate on the ground, with only trousers and a shirt on. And Pahóm dreamt that he looked more attentively to see what sort of a man it was that was lying there, and he saw that the man was dead, and that it was himself! He awoke horror-struck.

"What things one does dream," thought he.

Looking round he saw through the open door that the dawn was breaking.

"It's time to wake them up," thought he. "We ought to be starting."

He got up, roused his man (who was sleeping in his cart), bade him harness; and went to call the Bashkírs.

"It's time to go to the steppe to measure the land," he said.

The Bashkírs rose and assembled, and the Chief came too. Then they began drinking kumiss again, and offered Pahóm some tea, but he would not wait.

"If we are to go, let us go. It is high time," said he.

VIII

The Bashkírs got ready and they all started: some mounted on horses, and some in carts. Pahóm drove in his own small cart with his servant and took a spade with him. When they reached the steppe, the morning red was beginning to kindle. They ascended a hillock (called by the Bashkírs a *shikhan*) and dismounting from their carts and their horses, gathered in one spot. The Chief came up to Pahóm and stretching out his arms towards the plain:

"See," said he, "all this, as far as your eye can reach, is ours. You may have any part of it you like."

Pahóm's eyes glistened: it was all virgin soil, as flat as the palm of your hand, as black as the seed of a poppy, and in the hollows different kinds of grasses grew breast high.

The Chief took off his fox-fur cap, placed it on the ground and said:

"This will be the mark. Start from here, and return here again. All the land you go round shall be yours."

Pahóm took out his money and put it on the cap. Then he took off his outer coat, remaining in his sleeveless under-coat. He unfastened his girdle and tied it tight below his stomach, put a little bag of bread into the breast of his coat, and tying a flask of water to his girdle, he drew up the tops of his boots, took the spade from his man, and stood ready to start. He considered for some moments which way he had better go—it was tempting everywhere.

"No matter," he concluded, "I will go towards the rising sun."

He turned his face to the east, stretched himself, and waited for the sun to appear above the rim.

"I must lose no time," he thought, "and it is easier walking while it is still cool."

The sun's rays had hardly flashed above the horizon, before Pahóm, carrying the spade over his shoulder, went down into the steppe.

Pahóm started walking neither slowly nor quickly. After having gone a thousand yards he stopped, dug a hole, and placed pieces of turf one on another to make it more visible. Then he went on; and now that he had walked off his stiffness he quickened his pace. After a while he dug another hole.

Pahóm looked back. The hillock could be distinctly seen in the sunlight, with the people on it, and the glittering tires of the cart-wheels. At a rough guess Pahóm concluded that he had walked three miles. It was growing warmer; he took off his under-coat, flung it across his shoulder, and went on again. It had grown quite warm now; he looked at the sun, it was time to think of breakfast.

"The first shift is done, but there are four in a day, and it is too soon yet to turn. but I will just take off my boots," said he to himself.

He sat down, took off his boots, stuck them into his girdle, and went on. It   100
was easy walking now.

"I will go on for another three miles," thought he, "and then turn to the left. This spot is so fine, that it would be a pity to lose it. The further one goes, the better the land seems."

He went straight on for a while, and when he looked round, the hillock was scarcely visible and the people on it looked like black ants, and he could just see something glistening there in the sun.

"Ah," thought Pahóm, "I have gone far enough in this direction, it is time to turn. Besides I am in a regular sweat, and very thirsty."

He stopped, dug a large hole, and heaped up pieces of turf. Next he untied his flask, had a drink, and then turned sharply to the left. He went on and on; the grass was high, and it was very hot.

Pahóm began to grow tired: he looked at the sun and saw that it was noon.   105
"Well," he thought, "I must have a rest."

He sat down, and ate some bread and drank some water; but he did not lie down, thinking that if he did he might fall asleep. After sitting a little while, he went on again. At first he walked easily: the food had strengthened him; but it had become terribly hot and he felt sleepy, still he went on, thinking: "An hour to suffer, a life-time to live."

He went a long way in this direction also, and was about to turn to the left again, when he perceived a damp hollow: "It would be a pity to leave that out," he thought. "Flax would do well there." So he went on past the hollow, and dug a hole on the other side of it before he turned the corner. Pahóm looked towards the hillock. The heat made the air hazy: it seemed to be quivering, and through the haze the people on the hillock could scarcely be seen.

"Ah!" thought Pahóm, "I have made the sides too long; I must make this one shorter." And he went along the third side, stepping faster. He looked at the sun: it was nearly half-way to the horizon, and he had not yet done two miles of the third side of the square. He was still ten miles from the goal.

"No," he thought, "though it will make my land lop-sided, I must hurry back   110
in a straight line now. I might go too far, and as it is I have a great deal of land."

So Pahóm hurriedly dug a hole, and turned straight towards the hillock.

IX

Pahóm went straight towards the hillock, but he now walked with difficulty. He was done up with the heat, his bare feet were cut and bruised, and his legs began to fail. He longed to rest, but it was impossible if he meant to get back before sunset. The sun waits for no man, and it was sinking lower and lower.

"Oh dear," he thought, "if only I have not blundered trying for too much! What if I am too late?"

He looked towards the hillock and at the sun. He was still far from his goal, and the sun was already near the rim.

115   Pahóm walked on and on; it was very hard walking but he went quicker and quicker. He pressed on, but was still far from the place. He began running, threw away his coat, his boots, his flask, and his cap, and kept only the spade which he used as a support.

"What shall I do," he thought again, "I have grasped too much and ruined the whole affair. I can't get there before the sun sets."

And this fear made him still more breathless. Pahóm went on running, his soaking shirt and trousers stuck to him and his mouth was parched. His breast was working like a blacksmith's bellows, his heart was beating like a hammer, and his legs were giving way as if they did not belong to him. Pahóm was seized with terror lest he should die of the strain.

Though afraid of death, he could not stop. "After having run all that way they will call me a fool if I stop now," thought he. And he ran on and on, and drew near and heard the Bashkírs yelling and shouting to him, and their cries inflamed his heart still more. He gathered his last strength and ran on.

The sun was close to the rim, and cloaked in mist looked large, and red as blood. Now, yes now, it was about to set! The sun was quite low, but he was also quite near his aim. Pahóm could already see the people on the hillock waving their arms to hurry him up. He could see the fox-fur cap on the ground and the money on it, and the Chief sitting on the ground holding his sides. And Pahóm remembered his dream.

120   "There is plenty of land," thought he, "but will God let me live on it? I have lost my life, I have lost my life! I shall never reach that spot!"

Pahóm looked at the sun, which had reached the earth: one side of it had already disappeared. With all his remaining strength he rushed on, bending his body forward so that his legs could hardly follow fast enough to keep him from falling. Just as he reached the hillock it suddenly grew dark. He looked up—the sun had already set! He gave a cry: "All my labor has been in vain," thought he, and was about to stop, but he heard the Bashkírs still shouting, and remembered that though to him, from below, the sun seemed to have set, they on the hillock could still see it. He took a long breath and ran up the hillock. It was still light there. He reached the top and saw the cap. Before it sat the Chief laughing and holding his sides. Again Pahóm remembered his dream, and he uttered a cry: his legs gave way beneath him, he fell forward and reached the cap with his hands.

"Ah, that's a fine fellow!" exclaimed the Chief. "He has gained much land!"

Pahóm's servant came running up and tried to raise him, but he saw that blood was flowing from his mouth. Pahóm was dead!

The Bashkírs clicked their tongues to show their pity.

125   His servant picked up the spade and dug a grave long enough for Pahóm to lie in, and buried him in it. Six feet from his head to his heels was all he needed.

1886

KATHERINE MANSFIELD

Her First Ball

Exactly when the ball began Leila would have found it hard to say. Perhaps her first real partner was the cab. It did not matter that she shared the cab with the Sheridan girls and their brother. She sat back in her own little corner of it, and the bolster on which her hand rested felt like the sleeve of an unknown young man's dress suit; and away they bowled, past waltzing lampposts and houses and fences and trees.

"Have you really never been to a ball before, Leila? But, my child, how too weird—" cried the Sheridan girls.

"Our nearest neighbor was fifteen miles," said Leila softly, gently opening and shutting her fan.

Oh, dear, how hard it was to be indifferent like the others! She tried not to smile too much; she tried not to care. But every single thing was so new and exciting . . . Meg's tuberoses, Jose's long loop of amber, Laura's little dark head, pushing above her white fur like a flower through snow. She would remember for ever. It even gave her a pang to see her cousin Laurie throw away the wisps of tissue paper he pulled from the fastening of his new gloves. She would like to have kept those wisps as a keepsake, as a remembrance. Laurie leaned forward and put his hand on Laura's knee.

"Look here, darling," he said. "The third and the ninth as usual, Twig?"   5

Oh, how marvellous to have a brother! In her excitement Leila felt that if there had been time, if it hadn't been impossible, she couldn't have helped crying because she was an only child, and no brother had ever said "Twig?" to her; no sister would ever say, as Meg said to Jose that moment, "I've never known your hair go up more successfully than it has tonight!"

But, of course, there was no time. They were at the drill hall already; there were cabs in front of them and cabs behind. The road was bright on either side with moving fan-like lights, and on the pavement gay couples seemed to float through the air; little satin shoes chased each other like birds.

"Hold on to me, Leila; you'll get lost," said Laura.

"Come on, girls, let's make a dash for it," said Laurie.

Leila put two fingers on Laura's pink velvet cloak, and they were somehow   10
lifted past the big gold lantern, carried along the passage, and pushed into the little room marked "Ladies." Here the crowd was so great there was hardly space to take off their things; the noise was deafening. Two benches on either side were stacked high with wraps. Two old women in white aprons ran up and down tossing fresh armfuls. And everybody was pressing forward trying to get at the little dressing table and mirror at the far end.

A great quivering jet of gas lighted the ladies' room. It couldn't wait; it was dancing already. When the door opened again and there came a burst of tuning from the drill hall, it leaped almost to the ceiling.

Dark girls, fair girls were patting their hair, tying ribbons again, tucking handkerchiefs down the front of their bodices, smoothing marble-white gloves. And because they were all laughing it seemed to Leila that they were all lovely.

"Aren't there any invisible hairpins?" cried a voice. "How most extraordinary! I can't see a single invisible hairpin."

"Powder my back, there's a darling," cried some one else.

15   "But I must have a needle and cotton. I've torn simply miles and miles of the frill," wailed a third.

Then, "Pass them along, pass them along!" The straw basket of programs was tossed from arm to arm. Darling little pink-and-silver programs, with pink pencils and fluffy tassels. Leila's fingers shook as she took one out of the basket. She wanted to ask someone, "Am I meant to have one too?" but she had just time to read: "Waltz 3. *Two, Two in a Canoe*. Polka 4. *Making the Feathers Fly*," when Meg cried, "Ready, Leila?" and they pressed their way through the crush in the passage towards the big double doors of the drill hall.

Dancing had not begun yet, but the band had stopped tuning, and the noise was so great it seemed that when it did begin to play it would never be heard. Leila, pressing close to Meg, looking over Meg's shoulder, felt that even the little quivering colored flags strung across the ceiling were talking. She quite forgot to be shy; she forgot how in the middle of dressing she had sat down on the bed with one shoe off and one shoe on and begged her mother to ring up her cousins and say she couldn't go after all. And the rush of longing she had had to be sitting on the veranda of their forsaken upcountry home, listening to the baby owls crying "More pork" in the moonlight, was changed to a rush of joy so sweet that it was hard to bear alone. She clutched her fan, and, gazing at the gleaming, golden floor, the azaleas, the lanterns, the stage at one end with its red carpet and gilt chairs and the band in a corner, she thought breathlessly, "How heavenly; how simply heavenly!"

All the girls stood grouped together at one side of the doors, the men at the other, and the chaperones in dark dresses, smiling rather foolishly, walked with little careful steps over the polished floor towards the stage.

"This is my little country cousin Leila. Be nice to her. Find her partners; she's under my wing," said Meg, going up to one girl after another.

20   Strange faces smiled at Leila—sweetly, vaguely. Strange voices answered, "Of course, my dear." But Leila felt the girls didn't really see her. They were looking towards the men. Why didn't the men begin? What were they waiting for? There they stood, smoothing their gloves, patting their glossy hair and smiling among themselves. Then, quite suddenly, as if they had only just made up their minds that that was what they had to do, the men came gliding over the parquet. There was a joyful flutter among the girls. A tall, fair man flew up to Meg, seized her program, scribbled something; Meg passed him on to Leila. "May I have the pleasure?" He ducked and smiled. There came a dark man wearing an eyeglass, then cousin Laurie with a friend, and Laura with a little freckled fellow whose tie was crooked. Then quite an old man—fat, with a big bald patch on his head—took her program and murmured, "Let me see, let me see!" And he was a long time comparing his program, which looked black with

names, with hers. It seemed to give him so much trouble that Leila was ashamed. "Oh, please don't bother," she said eagerly. But instead of replying the fat man wrote something, glanced at her again. "Do I remember this bright little face?" he said softly. "Is it known to me of yore?" At that moment the band began playing; the fat man disappeared. He was tossed away on a great wave of music that came flying over the gleaming floor, breaking the groups up into couples, scattering them, sending them spinning. . . .

Leila had learned to dance at boarding school. Every Saturday afternoon the boarders were hurried off to a little corrugated iron mission hall where Miss Eccles (of London) held her "select" classes. But the difference between that dusty-smelling hall—with calico texts on the walls, the poor terrified little woman in a brown velvet toque with rabbit's ears thumping the cold piano, Miss Eccles poking the girls' feet with her long white wand—and this was so tremendous that Leila was sure if her partner didn't come and she had to listen to that marvelous music and to watch the others sliding, gliding over the golden floor, she would die at least, or faint, or lift her arms and fly out of one of those dark windows that showed the stars.

"Ours, I think—" Some one bowed, smiled, and offered her his arm; she hadn't to die after all. Some one's hand pressed her waist, and she floated away like a flower that is tossed into a pool.

"Quite a good floor, isn't it?" drawled a faint voice close to her ear.

"I think it's most beautifully slippery," said Leila.

"Pardon!" The faint voice sounded surprised. Leila said it again. And there was a tiny pause before the voice echoed. "Oh, quite!" and she was swung round again.   25

He steered so beautifully. That was the great difference between dancing with girls and men, Leila decided. Girls banged into each other, and stamped on each other's feet; the girl who was gentleman always clutched you so.

The azaleas were separate flowers no longer; they were pink and white flags streaming by.

"Were you at the Bells' last week?" the voice came again. It sounded tired. Leila wondered whether she ought to ask him if he would like to stop.

"No, this is my first dance," said she.

Her partner gave a little gasping laugh. "Oh, I say," he protested.   30

"Yes, it is really the first dance I've ever been to." Leila was most fervent. It was such a relief to be able to tell somebody. "You see, I've lived in the country all my life up until now. . . ."

At that moment the music stopped, and they went to sit on two chairs against the wall. Leila tucked her pink satin feet under and fanned herself, while she blissfully watched the other couples passing and disappearing through the swing doors.

"Enjoying yourself, Leila?" asked Jose, nodding her golden head.

Laura passed and gave her the faintest little wink; it made Leila wonder for a moment whether she was quite grown up after all. Certainly her partner did not say very much. He coughed, tucked his handkerchief away, pulled down his waistcoat, took a minute thread off his sleeve. But it didn't matter. Almost immediately the band started, and her second partner seemed to spring from the ceiling.

35   "Floor's not bad," said the new voice. Did one always begin with the floor? And then, "Were you at the Neaves' on Tuesday?" And again Leila explained. Perhaps it was a little strange that her partners were not more interested. For it was thrilling. Her first ball! she was only at the beginning of everything. It seemed to her that she had never known what the night was like before. Up till now it had been dark, silent, beautiful very often—oh, yes—but mournful somehow. Solemn. And now it would never be like that again—it had opened dazzling bright.

"Care for an ice?" said her partner. And they went through the swing doors, down the passage, to the supper room. Her cheeks burned, she was fearfully thirsty. How sweet the ices looked on little glass plates, and how cold the frosted spoon was, iced too! And when they came back to the hall there was the fat man waiting for her by the door. It gave her quite a shock again to see how old he was; he ought to have been on the stage with the fathers and mothers. And when Leila compared him with her other partners he looked shabby. His waistcoat was creased, there was a button off his glove, his coat looked as if it was dusty with French chalk.

"Come along, little lady," said the fat man. He scarcely troubled to clasp her, and they moved away so gently, it was more like walking than dancing. But he said not a word about the floor. "Your first dance, isn't it?" he murmured.

"How *did* you know?"

"Ah," said the fat man, "that's what it is to be old!" He wheezed faintly as he steered her past an awkward couple. "You see, I've been doing this kind of thing for the last thirty years."

40   "Thirty years?" cried Leila. Twelve years before she was born!

"It hardly bears thinking about, does it?" said the fat man gloomily. Leila looked at his bald head, and she felt quite sorry for him.

"I think it's marvelous to be still going on," she said kindly.

"Kind little lady," said the fat man, and he pressed her a little closer, and hummed a bar of the waltz. "Of course," he said, "you can't hope to last anything like as long as that. No-o," said the fat man, "long before that you'll be sitting up there on the stage, looking on, in your nice black velvet. And these pretty arms will have turned into little short fat ones, and you'll beat time with such a different kind of fan—a black bony one." The fat man seemed to shudder. "And you'll smile away like the poor old dears up there, and point to your daughter, and tell the elderly lady next to you how some dreadful man tried to kiss her at the club ball. And your heart will ache, ache"—the fat man squeezed her closer still, as if he really was sorry for that poor heart—"because no one wants to kiss you now. And you'll say how unpleasant these polished floors are to walk on, how dangerous they are. Eh, Mademoiselle Twinkletoes?" said the fat man softly.

Leila gave a light little laugh, but she did not feel like laughing. Was it—could it all be true? It sounded terribly true. Was this first ball only the beginning of her last ball after all? At that the music seemed to change; it sounded sad, sad it rose upon a great sigh. Oh, how quickly things changed! Why didn't happiness last for ever? For ever wasn't a bit too long.

"I want to stop," she said in a breathless voice. The fat man led her to the door. 45

"No," she said. "I won't go outside. I won't sit down. I'll just stand here, thank you." She leaned against the wall, tapping with her foot, pulling up her gloves and trying to smile. But deep inside her a little girl threw her pinafore over her head and sobbed. Why had he spoiled it all?

"I say, you know," said the fat man, "you mustn't take me seriously, little lady."

"As if I should!" said Leila, tossing her small dark head and sucking her underlip. . . .

Again the couples paraded. The swing doors opened and shut. Now new music was given out by the bandmaster. But Leila didn't want to dance any more. She wanted to be home, or sitting on the veranda listening to those baby owls. When she looked through the dark windows at the stars, they had long beams like wings. . . .

But presently a soft, melting, ravishing tune began, and a young man with 50 curly hair bowed before her. She would have to dance, out of politeness, until she could find Meg. Very stiffly she walked into the middle; very haughtily she put her hand on his sleeve. But in one minute, in one turn, her feet glided, glided. The lights, the azaleas, the dresses, the pink faces, the velvet chairs, all became one beautiful flying wheel. And when her next partner bumped her into the fat man and he said, "Pardon," she smiled at him more radiantly than ever. She didn't even recognize him again.

1922

ANGELA CARTER

A Souvenir of Japan

When I went outside to see if he was coming home, some children dressed ready for bed in cotton nightgowns were playing with sparklers in the vacant lot on the corner. When the sparks fell down in beards of stars, the smiling children cooed softly. Their pleasure was very pure because it was so restrained. An old woman said: "And so they pestered their father until he bought them fireworks." In their language, fireworks are called *hannabi*, which means "flower fire." All through summer, every evening, you can see all kinds of fireworks, from the humblest to the most elaborate, and once we rode the train out of Shinjuku for an hour to watch one of the public displays which are held over rivers so that the dark water multiplies the reflections.

By the time we arrived at our destination, night had already fallen. We were in the suburbs. Many families were on their way to enjoy the fireworks. Their mothers had scrubbed and dressed up the smallest children to celebrate the treat. The little girls were especially immaculate in pink and white cotton kimonos tied with fluffy sashes like swatches of candy floss. Their hair had been most beautifully brushed, arranged in sleek, twin bunches and decorated with twists of gold and silver thread. These children were all on their best behavior, because they were staying up late, and held their parents' hands with a charming propriety. We followed the family parties until we came to some fields by the river and saw, high in the air, fireworks already opening out like variegated parasols. They were visible from far away and, as we took the path that led through the fields towards their source, they seemed to occupy more and more of the sky.

Along the path were stalls where shirtless cooks with sweatbands round their heads roasted corncobs and cuttlefish over charcoal. We bought cuttlefish on skewers and ate them as we walked along. They had been basted with soy sauce and were very good. There were also stalls selling goldfish in plastic bags and others for big balloons with rabbit ears. It was like a fairground—but such a well-ordered fair! Even the patrolling policemen carried colored paper lanterns instead of torches.[1] Everything was altogether quietly festive. Ice-cream sellers wandered among the crowd, ringing handbells. Their boxes of wares smoked with cold and they called out in plaintive voices, "Icy, icy, icy cream!" When young lovers dispersed discreetly down the tracks in the sedge, the shadowy, indefatigable salesmen pursued them with bells, lamps and mournful cries.

By now, a great many people were walking towards the fireworks but their steps fell so softly and they chatted in such gentle voices there was no more noise than a warm, continual, murmurous humming, the cozy sound of shared happiness, and the night filled with a muted, bourgeois yet authentic magic. Above our heads, the fireworks hung dissolving earrings on the night. Soon we lay down in a stubbled field to watch the fireworks. But, as I expected, he very quickly grew restive.

5 "Are you happy?" he asked. "Are you sure you're happy?" I was watching the fireworks and did not reply at first although I knew how bored he was and, if he was himself enjoying anything, it was only the idea of my pleasure—or, rather, the idea that he enjoyed my pleasure, since this would be a proof of love. I became guilty and suggested we return to the heart of the city. We fought a silent battle of self-abnegation and I won it, for I had the stronger character. Yet the last thing in the world that I wanted was to leave the scintillating river and the gentle crowd. But I knew his real desire was to return and so return we did, although I do not know if it was worth my small victory of selflessness to bear his remorse at cutting short my pleasure, even if to engineer this remorse had, at some subterranean level, been the whole object of the outing.

Nevertheless, as the slow train nosed back into the thickets of neon, his natural liveliness returned. He could not lose his old habit of walking through the streets with a sense of expectation, as if a fateful encounter might be just around the corner, for, the longer one stayed out, the longer something remarkable might happen and, even if nothing ever did, the chance of it appeased the sweet ache of his boredom for a little while. Besides, his duty by me was done. He had taken me out for the evening and now he wanted to be rid of me. Or so

1. Flashlights (British).

I saw it. The word for wife, *okusan*, means the person who occupies the inner room and rarely, if ever, comes out of it. Since I often appeared to be his wife, I was frequently subjected to this treatment, though I fought against it bitterly.

But I usually found myself waiting for him to come home knowing, with a certain resentment, that he would not; and that he would not even telephone me to tell me he would be late, either, for he was far too guilty to do so. I had nothing better to do than to watch the neighborhood children light their sparklers and giggle; the old woman stood beside me and I knew she disapproved of me. The entire street politely disapproved of me. Perhaps they thought I was contributing to the delinquency of a juvenile for he was obviously younger than I. The old woman's back was bowed almost to a circle from carrying, when he was a baby, the father who now supervised the domestic fireworks in his evening *déshabillé* of loose, white, crepe drawers, naked to the waist. Her face had the seamed reserve of the old in this country. It was a neighborhood poignantly rich in old ladies.

At the corner shop, they put an old lady outside on an upturned beer crate each morning, to air. I think she must have been the household grandmother. She was so old she had lapsed almost entirely into a somnolent plant life. She was of neither more nor less significance to herself or to the world than the pot of morning glories which blossomed beside her and perhaps she had less significance than the flowers, which would fade before lunch was ready. They kept her very clean. They covered her pale cotton kimono with a spotless pinafore trimmed with coarse lace and she never dirtied it because she did not move. Now and then, a child came out to comb her hair. Her consciousness was quite beclouded by time and, when I passed by, her rheumy eyes settled upon me always with the same, vague, disinterested wonder, like that of an Eskimo watching a train. When she whispered, *Irrasyaimase*, the shopkeeper's word of welcome, in the ghostliest of whispers, like the rustle of a paper bag, I saw her teeth were rimmed with gold.

The children lit sparklers under a mouse-colored sky and, because of the pollution in the atmosphere, the moon was mauve. The cicadas throbbed and shrieked in the backyards. When I think of this city, I shall always remember the cicadas who whirr relentlessly all through the summer nights, rising to a piercing crescendo in the subfusc dawn. I have heard cicadas even in the busiest streets, though they thrive best in the back alleys, where they ceaselessly emit that scarcely tolerable susurration which is like a shrill intensification of extreme heat.

A year before, on such a throbbing, voluptuous, platitudinous, subtropical night, we had been walking down one of these shady streets together, in and out of the shadows of the willow trees, looking for somewhere to make love. Morning glories climbed the lattices which screened the low, wooden houses, but the darkness hid the tender colors of these flowers, which the Japanese prize because they fade so quickly. He soon found a hotel, for the city is hospitable to lovers. We were shown into a room like a paper box. It contained nothing but a mattress spread on the floor. We lay down immediately and began to kiss one another. Then a maid soundlessly opened the sliding door and, stepping out of her slippers, crept in on stockinged feet, breathing apologies. She carried a tray which contained two cups of tea and a plate of candies. She put the tray down on the matted floor beside us and backed, bowing and apologizing, from the room while our uninterrupted kiss continued. He started to unfasten my shirt and then she came back again. This time, she carried an armful of towels. I was stripped stark naked when she returned for a third time to bring the receipt for his money. She was clearly a most respectable woman and, if she was embarrassed, she did not show it by a single word or gesture.

I learned his name was Taro. In a toy store, I saw one of those books for children with pictures which are cunningly made of paper cut-outs so that, when you turn the page, the picture springs up in the three stylized dimensions of a backdrop in Kabuki. It was the story of Momotaro, who was born from a peach. Before my eyes, the paper peach split open and there was the baby, where the stone should have been. He, too, had the inhuman sweetness of a child born from something other than a mother, a passive, cruel sweetness I did not immediately understand, for it was that of the repressed masochism which, in my country, is usually confined to women.

Sometimes he seemed to possess a curiously unearthly quality when he perched upon the mattress with his knees drawn up beneath his chin in the attitude of a pixie on a doorknocker. At these times, his face seemed somehow both too flat and too large for his elegant body which had such curious, androgynous grace with its svelte, elongated spine, wide shoulders and unusually well developed pectorals, almost like the breasts of a girl approaching puberty. There was a subtle lack of alignment between face and body and he seemed almost goblin, as if he might have borrowed another person's head, as Japanese goblins do, in order to perform some devious trick. These impressions of a weird visitor were fleeting yet haunting. Sometimes, it was possible for me to believe he had practiced an enchantment upon me, as foxes in this country may, for, here, a fox can masquerade as human and at the best of times the high cheekbones gave to his face the aspect of a mask.

His hair was so heavy his neck drooped under its weight and was of a black so deep it turned purple in sunlight. His mouth also was purplish and his blunt, bee-stung lips those of Gauguin's Tahitians. The touch of his skin was as smooth as water as it flows through the fingers. His eyelids were retractable, like those of a cat, and sometimes disappeared completely. I should have liked to have had him embalmed and been able to keep him beside me in a glass coffin, so that I could watch him all the time and he would not have been able to get away from me.

As they say, Japan is a man's country. When I first came to Tokyo, cloth carps fluttered from poles in the gardens of the families fortunate enough to have borne boy children, for it was the time of the annual festival, Boys Day. At least they do not disguise the situation. At least one knows where one is. Our polarity was publicly acknowledged and socially sanctioned. As an example of the use of the word *dewa*, which occasionally means, as far as I can gather, "in," I once found in a textbook a sentence which, when translated, read: "In a society where men dominate, they value women only as the object of men's passions."

If the only conjunction possible to us was that of the death-defying double-somersault of love, it is, perhaps, a better thing to be valued only as an object of passion than never to be valued at all. I had never been so absolutely the mysterious other. I had become a kind of phoenix, a fabulous beast; I was an outlandish jewel. He found me, I think, inexpressibly exotic. But I often felt like a female impersonator in Japan.

In the department store there was a rack of dresses labeled: "For Young and Cute Girls Only." When I looked at them, I felt as gross as Glumdalclitch.[2] I wore men's sandals because they were the only kind that fitted me and, even so, I had to take the largest size. My pink cheeks, blue eyes and blatant yellow hair made of me, in the visual orchestration of this city in which all heads were dark, eyes brown and skin monotone, an instrument which played upon an alien scale. In a sober harmony of subtle plucked instruments and wistful flutes, I blared. I proclaimed myself like in a perpetual fanfare. He was so delicately put together that I thought his skeleton must have the airy elegance of a bird's and I was sometimes afraid that I might smash him. He told me that when he was in bed with me, he felt like a small boat upon a wide, stormy sea.

We pitched our tent in the most unlikely surroundings. We were living in a room furnished only by passion amongst homes of the most astounding respectability. The sounds around us were the swish of brooms upon *tatami* matting and the clatter of demotic Japanese. On all the window ledges, prim flowers bloomed in pots. Every morning, the washing came out on the balconies at seven. Early one morning, I saw a man washing the leaves of his tree. Quilts and mattresses went out to air at eight. The sunlight lay thick enough on these unpaved alleys to lay the dust and somebody always seemed to be practicing Chopin in one or another of the flimsy houses, so lightly glued together from plywood it seemed they were sustained only by willpower. Once I was at home, however, it was as if I occupied the inner room and he did not expect me to go out of it, although it was I who paid the rent.

Yet, when he was away from me, he spent much of the time savoring the most annihilating remorse. But this remorse or regret was the stuff of life to him and out he would go again the next night, or, if I had been particularly angry, he would wait until the night after that. And, even if he fully intended to come back early and had promised me he would do so, circumstances always somehow denied him and once more he would contrive to miss the last train. He and his friends spent their nights in a desultory progression from coffee shop to bar to *pachinko* parlor to coffee shop again, with the radiant aimlessness of the pure existential hero. They were connoisseurs of boredom. They savored the various bouquets of the subtly differentiated boredoms which rose from the long, wasted hours at the dead end of night. When it was time for the first train in the morning, he would go back to the mysteriously deserted, Piranesi[3] perspectives of the station, discolored by dawn, exquisitely tortured by the notion—which

2. In Jonathan Swift's *Gulliver's Travels*, Glumdalclitch is a giantess of Brobdingnag. She is Gulliver's nurse and, though only nine years old, is nearly 40 feet tall.   3. Giambattista Piranesi (1720–1778), Italian printmaker famous for exaggerated (oversized), dramatic, mysterious, almost dreamlike prints of Roman architecture and ruins.

probably contained within it a damped-down spark of hope—that, this time, he might have done something irreparable.

I speak as if he had no secrets from me. Well, then, you must realize that I was suffering from love and I knew him as intimately as I knew my own image in a mirror. In other words, I knew him only in relation to myself. Yet, on those terms, I knew him perfectly. At times, I thought I was inventing him as I went along, however, so you will have to take my word for it that we existed. But I do not want to paint our circumstantial portraits so that we both emerge with enough well-rounded, spuriously detailed actuality that you are forced to believe in us. I do not want to practice such sleight of hand. You must be content only with glimpses of our outlines, as if you had caught sight of our reflections in the looking-glass of somebody else's house as you passed by the window. His name was not Taro. I only called him Taro so that I could use the conceit of the peach boy, because it seemed appropriate.

Speaking of mirrors, the Japanese have a great respect for them and, in old-fashioned inns, one often finds them hooded with fabric covers when not in use. He said: "Mirrors make a room uncozy." I am sure there is more to it than that although they love to be cozy. One must love coziness if one is to live so close together. But, as if in celebration of the thing they feared, they seemed to have made the entire city into a cold hall of mirrors which continually proliferated whole galleries of constantly changing appearances, all marvelous but none tangible. If they did not lock up the real looking-glasses, it would be hard to tell what was real and what was not. Even buildings one had taken for substantial had a trick of disappearing overnight. One morning, we woke to find the house next door reduced to nothing but a heap of sticks and a pile of newspapers neatly tied with string, left out for the garbage collector.

I would not say that he seemed to me to possess the same kind of insubstantiality although his departure usually seemed imminent, until I realized he was as erratic but as inevitable as the weather. If you plan to come and live in Japan, you must be sure you are stoical enough to endure the weather. No, it was not insubstantiality; it was a rhetoric valid only on its own terms. When I listened to his protestations, I was prepared to believe he believed in them, although I knew perfectly well they meant nothing. And that isn't fair. When he made them, he believed in them implicitly. Then, he was utterly consumed by conviction. But his dedication was primarily to the idea of himself in love. This idea seemed to him magnificent, even sublime. He was prepared to die for it, as one of Baudelaire's dandies[4] might have been prepared to kill himself in order to preserve himself in the condition of a work of art, for he wanted to make this experience a masterpiece of experience which absolutely transcended the everyday. And this would annihilate the effects of the cruel drug, boredom, to which he was addicted although, perhaps, the element of boredom which is implicit in an affair so isolated from the real world was its principal appeal for him. But I had

4. Charles Baudelaire (1821–1867), 19th-century French writer who lived a life of excess and debauchery, and took such a lifestyle, the life of a "dandy," as a theme for his infamous poetic work, *Les fleurs du mal (The Flowers of Evil)* (1857).

no means of knowing how far his conviction would take him. And I used to turn over in my mind from time to time the question: how far does a pretense of feeling, maintained with absolute conviction, become authentic?

This country has elevated hypocrisy to the level of the highest style. To look at a samurai, you would not know him for a murderer, or a geisha for a whore. The magnificence of such objects hardly pertains to the human. They live only in a world of icons and there they participate in rituals which transmute life itself to a series of grand gestures, as moving as they are absurd. It was as if they all thought, if we believe in something hard enough, it will come true and, lo and behold! they had and it did. Our street was in essence a slum but, in appearance, it was a little enclave of harmonious quiet and, *mirabile dictu*, it was the appearance which was the reality, because they all behaved so well, kept everything so clean and lived with such rigorous civility. What terrible discipline it takes to live harmoniously. They had crushed all their vigor in order to live harmoniously and now they had the wistful beauty of flowers pressed dry in an enormous book.

But repression does not necessarily give birth only to severe beauties. In its programmed interstices, monstrous passions bloom. They torture trees to make them look more like the formal notion of a tree. They paint amazing pictures on their skins with awl and gouge, sponging away the blood as they go; a tattooed man is a walking masterpiece of remembered pain. They boast the most passionate puppets in the world who mimic love suicides in a stylized fashion, for here there is no such comfortable formula as "happy ever after." And, when I remembered the finale of the puppet tragedies, how the wooden lovers cut their throats together, I felt the beginnings of unease, as if the hieratic imagery of the country might overwhelm me, for his boredom had reached such a degree that he was insulated against everything except the irritation of anguish. If he valued me as an object of passion, he had reduced the word to its root, which derives from the Latin, *patior*, I suffer. He valued me as an instrument which would cause him pain.

So we lived under a disoriented moon which was as angry a purple as if the sky had bruised its eye, and, if we made certain genuine intersections, these only took place in darkness. His contagious conviction that our love was unique and desperate infected me with an anxious sickness; soon we would learn to treat one another with the circumspect tenderness of comrades who are amputees, for we were surrounded by the most moving images of evanescence, fireworks, morning glories, the old, children. But the most moving of these images were the intangible reflections of ourselves we saw in one another's eyes, reflections of nothing but appearances, in a city dedicated to seeming, and, try as we might to possess the essence of each other's otherness, we would inevitably fail.

1974

▼   ▼   ▼

THEME A Glossary

allusion: reference in a story to history, the Bible, literature, painting, music, and so on, that suggests the meaning or generalized relevance of details in the story

message: a misleading term for *theme,* or the central idea or statement of a story, misleading because it suggests a simple, packaged statement that preexists and for the simple communication of which the story is written

parable: a short fiction that illustrates an explicit moral lesson

plot summary: a description of the arrangement of the action in the order in which it actually appears in a story; the term is popularly used to mean the description of the history, or chronological order, of the action as it would have appeared in reality. It is important to indicate exactly in which sense you are using the term

subject: the concrete and literal description of what a story is about

theme: a generalized, abstract paraphrase of the inferred central or dominant idea of a story

QUESTIONS

1. How much land *does* a man—or woman—need? What do you mean by "need"?

2. Leila, in "Her First Ball," soon shakes off the gloomy thoughts offered her by her older partner. Is she just an empty-headed girl too shallow to think of serious things, or is she just young and healthy, enjoying life?

3. "A Souvenir of Japan" is at once, a love story, an analysis of Japanese culture as seen by an outsider, and a questioning of the nature of feelings and perception—are they "real" or constructed? The third sentence of the story sets up its subtleties, twists, paradoxes: "[The children's] pleasure was very pure because it was so restrained." Go through the story and find several instances of such arresting, puzzling statements. How does paragraph 18, in which the narrator analyzes how she is telling the story, relate to the theme? How do the fireworks of the first paragraph relate to the theme?

WRITING SUGGESTIONS

1. Compare Hawthorne's and Tolstoy's devils, their disguises, and how they function, and analyze what these figures imply about God and virtue in the two stories.

2. Land works well as a symbol of material wealth and as a symbol of the vanity of human wishes, the inevitable end of life, and therefore of the need for spiritual values. "How Many BMWs Does a Man Need" does not quite make it (but you could try a parody along those lines). Can you find a contemporary symbol that can work the way land does for Tolstoy? If you can, write an imitation or parody, calling it, perhaps, "How Much —— Does a Person Need?"

3. Rewrite "Her First Ball" using another focus and voice.

4. Write a narrative or an essay on one of the provocative phrases or sentences in "A Souvenir of Japan," such as "he . . . had the inhuman sweetness of a child born from something other than a mother, a passive, cruel sweetness I did not immediately understand, for it was that of the repressed maochism which, in my country, is usually confined to women" (par. 11); "how far does a pretense of feeling, maintained with absolute conviction, become authentic?" (par. 20); "soon we would learn to treat one another with the circumspect tenderness of comrades who are amputees" (par. 23).

7 THE WHOLE TEXT

> I feel that discussing story-writing in terms of plot, character,
> and theme is like trying to describe the expression on a face by
> saying where the eyes, nose, and mouth are.
> —FLANNERY O'CONNOR, "Writing Short Stories"

Plot, point of view, character, symbol, and theme are useful concepts. But they do not really exist as discrete parts or constituents of a finished work. In "How Much Land Does a Man Need?", for example, Pahóm's greed is a constituent both of his character and of the story's theme.

Analyzing a story means breaking it down into pieces we can handle. Analyzing may require talking or writing about a story in terms of its "elements," but we must remain aware of the arbitrariness of those distinctions and of the inextricable, organic integrity of the story itself. As you read the stories that follow in this chapter, apply all that you have learned about the history, the structure, and the elements of fiction, but be especially alert as to how the elements interact. Notice how after taking it apart in order to analyze it, we can put the story back together.

JOSEPH CONRAD

The Secret Sharer

I

On my right hand there were lines of fishing-stakes resembling a mysterious system of half-submerged bamboo fences, incomprehensible in its division of the domain of tropical fishes, and crazy[1] of aspect as if abandoned for ever by some nomad tribe of fishermen now gone to the other end of the ocean; for there was no sign of human habitation as far as the eye could reach. To the left a group of barren islets, suggesting ruins of stone walls, towers, and blockhouses, had its foundations set in a blue sea that itself looked solid, so still and stable did it lie below my feet; even the track of light from the westering sun shone smoothly, without that animated glitter which tells of an imperceptible ripple.

1. Irregular, rickety.

And when I turned my head to take a parting glance at the tug which had just left us anchored outside the bar, I saw the straight line of the flat shore joined to the stable sea, edge to edge, with a perfect and unmarked closeness, in one leveled floor half brown, half blue under the enormous dome of the sky. Corresponding in their insignificance to the islets of the sea, two small clumps of trees, one on each side of the only fault in the impeccable joint, marked the mouth of the river Meinam[2] we had just left on the first preparatory stage of our homeward journey; and, far back on the inland level, a larger and loftier mass, the grove surrounding the great Paknam pagoda, was the only thing on which the eye could rest from the vain task of exploring the monotonous sweep of the horizon. Here and there gleams as of a few scattered pieces of silver marked the windings of the great river; and on the nearest of them, just within the bar, the tug steaming right into the land became lost to my sight, hull and funnel and masts, as though the impassive earth had swallowed her up without an effort, without a tremor. My eye followed the light cloud of her smoke, now here, now there, above the plain, according to the devious curves of the stream, but always fainter and farther away, till I lost it at last behind the mitre-shaped hill of the great pagoda. And then I was left alone with my ship, anchored at the head of the Gulf of Siam.

She floated at the starting-point of a long journey, very still in an immense stillness, the shadows of her spars flung far to the eastward by the setting sun. At that moment I was alone on her decks. There was not a sound in her—and around us nothing moved, nothing lived, not a canoe on the water, not a bird in the air, not a cloud in the sky. In this breathless pause at the threshold of a long passage we seemed to be measuring our fitness for a long and arduous enterprise, the appointed task of both our existences to be carried out, far from all human eyes, with only sky and sea for spectators and for judges.

There must have been some glare in the air to interfere with one's sight, because it was only just before the sun left us that my roaming eyes made out beyond the highest ridge of the principal islet of the group something which did away with the solemnity of perfect solitude. The tide of darkness flowed on swiftly; and with tropical suddenness a swarm of stars came out above the shadowy earth, while I lingered yet, my hand resting lightly on my ship's rail as if on the shoulder of a trusted friend. But, with all that multitude of celestial bodies staring down at one, the comfort of quiet communion with her was gone for good. And there were also disturbing sounds by this time—voices, footsteps forward; the steward flitted along the main deck, a busily ministering spirit; a hand-bell tinkled urgently under the poop deck. . . .

I found my two officers waiting for me near the supper table, in the lighted cuddy. We sat down at once, and as I helped the chief mate, I said:

"Are you aware that there is a ship anchored inside the islands? I saw her mast-heads above the ridge as the sun went down."

He raised sharply his simple face, overcharged by a terrible growth of

5

2. The Menan (Chao Phraya) runs through Bangkok, Thailand, into the Gulf of Siam. The Paknam Pagoda stands at the mouth of the river.

whisker, and emitted his usual ejaculations, "Bless my soul, sir! You don't say so!"

My second mate was a round-cheeked, silent young man, grave beyond his years, I thought; but as our eyes happened to meet I detected a slight quiver on his lips. I looked down at once. It was not my part to encourage sneering on board my ship. It must be said, too, that I knew very little of my officers. In consequence of certain events of no particular significance, except to myself, I had been appointed to the command only a fortnight before. Neither did I know much of the hands forward. All these people had been together for eighteen months or so, and my position was that of the only stranger on board. I mention this because it has some bearing on what is to follow. But what I felt most was my being a stranger to the ship; and if all the truth must be told, I was somewhat of a stranger to myself. The youngest man on board (barring the second mate), and untried as yet by a position of the fullest responsibility, I was willing to take the adequacy of the others for granted. They had simply to be equal to their tasks; but I wondered how far I should turn out faithful to that ideal conception of one's own personality every man sets up for himself secretly.

Meantime the chief mate, with an almost visible effect of collaboration on the part of his round eyes and frightful whiskers, was trying to evolve a theory of the anchored ship. His dominant trait was to take all things into earnest consideration. He was of a painstaking turn of mind. As he used to say, he "liked to account to himself" for practically everything that came in his way, down to a miserable scorpion he had found in his cabin a week before. The why and the wherefore of that scorpion—how it got on board and came to select his room rather than the pantry (which was a dark place and more what a scorpion would be partial to), and how on earth it managed to drown itself in the inkwell of his writing-desk—had exercised him infinitely. The ship within the islands was much more easily accounted for; and just as we were about to rise from table he made his pronouncement. She was, he doubted not, a ship from home lately arrived. Probably she drew too much water to cross the bar except at the top of spring tides. Therefore she went into that natural harbor to wait for a few days in preference to remaining in an open roadstead.

"That's so," confirmed the second mate suddenly, in his slightly hoarse voice. "She draws over twenty feet. She's the Liverpool ship *Sephora* with a cargo of coal. Hundred and twenty-three days from Cardiff."

We looked at him in surprise.

"The tugboat skipper told me when he come on board for your letters, sir," explained the young man. "He expects to take her up the river the day after tomorrow."

After thus overwhelming us with the extent of his information he slipped out of the cabin. The mate observed regretfully that he "could not account for that young fellow's whims." What prevented him telling us all about it at once, he wanted to know.

I detained him as he was making a move. For the last two days the crew had had plenty of hard work, and the night before they had very little sleep. I felt painfully that I—a stranger—was doing something unusual when I directed him to let all hands turn in without setting an anchor-watch.[3] I proposed to keep on deck myself till one o'clock or thereabouts. I would get the second mate to relieve me at that hour.

"He will turn out the cook and the steward at four," I concluded, "and then give you a call. Of course at the slightest sign of any sort of wind we'll have the hands up and make a start at once."

He concealed his astonishment. "Very well, sir." Outside the cuddy he put his head in the second mate's door to inform him of my unheard-of caprice to take a five hours' anchor-watch on myself. I heard the other raise his voice incredulously—"What? The captain himself?" Then a few more murmurs, a door closed, then another. A few moments later I went on deck.

15

My strangeness, which had made me sleepless, had prompted that unconventional arrangement, as if I had expected in those solitary hours of the night to get on terms with the ship of which I knew nothing, manned by men of whom I knew very little more. Fast alongside a wharf, littered like any ship in port with a tangle of unrelated things, invaded by unrelated shore people, I had hardly seen her yet properly. Now, as she lay cleared for sea, the stretch of her main deck seemed to me very fine under the stars. Very fine, very roomy for her size, and very inviting. I descended the poop and paced the waist, my mind picturing to myself the coming passage through the Malay Archipelago, down the Indian Ocean, and up the Atlantic. All its phases were familiar enough to me, every characteristic, all the alternatives which were likely to face me on the high seas—everything! . . . except the novel responsibility of command. But I took heart from the reasonable thought that the ship was like other ships, the men like other men, and that the sea was not likely to keep any special surprises expressly for my discomfiture.

Arrived at that comforting conclusion, I bethought myself of a cigar and went below to get it. All was still down there. Everybody at the after end of the ship was sleeping profoundly. I came out again on the quarter-deck, agreeably at ease in my sleeping suit on that warm, breathless night, barefooted, a glowing cigar in my teeth, and, going forward, I was met by the profound silence of the fore end of the ship. Only as I passed the door of the forecastle I heard a deep, quiet, trustful sigh of some sleeper inside. And suddenly I rejoiced in the great security of the sea as compared with the unrest of the land, in my choice of that untempted life presenting no disquieting problems, invested with an elementary moral beauty by the absolute straightforwardness of its appeal and by the singleness of its purpose.

The riding-light[4] in the fore-rigging burned with a clear, untroubled, as if symbolic, flame, confident and bright in the mysterious shades of the night. Passing on my way aft along the other side of the ship, I observed that the rope side-ladder, put over, no doubt, for the master of the tug when he came to fetch away our letters, had not been hauled in as it should have been. I became annoyed at this, for exactitude in small matters is the very soul of discipline.

3. A detachment of seamen kept on deck while the ship lies at anchor.   4. Special light displayed by ship while ("riding") at anchor.

Then I reflected that I had myself peremptorily dismissed my officers from duty, and by my own act had prevented the anchor-watch being formally set and things properly attended to. I asked myself whether it was wise ever to interfere with the established routine of duties even from the kindest of motives. My action might have made me appear eccentric. Goodness only knew how that absurdly whiskered mate would "account" for my conduct, and what the whole ship thought of that informality of their new captain. I was vexed with myself.

Not from compunction certainly, but, as it were mechanically, I proceeded to get the ladder in myself. Now a side-ladder of that sort is a light affair and comes in easily, yet my vigorous tug, which should have brought it flying on board, merely recoiled upon my body in a totally unexpected jerk. What the devil! . . . I was so astounded by the immovableness of that ladder that I remained stockstill, trying to account for it to myself like that imbecile mate of mine. In the end, of course, I put my head over the rail.

20   The side of the ship made an opaque belt of shadow on the darkling glassy shimmer of the sea. But I saw at once something elongated and pale floating very close to the ladder. Before I could form a guess a faint flash of phosphorescent light, which seemed to issue suddenly from the naked body of a man, flickered in the sleeping water with the elusive, silent play of summer lightning in a night sky. With a gasp I saw revealed to my stare a pair of feet, the long legs, a broad livid back immersed right up to the neck in a greenish cadaverous glow. One hand, awash, clutched the bottom rung of the ladder. He was complete but for the head. A headless corpse! The cigar dropped out of my gaping mouth with a tiny plop and a short hiss quite audible in the absolute stillness of all things under heaven. At that I suppose he raised up his face, a dimly pale oval in the shadow of the ship's side. But even then I could only barely make out down there the shape of his black-haired head. However, it was enough for the horrid, frost-bound sensation which had gripped me about the chest to pass off. The moment of vain exclamations was past too. I only climbed on the spare spar and leaned over the rail as far as I could, to bring my eyes nearer to that mystery floating alongside.

As he hung by the ladder, like a resting swimmer, the sea-lightning played about his limbs at every stir; and he appeared in it ghastly, silvery, fish-like. He remained as mute as a fish, too. He made no motion to get out of the water, either. It was inconceivable that he should not attempt to come on board, and strangely troubling to suspect that perhaps he did not want to. And my first words were prompted by just that troubled incertitude.

"What's the matter?" I asked in my ordinary tone, speaking down to the face upturned exactly under mine.

"Cramp," it answered, no louder. Then slightly anxious, "I say, no need to call any one."

25   "I was not going to," I said.

"Are you alone on deck?"

"Yes."

I had somehow the impression that he was on the point of letting go the ladder to swim away beyond my ken—mysterious as he came. But, for the moment, this being appearing as if he had risen from the bottom of the sea (it was certainly the nearest land to the ship) wanted only to know the time. I told him. And he, down there, tentatively:

"I suppose your captain's turned in?"   30

"I am sure he isn't," I said.

He seemed to struggle with himself, for I heard something like the low, bitter murmur of doubt. "What's the good?" His next words came out with a hesitating effort.

"Look here, my man. Could you call him out quietly?"

I thought the time had come to declare myself.

"I am the captain."

I heard a "By Jove!" whispered at the level of the water. The phosphores-   35
cence flashed in the swirl of the water all about his limbs, his other hand seized the ladder.

"My name's Leggatt."

The voice was calm and resolute. A good voice. The self-possession of that man had somehow induced a corresponding state in myself. It was very quietly that I remarked:

"You must be a good swimmer."

"Yes. I've been in the water practically since nine o'clock. The question for me now is whether I am to let go this ladder and go on swimming till I sink from exhaustion or—to come on board here."

I felt this was no mere formula of desperate speech, but a real alternative in   40
the view of a strong soul. I should have gathered from this that he was young; indeed, it is only the young who are ever confronted by such clear issues. But at the time it was pure intuition on my part. A mysterious communication was established already between us two—in the face of that silent, darkened tropical sea. I was young, too; young enough to make no comment. The man in the water began suddenly to climb up the ladder, and I hastened away from the rail to fetch some clothes.

Before entering the cabin I stood still, listening in the lobby at the foot of the stairs. A faint snore came through the closed door of the chief mate's room. The second mate's door was on the hook, but the darkness in there was abso-lutely soundless. He, too, was young and could sleep like a stone. Remained the steward, but he was not likely to wake up before he was called. I got a sleeping suit out of my room, and, coming back on deck, saw the naked man from the sea sitting on the main-hatch, glimmering white in the darkness, his elbows on his knees and his head in his hands. In a moment he had concealed his damp body in a sleeping suit of the same gray-stripe pattern as the one I was wearing, and followed me like my double on the poop. Together we moved right aft, barefooted, silent.

"What is it?" I asked in a deadened voice, taking the lighted lamp out of the binnacle, and raising it to his face.

"An ugly business."

He had rather regular features; a good mouth; light eyes under somewhat heavy, dark eyebrows; a smooth, square forehead; no growth on his cheeks; a small, brown mustache, and a well-shaped, round chin. His expression was concentrated, meditative, under the inspecting light of the lamp I held up to his face; such as a man thinking hard in solitude might wear. My sleeping suit was just right for his size. A well-knit young fellow of twenty-five at most. He caught his lower lip with the edge of white, even teeth.

"Yes," I said, replacing the lamp in the binnacle. The warm, heavy tropical night closed upon his head again.

"There's a ship over there," he murmured.

"Yes, I know. The *Sephora*. Did you know of us?"

"Hadn't the slightest idea. I am the mate of her—" He paused and corrected himself. "I should say I *was*."

"Aha! Something wrong?"

"Yes. Very wrong indeed. I've killed a man."

"What do you mean? Just now?"

"No, on the passage. Weeks ago. Thirty-nine south. When I say a man—"

"Fit of temper," I suggested confidently.

The shadowy, dark head, like mine, seemed to nod imperceptibly above the ghostly gray of my sleeping suit. It was, in the night, as though I had been faced by my own reflection in the depths of a sombre and immense mirror.

"A pretty thing to have to own up to for a Conway[5] boy," murmured my double distinctly.

"You're a Conway boy?"

"I am," he said, as if startled. Then, slowly . . . "Perhaps you too . . ."

It was so; but being a couple of years older I had left before he joined. After a quick interchange of dates a silence fell; and I thought suddenly of my absurd mate with his terrific whiskers and the "Bless my soul—you don't say so" type of intellect. My double gave me an inkling of his thoughts by saying:

"My father's a parson in Norfolk. Do you see me before a judge and jury on that charge? For myself I can't see the necessity. There are fellows that an angel from heaven—And I am not that. He was one of those creatures that are just simmering all the time with a silly sort of wickedness. Miserable devils that have no business to live at all. He wouldn't do his duty and wouldn't let anybody else do theirs. But what's the good of talking! You know well enough the sort of ill-conditioned snarling cur . . ."

He appealed to me as if our experiences had been as identical as our clothes. And I knew well enough the pestiferous danger of such a character where there are no means of legal repression. And I knew well enough also that my double there was no homicidal ruffian. I did not think of asking him for details, and he told me the story roughly in brusque, disconnected sentences. I needed no more. I saw it all going on as though I were myself inside that other sleeping suit.

"It happened while we were setting a reefed foresail, at dusk. Reefed foresail! You understand the sort of weather. The only sail we had left to keep the ship running; so you may guess what it had been like for days. Anxious sort of job,

5. The wooden battleship *Conway*, which was used to train young officers for the Royal Navy and merchant service.

that. He gave me some of his cursed insolence at the sheet.[6] I tell you I was overdone with this terrific weather that seemed to have no end to it. Terrific, I tell you—and a deep ship. I believe the fellow himself was half crazed with funk. It was no time for gentlemanly reproof, so I turned round and felled him like an ox. He up and at me. We closed just as an awful sea made for the ship. All hands saw it coming and took to the rigging, but I had him by the throat, and went on shaking him like a rat, the men above us yelling. 'Look out! Look out!' Then a crash as if the sky had fallen on my head. They say that for over ten minutes hardly anything was to be seen of the ship—just the three masts and a bit of the forecastle head and of the poop all awash driving along in a smother of foam. It was a miracle that they found us, jammed together behind the forebits. It's clear that I meant business, because I was holding him by the throat still when they picked us up. He was black in the face. It was too much for them. It seems they rushed us aft together, gripped as we were, screaming 'Murder!' like a lot of lunatics, and broke into the cuddy. And the ship running for her life, touch and go all the time, any minute her last in a sea fit to turn your hair gray only a-looking at it. I understand that the skipper, too, started raving like the rest of them. The man had been deprived of sleep for more than a week, and to have this spring on him at the height of a furious gale nearly drove him out of his mind. I wonder they didn't fling me overboard after getting the carcass of their precious shipmate out of my fingers. They had rather a job to separate us, I've been told. A sufficiently fierce story to make an old judge and a respectable jury sit up a bit. The first thing I heard when I came to myself was the maddening howling of that endless gale, and on that the voice of the old man. He was hanging on to my bunk, staring into my face out of his sou'wester.

" 'Mr. Leggatt, you have killed a man. You can act no longer as chief mate of this ship.' "

His care to subdue his voice made it sound monotonous. He rested a hand on the end of the skylight to steady himself with, and all that time did not stir a limb, so far as I could see. "Nice little tale for a quiet tea party," he concluded in the same tone.

One of my hands, too, rested on the end of the skylight; neither did I stir a limb, so far as I knew. We stood less than a foot from each other. It occurred to me that if old "Bless my soul—you don't say so" were to put his head up the companion and catch sight of us, he would think he was seeing double, or imagine himself come upon a scene of weird witchcraft: the strange captain having a quiet confabulation by the wheel with his own gray ghost. I became very much concerned to prevent anything of the sort. I heard the other's soothing undertone:

"My father's a parson in Norfolk," it said. Evidently he had forgotten he had told me this important fact before. Truly a nice little tale.

"You had better slip down into my stateroom now," I said, moving off stealthily. My double followed my movements; our bare feet made no sound; I let him

65

6. Rope or chain attached to lower corner of sail used for shortening or slackening it.

in, closed the door with care, and, after giving a call to the second mate, returned on deck for my relief.

"Not much sign of any wind yet," I remarked when he approached.

"No, sir. Not much," he assented sleepily in his hoarse voice, with just enough deference, no more, and barely suppressing a yawn.

"Well, that's all you have to look out for. You have got your orders."

"Yes, sir."

I paced a turn or two on the poop and saw him take up his position face forward with his elbow in the ratlines of the mizzen-rigging before I went below. The mate's faint snoring was still going on peacefully. The cuddy lamp was burning over the table on which stood a vase with flowers, a polite attention from the ship's provision merchant—the last flowers we should see for the next three months at the very least. Two bunches of bananas hung from the beam symmetrically, one on each side of the rudder-casing. Everything was as before in the ship—except that two of her captain's sleeping suits were simultaneously in use, one motionless in the cuddy, the other keeping very still in the captain's stateroom.

It must be explained here that my cabin had the form of the capital letter L, the door being within the angle and opening into the short part of the letter. A couch was to the left, the bedplace to the right; my writing-desk and the chronometers' table faced the door. But any one opening it, unless he stepped right inside, had no view of what I call the long (or vertical) part of the letter. It contained some lockers surmounted by a bookcase; and a few clothes, a thick jacket or two, caps, oilskin coat, and such-like, hung on hooks. There was at the bottom of that part a door opening into my bathroom, which could be entered also directly from the saloon. But that way was never used.

The mysterious arrival had discovered the advantage of this particular shape. Entering my room, lighted strongly by a big bulkhead lamp swung on gimbals above my writing-desk, I did not see him anywhere till he stepped out quietly from behind the coats hung in the recessed part.

"I heard somebody moving about, and went in there at once," he whispered. I, too, spoke under my breath.

"Nobody is likely to come in here without knocking and getting permission."

He nodded. His face was thin and the sunburn faded, as though he had been ill. And no wonder. He had been, I heard presently, kept under arrest in his cabin for nearly nine weeks. But there was nothing sickly in his eyes or in his expression. He was not a bit like me, really; yet, as we stood leaning over my bedplace, whispering side by side, with our dark heads together and our backs to the door, anybody bold enough to open it stealthily would have been treated to the uncanny sight of a double captain busy talking in whispers with his other self.

"But all this doesn't tell me how you came to hang on to our side-ladder," I inquired, in the hardly audible murmurs we used, after he had told me something more of the proceedings on board the *Sephora* once the bad weather was over.

"When we sighted Java Head[7] I had had time to think all those matters out several times over. I had six weeks of doing nothing else, and with only an hour or so every evening for a tramp on the quarterdeck."

He whispered, his arms folded on the side of my bedplace, staring through the open port. And I could imagine perfectly the manner of this thinking out— a stubborn if not a steadfast operation; something of which I should have been perfectly incapable.

"I reckoned it would be dark before we closed with the land," he continued, so low that I had to strain my hearing, near as we were to each other, shoulder touching shoulder almost. "So I asked to speak to the old man. He always seemed very sick when he came to see me—as if he could not look me in the face. You know, that foresail saved the ship. She was too deep to have run long under bare poles. And it was I that managed to set it for him. Anyway, he came. When I had him in my cabin—he stood by the door looking at me as if I had the halter round my neck already—I asked him right away to leave my cabin door unlocked at night while the ship was going through Sunda Straits. There would be the Java coast within two or three miles, off Anjer Point. I wanted nothing more. I've had a prize for swimming my second year in the Conway."

"I can believe it," I breathed out.

"God only knows why they locked me in every night. To see some of their faces you'd have thought they were afraid I'd go about at night strangling people. Am I a murdering brute? Do I look it? By Jove! if I had been he wouldn't have trusted himself like that into my room. You'll say I might have chucked him aside and bolted out, there and then—it was dark already. Well, no. And for the same reason I wouldn't think of trying to smash the door. There would have been a rush to stop me at the noise, and I did not mean to get into a confounded scrimmage. Somebody else might have got killed—for I would not have broken out only to get chucked back, and I did not want any more of that work. He refused, looking more sick than ever. He was afraid of the men, and also of that old second mate of his who had been sailing with him for years—a gray-headed old humbug; and his steward, too, had been with him devil knows how long— seventeen years or more—a dogmatic sort of loafer who hated me like poison, just because I was the chief mate. No chief mate ever made more than one voyage in the *Sephora*, you know. Those two old chaps ran the ship. Devil only knows what the skipper wasn't afraid of (all his nerve went to pieces altogether in that hellish spell of bad weather we had)—of what the law would do to him— of his wife, perhaps. Oh yes! she's on board. Though I don't think she would have meddled. She would have been only too glad to have me out of the ship in any way. The 'brand of Cain'[8] business, don't you see? That's all right. I was ready enough to go off wandering on the face of the earth—and that was price enough to pay for an Abel of that sort. Anyhow, he wouldn't listen to me. 'This

7. A famous landmark for clipper ships engaged in the China trade on the western end of Java, the southern entrance to the Sunda Straits mentioned below; the killing thus took place some 1,500 miles south of the present scene.   8. Genesis 4:14–15.

thing must take its course. I represent the law here.' He was shaking like a leaf. 'So you won't?' 'No!' 'Then I hope you will be able to sleep on that," I said, and turned my back on him. 'I wonder that *you* can,' cries he, and locks the door.

"Well, after that, I couldn't. Not very well. That was three weeks ago. We have had a slow passage through the Java Sea; drifted about Carimata[9] for ten days. When we anchored here they thought, I suppose, it was all right. The nearest land (and that's five miles) is the ship's destination; the consul would soon set about catching me; and there would have been no object in bolting to these islets there. I don't suppose there's a drop of water on them. I don't know how it was, but tonight that steward, after bringing me my supper, went out to let me eat it, and left the door unlocked. And I ate it—all there was, too. After I had finished I strolled out on the quarterdeck. I don't know that I meant to do anything. A breath of fresh air was all I wanted, I believe. Then a sudden temptation came over me. I kicked off my slippers and was in the water before I had made up my mind fairly. Somebody heard the splash and they raised an awful hullabaloo. 'He's gone! Lower the boats! He's committed suicide! No, he's swimming.' Certainly I was swimming. It's not easy for a swimmer like me to commit suicide by drowning. I landed on the nearest islet before the boat left the ship's side. I heard them pulling about in the dark, hailing, and so on, but after a bit they gave up. Everything quieted down and the anchorage became as still as death. I sat down on a stone and began to think. I felt certain they would start searching for me at daylight. There was no place to hide on those stony things—and if there had been, what would have been the good? But now I was clear of that ship I was not going back. So after a while I took off all my clothes, tied them up in a bundle with a stone inside, and dropped them in the deep water on the outer side of that islet. That was suicide enough for me. Let them think what they liked, but I didn't mean to drown myself. I meant to swim till I sank—but that's not the same thing. I struck out for another of these little islands, and it was from that one that I first saw your riding-light. Something to swim for. I went on easily, and on the way I came upon a flat rock a foot or two above water. In the daytime, I dare say, you might make it out with a glass from your poop. I scrambled up on it and rested myself for a bit. Then I made another start. That last spell must have been over a mile."

85 His whisper was getting fainter and fainter, and all the time he stared straight out through the porthole, in which there was not even a star to be seen. I had not interrupted him. There was something that made comment impossible, in his narrative, or perhaps in himself; a sort of feeling, a quality, which I can't find a name for. And when he ceased, all I found was a futile whisper, "So you swam for our light?"

"Yes—straight for it. It was something to swim for. I couldn't see any stars low down because the coast was in the way, and I couldn't see the land, either. The water was like glass. One might have been swimming in a confounded thousand feet deep cistern with no place for scrambling out anywhere; but what

---

9. The Karimata Islands in the straits between Borneo and Sumatra, some 300 miles northeast of the Sunda Straits.

I didn't like was the notion of swimming round and round like a crazed bullock before I gave out; and as I didn't mean to go back . . . No. Do you see me being hauled back, stark naked, off one of these little islands by the scruff of the neck and fighting like a wild beast? Somebody would have got killed for certain, and I did not want any of that. So I went on. Then your ladder—"

"Why didn't you hail the ship?" I asked, a little louder.

He touched my shoulder lightly. Lazy footsteps came right over our heads and stopped. The second mate had crossed from the other side of the poop and might have been hanging over the rail, for all we knew.

"He couldn't hear us talking—could he?" My double breathed into my very ear anxiously.

His anxiety was an answer, a sufficient answer, to the question I had put to him. An answer containing all the difficulty of that situation. I closed the port-hole quietly, to make sure. A louder word might have been overheard.

"Who's that?" he whispered then.

"My second mate. But I don't know much more of the fellow than you do."

And I told him a little about myself. I had been appointed to take charge while I least expected anything of the sort, not quite a fortnight ago. I didn't know either the ship or the people. Hadn't had the time in port to look about me or size anybody up. And as to the crew, all they knew was that I was appointed to take the ship home. For the rest, I was almost as much of a stranger on board as himself, I said. And at the moment I felt it most acutely. I felt that it would take very little to make me a suspect person in the eyes of the ship's company.

He had turned about meantime; and we, the two strangers in the ship, faced each other in identical attitudes.

"Your ladder—" he murmured, after a silence. "Who'd have thought of finding a ladder hanging over at night in a ship anchored out here! I felt just then a very unpleasant faintness. After the life I've been leading for nine weeks, anybody would have got out of condition. I wasn't capable of swimming round as far as your rudder-chains. And, lo and behold! there was a ladder to get hold of. After I gripped it I said to myself, 'What's the good?' When I saw a man's head looking over I thought I would swim away presently and leave him shouting— in whatever language it was. I didn't mind being looked at. I—I liked it. And then you speaking to me so quietly—as if you had expected me—made me hold on a little longer. It had been a confounded lonely time—I don't mean while swimming. I was glad to talk a little to somebody that didn't belong to the *Sephora*. As to asking for the captain, that was a mere impulse. It could have been no use, with all the ship knowing about me and the other people pretty certain to be round here in the morning. I don't know—I wanted to be seen, to talk with somebody, before I went on. I don't know what I would have said. . . . 'Fine night, isn't it?' or something of the sort."

"Do you think they will be round here presently?" I asked, with some incredulity.

"Quite likely," he said faintly.

He looked extremely haggard all of a sudden. His head rolled on his shoulders.

"H'm. We shall see then. Meantime get into that bed," I whispered. "Want help? There."

100   It was a rather high bedplace with a set of drawers underneath. This amazing swimmer really needed the lift I gave him by seizing his leg. He tumbled in, rolled over on his back, and flung one arm across his eyes. And then, with his face nearly hidden, he must have looked exactly as I used to look in that bed. I gazed upon my other self for a while before drawing across carefully the two green serge curtains which ran on a brass rod. I thought for a moment of pinning them together for greater safety, but I sat down on the couch, and once there I felt unwilling to rise and hunt for a pin. I would do it in a moment. I was extremely tired, in a peculiarly intimate way, by the strain of stealthiness, by the effort of whispering, and the general secrecy of this excitement. It was three o'clock by now, and I had been on my feet since nine, but I was not sleepy; I could not have gone to sleep. I sat there, fagged out, looking at the curtains, trying to clear my mind of the confused sensation of being in two places at once, and greatly bothered by an exasperating knocking in my head. It was a relief to discover suddenly that it was not in my head at all, but on the outside of the door. Before I could collect myself, the words "Come in" were out of my mouth, and the steward entered with a tray, bringing in my morning coffee. I had slept, after all, and I was so frightened that I shouted, "This way! I am here, steward," as though he had been miles away. He put down the tray on the table next the couch and only then said, very quietly, "I can see you are here, sir." I felt him give me a keen look, but I dared not meet his eyes just then. He must have wondered why I had drawn the curtains of my bed before going to sleep on the couch. He went out, hooking the door open as usual.

I heard the crew washing decks above me. I knew I would have been told at once if there had been any wind. Calm, I thought, and I was doubly vexed. Indeed, I felt dual more than ever. The steward reappeared suddenly in the doorway. I jumped up from the couch so quickly that he gave a start.

"What do you want here?"

"Close your port, sir—they are washing decks."

"It is closed," I said, reddening.

105   "Very well, sir." But he did not move from the doorway and returned my stare in an extraordinary, equivocal manner for a time. Then his eyes, wavered, all his expression changed, and in a voice unusually gentle, almost coaxingly.

"May I come in to take the empty cup away, sir?"

"Of course!" I turned my back on him while he popped in and out. Then I unhooked and closed the door and even pushed the bolt. This sort of thing could not go on very long. The cabin was as hot as an oven, too. I took a peep at my double, and discovered that he had not moved; his arm was still over his eyes; but his chest heaved, his hair was wet, his chin glistened with perspiration. I reached over him and opened the port.

"I must show myself on deck," I reflected.

Of course, theoretically, I could do what I liked, with no one to say nay to me within the whole circle of the horizon; but to lock my cabin door and take the key away I did not dare. Directly I put my head out of the companion I saw the group of my two officers, the second mate barefooted, the chief mate in long india-rubber boots, near the break of the poop, and the steward half-way down the poop ladder talking to them eagerly. He happened to catch sight of me and dived, the second ran down on the main deck shouting some order or other, and the chief mate came to meet me, touching his cap.

There was a sort of curiosity in his eye that I did not like. I don't know whether the steward had told them that I was "queer" only, or downright drunk, but I know the man meant to have a good look at me. I watched him coming with a smile which, as he got into point-blank range, took effect and froze his very whiskers. I did not give him time to open his lips.

"Square the yards by lifts and braces before the hands go to breakfast."

It was the first particular order I had given on board that ship; and I stayed on deck to see it executed too. I had felt the need of asserting myself without loss of time. That sneering young cub got taken down a peg or two on that occasion, and I also seized the opportunity of having a good look at the face of every foremast man as they filed past me to go to the after braces. At breakfast time, eating nothing myself, I presided with such frigid dignity that the two mates were only too glad to escape from the cabin as soon as decency permitted; and all the time the dual working of my mind distracted me almost to the point of insanity. I was constantly watching myself, my secret self, as dependent on my actions as my own personality, sleeping in that bed, behind that door which faced me as I sat at the head of the table. It was very much like being mad, only it was worse, because one was aware of it.

I had to shake him for a solid minute, but when at last he opened his eyes it was in the full possession of his senses, with an inquiring look.

"All's well so far," I whispered. "Now you must vanish into the bathroom."

He did so, as noiseless as a ghost, and I then rang for the steward, and facing him boldly, directed him to tidy up my stateroom while I was having my bath— "and be quick about it." As my tone admitted of no excuses, he said, "Yes, sir," and ran off to fetch his dustpan and brushes. I took a bath and did most of my dressing, splashing, and whistling softly for the steward's edification, while the secret sharer of my life stood drawn bolt upright in that little space, his face looking very sunken in daylight, his eyelids lowered under the stern, dark line of his eyebrows drawn together by a slight frown.

When I left him there to go back to my room the steward was finishing dusting. I sent for the mate and engaged him in some insignificant conversation. It was, as it were, trifling with the terrific character of his whiskers; but my object was to give him an opportunity for a good look at my cabin. And then I could at last shut, with a clear conscience, the door of my stateroom and get my double back into the recessed part. There was nothing else for it. He had to sit still on a small folding stool, half smothered by the heavy coats hanging there. We listened to the steward going into the bathroom out of the saloon, filling the water-bottles there, scrubbing the bath, setting things to rights, whisk, bang, clatter— out again into the saloon—turn the key—click. Such was my scheme for keeping my second self invisible. Nothing better could be contrived under the circumstances. And there we sat: I at my writing-desk ready to appear busy with

110

115

some papers, he behind me, out of sight of the door. It would not have been prudent to talk in daytime; and I could not have stood the excitement of that queer sense of whispering to myself. Now and then, glancing over my shoulder, I saw him far back there, sitting rigidly on the low stool, his bare feet close together, his arms folded, his head hanging on his breast—and perfectly still. Anybody would have taken him for me.

I was fascinated by it myself. Every moment I had to glance over my shoulder. I was looking at him when a voice outside the door said:

"Beg pardon, sir."

"Well!" . . . I kept my eyes on him, and so when the voice outside the door announced, "There's a ship's boat coming our way, sir," I saw him give a start—the first movement he had made for hours. But he did not raise his bowed head.

"All right. Get the ladder over."

I hesitated. Should I whisper something to him? But what? His immobility seemed to have been never disturbed. What could I tell him he did not know already? . . . Finally I went on deck.

II

The skipper of the *Spehora* had a thin, red whisker all round his face, and the sort of complexion that goes with hair of that color; also the particular, rather smeary shade of blue in the eyes. He was not exactly a showy figure; his shoulders were high, his stature but middling—one leg slightly more bandy than the other. He shook hands, looking vaguely around. A spiritless tenacity was his main characteristic, I judged. I behaved with a politeness which seemed to disconcert him. Perhaps he was shy. He mumbled to me as if he were ashamed of what he was saying; gave his name (it was something like Archbold—but at this distance of years I hardly am sure), his ship's name, and a few other particulars of that sort, in the manner of a criminal making a reluctant and doleful confession. He had had terrible weather on the passage out—terrible—terrible—wife aboard, too.

By this time we were seated in the cabin and the steward brought in a tray with a bottle and glasses. "Thanks! No." Never took liquor. Would have some water, though. He drank two tumblerfuls. Terrible thirsty work. Ever since daylight had been exploring the islands round his ship.

"What was that for—fun?" I asked with an appearance of polite interest.

"No!" He sighed. "Painful duty."

As he persisted in his mumbling and I wanted my double to hear every word, I hit upon the notion of informing him that I regretted to say I was hard of hearing.

"Such a young man too!" he nodded, keeping his smeary, blue, unintelligent eyes fastened upon me. "What was the cause of it—some disease?" he inquired, without the least sympathy and as if he thought that, if so, I'd got no more than I deserved.

"Yes; disease," I admitted in a cheerful tone which seemed to shock him. But my point was gained, because he had to raise his voice to give me his tale.

It is not worth while to record that version. It was just over two months since all this had happened, and he had thought so much about it that he seemed completely muddled as to its bearings, but still immensely impressed.

"What would you think of such a thing happening on board your own ship? I've had the *Sephora* for these fifteen years. I am a well-known shipmaster."

He was densely distressed—and perhaps I should have sympathized with him if I had been able to detach my mental vision from the unsuspected sharer of my cabin as though he were my second self. There he was on the other side of the bulkhead, four or five feet from us, no more, as we sat in the saloon. I looked politely at Captain Archbold (if that was his name), but it was the other I saw, in a gray sleeping suit, seated on a low stool, his bare feet close together, his arms folded, and every word said between us falling into the ears of his dark head bowed on his chest.

"I have been at sea now, man and boy, for seven and thirty years, and I've never heard of such a thing happening in an English ship. And that it should be my ship. Wife on board, too."

I was hardly listening to him.

"Don't you think," I said, "that the heavy sea which, you told me, came aboard just then might have killed the man? I have seen the sheer weight of a sea kill a man very neatly, by simply breaking his neck."

"Good God!" he uttered impressively, fixing his smeary blue eyes on me. "The sea! No man killed by the sea ever looked like that." He seemed positively scandalized at my suggestion. And as I gazed at him, certainly not prepared for anything original on his part, he advanced his head close to mine and thrust his tongue out at me so suddenly that I couldn't help starting back.

After scoring over my calmness in this graphic way he nodded wisely. If I had seen the sight, he assured me, I would never forget it as long as I lived. The weather was too bad to give the corpse a proper sea burial. So next day at dawn they took it up on the poop, covering its face with a bit of bunting; he read a short prayer, and then, just as it was, in its oilskins and long boots, they launched it amongst those mountainous seas that seemed ready every moment to swallow up the ship herself and the terrified lives on board of her.

"That reefed foresail saved you," I threw in.

"Under God—it did," he exclaimed fervently. "It was by a special mercy, I firmly believe, that it stood some of those hurricane squalls."

"It was the setting of that sail which—" I began.

"God's own hand in it," he interrupted me. "Nothing less could have done it. I don't mind telling you that I hardly dared give the order. It seemed impossible that we could touch anything without losing it, and then our last hope would have been gone."

The terror of that gale was on him yet. I let him go on for a bit, then said casually—as if returning to a minor subject:

"You were very anxious to give up your mate to the shore people, I believe?"

He was. To the law. His obscure tenacity on that point had in it something incomprehensible and a little awful; something, as it were, mystical, quite apart from his anxiety that he should not be suspected of "countenancing any doings

130

135

140

of that sort." Seven and thirty virtuous years at sea, of which over twenty of immaculate command, and the last fifteen in the *Sephora*, seemed to have laid him under some pitiless obligation.

"And you know," he went on, groping shamefacedly amongst his feelings, "I did not engage that young fellow. His people had some interest with my owners. I was in a way forced to take him on. He looked very smart, very gentlemanly, and all that. But do you know—I never liked him, somehow. I am a plain man. You see, he wasn't exactly the sort for the chief mate of a ship like the *Sephora*."

I had become so connected in thoughts and impressions with the secret sharer of my cabin that I felt as if I, personally, were being given to understand that I, too, was not the sort that would have done for the chief mate of a ship like the *Sephora*. I had no doubt of it in my mind.

145   "Not at all the style of man. You understand," he insisted superfluously, looking hard at me.

I smiled urbanely. He seemed at a loss for a while.

"I suppose I must report a suicide."

"Beg pardon?"

"Sui-cide! That's what I'll have to write to my owners directly I get in."

150   "Unless you manage to recover him before tomorrow," I assented dispassionately. . . . "I mean, alive."

He mumbled something which I really did not catch, and I turned my ear to him in a puzzled manner. He fairly bawled:

"The land—I say, the mainland is at least seven miles off my anchorage."

"About that."

My lack of excitement, of curiosity, of surprise, of any sort of pronounced interest, began to arouse his distrust. But except for the felicitous pretense of deafness I had not tried to pretend anything. I had felt utterly incapable of playing the part of ignorance properly, and therefore was afraid to try. It is also certain that he had brought some ready-made suspicions with him, and that he viewed my politeness as a strange and unnatural phenomenon. And yet how else could I have received him? Not heartily! That was impossible for psychological reasons, which I need not state here. My only object was to keep off his inquiries. Surlily? Yes, but surliness might have provoked a point-blank question. From its novelty to him and from its nature, punctilious courtesy was the manner best calculated to restrain the man. But there was the danger of his breaking through my defense bluntly. I could not, I think, have met him by a direct lie, also for psychological (not moral) reasons. If he had only known how afraid I was of his putting my feeling of identity with the other to the test! But, strangely enough (I thought of it only afterward), I believe that he was not a little disconcerted by the reverse side of that weird situation, by something in me that reminded him of the man he was seeking—suggested a mysterious similitude to the young fellow he had distrusted and disliked from the first.

155   However that might have been the silence was not very prolonged. He took another oblique step.

"I reckon I had no more than a two-mile pull to your ship. Not a bit more."

"And quite enough, too, in this awful heat," I said.

Another pause full of mistrust followed. Necessity, they say, is mother of invention, but fear, too, is not barren of ingenious suggestions. And I was afraid he would ask me point-blank for news of my other self.

"Nice little saloon, isn't it?" I remarked, as if noticing for the first time the way his eyes roamed from one closed door to the other. "And very well fitted out, too. Here, for instance," I continued, reaching over the back of my seat negligently and flinging the door open, "is my bathroom."

He made an eager movement, but hardly gave it a glance. I got up, shut the door of the bathroom, and invited him to have a look round, as if I were very proud of my accommodation. He had to rise and be shown round, but he went through the business without any raptures whatever.

"And now we'll have a look at my stateroom," I declared, in a voice as loud as I dared to make it, crossing the cabin to the starboard side with purposely heavy steps.

He followed me in and gazed around. My intelligent double had vanished. I played my part.

"Very convenient—isn't it?"

"Very nice. Very comf . . ." He didn't finish, and went out brusquely as if to escape from some unrighteous wiles of mine. But it was not to be. I had been too frightened not to feel vengeful; I felt I had him on the run, and I meant to keep him on the run. My polite insistence must have had something menacing in it, because he gave in suddenly. And I did not let him off a single item: mates' rooms, pantry, storerooms, the very sail-locker, which was also under the poop— he had to look into them all. When at last I showed him out on the quarter-deck he drew a long, spiritless sigh, and mumbled dismally that he must really be going back to his ship now. I desired my mate, who had joined us, to see to the captain's boat.

The man of whiskers gave a blast on the whistle which he used to wear hanging round his neck, and yelled, "*Sephora's* away!" My double down there in my cabin must have heard, and certainly could not feel more relieved than I. Four fellows came running out from somewhere forward and went over the side, while my own men, appearing on deck too, lined the rail. I escorted my visitor to the gangway ceremoniously, and nearly overdid it. He was a tenacious beast. On the very ladder he lingered, and in that unique, guiltily conscientious manner of sticking to the point:

"I say . . . you . . . you don't think that—"

I covered his voice loudly.

"Certainly not. . . . I am delighted. Goodbye."

I had an idea of what he meant to say, and just saved myself by the privilege of defective hearing. He was too shaken generally to insist, but my mate, close witness of that parting, looked mystified and his face took on a thoughtful cast. As I did not want to appear as if I wished to avoid all communication with my officers, he had the opportunity to address me.

"Seems a very nice man. His boat's crew told our chaps a very extraordinary story, if what I am told by the steward is true. I suppose you had it from the captain, sir?"

"Yes. I had a story from the captain."

"A very horrible affair—isn't it, sir?"

"It is."

"Beats all these tales we hear about murders in Yankee ships."

175 "I don't think it beats them. I don't think it resembles them in the least."

"Bless my soul—you don't say so! But of course I've no acquaintance whatever with American ships, not I, so I couldn't go against your knowledge. It's horrible enough for me. . . . But the queerest part is that those fellows seemed to have some idea the man was hidden aboard here. They had really. Did you ever hear of such a thing?"

"Preposterous—isn't it?"

We were walking to and fro athwart the quarter-deck. No one of the crew forward could be seen (the day was Sunday), and the mate pursued:

"There was some little dispute about it. Our chaps took offense. 'As if we would harbor a thing like that,' they said. 'Wouldn't you like to look for him in our coal-hole?' Quite a tiff. But they made it up in the end. I suppose he did drown himself. Don't you, sir?"

180 "I don't suppose anything."

"You have no doubt in the matter, sir?"

"None whatever."

I left him suddenly. I felt I was producing a bad impression, but with my double down there it was most trying to be on deck. And it was almost as trying to be below. Altogether a nerve-trying situation. But on the whole I felt less torn in two when I was with him. There was no one in the whole ship whom I dared take into my confidence. Since the hands had got to know his story, it would have been impossible to pass him off for any one else, and an accidental discovery was to be dreaded now more than ever. . . .

The steward being engaged in laying the table for dinner, we could talk only with our eyes when I first went down. Later in the afternoon we had a cautious try at whispering. The Sunday quietness of the ship was against us; the stillness of air and water around her was against us; the elements, the men were against us—everything was against us in our secret partnership; time itself—for this could not go on for ever. The very trust in Providence was, I supposed, denied to his guilt. Shall I confess that this thought cast me down very much? And as to the chapter of accidents which counts for so much in the book of success, I could only hope that it was closed. For what favorable accident could be expected?

185 "Did you hear everything?" were my first words as soon as we took up our position side by side, leaning over my bedplace.

He had. And the proof of it was his earnest whisper, "The man told you he hardly dared to give the order."

I understood the reference to be to that saving foresail.

"Yes. He was afraid of it being lost in the setting."

"I assure you he never gave the order. He may think he did, but he never gave it. He stood there with me on the break of the poop after the maintopsail blew away, and whimpered about our last hope—positively whimpered about it and nothing else—and the night coming on! To hear one's skipper go on like that in such weather was enough to drive any fellow out of his mind. It worked me up into a sort of desperation. I just took it into my own hands and went away from him, boiling, and—But what's the use telling you? *You* know! . . . Do you think that if I had not been pretty fierce with them I should have got the men to do anything? Not it! The boss'en[1] perhaps? Perhaps! It wasn't a heavy sea—it was a sea gone mad! I suppose the end of the world will be something like that; and a man may have the heart to see it coming once and be done with it—but to have to face it day after day . . . I don't blame anybody. I was precious little better than the rest. Only—I was an officer of that old coal-wagon, anyhow. . . ."

"I quite understand," I conveyed that sincere assurance into his ear. He was out of breath with whispering; I could hear him pant slightly. It was all very simple. The same strung-up force which had given twenty-four men a chance, at least, for their lives had, in a sort of recoil, crushed an unworthy mutinous existence.

But I had no leisure to weigh the merits of the matter—footsteps in the saloon, a heavy knock. "There's enough wind to get under way with, sir." Here was the call of a new claim upon my thoughts and even upon my feelings.

"Turn the hands up," I cried through the door. "I'll be on deck directly."

I was going out to make the acquaintance of my ship. Before I left the cabin our eyes met—the eyes of the only two strangers on board. I pointed to the recessed part where the little camp-stool awaited him and laid my finger on my lips. He made a gesture—somewhat vague—a little mysterious, accompanied by a faint smile, as if of regret.

This is not the place to enlarge upon the sensations of a man who feels for the first time a ship move under his feet to his own independent word. In my case they were not unalloyed. I was not wholly alone with my command; for there was that stranger in my cabin. Or, rather, I was not completely and wholly with her. Part of me was absent. That mental feeling of being in two places at once affected me physically as if the mood of secrecy had penetrated my very soul. Before an hour had elapsed since the ship had begun to move, having occasion to ask the mate (he stood by my side) to take a compass bearing of the Pagoda, I caught myself reaching up to his ear in whispers. I say I caught myself, but enough had escaped to startle the man. I can't describe it otherwise than by saying that he shied. A grave, preoccupied manner, as though he were in possession of some perplexing intelligence, did not leave him henceforth. A little later I moved away from the rail to look at the compass with such a stealthy gait that the helmsman noticed it—and I could not help noticing the unusual roundness of his eyes. These are trifling instances, though it's to no commander's advantage to be suspected of ludicrous eccentricities. But I was also more seriously affected. There are to a seaman certain words, gestures, that should in given conditions come as naturally, as instinctively, as the winking of a menaced eye. A certain order should spring on to his lips without thinking; a certain sign should get itself made, so to speak, without reflection. But all unconscious alert-

190

---

1. *Bosun* or *boatswain*, petty officer in charge of deck crew and of rigging.

ness had abandoned me. I had to make an effort of will to recall myself back (from the cabin) to the conditions of the moment. I felt that I was appearing an irresolute commander to those people who were watching me more or less critically.

195 And, besides, there were the scares. On the second day out, for instance, coming off the deck in the afternoon (I had straw slippers on my bare feet) I stopped at the open pantry door and spoke to the steward. He was doing something there with his back to me. At the sound of my voice he nearly jumped out of his skin, as the saying is, and incidentally broke a cup.

"What on earth's the matter with you?" I asked, astonished.

He was extremely confused. "Beg your pardon, sir. I made sure you were in your cabin."

"You see I wasn't."

"No, sir. I could have sworn I had heard you moving in there not a moment ago. It's most extraordinary . . . very sorry, sir."

200 I passed on with an inward shudder. I was so identified with my secret double that I did not even mention the fact in those scanty, fearful whispers we exchanged. I suppose he had made some slight noise of some kind or other. It would have been miraculous if he hadn't at one time or another. And yet, haggard as he appeared, he looked always perfectly self-controlled, more than calm—almost invulnerable. On my suggestion he remained almost entirely in the bathroom, which, upon the whole, was the safest place. There could be really no shadow of an excuse for any one ever wanting to go in there, once the steward had done with it. It was a very tiny place. Sometimes he reclined on the floor, his legs bent, his head sustained on one elbow. At others I would find him on the camp-stool, sitting in his gray sleeping suit and with his cropped dark hair like a patient, unmoved convict. At night I would smuggle him into my bedplace, and we would whisper together, with the regular footfalls of the officer of the watch passing and repassing over our heads. It was an infinitely miserable time. It was lucky that some tins of fine preserves were stowed in a locker in my stateroom; hard bread I could always get hold of; and so he lived on stewed chicken, pâté de foie gras, asparagus, cooked oysters, sardines—on all sorts of abominable sham-delicacies out of tins. My early morning coffee he always drank; and it was all I dared do for him in that respect.

Every day there was the horrible maneuvering to go through so that my room and then the bathroom should be done in the usual way. I came to hate the sight of the steward, to abhor the voice of that harmless man. I felt that it was he who would bring on the disaster of discovery. It hung like a sword over our heads.

The fourth day out, I think (we were then working down the east side of the Gulf of Siam, tack for tack,[2] in light winds and smooth water)—the fourth day, I say, of this miserable juggling with the unavoidable, as we sat at our evening meal, that man, whose slightest movement I dreaded, after putting down the dishes ran up on deck busily. This could not be dangerous. Presently he came

---

2. By a series of shiftings back and forth of sails.

down again; and then it appeared that he had remembered a coat of mine which I had thrown over a rail to dry after having been wetted in a shower which had passed over the ship in the afternoon. Sitting stolidly at the head of the table I became terrified at the sight of the garment on his arm. Of course he made for my door. There was no time to lose.

"Steward!" I thundered. My nerves were so shaken that I could not govern my voice and conceal my agitation. This was the sort of thing that made my terrifically whiskered mate tap his forehead with his forefinger. I had detected him using that gesture while talking on deck with a confidential air to the carpenter. It was too far to hear a word, but I had no doubt that this pantomime could only refer to the strange new captain.

"Yes, sir," the pale-faced steward turned resignedly to me. It was this maddening course of being shouted at, checked without rhyme or reason, arbitrarily chased out of my cabin, suddenly called into it, sent flying out of his pantry on incomprehensible errands, that accounted for the growing wretchedness of his expression.

"Where are you going with that coat?"   205

"To your room, sir."

"Is there another shower coming?"

"I'm sure I don't know, sir. Shall I go up again and see, sir?"

"No! never mind."

My object was attained, as of course my other self in there would have heard   210
everything that passed. During this interlude my two officers never raised their eyes off their respective plates; but the lip of that confounded cub, the second mate, quivered visibly.

I expected the steward to hook my coat on and come out at once. He was very slow about it; but I dominated my nervousness sufficiently not to shout after him. Suddenly I became aware (it could be heard plainly enough) that the fellow for some reason or other was opening the door of the bathroom. It was the end. The place was literally not big enough to swing a cat in. My voice died in my throat and I went stony all over. I expected to hear a yell of surprise and terror, and made a movement, but had not the strength to get on my legs. Everything remained still. Had my second self taken the poor wretch by the throat? I don't know what I could have done next moment if I had not seen the steward come out of my room, close the door, and then stand quietly by the sideboard.

"Saved," I thought. "But, no! Lost! Gone! He was gone!"

I laid my knife and fork down and leaned back in my chair. My head swam. After a while, when sufficiently recovered to speak in a steady voice, I instructed my mate to put the ship round at eight o'clock himself.

"I won't come on deck," I went on. "I think I'll turn in, and unless the wind shifts I don't want to be disturbed before midnight. I feel a bit seedy."

"You did look middling bad a little while ago," the chief mate remarked   215
without showing any great concern.

They both went out, and I stared at the steward clearing the table. There was nothing to be read on that wretched man's face. But why did he avoid my eyes? I asked myself. Then I thought I should like to hear the sound of his voice.

"Steward!"

"Sir!" Startled as usual.

"Where did you hang up that coat?"

220   "In the bathroom, sir." The usual anxious tone. "It's not quite dry yet, sir."

For some time longer I sat in the cuddy. Had my double vanished as he had come? But of his coming there was an explanation, whereas his disappearance would be inexplicable. . . . I went slowly into my dark room, shut the door, lighted the lamp, and for a time dared not turn round. When at last I did I saw him standing bolt upright in the narrow recessed part. It would not be true to say I had a shock, but an irresistible doubt of his bodily existence flitted through my mind. Can it be, I asked myself, that he is not visible to other eyes than mine? It was like being haunted. Motionless, with a grave face, he raised his hands slightly at me in a gesture which meant clearly, "Heavens! what a narrow escape!" Narrow indeed. I think I had come creeping quietly as near insanity as any man who has not actually gone over the border. That gesture restrained me, so to speak.

The mate with the terrific whiskers was now putting the ship on the other tack. In the moment of profound silence which follows upon the hands going to their stations I heard on the poop his raised voice: "Hard alee!"[3] and the distant shout of the order repeated on the main deck. The sails, in that light breeze, made but a faint fluttering noise. It ceased. The ship was coming round slowly; I held my breath in the renewed stillness of expectation; one wouldn't have thought that there was a single living soul on her decks. A sudden brisk shout, "Mainsail haul!" broke the spell, and in the noisy cries and rush overhead of the men running away with the main brace we two, down in my cabin, came together in our usual position by the bedplace.

He did not wait for my question. "I heard him fumbling here and just managed to squat myself down in the bath," he whispered to me. "The fellow only opened the door and put his arm in to hang the coat up. All the same. . . ."

"I never thought of that," I whispered back, even more appalled than before at the closeness of the shave, and marveling at that something unyielding in his character which was carrying him through so finely. There was no agitation in his whisper. Whoever was being driven distracted, it was not he. He was sane. And the proof of his sanity was continued when he took up the whispering again.

225   "It would never do for me to come to life again."

It was something that a ghost might have said. But what he was alluding to was his old captain's reluctant admission of the theory of suicide. It would obviously serve his turn—if I had understood at all the view which seemed to govern the unalterable purpose of his action.

"You must maroon me as soon as ever you can get amongst these islands off the Cambodje[4] shore," he went on.

"Maroon you! We are not living in a boy's adventure tale," I protested. His scornful whispering took me up.

"We aren't indeed! There's nothing of a boy's tale in this. But there's nothing

3. I.e., put the helm all the way over to the side away from the wind.   4. Cambodian.

else for it. I want no more. You don't suppose I am afraid of what can be done to me? Prison or gallows or whatever they may please. But you don't see me coming back to explain such things to an old fellow in a wig and twelve respectable tradesmen, do you? What can they know whether I am guilty or not—or of *what* I am guilty, either? That's my affair. What does the Bible say? 'Driven off the face of the earth.'[5] Very well. I am off the face of the earth now. As I came at night so I shall go."

"Impossible!" I murmured. "You can't."   230

"Can't? . . . . Not naked like a soul on the Day of Judgment. I shall freeze on to this sleeping suit. The Last Day is not yet—and . . . you have understood thoroughly. Didn't you?"

I felt suddenly ashamed of myself. I may say truly that I understood—and my hesitation in letting that man swim away from my ship's side had been a mere sham sentiment, a sort of cowardice.

"It can't be done now till next night," I breathed out. "The ship is on the offshore tack and the wind may fail us."

"As long as I know that you understand," he whispered. "But of course you do. It's a great satisfaction to have got somebody to understand. You seem to have been there on purpose." And in the same whisper, as if we two whenever we talked had to say things to each other which were not fit for the world to hear, he added, "It's very wonderful."

We remained side by side talking in our secret way—but sometimes silent   235 or just exchanging a whispered word or two at long intervals. And as usual he stared through the port. A breath of wind came now and again into our faces. The ship might have been moored in dock, so gently and on an even keel she slipped through the water, that did not murmur even at our passage, shadowy and silent like a phantom sea.

At midnight I went on deck, and to my mate's great surprise put the ship round on the other tack. His terrible whiskers flitted round me in silent criticism. I certainly should not have done it if it had been only a question of getting out of that sleepy gulf as quickly as possible. I believe he told the second mate, who relieved him, that it was a great want of judgment. The other only yawned. That intolerable cub shuffled about so sleepily and lolled against the rails in such a slack, improper fashion that I came down on him sharply.

"Aren't you properly awake yet?"

"Yes, sir! I am awake."

"Well, then, be good enough to hold yourself as if you were. And keep a look out. If there's any current we'll be closing with some islands long before daylight."

The east side of the gulf is fringed with islands, some solitary, others in   240 groups. On the blue background of the high coast they seem to float on silvery patches of calm water, arid and gray, or dark green and rounded like clumps of evergreen bushes, with the larger ones, a mile or two long, showing the outlines of ridges, ribs of gray rock under the dank mantle of matted leafage. Unknown

5. Genesis 4:14.

to trade, to travel, almost to geography, the manner of life they harbor is an unsolved secret. There must be villages—settlements of fishermen at least—on the largest of them, and some communication with the world is probably kept up by native craft. But all that forenoon, as we headed for them, fanned along by the faintest of breezes, I saw no sign of man or canoe in the field of the telescope I kept on pointing at the scattered group.

At noon I gave no orders for a change of course, and the mate's whiskers became much concerned and seemed to be offering themselves unduly to my notice. At last I said:

"I am going to stand right in. Quite in—as far as I can take her."

The stare of extreme surprise imparted an air of ferocity also to his eyes, and he looked truly terrific for a moment.

"We're not doing well in the middle of the gulf," I continued casually. "I am going to look for the land breezes tonight."

"Bless my soul! Do you mean, sir, in the dark amongst the lot of all them islands and reefs and shoals?"

"Well, if there are any regular land breezes at all on this coast one must get close inshore to find them—mustn't one?"

"Bless my soul!" he exclaimed again under his breath. All that afternoon he wore a dreamy, comtemplative appearance which in him was a mark of perplexity. After dinner I went into my stateroom as if I meant to take some rest. There we two bent our dark heads over a half-unrolled chart lying on my bed.

"There," I said. "It's got to be Koh-ring.[6] I've been looking at it ever since sunrise. It has got two hills and a low point. It must be inhabited. And on the coast opposite there is what looks like the mouth of a biggish river—with some town, no doubt, not far up. It's the best chance for you that I can see."

"Anything. Koh-ring let it be."

He looked thoughtfully at the chart as if surveying chances and distances from a lofty height—and following with his eyes his own figure wandering on the blank land of Cochin-China, and then passing off that piece of paper clean out of sight into uncharted regions. And it was as if the ship had two captains to plan her course for her. I had been so worried and restless running up and down that I had not had the patience to dress that day. I had remained in my sleeping suit, with straw slippers and a soft floppy hat. The closeness of the heat in the gulf had been most oppressive, and the crew were used to see me wandering in that airy attire.

"She will clear the south point as she heads now," I whispered into his ear. "Goodness only knows when, though—but certainly after dark. I'll edge her in to half a mile, as far as I may be able to judge in the dark . . ."

"Be careful," he murmured warningly—and I realized suddenly that all my future, the only future for which I was fit, would perhaps go irretrievably to pieces in any mishap to my first command.

I could not stop a moment longer in the room. I motioned him to get out of

6. *Koh* or *Ko* means *island*; there are a large number of islands with that prefix at the head of the Gulf of Siam, but not, apparently, a Koh-ring.

sight and made my way on the poop. That unplayful cub had the watch. I walked up and down for a while thinking things out, then beckoned him over.

"Send a couple of hands to open the two quarter-deck ports," I said mildly.

He actually had the impudence, or else so forgot himself in his wonder at such an incomprehensible order, as to repeat:

"Open the quarter-deck ports! What for, sir?"

"The only reason you need concern yourself about is because I tell you to do so. Have them opened wide and fastened properly."

He reddened and went off, but I believe made some jeering remark to the carpenter as to the sensible practice of ventilating a ship's quarter-deck. I know he popped into the mate's cabin to impart the fact to him, because the whiskers came on deck, as it were by chance, and stole glances at me from below—for signs of lunacy or drunkenness, I suppose.

A little before supper, feeling more restless than ever, I rejoined, for a moment, my second self. And to find him sitting so quietly was surprising, like something against nature, inhuman.

I developed my plan in a hurried whisper.

"I shall stand in as close as I dare and then put her round. I shall presently find means to smuggle you out of here into the sail-locker, which communicates with the lobby. But there is an opening, a sort of square for hauling the sails out, which gives straight on the quarterdeck and which is never closed in fine weather, so as to give air to the sails. When the ship's way is deadened in stays[7] and all the hands are aft at the main braces you shall have a clear road to slip out and get overboard through the open quarter-deck port. I've had them both fastened up. Use a rope's end to lower yourself into the water so as to avoid a splash—you know. It could be heard and cause some beastly complication."

He kept silent for a while, then whispered, "I understand."

"I won't be there to see you go," I began with an effort. "The rest . . . I only hope I have understood too."

"You have. From first to last"—and for the first time there seemed to be a faltering, something strained in his whisper. He caught hold of my arm, but the ringing of the supper bell made me start. He didn't though; he only released his grip.

After supper I didn't come below again till well past eight o'clock. The faint, steady breeze was loaded with dew; and the wet, darkened sails held all there was of propelling power in it. The night, clear and starry, sparkled darkly, and the opaque, lightless patches shifting slowly amongst the low stars were the drifting islets. On the port bow there was a big one more distant and shadowily imposing by the great space of sky it eclipsed.

On opening the door I had a back view of my very own self looking at a chart. He had come out of the recess and was standing near the table.

"Quite dark enough," I whispered.

He stepped back and leaned against my bed with a level, quiet glance. I sat

7. When the ship's forward motion is slowed or stopped while its head is being turned toward the wind for the purpose of shifting the sail

on the couch. We had nothing to say to each other. Over our heads the officer of the watch moved here and there. Then I heard him move quickly. I knew what that meant. He was making for the companion; and presently his voice was outside my door.

"We are drawing in pretty fast, sir. Land looks rather close."

270 "Very well," I answered. "I am coming on deck directly."

I waited till he was gone out of the cuddy, then rose. My double moved too. The time had come to exchange our last whispers, for neither of us was ever to hear each other's natural voice.

"Look here!" I opened a drawer and took out three sovereigns. "Take this, anyhow. I've got six and I'd give you the lot, only I must keep a little money to buy some fruit and vegetables for the crew from native boats as we go through Sunda Straits."

He shook his head.

"Take it," I urged him, whispering desperately. "No one can tell what . . ."

275 He smiled and slapped meaningly the only pocket of the sleeping jacket. It was not safe, certainly. But I produced a large old silk handkerchief of mine, and tying the three pieces of gold in a corner, pressed it on him. He was touched, I suppose, because he took it at last and tied it quickly round his waist under the jacket, on his bare skin.

Our eyes met; several seconds elapsed, till, our glances still mingled, I extended my hand and turned the lamp out. Then I passed through the cuddy, leaving the door of my room wide open. . . . "Steward!"

He was still lingering in the pantry in the greatness of his zeal, giving a rub-up to a plated cruet stand the last thing before going to bed. Being careful not to wake up the mate, whose room was opposite, I spoke in an undertone.

He looked round anxiously. "Sir!"

"Can you get me a little hot water from the galley?"

280 "I am afraid, sir, the galley fire's been out for some time now."

"Go and see."

He fled up the stairs.

"Now," I whispered loudly into the saloon—too loudly, perhaps, but I was afraid I couldn't make a sound. He was by my side in an instant—the double captain slipped past the stairs—through a tiny dark passage . . . a sliding door. We were in the sail-locker, scrambling on our knees over the sails. A sudden thought struck me. I saw myself wandering barefooted, bareheaded, the sun beating on my dark poll. I snatched off my floppy hat and tried hurriedly in the dark to ram it on my other self. He dodged and fended off silently. I wonder what he thought had come to me before he understood and suddenly desisted. Our hands met gropingly, lingered united in a steady, motionless clasp for a second. . . . No word was breathed by either of us when they separated.

I was standing quietly by the pantry door when the steward returned.

285 "Sorry, sir. Kettle barely warm. Shall I light the spirit-lamp?"

"Never mind."

I came out on deck slowly. It was now a matter of conscience to shave the land as close as possible—for now he must go overboard whenever the ship was put in stays. Must! There could be no going back for him. After a moment I walked over to leeward and my heart flew into my mouth at the nearness of the land on the bow. Under any other circumstances I would not have held on a minute longer. The second mate had followed me anxiously.

I looked on till I felt I could command my voice.

"She will weather," I said then in a quiet tone.

"Are you going to try that, sir?" he stammered out incredulously.

I took no notice of him and raised my tone just enough to be heard by the helmsman.

"Keep her good full."[8]

"Good full, sir."

The wind fanned my cheek, the sails slept, the world was silent. The strain of watching the dark loom of the land grow bigger and denser was too much for me. I had to shut my eyes—because the ship must go closer. She must! The stillness was intolerable. Were we standing still?

When I opened my eyes the second view started my heart with a thump. The black southern hill of Koh-ring seemed to hang right over the ship like a towering fragment of the everlasting night. On that enormous mass of blackness there was not a gleam to be seen, not a sound to be heard. It was gliding irresistibly towards us and yet seemed already within reach of the hand. I saw the vague figures of the watch grouped in the waist, gazing in awed silence.

"Are you going on, sir?" inquired an unsteady voice at my elbow.

I ignored it. I had to go on.

"Keep her full. Don't check her way. That won't do now," I said warningly.

"I can't see the sails very well," the helmsman answered me, in strange, quavering tones.

Was she close enough? Already she was, I won't say in the shadow of the land, but in the very blackness of it, already swallowed up as it were, gone too close to be recalled, gone from me altogether.

"Give the mate a call," I said to the young man who stood at my elbow as still as death. "And turn all hands up."

My tone had a borrowed loudness reverberated from the height of the land. Several voices cried out together, "We are all on deck, sir."

Then stillness again, with the great shadow gliding closer, towering higher, without a light, without a sound. Such a hush had fallen on the ship that she might have been a bark of the dead floating in slowly under the very gate of Erebus.

"My God! Where are we?"

It was the mate moaning at my elbow. He was thunderstruck, and as it were deprived of the moral support of his whiskers. He clapped his hands and absolutely cried out, "Lost!"

"Be quiet," I said sternly.

He lowered his tone, but I saw the shadowy gesture of his despair. "What are we doing here?"

8. I.e., keep the ship's sails filled with wind.

"Looking for the land wind."

He made as if to tear his hair, and addressed me recklessly.

"She will never get out. You have done it, sir. I knew it'd end in something like this. She will never weather, and you are too close now to stay. She'll drift ashore before she's round. O my God!"

I caught his arm as he was raising it to batter his poor devoted head, and shook it violently.

"She's ashore already," he wailed, trying to tear himself away.

"Is she? . . . Keep good full there!"

"Good full, sir," cried the helmsman in a frightened, thin, childlike voice.

I hadn't let go the mate's arm and went on shaking it. "Ready about,[9] do you hear? You go forward"—shake—"and stop there"—shake—"and hold your noise"—shake—"and see these head-sheets properly overhauled"—shake, shake—shake.

And all the time I dared not look towards the land lest my heart should fail me. I released my grip at last and he ran forward as if fleeing for dear life.

I wondered what my double there in the sail-locker thought of this commotion. He was able to hear everything—and perhaps he was able to understand why, on my conscience, it had to be thus close—no less. My first order "Hard alee!" re-echoed ominously under the towering shadow of Koh-ring as if I had shouted in a mountain gorge. And then I watched the land intently. In that smooth water and light wind it was impossible to feel the ship coming-to.[1] No! I could not feel her. And my second self was making now ready to slip out and lower himself overboard. Perhaps he was gone already. . . ?

The great black mass brooding over our very mast-heads began to pivot away from the ship's side silently. And now I forgot the secret stranger ready to depart, and remembered only that I was a total stranger to the ship. I did not know her. Would she do it? How was she to be handled?

I swung the mainyard and waited helplessly. She was perhaps stopped, and her very fate hung in the balance, with the black mass of Koh-ring like the gate of the everlasting night towering over her taffrail. What would she do now? Had she way on her[2] yet? I stepped to the side swiftly, and on the shadowy water I could see nothing except a faint phosphorescent flash revealing the glassy smoothness of the sleeping surface. It was impossible to tell—and I had not learned yet the feel of my ship. Was she moving? What I needed was something easily seen, a piece of paper, which I could throw overboard and watch. I had nothing on me. To run down for it I didn't dare. There was no time. All at once my strained, yearning stare distinguished a white object floating within a yard of the ship's side—white, on the black water. A phosphorescent flash passed under it. What was that thing? . . . I recognized my own floppy hat. It must have fallen off his head . . . and he didn't bother. Now I had what I wanted—the saving mark for my eyes. But I hardly thought of my other self, now gone from the

9. I.e., be ready to shift the sails (tack). The head-sheets, below, are the lines attached to the sails of the forward mast, and to overhaul is to slacken a rope by pulling it in the opposite direction to that used in hoisting a sail and thus loosening the blocks.　　1. Coming to a standstill.　　2. Was she moving?

ship, to be hidden for ever from all friendly faces, to be a fugitive and a vagabond on the earth, with no brand of the curse on his sane forehead to stay a slaying hand . . . too proud to explain.

And I watched the hat—the expression of my sudden pity for his mere flesh. It had been meant to save his homeless head from the dangers of the sun. And now—behold—it was saving the ship, by serving me for a mark to help out the ignorance of my strangeness. Ha! It was drifting forward, warning me just in time that the ship had gathered sternway.

"Shift the helm," I said in a low voice to the seaman standing still like a statue.

The man's eyes glistened wildly in the binnacle light as he jumped round to the other side and spun round the wheel.

I walked to the break of the poop. On the overshadowed deck all hands stood by the forebraces waiting for my order. The stars ahead seemed to be gliding from right to left. And all was so still in the world that I heard the quiet remark, "She's round," passed in a tone of intense relief between two seamen.

"Let go and haul."

The foreyards ran round with a great noise, amidst cheery cries. And now the frightful whiskers made themselves heard giving various orders. Already the ship was drawing ahead. And I was alone with her. Nothing! no one in the world should stand now between us, throwing a shadow on the way of silent knowledge and mute affection; the perfect communion of a seaman with his first command.

Walking to the taffrail, I was in time to make out, on the very edge of a darkness thrown by a towering black mass like the very gateway of Erebus—yes, I was in time to catch an evanescent glimpse of my white hat left behind to mark the spot where the secret sharer of my cabin and of my thoughts, as though he were my second self, had lowered himself into the water to take his punishment: a free man, a proud swimmer striking out for a new destiny.

1912

The first paragraph of the story clearly functions as exposition, especially in describing the setting, the place and time of day. Its last sentence suggests something of the situation—the speaker is alone with *his* ship. It also establishes the focus and voice. In the description of the scene in the Gulf of Siam, there are some words that, though appropriate, are not necessarily inevitable. These are words that might not be used by just any narrator or in just any circumstances and so may characterize the speaker or his situation. In the first sentence alone you may notice "mysterious," "incomprehensible," even "crazy," which, though it deals with the physical irregularity of the fences, also suggests the irrational. These words arouse suspense and so further the plot, but they may also suggest something of the theme. And, since another speaker would be likely to see things somewhat differently and use different words, his choices may also characterize the speaker. Some of the details of the paragraph may also be symbolic.

1. How does the second paragraph further advance the description of set-ting, of situation, of theme? Are any of the details here symbolic or potentially symbolic? The last sentence of this paragraph seems to relate directly to theme, though it may also help characterize the narrator. There are many such sen-tences in the story—an example might be "And suddenly I rejoiced in the great security of the sea . . ." (par. 17). Collect five or six such sentences and see how they relate not only to theme but to other elements.

2. How does paragraph 7 characterize the second mate, explain the narra-tor's situation, and further arouse suspense and further define the theme?

3. How does the description of the episode with the scorpion (par. 8) char-acterize the chief mate, and, when looked back upon later, further the plot and suspense? How does the chief mate's propensity for logical explanations relate to the theme?

4. How does the "unconventional arrangement" of the narrator-captain's standing the first anchor-watch relate to his character? to the plot? to the theme(s)?

5. When the narrator notices that the rope side-ladder has not been hauled in, he blames himself for having disturbed the ship's routine and conjectures about how he will look in the eyes of the officers and crew and how his con-duct will be "accounted" for by the chief mate. All this relates to the characters of the two men, the plot or suspense, and the theme. It is just then that "the secret sharer" appears at the very end of that same ladder. Is he, then, in some way symbolic? If so, how? In the light of all that follows, is it good or bad to break the rules? Does following or breaking rules seem to have anything to do with being a captain? Explain.

6. What is the effect of paragraph 20, in which "something elongated and pale" appears at the bottom of the ladder? How many elements are involved in that description (including the first sentence of the next paragraph)?

7. When Leggatt is aboard and dressed in the captain's sleeping suit, he is described as looking like the captain's "double." That, plus Leggatt's arriving from the sea naked, looking like a fish, being phosphorescent and oblong, together with the title of the story, and the narrator's seeing his first command as a test, has led a substantial number of critics and other readers to view these details as Freudian symbols and to attribute to this story a Freudian, or at least a psychological, theme. Make out the best case you can for such a reading of the story. What happens to the specifics of the situation, the characters, the plot? Which details are symbolic in your version and which are not? Now

make out the best case *against* such a reading. If you are so committed to one position or the other that you cannot see how there can be another side, pair yourself off with someone else in the class who has made the best counterargument.

8. When Leggatt tells his story there is a shift in the focus and voice. How does this story within a story function in the plot of "The Secret Sharer"? How does it help define the character of Leggatt? How does it relate to the theme of "the double" in the larger story?

9. Why does the captain hide Leggatt rather than turn him in? How do all the elements of the story contribute to your answering this question?

10. The captain of the *Sephora* tells his version of Leggatt's crime, but the narrator says, "It is not worth while to record that version. It was just over two months since all this had happened, and . . . he seemed completely muddled . . ." (par. 128). Yet the narrator is telling his and Leggatt's story at a "distance of years," and there is a bit of Archbold's story in the paragraphs that follow. Write a fuller (two- or three-page) version of how the *Sephora* captain would tell the story. How does this shift in focus and voice affect the plot? the characterization of the captain of the *Sephora?* of Leggatt? of the narrator of "The Secret Sharer"? the theme?

11. Archbold believes Leggatt was too gentlemanly to be chief mate of the *Sephora,* and the narrator, so identified now with Leggatt, thinks Archbold would not consider the narrator himself a suitable chief mate (much less captain). How would you analyze this notion in terms of focus? character? symbol? theme?

12. There seems to be a turn in the story after Archbold leaves: ironically, Leggatt seems more of a burden to the narrator, who now seems to see himself in his role as captain: "I was not wholly alone with my command; for there was that stranger in my cabin. . . . Part of me was absent" (par. 194). What is the effect of this feeling of split identity on the plot? How does it relate to focus? The whole story can be read as the initiation of the narrator into leadership or captaincy. How does Leggatt figure in that initiation theme? How does his character relate to it? Is he a symbol? If you think he is, of what is he a symbol? How do the final episode and final two paragraphs of the story relate to this portion of the plot, this view of Leggatt, this theme? Can you imagine this story— the story of a new captain taking over command of a strange ship, with mates not of his own choosing and not of his own "kind," of the strained relations between the new captain and the other officers, of his routine and unroutine orders, of his emotional state, and of his first daring act of seamanship, of all this—without any mention of, or presence of, or story of, a Leggatt, a secret

sharer? Write a brief synopsis of such a story. Is there some way in which you might still call it "The Secret Sharer"? Who has the secret and with whom does he share it?

13. How does the captain's giving Leggatt his hat figure in the plot? What does it suggest about the narrator's character and feelings? Of what, if anything, might it be a symbol?

14. Write a sequel to "The Secret Sharer" about what happens to Leggatt after he leaves the ship, using as much evidence as you can from the elements and details of Conrad's story but with a new focus and voice.

The story that follows is funnier than, but just as serious as, "The Secret Sharer." It is the title story, or chapter, of a work that calls itself a novel but can also be seen as a collection of related but separable stories (indeed, many of the chapters were first published separately as stories, and a new edition of *Love Medicine* adds four new stories or chapters and rearranges the original sequence). Reading the whole novel or collection may enrich your understanding and enjoyment of the parts but this story is, as you will see, quite wonderful, enjoyable, and understandable by itself. It is a somewhat unfamiliar world you will be entering; though nearer to us in time and space, it is perhaps even stranger than the world of "The Secret Sharer." Stop reading after paragraph 18, look at item 1 below (p. 294), and get your bearings.

LOUISE ERDRICH
_____

Love Medicine

I never really done much with my life, I suppose. I never had a television. Grandma Kashpaw had one inside her apartment at the Senior Citizens, so I used to go there and watch my favorite shows. For a while she used to call me the biggest waste on the reservation and hark back to how she saved me from my own mother, who wanted to tie me in a potato sack and throw me in a slough. Sure, I was grateful to Grandma Kashpaw for saving me like that, for raising me, but gratitude gets old. After a while, stale. I had to stop thanking her. One day I told her I had paid her back in full by staying at her beck and call. I'd do anything for Grandma. She knew that. Besides, I took care of Grandpa like nobody else could, on account of what a handful he'd gotten to be.

But that was nothing. I know the tricks of mind and body inside out without ever having trained for it, because I got the touch. It's a thing you got to be born with. I got secrets in my hands that nobody ever knew to ask. Take Grandma Kashpaw with her tired veins all knotted up in her legs like clumps of blue snails. I take my fingers and I snap them on the knots. The medicine flows out of me. The touch. I run my fingers up the maps of those rivers of veins or I knock very gentle above their hearts or I make a circling motion on their stomachs, and it helps them. They feel much better. Some women pay me five dollars.

I couldn't do the touch for Grandpa, though. He was a hard nut. You know, some people fall right through the hole in their lives. It's invisible, but they come to it after time, never knowing where. There is this woman here, Lulu Lamartine, who always had a thing for Grandpa. She loved him since she was a girl and always said he was a genius. Now she says that his mind got so full it exploded.

How can I doubt that? I know the feeling when your mental power builds up too far. I always used to say that's why the Indians got drunk. Even statistically we're the smartest people on the earth. Anyhow with Grandpa I couldn't hardly believe it, because all my youth he stood out as a hero to me. When he started getting toward second childhood he went through different moods. He would stand in the woods and cry at the top of his shirt. It scared me, scared everyone, Grandma worst of all.

Yet he was so smart—do you believe it?—that he *knew* he was getting foolish.   5

He said so. He told me that December I failed school and come back on the train to Hoopdance. I didn't have nowhere else to go. He picked me up there and he said it straight out: "I'm getting into my second childhood." And then he said something else I still remember: "I been chosen for it. I couldn't say no." So I figure that a man so smart all his life—tribal chairman and the star of movies and even pictured in the statehouse and on cans of snuff—would know what he's doing by saying yes. I think he was called to second childhood like anybody else gets a call for the priesthood or the army or whatever. So I really did not listen too hard when the doctor said this was some kind of disease old people got eating too much sugar. You just can't tell me that a man who went to Washington and gave them bureaucrats what for could lose his mind from eating too much Milky Way. No, he put second childhood on himself.

Behind those songs he sings out in the middle of Mass, and back of those stories that everybody knows by heart, Grandpa is thinking hard about life. I know the feeling. Sometimes I'll throw up a smokescreen to think behind. I'll hitch up to Winnipeg and play the Space Invaders for six hours, but all the time there and back I will be thinking some fairly deep thoughts that surprise even me, and I'm used to it. As for him, if it was just the thoughts there wouldn't be no problem. Smokescreen is what irritates the social structure, see, and Grandpa has done things that just distract people to the point they want to throw him in the cookie jar where they keep the mentally insane. He's far from that, I know for sure, but even Grandma had trouble keeping her patience once he started sneaking off to Lamartine's place. He's not supposed to have his candy, and Lulu feeds it to him. That's *one* of the reasons why he goes.

Grandma tried to get me to put the touch on Grandpa soon after he began stepping out. I didn't want to, but before Grandma started telling me again what a bad state my bare behind was in when she first took me home, I thought I should at least pretend.

I put my hands on either side of Grandpa's head. You wouldn't look at him and say he was crazy. He's a fine figure of a man, as Lamartine would say, with all his hair and half his teeth, a beak like a hawk, and cheeks like the blades of a hatchet. They put his picture on all the tourist guides to North Dakota and even copied his face for artistic paintings. I guess you could call him a monument all of himself. He started grinning when I put my hands on his templates, and I knew right then he knew how come I touched him. I knew the smokescreen was going to fall.

And I was right: just for a moment it fell.

"Let's pitch whoopee," he said across my shoulder to Grandma.

They don't use that expression much around here anymore, but for damn sure it must have meant something. It got her goat right quick.

She threw my hands off his head herself and stood in front of him, overmatching him pound for pound, and taller too, for she had a growth spurt in middle age while he had shrunk, so now the length and breadth of her surpassed him. She glared up and spoke her piece into his face about how he was off at all hours tomcatting and chasing Lamartine again and making a damn old fool of himself.

"And you got no more whoopee to pitch anymore anyhow!" she yelled at last, surprising me so my jaw just dropped, for us kids all had pretended for so long that those rustling sounds we heard from their side of the room at night never happened. She sure had pretended it, up till now, anyway. I saw that tears were in her eyes. And that's when I saw how much grief and love she felt for him. And it gave me a real shock to the system. You see I thought love got easier over the years so it didn't hurt so bad when it hurt, or feel so good when it felt good. I thought it smoothed out and old people hardly noticed it. I thought it curled up and died, I guess. Now I saw it rear up like a whip and lash.

She loved him. She was jealous. She mourned him like the dead.

And he just smiled into the air, trapped in the seams of his mind.

So I didn't know what to do. I was in a laundry then. They was like parents to me, the way they had took me home and reared me. I could see her point for wanting to get him back the way he was so at least she could argue with him, sleep with him, not be shamed out by Lamartine. She'd always love him. That hit me like a ton of bricks. For one whole day I felt this odd feeling that cramped my hands. When you have the touch, that's where longing gets you. I never loved like that. It made me feel all inspired to see them fight, and I wanted to go out and find a woman who I would love until one of us died or went crazy. But I'm not like that really. From time to time I heal a person all up good inside, however when it comes to the long shot I doubt that I got staying power.

And you need that, staying power, going out to love somebody. I knew this quality was not going to jump on me with no effort. So I turned my thoughts back to Grandma and Grandpa. I felt her side of it with my hands and my tangled guts, and I felt his side of it within the stretch of my mentality. He had gone out to lunch one day and never came back. He was fishing in the middle of Lake Turcot. And there was big thoughts on his line, and he kept throwing them back for even bigger ones that would explain to him, say, the meaning of how we got here and why we have to leave so soon. All in all, I could not see myself treating Grandpa with the touch, bringing him back, when the real part of him had chose to be off thinking somewhere. It was only the rest of him that stayed around causing trouble, after all, and we could handle most of it without any problem.

Besides, it was hard to argue with his reasons for doing some things. Take Holy Mass. I used to go there just every so often, when I got frustrated mostly, because even though I know the Higher Power dwells everyplace, there's something very calming about the cool greenish inside of our mission. Or so I thought, anyway. Grandpa was the one who stripped off my delusions in this matter, for it was he who busted right through what Father Upsala calls the sacred serenity of the place.

We filed in that time. Me and Grandpa. We sat down in our pews. Then the rosary got started up pre-Mass and that's when Grandpa filled up his chest and opened his mouth and belted out them words.

HAIL MARIE FULL OF GRACE.

He had a powerful set of lungs.

And he kept on like that. He did not let up. He hollered and he yelled them prayers, and I guess people was used to him by now, because they only muttered theirs and did not quit and gawk like I did. I was getting red-faced, I admit. I give him the elbow once or twice, but that wasn't nothing to him. He kept on. He shrieked to heaven and he pleaded like a movie actor and he pounded his chest like Tarzan in the Lord I Am Not Worthies. I thought he might hurt himself. Then after a while I guess I got used to it, and that's when I wondered: how come?

So afterwards I out and asked him. "How come? How come you yelled?"

"God don't hear me otherwise," said Grandpa Kashpaw.

I sweat. I broke right into a little cold sweat at my hairline because I knew this was perfectly right and for years not one damn other person had noticed it. God's been going deaf. Since the Old Testament, God's been deafening up on us. I read, see. Besides the dictionary, which I'm constantly in use of, I had this Bible once. I read it. I found there was discrepancies between then and now. It struck me. Here God used to raineth bread from clouds, smite the Phillipines, sling fire down on red-light districts where people got stabbed. He even appeared in person every once in a while. God used to pay attention, is what I'm saying.

Now there's your God in the Old Testament and there is Chippewa Gods as well. Indian Gods, good and bad, like tricky Nanabozho or the water monster, Missepeshu, who lives over in Lake Turcot. That water monster was the last God I ever heard to appear. It had a weakness for young girls and grabbed one of the Blues off her rowboat. She got to shore all right, but only after this monster had its way with her. She's an old lady now. Old Lady Blue. She still won't let her family fish that lake.

Our Gods aren't perfect, is what I'm saying, but at least they come around. They'll do a favor if you ask them right. You don't have to yell. But you do have to know, like I said, how to ask in the right way. That makes problems, because to ask proper was an art that was lost to the Chippewas once the Catholics gained ground. Even now, I have to wonder if Higher Power turned it back, if we got to yell, or if we just don't speak its language.

I looked around me. How else could I explain what all I had seen in my short life—King smashing his fist in things, Gordie drinking himself down to the Bismarck hospitals, or Aunt June left by a white man to wander off in the snow. How else to explain the times my touch don't work, and farther back, to the oldtime Indians who was swept away in the outright germ warfare and dirty-dog killing of the whites. In those times, us Indians was so much kindlier than now.

30   We took them in.

Oh yes, I'm bitter as an old cutworm just thinking of how they done to us and doing still.

So Grandpa Kashpaw just opened my eyes a little there. Was there any sense relying on a God whose ears was stopped? Just like the government? I says then, right off, maybe we got nothing but ourselves. And that's not much, just personally speaking. I know I don't got the cold hard potatoes it takes to understand everything. Still, there's things I'd like to do. For instance, I'd like to help some people like my Grandpa and Grandma Kashpaw get back some happiness within the tail ends of their lives.

I told you once before I couldn't see my way clear to putting the direct touch on Grandpa's mind, and I kept my moral there, but something soon happened to make me think a little bit of mental adjustment wouldn't do him and the rest of us no harm.

It was after we saw him one afternoon in the sunshine courtyard of the Senior Citizens with Lulu Lamartine. Grandpa used to like to dig there. He had his little dandelion fork out, and he was prying up them dandelions right and left while Lamartine watched him.

35   "He's scratching up the dirt, all right," said Grandma, watching Lamartine watch Grandpa out the window.

Now Lamartine was about half the considerable size of Grandma, but you would never think of sizes anyway. They were different in an even more notice-able way. It was the difference between a house fixed up with paint and picky fence, and a house left to weather away into the soft earth, is what I'm saying. Lamartine was jacked up, latticed, shuttered, and vinyl sided, while Grandma sagged and bulged on her slipped foundations and let her hair go the silver gray of rain-dried lumber. Right now, she eyed the Lamartine's pert flowery dress with such a look it despaired me. I knew what this could lead to with Grandma. Alternating tongue storms and rock-hard silences was hard on a man, even one who didn't notice, like Grandpa. So I went fetching him.

But he was gone when I popped through the little screen door that led out on the courtyard. There was nobody out there either, to point which way they went. Just the dandelion fork quibbling upright in the ground. That gave me an idea. I snookered over to the Lamartine's door and I listened in first, then knocked. But nobody. So I went walking through the lounges and around the card tables. Still nobody. Finally it was my touch that led me to the laundry room. I cracked the door. I went in. There they were. And he was really loving her up good, boy, and she was going hell for leather. Sheets was flapping on the lines above, and washcloths, pillowcases, shirts was also flying through the air, for they was trying to clear out a place for themselves in a high-heaped but shallow laundry cart. The washers and dryers was all on, chock full of quarters, shaking and moaning. I couldn't hear what Grandpa and the Lamartine was billing and cooing, and they couldn't hear me.

I didn't know what to do, so I went inside and shut the door.

The Lamartine wore a big curly light-brown wig. Looked like one of them squeaky little white-people dogs. Poodles they call them. Anyway, that wig is what saved us from the worse. For I could hardly shout and tell them I was in there, no more could I try and grab him. I was trapped where I was. There was nothing I could really do but hold the door shut. I was scared of somebody else upsetting in and really getting an eyeful. Turned out though, in the heat of the clinch, as I was trying to avert my eyes you see, the Lamartine's curly wig jumped off her head. And if you ever been in the midst of something and had a big change like that occur in the someone, you can't help know how it devastates your basic urges. Not only that, but her wig was almost with a life of its own. Grandpa's eyes were bugging at the change already, and swear to God if the thing didn't rear up and pop him in the face like it was going to start something. He scrambled up, Grandpa did, and the Lamartine jumped up after him all addled looking. They just stared at each other, huffing and puffing, with quizzical expression. The surprise seemed to drive all sense completely out of Grandpa's mind.

"The letter was what started the fire," he said. "I never would have done it."

"What letter?" said the Lamartine. She was stiff-necked now, and elegant, even bald, like some alien queen. I gave her back the wig. The Lamartine replaced it on her head, and whenever I saw her after that, I couldn't help thinking of her bald, with special powers, as if from another planet.

"That was a close call," I said to Grandpa after she had left.

But I think he had already forgot the incident. He just stood there all quiet and thoughtful. You really wouldn't think he was crazy. He looked like he was just about to say something important, explaining himself. He said something, all right, but it didn't have nothing to do with anything that made sense.

He wondered where the heck he put his dandelion fork. That's when I decided about the mental adjustment.

Now what was mostly our problem was not so much that he was not all there, but that what was there of him often hankered after Lamartine. If we could put a stop to that, I thought, we might be getting someplace. But here, see, my touch was of no use. For what could I snap my fingers at to make him faithful to Grandma? Like the quality of staying power, this faithfulness was invisible. I know it's something that you got to acquire, but I never known where from. Maybe there's no rhyme or reason to it, like my getting the touch, and then again maybe it's a kind of magic.

It was Grandma Kashpaw who thought of it in the end. She knows things. Although she will not admit she has a scrap of Indian blood in her, there's no doubt in my mind she's got some Chippewa. How else would you explain the way she'll be sitting there, in front of her TV story, rocking in her armchair and suddenly she turns on me, her brown eyes hard as lake-bed flint.

"Lipsha Morrissey," she'll say, "you went out last night and got drunk."

How did she know that? I'll hardly remember it myself. Then she'll say she just had a feeling or ache in the scar of her hand or a creak in her shoulder. She is constantly being told things by little aggravations in her joints or by her household appliances. One time she told Gordie never to ride with a crazy Lamartine boy. She had seen something in the polished-up tin of her bread toaster. So he didn't. Sure enough, the time came we heard how Lyman and Henry went out of control in their car, ending up in the river. Lyman swam to the top, but Henry never made it.

Thanks to Grandma's toaster, Gordie was probably spared.

50   Someplace in the blood Grandma Kashpaw knows things. She also remembers things, I found. She keeps things filed away. She's got a memory like them video games that don't forget your score. One reason she remembers so many details about the trouble I gave her in early life is so she can flash back her total when she needs to.

Like now. Take the love medicine. I don't know where she remembered that from. It came tumbling from her mind like an asteroid off the corner of the screen.

Of course she starts out by mentioning the time I had this accident in church and did she leave me there with wet overhalls? No she didn't. And ain't I glad? Yes I am. Now what you want now, Grandma?

But when she mentions them love medicines, I feel my back prickle at the danger. These love medicines is something of an old Chippewa specialty. No other tribe has got them down so well. But love medicines is not for the layman to handle. You don't just go out and get one without paying for it. Before you get one, even, you should go through one hell of a lot of mental condensation. You got to think it over. Choose the right one. You could really mess up your life grinding up the wrong little thing.

So anyhow, I said to Grandma I'd give this love medicine some thought. I knew the best thing was to go ask a specialist like Old Man Pillager, who lives up in a tangle of bush and never shows himself. But the truth is I was afraid of him, like everyone else. He was known for putting the twisted mouth on people, seizing up their hearts. Old Man Pillager was serious business, and I have always thought it best to steer clear of that whenever I could. That's why I took the powers in my own hands. That's why I did what I could.

55   I put my whole mentality to it, nothing held back. After a while I started to remember things I'd heard gossiped over.

I heard of this person once who carried a charm of seeds that looked like baby pearls. They was attracted to a metal knife, which made them powerful. But I didn't know where them seeds grew. Another love charm I heard about I couldn't go along with, because how was I suppose to catch frogs in the act, which it required. Them little creatures is slippery and fast. And then the powerfullest of all, the most extreme, involved nail clips and such. I wasn't anywhere near asking Grandma to provide me all the little body bits that this last love recipe called for. I went walking around for days just trying to think up something that would work.

Well I got it. If it hadn't been the early fall of the year, I never would have got it. But I was sitting underneath a tree one day down near the school just watching people's feet go by when something tells me, look up! Look up! So I look up, and I see two honkers, Canada geese, the kind with little masks on their faces, a bird what mates for life. I see them flying right over my head naturally preparing to land in some slough on the reservation, which they certainly won't get off of alive.

It hits me, anyway. Them geese, they mate for life. And I think to myself, just what if I went out and got a pair? And just what if I fed some part—say the goose heart—of the female to Grandma and Grandpa ate the other heart? Wouldn't that work? Maybe it's all invisible, and then maybe again it's magic. Love is a stony road. We know that for sure. If it's true that the higher feelings of devotion get lodged in the heart like people say, then we'd be home free. If not, eating goose heart couldn't harm nobody anyway. I thought it was worth my effort, and Grandma Kashpaw thought so, too. She had always known a good idea when she heard one. She borrowed me Grandpa's gun.

So I went out to this particular slough, maybe the exact same slough I never got thrown in by my mother, thanks to Grandma Kashpaw, and I hunched down in a good comfortable pile of rushes. I got my gun loaded up. I ate a few of these soft baloney sandwiches Grandma made me for lunch. And then I waited. The cattails blown back and forth above my head. Them stringy blue herons was spearing up their prey. The thing I know how to do best in this world, the thing I been training for all my life, is to wait. Sitting there and sitting there was no hardship on me. I got to thinking about some funny things that happened. There was this one time that Lulu Lamartine's little blue tweety bird, a paraclete, I guess you'd call it, flown up inside her dress and got lost within there. I recalled her running out into the hallway trying to yell something, shaking. She was doing a right good jig there, cutting the rug for sure, and the thing is it *never* flown out. To this day people speculate where it went. They fear she might perhaps of crushed it in her corsets. It sure hasn't ever yet been seen alive. I thought of funny things for a while, but then I used them up, and strange things that happened started weaseling their way into my mind.

I got to thinking quite naturally of the Lamartine's cousin named Wristwatch. I never knew what his real name was. They called him Wristwatch because he got his father's broken wristwatch as a young boy when his father passed on. Never in his whole life did Wristwatch take his father's watch off. He didn't care if it worked, although after a while he got sensitive when people asked what time it was, teasing him. He often put it to his ear like he was listening to the tick. But it was broken for good and forever, people said so, at least that's what they thought.

Well I saw Wristwatch smoking in his pickup one afternoon and by nine that evening he was dead.

He died sitting at the Lamartine's table, too. As she told it, Wristwatch had just eaten himself a good-size dinner and she said would he take seconds on the hot dish when he fell over to the floor. They turnt him over. He was gone. But here's the strange thing: when the Senior Citizen's orderly took the pulse he noticed that the wristwatch Wristwatch wore was now working. The moment he died the wristwatch started keeping perfect time. They buried him with the watch still ticking on his arm.

I got to thinking. What if some gravediggers dug up Wristwatch's casket in two hundred years and that watch was still going? I thought what question they would ask and it was this: Whose hand wound it?

I started shaking like a piece of grass at just the thought.

65   Not to get off the subject or nothing. I was still hunkered in the slough. It was passing late into the afternoon and still no honkers had touched down. Now I don't need to tell you that the waiting did not get to me, it was the chill. The rushes was very soft, but damp. I was getting cold and debating to leave, when they landed. Two geese swimming here and there as big as life, looking deep into each other's little pinhole eyes. Just the ones I was looking for. So I lifted Grandpa's gun to my shoulder and I aimed perfectly, and *blam! Blam!* I delivered two accurate shots. But the thing is, them shots missed. I couldn't hardly believe it. Whether it was that the stock had warped or the barrel got bent someways, I don't quite know, but anyway them geese flown off into the dim sky, and Lipsha Morrissey was left there in the rushes with evening fallen and his two cold hands empty. He had before him just the prospect of another day of bone-cracking chill in them rushes, and the thought of it got him depressed.

Now it isn't my style, in no way, to get depressed.

So I said to myself, Lipsha Morrissey, you're a happy S.O.B. who could be covered up with weeds by now down at the bottom of this slough, but instead you're alive to tell the tale. You might have problems in life, but you still got the touch. You got the power, Lipsha Morrissey. Can't argue that. So put your mind to it and figure out how not to be depressed.

I took my advice. I put my mind to it. But I never saw at the time how my thoughts led me astray toward a tragic outcome none could have known. I ignored all the danger, all the limits, for I was tired of sitting in the slough and my feet were numb. My face was aching. I was chilled, so I played with fire. I told myself love medicine was simple. I told myself the old superstitions was just that—strange beliefs. I told myself to take the ten dollars Mary MacDonald had paid me for putting the touch on her arthritis joint, and the other five I hadn't spent yet from winning bingo last Thursday. I told myself to go down to the Red Owl store.

And here is what I did that made the medicine backfire. I took an evil short-cut. I looked at birds that was dead and froze.

70   All right. So now I guess you will say, "Slap a malpractice suit on Lipsha Morrissey."

I heard of those suits. I used to think it was a color clothing quack doctors had to wear so you could tell them from the good ones. Now I know better that it's law.

As I walked back from the Red Owl with the rock-hard, heavy turkeys, I argued to myself about malpractice. I thought of faith. I thought to myself that faith could be called belief against the odds and whether or not there's any proof. How does that sound? I thought how we might have to yell to be heard by Higher Power, but that's not saying it's not *there*. And that is faith for you. It's belief even when the goods don't deliver. Higher Power makes promises we all know they can't back up, but anybody ever go and slap an old malpractice suit on God? Or the U.S. government? No they don't. Faith might be stupid, but it gets us through. So what I'm heading at is this. I finally convinced myself that the real actual power to the love medicine was not the goose heart itself but the faith in the cure.

I didn't believe it, I knew it was wrong, but by then I had waded so far into my lie I was stuck there. And then I went one step further.

The next day, I cleaned the hearts away from the paper packages of gizzards inside the turkeys. Then I wrapped them hearts with a clean hankie and brung them both to get blessed up at the mission. I wanted to get official blessings from the priest, but when Father answered the door to the rectory, wiping his hands on a little towel, I could tell he was a busy man.

"Booshoo,[1] Father," I said. "I got a slight request to make of you this after-   75
noon."

"What is it?" he said.

"Would you bless this package?" I held out the hankie with the hearts tied inside it.

He looked at the package, questioning it.

"It's turkey hearts," I honestly had to reply.

A look of annoyance crossed his face.   80

"Why don't you bring this matter over to Sister Martin," he said. "I have duties."

And so, although the blessing wouldn't be as powerful, I went over to the Sisters with the package.

I rung the bell, and they brought Sister Martin to the door. I had her as a music teacher, but I was always so shy then. I never talked out loud. Now, I had grown taller than Sister Martin. Looking down, I saw that she was not feeling up to snuff. Brown circles hung under her eyes.

"What's the matter?" she said, not noticing who I was.

"Remember me, Sister?"   85

She squinted up at me.

"Oh yes," she said after a moment. "I'm sorry, you're the youngest of the Kashpaws. Gordie's brother."

Her face warmed up.

"Lipsha," I said, "that's my name."

"Well, Lipsha," she said, smiling broad at me now, "what can I do for   90
you?"

They always said she was the kindest-hearted of the Sisters up the hill, and

---

1. *Bonjour*, French for "good day."

she was. She brought me back into their own kitchen and made me take a big yellow wedge of cake and a glass of milk.

"Now tell me," she said, nodding at my package. "What have you got wrapped up so carefully in those handkerchiefs?"

Like before, I answered honestly.

"Ah," said Sister Martin. "Turkey hearts." She waited.

95 "I hoped you could bless them."

She waited some more, smiling with her eyes. Kindhearted though she was, I began to sweat. A person could not pull the wool down over Sister Martin. I stumbled through my mind for an explanation, quick, that wouldn't scare her off.

"They're a present," I said, "for Saint Kateri's statue."

"She's not a saint yet."

"I know," I stuttered on, "in the hopes they will crown her."

100 "Lipsha," she said, "I never heard of such a thing."

So I told her. "Well the truth is," I said, "it's a kind of medicine."

"For what?"

"Love."

"Oh Lipsha," she said after a moment, "you don't need any medicine. I'm sure any girl would like you exactly the way you are."

105 I just sat there. I felt miserable, caught in my pack of lies.

"Tell you what," she said, seeing how bad I felt, "my blessing won't make any difference anyway. But there is something you can do."

I looked up at her hopeless.

"Just be yourself."

I looked down at my plate. I knew I wasn't much to brag about right then, and I shortly became even less. For as I walked out the door I stuck my fingers in the cup of holy water that was sacred from their touches. I put my fingers in and blessed the hearts, quick, with my own hand.

110 I went back to Grandma and sat down in her little kitchen at the Senior Citizens. I unwrapped them hearts on the table, and her hard agate eyes went soft. She said she wasn't even going to cook those hearts up but eat them raw so their power would go down strong as possible.

I couldn't hardly watch when she munched hers. Now that's true love. I was worried about how she would get Grandpa to eat his, but she told me she'd think of something and don't worry. So I did not. I was supposed to hide off in her bedroom while she put dinner on a plate for Grandpa and fixed up the heart so he'd eat it. I caught a glint of the plate she was making for him. She put that heart smack on a piece of lettuce like in a restaurant and then attached to it a little heap of boiled peas.

He sat down. I was listening in the next room.

She said, "Why don't you have some mash potato?" So he had some mash potato. Then she gave him a little piece of boiled meat. He ate that. Then she said, "Why you didn't never touch your salad yet. See that heart? I'm feeding you it because the doctor said your blood needs building up."

I couldn't help it, at that point I peeked through a crack in the door.

I saw Grandpa picking at that heart on his plate with a certain look. He   115
didn't look appetized at all, is what I'm saying. I doubted our plan was going to
work. Grandma was getting worried, too. She told him one more time, loudly,
that he had to eat that heart.

"Swallow it down," she said. "You'll hardly notice it."

He just looked at her straight on. The way he looked at her made me think
I was going to see the smokescreen drop a second time, and sure enough it
happened.

"What you want me to eat this for so bad?" he asked her uncannily.

Now Grandma knew the jig was up. She knew that he knew she was working
medicine. He put his fork down. He rolled the heart around his saucer plate.

"I don't want to eat this," he said to Grandma. "It don't look good."   120

"Why it's fresh grade-A," she told him. "One hundred percent."

He didn't ask percent what, but his eyes took on an even more warier look.

"Just go on and try it," she said, taking the salt shaker up in her hand. She
was getting annoyed. "Not tasty enough? You want me to salt it for you?" She
waved the shaker over his plate.

"All right, skinny white girl!" She had got Grandpa mad. Oopsy-daisy, he
popped the heart into his mouth. I was about to yawn loudly and come out of
the bedroom. I was about ready for this crash of wills to be over, when I saw he
was still up to his old tricks. First he rolled it into one side of his cheek.
"Mmmmm," he said. Then he rolled it into the other side of his cheek.
"Mmmmmmm," again. Then he stuck his tongue out with the heart on it and
put it back, and there was no time to react. He had pulled Grandma's leg once
too far. Her goat was got. She was so mad she hopped up quick as a wink and
slugged him between the shoulderblades to make him swallow.

Only thing is, he choked.   125

He choked real bad. A person can choke to death. You ever sit down at a
restaurant table and up above you there is a list of instructions what to do if
something slides down the wrong pipe? It sure makes you chew slow, that's for
damn sure. When Grandpa fell off his chair better believe me that little graphic
illustrated poster fled into my mind. I jumped out the bedroom. I done everything within my power that I could do to unlodge what was choking him. I
squeezed underneath his ribcage. I socked him in the back. I was desperate. But
here's the factor of decision: he wasn't choking on the heart alone. There was
more to it than that. It was other things that choked him as well. It didn't seem
like he wanted to struggle or fight. Death came and tapped his chest, so he went
just like that. I'm sorry all through my body at what I done to him with that
heart, and there's those who will say Lipsha Morrissey is just excusing himself
off the hook by giving song and dance about how Grandpa gave up.

Maybe I can't admit what I did. My touch had gone worthless, that is true.
But here is what I seen while he lay in my arms.

You hear a person's life will flash before their eyes when they're in danger.
It was him in danger, not me, but it was *his* life come over me. I saw him dying,
and it was like someone pulled the shade down in a room. His eyes clouded

over and squeezed shut, but just before that I looked in. He was still fishing in the middle of Lake Turcot. Big thoughts was on his line and he had half a case of beer in the boat. He waved at me, grinned, and then the bobber went under.

Grandma had gone out of the room crying for help. I bunched my force up in my hands and I held him. I was so wound up I couldn't even breathe. All the moments he had spent with me, all the times he had hoisted me on his shoulders or pointed into the leaves was concentrated in that moment. Time was flashing back and forth like a pinball machine. Lights blinked and balls hopped and rubber bands chirped, until suddenly I realized the last ball had gone down the drain and there was nothing. I felt his force leaving him, flowing out of Grandpa never to return. I felt his mind weakening. The bobber going under in the lake. And I felt the touch retreat back into the darkness inside my body, from where it came.

130   One time, long ago, both of us were fishing together. We caught a big old snapper what started towing us around like it was a motor. "This here fishline is pretty damn good," Grandpa said. "Let's keep this turtle on and see where he takes us." So we rode along behind that turtle, watching as from time to time it surfaced. The thing was just about the size of a washtub. It took us all around the lake twice, and as it was traveling, Grandpa said something as a joke. "Lipsha," he said, "we are glad your mother didn't want you because we was always looking for a boy like you who would tow us around the lake."

"I ain't no snapper. Snappers is so stupid they stay alive when their head's chopped off," I said.

"That ain't stupidity," said Grandpa. "Their brain's just in their heart, like yours is."

When I looked up, I knew the fuse had blown between my heart and my mind and that a terrible understanding was to be given.

Grandma got back into the room and I saw her stumble. And then she went down too. It was like a house you can't hardly believe has stood so long, through years of record weather, suddenly goes down in the worst yet. It makes sense, is what I'm saying, but you still can't hardly believe it. You think a person you know has got through death and illness and being broke and living on commodity rice will get through anything. Then they fold and you see how fragile were the stones that underpinned them. You see how instantly the ground can shift you thought was solid. You see the stop signs and the yellow dividing markers of roads you traveled and all the instructions you had played according to vanish. You see how all the everyday things you counted on was just a dream you had been having by which you run your whole life. She had been over me, like a sheer overhang of rock dividing Lipsha Morrissey from outer space. And now she went underneath. It was as though the banks gave way on the shores of Lake Turcot, and where Grandpa's passing was just the bobber swallowed under by his biggest thought, her fall was the house and the rock under it sliding after, sending half the lake splashing up to the clouds.

135   Where there was nothing.

You play them games never knowing what you see. When I fell into the dream alongside of both of them I saw that the dominions I had defended myself from anciently was but delusions of the screen. Blips of light. And I was scot-free now, whistling through space.

I don't know how I come back. I don't know from where. They was slapping my face when I arrived back at Senior Citizens and they was oxygenating her. I saw her chest move, almost unwilling. She sighed the way she would when somebody bothered her in the middle of a row of beads she was counting. I think it irritated her to no end that they brought her back. I knew from the way she looked after they took the mask off, she was not going to forgive them disturbing her restful peace. Nor was she forgiving Lipsha Morrissey. She had been stepping out onto the road of death, she told the children later at the funeral. I asked was there any stop signs or dividing markers on that road, but she clamped her lips in a vise the way she always done when she was mad.

Which didn't bother me. I knew when things had cleared out she wouldn't have no choice. I was not going to speculate where the blame was put for Grandpa's death. We was in it together. She had slugged him between the shoulders. My touch had failed him, never to return.

All the blood children and the took-ins, like me, came home from Minneapolis and Chicago, where they had relocated years ago. They stayed with friends on the reservation or with Aurelia or slept on Grandma's floor. They were struck down with grief and bereavement to be sure, every one of them. At the funeral I sat down in the back of the church with Albertine. She had gotten all skinny and ragged haired from cramming all her years of study into two or three. She had decided that to be a nurse was not enough for her so she was going to be a doctor. But the way she was straining her mind didn't look too hopeful. Her eyes were bloodshot from driving and crying. She took my hand. From the back we watched all the children and the mourners as they hunched over their prayers, their hands stuffed full of Kleenex. It was someplace in that long sad service that my vision shifted. I began to see things different, more clear. The family kneeling down turned to rocks in a field. It struck me how strong and reliable grief was, and death. Until the end of time, death would be our rock.

So I had perspective on it all, for death gives you that. All the Kashpaw children had done various things to me in their lives—shared their folks with me, loaned me cash, beat me up in secret—and I decided, because of death, then and there I'd call it quits. If I ever saw King again, I'd shake his hand. Forgiving somebody else made the whole thing easier to bear.

Everybody saw Grandpa off into the next world. And then the Kashpaws had to get back to their jobs, which was numerous and impressive. I had a few beers with them and I went back to Grandma, who had sort of got lost in the shuffle of everybody being sad about Grandpa and glad to see one another.

Zelda had sat beside her the whole time and was sitting with her now. I wanted to talk to Grandma, say how sorry I was, that it wasn't her fault, but only mine. I would have, but Zelda gave me one of her looks of strict warning as if to say, "I'll take care of Grandma. Don't horn in on the women."

If only Zelda knew, I thought, the sad realities would change her. But of course I couldn't tell the dark truth.

It was evening, late. Grandma's light was on underneath a crack in the door. About a week had passed since we buried Grandpa. I knocked first but there wasn't no answer, so I went right in. The door was unlocked. She was there but she didn't notice me at first. Her hands were tied up in her rosary, and her gaze was fully absorbed in the easy chair opposite her, the one that had always been Grandpa's favorite. I stood there, staring with her, at the little green nubs in the cloth and plastic armrest covers and the sad little hair-tonic stain he had made on the white doily where he laid his head. For the life of me I couldn't figure what she was staring at. Thin space. Then she turned.

145   "He ain't gone yet,' she said.

Remember that chill I luckily didn't get from waiting in the slough? I got it now. I felt it start from the very center of me, where fear hides, waiting to attack. It spiraled outward so that in minutes my fingers and teeth were shaking and clattering. I knew she told the truth. She seen Grandpa. Whether or not he had been there is not the point. She had *seen* him, and that meant anybody else could see him, too. Not only that but, as is usually the case with these here ghosts, he had a certain uneasy reason to come back. And of course Grandma Kashpaw had scanned it out.

I sat down. We sat together on the couch watching his chair out of the corner of our eyes. She had found him sitting in his chair when she walked in the door.

"It's the love medicine, my Lipsha," she said. "It was stronger than we thought. He came back even after death to claim me to his side."

I was afraid. "We shouldn't have tampered with it," I said. She agreed. For a while we sat still. I don't know what she thought, but my head felt screwed on backward. I couldn't accurately consider the situation, so I told Grandma to go to bed. I would sleep on the couch keeping my eye on Grandpa's chair. Maybe he would come back and maybe he wouldn't. I guess I feared the one as much as the other, but I got to thinking, see, as I lay there in darkness, that perhaps even through my terrible mistakes some good might come. If Grandpa did come back, I thought he'd return in his right mind. I could talk with him. I could tell him it was all my fault for playing with power I did not understand. Maybe he'd forgive me and rest in peace. I hoped this. I calmed myself and waited for him all night.

150   He fooled me though. He knew what I was waiting for, and it wasn't what he was looking to hear. Come dawn I heard a blood-splitting cry from the bedroom and I rushed in there. Grandma turnt the lights on. She was sitting on the edge of the bed and her face looked harsh, pinched-up, gray.

"He was here," she said. "He came and laid down next to me in bed. And he touched me."

Her heart broke down. She cried. His touch was so cold. She laid back in bed after a while, as it was morning, and I went to the couch. As I lay there, falling asleep, I suddenly felt Grandpa's presence and the barrier between us like a swollen river. I felt how I had wronged him. How awful was the place where I had sent him. Behind the wall of death, he'd watched the living eat and cry and get drunk. He was lonesome, but I understood he meant no harm.

"Go back," I said to the dark, afraid and yet full of pity. "You got to be with your own kind now," I said. I felt him retreating, like a sigh, growing less. I felt his spirit as it shrunk back through the walls, the blinds, the brick courtyard of Senior Citizens. "Look up Aunt June," I whispered as he left.

I slept late the next morning, a good hard sleep allowing the sun to rise and warm the earth. It was past noon when I awoke. There is nothing, to my mind, like a long sleep to make those hard decisions that you neglect under stress of wakefulness. Soon as I woke up that morning, I saw exactly what I'd say to Grandma. I had gotten humble in the past week, not just losing the touch but getting jolted into the understanding that would prey on me from here on out. Your life feels different on you, once you greet death and understand your heart's position. You wear your life like a garment from the mission bundle sale ever after—lightly because you realize you never paid nothing for it, cherishing because you know you won't ever come by such a bargain again. Also you have the feeling someone wore it before you and someone will after. I can't explain that, not yet, but I'm putting my mind to it.

"Grandma," I said, "I got to be honest about the love medicine."   155

She listened. I knew from then on she would be listening to me the way I had listened to her before. I told her about the turkey hearts and how I had them blessed. I told her what I used as love medicine was purely a fake, and then I said to her what my understanding brought me.

"Love medicine ain't what brings him back to you, Grandma. No, it's something else. He loved you over time and distance, but he went off so quick he never got the chance to tell you how he loves you, how he doesn't blame you, how he understands. It's true feeling, not no magic. No supermarket heart could have brung him back."

She looked at me. She was seeing the years and days I had no way of knowing, and she didn't believe me. I could tell this. Yet a look came on her face. It was like the look of mothers drinking sweetness from their children's eyes. It was tenderness.

"Lipsha," she said, "you was always my favorite."

She took the beads off the bedpost, where she kept them to say at night, and   160 she told me to put out my hand. When I did this, she shut the beads inside of my fist and held them there a long minute, tight, so my hand hurt. I almost cried when she did this. I don't really know why. Tears shot up behind my eyelids, and yet it was nothing. I didn't understand, except her hand was so strong, squeezing mine.

The earth was full of life and there were dandelions growing out the window, thick as thieves, already seeded, fat as big yellow plungers. She let my hand go. I got up. "I'll go out and dig a few dandelions," I told her.

Outside, the sun was hot and heavy as a hand on my back. I felt it flow down my arms, out my fingers, arrowing through the ends of the fork into the earth.

With every root I prized up there was return, as if I was kin to its secret lesson. The touch got stronger as I worked through the grassy afternoon. Uncurling from me like a seed out of the blackness where I was lost, the touch spread. The spiked leaves full of bitter mother's milk. A buried root. A nuisance people dig up and throw in the sun to wither. A globe of frail seeds that's indestructible.

1982

---

1. In the first dramatized scene, Lipsha, the narrator, at Grandma Kashpaw's request, tries to "put the touch" on Grandpa. By this time, some seventeen or eighteen paragraphs into the story, focus and voice and the setting and situation have been established; you should be getting a good idea of Lipsha's character, and you should be forming some fairly definite expectations about the plot, and, with the help of the title, you should have some glimmers about the developing theme. Write down what you have observed of the structure and elements of the story and what you expect to happen. As you read on, note how your expectations are fulfilled or modified: in what ways are these surprises or changes in expectations related to plot? character? theme? how do they define the world of the fiction? differ from your prior view of the world? To what extent are they convincing?

2. Voice is a dominant element in this story, and it is in large measure through Lipsha's voice that we infer his character. His language is ungrammatical—the story opens with "I never really *done* much . . ." and is full of phrases like "I don't got"—and his malapropisms (ludicrous misuse of words)—"templates" for "temples," "laundry" for "quandary," and "Phillipines" for "Philistines"—tend to undercut his apparent confidence in his literary skills ("Besides the dictionary, which I'm constantly in use of, I had this Bible once. I read it." [par. 26]). His limitations, skillfully indicated, extend to his somewhat naive view of reality—or causality: for example, his version of why Grandpa has symptoms of senility, his "thoughtful" acceptance of Grandpa's illuminating insight that God is going deaf. These errors, attitudes, and views, however, are endearing and often quite funny. Some of them will turn out, in strange ways, to seem almost wise. His kindness and good nature show through the errors and naivete, and he is capable of insights that, though naive and tender, are not ludicrous: "I thought love got easier over the years so it didn't hurt so bad when it hurt, or feel so good when it felt good" (par. 14); "From time to time I heal a person all up good inside, however when it comes to the long shot I doubt I got staying power. / And you need that, staying power, going out to love

somebody" (pars. 17 and 18). His voice reveals character and theme, and his character is instrumental in this plot. A challenging topic for a paper might be to show not only how the theme is presented in this story through a character who is not well educated or intellectually profound, but how the character's very limitations contribute meaning and force to that theme.

3. How is "love medicine" related to the plot? to Grandma's and Lipsha's characters? to theme? In what way(s) may it be considered a symbol?

4. Lipsha tells the stories of Lulu's "tweety bird" that disappeared up her dress and of Wristwatch, whose broken watch started keeping time after its owner dropped dead. He then says, "Not to get off the subject or nothing" (par. 65). Are these stories off the subject? How do they arouse expectations? How do they function in the plot? What do they tell you of Lipsha's character? of the nature of the people on the reservation? Are they related to the theme? if so, how? When he thinks of Wristwatch's grave being dug up in two hundred years, the watch still running, and the diggers asking, "Whose hand wound it?" he says he "started shaking like a piece of grass at just the thought" (par. 64). Is it with awe and fear or with laughter? Do you find it awesome or funny? If there is a difference between how you feel and how you believe Lipsha feels, what is the effect? What is the relationship of this difference to plot, character, voice, and the other elements of the story? How is this episode related to the "subject" he does not mean to be getting off of when the story continues: for example, he says he fires two "accurate" shots at the geese but the shots miss; how does this affect your view of his "reliability" and thus your reading of character? plot? theme? How does it affect your reading of his glance forward, "I never saw at the time how my thoughts led me astray toward a tragic outcome none could have known" (par. 68)? There is a death involved. Is it "tragic"? How do you respond to it? He says he took "an evil shortcut" in practicing love medicine: does that mean that he has discovered that the old beliefs are not "superstitions" or "strange" as he thought at the time?

5. Toward the end of the story, Lipsha tells Grandma that it was not "love medicine" that brought Grandpa's ghost back to her but love itself, not magic but feeling. Grandma looks at him tenderly and says, " 'Lipsha, . . . you was always my favorite' " (par. 159). Explain this passage in terms of the plot (but be sure to remember Lulu); in terms of Lipsha's character; in terms of Grandma's; in terms of theme (and you might even want to think of "love medicine" as symbol).

Like "Love Medicine," "The Watcher" is also told in the first person and is funny and serious. Charlie is only eleven when the incidents occur, but the voice is that of an older Charlie. His language, like Lipsha's, is the chief source of the humor, but his is not ungrammatical or sprinkled with malapropisms; rather, it is sophisticated, wry, and a bit sardonic. It fits the serious aspects of the story, which is not, as in "Love Medicine," about love. Just as you did in reading "Love Medicine," you might stop at an early point in the story (here I suggest paragraph 27) and take stock of your responses thus far, your attitude toward the narrator, and what, if anything, you are anticipating.

GUY VANDERHAEGHE

The Watcher

I suppose it was having a bad chest that turned me into an observer, a watcher, at an early age.

"Charlie has my chest," my mother often informed friends. "A real weakness there," she would add significantly, thumping her own wishbone soundly.

I suppose I had. Family lore had me narrowly escaping death from pneumonia at the age of four. It seems I spent an entire Sunday in delirium, soaking the sheets. Dr. Carlyle was off at the reservoir rowing in his little skiff and couldn't be reached—something for which my mother illogically refused to forgive him. She was a woman who nursed and tenaciously held dark grudges. Forever after that incident the doctor was slightlingly and coldly dismissed in conversation as a "man who betrayed the public's trust."

Following that spell of pneumonia, I regularly suffered from bouts of bronchitis, which often landed me in hospital in Fortune, forty miles away. Compared with the oxygen tent and the whacking great needles that were buried in my skinny rump there, being invalided at home was a piece of cake. Coughing and hacking, I would leaf through catalogues and read comic books until my head swam with print-fatigue. My diet was largely of my own whimsical choosing—hot chocolate and graham wafers were supplemented by sticky sweet coughdrops, which I downed one after the another until my stomach could take no more, revolted, and tossed up the whole mess.

5   With the first signs of improvement in my condition my mother moved her baby to the living-room chesterfield, where she and the radio could keep me company. The electric kettle followed me and was soon burbling in the corner, jetting steam into the air to keep my lungs moist and pliable. Because I was neither quite sick nor quite well, these were the best days of my illnesses. My stay at home hadn't yet made me bored and restless, my chest no longer hurt when I breathed, and that loose pocket of rattling phlegm meant I didn't have to worry about going back to school just yet. So I luxuriated in this steamy equatorial climate, tended by a doting mother as if I were a rare tropical orchid.

My parents didn't own a television and so my curiosity and attention were focused on my surroundings during my illnesses. I tried to squeeze every bit of juice out of them. Sooner than most children I learned that if you kept quiet and still and didn't insist on drawing attention to yourself as many kids did, adults were inclined to regard you as being one with the furniture, as significant and sentient as a hassock. By keeping mum I was treated to illuminating glances into an adult world of conventional miseries and scandals.

I wasn't sure at the age of six what a miscarriage was, but I knew that Ida Thompson had had one and that now her plumbing was buggered. And watching old lady Kuznetzky hang her washing, through a living-room window trickling with condensed kettle steam, I was able to confirm for myself the rumour that the old girl eschewed panties. As she bent over to rummage in her laundry basket I caught a brief glimpse of huge, white buttocks that shimmered in the pale spring sunshine.

I also soon knew (how I don't remember exactly) that Norma Ruggs had business with the Liquor Board Store when she shuffled by our window every day at exactly 10:50 a.m. She was always at the store door at 11:00 when they unlocked and opened up for business. At 11:15 she trudged home again, a pint of ice cream in one hand, a brown paper bag disguising a bottle of fortified wine in the other, and her blotchy complexion painted a high colour of shame.

"Poor old girl," my mother would say whenever she caught sight of Norma passing by in her shabby coat and sloppy man's overshoes. They had been in high school together, and Norma had been class brain and valedictorian. She had been an obliging, dutiful girl and still was. For the wine wasn't Norma's — the ice cream was her only vice. The booze was her husband's, a vet who had come back from the war badly crippled.

All this careful study of adults may have made me old before my time. In any case it seemed to mark me in some recognizable way as being "different" or "queer for a kid." When I went to live with my grandmother in July of 1959 she spotted it right away. Of course, she was only stating the obvious when she declared me skinny and delicate, but she also noted in her vinegary voice that my eyes had a bad habit of never letting her go, and that I was the worst case of little pitchers having big ears that she had ever come across.

I ended up at my grandmother's because in May of that year my mother's bad chest finally caught up with her, much to her and everyone else's surprise. It had been pretty generally agreed by all her acquaintances that Mabel Bradley's defects in that regard were largely imagined. Not so. A government-sponsored X-ray programme discovered tuberculosis, and she was packed off, pale and drawn with worry, for a stay in the sanatorium at Fort Qu'Appelle.

For roughly a month, until the school year ended, my father took charge of me and the house. He was a desolate, lanky, drooping weed of a man who had married late in life but nevertheless had been easily domesticated. I didn't like him much.

My father was badly wrenched by my mother's sickness and absence. He scrawled her long, untidy letters with a stub of gnawed pencil, and once he got shut of me, visited her every weekend. He was a soft and sentimental man whose eyes ran to water at the drop of a hat, or more accurately, death of a cat. Unlike his mother, my Grandma Bradley, he hadn't a scrap of flint or hard-headed common sense in him.

But then neither had any of his many brothers and sisters. It was as if the old girl had unflinchingly withheld the genetic code for responsibility and practicality from her pin-headed offspring. Life for her children was a series of thundering defeats, whirlwind calamities, or, at best, hurried strategic retreats. Businesses crashed and marriages failed, for they had—my father excepted—a taste for the unstable in partners marital and fiscal.

15   My mother saw no redeeming qualities in any of them. By and large they drank too much, talked too loudly, and raised ill-mannered children—monsters of depravity whose rudeness provided my mother with endless illustrations of what she feared I might become. "You're eating just like a pig," she would say, "exactly like your cousin Elvin." Or to my father, "You're neglecting the belt. He's starting to get as lippy as that little snot Muriel."

And in the midst, in the very eye of this familial cyclone of mishap and discontent, stood Grandma Bradley, as firm as a rock. Troubles of all kinds were laid on her doorstep. When my cousin Criselda suddenly turned big-tummied at sixteen and it proved difficult to ascertain with any exactitude the father, or even point a finger of general blame in the direction of a putative sire, she was shipped off to Grandma Bradley until she delivered. Uncle Ernie dried out on Grandma's farm and Uncle Ed hid there from several people he had sold prefab, assemble-yourself, crop-duster airplanes to.

So it was only family tradition that I should be deposited there. When domestic duties finally overwhelmed him, and I complained too loudly about fried-egg sandwiches for dinner *again*, my father left the bacon rinds hardening and curling grotesquely on unwashed plates, the slut's wool eddying along the floor in the currents of a draft, and drove the one hundred and fifty miles to the farm, *right then and there*.

My father, a dangerous man behind the wheel, took any extended trip seriously, believing the highways to be narrow, unnavigable ribbons of carnage. This trip loomed so dangerously in his mind that, rather than tear a hand from the wheel, or an eye from the road, he had me, *chronic sufferer of lung disorders*, light his cigarettes and place them carefully in his dry lips. My mother would have killed him.

"You'll love it at Grandma's," he kept saying unconvincingly, "you'll have a real boy's summer on the farm. It'll build you up, the chores and all that. And good fun too. You don't know it now, but you are living the best days of your life right now. What I wouldn't give to be a kid again. You'll love it there. There's chickens and *everything*."

20   It wasn't exactly a lie. There were chickens. But the *everything*—as broad and overwhelming and suggestive of possibilities as my father tried to make it sound—didn't cover much. It certainly didn't comprehend a pony or a dog as I had hoped, chickens being the only livestock on the place.

It turned out that my grandmother, although she had spent most of her life on that particular piece of ground and eventually died there, didn't care much for the farm and was entirely out of sympathy with most varieties of animal life. She did keep chickens for the eggs, although she admitted that her spirits lifted considerably in the fall when it came time to butcher the hens.

Her flock was a garrulous, scraggly crew that spent their days having dust baths in the front yard, hiding their eggs, and, fleet and ferocious as hunting cheetahs, running down scuttling lizards which they trampled and pecked to death while their shiny, expressionless eyes shifted dizzily in their stupid heads. The only one of these birds I felt any compassion for was Stanley the rooster, a bedraggled male who spent his days tethered to a stake by a piece of bailer twine looped around his leg. Poor Stanley crowed heart-rendingly in his captivity: his comb drooped pathetically, and he was utterly crestfallen as he lecherously eyed his bantam beauties daintily scavenging. Grandma kept him in this unnatural bondage to prevent him fertilizing the eggs and producing blood spots in the yolks. Being a finicky eater I approved this policy, but nevertheless felt some guilt over Stanley.

No, the old Bradley homestead, all that encompassed by my father's *every-thing*, wasn't very impressive. The two-storey house, though big and solid, needed paint and shingles. A track had been worn in the kitchen linoleum clean through to the floorboards and a long rent in the screen door had been stitched shut with waxed thread. The yard was little more than a tangle of thigh-high ragweed and sowthistle to which the chickens repaired for shade. A windbreak of spruce on the north side of the house was dying from lack of water and the competition from Scotch thistle. The evergreens were no longer green; their sere needles fell away from the branches at the touch of a hand.

The abandoned barn out back was flanked by two mountainous rotted piles of manure which I remember sprouting button mushrooms after every warm soaker of a rain. That pile of shit was the only useful thing in a yard full of junk: wrecked cars, old wagon wheels, collapsing sheds. The barn itself was mightily decayed. The paint had been stripped from its planks by rain, hail, and dry, blistering winds, and the roof sagged like a tired nag's back. For a small boy it was an ominous place on a summer day. The air was still and dark and heavy with heat. At the sound of footsteps rats squeaked and scrabbled in the empty mangers, and the sparrows which had spattered the rafters white with their dung whirred about and fluted ghostly cries.

In 1959 Grandma Bradley would have been sixty-nine, which made her a child of the gay nineties—although the supposed gaiety of that age didn't seem to have made much impress upon the development of her character. Physically she was an imposing woman. Easily six feet tall, she carried a hundred and eighty pounds on her generous frame without prompting speculation as to what she had against girdles. She could touch the floor effortlessly with the flat of her palms and pack an eighty-pound sack of chicken feed on her shoulder. She dyed her hair auburn in defiance of local mores, and never went to town to play bridge, whist, or canasta without wearing a hat and getting dressed to the teeth. Grandma loved card games of all varieties and considered anyone who didn't a mental defective.

25

A cigarette always smouldered in her trap. She smoked sixty a day and rolled them thin as knitting needles in an effort at economy. These cigarettes were so wispy and delicate they tended to get lost between her swollen fingers.

And above all she believed in plain speaking. She let me know that as my father's maroon Meteor pulled out of the yard while we stood waving goodbye on the front steps.

"Let's get things straight from the beginning," she said without taking her eyes off the car as it bumped toward the grid road. "I don't chew my words twice. If you're like any of the rest of them I've had here, you've been raised as wild as a goddamn Indian. Not one of my grandchildren have been brought up to mind. Well, you'll mind around here. I don't jaw and blow hot air to jaw and blow hot air. I belted your father when he needed it, and make no mistake I'll belt you. Is that understood?"

"Yes," I said with a sinking feeling as I watched my father's car disappear down the road, swaying from side to side as its suspension was buffeted by pot-holes.

"These bloody bugs are eating me alive," she said, slapping her arm. "I'm going in."

I trailed after her as she slopped back into the house in a pair of badly mauled, laceless sneakers. The house was filled with a half-light that changed its texture with every room. The venetian blinds were drawn in the parlour and some flies carved Immelmanns in the dark air that smelled of cellar damp. Others battered their bullet bodies *tip-tap, tip-tap* against the window-panes.

In the kitchen my grandmother put the kettle on the stove to boil for tea. After she had lit one of her matchstick smokes, she inquired through a blue haze if I was hungry.

"People aren't supposed to smoke around me," I informed her. "Because of my chest. Dad can't even smoke in our house."

"That so?" she said genially. Her cheeks collapsed as she drew on her butt. I had a hint there, if I'd only known it, of how she'd look in her coffin. "You won't like it here then," she said. "I smoke all the time."

I tried a few unconvincing coughs. I was ignored. She didn't respond to the same signals as my mother.

"My mother has a bad chest, too," I said. "She's in a TB sanatorium."

"So I heard," my grandmother said, getting up to fetch the whistling kettle. "Oh, I suspect she'll be as right as rain in no time with a little rest. TB isn't what it used to be. Not with all these new drugs." She considered. "That's not to say though that your father'll ever hear the end of it. Mabel was always a silly little shit that way."

I almost fell off my chair. I had never thought I'd live to hear the day my mother was called a silly little shit.

"Drink tea?" asked Grandma Bradley, pouring boiling water into a brown teapot.

I shook my head.

"How old are you anyway?" she asked.

"Eleven."

"You're old enough then," she said, taking down a cup from the shelf. "Tea gets the kidneys moving and carries off the poisons in the blood. That's why all the Chinese live to be so old. They all live to be a hundred."

"I don't know if my mother would like it," I said. "Me drinking tea."

"You worry a lot for a kid," she said, "don't you?"   45

I didn't know how to answer that. It wasn't a question I had ever considered. I tried to shift the conversation.

"What's there for a kid to do around here?" I said in an unnaturally inquisitive voice.

"Well, we could play cribbage."

"I don't know how to play cribbage."

She was genuinely shocked. "What!" she exclaimed. "Why, you're eleven   50
years old! Your father could count a cribbage hand when he was five. I taught all my kids to."

"I never learned how," I said. "We don't even have a deck of cards at our house. My father hates cards. Says he had too much of them as a boy."

At this my grandmother arched her eyebrows. "Is that a fact? Well, hoity-toity."

"So, since I don't play cards," I continued in a strained manner I imagined was polite, "what could I do—I mean, for fun?"

"Make your own fun," she said. "I never considered fun such a problem. Use your imagination. Take a broomstick and make like Nimrod."

"Who's Nimrod?" I asked.   55

"Pig ignorant," she said under her breath, and then louder, directly to me, "Ask me no questions and I'll tell you no lies. Drink your tea."

And that, for the time being, was that.

It's all very well to tell someone to make their own fun. It's the making of it that is the problem. In a short time I was a very bored kid. There was no one to play with, no horses to ride, no gun to shoot gophers, no dog for company. There was nothing to read except the *Country Guide* and *Western Producer*. There was nothing or nobody interesting to watch. I went through my grandmother's drawers but found nothing as surprising there as I had discovered in my parents'.

Most days it was so hot that the very idea of fun boiled out of me and evaporated. I moped and dragged myself listlessly around the house in the loose-jointed, water-boned way kids have when they can't stand anything, not even their precious selves.

On my better days I tried to take up with Stanley the rooster. Scant chance   60
of that. Tremors of panic ran through his body at my approach. He tugged desperately on the twine until he jerked his free leg out from under himself and collapsed in the dust, his heart bumping the tiny crimson scallops of his breast feathers, the black pellets of his eyes glistening, all the while shitting copiously. Finally, in the last extremes of chicken terror, he would allow me to stroke his yellow beak and finger his comb.

I felt sorry for the captive Stanley and several times tried to take him for a walk, to give him a chance to take the air and broaden his limited horizons. But this prospect alarmed him so much that I was always forced to return him to his stake in disgust while he fluttered, squawked and flopped.

So fun was a commodity in short supply. That is, until something interesting turned up during the first week of August. Grandma Bradley was dredging little watering canals with a hoe among the corn stalks on a bright blue Monday morning, and I was shelling peas into a colander on the front stoop, when a black car nosed diffidently up the road and into the yard. Then it stopped a good twenty yards short of the house as if its occupants weren't sure of their welcome. After some time, the doors opened and a man and woman got carefully out.

The woman wore turquoise-blue pedal-pushers, a sloppy black turtleneck sweater, and a gash of scarlet lipstick swiped across her white, vivid face. This was my father's youngest sister, Aunt Evelyn.

The man took her gently and courteously by the elbow and balanced her as she edged up the front yard in her high heels, careful to avoid turning an ankle on a loose stone, or in an old tyre track.

65 The thing which immediately struck me about the man was his beard—the first I had ever seen. Beards weren't popular in 1959—not in our part of the world. His was a randy, jutting, little goat's-beard that would have looked wicked on any other face but his. He was very tall and his considerable height was accented by a lack of corresponding breadth to his body. He appeared to have been racked and stretched against his will into an exceptional and unnatural anatomy. As he walked and talked animatedly, his free hand fluttered in front of my aunt. It sailed, twirled and gambolled on the air. Like a butterfly enticing a child, it seemed to lead her hypnotized across a yard fraught with perils for city-shod feet.

My grandmother laid down her hoe and called sharply to her daughter.

"Evvie!" she called. "Over here, Evvie!"

At the sound of her mother's voice my aunt's head snapped around and she began to wave jerkily and stiffly, striving to maintain a tottering balance on her high-heeled shoes. It wasn't hard to see that there was something not quite right with her. By the time my grandmother and I reached the pair, Aunt Evelyn was in tears, sobbing hollowly and jamming the heel of her palm into her front teeth.

The man was speaking calmly to her. "Control. Control. Deep, steady breaths. Think sea. Control. Control. Control. Think sea, Evelyn. Deep. Deep. Deep," he muttered.

70 "What the hell is the matter, Evelyn?" my grandmother asked sharply. "And who is *he?*"

"Evelyn is a little upset," the man said, keeping his attention focused on my aunt. "She's having one of her anxiety attacks. If you'd just give us a moment we'll clear this up. She's got to learn to handle stressful situations." He inclined his head in a priestly manner and said, "Be with the sea, Evelyn. Deep. Deep. Sink in the sea."

"It's her damn nerves again," said my grandmother.

"Yes," the man said benignly, with a smile of blinding condescension. "Sort of."

"She's been as nervous as a cut cat all her life," said my grandmother, mostly to herself.

"Momma," said Evelyn, weeping. "Momma."

"Slide beneath the waves, Evelyn. Down, down, down to the beautiful pearls," the man chanted softly. This was really something.

My grandmother took Aunt Evelyn by her free elbow, shook it, and said sharply, "Evelyn, shut up!" Then she began to drag her briskly toward the house. For a moment the man looked as if he had it in mind to protest, but in the end he meekly acted as a flanking escort for Aunt Evelyn as she was marched into the house. When I tried to follow, my grandmother gave me one of her looks and said definitely, "You find something to do out here."

I did. I waited a few minutes and then duck-walked my way under the parlour window. There I squatted with my knobby shoulder blades pressed against the siding and the sun beating into my face.

My grandmother obviously hadn't wasted any time with the social niceties. They were fairly into it.

"Lovers?" said my grandmother. "Is that what it's called now? Shack-up, you mean."

"Oh, Momma," said Evelyn, and she was crying, "it's all right. We're going to get married."

"You believe that?" said my grandmother. "You believe that geek is going to marry you?"

"Thompson," said the geek, "my name is Thompson, Robert Thompson, and we'll marry as soon as I get my divorce. Although Lord only knows when that'll be."

"That's right," said my grandmother, "Lord only knows." Then to her daughter, "You got another one. A real prize off the midway, didn't you? Evelyn, you're a certifiable lunatic."

"I didn't expect this," said Thompson. "We came here because Evelyn has had a bad time of it recently. She hasn't been eating or sleeping properly and consequently she's got herself run down. She finds it difficult to control her emotions, don't you, darling?"

I thought I heard a mild yes.

"So," said Thompson, continuing, "we decided Evelyn needs some peace and quiet before I go back to school in September."

"School," said my grandmother. "Don't tell me you're some kind of teacher?" She seemed stunned by the very idea.

"No," said Aunt Evelyn, and there was a tremor of pride in her voice that testified to her amazement that she had been capable of landing such a rare and remarkable fish. "Not a teacher. Robert's a graduate student of American Literature at the University of British Columbia."

"Hoity-toity," said Grandmother. "A graduate student. A graduate student of American Literature."

"Doctoral programme," said Robert.

"And did you ever ask yourself, Evelyn, what the hell this genius is doing with you? Or is it just the same old problem with you—elevator panties? Some guy comes along and pushes the button. Up, down. Up, down."

The image this created in my mind made me squeeze my knees together deliciously and stifle a giggle.

"Mother," said Evelyn, continuing to bawl.

95 "Guys like this don't marry barmaids," said my grandmother.

"Cocktail hostess," corrected Evelyn. "I'm a cocktail hostess."

"You don't have to make any excuses, dear," said Thompson pompously. "Remember what I told you. You're past the age of being judged."

"What the hell is that supposed to mean?" said my grandmother. "And by the way, don't start handing out orders in my house. You won't be around long enough to make them stick."

"That remains to be seen," said Thompson.

100 "Let's go, Robert," said Evelyn nervously.

"Go on upstairs, Evelyn. I want to talk to your mother."

"You don't have to go anywhere," said my grandmother. "You can stay put."

"Evelyn, go upstairs." There was a pause and then I heard the sound of a chair creaking, then footsteps.

"Well," said my grandmother at last, "round one. Now for round two—get the hell out of my house."

105 "Can't do that."

"Why the hell not?"

"It's very difficult to explain," he said.

"Try."

"As you can see for yourself, Evelyn isn't well. She is very highly strung at the moment. I believe she is on the verge of a profound personality adjustment, a breakthrough." He paused dramatically. "Or breakdown."

110 "It's times like this that I wished I had a dog on the place to run off undesirables."

"The way I read it," said Thompson, unperturbed, "is that at the moment two people bulk very large in Evelyn's life. You and me. She needs the support and love of us both. You're not doing your share."

"I ought to slap your face."

"She has come home to try to get a hold of herself. We have to bury our dislikes for the moment. She needs to be handled very carefully."

"You make her sound like a trained bear. *Handled.* What that girl needs is a good talking to, and I am perfectly capable of giving her that."

115 "No, Mrs. Bradley," Thompson said firmly in that maddeningly self-assured tone of his. "If you don't mind me saying so, I think that's part of her problem. It's important now for you to just let Evelyn *be.*"

"Get out of my house," said my grandmother, at the end of her tether.

"I know it's difficult for you to understand," he said smoothly, "but if you understood the psychology of this you would see it's impossible for me to go; or for that matter, for Evelyn to go. If I leave she'll feel *I've* abandoned her. It can't be done. We're faced with a real psychological balancing act here."

"Now I've heard everything," said my grandmother. "Are you telling me you'd have the gall to move into a house where you're not wanted and just . . . just *stay there?*"

"Yes," said Thompson. "And I think you'll find me quite stubborn on this particular point."

"My God," said my grandmother. I could tell by her tone of voice that she had never come across anyone like Mr. Thompson before. At a loss for a suitable reply, she simply reiterated, "My God."   120

"I'm going upstairs now," said Thompson. "Maybe you could get the boy to bring in our bags while I see how Evelyn is doing. The car isn't locked." The second time he spoke his voice came from further away; I imagined him paused in the doorway. "Mrs. Bradley, please let's make this stay pleasant for Evelyn's sake."

She didn't bother answering him.

When I barged into the house some time later with conspicuous noisiness, I found my grandmother standing at the bottom of the stairs staring up the steps. "Well, I'll be damned," she said under her breath. "I've never seen anything like that. Goddamn freak." She even repeated it several times under her breath. "Goddamn freak. Goddamn freak."

Who could blame me if, after a boring summer, I felt my chest tighten with anticipation. Adults could be immensely interesting and entertaining if you knew what to watch for.

At first things were disappointingly quiet. Aunt Evelyn seldom set forth out-   125
side the door of the room she and her man inhabited by squatters' right. There was an argument, short and sharp, between Thompson and Grandmother over this. The professor claimed no one had any business prying into what Evelyn did up there. She was an adult and had the right to her privacy and her own thoughts. My grandmother claimed *she* had a right to know what was going on up there, even if nobody else thought she did.

I could have satisfied her curiosity on that point. Not much was going on up there. Several squints through the keyhole had revealed Aunt Evelyn lolling about the bedspread in a blue housecoat, eating soda crackers and sardines, and reading a stack of movie magazines she had me lug out of the trunk of the car.

Food, you see, was beginning to become something of a problem for our young lovers. Grandma rather pointedly set only three places for meals, and Evelyn, out of loyalty to her boyfriend, couldn't very well sit down and break bread with us. Not that Thompson didn't take such things in his stride. He sauntered casually and conspicuously about the house as if he owned it, even going so far as to poke his head in the fridge and rummage in it like some pale, hairless bear. At times like that my grandmother was capable of looking through him as if he didn't exist.

On the second day of his stay Thompson took up with me, which was all right as far as I was concerned. I had no objection. Why he decided to do this I'm not sure exactly. Perhaps he was looking for some kind of an ally, no matter how weak. Most likely he wanted to get under the old lady's skin. Or maybe he just couldn't bear not having anyone to tell how wonderful he was. Thompson was that kind of a guy.

I was certainly let in on the secret. He was a remarkable fellow. He dwelt at great length on those things which made him such an extraordinary human being. I may have gotten the order of precedence all wrong, but if I remember correctly there were three things which made Thompson very special and different from all the other people I would ever meet, no matter how long or hard I lived.

130   First, he was going to write a book about a poet called Allen Ginsberg[1] which was going to knock the socks off everybody who counted. It turned out he had actually met this Ginsberg the summer before in San Francisco and asked him if he could write a book about him and Ginsberg had said, Sure, why the hell not? The way Thompson described what it would be like when he published this book left me with the impression that he was going to spend most of the rest of his life riding around on people's shoulders and being cheered by a multitude of admirers.

Second, he confessed to knowing a tremendous amount about what made other people tick and how to adjust their mainsprings when they went kaflooey. He knew all this because at one time his own mainspring had gotten a little out of sorts. But now he was a fully integrated personality with a highly creative mind and a strong intuitive sense. That's why he was so much help to Aunt Evelyn in her time of troubles.

Third, he was a Buddhist.

The only one of these things which impressed me at the time was the bit about being a Buddhist. However, I was confused, because in the *Picture Book of the World's Great Religions* which we had at home, all the Buddhists were bald, and Thompson had a hell of a lot of hair, more than I had ever seen on a man. But even though he wasn't bald, he had an idol. A little bronze statue with the whimsical smile and slightly crossed eyes which he identified as Padmasambhava.[2] He told me that it was a Tibetan antique he had bought in San Francisco as an object of veneration and an aid to his meditations. I asked him what a meditation was and he offered to teach me one. So I learned to recite with great seriousness and flexible intonation one of his Tibetan meditations, while my grandmother glared across her quintessentially Western parlour with unbelieving eyes.

I could soon deliver. "A king must go when his time has come. His wealth, his friends and his relatives cannot go with him. Wherever men go, wherever they stay, the effect of their past acts follows them like a shadow. Those who are in the grip of desire, the grip of existence, the grip of ignorance, move helplessly round through the spheres of life, as men or gods or as wretches in the lower regions."

135   Not that an eleven-year-old could make much of any of *that*.

---

1. American poet (b. 1926) whose epic poem *Howl* (1956) is a significant product of the Beat movement.   2. Legendary Buddhist mystic who introduced Tantric Buddhism to Tibet. His followers emphasize Tantric ritual, worship, and yoga.

Which is not to say that even an eleven-year-old could be fooled by Robert Thompson. In his stubbornness, egoism and blindness he was transparently un-Buddhalike. To watch him and my grandmother snarl and snap their teeth over that poor, dry bone, Evelyn, was evidence enough of how firmly bound we all are to the wretched wheel of life and its stumbling desires.

No, even his most effective weapon, his cool benevolence, that patina of patience and forbearance which Thompson displayed to Grandmother, could crack.

One windy day when he had coaxed Aunt Evelyn out for a walk I followed them at a distance. They passed the windbreak of spruce, and at the sagging barbed-wire fence he gallantly manipulated the wires while my aunt floundered over them in an impractical dress and crinoline. It was the kind of dippy thing she would decide to wear on a hike.

Thompson strode along through the rippling grass like a wading heron, his baggy pant-legs flapping and billowing in the wind. My aunt moved along gingerly behind him, one hand modestly pinning down her wind-teased dress in the front, the other hand plastering the back of it to her behind.

It was only when they stopped and faced each other that I realized that all 140 the time they had been traversing the field they had been arguing. A certain vaguely communicated agitation in the attitude of her figure, the way his arm stabbed at the featureless wash of sky, implied a dispute. She turned toward the house and he caught her by the arm and jerked it. In a fifties calendar fantasy her dress lifted in the wind, exposing her panties. I sank in the grass until their seed tassels trembled against my chin. I wasn't going to miss watching this for the world.

She snapped and twisted on the end of his arm like a fish on a line. Her head was flung back in an exaggerated, antique display of despair; her head rolled grotesquely from side to side as if her neck were broken.

Suddenly Thompson began striking awkwardly at her exposed buttocks and thighs with the flat of his hand. The long, gangly arm slashed like a flail as she scampered around him, the radius of her escape limited by the distance of their linked arms.

From where I knelt in the grass I could hear nothing. I was too far off. As far as I was concerned there were no cries and no pleading. The whole scene, as I remember it, was shorn of any of the personal idiosyncrasies which manifest themselves in violence. It appeared a simple case of retribution.

That night, for the first time, my aunt came down to supper and claimed her place at the table with queenly graciousness. She wore shorts, too, for the first time, and gave a fine display of mottled, discoloured thighs which reminded me of bruised fruit. She made sure, almost as if by accident, that my grandmother had a good hard look at them.

Right out of the blue my grandmother said, "I don't want you hanging 145 around that man any more. You stay away from him."

"Why?" I asked rather sulkily. He was the only company I had. Since my aunt's arrival Grandmother had paid no attention to me whatsoever.

It was late afternoon and we were sitting on the porch watching Evelyn squeal as she swung in the tyre swing Thompson had rigged up for me in the barn. He had thrown a length of stray rope over the runner for the sliding door and hung a tyre from it. I hadn't the heart to tell him I was too old for tyre swings.

Aunt Evelyn seemed to be enjoying it though. She was screaming and girlishly kicking up her legs. Thompson couldn't be seen. He was deep in the settled darkness of the barn, pushing her back and forth. She disappeared and reappeared according to the arc which she travelled through. Into the barn, out in the sun. Light, darkness. Light, darkness.

Grandma ignored my question. "Goddamn freak," she said, scratching a match on the porch rail and lighting one of her rollies. "Wait and see, he'll get his wagon fixed."

150 "Aunt Evelyn likes him," I noted pleasantly, just to stir things up a bit.

"Your Aunt Evelyn's screws are loose," she said sourly. "And he's the son of a bitch who owns the screwdriver that loosened them."

"He must be an awful smart fellow to be studying to be a professor at a university," I commented. It was the last dig I could chance.

"One thing I know for sure," snapped my grandmother. "He isn't smart enough to lift the toilet seat when he pees. There's evidence enough for that."

After hearing that, I took to leaving a few conspicuous droplets of my own as a matter of course on each visit. Every little bit might help things along.

155 I stood in his doorway and watched Thompson meditate. And don't think that, drenched in *satori*[3] as he was, he didn't know it. He put on quite a performance sitting on the floor in his underpants. When he came out of his trance he pretended to be surprised to see me. While he dressed we struck up a conversation.

"You know, Charlie," he said while he put on his sandals (I'd never seen a grown man wear sandals in my entire life), "you remind me of my little Padma-sambhava," he said, nodding to the idol squatting on his dresser. "For a while, you know, I thought it was the smile, but it isn't. It's the eyes."

"Its eyes are crossed," I said, none too flattered at the comparison.

"No they're not," he said good-naturedly. He tucked his shirt-tail into his pants. "The artist, the maker of that image, set them fairly close together to suggest—aesthetically speaking—the intensity of inner vision, its concentration." He picked up the idol and, looking at it, said, "These are very watchful eyes, very knowing eyes. Your eyes are something like that. From your eyes I could tell you're an intelligent boy." He paused, set Padma-sambhava back on the dresser, and asked. "Are you?"

I shrugged.

160 "Don't be afraid to say if you are," he said. "False modesty can be as corrupting as vanity. It took me twenty-five years to learn that."

---

3. A state of enlightenment in Buddhism, achieved by intensive meditation.

"I usually get all A's on my report card," I volunteered.

"Well, that's something," he said, looking around the room for his belt. He picked a sweater off a chair and peered under it. "Then you see what's going on around here, don't you?" he asked. "You see what your grandmother is mistakenly trying to do?"

I nodded.

"That's right," he said. "You're a smart boy." He sat down on the bed. "Come here."

I went over to him. He took hold of me by the arms and looked into my eyes with all the sincerity he could muster. "You know, being intelligent means responsibilities. It means doing something worth while with your life. For instance, have you given any thought as to what you would like to be when you grow up?"

"A spy," I said.

The silly bugger laughed.

It was the persistent, rhythmic thud that first woke me, and once wakened, I picked up the undercurrent of muted clamour, of stifled struggle. The noise seeped through the beaverboard wall of the adjoining bedroom into my own, a storm of hectic urgency and violence. The floorboards of the old house squeaked; I heard what sounded like a strangled curse and moan, then a fleshy, meaty concussion which I took to be a slap. Was he killing her at last? Choking her with the silent, poisonous care necessary to escape detection?

I remembered Thompson's arm flashing frenziedly in the sunlight. My aunt's discoloured thighs. My heart creaked in my chest with fear. And after killing her? Would the madman stop? Or would he do us all in, one by one?

I got out of bed on unsteady legs. The muffled commotion was growing louder, more distinct. I padded into the hallway. The door to their bedroom was partially open, and a light showed. Terror made me feel hollow; the pit of my stomach ached.

They were both naked, something which I hadn't expected, and which came as quite a shock. What was perhaps even more shocking was the fact that they seemed not only oblivious of me, but of each other as well. She was slung around so that her head was propped on a pillow resting on the footboard of the bed. One smooth leg was draped over the edge of the bed and her heel was beating time on the floorboards (the thud which woke me) as accompaniment to Thompson's plunging body and the soft, liquid grunts of expelled air which he made with every lunge. One of her hands gripped the footboard and her knuckles were white with strain.

I watched until the critical moment, right through the growing frenzy and ardour. They groaned and panted and heaved and shuddered and didn't know themselves. At the very last he lifted his bony, hatchet face with the jutting beard to the ceiling and closed his eyes; for a moment I thought he was praying as his lips moved soundlessly. But then he began to whimper and his mouth fell open and he looked stupider and weaker than any human being I had ever seen before in my life.

"Like pigs at the trough," my grandmother said at breakfast. "With the boy up there too."

My aunt turned a deep red, and then flushed again so violently that her thin lips appeared to turn blue.

I kept my head down and went on shovelling porridge. Thompson still wasn't invited to the table. He was leaning against the kitchen counter, his bony legs crossed at the ankles, eating an apple he had helped himself to.

"He didn't hear anything," my aunt said uncertainly. She whispered conspiratorially across the table to Grandmother. "Not at that hour. He'd been asleep for hours."

I thought it wise, even though it meant drawing attention to myself, to establish my ignorance. "Hear what?" I inquired innocently.

"It wouldn't do any harm if he had," said Thompson, calmly biting and chewing the temptress's fruit.

"You wouldn't see it, would you?" said Grandma Bradley. "It wouldn't matter to you what he heard? You'd think that was manly."

"Manly has nothing to do with it. Doesn't enter into it," said Thompson in that cool way he had. "It's a fact of life, something he'll have to find out about sooner or later."

Aunt Evelyn began to cry. "Nobody is ever pleased with me," she spluttered. "I'm going crazy trying to please you both. I can't do it." She began to pull nervously at her hair. "He made me," she said finally in a confessional, humble tone to her mother.

"Evelyn," said my grandmother, "you have a place here. I would never send you away. I want you here. But he has to go. I want him to go. If he is going to rub my nose in it that way he has to go. I won't have that man under my roof."

"Evelyn isn't apologizing for anything," Thompson said. "And she isn't running away either. You can't force her to choose. It isn't healthy or fair."

"There have been other ones before you," said Grandma. "This isn't anything new for Evelyn."

"Momma!"

"I'm aware of that," he said stiffly, and his face vibrated with the effort to smile. "Provincial mores have never held much water with me. I like to think I'm above all that."

Suddenly my grandmother spotted me. "What are you gawking at!" she shouted. "Get on out of here!"

I didn't budge an inch.

"Leave him alone," said Thompson.

"You'll be out of here within a week," said Grandmother. "I swear."

"No," he said smiling. "When I'm ready."

"You'll go home and go with your tail between your legs. Last night was the last straw," she said. And by God you could tell she meant it.

Thompson gave her his beatific Buddha-grin and shook his head from side to side, very, very slowly.

A thunderstorm was brewing. The sky was a stew of dark, swollen clouds and a strange apple-green light. The temperature stood in the mid-nineties, not a breath of breeze stirred, my skin crawled and my head pounded above my eyes and through the bridge of my nose. There wasn't a thing to do except sit on the bottom step of the porch, keep from picking up a sliver in your ass, and scratch the dirt with a stick. My grandmother had put her hat on and driven into town on some unexplained business. Thompson and my aunt were upstairs in their bedroom, sunk in a stuporous, sweaty afternoon's sleep.

Like my aunt and Thompson, all the chickens had gone to roost to wait for rain. The desertion of his harem had thrown the rooster into a flap. Stanley trotted neurotically around his tethering post, stopping every few circuits to beat his bedraggled pinions and crow lustily in masculine outrage. I watched him for a bit without much curiosity, and then climbed off the step and walked toward him, listlessly dragging my stick in my trail. 195

"Here Stanley, Stanley," I called, not entirely sure how to summon a rooster, or instil in him confidence and friendliness.

I did neither. My approach only further unhinged Stanley. His stride lengthened, the tempo of his pace increased, and his head began to dart abruptly from side to side in furtive despair. Finally, in a last desperate attempt to escape, Stanley upset himself trying to fly. He landed in a heap of disarranged, stiff, glistening feathers. I put my foot on his string and pinned him to the ground.

"Nice pretty, pretty Stanley," I said coaxingly, adopting the tone that a neighbour used with her budgie, since I wasn't sure how one talked to a bird. I slowly extended my thumb to stroke his bright-red neck feathers. Darting angrily, he struck the ball of my thumb with a snappish peck and simultaneously hit my wrist with his heel spur. He didn't hurt me, but he did startle me badly. So badly I gave a little yelp. Which made me feel foolish and more than a little cowardly.

"You son of a bitch," I said, reaching down slowly and staring into one unblinking glassy eye in which I could see my face looming larger and larger. I caught the rooster's legs and held them firmly together. Stanley crowed defiantly and showed me his wicked little tongue.

"Now, Stanley," I said, "relax, I'm just going to stroke you. I'm just going to stroke you. I'm just going to pet Stanley." 200

No deal. He struck furiously again with a snake-like agility, and bounded in my hand, wings beating his poultry smell into my face. A real fighting cock at last. Maybe it was the weather. Perhaps his rooster pride and patience would suffer no more indignities.

The heat, the sultry menace of the gathering storm, made me feel prickly, edgy. I flicked my middle finger smartly against his tiny chicken skull, hard enough to rattle his pea-sized brain. "You like that, buster?" I asked him, and snapped him another one for good measure. He struck back again, his comb red, crested, and rubbery with fury.

I was angry myself. I turned him upside down and left him dangling, his wings drumming against the legs of my jeans. Then I righted him abruptly; he looked dishevelled, seedy and dazed.

"OK, Stanley," I said, feeling the intoxication of power. "I'm boss here, and you behave." There was a gleeful edge to my voice, which surprised me a little.

I realized I was hoping this confrontation would escalate. Wishing that he would provoke me into something.

205 Strange images came into my head: the bruises on my aunt's legs; Thompson's face drained of life, lifted like an empty receptacle toward the ceiling, waiting to be filled, the tendons of his neck stark and rigid with anticipation.

I was filled with anxiety, the heat seemed to stretch me, to tug at my nerves and my skin. Two drops of sweat, as large and perfectly formed as tears, rolled out of my hairline and splashed on to the rubber toes of my runners.

"Easy, Stanley," I breathed to him, "easy," and my hand crept deliberately towards him. This time he pecked me in such a way, directly on the knuckle, that it actually hurt. I took up my stick and rapped him on the beak curtly, the prim admonishment of a schoolmarm. I didn't hit him very hard, but it was hard enough to split the length of his beak with a narrow crack. The beak fissured like the nib of a fountain pen. Stanley squawked, opened and closed his beak spasmodically, bewildered by the pain. A bright jewel of blood bubbled out of the split and gathered to a trembling bead.

"There," I said excitedly, "now you've done it. How are you going to eat with a broken beak? You can't eat anything with a broken beak. You'll starve, you stupid goddamn chicken."

A wind that smelled of rain had sprung up. It ruffled his feathers until they moved with a barely discernible crackle.

210 "Poor Stanley," I said, and at last, numbed by the pain, he allowed me to stroke the gloss of his lacquer feathers.

I wasn't strong enough or practised enough to do a clean and efficient job of wringing his neck, but I succeeded in finishing him off after two clumsy attempts. Then because I wanted to leave the impression that a skunk had made off with him, I punched a couple of holes in his breast with my jack knife and tried to dribble some blood on the ground. Poor Stanley produced only a few meagre spots; this corpse refused to bleed in the presence of its murderer. I scattered a handful of his feathers on the ground and buried him in the larger of the two manure piles beside the barn.

"I don't think any skunk got that rooster," my grandmother said suspiciously, nudging at a feather with the toe of her boot until, finally disturbed, it was wafted away by the breeze.

Something squeezed my heart. How did she know?

"Skunks hunt at night," she said. "Must have been somebody's barn cat."

215 "You come along with me," my grandmother said. She was standing in front of the full-length hall mirror, settling on her hat, a deadly-looking hat pin poised above her skull. "We'll go into town and you can buy a comic book at the drugstore."

It was Friday and Friday was shopping day. But Grandma didn't wheel her battered De Soto to the kerb in front of the Brite Spot Grocery, she parked it in front of Maynard & Pritchard, Barristers and Solicitors.

"What are we doing here?" I asked.

Grandma was fumbling nervously with her purse. Small-town people don't like to be seen going to the lawyer's. "Come along with me. Hurry up."

"Why do I have to come?"

"Because I don't want you making a spectacle of yourself for the half-wits and loungers to gawk at," she said. "Let's not give them too much to wonder about."

Maynard & Pritchard, Barristers and Solicitors, smelled of wax and varnish and probity. My grandmother was shown into an office with a frosted pane of glass in the door and neat gilt lettering that announced it was occupied by D. F. Maynard, QC. I was ordered to occupy a hard chair, which I did, battering my heels on the rungs briskly enough to annoy the secretary into telling me to stop it.

My grandmother wasn't closeted long with her Queen's Counsel before the door opened and he glided after her into the passageway. Lawyer Maynard was the neatest man I had ever seen in my life. His suit fit him like a glove.

"The best I can do," he said, "is send him a registered letter telling him to remove himself from the premises, but it all comes to the same thing. If that doesn't scare him off, you'll have to have recourse to the police. That's all there is to it. I told you that yesterday and you haven't told me anything new today, Edith, that would make me change my mind. Just let him know you won't put up with him any more."

"No police," she said. "I don't want the police digging in my family's business and Evelyn giving one of her grand performances for some baby-skinned constable straight out of the depot. All I need is to get her away from him for a little while, then I could tune her in. I could get through to her in no time at all."

"Well," said Maynard, shrugging, "we could try the letter, but I don't think it would do any good. He has the status of a guest in your home; just tell him to go."

My grandmother was showing signs of exasperation. "But he *doesn't* go. That's the point. I've told him and told him. But he *won't.*"

"Mrs. Bradley," said the lawyer emphatically, "Edith, as a friend, don't waste your time. The police."

"I'm through wasting my time," she said.

Pulling away from the lawyer's office, my grandmother began a spirited conversation with herself. A wisp of hair had escaped from under her hat, and the dye winked a metallic red light as it jiggled up and down in the hot sunshine.

"I've told him and told him. But he won't listen. The goddamn freak thinks we're involved in a christly debating society. He thinks I don't mean business. But I mean business. I do. There's more than one way to skin a cat or scratch a dog's ass. We'll take the wheels off his little red wagon and see how she pulls."

"What about my comic book?" I said, as we drove past the Rexall.

"Shut up."

Grandma drove the De Soto to the edge of town and stopped it at the Ogdens' place. It was a service station, or rather had been until the BA company had taken out their pumps and yanked the franchise, or whatever you call it, on the two brothers. Since then everything had gone steadily downhill. Cracks in the window-panes had been taped with masking tape, and the roof had been patched with flattened tin cans and old licence plates. The building itself was surrounded by an acre of wrecks, sulking hulks rotten with rust, the guts of their upholstery spilled and gnawed by rats and mice.

But the Ogden brothers still carried on a business after a fashion. They stripped their wrecks for parts and were reputed to be decent enough mechanics whenever they were sober enough to turn a wrench or thread a bolt. People brought work to them whenever they couldn't avoid it, and the rest of the year gave them a wide berth.

235   The Ogdens were famous for two things: their meanness and their profligacy as breeders. The place was always aswarm with kids who never seemed to wear pants except in the most severe weather, and tottered about the premises, their legs smeared with grease, shit, or various combinations of both.

"Wait here," my grandmother said, slamming the car door loudly enough to bring the two brothers out of their shop. Through the open door I saw a motor suspended on an intricate system of chains and pulleys.

The Ogdens stood with their hands in the pockets of their bib overalls while my grandmother talked to them. They were quite a sight. They didn't have a dozen teeth in their heads between them, even though the oldest brother couldn't have been more than forty. They just stood there, one sucking on a cigarette, the other on a Coke. Neither one moved or changed his expression, except once, when a tow-headed youngster piddled too close to Grandma. He was lazily and casually slapped on the side of the head by the nearest brother and ran away screaming, his stream cavorting wildly in front of him.

At last, their business concluded, the boys walked my grandmother back to the car.

"You'll get to that soon?" she said, sliding behind the wheel.

240   "Tomorrow all right?" said one. His words sounded all slack and chewed, issuing from his shrunken, old man's mouth.

"The sooner the better. I want that seen to, Bert."

"What seen to?" I asked.

"Bert and his brother Elwood are going to fix that rattle that's been plaguing me."

"Sure thing," said Elwood. "Nothing but clear sailing."

245   "What rattle?" I said.

"What rattle? What rattle? The one in the glove compartment," she said, banging it with the heel of her hand. "That rattle. You hear it?"

Thompson could get very edgy some days. "I should be working on my dissertation," he said, coiled in the big chair. "I shouldn't be wasting my time in this shit-hole. I should be working!"

"So why aren't you?" said Evelyn. She was spool knitting. That and reading movie magazines were the only things she ever did.

"How the christ do I work without a library? You see a goddamn library within a hundred miles of this place?"

"Why do you need a library?" she said calmly. "Can't you write?" 250

"Write?" he said, looking at the ceiling. "Write, she says. What the hell do you know about it? What the hell do *you* know about it?"

"I can't see why you can't write."

"Before you write, you research. That's what you do, you *research*."

"So bite my head off. It wasn't my idea to come here."

"It wasn't me that lost my goddamn job. How the hell were we supposed to 255 pay the rent?"

"You could have got a job."

"I'm a student. Anyway, I told you, if I get a job my wife gets her hooks into me for support. I'll starve to death before I support that bitch."

"We could go back."

"How many times does it have to be explained to you? I don't get my scholarship cheque until the first of September. We happen to be broke. Absolutely. In fact, you're going to have to hit the old lady up for gas and eating money to get back to the coast. We're stuck here. Get that into your empty fucking head. The Lord Buddha might have been able to subsist on a single bean a day; I can't."

My grandmother came into the room. The conversation stopped. 260

"Do you think," she said to Thompson, "I could ask you to do me a favour?"

"Why, Mrs. Bradley," he said, smiling, "whatever do you mean?"

"I was wondering whether you could take my car into town to Ogdens' to get it fixed."

"Oh," said Thompson. "I don't know where it is. I don't think I'm your man."

"Ask anyone where it is. They can tell you. It isn't hard to find." 265

"Why would you ask me to do you a favour, Mrs. Bradley?" inquired Thompson complacently. Hearing his voice was like listening to someone drag their nails down a blackboard.

"Well, you can be goddamn sure I wouldn't," said Grandma, trying to keep a hold of herself, "except that I'm right in the middle of doing my pickling and canning. I thought you might be willing to move your lazy carcass to do something around here. Every time I turn around I seem to be falling over those legs of yours." She looked at the limbs in question as if she would like to dock them somewhere in the vicinity of the knee.

"No, I don't think I can," said Thompson easily, stroking his goat beard. "And why the hell can't you?"

"Oh, let's just say I don't trust you, Mrs. Bradley. I don't like to leave you 270 alone with Evelyn. Lord knows what ideas you might put in her head."

"Or take out."

"That's right. Or take out," said Thompson with satisfaction. "You can't imagine the trouble it took me to get them in there." He turned to Evelyn. "She can't imagine the trouble, can she, dear?"

Evelyn threw her spool knitting on the floor and walked out of the room.

"Evelyn's mad and I'm glad," shouted Thompson at her back. "And I know how to tease her!"

"Charlie, come here," said Grandma. I went over to her. She took me firmly 275 by the shoulder. "From now on," said my grandma, "my family is off limits to you. I don't want to see you talking to Charlie here, or to come within sniffing distance of Evelyn."

"What do you think of that idea, Charlie?" said Thompson. "Are you still my friend or what?"

I gave him a wink my grandma couldn't see. He thought that was great; he laughed like a madman. "Superb," he said. "Superb. There's no flies on Charlie. What a diplomat."

"What the hell is the matter with you, Mr. Beatnik?"[4] asked Grandma, annoyed beyond bearing. "What's so goddamn funny?"

"Ha, ha!" roared Thompson. "What a charming notion! Me a beatnik!"

280   Grandma Bradley held the mouthpiece of the phone very close to her lips as she spoke into it. "No, it can't be brought in. You'll have to come out here to do the job."

She listened with an intent expression on her face. Spotting me pretending to look in the fridge, she waved me out of the kitchen with her hand. I dragged myself out and stood quietly in the hallway.

"This is a party line," she said, "remember that."

Another pause while she listened.

"OK," she said and hung up.

285   I spent some of my happiest hours squatting in the corn patch. I was completely hidden in there; even when I stood, the maturing stalks reached a foot or more above my head. It was a good place. On the hottest days it was relatively cool in that thicket of green where the shade was dark and deep and the leaves rustled and scraped and sawed drily overhead.

Nobody ever thought to look for me there. They could bellow their bloody lungs out for me and I could just sit and watch them getting uglier and uglier about it all. There was some satisfaction in that. I'd just reach up and pluck myself a cob. I loved raw corn. The newly formed kernels were tiny, pale pearls of sweetness that gushed juice. I'd munch and munch and smile and smile and think, why don't you drop dead?

It was my secret place, my sanctuary, where I couldn't be found or touched by them. But all the same, if I didn't let them intrude on me—that didn't mean I didn't want to keep tabs on things.

At the time I was watching Thompson stealing peas at the other end of the garden. He was like some primitive man who lived in a gathering culture. My grandma kept him so hungry he was constantly prowling for food: digging in cupboards, rifling the refrigerator, scrounging in the garden.

Clad only in Bermuda shorts he was a sorry sight. His bones threatened to rupture his skin and jut out every which way. He sported a scrub-board chest with two old pennies for nipples, and a wispy garland of hair decorated his

---

4. A derisive term for adherents to the 1950's Beat movement, a social and literary rebellion against "square" conventions.

sunken breastbone. His legs looked particularly rackety; all gristle, knobs and sinew.

We both heard the truck at the same time. It came bucking up the approach, spurting gravel behind it. Thompson turned around, shaded his eyes and peered at it. He wasn't much interested. He couldn't get very curious about the natives.

The truck stopped and a man stepped out on to the runningboard of the '51 IHC. He gazed around him, obviously looking for something or someone. This character had a blue handkerchief sprinkled with white polka dots tied in a triangle over his face. Exactly like an outlaw in an Audie Murphy[5] Western. A genuine goddamn Jesse James.

He soon spotted Thompson standing half-naked in the garden, staring stupidly at this strange sight, his mouth bulging with peas. The outlaw ducked his head back into the cab of the truck, said something to the driver, and pointed. The driver then stepped out on to his runningboard and, standing on tippy-toe, peered over the roof of the cab at Thompson. He too wore a handkerchief tied over his mug, but his was red.

Then they both got down from the truck and began to walk very quickly toward Thompson with long, menacing strides.

"Fellows?" said Thompson.

At the sound of his voice the two men broke into a stiff-legged trot, and the one with the red handkerchief, while still moving, stooped down smoothly and snatched up the hoe that lay at the edge of the garden

"What the hell is going on here, boys?" said Thompson, his voice pitched high with concern.

The man with the blue mask reached Thompson first. One long arm, a dirty clutch of fingers on its end, snaked out and caught him by the hair and jerked his head down. Then he kicked him in the pit of the stomach with his work boots.

"OK, fucker," he shouted, "too fucking smart to take a fucking hint?" and he punched him on the side of the face with several short, snapping blows that actually tore Thompson's head out of his grip. Thompson toppled over clumsily and fell in the dirt. "Get fucking lost," Blue Mask said more quietly.

"Evelyn!" yelled Thompson to the house. "Jesus Christ, Evelyn!"

I crouched lower in the corn patch and began to tremble. I was certain they were going to kill him.

"Shut up," said the man with the hoe. He glanced at the blade for a second, considered, then rotated the handle in his hands and hit Thompson a quick chop on the head with the blunt side. "Shut your fucking yap," he repeated.

"Evelyn! Evelyn! Oh God!" hollered Thompson, "I'm being murdered! For God's sake, somebody help me!" The side of his face was slick with blood.

"I told you shut up, cock sucker," said Red Mask, and kicked him in the ribs several times. Thompson groaned and hugged himself in the dust.

5. World War II's most decorated GI, Murphy (1924–1971) went on to star in low-budget Western films as a baby-faced hero.

"Now you get lost, fucker," said the one with the hoe, "because if you don't stop bothering nice people we'll drive a spike in your skull."

305   "Somebody help me!" Thompson yelled at the house.

"Nobody there is going to help you," Blue Mask said. "You're all on your own, smart arse."

"You bastards," said Thompson, and spat ineffectually in their direction.

For his defiance he got struck a couple of chopping blows with the hoe. The last one skittered off his collar-bone with a sickening crunch.

"That's enough," said Red Mask, catching the handle of the hoe. "Come on."

310   The two sauntered back toward the truck, laughing. They weren't in any hurry to get out of there. Thompson lay on his side staring at their retreating backs. His face was wet with tears and blood.

The man with the red mask looked back over his shoulder and wiggled his ass at Thompson in an implausible imitation of effeminacy. "Was it worth it, tiger?" he shouted. "Getting your ashes hauled don't come cheap, do it?"

This set them off again. Passing me they pulled off their masks and stuffed them in their pockets. They didn't have to worry about Thompson when they had their backs to him; he couldn't see their faces. But I could. No surprise. They were the Ogden boys.

When the truck pulled out of the yard, its gears grinding, I burst out of my hiding place and ran to Thompson, who had got to his knees and was trying to stop the flow of blood from his scalp with his fingers. He was crying. Another first for Thompson. He was the first man I'd seen cry. It made me uncomfortable.

"The sons of bitches broke my ribs," he said, panting with shallow breaths. "God, I hope they didn't puncture a lung."

"Can you walk?" I asked.

315   "Don't think I don't know who's behind this," he said, getting carefully to his feet. His face was white. "You saw them," he said. "You saw their faces from the corn patch. We got the bastards."

He leaned a little on me as we made our way to the house. The front door was locked. We knocked. No answer. "Let me in, you old bitch!" shouted Thompson.

"Evelyn, open the goddamn door!" Silence. I couldn't hear a thing move in the house. It was as if they were all dead in there. It frightened me.

He started to kick the door. A panel splintered. "Open this door! Let me in, you old slut, or I'll kill you!"

Nothing.

320   "You better go," I said nervously. I didn't like this one little bit. "Those guys might come back and kill you."

"Evelyn!" he bellowed. "Evelyn!"

He kept it up for a good five minutes, alternately hammering and kicking the door, pleading with and threatening the occupants. By the end of that time he was sweating with exertion and pain. He went slowly down the steps, sobbing, beaten. "You saw them," he said, "we have the bastards dead to rights."

He winced when he eased his bare flesh on to the hot seat-covers of the car.

"I'll be back," he said, starting the motor of the car. "This isn't the end of   325
this."

When Grandma was sure he had gone, the front door was unlocked and I
was let in. I noticed my grandmother's hands trembled a touch when she lit her
cigarette.

"You can't stay away from him, can you?" she said testily.

"You didn't have to do that," I said. "He was hurt. You ought to have let him
in."

"I ought to have poisoned him a week ago. And don't talk about things you
don't know anything about."

"Sometimes," I said, "all of you get on my nerves."   330

"Kids don't have nerves. Adults have nerves. They're the only ones entitled
to them. And don't think I care a plugged nickel what does, or doesn't, get on
your nerves."

"Where's Aunt Evelyn?"

"Your Aunt Evelyn is taken care of," she replied.

"Why wouldn't she come to the door?"

"She had her own road to Damascus.[6] She has seen the light. Everything   335
has been straightened out," she said. "Everything is back to normal."

He looked foolish huddled in the back of the police car later that evening.
When the sun began to dip, the temperature dropped rapidly, and he was obviously cold dressed only in his Bermuda shorts. Thompson sat all hunched up to
relieve the strain on his ribs, his hands pressed between his knees, shivering.

My grandmother and the constable spoke quietly by the car for some time;
occasionally Thompson poked his head out the car window and said something.
By the look on the constable's face when he spoke to Thompson, it was obvious
he didn't care for him too much. Thompson had that kind of effect on people.
Several times during the course of the discussion the constable glanced my way.

I edged a little closer so I could hear what they were saying.

"He's mad as a hatter," said my grandmother. "I don't know anything about
two men. If you ask me, all this had something to do with drugs. My daughter
says that this man takes drugs. He's some kind of beatnik."

"Christ," said Thompson, drawing his knees up as if to scrunch himself into   340
a smaller, less noticeable package, "the woman is insane."

"One thing at a time, Mrs. Bradley," said the RCMP constable.

"My daughter is finished with him," she said. "He beats her, you know. I
want him kept off my property."

"I want to speak to Evelyn," Thompson said. He looked bedraggled and
frightened. "Evelyn and I will leave this minute if this woman wants. But I've
got to talk to Evelyn."

"My daughter doesn't want to see you, mister. She's finished with you," said

---

6. According to biblical legend, Saul (later Paul), was on his way to Damascus to subdue the Christians there when he was stopped by a vision of Jesus. He was temporarily blinded, and his conversion
was immediate.

Grandma Bradley, shifting her weight from side to side. She turned her attention to the constable. "He beats her," she said, "bruises all over her. Can you imagine?"

345 "The boy knows," said Thompson desperately. "He saw them. How many times do I have to tell you?" He piped his voice to me. "Didn't you, Charlie? You saw them, didn't you?"

"Charlie?" said my grandmother. This was news to her.

I stood very still.

"Come here, son," said the constable.

I walked slowly over to them.

350 "Did you see the faces of the men?" the constable asked, putting a hand on my shoulder. "Do you know the men? Are they from around here?"

"How would he know?" said my grandmother. "He's a stranger."

"He knows them. At least he saw them," said Thompson. "My little Padmasambhava never misses a trick," he said, trying to jolly me. "You see everything, don't you, Charlie? You remember everything, don't you?"

I looked at my grandmother, who stood so calmly and commandingly, waiting.

"Hey, don't look to her for the answers," said Thompson nervously. "Don't be afraid of her. You remember everything, don't you?"

355 He had no business begging me. I had watched their game from the sidelines long enough to know the rules. At one time he had imagined himself a winner. And now he was asking me to save him, to take a risk, when I was more completely in her clutches than he would ever be. He forgot I was a child. I depended on her.

Thompson, I saw, was powerless. He couldn't protect me. God, I remembered more than he dreamed. I remembered how his lips had moved soundlessly, his face pleading with the ceiling, his face blotted of everything but abject urgency. Praying to a simpering, cross-eyed idol. His arm flashing as he struck my aunt's bare legs. Crawling in the dirt, covered with blood.

He had taught me that "Those who are in the grip of desire, the grip of existence, the grip of ignorance, move helplessly round through the spheres of life, as men or gods or as wretches in the lower regions." Well, he was helpless now. But he insisted on fighting back and hurting the rest of us. The weak ones like Evelyn and me.

I thought of Stanley the rooster and how it had felt when the tendons separated, the gristle parted and the bones crunched under my twisting hands.

"I don't know what he's talking about," I said to the constable softly. "I didn't see anybody."

360 "Clear out," said my grandmother triumphantly. "Beat it."

"You dirty little son of a bitch," he said to me. "You mean little bugger."

He didn't understand much. He had forced me into the game, and now that I was a player and no longer a watcher he didn't like it. The thing was that I was good at the game. But he, being a loser, couldn't appreciate that.

Then suddenly he said, "Evelyn." He pointed to the upstairs window of the house and tried to get out of the back seat of the police car. But of course he couldn't. They take the handles off the back doors. Nobody can get out unless they are let out.

"Goddamn it!" he shouted. "Let me out! She's waving to me! She wants me!"

I admit that the figure was hard to make out at that distance. But any damn fool could see she was only waving goodbye.

365

1982

QUESTIONS

1. What is the focus of the narration? the voice? What expectations of plot, theme, character are aroused by the first fifteen or eighteen paragraphs? What are your early interpretations of the title? Trace "watching" through the story and its relation to character, plot, and theme.

2. For some time the narrator summarizes his childhood and gives brief character sketches of members of his family. How would you describe the narrator's characterizations—are they jovial? sympathetic? loving? critical? sardonic? nasty? What do you think of the narrator during these early (twenty to thirty) paragraphs? Does your view of him change in the course of the story? If so, how many times, in what ways, and when? How does the narrator's character relate to the incidents of the story (plot) and theme?

3. Though there is a brief scene with the father in paragraphs 18 and 19, the first lengthy, fully discriminated scene takes place in paragraphs 28 to 57. How does the scene contribute to the picture of the setting? characterization? theme?

4. It is not until paragraph 62 that "something interesting turned up"—the arrival of Aunt Evelyn and Robert Thompson. Did the first sixty-plus paragraphs hold your interest despite the absence of incident? If so, how? What expectations, if any, did those first paragraphs engender? What expectations or curiosity is aroused by the new arrivals? How does it contribute to the characterization of the narrator (Charlie)? Grandma Bradley? What are your first responses to and opinions of Aunt Evelyn? Thompson? What is the tone of the scene? What conflict is building? Whose side are you on in the ensuing argument? Why? Whose side is the narrator on? How do you know?

5. How does the narrator know what Evelyn does during the day? How does he know that Thompson beats her? What resemblance does Thompson see between Charlie and Padma-sambhava? Why does Charlie think Thompson a "silly bugger" when he laughs at what Charlie tells him he wants to be when

he grows up (par. 167)? How is this related to Thompson's character? Charlie's situation? the theme?

6. On the evening of the day Thompson whipped Evelyn, why does she come down to dinner in shorts (par. 144)? What does that tell you about her character? about Thompson? What expectations are aroused? In paragraphs 190 and 191, Grandma says Thompson will be out of the house in a week, but he says he won't. Who do you think will prove to be right? Why? What did you expect Grandma to do to get rid of Thompson? How was your expectation related to the characters? to plot? to theme?

7. How does paragraph 194 contribute to setting? expectations? characterization? How is the scene between Charlie and Stanley that follows related to details earlier in the story? What is the effect of the scene on the characterization of Charlie? on the theme? Is Stanley a symbol? Explain, by indicating what you mean by "symbol" and, if you think he is a symbol, what it is he symbolizes.

8. How is paragraph 355 related to plot? Charlie's character? theme?

9. How many previous scenes and details are echoed or brought to bear on the final scene (paragraphs 336 to the end of story)? How does that scene derive from and impinge upon the characterization of Charlie? How does it bring out, reinforce, or define the theme?

WRITING SUGGESTIONS

1. Show how the discussion of "The Country Husband" or "Sonny's Blues" in the chapter on plot would be modified and expanded by writing a essay on the whole text of the story.

2. Write a brief analytical essay on "The Secret Sharer" in terms of symbol or "Love Medicine" in terms of theme. How does the discussion of theme in this chapter's student essay differ from your treatment of an isolated element in one of these two stories?

3. Write an essay on the whole text of "The Real Thing," "The Yellow Wallpaper," or "A Hunger Artist" (all stories in *Reading More Fiction*).

STUDENT WRITING

Daniel Bronson's paper is a whole-text response to one of the earlier stories in the text, "A Rose for Emily." In his paper, Daniel traces the theme of resistance to change in the story, which he supports with examples from the text.

"Like the Sand of the Hourglass . . ."

Daniel Bronson

The year 1865 saw the end of the Civil War between the Union and the Confederacy, and saw the beginning of a "New South." With the many changes pressed upon the South, the so-called "Old South" could no longer exist. For example, people could not own slaves as they had in the past, and they couldn't survive anymore simply by belonging to a family with an "august name." These changes didn't happen overnight however; they took many years to occur. In William Faulkner's "A Rose for Emily," we are shown the transition from Old South to New South as it takes place in the little town of Jefferson, and we see how Miss Emily Grierson, survivor of the Old South, resists these changes.

Jefferson was once inhabited by many well-off families who were members of the Old South's aristocratic class. As time, and the

Reconstruction, marched on, these families slowly disappeared. Eventually, the last true living legacy of the Old South in Jefferson was Miss Emily Grierson. She had been raised to be a Southern Belle, an upstanding member of society, and she clung to her world of the Old South. She kept a black servant, Tobe, who did everything for her, just as if he were a slave, and she lived in "a big, squarish frame house that had once been white, decorated with cupolas and spires and scrolled balconies in the heavily lightsome style of the seventies, set on what had once been our most select street" (par. 2). With the infiltration of the New South, however, "garages and cotton gins . . . encroached and obliterated even the august names of that neighborhood" (par. 2). Yet the house remained, "lifting its stubborn and coquettish decay above the cotton wagons and the gasoline pumps," just as its willful inhabitant "carried her head high . . . even when we believed that she was fallen" (par. 33).

The house was all that Miss Emily really had left after her father died. When he passed away, Miss Emily spent three days denying his death and not letting the doctors and ministers dispose of the body. Though it is not told first in the story, this was the first time Miss Emily had rejected the truth in order to retain her world of the past: a world in which other members of the Old South, such as Colonel Sartoris, lived on after they too had died.

Colonel Sartoris also represented the Old South, and he protected Emily when her father died. As mayor of Jefferson at the time, he remitted her taxes, and since no aristocratic woman such as Miss Emily could possibly lower herself to accept charity, came up with a story of how her father had loaned money to Jefferson and this was how Miss Emily was to be repaid. "Only a man of Colonel Sartoris' generation and thought could have invented it, and only a woman could have believed it" (par. 3). So when Miss Emily was later approached by members of the generation of city authorities who wanted her taxes, she held onto the past and told them repeatedly to see Colonel Sartoris, even though he had been dead for almost ten years. Furthermore, when city authorities asked her whether or not she received "a notice from the sheriff, signed by him," she remarks, "Perhaps he considers himself the sheriff" (pars. 9, 10). Obviously, Miss Emily didn't accept that whoever was the new sheriff was really the sheriff. As far as she was concerned, the sheriff was still the same person it was several years ago.

We are shown not only the government of the Old South Jefferson, when it sided with Miss Emily, and the government of the New South Jefferson, when it was against Miss Emily, but we

also catch a glimpse of Jefferson's government
when it was still under transition. About two
years after her father's death, a smell developed
around Miss Emily's house. The "member of the
rising generation" on the Board of Aldermen said
that the solution to the problem was "'simple
enough. . . . Send her word to have her place
cleaned up. Give her a certain time to do it in,
and if she don't . . .'" At that point the
remaining Old South revealed itself when the
eighty-year-old mayor, Judge Stevens, irately
asked, "will you accuse a lady to her face of
smelling bad?" (pars. 22, 23). It is apparent
that though there were some old-timers left, just
as Jefferson changed, so did its people.

Members of the Old South were very honorable,
graceful and above all, dignified. They had great
respect for each other and for each other's
feelings, and were quick to help one another
whenever possible. Most importantly however, they
always retained their dignity, no matter what.
Miss Emily preserved her world of the Old South
by hanging on to her dignity. It was because her
dignity was so essential to her that a major
conflict arose when Miss Emily met Homer Barron.
Homer was a personification of Reconstruction and
was Miss Emily's opposite in every way. He was a
Yankee, a solicializer, a member of the vulgar,
haphazard post-war generation, and "a day
laborer," having been hired to build Jefferson's

sidewalks and thereby contribute to the
urbanization of the town.

When opposites attracted however, Miss Emily
put her dignity on the line and was seen "on
Sunday afternoons driving in the yellow-wheeled
buggy and the matched team of bays from the
livery stable" with Homer (par. 30). The ladies
of the town said, "'Of course a Grierson would
not think seriously of a Northerner,'" and the
"older people," those of the Old South, "said
that even grief could not cause a real lady to
forget *noblesse oblige*--without calling it
noblesse oblige." (par. 31). As time passed,
Homer and Miss Emily were seen again and again,
until finally, "some of the ladies began to say
that it was a disgrace to the town and a bad
example to the young people. The men did not want
to interfere, but at last the ladies forced the
Baptist minister . . . to call upon her" (par.
44). Then "the minister's wife wrote to Miss
Emily's relations in Alabama" (par. 44). When
they arrived, Miss Emily realized she had to do
something to preserve her dignity and pride that
kept her Old South alive.

Her choices were few: marry Homer, or separate
from him completely. At first it appeared that
Miss Emily and Homer were either married or
getting ready to be married, for she "ordered a
man's toilet set in silver, with the letters H.B.
on each piece" and she "bought a complete outfit

of men's clothing, including a nightshirt" (par. 45). Unfortunately, while this may have kept her reputation from being tarnished as far as the New South people were concerned, it was still not enough for Miss Emily's Old South dignity. It demanded that she never demean herself to being married to a Northerner. Therefore, in order to keep Homer, but not what he was or what he stood for, Miss Emily killed him, then kept him in a bed where she could be with him when she chose without "compromising her dignity." This violence and necrophilia reflect her wish to hold onto the South's dead past as well as her own and the price she pays to do so.

Miss Emily retained her sense of her dignity and her private version of the world of the Old South for the rest of her life. She was a "monument," "a tradition, a duty, and a care" (pars. 1, 3). Living secluded, she surrounded herself as best as she could by locking herself in her old house with only her memories and her black servant. When she died, she did so in dignity, "in a heavy walnut bed with a curtain, her gray head propped on a pillow" (par. 53). With her death went her Old South world as well, leaving behind only "the very old men--some in their brushed Confederate uniforms" to remind the New South of the past (par. 55) and to offer a rose of remembrance and respect for Emily.

Exploring Contexts

8 THE AUTHOR'S WORK AS CONTEXT: D. H. LAWRENCE AND FLANNERY O'CONNOR

Even if it were desirable to read a story as a thing in itself, separate from everything else we had ever read or seen and from everything else the author had written, this is in practice impossible. We can *first* look into Chapman's Homer or Faulkner's fiction only once. After we read a second and then a third story by an author, we begin to recognize the voice and have a sense of familiarity, as we would with a growing acquaintance. Each story is part of the author's entire body of work—the **canon**—which, taken together, forms something like a huge single entity, a vision, a world, a "superwork."

The author's voice and vision soon create in us certain expectations—of action, structure, characterization, world view, language. We come to expect short sentences from Hemingway, long ones from Faulkner, a certain amount of violence from both. We are not surprised if a Conrad story is set in Africa or Asia or aboard ship, but we are surprised if a Faulkner story takes place outside Mississippi (his portion of which, we soon learn, he calls Yoknapatawpha).

When we find an author's vision attractive or challenging, we naturally want to find out more about it, reading not only the literary works in the canon but the author's nonfictional prose—essays, letters, anything we can find that promises a fuller or clearer view of that unique way of looking at the world.

Such knowledge is helpful—within limits. D. H. Lawrence warned us to trust the tale and not the teller. A statement of beliefs or of intentions is not necessarily the same as what a given work may show or achieve; and, on the other hand, writers often embody in their art what they cannot articulate, what indeed may not be expressible, in discursive prose.

In this chapter we will look briefly but closely at the work of two writers, D. H. Lawrence and Flannery O'Connor. We will look both at differences between works by the same writer and at similarities.

The two short stories and brief selections from Lawrence's letters and criticism in this chapter are meant to make you feel more at home (and interested) in Lawrence's world and to raise questions about the relationship of the individual work to an author's work as a whole. Of course, a couple of short stories and a few pages of nonfiction alone cannot adequately represent the career of a writer who was a novelist, poet, critic, and essayist as well as short-story writer, nor can two stories represent the richness and variety of the fifty or more that he published over many years. However, as the stories come from different decades, they do represent somewhat the continuities and changes during his career. "Odour of Chrysanthemums" is characteristically set in the coal-mining region of his native English Midlands, the scene of many of his novels, including three of the most famous, which also span his career—*Sons and Lovers* (1913), *The Rainbow* (1915), and *Lady Chatterly's Lover* (1928). Though we have included brief excerpts from "Nottingham and the Mining Countryside" and from his "Autobiographical Sketch" (and the selection from "Women Are So Cocksure" may seem related to "Odour of Chrysanthemums" in another respect), there is no way in so few selections to represent both Lawrence's emphasis on the Midlands and the scope of his settings—his stories take place all over Western Europe, in the Americas, and in Australia. The London setting of "The Rocking-Horse Winner" only faintly indicates Lawrence's growing cosmopolitanism socially as well as geographically. It also suggests, though superficially, his developing interest in the superreal and the mythic—concerns most fully developed in *The Plumed Serpent* (1926) and *The Man Who Died* (1929)—and his movement in content and style away from nineteenth-century notions of realism.

It may be useful to see the first story here (one of Lawrence's very first stories) through the eyes of its first "professional" reader as he remembers the experience. Not long before World War I, a young woman sent to Ford Madox Ford, then editor of *The English Review*, three poems and a short story written by a schoolmaster friend of hers, the then-unknown D. H. Lawrence. Ford read the story first and, he recalls, knew immediately that he had a genius on his hands, "a big one." The very title, "Odour of Chrysanthemums," Ford noted, "makes an impact on the mind," indicates that the writer is observant (not many people realize that chrysanthemums have an odor), and sets the dark autumnal tone of the story. From the very first sentence, Ford goes on to say,

> . . . you know that this fellow with the power of observation is going to write whatever he writes about from the inside. The "Number 4" shows that. He will be the sort of fellow who knows that for the sort of people who work about engines, engines have a sort of individuality. He had to give the engine the personality of a number. . . . "With seven full wagons". . . . The "seven" is good. The ordinary careless writer would say "some small wagons." This man knows what he wants. He sees the scene of his story exactly. He has an authoritative mind.
>
> "It appeared round the corner with loud threats of speed." . . . Good writing; slightly, but not *too* arresting. . . . "But the colt that it startled from among the gorse . . . out-distanced it at a canter." Good again. This fellow does not "state." He doesn't say: "It was coming slowly," or—what would have been a little better—"at seven miles an hour." Because even "seven miles an hour" means nothing definite for the untrained mind. It might mean something for a trainer or pedestrian racers. The imaginative writer writes for all humanity; he does not limit his desired readers to specialists. . . . But anyone knows that an engine that makes a great deal of noise and yet cannot overtake a colt at a canter must be a ludicrously ineffective machine. We know then that this fellow knows his job.
>
> . . . . [T]his man knows. He knows how to open a story with a sentence of the right cadence for holding the attention. He knows how to construct a paragraph. He knows the life he is writing about. . . . You can trust him for the rest. . . .
>
> —from "Before the Wars," *Selected Memories, The Bodley Head Ford Madox Ford* (London, 1962), I, 322–23

In that strange and strangely different story, "The Rocking-Horse Winner," written at the other end of Lawrence's career and published posthumously in 1932, you will find the same precision of detail and the same "inside view," in the first description of Paul's riding the horse, for example; in the description of the horse's "lowered face" ("Its red mouth was slightly open, its big eye was wide and glassy-bright" [par. 42]); and in the precise accounting of the races, the odds, the money.

Ford read "Odour of Chrysanthemums" outside the context available to us. He did not know anything of the author and had read nothing else by him. Ford was an excellent editor (as well as writer) and to his credit spotted Lawrence's genius, a genius quite different from his own. Lawrence's mastery of detail made Ford trust him, but what he trusted him for seems to have been

knowledge of the "other ninety-nine hundredths" of the population, the working class. An English writer of genius with knowledge of the working class was
no doubt rare and notable in those prewar days, and Lawrence's early works
are full of details of the lives of miners and their families. But Lawrence, we
now know, considered not class but the man-woman relationship the "great
relationship of humanity," all others being subsidiary. Because we know that,
know of Lawrence's notoriety for describing sexual relations, know his later
works in which sexual relations are the major or basic concern—and perhaps
because of the emphasis on sex in our own time—in reading "Odour of Chrysanthemums" we focus our attention less on the picture of the working class
than on the strange relationship between the Bateses. The class element is still
in the story, but the context of Lawrence's other works and utterances high-
lights this other human relationship.

Though Ford stressed Lawrence's power of observation in terms of the outside of things, he does say that "this fellow . . . is going to write whatever he
writes about from the inside." It is not just Lawrence's powers of observation
but his penetration to the inside of his characters' beings, to the shockingly
original but convincing motives and feelings he finds there, and his insight
into relationships, particularly love relationships, that mark his best work.
Unfortunately, there is not space here to represent his more positive, fully
developed, and explicit incarnations of man-woman love, found particularly in
his novels *Women in Love* (1920) and *Lady Chatterley's Lover*. We can briefly
indicate, however, what woman-man love is not in "Odour of Chrysanthemums":

> Was this what it all meant—utter, intact separateness, obscured by heat of living? . . .
> There had been nothing between them, and yet they had come together, exchanging
> their nakedness repeatedly. Each time he had taken her, they had been two isolated
> beings, far apart as now [when he was dead]. . . . I have been fighting a husband who
> did not exist. *He* existed all the time . . . apart all the while, living as she never lived,
> feeling as she never felt.

(par. 218)

and what parent-child love is by what it is not in "The Rocking-Horse Winner":

> . . . when her children were present, she always felt the center of her heart go hard.
> This troubled her, and in her manner she was all the more gentle and anxious for
> her children, as if she loved them very much. Only she herself knew that at the
> center of her heart was a hard little place that could not feel love, no, not for anybody.
> Everybody else said of her: "She is such a good mother. She adores her children."
> Only she herself, and her children themselves, knew it was not so.

(par. 1)

In this chapter we have also included two of Flannery O'Connor's stories, both from her posthumous volume, *Everything That Rises Must Converge*, and so representative at least of the final years of her brief career. (She died at thirty-nine, having published some thirty-one stories, two novels, essays, and reviews.) The title story of that final volume is perhaps the more characteristic, for O'Connor frequently turned her piercingly accurate vision on the middle-aged and elderly, especially women, and on southern culture. Both these stories center, as many of her others do, on a sudden revelation of a truth about the self, shedding a new and unflattering light on one's attitudes, behaviors, beliefs. The exposure often involves snobbery, racism, or self-righteousness, often in false religious or falsely humanistic form. The first two are exemplified in "Everything That Rises Must Converge," self-righteousness and the falsely humanistic in "The Lame Shall Enter First." Her settings and situations are not so varied as Lawrence's, her world is narrower, and her focus fiercely concentrated. Like Lawrence, however, O'Connor has a keen eye for realistic detail and for her characters' self-deception. Violence is often in or near the surface of her fiction; as in Faulkner, it is used to shake up the reader and make him or her look beyond the conventional and the ordinary into a kind of truth, often an uncomfortable truth that lies within. Though O'Connor is a deeply religious and serious writer, her stories are replete with irony and wit, and are sometimes downright funny. Indeed, as you will see, she is not above using comic pratfalls seriously.

The central, sometimes obsessive concerns and assumptions that permeate an author's work not only relate the individual stories to each other, mutually illuminating and enriching them, but they also serve as the author's trademark. It is not difficult to recognize or even parody a story by Lawrence or O'Connor.

Embodying these larger concerns and underlying such larger structures as plot, focus, and voice are the basic characteristics of the author's language, such as **diction,** the choice and use of words; sentence structure; **rhetorical tropes,** figures of thought and speech; **imagery;** and **rhythm**—in other words, the author's **style.**

Perhaps because of the uniqueness of style, the vocabulary for discussing stylistic elements is not very precise or accessible. We can broadly characterize diction as **formal** ("The Cask of Amontillado") or informal (most of the stories in this collection), and within the broad term **informal** we can identify a level of language that approximates the speech of ordinary people and call it **colloquial** ("Why I Live at the P.O."). But to characterize precisely an author's diction so that it adequately describes his or her work and marks it off from the work of contemporaries is a very difficult task indeed. We can note Faulkner's long sentences, but it is hard to get much definition in the stylistic fingerprint of an author merely by measuring the lengths of sentences or tabulating connectives (though these qualities no doubt do subliminally contribute to the effect of the works on readers and do help to identify the author).

Diction and sentence structure contribute to the **tone** of a work, or the implied attitude or stance of the author toward the characters and events, an aspect somewhat analogous to tone of voice. When what is being said and the tone are consistent, it is difficult to separate one from the other; when there seems to be a discrepancy we have some words that are useful to describe the difference. If the language seems exaggerated, we call it **overstatement** or **hyperbole.** Sometimes it will be the narrator, sometimes a character, who uses language so intensive or exaggerated that we must read it at a discount, as it were, and judge the speaker's accuracy or honesty in the process. When Julian's mother, in "Everything That Rises Must Converge," says, " 'I've always had a great deal of respect for my colored friends. . . . I'd do anything in the world for them . . .' " (par. 32), we know she protests too much, that she is exaggerating, and we see her racism through or underneath her language. When Sister in "Why I Live at the P.O." says, ". . . I do not enjoy being referred to as a hussy by my own grandfather," we know that she means to express her dislike of being called a hussy much more forcefully than she does. She is indulging in a bit of obvious **understatement** or **litotes.** When a word or expression carries not only its literal meaning, but a different meaning for the speaker as well, we have an example of **verbal irony.** When Fortunato says, "I shall not die of a cough," Montresor's "True—true" may seem reassuring but we learn later in the story why it is both accurate and ominous. There are also nonverbal forms of irony, the most common of which is **dramatic irony,** in which a character holds a position or has an expectation that is reversed or fulfilled in an unexpected way. Knowing her husband's habit of drinking himself into unconsciousness, Elizabeth Bates expects him to be brought home like a log. How is her expectation fulfilled? She had also said bitterly, "But he needn't come rolling in here in his pit-dirt, for *I* won't wash him," and yet she does. Why is her determination altered? As you read through, or look back over "Odour of Chrysanthemums," watch for other reversed or unexpectedly fulfilled expectations.

Another, highly emphasized element of style is **imagery.** In its broadest sense imagery includes any sensory detail or evocation in a work. Note how much more imagery in that sense we find in "Fenstad's Mother" than in, say, "The Zebra Storyteller." Imagery in this broad sense, however, is so prevalent in literature that it would take exhaustive statistics to differentiate styles by counting the number of sensory elements per hundred or thousand words, categorizing the images as primarily visual, tactile, etc. In a more restricted sense imagery refers to figurative language (see Chapter 5 on symbols), particularly that which defines an abstraction or any emotional or psychological state with a sensory comparison. The opening paragraph of "Odour of Chrysanthemums" illustrates the broader definition of imagery, and this passage from later in the same story may represent the figurative sense: "Life with its smoky burning gone from him, had left him apart. . . . In her womb was ice of fear. . . ."

We might say that if an author's vision gives us his or her profile, the style gives us a fingerprint—though the fingerprint is unique and definitive, it is also harder to come by than a glimpse of a profile. Ultimately, however, vision and style are less distinguishable from each other than the profile-fingerprint image suggests. For vision and style, just like history and structure, do more than interact: they are inextricably fused or compounded. Let us look back at the Ford passage. He says this of "the gorse, which still flickered indistinctly in the raw afternoon" (though he misquotes it slightly and rather loosely calls it a phrase):

> . . .Good too, distinctly good. This is the just-sufficient observation of Nature that gives you, in a single phrase, landscape, time of day, weather, season.

Is this vision or style? The observation of Nature is clearly vision, but expressing that vision economically, tautly, is style. The two merge.

Whatever else this passage is, it is vintage, typical Lawrence. Perhaps it would take more than just these ten words, but surely in a paragraph or two we know we're in the fictional world that he perceived and that he embodied in his stories, novels, and poems in a language of his own created out of that language we share.

▼ ▼ ▼

D. H. LAWRENCE

Odour of Chrysanthemums

I

The small locomotive engine, Number 4, came clanking, stumbling down from Selston with seven full waggons. It appeared round the corner with loud threats of speed, but the colt that it startled from among the gorse, which still flickered indistinctly in the raw afternoon, outdistanced it at a canter. A woman, walking up the railway line to Underwood, drew back into the hedge, held her basket aside, and watched the footplate of the engine advancing. The trucks thumped heavily past, one by one, with slow inevitable movement, as she stood insignificantly trapped between the jolting black waggons and the hedge; then they curved away towards the coppice where the withered oak leaves dropped noiselessly, while the birds, pulling at the scarlet hips beside the track, made off into the dusk that had already crept into the spinney. In the open, the smoke from the engine sank and cleaved to the rough grass. The fields were dreary and forsaken, and in the marshy strip that led to the whimsey, a reedy pit-pond, the fowls had already abandoned their run among the alders, to roost in the tarred fowl-house. The pit-bank loomed up beyond the pond, flames like red sores licking its ashy sides, in the afternoon's stagnant light. Just beyond rose the tapering chimneys and the clumsy black headstocks of Brinsley Colliery. The two wheels were spinning fast up against the sky, and the winding-engine rapped out its little spasms. The miners were being turned up.

The engine whistled as it came into the wide bay of railway lines beside the colliery, where rows of trucks stood in harbour.

Miners, single, trailing and in groups, passed like shadows diverging home. At the edge of the ribbed level of sidings squat a low cottage, three steps down from the cinder track. A large bony vine clutched at the house, as if to claw down the tiled roof. Round the bricked yard grew a few wintry primroses. Beyond, the long garden sloped down to a bush-covered brook course. There were some twiggy apple trees, winter-crack trees, and ragged cabbages. Beside the path hung dishevelled pink chrysanthemums, like pink cloths hung on bushes. A woman came stooping out of the felt-covered fowl-house, half-way down the garden. She closed and padlocked the door, then drew herself erect, having brushed some bits from her white apron.

She was a tall woman of imperious mien, handsome, with definite black eyebrows. Her smooth black hair was parted exactly. For a few moments she stood steadily watching the miners as they passed along the railway: then she turned towards the brook course. Her face was calm and set, her mouth was closed with disillusionment. After a moment she called:

5 "John!" There was no answer. She waited, and then said distinctly:

"Where are you?"

"Here!" replied a child's sulky voice from among the bushes. The woman looked piercingly through the dusk.

"Are you at that brook?" she asked sternly.

For answer the child showed himself before the raspberry-canes that rose like whips. He was a small, sturdy boy of five. He stood quite still, defiantly.

10 "Oh!" said the mother, conciliated. "I thought you were down at that wet brook—and you remember what I told you—"

The boy did not move or answer.

"Come, come on in," she said more gently, "it's getting dark. There's your grandfather's engine coming down the line!"

The lad advanced slowly, with resentful, taciturn movement. He was dressed in trousers and waistcoat of cloth that was too thick and hard for the size of the garments. They were evidently cut down from a man's clothes.

As they went slowly towards the house he tore at the ragged wisps of chrysan-themums and dropped the petals in handfuls along the path.

"Don't do that—it does look nasty," said his mother. He refrained, and she, suddenly pitiful, broke off a twig with three or four wan flowers and held them against her face. When mother and son reached the yard her hand hesitated, and instead of laying the flower aside, she pushed it in her apron-band. The mother and son stood at the foot of the three steps looking across the bay of lines at the passing home of the miners. The trundle of the small train was imminent. Suddenly the engine loomed past the house and came to a stop opposite the gate.

The engine-driver, a short man with round grey beard, leaned out of the cab high above the woman.

"Have you got a cup of tea?" he said in a cheery, hearty fashion.

It was her father. She went in, saying she would mash.[1] Directly, she returned.

"I didn't come to see you on Sunday," began the little grey-bearded man.

"I didn't expect you," said his daughter.

The engine-driver winced; then, reassuming his cheery, airy manner, he said:

"Oh, have you heard then? Well, and what do you think——?"

"I think it is soon enough," she replied.

At her brief censure the little man made an impatient gesture, and said coax-ingly, yet with dangerous coldness:

"Well, what's a man to do? It's no sort of life for a man of my years, to sit at my own hearth like a stranger. And if I'm going to marry again it may as well be soon as late—what does it matter to anybody?"

The woman did not reply, but turned and went into the house. The man in the engine-cab stood assertive, till she returned with a cup of tea and a piece of bread and butter on a plate. She went up the steps and stood near the footplate of the hissing engine.

"You needn't 'a' brought me bread an' butter," said her father. "But a cup of tea"—he sipped appreciatively—"it's very nice." He sipped for a moment or two, then: "I hear as Walter's got another bout on," he said.

"When hasn't he?" said the woman bitterly.

"I heered tell of him in the 'Lord Nelson'[2] braggin' as he was going to spend that b—— afore he went: half a sovereign[3] that was."

"When?" asked the woman.

"A' Sat'day night—I know that's true."

"Very likely," she laughed bitterly. "He gives me twenty-three shillings."

"Aye, it's a nice thing, when a man can do nothing with his money but make a beast of himself!" said the grey-whiskered man. The woman turned her head away. Her father swallowed the last of his tea and handed her the cup.

"Aye," he sighed, wiping his mouth. "It's a settler, it is——"

1. Prepare (tea).   2. A public house, pub.   3. A sovereign was about half a week's wage; there are 20 shillings (see below) to the pound.

35   He put his hand on the lever. The little engine strained and groaned, and the train rumbled towards the crossing. The woman again looked across the metals. Darkness was settling over the spaces of the railway and trucks: the miners, in grey sombre groups, were still passing home. The winding-engine pulsed hurriedly, with brief pauses. Elizabeth Bates looked at the dreary flow of men, then she went indoors. Her husband did not come.

The kitchen was small and full of firelight; red coals piled glowing up the chimney mouth. All the life of the room seemed in the white, warm hearth and the steel fender reflecting the red fire. The cloth was laid for tea; cups glinted in the shadows. At the back, where the lowest stairs protruded into the room, the boy sat struggling with a knife and a piece of white wood. He was almost hidden in the shadow. It was half-past four. They had but to await the father's coming to begin tea. As the mother watched her son's sullen little struggle with the wood, she saw herself in his silence and pertinacity; she saw the father in her child's indifference to all but himself. She seemed to be occupied by her husband. He had probably gone past his home, slunk past his own door, to drink before he came in, while his dinner spoiled and wasted in waiting. She glanced at the clock, then took the potatoes to strain them in the yard. The garden and fields beyond the brook were closed in uncertain darkness. When she rose with the saucepan, leaving the drain steaming into the night behind her, she saw the yellow lamps were lit along the high road that went up the hill away beyond the space of the railway lines and the field.

Then again she watched the men trooping home, fewer now and fewer.

Indoors the fire was sinking and the room was dark red. The woman put her saucepan on the hob, and set a batter pudding near the mouth of the oven. Then she stood unmoving. Directly, gratefully, came quick young steps to the door. Someone hung on the latch a moment, then a little girl entered and began pulling off her outdoor things, dragging a mass of curls, just ripening from gold to brown, over her eyes with her hat.

Her mother chid her for coming late from school, and said she would have to keep her at home the dark winter days.

40   "Why, mother, it's hardly a bit dark yet. The lamp's not lighted, and my father's not home."

"No, he isn't. But it's a quarter to five! Did you see anything of him?"

The child became serious. She looked at her mother with large, wistful blue eyes.

"No, mother, I've never seen him. Why? Has he come up an' gone past, to Old Brinsley? He hasn't, mother, 'cos I never saw him."

"He'd watch that," said the mother bitterly, "he'd take care as you didn't see him. But you may depend upon it, he's seated in the 'Prince o' Wales.' He wouldn't be this late."

45   The girl looked at her mother piteously.

"Let's have our teas, mother, should we?" said she.

The mother called John to table. She opened the door once more and looked out across the darkness of the lines. All was deserted: she could not hear the winding-engines.

"Perhaps," she said to herself, "he's stopped to get some ripping[4] done."

They sat down to tea. John, at the end of the table near the door, was almost lost in the darkness. Their faces were hidden from each other. The girl crouched against the fender slowly moving a thick piece of bread before the fire. The lad, his face a dusky mark on the shadow, sat watching her who was transfigured in the red glow.

"I do think it's beautiful to look in the fire," said the child.   50

"Do you?" said her mother. "Why?"

"It's so red, and full of little caves—and it feels so nice, and you can fair smell it."

"It'll want mending directly," replied her mother, "and then if your father comes he'll carry on and say there never is a fire when a man comes home sweating from the pit.—A public-house is always warm enough."

There was silence till the boy said complainingly: "Make haste, our Annie."

"Well, I am doing! I can't make the fire do it no faster, can I?"   55

"She keeps wafflin'[5] it about so's to make 'er slow," grumbled the boy.

"Don't have such an evil imagination, child," replied the mother.

Soon the room was busy in the darkness with the crisp sound of crunching. The mother ate very little. She drank her tea determinedly, and sat thinking. When she rose her anger was evident in the stern unbending of her head. She looked at the pudding in the fender, and broke out:

"It is a scandalous thing as a man can't even come home to his dinner! If it's crozzled[6] up to a cinder I don't see why I should care. Past his very door he goes to get to a public-house, and here I sit with his dinner waiting for him——"

She went out. As she dropped piece after piece of coal on the red fire, the   60 shadows fell on the walls, till the room was almost in total darkness.

"I canna see," grumbled the invisible John. In spite of herself, the mother laughed.

"You know the way to your mouth," she said. She set the dustpan outside the door. When she came again like a shadow on the hearth, the lad repeated, complaining sulkily:

"I canna see."

"Good gracious!" cried the mother irritably, "you're as bad as your father if it's a bit dusk!"

Nevertheless she took a paper spill from a sheaf on the mantelpiece and   65 proceeded to light the lamp that hung from the ceiling in the middle of the room. As she reached up, her figure displayed itself just rounding with maternity.

"Oh, mother——!" exclaimed the girl.

"What?" said the woman, suspended in the act of putting the lamp-glass over the flame. The copper reflector shone handsomely on her, as she stood with uplifted arm, turning to face her daughter:

"You've got a flower in your apron!" said the child, in a little rapture at this unusual event.

4. Coal-mining term for taking down the roof of an underground road in order to make it higher.
5. Waving.   6. Shriveled.

"Goodness me!" exclaimed the woman, relieved. "One would think the house was afire." She replaced the glass and waited a moment before turning up the wick. A pale shadow was seen floating vaguely on the floor.

70 "Let me smell!" said the child, still rapturously, coming forward and putting her face to her mother's waist.

"Go along, silly!" said the mother, turning up the lamp. The light revealed their suspense so that the woman felt it almost unbearable. Annie was still bending at her waist. Irritably, the mother took the flowers out from her apron-band.

"Oh, mother—don't take them out!" Annie cried, catching her hand and trying to replace the sprig.

"Such nonsense!" said the mother, turning away. The child put the pale chrysanthemums to her lips, murmuring:

"Don't they smell beautiful!"

75 Her mother gave a short laugh.

"No," she said, "not to me. It was chrysanthemums when I married him, and chrysanthemums when you were born, and the first time they ever brought him home drunk, he'd got brown chrysanthemums in his button-hole."

She looked at the children. Their eyes and their parted lips were wondering. The mother sat rocking in silence for some time. Then she looked at the clock.

"Twenty minutes to six!" In a tone of fine bitter carelessness she continued: "Eh, he'll not come now till they bring him. There he'll stick! But he needn't come rolling in here in his pit-dirt, for *I* won't wash him. He can lie on the floor——Eh, what a fool I've been, what a fool! And this is what I came here for, to this dirty hole, rats and all, for him to slink past his very door. Twice last week—he's begun now——"

She silenced herself, and rose to clear the table.

80 While for an hour or more the children played, subduedly intent, fertile of imagination, united in fear of the mother's wrath, and in dread of their father's home-coming, Mrs. Bates sat in her rocking-chair making a "singlet" of thick cream-coloured flannel, which gave a dull wounded sound as she tore off the grey edge. She worked at her sewing with energy, listening to the children, and her anger wearied itself, lay down to rest, opening its eyes from time to time and steadily watching, its ears raised to listen. Sometimes even her anger quailed and shrank, and the mother suspended her sewing, tracing the footsteps that thudded along the sleepers outside; she would lift her head sharply to bid the children "hush," but she recovered herself in time, and the footsteps went past the gate, and the children were not flung out of their playworld.

But at last Annie sighed, and gave in. She glanced at her waggon of slippers, and loathed the game. She turned plaintively to her mother.

"Mother!"—but she was inarticulate.

John crept out like a frog from under the sofa. His mother glanced up.

"Yes," she said, "just look at those shirtsleeves!"

85 The boy held them out to survey them, saying nothing. Then somebody called in a hoarse voice away down the line, and suspense bristled in the room, till two people had gone by outside, talking.

"It is time for bed," said the mother.

"My father hasn't come," wailed Annie plaintively. But her mother was primed with courage.

"Never mind. They'll bring him when he does come—like a log." She meant there would be no scene. "And he may sleep on the floor till he wakes himself. I know he'll not go to work tomorrow after this!"

The children had their hands and faces wiped with a flannel.[7] They were very quiet. When they had put on their nightdresses, they said their prayers, the boy mumbling. The mother looked down at them, at the brown silken bush of intertwining curls in the nape of the girl's neck, at the little black head of the lad, and her heart burst with anger at their father who caused all three such distress. The children hid their faces in her skirts for comfort.

When Mrs. Bates came down, the room was strangely empty, with a tension of expectancy. She took up her sewing and stitched for some time without raising her head. Meantime her anger was tinged with fear.   90

II

The clock struck eight and she rose suddenly, dropping her sewing on her chair. She went to the stairfoot door, opened it, listening. Then she went out, locking the door behind her.

Something scuffled in the yard, and she started though she knew it was only the rats with which the place was overrun. The night was very dark. In the great bay of railway lines, bulked with trucks, there was no trace of light, only away back she could see a few yellow lamps at the pit-top, and the red smear of the burning pit-bank on the night. She hurried along the edge of the track, then, crossing the converging lines, came to the stile by the white gates, whence she emerged on the road. Then the fear which had led her shrank. People were walking up to New Brinsley; she saw the lights in the houses; twenty yards further on were the broad windows of the "Prince of Wales," very warm and bright, and the loud voices of men could be heard distinctly. What a fool she had been to imagine that anything had happened to him! He was merely drinking over there at the "Prince of Wales." She faltered. She had never yet been to fetch him, and she never would go. So she continued her walk towards the long straggling line of houses, standing blank on the highway. She entered a passage between the dwellings.

"Mr. Rigley?—Yes! Did you want him? No, he's not in at this minute."

The raw-boned woman leaned forward from her dark scullery and peered at the other, upon whom fell a dim light through the blind of the kitchen window.

"Is it Mrs. Bates?" she asked in a tone tinged with respect.   95

"Yes. I wondered if your Master was at home. Mine hasn't come yet."

" 'Asn't 'e! Oh, Jack's been 'ome an 'ad 'is dinner an' gone out. 'E's just gone for 'alf an hour afore bedtime. Did you call at the 'Prince of Wales'?"

"No——"

"No, you didn't like——! It's not very nice." The other woman was indulgent.

---

7. Washrag.

There was an awkward pause. "Jack never said nothink about—about your Mester," she said.

"No!—I expect he's stuck in there!"

Elizabeth Bates said this bitterly, and with recklessness. She knew that the woman across the yard was standing at her door listening, but she did not care. As she turned:

"Stop a minute! I'll just go an' ask Jack if 'e knows anythink," said Mrs. Rigley.

"Oh, no—I wouldn't like to put—!"

"Yes, I will, if you will just step inside an' see as th' childer doesn't come downstairs and set theirselves afire."

Elizabeth Bates, murmuring a remonstrance, stepped inside. The other woman apologized for the state of the room.

The kitchen needed apology. There were little frocks and trousers and childish undergarments on the squab[8] and on the floor, and a litter of playthings everywhere. On the black American cloth[9] of the table were pieces of bread and cake, crusts, slops, and a teapot with cold tea.

"Eh, ours is just as bad," said Elizabeth Bates, looking at the woman, not at the house. Mrs. Rigley put a shawl over her head and hurried out, saying:

"I shanna be a minute."

The other sat, noting with faint disapproval the general untidiness of the room. Then she fell to counting the shoes of various sizes scattered over the floor. There were twelve. She sighed and said to herself, "No wonder!"—glancing at the litter. There came the scratching of two pairs of feet on the yard, and the Rigleys entered. Elizabeth Bates rose. Rigley was a big man, with very large bones. His head looked particularly bony. Across his temple was a blue scar, caused by a wound got in the pit, a wound in which the coal-dust remained blue like tattooing.

" 'Asna 'e come whoam yit?" asked the man, without any form of greeting, but with deference and sympathy. "I couldna say wheer he is—'e's non ower theer!"—he jerked his head to signify the "Prince of Wales."

" 'E's 'appen[1] gone up to th' 'Yew,' " said Mrs. Rigley.

There was another pause. Rigley had evidently something to get off his mind:

"Ah left 'im finishin' a stint," he began. "Loose-all[2] 'ad bin gone about ten minutes when we com'n away, an' I shouted, 'Are ter comin', Walt?' an' 'e said 'Go on, Ah shanna be but a 'ef a minnit,' so we com'n ter th' bottom, me an' Browers, thinkin' as 'e wor just behint, an' 'ud come up i' th' next bantle[3]—"

He stood perplexed, as if answering a charge of deserting his mate. Elizabeth Bates, now again certain of disaster, hastened to reassure him:

"I expect 'e's gone up to th' 'Yew Tree,' as you say. It's not the first time. I've fretted myself into a fever before now. He'll come home when they carry him."

"Ay, isn't it too bad!" deplored the other woman.

---

8. Sofa.   9. Enameled oilcloth.   1. Perhaps.   2. Signal to quit work and come to the surface.   3. An open seat or car of the lift or elevator that takes the miners to the surface.

"I'll just step up to Dick's an' see if 'e *is* theer," offered the man, afraid of appearing alarmed, afraid of taking liberties.

"Oh, I wouldn't think of bothering you that far," said Elizabeth Bates, with emphasis, but he knew she was glad of his offer.

As they stumbled up the entry, Elizabeth Bates heard Rigley's wife run across the yard and open her neighbour's door. At this, suddenly all the blood in her body seemed to switch away from her heart.

"Mind!" warned Rigley. "Ah've said many a time as Ah'd fill up them ruts in this entry, sumb'dy 'll be breakin' their legs yit."

She recovered herself and walked quickly along with the miner.

"I don't like leaving the children in bed, and nobody in the house," she said.

"No, you dunna!" he replied courteously. They were soon at the gate of the cottage.

"Well, I shanna be many minnits. Dunna you be frettin' now, 'e'll be all right," said the butty.[4]

"Thank you very much, Mr. Rigley," she replied.

"You're welcome!" he stammered, moving away. "I shanna be many minnits."

The house was quiet. Elizabeth Bates took off her hat and shawl, and rolled back the rug. When she had finished, she sat down. It was a few minutes past nine. She was startled by the rapid chuff of the winding-engine at the pit, and the sharp whirr of the brakes on the rope as it descended. Again she felt the painful sweep of her blood, and she put her hand to her side, saying aloud, "Good gracious!—it's only the nine o'clock deputy going down," rebuking herself.

She sat still, listening. Half an hour of this, and she was wearied out.

"What am I working up like this for?" she said pitiably to herself, "I s'll only be doing myself some damage."

She took out her sewing again.

At a quarter to ten there were footsteps. One person! She watched for the door to open. It was an elderly woman, in a black bonnet and a black woollen shawl—his mother. She was about sixty years old, pale, with blue eyes, and her face all wrinkled and lamentable. She shut the door and turned to her daughter-in-law peevishly.

"Eh, Lizzie, whatever shall we do, whatever shall we do!" she cried.

Elizabeth drew back a little, sharply.

"What is it, mother?" she said.

The elder woman seated herself on the sofa.

"I don't know, child, I can't tell you!"—she shook her head slowly. Elizabeth sat watching her, anxious and vexed.

"I don't know," replied the grandmother, sighing very deeply. "There's no end to my troubles, there isn't. The things I've gone through, I'm sure it's enough ——!" She wept without wiping her eyes, the tears running.

"But, mother," interrupted Elizabeth, "what do you mean? What is it?"

---

4. Buddy, fellow worker.

The grandmother slowly wiped her eyes. The fountains of her tears were stopped by Elizabeth's directness. She wiped her eyes slowly.

140   "Poor child! Eh, you poor thing!" she moaned. "I don't know what we're going to do, I don't—and you as you are—it's a thing, it is indeed!"

Elizabeth waited.

"Is he dead?" she asked, and at the words her heart swung violently, though she felt a slight flush of shame at the ultimate extravagance of the question. Her words sufficiently frightened the old lady, almost brought her to herself.

"Don't say so, Elizabeth! We'll hope it's not as bad as that; no, may the Lord spare us that, Elizabeth. Jack Rigley came just as I was sittin' down to a glass afore going to bed, an' 'e said, ' 'Appen you'll go down th' line, Mrs. Bates. Walt's had an accident. 'Appen you'll go an' sit wi' 'er till we can get him home.' I hadn't time to ask him a word afore he was gone. An' I put my bonnet on an' come straight down, Lizzie. I thought to myself, 'Eh, that poor blessed child, if anybody should come an' tell her of a sudden, there's no knowin'; what'll 'appen to 'er.' You mustn't let it upset you, Lizzie—or you know what to expect. How long is it, six months—or is it five, Lizzie? Ay!"—the old woman shook her head—"time slips on, it slips on! Ay!"

Elizabeth's thoughts were busy elsewhere. If he was killed—would she be able to manage on the little pension and what she could earn?—she counted up rapidly. If he was hurt—they wouldn't take him to the hospital—how tiresome he would be to nurse!—but perhaps she'd be able to get him away from the drink and his hateful ways. She would—while he was ill. The tears offered to come to her eyes at the picture. But what sentimental luxury was this she was beginning?—She turned to consider the children. At any rate she was absolutely necessary for them. They were her business.

145   "Ay!" repeated the old woman, "it seems but a week or two since he brought me his first wages. Ay—he was a good lad, Elizabeth, he was, in his way. I don't know why he got to be such a trouble, I don't. He was a happy lad at home, only full of spirits. But there's no mistake he's been a handful of trouble, he has! I hope the Lord'll spare him to mend his ways. I hope so, I hope so. You've had a sight o' trouble with him, Elizabeth, you have indeed. But he was a jolly enough lad wi' me, he was, I can assure you. I don't know how it is. . . ."

The old woman continued to muse aloud, a monotonous irritating sound, while Elizabeth thought concentratedly, startled once, when she heard the winding-engine chuff quickly, and the brakes skirr with a shriek. Then she heard the engine more slowly, and the brakes made no sound. The old woman did not notice. Elizabeth waited in suspense. The mother-in-law talked, with lapses into silence.

"But he wasn't your son, Lizzie, an' it makes a difference. Whatever he was, I remember him when he was little, an' I learned to understand him and to make allowances. You've got to make allowances for them—"

It was half-past ten, and the old woman was saying: "But it's trouble from beginning to end; you're never too old for trouble, never too old for that——" when the gate banged back, and there were heavy feet on the steps.

"I'll go, Lizzie, let me go," cried the old woman, rising. But Elizabeth was at the door. It was a man in pit-clothes.

"They're bringin' 'im, Missis," he said. Elizabeth's heart halted a moment. 150 Then it surged on again, almost suffocating her.

"Is he—is it bad?" she asked.

The man turned away, looking at the darkness:

"The doctor says 'e'd been dead hours. 'E saw 'im i' th' lamp-cabin."

The old woman, who stood just behind Elizabeth, dropped into a chair and folded her hands, crying: "Oh, my boy, my boy!"

"Hush!" said Elizabeth, with a sharp twitch of a frown. "Be still, mother, 155 don't waken th' children: I wouldn't have them down for anything!"

The old woman moaned softly, rocking herself. The man was drawing away. Elizabeth took a step forward.

"How was it?" she asked.

"Well, I couldn't say for sure," the man replied, very ill at ease. " 'E wor finishin' a stint an' th' butties 'ad gone, an' a lot o' stuff come down atop 'n 'im."

"And crushed him?" cried the widow, with a shudder.

"No," said the man, "it fell at th' back of 'im. 'E wor under th' face, an' it 160 niver touched 'im. It shut 'im in. It seems 'e wor smothered."

Elizabeth shrank back. She heard the old woman behind her cry:

"What?—what did 'e say it was?"

The man replied, more loudly: "'E wor smothered!"

Then the old woman wailed aloud, and this relieved Elizabeth.

"Oh, mother," she said, putting her hands on the old woman, "don't waken 165 th' children, don't waken th' children."

She wept a little, unknowing, while the old mother rocked herself and moaned. Elizabeth remembered that they were bringing him home, and she must be ready. "They'll lay him in the parlour," she said to herself, standing a moment pale and perplexed.

Then she lighted a candle and went into the tiny room. The air was cold and damp, but she could not make a fire, there was no fireplace. She set down the candle and looked round. The candlelight glittered on the lustre-glasses,[5] on the two vases that held some of the pink chrysanthemums, and on the dark mahogany. There was a cold, deathly smell of chrysanthemums in the room. Elizabeth stood looking at the flowers. She turned away, and calculated whether there would be room to lay him on the floor, between the couch and the chiffonier. She pushed the chairs aside. There would be room to lay him down and to step round him. Then she fetched the old red tablecloth, and another old cloth, spreading them down to save her bit of carpet. She shivered on leaving the parlour; so, from the dresser-drawer she took a clean shirt and put it at the fire to air. All the time her mother-in-law was rocking herself in the chair and moaning.

5. Glass pendants around the edge of an ornamental vase.

"You'll have to move from there, mother," said Elizabeth. "They'll be bringing him in. Come in the rocker."

The old mother rose mechanically, and seated herself by the fire, continuing to lament. Elizabeth went into the pantry for another candle, and there, in the little penthouse[6] under the naked tiles, she heard them coming. She stood still in the pantry doorway, listening. She heard them pass the end of the house, and come awkwardly down the three steps, a jumble of shuffling footsteps and muttering voices. The old woman was silent. The men were in the yard.

170   Then Elizabeth heard Matthews, the manager of the pit, say: "You go in first, Jim. Mind!"

The door came open, and the two women saw a collier backing into the room, holding one end of a stretcher, on which they could see the nailed pit-boots of the dead man. The two carriers halted, the man at the head stooping to the lintel of the door.

"Wheer will you have him?" asked the manager, a short, white-bearded man.

Elizabeth roused herself and came from the pantry carrying the unlighted candle.

"In the parlour," she said.

175   "In there, Jim!" pointed the manager, and the carriers backed round into the tiny room. The coat with which they had covered the body fell off as they awkwardly turned through the two doorways, and the women saw their man, naked to the waist, lying stripped for work. The old woman began to moan in a low voice of horror.

"Lay th' stretcher at th' side," snapped the manager, "an' put 'im on th' cloths. Mind now, mind! Look you now——!"

One of the men had knocked off a vase of chrysanthemums. He stared awkwardly, then they set down the stretcher. Elizabeth did not look at her husband. As soon as she could get in the room, she went and picked up the broken vase and the flowers.

"Wait a minute!" she said.

The three men waited in silence while she mopped up the water with a duster.

180   "Eh, what a job, what a job, to be sure!" the manager was saying, rubbing his brow with trouble and perplexity. "Never knew such a thing in my life, never! He'd no business to ha' been left. I never knew such a thing in my life! Fell over him clean as a whistle, an' shut him in. Not four foot of space, there wasn't—yet it scarce bruised him."

He looked down at the dead man, lying prone, half naked, all grimed with coal-dust.

" ' 'Sphyxiated,' the doctor said. It *is* the most terrible job I've ever known. Seems as if it was done o' purpose. Clean over him, an' shut 'im in, like a mouse-trap"—he made a sharp, descending gesture with his hand.

The colliers standing by jerked aside their heads in hopeless comment.

The horror of the thing bristled upon them all.

---

6. Structure, usually with a sloping roof, attached to house.

Then they heard the girl's voice upstairs calling shrilly: "Mother, mother— 185
who is it? Mother, who is it?"

Elizabeth hurried to the foot of the stairs and opened the door:

"Go to sleep!" she commanded sharply. "What are you shouting about? Go
to sleep at once—there's nothing——"

Then she began to mount the stairs. They could hear her on the boards, and
on the plaster floor of the little bedroom. They could hear her distinctly:

"What's the matter now?—what's the matter with you, silly thing?"—her
voice was much agitated, with an unreal gentleness.

"I thought it was some men come," said the plaintive voice of the child. 190
"Has he come?"

"Yes, they've brought him. There's nothing to make a fuss about. Go to sleep
now, like a good child."

They could hear her voice in the bedroom, they waited whilst she covered
the children under the bedclothes.

"Is he drunk?" asked the girl, timidly, faintly.

"No! No—he's not! He's—he's asleep."

"Is he asleep downstairs?" 195

"Yes—and don't make a noise."

There was silence for a moment, then the men heard the frightened child
again:

"What's that noise?"

"It's nothing, I tell you, what are you bothering for?"

The noise was the grandmother moaning. She was oblivious of everything, 200
sitting on her chair rocking and moaning. The manager put his hand on her
arm and bade her "Sh-sh!!"

The old woman opened her eyes and looked at him. She was shocked by
this interruption, and seemed to wonder.

"What time is it?"—the plaintive thin voice of the child, sinking back unhappily into sleep, asked this last question.

"Ten o'clock," answered the mother more softly. Then she must have bent
down and kissed the children.

Matthews beckoned to the men to come away. They put on their caps, and
took up the stretcher. Stepping over the body, they tiptoed out of the house.
None of them spoke till they were far from the wakeful children.

When Elizabeth came down she found her mother alone on the parlour 205
floor, leaning over the dead man, the tears dropping on him.

"We must lay him out," the wife said. She put on the kettle, then returning
knelt at the feet, and began to unfasten the knotted leather laces. The room was
clammy and dim with only one candle, so that she had to bend her face almost
to the floor. At last she got off the heavy boots and put them away.

"You must help me now," she whispered to the old woman. Together they
stripped the man.

When they arose, saw him lying in the naïve dignity of death, the women
stood arrested in fear and respect. For a few moments they remained still, looking down, the old mother whimpering. Elizabeth felt countermanded. She saw

him, how utterly inviolable he lay in himself. She had nothing to do with him. She could not accept it. Stooping, she laid her hand on him, in claim. He was still warm, for the mine was hot where he had died. His mother had his face between her hands, and was murmuring incoherently. The old tears fell in succession as drops from wet leaves; the mother was not weeping, merely her tears flowed. Elizabeth embraced the body of her husband, with cheek and lips. She seemed to be listening, inquiring, trying to get some connection. But she could not. She was driven away. He was impregnable.

She rose, went into the kitchen, where she poured warm water into a bowl, brought soap and flannel and a soft towel.

210   "I must wash him," she said.

Then the old mother rose stiffly, and watched Elizabeth as she carefully washed his face, carefully brushing the big blonde moustache from his mouth with the flannel. She was afraid with a bottomless fear, so she ministered to him. The old woman, jealous, said:

"Let me wipe him!"—and she kneeled on the other side drying slowly as Elizabeth washed, her big black bonnet sometimes brushing the dark head of her daughter. They worked thus in silence for a long time. They never forgot it was death, and the touch of the man's dead body gave them strange emotions, different in each of the women; a great dread possessed them both, the mother felt the lie was given to her womb, she was denied; the wife felt the utter isolation of the human soul, the child within her was a weight apart from her.

At last it was finished. He was a man of handsome body, and his face showed no traces of drink. He was blonde, full-fleshed, with fine limbs. But he was dead.

"Bless him," whispered his mother, looking always at his face, and speaking out of sheer terror. "Dear lad—bless him!" She spoke in a faint sibilant ecstasy of fear and mother love.

215   Elizabeth sank down again to the floor, and put her face against his neck, and trembled and shuddered. But she had to draw away again. He was dead, and her living flesh had no place against his. A great dread and weariness held her: she was so unavailing. Her life was gone like this.

"White as milk he is, clear as a twelve-month baby, bless him, the darling!" the old mother murmured to herself. "Not a mark on him, clear and clean and white, beautiful as ever a child was made," she murmured with pride. Elizabeth kept her face hidden.

"He went peaceful, Lizzie—peaceful as sleep. Isn't he beautiful, the lamb? Ay—he must ha' made his peace, Lizzie. 'Appen he made it all right, Lizzie, shut in there. He'd have time. He wouldn't look like this if he hadn't made his peace. The lamb, the dear lamb. Eh, but he had a hearty laugh. I loved to hear it. He had the heartiest laugh, Lizzie, as a lad——"

Elizabeth looked up. The man's mouth was fallen back, slightly open under the cover of the moustache. The eyes, half shut, did not show glazed in the obscurity. Life with its smoky burning gone from him, had left him apart and utterly alien to her. And she knew what a stranger he was to her. In her womb was ice of fear, because of this separate stranger with whom she had been living as one flesh. Was this what it all meant—utter, intact separateness, obscured by heat of living? In dread she turned her face away. The fact was too deadly. There had been nothing between them, and yet they had come together, exchanging their nakedness repeatedly. Each time he had taken her, they had been two isolated beings, far apart as now. He was no more responsible than she. The child was like ice in her womb. For as she looked at the dead man, her mind, cold and detached, said clearly: "Who am I? What have I been doing? I have been fighting a husband who did not exist. *He* existed all the time. What wrong have I done? What was that I have been living with? There lies the reality, this man."—And her soul died in her for fear: she knew she had never seen him, he had never seen her, they had met in the dark and had fought in the dark, not knowing whom they met nor whom they fought. And now she saw, and turned silent in seeing. For she had been wrong. She had said he was something he was not; she had felt familiar with him. Whereas he was apart all the while, living as she never lived, feeling as she never felt.

In fear and shame she looked at his naked body, that she had known falsely. And he was the father of her children. Her soul was torn from her body and stood apart. She looked at his naked body and was ashamed, as if she had denied it. After all, it was itself. It seemed awful to her. She looked at his face, and she turned her own face to the wall. For his look was other than hers, his way was not her way. She had denied him what he was—she saw it now. She had refused him as himself.—And this had been her life, and his life.—She was grateful to death, which restored the truth. And she knew she was not dead.

And all the while her heart was bursting with grief and pity for him. What had he suffered? What stretch of horror for this helpless man! She was rigid with agony. She had not been able to help him. He had been cruelly injured, this naked man, this other being, and she could make no reparation. There were the children—but the children belonged to life. This dead man had nothing to do with them. He and she were only channels through which life had flowed to issue in the children. She was a mother—but how awful she knew it now to have been a wife. And he, dead now, how awful he must have felt it to be a husband. She felt that in her next world he would be a stranger to her. If they met there, in the beyond, they would only be ashamed of what had been before. The children had come, for some mysterious reason, out of both of them. But the children did not unite them. Now he was dead, she knew how eternally he was apart from her, how eternally he had nothing more to do with her. She saw this episode of her life closed. They had denied each other in life. Now he had withdrawn. An anguish came over her. It was finished then: it had become hopeless between them long before he died. Yet he had been her husband. But how little!

"Have you got his shirt, 'Lizabeth?"

Elizabeth turned without answering, though she strove to weep and behave as her mother-in-law expected. But she could not, she was silenced. She went into the kitchen and returned with the garment.

"It is aired," she said, grasping the cotton shirt here and there to try. She was almost ashamed to handle him; what right had she or anyone to lay hands on him; but her touch was humble on his body. It was hard work to clothe him.

220

He was so heavy and inert. A terrible dread gripped her all the while: that he could be so heavy and utterly inert, unresponsive, apart. The horror of the distance between them was almost too much for her—it was so infinite a gap she must look across.

At last it was finished. They covered him with a sheet and left him lying, with his face bound. And she fastened the door of the little parlour, lest the children should see what was lying there. Then, with peace sunk heavy on her heart, she went about making tidy the kitchen. She knew she submitted to life, which was her immediate master. But from death, her ultimate master, she winced with fear and shame.

1914

D. H. LAWRENCE

The Rocking-Horse Winner

There was a woman who was beautiful, who started with all the advantages, yet she had no luck. She married for love, and the love turned to dust. She had bonny children, yet she felt they had been thrust upon her, and she could not love them. They looked at her coldly, as if they were finding fault with her. And hurriedly she felt she must cover up some fault in herself. Yet what it was that she must cover up she never knew. Nevertheless, when her children were present, she always felt the centre of her heart go hard. This troubled her, and in her manner she was all the more gentle and anxious for her children, as if she loved them very much. Only she herself knew that at the centre of her heart was a hard little place that could not feel love, no, not for anybody. Everybody else said of her: "She is such a good mother. She adores her children." Only she herself, and her children themselves, knew it was not so. They read it in each other's eyes.

There were a boy and two little girls. They lived in a pleasant house, with a garden, and they had discreet servants, and felt themselves superior to anyone in the neighbourhood.

Although they lived in style, they felt always an anxiety in the house. There was never enough money. The mother had a small income, and the father had a small income, but not nearly enough for the social position which they had to keep up. The father went in to town to some office. But though he had good prospects, these prospects never materialized. There was always the grinding sense of the shortage of money, though the style was always kept up.

At last the mother said: "I will see if *I* can't make something." But she did not know where to begin. She racked her brains, and tried this thing and the other, but could not find anything successful. The failure made deep lines come into her face. Her children were growing up, they would have to go to school. There must be more money, there must be more money. The father, who was always very handsome and expensive in his tastes, seemed as if he never *would* be able to do anything worth doing. And the mother, who had a great belief in herself, did not succeed any better, and her tastes were just as expensive.

And so the house came to be haunted by the unspoken phrase: *There must be more money! There must be more money!* The children could hear it all the time, though nobody said it aloud. They heard it at Christmas, when the expensive and splendid toys filled the nursery. Behind the shining modern rocking-horse, behind the smart doll's-house, a voice would start whispering: "There *must* be more money! There *must* be more money!" And the children would stop playing, to listen for a moment. They would look into each other's eyes, to see if they had all heard. And each one saw in the eyes of the other two that they too had heard. "There *must* be more money! There *must* be more money!"

It came whispering from the springs of the still-swaying rocking-horse, and even the horse, bending his wooden, champing head, heard it. The big doll, sitting so pink and smirking in her new pram,[1] could hear it quite plainly, and seemed to be smirking all the more self-consciously because of it. The foolish puppy, too, that took the place of the teddy-bear, he was looking so extraordinarily foolish for no other reason but that he heard the secret whisper all over the house: "There *must* be more money!"

Yet nobody ever said it aloud. The whisper was everywhere, and therefore no one spoke it. Just as no one ever says: "We are breathing!" in spite of the fact that breath is coming and going all the time.

"Mother," said the boy Paul one day, "why don't we keep a car of our own? Why do we always use uncle's, or else a taxi?"

"Because we're the poor members of the family," said the mother.

"But why *are* we, mother?"

"Well—I suppose," she said slowly and bitterly, "it's because your father has no luck."

The boy was silent for some time.

"Is luck money, mother?" he asked rather timidly.

"No, Paul. Not quite. It's what causes you to have money."

"Oh!" said Paul vaguely. "I thought when Uncle Oscar said *filthy lucker*, it meant money."

"*Filthy lucre* does mean money," said the mother. "But it's lucre, not luck."

"Oh!" said the boy. "Then what *is* luck, mother?"

"It's what causes you to have money. If you're lucky you have money. That's why it's better to be born lucky than rich. If you're rich, you may lose your money. But if you're lucky, you will always get more money."

"Oh! Will you? And is father not lucky?"

"Very unlucky, I should say," she said bitterly.

The boy watched her with unsure eyes.

"Why?" he asked.

"I don't know. Nobody ever knows why one person is lucky and another unlucky."

"Don't they? Nobody at all? Does *nobody* know?"

"Perhaps God. But He never tells."

1. Baby carriage.

"He ought to, then. And aren't you lucky either, mother?"

"I can't be, if I married an unlucky husband."

"But by yourself, aren't you?"

"I used to think I was, before I married. Now I think I am very unlucky indeed."

"Why?"

"Well—never mind! Perhaps I'm not really," she said.

The child looked at her, to see if she meant it. But he saw, by the lines of her mouth, that she was only trying to hide something from him.

"Well, anyhow," he said stoutly, "I'm a lucky person."

"Why?" said his mother, with a sudden laugh.

He stared at her. He didn't even know why he had said it.

"God told me," he asserted, brazening it out.

"I hope He did, dear!" she said, again with a laugh, but rather bitter.

"He did, mother!"

"Excellent!" said the mother, using one of her husband's exclamations.

The boy saw she did not believe him; or, rather, that she paid no attention to his assertion. This angered him somewhat, and made him want to compel her attention.

He went off by himself, vaguely, in a childish way, seeking for the clue to "luck." Absorbed, taking no heed of other people, he went about with a sort of stealth, seeking inwardly for luck. He wanted luck, he wanted it, he wanted it. When the two girls were playing dolls in the nursery, he would sit on his big rocking-horse, charging madly into space, with a frenzy that made the little girls peer at him uneasily. Wildly the horse careered, the waving dark hair of the boy tossed, his eyes had a strange glare in them. The little girls dared not speak to him.

When he had ridden to the end of his mad little journey, he climbed down and stood in front of his rocking-horse, staring fixedly into its lowered face. Its red mouth was slightly open, its big eye was wide and glassy-bright.

"Now!" he would silently command the snorting steed. "Now, take me to where there is luck! Now take me!"

And he would slash the horse on the neck with the little whip he had asked Uncle Oscar for. He *knew* the horse could take him to where there was luck, if only he forced it. So he would mount again, and start on his furious ride, hoping at last to get there. He knew he could get there.

"You'll break your horse, Paul!" said the nurse.

"He's always riding like that! I wish he'd leave off!" said his elder sister Joan.

But he only glared down on them in silence. Nurse gave him up. She could make nothing of him. Anyhow he was growing beyond her.

One day his mother and his Uncle Oscar came in when he was on one of his furious rides. He did not speak to them.

"Hallo, you young jockey! Riding a winner?" said his uncle.

"Aren't you growing too big for a rocking-horse? You're not a very little boy any longer, you know," said his mother.

But Paul only gave a blue glare from his big, rather close-set eyes. He would speak to nobody when he was in full tilt. His mother watched him with an anxious expression on her face.

At last he suddenly stopped forcing his horse into the mechanical gallop, and slid down.

"Well, I got there!" he announced fiercely, his blue eyes still flaring, and his sturdy long legs straddling apart.

"Where did you get to?" asked his mother.

"Where I wanted to go," he flared back at her.   55

"That's right, son!" said Uncle Oscar. "Don't you stop till you get there. What's the horse's name?"

"He doesn't have a name," said the boy.

"Gets on without all right?" asked the uncle.

"Well, he has different names. He was called Sansovino last week."

"Sansovino, eh? Won the Ascot.[2] How did you know his name?"   60

"He always talks about horse-races with Bassett," said Joan.

The uncle was delighted to find that his small nephew was posted with all the racing news. Bassett, the young gardener, who had been wounded in the left foot in the war[3] and had got his present job through Oscar Cresswell, whose batman he had been, was a perfect blade of the "turf."[4] He lived in the racing events, and the small boy lived with him.

Oscar Cresswell got it all from Bassett.

"Master Paul comes and asks me, so I can't do more than tell him, sir," said Bassett, his face terribly serious, as if he were speaking of religious matters.

"And does he ever put anything on a horse he fancies?"   65

"Well—I don't want to give him away—he's a young sport, a fine sport, sir. Would you mind asking him himself? He sort of takes a pleasure in it, and perhaps he'd feel I was giving him away, sir, if you don't mind."

Bassett was serious as a church.

The uncle went back to his nephew and took him off for a ride in the car.

"Say, Paul, old man, do you ever put anything on a horse?" the uncle asked.

The boy watched the handsome man closely.   70

"Why, do you think I oughtn't to?" he parried.

"Not a bit of it! I thought perhaps you might give me a tip for the Lincoln."

The car sped on into the country, going down to Uncle Oscar's place in Hampshire.

"Honour bright?" said the nephew.

"Honour bright, son!" said the uncle.   75

"Well, then, Daffodil."

"Daffodil! I doubt it, sonny. What about Mirza?"

"I only know the winner," said the boy. "That's Daffodil."

"Daffodil, eh?"

2. A race run at a course of that name in Berkshire. Other races mentioned in the story are Lincolnshire Handicap, then run at Lincoln Downs; the St. Leger Stakes, run at Doncaster; the Grand National Steeplechase, run at Aintree, the most famous steeplechase in the world; the famous Derby, a mile-and-a-half race for three-year-olds run at Epsom Downs.   3. World War I, 1914–18.   4. Dashing young horseplayer. *Batman*: British officer's orderly.

80 There was a pause. Daffodil was an obscure horse comparatively.

"Uncle!"

"Yes, son?"

"You won't let it go any further, will you? I promised Bassett."

"Bassett be damned, old man! What's he got to do with it?"

85 "We're partners. We've been partners from the first. Uncle, he lent me my first five shillings, which I lost. I promised him, honour bright, it was only between me and him; only you gave me that ten-shilling note I started winning with, so I thought you were lucky. You won't let it go any further, will you?"

The boy gazed at his uncle from those big, hot, blue eyes, set rather close together. The uncle stirred and laughed uneasily.

"Right you are, son! I'll keep your tip private. Daffodil, eh? How much are you putting on him?"

"All except twenty pounds," said the boy. "I keep that in reserve."

The uncle thought it a good joke.

90 "You keep twenty pounds in reserve, do you, you young romancer? What are you betting, then?"

"I'm betting three hundred," said the boy, gravely. "But it's between you and me, Uncle Oscar! Honour bright?"

The uncle burst into a roar of laughter.

"It's between you and me all right, you young Nat Gould,"[5] he said, laughing. "But where's your three hundred?"

"Bassett keeps it for me. We're partners."

95 "You are, are you! And what is Bassett putting on Daffodil?"

"He won't go quite as high as I do, I expect. Perhaps he'll go a hundred and fifty."

"What, pennies?" laughed the uncle.

"Pounds," said the child, with a surprised look at his uncle. "Bassett keeps a bigger reserve than I do."

Between wonder and amusement Uncle Oscar was silent. He pursued the matter no further, but he determined to take his nephew with him to the Lincoln races.

100 "Now, son," he said, "I'm putting twenty on Mirza, and I'll put five for you on any horse you fancy. What's your pick?"

"Daffodil, uncle."

"No, not the fiver on Daffodil!"

"I should if it was my own fiver," said the child.

"Good! Good! Right you are! A fiver for me and a fiver for you on Daffodil."

105 The child had never been to a race-meeting before, and his eyes were blue fire. He pursed his mouth tight, and watched. A Frenchman just in front had put his money on Lancelot. Wild with excitement, he flayed his arms up and down, yelling *Lancelot! Lancelot!* in his French accent.

Daffodil came in first, Lancelot second, Mirza third. The child, flushed and

5. Nathaniel Gould (1857–1919), novelist and journalist whose writings in both genres concerned horse-racing.

with eyes blazing, was curiously serene. His uncle brought him four five-pound notes, four to one.

"What am I to do with these?" he cried, waving them before the boy's eyes.

"I suppose we'll talk to Bassett," said the boy. "I expect I have fifteen hundred now; and twenty in reserve; and this twenty."

His uncle studied him for some moments.

"Look here, son!" he said. "You're not serious about Bassett and that fifteen hundred, are you?"

"Yes, I am. But it's between you and me, uncle. Honour bright!"

"Honour bright all right, son! But I must talk to Bassett."

"If you'd like to be a partner, uncle, with Bassett and me, we could all be partners. Only, you'd have to promise, honour bright, uncle, not to let it go beyond us three. Bassett and I are lucky, and you must be lucky, because it was your ten shillings I started winning with. . . ."

Uncle Oscar took both Bassett and Paul into Richmond Park for an afternoon, and there they talked.

"It's like this, you see, sir," Bassett said. "Master Paul would get me talking about racing events, spinning yarns, you know, sir. And he was always keen on knowing if I'd made or if I'd lost. It's about a year since, now, that I put five shillings on Blush of Dawn for him—and we lost. Then the luck turned, with the ten shillings he had from you, that we put on Singhalese. And since that time, it's been pretty steady, all things considering. What do you say, Master Paul?"

"We're all right when we're sure," said Paul. "It's when we're not quite sure that we go down."

"Oh, but we're careful then," said Bassett.

"But when are you *sure*?" smiled Uncle Oscar.

"It's Master Paul, sir," said Bassett, in a secret, religious voice. "It's as if he had it from heaven. Like Daffodil, now, for the Lincoln. That was as sure as eggs."

"Did you put anything on Daffodil?" asked Oscar Cresswell.

"Yes, sir. I made my bit."

"And my nephew?"

Bassett was obstinately silent, looking at Paul.

"I made twelve hundred, didn't I, Bassett? I told uncle I was putting three hundred on Daffodil."

"That's right," said Bassett, nodding.

"But where's the money?" asked the uncle.

"I keep it safe locked up, sir. Master Paul he can have it any minute he likes to ask for it."

"What, fifteen hundred pounds?"

"And twenty! And *forty*, that is, with the twenty he made on the course."

"It's amazing!" said the uncle.

"If Master Paul offers you to be partners, sir, I would, if I were you; if you'll excuse me," said Bassett.

Oscar Cresswell thought about it.

"I'll see the money," he said.

They drove home again, and sure enough, Bassett came round to the garden-house with fifteen hundred pounds in notes. The twenty pounds reserve was left with Joe Glee, in the Turf Commission deposit.

"You see, it's all right, uncle, when I'm *sure!* Then we go strong, for all we're worth. Don't we, Bassett?"

"We do that, Master Paul"

"And when are you sure?" said the uncle, laughing.

"Oh, well, sometimes I'm *absolutely* sure, like about Daffodil," said the boy; "and sometimes I have an idea; and sometimes I haven't even an idea, have I, Bassett? Then we're careful, because we mostly go down."

"You do, do you! And when you're sure, like about Daffodil, what makes you sure, sonny?"

"Oh, well, I don't know," said the boy uneasily. "I'm sure, you know, uncle; that's all."

"It's as if he had it from heaven, sir," Bassett reiterated.

"I should say so!" said the uncle.

But he became a partner. And when the Leger was coming on, Paul was "sure" about Lively Spark, which was a quite inconsiderable horse. The boy insisted on putting a thousand on the horse, Bassett went for five hundred, and Oscar Cresswell two hundred. Lively Spark came in first, and the betting had been ten to one against him. Paul had made ten thousand.

"You see," he said, "I was absolutely sure of him."

Even Oscar Cresswell had cleared two thousand.

"Look here, son," he said, "this sort of thing makes me nervous."

"It needn't, uncle! Perhaps I shan't be sure again for a long time."

"But what are you going to do with your money?" asked the uncle.

"Of course," said the boy, "I started it for mother. She said she had no luck, because father is unlucky, so I thought if *I* was lucky, it might stop whispering."

"What might stop whispering?"

"Our house. I *hate* our house for whispering."

"What does it whisper?"

"Why—why"—the boy fidgeted—"why, I don't know. But it's always short of money, you know, uncle."

"I know it, son, I know it."

"You know people send mother writs, don't you, uncle?"

"I'm afraid I do," said the uncle.

"And then the house whispers, like people laughing at you behind your back. It's awful, that is! I thought if I was lucky . . ."

"You might stop it," added the uncle.

The boy watched him with big blue eyes, that had an uncanny cold fire in them, and he said never a word.

"Well, then!" said the uncle. "What are we doing?"

"I shouldn't like mother to know I was lucky," said the boy.

"Why not, son?"

"She'd stop me."

"I don't think she would."

"Oh!"—and the boy writhed in an odd way—"I *don't* want her to know, uncle." 165

"All right, son! We'll manage it without her knowing."

They managed it very easily. Paul, at the other's suggestion, handed over five thousand pounds to his uncle, who deposited it with the family lawyer, who was then to inform Paul's mother that a relative had put five thousand pounds into his hands, which sum was to be paid out a thousand pounds at a time, on the mother's birthday, for the next five years.

"So she'll have a birthday present of a thousand pounds for five successive years," said Uncle Oscar. "I hope it won't make it all the harder for her later."

Paul's mother had her birthday in November. The house had been "whispering" worse than ever lately, and, even in spite of his luck, Paul could not bear up against it. He was very anxious to see the effect of the birthday letter, telling his mother about the thousand pounds.

When there were no visitors, Paul now took his meals with his parents, as he 170 was beyond the nursery control. His mother went into town nearly every day. She had discovered that she had an odd knack of sketching furs and dress materials, so she worked secretly in the studio of a friend who was the chief "artist" for the leading drapers. She drew the figures of ladies in furs and ladies in silk and sequins for the newspaper advertisements. This young woman artist earned several thousand pounds a year, but Paul's mother only made several hundreds, and she was again dissatisfied. She so wanted to be first in something, and she did not succeed, even in making sketches for drapery advertisements.

She was down to breakfast on the morning of her birthday. Paul watched her face as she read her letters. He knew the lawyer's letter. As his mother read it, her face hardened and became more expressionless. Than a cold, determined look came on her mouth. She hid the letter under the pile of others, and said not a word about it.

"Didn't you have anything nice in the post for your birthday, mother?" said Paul.

"Quite moderately nice," she said, her voice cold and absent.

She went away to town without saying more.

But in the afternoon Uncle Oscar appeared. He said Paul's mother had had 175 a long interview with the lawyer, asking if the whole five thousand could not be advanced at once, as she was in debt.

"What do you think, uncle?" said the boy.

"I leave it to you, son."

"Oh, let her have it, then! We can get some more with the other," said the boy.

"A bird in the hand is worth two in the bush, laddie!" said Uncle Oscar.

"But I'm sure to *know* for the Grand National; or the Lincolnshire; or else 180 the Derby. I'm sure to know for *one* of them," said Paul.

So Uncle Oscar signed the agreement, and Paul's mother touched the whole five thousand. Then something very curious happened. The voices in the house suddenly went mad, like a chorus of frogs on a spring evening. There were certain new furnishings, and Paul had a tutor. He was *really* going to Eton, his father's school, in the following autumn. There were flowers in the winter, and a blossoming of the luxury Paul's mother had been used to. And yet the voices in the house, behind the sprays of mimosa and almond blossom, and from under the piles of iridescent cushions, simply trilled and screamed in a sort of ecstasy: "There *must* be more money! Oh-h-h; there *must* be more money Oh, now, now-w! Now-w-w—there *must* be more money!—more than ever! More than ever!"

It frightened Paul terribly. He studied away at his Latin and Greek with his tutors. But his intense hours were spent with Bassett. The Grand National had gone by: he had not "known," and had lost a hundred pounds. Summer was at hand. He was in agony for the Lincoln. But even for the Lincoln he didn't "know," and he lost fifty pounds. He became wild-eyed and strange, as if something were going to explode in him.

"Let it alone, son! Don't you bother about it!" urged Uncle Oscar. But it was as if the boy couldn't really hear what his uncle was saying.

"I've got to know for the Derby! I've got to know for the Derby!" the child reiterated, his big blue eyes blazing with a sort of madness.

185   His mother noticed how overwrought he was.

"You'd better go to the seaside. Wouldn't you like to go now to the seaside, instead of waiting? I think you'd better," she said, looking down at him anxiously, her heart curiously heavy because of him.

But the child lifted his uncanny blue eyes.

"I couldn't possibly go before the Derby, mother!" he said. "I couldn't possibly!"

"Why not?" she said, her voice becoming heavy when she was opposed. "Why not? You can still go from the seaside to see the Derby with your Uncle Oscar, if that's what you wish. No need for you to wait here. Besides, I think you care too much about these races. It's a bad sign. My family has been a gambling family, and you won't know till you grow up how much damage it has done. But it has done damage. I shall have to send Bassett away, and ask Uncle Oscar not to talk racing to you, unless you promise to be reasonable about it; go away to the seaside and forget it. You're all nerves!"

190   "I'll do what you like, mother, so long as you don't send me away till after the Derby," the boy said.

"Send you away from where? Just from this house?"

"Yes," he said, gazing at her.

"Why, you curious child, what makes you care about this house so much, suddenly? I never knew you loved it."

He gazed at her without speaking. He had a secret within a secret, something he had not divulged, even to Bassett or to his Uncle Oscar.

195   But his mother, after standing undecided and a little bit sullen for some moments, said:

"Very well, then! Don't go to the seaside till after the Derby, if you don't wish it. But promise me you won't let your nerves go to pieces. Promise you won't think so much about horse-racing and events, as you call them!"

"Oh, no," said the boy casually. "I won't think much about them, mother. You needn't worry. I wouldn't worry, mother, if I were you."

"If you were me and I were you," said his mother, "I wonder what we *should* do!"

"But you know you needn't worry, mother, don't you?" the boy repeated.

"I should be awfully glad to know it," she said wearily.   200

"Oh, well, you *can*, you know. I mean, you *ought* to know you needn't worry," he insisted.

"Ought I? Then I'll see about it," she said.

Paul's secret of secrets was his wooden horse, that which had no name. Since he was emancipated from a nurse and a nursery-governess, he had had his rocking-horse removed to his own bedroom at the top of the house.

"Surely, you're too big for a rocking-horse!" his mother had remonstrated.

"Well, you see, mother, till I can have a *real* horse, I like to have *some* sort   205
of animal about," had been his quaint answer.

"Do you feel he keeps you company?" she laughed.

"Oh, yes! He's very good, he always keeps me company, when I'm there," said Paul.

So the horse, rather shabby, stood in an arrested prance in the boy's bedroom.

The Derby was drawing near, and the boy grew more and more tense. He hardly heard what was spoken to him, he was very frail, and his eyes were really uncanny. His mother had sudden strange seizures of uneasiness about him. Sometimes, for half-an-hour, she would feel a sudden anxiety about him that was almost anguish. She wanted to rush to him at once, and know he was safe.

Two nights before the Derby, she was at a big party in town, when one of   210
her rushes of anxiety about her boy, her first-born, gripped her heart till she could hardly speak. She fought with the feeling, might and main, for she believed in common-sense. But it was too strong. She had to leave the dance and go downstairs to telephone to the country. The children's nursery-governess was terribly surprised and startled at being rung up in the night.

"Are the children all right, Miss Wilmot?"

"Oh, yes, they are quite all right."

"Master Paul? Is he all right?"

"He went to bed as right as a trivet. Shall I run up and look at him?"

"No," said Paul's mother reluctantly. "No! Don't trouble. It's all right. Don't   215
sit up. We shall be home fairly soon." She did not want her son's privacy intruded upon.

"Very good," said the governess.

It was about one o'clock when Paul's mother and father drove up to their house. All was still. Paul's mother went to her room and slipped off her white fur cloak. She had told her maid not to wait up for her. She heard her husband downstairs, mixing a whisky-and-soda.

And then, because of the strange anxiety at her heart, she stole upstairs to her son's room. Noiselessly she went along the upper corridor. Was there a faint noise? What was it?

She stood, with arrested muscles, outside his door, listening. There was a strange, heavy, and yet not loud noise. Her heart stood still. It was a soundless noise, yet rushing and powerful. Something huge, in violent, hushed motion. What was it? What in God's name was it? She ought to know. She felt that she knew the noise. She knew what it was.

220   Yet she could not place it. She couldn't say what it was. And on and on it went, like a madness.

Softly, frozen with anxiety and fear, she turned the door-handle.

The room was dark. Yet in the space near the window, she heard and saw something plunging to and fro. She gazed in fear and amazement.

Then suddenly she switched on the light, and saw her son, in his green pyjamas, madly surging on the rocking-horse. The blaze of light suddenly lit him up, as he urged the wooden horse, and lit her up, as she stood, blonde, in her dress of pale green and crystal, in the doorway.

"Paul!" she cried. "Whatever are you doing?"

225   "It's Malabar!" he screamed, in a powerful, strange voice. "It's Malabar!"

His eyes blazed at her for one strange and senseless second, as he ceased urging his wooden horse. Then he fell with a crash to the ground, and she, all her tormented motherhood flooding upon her, rushed to gather him up.

But he was unconscious, and unconscious he remained, with some brain-fever. He talked and tossed, and his mother sat stonily by his side.

"Malabar! It's Malabar! Bassett, Bassett, I *know*! It's Malabar!"

So the child cried, trying to get up and urge the rocking-horse that gave him his inspiration.

230   "What does he mean by Malabar?" asked the heart-frozen mother.

"I don't know," said the father stonily.

"What does he mean by Malabar?" she asked her brother Oscar.

"It's one of the horses running for the Derby," was the answer.

And, in spite of himself, Oscar Cresswell spoke to Bassett, and himself put a thousand on Malabar: at fourteen to one.

235   The third day of the illness was critical: they were waiting for a change. The boy, with his rather long, curly hair, was tossing ceaselessly on the pillow. He neither slept nor regained consciousness, and his eyes were like blue stones. His mother sat, feeling her heart had gone, turned actually into a stone.

In the evening, Oscar Cresswell did not come, but Bassett sent a message, saying could he come up for one moment, just one moment? Paul's mother was very angry at the intrusion, but on second thought she agreed. The boy was the same. Perhaps Bassett might bring him to consciousness.

The gardener, a shortish fellow with a little brown moustache, and sharp little brown eyes, tip-toed into the room, touched his imaginary cap to Paul's mother, and stole to the bedside, staring with glittering, smallish eyes, at the tossing, dying child.

"Master Paul!" he whispered. "Master Paul! Malabar came in first all right, a clean win. I did as you told me. You've made over seventy thousand pounds, you have; you've got over eighty thousand. Malabar came in all right, Master Paul."

"Malabar! Malabar! Did I say Malabar, mother? Did I say Malabar? Do you think I'm lucky, mother? I knew Malabar, didn't I? Over eighty thousand pounds! I call that lucky, don't you, mother? Over eighty thousand pounds! I knew, didn't I know I knew! Malabar came in all right. If I ride my horse till I'm sure, then I tell you, Bassett, you can go as high as you like. Did you go for all you were worth, Bassett?"

"I went a thousand on it, Master Paul."

240

"I never told you, mother, that if I can ride my horse, and *get there*, then I'm absolutely sure—oh absolutely! Mother, did I ever tell you? I *am* lucky!"

"No, you never did," said the mother.

But the boy died in the night.

And even as he lay dead, his mother heard her brother's voice saying to her: "My God, Hester, you're eighty-odd thousand to the good, and a poor devil of a son to the bad. But, poor devil, poor devil, he's best gone out of a life where he rides his rocking-horse to find a winner."

1932

D. H. LAWRENCE

Passages from Essays and Letters

from "Nottingham and the Mining Countryside"

I was born . . . in Eastwood, a mining village of some three thousand souls, about eight miles from Nottingham. . . . It is hilly country. . . . To me it seemed, and still seems, an extremely beautiful countryside, just between the red sand-stone and the oak-trees of Nottingham, and the cold limestone, the ash-trees, the stone fences of Derbyshire. To me, as a child and a young man, it was still the old England of the forest and agricultural past; there were no motorcars, the mines were, in a sense, an accident in the landscape, and Robin Hood and his merry men were not very far away.

. . . The people lived almost entirely by instinct, men of my father's age could not really read. And the pit did not mechanize men. . . . My father loved the pit. He was hurt badly, more than once, but he would never stay away. He loved the contact, the intimacy, as men in the war loved the intense male comradeship of the dark days.

Now the colliers had also an instinct for beauty. The colliers' wives had not. The colliers were deeply alive, instinctively. But they had no daytime ambition, and no daytime intellect. They avoided, really, the rational aspect of life. . . . They didn't even care very profoundly about wages. It was the women, naturally, who nagged on this score. . . . The collier went to the pub and drank in order to continue the intimacy with his mates.

. . . Life for him did not consist of facts, but in a flow. Very often he loved his garden. And very often he had a genuine love of the beauty of flowers. . . .

. . . Most women love flowers as possessions, and as trimmings. They can't look at a flower, and wonder a moment, and pass on. If they see a flower that arrests their attention, they must at once pick it, pluck it. Possession! A possession! Something added on to *me!*

from "Love"

. . . the love between a man and a woman . . . is dual. It is the melting into pure communion, and it is the friction of sheer sensuality, both. In pure communion I become whole in love. And in pure, fierce passion of sensuality, I am burned into essentiality. I am driven from the matrix unto sheer separate distinction. I become my single self, inviolable and unique, as the gems were perhaps once driven into themselves out of the confusion of earths. . . .

from "Women Are So Cocksure"

. . . [My mother] was convinced . . . that a man ought not to drink beer. This conviction developed from the fact, naturally, that my father drank beer. He sometimes drank too much. He sometimes boozed away the money necessary for the young family: When my father came in tipsy, she saw scarlet.

from "Art and Morality"

Apples are always apples! says Vox Populi, Vox Dei.[1]

Sometimes they're sin, sometimes they're a knock on the head, sometimes they're a bellyache, sometimes they're part of a pie, sometimes they're sauce for a goose. . . .

What art has got to do, and will go on doing, is to reveal things in their different relationships. That is to say, you've got to see in the apples the bellyache. Sir Isaac's knock on the cranium, the vast, moist wall through which the insect bores to lay her eggs in the middle, and the untasted, unknown quality which Eve saw hanging on a tree.

from "Morality and the Novel"

The business of art is to reveal the relation between man and his circumambient universe, at the living moment. As mankind is always struggling in the toils of old relationships, art is always ahead of the "times," which themselves are always far in the rear of the living moment.

When van Gogh paints sunflowers, he reveals, or achieves, the vivid relation between himself, as man, and the sunflowers, as sunflower, at that quick moment of time. His painting does not represent the sunflower itself. We shall

---

1. The voice of the people [is] the voice of God.

never know what the sunflower itself is. And the camera will *visualize* the sunflower far more perfectly than van Gogh can.

The vision on the canvas is a third thing, utterly intangible and inexplicable, the offspring of the sunflower itself and van Gogh himself. . . .

. . . The novel is the highest example of subtle interrelatedness that man has discovered. Everything is true in its own time, place, and circumstance, and untrue outside of its own place, time, circumstance. If you try to nail anything down, in the novel, either it kills the novel, or the novel gets up and walks away with the nail.

. . . Love is a great emotion. But if you set out to write a novel, and you yourself are in the throes of the great predilection for love, love as the supreme, the only emotion worth living for, then you will write an immoral novel.

Because *no* emotion is supreme, or exclusively worth living for. *All* emotions go to the achieving of a living relationship between a human being and the other human being or creature or thing he becomes purely related to. All emotions, including love and hate, and rage and tenderness, go to the adjusting of the oscillating, unestablished balance between two people who amount to anything . . .

A new relation, a new relatedness hurts somewhat in the attaining; and will always hurt. So life will always hurt. . . .

Each time we strive to a new relation, with anyone or anything, it is bound to hurt somewhat. Because it means the struggle with and the displacing of old connections, and this is never pleasant. And, moreover, between living things at least, an adjustment means also a fight, for each party, inevitably, must "seek its own" in the other, and be denied. When, in the two parties, each of them seeks his own, her own, absolutely, then it is a fight to the death. And this is true of the thing called "passion . . ."

The great relationship for humanity will always be the relation between man and woman. The relation between man and man, woman and woman, parent and child, will always be subsidiary.

And the relation between man and woman will change forever, and will forever be the new central clue to human life. It is the *relation itself* which is the quick and the central clue to life, not the man, nor the woman, nor the children that result from the relationship, as a contingency.

from "Why the Novel Matters"

We have curious ideas of ourselves. We think of ourselves as a body with a spirit in it, or a body with a soul in it, or a body with a mind in it. . . .

It is a funny sort of superstition. Why should I look at my hand, as it so cleverly writes these words, and decide that it is a mere nothing compared to the mind that directs it? Why should I imagine that there is a *me* which is more *me* than my hand is? Since my hand is absolutely alive, me alive . . .

And that's what you learn, when you're a novelist. And that's what you are liable *not* to know, if you're a parson, or a philosopher, or a scientist, or a stupid person.

Now I absolutely flatly deny that I am a soul, or a body, or a mind, or an intelligence, or a brain, or a nervous system, or a bunch of glands, or any of the rest of these bits of me. The whole is greater than the part. And therefore, I, who am man alive, am greater than my soul, or spirit, or body, or mind, or consciousness, or anything else that is merely a part of me. I am man a man, and alive. I am man alive, and as long as I can, I intend to go on being man alive.

For this reason I am a novelist. And being a novelist, I consider myself superior to the saint, the scientist, the philosopher, and the poet, who are all great masters of different bits of man alive, but never get the whole [thing] . . .

We should ask for no absolutes, or absolute. . . . There is no absolute good, there is nothing absolutely right. All things flow and change, and even change is not absolute. . . .

. . . If the one I love remains unchanged and unchanging, I shall cease to love her. It is only because she changes and startles me into change and defies my inertia, and is herself staggered in her inertia by my changing, that I can continue to love her. If she stayed put, I might as well love the pepper-pot . . .

In life, there is right and wrong, good and bad, all the time. But what is right in one case is wrong in another. And in the novel you see one man becoming a corpse, because of his so-called goodness, another going dead because of his so-called wickedness. Right and wrong is an instinct: but an instinct of the whole consciousness in a man, bodily, mental, spiritual at once. And only in the novel are *all* things given full play, or at least, they may be given full play, when we realize that life itself, and not inert safety, is the reason for living. For out of the full play of all things emerges the only thing that is anything, the wholeness of a man, the wholeness of a woman, man alive, and live woman.

from "Autobiographical Sketch"

They ask me; "Did you find it very hard to get on and to become a success?" And I have to admit that if I can be said to have got on, and if I can be called a success, then I *did not* find it hard.

I never starved in a garret, nor waited in anguish for the post to bring me an answer from editor or publisher, nor did I struggle in sweat and blood to bring forth mighty works, nor did I ever wake up and find myself famous.

. . . My father was a collier, and only a collier, nothing praise-worthy about him. He wasn't even respectable, in so far as he got drunk rather frequently, never went near a chapel, and was usually rather rude to his little immediate bosses at the pit . . .

My mother was, I suppose, superior. She came from town, and belonged really to the lower bourgeoisie. She spoke King's English, without an accent, and never in her life could even imitate a sentence of the dialect which my father spoke, and which we children spoke out of doors . . .

. . . I have *wanted* to feel truly friendly with some, at least, of my fellow-men. Yet I have never quite succeeded. Whether I got on *in* the world is a question; but I certainly don't get on very well *with* the world. And whether I am a worldly success or not I really don't know. But I feel, somehow, not much of a human success.

By which I mean that I don't feel there is any very cordial or fundamental contact between me and society, or me and other people. There is a breach. And my contact is with something that is nonhuman, nonvocal . . .

[Why?] The answer, as far as I can see, has something to do with class. Class makes a gulf, across which all the best human flow is lost. It is not exactly the triumph of the middle classes that has made the deadness, but the triumph of the middle-class *thing*.

As a man from the working class, I feel that the middle class cut off some of my vital vibration when I am with them. I admit them charming and educated and good people often enough. *But they just stop some part of me from working.* . . .

Then why don't I live with my working people? Because their vibration is limited in another direction. They are narrow, but still fairly deep and passionate, whereas the middle class is broad and shallow and passionless . . .

I cannot make the transfer from my own class into the middle class. I cannot, not for anything in the world, forfeit my passional consciousness and my old blood-affinity with my fellow-men and the animals and the land, for that other thin, spurious mental conceit which is all that is left of the mental consciousness once it has made itself exclusive.

from the Letters

TO A. W. MCLEOD, 26 APRIL 1913

I am so sure that only through a readjustment between men and women, and a making free and healthy of this sex, will she [England] get out of her present atrophy. Oh, Lord, and if I don't "subdue my art to a metaphysic," as somebody very beautifully said of Hardy, I do write because I want folk—English folk—to alter, and have more sense.

TO A. W. MCLEOD, 2 JUNE 1914

I think the only re-sourcing of art, revivifying it, is to make it more the joint work of man and woman. I think *the* one thing to do, is for men to have courage to draw nearer to women, expose themselves to them, and be altered by them; and for women to accept and admit men. That is the start—by bringing themselves together, men and women—revealing themselves to each other, gaining great blind knowledge and suffering and joy, which it will take a big further lapse of civilization to exploit and work out. Because the source of all life and knowledge is in man and woman, and the source of all living is in the inter-change and the meeting and mingling of these two: man-life and woman-life, man-knowledge and woman-knowledge, man-being and woman-being.

TO J. B. PINKER, 16 DECEMBER 1915

. . . Tell Arnold Bennett[2] that all rules of construction hold good only for novels which are copies of other novels. A book which is not a copy of other books has its own construction, and what he calls faults, he being an old imita-tor, I call characteristics.

TO ROLF GARDINER, 9 AUGUST 1924

What we need is to smash a few big holes in European suburbanity, let in a little real fresh air.

TO LADY OTTOLINE MORRELL, 5 FEBRUARY 1929

. . . Don't you think it's nonsense when Murry says that my world is not the ordinary man's world and that I am a sort of animal with a sixth sense? Seems to me more likely he's a sort of animal with only four senses—the real sense of touch missing. They all seem determined to make a freak of me—to save their own short-failings, and make them "normal."

▼ ▼ ▼

FLANNERY O'CONNOR

The Lame Shall Enter First

Sheppard sat on a stool at the bar that divided the kitchen in half, eating his cereal out of the individual pasteboard box it came in. He ate mechanically, his eyes on the child, who was wandering from cabinet to cabinet in the panelled kitchen, collecting the ingredients for his breakfast. He was a stocky blond boy of ten. Sheppard kept his intense blue eyes fixed on him. The boy's future was written in his face. He would be a banker. No, worse. He would operate a small loan company. All he wanted for the child was that he be good and unselfish and neither seemed likely. Sheppard was a young man whose hair was already white. It stood up like a narrow brush halo over his pink sensitive face.

The boy approached the bar with the jar of peanut butter under his arm, a plate with a quarter of a small chocolate cake on it in one hand and the ketchup bottle in the other. He did not appear to notice his father. He climbed up on the stool and began to spread peanut butter on the cake. He had very large

2. An early 20th-century novelist (1867–1931) whose major works—*The Old Wives' Tale* (1908) and *The Clayhanger Trilogy* (1910–15)—treat the middle classes in the pottery country of the English Midlands in a naturalistic manner (usually criticizing the money-grubbing, social-climbing selfish-ness of the society). In his later years he more or less turned into a hack, though a clever one, and it is to Bennett as a very popular, successful hack that Lawrence is referring.

round ears that leaned away from his head and seemed to pull his eyes slightly too far apart. His shirt was green but so faded that the cowboy charging across the front of it was only a shadow.

"Norton," Sheppard said, "I saw Rufus Johnson yesterday. Do you know what he was doing?"

The child looked at him with a kind of half attention, his eyes forward but not yet engaged. They were a paler blue than his father's as if they might have faded like the shirt; one of them listed, almost imperceptibly, toward the outer rim.

"He was in an alley," Sheppard said, "and he had his hand in a garbage can. He was trying to get something to eat out of it." He paused to let this soak in. "He was hungry," he finished, and tried to pierce the child's conscience with his gaze.

The boy picked up the piece of chocolate cake and began to gnaw it from one corner.

"Norton," Sheppard said, "do you have any idea what it means to share?"

A flicker of attention. "Some of it's yours," Norton said

"Some of it's *his*," Sheppard said heavily. It was hopeless. Almost any fault would have been preferable to selfishness—a violent temper, even a tendency to lie.

The child turned the bottle of ketchup upside down and began thumping ketchup onto the cake.

Sheppard's look of pain increased. "You are ten and Rufus Johnson is fourteen," he said. "Yet I'm sure your shirts would fit Rufus." Rufus Johnson was a boy he had been trying to help at the reformatory for the past year. He had been released two months ago. "When he was in the reformatory, he looked pretty good, but when I saw him yesterday, he was skin and bones. He hasn't been eating cake with peanut butter on it for breakfast."

The child paused. "It's stale," he said. "That's why I have to put stuff on it."

Sheppard turned his face to the window at the end of the bar. The side lawn, green and even, sloped fifty feet or so down to a small suburban wood. When his wife was living, they had often eaten outside, even breakfast, on the grass. He had never noticed then that the child was selfish. "Listen to me," he said, turning back to him, "look at me and listen."

The boy looked at him. At least his eyes were forward.

"I gave Rufus a key to this house when he left the reformatory—to show my confidence in him and so he would have a place he could come to and feel welcome any time. He didn't use it, but I think he'll use it now because he's seen me and he's hungry. And if he doesn't use it, I'm going out and find him and bring him here. I can't see a child eating out of garbage cans."

The boy frowned. It was dawning upon him that something of his was threatened.

Sheppard's mouth stretched in disgust. "Rufus's father died before he was born," he said. "His mother is in the state penitentiary. He was raised by his grandfather in a shack without water or electricity and the old man beat him every day. How would you like to belong to a family like that?"

"I don't know," the child said lamely.

"Well, you might think about it sometime," Sheppard said.

Sheppard was City Recreational Director. On Saturdays he worked at the reformatory as a counselor, receiving nothing for it but the satisfaction of knowing he was helping boys no one else cared about. Johnson was the most intelligent boy he had worked with and the most deprived.

Norton turned what was left of the cake over as if he no longer wanted it.

"Maybe he won't come," the child said and his eyes brightened slightly.

"Think of everything you have that he doesn't!" Sheppard said. "Suppose you had to root in garbage cans for food? Suppose you had a huge swollen foot and one side of you dropped lower than the other when you walked?"

The boy looked blank, obviously unable to imagine such a thing.

"You have a healthy body," Sheppard said, "a good home. You've never been taught anything but the truth. Your daddy gives you everything you need and want. You don't have a grandfather who beats you. And your mother is not in the state penitentiary."

The child pushed his plate away. Sheppard groaned aloud.

A knot of flesh appeared below the boy's suddenly distorted mouth. His face became a mass of lumps with slits for eyes. "If she was in the penitentiary," he began in a kind of racking bellow, "I could go to seeeeee her." Tears rolled down his face and the ketchup dribbled on his chin. He looked as if he had been hit in the mouth. He abandoned himself and howled.

Sheppard sat helpless and miserable, like a man lashed by some elemental force of nature. This was not a normal grief. It was all part of his selfishness. She had been dead for over a year and a child's grief should not last so long. "You're going on eleven years old," he said reproachfully.

The child began an agonizing high-pitched heaving noise.

"If you stop thinking about yourself and think what you can do for somebody else," Sheppard said, "then you'll stop missing your mother."

The boy was silent but his shoulders continued to shake. Then his face collapsed and he began to howl again.

"Don't you think I'm lonely without her too?" Sheppard said. "Don't you think I miss her at all? I do, but I'm not sitting around moping. I'm busy helping other people. When do you see me just sitting around thinking about my troubles?"

The boy slumped as if he were exhausted but fresh tears streaked his face.

"What are you going to do today?" Sheppard asked, to get his mind on something else.

The child ran his arm across his eyes. "Sell seeds," he mumbled.

Always selling something. He had four quart jars full of nickels and dimes he had saved and he took them out of his closet every few days and counted them. "What are you selling seeds for?"

"To win a prize."

"What's the prize?"

"A thousand dollars."

"And what would you do if you had a thousand dollars?"

"Keep it," the child said and wiped his nose on his shoulder.

"I feel sure you would," Sheppard said. "Listen," he said and lowered his voice to an almost pleading tone, "suppose by some chance you did win a thousand dollars. Wouldn't you like to spend it on children less fortunate than yourself? Wouldn't you like to give some swings and trapezes to the orphanage? Wouldn't you like to buy poor Rufus Johnson a new shoe?"

The boy began to back away from the bar. Then suddenly he leaned forward and hung with his mouth open over his plate. Sheppard groaned again. Everything came up, the cake, the peanut butter, the ketchup—a limp sweet batter. He hung over it gagging, more came, and he waited with his mouth open over the plate as if he expected his heart to come up next.

"It's all right," Sheppard said, "it's all right. You couldn't help it. Wipe your mouth and go lie down."

The child hung there a moment longer. Then he raised his face and looked blindly at his father.   45

"Go on," Sheppard said. "Go on and lie down."

The boy pulled up the end of his t-shirt and smeared his mouth with it. Then he climbed down off the stool and wandered out of the kitchen.

Sheppard sat there staring at the puddle of half-digested food. The sour odor reached him and he drew back. His gorge rose. He got up and carried the plate to the sink and turned the water on it and watched grimly as the mess ran down the drain. Johnson's sad thin hand rooted in garbage cans for food while his own child, selfish, unresponsive, greedy, had so much that he threw it up. He cut off the faucet with a thrust of his fist. Johnson had a capacity for real response and had been deprived of everything from birth; Norton was average or below and had had every advantage.

He went back to the bar to finish his breakfast. The cereal was soggy in the cardboard box but he paid no attention to what he was eating. Johnson was worth any amount of effort because he had the potential. He had seen it from the time the boy had limped in for his first interview.

Sheppard's office at the reformatory was a narrow closet with one window and a small table and two chairs in it. He had never been inside a confessional but he thought it must be the same kind of operation he had here, except that he explained, he did not absolve. His credentials were less dubious than a priest's; he had been trained for what he was doing.   50

When Johnson came in for his first interview, he had been reading over the boy's record—senseless destruction, windows smashed, city trash boxes set afire, tires slashed—the kind of thing he found where boys had been transplanted abruptly from the country to the city as this one had. He came to Johnson's I. Q. score. It was 140. He raised his eyes eagerly.

The boy sat slumped on the edge of his chair, his arms hanging between his thighs. The light from the window fell on his face. His eyes, steel-colored and very still, were trained narrowly forward. His thin dark hair hung in a flat forelock across the side of his forehead, not carelessly like a boy's, but fiercely like an old man's. A kind of fanatic intelligence was palpable in his face.

Sheppard smiled to diminish the distance between them.

The boy's expression did not soften. He leaned back in his chair and lifted a monstrous club foot to his knee. The foot was in a heavy black battered shoe with a sole four or five inches thick. The leather parted from it in one place and the end of an empty sock protruded like a gray tongue from a severed head. The case was clear to Sheppard instantly. His mischief was compensation for the foot.

55 "Well Rufus," he said, "I see by the record here that you don't have but a year to serve. What do you plan to do when you get out?"

"I don't make no plans," the boy said. His eyes shifted indifferently to something outside the window behind Sheppard in the far distance.

"Maybe you ought to," Sheppard said and smiled.

Johnson continued to gaze beyond him.

"I want to see you make the most of your intelligence," Sheppard said. "What's most important to you? Let's talk about what's important to *you*." His eyes dropped involuntarily to the foot.

60 "Study it and git your fill," the boy drawled.

Sheppard reddened. The black deformed mass swelled before his eyes. He ignored the remark and the leer the boy was giving him. "Rufus," he said, "you've got into a lot of senseless trouble but I think when you understand why you do these things, you'll be less inclined to do them." He smiled. They had so few friends, saw so few pleasant faces, that half his effectiveness came from nothing more than smiling at them. "There are a lot of things about yourself that I think I can explain to you," he said.

Johnson looked at him stonily. "I ain't asked for no explanation," he said. "I already know why I do what I do."

"Well good!" Sheppard said. "Suppose you tell me what's made you do the things you've done?"

A black sheen appeared in the boy's eyes. "Satan," he said. "He has me in his power."

65 Sheppard looked at him steadily. There was no indication on the boy's face that he had said this to be funny. The line of his thin mouth was set with pride. Sheppard's eyes hardened. He felt a momentary dull despair as if he were faced with some elemental warping of nature that had happened too long ago to be corrected now. This boy's questions about life had been answered by signs nailed on the pine trees: DOES SATAN HAVE YOU IN HIS POWER? REPENT OR BURN IN HELL. JESUS SAVES. He would know the Bible with or without reading it. His despair gave way to outrage. "Rubbish!" he snorted. "We're living in the space age! You're too smart to give me an answer like that."

Johnson's mouth twisted slightly. His look was contemptuous but amused. There was a glint of challenge in his eyes.

Sheppard scrutinized his face. Where there was intelligence anything was possible. He smiled again, a smile that was like an invitation to the boy to come into a school room with all its windows thrown open to the light. "Rufus," he said, "I'm going to arrange for you to have a conference with me once a week. Maybe there's an explanation for your explanation. Maybe I can explain your devil to you."

After that he had talked to Johnson every Saturday for the rest of the year. He talked at random, the kind of talk the boy would never have heard before. He talked a little above him to give him something to reach for. He roamed from simple psychology and the dodges of the human mind to astronomy and the space capsules that were whirling around the earth faster than the speed of sound and would soon encircle the stars. Instinctively he concentrated on the stars. He wanted to give the boy something to reach for besides his neighbor's goods. He wanted to stretch his horizons. He wanted him to *see* the universe, to see that the darkest parts of it could be penetrated. He would have given anything to be able to put a telescope in Johnson's hands.

Johnson said little and what he did say, for the sake of his pride, was in dissent or senseless contradiction, with the clubfoot raised always to his knee like a weapon ready for use, but Sheppard was not deceived. He watched his eyes and every week he saw something in them crumble. From the boy's face, hard but shocked, braced against the light that was ravaging him, he could see that he was hitting dead center.

Johnson was free now to live out of garbage cans and rediscover his old ignorance. The injustice of it was infuriating. He had been sent back to the grandfather; the old man's imbecility could only be imagined. Perhaps the boy had by now run away from him. The idea of getting custody of Johnson had occurred to Sheppard before, but the fact of the grandfather had stood in the way. Nothing excited him so much as thinking what he could do for such a boy. First he would have him fitted for a new orthopedic shoe. His back was thrown out of line every time he took a step. Then he would encourage him in some particular intellectual interest. He thought of the telescope. He could buy a second-hand one and they could set it up in the attic window. He sat for almost ten minutes thinking what he could do if he had Johnson here with him. What was wasted on Norton would cause Johnson to flourish. Yesterday when he had seen him with his hand in the garbage can, he had waved and started forward. Johnson had seen him, paused a split-second, then vanished with the swiftness of a rat, but not before Sheppard had seen his expression change. Something had kindled in the boy's eyes, he was sure of it, some memory of the lost light.

He got up and threw the cereal box in the garbage. Before he left the house, he looked into Norton's room to be sure he was not still sick. The child was sitting cross-legged on his bed. He had emptied the quart jars of change into one large pile in front of him, and was sorting it out by nickels and dimes and quarters.

That afternoon Norton was alone in the house, squatting on the floor of his room arranging packages of flower seeds in rows around himself. Rain slashed against the window panes and rattled in the gutters. The room had grown dark but every few minutes it was lit by silent lightning and the seed packages showed up gaily on the floor. He squatted motionless like a large pale frog in the midst of this potential garden. All at once his eyes became alert. Without warning the rain had stopped. The silence was heavy as if the downpour had been hushed by violence. He remained motionless, only his eyes turning.

Into the silence came the distinct click of a key turning in the front door lock. The sound was a very deliberate one. It drew attention to itself and held it as if it were controlled more by a mind than by a hand. The child leapt up and got into the closet.

The footsteps began to move in the hall. They were deliberate and irregular, a light and then a heavy one, then a silence as if the visitor had paused to listen himself or to examine something. In a minute the kitchen door screeked. The footsteps crossed the kitchen to the refrigerator. The closet wall and the kitchen wall were the same. Norton stood with his ear pressed against it. The refrigerator door opened. There was a prolonged silence.

75   He took off his shoes and then tiptoed out of the closet and stepped over the seed packages. In the middle of the room, he stopped and remained where he was, rigid. A thin bony-face boy in a wet black suit stood in his door, blocking his escape. His hair was flattened to his skull by the rain. He stood there like an irate drenched crow. His look went through the child like a pin and paralyzed him. Then his eyes began to move over everything in the room—the unmade bed, the dirty curtains on the one large window, a photograph of a wide-faced young woman that stood up in the clutter on top of the dresser.

The child's tongue suddenly went wild. "He's been expecting you, he's going to give you a new shoe because you have to eat out of garbage cans!" he said in a kind of mouse-like shriek.

"I eat out of garbage cans," the boy said slowly with a beady stare, "because I like to eat out of garbage cans. See?"

The child nodded.

"And I got ways of getting my own shoe. See?"

80   The child nodded, mesmerized.

The boy limped in and sat down on the bed. He arranged a pillow behind him and stretched his short leg out so that the big black shoe rested conspicuously on a fold of the sheet.

Norton's gaze settled on it and remained immobile. The sole was as thick as a brick.

Johnson wiggled it slightly and smiled. "If I kick somebody *once* with this," he said, "it learns them not to mess with me."

The child nodded.

85   "Go in the kitchen," Johnson said, "and make me a sandwich with some of that rye bread and ham and bring me a glass of milk."

Norton went off like a mechanical toy, pushed in the right direction. He made a large greasy sandwich with ham hanging out the sides of it and poured out a glass of milk. Then he returned to the room with the glass of milk in one hand and the sandwich in the other.

Johnson was leaning back regally against the pillow. "Thanks, waiter," he said and took the sandwich.

Norton stood by the side of the bed, holding the glass.

The boy tore into the sandwich and ate steadily until he finished it. Then he took the glass of milk. He held it with both hands like a child and when he lowered it for breath, there was a rim of milk around his mouth. He handed

Norton the empty glass. "Go get me one of them oranges in there, waiter," he said hoarsely.

Norton went to the kitchen and returned with the orange. Johnson peeled it with his fingers and let the peeling drop in the bed. He ate it slowly, spitting the seeds out in front of him. When he finished, he wiped his hands on the sheet and gave Norton a long appraising stare. He appeared to have been softened by the service. "You're his kid all right," he said. "You got the same stupid face."

The child stood there stolidly as if he had not heard.

"He don't know his left hand from his right," Johnson said with a hoarse pleasure in his voice.

The child cast his eyes a little to the side of the boy's face and looked fixedly at the wall.

"Yaketty yaketty yak," Johnson said, "and never says a thing."

The child's upper lip lifted slightly but he didn't say anything.

"Gas," Johnson said. "Gas."

The child's face began to have a wary look of belligerence. He backed away slightly as if he were prepared to retreat instantly. "He's good," he mumbled. "He helps people."

"Good!" Johnson said savagely. He thrust his head forward. "Listen here," he hissed, "I don't care if he's good or not. He ain't *right*!"

Norton looked stunned.

The screen door in the kitchen banged and someone entered. Johnson sat forward instantly. "Is that him?" he said.

"It's the cook," Norton said. "She comes in the afternoon."

Johnson got up and limped into the hall and stood in the kitchen door and Norton followed him.

The colored girl was at the closet taking off a bright red raincoat. She was a tall light-yellow girl with a mouth like a large rose that had darkened and wilted. Her hair was dressed in tiers on top of her head and leaned to the side like the Tower of Pisa.

Johnson made a noise through his teeth. "Well look at Aunt Jemima," he said.

The girl paused and trained an insolent gaze on them. They might have been dust on the floor.

"Come on," Johnson said, "let's see what all you got besides a nigger." He opened the first door to his right in the hall and looked into a pink-tiled bathroom. "A pink can!" he murmured.

He turned a comical face to the child. "Does he sit on that?"

"It's for company," Norton said, "but he sits on it sometimes."

"He ought to empty his head in it," Johnson said.

The door was open to the next room. It was the room Sheppard had slept in since his wife died. An ascetic-looking iron bed stood on the bare floor. A heap of Little League baseball uniforms was piled in one corner. Papers were scattered over a large roll-top desk and held down in various places by his pipes. Johnson stood looking into the room silently. He wrinkled his nose. "Guess who?" he said.

The door to the next room was closed but Johnson opened it and thrust his head into the semi-darkness within. The shades were down and the air was close with a faint scent of perfume in it. There was a wide antique bed and a mammoth dresser whose mirror glinted in the half light. Johnson snapped the light switch by the door and crossed the room to the mirror and peered into it. A silver comb and brush lay on the linen runner. He picked up the comb and began to run it through his hair. He combed it straight down on his forehead. Then he swept it to the side, Hitler fashion.

"Leave her comb alone!" the child said. He stood in the door, pale and breathing heavily as if he were watching sacrilege in a holy place.

Johnson put the comb down and picked up the brush and gave his hair a swipe with it.

"She's dead," the child said.

115 "I ain't afraid of dead people's things," Johnson said. He opened the top drawer and slid his hand in.

"Take your big fat dirty hands off my mother's clothes!" the child said in a high suffocated voice.

"Keep your shirt on, sweetheart," Johnson murmured. He pulled up a wrinkled red polka dot blouse and dropped it back. Then he pulled out a green silk kerchief and whirled it over his head and let it float to the floor. His hand continued to plow deep into the drawer. After a moment it came up gripping a faded corset with four dangling metal supporters. "Thisyer must be her saddle," he observed.

He lifted it gingerly and shook it. Then he fastened it around his waist and jumped up and down, making the metal supporters dance. He began to snap his fingers and turn his hips from side to side. "Gonter rock, rattle and roll," he sang. "Gonter rock, rattle and roll. Can't please that woman, to save my doggone soul." He began to move around, stamping the good foot down and slinging the heavy one to the side. He danced out the door, past the stricken child and down the hall toward the kitchen.

A half hour later Sheppard came home. He dropped his raincoat on a chair in the hall and came as far as the parlor door and stopped. His face was suddenly transformed. It shone with pleasure. Johnson sat, a dark figure, in a high-backed pink upholstered chair. The wall behind him was lined with books from floor to ceiling. He was reading one. Sheppard's eyes narrowed. It was a volume of the Encyclopedia Britannica. He was so engrossed in it that he did not look up. Sheppard held his breath. This was the perfect setting for the boy. He had to keep him here. He had to manage it somehow.

120 "Rufus!" he said, "it's good to see you boy!" and he bounded forward with his arm outstretched.

Johnson looked up, his face blank. "Oh hello," he said. He ignored the hand as long as he was able but when Sheppard did not withdraw it, he grudgingly shook it.

Sheppard was prepared for this kind of reaction. It was part of Johnson's make-up never to show enthusiasm.

"How are things?" he said. "How's your grandfather treating you?" He sat down on the edge of the sofa.

"He dropped dead," the boy said indifferently.

"You don't mean it!" Sheppard cried. He got up and sat down on the coffee table nearer the boy.   125

"Naw," Johnson said, "he ain't dropped dead. I wisht he had."

"Well where is he?" Sheppard muttered.

"He's gone with a remnant to the hills," Johnson said. "Him and some others. They're going to bury some Bibles in a cave and take two of different kinds of animals and all like that. Like Noah. Only this time it's going to be fire, not flood."

Sheppard's mouth stretched wryly. "I see," he said. Then he said, "In other words the old fool has abandoned you?"

"He ain't no fool," the boy said in an indignant tone.   130

"Has he abandoned you or not?" Sheppard asked impatiently.

The boy shrugged.

"Where's your probation officer?"

"I ain't supposed to keep up with him," Johnson said. "He's supposed to keep up with me."

Sheppard laughed. "Wait a minute," he said. He got up and went into the   135
hall and got his raincoat off the chair and took it to the hall closet to hang it up. He had to give himself time to think, to decide how he could ask the boy so that he would stay. He couldn't force him to stay. It would have to be voluntary. Johnson pretended not to like him. That was only to uphold his pride, but he would have to ask him in such a way that his pride could still be upheld. He opened the closet door and took out a hanger. An old gray winter coat of his wife's still hung there. He pushed it aside but it didn't move. He pulled it open roughly and winced as if he had seen the larva inside a cocoon. Norton stood in it, his face swollen and pale, with a drugged look of misery on it. Sheppard stared at him. Suddenly he was confronted with a possibility. "Get out of there," he said. He caught him by the shoulder and propelled him firmly into the parlor and over to the pink chair where Johnson was sitting with the encyclopedia in his lap. He was going to risk everything in one blow.

"Rufus," he said, "I've got a problem. I need your help."

Johnson looked up suspiciously.

"Listen," Sheppard said, "we need another boy in the house." There was a genuine desperation in his voice. "Norton here has never had to divide anything in his life. He doesn't know what it means to share. And I need somebody to teach him. How about helping me out? Stay here for a while with us, Rufus. I need your help." The excitement in his voice made it thin.

The child suddenly came to life. His face swelled with fury. "He went in her room and used her comb!" he screamed, yanking Sheppard's arm. "He put on her corset and danced with Leola, he . . ."

"Stop this!" Sheppard said sharply. "Is tattling all you're capable of? I'm not   140
asking you for a report on Rufus's conduct. I'm asking you to make him welcome here. Do you understand?

"You see how it is?" he asked, turning to Johnson.

Norton kicked the leg of the pink chair viciously, just missing Johnson's swollen foot. Sheppard yanked him back.

"He said you weren't nothing but gas!" the child shrieked.

A sly look of pleasure crossed Johnson's face.

145 Sheppard was not put back. These insults were part of the boy's defensive mechanism. "What about it, Rufus?" he said. "Will you stay with us for a while?"

Johnson looked straight in front of him and said nothing. He smiled slightly and appeared to gaze upon some vision of the future that pleased him.

"I don't care," he said and turned a page of the encyclopedia. "I can stand anywhere."

"Wonderful." Sheppard said. "Wonderful."

"He said," the child said in a throaty whisper, "you didn't know your left hand from your right."

150 There was a silence.

Johnson wet his finger and turned another page of the encyclopedia.

"I have something to say to both of you," Sheppard said in a voice without inflection. His eyes moved from one to the other of them and he spoke slowly as if what he was saying he would say only once and it behooved them to listen. "If it made any difference to me what Rufus thinks of me," he said, "then I wouldn't be asking him here. Rufus is going to help me out and I'm going to help him out and we're both going to help you out. I'd simply be selfish if I let what Rufus thinks of me interfere with what I can do for Rufus. If I can help a person, all I want is to do it. I'm above and beyond simple pettiness."

Neither of them made a sound. Norton stared at the chair cushion. Johnson peered closer at some fine print in the encyclopedia. Sheppard was looking at the tops of their heads. He smiled. After all, he had won. The boy was staying. He reached out and ruffled Norton's hair and slapped Johnson on the shoulder. "Now you fellows sit here and get acquainted," he said gaily and started toward the door. "I'm going to see what Leola left us for supper."

When he was gone, Johnson raised his head and looked at Norton. The child looked back at him bleakly. "God, kid," Johnson said in a cracked voice, "how do you stand it?" His face was stiff with outrage. "He thinks he's Jesus Christ!"

II

155 Sheppard's attic was a large unfinished room with exposed beams and no electric light. They had set the telescope up on a tripod in one of the dormer windows. It pointed now toward the dark sky where a sliver of moon, as fragile as an egg shell, had just emerged from behind a cloud with a brilliant silver edge. Inside, a kerosene lantern set on a trunk cast their shadows upward and tangled them, wavering slightly, in the joints overhead. Sheppard was sitting on a packing box, looking through the telescope, and Johnson was at his elbow, waiting to get at it. Sheppard had bought it for fifteen dollars two days before at a pawn shop.

"Quit hoggin it," Johnson said.

Sheppard got up and Johnson slid onto the box and put his eye to the instrument.

Sheppard sat down on a straight chair a few feet away. His face was flushed with pleasure. This much of his dream was a reality. Within a week he had made it possible for this boy's vision to pass through a slender channel to the stars. He looked at Johnson's bent back with complete satisfaction. The boy had on one of Norton's plaid shirts and some new khaki trousers he had bought him. The shoe would be ready next week. He had taken him to the brace shop the day after he came and had him fitted for a new shoe. Johnson was as touchy about the foot as if it were a sacred object. His face had been glum while the clerk, a young man with a bright pink bald head, measured the foot with his profane hands. The shoe was going to make the greatest difference in the boy's attitude. Even a child with normal feet was in love with the world after he had got a new pair of shoes. When Norton got a new pair, he walked around for days with his eyes on his feet.

Sheppard glanced across the room at the child. He was sitting on the floor against a trunk, trussed up in a rope he had found and wound around his legs from his ankles to his knees. He appeared so far away that Sheppard might have been looking at him through the wrong end of the telescope. He had had to whip him only once since Johnson had been with them—the first night when Norton had realized that Johnson was going to sleep in his mother's bed. He did not believe in whipping children, particularly in anger. In this case, he had done both and with good results. He had had no more trouble with Norton.

The child hadn't shown any positive generosity toward Johnson but what he couldn't help, he appeared to be resigned to. In the mornings Sheppard sent the two of them to the Y swimming pool, gave them money to get their lunch at the cafeteria and instructed them to meet him in the park in the afternoon to watch his Little League baseball practice. Every afternoon they had arrived at the park, shambling, silent, their faces closed each on his own thoughts as if neither were aware of the other's existence. At least he could be thankful there were no fights.

Norton showed no interest in the telescope. "Don't you want to get up and look through the telescope, Norton?" he said. It irritated him that the child showed no intellectual curiosity whatsoever. "Rufus is going to be way ahead of you."

Norton leaned forward absently and looked at Johnson's back.

Johnson turned around from the instrument. His face had begun to fill out again. The look of outrage had retreated from his hollow cheeks and was shored up now in the caves of his eyes, like a fugitive from Sheppard's kindness. "Don't waste your valuable time, kid," he said. "You seen the moon once, you seen it."

Sheppard was amused by these sudden turns of perversity. The boy resisted whatever he suspected was meant for his improvement and contrived when he was vitally interested in something to leave the impression he was bored. Sheppard was not deceived. Secretly Johnson was learning what he wanted him to learn—that his benefactor was impervious to insult and that there were no cracks in his armor of kindness and patience where a successful shaft could be

160

driven. "Some day you may go to the moon," he said. "In ten years men will probably be making round trips there on schedule. Why you boys may be space-men. Astronauts!"

"Astro-nuts," Johnson said.

165 "Nuts or nauts," Sheppard said, "it's perfectly possible that you, Rufus John-son, will go to the moon."

Something in the depths of Johnson's eyes stirred. All day his humor had been glum. "I ain't going to the moon and get there alive," he said, "and when I die I'm going to hell."

"It's at least possible to get to the moon," Sheppard said dryly. The best way to handle this kind of thing was with gentle ridicule. "We can see it. We know it's there. Nobody has given any reliable evidence there's a hell."

"The Bible has give the evidence," Johnson said darkly, "and if you die and go there you burn forever."

170 The child leaned forward.

"Whoever says it ain't a hell," Johnson said, "is contradicting Jesus. The dead are judged and the wicked are damned. They weep and gnash their teeth while they burn," he continued, "and it's everlasting darkness."

The child's mouth opened. His eyes appeared to grow hollow.

"Satan runs it," Johnson said.

Norton lurched up and took a hobbled step toward Sheppard. "Is she there?" he said in a loud voice. "Is she there burning up?" He kicked the rope off his feet. "Is she on fire?"

175 "Oh my God," Sheppard muttered. "No no," he said, "of course she isn't. Rufus is mistaken. Your mother isn't anywhere. She's not unhappy. She just isn't." His lot would have been easier if when his wife died he had told Norton she had gone to heaven and that some day he would see her again, but he could not allow himself to bring him up on a lie.

Norton's face began to twist. A knot formed in his chin.

"Listen," Sheppard said quickly and pulled the child to him, "your mother's spirit lives on in other people and it'll live on in you if you're good and generous like she was."

The child's pale eyes hardened in disbelief.

Sheppard's pity turned to revulsion. The boy would rather she be in hell than nowhere. "Do you understand?" he said. "She doesn't exist." He put his hand on the child's shoulder. "That's all I have to give you," he said in a softer, exasperated tone, "the truth."

180 Instead of howling, the boy wrenched himself away and caught Johnson by the sleeve. "Is she there, Rufus?" he said "Is she there, burning up?"

Johnson's eyes glittered. "Well," he said, "she is if she was evil. Was she a whore?"

"Your mother was not a whore," Sheppard said sharply. He had the sensation of driving a car without brakes. "Now let's have no more of this foolishness. We were talking about the moon."

"Did she believe in Jesus?" Johnson asked.

Norton looked blank. After a second he said, "Yes," as if he saw that this was necessary. "She did," he said. "All the time."

"She did not," Sheppard muttered.   185

"She did all the time," Norton said. "I heard her say she did all the time."

"She's saved," Johnson said.

The child still looked puzzled. "Where?" he said. "Where is she at?"

"On high," Johnson said.

"Where's that?" Norton gasped.   190

"It's in the sky somewhere," Johnson said, "but you got to be dead to get there. You can't go in no space ship." There was a narrow gleam in his eyes now like a beam holding steady on its target.

"Man's going to the moon," Sheppard said grimly, "is very much like the first fish crawling out of the water onto land billions and billions of years ago. He didn't have an earth suit. He had to grow his adjustments inside. He developed lungs."

"When I'm dead will I go to hell or where she is?" Norton asked.

"Right now you'd go where she is," Johnson said, "but if you live long enough, you'll go to hell."

Sheppard rose abruptly and picked up the lantern. "Close the window,   195
Rufus," he said. "It's time we went to bed."

On the way down the attic stairs he heard Johnson say in a loud whisper behind him, "I'll tell you all about it tomorrow, kid, when Himself has cleared out."

The next day when the boys came to the ball park, he watched them as they came from behind the bleachers and around the edge of the field. Johnson's hand was on Norton's shoulder, his head bent toward the younger boy's ear, and on the child's face there was a look of complete confidence, of dawning light. Sheppard's grimace hardened. This would be Johnson's way of trying to annoy him. But he would not be annoyed. Norton was not bright enough to be damaged much. He gazed at the child's dull absorbed little face. Why try to make him superior? Heaven and hell were for the mediocre, and he was that if he was anything.

The two boys came into the bleachers and sat down about ten feet away, facing him, but neither gave him any sign of recognition. He cast a glance behind him where the Little Leaguers were spread out in the field. Then he started for the bleachers. The hiss of Johnson's voice stopped as he approached.

"What have you fellows been doing today?" he asked genially.

"He's been telling me . . ." Norton started.   200

Johnson pushed the child in the ribs with his elbow. "We ain't been doing nothing," he said. His face appeared to be covered with a blank glaze but through it a look of complicity was blazoned forth insolently.

Sheppard felt his face grow warm, but he said nothing. A child in a Little League uniform had followed him and was nudging him in the back of the leg with a bat. He turned and put his arm around the boy's neck and went with him back to the game.

That night when he went to the attic to join the boys at the telescope, he found Norton there alone. He was sitting on the packing box, hunched over, looking intently through the instrument. Johnson was not there.

"Where's Rufus?" Sheppard asked.

"I said where's Rufus?" he said louder.

"Gone somewhere," the child said without turning around.

"Gone where?" Sheppard asked.

"He just said he was going somewhere. He said he was fed up looking at stars."

"I see," Sheppard said glumly. He turned and went back down the stairs. He searched the house without finding Johnson. Then he went to the living room and sat down. Yesterday he had been convinced of his success with the boy. Today he faced the possibility that he was failing with him. He had been over-lenient, too concerned to have Johnson like him. He felt a twinge of guilt. What difference did it make if Johnson liked him or not? What was that to him? When the boy came in, they would have a few things understood. As long as you stay here there'll be no going out at night by yourself, do you understand?

I don't have to stay here. It ain't nothing to me staying here.

Oh my God, he thought. He could not bring it to that. He would have to be firm but not make an issue of it. He picked up the evening paper. Kindness and patience were always called for but he had not been firm enough. He sat holding the paper but not reading it. The boy would not respect him unless he showed firmness. The doorbell rang and he went to answer it. He opened it and stepped back, with a pained disappointed face.

A large dour policeman stood on the stoop, holding Johnson by the elbow. At the curb a patrol car waited. Johnson looked very white. His jaw was thrust forward as if to keep from trembling.

"We brought him here first because he raised such a fit," the policeman said, "but now that you've seen him, we're going to take him to the station and ask him a few questions."

"What happened?" Sheppard muttered.

"A house around the corner from here," the policeman said. "A real smash job, dishes broken all over the floor, furniture turned upside down . . ."

"I didn't have a thing to do with it!" Johnson said. "I was walking along minding my own bidnis when this cop came up and grabbed me."

Sheppard looked at the boy grimly. He made no effort to soften his expression.

Johnson flushed. "I was just walking along," he muttered, but with no conviction in his voice.

"Come on, bud," the policeman said.

"You ain't going to let him take me, are you?" Johnson said. "You believe me, don't you?" There was an appeal in his voice that Sheppard had not heard there before.

This was crucial. The boy would have to learn that he could not be protected when he was guilty. "You'll have to go with him, Rufus," he said.

"You're going to let him take me and I tell you I ain't done a thing?" Johnson said shrilly.

Sheppard's face became harder as his sense of injury grew. The boy had failed him even before he had had a chance to give him the shoe. They were to have got it tomorrow. All his regret turned suddenly on the shoe; his irritation at the sight of Johnson doubled.

"You made out like you had all this confidence in me," the boy mumbled.

"I did have," Sheppard said. His face was wooden.   225

Johnson turned away with the policeman but before he moved, a gleam of pure hatred flashed toward Sheppard from the pits of his eyes.

Sheppard stood in the door and watched them get into the patrol car and drive away. He summoned his compassion. He would go to the station tomorrow and see what he could do about getting him out of trouble. The night in jail would not hurt him and the experience would teach him that he could not treat with impunity someone who had shown him nothing but kindness. Then they would go get the shoe and perhaps after a night in jail it would mean even more to the boy.

The next morning at eight o'clock the police sergeant called and told him he could come pick Johnson up. "We booked a nigger on that charge," he said. "Your boy didn't have nothing to do with it."

Sheppard was at the station in ten minutes, his face hot with shame. Johnson sat slouched on a bench in a drab outer office, reading a police magazine. There was no one else in the room. Sheppard sat down beside him and put his hand tentatively on his shoulder.

The boy glanced up—his lip curled—and back to the magazine.   230

Sheppard felt physically sick. The ugliness of what he had done bore in upon him with a sudden dull intensity. He had failed him at just the point where he might have turned him once and for all in the right direction. "Rufus," he said, "I apologize. I was wrong and you were right. I misjudged you."

The boy continued to read.

"I'm sorry."

The boy wet his finger and turned a page.

Sheppard braced himself. "I was a fool, Rufus," he said.   235

Johnson's mouth slid slightly to the side. He shrugged without raising his head from the magazine.

"Will you forget it, this time?" Sheppard said. "It won't happen again."

The boy looked up. His eyes were bright and unfriendly. "I'll forget it," he said, "but you better remember it." He got up and stalked toward the door. In the middle of the room he turned and jerked his arm at Sheppard and Sheppard jumped up and followed him as if the boy had yanked an invisible leash.

"Your shoe," he said eagerly, "today is the day to get your shoe!" Thank God for the shoe!

But when they went to the brace shop, they found that the shoe had been   240
made two sizes too small and a new one would not be ready for another ten days. Johnson's temper improved at once. The clerk had obviously made a mistake in the measurements but the boy insisted the foot had grown. He left the shop with a pleased expression, as if, in expanding, the foot had acted on some inspiration of its own. Sheppard's face was haggard.

After this he redoubled his efforts. Since Johnson had lost interest in the telescope, he bought a microscope and a box of prepared slides. If he couldn't impress the boy with immensity, he would try the infinitesimal. For two nights Johnson appeared absorbed in the new instrument, then he abruptly lost interest in it, but he seemed content to sit in the living room in the evening and read the encyclopedia. He devoured the encyclopedia as he devoured his dinner, steadily and without dint to his appetite. Each subject appeared to enter his head, be ravaged, and thrown out. Nothing pleased Sheppard more than to see the boy slouched on the sofa, his mouth shut, reading. After they had spent two or three evenings like this, he began to recover his vision. His confidence returned. He knew that some day he would be proud of Johnson.

On Thursday night Sheppard attended a city council meeting. He dropped the boys off at a movie on his way and picked them up on his way back. When they reached home, an automobile with a single red eye above its windshield was waiting in front of the house. Sheppard's lights as he turned into the driveway illuminated two dour faces in the car.

"The cops!" Johnson said. "Some nigger has broke in somewhere and they've come for me again."

"We'll see about that," Sheppard muttered. He stopped the car in the driveway and switched off the lights. "You boys go in the house and go to bed," he said. "I'll handle this."

245 He got out and strode toward the squad car. He thrust his head in the window. The two policemen were looking at him with silent knowledgeable faces. "A house on the corner of Shelton and Mills," the one in the driver's seat said. "It looks like a train run through it."

"He was in the picture show downtown," Sheppard said. "My boy was with him. He had nothing to do with the other one and he had nothing to do with this one. I'll be responsible."

"If I was you," the one nearest him said, "I wouldn't be responsible for any little bastard like him."

"I said I'd be responsible," Sheppard repeated coldly. "You people made a mistake the last time. Don't make another."

The policemen looked at each other. "It ain't our funeral," the one in the driver's seat said, and turned the key in the ignition.

250 Sheppard went in the house and sat down in the living room in the dark. He did not suspect Johnson and he did not want the boy to think he did. If Johnson thought he suspected him again, he would lose everything. But he wanted to know if his alibi was airtight. He thought of going to Norton's room and asking him if Johnson had left the movie. But that would be worse. Johnson would know what he was doing and would be incensed. He decided to ask Johnson himself. He would be direct. He went over in his mind what he was going to say and then he got up and went to the boy's door.

It was open as if he had been expected but Johnson was in bed. Just enough light came in from the hall for Sheppard to see his shape under the sheet. He came in and stood at the foot of the bed. "They've gone," he said. "I told them you had nothing to do with it and that I'd be responsible."

There was a muttered "Yeah," from the pillow.

Sheppard hesitated. "Rufus," he said, "you didn't leave the movie for anything at all, did you?"

"You make out like you got all this confidence in me!" a sudden outraged voice cried, "and you ain't got any! You don't trust me no more now than you did then!" The voice, disembodied, seemed to come more surely from the depths of Johnson than when his face was visible. It was a cry of reproach, edged slightly with contempt.

"I do have confidence in you," Sheppard said intensely. "I have every confidence in you. I believe in you and I trust you completely."   255

"You got your eye on me all the time," the voice said sullenly. "When you get through asking me a bunch of questions, you're going across the hall and ask Norton a bunch of them."

"I have no intention of asking Norton anything and never did," Sheppard said gently. "And I don't suspect you at all. You could hardly have got from the picture show downtown and out here to break in a house and back to the picture show in the time you had."

"That's why you believe me!" the boy cried, "—because you think I couldn't have done it."

"No, no!" Sheppard said. "I believe you because I believe you've got the brains and the guts not to get in trouble again. I believe you know yourself well enough now to know that you don't have to do such things. I believe that you can make anything of yourself that you set your mind to."

Johnson sat up. A faint light shone on his forehead but the rest of his face   260
was invisible. "And I could have broke in there if I'd wanted to in the time I had," he said.

"But I know you didn't," Sheppard said. "There's not the least trace of doubt in my mind."

There was a silence. Johnson lay back down. Then the voice, low and hoarse, as if it were being forced out with difficulty, said, "You don't want to steal and smash up things when you've got everything you want already."

Sheppard caught his breath. The boy was thanking him! He was thanking him! There was gratitude in his voice. There was appreciation. He stood there, smiling foolishly in the dark, trying to hold the moment in suspension. Involuntarily he took a step toward the pillow and stretched out his hand and touched Johnson's forehead. It was cold and dry like rusty iron.

"I understand. Good night, son," he said and turned quickly and left the room. He closed the door behind him and stood there, overcome with emotion.

Across the hall Norton's door was open. The child lay on the bed on his side,   265
looking into the light from the hall.

After this, the road with Johnson would be smooth.

Norton sat up and beckoned to him.

He saw the child but after the first instant, he did not let his eyes focus directly on him. He could not go in and talk to Norton without breaking Johnson's trust. He hesitated, but remained where he was a moment as if he saw nothing. Tomorrow was the day they were to go back for the shoe. It would be a climax to the good feeling between them. He turned quickly and went back into his own room.

The child sat for some time looking at the spot where his father had stood. Finally his gaze became aimless and he lay back down.

270   The next day Johnson was glum and silent as if he were ashamed that he had revealed himself. His eyes had a hooded look. He seemed to have retired within himself and there to be going through some crisis of determination. Sheppard could not get to the brace shop quickly enough. He left Norton at home because he did not want his attention divided. He wanted to be free to observe Johnson's reaction minutely. The boy did not seem pleased or even interested in the prospect of the shoe, but when it became an actuality, certainly then he would be moved.

The brace shop was a small concrete warehouse lined and stacked with the equipment of affliction. Wheel chairs and walkers covered most of the floor. The walls were hung with every kind of crutch and brace. Artificial limbs were stacked on the shelves, legs and arms and hands, claws and hooks, straps and human harnesses and unidentifiable instruments for unnamed deformities. In a small clearing in the middle of the room there was a row of yellow plastic-cushioned chairs and a shoe-fitting stool. Johnson slouched down in one of the chairs and set his foot up on the stool and sat with his eyes on it moodily. What was roughly the toe had broken open again and he had patched it with a piece of canvas; another place he had patched with what appeared to be the tongue of the original shoe. The two sides were laced with twine.

There was an excited flush on Sheppard's face; his heart was beating unnaturally fast.

The clerk appeared from the back of the shop with the new shoe under his arm. "Got her right this time!" he said. He straddled the shoe-fitting stool and held the shoe up, smiling as if he had produced it by magic.

It was a black slick shapeless object, shining hideously. It looked like a blunt weapon, highly polished.

275   Johnson gazed at it darkly.

"With this shoe," the clerk said, "you won't know you're walking. You'll think you're riding!" He bent his bright pink bald head and began gingerly to unlace the twine. He removed the old shoe as if he were skinning an animal still half alive. His expression was strained. The unsheathed mass of foot in the dirty sock made Sheppard feel queasy. He turned his eyes away until the new shoe was on. The clerk laced it up rapidly. "Now stand up and walk around," he said, "and see if that ain't power glide." He winked at Sheppard. "In that shoe," he said, "he won't know he don't have a normal foot."

Sheppard's face was bright with pleasure.

Johnson stood up and walked a few yards away. He walked stiffly with almost no dip in his short side. He stood for a moment, rigid, with his back to them.

"Wonderful!" Sheppard said. "Wonderful." It was as if he had given the boy a new spine.

280   Johnson turned around. His mouth was set in a thin icy line. He came back to the seat and removed the shoe. He put his foot in the old one and began lacing it up.

"You want to take it home and see if it suits you first?" the clerk murmured.

"No," Johnson said. "I ain't going to wear it at all."

"What's wrong with it?" Sheppard said, his voice rising.

"I don't need no new shoe," Johnson said. "And when I do, I got ways of getting my own." His face was stony but there was a glint of triumph in his eyes.

"Boy," the clerk said, "is your trouble in your foot or in your head?"   285

"Go soak your skull," Johnson said. "Your brains are on fire."

The clerk rose glumly but with dignity and asked Sheppard what he wanted done with the shoe, which he dangled dispiritedly by the lace.

Sheppard's face was a dark angry red. He was staring straight in front of him at a leather corset with an artificial arm attached.

The clerk asked him again.

"Wrap it up," Sheppard muttered. He turned his eyes to Johnson. "He's not   290
mature enough for it yet," he said. "I had thought he was less of a child."

The boy leered. "You been wrong before," he said.

That night they sat in the living room and read as usual. Sheppard kept himself glumly entrenched behind the Sunday New York *Times*. He wanted to recover his good humor, but every time he thought of the rejected shoe, he felt a new charge of irritation. He did not trust himself even to look at Johnson. He realized that the boy had refused the shoe because he was insecure. Johnson had been frightened by his own gratitude. He didn't know what to make of the new self he was becoming conscious of. He understood that something he had been was threatened and he was facing himself and his possibilities for the first time. He was questioning his identity. Grudgingly, Sheppard felt a slight return of sympathy for the boy. In a few minutes, he lowered his paper and looked at him.

Johnson was sitting on the sofa, gazing over the top of the encyclopedia. His expression was trancelike. He might have been listening to something far away. Sheppard watched him intently but the boy continued to listen, and did not turn his head. The poor kid is lost, Sheppard thought. Here he had sat all evening, sullenly reading the paper, and had not said a word to break the tension. "Rufus," he said.

Johnson continued to sit, stock-still, listening.

"Rufus," Sheppard said in a slow hypnotic voice, "you can be anything in   295
the world you want to be. You can be a scientist or an architect or an engineer or whatever you set your mind to, and whatever you set your mind to be, you can be the best of its kind." He imagined his voice penetrating to the boy in the black caverns of his psyche. Johnson leaned forward but his eyes did not turn. On the street a car door closed. There was a silence. Then a sudden blast from the door bell.

Sheppard jumped up and went to the door and opened it. The same policeman who had come before stood there. The patrol car waited at the curb.

"Lemme see that boy," he said.

Sheppard scowled and stood aside. "He's been here all evening," he said. "I can vouch for it."

The policeman walked into the living room. Johnson appeared engrossed in his book. After a second he looked up with an annoyed expression, like a great man interrupted at his work.

300 "What was that you were looking at in that kitchen window over on Winter Avenue about a half hour ago, bud?" the policeman asked.

"Stop persecuting this boy!" Sheppard said. "I'll vouch for the fact he was here. I was here with him."

"You heard him," Johnson said. "I been here all the time."

"It ain't everybody makes tracks like you," the policeman said and eyed the clubfoot.

"They couldn't be his tracks," Sheppard growled, infuriated. "He's been here all the time. You're wasting your own time and you're wasting ours." He felt the *ours* seal his solidarity with the boy. "I'm sick of this," he said. "You people are too damn lazy to go out and find whoever is doing these things. You come here automatically."

305 The policeman ignored this and continued looking through Johnson. His eyes were small and alert in his fleshy face. Finally he turned toward the door. "We'll get him sooner or later," he said, "with his head in a window and his tail out."

Sheppard followed him to the door and slammed it behind him. His spirits were soaring. This was exactly what he had needed. He returned with an expectant face.

Johnson had put the book down and was sitting there, looking at him slyly. "Thanks," he said.

Sheppard stopped. The boy's expression was predatory. He was openly leering.

"You ain't such a bad liar yourself," he said.

310 "Liar?" Sheppard murmured. Could the boy have left and come back? He felt himself sicken. Then a rush of anger sent him forward. "Did you leave?" he said furiously. "I didn't see you leave."

The boy only smiled.

"You went up in the attic to see Norton," Sheppard said.

"Naw," Johnson said, "that kid is crazy. He don't want to do nothing but look through that stinking telescope."

"I don't want to hear about Norton," Sheppard said harshly. "Where were you?"

315 "I was sitting on that pink can by my ownself," Johnson said. "There wasn't no witnesses."

Sheppard took out his handkerchief and wiped his forehead. He managed to smile.

Johnson rolled his eyes. "You don't believe in me," he said. His voice was cracked the way it had been in the dark room two nights before. "You make out like you got all this confidence in me but you ain't got any. When things get hot, you'll fade like the rest of them." The crack became exaggerated, comic. The mockery in it was blatant. "You don't believe in me. You ain't got no confidence," he wailed. "And you ain't any smarter than that cop. All that about tracks—that was a trap. There wasn't any tracks. That whole place is concreted in the back and my feet were dry."

Sheppard slowly put the handkerchief back in his pocket. He dropped down on the sofa and gazed at the rug beneath his feet. The boy's clubfoot was set within the circle of his vision. The pieced-together shoe appeared to grin at him with Johnson's own face. He caught hold of the edge of the sofa cushion and his knuckles turned white. A chill of hatred shook him. He hated the shoe, hated the foot, hated the boy. His face paled. Hatred choked him. He was aghast at himself.

He caught the boy's shoulder and gripped it fiercely as if to keep himself from falling. "Listen," he said, "you looked in that window to embarrass me. That was all you wanted—to shake my resolve to help you, but my resolve isn't shaken. I'm stronger than you are. I'm stronger than you are and I'm going to save you. The good will triumph."

"Not when it ain't true," the boy said. "Not when it ain't right."   320

"My resolve isn't shaken," Sheppard repeated. "I'm going to save you."

Johnson's look became sly again. "You ain't going to save me," he said. "You're going to tell me to leave this house. I did those other two jobs too—the first one as well as the one I done when I was supposed to be in the picture show."

"I'm not going to tell you to leave," Sheppard said. His voice was toneless, mechanical. "I'm going to save you."

Johnson thrust his head forward. "Save yourself," he hissed. "Nobody can save me but Jesus."

Sheppard laughed curtly. "You don't deceive me," he said. "I flushed that   325
out of your head in the reformatory. I saved you from that, at least."

The muscles in Johnson's face stiffened. A look of such repulsion hardened on his face that Sheppard drew back. The boy's eyes were like distorting mirrors in which he saw himself made hideous and grotesque. "I'll show you," Johnson whispered. He rose abruptly and started headlong for the door as if he could not get out of Sheppard's sight quick enough, but it was the door to the back hall he went through, not the front door. Sheppard turned on the sofa and looked behind him where the boy had disappeared. He heard the door to his room slam. He was not leaving. The intensity had gone out of Sheppard's eyes. They looked flat and lifeless as if the shock of the boy's revelation were only now reaching the center of his consciousness. "If he would only leave," he murmured. "If he would only leave now of his own accord."

The next morning Johnson appeared at the breakfast table in the grandfather's suit he had come in. Sheppard pretended not to notice but one look told him what he already knew, that he was trapped, that there could be nothing now but a battle of nerves and that Johnson would win it. He wished he had never laid eyes on the boy. The failure of his compassion numbed him. He got out of the house as soon as he could and all day he dreaded to go home in the evening. He had a faint hope that the boy might be gone when he returned. The grandfather's suit might have meant he was leaving. The hope grew in the afternoon. When he came home and opened the front door, his heart was pounding.

He stopped in the hall and looked silently into the living room. His expectant expression faded. His face seemed suddenly as old as his white hair. The two boys were sitting close together on the sofa, reading the same book. Norton's cheek rested against the sleeve of Johnson's black suit. Johnson's finger moved under the lines they were reading. The elder brother and the younger. Sheppard looked woodenly at this scene for almost a minute. Then he walked into the room and took off his coat and dropped it on a chair. Neither boy noticed him. He went on to the kitchen.

Leola left the supper on the stove every afternoon before she left and he put it on the table. His head ached and his nerves were taut. He sat down on the kitchen stool and remained there, sunk in his depression. He wondered if he could infuriate Johnson enough to make him leave of his own accord. Last night what had enraged him was the Jesus business. It might enrage Johnson, but it depressed him. Why not simply tell the boy to go? Admit defeat. The thought of facing Johnson again sickened him. The boy looked at him as if he were the guilty one, as if he were a moral leper. He knew without conceit that he was a good man, that he had nothing to reproach himself with. His feelings about Johnson now were involuntary. He would like to feel compassion for him. He would like to be able to help him. He longed for the time when there would be no one but himself and Norton in the house, when the child's simple selfishness would be all he had to contend with, and his own loneliness.

330   He got up and took three serving dishes off the shelf and took them to the stove. Absently he began pouring the butterbeans and the hash into the dishes. When the food was on the table, he called them in.

They brought the book with them. Norton pushed his place setting around to the same side of the table as Johnson's and moved his chair next to Johnson's chair. They sat down and put the book between them. It was a black book with red edges.

"What's that you're reading?" Sheppard asked, sitting down.

"The Holy Bible," Johnson said.

God give me strength, Sheppard said under his breath.

335   "We lifted it from a ten cent store," Johnson said.

"We?" Sheppard muttered. He turned and glared at Norton. The child's face was bright and there was an excited sheen to his eyes. The change that had come over the boy struck him for the first time. He looked alert. He had on a blue plaid shirt and his eyes were a brighter blue than he had ever seen them before. There was a strange new life in him, the sign of new and more rugged vices. "So now you steal?" he said, glowering. "You haven't learned to be generous but you have learned to steal."

"No he ain't," Johnson said. "I was the one lifted it. He only watched. He can't sully himself. It don't make any difference about me. I'm going to hell anyway."

Sheppard held his tongue.

"Unless," Johnson said, "I repent."

340   "Repent, Rufus," Norton said in a pleading voice. "Repent, hear? You don't want to go to hell."

"Stop talking this nonsense," Sheppard said, looking sharply at the child.

"If I do repent, I'll be a preacher," Johnson said. "If you're going to do it, it's no sense in doing it halfway."

"What are you going to be, Norton," Sheppard asked in a brittle voice, "a preacher too?"

There was a glitter of wild pleasure in the child's eyes. "A space man!" he shouted.

"Wonderful," Sheppard said bitterly.   345

"Those space ships ain't going to do you any good unless you believe in Jesus," Johnson said. He wet his finger and began to leaf through the pages of the Bible. "I'll read you where it says so," he said.

Sheppard leaned forward and said in a low furious voice, "Put that Bible up, Rufus, and eat your dinner."

Johnson continued searching for the passage.

"Put that Bible up!" Sheppard shouted.

The boy stopped and looked up. His expression was startled but pleased.   350

"That book is something for you to hide behind," Sheppard said. "It's for cowards, people who are afraid to stand on their own feet and figure things out for themselves."

Johnson's eyes snapped. He backed his chair a little way from the table. "Satan has you in his power," he said. "Not only me. You too."

Sheppard reached across the table to grab the book but Johnson snatched it and put it in his lap.

Sheppard laughed. "You don't believe in that book and you know you don't believe in it!"

"I believe it!" Johnson said. "You don't know what I believe and what I   355
don't."

Sheppard shook his head. "You don't believe it. You're too intelligent."

"I ain't too intelligent," the boy muttered. "You don't know nothing about me. Even if I didn't believe it, it would still be true."

"You don't believe it!" Sheppard said. His face was a taunt.

"I believe it!" Johnson said breathlessly. "I'll show you I believe it!" He opened the book in his lap and tore out a page of it and thrust it into his mouth. He fixed his eyes on Sheppard. His jaws worked furiously and the paper crackled as he chewed it.

"Stop this," Sheppard said in a dry, burnt-out voice. "Stop it."   360

The boy raised the Bible and tore out a page with his teeth and began grinding it in his mouth, his eyes burning.

Sheppard reached across the table and knocked the book out of his hand. "Leave the table," he said coldly.

Johnson swallowed what was in his mouth. His eyes widened as if a vision of splendor were opening up before him. "I've eaten it!" he breathed. "I've eaten it like Ezekiel and it was honey to my mouth!"[1]

"Leave this table," Sheppard said. His hands were clenched beside his plate.

---

1. Ezekiel 3:1–3. The Lord in a vision told Ezekiel to eat a roll and go speak to the captive Israelites; when he ate it "it was in my mouth as honey for sweetness."

365 "I've eaten it!" the boy cried. Wonder transformed his face. "I've eaten it like Ezekiel and I don't want none of your food after it nor no more ever."

"Go then," Sheppard said softly. "Go. Go."

The boy rose and picked up the Bible and started toward the hall with it. At the door he paused, a small black figure on the threshold of some dark apocalypse. "The devil has you in his power," he said in a jubilant voice and disappeared.

After supper Sheppard sat in the living room alone. Johnson had left the house but he could not believe that the boy had simply gone. The first feeling of release had passed. He felt dull and cold as at the onset of an illness and dread had settled in him like a fog. Just to leave would be too anticlimactic an end for Johnson's taste; he would return and try to prove something. He might come back a week later and set fire to the place. Nothing seemed too outrageous now.

He picked up the paper and tried to read. In a moment he threw it down and got up and went into the hall and listened. He might be hiding in the attic. He went to the attic door and opened it.

370 The lantern was lit, casting a dim light on the stairs. He didn't hear anything. "Norton," he called, "are you up there?" There was no answer. He mounted the narrow stairs to see.

Amid the strange vine-like shadows cast by the lantern, Norton sat with his eye to the telescope. "Norton," Sheppard said, "do you know where Rufus went?"

The child's back was to him. He was sitting hunched, intent, his large ears directly above his shoulders. Suddenly he waved his hand and crouched closer to the telescope as if he could not get near enough to what he saw.

"Norton!" Sheppard said in a loud voice.

The child didn't move.

375 "Norton!" Sheppard shouted.

Norton started. He turned around. There was an unnatural brightness about his eyes. After a moment he seemed to see that it was Sheppard. "I've found her!" he said breathlessly.

"Found who?" Sheppard said.

"Mamma!"

Sheppard steadied himself in the door way. The jungle of shadows around the child thickened.

380 "Come and look!" he cried. He wiped his sweaty face on the tail of his plaid shirt and then put his eye back to the telescope. His back became fixed in a rigid intensity. All at once he waved again.

"Norton," Sheppard said, "you don't see anything in the telescope but star clusters. Now you've had enough of that for one night. You'd better go to bed. Do you know where Rufus is?"

"She's there!" he cried, not turning around from the telescope. "She waved at me!"

"I want you in bed in fifteen minutes," Sheppard said. After a moment he said, "Do you hear me, Norton?"

The child began to wave frantically.

"I mean what I say," Sheppard said. "I'm going to call in fifteen minutes and see if you're in bed." 385

He went down the steps again and returned to the parlor. He went to the front door and cast a cursory glance out. The sky was crowded with the stars he had been fool enough to think Johnson could reach. Somewhere in the small wood behind the house, a bull frog sounded a low hollow note. He went back to his chair and sat a few minutes. He decided to go to bed. He put his hands on the arms of the chair and leaned forward and heard, like the first shrill note of a disaster warning, the siren of a police car, moving slowly into the neighborhood and nearer until it subsided with a moan outside the house.

He felt a cold weight on his shoulders as if an icy cloak had been thrown about him. He went to the door and opened it.

Two policemen were coming up the walk with a dark snarling Johnson between them, handcuffed to each. A reporter jogged alongside and another policeman waited in the patrol car.

"Here's your boy," the dourest of the policemen said. "Didn't I tell you we'd get him?"

Johnson jerked his arm down savagely. "I was waitin for you!" he said. "You wouldn't have got me if I hadn't of wanted to get caught. It was my idea." He was addressing the policemen but leering at Sheppard. 390

Sheppard looked at him coldly.

"Why did you want to get caught?" the reporter asked, running around to get beside Johnson. "Why did you deliberately want to get caught?"

The question and the sight of Sheppard seemed to throw the boy into a fury. "To show up that big tin Jesus!" he hissed and kicked his leg out at Sheppard. "He thinks he's God. I'd rather be in the reformatory than in his house, I'd rather be in the pen! The Devil has him in his power. He don't know his left hand from his right, he don't have as much sense as his crazy kid!" He paused and then swept on to his fantastic conclusion. "He made suggestions to me!"

Sheppard's face blanched. He caught hold of the door facing.

"Suggestions?" the reporter said eagerly, "what kind of suggestion?" 395

"Immor'l suggestions!" Johnson said. "What kind of suggestions do you think? But I ain't having none of it, I'm a Christian, I'm . . ."

Sheppard's face was tight with pain. "He knows that's not true," he said in a shaken voice. "He knows he's lying. I did everything I knew how for him. I did more for him than I did for my own child. I hoped to save him and I failed, but it was an honorable failure. I have nothing to reproach myself with. I made no suggestions to him."

"Do you remember the suggestions?" the reporter asked. "Can you tell us exactly what he said?"

"He's a dirty atheist," Johnson said. "He said there wasn't no hell."

400   "Well, they seen each other now," one of the policemen said with a knowing sigh. "Let's us go."

"Wait," Sheppard said. He came down one step and fixed his eyes on Johnson's eyes in a last desperate effort to save himself. "Tell the truth, Rufus," he said. "You don't want to perpetrate this lie. You're not evil, you're mortally confused. You don't have to make up for that foot, you don't have to . . ."

Johnson hurled himself forward. "Listen at him!" he screamed. "I lie and steal because I'm good at it! My foot don't have a thing to do with it! The lame shall enter first! The halt'll be gathered together. When I get ready to be saved, Jesus'll save me, not that lying stinking atheist, not that . . ."

"That'll be enough out of you," the policeman said and yanked him back. "We just wanted you to see we got him," he said to Sheppard, and the two of them turned around and dragged Johnson away, half turned and screaming back at Sheppard.

"The lame'll carry off the prey!" he screeched, but his voice was muffled inside the car. The reporter scrambled into the front seat with the driver and slammed the door and the siren wailed into the darkness.

405   Sheppard remained there, bent slightly like a man who has been shot but continues to stand. After a minute he turned and went back in the house and sat down in the chair he had left. He closed his eyes on a picture of Johnson in a circle of reporters at the police station, elaborating his lies. "I have nothing to reproach myself with," he murmured. His every action had been selfless, his one aim had been to save Johnson for some decent kind of service, he had not spared himself, he had sacrificed his reputation, he had done more for Johnson than he had done for his own child. Foulness hung about him like an odor in the air, so close that it seemed to come from his own breath. "I have nothing to reproach myself with," he repeated. His voice sounded dry and harsh. "I did more for him than I did for my own child." He was swept with a sudden panic. He heard the boy's jubilant voice. Satan has you in his power.

"I have nothing to reproach myself with," he began again. "I did more for him than I did for my own child." He heard his voice as if it were the voice of his accuser. He repeated the sentence silently.

Slowly his face drained of color. It became almost gray beneath the white halo of his hair. The sentence echoed in his mind, each syllable like a dull blow. His mouth twisted and he closed his eyes against the revelation. Norton's face rose before him, empty, forlorn, his left eye listing almost imperceptibly toward the outer rim as if it could not bear a full view of grief. His heart constricted with a repulsion for himself so clear and intense that he gasped for breath. He had stuffed his own emptiness with good works like a glutton. He had ignored his own child to feed his vision of himself. He saw the clear-eyed Devil, the sounder of hearts, leering at him from the eyes of Johnson. His image of himself shrivelled until everything was black before him. He sat there paralyzed, aghast.

He saw Norton at the telescope, all back and ears, saw his arm shoot up and wave frantically. A rush of agonizing love for the child rushed over him like a transfusion of life. The little boy's face appeared to him transformed; the image of his salvation; all light. He groaned with joy. He would make everything up to him. He would never let him suffer again. He would be mother and father. He jumped up and ran to his room, to kiss him, to tell him that he loved him, that he would never fail him again.

The light was on in Norton's room but the bed was empty. He turned and dashed up the attic stairs and at the top reeled back like a man on the edge of a pit. The tripod had fallen and the telescope lay on the floor. A few feet over it, the child hung in the jungle of shadows, just below the beam from which he had launched his flight into space.

1965

FLANNERY O'CONNOR

Everything That Rises Must Converge

Her doctor had told Julian's mother that she must lose twenty pounds on account of her blood pressure, so on Wednesday nights Julian had to take her downtown on the bus for a reducing class at the Y. The reducing class was designed for working girls over fifty, who weighed from 165 to 200 pounds. His mother was one of the slimmer ones, but she said ladies did not tell their age or weight. She would not ride the buses by herself at night since they had been integrated, and because the reducing class was one of her few pleasures, necessary for her health, and *free*, she said Julian could at least put himself out to take her, considering all she did for him. Julian did not like to consider all she did for him, but every Wednesday night he braced himself and took her.

She was almost ready to go, standing before the hall mirror, putting on her hat, while he, his hands behind him, appeared pinned to the door frame, waiting like Saint Sebastian for the arrows to begin piercing him.[1] The hat was new and had cost her seven dollars and a half. She kept saying, "Maybe I shouldn't have paid that for it. No, I shouldn't have. I'll take it off and return it tomorrow. I shouldn't have bought it."

Julian raised his eyes to heaven. "Yes, you should have bought it," he said. "Put it on and let's go." It was a hideous hat. A purple velvet flap came down on one side of it and stood up on the other; the rest of it was green and looked like a cushion with the stuffing out. He decided it was less comical than jaunty and pathetic. Everything that gave her pleasure was small and depressed him.

She lifted the hat one more time and set it down slowly on top of her head. Two wings of gray hair protruded on either side of her florid face, but her eyes, sky-blue, were as innocent and untouched by experience as they must have been when she was ten. Were it not that she was a widow who had struggled fiercely to feed and clothe and put him through school and who was supporting him

---

1. Discovered to be a Christian, Sebastian, Roman commander in Milan, was tied to a tree, shot with arrows, and left for dead. (He recovered but when he reasserted his faith he was clubbed to death.)

still, "until he got on his feet," she might have been a little girl that he had to take to town.

"It's all right, it's all right," he said. "Let's go." He opened the door himself and started down the walk to get her going. The sky was a dying violet and the houses stood out darkly against it, bulbous liver-colored monstrosities of a uniform ugliness though no two were alike. Since this had been a fashionable neighborhood forty years ago, his mother persisted in thinking they did well to have an apartment in it. Each house had a narrow collar of dirt around it in which sat, usually, a grubby child. Julian walked with his hands in his pockets, his head down and thrust forward and his eyes glazed with the determination to make himself completely numb during the time he would be sacrificed to her pleasure.

The door closed and he turned to find the dumpy figure, surmounted by the atrocious hat, coming toward him. "Well," she said, "you only live once and paying a little more for it, I at least won't meet myself coming and going."

"Some day I'll start making money," Julian said gloomily—he knew he never would—"and you can have one of those jokes whenever you take the fit." But first they would move. He visualized a place where the nearest neighbors would be three miles away on either side.

"I think you're doing fine," she said, drawing on her gloves. "You've only been out of school a year. Rome wasn't built in a day."

She was one of the few members of the Y reducing class who arrived in hat and gloves and who had a son who had been to college. "It takes time," she said, "and the world is in such a mess. This hat looked better on me than any of the others, though when she brought it out I said, 'Take that thing back. I wouldn't have it on my head,' and she said, 'Now wait till you see it on,' and when she put it on me, I said, 'We-ull,' and she said, 'If you ask me, that hat does something for you and you do something for the hat, and besides,' she said, 'with that hat, you won't meet yourself coming and going.'"

Julian thought he could have stood his lot better if she had been selfish, if she had been an old hag who drank and screamed at him. He walked along, saturated in depression, as if in the midst of his martyrdom he had lost his faith. Catching sight of his long, hopeless, irritated face, she stopped suddenly with a grief-stricken look, and pulled back on his arm. "Wait on me," she said. "I'm going back to the house and take this thing off and tomorrow I'm going to return it. I was out of my head. I can pay the gas bill with that seven-fifty."

He caught her arm in a vicious grip. "You are not going to take it back," he said. "I like it."

"Well," she said, "I don't think I ought . . ."

"Shut up and enjoy it," he muttered, more depressed than ever.

"With the world in the mess it's in," she said, "it's a wonder we can enjoy anything. I tell you, the bottom rail is on the top."

Julian sighed.

"Of course," she said, "if you know who are you, you can go anywhere." She said this every time he took her to the reducing class. "Most of them in it are not our kind of people," she said, "but I can be gracious to anybody. I know who I am."

"They don't give a damn for your graciousness," Julian said savagely. "Knowing who you are is good for one generation only. You haven't the foggiest idea where you stand now or who you are."

She stopped and allowed her eyes to flash at him. "I most certainly do know who I am," she said, "and if you don't know who you are, I'm ashamed of you."

"Oh hell," Julian said.

"Your great-grandfather was a former governor of this state," she said. "Your grandfather was a prosperous land-owner. Your grandmother was a Godhigh."

"Will you look around you," he said tensely, "and see where you are now?" and he swept his arm jerkily out to indicate the neighborhood, which the growing darkness at least made less dingy.

"You remain what you are," she said. "Your great-grandfather had a plantation and two hundred slaves."

"There are no more slaves," he said irritably.

"They were better off when they were," she said. He groaned to see that she was off on that topic. She rolled onto it every few days like a train on an open track. He knew every stop, every junction, every swamp along the way, and knew the exact point at which her conclusion would roll majestically into the station: "It's ridiculous. It's simply not realistic. They should rise, yes, but on their own side of the fence."

"Let's skip it," Julian said.

"The ones I feel sorry for," she said, "are the ones that are half white. They're tragic."

"Will you skip it?"

"Suppose we were half white. We would certainly have mixed feelings."

"I have mixed feelings now," he groaned.

"Well let's talk about something pleasant," she said. "I remember going to Grandpa's when I was a little girl. Then the house had double stairways that went up to what was really the second floor—all the cooking was done on the first. I used to like to stay down in the kitchen on account of the way the walls smelled. I would sit with my nose pressed against the plaster and take deep breaths. Actually the place belonged to the Godhighs but your grandfather Chestny paid the mortgage and saved it for them. They were in reduced circumstances," she said, "but reduced or not, they never forgot who they were."

"Doubtless that decayed mansion reminded them," Julian muttered. He never spoke of it without contempt or thought of it without longing. He had seen it once when he was a child before it had been sold. The double stairways had rotted and been torn down. Negroes were living in it. But it remained in his mind as his mother had known it. It appeared in his dreams regularly. He would stand on the wide porch, listening to the rustle of oak leaves, then wander through the high-ceilinged hall into the parlor that opened onto it and gaze at the worn rugs and faded draperies. It occurred to him that it was he, not she, who could have appreciated it. He preferred its threadbare elegance to anything he could name and it was because of it that all the neighborhoods they had lived in had been a torment to him—whereas she had hardly known the difference. She called her insensitivity "being adjustable."

"And I remember the old darky who was my nurse, Caroline. There was no better person in the world. I've always had a great respect for my colored friends," she said. "I'd do anything in the world for them and they'd . . ."

"Will you for God's sake get off that subject?" Julian said. When he got on a bus by himself, he made it a point to sit down beside a Negro, in reparation as it were for his mother's sins.

"You're mighty touchy tonight," she said. "Do you feel all right?"

35   "Yes I feel all right," he said. "Now lay off."

She pursed her lips. "Well, you certainly are in a vile humor," she observed. "I just won't speak to you at all."

They had reached the bus stop. There was no bus in sight and Julian, his hands still jammed in his pockets and his head thrust forward, scowled down the empty street. The frustration of having to wait on the bus as well as ride on it began to creep up his neck like a hot hand. The presence of his mother was borne in upon him as she gave a pained sigh. He looked at her bleakly. She was holding herself very erect under the preposterous hat, wearing it like a banner of her imaginary dignity. There was in him an evil urge to break her spirit. He suddenly unloosened his tie and pulled it off and put it in his pocket.

She stiffened. "Why must you look like *that* when you take me to town?" she said. "Why must you deliberately embarrass me?"

"If you'll never learn where you are," he said, "you can at least learn where I am."

40   "You look like a—thug," she said.

"Then I must be one," he murmured.

"I'll just go home," she said. "I will not bother you. If you can't do a little thing like that for me . . ."

Rolling his eyes upward, he put his tie back on. "Restored to my class," he muttered. He thrust his face toward her and hissed, "True culture is in the mind, the *mind*," he said, and tapped his head, "the mind."

"It's in the heart," she said, "and in how you do things and how you do things is because of who you *are*."

45   "Nobody in the damn bus cares who you are."

"I care who I am," she said icily.

The lighted bus appeared on top of the next hill and as it approached, they moved out into the street to meet it. He put his hand under her elbow and hoisted her up on the creaking step. She entered with a little smile, as if she were going into a drawing room where everyone had been waiting for her. While he put in the tokens, she sat down on one of the broad front seats for three which faced the aisle. A thin woman with protruding teeth and long yellow hair was sitting on the end of it. His mother moved up beside her and left room for Julian beside herself. He sat down and looked at the floor across the aisle where a pair of thin feet in red and white canvas sandals were planted.

His mother immediately began a general conversation meant to attract anyone who felt like talking. "Can it get any hotter?" she said and removed from her purse a folding fan, black with a Japanese scene on it, which she began to flutter before her.

"I reckon it might could," the woman with the protruding teeth said, "but I know for a fact my apartment couldn't get no hotter."

"It must get the afternoon sun," his mother said. She sat forward and looked up and down the bus. It was half filled. Everybody was white. "I see we have the bus to ourselves," she said. Julian cringed.

"For a change," said the woman across the aisle, the owner of the red and white canvas sandals. "I come on one the other day and they were thick as fleas—up front and all through."

"The world is in a mess everywhere," his mother said. "I don't know how we've let it get in this fix."

"What gets my goat is all those boys from good families stealing automobile tires," the woman with the protruding teeth said. "I told my boy, I said you may not be rich but you been raised right and if I ever catch you in any such mess, they can send you on to the reformatory. Be exactly where you belong."

"Training tells," his mother said. "Is your boy in high school?"

"Ninth grade," the woman said.

"My son just finished college last year. He wants to write but he's selling typewriters until he gets started," his mother said.

The woman leaned forward and peered at Julian. He threw her such a malevolent look that she subsided against the seat. On the floor across the aisle there was an abandoned newspaper. He got up and got it and opened it out in front of him. His mother discreetly continued the conversation in a lower tone but the woman across the aisle said in a loud voice, "Well that's nice. Selling typewriters is close to writing. He can go right from one to the other."

"I tell him," his mother said, "that Rome wasn't built in a day."

Behind the newspaper Julian was withdrawing into the inner compartment of his mind where he spent most of his time. This was a kind of mental bubble in which he established himself when he could not bear to be a part of what was going on around him. From it he could see out and judge but in it he was safe from any kind of penetration from without. It was the only place where he felt free of the general idiocy of his fellows. His mother had never entered it but from it he could see her with absolute clarity.

The old lady was clever enough and he thought that if she had started from any of the right premises, more might have been expected of her. She lived according to the laws of her own fantasy world, outside of which he had never seen her set foot. The law of it was to sacrifice herself for him after she had first created the necessity to do so by making a mess of things. If he had permitted her sacrifices, it was only because her lack of foresight had made them necessary. All of her life had been a struggle to act like a Chestny without the Chestny goods, and to give him everything she thought a Chestny ought to have; but since, said she, it was fun to struggle, why complain? And when you had won, as she had won, what fun to look back on the hard times! He could not forgive her that she had enjoyed the struggle and that she thought *she* had won.

What she meant when she said she had won was that she had brought him up successfully and had sent him to college and that he had turned out so well — good looking (her teeth had gone unfilled so that his could be straightened), intelligent (he realized he was too intelligent to be a success), and with a future ahead of him (there was of course no future ahead of him). She excused his gloominess on the grounds that he was still growing up and his radical ideas on his lack of practical experience. She said he didn't yet know a thing about "life," that he hadn't even entered the real world—when already he was as disenchanted with it as a man of fifty.

The further irony of all this was that in spite of her, he had turned out so well. In spite of going to only a third-rate college, he had, on his own initiative, come out with a first-rate education; in spite of growing up dominated by a small mind, he had ended up with a large one; in spite of all her foolish views, he was free of prejudice and unafraid to face facts. Most miraculous of all, instead of being blinded by love for her as she was for him, he had cut himself emotionally free of her and could see her with complete objectivity. He was not dominated by his mother.

The bus stopped with a sudden jerk and shook him from his meditation. A woman from the back lurched forward with little steps and barely escaped falling in his newspaper as she righted herself. She got off and a large Negro got on. Julian kept his paper lowered to watch. It gave him a certain satisfaction to see injustice in daily operation. It confirmed his view that with a few exceptions there was no one worth knowing within a radius of three hundred miles. The Negro was well dressed and carried a briefcase. He looked around and then sat down on the other end of the seat where the woman with the red and white canvas sandals was sitting. He immediately unfolded a newspaper and obscured himself behind it. Julian's mother's elbow at once prodded insistently into his ribs. "Now you see why I won't ride on these buses by myself," she whispered.

The woman with the red and white canvas sandals had risen at the same time the Negro sat down and had gone further back in the bus and taken the seat of the woman who had got off. His mother leaned forward and cast her an approving look.

65   Julian rose, crossed the aisle, and sat down in the place of the woman with the canvas sandals. From this position, he looked serenely across at his mother. Her face had turned an angry red. He stared at her, making his eyes the eyes of a stranger. He felt his tension suddenly lift as if he had openly declared war on her.

He would have liked to get in conversation with the Negro and to talk with him about art or politics or any subject that would be above the comprehension of those around them, but the man remained entrenched behind his paper. He was either ignoring the change of seating or had never noticed it. There was no way for Julian to convey his sympathy.

His mother kept her eyes fixed reproachfully on his face. The woman with the protruding teeth was looking at him avidly as if he were a type of monster new to her.

"Do you have a light?" he asked the Negro.

Without looking away from his paper, the man reached in his pocket and handed him a packet of matches.

"Thanks," Julian said. For a moment he held the matches foolishly. A NO SMOKING sign looked down upon him from over the door. This alone would not have deterred him; he had no cigarettes. He had quit smoking some months before because he could not afford it. "Sorry," he muttered and handed back the matches. The Negro lowered the paper and gave him an annoyed look. He took the matches and raised the paper again.

His mother continued to gaze at him but she did not take advantage of his momentary discomfort. Her eyes retained their battered look. Her face seemed to be unnaturally red, as if her blood pressure had risen. Julian allowed no glimmer of sympathy to show on his face. Having got the advantage, he wanted desperately to keep it and carry it through. He would have liked to teach her a lesson that would last her a while, but there seemed no way to continue the point. The Negro refused to come out from behind his paper.

Julian folded his arms and looked stolidly before him, facing her but as if he did not see her, as if he had ceased to recognize her existence. He visualized a scene in which, the bus having reached their stop, he would remain in his seat and when she said, "Aren't you going to get off?" he would look at her as a stranger who had rashly addressed him. The corner they got off on was usually deserted, but it was well lighted and it would not hurt her to walk by herself the four blocks to the Y. He decided to wait until the time came and then decide whether or not he would let her get off by herself. He would have to be at the Y at ten to bring her back, but he could leave her wondering if he was going to show up. There was no reason for her to think she could always depend on him.

He retired again into the high-ceilinged room sparsely settled with large pieces of antique furniture. His soul expanded momentarily but then he became aware of his mother across from him and the vision shriveled. He studied her coldly. Her feet in little pumps dangled like a child's and did not quite reach the floor. She was training on him an exaggerated look of reproach. He felt completely detached from her. At that moment he could with pleasure have slapped her as he would have slapped a particularly obnoxious child in his charge.

He began to imagine various unlikely ways by which he could teach her a lesson. He might make friends with some distinguished Negro professor or lawyer and bring him home to spend the evening. He would be entirely justified but her blood pressure would rise to 300. He could not push her to the extent of making her have a stroke, and moreover, he had never been successful at making any Negro friends. He had tried to strike up an acquaintance on the bus with some of the better types, with ones that looked like professors or ministers or lawyers. One morning he had sat down next to a distinguished-looking dark brown man who had answered his questions with a sonorous solemnity but who had turned out to be an undertaker. Another day he had sat down beside a cigar-smoking Negro with a diamond ring on his finger, but after a few stilted pleasantries, the Negro had rung the buzzer and risen, slipping two lottery tickets into Julian's hand as he climbed over him to leave.

70

75   He imagined his mother lying desperately ill and his being able to secure only a Negro doctor for her. He toyed with that idea for a few minutes and then dropped it for a momentary vision of himself participating as a sympathizer in a sit-in demonstration. This was possible but he did not linger with it. Instead, he approached the ultimate horror. He brought home a beautiful suspiciously Negroid woman. Prepare yourself, he said. There is nothing you can do about it. This is the woman I've chosen. She's intelligent, dignified, even good, and she's suffered and she hasn't thought it *fun*. Now persecute us, go ahead and persecute us. Drive her out of here, but remember, you're driving me too. His eyes were narrowed and through the indignation he had generated, he saw his mother across the aisle, purple-faced, shrunken to the dwarf-like proportions of her moral nature, sitting like a mummy beneath the ridiculous banner of her hat.

He was tilted out of his fantasy again as the bus stopped. The door opened with a sucking hiss and out of the dark a large, gaily dressed, sullen-looking colored woman got on with a little boy. The child, who might have been four, had on a short plaid suit and a Tyrolean hat with a blue feather in it. Julian hoped that he would sit down beside him and that the woman would push in beside his mother. He could think of no better arrangement.

As she waited for her tokens, the woman was surveying the seating possibilities—he hoped with the idea of sitting where she was least wanted. There was something familiar-looking about her but Julian could not place what it was. She was a giant of a woman. Her face was set not only to meet opposition but to seek it out. The downward tilt of her large lower lip was like a warning sign: DON'T TAMPER WITH ME. Her bulging figure was encased in a green crepe dress and her feet overflowed in red shoes. She had on a hideous hat. A purple velvet flap came down on one side of it and stood up on the other; the rest of it was green and looked like a cushion with the stuffing out. She carried a mammoth red pocketbook that bulged throughout as if it were stuffed with rocks.

To Julian's disappointment, the little boy climbed up on the empty seat beside his mother. His mother lumped all children, black and white, into the common category, "cute," and she thought little Negroes were on the whole cuter than little white children. She smiled at the little boy as he climbed on the seat.

Meanwhile the woman was bearing down upon the empty seat beside Julian. To his annoyance, she squeezed herself into it. He saw his mother's face change as the woman settled herself next to him and he realized with satisfaction that this was more objectionable to her than it was to him. Her face seemed almost gray and there was a look of dull recognition in her eyes, as if suddenly she had sickened at some awful confrontation. Julian saw that it was because she and the woman had, in a sense, swapped sons. Though his mother would not realize the symbolic significance of this, she would feel it. His amusement showed plainly on his face.

80   The woman next to him muttered something unintelligible to herself. He was conscious of a kind of bristling next to him, a muted growling like that of an angry cat. He could not see anything but the red pocketbook upright on the

bulging green thighs. He visualized the woman as she had stood waiting for her tokens—the ponderous figure, rising from the red shoes upward over the solid hips, the mammoth bosom, the haughty face, to the green and purple hat.

His eyes widened.

The vision of the two hats, identical, broke upon him with the radiance of a brilliant sunrise. His face was suddenly lit with joy. He could not believe that Fate had thrust upon his mother such a lesson. He gave a loud chuckle so that she would look at him and see that he saw. She turned her eyes on him slowly. The blue in them seemed to have turned a bruised purple. For a moment he had an uncomfortable sense of her innocence, but it lasted only a second before principle rescued him. Justice entitled him to laugh. His grin hardened until it said to her as plainly as if he were saying aloud: Your punishment exactly fits your pettiness. This should teach you a permanent lesson.

Her eyes shifted to the woman. She seemed unable to bear looking at him and to find the woman preferable. He became conscious again of the bristling presence at his side. The woman was rumbling like a volcano about to become active. His mother's mouth began to twitch slightly at one corner. With a sinking heart, he saw incipient signs of recovery on her face and realized that this was going to strike her suddenly as funny and was going to be no lesson at all. She kept her eyes on the woman and an amused smile came over her face as if the woman were a monkey that had stolen her hat. The little Negro was looking up at her with large fascinated eyes. He had been trying to attract her attention for some time.

"Carver!" the woman said suddenly. "Come heah!"

When he saw that the spotlight was on him at last, Carver drew his feet up and turned himself toward Julian's mother and giggled. 85

"Carver!" the woman said. "You heah me? Come heah!"

Carver slid down from the seat but remained squatting with his back against the base of it, his head turned slyly around toward Julian's mother, who was smiling at him. The woman reached a hand across the aisle and snatched him to her. He righted himself and hung backwards on her knees, grinning at Julian's mother. "Isn't he cute?" Julian's mother said to the woman with the protruding teeth.

"I reckon he is," the woman said without conviction.

The Negress yanked him upright but he eased out of her grip and shot across the aisle and scrambled, giggling wildly, onto the seat beside his love.

"I think he likes me," Julian's mother said, and smiled at the woman. It was the smile she used when she was being particularly gracious to an inferior. Julian saw everything was lost. The lesson had rolled off her like rain on a roof. 90

The woman stood up and yanked the little boy off the seat as if she were snatching him from contagion. Julian could feel the rage in her at having no weapon like his mother's smile. She gave the child a sharp slap across his leg. He howled once and then thrust his head into her stomach and kicked his feet against her shins. "Behave," she said vehemently.

The bus stopped and the Negro who had been reading the newspaper got off. The woman moved over and set the little boy down with a thump between herself and Julian. She held him firmly by the knee. In a moment he put his hands in front of his face and peeped at Julian's mother through his fingers.

"I see yoooooooo!" she said and put her hand in front of her face and peeped at him.

The woman slapped his hand down. "Quit yo' foolishness," she said, "before I knock the living Jesus out of you!"

95   Julian was thankful that the next stop was theirs. He reached up and pulled the cord. The woman reached up and pulled it at the same time. Oh my God, he thought. He had the terrible intuition that when they got off the bus together, his mother would open her purse and give the little boy a nickel. The gesture would be as natural to her as breathing. The bus stopped and the woman got up and lunged to the front, dragging the child, who wished to stay on, after her. Julian and his mother got up and followed. As they neared the door, Julian tried to relieve her of her pocketbook.

"No," she murmured, "I want to give the little boy a nickel."

"No!" Julian hissed. "No!"

She smiled down at the child and opened her bag. The bus door opened and the woman picked him up by the arm and descended with him, hanging at her hip. Once in the street she set him down and shook him.

Julian's mother had to close her purse while she got down the bus step but as soon as her feet were on the ground, she opened it again and began to rummage inside. "I can't find but a penny," she whispered, "but it looks like a new one."

100   "Don't do it!" Julian said fiercely between his teeth. There was a streetlight on the corner and she hurried to get under it so that she could better see into her pocketbook. The woman was heading off rapidly down the street with the child still hanging backward on her hand.

"Oh little boy!" Julian's mother called and took a few quick steps and caught up with them just beyond the lamppost. "Here's a bright new penny for you," and she held out the coin, which shone bronze in the dim light.

The huge woman turned and for a moment stood, her shoulders lifted and her face frozen with frustrated rage, and stared at Julian's mother. Then all at once she seemed to explode like a piece of machinery that had been given one ounce of pressure too much. Julian saw the black fist swing out with the red pocketbook. He shut his eyes and cringed as he heard the woman shout, "He don't take nobody's pennies!" When he opened his eyes, the woman was disappearing down the street with the little boy staring wide-eyed over her shoulder. Julian's mother was sitting on the sidewalk.

"I told you not to do that," Julian said angrily. "I told you not to do that!"

He stood over her for a minute, gritting his teeth. Her legs were stretched out in front of her and her hat was on her lap. He squatted down and looked her in the face. It was totally expressionless. "You got exactly what you deserved," he said. "Now get up."

105   He picked up her pocketbook and put what had fallen out back in it. He picked the hat up off her lap. The penny caught his eye on the sidewalk and he picked that up and let it drop before her eyes into the purse. Then he stood up

and leaned over and held his hands out to pull her up. She remained immobile. He sighed. Rising above them on either side were black apartment buildings, marked with irregular rectangles of light. At the end of the block a man came out of a door and walked off in the opposite direction. "All right," he said, "suppose somebody happens by and wants to know why you're sitting on the sidewalk?"

She took the hand and, breathing hard, pulled heavily up on it and then stood for a moment, swaying slightly as if the spots of light in the darkness were circling around her. Her eyes, shadowed and confused, finally settled on his face. He did not try to conceal his irritation. "I hope this teaches you a lesson," he said. She leaned forward and her eyes raked his face. She seemed trying to determine his identity. Then, as if she found nothing familiar about him, she started off with a headlong movement in the wrong direction.

"Aren't you going on to the Y?" he asked.

"Home," she muttered.

"Well, are we walking?"

For answer she kept going. Julian followed along, his hands behind him. He saw no reason to let the lesson she had had go without backing it up with an explanation of its meaning. She might as well be made to understand what had happened to her. "Don't think that was just an uppity Negro woman," he said. "That was the whole colored race which will no longer take your condescending pennies. That was your black double. She can wear the same hat as you, and to be sure," he added gratuitously (because he thought it was funny), "it looked better on her than it did on you. What all this means," he said, "is that the old world is gone. The old manners are obsolete and your graciousness is not worth a damn." He thought bitterly of the house that had been lost for him. "You aren't who you think you are," he said.

She continued to plow ahead, paying no attention to him. Her hair had come undone on one side. She dropped her pocketbook and took no notice. He stooped and picked it up and handed it to her but she did not take it.

"You needn't act as if the world had come to an end," he said, "because it hasn't. From now on you've got to live in a new world and face a few realities for a change. Buck up," he said, "it won't kill you."

She was breathing fast.

"Let's wait on the bus," he said.

"Home," she said thickly.

"I hate to see you behave like this," he said. "Just like a child. I should be able to expect more of you." He decided to stop where he was and make her stop and wait for a bus. "I'm not going any farther," he said stopping. "We're going on the bus."

She continued to go on as if she had not heard him. He took a few steps and caught her arm and stopped her. He looked into her face and caught his breath. He was looking into a face he had never seen before. "Tell Grandpa to come get me," she said.

He stared, stricken.

"Tell Caroline to come get me," she said.

Stunned, he let her go and she lurched forward again, walking as if one leg were shorter than the other. A tide of darkness seemed to be sweeping her from him. "Mother!" he cried. "Darling, sweetheart, wait!" Crumpling, she fell to the pavement. He dashed forward and fell at her side, crying, "Mamma, Mamma!" He turned her over. Her face was fiercely distorted. One eye, large and staring, moved slightly to the left as if it had become unmoored. The other remained fixed on him, raked his face again, found nothing and closed.

"Wait here, wait here!" he cried and jumped up and began to run for help toward a cluster of lights he saw in the distance ahead of him. "Help, help!" he shouted, but his voice was thin, scarcely a thread of sound. The lights drifted farther away the faster he ran and his feet moved numbly as if they carried him nowhere. The tide of darkness seemed to sweep him back to her, postponing from moment to moment his entry into the world of guilt and sorrow.

1965

FLANNERY O'CONNOR

Passages from Essays and Letters

from "The Fiction Writer and His Country"

. . . when I look at stories I have written I find that they are, for the most part, about people who are poor, who are afflicted in both mind and body, who have little—or at best a distorted—sense of spiritual purpose, and whose actions do not apparently give the reader a great assurance of the joy of life.

Yet how is this? For I am no disbeliever in spiritual purpose and no vague believer. I see from the standpoint of Christian orthodoxy. This means that for me the meaning of life is centered in our Redemption by Christ and what I see in the world I see in its relation to that.

Some may blame preoccupation with the grotesque on the fact that here we have a Southern writer and that this is just the type of imagination that Southern life fosters. . . . I find it hard to believe that what is observable behavior in one section can be entirely without parallel in another. At least, of late, Southern writers have had the opportunity of pointing out that none of us invented Elvis Presley and that that youth is himself probably less an occasion for concern than his popularity, which is not restricted to the Southern part of the country.

When you can assume that your audience holds the same beliefs you do, you can relax a little and use more normal means of talking to it; when you have to assume that it does not, then you have to make your vision apparent by shock—to the hard of hearing you shout, and for the almost-blind you draw large and startling figures.

from "The Grotesque in Southern Fiction"

All novelists are fundamentally seekers and describers of the real, but the realism of each novelist will depend on his view of the ultimate reaches of reality. . . . If the novelist is in tune with this [modern scientific] spirit, if he believes that actions are predetermined by psychic make-up or the economic situation or some other determinable factor, then he will be concerned above all with an accurate reproduction of the things that most immediately concern man, with the natural forces that he feels control his destiny. . . .

On the other hand, if the writer believes that our life is and will remain essentially mysterious, . . . then what he sees on the surface will be of interest to him only as he can go through it into an experience of mystery itself. . . . [F]or this kind of writer, the meaning of a story does not begin except at a depth where adequate motivation and adequate psychology and the various determinations have been exhausted. Such a writer will be interested in what we don't understand rather than in what we do.

from "The Nature and Aim of Fiction"[1]

. . . The beginning of human knowledge is through the senses, and the fiction writer begins where human perception begins. He appeals through the senses, and you cannot appeal to the senses with abstractions. . . . [F]iction is so very much an incarnational art.

Now the word *symbol* scares a good many people off, just as the word *art* does. They seem to feel that a symbol is some mysterious thing put in arbitrarily by the writer to frighten the common reader—sort of a literary Masonic grip that is only for the initiated. They seem to think that it is a way of saying something that you aren't actually saying, and so . . . they approach it as if it were a problem in algebra. Find *x*. And when they do find or think they find this abstraction, *x*, then they go off with an elaborate sense of satisfaction and the notion that they have "understood" the story. . . .

I think for the fiction writer himself, symbols are something he uses simply as a matter of course. You might say that these are details that, while having their essential place in the literal level of the story, operate in depth as well as on the surface, increasing the story in every direction.

People have a habit of saying, "What is the theme of your story?" and they expect you to give them a statement. . . . And when they've got a statement . . . , they go off happy and feel it is no longer necessary to read the story. . . . , but for the fiction writer himself the whole story is the meaning, because it is an experience, not an abstraction.

1. These selections and those that follow (from "Writing Short Stories") are composites, edited from O'Connor manuscripts by Sally and Robert Fitzgerald in *Mystery and Manners.*

from "Writing Short Stories"

. . . A story is a complete dramatic action—and in good stories, the characters are shown through the action and the action is controlled through the characters, and the result of this is meaning that derives from the whole presented experience.

. . . Nothing essential to the main experience can be left out of a short story. All the action has to be satisfactorily accounted for in terms of motivation, and there has to be a beginning, a middle, and an end, though not necessarily in that order.

. . . I prefer to talk about the meaning in a story rather than the theme of a story. People talk about the theme of a story as if the theme were like the string that a sack of chicken feed is tied with. They think that if you can pick out the theme, the way you pick the right thread in the chicken-feed sack, you can rip the story open and feed the chickens. But this is not the way meaning works in fiction.

When you can state the theme of a story, when you can separate it from the story itself, then you can be sure the story is not a very good one. The meaning of a story has to be embodied in it, has to be made concrete in it. A story is a way to say something that can't be said any other way, and it takes every word in the story to say what the meaning is. You tell a story because a statement would be inadequate.

An idiom characterizes a society, and when you ignore the idiom, you are very likely ignoring the whole social fabric that could make a meaningful character. You can't cut characters off from their society and say much about them as individuals. You can't say anything meaningful about the mystery of a personality unless you put that personality in a believable and significant social context.

from "On Her Own Work"

In most English classes the short story has become a kind of literary specimen to be dissected. Every time a story of mine appears in a Freshman anthology, I have a vision of it, with its little organs laid open, like a frog in a bottle.

I realize that a certain amount of this what-is-the-significance has to go on, but I think something has gone wrong in the process when, for so many students, the story becomes simply a problem to be solved, something which you evaporate to get Instant Enlightenment.

A story isn't any good unless it successfully resists paraphrase, unless it hangs on and expands in the mind. Properly, you analyze to enjoy, but it's equally true that to analyze with any discrimination, you have to have enjoyed already, and I think that the best reason to hear a story read is that it should stimulate that primary enjoyment.

I often ask myself what makes a story work, and what makes it hold up as a story, and I have decided that it is probably some action, some gesture of a character that is unlike any other in the story, one which indicates where the real heart of the story lies. This would have to be an action or a gesture which was both totally right and totally unexpected; it would have to be one that was both in character and beyond character; it would have to suggest both the world and eternity. The action or gesture I'm talking about would have to be on the anagogical level, that is, the level which has to do with the Divine life and our participation in it. It would be a gesture that transcended any neat allegory that might have been intended or any pat moral categories a reader could make. It would be a gesture which somehow made contact with mystery.

   ... in my own stories I have found that violence is strangely capable of returning my characters to reality and preparing them to accept their moment of grace ...

We hear many complaints about the prevalence of violence in modern fiction, and it is always assumed that this violence is a bad thing and meant to be an end in itself. With the serious writer, violence is never an end in itself. It is the extreme situation that best reveals what we are essentially ...

from "Novelist and Believer"

   ... Great fiction ... is not simply an imitation of feeling. The good novelist not only finds a symbol for feeling, he finds a symbol and a way of lodging it which tells the intelligent reader whether this feeling is adequate or inadequate, whether it is moral or immoral, whether it is good or evil. And his theology, even in its most remote reaches, will have a direct bearing on this.

   ... The artist penetrates the concrete world in order to find at its depths the image of its source, the image of ultimate reality. This in no way hinders his perception of evil but rather sharpens it, for only when the natural world is seen as good does evil become intelligible as a destructive force and a necessary result of our freedom.

from the Letters

TO A PROFESSOR OF ENGLISH, 28 MARCH 1961

The meaning of a story should go on expanding for the reader the more he thinks about it, but meaning cannot be captured in an interpretation. If teachers are in the habit of approaching a story as if it were a research problem for which any answer is believable so long as it is not obvious, then I think students will never learn to enjoy fiction. Too much interpretation is certainly worse than too little, and where feeling for a story is absent, theory will not supply it.

TO LOUISE AND TOM GOSSETT, 10 APRIL 1961

I have just read a review of my book [*The Violent Bear It Away*], long and damming [*sic*], which says it don't give us hope and courage and that all novels should give us hope and courage. I think if the novel is to give us virtue the selection of hope and courage is rather arbitrary—why not charity, peace, patience, joy, benignity, long-suffering and fear of the Lord? Or faith? The fact of the matter is that the modern mind opposes courage to faith. It also demands that the novel provide us with gifts that only religion can give. I don't think the novel can offend against the truth, but I think its truths are more particular than general. But this is a large subject and I ain't no aesthetician.

TO ROSLYN BARNES, 17 JUNE 1961

Can you tell me if the statement: "everything that rises must converge" is a true proposition in physics? I can easily see its moral, historical and evolutionary significance, but I want to know if it is also a correct physical statement.

TO "A", 22 JULY 1961

I had a story that I had written a first draft sort of on and Caroline thought as usual that it wasn't dramatic enough (and she was right) and told me all the things that I tell you when I read one of yours. She did think the structure was good and the situation. All I got to do is write the story. This one is called "The Lame Shall Enter First."

TO "A", 16 SEPTEMBER 1961

The thing I am writing now is surely going to convince Jack [the author John Hawkes] that I am of the Devil's party. It is out of hand right now but I am hoping I can bring it into line. It is a composite of all the eccentricities of my writing and for this reason may not be any good, maybe almost a parody. But what you start, you ought to carry through and if it is no good, I don't have to publish it. I am thinking of changing the title to "The Lame Will Carry Off the Prey."

TO JOHN HAWKES, 28 NOVEMBER 1961

You haven't convinced me that I write with the Devil's will or belong in the romantic tradition and I'm prepared to argue some more with you on this if I can remember where we left off at. I think the reason we can't agree on this is because there is a difference in our two devils. My Devil has a name, a history and a definite plan. His name is Lucifer, he's a fallen angel, his sin is pride, and his aim is the destruction of the Divine plan. Now I judge that your Devil is co-equal to God, not his creature: that pride is his virtue not his sin; and that his aim is not to destroy the Divine plan because there isn't any Divine plan to destroy. My Devil is objective and yours is subjective. You say one becomes "evil" when one leaves the herd. I say that depends entirely on what the herd is doing.

TO "A", 9 DECEMBER 1961

Some friends of mine in Texas wrote me that a friend of theirs went into a bookstore looking for a paperback copy of A *Good Man*. The clerk said, "We don't have that one but we have another by that author, called *The Bear That Ran Away With It.* I foresee the trouble I am going to have with "Everything That Rises Must Converge" — "Every Rabbit That Rises Is a Sage."

TO CECIL DAWKINS, 6 SEPTEMBER 1962

About the story ["The Lame Shall Enter First"] I certainly agree that it don't work and have never felt that it did, but in heaven's name where do you get the idea that Sheppard represents Freud? Freud never entered my mind and looking back over it, I can't make him fit now. The story is about a man who thought he was good and thought he was doing good when he wasn't. Freud was a great one, wasn't he, for bringing home to people the fact that they weren't what they thought they were, so if Freud were in this, which he is not, he would certainly be on the other side of the fence from Shepp. The story doesn't work because I don't know, don't sympathize, don't like Mr. Sheppard in the way that I know and like most of my other characters. This is a story, not a statement. I think you ought to look for simpler explanations of why things don't work and not mess around with philosophical ideas where they haven't been intended or don't apply. There's nothing in the story that could possibly suggest that Sheppard represents Freud. This is some theory of which you are possessed. I am wondering if this kind of theorizing could be what is interfering with your getting going on some writing. Don't mix up thought-knowledge with felt-knowledge. If Sheppard represents anything here, it is, as he realizes at the end of the story, the empty man who fills up his emptiness with good works.

TO "A", 3 NOVEMBER 1962

. . . In that story of mine ["The Lame Shall Enter First"] . . . the little boy wouldn't have been looking for his mother if she hadn't been a good one when she was alive. This of course could be debated, but it's nowhere suggested in the story that she wasn't a good one.

TO MARION MONTGOMERY, 16 JUNE 1963

I never wrote and thanked you for innerducing me at Georgia or for the copy of *The Sermon of Introduction*, but I liked them. They made up for my present lack of popularity with the *Atlanta Journal-Constitution* book page, that alert sheet of Sunday criticism. Did you ever see their mention of "Everything That Rises Must Converge"? Unsigned. I suspect somebody from Atlanta U. did it.

TO "A", 1 SEPTEMBER 1963

The topical is poison. I got away with it in "Everything That Rises" but only because I say a plague on everybody's house as far as the race business goes.

▼   ▼   ▼

THE AUTHOR'S WORK AS CONTEXT A Glossary

canon: an author's entire body of work

colloquial diction: level of language or vocabulary that is *informal* in that it is the language of ordinary people but tends to imitate or suggest ordinary spoken rather than written language

diction: choice of words; often generally characterized as *formal, informal,* or *colloquial;* an aspect of *style*

dramatic irony: the unexpected fulfillment or reversal of a character's expectations

formal diction: large, sophisticated, and traditional vocabulary

hyperbole: see *overstatement*

imagery: broadly thought of, the visual descriptions, or even any sensory impressions generated, in a work, but more narrowly and usually, the figurative language, including *metaphors, similes, analogies* (see *Symbols: A Glossary,* p. 210); an aspect of *style*

informal diction: level of language or vocabulary that characterizes the written language of ordinary people

litotes: see *understatement*

overstatement or **hyperbole:** language that is so intense or exaggerated it must be read "at a discount," as meaning less than it literally states

rhetorical tropes: figures of thought or speech; part of *style*

rhythm: the pattern of sound pulsations in the voice as one reads (or as the sound is imagined in the mind); an aspect of *style*

style: the basic characteristics of the language of an author (or an age); while sometimes considered the manner as opposed to the matter, as "ornament," it is now more often seen as organic or fused, with the substance, manner, and matter being as closely related as body and soul; indeed, much recent criticism suggests that there is no "meaning" prior to language, that to think or mean is to think or mean in language itself

tone: the implied attitude or stance of the author toward the characters and events, somewhat like "tone of voice"

understatement or **litotes:** language that obviously underrates something or portrays it as lesser than it is usually thought to be

verbal irony: a word or expression that carries not only its literal meaning but for the speaker has a different, sometimes even an opposite, meaning

QUESTIONS

1. What sensory details do you find in the opening paragraph of "Odour of Chrysanthemums"? later in the story? What expectations are aroused by the opening paragraph? When do you first begin to suspect that Walter Bates is not off drinking somewhere?

2. In what ways might the opening of "The Rocking-Horse Winner" prepare you for the surreal or supernatural events later in the story?

3. If you did not know that "Odour of Chrysanthemums" and "The Rocking-Horse Winner" were by the same author, what internal evidence (elements, views, language within the story) might suggest it? How does "The Rocking-Horse Winner" of 1932 differ from the 1914 story "Odour of Chrysanthemums"?

4. How does Sheppard explain why Norton throws up ("The Lame Shall Enter First," par. 48)? Why do you think Norton throws up (other than his putting peanut butter and ketchup on his cake!)?

5 . What internal evidence is there that "The Lame Shall Enter First" and "Everything That Rises Must Converge" are by the same author?

WRITING SUGGESTIONS

1. Describe the continuity and the change or development in Lawrence's work, assuming those two stories are typical of that work and time of publication.

2. Briefly retell the story of "Everything That Rises Must Converge" from the point of view, perhaps even in the voice, of the African-American woman who is wearing "*the* hat."

3. Compare the function of money in "The Rocking-Horse Winner" and "The Lame Shall Enter First."

9 CULTURE AS CONTEXT: BORDER STORIES

O ver the past two hundred years, the meaning of the word "culture" has changed from "enabling growth" (as in agri*culture*), to the arts or familiarity with the arts ("high culture," "a cultured person"), to a whole way of life ("Japanese culture"). In everyday use it sometimes is associated with "race," though it is usually distinguished from race in that culture is social rather than biological, learned from other members of the group or from experience rather than inherited through the genes (as "race," narrowly defined, is). Its current use is transitional and a sort of stopgap response to modern life: while it was used for a time to designate "primitive" groups (tribes) and their way of life, then applied to present-day national groups, it has been complicated by the worldwide spread of knowledge, experience, and interdependence of both material culture—clothing (jeans), tools, appliances, means of travel (cars and jets), and communication (television, computers, "the information highway")—and cultural ideas, like social and political organization (democracy, for example) or economic organization (such as the market economy), or tastes (like "American" popular music).

Often for the individual, the family, or larger groups, there is or seems to be a clash between the traditional culture of the group that has been passed on for generations or centuries and the practical pressures of survival (culture developed as a means of survival) in the modern world. As a result, we have developed the term "multiculturalism," whose definition and evaluation are intellectual and emotional battlegrounds.

As Americans, we tend to think ours is the only multicultural society and ours the only struggle to define what that means or should mean. We have become more and more conscious of how questionable the term "American culture" is or was, more and more aware that it represents not something clear and "natural," but the power structure of the nation. (This is not just a matter of race and gender: for some time "American" meant Northeastern, Christian [even Protestant], and at least second-generation.) In our new awareness we have taken what we used to consider "subcultures" into account, often with hyphens—African-American, Asian-American, and so on—though, of course, we are all immigrants (even Native Americans apparently came to this continent across the Bering Straits or some earlier bridge from Asia).

Multiculturalism implies rejection of the older idea of assimilation, of America as "melting pot," which meant, in effect, "Reject your group's culture and adopt ours" (that is, the culture of the majority or of those in power). But for some, multiculturalism strongly implies separatism as well, almost an adversarial stance toward other "subcultures," a last-ditch effort to retain the culture of the homeland or place of origin. So there is developing—influenced, interestingly, by forces in Eastern Europe after the breakup of the Soviet Union—what some call "transculturalism," a retention of something of the original, learned culture blended with other cultures and modern experience or "American" culture.

Whatever the outcome, it seems safe to say that our notions of "American" and of "culture" are in flux, even as world culture is in flux. (Notice, for example, that when June May gets to China—in "A Pair of Tickets"—her family takes her to a hotel much like a Hyatt Regency and orders hamburgers, french fries, and apple pie à la mode.) If culture is a means of survival and trans- or multiculturalism is the nature of contemporary culture, for survival's sake we must be aware not only of our own heritage but of that of others and of all our experiences of the here and now.

In this chapter this fluctuating cultural condition is represented by stories of Chicano/a experience, for Chicano culture is demonstrably, if not uniquely, a complex, fluctuating culture. Chicanos are not only Mexican Americans who speak traditional Spanish and recent English; they also combine Native American and Spanish (and thus Catholic) history and experience. But Chicanos live in the United States, most often (but far from always) near the Mexican border. This border position—geographical, linguistic, ethnic, cultural—is both unique, and, paradoxically, typical. We all live on the cultural border.

Rudolfo Anaya's "The Water People" delineates a religious borderline in Chicano culture that parallels the mixed Native American and Spanish "blood" or heritage, a border that runs between ancient native religions rooted in the natural world—a religion "moderns" may think of as legend or magic—and the Catholicism brought to the New World by the Spanish, now long a part of Chicano experience. These seemingly opposing visions of the world are variously negotiated but seldom ignored in Chicano culture. Here Ultima—a "good witch," who practices magic and herbal curing but goes to the Catholic church—suggests to Tony in a dream that these religious traditions, like Tony's divided blood or heritage, are part of one "great cycle that binds us all."

Juan Sánchez, in Richard Dokey's story, moves from Mexico to Mexicali and then almost four hundred miles north of the border to Twin Pines in the

Sierra Nevada mountains east of Stockton, seeking cooler, healthier air. His son, Jésus—born "miraculously" after the deaths of two earlier children and Juan's tubes having been tied—now grown, has a job in the Stockton cannery and brags to his father about the cannery's "greatness" and its "marvelous machines." His values are clearly not those of his father. He is proud of his room, though his father sees only its soiled bed and walls, the bare light bulb, the smell; proud of his "entertainment," a shabby pool hall and a movie house that leaves his father "beyond disappointment." A geographical, generational, and cultural border has been crossed, and Juan longs for Mexico, the home he had left with such hopes.

In "The Last of the Menu Girls" there are geographical and cultural borders as well, largely implicitly but explicitly in the Juan María section where the issue of illegal immigration is raised. Despite the specific location, the names, and the occasional Spanish phrases, this trenchant yet engaging story of "How I Spent My Summer Vacation" could have been set in any pocket of American culture, because the vibrant Chicano culture, though unique, is in its fluctuation and complexity typical of most modern American cultures.

▼ ▼ ▼

RUDOLFO ANAYA

The Water People

"Hey Toni-eeeeee. Hulooooo Antonioforous!"

A voice called.

At first I thought I was dreaming. I was fishing, and sitting on a rock; the sun beating on my back had made me sleepy. I had been thinking how Ultima's medicine had cured my uncle and how he was well and could work again. I had been thinking how the medicine of the doctors and of the priest had failed. In my mind I could not understand how the power of God could fail. But it had.

"Toni-eeeeee!" the voice called again.

I opened my eyes and peered into the green brush of the river. Silently, like a deer, the figure of Cico emerged. He was barefoot, he made no noise. He moved to the rock and squatted in front of me. I guess it was then that he decided to trust me with the secret of the golden carp.

"Cico?" I said. He nodded his dark, freckled face.

"Samuel told you about the golden carp," he said.

"Yes," I replied.

"Have you ever fished for carp?" he asked. "Here in the river, or anywhere?"

"No," I shook my head. I felt as if I was making a solemn oath.

"Do you want to see the golden carp?" he whispered.

"I have hoped to see him all summer," I said breathlessly.

"Do you believe the golden carp is a god?" he asked.

The commandment of the Lord said, Thou shalt have no other gods before me . . .

I could not lie. I knew he would find the lie in my eyes if I did. But maybe there were other gods? Why had the power of God failed to cure my uncle?

"I am a Catholic," I stuttered, "I can believe only in the God of the church—" I looked down. I was sorry because now he would not take me to see the golden carp. For a long time Cico did not speak.

"At least you are truthful, Tony," he said. He stood up. The quiet waters of the river washed gently southward. "We have never taken a non-believer to see him," he said solemnly.

"But I want to believe," I looked up and pleaded, "it's just that I have to believe in Him." I pointed across the river to where the cross of the church showed above the tree tops.

"Perhaps—" he mused for a long time. "Will you make an oath?" he asked.

"Yes," I answered. But the commandment said, Thou shalt not take the Lord's name in vain.

"Swear by the cross of the church that you will never hunt or kill a carp." He pointed to the cross. I had never sworn on the cross before. I knew that if you broke your oath it was the biggest sin a man could commit, because God was witness to the swearing on his name. But I would keep my promise! I would never break my oath!

"I swear," I said.

"Come!" Cico was off, wading across the river. I followed. I had waded across that river many times, but I never felt an urgency like today. I was excited about seeing the magical golden carp.

"The golden carp will be swimming down the creek today," Cico whispered. We scrambled up the bank and through the thick brush. We climbed the steep hill to the town and headed towards the school. I never came up this street to go to school and so the houses were not familiar to me. We paused at one place.

"Do you know who lives there?" Cico pointed at a green arbor. There was a fence with green vines on it, and many trees. Every house in town had trees, but I had never seen a place so green. It was thick like some of the jungles I saw in the movies in town.

"No," I said. We drew closer and peered through the dense curtain of green that surrounded a small adobe hut.

"Narciso," Cico whispered.

Narciso had been on the bridge the night Lupito was murdered. He had tried to reason with the men; he had tried to save Lupito's life. He had been called a drunk.

"My father and my mother know him," I said. I could not take my eyes from the garden that surrounded the small house. Every kind of fruit and vegetable I knew seemed to grow in the garden, and there was even more abundance here than on my uncles' farms.

30   "I know," Cico said, "they are from the llano[1]—"

"I have never seen such a place," I whispered. Even the air of the garden was sweet to smell.

"The garden of Narciso," Cico said with reverence, "is envied by all—Would you like to taste its fruits?"

"We can't," I said. It was a sin to take anything without permission.

"Narciso is my friend," Cico said. He reached through the green wall and a secret latch opened an ivy-laden door. We walked into the garden. Cico closed the door behind him and said, "Narciso is in jail. The sheriff found him drunk."

35   I was fascinated by the garden. I forgot about seeing the golden carp. The air was cool and clear, not dusty and hot like the street. Somewhere I heard the sound of gurgling water.

"Somewhere here there is a spring," Cico said, "I don't know where. That is what makes the garden so green. That and the magic of Narciso—"

I was bewildered by the garden. Everywhere I looked there were fruit-laden trees and rows and rows of vegetables. I knew the earth was fruitful because I had seen my uncles make it bear in abundance; but I never realized it could be like this! The ground was soft to walk on. The fragrance of sun-dazzling flowers was deep, and soft, and beautiful.

"The garden of Narciso," I whispered.

"Narciso is my friend," Cico intoned. He pulled some carrots from the soft, dark earth and we sat down to eat.

40   "I cannot," I said. It was silent and peaceful in the garden. I felt that someone was watching us.

"It is all right," Cico said.

And although I did not feel good about it, I ate the golden carrot. I had never eaten anything sweeter or juicier in my life.

"Why does Narciso drink?" I asked.

"To forget," Cico answered.

45   "Does he know about the golden carp?" I asked.

"The magic people all know about the coming day of the golden carp," Cico answered. His bright eyes twinkled. "Do you know how Narciso plants?" he asked.

"No," I answered. I had always thought farmers were sober men. I could not imagine a drunk man planting and reaping such fruits!

"By the light of the moon," Cico whispered.

"Like my uncles, the Lunas—"

50   "In the spring Narciso gets drunk," Cico continued. "He stays drunk until the bad blood of spring is washed away. Then the moon of planting comes over the elm trees and shines on the horde of last year's seeds—It is then that he gathers the seeds and plants. He dances as he plants, and he sings. He scatters the seeds by moonlight, and they fall and grow—The garden is like Narciso, it is drunk."

---

1. Plains. The Llano Estacado (or enclosed plain) stretches from Roswell, southeast New Mexico, to Lubbock, west Texas.

"My father knows Narciso," I said. The story Cico had told me was fascinating. It seemed that the more I knew about people the more I knew about the strange magic hidden in their hearts.

"In this town, everybody knows everybody," Cico said.

"Do you know everyone?" I asked.

"Uh-huh," he nodded.

"You know Jasón's Indian?" 55

"Yes."

"Do you know Ultima?" I asked.

"I know about her cure," he said. "It was good. Come on now, let's be on our way. The golden carp will be swimming soon—"

We slipped out of the coolness of the garden into the hot, dusty street. On the east side of the school building was a barren playground with a basketball goal. The gang was playing basketball in the hot sun.

"Does the gang know about the golden carp?" I asked as we approached the 60 group.

"Only Samuel," Cico said, "only Samuel can be trusted."

"Why do you trust me?" I asked. He paused and looked at me.

"Because you are a fisherman," he said. "There are no rules on who we trust, Tony, there is just a feeling. The Indian told Samuel the story; Narciso told me; now we tell you. I have a feeling someone, maybe Ultima, would have told you. We all share—"

"Hey!" Ernie called, "you guys want to play!" They ran towards us.

"Nah," Cico said. He turned away. He did not face them. 65

"Hi, Tony," they greeted me.

"Hey, you guys headed for Blue Lake? Let's go swimming," Florence suggested.

"It's too hot to play," Horse griped. He was dripping with sweat.

"Hey, Tony, is it true what they say? Is there a bruja at your house?" Ernie asked.

"¡A bruja!" "¡Chingada!" "¡A la veca!"[2] 70

"No," I said simply.

"My father said she cursed someone and three days later that person changed into a frog—"

"Hey! Is that the old lady that goes to church with your family!" Bones shrieked.

"Let's go," Cico said.

"Knock it off, you guys, are we going to play or not!" Red pleaded. Ernie 75 spun the basketball on his finger. He was standing close to me and grinning as the ball spun.

"Hey, Tony, can you make the ball disappear?" He laughed. The others laughed too.

"Hey, Tony, do some magic!" Horse threw a hold around my neck and locked me into his half-nelson.

---

2. Common obscenities. *Bruja:* witch.

"Yeah!" Ernie shouted in my face. I did not know why he hated me.

"Leave him alone, Horse," Red said.

80 "Stay out of it, Red," Ernie shouted, "you're a Protestant. You don't know about the brujas!"

"They turn to owls and fly at night," Abel shouted.

"You have to kill them with a bullet marked with a cross," Lloyd added. "It's the law."

"Do magic," Horse grunted in my ear. His half-nelson was tight now. My stomach felt sick.

"Voodoo!" Ernie spun the ball in my face.

85 "Okay!" I cried. It must have scared Horse because he let loose and jumped back. They were all still, watching me.

The heat and what I had heard made me sick. I bent over, wretched and vomited. The yellow froth and juice of the carrots splattered at their feet.

"Jesuschriss!" "¡Chingada!" "¡Puta!" "¡A la madre!"[3]

"Come on," Cico said. We took advantage of their surprise and ran. We were over the hill, past the last few houses, and at Blue Lake before they recovered from the astonishment I saw in their faces. We stopped to rest and laugh.

"That was great, Tony," Cico gasped, "that really put Ernie in his place—"

90 "Yeah," I nodded. I felt better after vomiting and running. I felt better about taking the carrots, but I did not feel good about what they had said about Ultima.

"Why are they like that?" I asked Cico. We skirted Blue Lake and worked our way through the tall, golden grass to the creek.

"I don't know," Cico answered, "except that people, grown-ups and kids, seem to want to hurt each other—and it's worse when they're in a group."

We walked on in silence. I had never been this far before so the land interested me. I knew that the waters of El Rito flowed from springs in the dark hills. I knew that those hills cradled the mysterious Hidden Lakes, but I had never been there. The creek flowed around the town, crossed beneath the bridge to El Puerto, then turned towards the river. There was a small reservoir there, and where the water emptied into the river the watercress grew thick and green. Ultima and I had visited the place in search of roots and herbs.

The water of El Rito was clear and clean. It was not muddy like the water of the river. We followed the footpath along the creek until we came to a thicket of brush and trees. The trail skirted around the bosque.

95 Cico paused and looked around. He pretended to be removing a splinter from his foot, but he was cautiously scanning the trail and the grass around us. I was sure we were alone; the last people we had seen were the swimmers at the Blue Lake a few miles back. Cico pointed to the path.

"The fishermen follow the trail around the brush," he whispered, "they hit the creek again just below the pond that's hidden in here." He squirmed into the thicket on hands and knees, and I followed. After a while we could stand up again and follow the creek to a place where an old beaver dam made a large pond.

---

3. Common obscenities.

It was a beautiful spot. The pond was dark and clear, and the water trickled and gurgled over the top of the dam. There was plenty of grass along the bank, and on all sides the tall brush and trees rose to shut off the world.

Cico pointed. "The golden carp will come through there." The cool waters of the creek came out of a dark, shadowy grotto of overhanging thicket, then flowed about thirty feet before they entered the large pond. Cico reached into a clump of grass and brought out a long, thin salt cedar branch with a spear at the end. The razor-sharp steel glistened in the sun. The other end of the spear had a nylon cord attached to it for retrieving.

"I fish for the black bass of the pond," Cico said. He took a position on a high clump of grass at the edge of the bank and motioned for me to sit by the bank, but away from him.

"How can you see him?" I asked. The waters of the pool were clear and pure, but dark from their depth and shadows of the surrounding brush. The sun was crystaline white in the clear, blue sky, but still there was the darkness of shadows in this sacred spot.

"The golden carp will scare him up," Cico whispered. "The black bass thinks he can be king of the fish, but all he wants is to eat them. The black bass is a killer. But the real king is the golden carp, Tony. He does not eat his own kind—"

Cico's eyes remained glued on the dark waters. His body was motionless, like a spring awaiting release. We had been whispering since we arrived at the pond, why I didn't know, except that it was just one of those places where one can communicate only in whispers, like church.

We sat for a long time, waiting for the golden carp. It was very pleasant to sit in the warm sunshine and watch the pure waters drift by. The drone of the summer insects and grasshoppers made me sleepy. The lush green of the grass was cool, and beneath the grass was the dark earth, patient, waiting . . .

To the northeast two hawks circled endlessly in the clear sky. There must be something dead on the road to Tucumcari,[4] I thought.

Then the golden carp came. Cico pointed and I turned to where the stream came out of the dark grotto of overhanging tree branches. At first I thought I must be dreaming. I had expected to see a carp the size of a river carp, perhaps a little bigger and slightly orange instead of brown. I rubbed my eyes and watched in astonishment.

"Behold the golden carp, Lord of the waters—" I turned and saw Cico standing, his spear held across his chest as if in acknowledgment of the presence of a ruler.

The huge, beautiful form glided through the blue waters. I could not believe its size. It was bigger than me! And bright orange! The sunlight glistened off his golden scales. He glided down the creek with a couple of small carp following, but they were like minnows compared to him.

"The golden carp," I whispered in awe. I could not have been more entranced if I had seen the Virgin, or God Himself. The golden carp had seen

100

105

4. City in east-central New Mexico.

me. It made a wide sweep, its back making ripples in the dark water. I could have reached out into the water and touched the holy fish!

"He knows you are a friend," Cico whispered.

110 Then the golden carp swam by Cico and disappeared into the darkness of the pond. I felt my body trembling as I saw the bright golden form disappear. I knew I had witnessed a miraculous thing, the appearance of a pagan god, a thing as miraculous as the curing of my uncle Lucas. And I thought, the power of God failed where Ultima's worked; and then a sudden illumination of beauty and understanding flashed through my mind. This is what I had expected God to do at my first holy communion! If God was witness to my beholding of the golden carp then I had sinned! I clasped my hands and was about to pray to the heavens when the waters of the pond exploded.

I turned in time to see Cico hurl his spear at the monstrous black bass that had broken the surface of the waters. The evil mouth of the black bass was open and red. Its eyes were glazed with hate as it hung in the air surrounded by churning water and a million diamond droplets of water. The spear whistled through the air, but the aim was low. The huge tail swished and contemptuously flipped it aside. Then the black form dropped into the foaming waters.

"Missed," Cico groaned. He retrieved his line slowly.

I nodded my head. "I can't believe what I have seen," I heard myself say, "are all the fish that big here—"

"No," Cico smiled, "they catch two and three pounders below the beaver dam, the black bass must weigh close to twenty—" He threw his spear and line behind the clump of grass and came to sit by me. "Come on, let's put our feet in the water. The golden carp will be returning—"

115 "Are you sorry you missed?" I asked as we slid our feet into the cool water.

"No," Cico said, "it's just a game."

The orange of the golden carp appeared at the edge of the pond. As he came out of the darkness of the pond the sun caught his shiny scales and the light reflected orange and yellow and red. He swam very close to our feet. His body was round and smooth in the clear water. We watched in silence at the beauty and grandeur of the great fish. Out of the corners of my eyes I saw Cico hold his hand to his breast as the golden carp glided by. Then with a switch of his powerful tail the golden carp disappeared into the shadowy water under the thicket.

I shook my head. "What will happen to the golden carp?"

"What do you mean?" Cico asked.

120 "There are many men who fish here—"

Cico smiled. "They can't see him, Tony, they can't see him. I know every man from Guadalupe[5] who fishes, and there ain't a one who has ever mentioned seeing the golden carp. So I guess the grown-ups can't see him—"

"The Indian, Narciso, Ultima—"

"They're different, Tony. Like Samuel, and me, and you—"

"I see," I said. I did not know what that difference was, but I did feel a strange

---

5. County in east-central New Mexico, west of Tucumcari.

brotherhood with Cico. We shared a secret that would always bind us.

"Where does the golden carp go?" I asked and nodded upstream.

"He swims upstream to the lakes of the mermaid, the Hidden Lakes—"

"The mermaid?" I questioned him.

"There are two deep, hidden lakes up in the hills," he continued, "they feed the creek. Some people say those lakes have no bottom. There's good fishing, but very few people go there. There's something strange about those lakes, like they are haunted. There's a strange power, it seems to watch you—"

"Like the *presence* of the river?" I asked softly. Cico looked at me and nodded.

"You've felt it," he said.

"Yes."

"Then you understand. But this thing at the lakes is stronger, or maybe not stronger, it just seems to want you more. The time I was there—I climbed to one of the overhanging cliffs, and I just sat there, watching the fish in the clear water—I didn't know about the power then, I was just thinking how good the fishing would be, when I began to hear strange music. It came from far away. It was a low, lonely murmuring, maybe like something a sad girl would sing. I looked around, but I was alone. I looked over the ledge of the cliff and the singing seemed to be coming from the water, and it seemed to be calling me—"

I was spellbound with Cico's whispered story. If I had not seen the golden carp perhaps I would not have believed him. But I had seen too much today to doubt him.

"I swear, Tony, the music was pulling me into the dark waters below! The only thing that saved me from plunging into the lake was the golden carp. He appeared and the music stopped. Only then could I tear myself away from that place. Man, I ran! Oh how I ran! I had never been afraid before, but I was afraid then. And it wasn't that the singing was evil, it was just that it called for me to join it. One more step and I'da stepped over the ledge and drowned in the waters of the lake—"

I waited a long time before I asked the next question. I waited for him to finish reliving his experience. "Did you see the mermaid?"

"No," he answered.

"Who is she?" I whispered.

"No one knows. A deserted woman—or just the wind singing around the edges of those cliffs. No one really knows. It just calls people to it—"

"Who?"

He looked at me carefully. His eyes were clear and bright, like Ultima's, and there were lines of age already showing.

"Last summer the mermaid took a shepherd. He was a man from Méjico, new here and working for a ranch beyond the hills. He had not heard the story about the lakes. He brought his sheep to water there, and he heard the singing. He made it back to town and even swore that he had seen the mermaid. He said it was a woman, resting on the water and singing a lonely song. She was half woman and half fish—He said the song made him want to wade out to the middle of the lake to help her, but his fear had made him run. He told everyone the story, but no one believed him. He ended up getting drunk in town and swearing he would prove his story by going back to the lakes and bringing back the mer-woman. He never returned. A week later the flock was found near the lakes. He had vanished—"

"Do you think the mermaid took him?" I asked.

"I don't know, Tony," Cico said and knit his brow, "there's a lot of things I don't know. But never go to the Hidden Lakes alone, Tony, never. It's not safe."

I nodded that I would honor his warning. "It is so strange," I said, "the things that happen. The things that I have seen, or heard about."

145 "Yes," he agreed.

"These things of the water, the mermaid, the golden carp. They are strange. There is so much water around the town, the river, the creek, the lakes—"

Cico leaned back and stared into the bright sky. "This whole land was once covered by a sea, a long time ago—"

"My name means sea," I pondered aloud.

"Hey, that's right," he said, "Márez means sea, it means you came from the ocean, Tony Márez arisen from the sea—"

150 "My father says our blood is restless, like the sea—"

"That is beautiful," he said. He laughed. "You know, this land belonged to the fish before it belonged to us. I have no doubt about the prophecy of the golden carp. He will come to rule again!"

"What do you mean?" I asked.

"What do I mean?" Cico asked quizzically. "I mean that the golden carp will come to rule again. Didn't Samuel tell you?"

"No," I shook my head.

155 "Well he told you about the people who killed the carp of the river and were punished by being turned into fish themselves. After that happened, many years later, a new people came to live in this valley. And they were no better than the first inhabitants, in fact they were worse. They sinned a lot, they sinned against each other, and they sinned against the legends they knew. And so the golden carp sent them a prophecy. He said that the sins of the people would weigh so heavy upon the land that in the end the whole town would collapse and be swallowed by water—"

I must have whistled in exclamation and sighed.

"Tony," Cico said, "this whole town is sitting over a deep, underground lake! Everybody knows that. Look." He drew on the sand with a stick. "Here's the river. The creek flows up here and curves into the river. The Hidden Lakes complete the other border. See?"

I nodded. The town was surrounded by water. It was frightening to know that! "The whole town!" I whispered in amazement.

"Yup," Cico said, "the whole town. The golden carp has warned us that the land cannot take the weight of the sins—the land will finally sink!"

160 "But you live in town!" I exclaimed.

He smiled and stood up. "The golden carp is my god, Tony. He will rule the new waters. I will be happy to be with my god—"

It was unbelievable, and yet it made a wild kind of sense! All the pieces fitted!

"Do the people of the town know?" I asked anxiously.

"They know," he nodded, "and they keep on sinning."

"But it's not fair to those who don't sin!" I countered.   165

"Tony," Cico said softly, "all men sin."

I had no answer to that. My own mother had said that losing your innocence and becoming a man was learning to sin. I felt weak and powerless in the knowledge of the impending doom.

"When will it happen?" I asked.

"No one knows," Cico answered. "It could be today, tomorrow, a week, a hundred years—but it will happen."

"What can we do?" I asked. I heard my voice tremble.   170

"Sin against no one," Cico answered.

I walked away from that haven which held the pond and the swimming waters of the golden carp feeling a great weight in my heart. I was saddened by what I had learned. I had seen beauty, but the beauty had burdened me with responsibility. Cico wanted to fish at the dam, but I was not in the mood for it. I thanked him for letting me see the golden carp, crossed the river, and trudged up the hill homeward.

I thought about telling everyone in town to stop their sinning, or drown and die. But they would not believe me. How could I preach to the whole town, I was only a boy. They would not listen. They would say I was crazy, or bewitched by Ultima's magic.

I went home and thought about what I had seen and the story Cico told. I went to Ultima and told her the story. She said nothing. She only smiled. It was as if she knew the story and found nothing fantastic or impending in it. "I would have told you the story myself," she nodded wisely, "but it is better that you hear the legend from someone your own age . . ."

"Am I to believe the story?" I asked. I was worried.   175

"Antonio," she said calmly and placed her hand on my shoulder, "I cannot tell you what to believe. Your father and your mother can tell you, because you are their blood, but I cannot. As you grow into manhood you must find your own truths—"

That night in my dreams I walked by the shore of a great lake. A bewitching melody filled the air. It was the song of the mer-woman! I looked into the dark depths of the lake and saw the golden carp, and all around him were the people he had saved. On the bleached shores of the lake the carcasses of sinners rotted.

Then a huge golden moon came down from the heavens and settled on the surface of the calm waters. I looked towards the enchanting light, expecting to see the Virgin of Guadalupe, but in her place I saw my mother!

Mother, I cried, you are saved! We are all saved!

Yes, my Antonio, she smiled, we who were baptized in the water of the moon   180
which was made holy by our Holy Mother the Church are saved.

Lies! my father shouted, Antonio was not baptized in the holy water of the moon, but in the salt water of the sea!

I turned and saw him standing on the corpse-strewn shore. I felt a searing pain spread through my body.

Oh please tell me which is the water that runs through my veins, I moaned; oh please tell me which is the water that washes my burning eyes!

It is the sweet water of the moon, my mother crooned softly, it is the water the Church chooses to make holy and place in its font. It is the water of your baptism.

185 *Lies, lies, my father laughed, through your body runs the salt water of the oceans. It is that water which makes you Márez and not Luna. It is the water that binds you to the pagan god of Cico, the golden carp!*

Oh, I cried, please tell me. The agony of pain was more than I could bear. The excruciating pain broke and I sweated blood.

There was a howling wind as the moon rose and its powers pulled at the still waters of the lake. Thunder split the air and the lightning bursts illuminated the churning, frothy tempest. The ghosts stood and walked upon the shore.

The lake seemed to respond with rage and fury. It cracked with the laughter of madness as it inflicted death upon the people. I thought the end had come to everything. The cosmic struggle of the two forces would destroy everything!

The doom which Cico had predicted was upon us! I clasped my hands and knelt to pray. The terrifying end was near. Then I heard a voice speak above the sound of the storm. I looked up and saw Ultima.

190 *Cease! she cried to the raging powers, and the power from the heavens and the power from the earth obeyed her. The storm abated.*

Stand, Antonio, she commanded, and I stood. You both know, she spoke to my father and my mother, that the sweet water of the moon which falls as rain is the same water that gathers into rivers and flows to fill the seas. Without the waters of the moon to replenish the oceans there would be no oceans. And the same salt waters of the oceans are drawn by the sun to the heavens, and in turn become again the waters of the moon. Without the sun there would be no waters formed to slake the dark earth's thirst.

The waters are one, Antonio. I looked into her bright, clear eyes and understood her truth.

You have been seeing only parts, she finished, and not looking beyond into the great cycle that binds us all.

Then there was peace in my dreams and I could rest.

1972

RICHARD DOKEY

Sánchez

That summer the son of Juan Sánchez went to work for the Flotill Cannery in Stockton. Juan drove with him to the valley in the old Ford.

While they drove, the boy, whose name was Jesús, told him of the greatness of the cannery, of the great aluminum buildings, the marvelous machines, and the belts of cans that never stopped running. He told him of the building on one side of the road where the cans were made and how the cans ran in a metal tube across the road to the cannery. He described the food machines, the sanitary precautions. He laughed when he spoke of the labeling. His voice was serious about the money.

When they got to Stockton, Jesús directed him to the central district of town, the skid row where the boy was to live while he worked for the Flotill. It was a cheap hotel on Center Street. The room smelled. There was a table with one chair. The floor was stained like the floor of a public urinal and the bed was soiled, as were the walls. There were no drapes on the windows. A pall spread out from the single light bulb overhead that was worked with a length of grimy string.

"I will not stay much in the room," Jesús said, seeing his father's face. "It is only for sleep. I will be working overtime, too. There is also the entertainment."

Jesús led him from the room and they went out into the street. Next to the hotel there was a vacant lot where a building had stood. The hole which was left had that recent, peculiar look of uprootedness. There were the remains of the foundation, the broken flooring, and the cracked bricks of tired red to which the gray blotches of mortar clung like dried phlegm. But the ground had not yet taken on the opaqueness of wear that the air and sun give it. It gleamed dully in the light and held to itself where it had been torn, as earth does behind a plow. Juan studied the hole for a time; then they walked up Center Street to Main, passing other empty lots, and then moved east toward Hunter Street. At the corner of Hunter and Main a wrecking crew was at work. An iron ball was suspended from the end of a cable and a tall machine swung the ball up and back and then whipped it forward against the building. The ball was very thick-looking, and when it struck the wall the building trembled, spurted dust, and seemed to cringe inward. The vertical lines of the building had gone awry. Juan shook each time the iron struck the wall.

"They are tearing down the old buildings," Jesús explained. "Redevelopment," he pronounced. "Even my building is to go someday."

Juan looked at his son. "And what of the men?" he asked. "Where do the men go when there are no buildings?"

Jesús, who was a head taller than his father, looked down at him and then shrugged in that Mexican way, the head descending and cocking while the shoulders rise as though on puppet strings. "¿Quien sabe?"[1]

"And the large building there?" Juan said, looking across the rows of parked cars in Hunter Square. "The one whose roof rubs the sky. Of what significance?"

"That is the new courthouse," Jesús said.

"There are no curtains on the windows."

"They do not put curtains on such windows," Jesús explained.

"No," sighed Juan, "that is true."

They walked north on Hunter past the new Bank of America and entered an

5

10

---

1. "Who knows?"

old building. They stood to one side of the entrance. Jesús smiled proudly and inhaled the stale air.

15   "This is the entertainment," he said.

Juan looked about. A bar was at his immediate left, and a bald man in a soiled apron stood behind it. Beyond the bar there were many thick-wooded tables covered with green material. Men crouched over them and cone-shaped lights hung low from the ceiling casting broad cones of light downward upon the men and tables. Smoke drifted and rolled in the light and pursued the men when they moved quickly. There was the breaking noise of balls striking together, the hard wooden rattle of the cues in the racks upon the wall, the humming slither of the scoring disks along the loose wires overhead, the explosive cursing of the men. The room was warm and dirty. Juan shook his head.

"I have become proficient at the game," Jesús said.

"This is the entertainment," Juan said, still moving his head.

Jesús turned and walked outside. Juan followed. The boy pointed across the parked cars past the courthouse to a marquee on Main Street. "There are also motion pictures," Jesús said.

20   Juan had seen a movie as a young man working in the fields near Fresno. He had understood no English then. He sat with his friends in the leather seats that had gum under the arms and watched the images move upon the white canvas. The images were dressed in expensive clothes. There was laughing and dancing. One of the men did kissing with two very beautiful women, taking turns with each when the other was absent. This had embarrassed Juan, the embracing and unhesitating submission of the women with so many unfamiliar people to watch. Juan loved his wife, was very tender and gentle with her before she died. He never went to another motion picture, even after he had learned English, and this kept him from the Spanish films as well.

"We will go to the cannery now," Jesús said, taking his father's arm. "I will show you the machines."

Juan permitted himself to be led away, and they moved back past the bank to where the men were destroying the building. A ragged hole, like a wound, had been opened in the wall. Juan stopped and watched. The iron ball came forward tearing at the hole, enlarging it, exposing the empty interior space that had once been a room. The floor of the room teetered at a precarious angle. The wood was splintered and very dry in the noon light.

"I do not think I will go to the cannery," Juan said.

The boy looked at his father like a child who has made a toy out of string and bottle caps only to have it ignored.

25   "But it is honorable work," Jesús said, suspecting his father. "And it pays well."

"Honor," Juan said. "Honor is a serious matter. It is not a question of honor. You are a man now. All that is needed is a room and a job at the Flotill. Your father is tired, that is all."

"You are disappointed," Jesús said, hanging his head.

"No," Juan said. "I am beyond disappointment. You are my son. Now you have a place in the world. You have the Flotill."

Nothing more was said, and they walked to the car. Juan got in behind the wheel. Jesús stood beside the door, his arms at his sides, the fingers spread. Juan looked up at him. The boy's eyes were big.

"You are my son," Juan said, "and I love you. Do not have disappointment.   30 I am not of the Flotill. Seeing the machines would make it worse. You understand, *niño?*"[2]

"*Sí*, Papa," Jesús said. He put a hand on his father's shoulder.

"It is a strange world, *niñito*," Juan said.

"I will earn money. I will buy a red car and visit you. All in Twin Pines will be envious of the son of Sánchez, and they will say that Juan Sánchez has a son of purpose."

"Of course, Jesús *mío*," Juan said. He bent and placed his lips against the boy's hand. "I will look for the bright car. I will write regardless." He smiled, showing yellowed teeth. "Goodbye, *querido*," he said. He started the car, raced the engine once too high, and drove off up the street.

When Juan Sánchez returned to Twin Pines, he drove the old Ford to the   35 top of Bear Mountain and pushed it over. He then proceeded systematically to burn all that was of importance to him, all that was of nostalgic value, and all else that meant nothing in itself, like the extra chest of drawers he had kept after his wife's death, the small table in the bedroom, and the faded mahogany stand in which he kept his pipe and tobacco and which sat next to the stuffed chair in the front room. He broke all the dishes, cups, plates, discarded all the cooking and eating utensils in the same way. The fire rose in the blue wind carrying dust wafers of ash in quick, breathless spirals and then released them in a panoply of diluted smoke, from which they drifted and spun and fell like burnt snow. The forks, knives, and spoons became very black with a flaky crust of oxidized metal. Then Juan burned his clothing, all that was unnecessary, and the smoke dampened and took on a thick smell. Finally he threw his wife's rosary into the flames. It was a cheap one, made of wood, and disappeared immediately. He went into his room then and lay down on the bed. He went to sleep.

When he woke, it was dark and cool. He stepped outside, urinated, and then returned, shutting the door. The darkness was like a mammoth held breath, and he felt very awake listening to the beating of his heart. He would not be able to sleep now, and so he lay awake thinking.

He thought of his village in Mexico, the baked white clay of the small houses spread like little forts against the stillness of the bare mountains, the men with their great wide hats, their wide, white pants, and their naked, brown-skinned feet, splayed against the fine dust of the road. He saw the village cistern and the women all so big and slow, always with child, enervated by the earth and the unbearable sun, the enervation passing into their very wombs like the acceptance, slow, silent blood. The men walked bent as though carrying the air or sky, slept against the buildings in the shade like old dogs, ate dry, hot food that dried them inside and seemed to bake the moisture from the flesh, so that the men and women while still young had faces like eroded fields and fingers like

2. Son. *Niñito*: dear son. *Querido*: dear one.

stringy, empty stream beds. It was a hard land. It took the life of his father and mother before he was twelve and the life of his aunt, with whom he then lived, before he was sixteen.

When he was seventeen he went to Mexicali because he had heard much of America and the money to be obtained there. They took him in a truck with other men to work in the fields around Bakersfield, then in the fields near Fresno. On his return to Mexicali he met La Belleza, as he came to call her: loveliness. He married her when he was nineteen and she only fifteen. The following year she had a baby girl. It was stillborn and the birth almost killed her, for the doctor said the passage was oversmall. The doctor cautioned him (warned him, really) La Belleza could not have children and live, and he went outside into the moonlight and wept.

He had heard much of the liveliness of the Sierra Nevada above what was called the Mother Lode, and because he feared the land, believed almost that it possessed the power to kill him—as it had killed his mother and father, his aunt, was, in fact, slow killing so many of his people—he wanted to run away from it to the high white cold of the California mountains, where he believed his heart would grow, his blood run and, perhaps, the passage of La Belleza might open. Two years later he was taken in the trucks to Stockton in the San Joaquin Valley to pick tomatoes, and he saw the Sierra Nevada above the Mother Lode.

40

It was from a distance, of course, and in the summer, so that there was no snow. But when he returned he told La Belleza about the blueness of the mountains in the warm, still dawn, the extension of them, the aristocracy of their unmoving height, and that they were only fifty miles away from where he had stood.

He worked very hard now and saved his money. He took La Belleza back to his village, where he owned the white clay house of his father. It was cheaper to live there while he waited, fearing the sun, the dust, and the dry, airless silence, for the money to accumulate. That fall La Belleza became pregnant again by an accident of passion and the pregnancy was very difficult. In the fifth month the doctor—who was an atheist—said that the baby would have to be taken or else the mother would die. The village priest, a very loud, dramatic man—an educated man who took pleasure in striking a pose—proclaimed the wrath of God in the face of such sacrilege. It was the child who must live, the priest cried. The pregnancy must go on. There was the immortal soul of the child to consider. But Juan decided for the atheist doctor, who did take the child. La Belleza lost much blood. At one point her heart had stopped beating. When the child was torn from its mother and Juan saw that it was a boy, he ran out of the clay house of his father and up the dusty road straight into a hideous red moon. He cursed the earth, the sky. He cursed his village, himself, the soulless indifference of the burnt mountains. He cursed God.

Juan was very afraid now, and though it cost more money, he had himself tied by the atheist doctor so that he could never again put the life of La Belleza in danger, for the next time, he knew with certainty, would kill her.

The following summer he went again on the trucks to the San Joaquin Valley. The mountains were still there, high and blue in the quiet dawn, turned to a milky pastel by the heat swirls and haze of midday. Sometimes at night he stepped outside the shacks in which the men were housed and faced the darkness. It was tragic to be so close to what you wanted, he would think, and be unable to possess it. So strong was the feeling in him, particularly during the hot, windless evenings, that he sometimes went with the other men into Stockton, where he stood on the street corners of skid row and talked, though he did not get drunk on cheap wine or go to the whores, as did the other men. Nor did he fight.

They rode in old tilted trucks covered with canvas and sat on rude benches staring out over the slats of the tail gate. The white glare of headlights crawled up and lay upon them, waiting to pass. They stared over the whiteness. When the lights swept out and by, the glass of the side windows shone. Behind the windows sometimes there would be the ghost flash of an upturned face, before the darkness clamped shut. Also, if one of the men had a relative who lived in the area, there was the opportunity to ride in a car.

He had done so once. He had watched the headlights of the car pale, then whiten the back of one of the trucks. He saw the faces of the men turned outward and the looks on the faces that seemed to float upon the whiteness of the light. The men sat forward, arms on knees, and looked over the glare into the darkness. After that he always rode in the trucks.

When he returned to his village after that season's harvest, he knew they could wait no longer. He purchased a dress of silk for La Belleza and in a secondhand store bought an American suit for himself. He had worked hard, sold his father's house, saved all his money, and on a bright day in early September they crossed the border at Mexicali and caught the Greyhound for Fresno.

Juan got up from his bed to go outside. He stood looking up at the stars. The stars were pinned to the darkness, uttering little flickering cries of light, and as always he was moved by the nearness and profusion of their agony. His mother had told him the stars were a kind of purgatory in which souls burned in cold, silent repentance. He had wondered after her death if the earth too were not a star burning in loneliness, and he could never look at them later without thinking this and believing that the earth must be the brightest of all stars. He walked over to the remains of the fire. A dull heat came from the ashes and a column of limp smoke rose and then bent against the night wind. He studied the ashes for a time and then looked over the tall pine shapes to the southern sky. It was there all right. He could feel the dry char of its heat, that deeper, dryer burning. He imagined it, of course. But it was there nevertheless. He went back into the cabin and lay down, but now his thoughts were only of La Belleza and the beautiful Sierra Nevada.

From Fresno all the way up the long valley to Stockton they had been full with pride and expectation. They had purchased oranges and chocolate bars and they ate them laughing. The other people on the bus looked at them, shook their heads, and slept or read magazines. He and La Belleza gazed out the window at the land.

In Stockton they were helped by a man named Eugenio Mendez. Juan had met him while picking tomatoes in the delta. Eugenio had eight children and a

45

very fat but very kind and tolerant wife named Anilla. He had helped them find a cheap room off Center Street, where they stayed while determining their next course of action. Eugenio had access to a car, and it was he who drove them finally to the mountains.

It was a day like no other day in his life: to be sitting in the car with La Belleza, to be in this moving car with his Belleza heading straight toward the high, lovely mountains. The car traveled from the flatness of the valley into the rolling brown swells of the foothills, where hundreds of deciduous and evergreen oaks grew, their puffball shapes like still pictures of exploding holiday rockets, only green, but spreading up and out and then around and down in nearly perfect canopies. At Jackson the road turned and began an immediate, constant climb upward.

It was as though his dream about it had materialized. He had never seen so many trees, great with dignity: pines that had gray bark twisted and stringy like hemp; others whose bark resembled dry, flat ginger cookies fastened with black glue about a drum, and others whose bark pulled easily away; and those called redwoods, standing stiff and tall, amber-hued with straight rolls of bark as thick as his fist, flinging out high above great arms of green. And the earth, rich red, as though the blood of scores of Indians had just flowed there and dried. Dark patches of shadow stunned with light, blue flowers, orange flowers, birds, even deer. They saw them all on that first day.

"¿A dónde vamos?" Eugenio had asked. "Where are we going?"

"Bellísima," Juan replied. "Into much loveliness."

They did not reach Twin Pines that day. But on their return a week later they inquired in Jackson about the opportunity of buying land or a house in the mountains. The man, though surprised, told them of the sawmill town of Twin Pines, where there were houses for sale.

Their continued luck on that day precipitated the feeling in Juan that it was indeed the materialization of a dream. He had been able in all those years to save two thousand dollars, and a man had a small shack for sale at the far edge of town. He looked carefully at Juan, at La Belleza and Eugenio and said "One thousand dollars," believing they could never begin to possess such a sum. When Juan handed him the money, the man was so struck that he made out a bill of sale. Juan Sanchez and his wife had their home in the Sierra.

When Juan saw the cabin close up, he knew the man had stolen their money. It was small, the roof slanted to one side, the door would not close evenly. The cabin was gradually falling downhill. But it was theirs and he could, with work, repair it. Hurriedly they drove back to Jackson, rented a truck, bought some cheap furniture and hauled it back to the cabin. When they had moved in, Juan brought forth a bottle of whiskey and for the first time in his life proceeded to get truly drunk.

Juan was very happy with La Belleza. She accepted his philosophy completely, understood his need, made it her own. In spite of the people of the town, they created a peculiar kind of joy. And anyway Juan had knowledge about the people.

Twin Pines had been founded, he learned, by one Benjamin Carter, who lived with his daughter in a magnificent house on the hill overlooking town. This Benjamin Carter was a very wealthy man. He had come to the mountains thirty years before to save his marriage, for he had been poor once and loved when he was poor, but then he grew very rich because of oil discovered on his father's Ohio farm and he went away to the city and became incapable of love in the pursuit of money and power. When he at last married the woman whom he had loved, a barrier had grown between them, for Ben Carter had changed but the woman had not. Then the woman became ill and Ben Carter promised her he would take her West, all the way West away from the city so that it could be as it had been in the beginning of their love. But the woman was with child. And so Ben Carter rushed to the California mountains, bought a thousand acres of land, and hurried to build his house before the rain and snows came. He hired many men and the house was completed, except for the interior work and the furnishings. All that winter men he had hired worked in the snow to finish the house while Ben Carter waited with his wife in the city. When it was early spring they set out for California, Ben Carter, his wife, and the doctor, who strongly advised against the rough train trip and the still rougher climb by horse and wagon from Jackson to the house. But the woman wanted the child born properly, so they went. The baby came the evening of their arrival at the house, and the woman died all night having it. It was this Ben Carter who lived with that daughter now in the great house on the hill, possessing her to the point, it was said about his madness, that he had murdered a young man who had shown interest in her.

Juan learned all this from a Mexican servant who had worked at the great house from the beginning, and when he told the story to La Belleza she wept because of its sadness. It was a tragedy of love, she explained, and Juan—soaring to the heights of his imagination—believed that the town, all one hundred souls, had somehow been infected with the tragedy, as they were touched by the shadow of the house itself, which crept directly up the highway each night when the sun set. This was why they left dead chickens and fish on the porch of the cabin or dumped garbage into the yard. He believed he understood something profound and so did nothing about these incidents, which, after all, might have been the pranks of boys. He did not want the infection to touch him, nor the deeper infection of their prejudice because he was Mexican. He was not indifferent. He was simply too much in love with La Belleza and the Sierra Nevada. Finally the incidents stopped.

Now the life of Juan Sánchez entered its most beautiful time. When the first snows fell he became delirious, running through the pines, shouting, rolling on the ground, catching the flakes in his open mouth, bringing them in his cupped hands to rub in the hair of La Belleza, who stood in the doorway of their cabin laughing at him. He danced, made up a song about snowflakes falling on a desert and then a prayer which he addressed to the Virgin of Snowflakes. That night while the snow fluttered like wings against the bedroom window, he celebrated the coming of the whiteness with La Belleza.

He understood that first year in the mountains that love was an enlargement of himself, that it enabled him to be somehow more than he had ever been

60

before, as though certain pores of his senses had only just been opened. Whereas before he had desired the Sierra Nevada for its beauty and contrast to his harsh fatherland, now he came to acquire a love for it, and he loved it as he loved La Belleza; he loved it as a woman. Also in that year he came to realize that there was a fear or dread about such love. It was more a feeling than anything else, something which reached thought now and then, particularly in those last moments before sleep. It was an absolutely minor thing. The primary knowledge was of the manner in which this love seemed to assimilate everything, rejecting all that would not yield. This love was a kind of blindness.

That summer Juan left La Belleza at times to pick the crops of the San Joaquin Valley. He had become good friends with the servant of the big house and this man had access to the owner's car, which he always drove down the mountain in a reckless but confident manner. After that summer Juan planned also to buy a car, not out of material desire, but simply because he believed this man would one day kill himself, and also because he did not wish to be dependent.

He worked in the walnuts near the town of Linden and again in the tomatoes of the rich delta. He wanted very much to have La Belleza with him, but that would have meant more money and a hotel room in the skid row, and that was impossible because of the pimps and whores, the drunks and criminals and the general despair, which the police always tapped at periodic intervals, as one does a vat of fermenting wine. The skid row was a place his love could not assimilate, but he could not ignore it because so many of his people were lost there. He stayed in the labor camps, which were also bad because of what the men did with themselves, but they were tolerable. He worked hard and as often as he could and gazed at the mountains, which he could always see clearly in the morning light. When tomato season was over he returned to La Belleza.

Though the town would never accept them as equals, it came that summer to tolerate their presence. La Belleza made straw baskets which she sold to the townspeople and which were desired for their beauty and intricacy of design. Juan carved animals, a skill he had acquired from his father, and these were also sold. The activity succeeded so well that Juan took a box of these things to Jackson, where they were readily purchased. The following spring he was able to buy the Ford.

65   Juan acquired another understanding that second year in the mountains. It was, he believed, that love, his love, was the single greatness of which he was capable, the thing which ennobled him and gave him honor. Love, he became convinced, was his only ability, the one success he had accomplished in a world of insignificance. It was a simple thing, after all, made so painfully simple each time he went to the valley to work with his face toward the ground, every time he saw the men in the fields and listened to their talk and watched them drive off to the skid row at night. After he had acquired this knowledge, the nights he had to spend away from La Belleza were occupied by a new kind of loneliness, as though a part of his body had been separated from the whole. He began also to understand something more of the fear or dread that seemed to trail behind love.

It happened late in the sixth year of their marriage. It was impossible, of course, and he spent many hours at the fire in their cabin telling La Belleza of the impossibility, for the doctor had assured him that all had been well tied. He had conducted himself on the basis of that assumption. But doctors can be wrong. Doctors can make mistakes. La Belleza was with child.

For the first five months the pregnancy was not difficult, and he came almost to believe that indeed the passage of La Belleza would open. He prayed to God. He prayed to the earth and sky. He prayed to the soul of his mother. But after the fifth month the true sickness began and he discarded prayer completely in favor of blasphemy. There was no God and never could be God in the face of such sickness, such unbelievable human sickness. Even when he had her removed to the hospital in Stockton, the doctors could not stop it, but it continued so terribly that he believed that La Belleza carried sickness itself in her womb.

After seven months the doctors decided to take the child. They brought La Belleza into a room with lights and instruments. They worked on her for a long time and she died there under the lights with the doctors cursing and perspiring above the large wound of her pain. They did not tell him of the child, which they had cleaned and placed in an incubator, until the next day. That night he sat in the Ford and tried to see it all, but he could only remember the eyes of La Belleza in the vortex of pain. They were of an almost eerie calmness. They had possessed calmness, as one possesses the truth. Toward morning he slumped sideways on the seat and went to sleep.

So he put her body away in the red earth of the town cemetery beyond the cabin. The pines came together overhead and in the heat of midday a shadow sprinkled with spires of light lay upon the ground so that the earth was cool and clean to smell. He did not even think of taking her back to Mexico, since, from the very beginning she had always been part of that dream he had dreamed. Now she would be always in the Sierra Nevada, with the orange and blue flowers, the quiet, deep whiteness of winter, and all that he ever was or could be was with her.

But he did not think these last thoughts then, as he did now. He had simply performed them out of instinct for their necessity, as he had performed the years of labor while waiting for the infant Jesús to grow to manhood. Jesús. Why had he named the boy Jesús? That, perhaps, had been instinct too. He had stayed after La Belleza's death for the boy, to be with him until manhood, to show him the loveliness of the Sierra Nevada, to instruct him toward true manhood. But Jesús. Ah, Jesús. Jesús the American. Jesús of the Flotill. Jesús understood nothing. Jesús, he believed, was forever lost to knowledge. That day with Jesús had been his own liberation.

For a truth had come upon him after the years of waiting, the ultimate truth that he understood only because La Belleza had passed through his life. Love was beauty, La Belleza and the Sierra Nevada, a kind of created or made thing. But there was another kind of love, a very profound, embracing love that he had felt of late blowing across the mountains from the south and that, he knew now, had always been there from the beginning of his life, disguised in the sun and wind. In this love there was blood and earth and, yes, even God, some kind of god, at least the power of a god. This love wanted him for its own. He understood it, that it had permitted him to have La Belleza and that without it there could have been no Belleza.

Juan placed an arm over his eyes and turned to face the wall. The old bed sighed. An image went off in his head and he remembered vividly the lovely body of La Belleza. In that instant the sound that loving had produced with the bed was alive in him like a forgotten melody, and his body seemed to swell and press against the ceiling. It was particularly cruel because it was so sudden, so intense, and came from so deep within him that he knew it must all still be alive somewhere, and that was the cruelest part of all. He wept softly and held the arm across his eyes.

In the dark morning the people of the town were awakened by the blaze of fire that was the house of Juan Sánchez. Believing that he had perished in the flames, several of the townspeople placed a marker next to the grave of his wife with his name on it. But, of course, on that score they were mistaken. Juan Sánchez had simply gone home.

1981

DENISE CHÁVEZ

The Last of the Menu Girls

NAME: Rocío Esquibel
AGE: Seventeen
PREVIOUS EXPERIENCE WITH THE SICK AND DYING: My Great Aunt
  Eutilia
PRESENT EMPLOYMENT: Work-study aide at Altavista Memorial

I never wanted to be a nurse. My mother's aunt died in our house, seventy-seven years old and crying in her metal crib: "Put a pillow on the floor. I can jump," she cried. "Go on, let me jump. I want to get away from here, far away."

Eutilia's mattress was covered with chipped clothlike sheaves of yellowed plastic. She wet herself, was a small child, undependable, helpless. She was an old lady with a broken hip, dying without having gotten down from that rented bed. Her blankets were sewn by my mother: corduroy patches, bright yellows, blues and greens, and still she wanted to jump!

"Turn her over, turn her over, turn her, wait a minute, wait—turn . . ."

Eutilia faced the wall. It was plastered white. The foamed, concrete turnings of some workman's trowel revealed daydreams: people's faces, white clouds, phantom pianos slowly playing half lost melodies, "Las Mañanitas," "Cielito Lindo,"[1] songs formulated in expectation, dissolved into confusion. Eutilia's

---

1. Literally, "Little Mornings," traditionally sung to a girl on her 15th birthday; familiar song, "Beautiful Little Sky," in which a girl's eyes are compared to the sky.

blurred faces, far off tunes faded into the white walls, into jagged, broken waves.

I never wanted to be a nurse, ever. All that gore and blood and grief. I was not as squeamish as my sister Mercy, who could not stand to put her hands into a sinkful of dirty dishes filled with floating food—wet bread, stringy vegetables and bits of softened meat. Still, I didn't like the touch, the smells. How could I? When I touched my mother's feet, I looked away, held my nose with one hand, the other with finger laced along her toes, pulling and popping them into place. "It really helps my arthritis, baby—you don't know. Pull my toes, I'll give you a dollar, find my girdle, and I'll give you two. Ouch. Ouch. Not so hard. There, that's good. Look at my feet. You see the veins? Look at them. Aren't they ugly? And up here, look where I had the operations . . . ugly, they stripped them and still they hurt me."

She rubbed her battered flesh wistfully, placed a delicate and lovely hand on her right thigh. Mother said proudly, truthfully, "I still have lovely thighs."

PREVIOUS EXPERIENCE WITH THE SICK AND DYING: Let me think . . .

Great Aunt Eutilia came to live with us one summer and seven months later she died in my father's old study, the walls lined with books, whatever answers were there—unread.

Great Aunt Eutilia smelled like the mercilessly sick. At first, a vague, softened aroma of tiredness and spilled food. And later, the full-blown emptyings of the dying: gas, putrefaction and fetid lucidity. Her body poured out long, held-back odors. She wet her diapers and sheets and knocked over medicines and glasses of tepid water, leaving in the air an unpleasant smell.

I danced around her bed in my dreams, naked, smiling, jubilant. It was an exultant adolescent dance for my dying aunt. It was necessary, compulsive. It was a primitive dance, a full moon offering that led me slithering into her room with breasts naked and oily at thirteen . . .

No one home but me.

Led me to her room, my father's refuge, those halcyon days now that he was gone—and all that remained were dusty books, cast iron bookends, reminders of the spaces he filled. Down the steps I leaped into Eutilia's faded and foggy consciousness where I whirled and danced and sang: I am your flesh and my mother's flesh and you are . . . are . . . Eutilia stared at me. I turned away.

I danced around Eutilia's bed. I hugged the screen door, my breasts indented in the meshed wire. In the darkness Eutilia moaned, my body wet, her body dry. Steamy we were, and full of prayers.

Could I have absolved your dying by my life? Could I have lessened your agony with my spirit-filled dance in the deep darkness? The blue fan stirred, then whipped nonstop the solid air; little razors sliced through consciousness and prodded the sick and dying woman, whose whitened eyes screeched: Ay! Ay! Let me jump, put a pillow, I want to go away . . . let me . . . let me . . .

10

15   One day while playing "Cielito Lindo" on the piano in the living room, Eutilia got up and fell to the side of the piano stool. Her foot caught on the rug, "¡Ay! ¡Ay! ¡Ay! ¡Ay! Canta y no llores . . ."[2]

All requests were silenced. Eutilia rested in her tattered hospital gown, having shredded it to pieces. She was surrounded by little white strips of raveled cloth. Uncle Toño, her babysitter, after watching the evening news, found her naked and in a bed of cloth. She stared at the ceiling, having played the piano far into the night. She listened to sounds coming from around the back of her head. Just listened. Just looked. Just shredded. Shredded the rented gown, shredded it. When the lady of the house returned and asked how was she, meaning, does she breathe, Toño answered, "Fine."

Christ on his crucifix! He'd never gone into the room to check on her. Later, when they found her, Toño cried, his cousin laughed. They hugged each other, then cried, then laughed, then cried. Eutilia's fingers never rested. They played beautiful tunes. She was a little girl in tatters in her metal bed with sideboards that went up and down, up and down . . .

The young girls danced they played they danced they filled out forms.

PREVIOUS EMPLOYMENT: None.

There was always a first job, as there was the first summer of the very first boyfriend. That was the summer of our first swamp cooler. The heat bore down and congealed sweat. It made rivulets trace the body's meridian and, before it stopped, was wiped away, never quite dismissed.

20   On the tops of the neighbors' houses old swamp coolers, with their jerky grating and droning moans, strained to ease the southern implacabilities. Whrr whrr cough whrr.

Regino Suárez climbed up and down the roof, first forgetting his hammer and then the cooler filter. His boy, Eliterio, stood at the bottom of the steps that led to the sun deck and squinted dumbly at the blazing sun. For several days Regino tramped over my dark purple bedroom. I had shut the curtains to both father and son and rested in violet contemplation of my first boyfriend.

Regino stomped his way to the other side of the house where Eutilia lay in her metal crib, trying to sleep, her weary eyes uncomprehending. The noise was upsetting, she could not play. The small blue fan wheezed freshness. Regino hammered and paced then climbed down. When lunchtime came, a carload of fat daughters drove Regino and the handsome son away.

If Eutilia could have read a book, it would have been the *Bible*, or maybe her novena to the Santo Niño de Atocha,[3] he was her boy . . .

PREVIOUS EXPERIENCE WITH THE SICK AND DYING:

This question reminds me of a story my mother told me about a very old woman, Doña Mercedes, who was dying of cancer. Doña Mercedes lived with

---

2. "Sing and don't cry."   3. Prayer to the Saint Niño, the holy child of Atocha.

her daughter, Corina, who was my mother's friend. The old woman lay in bed, day after day, moaning and crying softly, not actually crying out, but whimpering in a sad, hopeless way. "Don't move me," she begged when her daughter tried to change the sheets or bathe her. Every day this ordeal of maintenance became worse. It was a painful thing and full of dread for the old woman, the once fastidious and upright Doña Mercedes. She had been a lady, straight and imposing, and with a headful of rich dark hair. Her ancestors were from Spain. "You mustn't move me, Corina," Doña Mercedes pleaded, "never, please. Leave me alone, mi'jita,[4]" and so the daughter acquiesced. Cleaning around her tortured flesh and delicately wiping where they could, the two women attended to Doña Mercedes. She died in the daytime, as she had wanted.

When the young women went to lift the old lady from her death bed, they struggled to pull her from the sheets; and, when finally they turned her on her side, they saw huge gaping holes in her back where the cancer had eaten through the flesh. The sheets were stained, the bedsores lost in a red wash of bloody pus. Doña Mercedes' cancer had eaten its way through her back and onto those sheets. "Don't move me, please don't move me," she had cried.

The two young women stuffed piles of shredded disinfected rags soaked in Lysol into Doña Mercedes' chest cavity, filling it, and horrified, with cloths over their mouths, said the prayers for the dead. Everyone remembered her as tall and straight and very Spanish.

PRESENT EMPLOYMENT: Work-study aide at Altavista Memorial Hospital

I never wanted to be a nurse. Never. The smells. The pain. What was I to do then, working in a hospital, in that place of white women, whiter men with square faces? I had no skills. Once in the seventh grade I'd gotten a penmanship award. Swirling R's in boredom, the ABC's ad infinitum. Instead of dipping chocolate cones at the Dairy Queen next door to the hospital, I found myself a frightened girl in a black skirt and white blouse standing near the stairwell to the cafeteria.

I stared up at a painting of a dark-haired woman in a stiff nurse's cap and grey tunic, tending to men in old fashioned service uniforms. There was a beauty in that woman's face whoever she was. I saw myself in her, helping all of mankind, forgetting and absolving all my own sick, my own dying, especially relatives, all of them so far away, removed. I never wanted to be like Great Aunt Eutilia, or Doña Mercedes with the holes in her back, or my mother, her scarred legs, her whitened thighs.

MR. SMITH

Mr. Smith sat at his desk surrounded by requisition forms. He looked up to me with glassy eyes like filmy paperweights.

MOTHER OF GOD, MR. SMITH WAS A WALLEYED HUNCHBACK!

4. My "darling daughter."

"Mr. Smith, I'm Rocío Esquibel, the work-study student from the university and I was sent down here to talk to you about my job."

"Down here, down here," he laughed, as if it were a private joke. "Oh, yes, you must be the new girl. Menus," he mumbled. "Now just have a seat and we'll see what we can do. Would you like some iced tea?"

It was nine o'clock in the morning, too early for tea. "No, well, yes, that would be nice."

"It's good tea, everyone likes it. Here, I'll get you some." Mr. Smith got up, more hunchbacked than I'd imagined. He tiptoed out of the room whispering, "Tea, got to get this girl some tea."

35 There was a bit of the gruesome Golom[5] in him, a bit of the twisted spider in the dark. Was I to work for this gnome? I wanted to rescue souls, not play attendant to this crippled, dried up specimen, this cartilaginous insect with his misshapen head and eyes that peered out to me like the marbled eyes of statues one sees in museums. History preserves its freaks. God, was my job to do the same? No, never!

I faced Dietary Awards, Degrees in Food Management, menus for Low Salt and Fluids; the word Jello leaped out at every turn. I touched the walls. They were moist, never having seen the light.

In my dreams, Mr. Smith was encased in green Jello; his formaldehyde breath reminded me of other smells—decaying, saddened dead things; my great aunt, biology class in high school, my friend Dolores Casaus. Each of us held a tray with a dead frog pinned in place, served to us by a tall stoop-shouldered Viking turned farmer, our biology teacher Mr. Franke, pink-eyed, half blind. Dolores and I cut into the chest cavity and explored that small universe of dead cold fibers. Dolores stopped at the frog's stomach, then squeezed out its last meal, a green mash, spinach-colored, a viscous fluid—that was all that remained in that miniaturized, unresponding organ, all that was left of potential life.

Before Eutilia died she ate a little, mostly drank juice through bent and dripping hospital straws. The straws littered the floor where she'd knocked them over in her wild frenzy to escape. "Dioooooooos," she cried in that shrill voice. "Dios mío, Diosito, por favor. Ay, I won't tell your mamá, just help me get away . . . Diosito de mi vida . . . Diosito de mi corazón . . . agua, agua . . . por favor, por favor . . ."[6]

Mr. Smith returned with my iced tea.
40 "Sugar?"

Sugar, yes, sugar. Lots of it. Was I to spend all summer in this smelly cage? What was I to do? What? And for whom? I had no business here. It was summertime and my life stretched out magically in front of me: there was my boyfriend, my freedom. Senior year had been the happiest of my life; was it to change?

"Anytime you want to come down and get a glass of tea, you go right ahead.

5. In Jewish legend a man created by mystic rites.   6. "My God, oh, loving God, please. . . . Loving God of my life . . . Loving God of my heart . . . water, water . . . please, please."

We always have it on hand. Everyone likes my tea," he said with pride.

"About the job?" I asked.

Mr. Smith handed me a pile of green forms. They were menus.

In the center of the menu was listed the day of the week, and to the left and coming down in a neat order were the three meals, breakfast, lunch and dinner. Each menu had various choices for each meal. 45

LUNCH:

☐ Salisbury Steak	☐ Mashed potatoes and gravy
☐ Fish sticks	☐ Macaroni and cheese
☐ Enchiladas	☐ Broccoli and onions
☐ Rice almondine	

Drinks	*Dessert*
☐ Coffee	☐ Jello
☐ Tea	☐ Carrot cake
☐ 7-Up	☐ Ice Cream, vanilla
☐ Other	

"Here you see a menu for Friday, listing the three meals. Let's take lunch. You have a choice of Salisbury steak, enchiladas, they're really good, Trini makes them, she's been working for me for twenty years. Her son George Jr. works for me, too, probably his kids one day." At this possibility, Mr. Smith laughed at himself. "Oh, and fish sticks. You a . . . ?"

"Our Lady of the Holy Scapular."

"Sometimes I'll get a menu back with a thank you written on the side, 'Thanks for the liver, it was real good', or 'I haven't had rice pudding since I was a boy.' Makes me feel good to know we've made our patients happy."

Mr. Smith paused, reflecting on the positive aspects of his job. 50

"Mind you, these menus are only for people on regular diets, not everybody, but a lot of people. I take care of the other special diets, that doesn't concern you. I have a girl working for me now, Arlene Rutschman. You know . . ."

My mind raced forward, backward. Arlene Rutschman, the Arlene from Holy Scapular, Arlene of the soft voice, the limp mannerisms, the plain, too goodly face, Arlene, president of Our Lady's Sodality, in her white and navy blue beanie, her bobby socks and horn-rimmed glasses, the Arlene of the school dances with her perpetual escort, Bennie Lara, the toothy better-than-no-date date, the Arlene of the high grades, the muscular, yet turned-in legs, the curly unattractive hair, *that* Arlene, the dud?

"Yes, I know her."

"Good!"

"We went to school together." 55

"Wonderful!"

"She works here?"

"Oh, she's a nice girl. She'll help you, show you what to do, how to distribute the menus."

"Distribute the menus?"

60   "Now you just sit there, drink your tea and tell me about yourself."

This was the first of many conversations with Mr. Smith, the hunchbacked dietician, a man who was never anything but kind to me.

"Hey," he said proudly, "these are my kids. Norma and Bardwell. Norma's in Junior High, majoring in boys, and Bardwell is graduating from the Military Institute."

"Bardwell. That's an unusual name," I said as I stared at a series of 5 x 7's on Mr. Smith's desk.

"Bardwell, well, that was my father's name. Bardwell B. Smith. The Bard, they called him!" At this he chuckled to himself, myopically recalling his father, tracing with his strange eyes patterns of living flesh and bone.

65   "He used to recite."

The children looked fairly normal. Norma was slight, with a broad toothy smile. Bardwell, or Bobby, as he was called, was not unhandsome in his uniform, if it weren't for one ragged, splayed ear that slightly cupped forward, as if listening to something.

Mr. Smith's image was nowhere in sight. "Camera shy," he said. To the right of Mr. Smith's desk hung a plastic gold framed prayer beginning with the words: "Oh Lord of Pots and Pans." To the left, near a dried out water-cooler was a sign, "Bless This Mess."

Over the weeks I began to know something of Mr. Smith's convoluted life, its anchorings. His wife and children came to life, and Mr. Smith acquired a name: Marion, and a vague disconcerting sexuality. It was upsetting for me to imagine him fathering Norma and Bardwell. I stared into the framed glossies full of disbelief. Who was Mrs. Smith? What was she like?

Eutilia never had any children. She'd been married to José Esparza, a good man, a handsome man. They ran a store in Agua Tibia. They prospered, until one day, early in the morning, about three a.m., several men from El Otro Lado[7] called out to them in the house. "Don José, wake up! We need to buy supplies." Eutilia was afraid, said, "No, José, don't let them in." He told her, "Woman, what are we here for?" And she said, "But at this hour, José? At this hour?" Don José let them into the store. The two men came in carrying two sacks, one that was empty, and another that they said was full of money. They went through the store, picking out hats, clothing, tins of corned beef, and stuffing them into the empty sack. "So many things, José," Eutilia whispered, "*too* many things!" "Oh no," one man replied, "we have the money, don't you trust us, José?" "Cómo no, compadre,"[8] he replied easily. "We need the goods, don't be afraid, compadre." "Too many things, too many things," Eutilia sighed, huddled in the darkness in her robe. She was a small woman, with the body of a little girl. Eutilia looked at José, and it was then that they both knew. When the two men had loaded up, they turned to Don José, took out a gun, which was hidden in a sack, and said, "So sorry, compadre, but you know . . . stay there, don't follow

---

7. The other side (of the border, i.e. Mexico).   8. "Why not, friend."

us." Eutilia hugged the darkness, saying nothing for the longest time. José was a handsome man, but dumb.

The village children made fun of José Esparza, laughed at him and pinned   70
notes and pieces of paper to his pants. "Tonto, tonto"[9] and "I am a fool." He never saw these notes, wondered why they laughed.

"I've brought you a gift, a bag of rocks"; all fathers have said that to their children. Except Don José Esparza. He had no children, despite his looks. "At times a monkey can do better than a prince," la comadre[1] Lucaya used to say to anyone who would listen.

The bodies of patients twisted and moaned and cried out, and cursed, but for the two of us in that basement world, all was quiet save for the occasional clinking of an iced tea glass and the sporadic sound of Mr. Smith clearing his throat.

"There's no hurry," Mr. Smith always said. "Now you just take your time. Always in a hurry. A young person like you."

ARLENE RUTSCHMAN

"You're so lucky that you can speak Spanish," Arlene intoned. She stood tiptoes, held her breath, then knocked gently on the patient's door. No sound. A swifter knock. "I could never remember what a turnip was," she said.

"Whatjawant?" a voice bellowed.   75

"I'm the menu girl; can I take your order?"

Arlene's high tremulous little girl's voice trailed off, "Good morning, Mr. Samaniego! What'll it be? No, it's not today you leave, tomorrow, after lunch. Your wife is coming to get you. So, what'll it be for your third-to-the-last meal? Now we got poached or fried eggs. Poached. P-o-a-c-h-e-d. That's like a little hard in the middle, but a little soft on the outside. Firm. No, not like scrambled. Different. Okay, you want scrambled. Juice? We got grape or orange. You like grape? Two grape. And some coffee, black."

A tall Anglo man, gaunt and yellowed like an old newspaper, his eyes rubbed black like an old raccoon's, ranged the hallway. The man talked quietly to himself and smoked numbers of cigarettes as he weaved between attendants with half-filled urinals and lugubrious I.V.'s. He reminded me of my father's friends, angular Anglos in their late fifties, men with names like Bud or Earl, men who owned garages or steak houses, men with firm hairy arms, clear blue eyes and tattoos from the war.

"That's Mr. Ellis, 206." Arlene whispered, "jaundice."

"Oh," I said, curiously contemptuous and nervous at the same time,   80
unhappy and reeling from the phrase, "I'm the menu girl!" How'd I ever manage to get such a dumb job? At least the Candy Stripers wore a cute uniform, and they got to do fun things like deliver flowers and candy.

"Here comes Mrs. Samaniego. The wife."

---

9. "Stupid, stupid."   1. Daughter's godmother.

"Mr. Ellis's wife?" I said, with concern.

"No, Mr. Samaniego's wife, Donelda." Arlene pointed to a wizened and giggly old woman who was sneaking by the information desk, past the silver-haired volunteer, several squirmy grandchildren in tow. Visiting hours began at two p.m., but Donelda Samaniego had come early to beat the rush. From the hallway, Arlene and I heard loud smacks, much kidding and general merriment. The room smelled of tamales.

85   "Old Mr. Phillips in 304, that's the Medical Floor, he gets his cath[2] at eleven, so don't go ask him about his menu then. It upsets his stomach."

Mrs. Daniels in 210 told Arlene weakly, "Honey, yes, you, honey, who's the other girl? Who is she? You'll just have to come back later, I don't feel good. I'm a dying woman, can't you see that?" When we came back an hour later, Mrs. Daniels was asleep, snoring loudly.

Mrs. Gustafson, a sad wet-eyed, well-dressed woman in her late sixties, dismissed us from the shade of drawn curtains as her husband, G.P. "Gus" Gustafson, the judge, took long and fitful naps only to wake up again, then go back to sleep, beginning once more his inexorable round of disappearances.

"Yesterday I weighed myself in the hall and I'm getting fat. Oh, and you're so thin."

"The hips," I said, "the hips."

"You know, you remind me of that painting," Arlene said, thoughtfully.

90   "Which?"

"Not which, who. The one in the stairwell. Florence Nightingale, she looks like you."

"That's who that is!"

"The eyes."

"She does?"

95   "The eyes."

"The eyes?"

"And the hair."

"The eyes and the hair? Maybe the hair, but not the eyes."

"Yes."

100   "I don't think so."

"Oh yes! Every time I look at it."

"Me?"

Arlene and I sat talking at our table in the cafeteria, that later was to become *my* table. It faced the dining room. From that vantage point I could see everything and not be seen.

We talked, two friends almost, if only she weren't so, so, little girlish with ribbons. Arlene was still dating Bennie and was majoring in either home ec or biology. They seemed the same in my mind: babies, menus and frogs. Loathsome, unpleasant things.

105   It was there, in the coolness of the cafeteria, in that respite from the green forms, at our special table, drinking tea, laughing with Arlene, that I, still shy,

2. Catheter.

still judgmental, still wondering and still afraid, under the influence of caffeine, decided to stick it out. I would not quit the job.

"How's Mr. Prieto in 200?"

"He left yesterday, but he'll be coming back. He's dying."

"Did you see old Mr. Carter? They strapped him to the wheelchair finally."

"It was about time. He kept falling over."

"Mrs. Domínguez went to bland."[3]

"She was doing so well."

"You think so? She couldn't hardly chew. She kept choking."

"And that grouch, what's her name, the head nurse, Stevens in 214 . . ."

"She's the head nurse? I didn't know that—god, I filled out her menu for her . . . she was sleeping and I . . . no wonder she was mad . . . how did I know she was the head nurse?"

"It's okay. She's going home or coming back, I can't remember which. Esperanza González is gonna be in charge."

"She was real mad."

"Forget it, it's okay."

"The woman will never forgive me, I'll lose my job," I sighed.

I walked home past the Dairy Queen. It took five minutes at the most. I stopped midway at the ditch's edge, where the earth rose and where there was a concrete embankment on which to sit. To some this was the quiet place, where neighborhood lovers met on summer nights to kiss, and where older couples paused between their evening walks to rest. It was also the talking place, where all the neighbor kids discussed life while eating hot fudge sundae with nuts. The bench was large; four could sit on it comfortably. It faced an open field in the middle of which stood a huge apricot tree. Lastly, the bench was a stopping place, the "throne," we called it. We took off hot shoes and dipped our cramped feet into the cool ditch water, as we sat facing the southern sun at the quiet talking place, at our thrones, not thinking anything, eyes closed, but sun. The great red velvet sun.

One night I dreamt of food, wading through hallways of food, inside some dark evil stomach. My boyfriend waved to me from the ditch's bank. I sat on the throne, ran alongside his car, a blue Ford, in which he sat, on clear plastic seat covers, with that hungry Church-of-Christ smile of his. He drove away, and when he returned, the car was small and I was too big to get inside.

Eutilia stirred. She was tired. She did not recognize anyone. I danced around the bed, crossed myself, en el nombre del padre, del hijo y del espíritu santo,[4] crossed forehead, chin and breast, begged for forgiveness even as I danced.

And on waking, I remembered. *Nabos. Turnips.* But of course.

It seemed right to me to be working in a hospital, to be helping people, and yet: why was I only a menu girl? Once a menu was completed, another would

---

3. Bland diet.   4. In the name of the Father, of the Son, and of the Holy Ghost.

take its place and the next day another. It was a never ending round of food and more food. I thought of Judge Gustafson.

When Arlene took a short vacation to the Luray Caverns, I became the official menu girl. That week was the happiest of my entire summer.

125   That week I fell in love.

ELIZABETH RAINEY

130   Elizabeth Rainey, Room 240, was in for a D and C.[5] I didn't know what a D and C was, but I knew it was mysterious and to me, of course, this meant it had to do with sex. Elizabeth Rainey was propped up in bed with many pillows, a soft blue, homemade quilt at the foot of her bed. Her cheeks were flushed, her red lips quivering. She looked fragile, and yet her face betrayed a harsh indelicate bitterness. She wore a creme-colored gown on which her loose hair fell about her like a cape. She was a beautiful woman, full-bodied, with the translucent beauty certain women have in the midst of sorrow—clear and unadorned, her eyes bright with inexplicable and self-contained suffering.

She cried out to me rudely, as if I personally had offended her. "What do you want? Can't you see I want to be alone. Now close the door and go away! Go away!"

"I'm here to get your menu." I could not bring myself to say, I'm the menu girl.

"Go away, go away, I don't want anything. I don't want to eat. Close the door!"

Elizabeth Rainey pulled her face away from me and turned to the wall, and, with deep and self-punishing exasperation, grit her teeth, and from the depths of her self-loathing a small inarticulate cry escaped—"Oooooh."

I ran out, frightened by her pain, yet excited somehow. She was so beautiful and so alone. I wanted in my little girl's way to hold her, hold her tight and in my woman's way never to feel her pain, ever, whatever it was.

"Go away, go away," she said, her trembling mouth rimmed with pain, "go away!"

She didn't want to eat, told me to go away. How many people yelled to me to go away that summer, have yelled since then, countless people, of all ages, sick people, really sick people, dying people, people who were well and still rudely tied into their needs for privacy and space, affronted by these constant impositions from, of all people, the menu girl!

"Move over and move out, would you? Go away! Leave me alone!"

135   And yet, of everyone who told me to go away, it was this woman in her solitary anguish who touched me the most deeply. How could I, age seventeen, not knowing love, how could I presume to reach out to this young woman in her sorrow, touch her and say, "I know, I understand."

Instead, I shrank back into myself and trembled behind the door. I never went back into her room. How could I? It was too terrible a vision, for in her I

5. Dilation and curettage; expanding and cleaning the uterus by scraping.

saw myself, all life, all suffering. What I saw both chilled and burned me. I stood long in that darkened doorway, confused in the presence of human pain. I wanted to reach out . . . I wanted to . . . I wanted to . . . But *how?*

As long as I live I will carry Elizabeth Rainey's image with me: in a creme-colored gown she is propped up, her hair fanning pillows in a room full of deep sweet acrid and overspent flowers. Oh, I may have been that summer girl, but yes, I knew, I understood. I would have danced for her, Eutilia, had I but dared.

DOLORES CASAUS

Dolores of the frog entrails episode, who'd played my sister Ismene in the world literature class play,[6] was now a nurse's aide on the surgical floor, changing sheets, giving enemas and taking rectal temperatures.

It was she who taught me how to take blood pressure, wrapping the cuff around the arm, counting the seconds and then multiplying beats. As a friend, she was rude, impudent, delightful; as an aide, most dedicated. One day for an experiment, with me as a guinea pig, she took the blood pressure of my right leg. That day I hobbled around the hospital, the leg cramped and weak. In high school Dolores had been my double, my confidante and the best Ouija board partner I ever had. When we set our fingers to the board, the dial raced and spun, flinging out letters — notes from the long dead, the crying out. Together we contacted la Llorona[7] and would have unraveled *that* mystery if Sister Esperidiana hadn't caught us in the religion room during lunchtime communing with that distressed spirit who had so much to tell!

Dolores was engaged. She had a hope chest. She wasn't going to college because she had to work, and her two sisters-in-law, the Nurses González and González — Esperanza, male, and Bertha, female, were her supervisors.

As a favor to Dolores, González the Elder, Esperanza would often give her a left-over tray of "regular" food, the patient having checked out or on to other resting grounds. Usually I'd have gone home after the ritualistic glass of tea but one day, out of boredom perhaps, most likely out of curiosity, I hung around the surgical floor talking to Dolores, my only friend in all the hospital. I clung to her sense of wonder, her sense of the ludicrous, to her humor in the face of order, for even in that environment of restriction, I felt her still probing the whys and wherefores of science, looking for vestiges of irregularity with immense childlike curiosity.

The day of the left-over meal found Dolores and me in the laundry room, sandwiched between bins of feces and urine stained sheets to be laundered. There were also dripping urinals waiting to be washed. Hunched over a tray of fried chicken, mashed potatoes and gravy, lima beans and vanilla ice cream, we devoured crusty morsels of Mr. Smith's fried chicken breasts. The food was good. We fought over the ice cream. I resolved to try a few more meals before the summer ended, perhaps in a more pleasant atmosphere.

140

---

6. The Greek tragedy *Antigone*, by Sophocles. Dolores played Ismene, the weaker sister of Antigone, played by Rocío.   7. The Weeper, a dead woman's ghost, folklore.

That day, I lingered at the hospital longer than usual. I helped Dolores with Francisca Pacheco, turning the old woman on her side as we fitted the sheet on the mattress. "Cuidado, no me toquen,"[8] she cried. When Dolores took her temperature rectally, I left the room, but returned just as quickly, ashamed of my timidity. I was always the passing menu girl, too afraid to linger, too unwilling to see, too busy with summer illusions. Every day I raced to finish the daily menus, punching in my time card, greeting the beginning of what I considered to be my *real* day outside those long and smelly corridors where food and illness intermingled, leaving a sweet thick air of exasperation in my lungs. The "ooooh" of Elizabeth Rainey's anxious flesh.

The "ay ay ay" of Great Aunt Eutilia's phantom cries awaited me in my father's room. On the wall the portrait of his hero Napoleon hung, shielded by white sheets. The sun was too bright that summer for delicate fading eyes, the heat too oppressive. The blue fan raced to bring freshness to that acrid tomb full of ghosts.

145   I walked home slowly, not stopping at the quiet place. Compadre Regino Suárez was on the roof. The cooler leaked. Impatient with Regino and his hearty wave, his habit of never doing any job thoroughly, I remembered that I'd forgotten my daily iced tea. The sun was hot. All I wanted was to rest in the cool darkness of my purple room.

The inside of the house smelled of burnt food and lemons. My mother had left something on the stove again. To counteract the burnt smell she'd placed lemons all over the house. Lemons filled ashtrays and bowls, they lay solidly on tables and rested in hot corners. I looked in the direction of Eutilia's room. Quiet. She was sleeping. She'd been dead five years but, still, the room was hers. She was sleeping peacefully. I smelled the cleansing bitterness of lemons.

MRS. DANIELS

When I entered rooms and saw sick, dying women in their forties, I always remembered room 210, Mrs. Daniels, the mother of my cousin's future wife.

Mrs. Daniels usually lay in bed, whimpering like a little dog, moaning to her husband, who always stood nearby, holding her hand, saying softly, "Now, Martha, Martha. The little girl only wants to get your order."

"Send her away, goddammit!"

150   On those days that Mr. Daniels was absent, Mrs. Daniels whined for me to go away. "Leave me alone, can't you see I'm dying" she said and looked toward the wall. She looked so pale, sick, near death to me, but somehow I knew, not really having imagined death without the dying, not having felt the outrage and loathing, I knew and saw her outbursts for what they really were: deep hurts, deep distresses. I saw her need to release them, to fling them at others, dribbling pain / anguish / abuse, trickling away those vast torrential feelings of sorrow and hate and fear, letting them fall wherever they would, on whomever they might. I was her white wall. I was her whipping girl upon whom she spilled her dark-

8. "Watch out, don't touch me."

ened ashes. She cried out obscenely to me, sending me reeling from her room, that room of loathing and dread. That room anxious with worms.

Who of us has not heard the angry choked words of crying people, listened, not wanting to hear, then shut our ears, said enough, I don't want to. Who has not seen the fearful tear-streamed faces, known the blank eyes and felt the holding back, and, like smiling thoughtless children, said: "I was in the next room, I couldn't help hearing, I heard, I saw, you didn't know, did you? I know."

We rolled up the pain, assigned it a shelf, placed it in the hardened place, along with a certain self-congratulatory sense of wonder at the world's unfortunates like Mrs. Daniels. We were embarrassed to be alive.

JUAN MARIA / THE NOSE

"Cómo se dice[9] when was the last time you had a bowel movement?" Nurse Luciano asked. She was from Yonkers, a bright newlywed. Erminia, the ward secretary, a tall thin horsey woman with a postured Juárez hairdo of exaggerated sausage ringlets, replied through chapped lips, "Oh, who cares, he's sleeping."

"He's from México, huh?" Luciano said with interest.

"An illegal alien," Rosario retorted. She was Erminia's sister, the superintendent's secretary, with the look of a badly scarred bulldog. She'd stopped by to invite Erminia to join her for lunch.

"So where'd it happen?" Luciano asked.

"At the Guadalajara Bar on Main Street," Erminia answered, moistening her purple lips nervously. It was a habit of hers.

"Hey, I remember when we used to walk home from school. You remember, Rocío?" Dolores asked, "We'd try to throw each other through the swinging doors. It was real noisy in there."

"Father O'Kelley said drink was the defilement of men, the undoing of staunch, god-fearing women," I said.

"Our father has one now and then," Rosario replied, "that doesn't mean anything. It's because he was one of those aliens."

"Those kind of problems are bad around here I heard," Luciano said, "people sneaking across the border and all."

"Hell, you don't know the half of it," Nurse González said as she came up to the desk where we all stood facing the hallway. "It's an epidemic."

"I don't know, my mother always had maids, and they were all real nice except the one who stole her wedding rings. We had to track her all the way to Piedras Negras[1] and even then she wouldn't give them up," Erminia interjected.

"Still, it doesn't seem human the way they're treated at times."

"Some of them, they ain't human."

"Still, he was drunk, he wasn't full aware."

"Full aware, my ass," retorted Esperanza angrily, "he had enough money to buy booze. If that's not aware, I don't know what aware is. Ain't my goddam

9. "How do you say . . ."   1. Mexican town on the Texas border.

fault the bastard got into a fight and someone bit his nose off. Ain't *my* fault he's here and *we* gotta take care of him. Christ! If *that* isn't aware, I don't know what aware is!"

Esperanza González, head surgical floor nurse, the short but highly respected Esperanza of no esperanzas,[2] the Esperanza of the short-bobbed hair, the husky deferential voice, the commands, the no-nonsense orders and brisk-ness, Esperanza the future sister-in-law of Dolores, my only friend, Esperanza the dyke, who was later killed in a car accident on the way to somewhere, said: "Now get back to work all of you, we're just here to clean up the mess."

Later when Esperanza was killed my aunt said, "How nice. In the paper they called her lover her sister. How nice!"

170 "Hey, Erminia, lunch?" asked Rosario, almost sheepishly. "You hungry?"

"Coming, Rosario," yelled Erminia from the back office where she was get-ting her purse. "Coming!"

"God, I'm starving," Rosario said, "can you hear my stomach?"

"Go check Mr. Carter's cath, Dolores, will you?" said Esperanza in a softer tone.

"Well, I don't know, I just don't know," Luciano pondered. "It doesn't seem human, does it? I mean how in the world could anyone in their right mind bite off another person's nose? How? You know it, González, you're a tough rooster. If I didn't know you so well already, you'd scare the hell out of me. How long you been a nurse?"

175 "Too long, Luciano. Look, I ain't a new bride, that's liable to make a person soft. Me, I just clean up the mess."

"Luciano, what you know about people could be put on the head of a pin. You just leave these alien problems to those of us who were brought up around here and know what's going on. Me, I don't feel one bit sorry for that bastard," Esperanza said firmly. "Christ, Luciano, what do you expect, he don't speak no Engleesh!"

"His name is Juan María Mejía," I ventured.

Luciano laughed. Esperanza laughed. Dolores went off to Mr. Carter's room, and Rosario chatted noisily with Erminia as they walked toward the cafeteria.

"Hey, Rosario," Luciano called out, "what happened to the rings?"

180 It was enchilada day. Trini was very busy.

Juan María the Nose was sleeping in the hallway; all the other beds were filled. His hospital gown was awry, the grey sheet folded through sleep-deadened limbs. His hands were tightly clenched. The hospital screen barely concealed his twisted private sleep of legs akimbo, moist armpits and groin. It was a sleep of sleeping off, of hard drunken wanderings, with dreams of a bar, dreams of a fight. He slept the way little boys sleep, carelessly half exposed. I stared at him.

Esperanza complained and muttered under her breath, railing at the Anglo sons of bitches and at all the lousy wetbacks, at everyone, male and female, goddamn them and their messes. Esperanza was dark and squat, pura india[3] tortured by her very face. Briskly, she ordered Dolores and now me about. I had

---

2. Hope of no hopes.   **3.** Pure Indian. Slang for ugly woman.

graduated overnight, as if in a hazy dream, to assistant, but unofficial, ward secretary.

I stared across the hallway to Juan María the Nose. He faced the wall, a dangling I.V. at the foot of the bed. Esperanza González, R.N., looked at me.

"Well, and *who* are you?"

"I'm the menu, I mean, I *was* the menu . . ." I stammered. "I'm helping   185
Erminia."

"So get me some cigarettes. Camels. I'll pay you tomorrow when I get paid."

Yes, it was really González, male, who ran the hospital.

Arlene returned from the Luray Caverns with a stalactite charm bracelet for me. She announced to Mr. Smith and me that she'd gotten a job with an insurance company.

"I'll miss you, Rocío."

"Me, too, Arlene." God knows it was the truth. I'd come to depend on her,   190
our talks over tea. No one ever complimented me like she did.

"You never get angry, do you?" she said admiringly.

"Rarely," I said. But inside, I was always angry.

"What do you want to do?"

"Want to do?"

"Yeah."   195

I want to be someone else, somewhere else, someone important and responsible and sexy. I want to be sexy.

"I don't know. I'm going to major in drama."

"You're sweet," she said. "Everyone likes you. It's in your nature. You're the Florence Nightingale of Altavista Memorial, that's it!"

"Oh God, Arlene, I don't want to be a nurse, *ever!* I can't take the smells. No one in our family can stand smells."

"You look like that painting. I always did think it looked like you . . ."   200

"You did?"

"Yeah."

"Come on, you're making me sick, Arlene."

"Everyone likes you."

"Well . . ."   205

"So keep in touch. I'll see you at the University."

"Home ec?"

"Biology."

We hugged.

The weeks progressed. My hours at the hospital grew. I was allowed to check   210
in patients, to take their blood pressures and temperatures. I flipped through the patients' charts, memorizing names, room numbers, types of diet. I fingered the doctors' reports with reverence. Perhaps someday I would begin to write in them as Erminia did: "2:15 p.m., Mrs. Daniels, pulse normal, temp normal, Dr. Blasse checked patient, treatment on schedule, medication given to quiet patient."

One day I received a call at the ward desk. It was Mr. Smith.

"Ms. Esquibel? Rocío? This is Mr. Smith, you know, down in the cafeteria."

"Yes, Mr. Smith! How are you? Is there anything I can do? Are you getting the menus okay? I'm leaving them on top of your desk."

"I've been talking to Nurse González, surgical; she says they need you there full time to fill in and could I do without you?"

215 "Oh, I can do both jobs; it doesn't take that long, Mr. Smith."

"No, we're going by a new system. Rather, it's the old system. The aides will take the menu orders like they used to before Arlene came. So, you come down and see me, Rocío, have a glass of iced tea. I never see you any more since you moved up in the world. Yeah, I guess you're the last of the menu girls."

The summer passed. June, July, August, my birth month. There were serious days, hurried admissions, feverish errands, quick notes jotted in the doctor's charts. I began to work Saturdays. In my eagerness to "advance," I unwittingly had created more work for myself, work I really wasn't skilled to do.

My heart reached out to every person, dragged itself through the hallways with the patients, cried when they did, laughed when they did. I had no business in the job. I was too emotional.

Now when I walked into a room I knew the patient's history, the cause of illness. I began to study individual cases with great attention, turning to a copy of *The Family Physician*, which had its place among my father's old books in his abandoned study.

220 Gone were the idle hours of sitting in the cafeteria, leisurely drinking iced tea, gone were the removed reflections of the outsider.

My walks home were measured, pensive. I hid in my room those long hot nights, nights full of wrestling, injured dreams. Nothing seemed enough.

Before I knew it, it was the end of August, close to that autumnal time of setting out. My new life was about to begin. I had made that awesome leap into myself that steamy summer of illness and dread—confronting at every turn, the flesh, its lingering cries.

"Ay, Ay, Ay, Ay, Canta y no llores! Porque cantando se alegran, Cielito Lindo, los corazones . . ."[4] The little thin voice of an old woman sang from one of the back rooms. She pumped the gold pedals with fast furious and fervant feet, she smiled to the wall, its faces, she danced on the ceiling.

Let me jump.

225 "Goodbye, Dolores, it was fun."

"I'll miss you, Rocío! But you know, gotta save some money. I'll get back to school someday, maybe."

"What's wrong, Erminia? You mad?" I asked.

"I thought you were gonna stay and help me out here on the floor."

"Goddamn right!" complained Esperanza. "Someone told me this was your last day, so why didn't you tell me? Why'd I train you for, so you could leave us? To go to school? What for? So you can get those damned food stamps? It's a

---

4. "Sing and don't cry! Because singing brightens the heart; Beautiful Little Sky."

disgrace all those wetbacks and healthy college students getting our hard earned tax money. Makes me sick. Christ!" Esperanza shook her head with disgust.

"Hey, Erminia, you tell Rosario goodbye for me and Mrs. Luciano, too," I said sadly.

"Yeah, okay. They'll be here tomorrow," she answered tonelessly. I wanted to believe she was sad.

"I gotta say goodbye to Mr. Smith," I said, as I moved away.

"Make him come up and get some sun," González snickered. "Hell no, better not, he might get sunstroke and who'd fix my fried chicken?"

I climbed down the steps to the basement, past the cafeteria, past my special table, and into Mr. Smith's office, where he sat, adding numbers.

"Miss Esquibel, Rocío!"

"This is my last day, Mr. Smith. I wanted to come down and thank you. I'm sorry about . . ."

"Oh no, it worked out all right. It's nothing."

Did I see, from the corner of my eye, a set of Friday's menus he himself was tabulating—salisbury steak, macaroni and cheese . . .

"We'll miss you, Rocío. You were an excellent menu girl."

"It's been a wonderful summer."

"Do you want some tea?"

"No, I really don't have the time."

"I'll get . . ."

"No, thank you, Mr. Smith, I *really* have to go, but thanks. It's really good tea."

I extended my hand, and for the first time, we touched. Mr. Smith's eyes seemed fogged, distracted. He stood up and hobbled closer to my side. I took his grave cold hand, shook it softly, and turned to the moist walls. When I closed the door, I saw him in front of me, framed in paper, the darkness of that quiet room. Bless this mess.

Eutilia's voice echoed in the small room. Goodbye. Goodbye. And let me jump.

I turned away from the faces, the voices, now gone: Father O'Kelley, Elizabeth Rainey, Mrs. Luciano, Arlene Rutschman, Mrs. Daniels, Juan María the Nose, Mr. Samaniego and Donelda, his wife, their grandchildren, Mr. Carter, Earl Ellis, Dolores Casaus, Erminia and her sister, the bulldog. Esperanza González, Francisca Pacheco, Elweena Twinbaum, the silver-haired volunteer whose name I'd learned the week before I left Altavista Memorial. I'd made a list on a menu of all the people I'd worked with. To remember. It seemed right.

From the distance I heard Marion Smith's high voice: "Now you come back and see us!"

Above the stairs the painting of Florence Nightingale stared solidly into weary soldiers' eyes. Her look encompassed all the great unspeakable sufferings of every war. I thought of Arlene typing insurance premiums.

Farther away, from behind and around my head, I heard the irregular but joyful strains of "Cielito Lindo" played on a phantom piano by a disembodied but now peaceful voice that sang with great quivering emotion: De la sierra morena, Cielito Lindo . . . viene bajando . . .[5]

Regino fixed the cooler. I started school. Later that year I was in a car accident. I crashed into a brick wall at the cemetery. I walked to Dolores' house, holding my bleeding face in my hands. Dolores and her father argued all the way to the hospital. I sat quietly in the back seat. It was a lovely morning. So clear. When I woke up I was on the surgical floor. Everyone knew me. I had so many flowers in the room I could hardly breathe. My older sister, Ronelia, thought I'd lost part of my nose in the accident and she returned to the cemetery to look for it. It wasn't there.

Mr. Smith came to see me once. I started to cry.

"Oh no, no, no, now don't you do that, Rocío. You want some tea?"

No one took my menu order. I guess that system had finally died out. I ate the food, whatever it was, walked the hallways in my grey hospital gown slit in the back, railed at the well-being of others, cursed myself for being so stupid. I only wanted to be taken home, down the street, past the quiet-talking place, a block away, near the Dairy Queen, to the darkness of my purple room.

255   It was time.

PREVIOUS EMPLOYMENT: Altavista Memorial Hospital
SUPERVISORS: Mr. Marion Smith, Dietician, and Miss Esperanza González,
    R.N., Surgical Floor.
DATES: June 1966 to August 1966
IN A FEW SENTENCES GIVE A BRIEF DESCRIPTION OF YOUR JOB:
    As Ward Secretary, I was responsible for . . . let me think . . .

1986

▼   ▼   ▼

QUESTIONS

1. Why did Juan Sánchez want to leave his native village in Mexico? Why did he choose the Sierra Nevada above Stockton as his new home? How does the central district of Stockton appear to Juan? to Jesús? to you?

2. What element of Western religion and legend—classical as well as Christian—do you find in Cico's story of the golden carp? What religious overtones are there in Narciso's garden? How does the incident of Tony's harassment by his school friends relate to the religious and cultural themes of the story?

3. How did you feel about Mr. Smith when he was first introduced in "The Last of the Menu Girls"? What role did you expect him to play? How did your response to him change during the story? What is a "menu girl"? What signifi-

5. From the dark highlands, Beautiful Little Sky . . . you are coming down.

cance do you find in the fact that Rocío is the "last" of them? How do the Mexican Americans in the story feel about illegal immigration? Did you find the story depressing? uplifting? educational? what? Are you moved by stories that deal with sorrow, death, disease? Do you seek them out? avoid them? read them reluctantly, only when assigned or highly recommended? Did you see *Philadelphia?* Did you avoid seeing it? Why (or why not)?

WRITING SUGGESTIONS

1. Write a personal narrative centering on an incident or situation that involved your "mixed" heritage (even if that "mixture" is made up of ethnic ingredients as close as Mexican and Guatemalan, English and Scots, Blackfoot and Sioux, Italian and Irish). If you have had no such experience, search out members of your family or friends who may have, interview them, and write a narrative based on their experience.

2. Research the history of one of your ethnic strains and write a report of the "mixing" of that heritage over the centuries; e.g., the invasion of Russia and the Ukraine by Mongolians, of France by Germanic tribes, etc.

3. Using specific textual passages to support your position, write an essay on "Sánchez" about Jésus's parentage and the implication of his name; or, write about whether Juan going "home" means (1) he went back to Mexico, or (2) he committed suicide.

4. Write (a) an analytical character sketch of Rocío Esquibel ("The Last of the Menu Girls"), documenting it with specific references to and passages from the text, or (b) an account of what Rocío learned that summer, indicating as specifically as possible how her experience was affected by each of the patients and each of her friends at the hospital.

10 LITERARY KIND AS CONTEXT: INITIATION STORIES

Themes are useful for grouping stories together for comparison, both to highlight similarities and to reveal differences in history and structure and so to discover the uniqueness of the work. Types of characters—stereotypes—are useful for the same purpose: to show both the common qualities and the unique combination of qualities in a particular character in a story. Though all grouping and classification, used poorly, can blur distinctions and make all members of a group seem the same, when used well they do not blur but bring into focus the individuality of each member or being.

Literary criticism lacks the specific and agreed-on system of classification of biology, so that its terms are not so fixed as *phylum, genus, species*. In general, we use the term **genre** for the largest commonly agreed-on categories: fiction, poetry, drama. When I'm trying to be consistent, I use the term **subgenre** for the divisions of fiction—novel, novella, short story, and so on. A **kind** is a species or subcategory within a subgenre.

One kind of short story, so common that some maintain it is not a kind but is equivalent to the subgenre short story itself, is the **initiation** story, in which a character—often but not always a child or young person—first learns a significant truth about the universe, reality, society, people, himself or herself. Such a subject tends to dictate the main outlines of the story's action: it begins with the protagonist in a state of innocence or mistaken belief (exposition); it leads up to the moment of illumination or the discovery of the truth (rising action to climax or turning point), and ends usually with some indication of the result of that discovery (falling action to conclusion). This kind is particularly suitable to a short story because it lends itself to brief treatment: the illumination is more or less sudden—there is no need for lengthy development, for multiple scenes or settings, for much time to pass, for too many complications of action or a large cast of characters—yet it can encapsulate a whole life or important segment of a life and wide-ranging, significant themes.

If you've been reading this anthology from the beginning, you have already run into a number of initiation stories, and you may have some idea of what sorts of truths their protagonists discover. Young goodman Brown discovers the universality of evil in human beings. The captain in "The Secret Sharer" discovers that someone very much like him, virtually his double and therefore

454

probably he himself, is not only capable of murder but may, under certain circumstances and in his capacity as a captain or leader, consciously choose murder as the lesser of evils. Leila ("Her First Ball") comes across the truth that youth is fleeting (you cannot say she really learns it, since by the end of that very short story she has forgotten it). We have also seen that one may retreat from the truth physically or psychologically, as does Brown, or remain unchanged or revert to one's former state, as Leila does.

Since to the young all things seem possible—one can be a doctor, novelist, tennis star, saint, and swinger, serially or simultaneously—many of the truths learned in initiation stories have to do with limitation. The girl in "Boys and Girls" learns that she is "only a girl." Sometimes the child learns the difference between romance and reality, as does the boy in "Araby" or between words and reality in the adult world, as Hazel does in "Gorilla, My Love."

Sometimes, the initiation takes place as an unscheduled event, as in "Araby." At other times there is a ritual or **rite of passage,** such as a formal entry into society ("Her First Ball"). What do we usually think of as the purpose of a debut? How does the society intend to induct its new member? As you read "Her First Ball," think about these questions and watch how Leila's debut fulfills its ritual role, how it differs from it, and how it may induct Leila into society more truly than intended.

By the time you finish this chapter you should have some idea of the variations possible within the initiation story, and as you look back to such stories as "Sonny's Blues," "The Country Husband," "How Much Land Does a Man Need?", "Her First Ball," "Odour of Chrysanthemums," and many of the others, you should have a still better idea of the range of stories in this kind. Adults may be initiated as well as children and adolescents; the truths may be bitter or pleasing, cosmic, social, psychological; the initiates may change forever, retreat, shrug off what they have learned. By seeing all these stories as part of the large group of initiation stories you may the more readily notice the differences in the protagonists, the learning experiences, and the results of the initiations on the protagonists, whether they are permanent or temporary, lifedenying or life-enhancing. You may, in other words, have gone a long way toward defining the unique vision of the story, its precise and individual illumination of reality. And that's the function of classification in the first place.

▼   ▼   ▼

JAMES JOYCE

Araby

North Richmond Street, being blind,[1] was a quiet street except at the hour when the Christian Brothers' School set the boys free. An uninhabited house of two storeys stood at the blind end, detached from its neighbours in a square ground. The other houses of the street, conscious of decent lives within them, gazed at one another with brown imperturbable faces.

The former tenant of our house, a priest, had died in the back drawing-room. Air, musty from having been long enclosed, hung in all the rooms, and the waste room behind the kitchen was littered with old useless papers. Among these I found a few paper-covered books, the pages of which were curled and damp: *The Abbot*, by Walter Scott, *The Devout Communicant* and *The Memoirs of Vidocq*.[2] I liked the last best because its leaves were yellow. The wild garden behind the house contained a central apple tree and a few straggling bushes, under one of which I found the late tenant's rusty bicycle-pump. He had been a very charitable priest; in his will he had left all his money to institutions and the furniture of his house to his sister.

When the short days of winter came, dusk fell before we had well eaten our dinners. When we met in the street the houses had grown sombre. The space of sky above us was the colour of ever-changing violet and towards it the lamps of the street lifted their feeble lanterns. The cold air stung us and we played till our bodies glowed. Our shouts echoed in the silent street. The career of our play brought us through the dark muddy lanes behind the houses, where we ran the gauntlet of the rough tribes from the cottages, to the back doors of the dark dripping gardens where odours arose from the ashpits,[3] to the dark odorous stables where a coachman smoothed and combed the horse or shook music from the buckled harness. When we returned to the street, light from the kitchen windows had filled the areas. If my uncle was seen turning the corner, we hid in the shadow until we had seen him safely housed. Or if Mangan's sister came out on the doorstep to call her brother in to his tea, we watched her from our shadow peer up and down the street. We waited to see whether she would remain or go in and, if she remained, we left our shadow and walked up to Mangan's steps resignedly. She was waiting for us, her figure defined by the light from the half-opened door. Her brother always teased her before he obeyed, and I stood by the railings looking at her. Her dress swung as she moved her body, and the soft rope of her hair tossed from side to side.

1. Dead-end street.   2. The 1820 novel by Sir Walter Scott (1771–1834) is a romance about the Catholic Mary, Queen of Scots (1542–1587), who was beheaded; a Catholic religious tract: *The Devout Communicant: or Pious Meditations and Aspirations for the Three Days Before and Three Days After Receiving the Holy Eucharist* (1813); the "memoirs" were probably *not* written by François Vidocq (1775–1857), a French criminal who became chief of detectives and who died poor and disgraced for his part in a crime that he solved.   3. Where fireplace ashes were dumped.

Every morning I lay on the floor in the front parlour watching her door. The blind was pulled down to within an inch of the sash so that I could not be seen. When she came out on the doorstep my heart leaped. I ran to the hall, seized my books and followed her. I kept her brown figure always in my eye and, when we came near the point at which our ways diverged, I quickened my pace and passed her. This happened morning after morning. I had never spoken to her, except for a few casual words, and yet her name was like a summons to all my foolish blood.

Her image accompanied me even in places the most hostile to romance. On Saturday evenings when my aunt went marketing I had to go to carry some of the parcels. We walked through the flaring streets, jostled by drunken men and bargaining women, amid the curses of labourers, the shrill litanies of shop-boys who stood on guard by the barrels of pigs' cheeks, the nasal chanting of street-singers, who sang a *come-all-you* about O'Donovan Rossa,[4] or a ballad about the troubles in our native land. These noises converged in a single sensation of life for me: I imagined that I bore my chalice safely through a throng of foes. Her name sprang to my lips at moments in strange prayers and praises which I myself did not understand. My eyes were often full of tears (I could not tell why) and at times a flood from my heart seemed to pour itself out into my bosom. I thought little of the future. I did not know whether I would ever speak to her or not or, if I spoke to her, how I would tell her of my confused adoration. But my body was like a harp and her words and gestures were like fingers running upon the wires.

One evening I went into the back drawing-room in which the priest had died. It was a dark rainy evening and there was no sound in the house. Through one of the broken panes I heard the rain impinge upon the earth, the fine incessant needles of water playing in the sodden beds. Some distant lamp or lighted window gleamed below me. I was thankful that I could see so little. All my senses seemed to desire to veil themselves and, feeling that I was about to slip from them, I pressed the palms of my hands together until they trembled, murmuring: *"O love! O love!"* many times.

At last she spoke to me. When she addressed the first words to me I was so confused that I did not know what to answer. She asked me was I going to *Araby.*[5] I forgot whether I answered yes or no. It would be a splendid bazaar, she said; she would love to go.

"And why can't you?" I asked.

While she spoke she turned a silver bracelet round and round her wrist. She could not go, she said, because there would be a retreat that week in her convent. Her brother and two other boys were fighting for their caps and I was alone at the railings. She held one of the spikes, bowing her head towards me. The light from the lamp opposite our door caught the white curve of her neck, lit up

5

4. Jeremiah O'Donovan (1831–1915) was a militant Irish nationalist who fought on despite terms in prison and banishment. *Come-all-you:* A song, of which there were many, which began "Come, all you Irishmen." 5. A bazaar billed as a "Grand Oriental Fête," Dublin, May 1894.

her hair that rested there and, falling, lit up the hand upon the railing. It fell over one side of her dress and caught the white border of a petticoat, just visible as she stood at ease.

"It's well for you," she said.

"If I go," I said. "I will bring you something."

What innumerable follies laid waste my waking and sleeping thoughts after that evening! I wished to annihilate the tedious intervening days. I chafed against the work of school. At night in my bedroom and by day in the classroom her image came between me and the page I strove to read. The syllables of the word *Araby* were called to me through the silence in which my soul luxuriated and cast an Eastern enchantment over me. I asked for leave to go to the bazaar on Saturday night. My aunt was surprised and hoped it was not some Freemason[6] affair. I answered few questions in class. I watched my master's face pass from amiability to sternness; he hoped I was not beginning to idle. I could not call my wandering thoughts together. I had hardly any patience with the serious work of life which, now that it stood between me and my desire, seemed to me child's play, ugly monotonous child's play.

On Saturday morning I reminded my uncle that I wished to go to the bazaar in the evening. He was fussing at the hallstand, looking for the hat-brush, and answered me curtly:

"Yes, boy, I know."

As he was in the hall I could not go into the front parlour and lie at the window. I left the house in bad humour and walked slowly towards the school. The air was pitilessly raw and already my heart misgave me.

When I came home to dinner my uncle had not yet been home. Still it was early. I sat staring at the clock for some time and, when its ticking began to irritate me, I left the room. I mounted the staircase and gained the upper part of the house. The high, cold, empty, gloomy rooms liberated me and I went from room to room singing. From the front window I saw my companions playing below in the street. Their cries reached me weakened and indistinct and, leaning my forehead against the cool glass, I looked over at the dark house where she lived. I may have stood there for an hour, seeing nothing but a brown-clad figure cast by my imagination, touched discreetly by the lamplight at the curved neck, at the hand upon the railings and at the border below the dress.

When I came downstairs again I found Mrs. Mercer sitting at the fire. She was an old, garrulous woman, a pawnbroker's widow, who collected used stamps for some pious purpose. I had to endure the gossip of the tea-table. The meal was prolonged beyond an hour and still my uncle did not come. Mrs. Mercer stood up to go: she was sorry she couldn't wait any longer, but it was after eight o'clock and she did not like to be out late, as the night air was bad for her. When she had gone I began to walk up and down the room, clenching my fists. My aunt said:

"I'm afraid you may put off your bazaar for this night of Our Lord."

At nine o'clock I heard my uncle's latchkey in the hall door. I heard him

6. The Masons, or Freemasons, were considered enemies of the Catholics.

talking to himself and heard the hallstand rocking when it had received the weight of his overcoat. I could interpret these signs. When he was midway through his dinner I asked him to give me the money to go to the bazaar. He had forgotten.

"The people are in bed and after their first sleep now," he said.   20

I did not smile. My aunt said to him energetically:

"Can't you give him the money and let him go? You've kept him late enough as it is."

My uncle said he was very sorry he had forgotten. He said he believed in the old saying: "All work and no play makes Jack a dull boy." He asked me where I was going and, when I had told him a second time, he asked me did I know *The Arab's Farewell to his Steed*.[7] When I left the kitchen he was about to recite the opening lines of the piece to my aunt.

I held a florin[8] tightly in my hand as I strode down Buckingham Street towards the station. The sight of the streets thronged with buyers and glaring with gas recalled to me the purpose of my journey. I took my seat in a third-class carriage of a deserted train. After an intolerable delay the train moved out of the station slowly. It crept onward among ruinous houses and over the twinkling river. At Westland Row Station a crowd of people pressed to the carriage doors; but the porters moved them back, saying that it was a special train for the bazaar. I remained alone in the bare carriage. In a few minutes the train drew up beside an improvised wooden platform. I passed out on to the road and saw by the lighted dial of a clock that it was ten minutes to ten. In front of me was a large building which displayed the magical name.

I could not find any sixpenny entrance and, fearing that the bazaar would   25
be closed, I passed in quickly through a turnstile, handing a shilling to a weary-looking man. I found myself in a big hall girdled at half its height by a gallery. Nearly all the stalls were closed and the greater part of the hall was in darkness. I recognized a silence like that which pervades a church after a service. I walked into the centre of the bazaar timidly. A few people were gathered about the stalls which were still open. Before a curtain, over which the words *Café Chantant*[9] were written in coloured lamps, two men were counting money on a salver. I listened to the fall of the coins.

Remembering with difficulty why I had come I went over to one of the stalls and examined porcelain vases and flowered tea-sets. At the door of the stall a young lady was talking and laughing with two young gentlemen. I remarked their English accents and listened vaguely to their conversation.

"O, I never said such a thing!"

"O, but you did!"

"O, but I didn't!"

"Didn't she say that?"   30

"Yes. I heard her."

---

7. Or *The Arab's Farewell to His Horse*, sentimental 19th-century poem by Caroline Norton. The speaker has sold the horse.   8. Two-shilling piece; thus four times the "sixpenny entrance" fee. 9. Café with music.

"O, there's a . . . fib!"

Observing me, the young lady came over and asked me did I wish to buy anything. The tone of her voice was not encouraging; she seemed to have spoken to me out of a sense of duty. I looked humbly at the great jars that stood like eastern guards at either side of the dark entrance to the stall and murmured:

"No, thank you."

35   The young lady changed the position of one of the vases and went back to the two young men. They began to talk of the same subject. Once or twice the young lady glanced at me over her shoulder.

I lingered before her stall, though I knew my stay was useless, to make my interest in her wares seem the more real. Then I turned away slowly and walked down the middle of the bazaar. I allowed the two pennies to fall against the sixpence in my pocket. I heard a voice call from one end of the gallery that the light was out. The upper part of the hall was now completely dark.

Gazing up into the darkness I saw myself as a creature driven and derided by vanity; and my eyes burned with anguish and anger.

1914

TONI CADE BAMBARA

Gorilla, My Love

That was the year Hunca Bubba changed his name. Not a change up, but a change back, since Jefferson Winston Vale was the name in the first place. Which was news to me cause he'd been my Hunca Bubba my whole lifetime, since I couldn't manage Uncle to save my life. So far as I was concerned it was a change completely to somethin soundin very geographical weatherlike to me, like somethin you'd find in a almanac. Or somethin you'd run across when you sittin in the navigator seat with a wet thumb on the map crinkly in your lap, watchin the roads and signs so when Granddaddy Vale say "Which way, Scout," you got sense enough to say take the next exit or take a left or whatever it is. Not that Scout's my name. Just the name Granddaddy call whoever sittin in the navigator seat. Which is usually me cause I don't feature sittin in the back with the pecans. Now, you figure pecans all right to be sittin with. If you thinks so, that's your business. But they dusty sometime and make you cough. And they got a way of slidin around and dippin down sudden, like maybe a rat in the buckets. So if you scary like me, you sleep with the lights on and blame it on Baby Jason and, so as not to waste good electric, you study the maps. And that's how come I'm in the navigator seat most times and get to be called Scout.

So Hunca Bubba in the back with the pecans and Baby Jason, and he in love. And we got to hear all this stuff about this woman he in love with and all. Which really ain't enough to keep the mind alive, though Baby Jason got no better sense than to give his undivided attention and keep grabbin at the photograph which is just a picture of some skinny woman in a countrified dress with her hand shot up to her face like she shame fore cameras. But there's a movie house in the background which I ax about. Cause I am a movie freak from way back, even though it do get me in trouble sometime.

Like when me and Big Brood and Baby Jason was on our own last Easter and couldn't go to the Dorset cause we'd seen all the Three Stooges they was. And the RKO Hamilton was closed readying up for the Easter Pageant that night. And the West End, the Regun and the Sunset was too far, less we had grownups with us which we didn't. So we walk up Amsterdam Avenue to the Washington and *Gorilla, My Love* playin, they say, which suit me just fine, though the "my love" part kinda drag Big Brood some. As for Baby Jason, shoot, like Granddaddy say, he'd follow me into the fiery furnace if I say come on. So we go in and get three bags of Havmore potato chips which not only are the best potato chips but the best bags for blowin up and bustin real loud so the matron come trottin down the aisle with her chunky self, flashin that flashlight dead in your eye so you can give her some lip, and if she answer back and you already finish seein the show anyway, why then you just turn the place out. Which I love to do, no lie. With Baby Jason kickin at the seat in front, egging me on, and Big Brood mumblin bout what fiercesome things we goin do. Which means me. Like when the big boys come up on us talkin bout Lemme a nickel. It's me that hide the money. Or when the bad boys in the park take Big Brood's Spaudeen[1] way from him. It's me that jump on they back and fight awhile. And it's me that turns out the show if the matron get too salty.

So the movie come on and right away it's this churchy music and clearly not about no gorilla. Bout Jesus. And I am ready to kill, not cause I got anything gainst Jesus. Just that when you fixed to watch a gorilla picture you don't wanna get messed around with Sunday School stuff. So I am mad. Besides, we see this raggedy old brown film *King of Kings*[2] every year and enough's enough. Grownups figure they can treat you just anyhow. Which burns me up. There I am, my feet up and my Havmore potato chips really salty and crispy and two jawbreakers in my lap and the money safe in my shoe from the big boys, and there comes this Jesus stuff. So we all go wild. Yellin, booin, stompin and carrying on. Really to wake the man in the booth up there who musta went to sleep and put on the wrong reels. But no, cause he holler down to shut up and then he turn the sound up so we really gotta holler like crazy to even hear ourselves good. And the matron ropes off the children section and flashes her light all over the place and we yell some more and some kids slip under the rope and run up and down the aisle just to show it take more than some dusty ole velvet rope to tie us down. And I'm flingin the kid in front of me's popcorn. And Baby Jason kickin seats. And it's really somethin. Then here come the big and bad matron, the one they let out in case of emergency. And she totin that flashlight like she gonna use it on somebody. This here the colored matron Brandy and her friends call Thunderbuns. She do not play. She do not smile. So we shut up and watch the simple ass picture.

1. Probably refers to "Spaldeen," the small rubber ball made by the Spalding company and used for stick-ball.   2. Although there is a 1961 version of the film, this probably refers to the silent-movie version made in the 1920s.

5   Which is not so simple as it is stupid. Cause I realized that just about anybody in my family is better than this god they always talkin about. My daddy
wouldn't stand for nobody treatin any of us that way. My mama specially. And I
can just see it now, Big Brood up there on the cross talkin bout Forgive them
Daddy cause they don't know what they doin. And my Mama say Get on down
from there you big fool, whatcha think this is, playtime? And my Daddy yellin
to Granddaddy to get him a ladder cause Big Brood actin the fool, his mother
side of the family showin up. And my mama and her sister Daisy jumpin on
them Romans beatin them with they pocketbooks. And Hunca Bubba tellin
them folks on they knees they better get out the way and go get some help or
they goin to get trampled on. And Granddaddy Vale sayin Leave the boy alone,
if that's what he wants to do with his life we ain't got nothin to say about it.
Then Aunt Daisy givin him a taste of that pocketbook, fussin bout what a damn
fool old man Granddaddy is. Then everybody jumpin in his chest like the time
Uncle Clayton went in the army and come back with only one leg and Granddaddy say somethin stupid about that's life. And by this time Big Brood off the
cross and in the park playin handball or skully[3] or somethin. And the family in
the kitchen throwin dishes at each other, screamin bout if you hadn't done this
I wouldn't had to do that. And me in the parlor trying to do my arithmetic yellin
Shut it off.

Which is what I was yellin all by myself which make me a sittin target for
Thunderbuns. But when I yell We want our money back, that gets everybody in
chorus. And the movie windin up with this heavenly cloud music and the smart-
ass up there in his hole in the wall turns up the sound again to drown us out.
Then there comes Bugs Bunny which we already seen so we know we been had.
No gorilla my nuthin. And Big Brood say Awwww sheeet, we goin to see the
manager and get our money back. And I know from this we business. So I brush
the potato chips out of my hair which is where Baby Jason like to put em, and I
march myself up the aisle to deal with the manager who is a crook in the first
place for lyin out there sayin *Gorilla, My Love* playin. And I never did like the
man cause he oily and pasty at the same time like the bad guy in the serial, the
one that got a hideout behind a push-button bookcase and play "Moonlight
Sonata"[4] with gloves on. I knock on the door and I am furious. And I am alone,
too. Cause Big Brood suddenly got to go so bad even though my mama told us
bout goin in them nasty bathrooms. And I hear him sigh like he disgusted when
he get to the door and see only a little kid there. And now I'm really furious
cause I get so tired grownups messin over kids cause they little and can't take
em to court. What is it, he say to me like I lost my mittens or wet myself or am
somebody's retarded child. When in reality I am the smartest kid P.S. 186 ever
had in its whole lifetime and you can ax anybody. Even them teachers that don't
like me cause I won't sing them Southern songs or back off when they tell me
my questions are out of order. And cause my Mama come up there in a minute

---

3. A basketball game that tests shooting skill and can be played alone or as a contest between two
people.   4. Popular name for Beethoven's 14th Sonata. The man who plays this song with gloves
on refers to the ever-creepy *Phantom of the Opera*.

when them teachers start playin the dozens[5] behind colored folks. She stalks in with her hat pulled down bad and that Persian lamb coat draped back over one hip on account of she got her fist planted there so she can talk that talk which gets us all hypnotized, and teacher be comin undone cause she know this could be her job and her behind cause Mama got pull with the Board and bad by her own self anyhow.

So I kick the door open wider and just walk right by him and sit down and tell the man about himself and that I want my money back and that goes for Baby Jason and Big Brood too. And he still trying to shuffle me out the door even though I'm sittin which shows him for the fool he is. Just like them teachers do fore they realize Mama like a stone on that spot and ain't backin up. So he ain't gettin up off the money. So I was forced to leave, takin the matches from under his ashtray, and set a fire under the candy stand, which closed the raggedy ole Washington down for a week. My Daddy had the suspect it was me cause Big Brood got a big mouth. But I explained right quick what the whole thing was about and I figured it was even-steven. Cause if you say Gorilla, My Love, you supposed to mean it. Just like when you say you goin to give me a party on my birthday, you gotta mean it. And if you say me and Baby Jason can go South pecan haulin with Granddaddy Vale, you better not be comin up with no stuff about the weather look uncertain or did you mop the bathroom or any other trickified business. I mean even gangsters in the movies say My word is my bond. So don't nobody get away with nothin far as I'm concerned. So Daddy put his belt back on. Cause that's the way I was raised. Like my Mama say in one of them situations when I won't back down, Okay Badbird, you right. Your point is well-taken. Not that Badbird my name, just what she say when she tired arguin and know I'm right. And Aunt Jo, who is the hardest head in the family and worse even than Aunt Daisy, she say, You absolutely right Miss Muffin, which also ain't my real name but the name she gave me one time when I got some medicine shot in my behind and wouldn't get up off her pillows for nothin. And even Granddaddy Vale—who got no memory to speak of, so sometime you can just plain lie to him, if you want to be like that—he say, Well if that's what I said, then that's it. But this name business was different they said. It wasn't like Hunca Bubba had gone back on his word or anything. Just that he was thinkin bout gettin married and was usin his real name now. Which ain't the way I saw it at all.

So there I am in the navigator seat. And I turned to him and just plain ole ax him. I mean I come right on out with it. No sense goin all around that barn the old folks talk about. And like my mama say, Hazel—which is my real name and what she remembers to call me when she bein serious—when you got somethin on your mind, speak up and let the chips fall where they may. And if anybody don't like it, tell em to come see your mama. And Daddy look up from the paper and say, You hear your Mama good, Hazel. And tell em to come see me first. Like that. That's how I was raised.

5. Ritualized game or contest in which two participants exchange insults directed against each other's relatives.

So I turn clear round in the navigator seat and say, "Look here, Hunca Bubba or Jefferson Windsong Vale or whatever your name is, you gonna marry this girl?"

"Sure am," he say, all grins.

And I say, "Member that time you was baby-sittin me when we lived at four-o-nine and there was this big snow and Mama and Daddy got held up in the country so you had to stay for two days?"

And he say, "Sure do."

"Well. You remember how you told me I was the cutest thing that ever walked the earth?"

"Oh, you were real cute when you were little," he say, which is supposed to be funny. I am not laughin.

"Well. You remember what you said?"

And Granddaddy Vale squintin over the wheel and axin Which way, Scout. But Scout is busy and don't care if we all get lost for days.

"Watcha mean, Peaches?"

"My name is Hazel. And what I mean is you said you were going to marry *me* when I grew up. You were going to wait. That's what I mean, my dear Uncle Jefferson." And he don't say nuthin. Just look at me real strange like he never saw me before in life. Like he lost in some weird town in the middle of night and lookin for directions and there's no one to ask. Like it was me that messed up the maps and turned the road posts round. "Well, you said it, didn't you?" And Baby Jason lookin back and forth like we playin ping-pong. Only I ain't playin. I'm hurtin and I can hear that I am screamin. And Granddaddy Vale mumblin how we never gonna get to where we goin if I don't turn around and take my navigator job serious.

"Well, for cryin out loud, Hazel, you just a little girl. And I was just teasin."

" 'And I was just teasin,' " I say back just how he said it so he can hear what a terrible thing it is. Then I don't say nuthin. And he don't say nuthin. And Baby Jason don't say nuthin nohow. Then Granddaddy Vale speak up. "Look here, Precious, it was Hunca Bubba what told you them things. This here, Jefferson Winston Vale." And Hunca Bubba say, "That's right. That was somebody else. I'm a new somebody."

"You a lyin dawg," I say, when I meant to say treacherous dog, but just couldn't get hold of the word. It slipped away from me. And I'm crying and crumplin down in the seat and just don't care. And Granddaddy say to hush and steps on the gas. And I'm losin my bearins and don't even know where to look on the map cause I can't see for cryin. And Baby Jason cryin too. Cause he is my blood brother and understands that we must stick together or be forever lost, what with grown-ups playin change-up and turnin you round every which way so bad. And don't even say they sorry.

1972

ALICE MUNRO

Boys and Girls

My father was a fox farmer. That is, he raised silver foxes, in pens; and in the fall and early winter, when their fur was prime, he killed them and skinned them and sold their pelts to the Hudson's Bay Company or the Montreal Fur Traders. These companies supplied us with heroic calendars to hang, one on each side of the kitchen door. Against a background of cold blue sky and black pine forests and treacherous northern rivers, plumed adventurers planted the flags of England or of France; magnificent savages bent their backs to the portage.

For several weeks before Christmas, my father worked after supper in the cellar of our house. The cellar was white-washed, and lit by a hundred-watt bulb over the worktable. My brother Laird and I sat on the top step and watched. My father removed the pelt inside-out from the body of the fox, which looked surprisingly small, mean and rat-like, deprived of its arrogant weight of fur. The naked, slippery bodies were collected in a sack and buried at the dump. One time the hired man, Henry Bailey, had taken a swipe at me with this sack, saying, "Christmas present!" My mother thought that was not funny. In fact she disliked the whole pelting operation—that was what the killing, skinning, and preparation of the furs was called—and wished it did not have to take place in the house. There was the smell. After the pelt had been stretched inside-out on a long board my father scraped away delicately, removing the little clotted webs of blood vessels, the bubbles of fat; the smell of blood and animal fat, with the strong primitive odour of the fox itself, penetrated all parts of the house. I found it reassuringly seasonal, like the smell of oranges and pine needles.

Henry Bailey suffered from bronchial troubles. He would cough and cough until his narrow face turned scarlet, and his light blue, derisive eyes filled up with tears; then he took the lid off the stove, and, standing well back, shot out a great clot of phlegm—hsss—straight into the heart of the flames. We admired him for this performance and for his ability to make his stomach growl at will, and for his laughter, which was full of high whistlings and gurglings and involved the whole faulty machinery of his chest. It was sometimes hard to tell what he was laughing at, and always possible that it might be us.

After we had been sent to bed we could still smell fox and still hear Henry's laugh, but these things, reminders of the warm, safe, brightly lit downstairs world, seemed lost and diminished, floating on the stale cold air upstairs. We were afraid at night in the winter. We were not afraid of *outside* though this was the time of year when snowdrifts curled around our house like sleeping whales and the wind harassed us all night, coming up from the buried fields, the frozen swamp, with its old bugbear chorus of threats and misery. We were afraid of *inside*, the room where we slept. At this time the upstairs of our house was not finished. A brick chimney went up one wall. In the middle of the floor was a square hole, with a wooden railing around it; that was where the stairs came up.

On the other side of the stairwell were the things that nobody had any use for any more—a soldiery roll of linoleum, standing on end, a wicker baby carriage, a fern basket, china jugs and basins with cracks in them, a picture of the Battle of Balaclava,[1] very sad to look at. I had told Laird, as soon as he was old enough to understand such things, that bats and skeletons lived over there; whenever a man escaped from the county jail, twenty miles away, I imagined that he had somehow let himself in the window and was hiding behind the linoleum. But we had rules to keep us safe. When the light was on, we were safe as long as we did not step off the square of worn carpet which defined our bedroom-space; when the light was off no place was safe but the beds themselves. I had to turn out the light kneeling on the end of my bed, and stretching as far as I could to reach the cord.

5   In the dark we lay on our beds, our narrow life rafts, and fixed our eyes on the faint light coming up the stairwell, and sang songs. Laird sang "Jingle Bells," which he would sing any time, whether it was Christmas or not, and I sang "Danny Boy." I loved the sound of my own voice, frail and supplicating, rising in the dark. We could make out the tall frosted shapes of the windows now, gloomy and white. When I came to the part, *When I am dead, as dead I well may be*—a fit of shivering caused not by the cold sheets but by pleasurable emotion almost silenced me. *You'll kneel and say, an Ave there above me*—What was an Ave? Every day I forgot to find out.

Laird went straight from singing to sleep. I could hear his long, satisfied, bubbly breaths. Now for the time that remained to me, the most perfectly private and perhaps the best time of the whole day, I arranged myself tightly under the covers and went on with one of the stories I was telling myself from night to night. These stories were about myself, when I had grown a little older; they took place in a world that was recognizably mine, yet one that presented opportunities for courage, boldness and self-sacrifice, as mine never did. I rescued people from a bombed building (it discouraged me that the real war had gone on so far away from Jubilee). I shot two rabid wolves who were menacing the schoolyard (the teachers cowered terrified at my back). I rode a fine horse spiritedly down the main street of Jubilee, acknowledging the townspeople's gratitude for some yet-to-be-worked-out piece of heroism (nobody ever rode a horse there, except King Billy in the Orangemen's Day[2] parade). There was always riding and shooting in these stories, though I had only been on a horse twice—bareback because we did not own a saddle—and the second time I had slid right around and dropped under the horse's feet; it had stepped placidly over me. I really was learning to shoot, but I could not hit anything yet, not even tin cans on fence posts.

Alive, the foxes inhabited a world my father made for them. It was surrounded by a high guard fence, like a medieval town, with a gate that was pad-

1. An indecisive Crimean War battle fought on October 25, 1854.   2. The Orange Society is an Irish Protestant group named after William of Orange, who, as King William III of England, defeated the Catholic James II. The Society sponsors an annual procession on July 12 to commemorate the victory of William III at the Battle of the Boyne (1690).

locked at night. Along the streets of this town were ranged large, sturdy pens. Each of them had a real door that a man could go through, a wooden ramp along the wire, for the foxes to run up and down on, and a kennel—something like a clothes chest with airholes—where they slept and stayed in winter and had their young. There were feeding and watering dishes attached to the wire in such a way that they could be emptied and cleaned from the outside. The dishes were made of old tin cans, and the ramps and kennels of odds and ends of old lumber. Everything was tidy and ingenious; my father was tirelessly inventive and his favourite book in the world was *Robinson Crusoe*.[3] He had fitted a tin drum on a wheelbarrow, for bringing water down to the pens. This was my job in summer, when the foxes had to have water twice a day. Between nine and ten o'clock in the morning, and again after supper, I filled the drum at the pump and trundled it down through the barnyard to the pens, where I parked it, and filled my watering can and went along the streets. Laird came too, with his little cream and green gardening can, filled too full and knocking against his legs and slopping water on his canvas shoes. I had the real watering can, my father's, though I could only carry it three-quarters full.

The foxes all had names, which were printed on a tin plate and hung beside their doors. They were not named when they were born, but when they survived the first year's pelting and were added to the breeding stock. Those my father had named were called names like Prince, Bob, Wally and Betty. Those I had named were called Star or Turk, or Maureen or Diana. Laird named one Maud after a hired girl we had when he was little, one Harold after a boy at school, and one Mexico, he did not say why.

Naming them did not make pets out of them, or anything like it. Nobody but my father ever went into the pens, and he had twice had blood-poisoning from bites. When I was bringing them their water they prowled up and down on the paths they had made inside their pens, barking seldom—they saved that for nighttime, when they might get up a chorus of community frenzy—but always watching me, their eyes burning, clear gold, in their pointed, malevolent faces. They were beautiful for their delicate legs and heavy, aristocratic tails and the bright fur sprinkled on dark down their backs—which gave them their name—but especially for their faces, drawn exquisitely sharp in pure hostility, and their golden eyes.

Besides carrying water I helped my father when he cut the long grass, and the lamb's quarter and flowering money-musk, that grew between the pens. He cut with the scythe and I raked into piles. Then he took a pitchfork and threw fresh-cut grass all over the top of the pens, to keep the foxes cooler and shade their coats, which were browned by too much sun. My father did not talk to me unless it was about the job we were doing. In this he was quite different from my mother, who, if she was feeling cheerful, would tell me all sorts of things— the name of a dog she had had when she was a little girl, the names of boys she had gone out with later on when she was grown up, and what certain dresses of

10

---

3. Novel (1719) by Daniel Defoe about a man shipwrecked on a desert island; it goes into great detail about his ingenious contraptions.

hers had looked like—she could not imagine now what had become of them. Whatever thoughts and stories my father had were private, and I was shy of him and would never ask him questions. Nevertheless I worked willingly under his eyes, and with a feeling of pride. One time a feed salesman came down into the pens to talk to him and my father said, "Like to have you meet my new hired man." I turned away and raked furiously, red in the face with pleasure.

"Could of fooled me," said the salesman. "I thought it was only a girl."

After the grass was cut, it seemed suddenly much later in the year. I walked on stubble in the earlier evening, aware of the reddening skies, the entering silences, of fall. When I wheeled the tank out of the gate and put the padlock on, it was almost dark. One night at this time I saw my mother and father standing talking on the little rise of ground we called the gangway, in front of the barn. My father had just come from the meathouse; he had his stiff bloody apron on, and a pail of cut-up meat in his hand.

It was an odd thing to see my mother down at the barn. She did not often come out of the house unless it was to do something—hang out the wash or dig potatoes in the garden. She looked out of place, with her bare lumpy legs, not touched by the sun, her apron still on and damp across the stomach from the supper dishes. Her hair was tied up in a kerchief, wisps of it falling out. She would tie her hair up like this in the morning, saying she did not have time to do it properly, and it would stay tied up all day. It was true, too; she really did not have time. These days our back porch was piled with baskets of peaches and grapes and pears, bought in town, and onions and tomatoes and cucumbers grown at home, all waiting to be made into jelly and jam and preserves, pickles and chili sauce. In the kitchen there was a fire in the stove all day, jars clinked in boiling water, sometimes a cheesecloth bag was strung on a pole between two chairs, straining blue-black grape pulp for jelly. I was given jobs to do and I would sit at the table peeling peaches that had been soaked in the hot water, or cutting up onions, my eyes smarting and streaming. As soon as I was done I ran out of the house, trying to get out of earshot before my mother thought of what she wanted me to do next. I hated the hot dark kitchen in summer, the green blinds and the flypapers, the same old oilcloth table and wavy mirror and bumpy linoleum. My mother was too tired and preoccupied to talk to me, she had no heart to tell about the Normal School Graduation Dance; sweat trickled over her face and she was always counting under her breath, pointing at jars, dumping cups of sugar. It seemed to me that work in the house was endless, dreary and peculiarly depressing; work done out of doors, and in my father's service, was ritualistically important.

I wheeled the tank up to the barn, where it was kept, and I heard my mother saying, "Wait till Laird gets a little bigger, then you'll have a real help."

What my father said I did not hear. I was pleased by the way he stood listening, politely as he would to a salesman or a stranger, but with an air of wanting to get on with his real work. I felt my mother had no business down here and I wanted him to feel the same way. What did she mean about Laird? He was no help to anybody. Where was he now? Swinging himself sick on the swing, going around in circles, or trying to catch caterpillars. He never once stayed with me till I was finished.

"And then I can use her more in the house," I heard my mother say. She had a dead-quiet, regretful way of talking about me that always made me uneasy. "I just get my back turned and she runs off. It's not like I had a girl in the family at all."

I went and sat on a feed bag in the corner of the barn, not wanting to appear when this conversation was going on. My mother, I felt, was not to be trusted. She was kinder than my father and more easily fooled, but you could not depend on her, and the real reasons for the things she said and did were not to be known. She loved me, and she sat up late at night making a dress of the difficult style I wanted, for me to wear when school started, but she was also my enemy. She was always plotting. She was plotting now to get me to stay in the house more, although she knew I hated it (*because* she knew I hated it) and keep me from working for my father. It seemed to me she would do this simply out of perversity, and to try her power. It did not occur to me that she could be lonely, or jealous. No grown-up could be; they were too fortunate. I sat and kicked my heels monotonously against a feedbag, raising dust, and did not come out till she was gone.

At any rate, I did not expect my father to pay any attention to what she said. Who could imagine Laird doing my work—Laird remembering the padlock and cleaning out the watering-dishes with a leaf on the end of a stick, or even wheeling the tank without it tumbling over? It showed how little my mother knew about the way things really were.

I have forgotten to say what the foxes were fed. My father's bloody apron reminded me. They were fed horsemeat. At this time most farmers still kept horses, and when a horse got too old to work, or broke a leg or got down and would not get up, as they sometimes did, the owner would call my father, and he and Henry went out to the farm in the truck. Usually they shot and butchered the horse there, paying the farmer from five to twelve dollars. If they had already too much meat on hand, they would bring the horse back alive, and keep it for a few days or weeks in our stable, until the meat was needed. After the war the farmers were buying tractors and gradually getting rid of horses altogether, so it sometimes happened that we got a good healthy horse, that there was just no use for any more. If this happened in the winter we might keep the horse in our stable till spring, for we had plenty of hay and if there was a lot of snow—and the plow did not always get our road cleared—it was convenient to be able to go to town with a horse and cutter.[4]

The winter I was eleven years old we had two horses in the stable. We did not know what names they had had before, so we called them Mack and Flora. Mack was an old black workhorse, sooty and indifferent. Flora was a sorrel mare, a driver. We took them both out in the cutter. Mack was slow and easy to handle.

20

4. A small, light sleigh.

Flora was given to fits of violent alarm, veering at cars and even at other horses, but we loved her speed and high-stepping, her general air of gallantry and abandon. On Saturdays we went down to the stable and as soon as we opened the door on its cosy, animal-smelling darkness Flora threw up her head, rolled her eyes, whinnied despairingly and pulled herself through a crisis of nerves on the spot. It was not safe to go into her stall; she would kick.

This winter also I began to hear a great deal more on the theme my mother had sounded when she had been talking in front of the barn. I no longer felt safe. It seemed that in the minds of the people around me there was a steady undercurrent of thought, not to be deflected, on this one subject. The word *girl* had formerly seemed to me innocent and unburdened, like the world *child*; now it appeared that it was no such thing. A girl was not, as I had supposed, simply what I was; it was what I had to become. It was a definition, always touched with emphasis, with reproach and disappointment. Also it was a joke on me. Once Laird and I were fighting, and for the first time ever I had to use all my strength against him; even so, he caught and pinned my arm for a moment, really hurting me. Henry saw this, and laughed, saying, "Oh, that there Laird's gonna show you, one of these days!" Laird was getting a lot bigger. But I was getting bigger too.

My grandmother came to stay with us for a few weeks and I heard other things. "Girls don't slam doors like that." "Girls keep their knees together when they sit down." And worse still, when I asked some questions, "That's none of girls' business." I continued to slam the doors and sit as awkwardly as possible, thinking that by such measures I kept myself free.

When spring came, the horses were let out in the barnyard. Mack stood against the barn wall trying to scratch his neck and haunches, but Flora trotted up and down and reared at the fences, clattering her hooves against the rails. Snow drifts dwindled quickly, revealing the hard grey and brown earth, the familiar rise and fall of the ground, plain and bare after the fantastic landscape of winter. There was a great feeling of opening-out, of release. We just wore rubbers now, over our shoes; our feet felt ridiculously light. One Saturday we went out to the stable and found all the doors open, letting in the unaccustomed sunlight and fresh air. Henry was there, just idling around looking at his collection of calendars which were tacked up behind the stalls in a part of the stable my mother had probably never seen.

"Come to say goodbye to your old friend Mack?" Henry said. "Here, you give him a taste of oats." He poured some oats into Laird's cupped hands and Laird went to feed Mack. Mack's teeth were in bad shape. He ate very slowly, patiently shifting the oats around in his mouth, trying to find a stump of a molar to grind it on. "Poor old Mack," said Henry mournfully. "When a horse's teeth's gone, he's gone. That's about the way."

25   "Are you going to shoot him today?" I said. Mack and Flora had been in the stable so long I had almost forgotten they were going to be shot.

Henry didn't answer me. Instead he started to sing in a high, trembly, mocking-sorrowful voice, *Oh, there's no more work, for poor Uncle Ned, he's gone* where the good darkies go.[5] Mack's thick, blackish tongue worked diligently at Laird's hand. I went out before the song was ended and sat down on the gangway.

I had never seen them shoot a horse, but I knew where it was done. Last summer Laird and I had come upon a horse's entrails before they were buried. We had thought it was a big black snake, coiled up in the sun. That was around in the field that ran up beside the barn. I thought that if we went inside the barn, and found a wide crack or knothole to look through we would be able to see them do it. It was not something I wanted to see; just the same, if a thing really happened, it was better to see it, and know.

My father came down from the house, carrying the gun.

"What are you doing here?" he said.

"Nothing."

"Go on up and play around the house."

He sent Laird out of the stable. I said to Laird, "Do you want to see them shoot Mack?" and without waiting for an answer led him around to the front door of the barn, opened it carefully, and went in. "Be quiet or they'll hear us," I said. We could hear Henry and my father talking in the stable, then the heavy, shuffling steps of Mack being backed out of his stall.

In the loft it was cold and dark. Thin, crisscrossed beams of sunlight fell through the cracks. The hay was low. It was a rolling country, hills and hollows, slipping under our feet. About four feet up was a beam going around the walls. We piled hay up in one corner and I boosted Laird up and hoisted myself. The beam was not very wide; we crept along it with our hands flat on the barn walls. There were plenty of knotholes, and I found one that gave me the view I wanted—a corner of the barnyard, the gate, part of the field. Laird did not have a knothole and began to complain.

I showed him a widened crack between two boards. "Be quiet and wait. If they hear you you'll get us in trouble."

My father came in sight carrying the gun. Henry was leading Mack by the halter. He dropped it and took out his cigarette papers and tobacco; he rolled cigarettes for my father and himself. While this was going on Mack nosed around in the old, dead grass along the fence. Then my father opened the gate and they took Mack through. Henry led Mack way from the path to a patch of ground and they talked together, not loud enough for us to hear. Mack again began searching for a mouthful of fresh grass, which was not to be found. My father walked away in a straight line, and stopped short at a distance which seemed to suit him. Henry was walking away from Mack too, but sideways, still negligently holding on to the halter. My father raised the gun and Mack looked up as if he had noticed something and my father shot him.

Mack did not collapse at once but swayed, lurched sideways and fell, first on his side; then he rolled over on his back and, amazingly, kicked his legs for a few seconds in the air. At this Henry laughed, as if Mack had done a trick for

30

35

5. Lines from the Stephen Foster song "Old Uncle Ned."

him. Laird, who had drawn a long, groaning breath of surprise when the shot was fired, said out loud, "He's not dead." And it seemed to me it might be true. But his legs stopped, he rolled on his side again, his muscles quivered and sank. The two men walked over and looked at him in a businesslike way; they bent down and examined his forehead where the bullet had gone in, and now I saw his blood on the brown grass.

"Now they just skin him and cut him up," I said. "Let's go." My legs were a little shaky and I jumped gratefully down into the hay. "Now you've seen how they shoot a horse," I said in a congratulatory way, as if I had seen it many times before. "Let's see if any barn cat's had kittens in the hay." Laird jumped. He seemed young and obedient again. Suddenly I remembered how, when he was little, I had brought him into the barn and told him to climb the ladder to the top beam. That was in the spring, too, when the hay was low. I had done it out of a need for excitement, a desire for something to happen so that I could tell about it. He was wearing a little bulky brown and white checked coat, made down from one of mine. He went all the way up, just as I told him, and sat down on the top beam with the hay far below him on one side, and the barn floor and some old machinery on the other. Then I ran screaming to my father, "Laird's up on the top beam!" My father came, my mother came, my father went up the ladder talking very quietly and brought Laird down under his arm, at which my mother leaned against the ladder and began to cry. They said to me, "Why weren't you watching him?" but nobody ever knew the truth. Laird did not know enough to tell. But whenever I saw the brown and white checked coat hanging in the closet, or at the bottom of the rag bag, which was where it ended up, I felt a weight in my stomach, the sadness of unexorcized guilt.

I looked at Laird who did not even remember this, and I did not like the look on this thin, winter-pale face. His expression was not frightened or upset, but remote, concentrating. "Listen," I said, in an unusually bright and friendly voice, "you aren't going to tell, are you?"

"No," he said absently.

"Promise."

"Promise," he said. I grabbed the hand behind his back to make sure he was not crossing his fingers. Even so, he might have a nightmare; it might come out that way. I decided I had better work hard to get all thoughts of what he had seen out of his mind—which, it seemed to me, could not hold very many things at a time. I got some money I had saved and that afternoon we went into Jubilee and saw a show, with Judy Canova,[6] at which we both laughed a great deal. After that I thought it would be all right.

Two weeks later I knew they were going to shoot Flora. I knew from the night before, when I heard my mother ask if the hay was holding out all right, and my father said, "Well, after to-morrow there'll just be the cow, and we should be able to put her out to grass in another week." So I knew it was Flora's turn in the morning.

This time I didn't think of watching it. That was something to see just one

40

6. American comedian best known for her yodeling in hillbilly movies of the 1940s.

time. I had not thought about it very often since, but sometimes when I was busy, working at school, or standing in front of the mirror combing my hair and wondering if I would be pretty when I grew up, the whole scene would flash into my mind: I would see the easy, practised way my father raised the gun, and hear Henry laughing when Mack kicked his legs in the air. I did not have any great feeling of horror and opposition, such as a city child might have had; I was too used to seeing the death of animals as a necessity by which we lived. Yet I felt a little ashamed, and there was a new wariness, a sense of holding-off, in my attitude to my father and his work.

It was a fine day, and we were going around the yard picking up tree branches that had been torn off in winter storms. This was something we had been told to do, and also we wanted to use them to make a teepee. We heard Flora whinny, and then my father's voice and Henry's shouting, and we ran down to the barnyard to see what was going on.

The stable door was open. Henry had just brought Flora out, and she had broken away from him. She was running free in the barnyard, from one end to the other. We climbed up on the fence. It was exciting to see her running, whinnying, going up on her hind legs, prancing and threatening like a horse in a Western movie, an unbroken ranch horse, though she was just an old driver, an old sorrel mare. My father and Henry ran after her and tried to grab the dangling halter. They tried to work her into a corner, and they had almost succeeded when she made a run between them, wild-eyed, and disappeared around the corner of the barn. We heard the rails clatter down as she got over the fence, and Henry yelled, "She's into the field now!"

That meant she was in the long L-shaped field that ran up by the house. If she got around the center, heading towards the lane, the gate was open; the truck had been driven into the field this morning. My father shouted to me, because I was on the other side of the fence, nearest the lane, "Go shut the gate!"

I could run very fast. I ran across the garden, past the tree where our swing was hung, and jumped across a ditch into the lane. There was the open gate. She had not got out, I could not see her up on the road; she must have run to the other end of the field. The gate was heavy. I lifted it out of the gravel and carried it across the roadway. I had it half-way across when she came in sight, galloping straight towards me. There was just time to get the chain on. Laird came scrambling through the ditch to help me.

Instead of shutting the gate, I opened it as wide as I could. I did not make any decision to do this, it was just what I did. Flora never slowed down; she galloped straight past me, and Laird jumped up and down, yelling, "Shut it, shut it!" even after it was too late. My father and Henry appeared in the field a moment too late to see what I had done. They only saw Flora heading for the township road. They would think I had not got there in time.

They did not waste any time asking about it. They went back to the barn and got the gun and the knives they used, and put these in the truck; then they turned the truck around and came bouncing up the field toward us. Laird called to them, "Let me go too, let me go too!" and Henry stopped the truck and they took him in. I shut the gate after they were all gone.

50   I supposed Laird would tell. I wondered what would happen to me. I had never disobeyed my father before, and I could not understand why I had done it. Flora would not really get away. They would catch up with her in the truck. Or if they did not catch her this morning somebody would see her and telephone us this afternoon or tomorrow. There was no wild country here for her to run to, only farms. What was more, my father had paid for her, we needed the meat to feed the foxes, we needed the foxes to make our living. All I had done was make more work for my father who worked hard enough already. And when my father found out about it he was not going to trust me any more; he would know that I was not entirely on his side. I was on Flora's side, and that made me no use to anybody, not even to her. Just the same, I did not regret it; when she came running at me and I held the gate open, that was the only thing I could do.

I went back to the house, and my mother said, "What's all the commotion?" I told her that Flora had kicked down the fence and got away. "Your poor father," she said, "now he'll have to go chasing over the countryside. Well, there isn't any use planning dinner before one." She put up the ironing board. I wanted to tell her, but thought better of it and went upstairs and sat on my bed.

Lately I had been trying to make my part of the room fancy, spreading the bed with old lace curtains, and fixing myself a dressing-table with some leftovers of cretonne for a skirt. I planned to put up some kind of barricade between my bed and Laird's, to keep my section separate from his. In the sunlight, the lace curtains were just dusty rags. We did not sing at night any more. One night when I was singing Laird said, "You sound silly," and I went right on but the next night I did not start. There was not so much need to anyway, we were no longer afraid. We knew it was just old furniture over there, old jumble and confusion. We did not keep to the rules. I still stayed awake after Laird was asleep and told myself stories, but even in these stories something different was happening, mysterious alterations took place. A story might start off in the old way, with a spectacular danger, a fire or wild animals, and for a while I might rescue people; then things would change around, and instead, somebody would be rescuing me. It might be a boy from our class at school, or even Mr. Campbell, our teacher, who tickled girls under the arms. And at this point the story concerned itself at great length with what I looked like — how long my hair was, and what kind of dress I had on; by the time I had these details worked out the real excitement of the story was lost.

It was later than one o'clock when the truck came back. The tarpaulin was over the back, which meant there was meat in it. My mother had to heat dinner up all over again. Henry and my father had changed from their bloody overalls into ordinary working overalls in the barn, and they washed their arms and necks and faces at the sink, and splashed water on their hair and combed it. Laird lifted his arm to show off a streak of blood. "We shot old Flora," he said, "and cut her up in fifty pieces."

"Well I don't want to hear about it," my mother said. "And don't come to my table like that."

My father made him go and wash the blood off.   55

We sat down and my father said grace and Henry pasted his chewing-gum on the end of his fork, the way he always did; when he took it off he would have us admire the pattern. We began to pass the bowls of steaming, overcooked vegetables. Laird looked across the table at me and said proudly, distinctly, "Anyway it was her fault Flora got away."

"What?" my father said.

"She could of shut the gate and she didn't. She just open' it up and Flora run out."

"Is that right?" my father said.

Everybody at the table was looking at me. I nodded, swallowing food with   60 great difficulty. To my shame, tears flooded my eyes.

My father made a curt sound of disgust. "What did you do that for?"

I did not answer. I put down my fork and waited to be sent from the table, still not looking up.

But this did not happen. For some time nobody said anything, then Laird said matter-of-factly, "She's crying."

"Never mind," my father said. He spoke with resignation, even good humour, the words which absolved and dismissed me for good. "She's only a girl," he said.

I didn't protest that, even in my heart. Maybe it was true.   65

1968

▼　▼　▼

LITERARY KIND AS CONTEXT A Glossary

genre: the largest category for classifying literature—fiction, poetry, drama

initiation story: a *kind* of short story in which a character—often but not always a child or young person—first learns a significant, usually life-changing truth about the universe, society, people, himself or herself

kind: a species or subcategory within a *subgenre; initiation stories* are a subcategory of the subgenre short story

rite of passage: a ritual or ceremony marking an individual's passing from one stage or state to a more advance one, or an event in one's life that seems to have such significance; a formal initiation

subgenre: division within the category of a *genre;* novel, novella, and short story are subgenres of the genre fiction

QUESTIONS

1. What does the title literally denote in the story "Araby"? What does it suggest? How do both its denotative and connotative meanings function in the story?

2. What is the point of view (focus) in "Araby"? Are the words of the story the boy's? How does the difference between focus and voice define the nature of the initiation in the story?

3. What is the nature of the initiation in "Boys and Girls"? in "Gorilla, My Love"? How are the two initiation experiences similar? How do they differ?

4. The phrase "only a girl" appears twice in Alice Munro's story. How do the contexts differ? How do the implications of the phrase differ at each appearance (that is, what does it mean or suggest each time)?

WRITING SUGGESTIONS

1. Compare the use of the theme of romance-of-childhood versus realism-of-maturity in "Araby" and "Boys and Girls."

2. Using "Gorilla, My Love" as a model, write a personal narrative in which you describe an initiation in your own life, or a fictional event.

3. Find a pattern of words or images that recurs throughout one of the stories in this chapter. Relate the pattern to the story's theme, citing evidence from the story.

STUDENT WRITING

Teri Garrity's paper is one student's response to the third writing assignment. Teri discovered a pattern of blindness and light in "Araby," and, in her paper, relates the pattern to the larger theme of appearance and reality in the story. She substantiates her thesis by using concrete examples from the story.

To See the Light

Teri Garrity

Many times we encounter something or someone who appears to be more important to us than anything else. Often we lose track of those things that really are most worthy. Occasionally, we hurt others or ourselves in the process of discovering which things are of greatest significance in our lives. One of the main themes in James Joyce's story "Araby" seems to involve such a blindness to reality. From the blindness of North Richmond Street to the blindness of the boy during his maturation, Joyce effectively illustrates the complexities of a boy's rough transition into adulthood and the confusing feelings that accompany the transition. From these blindnesses, Joyce concludes the story with the boy's painful insight into reality.

Part of the transition from childhood to adulthood involves encountering new feelings. One of the deepest of these feelings is that of love and relationships. As the boy in the story matures, his feelings are not an exception. Although he believes his love is true, it is actually blind. That is, his love for Mangan's sister is purely physical. The first picture the reader is given of her describes ". . . her figure defined by the light from the half-opened door" (par. 3). This image of the girl reappears throughout the story. Consequently, the boy seems to be blind to all except the aura of light that accompanies her appearance. Furthermore, because he has never communicated with the girl, the boy's attraction is superficial. Each description of her is similar to the following: "Her dress swung as she moved her body, and the soft rope of her hair tossed from side to side" (par. 3). The reader is given only physical descriptions of Mangan's sister; thus, he is able to infer the boy's confusion between real and ideal love. In contrast, although the boy seems to be completely obsessed with the girl, he does not wish for her to know. For instance, he watches her out the window each day, but pulls the blind "down to within an inch of the sash so that I could not be seen" (par. 4). Even though he does not realize his own blindness, he seems to want the girl to be blind to his feelings. It is apparent, then, that the boy does not understand, or see, that there is more to a real love relationship than physical attraction. His blindness to this fact leads him to be blind about the most important things in life.

As the boy's desire becomes stronger, he begins to lose sight of the more "serious work of life" (par. 12). That is, he becomes blind to everything but the girl he adores. He "chafed against the work of school" (par. 12), and "answered few questions in class" (par. 12). He completely disregards these important duties since they "stood between me and my desire," and thus, "seemed to me child's play, ugly monotonous child's play" (par. 12). Although these serious things appear to him to be "child's play," it is, in fact, his obsessive infatuation that is childish. His inability to see this, or his blindness, causes him to also become blind to the reality that he is, indeed, still a child. He is no longer interested in his companions, and their cries become "weakened and indistinct" (par. 16). The thoughts that once occupied his mind, such as playing and shouting, are replaced with images of a blind obsession. His inability to see this reality causes him a great deal of confusion. He refers to his "confused adoration," and how he, "didn't understand," and "could not tell why" (par. 5). Although he cannot interpret these feelings, they seem to reveal that he is blind to his thoughts, to his future, and to reality.

Perhaps the worst part of the boy's blindness to reality is the fact that it results in self-deception. Because of his intense admiration for the girl, he views her as a "single sensation of life" (par. 5), and he imagines that his "body was like a harp and her words and gestures were like fingers running upon the wires" (par. 5). The girl does seem to be playing him like a musical instrument: she seems to be able to manipulate him in any way. He is under her complete control. He gives up everything he has and deceives himself into thinking that he has a relationship with her. Moreover, he becomes so obsessed with presenting her a gift from Araby that he also becomes blind to the fact that she is interested in the gift, not in him.

Although he is unaware of it, the boy seems to be slowly realizing that his love is, indeed, blind. He once observes that, "Some distant lamp or lighted window gleamed below me. I was thankful that I could see so little" (par. 6). This distant lamp seems to symbolize the realization (that he would soon encounter) of his false adoration. Moreover, his reference to blindness, or thankfulness that he could not see much, is his way of avoiding the painful truth of reality. However, the boy inevitably encounters this painful realization at Araby. When he comes upon the busy bazaar, he remembers "with difficulty" (par. 26), why he is there. The busy street seems to trigger his realization that he has so long been blind to the complexity and confusion associated with his infatuation. The final determinant in his realization is the conversation between the trio at the bazaar. He recognizes the triviality of the conversation and manages to relate it to his love. After examining the "great jars that stood like eastern guards at either side of the dark entrance" (par. 33), the boy utters, "No thank you" (par. 34). This seems to reveal that he has begun to overcome his blindness and realize the truth of the relationship. In addition, the fact that the salesclerk changes the position of one of the jars could represent an elimination of the "guards" and an opening of the dark tunnel into a light one. That is, it symbolizes an elimination of the boy's blindness.

As the boy leaves the bazaar, he sees the truth: "Gazing up into the darkness, I saw myself as a creature driven and derided by vanity; and my eyes burned with anguish and anger" (par. 37). This feeling symbolizes his complete realization of his self-deceit and the shame he has succumbed to. He is overcome with anger that he let his emotions control him and cause him to be blind to all else. This pattern of blindness--from the notion of real love to the important things in life to his self-deception--suggests that he is, in fact, involved in a conflict between appearance and reality. The boy's realization of the conflict is not only a painful cure for his blindness, but it is also a large step in the direction of adulthood.

11 FORM AS CONTEXT: THE SHORT SHORT STORY AND THE NOVEL

The short short story, a story of about two thousand words or less, though it has been around for a long time, has rather suddenly become quite popular. There have been many attempts to explain this phenomenon, explanations ranging from the shrinking attention span "caused" by television, to the hurried, fragmented nature of modern life, to our disenchantment with lengthy explanations of behavior by psychologists, politicians, and novelists. There have also been attempts to define the form generically. Its boundaries have been those of the anecdote, the vignette, the parable, the poem, the short story proper, yet all these borders have been contested.

Length is not just an aspect of form, however; it also contributes significantly to a story's effect and to your consequent response. You rarely read a full-length novel in a single sitting, so not only is there a momentary recapitulation in your mind as you pick up the narrative again—something like the excerpts from the previous episode in a television miniseries—but you have lived another period of your life outside of the narrative. When you sit down to read again you are not exactly the same repository of experiences as when you put the book down, and not only are you at a different point in your life, your mood may have drastically changed as well. The novel has advantages, however, in its duration and in the times of your readings and departures: you are likely to recall the characters, scenes, and incidents, in one order or another, in more or less accurate detail, from time to time during the period you are away from the text. The novel thereby gets a texture, layers of memories and views from different angles, that is rarely obtained by a short story, and never by a short short story. You usually read a short story in a single sitting, and though it has an immediate and concentrated impact and you pause a moment and savor its emotional and intellectual effect, you can rarely recall it in all its detail; yet rarely too do you immediately begin at the beginning and read it through once again. The effect of the short short story is stronger; even if the after-effect is of the same duration (and it often is longer, because its economy has left so much out that you have to supply a great deal yourself), it is stronger compared to the length of time of your reading. You can remember, if not all, at least almost all the details. Yet it is not uncommon for strongly impressed readers to immediately read the story again. So the differences between novels, short stories, and short short stories are not merely their formal length, but the different way you read and respond to them.

On a personal note: though I can read four or five short short stories in the time it takes me to read a short story, I find it unsatisfactory to read four or five short short stories in a row. Their effects are so strong and so concentrated that reading several overcharges my response system. I rehearse the story in my mind, recalling its details, often its words, and try to fill in the details the story's conciseness can only imply. So I'd advise taking a break, perhaps at least an hour, between reading each of the stories in this chapter. And when one of these stories affects you, you may want to write an account of your emotive and intellectual responses, what you recall, and what you force yourself to supply.

The stories in this chapter represent a sampling of short short stories the editors found emotionally or intellectually moving, stories that reverberated in the mind long after the story ended. (And note that there are other stories in the anthology that fit the definition: "The Zebra Storyteller," "No One's a Mystery," "Happy Endings," and hovering around or just over the border, "The Cask of Amontillado," "A Conversation with My Father," "Her First Ball," and "Araby".)

They also represent the limits and the variety of the form. Chopin's and Hemingway's stories share the ironic reversal that perhaps come from Maupassant, but Chopin's is, as its title suggests, limited to an hour of fictional time, while Hemingway's spans years, defying any unity or constricting of time the brevity of the narrative might lead you to expect. Jamaica Kincaid's "Girl" does not seem so much to span time as to compact it: the story is largely the words of mother to daughter (with two brief responses by the daughter). The near-monologue does not take place at one moment, however; rather, we can infer (there are no internal time-indicators)—in part from the repetition, in part from our memories of our own childhood—that its instructions were repeated time and time again over the years the girl was growing up. "A Very Old Man with Enormous Wings" represents the many short short tales that are fantasies—written in a literary mode involving the consciously unreal—about places, societies, or beings that never existed, do not exist, or do not yet exist, or with qualities that are beyond or counter to the ordinary or commonsensical. Often such fantasies tease us with the possibilities of allegory but are more than likely symbolic—untranslatable into "messages" or ordinary "meaning." They exist on their own terms, representing certain aspects of human experience in fantasy more precisely than might be done in discursive prose, scientific formulas, graphs, charts. I've saved the best for last. Is Yasunari Kawabata's "The Grasshopper and the Bell Cricket" a novel of fewer than fifteen hundred words, or is it an expanded haiku? All that you have learned of history and structure, focus and voice, characterization, symbol, and theme are needed to articulate the breadth and delicacy of this superb short short story.

▼   ▼   ▼

KATE CHOPIN

The Story of an Hour

Knowing that Mrs. Mallard was afflicted with a heart trouble, great care was taken to break to her as gently as possible the news of her husband's death.

It was her sister Josephine who told her, in broken sentences; veiled hints that revealed in half concealing. Her husband's friend Richards was there, too, near her. It was he who had been in the newspaper office when intelligence of the railroad disaster was received, with Brently Mallard's name leading the list of "killed." He had only taken the time to assure himself of its truth by a second telegram, and had hastened to forestall any less careful, less tender friend in bearing the sad message.

She did not hear the story as many women have heard the same, with a paralyzed inability to accept its significance. She wept at once, with sudden, wild abandonment, in her sister's arms. When the storm of grief had spent itself she went away to her room alone. She would have no one follow her.

There stood, facing the open window, a comfortable, roomy armchair. Into this she sank, pressed down by a physical exhaustion that haunted her body and seemed to reach into her soul.

5   She could see in the open square before her house the tops of trees that were all aquiver with the new spring life. The delicious breath of rain was in the air. In the street below a peddler was crying his wares. The notes of a distant song which some one was singing reached her faintly, and countless sparrows were twittering in the eaves.

There were patches of blue sky showing here and there through the clouds that had met and piled one above the other in the west facing her window.

She sat with her head thrown back upon the cushion of the chair, quite motionless, except when a sob came up into her throat and shook her, as a child who has cried itself to sleep continues to sob in its dreams.

She was young, with a fair, calm face, whose lines bespoke repression and even a certain strength. But now there was a dull stare in her eyes, whose gaze was fixed away off yonder on one of those patches of blue sky. It was not a glance of reflection, but rather indicated a suspension of intelligent thought.

There was something coming to her and she was waiting for it, fearfully. What was it? She did not know; it was too subtle and elusive to name. But she felt it, creeping out of the sky, reaching toward her through the sounds, the scents, the color that filled the air.

Now her bosom rose and fell tumultuously. She was beginning to recognize this thing that was approaching to possess her, and she was striving to beat it back with her will—as powerless as her two white slender hands would have been.

When she abandoned herself a little whispered word escaped her slightly parted lips. She said it over and over under her breath: "free, free, free!" The vacant stare and the look of terror that had followed it went from her eyes. They stayed keen and bright. Her pulses beat fast, and the coursing blood warmed and relaxed every inch of her body.

She did not stop to ask if it were or were not a monstrous joy that held her. A clear and exalted perception enabled her to dismiss the suggestion as trivial.

She knew that she would weep again when she saw the kind, tender hands folded in death; the face that had never looked save with love upon her, fixed and gray and dead. But she saw beyond that bitter moment a long procession of years to come that would belong to her absolutely. And she opened and spread her arms out to them in welcome.

There would be no one to live for her during those coming years; she would live for herself. There would be no powerful will bending hers in that blind persistence with which men and women believe they have a right to impose a private will upon a fellow-creature. A kind intention or a cruel intention made the act seem no less a crime as she looked upon it in that brief moment of illumination.

And yet she had loved him—sometimes. Often she had not. What did it matter! What could love, the unsolved mystery, count for in face of this possession of self-assertion which she suddenly recognized as the strongest impulse of her being!

"Free! Body and soul free!" she kept whispering.

Josephine was kneeling before the closed door with her lips to the keyhold, imploring for admission. "Louise, open the door! I beg; open the door—you will make yourself ill. What are you doing, Louise? For heaven's sake open the door."

"Go away. I am not making myself ill." No; she was drinking in a very elixir of life through that open window.

Her fancy was running riot along those days ahead of her. Spring days, and summer days, and all sorts of days that would be her own. She breathed a quick prayer that life might be long. It was only yesterday she had thought with a shudder that life might be long.

She arose at length and opened the door to her sister's importunities. There was a feverish triumph in her eyes, and she carried herself unwittingly like a goddess of Victory. She clasped her sister's waist, and together they descended the stairs. Richards stood waiting for them at the bottom.

Some one was opening the front door with a latchkey. It was Brently Mallard who entered, a little travel-stained, composedly carrying his grip-sack and umbrella. He had been far from the scene of accident, and did not even know there had been one. He stood amazed at Josephine's piercing cry; at Richards' quick motion to screen him from the view of his wife.

But Richards was too late.

When the doctors came they said she had died of heart disease—of joy that kills.

1891

ERNEST HEMINGWAY

A Very Short Story

One hot evening in Padua they carried him up onto the roof and he could look out over the top of the town. There were chimney swifts in the sky. After a while it got dark and the searchlights came out. The others went down and took the bottles with them. He and Luz could hear them below on the balcony. Luz sat on the bed. She was cool and fresh in the hot night.

Luz stayed on night duty for three months. They were glad to let her. When they operated on him she prepared him for the operating table; and they had a joke about friend or enema. He went under the anesthetic holding tight on to himself so he would not blab about anything during the silly, talky time. After he got on crutches he used to take the temperatures so Luz would not have to get up from the bed. There were only a few patients, and they all knew about it. They all liked Luz. As he walked back along the halls he thought of Luz in his bed.

Before he went back to the front they went into the Duomo[1] and prayed. It was dim and quiet, and there were other people praying. They wanted to get married, but there was not enough time for the banns, and neither of them had birth certificates. They felt as though they were married, but they wanted everyone to know about it, and to make it so they could not lose it.

Luz wrote him many letters that he never got until after the armistice. Fifteen came in a bunch to the front and he sorted them by the dates and read them all straight through. They were all about the hospital, and how much she loved him, and how it was impossible to get along without him, and how terrible it was missing him at night.

5   After the armistice they agreed he should go home to get a job so they might be married. Luz would not come home until he had a good job and could come to New York to meet her. It was understood he would not drink, and he did not want to see his friends or anyone in the States. Only to get a job and be married. On the train from Padua to Milan they quarreled about her not being willing to come home at once. When they had to say goodbye, in the station at Milan, they kissed goodbye, but were not finished with the quarrel. He felt sick about saying goodbye like that.

He went to America on a boat from Genoa. Luz went back to Pordenone to

1. Cathedral

open a hospital. It was lonely and rainy there, and there was a battalion of arditi quartered in the town. Living in the muddy, rainy town in the winter, the major of the battalion made love to Luz, and she had never known Italians before, and finally wrote to the States that theirs had been only a boy and girl affair. She was sorry, and she knew he would probably not be able to understand, but might someday forgive her, and be grateful to her, and she expected, absolutely unexpectedly, to be married in the spring. She loved him as always, but she realized now it was only a boy and girl love. She hoped he would have a great career and believed in him absolutely. She knew it was for the best.

The major did not marry her in the spring, or any other time. Luz never got an answer to the letter to Chicago about it. A short time after he contracted gonorrhea from a salesgirl in a loop[2] department store while riding in a taxicab through Lincoln Park.

1925

GABRIEL GARCÍA MÁRQUEZ

A Very Old Man with Enormous Wings[1]

A TALE FOR CHILDREN

On the third day of rain they had killed so many crabs inside the house that Pelayo had to cross his drenched courtyard and throw them into the sea, because the newborn child had a temperature all night and they thought it was due to the stench. The world had been sad since Tuesday. Sea and sky were a single ash-gray thing and the sands of the beach, which on March nights glimmered like powdered light, had become a stew of mud and rotten shellfish. The light was so weak at noon that when Pelayo was coming back to the house after throwing away the crabs, it was hard for him to see what it was that was moving and groaning in the rear of the courtyard. He had to go very close to see that it was an old man, a very old man, lying face down in the mud, who, in spite of his tremendous efforts, couldn't get up, impeded by his enormous wings.

Frightened by that nightmare, Pelayo ran to get Elisenda, his wife, who was putting compresses on the sick child, and he took her to the rear of the courtyard. They both looked at the fallen body with mute stupor. He was dressed like a ragpicker. There were only a few faded hairs left on his bald skull and very few teeth in his mouth, and his pitiful condition of a drenched great-grandfather had taken away any sense of grandeur he might have had. His huge buzzard wings, dirty and half-plucked, were forever entangled in the mud. They looked at him so long and so closely that Pelayo and Elisenda very soon overcame their surprise and in the end found him familiar. Then they dared speak to him, and he answered in an incomprehensible dialect with a strong sailor's voice. That

---

2. Chicago business and shopping district.   1. Translated by Gregory Rabassa.

was how they skipped over the inconvenience of the wings and quite intelligently concluded that he was a lonely castaway from some foreign ship wrecked by the storm. And yet, they called in a neighbor woman who knew everything about life and death to see him, and all she needed was one look to show them their mistake.

"He's an angel," she told them. "He must have been coming for the child, but the poor fellow is so old that the rain knocked him down."

On the following day everyone knew that a flesh-and-blood angel was held captive in Pelayo's house. Against the judgment of the wise neighbor woman, for whom angels in those times were the fugitive survivors of a celestial conspiracy, they did not have the heart to club him to death. Pelayo watched over him all afternoon from the kitchen, armed with his bailiff's club, and before going to bed he dragged him out of the mud and locked him up with the hens in the wire chicken coop. In the middle of the night, when the rain stopped, Pelayo and Elisenda were still killing crabs. A short time afterward the child woke up without a fever and with a desire to eat. Then they felt magnanimous and decided to put the angel on a raft with fresh water and provisions for three days and leave him to his fate on the high seas. But when they went out into the courtyard with the first light of dawn, they found the whole neighborhood in front of the chicken coop having fun with the angel, without the slightest reverence, tossing him things to eat through the openings in the wire as if he weren't a supernatural creature but a circus animal.

5   Father Gonzaga arrived before seven o'clock, alarmed at the strange news. By that time onlookers less frivolous than those at dawn had already arrived and they were making all kinds of conjectures concerning the captive's future. The simplest among them thought that he should be named mayor of the world. Others of sterner mind felt that he should be promoted to the rank of five-star general in order to win all wars. Some visionaries hoped that he could be put to stud in order to implant on earth a race of winged wise men who could take charge of the universe. But Father Gonzaga, before becoming a priest, had been a robust woodcutter. Standing by the wire, he reviewed his catechism in an instant and asked them to open the door so that he could take a close look at that pitiful man who looked more like a huge decrepit hen among the fascinated chickens. He was lying in a corner drying his open wings in the sunlight among the fruit peels and breakfast leftovers that the early risers had thrown him. Alien to the impertinences of the world, he only lifted his antiquarian eyes and murmured something in his dialect when Father Gonzaga went into the chicken coop and said good morning to him in Latin. The parish priest had his first suspicion of an imposter when he saw that he did not understand the language of God or know how to greet His ministers. Then he noticed that seen close up he was much too human: he had an unbearable smell of the outdoors, the back side of his wings was strewn with parasites and his main feathers had been mistreated by terrestrial winds, and nothing about him measured up to the proud dignity of angels. Then he came out of the chicken coop and in a brief sermon warned the curious against the risks of being ingenuous. He reminded them that the devil had the bad habit of making use of carnival tricks in order

to confuse the unwary. He argued that if wings were not the essential element in determining the difference between a hawk and an airplane, they were even less so in the recognition of angels. Nevertheless, he promised to write a letter to his bishop so that the latter would write to his primate so that the latter would write to the Supreme Pontiff in order to get the final verdict from the highest courts.

His prudence fell on sterile hearts. The news of the captive angel spread with such rapidity that after a few hours the courtyard had the bustle of a market-place and they had to call in troops with fixed bayonets to disperse the mob that was about to knock the house down. Elisenda, her spine all twisted from sweeping up so much marketplace trash, then got the idea of fencing in the yard and charging five cents admission to see the angel.

The curious came from far away. A traveling carnival arrived with a flying acrobat who buzzed over the crowd several times, but no one paid any attention to him because his wings were not those of an angel but, rather, those of a sidereal bat. The most unfortunate invalids on earth came in search of health: a poor woman who since childhood had been counting her heartbeats and had run out of numbers; a Portuguese man who couldn't sleep because the noise of the stars disturbed him; a sleepwalker who got up at night to undo the things he had done while awake; and many others with less serious ailments. In the midst of that shipwreck disorder that made the earth tremble, Pelayo and Elisenda were happy with fatigue, for in less than a week they had crammed their rooms with money and the line of pilgrims waiting their turn to enter still reached beyond the horizon.

The angel was the only one who took no part in his own act. He spent his time trying to get comfortable in his borrowed nest, befuddled by the hellish heat of the oil lamps and sacramental candles that had been placed along the wire. At first they tried to make him eat some mothballs, which, according to the wisdom of the wise neighbor woman, were the food prescribed for angels. But he turned them down, just as he turned down the papal lunches[2] that the penitents brought him, and they never found out whether it was because he was an angel or because he was an old man that in the end he ate nothing but eggplant mush. His only supernatural virtue seemed to be patience. Especially during the first days, when the hens pecked at him, searching for the stellar parasites that proliferated in his wings, and the cripples pulled out feathers to touch their defective parts with, and even the most merciful threw stones at him, trying to get him to rise so they could see him standing. The only time they succeeded in arousing him was when they burned his side with an iron for branding steers, for he had been motionless for so many hours that they thought he was dead. He awoke with a start, ranting in his hermetic language and with tears in his eyes, and he flapped his wings a couple of times, which brought on a whirlwind of chicken dung and lunar dust and a gale of panic that did not seem to be of this world. Although many thought that his reaction had been one not of rage but of pain, from then on they were careful not to annoy him,

---

2. Choice, extremely expensive meals.

because the majority understood that his passivity was not that of a hero taking his ease but that of a cataclysm in repose.

Father Gonzaga held back the crowd's frivolity with formulas of maidservant inspiration while awaiting the arrival of a final judgment on the nature of the captive. But the mail from Rome showed no sense of urgency. They spent their time finding out if the prisoner had a navel, if his dialect had any connection with Aramaic, how many times he could fit on the head of a pin, or whether he wasn't just a Norwegian with wings. Those meager letters might have come and gone until the end of time if a providential event had not put an end to the priest's tribulations.

It so happened that during those days, among so many other carnival attractions, there arrived in town the traveling show of the woman who had been changed into a spider for having disobeyed her parents. The admission to see her was not only less than the admission to see the angel, but people were permitted to ask her all manner of questions about her absurd state and to examine her up and down so that no one would ever doubt the truth of her horror. She was a frightful tarantula the size of a ram and with the head of a sad maiden. What was most heart-rending, however, was not her outlandish shape but the sincere affliction with which she recounted the details of her misfortune. While still practically a child she had sneaked out of her parents' house to go to a dance, and while she was coming back through the woods after having danced all night without permission, a fearful thunderclap rent the sky in two and through the crack came the lightning bolt of brimstone that changed her into a spider. Her only nourishment came from the meatballs that charitable souls chose to toss into her mouth. A spectacle like that, full of so much human truth and with such a fearful lesson, was bound to defeat without even trying that of a haughty angel who scarcely deigned to look at mortals. Besides, the few miracles attributed to the angel showed a certain mental disorder, like the blind man who didn't recover his sight but grew three new teeth, or the paralytic who didn't get to walk but almost won the lottery, and the leper whose sores sprouted sunflowers. Those consolation miracles, which were more like mocking fun, had already ruined the angel's reputation when the woman who had been changed into a spider finally crushed him completely. That was how Father Gonzaga was cured forever of his insomnia and Pelayo's courtyard went back to being as empty as during the time it had rained for three days and crabs walked through the bedrooms.

The owners of the house had no reason to lament. With the money they saved they built a two-story mansion with balconies and gardens and high netting so that crabs wouldn't get in during the winter, and with iron bars on the windows so that angels wouldn't get in. Pelayo also set up a rabbit warren close to town and gave up his job as bailiff for good, and Elisenda bought some satin pumps with high heels and many dresses of iridescent silk, the kind worn on Sunday by the most desirable women in those times. The chicken coop was the only thing that didn't receive any attention. If they washed it down with creolin[3]

3. A disinfectant.

and burned tears of myrrh inside it every so often, it was not in homage to the angel but to drive away the dungheap stench that still hung everywhere like a ghost and was turning the new house into an old one. At first, when the child learned to walk, they were careful that he not get too close to the chicken coop. But then they began to lose their fears and got used to the smell, and before the child got his second teeth he'd gone inside the chicken coop to play, where the wires were falling apart. The angel was no less standoffish with him than with other mortals, but he tolerated the most ingenious infamies with the patience of a dog who had no illusions. They both came down with chicken pox at the same time. The doctor who took care of the child couldn't resist the temptation to listen to the angel's heart, and he found so much whistling in the heart and so many sounds in his kidneys that it seemed impossible for him to be alive. What surprised him most, however, was the logic of his wings. They seemed so natural on that completely human organism that he couldn't understand why other men didn't have them too.

When the child began school it had been some time since the sun and rain had caused the collapse of the chicken coop. The angel went dragging himself about here and there like a stray dying man. They would drive him out of the bedroom with a broom and a moment later find him in the kitchen. He seemed to be in so many places at the same time that they grew to think that he'd been duplicated, that he was reproducing himself all through the house, and the exasperated and unhinged Elisenda shouted that it was awful living in that hell full of angels. He could scarcely eat and his antiquarian eyes had also become so foggy that he went about bumping into posts. All he had left were the bare cannulae of his last feathers. Pelayo threw a blanket over him and extended him the charity of letting him sleep in the shed, and only then did they notice that he had a temperature at night, and was delirious with the tongue twisters of an old Norwegian. That was one of the few times they became alarmed, for they thought he was going to die and not even the wise neighbor woman had been able to tell them what to do with dead angels.

And yet he not only survived his worst winter, but seemed improved with the first sunny days. He remained motionless for several days in the farthest corner of the courtyard, where no one would see him, and at the beginning of December some large, stiff feathers began to grow on his wings, the feathers of a scarecrow, which looked more like another misfortune of decrepitude. But he must have known the reason for those changes, for he was quite careful that no one should notice them, that no one should hear the sea chanteys that he sometimes sang under the stars. One morning Elisenda was cutting some bunches of onions for lunch when a wind that seemed to come from the high seas blew into the kitchen. Then she went to the window and caught the angel in his first attempts at flight. They were so clumsy that his fingernails opened a furrow in the vegetable patch and he was on the point of knocking the shed down with the ungainly flapping that slipped on the light and couldn't get a grip on the air. But he did manage to gain altitude. Elisenda let out a sign of relief, for herself and for him, when she saw him pass over the last houses, holding himself up in some way with the risky flapping of a senile vulture. She kept watching him even when she was through cutting the onions and she kept on watching until it was no longer possible for her to see him, because then he was no longer an annoyance in her life but an imaginary dot on the horizon of the sea.

1968

JAMAICA KINCAID

Girl

Wash the white clothes on Monday and put them on the stone heap; wash the color clothes on Tuesday and put them on the clothesline to dry; don't walk barehead in the hot sun; cook pumpkin fritters in very hot sweet oil; soak your little cloths right after you take them off; when buying cotton to make yourself a nice blouse, be sure that it doesn't have gum on it, because that way it won't hold up well after a wash; soak salt fish overnight before you cook it; is it true that you sing benna[1] in Sunday school?; always eat your food in such a way that it won't turn someone else's stomach; on Sundays try to walk like a lady and not like the slut you are so bent on becoming; don't sing benna in Sunday school; you mustn't speak to wharf-rat boys, not even to give directions; don't eat fruits on the street—flies will follow you; *but I don't sing benna on Sundays at all and never in Sunday school*; this is how to sew on a button; this is how to make a buttonhole for the button you have just sewed on; this is how to hem a dress when you see the hem coming down and so to prevent yourself from looking like the slut I know you are so bent on becoming; this is how you iron your father's khaki shirt so that it doesn't have a crease; this is how you iron your father's khaki pants so that they don't have a crease; this is how you grow okra— far from the house, because okra tree harbors red ants; when you are growing dasheen, make sure it gets plenty of water or else it makes your throat itch when you are eating it; this is how you sweep a corner; this is how you sweep a whole house; this is how you sweep a yard; this is how you smile to someone you don't like too much; this is how you smile to someone you don't like at all; this is how you smile to someone you like completely; this is how you set a table for tea; this is how you set a table for dinner; this is how you set a table for dinner with an important guest; this is how you set a table for lunch; this is how you set a table for breakfast; this is how to behave in the presence of men who don't know you very well, and this way they won't recognize immediately the slut I have warned you against becoming; be sure to wash every day, even if it is with your own spit; don't squat down to play marbles—you are not a boy, you know; don't pick people's flowers—you might catch something; don't throw stones at black-birds, because it might not be a blackbird at all; this is how to make a bread pudding; this is how to make doukona[2]; this is how to make pepper pot; this is how to make a good medicine for a cold; this is how to make a good medicine

---

1. Sing popular music, calypso.   2. A spicy pudding, often made from plantain and wrapped in a plantain or banana leaf.

to throw away a child before it even becomes a child; this is how to catch a fish; this is how to throw back a fish you don't like, and that way something bad won't fall on you; this is how to bully a man; this is how a man bullies you; this is how to love a man, and if this doesn't work there are other ways, and if they don't work don't feel too bad about giving up; this is how to spit up in the air if you feel like it, and this is how to move quick so that it doesn't fall on you; this is how to make ends meet; always squeeze bread to make sure it's fresh; *but what if the baker won't let me feel the bread?*; you mean to say that after all you are really going to be the kind of woman who the baker won't let near the bread?

1983

YASUNARI KAWABATA

The Grasshopper and the Bell Cricket[1]

Walking along the tile-roofed wall of the university, I turned aside and approached the upper school. Behind the white board fence of the school playground, from a dusky clump of bushes under the black cherry trees, an insect's voice could be heard. Walking more slowly and listening to that voice, and furthermore reluctant to part with it, I turned right so as not to leave the playground behind. When I turned to the left, the fence gave way to an embankment planted with orange trees. At the corner, I exclaimed with surprise. My eyes gleaming at what they saw up ahead, I hurried forward with short steps.

At the base of the embankment was a bobbing cluster of beautiful varicolored lanterns, such as one might see at a festival in a remote country village. Without going any farther, I knew that it was a group of children on an insect chase among the bushes of the embankment. There were about twenty lanterns. Not only were there crimson, pink, indigo, green, purple, and yellow lanterns, but one lantern glowed with five colors at once. There were even some little red store-bought lanterns. But most of the lanterns were beautiful square ones which the children had made themselves with love and care. The bobbing lanterns, the coming together of children on this lonely slope—surely it was a scene from a fairy tale?

One of the neighborhood children had heard an insect sing on this slope one night. Buying a red lantern, he had come back the next night to find the insect. The night after that, there was another child. This new child could not buy a lantern. Cutting out the back and front of a small carton and papering it, he placed a candle on the bottom and fastened a string to the top. The number of children grew to five, and then to seven. They learned how to color the paper that they stretched over the windows of the cutout cartons, and to draw pictures on it. Then these wise child-artists, cutting out round, three-cornered, and lozenge leaf shapes in the cartons, coloring each little window a different color, with circles and diamonds, red and green, made a single and whole decorative

1. Translated by Lane Dunlop.

pattern. The child with the red lantern discarded it as a tasteless object that could be bought at a store. The child who had made his own lantern threw it away because the design was too simple. The pattern of light that one had had in hand the night before was unsatisfying the morning after. Each day, with cardboard, paper, brush, scissors, penknife, and glue, the children made new lanterns out of their hearts and minds. Look at my lantern! Be the most unusually beautiful! And each night, they had gone out on their insect hunts. These were the twenty children and their beautiful lanterns that I now saw before me.

Wide-eyed, I loitered near them. Not only did the square lanterns have old-fashioned patterns and flower shapes, but the names of the children who had made them were cut out in squared letters of the syllabary. Different from the painted-over red lanterns, others (made of thick cutout cardboard) had their designs drawn onto the paper windows, so that the candle's light seemed to emanate from the form and color of the design itself. The lanterns brought out the shadows of the bushes like dark light. The children crouched eagerly on the slope wherever they heard an insect's voice.

"Does anyone want a grasshopper?" A boy, who had been peering into a bush about thirty feet away from the other children, suddenly straightened up and shouted.

"Yes! Give it to me!" Six or seven children came running up. Crowding behind the boy who had found the grasshopper, they peered into the bush. Brushing away their outstretched hands and spreading out his arms, the boy stood as if guarding the bush where the insect was. Waving the lantern in his right hand, he called again to the other children.

"Does anyone want a grasshopper? A grasshopper!"

"I do! I do!" Four or five more children came running up. It seemed you could not catch a more precious insect than a grasshopper. The boy called out a third time.

"Doesn't anyone want a grasshopper?"

Two or three more children came over.

"Yes. I want it."

It was a girl, who just now had come up behind the boy who'd discovered the insect. Lightly turning his body, the boy gracefully bent forward. Shifting the lantern to his left hand, he reached his right hand into the bush.

"It's a grasshopper."

"Yes. I'd like to have it."

The boy quickly stood up. As if to say "Here!" he thrust out his fist that held the insect at the girl. She, slipping her left wrist under the string of her lantern, enclosed the boy's fist with both hands. The boy quietly opened his fist. The insect was transferred to between the girl's thumb and index finger.

"Oh! It's not a grasshopper. It's a bell cricket." The girl's eyes shone as she looked at the small brown insect.

"It's a bell cricket! It's a bell cricket!" The children echoed in an envious chorus.

"It's a bell cricket. It's a bell cricket."

Glancing with her bright intelligent eyes at the boy who had given her the cricket, the girl opened the little insect cage hanging at her side and released the cricket in it.

"It's a bell cricket."

"Oh, it's a bell cricket," the boy who'd captured it muttered. Holding up the insect cage close to his eyes, he looked inside it. By the light of his beautiful many-colored lantern, also held up at eye level, he glanced at the girl's face.

Oh, I thought. I felt slightly jealous of the boy, and sheepish. How silly of me not to have understood his actions until now! Then I caught my breath in surprise. Look! It was something on the girl's breast which neither the boy who had given her the cricket, nor she who had accepted it, nor the children who were looking at them noticed.

In the faint greenish light that fell on the girl's breast, wasn't the name "Fujio" clearly discernible? The boy's lantern, which he held up alongside the girl's insect cage, inscribed his name, cut out in the green papered aperture, onto her white cotton kimono. The girl's lantern, which dangled loosely from her wrist, did not project its pattern so clearly, but still one could make out, in a trembling patch of red on the boy's waist, the name "Kiyoko." This chance interplay of red and green—if it was chance or play—neither Fujio nor Kiyoko knew about.

Even if they remembered forever that Fujio had given her the cricket and that Kiyoko had accepted it, not even in dreams would Fujio ever know that his name had been written in green on Kiyoko's breast or that Kiyoko's name had been inscribed in red on his waist, nor would Kiyoko ever know that Fujio's name had been inscribed in green on her breast or that her own name had been written in red on Fujio's waist.

Fujio! Even when you have become a young man, laugh with pleasure at a girl's delight when, told that it's a grasshopper, she is given a bell cricket; laugh with affection at a girl's chagrin when, told that it's a bell cricket, she is given a grasshopper.

Even if you have the wit to look by yourself in a bush away from the other children, there are not many bell crickets in the world. Probably you will find a girl like a grasshopper whom you think is a bell cricket.

And finally, to your clouded, wounded heart, even a true bell cricket will seem like a grasshopper. Should that day come, when it seems to you that the world is only full of grasshoppers, I will think it a pity that you have no way to remember tonight's play of light, when your name was written in green by your beautiful lantern on a girl's breast.

1988

If the brevity of the short short story suggests certain possibilities and limitations, the length of another fictional form, the novel, suggests another range of possible effects and response. The novel is so familiar and popular a form, we scarcely ever stop to ask ourselves just what the novel, as distinct from other fictional forms, is. Let's look at some of its characteristics.

The novel is a long narrative. Though it is arbitrary to say just where the long short story becomes the short novel, most fictional works of fewer than 15,000–20,000 words (about 20–25 pages in this book) will display the characteristic development and engender the characteristic range of response of the short story. Longer works than these will likely be called **short novels** (or, sometimes, **novellas** or **novelettes**), though there is a broad shadowy area between the short story and the short novel. In this volume, for example, "Sonny's Blues" and "Barn Burning" fall just short of 20 pages, "The Watcher" is just over 20, and "The Secret Sharer" is close to 30. We have treated these as short stories, but some or all could be, and have at one time or another been, called short novels. We would begin to call works of fiction of about 70,000 words, nearly 100 pages in this book, just plain "novels." We have chosen to represent novels with the short novel *Heart of Darkness*, by Joseph Conrad, which, at about 38,000 words, is clearly not a short story and perhaps just as clearly not a full-length novel.

What differentiates the novel from the short story is not only length but a combination as well of the number of characters, scenes, and incidents; duration and scope of the action; and complexity of the whole work or of one or more of its elements. *Heart of Darkness* is an initiation story, like those in Chapter 10, or like "Young Goodman Brown." Indeed, what may be considered a fundamental theme in both is the presence of evil in all of us, or Original Sin. Yet *Heart of Darkness* is six or seven times as long as "Young Goodman Brown," and is greater in scope and complexity. The Conrad novel has many more separate scenes and incidents, several more characters, and a journey that in time and space is many times longer than Brown's journey into the New England woods. While both narratives treat moral evil, *Heart of Darkness* treats political, social, and economic evil as well, and also raises issues of gender, race, and culture, and even more submerged but significant questions such as the efficacy of narrative or language, to what extent one can transmit knowledge gained from experience.

Though novels by virtue of their length are not necessarily better than short stories, sheer length does make a difference in the nature of the reading experience. Though we can sometimes read a short novel—or even a full-length novel—in a single sitting, most of the time we put it down one or more times after reading a while and pick it up later. So we live with a novel over a period of time, and while we are doing other things, characters, episodes, and scenes come back to us, or we see new shapes and possibilities or harden our expectations of what is to come or what it all amounts to. When we return to the novel, we re-enter its world, readjust our minds and imaginations to its reality, and give it what we might think of as stereo-imaginative depth or solidity. The novel is different from the shorter forms of fiction in a sense not only because of what *it is* but because of what *we* become as we read it.

There is also, of course, more to take in as we read, more to "process" or evaluate, more to select and remember; there are many more details to make into patterns and more patterns to project in anticipating what will happen next and in putting it all together to interpret what it all means. Reading the first part of "The Most Dangerous Game," we may have pieced together hints about superstition and the discovery of a Gothic castle in the middle of the jungle and anticipated that the story might have something to do with the supernatural or monstrous. We may also have stored the early conversation about hunting, so that when the Cossack colonel turns out to be a hunter and to know about the hero's reputation as a great hunter, we may have related the details and projected a pattern that guided our later reading. The sheer weight and variety of detail in *Heart of Darkness*, however, makes it all but impossible (at least for me) to hold all the possibly suggestive details in mind at one time and fit them all into a definitive pattern; we ignore or miss some details, forget others, cannot fit others into our best projected pattern, so each reading is to a greater or lesser degree a partial one, and every time we read the novel it is somewhat different. So we must go back and read the novel again, experience it again (or experience our new reading of it for the first time). And when we have finished, we are not finished with it. The duration of the experience, the variety and complexity of our mental and emotional activities each time we read a novel, the fact that a novel hardly ever can be taken entirely into our minds or held there the way we can hold a sonnet or a short story, can seldom be reconstructed and contemplated in its entirety and made our own—all of these qualities or potential qualities inhere in the rather obvious and trivial statement that "The novel is a long narrative."

The novel is a continuous narrative. There are long narratives that we don't call novels because they are not continuous. John Cheever's *The Housebreaker of Shady Hill*, for example (from which "The Country Husband" is taken), is a book-length work of fiction about people who live in a new, middle-class, commuter suburb of New York City just after World War II. But rather than one continuous narrative, the book is made up of a number of narratives, each about a different set of characters. This is clearly a collection of short stories, not a novel. *The Book of the Thousand Nights and a Night (The Arabian*

Nights) is a long narrative or series of narratives in prose, connected by a frame story: here Shahrazad seeks to stave off execution by keeping her husband enthralled from night to night by the stories she tells. Her stories make no continuous whole, involving different sets of characters, settings, actions, kinds of action, and even kinds of reality. The frame is insufficient to bind the work into a continuous narrative that could be called a novel. Dickens's *Pickwick Papers* begins with a comparable frame—the adventures of the members of the Pickwick Club—and is somewhat more fully bound together by the fact that most of the early episodes involve the club members and most of them follow, at least chronologically, one from the other. In the first half of the novel, however, there are a good many stories within the story, told by strangers, involving characters we have not heard of before and won't hear of again—some of the stories funny, some melodramatic, some realistic, some fantastic. But the frame does—even if at first just barely—hold the narrative together, and in the second half the "miscellany" becomes a novel, bound together by the continuing story of the famous Bardell v. Pickwick breach of promise suit and its consequences. The book emerges, as a result, as one of the looser and baggier of those loose, baggy monsters called Victorian novels, but a novel nevertheless. There are episodic novels in which a hero or heroine runs into one adventure after another without logical or necessary connection, and in some cases even without the change or development in the central character we find in such novels as Defoe's *Moll Flanders*.

Novels contain a number of characters and incidents, as we have mentioned earlier in connection with length. They vary greatly, however, not only in the number of characters and incidents, or the ratio of characters to incident, but also in the amount of emphasis on an individual character or characters and the tightness of the connection of the incidents. *Crime and Punishment* contains a fairly large number of characters and a rather large number of incidents, but it centers on a single character—the student Raskolnikov—and on a single action—his planning and carrying out a murder, and its consequences. Huckleberry Finn's numerous adventures as he travels down the Mississippi River are bound together not by a single action nor by any inherent logic in their sequence but by the river, by the central character and his language (unlike Raskolnikov, Huck tells his own story), and by the overall pattern of Huck's attempt to escape society and its attempt to trap him. *War and Peace* follows many characters both fictional and historical (including Napoleon) through many incidents before, during, and after the French invasion of Russia in 1812. The whole is woven together by the relationships of the characters, the story of the impact of the war and of Western culture on Russian society, and by the interconnected themes of private and public history, the individual's sense of free will and apparent historical necessity, chance and divine will.

The novel is a temporal genre. I have already stressed the fact that a novel because of its length offers a reading experience of some duration: it is read over a fairly extended period of time. Because of its length it also can cover in sufficient detail a rather long period of fictional time. It typically covers years and it is not unusual for a novel to span the major portion of a character's life. Even in James Joyce's *Ulysses* (1922), where the action is carefully restricted to less than a day, through various kinds of exposition, especially characters' memories and associations, we learn a good deal about the three main characters' pasts. Time is, indeed, one of the typical subjects of the novel. There are, for example, **historical novels**—novels set in the past that involve actual people or events of the past, that often investigate the nature of history or the effect of the past on the present or of historical forces on the individual—novels such as *War and Peace*, the novels of Sir Walter Scott, or *Gone With the Wind*. There are **fictional biographies** or **autobiographies** like *Sons and Lovers* and *David Copperfield*, which narrate the story of a character's life in third or first person. There are even novels that quite directly treat time itself: Marcel Proust's *Remembrance of Things Past* (whose French title literally means *In Search of Lost Time*) or another, more recent multivolume novel, Anthony Powell's *A Dance to the Music of Time*, not to mention such time-ridden novels as Thomas Wolfe's *Of Time and the River*.

The dominant novel kind, the **Bildungsroman** or **apprentice novel,** exemplified by Goethe's *Wilhelm Meister* (1796–1829), demands a rather extensive period of fictional time, for it traces the protagonist from youth to maturity, usually from his rejection of his family, his society, and religion and his roving search for a new order, purpose, and meaning in life, to his discovery of or return to a new home, society, and world view. If, as some would maintain, all short stories are initiation stories, it may as readily be claimed that all novels are *Bildungsroman.* Initiation, the sudden insight or illumination (what Joyce called an *epiphany*), is indeed eminently suited to the compact form of the short story, and so too the narrative of growth and change, of quest and development, is suited to the broader, more inclusive form and more leisurely pace of the novel.

The novel is a long continuous narrative in prose, with a number of characters and incidents, and informed by time. We cannot confidently go beyond this simple and somewhat superficial definition, for *the novel genre is a form in flux.* Indeed, it is not a genre in being but a genre-becoming; an evolutionary, adaptive, ever-changing form, like biological species seen in time-lapse photography. The Western novel was born about the time when an old order of the world—hierarchical and static, in which everything (serf, knight, king; all literary genres) had a fixed or ideal nature and a predetermined and proper place in a *vertical* Great Chain of Being—was toppling, and a new world view was arising—*horizontal*, dominated by time, history, process, evolution. It is no wonder that the characteristic and dominant genre of that world is dynamic and without an ideal or fixed form.

Though there were long narrative prose works in the classical periods which some would now call novels, there were no definitions of the novel as a genre then, as there were of comedy, tragedy, epic, pastoral, and other established forms, nor was there anything called the novel for centuries to come. During the Middle Ages in Italy, there were brief, more or less realistic tales like those in Boccaccio's *Decameron* that were called **novelle** (singular, *novella*). In Europe there was a still older form known as the **romance** (because it was chiefly written in the Romance languages) that recounted the high-flown, fanciful adventures of knights and princesses and other wondrous tales. In France, from about the middle of the seventeenth century to the middle of the eighteenth, the two streams merged into what we would at some point call novels: perhaps Mlle. de Scudéry's romances at the beginning of this period; perhaps the *Princesse de Clèves* (1678) and other relatively realistic works by Marguerite de la Vergne (Mme. de la Fayette); certainly Prévost's *Manon Lescaut* and Marivaux's *Marianne* in 1731. The narrative traditions of the Continent were fed in England by local narratives and traditions from the Arthurian legends through the moral allegories of John Bunyan (whose *Pilgrim's Progress* was published in 1678). Early in the eighteenth century Daniel Defoe conflated journalistic narrative, spiritual autobiography, and travel literature into works such as *Robinson Crusoe* (1719) and *Moll Flanders* (1722) that many consider the first "true" novels in English. Others, however, call Samuel Richardson's *Pamela; or, Virtue Rewarded* (1740–41) the first English novel. *Pamela* stimulated—or irritated—Henry Fielding into writing the story of Pamela's "virtuous brother," *Joseph Andrews* (1742), to be followed in 1749 by *Tom Jones*. By the middle of the eighteenth century, then, the English novel was well under way.

A century or so later it seemed quite reasonable to identify the novel genre with **verisimilitude** or **realism** in its many aspects. Looking back from the 1850s or '60s, the best fiction seemed to be that which had contributed to "the rise of realism," as with Defoe's use of concrete physical detail; Charlotte Brontë's unbeautiful heroines and unhandsome heroes; George Eliot's imperfect "heroes" and her villains more weak than evil (to use only English examples). The history of the novel seemed one of "progress" from the errantly romantic, the exaggerated and incredible, to increasingly broad, deep, and skill-ful representations of everyday life. Even Victor Hugo *(Les Misérables)* and Dickens could be excused for their melodrama because of their social realism. The demonic *Wuthering Heights* and *Moby-Dick* might be grudgingly admit-ted to have a certain amount of power, but they were so overblown, so awk-ward that they were not admitted into the best critical company.

The century that followed the 1850s and '60s seemed to confirm the graph of rising and widening realism. The "lower classes" were now admitted into the novel as other than rogues or clowns. **Naturalism** portrayed people and their actions as largely determined by their biological natures. Following Émile Zola, Stephen Crane found nature merely indifferent and valueless. Humanity's lofty ideals and values, for Thomas Hardy, were out of step with nature's law, having outstripped God's plan, if there was a God, if there was a plan. For Conrad, natural man or man in nature was corrupt; all values were artificial, like rules of a game, but it was man's necessity, role, and glory to make and live by such rules, no matter that they were inevitably fictions. The dark and desperate view of humanity and nature, and even the phoniness of civilization itself, seemed confirmed by the First World War, and this view manifested itself in the novels of Hemingway and Fitzgerald and the entire "Lost Generation."

Meanwhile, the whole conception of human reality—our perception of our inner selves and the relationship between our perceptions and the reality of the outside world—was undergoing the same kind of questioning and revision that was giving birth to the newest of the sciences, psychology. From the mid-nine-teenth to the mid-twentieth century the common assumption was that truth—about our motives, our "real selves"—lay deep within. If we could only strip away the outer layers of artificiality or pretense or hypocrisy, in look and lan-guage, and peer inside the human consciousness, we would really know truth. Over the years, George Eliot, Henry James, Marcel Proust analyzed the work-ings of their characters' minds and motives with increasing subtlety. Analysis is logical, and conventional language and narrative are satisfactory tools. Con-sciousness, however, is not essentially logical, and to reflect or represent its workings more unconventional methods are required. James Joyce, Virginia Woolf, and William Faulkner presented the mind at work not as a logical or systematic processor of stimuli and thoughts, but as a **stream of conscious-ness**—a rapid and ceaseless flow of perceptions, images, memories, and desires just on and just below the surface of the mind. Joyce represented this stream in *Ulysses* not only without logical analysis but in sentence fragments and some-what bewildering sequences and recurrences of images.

Ulysses seems child's play, however, compared to Joyce's next (and last) novel, *Finnegans Wake* (1939), which explores the nighttime world, the unconscious. One may analyze such a world in conventional, logical language, but to represent it accurately, Joyce felt obliged to reject analytical connectives, conventional syntax, and punctuation—the preconscious mind probably doesn't contain commas and subordinating conjunctions. He even had to dissolve and re-form words into something like perpetual puns, syllables suggesting simultaneously several words (sometimes in various languages). In such a world mere narrative sequence was of course the first thing to go.

For many readers—and writers—*Finnegans Wake* marked a dead end. Just as a half-century earlier Dostoevsky showed in *Notes from Underground* that the interior workings of the mind were as contradictory, confusing, and deceptive as spoken or social language, so Joyce's last novel seemed to suggest that to plumb the depths of consciousness was to reveal not some portable truth but chaos. There was quite soon in writers such as Alain Robbe-Grillet and other creators of **le nouveau roman** (the "new novel") a return from the depths of consciousness to the surface of experience. But the discouraging failure to reach truth by psychological analysis now extended to other structures—away with the artificiality of plot, which with its simple cause-effect assumptions did not represent but analyzed and thus distorted reality, and of character, which was a similar analytical distortion, presuming consistency, essence, unity in that bundle of contradictions known as a person. For an increasing number of novelists, the pretense that fiction somehow represented reality gave way.

Already in the nineteenth century "common sense" notions of realism were beginning to give way before the discovery of worlds beyond our unaided senses, observable through microscope and telescope, as well as skepticism about traditional histories and views of the world and more careful observation. Geologists had gradually come to believe that the Earth was much older than tradition suggested, had changed over time and was still changing, so that even the solid earth under our feet seemed a little less solid. Darwin, with his theory, based on observation and deduction, that species themselves were not fixed but moving and changing in time, furthered the notion of change and development, the instability of things and beings over time. With the rise of psychology toward the end of the century we became more and more aware that there were realities only dreamed of in our philosophies. When physics, the most advanced and scientific of the sciences, told us first that mass itself was a form of energy, and that science itself, if not exactly "subjective," was at least limited to what the human brain and its instruments can perceive and may be altered by our attempt to measure or examine, we were not so sure that reality was what existed "out there." There is no way that this revolution in what we consider reality and in our ways of knowing and our ability to know could not have affected that genre most sensitive to social and perceptual change, the novel. The novel tradition no longer looks like the story of the rise of realism. There is new interest in and respect for the romance, the Gothic, the grotesque, the fantastic. We admire Joyce less nowadays for his dear, dirty Dublin than for the music and mystery of his words and his vision, and Lawrence's sexual scenarios as much for their mystical implications as for their physical explicitness. We no longer seek to explain (or explain away) what seemed fantastic in Kafka, Dostoyevsky, Dickens, but seek in them instead a kind of profound perception of human and cosmic irrationality.

The novel of our time has given us this new perspective and made us review its roots. John Fowles in *The Magus* and Robert Coover in *The Universal Baseball Association*, for example, by the interpenetration of "reality" and fantasy, of fictions or games that may be real and reality that may be false, blur the borders of the regions of fact and fiction. Gabriel García Márquez so shifts time-schemes and juxtaposes people and events from different eras, and introduces the fantastic, the unnatural, the legendary and interweaves it so casually with the everyday, the borders are once more blurred. And it is now common in fiction for the author to intervene "in person" or as narrator, not merely to comment but to point out that you are reading fiction, an arbitrary and artificial world, and that he or she as maker of that fiction can change or "erase" events or characters and make it all otherwise.

We can, then, no longer assume that verisimilitude is a necessary characteristic of the novel, or that the history of the novel is a history of increasingly full and successful representation of everyday reality, unless we want to say, as some have, that the novel in our time is in decline, or as others have been saying for some time, that the novel as a form is dead and is to be replaced by some other form of prose narrative.

The novel, in its relatively brief history, has already taken for its own subject matter ghosts and governesses, gold and gods; all continents and classes; packing plants and Providence; baseball and Beelzebub. It has absorbed into itself the disciplines of history, sociology, anthropology, journalism, and psychology, among others; it has taken in when needed the forms of the sermon, travel literature, journalism, autobiography spiritual and confessional, biography and history complete with footnotes, essays familiar and formal, and analyses and processes from the causes of Napoleon's invasion of Russia, determinism and free will, to extracting sperm from a whale. It has been lyric and dramatic, comic and tragic, satiric and epic. Its very lack of generic definition has permitted it to adapt to the needs of each generation and decade for more than two centuries. Even now it is probing the heart—and the darkness.

JOSEPH CONRAD

Heart of Darkness

I

The *Nellie*, a cruising yawl, swung to her anchor without a flutter of the sails, and was at rest. The flood had made, the wind was nearly calm, and being bound down the river, the only thing for it was to come to and wait for the turn of the tide.

The sea-reach[1] of the Thames stretched before us like the beginning of an interminable waterway. In the offing the sea and the sky were welded together without a joint, and in the luminous space the tanned sails of the barges drifting up with the tide seemed to stand still in red clusters of canvas sharply peaked, with gleams of varnished sprits. A haze rested on the low shores that ran out to sea in vanishing flatness. The air was dark above Gravesend,[2] and farther back still seemed condensed into a mournful gloom, brooding motionless over the biggest, and the greatest, town on earth.

The Director of Companies was our captain and our host. We four affectionately watched his back as he stood in the bows looking to seaward. On the whole river there was nothing that looked half so nautical. He resembled a pilot, which to a seaman is trustworthiness personified. It was difficult to realize his work was not out there in the luminous estuary, but behind him, within the brooding gloom.

Between us there was, as I have already said somewhere, the bond of the sea. Besides holding our hearts together through long periods of separation, it had the effect of making us tolerant of each other's yarns—and even convictions. The Lawyer—the best of old fellows—had, because of his many years and many virtues, the only cushion on deck, and was lying on the only rug. The accountant had brought out already a box of dominoes, and was toying architecturally with the bones. Marlow sat cross-legged right aft, leaning against the mizzen-mast. He had sunken cheeks, a yellow complexion, a straight back, and ascetic aspect, and, with his arms dropped, the palms of hands outwards, resembled an idol. The director, satisfied the anchor had good hold, made his way aft and sat down amongst us. We exchanged a few words lazily. Afterwards there was silence on board the yacht. For some reason or other we did not begin that game of dominoes. We felt meditative, and fit for nothing but placid staring. The day was ending in a serenity of still and exquisite brilliance. The water shone pacifically; the sky, without a speck, was a benign immensity of unstained light; the very mist on the Essex marshes was like a gauzy and radiant fabric, hung from the wooded rises inland, and draping the low shores in diaphanous folds. Only

---

1. Straight course of an otherwise winding river as it approaches the sea.　2. Easternmost large town on the Thames before it reaches the sea, 26 miles from London.

the gloom to the west, brooding over the upper reaches, became more somber every minute, as if angered by the approach of the sun.

And at last, in its curved and imperceptible fall, the sun sank low, and from glowing white changed to a dull red without rays and without heat, as if about to go out suddenly, stricken to death by the touch of that gloom brooding over a crowd of men.

Forthwith a change came over the waters, and the serenity became less brilliant but more profound. The old river in its broad reach rested unruffled at the decline of day, after ages of good service done to the race that peopled its banks, spread out in the tranquil dignity of a waterway leading to the uttermost ends of the earth. We looked at the venerable stream not in the vivid flush of a short day that comes and departs forever, but in the august light of abiding memories. And indeed nothing is easier for a man who has, as the phrase goes, "followed the sea" with reverence and affection, than to evoke the great spirit of the past upon the lower reaches of the Thames. The tidal current runs to and fro in its unceasing service, crowded with memories of men and ships it had borne to the rest of home or to the battles of the sea. It had known and served all the men of whom the nation is proud, from Sir Francis Drake to Sir John Franklin,[3] knights all, titled and untitled—the great knights-errant of the sea. It had borne all the ships whose names are like jewels flashing in the night of time, from the *Golden Hind* returning with her round flanks full of treasure, to be visited by the Queen's Highness and thus pass out of the gigantic tale, to the *Erebus* and *Terror*, bound on other conquests—and that never returned. It had known the ships and the men. They had sailed from Deptford, from Greenwich, from Erith—the adventurers and the settlers; kings' ships and the ships of men on 'Change; captains, admirals, the dark "interlopers" of the Eastern trade, and the commissioned "Generals" of East India fleets. Hunters for gold or pursuers of fame, they all had gone out on that stream, bearing the sword, and often the torch, messengers of the might within the land, bearers of a spark from the sacred fire. What greatness had not floated on the ebb of that river into the mystery of an unknown earth! . . . The dreams of men, the seed of commonwealths, the germs of empires.

The sun set; the dusk fell on the stream, and lights began to appear along the shore. The Chapman lighthouse, a three-legged thing erect on a mud-flat, shone strongly. Lights of ships moved in the fairway—a great stir of lights going up and going down. And farther west on the upper reaches the place of the monstrous town was still marked ominously on the sky, a brooding gloom in sunshine, a lurid glare under the stars.

"And this also," said Marlow suddenly, "has been one of the dark places on the earth."

He was the only man of us who still "followed the sea." The worst that could

---

3. Drake (1545?–1596), admiral under Elizabeth I and first Englishman to sail around the world, sailed the *Golden Hind*; Franklin (1786–1847) led a party in the *Erebus* and *Terror* on an ill-fated search for the Northwest Passage, which none survived.

be said of him was that he did not represent his class. He was a seaman, but he was a wanderer, too, while most seamen lead, if one may so express it, a sedentary life. Their minds are of the stay-at-home order, and their home is always with them—the ship; and so is their country—the sea. One ship is very much like another, and the sea is always the same. In the immutability of their surroundings the foreign shores, the foreign faces, the changing immensity of life, glide past, veiled not by a sense of mystery but by a slightly disdainful ignorance; for there is nothing mysterious to a seaman unless it be the sea itself, which is the mistress of his existence and as inscrutable as Destiny. For the rest, after his hours of work, a casual stroll or a casual spree on shore suffices to unfold for him the secret of a whole continent, and generally he finds the secret not worth knowing. The yarns of seamen have a direct simplicity, the whole meaning of which lies within the shell of a cracked nut. But Marlow was not typical (if his propensity to spin yarns be excepted), and to him the meaning of an episode was not inside like a kernel but outside, enveloping the tale which brought it out only as a glow brings out a haze, in the likeness of one of these misty halos that sometimes are made visible by the spectral illumination of moonshine.

10   His remark did not seem at all surprising. It was just like Marlow. It was accepted in silence. No one took the trouble to grunt even; and presently he said, very slow—

"I was thinking of very old times, when the Romans first came here, nineteen hundred years ago—the other day. . . . Light came out of this river since—you say Knights? Yes; but it is like a running blaze on a plain, like a flash of lightning in the clouds. We live in the flicker—may it last as long as the old earth keeps rolling! But darkness was here yesterday. Imagine the feelings of a commander of a fine—what d'ye call 'em?—trireme in the Mediterranean, ordered suddenly to the north; run overland across the Gauls in a hurry; put in charge of one of these craft the legionaries—a wonderful lot of handy men they must have been, too—used to build, apparently by the hundred, in a month or two, if we may believe what we read. Imagine him here—the very end of the world, a sea the color of lead, a sky the color of smoke, a kind of ship about as rigid as a concertina—and going up this river with stores, or orders, or what you like. Sand-banks, marshes, forests, savages,—precious little to eat fit for a civilized man, nothing but Thames water to drink. No Falernian wine[4] here, no going ashore. Here and there a military camp lost in a wilderness, like a needle in a bundle of hay— cold, fog, tempests, disease, exile, and death,—death skulking in the air, in the water, in the bush. They must have been dying like flies here. Oh yes—he did it. Did it very well, too, no doubt, and without thinking much about it either, except afterwards to brag of what he had gone through in his time, perhaps. They were men enough to face the darkness. And perhaps he was cheered by keeping his eye on a chance of promotion to the fleet at Ravenna[5] by and by, if he had good friends in Rome and survived the awful climate. Or think of a decent young citizen in a toga—perhaps too much dice, you know—coming

---

4. Famous ancient wine from the city of Naples.   5. Roman naval base on the Adriatic (though now inland).

out here in the train of some prefect, or taxgatherer, or trader even, to mend his fortunes. Land in a swamp, march through the woods, and in some inland post feel the savagery, the utter savagery, had closed round him,—all that mysterious life of the wilderness that stirs in the forest, in the jungles, in the hearts of wild men. There's no initiation either into such mysteries. He has to live in the midst of the incomprehensible, which is also detestable. And it has a fascination, too, that goes to work upon him. The fascination of the abomination—you know, imagine the growing regrets, the longing to escape, the powerless disgust, the surrender, the hate."

He paused.

"Mind," he began again, lifting one arm from the elbow, the palm of the hand outwards, so that, with his legs folded before him, he had the pose of a Buddha preaching in European clothes and without a lotus-flower[6]—"Mind, none of us would feel exactly like this. What saves us is efficiency—the devotion to efficiency. But these chaps were not much account, really. They were no colonists; their administration was merely a squeeze, and nothing more, I suspect. They were conquerors, and for that you want only brute force—nothing to boast of, when you have it, since your strength is just an accident arising from the weakness of others. They grabbed what they could get for the sake of what was to be got. It was just robbery with violence, aggravated murder on a great scale, and men going at it blind—as is very proper for those who tackle a darkness. The conquest of the earth, which mostly means the taking it away from those who have a different complexion or slightly flatter noses than ourselves, is not a pretty thing when you look into it too much. What redeems it is the idea only. An idea at the back of it; not a sentimental pretense but an idea; and an unselfish belief in the idea—something you can set up, and bow down before, and offer a sacrifice to. . . ."

He broke off. Flames glided in the river, small green flames, red flames, white flames, pursuing, overtaking, joining, crossing each other—then separating slowly or hastily. The traffic of the great city went on in the deepening night upon the sleepless river. We looked on, waiting patiently—there was nothing else to do till the end of the flood; but it was only after a long silence, when he said, in a hesitating voice, "I suppose you fellows remember I did once turn fresh-water sailor for a bit," that we knew we were fated, before the ebb began to run, to hear one of Marlow's inconclusive experiences.

"I don't want to bother you much with what happened to me personally," he began, showing in this remark the weakness of many tellers of tales who seem so often unaware of what their audience would best like to hear; "yet to understand the effect of it on me you ought to know how I got out there, what I saw, how I went up that river to the place where I first met the poor chap. It was the farthest point of navigation and the culminating point of my experience. It seemed somehow to throw a kind of light on everything about me—and into my thoughts. It was somber enough, too—and pitiful—not extraordinary in any

15

6. Buddha is often depicted sitting on a lotus seat or standing on a lotus pedestal, the lotus flower representing spirituality, perfection, immortality, divine birth, and regeneration.

way—not very clear either. No, not very clear. And yet it seemed to throw a kind of light.

"I had then, as you remember, just returned to London after a lot of Indian Ocean, Pacific, China Seas—a regular dose of the East—six years or so, and I was loafing about, hindering you fellows in your work and invading your homes, just as though I had got a heavenly mission to civilize you. It was very fine for a time, but after a bit I did get tired of resting. Then I began to look for a ship—I should think the hardest work on earth. But the ships wouldn't even look at me. And I got tired of that game too.

"Now when I was a little chap I had a passion for maps. I would look for hours at South America, or Africa, or Australia, and lose myself in all the glories of exploration. At that time there were many blank spaces on the earth, and when I saw one that looked particularly inviting on a map (but they all look that) I would put my finger on it and say, When I grow up I will go there. The North Pole was one of these places, I remember. Well, I haven't been there yet, and shall not try now. The glamour's off. Other places were scattered about the Equator, and in every sort of latitude all over the two hemispheres. I have been in some of them, and . . . well, we won't talk about that. But there was one yet— the biggest, the most blank, so to speak—that I had a hankering after.

"True, by this time it was not a blank space any more. It had got filled since my childhood with rivers and lakes and names. It had ceased to be a blank space of delightful mystery—a white patch for a boy to dream gloriously over. It had become a place of darkness. But there was in it one river especially, a mighty big river, that you could see on the map, resembling an immense snake uncoiled, with its head in the sea, its body at rest curving afar over a vast country, and its tail lost in the depths of the land. And as I looked at the map of it in a shop-window, it fascinated me as a snake would a bird—a silly little bird. Then I remembered there was a big concern, a Company for trade on that river. Dash it all! I thought to myself, they can't trade without using some kind of craft on that lot of fresh water—steamboats! Why shouldn't I try to get charge of one? I went on along Fleet Street, but could not shake off the idea. The snake had charmed me.

"You understand it was a Continental concern, that Trading society; but I have a lot of relations living on the Continent, because it's cheap and not so nasty as it looks, they say.

20   "I am sorry to own I began to worry them. This was already a fresh departure for me. I was not used to getting things that way, you know. I always went my own road and on my own legs where I had a mind to go. I wouldn't have believed it of myself; but, then—you see—I felt somehow I must get there by hook or by crook. So I worried them. The men said, 'My dear fellow,' and did nothing. Then—would you believe it?—I tried the women. I, Charlie Marlow, set the women to work—to get a job. Heavens! Well, you see, the notion drove me. I had an aunt, a dear enthusiastic soul. She wrote: 'It will be delightful. I am ready to do anything, anything for you. It is a glorious idea. I know the wife of a very high personage in the Administration, and also a man who has lots of

influence with,' etc. etc. She was determined to make no end of fuss to get me appointed skipper of a river steamboat, if such was my fancy.

"I got my appointment—of course; and I got it very quick. It appears the Company had received news that one of their captains had been killed in a scuffle with the natives. This was my chance, and it made me the more anxious to go. It was only months and months afterwards, when I made the attempt to recover what was left of the body, that I heard the original quarrel arose from a misunderstanding about some hens. Yes, two black hens. Fresleven—that was the fellow's name, a Dane—thought himself wronged somehow in the bargain, so he went ashore and started to hammer the chief of the village with a stick. Oh, it didn't surprise me in the least to hear this, and at the same time to be told that Fresleven was the gentlest, quietest creature that ever walked on two legs. No doubt he was; but he had been a couple of years already out there engaged in the noble cause, you know, and he probably felt the need at last of asserting his self-respect in some way. Therefore he whacked the old nigger mercilessly, while a big crowd of his people watched him, thunderstruck, till some man—I was told the chief's son—in desperation at hearing the old chap yell, made a tentative jab with a spear at the white man—and of course it went quite easy between the shoulder blades. Then the whole population cleared into the forest, expecting all kinds of calamities to happen, while, on the other hand, the steamer Fresleven commanded left also in a bad panic, in charge of the engineer, I believe. Afterwards nobody seemed to trouble much about Fresleven's remains, till I got out and stepped into his shoes. I couldn't let it rest, though; but when an opportunity offered at last to meet my predecessor, the grass growing through his ribs was tall enough to hide his bones. They were all there. The supernatural being had not been touched after he fell. And the village was deserted, the huts gaped black, rotting, all askew within the fallen enclosures. A calamity had come to it, sure enough. The people had vanished. Mad terror had scattered them, men, women, and children, through the bush, and they had never returned. What became of the hens I don't know either. I should think the cause of progress got them, anyhow. However, through this glorious affair I got my appointment, before I had fairly begun to hope for it.

"I flew around like mad to get ready, and before forty-eight hours I was crossing the Channel to show myself to my employers, and sign the contract. In a very few hours I arrived in a city that always makes me think of a whited sepulcher. Prejudice no doubt. I had no difficulty in finding the Company's offices. It was the biggest thing in the town, and everybody I met was full of it. They were going to run an oversea empire, and make no end of coin by trade.

"A narrow and deserted street in deep shadow, high houses, innumerable windows with venetian blinds, a dead silence, grass sprouting between the stones, imposing carriage archways right and left, immense double doors standing ponderously ajar. I slipped through one of these cracks, went up a swept and ungarnished staircase, as arid as a desert, and opened the first door I came to. Two women, one fat and the other slim, sat on straw-bottomed chairs, knitting black wool. The slim one got up and walked straight at me—still knitting with downcast eyes—and only just as I began to think of getting out of her way, as you would for a somnambulist, stood still, and looked up. Her dress was as plain as an umbrella-cover, and she turned round without a word and preceded me into a waiting-room. I gave my name, and looked about. Deal table in the middle, plain chairs all around the walls, on one end a large shining map, marked with all the colors of a rainbow. There was a vast amount of red—good to see at any time, because one knows that some real work is done in there, a deuce of a lot of blue, a little green, smears of orange, and, on the East Coast, a purple patch, to show where the jolly pioneers of progress drink the jolly lager-beer.[7] However, I wasn't going into any of these. I was going into the yellow. Dead in the center. And the river was there—fascinating—deadly—like a snake. Ough! A door opened, a white-haired secretarial head, but wearing a compassionate expression, appeared, and a skinny forefinger beckoned me into the sanctuary. Its light was dim, and a heavy writing-desk squatted in the middle. From behind that structure came out an impression of pale plumpness in a frock-coat. The great man himself. He was five feet six, I should judge, and had his grip on the handle-end of ever so many millions. He shook hands, I fancy, murmured vaguely, was satisfied with my French. *Bon voyage.*

"In about forty-five seconds I found myself again in the waiting-room with the compassionate secretary, who, full of desolation and sympathy, made me sign some document. I believe I undertook amongst other things not to disclose any trade secrets. Well, I am not going to.

25

"I began to feel slightly uneasy. You know I am not used to such ceremonies, and there was something ominous in the atmosphere. It was just as though I had been let into some conspiracy—I don't know—something not quite right; and I was glad to get out. In the outer room the two women knitted black wool feverishly. People were arriving, and the younger one was walking back and forth introducing them. The old one sat on her chair. Her flat cloth slippers were propped up on a footwarmer, and a cat reposed on her lap. She wore a starched white affair on her head, had a wart on one cheek, and silver-rimmed spectacles hung on the tip of her nose. She glanced at me above the glasses. The swift and indifferent placidity of that look troubled me. Two youths with foolish and cheery countenances were being piloted over, and she threw at them the same quick glance of unconcerned wisdom. She seemed to know all about them and about me, too. An eerie feeling came over me. She seemed uncanny and fateful. Often far away there I thought of these two, guarding the door of Darkness, knitting black wool as for a warm pall, one introducing, introducing continuously to the unknown, the other scrutinizing the cheery and foolish faces with unconcerned old eyes. *Ave!* Old knitter of black wool. *Morituri te salutant.*[8] Not many of those she looked at ever saw her again—not half, by a long way.

"There was yet a visit to the doctor. 'A simple formality,' assured me the secretary, with an air of taking an immense part in all my sorrows. Accordingly

---

7. Though British territories or colonies are almost universally shown as red, there seems to be no fixed color system now or in the 19th century for indicating national holdings. Here the blue seems to be French; green, Portuguese; orange, German; purple, Dutch; yellow, the Congo Free State.
8. Gladiators' salutation to the Roman emperor: "Hail! . . . Those who are about to die salute you."

a young chap wearing his hat over the left eyebrow, some clerk I suppose—there must have been clerks in the business, though the house was as still as a house in a city of the dead—came from somewhere upstairs, and led me forth. He was shabby and careless, with inkstains on the sleeves of his jacket, and his cravat was large and billowy, under a chin shaped like the toe of an old boot. It was a little too early for the doctor, so I proposed a drink, and thereupon he developed a vein of joviality. As we sat over our vermouths he glorified the Company's business, and by and by I expressed casually my surprise at him not going out there. He became very cool and collected all at once. 'I am not such a fool as I look, quoth Plato to his disciples,' he said sententiously, emptied his glass with great resolution, and we rose.

"The old doctor felt my pulse, evidently thinking of something else the while. 'Good, good for there,' he mumbled, and then with a certain eagerness asked me whether I would let him measure my head. Rather surprised, I said Yes, when he produced a thing like calipers and got the dimensions back and front and every way, taking notes carefully. He was an unshaven little man in a threadbare coat like a gaberdine, with his feet in slippers, and I thought him a harmless fool. 'I always ask leave, in the interests of science, to measure the crania of those going out there,' he said. 'And when they come back, too?' I asked. 'Oh, I never see them,' he remarked; 'and, moreover, the changes take place inside, you know.' He smiled, as if at some quiet joke. 'So you are going out there. Famous.[9] Interesting too.' He gave me a searching glance, and made another note. 'Ever any madness in your family?' he asked, in a matter-of-fact tone. I felt very annoyed. 'Is that question in the interests of science, too?' 'It would be,' he said, without taking notice of my irritation, 'interesting for science to watch the mental changes of individuals, on the spot, but . . .' 'Are you an alienist?'[1] I interrupted. 'Every doctor should be—a little,' answered that original, imperturbably. 'I have a little theory which you Messieurs who go out there must help me to prove. This is my share in the advantages my country shall reap from the possession of such a magnificent dependency. The mere wealth I leave to others. Pardon my questions, but you are the first Englishman coming under my observation . . .' I hastened to assure him I was not in the least typical. 'If I were,' said I, 'I wouldn't be talking like this with you.' 'What you say is rather profound, and probably erroneous,' he said, with a laugh. 'Avoid irritation more than exposure to the sun. Adieu. How do you English say, eh? Good-by. Ah! Good-by. Adieu. In the tropics one must before everything keep calm.' . . . He lifted a warning forefinger. . . . '*Du calme, du calme. Adieu.*'

"One thing more remained to do—say good-by to my excellent aunt. I found her triumphant. I had a cup of tea—the last decent cup of tea for many days—and in a room that most soothingly looked just as you would expect a lady's drawing-room to look, we had a long quiet chat by the fireside. In the course of these confidences it became quite plain to me I had been represented to the wife of the high dignitary, and goodness knows to how many more people besides, as

9. Excellent, splendid.   1. Psychiatrist.

an exceptional and gifted creature—a piece of good fortune for the Company—a man you don't get hold of every day. Good heavens! and I was going to take charge of a two-penny-half-penny river-steamboat with a penny whistle attached! It appeared, however, I was also one of the Workers, with a capital—you know. Something like an emissary of light, something like a lower sort of apostle. There had been a lot of such rot let loose in print and talk just about that time, and the excellent woman, living right in the rush of all that humbug, got carried off her feet. She talked about 'weaning those ignorant millions from their horrid ways,' till, upon my word, she made me quite uncomfortable. I ventured to hint that the Company was run for profit.

" 'You forget, dear Charlie, that the laborer is worthy of his hire,'[2] she said, brightly. It's queer how out of touch with truth women are. They live in a world of their own, and there has never been anything like it, and never can be. It is too beautiful altogether, and if they were to set it up it would go to pieces before the first sunset. Some confounded fact we men have been living contentedly with ever since the day of creation would start up and knock the whole thing over.

30

"After this I got embraced, told to wear flannel, be sure to write often, and so on—and I left. In the street—I don't know why—a queer feeling came to me that I was an impostor. Odd thing that I, who used to clear out for any part of the world at twenty-four hours' notice, with less thought than most men give to the crossing of a street, had a moment—I won't say of hesitation, but of startled pause, before this commonplace affair. The best way I can explain it to you is by saying that, for a second or two, I felt as though, instead of going to the center of a continent, I were about to set off for the center of the earth.

"I left in a French steamer, and she called in every blamed port they have out there, for, as far as I could see, the sole purpose of landing soldiers and custom-house officers. I watched the coast. Watching a coast as it slips by the ship is like thinking about an enigma. There it is before you—smiling, frowning, inviting, grand, mean, insipid, or savage, and always mute with an air of whispering, Come and find out. This one was almost featureless, as if still in the making, with an aspect of monotonous grimness. The edge of a colossal jungle, so dark-green as to be almost black, fringed with white surf, ran straight, like a ruled line, far, far away along a blue sea whose glitter was blurred by a creeping mist. The sun was fierce, the land seemed to glisten and drip with steam. Here and there grayish-whitish specks showed up clustered inside the white surf, with a flag flying above them perhaps. Settlements some centuries old, and still no bigger than pinheads on the untouched expanse of their background. We pounded along, stopped, landed soldiers; went on, landed custom-house clerks to levy toll in what looked like a God-forsaken wilderness, with a tin shed and a flag-pole lost in it; landed more soldiers—to take care of the custom-house clerks, presumably. Some, I heard, got drowned in the surf; but whether they did or not, nobody seemed particularly to care. They were just flung out there, and on we went. Every day the coast looked the same, as though we had not

2. Words of Jesus in Luke 10:7.

moved; but we passed various places—trading places—with names like Gran' Bassam, Little Popo; names that seemed to belong to some sordid farce acted in front of a sinister backcloth. The idleness of a passenger, my isolation amongst all these men with whom I had no point of contact, the oily and languid sea, the uniform somberness of the coast, seemed to keep me away from the truth of things, within the toil of a mournful and senseless delusion. The voice of the surf heard now and then was a positive pleasure, like the speech of a brother. It was something natural, that had its reason, that had a meaning. Now and then a boat from the shore gave one a momentary contact with reality. It was paddled by black fellows. You could see from afar the white of their eyeballs glistening. They shouted, sang; their bodies streamed with perspiration; they had faces like grotesque masks—these chaps; but they had bone, muscle, a wild vitality, an intense energy of movement, that was as natural and true as the surf along their coast. They wanted no excuse for being there. They were a great comfort to look at. For a time I would feel I belonged still to a world of straightforward facts, but the feeling would not last long. Something would turn up to scare it away. Once, I remember, we came upon a man-of-war anchored off the coast. There wasn't even a shed there, and she was shelling the bush. It appears the French had one of their wars going on thereabouts. Her ensign dropped limp like a rag; the muzzles of the long six-inch guns stuck out all over the low hull; the greasy, slimy swell swung her up lazily and let her down, swaying her thin masts. In the empty immensity of earth, sky, and water, there she was, incomprehensible, firing into a continent. Pop, would go one of the six-inch guns; a small flame would dart and vanish, a little white smoke would disappear, a tiny projectile would give a feeble screech—and nothing happened. Nothing could happen. There was a touch of insanity in the proceeding, a sense of lugubrious drollery in the sight; and it was not dissipated by somebody on board assuring me earnestly there was a camp of natives—he called them enemies!—hidden out of sight somewhere.

"We gave her her letters (I heard the men in that lonely ship were dying of fever at the rate of three a day) and went on. We called at some more places with farcical names, where the merry dance of death and trade goes on in a still and earthy atmosphere as of an overheated catacomb; all along the formless coast bordered by dangerous surf, as if Nature herself had tried to ward off intruders; in and out of rivers, streams of death in life, whose banks were rotting into mud, whose waters, thickened into slime, invaded the contorted mangroves, that seemed to writhe at us in the extremity of an impotent despair. Nowhere did we stop long enough to get a particularized impression, but the general sense of vague and oppressive wonder grew upon me. It was like a weary pilgrimage amongst hints for nightmares.

"It was upward of thirty days before I saw the mouth of the big river. We anchored off the seat of the government. But my work would not begin till some two hundred miles farther on. So as soon as I could I made a start for a place thirty miles higher up.

"I had my passage on a little sea-going steamer. Her captain was a Swede, and knowing me for a seaman, invited me on the bridge. He was a young man,

lean, fair, and morose, with lanky hair and a shuffling gait. As we left the miserable little wharf, he tossed his head contemptuously at the shore. 'Been living
there?' he asked. I said, 'Yes.' 'Fine lot these government chaps—are they not?'
he went on, speaking English with great precision and considerable bitterness.
'It is funny what some people will do for a few francs a month. I wonder what
becomes of that kind when it goes up-country?' I said to him I expected to see
that soon. 'So-o-o!' he exclaimed. He shuffled athwart, keeping one eye ahead
vigilantly. 'Don't be too sure,' he continued. 'The other day I took up a man
who hanged himself on the road. He was a Swede, too.' 'Hanged himself! Why,
in God's name?' I cried. He kept on looking out watchfully. 'Who knows? The
sun was too much for him, or the country perhaps.'

35   "At last we opened a reach. A rocky cliff appeared, mounds of turned-up
earth by the shore, houses on a hill, others with iron roofs, amongst a waste of
excavations, or hanging to the declivity. A continuous noise of the rapids above
hovered over this scene of inhabited devastation. A lot of people, mostly black
and naked, moved about like ants. A jetty projected into the river. A blinding
sunlight drowned all this at times in a sudden recrudescence of glare. 'There's
your Company's station,' said the Swede, pointing to three wooden barrack-like
structures on the rocky slope. 'I will send your things up. Four boxes did you
say? So. Farewell.'

    "I came upon a boiler wallowing in the grass, then found a path leading up
the hill. It turned aside for the boulders, and also for an undersized railway-truck
lying there on its back with its wheels in the air. One was off. The thing looked
as dead as the carcass of some animal. I came upon more pieces of decaying
machinery, a stack of rusty nails. To the left a clump of trees made a shady spot,
where dark things seemed to stir feebly. I blinked, the path was steep. A horn
tooted to the right, and I saw the black people run. A heavy and dull detonation
shook the ground, a puff of smoke came out of the cliff, and that was all. No
change appeared on the face of the rock. They were building a railway. The
cliff was not in the way or anything; but this objectless blasting was all the work
going on.

    "A slight clinking behind me made me turn my head. Six black men
advanced in a file, toiling up the path. They walked erect and slow, balancing
small baskets full of earth on their heads, and the clink kept time with their
footsteps. Black rags were wound round their loins, and the short ends behind
waggled to and fro like tails. I could see every rib, the joints of their limbs were
like knots in a rope; each had an iron collar on his neck, and all were connected
together with a chain whose bights swung between them, rhythmically clinking.
Another report from the cliff made me think suddenly of that ship of war I had
seen firing into a continent. It was the same kind of ominous voice; but these
men could by no stretch of imagination be called enemies. They were called
criminals, and the outraged law, like the bursting shells, had come to them, an
insoluble mystery from the sea. All their meager breasts panted together, the
violently dilated nostrils quivered, the eyes stared stonily up-hill. They passed me
within six inches, without a glance, with that complete, deathlike indifference of
unhappy savages. Behind this raw matter one of the reclaimed, the product of

the new forces at work, strolled despondently, carrying a rifle by its middle. He had a uniform jacket with one button off, and seeing a white man on the path, hoisted his weapon to his shoulder with alacrity. This was simple prudence, white men being so much alike at a distance that he could not tell who I might be. He was speedily reassured, and with a large, white, rascally grin, and a glance at his charge, seemed to take me into partnership in his exalted trust. After all, I also was a part of the great cause of these high and just proceedings.

"Instead of going up, I turned and descended to the left. My idea was to let that chain-gang get out of sight before I climbed the hill. You know I am not particularly tender; I've had to strike and to fend off. I've had to resist and to attack sometimes—that's only one way of resisting—without counting the exact cost, according to the demands of such sort of life as I had blundered into. I've seen the devil of violence, and the devil of greed, and the devil of hot desire; but, by all the stars! these were strong, lusty, red-eyed devils, that swayed and drove men—men, I tell you. But as I stood on this hillside, I foresaw that in the blinding sunshine of that land I would become acquainted with a flabby, pretending, weak-eyed devil of a rapacious and pitiless folly. How insidious he could be, too, I was only to find out several months later and a thousand miles farther. For a moment I stood appalled, as though by a warning. Finally I descended the hill, obliquely, towards the trees I had seen.

"I avoided a vast artificial hole somebody had been digging on the slope, the purpose of which I found it impossible to divine. It wasn't a quarry or a sandpit, anyhow. It was just a hole. It might have been connected with the philanthropic desire of giving the criminals something to do. I don't know. Then I nearly fell into a very narrow ravine, almost no more than a scar in the hillside. I discovered that a lot of imported drainage-pipes for the settlement had been tumbled in there. There wasn't one that was not broken. It was a wanton smash-up. At last I got under the trees. My purpose was to stroll into the shade for a moment; but no sooner within than it seemed to me I had stepped into the gloomy circle of some Inferno. The rapids were near, and an uninterrupted, uniform, headlong, rushing noise filled the mournful stillness of the grove, where not a breath stirred, not a leaf moved, with a mysterious sound—as though the tearing pace of the launched earth had suddenly become audible.

"Black shapes crouched, lay, sat between the trees, leaning against the trunks, clinging to the earth, half coming out, half effaced within the dim light, in all the attitudes of pain, abandonment, and despair. Another mine on the cliff went off, followed by a slight shudder of the soil under my feet. The work was going on. The work! And this was the place where some of the helpers had withdrawn to die.

"They were dying slowly—it was very clear. They were not enemies, they were not criminals, they were nothing earthly now,—nothing but black shadows of disease and starvation, lying confusedly in the greenish gloom. Brought from all the recesses of the coast in all the legality of time contracts, lost in uncongenial surroundings, fed on unfamiliar food, they sickened, became inefficient, and were then allowed to crawl away and rest. These moribund shapes were free as air—and nearly as thin. I began to distinguish the gleam of the eyes under

40

the trees. Then, glancing down, I saw a face near my hand. The black bones reclined at full length with one shoulder against the tree, and slowly the eyelids rose and the sunken eyes looked up at me, enormous and vacant, a kind of blind, white flicker in the depths of the orbs, which died out slowly. The man seemed young—almost a boy—but you know with them it's hard to tell. I found nothing else to do but to offer him one of my good Swede's ship's biscuits I had in my pocket. The fingers closed slowly on it and held—there was no other movement and no other glance. He had tied a bit of white worsted round his neck—Why? Where did he get it? Was it a badge—an ornament—a charm—a propitiatory act? Was there any idea at all connected with it? It looked startling round his black neck, this bit of white thread from beyond the seas.

"Near the same tree two more bundles of acute angles sat with their legs drawn up. One, with his chin propped on his knees, stared at nothing, in an intolerable and appalling manner: his brother phantom rested its forehead, as if overcome with a great weariness; and all about others were scattered in every pose of contorted collapse, as in some picture of a massacre or a pestilence. While I stood horror-struck, one of these creatures rose to his hands and knees, and went off on all-fours towards the river to drink. He lapped out of his hand, then sat up in the sunlight, crossing his shins in front of him, and after a time let his woolly head fall on his breastbone.

"I didn't want any more loitering in the shade, and I made haste towards the station. When near the buildings I met a white man, in such an unexpected elegance of get-up that in the first moment I took him for a sort of vision. I saw a high starched collar, white cuffs, a light alpaca jacket, snowy trousers, a clear necktie, and varnished boots. No hat. Hair parted, brushed, oiled, under a green-lined parasol held in a big white hand. He was amazing, and had a penholder behind his ear.

"I shook hands with this miracle, and I learned he was the Company's chief accountant, and that all the bookkeeping was done at this station. He had come out for a moment, he said, 'to get a breath of fresh air.' The expression sounded wonderfully odd, with its suggestion of sedentary desk-life. I wouldn't have mentioned the fellow to you at all, only it was from his lips that I first heard the name of the man who is so indissolubly connected with the memories of that time. Moreover, I respected the fellow. Yes; I respected his collars, his vast cuffs, his brushed hair. His appearance was certainly that of a hairdresser's dummy; but in the great demoralization of the land he kept up his appearance. That's backbone. His starched collars and got-up shirt-fronts were achievements of character. He had been out nearly three years; and, later, I could not help asking him how he managed to sport such linen. He had just the faintest blush, and said modestly, 'I've been teaching one of the native women about the station. It was difficult. She had a distaste for the work.' Thus this man had verily accomplished something. And he was devoted to his books, which were in apple-pie order.

45

"Everything else in the station was in a muddle,—heads, things, buildings. Strings of dusty niggers with splay feet arrived and departed; a stream of manufactured goods, rubbishy cottons, beads, and brass-wire set into the depths of darkness, and in return came a precious trickle of ivory.

"I had to wait in the station for ten days—an eternity. I lived in a hut in the yard, but to be out of the chaos I would sometimes get into the accountant's office. It was built of horizontal planks, and so badly put together that, as he bent over his high desk, he was barred from neck to heels with narrow strips of sunlight. There was no need to open the big shutter to see. It was hot there, too; big flies buzzed fiendishly, and did not sting, but stabbed. I sat generally on the floor, while, of faultless appearance (and even slightly scented), perching on a high stool, he wrote, he wrote. Sometimes he stood up for exercise. When a trucklebed with a sick man (some invalid agent from up-country) was put in there, he exhibited a gentle annoyance. 'The groans of this sick person,' he said, 'distract my attention. And without that it is extremely difficult to guard against clerical errors in this climate.'

"One day he remarked, without lifting his head, 'In the interior you will no doubt meet Mr. Kurtz.' On my asking who Mr. Kurtz was, he said he was a first-class agent; and seeing my disappointment at this information, he added slowly, laying down his pen, 'He is a very remarkable person.' Further questions elicited from him that Mr. Kurtz was at present in charge of a trading post, a very important one, in the true ivory-country, at 'the very bottom of there. Sends in as much ivory as all the others put together. . . .' He began to write again. The sick man was too ill to groan. The flies buzzed in a great peace.

"Suddenly there was a growing murmur of voices and a great tramping of feet. A caravan had come in. A violent babble of uncouth sounds burst out on the other side of the planks. All the carriers were speaking together, and in the midst of the uproar the lamentable voice of the chief agent was heard 'giving it up'[3] tearfully for the twentieth time that day. . . . He rose slowly. 'What a fright-ful row,' he said. He crossed the room gently to look at the sick man, and returning, said to me, 'He does not hear.' 'What! Dead?' I asked, startled. 'No, not yet,' he answered, with great composure. Then, alluding with a toss of the head to the tumult in the station-yard, 'When one has got to make correct entries, one comes to hate those savages—hate them to the death.' He remained thoughtful for a moment. 'When you see Mr. Kurtz,' he went on, 'tell him for me that everything here'—he glanced at the desk—'is very satisfactory. I don't like to write to him—with those messengers of ours you never know who may get hold of your letter—at that Central Station.' He stared at me for a moment with his mild, bulging eyes. 'Oh, he will go far, very far,' he began again. 'He will be a somebody in the Administration before long. They, above—the Council in Europe, you know—mean him to be.'

"He turned to his work. The noise outside had ceased, and presently in going out I stopped at the door. In the steady buzz of flies the homeward-bound agent was lying flushed and insensible; the other, bent over his books, was making correct entries of perfectly correct transactions; and fifty feet below the doorstep I could see the still tree-tops of the grove of death.

"Next day I left that station at last, with a caravan of sixty men, for a two-hundred-mile tramp.

"No use telling you much about that. Paths, paths, everywhere; a stamped-

50

3. Giving up the ghost, or dying.

in network of paths spreading over the empty land, through long grass, through burnt grass, through thickets, down and up chilly ravines, up and down stony hills ablaze with heat; and a solitude, a solitude, nobody, not a hut. The population had cleared out a long time ago. Well, if a lot of mysterious niggers armed with all kinds of fearful weapons suddenly took to traveling on the road between Deal[4] and Gravesend, catching the yokels right and left to carry heavy loads for them, I fancy every farm and cottage thereabouts would get empty very soon. Only here the dwellings were gone, too. Still I passed through several abandoned villages. There's something pathetically childish in the ruins of grass walls. Day after day, with the stamp and shuffle of sixty pair of bare feet behind me, each pair under a sixty-pound load. Camp, cook, sleep, strike camp, march. Now and then a carrier dead in harness, at rest in the long grass near the path, with an empty water-gourd and his long staff lying by his side. A great silence around and above. Perhaps on some quiet night the tremor of far-off drums, sinking, swelling, a tremor vast, faint; a sound weird, appealing, suggestive, and wild—and perhaps with as profound a meaning as the sound of bells in a Christian country. Once a white man in an unbuttoned uniform, camping on the path with an armed escort of lank Zanzibaris,[5] very hospitable and festive—not to say drunk. Was looking after the upkeep of the road, he declared. Can't say I saw any road or any upkeep, unless the body of a middle-aged Negro, with a bullet-hole in the forehead, upon which I absolutely stumbled three miles farther on, may be considered as a permanent improvement. I had a white companion, too, not a bad chap, but rather too fleshy and with the exasperating habit of fainting on the hot hillsides, miles away from the least bit of shade and water. Annoying, you know, to hold your own coat like a parasol over a man's head while he is coming-to. I couldn't help asking him once what he meant by coming there at all. 'To make money, of course. What do you think?' he said, scornfully. Then he got fever, and had to be carried in a hammock slung under a pole. As he weighed sixteen stone[6] I had no end of rows with the carriers. They jibbed, ran away, sneaked off with their loads in the night—quite a mutiny. So, one evening, I made a speech in English with gestures, not one of which was lost to the sixty pairs of eyes before me, and the next morning I started the hammock off in front all right. An hour afterwards I came upon the whole concern wrecked in a bush—man, hammock, groans, blankets, horrors. The heavy pole had skinned his poor nose. He was very anxious for me to kill somebody, but there wasn't the shadow of a carrier near. I remembered the old doctor—'It would be interesting for science to watch the mental changes of individuals, on the spot.' I felt I was becoming scientifically interesting. However, all that is to no purpose. On the fifteenth day I came in sight of the big river again, and hobbled into the Central Station. It was on a backwater surrounded by scrub and forest, with a pretty border of smelly mud on one side, and on the three others enclosed by a crazy[7] fence of rushes. A neglected gap

---

4. Port near Dover.   5. Zanzibar, a British-controlled island off the east coast of Africa, supplied mercenaries for service throughout the continent.   6. I.e., 224 pounds; a stone, 14 pounds, is a standard British measure.   7. Irregular and/or shaky.

was all the gate it had, and the first glance at the place was enough to let you see the flabby devil was running that show. White men with long staves in their hands appeared languidly from amongst the buildings, strolling up to take a look at me, and then retired out of sight somewhere. One of them, a stout, excitable chap with black mustaches, informed me with great volubility and many digressions, as soon as I told him who I was, that my steamer was at the bottom of the river. I was thunderstruck. What, how, why? Oh, it was 'all right.' The 'manager himself' was there. All quite correct. 'Everybody had behaved splendidly! splendidly!'—'you must,' he said in agitation, 'go and see the general manager at once. He is waiting!'

"I did not see the real significance of that wreck at once. I fancy I see it now, but I am not sure—not at all. Certainly the affair was too stupid—when I think of it—to be altogether natural. Still . . . . But at the moment it presented itself simply as a confounded nuisance. The steamer was sunk. They had started two days before in a sudden hurry up the river with the manager on board, in charge of some volunteer skipper, and before they had been out three hours they tore the bottom out of her on stones, and she sank near the south bank. I asked myself what I was to do there, now my boat was lost. As a matter of fact, I had plenty to do in fishing my command out of the river. I had to set about it the very next day. That, and the repairs when I brought the pieces to the station, took some months.

"My first interview with the manager was curious. He did not ask me to sit down after my twenty-mile walk that morning. He was commonplace in complexion, in feature, in manners, and in voice. He was of middle size and of ordinary build. His eyes, of the usual blue, were perhaps remarkably cold, and he certainly could make his glance fall on one as trenchant and heavy as an ax. But even at these times the rest of his person seemed to disclaim the intention. Otherwise there was only an indefinable, faint expression of his lips, something stealthy—a smile—not a smile—I remember it, but I can't explain. It was unconscious, this smile was, though just after he had said something it got intensified for an instant. It came at the end of his speeches like a seal applied on the words to make the meaning of the commonest phrase appear absolutely inscrutable. He was a common trader, from his youth up employed in these parts—nothing more. He was obeyed, yet he inspired neither love nor fear, nor even respect. He inspired uneasiness. That was it! Uneasiness. Not a definite mistrust—just uneasiness—nothing more. You have no idea how effective such a . . . a . . . faculty can be. He had no genius for organizing, for initiative, or for order even. That was evident in such things as the deplorable state of the station. He had no learning, and no intelligence. His position had come to him—why? Perhaps because he was never ill. . . . He had served three terms of three years out there. . . . Because triumphant health in the general rout of constitutions is a kind of power in itself. When he went home on leave he rioted on a large scale—pompously. Jack[8] ashore—with a difference—in externals only. This one could gather from his casual talk. He originated nothing, he could keep the

8. Sailor.

routine going—that's all. But he was great. He was great by this little thing that it was impossible to tell what could control such a man. He never gave that secret away. Perhaps there was nothing within him. Such a suspicion made one pause—for out there there were no external checks. Once when various tropical diseases had laid low almost every 'agent' in the station, he was heard to say, 'Men who come out here should have no entrails.' He sealed the utterance with that smile of his, as though it had been a door opening into a darkness he had in his keeping. You fancied you had seen things—but the seal was on. When annoyed at meal-times by the constant quarrels of the white men about precedence, he ordered an immense round table to be made, for which a special house had to be built. This was the station's messroom. Where he sat was the first place—the rest were nowhere. One felt this to be his unalterable conviction. He was neither civil nor uncivil. He was quiet. He allowed his 'boy'—an overfed young Negro from the coast—to treat the white men, under his very eyes, with provoking insolence.

"He began to speak as soon as he saw me. I had been very long on the road. He could not wait. Had to start without me. The upriver stations had to be relieved. There had been so many delays already that he did not know who was dead and who was alive, and how they got on—and so on, and so on. He paid no attention to my explanations, and, playing with a stick of sealing-wax, repeated several times that the situation was 'very grave, very grave.' There were rumors that a very important station was in jeopardy, and its chief, Mr. Kurtz, was ill. Hoped it was not true. Mr. Kurtz was . . . I felt weary and irritable. Hang Kurtz, I thought. I interrupted him by saying I had heard of Mr. Kurtz on the coast. 'Ah! So they talk of him down there,' he murmured to himself. Then he began again, assuring me Mr. Kurtz was the best agent he had, an exceptional man, of the greatest importance to the Company; therefore I could understand his anxiety. He was, he said, 'very, very uneasy.' Certainly he fidgeted on his chair a good deal, exclaimed, 'Ah, Mr. Kurtz!' broke the stick of sealing-wax and seemed dumfounded by the accident. Next thing he wanted to know 'how long it would take to . . .' I interrupted him again. Being hungry, you know, and kept on my feet too, I was getting savage. 'How can I tell?' I said, 'I haven't even seen the wreck yet—some months, no doubt.' All this talk seemed to me so futile. 'Some months,' he said. 'Well, let us say three months before we can make a start. Yes. That ought to do the affair.' I flung out of his hut (he lived all alone in a clay hut with a sort of veranda) muttering to myself my opinion of him. He was a chattering idiot. Afterwards I took it back when it was borne in upon me startlingly with what extreme nicety he had estimated the time requisite for the 'affair.'

55 "I went to work the next day, turning, so to speak, my back on that station. In that way only it seemed to me I could keep my hold on the redeeming facts of life. Still, one must look about sometimes; and then I saw this station, these men strolling aimlessly about in the sunshine of the yard. I asked myself sometimes what it all meant. They wandered here and there with their absurd long staves in their hands, like a lot of faithless pilgrims bewitched inside a rotten fence. The word 'ivory' rang in the air, was whispered, was sighed. You would

think they were praying to it. A taint of imbecile rapacity blew through it all, like a whiff from some corpse. By Jove! I've never seen anything so unreal in my life. And outside, the silent wilderness surrounding this cleared speck on the earth struck me as something great and invincible, like evil or truth, waiting patiently for the passing away of this fantastic invasion.

"Oh, these months! Well, never mind. Various things happened. One evening a grass shed full of calico, cotton prints, beads, and I don't know what else, burst into a blaze so suddenly that you would have thought the earth had opened to let an avenging fire consume all that trash. I was smoking my pipe quietly by my dismantled steamer, and saw them all cutting capers in the light, with their arms lifted high, when the stout man with mustaches came tearing down to the river, a tin pail in his hand, assured me that everybody was 'behaving splendidly, splendidly,' dipped about a quart of water and tore back again. I noticed there was a hole in the bottom of his pail.

"I strolled up. There was no hurry. You see the thing had gone off like a box of matches. It had been hopeless from the very first. The flame had leaped high, driven everybody back, lighted up everything—and collapsed. The shed was already a heap of embers glowing fiercely. A nigger was being beaten near by. They said he had caused the fire in some way; be that as it may, he was screeching most horribly. I saw him, later, for several days, sitting in a bit of shade looking very sick and trying to recover himself: afterwards he arose and went out—and the wilderness without a sound took him into its bosom again. As I approached the glow from the dark I found myself at the back of two men, talking. I heard the name of Kurtz pronounced, then the words, 'take advantage of this unfortunate accident.' One of the men was the manager. I wished him a good evening. 'Did you ever see anything like it—eh? it is incredible,' he said, and walked off. The other man remained. He was a first-class agent, young, gentlemanly, a bit reserved, with a forked little beard and a hooked nose. He was standoffish with the other agents, and they on their side said he was the manager's spy among them. As to me, I had hardly ever spoken to him before. We got into talk, and by and by we strolled away from the hissing ruins. Then he asked me to his room, which was in the main building of the station. He struck a match, and I perceived that this young aristocrat had not only a silver-mounted dressing-case but also a whole candle all to himself. Just at that time the manager was the only man supposed to have any right to candles. Native mats covered the clay walls; a collection of spears, assegais, shields, knives was hung up in trophies. The business intrusted to this fellow was the making of bricks—so I had been informed; but there wasn't a fragment of a brick anywhere in the station, and he had been there more than a year—waiting. It seems he could not make bricks without something, I don't know what—straw[9], maybe. Anyways, it could not be found there, and as it was not likely to be sent from

9. In Exodus 5, the Hebrews, slaves of the Egyptians, had to make a certain number of bricks daily, the straw for the process supplied by the Egyptians, but the Pharaoh ordered the supplying of straw stopped while keeping the daily quota the same; not only was a good deal of time lost searching for straw, but little else than stubble could be found.

Europe, it did not appear clear to me what he was waiting for. An act of special creation perhaps. However, they were all waiting—all the sixteen or twenty pilgrims of them—for something; and upon my word it did not seem an uncongenial occupation, from the way they took it, though the only thing that ever came to them was disease—as far as I could see. They beguiled the time by backbiting and intriguing against each other in a foolish kind of way. There was an air of plotting about that station, but nothing came of it, of course. It was as unreal as everything else—as the philanthropic pretense of the whole concern, as their talk, as their government, as their show of work. The only real feeling was a desire to get appointed to a trading-post where ivory was to be had, so that they could earn percentages. They intrigued and slandered and hated each other only on that account,—but as to effectually lifting a little finger—oh, no. By heavens! there is something after all in the world allowing one man to steal a horse while another must not look at the halter. Steal a horse straight out. Very well. He has done it. Perhaps he can ride. But there is a way of looking at a halter that would provoke the most charitable of saints into a kick.

"I had no idea why he wanted to be sociable, but as we chatted in there it suddenly occurred to me the fellow was trying to get at something—in fact, pumping me. He alluded constantly to Europe, to the people I was supposed to know there—putting leading questions as to my acquaintances in the sepulchral city, and so on. His little eyes glittered like mica discs—with curiosity—though he tried to keep up a bit of superciliousness. At first I was astonished, but very soon I became awfully curious to see what he would find out from me. I couldn't possibly imagine what I had in me to make it worth his while. It was very pretty to see how he baffled himself, for in truth my body was full only of chills, and my head had nothing in it but that wretched steamboat business. It was evident he took me for a perfectly shameless prevaricator. At last he got angry, and, to conceal a movement of furious annoyance, he yawned. I rose. Then I noticed a small sketch in oils, on a panel, representing a woman, draped and blindfolded, carrying a lighted torch. The background was somber—almost black. The movement of the woman was stately, and the effect of the torchlight on the face was sinister.

"It arrested me, and he stood by civilly, holding an empty half-pint champagne bottle (medical comforts) with the candle stuck in it. To my question he said Mr. Kurtz had painted this—in this very station more than a year ago— while waiting for means to go to his trading-post. 'Tell me, pray,' said I, 'who is this Mr. Kurtz?'

" 'The chief of the Inner Station,' he answered in a short tone, looking away. 'Much obliged,' I said, laughing. 'And you are the brickmaker of the Central Station. Everyone knows that.' He was silent for a while. 'He is a prodigy,' he said at last. 'He is an emissary of pity, and science, and progress, and devil knows what else. We want,' he began to declaim suddenly, 'for the guidance of the cause intrusted to us by Europe, so to speak, higher intelligence, wide sympathies, a singleness of purpose.' 'Who says that?' I asked. 'Lots of them,' he replied. 'Some even write that; and so *he* comes here, a special being, as you ought to know.' 'Why ought I to know?' I interrupted, really surprised. He paid no attention. 'Yes. Today he is chief of the best station, next year he will be assistant-manager, two years more and . . . but I daresay you know what he will be in two years' time. You are of the new gang—the gang of virtue. The same people who sent him specially also recommended you. Oh, don't say no. I've my own eyes to trust.' Light dawned upon me. My dear aunt's influential acquaintances were producing an unexpected effect upon that young man. I nearly burst into a laugh. 'Do you read the Company's confidential correspondence?' I asked. He hadn't a word to say. It was great fun. 'When Mr. Kurtz,' I continued, severely, 'is General Manager, you won't have the opportunity.'

"He blew the candle out suddenly, and we went outside. The moon had risen. Black figures strolled about listlessly, pouring water on the glow, whence proceeded a sound of hissing; steam ascended in the moonlight, the beaten nigger groaned somewhere. 'What a row the brute makes!' said the indefatigable man with the mustaches, appearing near us. 'Serves him right. Transgression—punishment—bang! Pitiless, pitiless. That's the only way. This will prevent all conflagrations for the future. I was just telling the manager. . . .' He noticed my companion, and became crestfallen all at once. 'Not in bed yet,' he said, with a kind of servile heartiness; 'it's so natural. Ha! Danger—agitation.' He vanished. I went on to the river-side, and the other followed me. I heard a scathing murmur at my ear, 'Heap of muffs—go to.' The pilgrims could be seen in knots gesticulating, discussing. Several had still their staves in their hands. I verily believe they took these sticks to bed with them. Beyond the fence the forest stood up spectrally in the moonlight, and through the dim stir, through the faint sounds of that lamentable courtyard, the silence of the land went home to one's very heart—its mystery, its greatness, the amazing reality of its concealed life. The hurt nigger moaned feebly somewhere near by, and then fetched a deep sigh that made me mend my pace away from there. I felt a hand introducing itself under my arm. 'My dear sir,' said the fellow, 'I don't want to be misunderstood, and especially by you, who will see Mr. Kurtz long before I can have that pleasure. I wouldn't like him to get a false idea of my disposition. . . .'

"I let him run on, this papier-mâché Mephistopheles, and it seemed to me that if I tried I could poke my forefinger through him, and would find nothing inside but a little loose dirt, maybe. He, don't you see, had been planning to be assistant-manager by and by under the present man, and I could see that the coming of that Kurtz had upset them both not a little. He talked precipitately, and I did not try to stop him. I had my shoulders against the wreck of my steamer, hauled up on the slope like a carcass of some big river animal. The smell of mud, of primeval mud, by Jove! was in my nostrils, the high stillness of primeval forest was before my eyes; there were shiny patches on the black creek. The moon had spread over everything a thin layer of silver—over the rank grass, over the mud, upon the wall of matted vegetation standing higher than the wall of a temple, over the great river I could see through a somber gap glittering, glittering, as it flowed broadly by without a murmur. All this was great, expectant, mute, while the man jabbered about himself. I wondered whether the stillness on the face of the immensity looking at us two were meant as an appeal or as a menace. What were we who had strayed in here? Could we handle that dumb thing, or would it handle us? I felt how big, how confoundedly big, was that thing that couldn't talk, and perhaps was deaf as well. What was in there? I could see a little ivory coming out from there, and I had heard Mr. Kurtz was in there. I had heard enough about it, too—God knows! Yet somehow it didn't bring any image with it—no more than if I had been told an angel or a fiend was in there. I believed it in the same way one of you might believe there are inhabitants in the planet Mars. I knew once a Scotch sailmaker who was certain, dead sure, there were people in Mars. If you asked him for some idea how they looked and behaved, he would get shy and mutter something about 'walking on all-fours.' If you as much as smiled, he would—though a man of sixty—offer to fight you. I would not have gone so far as to fight for Kurtz, but I went for him near enough to a lie. You know I hate, detest, and can't bear a lie, not because I am straighter than the rest of us, but simply because it appalls me. There is a taint of death, a flavor of mortality in lies—which is exactly what I hate and detest in the world—what I want to forget. It makes me miserable and sick, like biting something rotten would do. Temperament, I suppose. Well, I went near enough to it by letting the young fool there believe anything he liked to imagine as to my influence in Europe. I became in an instant as much of a pretence as the rest of the bewitched pilgrims. This simply because I had a notion it some-how would be of help to that Kurtz whom at the time I did not see—you under-stand. He was just a word for me. I did not see the man in the name any more than you do. Do you see him? Do you see the story? Do you see anything? It seems to me I am trying to tell you a dream—making a vain attempt, because no relation of a dream can convey the dream-sensation, that commingling of absurdity, surprise, and bewilderment in a tremor of struggling revolt, that notion of being captured by the incredible which is of the very essence of dreams. . . ."

He was silent for a while.

". . . No, it is impossible; it is impossible to convey the life-sensation of any given epoch of one's existence—that which makes its truth, its meaning—its subtle and penetrating essence. It is impossible. We live, as we dream—alone. . . ."

He paused again as if reflecting, then added—

"Of course in this you fellows see more than I could then. You see me, whom you know. . . ."

It had become so pitch dark that we listeners could hardly see one another. For a long time already he, sitting apart, had been no more to us than a voice. There was not a word from anybody. The others might have been asleep, but I was awake. I listened, I listened on the watch for the sentence, for the word, that would give me the clew to the faint uneasiness inspired by this narrative that seemed to shape itself without human lips in the heavy night-air of the river.

". . . Yes—I let him run on," Marlow began again, "and think what he pleased about the powers that were behind me. I did! And there was nothing behind me! There was nothing but that wretched, old, mangled steamboat I was leaning against, while he talked fluently about 'the necessity for every man to get on.' 'And when one comes out here, you conceive, it is not to gaze at the moon.' Mr. Kurtz was a 'universal genius,' but even a genius would find it easier to work with 'adequate tools—intelligent men.' He did not make bricks—why, there was a physical impossibility in the way—as I was well aware; and if he did secretarial work for the manager, it was because 'no sensible man rejects wantonly the confidence of his superiors.' Did I see it? I saw it. What more did I want? What I really wanted was rivets, by heaven! Rivets. To get on with the work—to stop the hole. Rivets I wanted. There were cases of them down at the coast—cases—piled up—burst—split! You kicked a loose rivet at every second step in that station yard on the hillside. Rivets had rolled into the grove of death. You could fill your pockets with rivets for the trouble of stooping down—and there wasn't one rivet to be found where it was wanted. We had plates that would do, but nothing to fasten them with. And every week the messenger, a lone Negro, letter-bag on shoulder and staff in hand, left our station for the coast. And several times a week a coast caravan came in with trade goods— ghastly glazed calico that made you shudder only to look at it; glass beads, valued about a penny a quart, confounded spotted cotton handkerchiefs. And no rivets. Three carriers could have brought all that was wanted to set that steamboat afloat.

"He was becoming confidential now, but I fancy my unresponsive attitude must have exasperated him at last, for he judged it necessary to inform me he feared neither God nor devil, let alone any mere man. I said I could see that very well, but what I wanted was a certain quantity of rivets—and rivets were what really Mr. Kurtz wanted, if he had only known it. Now letters went to the coast every week. . . . 'My dear sir,' he cried, 'I write from dictation.' I demanded rivets. There was a way—for an intelligent man. He changed his manner; became very cold, and suddenly began to talk about a hippopotamus; wondered whether sleeping on board the steamer (I stuck to my salvage night and day) I wasn't disturbed. There was an old hippo that had the bad habit of getting out on the bank and roaming at night over the station grounds. The pilgrims used to turn out in a body and empty every rifle they could lay hands on at him. Some even had sat up o' nights for him. All this energy was wasted, though. 'That animal has a charmed life,' he said; 'but you can say this only of brutes in this country. No man—you apprehend me?—no man here bears a charmed life.' He stood there for a moment in the moonlight with his delicate hooked nose set a little askew, and his mica eyes glittering without a wink, then, with a curt good night, he strode off. I could see he was disturbed and considerably puzzled, which made me feel more hopeful than I had been for days. It was a great comfort to turn from that chap to my influential friend, the battered, twisted, ruined, tin-pot steamboat. I clambered on board. She rang under my feet like an empty Huntley & Palmer biscuit-tin kicked along a gutter; she was nothing so solid in make, and rather less pretty in shape, but I had expended enough hard work on her to make me love her. No influential friend would have served me better. She had given me a chance to come out a bit—to find out what I could do. No, I don't like work. I had rather laze about and think of all the fine things that can be done. I don't like work—no man does—but I like what is in the work,—the chance to find yourself. Your own reality—for yourself, not for others—what no other man can ever know. They can only see the mere show, and never can tell what it really means.

70   "I was not surprised to see somebody sitting aft, on the deck, with his legs dangling over the mud. You see I rather chummed with the few mechanics there were in that station, whom the other pilgrims naturally despised—on account of their imperfect manners, I suppose. This was the foreman—a boiler-maker by trade—a good worker. He was a lank, bony, yellow-faced man, with big intense eyes. His aspect was worried, and his head was as bald as the palm of my hand; but his hair in falling seemed to have stuck to his chin, and had prospered in the new locality, for his beard hung down to his waist. He was a widower with six young children (he had left them in charge of a sister of his to come out there), and the passion of his life was pigeon-flying. He was an enthusiast and a connoisseur. He would rave about pigeons. After work hours he used sometimes to come over from his hut for a talk about his children and his pigeons; at work, when he had to crawl in the mud under the bottom of the steamboat, he would tie up that beard of his in a kind of white serviette he brought for the purpose. It had loops to go over his ears. In the evening he could be seen squatted on the bank rinsing that wrapper in the creek with great care, then spreading it solemnly on a bush to dry.

    "I slapped him on the back and shouted, 'We shall have rivets!' He scrambled to his feet exclaiming, 'No! Rivets!' as though he couldn't believe his ears. Then in a low voice, 'You . . . eh?' I don't know why we behaved like lunatics. I put my finger to the side of my nose and nodded mysteriously. 'Good for you!' he cried, snapped his fingers above his head, lifting one foot. I tried a jig. We capered on the iron deck. A frightful clatter came out of that hulk, and the virgin forest on the other bank of the creek sent it back in a thundering roll upon the sleeping station. It must have made some of the pilgrims sit up in their hovels. A dark figure obscured the lighted doorway of the manager's hut, vanished, then, a second or so after, the doorway itself vanished, too. We stopped, and the silence driven away by the stamping of our feet flowed back again from the recesses of the land. The great wall of vegetation, an exuberant and entangled mass of trunks, branches, leaves, boughs, festoons, motionless in the moonlight, was like a rioting invasion of soundless life, a rolling wave of plants, piled up, crested, ready to topple over the creek, to sweep every little man of us out of his little existence. And it moved not. A deadened burst of mighty splashes and snorts reached us from afar as though an ichthyosaurus had been taking a bath of glitter in the great river. 'After all,' said the boilermaker in a reasonable tone, 'why shouldn't we get the rivets?' Why not, indeed! I did not know of any reason why we shouldn't. 'They'll come in three weeks,' I said, confidently.

    "But they didn't. Instead of rivets there came an invasion, an infliction, a visitation. It came in sections during the next three weeks, each section headed by a donkey carrying a white man in new clothes and tan shoes, bowing from that elevation right and left to the impressed pilgrims. A quarrelsome band of footsore sulky niggers trod on the heels of the donkeys; a lot of tents, campstools, tin boxes, white cases, brown bales would be shot down in the courtyard, and the air of mystery would deepen a little over the muddle of the station. Five such installments came, with their absurd air of disorderly flight with the loot of innumerable outfit shops and provision stores, that, one would think, they were lugging, after a raid, into the wilderness for equitable division. It was an extricable mess of things decent in themselves but that human folly made look like the spoils of thieving.

"This devoted band called itself the Eldorado Exploring Expedition, and I believe they were sworn to secrecy. Their talk, however, was the talk of sordid buccaneers: it was reckless without hardihood, greedy without audacity, and cruel without courage; there was not an atom of foresight or of serious intention in the whole batch of them, and they did not seem aware these things are wanted for the work of the world. To tear treasure out of the bowels of the land was their desire, with no more moral purpose at the back of it than there is in burglars breaking into a safe. Who paid the expenses of the noble enterprise I don't know; but the uncle of our manager was leader of that lot.

"In exterior he resembled a butcher in a poor neighborhood, and his eyes had a look of sleepy cunning. He carried his fat paunch with ostentation on his short legs, and during the time his gang infested the station spoke to no one but his nephew. You could see these two roaming about all day long with their heads close together in an everlasting confab.

"I had given up worrying myself about the rivets. One's capacity for that kind of folly is more limited than you would suppose. I said Hang!—and let things slide. I had plenty of time for meditation, and now and then I would give some thought to Kurtz. I wasn't very interested in him. No. Still, I was curious to see whether this man, who had come out equipped with moral ideas of some sort, would climb to the top after all and how he would set about his work when there."

75

II

"One evening as I was lying flat on the deck of my steamboat, I heard voices approaching—and there were the nephew and the uncle strolling along the bank. I laid my head on my arm again, and had nearly lost myself in a doze, when somebody said in my ear, as it were: 'I am as harmless as a little child, but I don't like to be dictated to. Am I the manager—or am I not? I was ordered to send him there. It's incredible.' . . . I became aware that the two were standing on the shore alongside the forepart of the steamboat, just below my head. I did not move; it did not occur to me to move: I was sleepy. 'It *is* unpleasant,' grunted the uncle. 'He has asked the Administration to be sent there,' said the other, 'with the idea of showing what he could do; and I was instructed accordingly. Look at the influence that man must have. Is it not frightful?' They both agreed it was frightful, then made several bizarre remarks: 'Make rain and fine weather—one man—the Council—by the nose'—bits of absurd sentences that got the better of my drowsiness, so that I had pretty near the whole of my wits about me when the uncle said, 'The climate may do away with this difficulty for you. Is he alone there?' 'Yes,' answered the manager; 'he sent his assistant down the river with a note to me in these terms: "Clear this poor devil out of the country, and don't bother sending more of that sort. I had rather be alone than have the kind of men you can dispose of with me." It was more than a year ago. Can you imagine such impudence?' 'Anything since then?' asked the other, hoarsely. 'Ivory,' jerked the nephew; 'lots of it—prime sort—lots—most annoying, from him.' 'And with that?' questioned the heavy rumble. 'Invoice,' was the reply fired out, so to speak. Then silence. They had been talking about Kurtz.

"I was broad awake by this time, but, lying perfectly at ease, remained still, having no inducement to change my position. 'How did that ivory come all this way?' growled the elder man, who seemed very vexed. The other explained that it had come with a fleet of canoes in charge of an English half-caste clerk Kurtz had with him; that Kurtz had apparently intended to return himself, the station being by that time bare of goods and stores, but after coming three hundred miles, had suddenly decided to go back, which he started to do alone in a small dugout with four paddlers, leaving the half-caste to continue down the river with the ivory. The two fellows there seemed astounded at anybody attempting such a thing. They were at a loss for an adequate motive. As to me, I seemed to see Kurtz for the first time. It was a distinct glimpse: the dugout, four paddling savages, and the lone white man turning his back suddenly on the headquarters, on relief, on thoughts of home—perhaps; setting his face towards the depths of the wilderness, towards his empty and desolate station. I did not know the motive. Perhaps he was just simply a fine fellow who stuck to his work for its own sake. His name, you understand, had not been pronounced once. He was 'that man.' The half-caste, who, as far as I could see, had conducted a difficult trip with great prudence and pluck, was invariably alluded to as 'that scoundrel.' The 'scoundrel' had reported that the 'man' had been very ill—had recovered imperfectly. . . . The two below me moved away then a few paces, and strolled back and forth at some little distance. I heard: 'Military post—doctor—two hundred miles—quite alone now—unavoidable delays—nine months—no news— strange rumors.' They approached again, just as the manager was saying, 'No one, as far as I know, unless a species of wandering trader—a pestilential fellow, snapping ivory from the natives.' Who was it they were talking about now? I gathered in snatches that this was some man supposed to be in Kurtz's district, and of whom the manager did not approve. 'We will not be free from unfair competition till one of these fellows is hanged for an example,' he said. 'Certainly,' grunted the other; 'get him hanged! Why not? Anything—anything can be done in this country. That's what I say; nobody here, you understand, *here*, can endanger your position. And why? You stand the climate—you outlast them all. The danger is in Europe; but there before I left I took care to—' They moved off and whispered, then their voices rose again. 'The extraordinary series of delays is not my fault. I did my best.' The fat man sighed. 'Very sad.' 'And the pestiferous absurdity of his talk,' continued the other; 'he bothered me enough when he was here. "Each station should be like a beacon on the road towards better things, a center for trade, of course, but also for humanizing, improving, instructing." Conceive you—that ass! And he wants to be manager! No, it's—' Here he got choked by excessive indignation, and I lifted my head the least bit.

I was surprised to see how near they were—right under me. I could have spat upon their hats. They were looking on the ground, absorbed in thought. The manager was switching his leg with a slender twig: his sagacious relative lifted his head. 'You have been well since you came out this time?' he asked. The other gave a start. 'Who? I? Oh! Like a charm—like a charm. But the rest—oh, my goodness! All sick. They die so quick, too, that I haven't the time to send them out of the country—it's incredible!' 'H'm. Just so,' grunted the uncle. 'Ah! my boy, trust to this—I say, trust to this.' I saw him extend his short flipper of an arm for a gesture that took in the forest, the creek, the mud, the river,—seemed to beckon with a dishonoring flourish before the sunlit face of the land a treacherous appeal to the lurking death, to the hidden evil, to the profound darkness of its heart. It was so startling that I leaped to my feet and looked back at the edge of the forest, as though I had expected an answer of some sort to that black display of confidence. You know the foolish notions that come to one sometimes. The high stillness confronted these two figures with its ominous patience, waiting for the passing away of a fantastic invasion.

"They swore aloud together—out of sheer fright, I believe—then pretending not to know anything of my existence, turned back to the station. The sun was low; and leaning forward side by side, they seemed to be tugging painfully uphill their two ridiculous shadows of unequal length, that trailed behind them slowly over the tall grass without bending a single blade.

"In a few days the Eldorado Expedition went into the patient wilderness, that closed upon it as the sea closes over a diver. Long afterwards the news came that all the donkeys were dead. I know nothing as to the fate of the less valuable animals. They, no doubt, like the rest of us, found what they deserved. I did not inquire. I was then rather excited at the prospect of meeting Kurtz very soon. When I say very soon I mean it comparatively. It was just two months from the day we left the creek when we came to the bank below Kurtz's station.

"Going up that river was like traveling back to the earliest beginnings of the world, when vegetation rioted on the earth and the big trees were kings. An empty stream, a great silence, an impenetrable forest. The air was warm, thick, heavy, sluggish. There was no joy in the brilliance of sunshine. The long stretches of the waterway ran on, deserted, into the gloom of overshadowed distances. On silvery sandbanks hippos and alligators sunned themselves side by side. The broadening waters flowed through a mob of wooded islands; you lost your way on that river as you would in a desert, and butted all day long against shoals, trying to find the channel, till you thought yourself bewitched and cut off forever from everything you had known once—somewhere—far away—in another existence perhaps. There were moments when one's past came back to one, as it will sometimes when you have not a moment to spare to yourself; but it came in the shape of an unrestful and noisy dream, remembered with wonder amongst the overwhelming realities of this strange world of plants, and water, and silence. And this stillness of life did not in the least resemble a peace. It was the stillness of an implacable force brooding over an inscrutable intention. It looked at you with a vengeful aspect. I got used to it afterwards; I did not see it any more; I had no time. I had to keep guessing at the channel; I had to discern,

80

mostly by inspiration, the signs of hidden banks; I watched for sunken stones; I was learning to clap my teeth smartly before my heart flew out, when I shaved by a fluke some infernal sly old snag that would have ripped the life out of the tin-pot steamboat and drowned all the pilgrims; I had to keep a lookout for the signs of dead wood we could cut up in the night for next day's steaming. When you have to attend to things of that sort, to the mere incidents of the surface, the reality—the reality, I tell you—fades. The inner truth is hidden—luckily, luckily. But I felt it all the same; I felt often its mysterious stillness watching me at my monkey tricks, just as it watches you fellows performing on your respective tight-ropes for—what is it? half-a-crown a tumble—"

"Try to be civil, Marlow," growled a voice, and I knew there was at least one listener awake besides myself.

"I beg your pardon. I forgot the heartache which makes up the rest of the price. And indeed what does the price matter, if the trick be well done? You do your tricks very well. And I didn't do badly either, since I managed not to sink that steamboat on my first trip. It's a wonder to me yet. Imagine a blindfolded man set to drive a van over a bad road. I sweated and shivered over that business considerably, I can tell you. After all, for a seaman, to scrape the bottom of the thing that's supposed to float all the time under his care is the unpardonable sin. No one may know of it, but you never forget the thump—eh? A blow on the very heart. You remember it, you dream of it, you wake up at night and think of it—years after—and go hot and cold all over. I don't pretend to say that steamboat floated all the time. More than once she had to wade for a bit, with twenty cannibals splashing around and pushing. We had enlisted some of these chaps on the way for a crew. Fine fellows—cannibals—in their place. They were men one could work with, and I am grateful to them. And, after all, they did not eat each other before my face: they had brought along a provision of hippo-meat which went rotten, and made the mystery of the wilderness stink in my nostrils. Phoo! I can sniff it now. I had the manager on board and three or four pilgrims with their staves—all complete. Sometimes we came upon a station close by the bank, clinging to the skirts of the unknown, and the white men rushing out of a tumble-down hovel, with great gestures of joy and surprise and welcome, seemed very strange—had the appearance of being held there captive by a spell. The word ivory would ring in the air for a while—and on we went again into the silence, along empty reaches, round the still bends, between the high walls of our winding way, reverberating in hollow claps the ponderous beat of the stern-wheel. Trees, trees, millions of trees, massive, immense, running up high; and at their foot, hugging the bank against the stream, crept the little begrimed steamboat, like a sluggish beetle crawling on the floor of a lofty portico. It made you feel very small, very lost, and yet it was not altogether depressing, that feeling. After all, if you were small, the grimy beetle crawled on—which was just what you wanted it to do. Where the pilgrims imagined it crawled to I don't know. To some place where they expected to get something, I bet! For me it crawled towards Kurtz—exclusively; but when the steam-pipes started leaking we crawled very slow. The reaches opened before us and closed behind, as if the forest had stepped leisurely across the water to bar the way for our return. We penetrated deeper and deeper into the heart of darkness. It was very quiet there. At night sometimes the roll of drums behind the curtain of trees would run up the river and remain sustained faintly, as if hovering in the air high over our heads, till the first break of day. Whether it meant war, peace, or prayer we could not tell. The dawns were heralded by the descent of a chill stillness; the woodcutters slept, their fires burned low; the snapping of a twig would make you start. We were wanderers on a prehistoric earth, on an earth that wore the aspect of an unknown planet. We could have fancied ourselves the first men taking possession of an accursed inheritance, to be subdued at the cost of profound anguish and of excessive toil. But suddenly, as we struggled round a bend, there would be a glimpse of rush walls, of peaked grass-roofs, a burst of yells, a whirl of black limbs, a mass of hands clapping, of feet stamping, of bodies swaying, of eyes rolling, under the droop of heavy and motionless foliage. The steamer toiled along slowly on the edge of a black and incomprehensible frenzy. The prehistoric man was cursing us, praying to us, welcoming us—who could tell? We were cut off from the comprehension of our surroundings; we glided past like phantoms, wondering and secretly appalled, as sane men would be before an enthusiastic outbreak in a madhouse. We could not understand because we were too far and could not remember, because we were traveling in the night of first ages, of those ages that are gone, leaving hardly a sign—and no memories.

"The earth seemed unearthly. We are accustomed to look upon the shackled form of a conquered monster, but there—there you could look at a thing monstrous and free. It was unearthly, and the men were—No, they were not inhuman. Well, you know, that was the worst of it—this suspicion of their not being inhuman. It would come slowly to one. They howled and leaped, and spun, and made horrid faces; but what thrilled you was just the thought of their humanity—like yours—the thought of your remote kinship with this wild and passionate uproar. Ugly. Yes, it was ugly enough; but if you were man enough you would admit to yourself that there was in you just the faintest trace of a response to the terrible frankness of that noise, a dim suspicion of there being a meaning in it which you—you so remote from the night of first ages—could comprehend. And why not? The mind of man is capable of anything—because everything is in it, all the past as well as all the future. What was there after all? Joy, fear, sorrow, devotion, valor, rage—who can tell?—but truth—truth stripped of its cloak of time. Let the fool gape and shudder—the man knows, and can look on without a wink. But he must at least be as much of a man as these on the shore. He must meet that truth with his own true stuff—with his own inborn strength. Principles won't do. Acquisitions, clothes, pretty rags—rags that would fly off at the first good shake. No; you want a deliberate belief. An appeal to me in this fiendish row—is there? Very well; I hear; I admit, but I have a voice too, and for good or evil mine is the speech that cannot be silenced. Of course, a fool, what with sheer fright and fine sentiments, is always safe. Who's that grunting? You wonder I didn't go ashore for a howl and a dance? Well, no—I didn't. Fine sentiments, you say? Fine sentiments, be hanged! I had no time. I had to mess about with white-lead[1] and strips of woolen blanket helping to put bandages on those leaky steam-pipes—I tell you. I had to watch the steering, and circumvent those snags, and get the tin-pot along by hook or by crook. There was surface-truth enough in these things to save a wiser man. And between whiles I had to look after the savage who was fireman. He was an improved specimen; he could fire up a vertical boiler.[2] He was there below me, and, upon my word, to look at him was as edifying as seeing a dog in a parody of breeches and a feather hat, walking on his hindlegs. A few months of training had done for that really fine chap. He squinted at the steam-gauge and at the water-gauge with an evident effort of intrepidity—and he had filed teeth, too, the poor devil, and the wool of his pate shaved into queer patterns, and three ornamental scars on each of his cheeks. He ought to have been clapping his hands and stamping his feet on the bank, instead of which he was hard at work, a thrall to strange witchcraft, full of improving knowledge. He was useful because he had been instructed; and what he knew was this—that should the water in that transparent thing disappear, the evil spirit inside the boiler would get angry through the greatness of his thirst, and take a terrible vengeance. So he sweated and fired up and watched the glass fearfully (with an impromptu charm, made of rags, tied to his arm, and a piece of polished bone, as big as a watch, stuck flatways through his lower lip), while the wooden banks slipped past us slowly, the short noise was left behind, the interminable miles of silence—and we crept on, towards Kurtz. But the snags were thick, the water was treacherous and shallow, the boiler seemed indeed to have a sulky devil in it, and thus neither that fireman nor I had any time to peer into our creepy thoughts.

"Some fifty miles below the Inner Station we came upon a hut of reeds, an inclined and melancholy pole, with the unrecognizable tatters of what had been a flag of some sort flying from it, and a neatly stacked woodpile. This was unexpected. We came to the bank, and on the stack of firewood found a flat piece of board with some faded pencil-writing on it. When deciphered it said: 'Wood for you. Hurry up. Approach cautiously.' There was a signature, but it was illegible—not Kurtz—a much longer word. 'Hurry up.' Where? Up the river? 'Approach cautiously.' We had not done so. But the warning could not have been meant for the place where it could be only found after approach. Something was wrong above. But what—and how much? That was the question. We commented adversely upon the imbecility of that telegraphic style. The bush around said nothing, and would not let us look very far, either. A torn curtain of red twill hung in the doorway of the hut, and flapped sadly in our faces. The dwelling was dismantled; but we could see a white man had lived there not very long ago. There remained a rude table—a plank on two posts; a heap of rubbish reposed in a dark corner, and by the door I picked up a book. It had lost its covers, and the pages had been thumbed into a state of extremely dirty softness; but the back had been lovingly stitched afresh with white cotton thread, which looked clean yet. It was an extraordinary find. Its title was, *An Inquiry into some*

1. Putty.   2. An upright, simple, easily fired boiler.

Points of Seamanship, by a man Towser, Towson — some such name — Master in his Majesty's Navy. The matter looked dreary reading enough, with illustrative diagrams and repulsive tables of figures, and the copy was sixty years old. I handled this amazing antiquity with the greatest possible tenderness, lest it should dissolve in my hands. Within, Towson or Towser was inquiring earnestly into the breaking strain of ships' chains and tackle, and other such matters. Not a very enthralling book; but at the first glance you could see there a singleness of intention, an honest concern for the right way of going to work, which made these humble pages, thought out so many years ago, luminous with another than a professional light. The simple old sailor, with his talk of chains and purchases,[3] made me forget the jungle and the pilgrims in a delicious sensation of having come upon something unmistakably real. Such a book being there was wonderful enough; but still more astounding were the notes penciled in the margin, and plainly referring to the text. I couldn't believe my eyes! They were in cipher! Yes, it looked like cipher. Fancy a man lugging with him a book of that description into this nowhere and studying it — and making notes — in cipher at that! It was an extravagant mystery.

"I had been dimly aware for some time of a worrying noise, and when I lifted my eyes I saw the woodpile was gone, and the manager, aided by all the pilgrims, was shouting at me from the river-side. I slipped the book into my pocket. I assure you to leave off reading was like tearing myself away from the shelter of an old and solid friendship.

"I started the lame engine ahead. 'It must be this miserable trader — this intruder,' exclaimed the manager, looking back malevolently at the place we had left. 'He must be English,' I said. 'It will not save him from getting into trouble if he is not careful,' muttered the manager darkly. I observed with assumed innocence that no man was safe from trouble in this world.

"The current was more rapid now, the steamer seemed at her last gasp, the stern-wheel flopped languidly, and I caught myself listening on tiptoe for the next beat of the float,[4] for in sober truth I expected the wretched thing to give up every moment. It was like watching the last flickers of a life. But still we crawled. Sometimes I would pick out a tree a little way ahead to measure our progress towards Kurtz by, but I lost it invariably before we got abreast. To keep the eyes so long on one thing was too much for human patience. The manager displayed a beautiful resignation. I fretted and fumed and took to arguing with myself whether or no I would talk openly with Kurtz; but before I could come to any conclusion it occurred to me that my speech or my silence, indeed any action of mine, would be a mere futility. What did it matter what anyone knew or ignored? What did it matter who was manager? One gets sometimes such a flash of insight. The essentials of this affair lay deep under the surface, beyond my reach, and beyond my power of meddling.

"Towards the evening of the second day we judged ourselves about eight miles from Kurtz's station. I wanted to push on; but the manager looked grave, and told me the navigation up there was so dangerous that it would be advisable,

85

---

3. Levers, or system of pulleys.   4. Blade on paddle-wheel.

the sun being very low already, to wait where we were till next morning. Moreover, he pointed out that if the warning to approach cautiously were to be followed, we must approach in daylight—not at dusk, or in the dark. This was sensible enough. Eight miles meant nearly three hours' steaming for us, and I could also see suspicious ripples at the upper end of the reach. Nevertheless, I was annoyed beyond expression at the delay, and most unreasonably, too, since one night more could not matter much after so many months. As we had plenty of wood, and caution was the word, I brought up in the middle of the stream. The reach was narrow, straight, with high sides like a railway cutting. The dusk came gliding into it long before the sun had set. The current ran smooth and swift, but a dumb immobility sat on the banks. The living trees, lashed together by the creepers and every living bush of the undergrowth, might have been changed into stone, even to the slenderest twig, to the lightest leaf. It was not sleep—it seemed unnatural, like a state of trance. Not the faintest sound of any kind could be heard. You looked on amazed, and began to suspect yourself of being deaf—then the night came suddenly, and struck you blind as well. About three in the morning some large fish leaped, and the loud splash made me jump as though a gun had been fired. When the sun rose there was a white fog, very warm and clammy, and more blinding than the night. It did not shift or drive; it was just there, standing all around you like something solid. At eight or nine, perhaps, it lifted as a shutter lifts. We had a glimpse of the towering multitude of trees, of the immense matted jungle, with the blazing little ball of the sun hanging over it—all perfectly still—and then the white shutter came down again, smoothly, as if sliding in greased grooves. I ordered the chain, which we had begun to heave in, to be paid out again. Before it stopped running with a muffled rattle, a cry, a very loud cry, as of infinite desolation, soared slowly in the opaque air. It ceased. A complaining clamor, modulated in savage discords, filled our ears. The sheer unexpectedness of it made my hair stir under my cap. I don't know how it struck the others: to me it seemed as though the mist itself had screamed, so suddenly, and apparently from all sides at once, did this tumultuous and mournful uproar arise. It culminated in a hurried outbreak of almost intolerably excessive shrieking, which stopped short, leaving us stiffened in a variety of silly attitudes, and obstinately listening to the nearly as appalling and excessive silence. 'Good God! What is the meaning—' stammered at my elbow one of the pilgrims,—a little fat man, with sandy hair and red whiskers, who wore side-spring boots, and pink pajamas tucked into his socks. Two others remained open-mouthed a whole minute, then dashed into the little cabin, to rush out incontinently and stand darting scared glances, with Winchesters at 'ready' in their hands. What we could see was just the steamer we were on, her outlines blurred as though she had been on the point of dissolving, and a misty strip of water, perhaps two feet broad, around her—and that was all. The rest of the world was nowhere, as far as our eyes and ears were concerned. Just nowhere. Gone, disappeared; swept off without leaving a whisper or a shadow behind.

"I went forward, and ordered the chain to be hauled in short, so as to be ready to trip the anchor and move the steamboat at once if necessary. 'Will they attack?' whispered an awed voice. 'We will be all butchered in this fog,' murmured another. The faces twitched with the strain, the hands trembling slightly, the eyes forgot to wink. It was very curious to see the contrast of expressions of the white men and of the black fellows of our crew, who were as much strangers to that part of the river as we, though their homes were only eight hundred miles away. The whites, of course, greatly discomposed, had besides a curious look of being painfully shocked by such an outrageous row. The others had an alert, naturally interested expression; but their faces were essentially quiet, even those of the one or two who grinned as they hauled at the chain. Several exchanged short, grunting phrases, which seemed to settle the matter to their satisfaction. Their headman, a young, broad-chested black, severely draped in dark-blue fringed cloths, with fierce nostrils and his hair all done up artfully in oily ringlets, stood near me. 'Aha!' I said, just for good fellowship's sake. 'Catch 'em,' he snapped, with a bloodshot widening of his eyes and a flash of sharp teeth— 'catch 'im. Give 'im to us.' 'To you, eh?' I asked; 'what would you do with them?' 'Eat 'em!' he said, curtly, and, leaning his elbow on the rail, looked out into the fog in a dignified and profoundly pensive attitude. I would no doubt have been properly horrified, had it not occurred to me that he and his chaps must be very hungry: that they must have been growing increasingly hungry for at least this month past. They had been engaged for six months (I don't think a single one of them had any clear idea of time, as we at the end of countless ages have. They still belonged to the beginnings of time—had no inherited experience to teach them as it were), and of course, as long as there was a piece of paper written over in accordance with some farcical law or other made down the river, it didn't enter anybody's head to trouble how they would live. Certainly they had brought with them some rotten hippo-meat, which couldn't have lasted very long, anyway, even if the pilgrims hadn't, in the midst of a shocking hullabaloo, thrown a considerable quantity of it overboard. It looked like a high-handed proceeding; but it was really a case of legitimate self-defense. You can't breathe dead hippo waking, sleeping, and eating, and at the same time keep your precarious grip on existence. Besides that, they had given them every week three pieces of brass wire, each about nine inches long; and the theory was they were to buy their provisions with that currency in riverside villages. You can see how *that* worked. There were either no villages, or the people were hostile, or the director, who like the rest of us fed out of tins, with an occasional old he-goat thrown in, didn't want to stop the steamer for some more or less recondite reason. So, unless they swallowed the wire itself, or made loops of it to snare the fishes with, I don't see what good their extravagant salary could be to them. I must say it was paid with a regularity worthy of a large and honorable trading company. For the rest, the only thing to eat—though it didn't look eatable in the least—I saw in their possession was a few lumps of some stuff like half-cooked dough, of a dirty lavender color, they kept wrapped in leaves, and now and then swallowed a piece of, but so small that it seemed done more for the looks of the thing than for any serious purpose of sustenance. Why in the name of all the gnawing devils of hunger they didn't go for us—they were thirty to five—and have a good tuck-in[5] for once, amazes me now when I think of it. They were big powerful men, with not much capacity to weigh the consequences, with courage, with strength, even yet, though their skins were no longer glossy and their muscles no longer hard. And I saw that something restraining, one of those human secrets that baffle probability, had come into play there. I looked at them with a swift quickening of interest—not because it occurred to me I might be eaten by them before very long, though I own to you that just then I perceived—in a new light, as it were—how unwholesome the pilgrims looked, and I hoped, yes, I positively hoped, that my aspect was not so—what shall I say?—so—unappetizing: a touch of fantastic vanity which fitted well with the dream-sensation that pervaded all my days at that time. Perhaps I had a little fever, too. One can't live with one's finger everlastingly on one's pulse. I had often 'a little fever,' or a little touch of other things—the playful paw-strokes of the wilderness, the preliminary trifling before the more serious onslaught which came in due course. Yes; I looked at them as you would on any human being, with a curiosity of their impulses, motives, capacities, weaknesses, when brought to the test of an inexorable physical necessity. Restraint! What possible restraint? Was it superstition, disgust, patience, fear—or some kind of primitive honor? No fear can stand up to hunger, no patience can wear it out, disgust simply does not exist where hunger is; and as to superstition, beliefs, and what you may call principles, they are less than chaff in a breeze. Don't you know the devilry of lingering starvation, its exasperating torment, its black thoughts, its somber and brooding ferocity? Well, I do. It takes a man all his inborn strength to fight hunger properly. It's really easier to face bereavement, dishonor, and the perdition of one's soul—than this kind of prolonged hunger. Sad, but true. And these chaps, too, had no earthly reason for any kind of scruple. Restraint! I would just as soon have expected restraint from a hyena prowling amongst the corpses of a battlefield. But there was the fact facing me—the fact dazzling, to be seen, like the foam on the depths of the sea, like a ripple on an unfathomable enigma, a mystery greater—when I thought of it—than the curious, inexplicable note of desperate grief in this savage clamor that had swept by us on the river-bank, behind the blind whiteness of the fog.

90   "Two pilgrims were quarreling in hurried whispers as to which bank. 'Left.' 'No, no; how can you? Right, right, of course.' 'It is very serious,' said the manager's voice behind me; 'I would be desolated if anything should happen to Mr. Kurtz before we came up.' I looked at him, and had not the slightest doubt he was sincere. He was just the kind of man who would wish to preserve appearances. That was his restraint. But when he muttered something about going on at once, I did not even take the trouble to answer him. I knew, and he knew, that it was impossible. Were we to let go our hold of the bottom, we would be absolutely in the air—in space. We wouldn't be able to tell where we were going to—whether up or down stream, or across—till we fetched against one bank or the other,—and then we wouldn't know at first which it was. Of course I made

5. Meal.

no move. I had no mind for a smash-up. You couldn't imagine a more deadly place for a shipwreck. Whether drowned at once or not, we were sure to perish speedily in one way or another. 'I authorize you to take all the risks,' he said, after a short silence. 'I refuse to take any,' I said, shortly; which was just the answer he expected, though its tone might have surprised him. 'Well, I must defer to your judgment. You are captain,' he said, with marked civility. I turned my shoulder to him in sign of my appreciation, and looked into the fog. How long would it last? It was the most hopeless lookout. The approach to this Kurtz grubbing for ivory in the wretched bush was beset by as many dangers as though he had been an enchanted princess sleeping in a fabulous castle. 'Will they attack, do you think?' asked the manager, in a confidential tone.

"I did not think they would attack, for several obvious reasons. The thick fog was one. If they left the bank in their canoes they would get lost in it, as we would be if we attempted to move. Still, I had also judged the jungle of both banks quite impenetrable—and yet eyes were in it, eyes that had seen us. The river-side bushes were certainly very thick; but the undergrowth behind was evidently penetrable. However, during the short lift I had seen no canoes any-where in the reach—certainly not abreast of the steamer. But what made the idea of attack inconceivable to me was the nature of the noise—of the cries we had heard. They had not the fierce character boding immediate hostile inten-tion. Unexpected, wild, and violent as they had been, they had given me an irresistible impression of sorrow. The glimpse of the steamboat had for some reason filled those savages with unrestrained grief. The danger, if any, I expounded, was from our proximity to a great human passion let loose. Even extreme grief may ultimately vent itself in violence—but more generally takes the form of apathy. . . .

"You should have seen the pilgrims stare! They had no heart to grin, or even to revile me: but I believe they thought me gone mad—with fright, maybe. I delivered a regular lecture. My dear boys, it was no good bothering. Keep a look-out? Well, you may guess I watched the fog for the signs of lifting as a cat watches a mouse; but for anything else our eyes were of no more use to us than if we had been buried miles deep in a heap of cotton-wool. It felt like it, too—choking, warm, stifling. Besides, all I said, though it sounded extravagant, was absolutely true to fact. What we afterwards alluded to as an attack was really an attempt at repulse. The action was very far from being aggressive—it was not even defensive, in the usual sense: it was undertaken under the stress of despera-tion, and in its essence was purely protective.

"It developed itself, I should say, two hours after the fog lifted, and its com-mencement was at a spot, roughly speaking, about a mile and a half below Kurtz's station. We had just floundered and flopped round a bend, when I saw an islet, a mere grassy hummock of bright green, in the middle of the stream. It was the only thing of the kind; but as we opened the reach more, I perceived it was the head of a long sandbank, or rather of a chain of shallow patches stretch-ing down the middle of the river. They were discolored, just awash, and the whole lot was seen just under the water, exactly as a man's backbone is seen running down the middle of his back under the skin. Now, as far as I did see, I could go to the right or to the left of this. I didn't know either channel, of course. The banks looked pretty well alike, the depth appeared the same; but as I had been informed the station was on the west side, I naturally headed for the western passage.

"No sooner had we fairly entered it than I became aware it was much narrower than I had supposed. To the left of us there was the long uninterrupted shoal, and to the right a high, steep bank heavily overgrown with bushes. Above the bush the trees stood in serried ranks. The twigs overhung the current thickly, and from distance to distance a large limb of some tree projected rigidly over the stream. It was then well on in the afternoon, the face of the forest was gloomy, and a broad strip of shadow had already fallen on the water. In this shadow we steamed up—very slowly, as you may imagine. I sheered her well inshore—the water being deepest near the bank, as the sounding-pole informed me.

95
"One of my hungry and forbearing friends was sounding in the bows just below me. This steamboat was exactly like a decked scow. On the deck, there were two little teak-wood houses, with doors and windows. The boiler was in the fore-end, and the machinery right astern. Over the whole there was a light roof, supported on stanchions. The funnel projected through that roof, and in front of the funnel a small cabin built of light planks served for a pilot-house. It contained a couch, two campstools, a loaded Martini-Henry[6] leaning in one corner, a tiny table, and the steering-wheel. It had a wide door in front and a broad shutter at each side. All these were always thrown open, of course. I spent my days perched up there on the extreme fore-end of that roof, before the door. At night I slept, or tried to, on the couch. An athletic black belonging to some coast tribe, and educated by my poor predecessor, was the helmsman. He sported a pair of brass earrings, wore a blue cloth wrapper from the waist to the ankles, and thought all the world of himself. He was the most unstable kind of fool I had ever seen. He steered with no end of a swagger while you were by; but if he lost sight of you, he became instantly the prey of an abject funk, and would let that cripple of a steamboat get the upper hand of him in a minute.

"I was looking down at the sounding-pole, and feeling much annoyed to see at each try a little more of it stick out of that river, when I saw my poleman give up the business suddenly, and stretch himself flat on the deck, without even taking the trouble to haul his pole in. He kept hold on it though, and it trailed in the water. At the same time the fireman, whom I could also see below me, sat down abruptly before his furnace and ducked his head. I was amazed. Then I had to look at the river mighty quick, because there was a snag in the fairway. Sticks, little sticks, were flying about—thick: they were whizzing before my nose, dropping below me, striking behind me against my pilot-house. All this time the river, the shore, the woods, were very quiet—perfectly quiet. I could only hear the heavy splashing thump of the stern-wheel and the patter of these things. We cleared the snag clumsily. Arrows, by Jove! We were being shot at! I stepped in quickly to close the shutter on the land-side. That fool-helmsman, his hands on

6. Breech-action rifle.

the spokes, was lifting his knees high, stamping his feet, champing his mouth, like a reined-in horse. Confound him! And we were staggering within ten feet of the bank. I had to lean right out to swing the heavy shutter, and I saw a face amongst the leaves on the level with my own, looking at me very fierce and steady; and then suddenly, as though a veil had been removed from my eyes, I made out, deep in the tangled gloom, naked breasts, arms, legs, glaring eyes,— the bush was swarming with human limbs in movement, glistening, of bronze color. The twigs shook, swayed, and rustled, the arrows flew out of them, and then the shutter came to. 'Steer her straight,' I said to the helmsman. He held his head rigid, face forward; but his eyes rolled, he kept on lifting and setting down his feet gently, his mouth foamed a little. 'Keep quiet!' I said in a fury. I might just as well have ordered a tree not to sway in the wind. I darted out. Below me there was a great scuffle of feet on the iron deck; confused exclamations; a voice screamed, 'Can you turn back?' I caught sight of a V-shaped ripple on the water ahead. What? Another snag! A fusillade burst out under my feet. The pilgrims had opened with their Winchesters, and were simply squirting lead into that bush. A deuce of a lot of smoke came up and drove slowly forward. I swore at it. Now I couldn't see the ripple or the snag either. I stood in the doorway, peering, and the arrows came in swarms. They might have been poisoned, but they looked as though they wouldn't kill a cat. The bush began to howl. Our wood-cutters raised a warlike whoop; the report of a rifle just at my back deafened me. I glanced over my shoulder, and the pilot-house was yet full of noise and smoke when I made a dash at the wheel. The fool-nigger had dropped everything to throw the shutter open and let off that Martini-Henry. He stood before the wide opening, glaring, and I yelled at him to come back, while I straightened the sudden twist out of that steamboat. There was no room to turn even if I had wanted to, the snag was somewhere very near ahead in that confounded smoke, there was no time to lose, so I just crowded her into the bank— right into the bank, where I knew the water was deep.

"We tore slowly along the overhanging bushes in a whirl of broken twigs and flying leaves. The fusillade below stopped short, as I had foreseen it would when the squirts got empty. I threw my head back to a glinting whizz that traversed the pilot-house, in at one shutter-hole and out at the other. Looking past that mad helmsman, who was shaking the empty rifle and yelling at the shore, I saw vague forms of men running bent double, leaping, gliding, distinct, incomplete, evanescent. Something big appeared in the air before the shutter, the rifle went overboard, and the man stepped back swiftly, looked at me over his shoulder in an extraordinary, profound, familiar manner, and fell upon my feet. The side of his head hit the wheel twice, and the end of what appeared a long cane clattered round and knocked over a little campstool. It looked as though after wrenching that thing from somebody ashore he had lost his balance in the effort. The thin smoke had blown away, we were clear of the snag, and looking ahead I could see that in another hundred yards or so I would be free to sheer off, away from the bank; but my feet felt so very warm and wet that I had to look down. The man had rolled on his back and stared straight up at me; both his hands clutched that cane. It was the shaft of a spear that, either thrown or lunged through the opening, had caught him in the side just below the ribs; the blade had gone in out of sight, after making a frightful gash; my shoes were full; a pool of blood lay very still, gleaming dark-red under the wheel; his eyes shone with an amazing luster. The fusillade burst out again. He looked at me anxiously, gripping the spear like something precious, with an air of being afraid I would try to take it away from him. I had to make an effort to free my eyes from his gaze and attend to steering. With one hand I felt above my head for the line of the steam-whistle, and jerked out screech after screech hurriedly. The tumult of angry and warlike yells was checked instantly, and then from the depths of the woods went out such a tremulous and prolonged wail of mournful fear and utter despair as may be imagined to follow the flight of the last hope from the earth. There was a great commotion in the bush; the shower of arrows stopped, a few dropping shots rang out sharply—then silence, in which the languid beat of the stern-wheel came plainly to my ears. I put the helm hard a-starboard at the moment when the pilgrim in pink pajamas, very hot and agitated, appeared in the doorway. 'The manager sends me—' he began in an official tone, and stopped short. 'Good God!' he said, glaring at the wounded man.

"We two whites stood over him, and his lustrous and inquiring glance enveloped us both. I declare it looked as though he would presently put to us some question in an understandable language; but he died without uttering a sound, without moving a limb, without twitching a muscle. Only in the very last moment, as though in response to some sign we could not see, to some whisper we could not hear, he frowned heavily, and that frown gave to his black death-mask an inconceivably somber, brooding, and menacing expression. The luster of inquiring glance faded swiftly into vacant glassiness. 'Can you steer?' I asked the agent eagerly. He looked very dubious; but I made a grab at his arm, and he understood at once I meant him to steer whether or no. To tell you the truth, I was morbidly anxious to change my shoes and socks. 'He is dead,' murmured the fellow, immensely impressed. 'No doubt about it,' said I tugging like mad at the shoe-laces. 'And by the way, I suppose Mr. Kurtz is dead as well by this time.'

"For the moment that was the dominant thought. There was a sense of extreme disappointment, as though I had found out I had been striving after something altogether without a substance. I couldn't have been more disgusted if I had traveled all this way for the sole purpose of talking with Mr. Kurtz. Talking with . . . I flung one shoe overboard, and became aware that that was exactly what I had been looking forward to—a talk with Kurtz. I made the strange discovery that I had never imagined him as doing, you know, but as discoursing. I didn't say to myself, 'Now I will never see him,' or 'Now I will never shake him by the hand,' but, 'Now I will never hear him.' The man presented himself as a voice. Not of course that I did not connect him with some sort of action. Hadn't I been told in all the tones of jealousy and admiration that he had collected, bartered, swindled, or stolen more ivory than all the other agents together? That was not the point. The point was in his being a gifted creature, and that of all his gifts the one that stood out preeminently, that carried with it a sense of real presence, was his ability to talk, his words—the gift of expression, the bewildering, the illuminating, the most exalted and the most contemptible, the pulsating stream of light, or the deceitful flow from the heart of an impenetrable darkness.

"The other shoe went flying unto the devil-god of that river. I thought, by Jove! it's all over. We are too late; he has vanished—the gift has vanished, by means of some spear, arrow, or club. I will never hear that chap speak after all,—and my sorrow had a startling extravagance of emotion, even such as I had noticed in the howling sorrow of these savages in the bush. I couldn't have felt more lonely desolation somehow, had I been robbed of a belief or had missed my destiny in life. . . . Why do you sigh in this beastly way, somebody? Absurd? Well, absurd. Good Lord! mustn't a man ever—Here, give me some tobacco." . . .

There was a pause of profound stillness, then a match flared, and Marlow's lean face appeared, worn, hollow, with downward folds and drooped eyelids, with an aspect of concentrated attention; and as he took vigorous draws at his pipe, it seemed to retreat and advance out of the night in the regular flicker of the tiny flame. The match went out.

"Absurd!" he cried. "This is the worst of trying to tell . . . . Here you all are, each moored with two good addresses, like a hulk with two anchors, a butcher round one corner, a policeman round another, excellent appetites, and tempera-ture normal—you hear—normal from year's end to year's end. And you say, Absurd! Absurd be—exploded! Absurd! My dear boys, what can you expect from a man who out of sheer nervousness had just flung overboard a pair of new shoes? Now I think of it, it is amazing I did not shed tears. I am, upon the whole, proud of my fortitude. I was cut to the quick at the idea of having lost the inestimable privilege of listening to the gifted Kurtz. Of course I was wrong. The privilege was waiting for me. Oh yes, I heard more than enough. And I was right, too. A voice. He was very little more than a voice. And I heard—him—it—this voice—other voices—all of them were so little more than voices—and the memory of that time itself lingers around me, impalpable, like a dying vibra-tion of one immense jabber, silly, atrocious, sordid, savage, or simply mean, without any kind of sense. Voices, voices—even the girl herself—now—"

He was silent for a long time.

"I laid the ghost of his gifts at last with a lie," he began, suddenly. "Girl! What? Did I mention a girl? Oh, she is out of it—completely. They—the women I mean—are out of it—should be out of it. We must help them to stay in that beautiful world of their own, lest ours gets worse. Oh, she had to be out of it. You should have heard the disinterred body of Mr. Kurtz saying, 'My Intended.' You would have perceived directly then how completely she was out of it. And the lofty frontal bone of Mr. Kurtz! They say the hair goes on growing sometimes, but this—ah—specimen, was impressively bald. The wilderness had patted him on the head, and, behold, it was like a ball—an ivory ball; it had caressed him, and—lo!—he had withered; it had taken him, loved him, embraced him, got into his veins, consumed his flesh, and sealed his soul to its own by the inconceivable ceremonies of some devilish initiation. He was its spoiled and pampered favorite. Ivory? I should think so. Heaps of it, stacks of it.

100

The old mud shanty was bursting with it. You would think here was not a single tusk left either above or below the ground in the whole country. 'Mostly fossil,' the manager had remarked, disparagingly. It was no more fossil than I am; but they call it fossil when it is dug up. It appears these niggers do bury the tusks sometimes—but evidently they couldn't bury this parcel deep enough to save the gifted Mr. Kurtz from his fate. We filled the steamboat with it, and had to pile a lot on the deck. Thus he could see and enjoy as long as he could see, because the appreciation of this favor had remained with him to the last. You should have heard him say, 'My ivory.' Oh yes, I heard him. 'My Intended, my ivory, my station, my river, my—' everything belonged to him. It made me hold my breath in expectation of hearing the wilderness burst into a prodigious peal of laughter that would shake the fixed stars in their places. Everything belonged to him—but that was a trifle. The thing was to know what he belonged to, how many powers of darkness claimed him for their own. That was the reflection that made you creepy all over. It was impossible—it was not good for one either—trying to imagine. He had taken a high seat amongst the devils of the land—I mean literally. You can't understand. How could you?—with solid pavement under your feet, surrounded by kind neighbors ready to cheer you or to fall on you, stepping delicately between the butcher and the policeman, in the holy terror of scandal and gallows and lunatic asylums—how can you imagine what particular region of the first ages a man's untrammeled feet may take him into by the way of solitude—utter solitude without a policeman—by the way of silence—utter silence, where no warning voice of a kind neighbor can be heard whispering of public opinion? These little things make all the great difference. When they are gone you must fall back upon your own innate strength, upon your own capacity for faithfulness. Of course you may be too much of a fool to go wrong—too dull even to know you are being assaulted by the powers of darkness. I take it, no fool ever made a bargain for his soul with the devil: the fool is too much of a fool, or the devil too much of a devil—I don't know which. Or you may be such a thunderingly exalted creature as to be altogether deaf and blind to anything but heavenly sights and sounds. Then the earth for you is only a standing place—and whether to be like this is your loss or your gain I won't pretend to say. But most of us are neither one nor the other. The earth for us is a place to live in, where we must put up with sights, with sounds, with smells, too, by Jove!—breathe dead hippo, so to speak, and not be contaminated. And there, don't you see? your strength comes in, the faith in your ability for the digging of unostentatious holes to bury the stuff in—your power of devotion, not to yourself, but to an obscure, back-breaking business. And that's difficult enough. Mind, I am not trying to excuse or even explain—I am trying to account to myself for—for—Mr. Kurtz—for the shade of Mr. Kurtz. This initiated wraith from the back of Nowhere honored me with its amazing confidence before it vanished altogether. This was because it could speak English to me. The original Kurtz had been educated partly in England, and—as he was good enough to say himself—his sympathies were in the right place. His mother was half-English, his father was half-French. All Europe contributed to the making of Kurtz; and by and by I learned that, most appropriately, the International

Society for the Suppression of Savage Customs had intrusted him with the making of a report, for its future guidance. And he had written it, too. I've seen it. I've read it. It was eloquent, vibrating with eloquence, but too high-strung, I think. Seventeen pages of close writing he had found time for! But this must have been before his—let us say—nerves, went wrong, and caused him to preside at certain midnight dances ending with unspeakable rites, which—as far as I reluctantly gathered from what I heard at various times—were offered up to him—do you understand?—to Mr. Kurtz himself. But it was a beautiful piece of writing. The opening paragraph, however, in the light of later information, strikes me now as ominous. He began with the argument that we whites, from the point of development we had arrived at, 'must necessarily appear to them [savages] in the nature of supernatural beings—we approach them with the might as of a deity,' and so on, and so on. 'By the simple exercise of our will we can exert a power for good practically unbounded,' etc., etc. From that point he soared and took me with him. The peroration was magnificent, though difficult to remember, you know. It gave me the notion of an exotic Immensity ruled by an august Benevolence. It made me tingle with enthusiasm. This was the unbounded power of eloquence—of words—of burning noble words. There were no practical hints to interrupt the magic current of phrases, unless a kind of note at the foot of the last page, scrawled evidently much later, in an unsteady hand, may be regarded as the exposition of a method. It was very simple, and at the end of that moving appeal to every altruistic sentiment it blazed at you, luminous and terrifying, like a flash of lightning in a serene sky: 'Exterminate all the brutes!' The curious part was that he had apparently forgotten all about that valuable postscriptum, because, later on, when he in a sense came to himself, he repeatedly entreated me to take good care of 'my pamphlet' (he called it), as it was sure to have in the future a good influence upon his career. I had full information about all these things, and, besides, as it turned out, I was to have the care of his memory. I've done enough for it to give me the indisputable right to lay it, if I choose, for an everlasting rest in the dust-bin of progress, amongst all the sweepings and, figuratively speaking, all the dead cats of civilization. But then, you see, I can't choose. He won't be forgotten. Whatever he was, he was not common. He had the power to charm or frighten rudimentary souls into an aggravated witch-dance in his honor; he could also fill the small souls of the pilgrims with bitter misgivings: he had one devoted friend at least, and he had conquered one soul in the world that was neither rudimentary nor tainted with self-seeking. No; I can't forget him, though I am not prepared to affirm the fellow was exactly worth the life we lost in getting to him. I missed my late helmsman awfully,—I missed him even while his body was still lying in the pilot-house. Perhaps you will think it passing strange this regret for a savage who was no more account than a grain of sand in a black Sahara. Well, don't you see, he had done something, he had steered; for months I had him at my back—a help—an instrument. It was a kind of partnership. He steered for me—I had to look after him, I worried about his deficiencies, and thus a subtle bond had been created, of which I only became aware when it was suddenly broken. And the intimate profundity of that look he gave me when he received his hurt remains to this day in my memory—like a claim of distant kinship affirmed in a supreme moment.

105   "Poor fool! If he had only left that shutter alone. He had no restraint, no restraint—just like Kurtz—a tree swayed by the wind. As soon as I had put on a dry pair of slippers, I dragged him out, after first jerking the spear out of his side, which operation I confess I performed with my eyes shut tight. His heels leaped together over the little doorstep; his shoulders were pressed to my breast; I hugged him from behind desperately. Oh! he was heavy, heavy; heavier than any man on earth, I should imagine. Then without more ado I tipped him overboard. The current snatched him as though he had been a wisp of grass, and I saw the body roll over twice before I lost sight of it forever. All the pilgrims and the manager were then congregated on the awning-deck about the pilot-house, chattering at each other like a flock of excited magpies, and there was a scandalized murmur at my heartless promptitude. What they wanted to keep that body hanging about for I can't guess. Embalm it, maybe. But I had also heard another, and a very ominous, murmur on the deck below. My friends the wood-cutters were likewise scandalized, and with a better show of reason—though I admit that the reason itself was quite inadmissible. Oh, quite! I had made up my mind that if my late helmsman was to be eaten, the fishes alone should have him. He had been a very second-rate helmsman while alive, but now he was dead he might have become a first-class temptation, and possibly cause some startling trouble. Besides, I was anxious to take the wheel, the man in pink pajamas showing himself a hopeless duffer at the business.

"This I did directly the simple funeral was over. We were going half-speed, keeping right in the middle of the stream, and I listened to the talk about me. They had given up Kurtz, they had given up the station; Kurtz was dead, and the station had been burnt—and so on—and so on. The red-haired pilgrim was beside himself with the thought that at least this poor Kurtz had been properly avenged. 'Say! We must have made a glorious slaughter of them in the bush. Eh? What do you think? Say?' He positively danced, the bloodthirsty little gingery beggar.[7] And he had nearly fainted when he saw the wounded man! I could not help saying, 'You made a glorious lot of smoke, anyhow.' I had seen, from the way the tops of the bushes rustled and flew, that almost all the shots had gone too high. You can't hit anything unless you take aim and fire from the shoulder; but these chaps fired from the hip with their eyes shut. The retreat, I maintained—and I was right—was caused by the screeching of the steam-whistle. Upon this they forgot Kurtz, and began to howl at me with indignant protests.

"The manager stood by the wheel murmuring confidentially about the necessity of getting well away down the river before dark at all events, when I saw in the distance a clearing on the river-side and the outlines of some sort of building. 'What's this?' I asked. He clapped his hands in wonder. 'The station!' he cried. I edged in at once, still going half-speed.

"Through my glasses I saw the slope of a hill interspersed with rare trees and

---

7. Red-haired scoundrel.

perfectly free from undergrowth. A long decaying building on the summit was half buried in the high grass; the large holes in the peaked roof gaped black from afar; the jungle and the woods made a background. There was no enclosure or fence of any kind; but there had been one apparently, for near the house half-a-dozen slim posts remained in a row, roughly trimmed, and with their upper ends ornamented with round carved balls. The rails, or whatever there had been between, had disappeared. Of course the forest surrounded all that. The river-bank was clear, and on the water-side I saw a white man under a hat like a cart-wheel beckoning persistently with his whole arm. Examining the edge of the forest above and below, I was almost certain I could see movements—human forms gliding here and there. I steamed past prudently, then stopped the engines and let her drift down. The man on the shore began to shout, urging us to land. 'We have been attacked,' screamed the manager. 'I know—I know. It's all right,' yelled back the other, as cheerful as you please. 'Come along. It's all right. I am glad.'

"His aspect reminded me of something I had seen—something funny I had seen somewhere. As I maneuvered to get alongside, I was asking myself, 'What does this fellow look like?' Suddenly I got it. He looked like a harlequin. His clothes had been made of some stuff that was brown holland probably, but it was covered with patches all over, with bright patches, blue, red, and yellow,— patches on the back, patches on the front, patches on elbows, on knees; colored binding around his jacket, scarlet edging at the bottom of his trousers; and the sunshine made him look extremely gay and wonderfully neat withal, because you could see how beautifully all this patching had been done. A beardless, boyish face, very fair, no features to speak of, nose peeling, little blue eyes, smiles and frowns chasing each other over that open countenance like sunshine and shadow on a windswept plain. 'Look out, captain!' he cried; 'there's a snag lodged in here last night.' What! Another snag? I confess I swore shamefully. I had nearly holed my cripple, to finish off that charming trip. The harlequin on the bank turned his little pug-nose up to me. 'You English?' he asked, all smiles. 'Are you?' I shouted from the wheel. The smiles vanished, and he shook his head as if sorry for my disappointment. Then he brightened up. 'Never mind!' he cried, encouragingly. 'Are we in time?' I asked. 'He is up there,' he replied, with a toss of the head up the hill, and becoming gloomy all of a sudden. His face was like the autumn sky, overcast one moment and bright the next.

"When the manager, escorted by the pilgrims, all of them armed to the teeth, had gone to the house this chap came on board. 'I say, I don't like this. These natives are in the bush,' I said. He assured me earnestly it was all right. 'They are simple people,' he added; 'well, I am glad you came. It took me all my time to keep them off.' 'But you said it was all right,' I cried. 'Oh, they meant no harm,' he said; and as I stared he corrected himself, 'Not exactly.' Then viva-ciously, 'My faith, your pilot-house wants a clean-up!' In the next breath he advised me to keep enough steam on the boiler to blow the whistle in case of any trouble. 'One good screech will do more for you than all your rifles. They are simple people,' he repeated. He rattled away at such a rate he quite over-whelmed me. He seemed to be trying to make up for lots of silence, and actually

110

hinted, laughing, that such was the case. 'Don't you talk with Mr. Kurtz?' I said. 'You don't talk with that man—you listen to him,' he exclaimed with severe exaltation. 'But now—' He waved his arm, and in the twinkling of an eye was in the uttermost depths of despondency. In a moment he came up again with a jump, possessed himself of both my hands, shook them continuously, while he gabbled: 'Brother sailor . . . honor . . . pleasure . . . delight . . . introduce myself . . . Russian . . . son of an arch-priest . . . Government of Tambov. . . . What? Tobacco! English tobacco; the excellent English tobacco! Now, that's brotherly. Smoke? Where's a sailor that does not smoke?'

"The pipe soothed him, and gradually I made out he had run away from school, had gone to sea in a Russian ship; ran away again; served some time in English ships; was now reconciled with the arch-priest. He made a point of that. 'But when one is young one must see things, gather experience, ideas; enlarge the mind.' 'Here!' I interrupted. 'You can never tell! Here I met Mr. Kurtz,' he said, youthfully solemn and reproachful. I held my tongue after that. It appears he had persuaded a Dutch trading-house on the coast to fit him out with stores and goods, and had started for the interior with a light heart, and no more idea of what would happen to him than a baby. He had been wandering about that river for nearly two years alone, cut off from everybody and everything. 'I am not so young as I look. I am twenty-five,' he said. 'At first old Van Shuyten would tell me to go to the devil,' he narrated with keen enjoyment; 'but I stuck to him, and talked and talked, till at last he got afraid I would talk the hind-leg off his favorite dog, so he gave me some cheap things and a few guns, and told me he hoped he would never see my face again. Good old Dutchman, Van Shuyten. I've sent him one small lot of ivory a year ago, so that he can't call me a little thief when I get back. I hope he got it. And for the rest I don't care. I had some wood stacked for you. That was my old house. Did you see?'

"I gave him Towson's book. He made as though he would kiss me, but restrained himself. 'The only book I had left, and I thought I had lost it,' he said, looking at it ecstatically. 'So many accidents happen to a man going about alone, you know. Canoes get upset sometimes—and sometimes you've got to clear out so quick when the people get angry.' He thumbed the pages. 'You made notes in Russian?' I asked. He nodded. 'I thought they were written in cipher,' I said. He laughed, then became serious. 'I had lots of trouble to keep these people off,' he said. 'Did they want to kill you?' I asked. 'Oh no!' he cried, and checked himself. 'Why did they attack us?' I pursued. He hesitated, then said shame-facedly, 'They don't want him to go.' 'Don't they?' I said curiously. He nodded a nod full of mystery and wisdom. 'I tell you,' he cried, 'this man has enlarged my mind.' He opened his arms wide, staring at me with his little blue eyes that were perfectly round."

III

"I looked at him, lost in astonishment. There he was before me, in motley, as though he had absconded from a troupe of mimes, enthusiastic, fabulous. His very existence was improbable, inexplicable, and altogether bewildering. He was an insoluble problem. It was inconceivable how he had existed, how he had succeeded in getting so far, how he had managed to remain—why he did not instantly disappear. 'I went a little farther,' he said, 'then still a little farther—till I had gone so far that I don't know how I'll ever get back. Never mind. Plenty time. I can manage. You take Kurtz away quick—quick—I tell you.' The glamour of youth enveloped his parti-colored rags, his destitution, his loneliness, the essential desolation of his futile wanderings. For months—for years—his life hadn't been worth a day's purchase; and there he was gallantly, thoughtlessly alive, to all appearance indestructible solely by the virtue of his few years and of his unreflecting audacity. I was seduced into something like admiration—like envy. Glamour urged him on, glamour kept him unscathed. He surely wanted nothing from the wilderness but space to breathe in and to push on through. His need was to exist, and to move onwards at the greatest possible risk, and with a maximum of privation. If the absolutely pure, uncalculating, unpractical spirit of adventure had ever ruled a human being, it ruled this be-patched youth. I almost envied him the possession of this modest and clear flame. It seemed to have consumed all thought of self so completely, that even while he was talking to you, you forgot that it was he—the man before your eyes—who had gone through these things. I did not envy him his devotion to Kurtz, though. He had not meditated over it. It came to him and he accepted it with a sort of eager fatalism. I must say that to me it appeared about the most dangerous thing in every way he had come upon so far.

"They had come together unavoidably, like two ships becalmed near each other, and lay rubbing sides at last. I suppose Kurtz wanted an audience, because on a certain occasion, when encamped in the forest, they had talked all night, or more probably Kurtz had talked. 'We talked of everything,' he said, quite transported at the recollection. 'I forgot there was such a thing as sleep. The night did not seem to last an hour. Everything! Everything! . . . Of love, too.' 'Ah, he talked to you of love!' I said, much amused. 'It isn't what you think,' he cried, almost passionately. 'It was in general. He made me see things—things.'

"He threw his arms up. We were on deck at the time, and the headman of my wood-cutters, lounging near by, turned upon him his heavy and glittering eyes. I looked around, and I don't know why, but I assure you that never, never before, did this land, this river, this jungle, the very arch of this blazing sky, appear to me so hopeless and so dark, so impenetrable to human thought, so pitiless to human weakness. 'And, ever since, you have been with him, of course?' I said.

"On the contrary. It appears their intercourse had been very much broken by various causes. He had, as he informed me proudly, managed to nurse Kurtz through two illnesses (he alluded to it as you would to some risky feat), but as a rule Kurtz wandered alone far in the depths of the forest. 'Very often coming to this station, I had to wait days and days before he would turn up,' he said. 'Ah, it was worth waiting for!—sometimes.' 'What was he doing? exploring or what?' I asked. 'Oh, yes, of course'; he had discovered lots of villages, a lake, too—he did not know exactly in what direction; it was dangerous to inquire too much— but mostly his expeditions had been for ivory. 'But he had no goods to trade

115

with by that time,' I objected. 'There's a good lot of cartridges left even yet,' he answered, looking away. 'To speak plainly, he raided the country,' I said. He nodded. 'Not alone, surely!' He muttered something about the villages round that lake. 'Kurtz got the tribe to follow him, did he?' I suggested. He fidgeted a little. 'They adored him,' he said. The tone of these words was so extraordinary that I looked at him searchingly. It was curious to see his mingled eagerness and reluctance to speak of Kurtz. The man filled his life, occupied his thoughts, swayed his emotions. 'What can you expect?' he burst out; 'he came to them with thunder and lightning, you know—and they had never seen anything like it—and very terrible. He could be very terrible. You can't judge Mr. Kurtz as you would an ordinary man. No, no, no! Now—just to give you an idea—I don't mind telling you, he wanted to shoot me, too, one day—but I don't judge him.' 'Shoot you!' I cried. 'What for?' 'Well, I had a small lot of ivory the chief of that village near my house gave me. You see I used to shoot game for them. Well, he wanted it, and wouldn't hear reason. He declared he would shoot me unless I gave him the ivory and then cleared out of the country, because he could do so, and had a fancy for it, and there was nothing on earth to prevent him killing whom he jolly well pleased. And it was true, too. I gave him the ivory. What did I care! But I didn't clear out. No, no. I couldn't leave him. I had to be careful, of course, till we got friendly again for a time. He had his second illness then. Afterwards I had to keep out of the way; but I didn't mind. He was living for the most part in those villages on the lake. When he came down to the river, some-times he would take to me, and sometimes it was better for me to be careful. This man suffered too much. He hated all this, and somehow he couldn't get away. When I had a chance I begged him to try and leave while there was time; I offered to go back with him. And he would say yes, and then he would remain; go off on another ivory hunt; disappear for weeks; forget himself amongst these people—forget himself—you know.' 'Why! he's mad,' I said. He protested indig-nantly. Mr. Kurtz couldn't be mad. If I had heard him talk, only two days ago, I wouldn't dare hint at such a thing. . . . I had taken up my binoculars while we talked, and was looking at the shore, sweeping the limit of the forest at each side and at the back of the house. The consciousness of there being people in that bush, so silent, so quiet—as silent and quiet as the ruined house on the hill—made me uneasy. There was no sign on the face of nature of this amazing tale that was not so much told as suggested to me in desolate exclamations, com-pleted by shrugs, in interrupted phrases, in hints ending in deep sighs. The woods were unmoved, like a mask—heavy, like the closed door of a prison—they looked with their air of hidden knowledge, of patient expectation, of unap-proachable silence. The Russian was explaining to me that it was only lately that Mr. Kurtz had come down to the river, bringing along with him all the fighting men of that lake tribe. He had been absent for several months—getting himself adored, I suppose—and had come down unexpectedly, with the intention to all appearance of making a raid either across the river or down stream. Evidently the appetite for more ivory had got the better of the—what shall I say?—less material aspirations. However he had got much worse suddenly. 'I heard he was lying helpless, and so I came up—took my chance,' said the Russian. 'Oh, he is bad, very bad.' I directed my glass to the house. There were no signs of life, but there was the ruined roof, the long mud wall peeping above the grass, with three little square window-holes, no two of the same size; all this brought within reach of my hand, as it were. And then I made a brusque movement, and one of the remaining posts of that vanished fence leaped up in the field of my glass. You remember I told you I had been struck at the distance by certain attempts at ornamentation, rather remarkable in the ruinous aspect of the place. Now I had suddenly a nearer view, and its first result was to make me throw my head back as if before a blow. Then I went carefully from post to post with my glass, and I saw my mistake. These round knobs were not ornamental but symbolic; they were expressive and puzzling, striking and disturbing—food for thought and also for vultures if there had been any looking down from the sky; but at all events for such ants as were industrious enough to ascend the pole. They would have been even more impressive, those heads on the stakes, if their faces had not been turned to the house. Only one, the first I had made out, was facing my way. I was not so shocked as you may think. The start back I had given was really nothing but a movement of surprise. I had expected to see a knob of wood there, you know. I returned deliberately to the first I had seen—and there it was, black, dried, sunken, with closed eyelids,—a head that seemed to sleep at the top of that pole, and with the shrunken dry lips showing a narrow white line of the teeth, was smiling, too, smiling continuously at some endless and jocose dream of that eternal slumber.

"I am not disclosing any trade secrets. In fact, the manager said afterwards that Mr. Kurtz's methods had ruined the district. I have no opinion on that point, but I want you clearly to understand that there was nothing exactly profitable in these heads being there. They only showed that Mr. Kurtz lacked restraint in the gratification of his various lusts, that there was something wanting in him—some small matter which, when the pressing need arose, could not be found under his magnificent eloquence. Whether he knew of this deficiency himself I can't say. I think the knowledge came to him at last—only at the very last. But the wilderness had found him out early, and had taken on him a terrible vengeance for the fantastic invasion. I think it had whispered to him things about himself which he did not know, things of which he had no conception till he took counsel with this great solitude—and the whisper had proved irresistibly fascinating. It echoed loudly within him because he was hollow at the core. . . . I put down the glass, and the head that had appeared near enough to be spoken to seemed at once to have leaped away from me into inaccessible distance.

"The admirer of Mr. Kurtz was a bit crestfallen. In a hurried indistinct voice he began to assure me he had not dared to take these—say, symbols—down. He was not afraid of the natives; they would not stir till Mr. Kurtz gave the word. His ascendancy was extraordinary. The camps of these people surrounded the place, and the chiefs came every day to see him. They would crawl. . . . 'I don't want to know anything of the ceremonies used when approaching Mr. Kurtz,' I shouted. Curious, this feeling that came over me that such details would be more intolerable than those heads drying on the stakes under Mr. Kurtz's windows. After all, that was only a savage sight, while I seemed at one bound to have been transported into some lightless region of subtle horrors, where pure, uncomplicated savagery was a positive relief, being something that had a right to exist—obviously—in the sunshine. The young man looked at me with surprise. I suppose it did not occur to him that Mr. Kurtz was no idol of mine. He forgot I hadn't heard any of these splendid monologues on, what was it? on love, justice, conduct of life—or what not. If it had come to crawling before Mr. Kurtz, he crawled as much as the veriest savage of them all. I had no idea of the conditions, he said: these heads were the heads of rebels. I shocked him excessively by laughing. Rebels! What would be the next definition I was to hear? There had been enemies, criminals, workers—and these were rebels. Those rebellious heads looked very subdued to me on their sticks. 'You don't know how such a life tries a man like Kurtz,' cried Kurtz's last disciple. 'Well, and you?' I said. 'I! I! I am a simple man. I have no great thoughts. I want nothing from anybody. How can you compare me to . . . ?' His feelings were too much for speech, and suddenly he broke down. 'I don't understand,' he groaned. 'I've been doing my best to keep him alive, and that's enough. I had no hand in all this. I have no abilities. There hasn't been a drop of medicine or a mouthful of invalid food for months here. He was shamefully abandoned. A man like this, with such ideas. Shamefully! Shamefully! I—I—haven't slept for the last ten nights. . . .'

"His voice lost itself in the calm of the evening. The long shadows of the forest had slipped downhill while we talked, had gone far beyond the ruined hovel, beyond the symbolic row of stakes. All this was in the gloom, while we down there were yet in the sunshine, and the stretch of the river abreast of the clearing glittered in a still and dazzling splendor, with a murky and overshadowed bend above and below. Not a living soul was seen on the shore. The bushes did not rustle.

120   "Suddenly round the corner of the house a group of men appeared, as though they had come up from the ground. They waded waist-deep in the grass, in a compact body, bearing an improvised stretcher in their midst. Instantly, in the emptiness of the landscape, a cry arose whose shrillness pierced the still air like a sharp arrow flying straight to the very heart of the land; and, as if by enchantment, streams of human beings—of naked human beings—with spears in their hands, with bows, with shields, with wild glances and savage movements, were poured into the clearing by the dark-faced and pensive forest. The bushes shook, the grass swayed for a time, and then everything stood still in attentive immobility.

" 'Now, if he does not say the right thing to them we are all done for,' said the Russian at my elbow. The knot of men with the stretcher had stopped, too, halfway to the steamer, as if petrified. I saw the man on the stretcher sit up, lank and with an uplifted arm, above the shoulders of the bearers. 'Let us hope that the man who can talk so well of love in general will find some particular reason to spare us this time,' I said. I resented bitterly the absurd danger of our situation, as if to be at the mercy of that atrocious phantom had been a dishonoring necessity. I could not hear a sound, but through my glasses I saw the thin arm extended commandingly, the lower jaw moving, the eyes of that apparition shining darkly far in its bony head that nodded with grotesque jerks. Kurtz—Kurtz—

that means short in German—don't it? Well, the name was as true as everything else in his life—and death. He looked at least seven feet long. His covering had fallen off, and his body emerged from it pitiful and appalling as from a winding-sheet. I could see the cage of his ribs all astir, the bones of his arm waving. It was as though an animated image of death carved out of old ivory had been shaking its hand with menaces at a motionless crowd of men made of dark and glittering bronze. I saw him open his mouth wide—it gave him a weirdly vora-cious aspect, as though he had wanted to swallow all the air, all the earth, all the men before him. A deep voice reached me faintly. He must have been shouting. He fell back suddenly. The stretcher shook as the bearers staggered forward again, and almost at the same time I noticed that the crowd of savages was vanishing without any perceptible movement of retreat, as if the forest that had ejected these beings so suddenly had drawn them in again as the breath is drawn in a long aspiration.

"Some of the pilgrims behind the stretcher carried his arms—two shotguns, a heavy rifle, and a light revolver-carbine—the thunderbolts of that pitiful Jupi-ter. The manager bent over him murmuring as he walked beside his head. They laid him down in one of the little cabins—just a room for a bedplace and a campstool or two, you know. We had brought his belated correspondence, and a lot of torn envelopes and open letters littered his bed. His hand roamed feebly amongst these papers. I was struck by the fire in his eyes and the composed languor of his expression. It was not so much the exhaustion of disease. He did not seem in pain. This shadow looked satiated and calm, as though for the moment it had had its fill of all the emotions.

"He rustled one of the letters, and looking straight in my face said, 'I am glad.' Somebody had been writing to him about me. These special recommen-dations were turning up again. The volume of tone he emitted without effort, almost without the trouble of moving his lips, amazed me. A voice! a voice! It was grave, profound, vibrating, while the man did not seem capable of a whisper. However, he had enough strength in him—factitious no doubt—to very nearly make an end of us, as you shall hear directly.

"The manager appeared silently in the doorway; I stepped out at once and he drew the curtain after me. The Russian, eyed curiously by the pilgrims, was staring at the shore. I followed the direction of his glance.

"Dark human shapes could be made out in the distance, flitting indistinctly against the gloomy border of the forest, and near the river two bronze figures, leaning on tall spears, stood in the sunlight under fantastic headdresses of spot-ted skins, war-like and still in statuesque repose. And from right to left along the lighted shore moved a wild and gorgeous apparition of a woman.

"She walked with measured steps, draped in striped and fringed cloths, tread-ing the earth proudly, with a slight jingle and flash of barbarous ornaments. She carried her head high; her hair was done in the shape of a helmet; she had brass leggings to the knee, brass wire gauntlets to the elbow, a crimson spot on her tawny cheek, innumerable necklaces of glass beads on her neck; bizarre things, charms, gifts of witch-men, that hung about her, glittered and trembled at every step. She must have had the value of several elephant tusks upon her. She was

125

savage and superb, wild-eyed and magnificent; there was something ominous and stately in her deliberate progress. And in the hush that had fallen suddenly upon the whole sorrowful land, the immense wilderness, the colossal body of the fecund and mysterious life seemed to look at her, pensive, as though it had been looking at the image of its own tenebrous and passionate soul.

"She came abreast of the steamer, stood still, and faced us. Her long shadow fell to the water's edge. Her face had a tragic and fierce aspect of wild sorrow and of dumb pain mingled with the fear of some struggling, half-shaped resolve. She stood looking at us without a stir, and like the wilderness itself, with an air of brooding over an inscrutable purpose. A whole minute passed, and then she made a step forward. There was a low jingle, a glint of yellow metal, a sway of fringed draperies, and she stopped as if her heart had failed her. The young fellow by my side growled. The pilgrims murmured at my back. She looked at us all as if her life had depended upon the unswerving steadiness of her glance. Suddenly she opened her bared arms and threw them up rigid above her head, as though in an uncontrollable desire to touch the sky, and at the same time the swift shadows darted out on the earth, swept around on the river, gathering the steamer into a shadowy embrace. A formidable silence hung over the scene.

"She turned away slowly, walked on, following the bank, and passed into the bushes to the left. Once only her eyes gleamed back at us in the dusk of the thickets before she disappeared.

" 'If she had offered to come aboard I really think I would have tried to shoot her,' said the man of patches, nervously. 'I have been risking my life every day for the last fortnight to keep her out of the house. She got in one day and kicked up a row about those miserable rags I picked up in the storeroom to mend my clothes with. I wasn't decent. At least it must have been that, for she talked like a fury to Kurtz for an hour, pointing at me now and then. I don't understand the dialect of this tribe. Luckily for me, I fancy Kurtz felt too ill that day to care, or there would have been mischief. I don't understand. . . . No—it's too much for me. Ah, well, it's all over now.'

"At this moment I heard Kurtz's deep voice behind the curtain: 'Save me!—save the ivory, you mean. Don't tell me. Save *me!* Why, I've had to save you. You are interrupting my plans now. Sick! Sick! Not so sick as you would like to believe. Never mind. I'll carry my ideas out yet—I will return. I'll show you what can be done. You with your little peddling notions—you are interfering with me. I will return. I . . . '

"The manager came out. He did me the honor to take me under the arm and lead me aside. 'He is very low, very low,' he said. He considered it necessary to sigh, but neglected to be consistently sorrowful. 'We have done all we could for him—haven't we? But there is no disguising the fact, Mr. Kurtz has done more harm than good to the Company. He did not see the time was not ripe for vigorous action. Cautiously, cautiously—that's my principle. We must be cautious yet. The district is closed to us for a time. Deplorable! Upon the whole, the trade will suffer. I don't deny there is a remarkable quantity of ivory—mostly fossil. We must save it, at all events—but look how precarious the position is—and why? Because the method is unsound.' 'Do you,' said I, looking at the shore,

'call it "unsound method"?' 'Without doubt,' he exclaimed hotly. 'Don't you?'
... 'No method at all,' I murmured after a while. 'Exactly,' he exulted. 'I anticipated this. Shows a complete want of judgment. It is my duty to point it out in
the proper quarter.' 'Oh,' said I, 'that fellow—what's his name?—the brickmaker, will make a readable report for you.' He appeared confounded for a
moment. It seemed to me I had never breathed an atmosphere so vile, and I
turned mentally to Kurtz for relief—positively for relief. 'Nevertheless I think
Mr. Kurtz is a remarkable man,' I said with emphasis. He started, dropped on
me a cold heavy glance, said very quietly, 'he *was*,' and turned his back on me.
My hour of favor was over; I found myself lumped along with Kurtz as a partisan
of methods for which the time was not ripe: I was unsound! Ah! but it was
something to have at least a choice of nightmares.

"I had turned to the wilderness really, not to Mr. Kurtz, who, I was ready to
admit, was as good as buried. And for a moment it seemed to me as if I also
were buried in a vast grave full of unspeakable secrets. I felt an intolerable
weight oppressing my breast, the smell of the damp earth, the unseen presence
of victorious corruption, the darkness of an impenetrable night. . . . The Russian
tapped me on the shoulder. I heard him mumbling and stammering something
about 'brother seaman—couldn't conceal—knowledge of matters that would
affect Mr. Kurtz's reputation.' I waited. For him evidently Mr. Kurtz was not in
his grave; I suspect that for him Mr. Kurtz was one of the immortals. 'Well!' said
I at last, 'speak out. As it happens, I am Mr. Kurtz's friend—in a way.'

"He stated with a good deal of formality that had we not been 'of the same
profession,' he would have kept the matter to himself without regard to consequences. 'He suspected there was an active ill will towards him on the part of
these white men that—' 'You are right,' I said, remembering a certain conversation I had overheard. 'The manager thinks you ought to be hanged.' He showed
a concern at this intelligence which amused me at first. 'I had better get out of
the way quietly,' he said, earnestly. 'I can do no more for Kurtz now, and they
would soon find some excuse. What's to stop them? There's a military post three
hundred miles from here.' 'Well, upon my word,' said I, 'perhaps you had better
go if you have any friends amongst the savages near by.' 'Plenty,' he said. 'They
are simple people—and I want nothing, you know.' He stood biting his lip, then:
'I don't want any harm to happen to these whites here, but of course I was
thinking of Mr. Kurtz's reputation—but you are a brother seaman and—' 'All
right,' said I, after a time. 'Mr. Kurtz's reputation is safe with me.' I did not know
how truly I spoke.

"He informed me, lowering his voice, that it was Kurtz who had ordered the
attack to be made on the steamer. 'He hated sometimes the idea of being taken
away—and then again . . . But I don't understand these matters. I am a simple
man. He thought it would scare you away—that you would give it up, thinking
him dead. I could not stop him. Oh, I had an awful time of it this last month.'
'Very well,' I said. 'He is all right now.' 'Ye-e-es,' he muttered, not very convinced apparently. 'Thanks,' said I; 'I shall keep my eyes open.' 'But quiet—eh?'
he urged, anxiously. 'It would be awful for his reputation if anybody here—' I
promised a complete discretion with great gravity. 'I have a canoe and three

black fellows waiting not very far. I am off. Could you give me a few Martini-Henry cartridges?' I could, and did, with proper secrecy. He helped himself, with a wink at me, to a handful of my tobacco. 'Between sailors—you know—good English tobacco.' At the door of the pilot-house he turned round—'I say, haven't you a pair of shoes you could spare?' He raised one leg. 'Look.' The soles were tied with knotted strings sandal-wise under his bare feet. I rooted out an old pair, at which he looked with admiration before tucking them under his left arm. One of his pockets (bright red) was bulging with cartridges, from the other (dark blue) peeped 'Towson's Inquiry,' etc., etc. He seemed to think himself excellently well equipped for a renewed encounter with the wilderness. 'Ah! I'll never, never meet such a man again. You ought to have heard him recite poetry—his own, too, it was, he told me. Poetry!' He rolled his eyes at the recollection of these delights. 'Oh, he enlarged my mind!' 'Good-by,' said I. He shook hands and vanished in the night. Sometimes I ask myself whether I had ever really seen him—whether it was possible to meet such a phenomenon! . . .

135   "When I woke up shortly after midnight his warning came to my mind with its hint of danger that seemed, in the starred darkness, real enough to make me get up for the purpose of having a look round. On the hill a big fire burned, illuminating fitfully a crooked corner of the station-house. One of the agents with a picket of a few of our blacks, armed for the purpose, was keeping guard over the ivory; but deep within the forest, red gleams that wavered, that seemed to sink and rise from the ground amongst confused columnar shapes of intense blackness, showed the exact position of the camp where Mr. Kurtz's adorers were keeping their uneasy vigil. The monotonous beating of a big drum filled the air with muffled shocks and a lingering vibration. A steady droning sound of many men chanting each to himself some weird incantation came out from the black, flat wall of the woods as the humming of bees comes out of a hive, and had a strange narcotic effect upon my half-awake senses. I believe I dozed off leaning over the rail, till an abrupt burst of yells, an overwhelming outbreak of a pent-up and mysterious frenzy, woke me up in a bewildered wonder. It was cut short all at once, and the low droning went on with an effect of audible and soothing silence. I glanced casually into the little cabin. A light was burning within, but Mr. Kurtz was not there.

    "I think I would have raised an outcry if I had believed my eyes. But I didn't believe them at first—the thing seemed so impossible. The fact is I was completely unnerved by a sheer blank fright, pure abstract terror, unconnected with any distinct shape of physical danger. What made this emotion so overpowering was—how shall I define it?—the moral shock I received, as if something altogether monstrous, intolerable to thought and odious to the soul, had been thrust upon me unexpectedly. This lasted of course the merest fraction of a second, and then the usual sense of commonplace, deadly danger, the possibility of a sudden onslaught and massacre, or something of the kind, which I saw impending, was positively welcome and composing. It pacified me, in fact, so much, that I did not raise an alarm.

    "There was an agent buttoned up inside an ulster and sleeping on a chair on deck within three feet of me. The yells had not awakened him; he snored very slightly; I left him to his slumbers and leaped ashore. I did not betray Mr. Kurtz—it was ordered I should never betray him—it was written I should be loyal to the nightmare of my choice. I was anxious to deal with this shadow by myself alone,—and to this day I don't know why I was so jealous of sharing with anyone the peculiar blackness of that experience.

"As soon as I got on the bank I saw a trail—a broad trail through the grass. I remember the exultation with which I said to myself, 'He can't walk—he is crawling on all-fours—I've got him.' The grass was wet with dew. I strode rapidly with clenched fists. I fancy I had some vague notion of falling upon him and giving him a drubbing. I don't know. I had some imbecile thoughts. The knitting old woman with the cat obtruded herself upon my memory as a most improper person to be sitting at the other end of such an affair. I saw a row of pilgrims squirting lead in the air out of Winchesters held to the hip. I thought I would never get back to the steamer, and imagined myself living alone and unarmed in the woods to an advanced age. Such silly things—you know. And I remember I confounded the beat of the drum with the beating of my heart, and was pleased at its calm regularity.

"I kept to the track though—then stopped to listen. The night was very clear; a dark blue space, sparkling with dew and starlight, in which black things stood very still. I thought I could see a kind of motion ahead of me. I was strangely cocksure of everything that night. I actually left the track and ran in a wide semicircle (I verily believe chuckling to myself) so as to get in front of that stir, of that motion I had seen—if indeed I had seen anything. I was circumventing Kurtz as though it had been a boyish game.

"I came upon him, and, if he had not heard me coming, I would have fallen over him too, but he got up in time. He rose, unsteady, long, pale, indistinct, like a vapor exhaled by the earth, and swayed slightly, misty and silent before me; while at my back the fires loomed between the trees, and the murmur of many voices issued from the forest. I had cut him off cleverly; but when actually confronting him I seemed to come to my senses, I saw the danger in its right proportion. It was by no means over yet. Suppose he began to shout? Though he could hardly stand, there was still plenty of vigor in his voice. 'Go away— hide yourself,' he said, in that profound tone. It was very awful. I glanced back. We were within thirty yards from the nearest fire. A black figure stood up, strode on long black legs, waving long black arms, across the glow. It had horns— antelope horns, I think—on its head. Some sorcerer, some witchman, no doubt: it looked fiend-like enough. 'Do you know what you are doing?' I whispered. 'Perfectly,' he answered, raising his voice for that single word: it sounded to me far off and yet loud, like a hail through a speaking-trumpet. If he makes a row we are lost, I thought to myself. This clearly was not a case for fisticuffs, even apart from the very natural aversion I had to beat that Shadow—this wandering and tormented thing. 'You will be lost,' I said—'utterly lost.' One gets sometimes such a flash of inspiration, you know. I did say the right thing, though indeed he could not have been more irretrievably lost than he was at this very moment, when the foundations of our intimacy were being laid—to endure—to endure— even to the end—even beyond.

140

" 'I had immense plans,' he muttered irresolutely. 'Yes,' said I; 'but if you try to shout I'll smash your head with—' There was not a stick or a stone near. 'I will throttle you for good,' I corrected myself. 'I was on the threshold of great things,' he pleaded, in a voice of longing, with a wistfulness of tone that made my blood run cold. 'And now for this stupid scoundrel—' 'Your success in Europe is assured in any case,' I affirmed, steadily. I did not want to have the throttling of him, you understand—and indeed it would have been very little use for any practical purpose. I tried to break the spell—the heavy, mute spell of the wilderness—that seemed to draw him to its pitiless breast by the awakening of forgotten and brutal instincts, by the memory of gratified and monstrous passions. This alone, I was convinced, had driven him out to the edge of the forest, to the bush, towards the gleam of fires, the throb of drums, the drone of weird incantations; this alone had beguiled his unlawful soul beyond the bounds of permitted aspirations. And, don't you see, the terror of the position was not in being knocked on the head—though I had a very lively sense of that danger, too—but in this, that I had to deal with a being to whom I could not appeal in the name of anything high or low. I had, even like the niggers, to invoke him— himself—his own exalted and incredible degradation. There was nothing either above or below him, and I knew it. He had kicked himself loose of the earth. Confound the man! he had kicked the very earth to pieces. He was alone, and I before him did not know whether I stood on the ground or floated in the air. I've been telling you what we said—repeating the phrases we pronounced—but what's the good? They were common everyday words—the familiar, vague sounds exchanged on every waking day of life. But what of that? They had behind them, to my mind, the terrific suggestiveness of words heard in dreams, of phrases spoken in nightmares. Soul! If anybody had ever struggled with a soul, I am the man. And I wasn't arguing with a lunatic either. Believe me or not, his intelligence was perfectly clear—concentrated, it is true, upon himself with horrible intensity, yet clear; and therein was my only chance—barring, of course, the killing him there and then, which wasn't so good, on account of unavoidable noise. But his soul was mad. Being alone in the wilderness, it had looked within itself, and, by heavens! I tell you, it had gone mad. I had—for my sins, I suppose—to go through the ordeal of looking into it myself. No eloquence could have been so withering to one's belief in mankind as his final burst of sincerity. He struggled with himself, too. I saw it,—I heard it. I saw the inconceivable mystery of a soul that knew no restraint, no faith, and no fear, yet struggling blindly with itself. I kept my head pretty well; but when I had him at last stretched on the couch, I wiped my forehead, while my legs shook under me as though I had carried half a ton on my back down that hill. And yet I had only supported him, his bony arm clasped round my neck—and he was not much heavier than a child.

"When next day we left at noon, the crowd, of whose presence behind the curtain of trees I had been acutely conscious all the time, flowed out of the woods again, filled the clearing, covered the slope with a mass of naked, breathing, quivering, bronze bodies. I steamed up a bit, then swung downstream, and two thousand eyes followed the evolutions of the splashing, thumping, fierce river-demon beating the water with its terrible tail and breathing black smoke into the air. In front of the first rank, along the river, three men, plastered with bright red earth from head to foot, strutted to and fro restlessly. When we came abreast again, they faced the river, stamped their feet, nodded their horned heads, swayed their scarlet bodies; they shook towards the fierce river-demon a bunch of black feathers, a mangy skin with a pendent tail—something that looked like a dried gourd; they shouted periodically together strings of amazing words that resembled no sounds of human language; and the deep murmurs of the crowd, interrupted suddenly, were like the responses of some satanic litany.

"We had carried Kurtz into the pilot-house: there was more air there. Lying on the couch, he stared through the open shutter. There was an eddy in the mass of human bodies, and the woman with helmeted head and tawny cheeks rushed out to the very brink of the stream. She put out her hands, shouted something, and all that wild mob took up the shout in a roaring chorus of articulated, rapid, breathless utterance.

" 'Do you understand this?' I asked.

"He kept on looking out past me with fiery, longing eyes, with a mingled expression of wistfulness and hate. He made no answer, but I saw a smile, a smile of indefinable meaning, appear on his colorless lips that a moment after twitched convulsively. 'Do I not?' he said slowly, gasping, as if the words had been torn out of him by a supernatural power.

"I pulled the string of the whistle, and I did this because I saw the pilgrims on deck getting out their rifles with an air of anticipating a jolly lark. At the sudden screech there was a movement of abject terror through that wedged mass of bodies. 'Don't! don't you frighten them away,' cried someone on deck disconsolately. I pulled the string time after time. They broke and ran, they leaped, they crouched, they swerved, they dodged the flying terror of the sound. The three red chaps had fallen flat, face down on the shore, as though they had been shot dead. Only the barbarous and superb woman did not so much as flinch, and stretched tragically her bare arms after us over the somber and glittering river.

"And then that imbecile crowd down on the deck started their little fun, and I could see nothing more for smoke.

"The brown current ran swiftly out of the heart of darkness, bearing us down towards the sea with twice the speed of our upward progress; and Kurtz's life was running swiftly, too, ebbing, ebbing out of his heart into the sea of inexorable time. The manager was very placid, he had no vital anxieties now, he took us both in with a comprehensive and satisfied glance: the 'affair' had come off as well as could be wished. I saw the time approaching when I would be left alone of the party of 'unsound method.' The pilgrims looked upon me with disfavor. I was, so to speak, numbered with the dead. It is strange how I accepted this unforeseen partnership, this choice of nightmares forced upon me in the tenebrous land invaded by these mean and greedy phantoms.

"Kurtz discoursed. A voice! a voice! It rang deep to the very last. It survived his strength to hide in the magnificent folds of eloquence the barren darkness of his heart. Oh, he struggled! he struggled! The wastes of his weary brain were haunted by shadowy images now—images of wealth and fame revolving obsequiously round his unextinguishable gift of noble and lofty expression. My Intended, my station, my career, my ideas—these were the subjects for the occasional utterances of elevated sentiments. The shade of the original Kurtz frequented the bedside of the hollow sham, whose fate it was to be buried presently in the mold of primeval earth. But both the diabolic love and the unearthly hate of the mysteries it had penetrated fought for the possession of that soul satiated with primitive emotions, avid of lying fame, of sham distinction, of all the appearances of success and power.

150   "Sometimes he was contemptibly childish. He desired to have kings meet him at railway stations on his return from some ghastly Nowhere, where he intended to accomplish great things. 'You show them you have in you something that is really profitable, and then there will be no limits to the recognition of your ability,' he would say. 'Of course you must take care of the motives—right motives—always.' The long reaches that were like one and the same reach, monotonous bends that were exactly alike, slipped past the steamer with their multitude of secular[8] trees looking patiently after this grimy fragment of another world, the forerunner of change, of conquest, of trade, of massacres, of blessings. I looked ahead—piloting. 'Close the shutter,' said Kurtz suddenly one day; 'I can't bear to look at this.' I did so. There was a silence. 'Oh, but I will wring your heart yet!' he cried at the invisible wilderness.

"We broke down—as I had expected—and had to lie up for repairs at the head of an island. This delay was the first thing that shook Kurtz's confidence. One morning he gave me a packet of papers and a photograph—the lot tied together with a shoestring. 'Keep this for me,' he said. 'This noxious fool' (meaning the manager) 'is capable of prying into my boxes when I am not looking.' In the afternoon I saw him. He was lying on his back with closed eyes, and I withdrew quietly, but I heard him mutter, 'Live rightly, die, die. . . .' I listened. There was nothing more. Was he rehearsing some speech in his sleep, or was it a fragment of a phrase from some newspaper article? He had been writing for the papers and meant to do so again, 'for the furthering of my ideas. It's a duty.'

"His was an impenetrable darkness. I looked at him as you peer down at a man who is lying at the bottom of a precipice where the sun never shines. But I had not much time to give him, because I was helping the engine-driver to take to pieces the leaky cylinders, to straighten a bent connecting-rod, and in other such matters. I lived in an infernal mess of rust, filings, nuts, bolts, spanners, hammers, ratchet-drills—things I abominate, because I don't get on with them. I tended the little forge we fortunately had aboard; I toiled wearily in a wretched scrap-heap—unless I had the shakes too bad to stand.

"One evening coming in with a candle I was startled to hear him say a little tremulously, 'I am lying here in the dark waiting for death.' The light was within a foot of his eyes. I forced myself to murmur, 'Oh, nonsense!' and stood over him as if transfixed.

8. Ancient.

"Anything approaching the change that came over his features I have never seen before, and hope never to see again. Oh, I wasn't touched. I was fascinated. It was as though a veil had been rent. I saw on that ivory face the expression of somber pride, of ruthless power, of craven terror—of an intense and hopeless despair. Did he live his life again in every detail of desire, temptation, and surrender during that supreme moment of complete knowledge? He cried in a whisper at some image, at some vision—he cried out twice, a cry that was no more than a breath—

" 'The horror! The horror!'   155

"I blew the candle out and left the cabin. The pilgrims were dining in the mess-room, and I took my place opposite the manager, who lifted his eyes to give me a questioning glance, which I successfully ignored. He leaned back, serene, with that peculiar smile of his sealing the unexpressed depths of his meanness. A continuous shower of small flies streamed upon the lamp, upon the cloth, upon our hands and faces. Suddenly the manager's boy put his insolent black head in the doorway, and said in a tone of scathing contempt—

" 'Mistah Kurtz—he dead.'

"All the pilgrims rushed out to see. I remained, and went on with my dinner. I believe I was considered brutally callous. However, I did not eat much. There was a lamp in there—light, don't you know—and outside it was so beastly, beastly dark. I went no more near the remarkable man who had pronounced a judgment upon the adventures of his soul on this earth. The voice was gone. What else had been there? But I am of course aware that next day the pilgrims buried something in a muddy hole.

"And then they very nearly buried me.

"However, as you see, I did not go to join Kurtz there and then. I did not. I   160
remained to dream the nightmare out to the end, and to show my loyalty to Kurtz once more. Destiny. My destiny! Droll thing life is—that mysterious arrangement of merciless logic for a futile purpose. The most you can hope from it is some knowledge of yourself—that comes too late—a crop of unextinguishable regrets. I have wrestled with death. It is the most unexciting contest you can imagine. It takes place in an impalpable grayness, with nothing underfoot, with nothing around, without spectators, without clamor, without glory, without the great desire of victory, without the great fear of defeat, in a sickly atmosphere of tepid skepticism, without much belief in your own right, and still less in that of your adversary. If such is the form of ultimate wisdom, then life is a greater riddle than some of us think it to be. I was within a hair's breadth of the last opportunity for pronouncement, and I found with humiliation that probably I would have nothing to say. This is the reason why I affirm that Kurtz was a remarkable man. He had something to say. He said it. Since I had peeped over the edge myself, I understand better the meaning of his stare, that could not see the flame of the candle, but was wide enough to embrace the whole universe, piercing enough to penetrate all the hearts that beat in the darkness. He had summed up—he had judged. 'The horror!' He was a remarkable man. After all, this was the expression of some sort of belief; it had candor, it had conviction, it had a vibrating note of revolt in its whisper, it had the appalling

face of a glimpsed truth—the strange commingling of desire and hate. And it is not my own extremity I remember best—a vision of grayness without form filled with physical pain, and a careless contempt for the evanescence of all things— even of this pain itself. No! It is his extremity that I seem to have lived through. True, he had made that last stride, he had stepped over the edge, while I had been permitted to draw back my hesitating foot. And perhaps in this is the whole difference; perhaps all the wisdom, and all truth, and all sincerity, are just compressed into that inappreciable moment of time in which we step over the threshold of the invisible. Perhaps! I like to think my summing-up would not have been a word of careless contempt. Better his cry—much better. It was an affirmation, a moral victory paid for by innumerable defeats, by abominable terrors, by abominable satisfactions. But it was a victory! That is why I have remained loyal to Kurtz to the last, and even beyond, when a long time after I heard once more, not his own voice, but the echo of his magnificent eloquence thrown to me from a soul as translucently pure as a cliff of crystal.

"No, they did not bury me, though there is a period of time which I remember mistily, with a shuddering wonder, like a passage through some inconceivable world that had no hope in it and no desire. I found myself back in the sepulchral city resenting the sight of people hurrying through the streets to filch a little money from each other, to devour their infamous cookery, to gulp their unwholesome beer, to dream their insignificant and silly dreams. They trespassed upon my thoughts. They were intruders whose knowledge of life was to me an irritating pretense, because I felt so sure they could not possibly know the things I knew. Their bearing, which was simply the bearing of commonplace individuals going about their business in the assurance of perfect safety, was offensive to me like the outrageous flauntings of folly in the face of a danger it is unable to comprehend. I had no particular desire to enlighten them, but I had some difficulty in restraining myself from laughing in their faces, so full of stupid importance. I daresay I was not very well at that time. I tottered about the streets—there were various affairs to settle—grinning bitterly at perfectly respectable persons. I admit my behavior was inexcusable, but then my temperature was seldom normal in these days. My dear aunt's endeavors to 'nurse up my strength' seemed altogether beside the mark. It was not my strength that wanted nursing, it was my imagination that wanted soothing. I kept the bundle of papers given me by Kurtz, not knowing exactly what to do with it. His mother had died lately, watched over, as I was told, by his Intended. A clean-shaven man, with an official manner and wearing gold-rimmed spectacles, called on me one day and made inquiries, at first circuitous, afterwards suavely pressing, about what he was pleased to denominate certain 'documents.' I was not surprised, because I had had two rows with the manager on the subject out there. I had refused to give up the smallest scrap out of that package, and I took the same attitude with the spectacled man. He became darkly menacing at last, and with much heat argued that the Company had the right to every bit of information about its 'territories.' And said he, 'Mr. Kurtz's knowledge of unexplored regions must have been necessarily extensive and peculiar—owing to his great abilities and to the deplorable circumstances in which he had been placed: therefore—' I assured him Mr. Kurtz's knowledge, however extensive, did not bear upon the problems of commerce or administration. He invoked then the name of science. 'It would be an incalculable loss if,' etc., etc. I offered him the report on the 'Suppression of Savage Customs,' with the postscriptum torn off. He took it up eagerly, but ended by sniffing at it with an air of contempt. 'This is not what we had a right to expect,' he remarked. 'Expect nothing else,' I said. 'There are only private letters.' He withdrew upon some threat of legal proceedings, and I saw him no more; but another fellow, calling himself Kurtz's cousin, appeared two days later, and was anxious to hear all the details about his dear relative's last moments. Incidentally he gave me to understand that Kurtz had been essentially a great musician. 'There was the making of an immense success,' said the man, who was an organist, I believe, with lank gray hair flowing over a greasy coat-collar. I had no reason to doubt his statement; and to this day I am unable to say what was Kurtz's profession, whether he ever had any— which was the greatest of his talents. I had taken him for a painter who wrote for the papers, or else for a journalist who could paint—but even the cousin (who took snuff during the interview) could not tell me what he had been— exactly. He was a universal genius—on that point I agreed with the old chap, who thereupon blew his nose noisily into a large cotton handkerchief and with-drew in senile agitation, bearing off some family letters and memoranda without importance. Ultimately a journalist anxious to know something of the fate of his 'dear colleague' turned up. This visitor informed me Kurtz's proper sphere ought to have been politics 'on the popular side.' He had furry straight eyebrows, bristly hair cropped short, an eye-glass on a broad ribbon, and, becoming expansive, confessed his opinion that Kurtz really couldn't write a bit—'But heavens! how that man could talk. He electrified large meetings. He had faith—don't you see?—he had the faith. He could get himself to believe anything—anything. He would have been a splendid leader of an extreme party.' 'What party?' I asked. 'Any party,' answered the other. 'He was an—an—extremist.' Did I not think so? I assented. Did I know, he asked, with a sudden flash of curiosity, 'what it was that had induced him to go out there?' 'Yes,' said I, and forthwith handed him the famous Report for publication, if he thought fit. He glanced through it hur-riedly, mumbling all the time, judged 'it would do,' and took himself off with this plunder.

"Thus I was left at last with a slim packet of letters and the girl's portrait. She struck me as beautiful—I mean she had a beautiful expression. I know that the sunlight can be made to lie, too, yet one felt that no manipulation of light and pose could have conveyed the delicate shade of truthfulness upon those features. She seemed ready to listen without mental reservation, without suspicion, with-out a thought for herself. I concluded I would go and give her back her portrait and those letters myself. Curiosity? Yes; and also some other feeling perhaps. All that had been Kurtz's had passed out of my hands: his soul, his body, his station, his plans, his ivory, his career. There remained only this memory and his Intended—and I wanted to give that up, too, to the past, in a way—to surrender personally all that remained of him with me to that oblivion which is the last word of our common fate. I don't defend myself. I had no clear perception of what it was I really wanted. Perhaps it was an impulse of unconscious loyalty, or the fulfillment of one of those ironic necessities, that lurk in the facts of human existence. I don't know. I can't tell. But I went.

"I thought his memory was like the other memories of the dead that accumulate in every man's life—a vague impress on the brain of shadows that had fallen on it in their swift and final passage; but before the high and ponderous door, between the tall houses of a street as still and decorous as a well-kept alley in a cemetery, I had a vision of him on the stretcher, opening his mouth voraciously, as if to devour all the earth with all its mankind. He lived then before me; he lived as much as he had ever lived—a shadow insatiable of splendid appearances, of frightful realities; a shadow darker than the shadow of the night, and draped nobly in the folds of a gorgeous eloquence. The vision seemed to enter the house with me—the stretcher, the phantom-bearers, the wild crowd of obedient worshipers, the gloom of the forests, the glitter of the reach between the murky bends, the beat of the drum, regular and muffled like the beating of a heart—the heart of a conquering darkness. It was a moment of triumph for the wilderness, an invading and vengeful rush which, it seemed to me, I would have to keep back alone for the salvation of another soul. And the memory of what I had heard him say afar there, with the horned shapes stirring at my back, in the glow of fires, within the patient woods, those broken phrases came back to me, were heard again in their ominous and terrifying simplicity. I remembered his abject pleading, his abject threats, the colossal scale of his vile desires, the meanness, the torment, the tempestuous anguish of his soul. And later on I seem to see his collected languid manner, when he said one day, 'This lot of ivory now is really mine. The Company did not pay for it. I collected it myself at a very great personal risk. I am afraid they will try to claim it as theirs though. H'm. It is a difficult case. What do you think I ought to do—resist? Eh? I want no more than justice.' . . . He wanted no more than justice—no more than justice. I rang the bell before a mahogany door on the first floor, and while I waited he seemed to stare at me out of the glossy panel—stare with that wide and immense stare embracing, condemning, loathing all the universe. I seemed to hear the whispered cry, 'The horror! The horror!'

"The dusk was falling. I had to wait in a lofty drawing-room with three long windows from floor to ceiling that were like three luminous and bedraped columns. The bent gilt legs and backs of the furniture shone in indistinct curves. The tall marble fireplace had a cold and monumental whiteness. A grand piano stood massively in a corner; with dark gleams on the flat surfaces like a somber and polished sarcophagus. A high door opened—closed. I rose.

165 "She came forward, all in black, with a pale head, floating towards me in the dusk. She was in mourning. It was more than a year since his death, more than a year since the news came; she seemed as though she would remember and mourn forever. She took both my hands in hers and murmured, 'I had heard you were coming.' I noticed she was not very young—I mean not girlish. She

had a mature capacity for fidelity, for belief, for suffering. The room seemed to have grown darker, as if all the sad light of the cloudy evening had taken refuge on her forehead. This fair hair, this pale visage, this pure brow, seemed surrounded by an ashy halo from which the dark eyes looked out at me. Their glance was guileless, profound, confident, and trustful. She carried her sorrowful head as though she were proud of that sorrow, as though she would say, I—I alone know how to mourn him as he deserves. But while we were still shaking hands, such a look of awful desolation came upon her face that I perceived she was one of those creatures that are not the playthings of Time. For her he had died only yesterday. And, by Jove! the impression was so powerful that for me, too, he seemed to have died only yesterday—nay, this very minute. I saw her and him in the same instant of time—his death and her sorrow—I saw her sorrow in the very moment of his death. Do you understand? I saw them together—I heard them together. She had said, with a deep catch of the breath, 'I have survived' while my strained ears seemed to hear distinctly, mingled with her tone of despairing regret, the summing up whisper of his eternal condemnation. I asked myself what I was doing there, with a sensation of panic in my heart as though I had blundered into a place of cruel and absurd mysteries not fit for a human being to behold. She motioned me to a chair. We sat down. I laid the packet gently on the little table, and she put her hand over it. . . . 'You knew him well,' she murmured, after a moment of mourning silence.

" 'Intimacy grows quickly out there,' I said. 'I knew him as well as it is possible for one man to know another.'

" 'And you admired him,' she said. 'It was impossible to know him and not to admire him. Was it?'

" 'He was a remarkable man,' I said, unsteadily. Then before the appealing fixity of her gaze, that seemed to watch for more words on my lips, I went on, 'It was impossible not to —'

" 'Love him,' she finished eagerly, silencing me into an appalled dumbness. 'How true! how true! But when you think that no one knew him so well as I! I had all his noble confidence. I knew him best.'

" 'You knew him best,' I repeated. And perhaps she did. But with every word spoken the room was growing darker, and only her forehead, smooth and white, remained illumined by the unextinguishable light of belief and love.

" 'You were his friend,' she went on. 'His friend,' she repeated, a little louder. 'You must have been, if he had given you this, and sent you to me. I feel I can speak to you—and oh! I must speak. I want you—you have heard his last words—to know I have been worthy of him. . . . It is not pride. . . . Yes! I am proud to know I understood him better than anyone on earth—he told me so himself. And since his mother died I have had no one—no one—to—to—'

"I listened. The darkness deepened. I was not even sure whether he had given me the right bundle. I rather suspect he wanted me to take care of another batch of his papers which, after his death, I saw the manager examining under the lamp. And the girl talked, easing her pain in the certitude of my sympathy; she talked as thirsty men drink. I had heard that her engagement with Kurtz had

170

been disapproved by her people. He wasn't rich enough or something. And indeed I don't know whether he had not been a pauper all his life. He had given me some reason to infer that it was his impatience of comparative poverty that drove him out there.

" '. . . Who was not his friend who had heard him speak once?' she was saying. 'He drew men towards him by what was best in them.' She looked at me with intensity. 'It is the gift of the great,' she went on, and the sound of her low voice seemed to have the accompaniment of all the other sounds, full of mystery, desolation, and sorrow, I had ever heard—the ripple of the river, the soughing of the trees swayed by the wind, the murmurs of the crowds, the faint ring of incomprehensible words cried from afar, the whisper of a voice speaking from beyond the threshold of an eternal darkness. 'But you have heard him! You know!' she cried.

" 'Yes, I know,' I said with something like despair in my heart, but bowing my head before the faith that was in her, before that great and saving illusion that shone with an unearthly glow in the darkness, in the triumphant darkness from which I could not have defended her—from which I could not even defend myself.

175   " 'What a loss to me—to us!'—she corrected herself with beautiful generosity; then added in a murmur, 'To the world.' By the last gleams of twilight I could see the glitter of her eyes, full of tears—of tears that would not fall.

" 'I have been very happy—very fortunate—very proud,' she went on. 'Too fortunate. Too happy for a little while. And now I am unhappy for—for life.'

"She stood up; her fair hair seemed to catch all the remaining light in a glimmer of gold. I rose, too.

" 'And of all this,' she went on, mournfully, 'of all his promise, and of all his greatness, of his generous mind, of his noble heart, nothing remains—nothing but a memory. You and I—'

" 'We shall always remember him,' I said, hastily.

180   " 'No!' she cried. 'It is impossible that all this should be lost—that such a life should be sacrificed to leave nothing—but sorrow. You know what vast plans he had. I knew of them, too—I could not perhaps understand—but others knew of them. Something must remain. His words, at least, have not died.'

" 'His words will remain,' I said.

" 'And his example,' she whispered to herself. 'Men looked up to him—his goodness shone in every act. His example—'

" 'True,' I said; 'his example too. Yes, his example. I forgot that.'

" 'But I do not. I cannot—I cannot believe—not yet. I cannot believe that I shall never see him again, that nobody will see him again, never, never, never.'

185   "She put out her arms as if after a retreating figure, stretching them black and with clasped pale hands across the fading and narrow sheen of the window. Never see him! I saw him clearly enough then. I shall see this eloquent phantom as long as I live, and I shall see her, too, a tragic and familiar Shade, resembling in this gesture another one, tragic also, and bedecked with powerless charms, stretching bare brown arms over the glitter of the infernal stream, the stream of darkness. She said suddenly very low, 'He died as he lived.'

" 'His end,' said I, with dull anger stirring in me, 'was in every way worthy of his life.'

" 'And I was not with him,' she murmured. My anger subsided before a feeling of infinite pity.

" 'Everything that could be done—' I mumbled.

" 'Ah, but I believed in him more than anyone on earth—more than his own mother, more than—himself. He needed me! Me! I would have treasured every sigh, every word, every sign, every glance.'

"I felt like a chill grip on my chest. 'Don't,' I said, in a muffled voice.   190

" 'Forgive me. I—I—have mourned so long in silence—in silence. . . . You were with him—to the last? I think of his loneliness. Nobody near to understand him as I would have understood. Perhaps no one to hear. . . .'

" 'To the very end,' I said shakily. 'I heard his very last words. . . .' I stopped in a fright.

" 'Repeat them,' she murmured in a heart-broken tone. 'I want—I want—something—something—to—live with.'

"I was on the point of crying at her, 'Don't you hear them?' The dusk was repeating them in a persistent whisper all around us, in a whisper that seemed to swell menacingly like the first whisper of a rising wind. 'The horror! The horror!'

" 'His last word—to live with,' she insisted. 'Don't you understand I loved   195
him—I loved him—I loved him!'

"I pulled myself together and spoke slowly.

" 'The last word he pronounced was—your name.'

"I heard a light sigh and then my heart stood still, stopped dead short by an exulting and terrible cry, by the cry of inconceivable triumph and of unspeakable pain. 'I knew it—I was sure!' . . . She knew. She was sure. I heard her weeping, she had hidden her face in her hands. It seemed to me that the house would collapse before I could escape, that the heavens would fall upon my head. But nothing happened. The heavens do not fall for such a trifle. Would they have fallen, I wonder, if I had rendered Kurtz that justice which was his due? Hadn't he said he wanted only justice? But I couldn't. I could not tell her. It would have been too dark—too dark altogether. . . ."

Marlow ceased, and sat apart, indistinct and silent, in the pose of a meditating Buddha. Nobody moved for a time. "We have lost the first of the ebb," said the Director, suddenly. I raised my head. The offing was barred by a black bank of clouds, and the tranquil waterway leading to the uttermost ends of the earth flowed somber under an overcast sky—seemed to lead into the heart of an immense darkness.

1899

▼ ▼ ▼

QUESTIONS

1. How do the details in paragraphs 5–10 in "The Story of an Hour" prepare for the reversal that comes in paragraph 11? Did you find the turn surprising? convincing?

2. What details in the first four paragraphs of "A Very Short Story" make the characters' love seem real and convincing? There is a reversal in the sixth paragraph that makes this story's effect something like that of "The Story of an Hour." What is the effect of the final paragraph?

3. What humorous elements do you find in "A Very Old Man with Enormous Wings"? How do they function? Is the old man a symbol? If so, does he "stand for" something you can name or paraphrase? If you cannot say what he stands for, how can he be a symbol? If we do not read this story symbolically, how can we deal with its fantastic elements? take the story seriously as "literature"?

4. What images of the characters of the girl and her mother emerge from your reading of "Girl"? How are those images created?

5. What does the narrator contribute to the meaning and effect of "The Grasshopper and the Bell Cricket"? (Try to imagine the story without him.) What is the effect of the relatively lengthy description of the varied lanterns? To what extent are the meanings of "grasshopper" and "bell cricket" paraphrasable? What is the tone, effect, and meaning of the last two paragraphs?

6. In *Heart of Darkness*, what expectations are engendered by each of the following, and how are these expectations fulfilled?

    a. the interview for the job

    b. the visit to the doctor

    c. the apparently meaningless shelling of the African continent, the useless blasting of the cliffs, the purposeless digging of holes

    d. the overheard conversation between the manager of the Central Station and his uncle.

7. Why is Kurtz described by Marlow as "the nightmare of my choice"? What kinds of rites, lusts, monstrous passions, forgotten and brutal instincts do you imagine Kurtz indulging in? What evidence is there for defining them? If they are somewhat vague, what is the effect of this vagueness? In what sense is Kurtz's final judgment—"The horror!"—a victory?

8. Why does the story go on after Kurtz's death and Marlow's return? What ironies are there in Marlow's conversation with the Intended? Why does Marlow lie to her? Is Marlow's (Conrad's?) attitude sexist? The African woman at

Kurtz's station is certainly at the heart of darkness, so why must the Intended be protected from the truth? Is the story, then, racist? What evidence is there in the story of racism?

9. Early in the story, Marlow says that what saves us "is the devotion to efficiency," and what redeems conquest "is the idea . . . at the back of it; not a sentimental pretense but an idea; and an unselfish belief in the idea. . . ." He later praises the chief accountant's keeping up appearances by his European dress as evidence of character, having backbone amid "the great demoralization of the land." Is he then criticizing the colonial exploitation only for its inefficiency and its "philanthropic pretense"? How would you summarize the implied attitude of the story toward imperialism?

10. Marlow, we are told, believes that "the meaning of an episode was not inside like a kernel but outside, enveloping the tale which brought it out only as a glow brings out a haze," and he later compares telling his story to "trying to tell you a dream—making a vain attempt, because no relation of a dream can convey the dream sensation, that commingling of absurdity, surprise, and bewilderment in a tremor of struggling revolt . . . ," and he ends by saying, "We live, as we dream—alone." How are these comments related to the focus of narration (including the frame)? To what extent can it be said that not only is the action here the telling of the story but the story itself is *about* the telling of a story (or the telling of a truth)?

WRITING SUGGESTIONS

1. Write a personal essay either about grief and its complexities or about another experience in which an initial and expected emotion gave way to something like its opposite.

2. Compare the ending of "A Very Short Story" to that of "The Jewelry."

3. Write a personal essay called "Boy" or "Another Girl" that deals with the oft-repeated and multiple instructions, advice, and commands of a parent (not necessarily a mother).

4. The introduction to the chapter suggests that all you have learned about the elements of fiction may be, perhaps must be, brought to bear on Kawabata's story. Write an analysis of this story as if for the earlier chapter called "The Whole Text."

5. Write a personal essay—with yourself as either protagonist or, as in the

case of Marlow, narrator—about an experience (real or imaginary) that shook up one of your important basic beliefs.

6. Write an argumentative essay on the question (a) whether Conrad's novel is sexist, or (b) whether it is racist. (See questions 8 and 9 above for some hints.)

7. Write an analytical essay, stressing but not limited to focus and voice, on how the narrative and thematic elements of *Heart of Darkness* would be changed if Marlow's story were told in the third person and there were no frame. (See question 10 above.)

Evaluating Fiction

T o evaluate a work of literature—to determine its worth or quality—is
one of the most fundamental, significant, and difficult activities in literary study. It is impossible to dodge such questions as "Is this story
good?" "Is it great?" "Is it better than that one? . . . that other one?" "Is it worth
reading? studying?" It is equally impossible to answer such questions definitively, for all time and for all readers.

It is, however, usually possible to answer the question, "Do you like this
story?" and often possible to answer "Do you like this one more than or less
than that other?" Whether you like a story or not when you first read it is therefore probably the proper place to *begin*. But it is a dangerous place to *stop* the
process of evaluation. If our appreciation and understanding of literature is to
grow, and if we are not content simply to accept without question the authority
of "those who know best," we must learn to isolate, analyze, and articulate
what it is *we* like about a story and to search out in our minds and experience
the reasons *we* like it. We must listen to other readers' responses too, responses
that may reinforce our own, may show us things to appreciate in the story that
we missed, or may challenge the viability of our reasons, if not that of our
responses.

Let us begin by reading a story together. Let's see how we like it, and what
we can say about it.

RICHARD CONNELL

The Most Dangerous Game

"Off there to the right—somewhere—is a large island," said Whitney. "It's rather
a mystery—"

"What island is it?" Rainsford asked.

"The old charts call it 'Ship-Trap Island,' " Whitney replied. "A suggestive name, isn't it? Sailors have a curious dread of the place. I don't know why. Some superstition—"

"Can't see it," remarked Rainsford, trying to peer through the dank tropical night that was palpable as it pressed its thick warm blackness in upon the yacht.

"You've good eyes," said Whitney, with a laugh, "and I've seen you pick off a moose moving in the brown fall bush at four hundred yards, but even you can't see four miles or so through a moonless Caribbean night."

"Nor four yards," admitted Rainsford. "Ugh! It's like moist black velvet."

"It will be light in Rio," promised Whitney. "We should make it in a few days. I hope the jaguar guns have come from Purdey's. We should have some good hunting up the Amazon. Great sport, hunting."

"The best sport in the world," agreed Rainsford.

"For the hunter," amended Whitney. "Not for the jaguar."

"Don't talk rot, Whitney," said Rainsford. "You're a big-game hunter, not a philosopher. Who cares how a jaguar feels?"

"Perhaps the jaguar does," observed Whitney.

"Bah! They've no understanding."

"Even so, I rather think they understand one thing—fear. The fear of pain and the fear of death."

"Nonsense," laughed Rainsford. "This hot weather is making you soft, Whitney. Be a realist. The world is made up of two classes—the hunters and the huntees. Luckily, you and I are hunters. Do you think we've passed that island yet?"

"I can't tell in the dark. I hope so."

"Why?" asked Rainsford.

"The place has a reputation—a bad one."

"Cannibals?" suggested Rainsford.

"Hardly. Even cannibals wouldn't live in such a God-forsaken place. But it's gotten into sailor lore, somehow. Didn't you notice that the crew's nerves seemed a bit jumpy today?"

"They were a bit strange, now you mention it. Even Captain Nielsen—"

"Yes, even that tough-minded old Swede, who'd go up to the devil himself and ask him for a light. Those fishy blue eyes held a look I never saw there before. All I could get out of him was: 'This place has an evil name among seafaring men, sir.' Then he said to me, very gravely: 'Don't you feel anything?'—as if the air about us was actually poisonous. Now, you mustn't laugh when I tell you this—I did feel something like a sudden chill.

"There was no breeze. The sea was as flat as a plate-glass window. We were drawing near the island then. What I felt was a—a mental chill; a sort of sudden dread."

"Pure imagination," said Rainsford. "One superstitious sailor can taint the whole ship's company with his fear."

"Maybe. But sometimes I think sailors have an extra sense that tells them when they are in danger. Sometimes I think evil is a tangible thing—with wave lengths, just as sound and light have. An evil place can, so to speak, broadcast vibrations of evil. Anyhow, I'm glad we're getting out of this zone. Well, I think I'll turn in now, Rainsford."

"I'm not sleepy," said Rainsford. "I'm going to smoke another pipe up on the after deck." 25

"Good night, then, Rainsford. See you at breakfast."

"Right. Good night, Whitney."

There was no sound in the night as Rainsford sat there, but the muffled throb of the engine that drove the yacht swiftly through the darkness, and the swish and ripple of the wash of the propeller.

Rainsford, reclining in a steamer chair, indolently puffed on his favorite brier. The sensuous drowsiness of the night was on him. "It's so dark," he thought, "that I could sleep without closing my eyes; the night would be my eyelids—"

An abrupt sound startled him. Off to the right he heard it, and his ears, expert in such matters, could not be mistaken. Again he heard the sound, and again. Somewhere, off in the blackness, some one had fired a gun three times. 30

Rainsford sprang up and moved quickly to the rail, mystified. He strained his eyes in the direction from which the reports had come, but it was like trying to see through a blanket. He leaped upon the rail and balanced himself there, to get greater elevation; his pipe, striking a rope, was knocked from his mouth. He lunged for it; a short, hoarse cry came from his lips as he realized he had reached too far and had lost his balance. The cry was pinched off short as the bloodwarm waters of the Caribbean Sea closed over his head.

He struggled up to the surface and tried to cry out, but the wash from the speeding yacht slapped him in the face and the salt water in his open mouth made him gag and strangle. Desperately he struck out with strong strokes after the receding lights of the yacht, but he stopped before he had swum fifty feet. A certain cool-headedness had come to him; it was not the first time he had been in a tight place. There was a chance that his cries could be heard by some one aboard the yacht, but that chance was slender, and grew more slender as the yacht raced on. He wrestled himself out of his clothes, and shouted with all his power. The lights of the yacht became faint and ever-vanishing fireflies; then they were blotted out entirely by the night.

Rainsford remembered the shots. They had come from the right, and doggedly he swam in that direction, swimming with slow, deliberate strokes, conserving his strength. For a seemingly endless time he fought the sea. He began to count his strokes; he could do possibly a hundred more and then—

Rainsford heard a sound. It came out of the darkness, a high screaming sound, the sound of an animal in an extremity of anguish and terror.

He did not recognize the animal that made the sound; he did not try to; with fresh vitality he swam toward the sound. He heard it again; then it was cut short by another noise, crisp, staccato. 35

"Pistol shot," muttered Rainsford, swimming on.

Ten minutes of determined effort brought another sound to his ears—the most welcome he had ever heard—the muttering and growling of the sea breaking on a rocky shore. He was almost on the rocks before he saw them; on a night less calm he would have been shattered against them. With his remaining strength he dragged himself from the swirling waters. Jagged crags appeared to jut into the opaqueness; he forced himself upward, hand over hand. Gasping, his hands raw, he reached a flat place at the top. Dense jungle came down to the very edge of the cliffs. What perils that tangle of trees and underbrush might hold for him did not concern Rainsford just then. All he knew was that he was safe from his enemy, the sea, and that utter weariness was on him. He flung himself down at the jungle edge and tumbled headlong into the deepest sleep of his life.

When he opened his eyes he knew from the position of the sun that it was late in the afternoon. Sleep had given him new vigor; a sharp hunger was picking at him. He looked about him, almost cheerfully.

"Where there are pistol shots, there are men. Where there are men, there is food," he thought. But what kind of men, he wondered, in so forbidding a place? An unbroken front of snarled and ragged jungle fringed the shore.

40 He saw no sign of a trail through the closely knit web of weeds and trees; it was easier to go along the shore, and Rainsford floundered along by the water. Not far from where he had landed, he stopped.

Some wounded thing, by the evidence a large animal, had thrashed about in the underbrush; the jungle weeds were crushed down and the moss was lacerated; one patch of weeds was stained crimson. A small, glittering object not far away caught Rainsford's eye and he picked it up. It was an empty cartridge.

"A twenty-two," he remarked. "That's odd. It must have been a fairly large animal too. The hunter had his nerve with him to tackle it with a light gun. It's clear that the brute put up a fight. I suppose the first three shots I heard was when the hunter flushed his quarry and wounded it. The last shot was when he trailed it here and finished it."

He examined the ground closely and found what he had hoped to find—the print of hunting boots. They pointed along the cliff in the direction he had been going. Eagerly, he hurried along, now slipping on a rotten log or a loose stone, but making headway; night was beginning to settle down on the island.

Bleak darkness was blacking out the sea and jungle when Rainsford sighted the lights. He came upon them as he turned a crook in the coast line, and his first thought was that he had come upon a village, for there were many lights. But as he forged along he saw to his great astonishment that all the lights were in one enormous building—a lofty structure with pointed towers plunging upward into the gloom. His eyes made out the shadowy outlines of a palatial château; it was set on a high bluff, and on three sides of it cliffs dived down to where the sea licked greedy lips in the shadows.

45 "Mirage," thought Rainsford. But it was no mirage, he found, when he opened the tall spiked iron gate. The stone steps were real enough; the massive door with a leering gargoyle for a knocker was real enough; yet about it all hung an air of unreality.

He lifted the knocker, and it creaked up stiffly, as if it had never before been used. He let it fall, and it startled him with its booming loudness. He thought he heard steps within; the door remained closed. Again Rainsford lifted the heavy knocker, and let it fall. The door opened then, opened as suddenly as if it were on a spring, and Rainsford stood blinking in the river of glaring gold light that poured out. The first thing Rainsford's eyes discerned was the largest man Rainsford had ever seen—a gigantic creature, solidly made and blackbearded to the waist. In his hand the man held a long-barreled revolver, and he was pointing it straight at Rainsford's heart.

Out of the snarl of beard two small eyes regarded Rainsford.

"Don't be alarmed," said Rainsford, with a smile which he hoped was disarming. "I'm no robber. I fell off a yacht. My name is Sanger Rainsford of New York City."

The menacing look in the eyes did not change. The revolver pointed as rigidly as if the giant were a statue. He gave no sign that he understood Rainsford's words, or that he had even heard them. He was dressed in uniform, a black uniform trimmed with gray astrakhan.

"I'm Sanger Rainsford of New York," Rainsford began again. "I fell off a yacht. I am hungry." 50

The man's only answer was to raise with his thumb the hammer of his revolver. Then Rainsford saw the man's free hand go to his forehead in a military salute, and he saw him click his heels together and stand at attention. Another man was coming down the broad marble steps, an erect, slender man in evening clothes. He advanced to Rainsford and held out his hand.

In a cultivated voice marked by a slight accent that gave it added precision and deliberateness, he said: "It is a very great pleasure and honor to welcome Mr. Sanger Rainsford, the celebrated hunter, to my home."

Automatically Rainsford shook the man's hand.

"I've read your book about hunting snow leopards in Tibet, you see" explained the man. "I am General Zaroff."

Rainsford's first impression was that the man was singularly handsome; his 55 second was that there was an original, almost bizarre quality about the general's face. He was a tall man past middle age, for his hair was a vivid white; but his thick eyebrows and pointed military mustache were as black as the night from which Rainsford had come. His eyes, too, were black and very bright. He had high cheek bones, a sharp-cut nose, a spare, dark face, the face of a man used to giving orders, the face of an aristocrat. Turning to the giant in uniform, the general made a sign. The giant put away his pistol, saluted, withdrew.

"Ivan is an incredibly strong fellow," remarked the general, "but he has the misfortune to be deaf and dumb. A simple fellow, but, I'm afraid, like all his race, a bit of a savage."

"Is he Russian?"

"He is a Cossack," said the general, and his smile showed red lips and pointed teeth. "So am I."

"Come," he said, "we shouldn't be chatting here. We can talk later. Now you want clothes, food, rest. You shall have them. This is a most restful spot."

Ivan had reappeared, and the general spoke to him with lips that moved but 60 gave forth no sound.

"Follow Ivan, if you please, Mr. Rainsford," said the general. "I was about to have my dinner when you came. I'll wait for you. You'll find that my clothes will fit you, I think."

It was to a huge, beam-ceilinged bedroom with a canopied bed big enough for six men that Rainsford followed the silent giant. Ivan laid out an evening suit, and Rainsford, as he put it on, noticed that it came from a London tailor who ordinarily cut and sewed for none below the rank of duke.

The dining room to which Ivan conducted him was in many ways remarkable. There was a medieval magnificence about it; it suggested a baronial hall of feudal times with its oaken panels, its high ceiling, its vast refectory table where twoscore men could sit down to eat. About the hall were the mounted heads of many animals—lions, tigers, elephants, moose, bears; larger or more perfect specimens Rainsford had never seen. At the great table the general was sitting, alone.

"You'll have a cocktail, Mr. Rainsford," he suggested. The cocktail was surpassingly good; and, Rainsford noted, the table appointments were of the finest—the linen, the crystal, the silver, the china.

65   They were eating *borsch*, the rich, red soup with whipped cream so dear to Russian palates. Half apologetically General Zaroff said: "We do our best to preserve the amenities of civilization here. Please forgive any lapses. We are well off the beaten track, you know. Do you think the champagne has suffered from its long ocean trip?"

"Not in the least," declared Rainsford. He was finding the general a most thoughtful and affable host, a true cosmopolite. But there was one small trait of the general's that made Rainsford uncomfortable. Whenever he looked up from his plate he found the general studying him, appraising him narrowly.

"Perhaps," said General Zaroff, "you were surprised that I recognized your name. You see, I read all books on hunting published in English, French, and Russian. I have but one passion in my life, Mr. Rainsford, and it is the hunt."

"You have some wonderful heads here," said Rainsford as he ate a particularly well cooked filet mignon. "That Cape buffalo is the largest I ever saw."

"Oh, that fellow. Yes, he was a monster."

70   "Did he charge you?"

"Hurled me against a tree," said the general. "Fractured my skull. But I got the brute."

"I've always thought," said Rainsford, "that the Cape buffalo is the most dangerous of all big game."

For a moment the general did not reply; he was smiling his curious redlipped smile. Then he said slowly: "No. You are wrong, sir. The Cape buffalo is not the most dangerous big game." He sipped his wine. "Here in my preserve on this island," he said in the same slow tone, "I hunt more dangerous game."

Rainsford expressed his surprise. "Is there big game on this island?"

75   The general nodded. "The biggest."

"Really?"

"Oh, it isn't here naturally, of course. I have to stock the island."

"What have you imported, general?" Rainsford asked. "Tigers?"

The general smiled. "No," he said. "Hunting tigers ceased to interest me some years ago. I exhausted their possibilities, you see. No thrill left in tigers, no real danger. I live for danger, Mr. Rainsford."

The general took from his pocket a gold cigarette case and offered his guest a long black cigarette with a silver tip; it was perfumed and gave off a smell like incense.

80

"We will have some capital hunting, you and I," said the general. "I shall be most glad to have your society."

"But what game—" began Rainsford.

"I'll tell you," said the general. "You will be amused, I know. I think I may say, in all modesty, that I have done a rare thing. I have invented a new sensation. May I pour you another glass of port, Mr. Rainsford?"

"Thank you, general."

The general filled both glasses, and said: "God makes some men poets. Some He makes kings, some beggars. Me He made a hunter. My hand was made for the trigger, my father said. He was a very rich man with a quarter of a million acres in the Crimea, and he was an ardent sportsman. When I was only five years old he gave me a little gun, specially made in Moscow for me, to shoot sparrows with. When I shot some of his prize turkeys with it, he did not punish me; he complimented me on my marksmanship. I killed my first bear in the Caucasus when I was ten. My whole life has been one prolonged hunt. I went into the army—it was expected of noblemen's sons—and for a time commanded a division of Cossack cavalry, but my real interest was always the hunt. I have hunted every kind of game in every land. It would be impossible for me to tell you how many animals I have killed."

85

The general puffed at his cigarette.

"After the debacle in Russia[1] I left the country, for it was imprudent for an officer of the Czar to stay there. Many noble Russians lost everything. I, luckily, had invested heavily in American securities, so I shall never have to open a tea room in Monte Carlo or drive a taxi in Paris. Naturally, I continued to hunt—grizzlies in your Rockies, crocodiles in the Ganges, rhinoceroses in East Africa. It was in Africa that the Cape buffalo hit me and laid me up for six months. As soon as I recovered I started for the Amazon to hunt jaguars, for I had heard they were unusually cunning. They weren't." The Cossack sighed. "They were no match at all for a hunter with his wits about him, and a high-powered rifle. I was bitterly disappointed. I was lying in my tent with a splitting headache one night when a terrible thought pushed its way into my mind. Hunting was beginning to bore me! And hunting, remember, had been my life. I have heard that in America business men often go to pieces when they give up the business that has been their life."

"Yes, that's so," said Rainsford.

The general smiled. "I had no wish to go to pieces," he said. "I must do something. Now, mine is an analytical mind, Mr. Rainsford. Doubtless that is why I enjoy the problems of the chase."

1. The Revolution of 1917, which overthrew the Czar and prepared the way for Communist rule.

90   "No doubt, General Zaroff."

"So," continued the general, "I asked myself why the hunt no longer fascinated me. You are much younger than I am, Mr. Rainsford, and have not
hunted as much, but you perhaps can guess the answer."

"What was it?"

"Simply this: hunting had ceased to be what you call 'a sporting proposition.'
It had become too easy. I always got my quarry. Always. There is no greater bore
than perfection."

The general lit a fresh cigarette.

95   "No animal had a chance with me any more. That is no boast; it is a mathematical certainty. The animal had nothing but his legs and his instinct. Instinct
is no match for reason. When I thought of this it was a tragic moment for me, I
can tell you."

Rainsford leaned across the table, absorbed in what his host was saying.

"It came to me as an inspiration what I must do," the general went on.

"And that was?"

The general smiled the quiet smile of one who had faced an obstacle and
surmounted it with success. "I had to invent a new animal to hunt," he said.

100   "A new animal? You're joking."

"Not at all," said the general. "I never joke about hunting. I needed a new
animal. I found one. So I bought this island, built this house, and here I do my
hunting. The island is perfect for my purposes—there are jungles with a maze
of trails in them, hills, swamps—"

"But the animal, General Zaroff?"

"Oh," said the general, "it supplies me with the most exciting hunting in the
world. No other hunting compares with it for an instant. Every day I hunt, and
I never grow bored now, for I have a quarry with which I can match my wits."

Rainsford's bewilderment showed in his face.

105   "I wanted the ideal animal to hunt," explained the general. "So I said: 'What
are the attributes of an ideal quarry?' And the answer was, of course: 'It must
have courage, cunning, and, above all, it must be able to reason.'"

"But no animal can reason," objected Rainsford.

"My dear fellow," said the general, "there is one that can."

"But you can't mean—" gasped Rainsford.

"And why not?"

110   "I can't believe you are serious, General Zaroff. This is a grisly joke."

"Why should I not be serious? I am speaking of hunting."

"Hunting? Good God, General Zaroff, what you speak of is murder."

The general laughed with entire good nature. He regarded Rainsford quizzically. "I refuse to believe that so modern and civilized a young man as you
seem to be harbors romantic ideas about the value of human life. Surely your
experiences in the war—"

"Did not make me condone cold-blooded murder," finished Rainsford stiffly.

115   Laughter shook the general. "How extraordinarily droll you are!" he said.
"One does not expect nowadays to find a young man of the educated class, even
in America, with such a naïve, and, if I may say so, mid-Victorian point of view.

It's like finding a snuff-box in a limousine. Ah, well, doubtless you had Puritan ancestors. So many Americans appear to have had. I'll wager you'll forget your notions when you go hunting with me. You've a genuine new thrill in store for you, Mr. Rainsford."

"Thank you, I'm a hunter, not a murderer."

"Dear me," said the general, quite unruffled, "again that unpleasant word. But I think I can show you that your scruples are quite ill founded."

"Yes?"

"Life is for the strong, to be lived by the strong, and, if need be, taken by the strong. The weak of the world were put here to give the strong pleasure. I am strong. Why should I not use my gift? If I wish to hunt, why should I not? I hunt the scum of the earth—sailors from tramp ships—lascars, blacks, Chinese, whites, mongrels—a thoroughbred horse or hound is worth more than a score of them."

"But they are men," said Rainsford hotly.   120

"Precisely," said the general. "That is why I use them. It gives me pleasure. They can reason, after a fashion. So they are dangerous."

"But where do you get them?"

The general's left eyelid fluttered down in a wink. "This island is called Ship-Trap," he answered. "Sometimes an angry god of the high seas sends them to me. Sometimes, when Providence is not so kind, I help Providence a bit. Come to the window with me."

Rainsford went to the window and looked out toward the sea.

"Watch! Out there!" exclaimed the general, pointing into the night. Rains-   125
ford's eyes saw only blackness, and then, as the general pressed a button, far out to sea Rainsford saw the flash of lights.

The general chuckled. "They indicate a channel," he said, "where there's none: giant rocks with razor edges crouch like a sea monster with wide-open jaws. They can crush a ship as easily as I crush this nut." He dropped a walnut on the hardwood floor and brought his heel grinding down on it. "Oh, yes," he said, casually, as if in answer to a question, "I have electricity. We try to be civilized here."

"Civilized? And you shoot down men?"

A trace of anger was in the general's black eyes, but it was there for but a second, and he said, in his most pleasant manner: "Dear me, what a righteous young man you are! I assure you I do not do the thing you suggest. That would be barbarous. I treat these visitors with every consideration. They get plenty of good food and exercise. They get into splendid physical condition. You shall see for yourself tomorrow."

"What do you mean?"

"We'll visit my training school," smiled the general. "It's in the cellar. I have   130
about a dozen pupils down there now. They're from the Spanish bark San Lucar that had the bad luck to go on the rocks out there. A very inferior lot, I regret to say. Poor specimens and more accustomed to the deck than to the jungle."

He raised his hand, and Ivan, who served as waiter, brought thick Turkish coffee. Rainsford, with an effort, held his tongue in check.

"It's a game, you see," pursued the general blandly. "I suggest to one of them that we go hunting. I give him a supply of food and an excellent hunting knife. I give him three hours' start. I am to follow, armed only with a pistol of the smallest caliber and range. If my quarry eludes me for three whole days, he wins the game. If I find him"—the general smiled—"he loses."

"Suppose he refuses to be hunted?"

"Oh," said the general, "I give him his option, of course. He need not play that game if he doesn't wish to. If he does not wish to hunt, I turn him over to Ivan. Ivan once had the honor of serving as official knouter to the Great White Czar,[2] and he has his own ideas of sport. Invariably, Mr. Rainsford, invariably they choose the hunt."

135   "And if they win?"

The smile on the general's face widened. "To date I have not lost," he said.

Then he added, hastily: "I don't wish you to think me a braggart, Mr. Rainsford. Many of them afford only the most elementary sort of problem. Occasionally I strike a tartar. One almost did win. I eventually had to use the dogs."

"The dogs?"

"This way, please. I'll show you."

140   The general steered Rainsford to a window. The lights from the windows sent a flickering illumination that made grotesque patterns on the courtyard below, and Rainsford could see moving about there a dozen or so huge black shapes; as they turned toward him, their eyes glittered greenly.

"A rather good lot, I think," observed the general. "They are let out at seven every night. If anyone should try to get into my house—or out of it—something extremely regrettable would occur to him." He hummed a snatch of song from the Folies Bergère.[3]

"And now," said the general, "I want to show you my new collection of heads. Will you come with me to the library?"

"I hope," said Rainsford, "that you will excuse me tonight, General Zaroff. I'm really not feeling at all well."

"Ah, indeed?" the general inquired solicitously. "Well, I suppose that's only natural, after your long swim. You need a good, restful night's sleep. Tomorrow you'll feel like a new man, I'll wager. Then we'll hunt, eh? I've one rather promising prospect—"

145   Rainsford was hurrying from the room.

"Sorry you can't go with me tonight," called the general. "I expect rather fair sport—a big, strong black. He looks resourceful—Well, good night, Mr. Rainsford; I hope you have a good night's rest."

The bed was good, and the pajamas of the softest silk, and he was tired in every fiber of his being, but nevertheless Rainsford could not quiet his brain with the opiate of sleep. He lay, eyes wide open. Once he thought he heard stealthy steps in the corridor outside his room. He sought to throw open the

---

2. Probably Nicholas II (1868–1918), who was overthrown by the Revolution and executed; "White" designates those opposed to the Communists, or "Reds."   3. Paris theater and music hall.

door; it would not open. He went to the window and looked out. His room was high up in one of the towers. The lights of the château were out now; and it was dark and silent, but there was a fragment of sallow moon, and by its wan light he could see, dimly, the courtyard; there, weaving in and out in the pattern of shadow, were black, noiseless forms; the hounds heard him at the window and looked up, expectantly, with their green eyes. Rainsford went back to bed and lay down. By many methods he tried to put himself to sleep. He had achieved a doze when, just as morning began to come, he heard, far off in the jungle, the faint report of a pistol.

General Zaroff did not appear until luncheon. He was dressed faultlessly in the tweeds of a country squire. He was solicitous about the state of Rainsford's health.

"As for me," sighed the general, "I do not feel so well. I am worried, Mr. Rainsford. Last night I detected traces of my old complaint."

To Rainsford's questioning glance the general said: "Ennui. Boredom."   150

Then, taking a second helping of *crêpes suzette*, the general explained: "The hunting was not good last night. The fellow lost his head. He made a straight trail that offered no problems at all. That's the trouble with these sailors; they have dull brains to begin with, and they do not know how to get about in the woods. They do excessively stupid and obvious things. It's most annoying. Will you have another glass of Chablis, Mr. Rainsford?"

"General," said Rainsford firmly, "I wish to leave this island at once."

The general raised his thickets of eyebrows; he seemed hurt. "But, my dear fellow," the general protested, "you've only just come. You've had no hunting—"

"I wish to go today," said Rainsford. He saw the dead black eyes of the general on him, studying him. General Zaroff's face suddenly brightened.

He filled Rainsford's glass with venerable Chablis from a dusty bottle.   155

"Tonight," said the general, "we will hunt—you and I."

Rainsford shook his head. "No, general," he said, "I will not hunt."

The general shrugged his shoulders and delicately ate a hothouse grape. "As you wish, my friend," he said. "The choice rests entirely with you. But may I not venture to suggest that you will find my idea of sport more diverting than Ivan's?"

He nodded toward the corner to where the giant stood, scowling, his thick arms crossed on his hogshead of a chest.

"You don't mean—" cried Rainsford.   160

"My dear fellow," said the general, "have I not told you I always mean what I say about hunting? This is really an inspiration. I drink to a foeman worthy of my steel—at last."

The general raised his glass, but Rainsford sat staring at him.

"You'll find this game worth playing," the general said enthusiastically. "Your brain against mine. Your woodcraft against mine. Your strength and stamina against mine. Outdoor chess! And the stake is not without value, eh?"

"And if I win—" began Rainsford huskily.

165   "I'll cheerfully acknowledge myself defeated if I do not find you by midnight of the third day," said General Zaroff. "My sloop will place you on the mainland near a town."

    The general read what Rainsford was thinking.

    "Oh, you can trust me," said the Cossack. "I will give you my word as a gentleman and a sportsman. Of course you, in turn, must agree to say nothing of your visit here."

    "I'll agree to nothing of the kind," said Rainsford.

    "Oh," said the general, "in that case—But why discuss that now? Three days hence we can discuss it over a bottle of Veuve Cliquot,[4] unless—"

170   The general sipped his wine.

    Then a businesslike air animated him. "Ivan," he said to Rainsford, "will supply you with hunting clothes, food, a knife. I suggest you wear moccasins; they leave a poorer trail. I suggest too that you avoid the big swamp in the southeast corner of the island. We call it Death Swamp. There's quicksand there. One foolish fellow tried it. The deplorable part of it was that Lazarus followed him. You can imagine my feelings, Mr. Rainsford. I loved Lazarus; he was the finest hound in my pack. Well, I must beg you to excuse me now. I always take a siesta after lunch. You'll hardly have time for a nap, I fear. You'll want to start, no doubt. I shall not follow till dusk. Hunting at night is so much more exciting than by day, don't you think? Au revoir, Mr. Rainsford, au revoir."

    General Zaroff, with a deep, courtly bow, strolled from the room.

    From another door came Ivan. Under one arm he carried khaki hunting clothes, a haversack of food, a leather sheath containing a long-bladed hunting knife; his right hand rested on a cocked revolver thrust in the crimson sash about his waist. . . .

    Rainsford had fought his way through the bush for two hours. "I must keep my nerve. I must keep my nerve," he said through tight teeth.

175   He had not been entirely clear-headed when the château gates snapped shut behind him. His whole idea at first was to put distance between himself and General Zaroff, and, to this end, he had plunged along, spurred on by the sharp rowels of something very like panic. Now he had got a grip on himself, had stopped, and was taking stock of himself and the situation.

    He saw that straight flight was futile; inevitably it would bring him face to face with the sea. He was in a picture with a frame of water, and his operations, clearly, must take place within that frame.

    "I'll give him a trail to follow," muttered Rainsford, and he struck off from the rude paths he had been following into the trackless wilderness. He executed a series of intricate loops; he doubled on his trail again and again, recalling all the lore of the fox hunt, and all the dodges of the fox. Night found him leg-weary, with hands and face lashed by the branches, on a thickly wooded ridge. He knew it would be insane to blunder on through the dark, even if he had the strength. His need for rest was imperative and he thought: "I have played the

4. A fine champagne; Chablis, above, is a very dry white Burgundy table wine.

fox, now I must play the cat of the fable."[5] A big tree with a thick trunk and outspread branches was nearby, and, taking care to leave not the slightest mark, he climbed up into the crotch, and stretching out on one of the broad limbs, after a fashion, rested. Rest brought him new confidence and almost a feeling of security. Even so zealous a hunter as General Zaroff could not trace him there, he told himself; only the devil himself could follow that complicated trail through the jungle after dark. But, perhaps, the general was a devil—

An apprehensive night crawled slowly by like a wounded snake, and sleep did not visit Rainsford, although the silence of a dead world was on the jungle. Toward morning when a dingy gray was varnishing the sky, the cry of some startled bird focused Rainsford's attention in that direction. Something was coming through the bush, coming slowly, carefully, coming by the same winding way Rainsford had come. He flattened himself down on the limb, and through a screen of leaves almost as thick as tapestry, he watched. The thing that was approaching was a man.

It was General Zaroff. He made his way along with his eyes fixed in utmost concentration on the ground before him. He paused, almost beneath the tree, dropped to his knees and studied the ground. Rainsford's impulse was to hurl himself down like a panther, but he saw that the general's right hand held something metallic—a small automatic pistol.

The hunter shook his head several times, as if he were puzzled. Then he straightened up and took from his case one of his black cigarettes; its pungent incense-like smoke floated up to Rainsford's nostrils.   180

Rainsford held his breath. The general's eyes had left the ground and were traveling inch by inch up the tree. Rainsford froze there, every muscle tensed for a spring. But the sharp eyes of the hunter stopped before they reached the limb where Rainsford lay; a smile spread over his brown face. Very deliberately he blew a smoke ring into the air; then he turned his back on the tree and walked carelessly away, back along the trail he had come. The swish of the underbrush against his hunting boots grew fainter and fainter.

The pent-up air burst hotly from Rainsford's lungs. His first thought made him feel sick and numb. The general could follow a trail through the woods at night; he could follow an extremely difficult trail; he must have uncanny powers; only by the merest chance had the Cossack failed to see his quarry.

Rainsford's second thought was even more terrible. It sent a shudder of cold horror through his whole being. Why had the general smiled? Why had he turned back?

Rainsford did not want to believe what his reason told him was true, but the truth was as evident as the sun that had by now pushed through the morning mists. The general was playing with him! The general was saving him for another day's sport! The Cossack was the cat; he was the mouse.[6] Then it was that Rainsford knew the full meaning of terror.

---

5. The fox boasts of his many tricks to elude the hounds; the cat responds he knows only one—to climb the nearest tree—but that this is worth more than all the fox's tricks.   6. A cat, sure of his prey, plays with a mouse before killing him.

185 "I will not lose my nerve. I will not."

He slid down the tree, and struck off again into the woods. His face was set and he forced the machinery of his mind to function. Three hundred yards from his hiding place he stopped where a huge dead tree leaned precariously on a smaller, living one. Throwing off his sack of food, Rainsford took his knife from its sheath and began to work with all his energy.

The job was finished at last, and he threw himself down behind a fallen log a hundred feet away. He did not have to wait long. The cat was coming again to play with the mouse.

Following the trail with the sureness of a bloodhound, came General Zaroff. Nothing escaped those searching black eyes, no crushed blade of grass, no bent twig, no mark, no matter how faint, in the moss. So intent was the Cossack on his stalking that he was upon the thing Rainsford had made before he saw it. His foot touched the protruding bough that was the trigger. Even as he touched it, the general sensed his danger and leaped back with the agility of an ape. But he was not quite quick enough; the dead tree, delicately adjusted to rest on the cut living one, crashed down and struck the general a glancing blow on the shoulder as it fell; but for his alertness, he must have been smashed beneath it. He staggered, but he did not fall; nor did he drop his revolver. He stood there, rubbing his injured shoulder, and Rainsford, with fear again gripping his heart, heard the general's mocking laugh ring through the jungle.

"Rainsford," called the general, "if you are within sound of my voice, as I suppose you are, let me congratulate you. Not many men know how to make a Malay man-catcher. Luckily, for me, I too have hunted in Malacca. You are proving interesting, Mr. Rainsford. I am going now to have my wound dressed; it's only a slight one. But I shall be back. I shall be back."

190 When the general, nursing his bruised shoulder, had gone, Rainsford took up his flight again. It was flight now, a desperate, hopeless flight, that carried him on for some hours. Dusk came, then darkness, and still he pressed on. The ground grew softer under his moccasins; the vegetation grew ranker, denser; insects bit him savagely. Then, as he stepped forward, his foot sank into the ooze. He tried to wrench it back, but the muck sucked viciously at his foot as if it were a giant leech. With a violent effort, he tore his foot loose. He knew where he was now. Death Swamp and its quicksand.

His hands were tight closed as if his nerve were something tangible that someone in the darkness was trying to tear from his grip. The softness of the earth had given him an idea. He stepped back from the quicksand a dozen feet or so and, like some huge prehistoric beaver, he began to dig.

Rainsford had dug himself in in France[7] when a second's delay meant death. That had been a placid pastime compared to his digging now. The pit grew deeper; when it was above his shoulders, he climbed out and from some hard saplings cut stakes and sharpened them to a fine point. These stakes he planted in the bottom of the pit with the points sticking up. With flying fingers he wove

7. During World War I he had quickly dug a hole or trench to shelter himself from exploding shells, bullets, etc.

a rough carpet of weeds and branches and with it he covered the mouth of the pit. Then, wet with sweat and aching with tiredness, he crouched behind the stump of a lightning-charred tree.

He knew his pursuer was coming; he heard the padding sound of feet on the soft earth, and the night breeze brought him the perfume of the general's cigarette. It seemed to Rainsford that the general was coming with unusual swiftness; he was not feeling his way along, foot by foot. Rainsford, crouching there, could not see the general, nor could he see the pit. He lived a year in a minute. Then he felt an impulse to cry aloud with joy, for he heard the sharp crackle of the breaking branches as the cover of the pit gave way; he heard the sharp scream of pain as the pointed stakes found their mark. He leaped up from his place of concealment. Then he cowered back. Three feet from the pit a man was standing, with an electric torch in his hand.

"You've done well, Rainsford," the voice of the general called. "Your Burmese tiger pit has claimed one of my best dogs. Again you score. I think, Mr. Rainsford, I'll see what you can do against my whole pack. I'm going home for a rest now. Thank you for a most amusing evening."

At daybreak Rainsford, lying near the swamp, was awakened by a sound that made him know that he had new things to learn about fear. It was a distant sound, faint and wavering, but he knew it. It was the baying of a pack of hounds.

Rainsford knew he could do one of two things. He could stay where he was and wait. That was suicide. He could flee. That was postponing the inevitable. For a moment he stood there, thinking. An idea that held a wild chance came to him, and, tightening his belt, he headed away from the swamp.

The baying of the hounds drew nearer, then still nearer, nearer, ever nearer. On a ridge Rainsford climbed a tree. Down a watercourse, not a quarter of a mile away, he could see the bush moving. Straining his eyes, he saw the lean figure of General Zaroff; just ahead of him Rainsford made out another figure whose wide shoulders surged through the tall jungle weeds; it was the giant Ivan, and he seemed pulled forward by some unseen force; Rainsford knew that Ivan must be holding the pack in leash.

They would be on him any minute now. His mind worked frantically. He thought of a native trick he had learned in Uganda. He slid down the tree. He caught hold of a springy young sapling and to it he fastened his hunting knife, with the blade pointing down the trail; with a bit of wild grapevine he tied back the sapling. Then he ran for his life. The hounds raised their voices as they hit the fresh scent. Rainsford knew now how an animal at bay feels.

He had to stop to get his breath. The baying of the hounds stopped abruptly, and Rainsford's heart stopped too. They must have reached the knife.

He shinnied excitedly up a tree and looked back. His pursuers had stopped. But the hope that was in Rainsford's brain when he climbed died, for he saw in the shallow valley that General Zaroff was still on his feet. But Ivan was not. The knife, driven by the recoil of the springing tree, had not wholly failed.

Rainsford had hardly tumbled to the ground when the pack took up the cry again.

"Nerve, nerve, nerve!" he panted, as he dashed along. A blue gap showed between the trees dead ahead. Ever nearer drew the hounds. Rainsford forced himself on toward that gap. He reached it. It was the shore of the sea. Across a cove he could see the gloomy gray stone of the château. Twenty feet below him the sea rumbled and hissed. Rainsford hesitated. He heard the hounds. Then he leaped far out into the sea. . . .

When the general and his pack reached the place by the sea, the Cossack stopped. For some minutes he stood regarding the blue-green expanse of water. He shrugged his shoulders. Then he sat down, took a drink of brandy from a silver flask, lit a perfumed cigarette, and hummed a bit from "Madame Butterfly."[8]

General Zaroff had an exceedingly good dinner in his great paneled dining hall that evening. With it he had a bottle of Pol Roger and half a bottle of Chambertin.[9] Two slight annoyances kept him from perfect enjoyment. One was the thought that it would be difficult to replace Ivan; the other was that his quarry had escaped him; of course the American hadn't played the game—so thought the general as he tasted his after-dinner liqueur. In his library he read, to soothe himself, from the works of Marcus Aurelius.[1] At ten he went up to his bedroom. He was deliciously tired, he said to himself, as he locked himself in. There was a little moonlight so, before turning on his light, he went to the window and looked down at the courtyard. He could see the great hounds, and he called: "Better luck another time," to them. Then he switched on the light.

205   A man, who had been hiding in the curtains of the bed, was standing there.

"Rainsford!" screamed the general. "How in God's name did you get here?"

"Swam," said Rainsford. "I found it quicker than walking through the jungle."

The general sucked in his breath and smiled. "I congratulate you," he said. "You have won the game."

Rainsford did not smile. "I am still a beast at bay," he said, in a low, hoarse voice. "Get ready, General Zaroff."

210   The general made one of his deepest bows. "I see," he said. "Splendid! One of us is to furnish a repast for the hounds. The other will sleep in this very excellent bed. On guard, Rainsford. . . ."

He had never slept in a better bed, Rainsford decided.

1924

A good many readers like "The Most Dangerous Game." In classes I teach it is often a favorite, or even *the* favorite. Yet other readers have urged me to

8. Opera (1904) by Giacomo Puccini (1858–1924).   9. Pol Roger is champagne, Chambertin is a highly esteemed red Burgundy wine.   1. Roman emperor (A.D. 161–180), Stoic philosopher, writer, and humanitarian.

drop this story from the anthology because it is "unworthy," not really Literature. Is this simply ignorance on the one hand or snobbery on the other?

Here are two brief papers, somewhat like those a student might write in
class, the first supporting "The Most Dangerous Game," the second
responding to the first.

Why "The Most Dangerous Game" Is Good Literature

Thaddeus Smith

"The Most Dangerous Game" by Richard Connell
is exciting. Things happen in it, and you want to
read on because you want to find out what will
happen next and how it will come out. Too often
the things we need to read for class are boring,
nothing happens, or, if something does happen, it
happens inside somebody's head. But here things
happen outside; I mean, there's real action.

Not only is there action, but that action is
important, a real life-and-death struggle. This
story is not just about whether somebody used the
wrong fork or had a good time or didn't have a
good time at a party.

The good guy wins, the story ends happily, and
when you finish reading it, you feel good about
things. Sometimes in class I think only real
downers are supposed to be good stories, like
life always has to be full of gloom and doom. Now
all of us die sooner or later, of course, but
that's only the end, a minute or a month or
something, and there's all the rest of the time

when we're not dead and not really in the process of dying. That's life, and that's what a good story should be about.

"The Most Dangerous Game" is fun to read. Sometimes I think that what are supposed to be the "good" stories are the ones I don't like. But popular stories can be good: there have been several movies made of "The Most Dangerous Game" and several stories adapted from it with just a few things changed. But, I'm told, the world of literature isn't a democracy--you don't vote for what's Literature. When I say I like Stephen King--and I'm sure not the only one, because he sells lots and lots of books--teachers or English majors say wait fifty years and see if his stuff is still around.

Well, "The Most Dangerous Game" is over sixty-five years old, older than at least three-quarters of the stories in this anthology, so it's stood the test of time, whatever that is.

Why "The Most Dangerous Game" Is Not Good Literature

Sara Rosen

Though "The Most Dangerous Game" may be "a good read," at least the first time through, and I have nothing against someone reading it or even liking it in its way, I don't think it ought to be in *The Norton Introduction to Fiction.* Being in the anthology gives it a status it does not deserve. It makes it the subject of serious study by college students, and college students ought to be engaged in more challenging and thought-provoking reading material, even if outside of class they are reading Stephen King and the likes of "The Most Dangerous Game."

Though it's true that a life-and-death struggle is important—for the person involved--it has no relevance for us, no outreach: it does not relate to our experience nor does it really illuminate anything about our experience or the way we look at life. I don't mean that a worthy story must have a "message," necessarily, but it should have a "theme," something that explores a significant area of human experience and understanding.

I admit that there is something like suspense in Connell's story, but that is not enough. There's nothing wrong with suspense in itself--expectations of one sort or another are part of every good work--but here the suspense is manipulated at the price of consistency. Note how we're seeing things from Rainsford's perspective (not through his eyes and mind exactly, not in the first person, but over his shoulder) until near the end when he leaps into the sea. At that point, when we're supposed to want most to know what happens next, there's the more or less

artificial suspense added by three dots and a
break on the page, and then we're not with
Rainsford but Zaroff, just to make us wonder if
Rainsford did indeed die. It's a cheap trick.
Besides, don't we know from the beginning that in
this kind of story the hero never dies, so isn't
the suspense really phony? What's wrong with
stories like this is the unrealistic, wish-
fulfilling way it looks at reality: it tells us
that good guys always finish first; they win
because they're good.

 While good guys do sometimes finish first, and
plenty of good stories end happily, more or less,
like "Sonny Blues," and "The Secret Sharer," life
is not always like that, and this victory seems a
little too easy.

 Finally, Rainsford has no "character"; he's
just a good guy because he's an American and his
life is threatened by a bad guy who's a Russian;
and the bad guy is just a bad guy, with no
redeeming human qualities--it's all about guys in
white hats versus guys in black hats.

These are not polished and conclusive arguments, of course. Had the
writer of the first paper read the response, he might have had more to say.
About the alleged absence of theme in "The Most Dangerous Game," for
example:

There is a theme in Connell's story. It is a
very important one, one that you have to think

about, and that some people will agree with,
though it is not a theme that you necessarily
have to agree with in order to appreciate the
story. Notice it is set just after the Russian
Revolution, and Zaroff (the "son of the czar") is
a cruel aristocrat from the czarist regime who
believes in power, believes that might-makes-
right, and believes some people are better than
others and have a right to do what they will with
their "inferiors," even kill them for pleasure.
Rainsford at the beginning is a hunter/exploiter,
never thinking what the "inferior" beast, the
hunted, feels like. Having been put in the place
of the hunted he will no doubt learn to have more
reverence for life, more sympathy for the
underdog.

The opponent, hearing this contention that there is a significant theme in the story, might well respond that the theme as described is too pat, and that it is presented through too convenient (as well as unbelievable) a situation, too much of a set-up.

This, then, is only one example of the kinds of arguments readers can use to support their judgments. We need to go on from there to consider what we read for ("a good read," "an illumination of human life and experience"), and what we mean by "the reader," the one judging the story to be "good."

Let us assume for the moment that "the readers" can be represented roughly by the people in this class—you, those who agree you about stories, and those who, though they are more or less like you, do not always agree with you. We said earlier that if our appreciation and understanding of literature is to grow, and if we are not to merely accept what those considered "authorities" say is good or great, we must learn to isolate, analyze, and articulate what *we* like (or dislike) in a story. And, we said, we must listen to those with other responses as they articulate their reasons.

Now for the test. The next story is by a Nobel laureate and much revered writer, William Faulkner, and this is one of his most admired stories. It has some of the same attractive qualities as "The Most Dangerous Game"—conflict, action, suspense—but there are those who find it critically flawed. Regardless of which side we are on, we must take seriously both those who have reservations and questions and the author's and the story's established reputation. But first, we must read it.

WILLIAM FAULKNER

Barn Burning

The store in which the Justice of the Peace's court was sitting smelled of cheese. The boy, crouched on his nail keg at the back of the crowded room, knew he smelled cheese, and more: from where he sat he could see the ranked shelves close-packed with the solid, squat, dynamic shapes of tin cans whose labels his stomach read, not from the lettering which meant nothing to his mind but from the scarlet devils and the silver curve of fish—this, the cheese which he knew he smelled and the hermetic meat which his intestines believed he smelled coming in intermittent gusts momentary and brief between the other constant one, the smell and sense just a little of fear because mostly of despair and grief, the old fierce pull of blood. He could not see the table where the Justice sat and before which his father and his father's enemy (*our enemy* he thought in that despair; *ourn! mine and hisn both! He's my father!*) stood, but he could hear them, the two of them that is, because his father had said no word yet:

"But what proof have you, Mr. Harris?"

"I told you. The hog got into my corn. I caught it up and sent it back to him. He had no fence that would hold it. I told him so, warned him. The next time I put the hog in my pen. When he came to get it I gave him enough wire to patch up his pen. The next time I put the hog up and kept it. I rode down to his house and saw the wire I gave him still rolled on to the spool in his yard. I told him he could have the hog when he paid me a dollar pound fee. That evening a nigger came with the dollar and got the hog. He was a strange nigger. He said, 'He say to tell you wood and hay kin burn.' I said, 'What?' 'That whut he say to tell you,' the nigger said. 'Wood and hay kin burn.' That night my barn burned. I got the stock out but I lost the barn."

"Where is the nigger? Have you got him?"

5 "He was a strange nigger, I tell you. I don't know what became of him."

"But that's not proof. Don't you see that's not proof?"

"Get that boy up here. He knows." For a moment the boy thought too that the man meant his older brother until Harris said, "Not him. The little one. The boy," and, crouching, small for his age, small and wiry like his father, in patched and faded jeans even too small for him, with straight, uncombed, brown hair and eyes gray and wild as storm scud, he saw the men between himself and the table part and become a lane of grim faces, at the end of which he saw the

Justice, a shabby, collarless, graying man in spectacles, beckoning him. He felt no floor under his bare feet; he seemed to walk beneath the palpable weight of the grim turning faces. His father, stiff in his black Sunday coat donned not for the trial but for the moving, did not even look at him. *He aims for me to lie*, he thought, again with that frantic grief and despair. *And I will have to do hit.*

"What's your name, boy?" the Justice said.

"Colonel Sartoris Snopes," the boy whispered.

"Hey?" the Justice said. "Talk louder. Colonel Sartoris? I reckon anybody named for Colonel Sartoris in this country can't help but tell the truth, can they?" The boy said nothing. *Enemy! Enemy!* he thought; for a moment he could not even see, could not see that the Justice's face was kindly nor discern that his voice was troubled when he spoke to the man named Harris: "Do you want me to question this boy?" But he could hear, and during those subsequent long seconds while there was absolutely no sound in the crowded little room save that of quiet and intent breathing it was as if he had swung outward at the end of a grape vine, over a ravine, and at the top of the swing had been caught in a prolonged instant of mesmerized gravity, weightless in time.

"No!" Harris said violently, explosively. "Damnation! Send him out of here!" Now time, the fluid world, rushed beneath him again, the voices coming to him again through the smell of cheese and sealed meat, the fear and despair and the old grief of blood:

"This case is closed. I can't find against you, Snopes, but I can give you advice. Leave this country and don't come back to it."

His father spoke for the first time, his voice cold and harsh, level, without emphasis: "I aim to. I don't figure to stay in a country among people who . . ." he said something unprintable and vile, addressed to no one.

"That'll do," the Justice said. "Take your wagon and get out of this country before dark. Case dismissed."

His father turned, and he followed the stiff black coat, the wiry figure walking a little stiffly from where a Confederate provost's man's[1] musket ball had taken him in the heel on a stolen horse thirty years ago, followed the two backs now, since his older brother had appeared from somewhere in the crowd, no taller than the father but thicker, chewing tobacco steadily, between the two lines of grim-faced men and out of the store and across the worn gallery and down the sagging steps and among the dogs and half-grown boys in the mild May dust, where as he passed a voice hissed:

"Barn burner!"

Again he could not see, whirling; there was a face in a red haze, moonlike, bigger than the full moon, the owner of it half again his size, he leaping in the red haze toward the face, feeling no blow, feeling no shock when his head struck the earth, scrabbling up and leaping again, feeling no blow this time either and tasting no blood, scrabbling up to see the other boy in full flight and himself already leaping into pursuit as his father's hand jerked him back, the harsh, cold voice speaking above him: "Go get in the wagon."

It stood in a grove of locusts and mulberries across the road. His two hulking

1. Military policeman.

sisters in their Sunday dresses and his mother and her sister in calico and sun-bonnets were already in it, sitting on and among the sorry residue of the dozen and more movings which even the boy could remember—the battered stove, the broken beds and chairs, the clock inlaid with mother-of-pearl, which would not run, stopped at some fourteen minutes past two o'clock of a dead and forgotten day and time, which had been his mother's dowry. She was crying, though when she saw him she drew her sleeve across her face and began to descend from the wagon. "Get back," the father said.

"He's hurt. I got to get some water and wash his . . ."

20   "Get back in the wagon," his father said. He got in too, over the tail-gate. His father mounted to the seat where the older brother already sat and struck the gaunt mules two savage blows with the peeled willow, but without heat. It was not even sadistic; it was exactly that same quality which in later years would cause his descendants to overrun the engine before putting a motor car into motion, striking and reining back in the same movement. The wagon went on, the store with its quiet crowd of grimly watching men dropped behind; a curve in the road hid it. *Forever* he thought. *Maybe he's done satisfied now, now that he has* . . . stopping himself, not to say it aloud even to himself. His mother's hand touched his shoulder.

"Does hit hurt?" she said.

"Naw," he said. "Hit don't hurt. Lemme be."

"Can't you wipe some of the blood off before hit dries?"

"I'll wash to-night," he said. "Lemme be, I tell you."

25   The wagon went on. He did not know where they were going. None of them ever did or ever asked, because it was always somewhere, always a house of sorts waiting for them a day or two days or even three days away. Likely his father had already arranged to make a crop on another farm before he . . . Again he had to stop himself. He (the father) always did. There was something about his wolf-like independence and even courage when the advantage was at least neutral which impressed strangers, as if they got from his latent ravening ferocity not so much a sense of dependability as a feeling that his ferocious conviction in the rightness of his own actions would be of advantage to all whose interest lay with his.

That night they camped, in a grove of oaks and beeches where a spring ran. The nights were still cool and they had a fire against it, of a rail lifted from a nearby fence and cut into lengths—a small fire, neat, niggard almost, a shrewd fire; such fires were his father's habit and custom always, even in freezing weather. Older, the boy might have remarked this and wondered why not a big one; why should not a man who had not only seen the waste and extravagance of war, but who had in his blood an inherent voracious prodigality with material not his own, have burned everything in sight? Then he might have gone a step farther and thought that that was the reason: that niggard blaze was the living fruit of nights passed during those four years in the woods hiding from all men, blue or gray,[2] with his strings of horses (captured horses, he called them). And

2. The colors of the Union and Confederate Civil War (1861–65) uniforms, respectively.

older still, he might have divined the true reason: that the element of fire spoke to some deep mainspring of his father's being, as the element of steel or of powder spoke to other men, as the one weapon for the preservation of integrity, else breath were not worth the breathing, and hence to be regarded with respect and used with discretion.

But he did not think this now and he had seen those same niggard blazes all his life. He merely ate his supper beside it and was already half asleep over his iron plate when his father called him, and once more he followed the stiff back, the stiff and ruthless limp, up the slope and on to the starlit road where, turning, he could see his father against the stars but without face or depth—a shape black, flat, and bloodless as though cut from tin in the iron folds of the frockcoat which had not been made for him, the voice harsh like tin and without heat like tin:

"You were fixing to tell them. You would have told him." He didn't answer. His father struck him with the flat of his hand on the side of the head, hard but without heat, exactly as he had struck the two mules at the store, exactly as he would strike either of them with any stick in order to kill a horse fly, his voice still without heat or anger: "You're getting to be a man. You got to learn. You got to learn to stick to your own blood or you ain't going to have any blood to stick to you. Do you think either of them, any man there this morning, would? Don't you know all they wanted was a chance to get at me because they knew I had them beat? Eh?" Later, twenty years later, he was to tell himself, "If I had said they wanted only truth, justice, he would have hit me again." But now he said nothing. He was not crying. He just stood there. "Answer me," his father said.

"Yes," he whispered. His father turned.

"Get on to bed. We'll be there tomorrow." 30

Tomorrow they were there. In the early afternoon the wagon stopped before a paintless two-room house identical almost with the dozen others it had stopped before even in the boy's ten years, and again, as on the other dozen occasions, his mother and aunt got down and began to unload the wagon, although his two sisters and his father and brother had not moved.

"Likely hit ain't fitten for hawgs," one of the sisters said.

"Nevertheless, fit it will and you'll hog it and like it," his father said. "Get out of them chairs and help your Ma unload."

The two sisters got down, big, bovine, in a flutter of cheap ribbons; one of them drew from the jumbled wagon bed a battered lantern, the other a worn broom. His father handed the reins to the older son and began to climb stiffly over the wheel. "When they get unloaded, take the team to the barn and feed them." Then he said, and at first the boy thought he was still speaking to his brother: "Come with me."

"Me?" he said. 35

"Yes," his father said. "You."

"Abner," his mother said. His father paused and looked back—the harsh level stare beneath the shaggy, graying, irascible brows.

"I reckon I'll have a word with the man that aims to begin to-morrow owning me body and soul for the next eight months."

They went back up the road. A week ago—or before last night, that is—he would have asked where they were going, but not now. His father had struck him before last night but never before had he paused afterward to explain why; it was as if the blow and the following calm, outrageous voice still rang, repercussed, divulging nothing to him save the terrible handicap of being young, the light weight of his few years, just heavy enough to prevent his soaring free of the world as it seemed to be ordered but not heavy enough to keep him footed solid in it, to resist it and try to change the course of its events.

Presently he could see the grove of oaks and cedars and the other flowering trees and shrubs, where the house would be, though not the house yet. They walked beside a fence massed with honeysuckle and Cherokee roses and came to a gate swinging open between two brick pillars, and now, beyond a sweep of drive, he saw the house for the first time and at that instant he forgot his father and the terror and despair both, and even when he remembered his father again (who had not stopped) the terror and despair did not return. Because, for all the twelve movings, they had sojourned until now in a poor country, a land of small farms and fields and houses, and he had never seen a house like this before. *Hit's big as a courthouse* he thought quietly, with a surge of peace and joy whose reason he could not have thought into words, being too young for that: *They are safe from him. People whose lives are a part of this peace and dignity are beyond his touch, he no more to them than a buzzing wasp: capable of stinging for a little moment but that's all; the spell of this peace and dignity rendering even the barns and stable and cribs which belong to it impervious to the puny flames he might contrive* . . . this, the peace and joy, ebbing for an instant as he looked again at the stiff black back, the stiff and implacable limp of the figure which was not dwarfed by the house, for the reason that it had never looked big anywhere and which now, against the serene columned backdrop, had more than ever that impervious quality of something cut ruthlessly from tin, depthless, as though, sidewise to the sun, it would cast no shadow. Watching him, the boy remarked the absolutely undeviating course which his father held and saw the stiff foot come squarely down in a pile of fresh droppings where a horse had stood in the drive and which his father could have avoided by a simple change of stride. But it ebbed only for a moment, though he could not have thought this into words either, walking on in the spell of the house, which he could even want but without envy, without sorrow, certainly never with that ravening and jealous rage which unknown to him walked in the ironlike black coat before him: *Maybe he will feel it too. Maybe it will even change him now from what maybe he couldn't help but be.*

They crossed the portico. Now he could hear his father's stiff foot as it came down on the boards with clocklike finality, a sound out of all proportion to the displacement of the body it bore and which was not dwarfed either by the white door before it, as though it had attained to a sort of vicious and ravening minimum not to be dwarfed by anything—the flat, wide, black hat, the formal coat of broadcloth which had once been black but which had now that friction-glazed greenish cast of the bodies of old house flies, the lifted sleeve which was too large, the lifted hand like a curled claw. The door opened so promptly that the boy knew the Negro must have been watching them all the time, an old man with neat grizzled hair, in a linen jacket, who stood barring the door with his body, saying, "Wipe yo foots, white man, fo you come in here. Major ain't home nohow."

"Get out of my way, nigger," his father said, without heat too, flinging the door back and the Negro also and entering, his hat still on his head. And now the boy saw the prints of the stiff foot on the doorjamb and saw them appear on the pale rug behind the machinelike deliberation of the foot which seemed to bear (or transmit) twice the weight which the body compassed. The Negro was shouting "Miss Lula! Miss Lula!" somewhere behind them, then the boy, deluged as though by a warm wave by a suave turn of carpeted stair and a pendant glitter of chandeliers and a mute gleam of gold frames, heard the swift feet and saw her too, a lady—perhaps he had never seen her like before either—in a gray, smooth gown with lace at the throat and an apron tied at the waist and the sleeves turned back, wiping cake or biscuit dough from her hands with a towel as she came up the hall, looking not at his father at all but at the tracks on the blond rug with an expression of incredulous amazement.

"I tried," the Negro cried. "I tole him to . . ."

"Will you please go away?" she said in a shaking voice. "Major de Spain is not at home. Will you please go away?"

His father had not spoken again. He did not speak again. He did not even look at her. He just stood stiff in the center of the rug, in his hat, the shaggy iron-gray brows twitching slightly above the pebble-colored eyes as he appeared to examine the house with brief deliberation. Then with the same deliberation he turned; the boy watched him pivot on the good leg and saw the stiff foot drag round the arc of the turning, leaving a final long and fading smear. His father never looked at it, he never once looked down at the rug. The Negro held the door. It closed behind them, upon the hysteric and indistinguishable woman-wail. His father stopped at the top of the steps and scraped his boot clean on the edge of it. At the gate he stopped again. He stood for a moment, planted stiffly on the stiff foot, looking back at the house. "Pretty and white, ain't it?" he said. "That's sweat. Nigger sweat. Maybe it ain't white enough yet to suit him. Maybe he wants to mix some white sweat with it." 45

Two hours later the boy was chopping wood behind the house within which his mother and aunt and the two sisters (the mother and aunt, not the two girls, he knew that; even at this distance and muffled by walls the flat loud voices of the two girls emanated an incorrigible idle inertia) were setting up the stove to prepare a meal, when he heard the hooves and saw the linen-clad man on a fine sorrel mare, whom he recognized even before he saw the rolled rug in front of the Negro youth following on a fat bay carriage horse—a suffused, angry face vanishing, still at full gallop, beyond the corner of the house where his father and brother were sitting in the two tilted chairs; and a moment later, almost before he could have put the axe down, he heard the hooves again and watched the sorrel mare go back out of the yard, already galloping again. Then his father began to shout one of the sisters' names, who presently emerged backward from the kitchen door dragging the rolled rug along the ground by one end while the other sister walked behind it.

"If you ain't going to tote, go on and set up the wash pot," the first said.

"You, Sarty!" the second shouted. "Set up the wash pot!" His father appeared at the door, framed against that shabbiness, as he had been against that other bland perfection, impervious to either, the mother's anxious face at his shoulder.

"Go on," the father said. "Pick it up." The two sisters stooped, broad, lethargic; stooping, they presented an incredible expanse of pale cloth and a flutter of tawdry ribbons.

50 "If I thought enough of a rug to have to git hit all the way from France I wouldn't keep hit where folks coming in would have to tromp on hit," the first said. They raised the rug.

"Abner," the mother said. "Let me do it."

"You go back and git dinner," his father said. "I'll tend to this."

From the woodpile through the rest of the afternoon the boy watched them, the rug spread flat in the dust beside the bubbling wash-pot, the two sisters stooping over it with that profound and lethargic reluctance, while the father stood over them in turn, implacable and grim, driving them though never raising his voice again. He could smell the harsh homemade lye they were using; he saw his mother come to the door once and look toward them with an expression not anxious now but very like despair; he saw his father turn, and he fell to with the axe and saw from the corner of his eye his father raise from the ground a flattish fragment of field stone and examine it and return to the pot, and this time his mother actually spoke: "Abner. Abner. Please don't. Please, Abner."

Then he was done too. It was dusk; the whippoorwills had already begun. He could smell coffee from the room where they would presently eat the cold food remaining from the mid-afternoon meal, though when he entered the house he realized they were having coffee again probably because there was a fire on the hearth, before which the rug now lay spread over the backs of the two chairs. The tracks of his father's foot were gone. Where they had been were now long, water-cloudy scoriations resembling the sporadic course of a Lilliputian mowing machine.

55 It still hung there while they ate the cold food and then went to bed, scattered without order or claim up and down the two rooms, his mother in one bed, where his father would later lie, the older brother in the other, himself, the aunt, and the two sisters on pallets on the floor. But his father was not in bed yet. The last thing the boy remembered was the depthless, harsh silhouette of the hat and coat bending over the rug and it seemed to him that he had not even closed his eyes when the silhouette was standing over him, the fire almost dead behind it, the stiff foot prodding him awake. "Catch up the mule," his father said.

When he returned with the mule his father was standing in the black door, the rolled rug over his shoulder. "Ain't you going to ride?" he said.

"No. Give me your foot."

He bent his knee into his father's hand, the wiry, surprising power flowed smoothly, rising, he rising with it, on to the mule's bare back (they had owned a saddle once; the boy could remember it though not when or where) and with the same effortlessness his father swung the rug up in front of him. Now in the starlight they retraced the afternoon's path, up the dusty road rife with honey-suckle, through the gate and up the black tunnel of the drive to the lightless house, where he sat on the mule and felt the rough warp of the rug drag across his thighs and vanish.

"Don't you want me to help?" he whispered. His father did not answer and now he heard again that stiff foot striking the hollow portico with that wooden and clocklike deliberation, that outrageous overstatement of the weight it car-ried. The rug, hunched, not flung (the boy could tell that even in the darkness) from his father's shoulder struck the angle of wall and floor with a sound unbe-lievably loud, thunderous, then the foot again, unhurried and enormous; a light came on in the house and the boy sat, tense, breathing steadily and quietly and just a little fast, though the foot itself did not increase its beat at all, descending the steps now; now the boy could see him.

"Don't you want to ride now?" he whispered. "We kin both ride now," the light within the house altering now, flaring up and sinking. *He's coming down the stairs now*, he thought. He had already ridden the mule up beside the horse block; presently his father was up behind him and he doubled the reins over and slashed the mule across the neck, but before the animal could begin to trot the hard, thin arm came round him, the hard, knotted hand jerking the mule back to a walk.

In the first red rays of the sun they were in the lot, putting plow gear on the mules. This time the sorrel mare was in the lot before he heard it at all, the rider collarless and even bareheaded, trembling, speaking in a shaking voice as the woman in the house had done, his father merely looking up once before stooping again to the hame he was buckling, so that the man on the mare spoke to his stooping back:

"You must realize you have ruined that rug. Wasn't there anybody here, any of your women . . ." he ceased, shaking, the boy watching him, the older brother leaning now in the stable door, chewing, blinking slowly and steadily at nothing apparently. "It cost a hundred dollars. But you never had a hundred dollars. You never will. So I'm going to charge you twenty bushels of corn against your crop. I'll add it in your contract and when you come to the commissary you can sign it. That won't keep Mrs. de Spain quiet but maybe it will teach you to wipe your feet off before you enter her house again."

Then he was gone. The boy looked at his father, who still had not spoken or even looked up again, who was now adjusting the logger-head in the hame.

"Pap," he said. His father looked at him—the inscrutable face, the shaggy brows beneath which the gray eyes glinted coldly. Suddenly the boy went toward him, fast, stopping as suddenly. "You done the best you could!" he cried. "If he wanted hit done different why didn't he wait and tell you how? He won't git no twenty bushels! He won't git none! We'll gether hit and hide hit! I kin watch . . ."

"Did you put the cutter back in that straight stock like I told you?"

"No, sir," he said.

"Then go do it."

60

65

That was Wednesday. During the rest of that week he worked steadily, at what was within his scope and some which was beyond it, with an industry that did not need to be driven nor even commanded twice; he had this from his mother, with the difference that some at least of what he did he liked to do, such as splitting wood with the half-size axe which his mother and aunt had earned, or saved money somehow, to present him with at Christmas. In company with the two older women (and on one afternoon, even one of the sisters), he built pens for the shoat and the cow which were a part of his father's contract with the landlord, and one afternoon, his father being absent, gone somewhere on one of the mules, he went to the field.

They were running a middle buster[3] now, his brother holding the plow straight while he handled the reins, and walking beside the straining mule, the rich black soil shearing cool and damp against his bare ankles, he thought *Maybe this is the end of it. Maybe even that twenty bushels that seems hard to have to pay for just a rug will be a cheap price for him to stop forever and always from being what he used to be*; thinking, dreaming now, so that his brother had to speak sharply to him to mind the mule: *Maybe he even won't collect the twenty bushels. Maybe it will all add up and balance and vanish—corn, rug, fire; the terror and grief, the being pulled two ways like between two teams of horses— gone, done with for ever and ever.*

70   Then it was Saturday; he looked up from beneath the mule he was harnessing and saw his father in the black coat and hat. "Not that," his father said. "The wagon gear." And then, two hours later, sitting in the wagon bed behind his father and brother on the seat, the wagon accomplished a final curve, and he saw the weathered paintless store with its tattered tobacco- and patent-medicine posters and the tethered wagons and saddle animals below the gallery. He mounted the gnawed steps behind his father and brother, and there again was the lane of quiet, watching faces for the three of them to walk through. He saw the man in spectacles sitting at the plank table and he did not need to be told this was a Justice of the Peace; he sent one glare of fierce, exultant, partisan defiance at the man in collar and cravat now, whom he had seen but twice before in his life, and that on a galloping horse, who now wore on his face an expression not of rage but of amazed unbelief which the boy could not have known was at the incredible circumstance of being sued by one of his own tenants, and came and stood against his father and cried at the Justice: "He ain't done it! He ain't burnt . . ."

"Go back to the wagon," his father said.

"Burnt?" the Justice said. "Do I understand this rug was burned too?"

"Does anybody here claim it was?" his father said. "Go back to the wagon." But he did not, he merely retreated to the rear of the room, crowded as that other had been, but not to sit down this time, instead, to stand pressing among the motionless bodies, listening to the voices:

"And you claim twenty bushels of corn is too high for the damage you did to the rug?"

---

3. A double moldboard plow that throws a ridge of earth both ways.

"He brought the rug to me and said he wanted the tracks washed out of it. I washed the tracks out and took the rug back to him." 75

"But you didn't carry the rug back to him in the same condition it was in before you made the tracks on it."

His father did not answer, and now for perhaps half a minute there was no sound at all save that of breathing, the faint, steady suspiration of complete and intent listening.

"You decline to answer that, Mr. Snopes?" Again his father did not answer. "I'm going to find against you, Mr. Snopes. I'm going to find that you were responsible for the injury to Major de Spain's rug and hold you liable for it. But twenty bushels of corn seems a little high for a man in your circumstances to have to pay. Major de Spain claims it cost a hundred dollars. October corn will be worth about fifty cents. I figure that if Major de Spain can stand a ninety-five dollar loss on something he paid cash for, you can stand a five-dollar loss you haven't earned yet. I hold you in damages to Major de Spain to the amount of ten bushels of corn over and above your contract with him, to be paid to him out of your crop at gathering time. Court adjourned."

It had taken no time hardly, the morning was but half begun. He thought they would return home and perhaps back to the field, since they were late, far behind all other farmers. But instead his father passed on behind the wagon, merely indicating with his hand for the older brother to follow with it, and crossed the road toward the blacksmith shop opposite, pressing on after his father, overtaking him, speaking, whispering up at the harsh, calm face beneath the weathered hat: "He won't git no ten bushels neither. He won't git one. We'll ..." until his father glanced for an instant down at him, the face absolutely calm, the grizzled eyebrows tangled above the cold eyes, the voice almost pleasant, almost gentle:

"You think so? Well, we'll wait till October anyway." 80

The matter of the wagon—the setting of a spoke or two and the tightening of the tires—did not take long either, the business of the tires accomplished by driving the wagon into the spring branch behind the shop and letting it stand there, the mules nuzzling into the water from time to time, and the boy on the seat with the idle reins, looking up the slope and through the sooty tunnel of the shed where the slow hammer rang and where his father sat on an upended cypress bolt, easily, either talking or listening, still sitting there when the boy brought the dripping wagon up out of the branch and halted it before the door.

"Take them on to the shade and hitch," his father said. He did so and returned. His father and the smith and a third man squatting on his heels inside the door were talking, about crops and animals; the boy, squatting too in the ammoniac dust and hoof-parings and scales of rust, heard his father tell a long and unhurried story out of the time before the birth of the older brother even when he had been a professional horsetrader. And then his father came up beside him where he stood before a tattered last year's circus poster on the other side of the store, gazing rapt and quiet at the scarlet horses, the incredible poisings and convolutions of tulle and tights and the painted leers of comedians, and said, "It's time to eat."

But not at home. Squatting beside his brother against the front wall, he watched his father emerge from the store and produce from a paper sack a segment of cheese and divide it carefully and deliberately into three with his pocket knife and produce crackers from the same sack. They all three squatted on the gallery and ate, slowly, without talking; then in the store again, they drank from a tin dipper tepid water smelling of the cedar bucket and of living beech trees. And still they did not go home. It was a horse lot this time, a tall rail fence upon and along which men stood and sat and out of which one by one horses were led, to be walked and trotted and then cantered back and forth along the road while the slow swapping and buying went on and the sun began to slant westward, they—the three of them—watching and listening, the older brother with his muddy eyes and his steady, inevitable tobacco, the father commenting now and then on certain of the animals, to no one in particular.

It was after sundown when they reached home. They ate supper by lamplight, then, sitting on the doorstep, the boy watched the night fully accomplish, listening to the whippoorwills and the frogs, when he heard his mother's voice: "Abner! No! No! Oh, God. Oh, God. Abner!" and he rose, whirled, and saw the altered light through the door where a candle stub now burned in a bottle neck on the table and his father, still in the hat and coat, at once formal and burlesque as though dressed carefully for some shabby and ceremonial violence, emptying the reservoir of the lamp back into the five-gallon kerosene can from which it had been filled, while the mother tugged at his arm until he shifted the lamp to the other hand and flung her back, not savagely or viciously, just hard, into the wall, her hands flung out against the wall for balance, her mouth open and in her face the same quality of hopeless despair as had been in her voice. Then his father saw him standing in the door.

85   "Go to the barn and get that can of oil we were oiling the wagon with," he said. The boy did not move. Then he could speak.

"What . . ." he cried. "What are you . . ."

"Go get that oil," his father said. "Go."

Then he was moving, running, outside the house, toward the stable: this the old habit, the old blood which he had not been permitted to choose for himself, which had been bequeathed him willy nilly and which had run for so long (and who knew where, battening on what of outrage and savagery and lust) before it came to him. *I could keep on,* he thought. *I could run on and on and never look back, never need to see his face again. Only I can't. I can't,* the rusted can in his hand now, the liquid sploshing in it as he ran back to the house and into it, into the sound of his mother's weeping in the next room, and handed the can to his father.

"Ain't you going to even send a nigger?" he cried. "At least you sent a nigger before!"

90   This time his father didn't strike him. The hand came even faster than the blow had, the same hand which had set the can on the table with almost excruciating care flashing from the can toward him too quick for him to follow it, gripping him by the back of his shirt and on to tiptoe before he had seen it quit the can, the face stooping at him in breathless and frozen ferocity, the cold,

dead voice speaking over him to the older brother, who leaned against the table, chewing with that steady, curious, sidewise motion of cows:

"Empty the can into the big one and go on. I'll catch up with you."

"Better tie him up to the bedpost," the brother said.

"Do like I told you," the father said. Then the boy was moving, his bunched shirt and the hard, bony hand between his shoulder-blades, his toes just touching the floor, across the room and into the other one, past the sisters sitting with spread heavy thighs in the two chairs over the cold hearth, and to where his mother and aunt sat side by side on the bed, the aunt's arms about his mother's shoulders.

"Hold him," the father said. The aunt made a startled movement. "Not you," the father said. "Lennie. Take hold of him. I want to see you do it." His mother took him by the wrist. "You'll hold him better than that. If he gets loose don't you know what he is going to do? He will go up yonder." He jerked his head toward the road. "Maybe I'd better tie him."

"I'll hold him," his mother whispered.   95

"See you do then." Then his father was gone, the stiff foot heavy and measured upon the boards, ceasing at last.

Then he began to struggle. His mother caught him in both arms, he jerking and wrenching at them. He would be stronger in the end, he knew that. But he had no time to wait for it. "Lemme go!" he cried. "I don't want to have to hit you!"

"Let him go!" the aunt said. "If he don't go, before God, I am going up there myself!"

"Don't you see I can't?" his mother cried. "Sarty! Sarty! No! No! Help me, Lizzie!"

Then he was free. His aunt grasped at him but it was too late. He whirled,   100
running, his mother stumbled forward on to her knees behind him, crying to the nearer sister: "Catch him, Net! Catch him!" But that was too late too, the sister (the sisters were twins, born at the same time, yet either of them now gave the impression of being, encompassing as much living meat and volume and weight as any other two of the family) not yet having begun to rise from the chair, her head, face, alone merely turned, presenting to him in the flying instant an astonishing expanse of young female features untroubled by any surprise even, wearing only an expression of bovine interest. Then he was out of the room, out of the house, in the mild dust of the starlit road and the heavy rifeness of honeysuckle, the pale ribbon unspooling with terrific slowness under his running feet, reaching the gate at last and turning in, running, his heart and lungs drumming, on up the drive toward the lighted house, the lighted door. He did not knock, he burst in, sobbing for breath, incapable for the moment of speech; he saw the astonished face of the Negro in the linen jacket without knowing when the Negro had appeared.

"De Spain!" he cried, panted. "Where's . . ." then he saw the white man too emerging from a white door down the hall. "Barn!" he cried. "Barn!"

"What?" the white man said. "Barn?"

"Yes!" the boy cried. "Barn!"

"Catch him!" the white man shouted.

105 But it was too late this time too. The Negro grasped his shirt, but the entire sleeve, rotten with washing, carried away, and he was out that door too and in the drive again, and had actually never ceased to run even while he was screaming into the white man's face.

Behind him the white man was shouting, "My horse! Fetch my horse!" and he thought for an instant of cutting across the park and climbing the fence into the road, but he did not know the park nor how high the vine-massed fence might be and he dared not risk it. So he ran on down the drive, blood and breath roaring; presently he was in the road again though he could not see it. He could not hear either: the galloping mare was almost upon him before he heard her, and even then he held his course, as if the very urgency of his wild grief and need must in a moment more find his wings, waiting until the ultimate instant to hurl himself aside and into the weed-choked roadside ditch as the horse thundered past and on, for an instant in furious silhouette against the stars, the tranquil early summer night sky which, even before the shape of the horse and rider vanished, stained abruptly and violently upward: a long, swirling roar incredible and soundless, blotting the stars, and he springing up and into the road again, running again, knowing it was too late yet still running even after he heard the shot and, an instant later, two shots, pausing now without knowing he had ceased to run, crying "Pap! Pap!", running again before he knew he had begun to run, stumbling, tripping over something and scrabbling up again without ceasing to run, looking backward over his shoulder at the glare as he got up, running on among the invisible trees, panting, sobbing, "Father! Father!"

At midnight he was sitting on the crest of a hill. He did not know it was midnight and he did not know how far he had come. But there was no glare behind him now and he sat now, his back toward what he had called home for four days anyhow, his face toward the dark woods which he would enter when breath was strong again, small, shaking steadily in the chill darkness, hugging himself into the remainder of his thin, rotten shirt, the grief and despair now no longer terror and fear but just grief and despair. *Father. My father,* he thought. "He was brave!" he cried suddenly, aloud but not loud, no more than a whisper: "He was! He was in the war! He was in Colonel Sartoris' cav'ry!" not knowing that his father had gone to that war a private in the fine old European sense, wearing no uniform, admitting the authority of and giving fidelity to no man or army or flag, going to war as Malbrouck[4] himself did: for booty—it meant nothing and less than nothing to him if it were enemy booty or his own.

The slow constellations wheeled on. It would be dawn and then sun-up after a while and he would be hungry. But that would be to-morrow and now he was only cold, and walking would cure that. His breathing was easier now and he decided to get up and go on, and then he found that he had been asleep because he knew it was almost dawn, the night almost over. He could tell that from the whippoorwills. They were everywhere now among the dark trees below him,

---

4. The duke of Marlborough (1650–1722), an English general whose name became distorted as Malbrough and Malbrouch in English and French popular songs celebrating his exploits.

constant and inflectioned and ceaseless, so that, as the instant for giving over to the day birds drew nearer and nearer, there was no interval at all between them. He got up. He was a little stiff, but walking would cure that too as it would the cold, and soon there would be the sun. He went on down the hill, toward the dark woods within which the liquid silver voices of the birds called unceasing— the rapid and urgent beating of the urgent and quiring heart of the late spring night. He did not look back.

1939

The reservations I hear most often can be summarized as three "charges":

1. Faulkner's style is bad. His sentences are often too long and complicated, vague, unnecessarily wordy, and sometimes hard to read.

2. The structure of the story seems almost haphazard: it wanders off the subject or out of focus.

3. The reasons the story gives—and insists upon—for people acting the way they do are unrealistic and shallow.

Can a story with a dubious style, form, theme, and vision of human actions and motives be good, much less great? Should I, must I, like it, or at least recognize its "literary value"?

Let us see a few examples of what those who find the story flawed might isolate, analyze, and articulate. We can begin with Faulkner's awkward and obscure style and pick out an early sentence—the second sentence of the story—as evidence:

> The boy, crouched on his nail keg at the back of the crowded room, knew he smelled cheese, and more: from where he sat he could see the ranked shelves close-packed with the solid, squat, dynamic shapes of tin cans whose labels his stomach read, not from the lettering which meant nothing to his mind but from the scarlet devils and the silver curve of fish—this, the cheese which he knew he smelled and the hermetic meat which his intestines believed he smelled coming in intermittent gusts momentary and brief between the other constant one, the smell and sense just a little of fear because mostly of despair and grief, the old fierce pull of blood.

Even those who do not mind taking some pains in reading will probably acknowledge that this sentence is not immediately clear. The chief problem is how to relate the final phrase "the old fierce pull of blood" to the rest of the sentence, and so to discover what the sentence as a whole means. After a little work, you may decide that what the sentence says is that there is not only the smell of cheese and the imagined smell of canned meat but also the smell of despair and grief and even some smell of fear; and that despair, grief, and fear are in the boy's "blood," that is, inherited, in his genes. We still cannot be sure whether this implies that acquired traits or experiences are hereditary or whether "blood" means something else, and we still cannot be sure whether the smell of fear is imaginary—like the smell of the meat in the cans—or real—like the smell of the cheese (perhaps the smell of the sweat that comes with fear, or the odor some say fear gives off). But even if we have been successful in our unraveling of the meaning, what is the value of a sentence that has to be worked over so much and whose meaning even then is doubtful?

Now as to the matter of form. One reason "The Most Dangerous Game" is just a slick adventure story, some people say, is that everything in it is manipulated to heighten suspense. But if we criticize Connell for shifting focus for his own purposes, what can we say about the shifting of the focus in "Barn Burning"? One such shift occurs when the narrator is explaining why the man who burns other people's barns lights only a small neat fire when it is for his own use:

> Older, the boy might have remarked this and wondered why not a big one; why should not a man who had not only seen the waste and extravagance of war, but who had in his blood an inherent voracious prodigality with material not his own, have burned everything in sight? Then he might have gone a step farther and thought that that was the reason: that niggard blaze was the living fruit of nights passed during those four years in the woods hiding from all men, blue or gray, with his strings of horses (captured horses, he called them). And older still, he might have divined the true reason: that the element of fire spoke to some deep mainspring of his father's being, as the element of steel or of powder spoke to other men, as the one weapon for the preservation of integrity, else breath were not worth the breathing, and hence to be regarded with respect and used with discretion.

Is it okay to shift the focus temporally like this because the purpose of the shift is not "merely" to enhance the suspense but to clarify the meaning, to reveal "the true reason"?

Besides shifting to a time outside the story's present, sometimes the focus moves away from the boy's consciousness, which, like Rainsford's in "The Most Dangerous Game," dominates the rest of the story. When the father climbs aboard the wagon and immediately starts hitting the mules with a willow switch, the narrator comments,

> It was not even sadistic; it was exactly the same quality which in later years would cause his descendants to overrun the engine before putting a motor car into motion, striking and reining back in the same movement.

The time moves backward as well as forward and it always seems to do so in order to clarify or emphasize the meaning or illustrate the concept of "blood"—inborn, inherited habits or feelings. So, when his father tells him to get a can of oil the boy knows will be used to burn still another barn, despite the boy's repugnance at the act, he does it:

> Then he was moving, running, outside the house, toward the stable: this the old habit, the old blood which he had not been permitted to choose for himself, which had been bequeathed him willy nilly and which had run for so long (and who knew where, battening on what of outrage and savagery and lust) before it came to him. *I could keep on*, he thought. *I could run on and on and never look back, never need to see his face again. Only I can't. I can't, . . .*

This passage leads us directly into the third reservation or question, that having to do with the story's vision of the springs of human action. Can we accept that such habits, such capacities or incapacities, are bred into the "blood"? Can we even accept that this is a concept to be taken seriously, even if we cannot accept it? And if it is a serious concept, to what does it lead? to genetic determinism of one kind or another? to justifying "class"? to racism?

And, to go back to the earlier passage about the fire: what does it mean that "the element of fire spoke to some deep mainspring of his father's being, as the element of steel or powder spoke to other men"? And how is it that fire, swords, guns—violence—can be weapons "for the preservation of integrity," without which life is not worth living? What "integrity" is the father so intent on preserving? And what kind of "discretion" does the father show in his use of fire? What makes whether we accept the meaning of this passage crucial is that it is not embedded in the fiction, as part of the action and thoughts of the characters—the boy, let us say—but it is separated from them by the shift in focus and by the flat statement that we are being given the "true reason"; so it has the authority of the story / author and we either have to believe it or discount the whole vision of the story.

And if we look beneath the surface of these "true reasons" and the "pull of blood" and look at the events of the story itself, we begin to suspect a "hidden agenda," an ideology that determines what the characters are seen to do and why.

Why is it that the boy overcomes or betrays the "pull of blood" only when the "aristocratic" Major de Spain's barn is to be burned? Is the blood of the highborn somehow more valuable than that of the low? (Though a Snopes, the boy's first name is that of the aristocrat Colonel Sartoris.) Is some blood better than others? some loyalties better than others? Or is property a higher good than blood?

The selection of certain key passages or incidents, the analysis and interpretation of the text, can be used to directly confront these critical comments and questions, as well as to explore other, more positive areas of the story and its accomplishment. And the objections themselves can be examined in terms of what unspoken assumptions they make about what makes a story good, and what agendas they hide.

The long second sentence of "Barn Burning" does indeed put extraordinary emphasis on "blood." The concept here embodied in the word "blood" can stand such emphasis, even demands it, for "blood" is one of the forces that conflict within the boy. Therefore the sentence, though it may seem difficult, really gives ready access to the meaning of the story by calling attention to one of its key elements. Part of its length, too, consists in magnificent particularizing detail, the kind that convinces you that the author knows what he is talking about, and really "sees" the scene. (See the comments Ford Madox Ford makes on the first sentence in "Odour of Chrysanthemums"; you can make the same kind of analysis of this sentence.) The density of detail is also necessary in realizing (making real) the boy's sensations. The detail and the focus of the sentence also indicate where the significant action of the story is to take place—that is, inside the boy—and so we are made to understand and perhaps feel with him. Finally, the move from the smell of cheese to the "smell" of canned meat, to that of fear, is crucial: the smell of cheese is real. The smell of meat is inside the can and though it cannot actually be smelled while the can is intact it is real and is there. So what this suggests is that the boy's sensory imagination does not falsify, it just penetrates into things beyond the immediate present sense perceptions. This gives reality to the smell of despair, grief, fear—not necessarily real to the senses, but really there beneath the surface, real to the imagination. What the sentence does, then, is open up our notions of reality to include not just what the senses tell us, but what the imagination can sense. And since it does so through sensory images that gradually shade off into the imaginative, we are not just told that the imaginative is valid but we are made to feel that this is so. Thus the sentence that seemed unnecessarily long, complex, and difficult turns out to be functional. It does what no short sentence or series of sentences would be likely to manage.

Complexity, even obscurity, is not in all cases "bad"—as the criticism of the sentence seemed to assume. The literary value of language and detail does not necessarily follow rules of usage but questions of function—whether they work to create, reveal, intensify, the meaning and effect of the story.

Before going on to address the issue of the structure or theme of "Barn Burning," it may be appropriate to suggest that it is precisely in this merging of the physical and the imaginative, moral or psychological, that one of the strengths of the story—and of Faulkner—lies. The force that opposes blood, we soon learn, is the boy's sense of right and wrong. His father is accused of maliciously burning down Mr. Harris's barn. The boy knows his father is guilty. But when Harris demands the boy be called before the judge, the boy knows that because his ties to his father are those of "blood," he must lie. When the judge asks if Harris really wants the boy questioned there is a pause. For a boy,

> . . . it was as if he had swung outward at the end of a grape vine, over a ravine, and at the top of the swing had been caught in a prolonged instant of mesmerized gravity, weightless in time.

Most readers would acknowledge the appropriateness of the image both to the feeling of suspense and to the experience of the boy, and the intervention of the image suspends the meaning and imitates the boy's suspense. When Harris says the boy does not have to testify, "the smell of cheese and sealed meat, the fear and despair and the old grief of blood" return to the boy's consciousness. The importance and meaning of fear, despair, and grief in the "blood" is now a little clearer.

Faulkner's complexity, "idiosyncrasies" (what some call "flaws"), and difficulty (sometimes called "obscurity") usually come from this interpenetration of imagination and sensory reality or other things that we usually keep separate, like past and present. Each episode, character, detail, is saturated with the full world of his fiction, and its function seems to be primarily to embody that world rather than to further the plot or make a statement. The present is informed by the past and informs the future. Characters (Major de Spain) and names (Colonel Sartoris) that are minor or casual here are central elsewhere in Faulkner's canon, like actors in a repertory theater. The fiction is all one seamless, interconnected, timeless world. The interpenetration of community and generations is essential to the vision.

This gives both a smaller and larger role to the concept of "blood." "Blood" alone—inherited traits, customs, motives—does not determine behavior, but it is one of the multitude of communal and traditional forces that condition behavior. Though "blood" can explain many acts and impulses, its force does not eliminate free will. The boy does, after all, choose to warn the Major of his father's intention, chooses morality over blood. To claim that it was only Major de Spain's class or property that moved the boy to consider betraying his father is to ignore the fact that the story opens with his being on the verge of doing so in the Harris case. The father's crimes went well beyond the destruction of property; indeed it was the primacy of property over principles in his scheme of values that led him to serve neither North nor South but Mammon (by being a nonpartisan horse thief) during the Civil War.

Explaining the function of what may at first have seemed defects does not close the discussion about the merits of a work or the nature and function of literature. The discussion of the value of "Barn Burning" does not necessarily end here.

Until now, we have depersonalized the evaluations, assuming that the pros and cons are intellectual positions that have little or nothing to do with an individual reader, and that the "evidence" is always in the story. But already we have seen that some of the response to Faulkner is ideological, based on social or political values that have little to do with whether the focus shifts or the sentences are too long. We must admit that not all evidence of value is "on the page"; some beauty is in the eyes of the beholder. Let us keep in mind to be aware of our own responses and try at the same time to account for those responses in terms of both the narrative strategies and our own prejudices or predispositions.

BHARATI MUKHERJEE

The Management of Grief

A woman I don't know is boiling tea the Indian way in my kitchen. There are a lot of women I don't know in my kitchen, whispering, and moving tactfully. They open doors, rummage through the pantry, and try not to ask me where things are kept. They remind me of when my sons were small, on Mother's Day or when Vikram and I were tired, and they would make big, sloppy omelets. I would lie in bed pretending I didn't hear them.

Dr. Sharma, the treasurer of the Indo-Canada Society, pulls me into the hallway. He wants to know if I am worried about money. His wife, who has just come up from the basement with a tray of empty cups and glasses, scolds him. "Don't bother Mrs. Bhave with mundane details." She looks so monstrously pregnant her baby must be days overdue. I tell her she shouldn't be carrying heavy things. "Shaila," she says, smiling, "this is the fifth." Then she grabs a teenager by his shirttails. He slips his Walkman off his head. He has to be one of her four children, they have the same domed and dented foreheads. "What's the official word now?" she demands. The boy slips the headphones back on. "They're acting evasive, Ma. They're saying it could be an accident or a terrorist bomb."

All morning, the boys have been muttering, Sikh Bomb, Sikh Bomb. The men, not using the word, bow their heads in agreement. Mrs. Sharma touches her forehead at such a word. At least they've stopped talking about space debris and Russian lasers.

Two radios are going in the dining room. They are tuned to different stations. Someone must have brought the radios down from my boys' bedrooms. I haven't gone into their rooms since Kusum came running across the front lawn in her bathrobe. She looked so funny, I was laughing when I opened the door.

The big TV in the den is being whizzed through American networks and cable channels. 5

"Damn!" some man swears bitterly. "How can these preachers carry on like nothing's happened?" I want to tell him we're not that important. You look at the audience, and at the preacher in his blue robe with his beautiful white hair, the potted palm trees under a blue sky, and you know they care about nothing.

The phone rings and rings. Dr. Sharma's taken charge. "We're with her," he keeps saying. "Yes, yes, the doctor has given calming pills. Yes, yes, pills are having necessary effect." I wonder if pills alone explain this calm. Not peace, just a deadening quiet. I was always controlled, but never repressed. Sound can reach me, but my body is tensed, ready to scream. I hear their voices all around me. I hear my boys and Vikram cry, "Mommy, Shaila!" and their screams insulate me, like headphones.

The woman boiling water tells her story again and again. "I got the news first. My cousin called from Halifax before six A.M., can you imagine? He'd gotten up for prayers and his son was studying for medical exams and he heard on a rock channel that something had happened to a plane. They said first it had disappeared from the radar, like a giant eraser just reached out. His father called me, so I said to him, what do you mean, 'something bad'? You mean a hijacking? And he said, *behn*,[1] there is no confirmation of anything yet, but check with your neighbors because a lot of them must be on that plane. So I called poor Kusum straightaway. I knew Kusum's husband and daughter were booked to go yesterday."

Kusum lives across the street from me. She and Satish had moved in less than a month ago. They said they needed a bigger place. All these people, the Sharmas and friends from the Indo-Canada Society had been there for the housewarming. Satish and Kusum made homemade tandoori on their big gas grill and even the white neighbors piled their plates high with that luridly red, charred, juicy chicken. Their younger daughter had danced, and even our boys had broken away from the Stanley Cup telecast to put in a reluctant appearance. Everyone took pictures for their albums and for the community newspapers— another of our families had made it big in Toronto—and now I wonder how many of those happy faces are gone. "Why does God give us so much if all along He intends to take it away?" Kusum asks me.

I nod. We sit on carpeted stairs, holding hands like children. "I never once 10 told him that I loved him," I say. I was too much the well brought up woman. I was so well brought up I never felt comfortable calling my husband by his first name.

1. No.

"It's all right," Kusum says. "He knew. My husband knew. They felt it. Modern young girls have to say it because what they feel is fake."

Kusum's daughter, Pam, runs in with an overnight case. Pam's in her McDonald's uniform. "Mummy! You have to get dressed!" Panic makes her cranky. "A reporter's on his way here."

"Why?"

"You want to talk to him in your bathrobe?" She starts to brush her mother's long hair. She's the daughter who's always in trouble. She dates Canadian boys and hangs out in the mall, shopping for tight sweaters. The younger one, the goody-goody one according to Pam, the one with a voice so sweet that when she sang *bhajans*[2] for Ethiopian relief even a frugal man like my husband wrote out a hundred dollar check, *she* was on that plane. *She* was going to spend July and August with grandparents because Pam wouldn't go. Pam said she'd rather waitress at McDonald's. "If it's a choice between Bombay and Wonderland, I'm picking Wonderland," she'd said.

"Leave me alone," Kusum yells. "You know what I want to do? If I didn't have to look after you now, I'd hang myself."

Pam's young face goes blotchy with pain. "Thanks," she says, "don't let me stop you."

"Hush," pregnant Mrs. Sharma scolds Pam. "Leave your mother alone. Mr. Sharma will tackle the reporters and fill out the forms. He'll say what has to be said."

Pam stands her ground. "You think I don't know what Mummy's thinking? *Why her?* that's what. That's sick! Mummy wishes my little sister were alive and I were dead."

Kusum's hand in mine is trembly hot. We continue to sit on the stairs.

She calls before she arrives, wondering if there's anything I need. Her name is Judith Templeton and she's an appointee of the provincial government. "Multiculturalism?" I ask, and she says, "partially," but that her mandate is bigger. "I've been told you knew many of the people on the flight," she says. "Perhaps if you'd agree to help us reach the others. . . ?"

She gives me time at least to put on tea water and pick up the mess in the front room. I have a few *samosas*[3] from Kusum's housewarming that I could fry up, but then I think, why prolong this visit?

Judith Templeton is much younger than she sounded. She wears a blue suit with a white blouse and a polka dot tie. Her blond hair is cut short, her only jewelry is pearl drop earrings. Her briefcase is new and expensive looking, a gleaming cordovan leather. She sits with it across her lap. When she looks out the front windows onto the street, her contact lenses seem to float in front of her light blue eyes.

"What sort of help do you want from me?" I ask. She has refused the tea, out of politeness, but I insist, along with some slightly stale biscuits.

2. Hymns.   3. Fried turnovers filled with meat or vegetable mixtures.

"I have no experience," she admits. "That is, I have an MSW and I've worked in liaison with accident victims, but I mean I have no experience with a tragedy of this scale—"

"Who could?" I ask.   25

"—and with the complications of culture, language, and customs. Someone mentioned that Mrs. Bhave is a pillar—because you've taken it more calmly."

At this, perhaps, I frown, for she reaches forward, almost to take my hand. "I hope you understand my meaning, Mrs. Bhave. There are hundreds of people in Metro directly affected, like you, and some of them speak no English. There are some widows who've never handled money or gone on a bus, and there are old parents who still haven't eaten or gone outside their bedrooms. Some houses and apartments have been looted. Some wives are still hysterical. Some husbands are in shock and profound depression. We want to help, but our hands are tied in so many ways. We have to distribute money to some people, and there are legal documents—these things can be done. We have interpreters, but we don't always have the human touch, or maybe the right human touch. We don't want to make mistakes, Mrs. Bhave, and that's why we'd like to ask you to help us."

"More mistakes, you mean," I say.

"Police matters are not in my hands," she answers.

"Nothing I can do will make any difference," I say. "We must all grieve in   30
our own way."

"But you are coping very well. All the people said, Mrs. Bhave is the strongest person of all. Perhaps if the others could see you, talk with you, it would help them."

"By the standards of the people you call hysterical, I am behaving very oddly and very badly, Miss Templeton." I want to say to her, *I wish I could scream, starve, walk into Lake Ontario, jump from a bridge.* "They would not see me as a model. I do not see myself as a model."

I am a freak. No one who has ever known me would think of me reacting this way. This terrible calm will not go away.

She asks me if she may call again, after I get back from a long trip that we all must make. "Of course," I say. "Feel free to call, anytime."

Four days later, I find Kusum squatting on a rock overlooking a bay in Ire-   35
land. It isn't a big rock, but it juts sharply out over water. This is as close as we'll ever get to them. June breezes balloon out her sari and unpin her knee-length hair. She has the bewildered look of a sea creature whom the tides have stranded.

It's been one hundred hours since Kusum came stumbling and screaming across my lawn. Waiting around the hospital, we've heard many stories. The police, the diplomats, they tell us things thinking that we're strong, that knowledge is helpful to the grieving, and maybe it is. Some, I know, prefer ignorance, or their own versions. The plane broke into two, they say. Unconsciousness was instantaneous. No one suffered. My boys must have just finished their breakfasts.

They loved eating on planes, they loved the smallness of plates, knives, and forks. Last year they saved the airline salt and pepper shakers. Half an hour more and they would have made it to Heathrow.

Kusum says that we can't escape our fate. She says that all those people—our husbands, my boys, her girl with the nightingale voice, all those Hindus, Christians, Sikhs, Muslims, Parsis, and atheists on that plane—were fated to die together off this beautiful bay. She learned this from a swami in Toronto.

I have my Valium.

Six of us "relatives"—two widows and four widowers—choose to spend the day today by the waters instead of sitting in a hospital room and scanning photographs of the dead. That's what they call us now: relatives. I've looked through twenty-seven photos in two days. They're very kind to us, the Irish are very understanding. Sometimes understanding means freeing a tourist bus for this trip to the bay, so we can pretend to spy our loved ones through the glassiness of waves or in sunspeckled cloud shapes.

40   I could die here, too, and be content.

"What is that, out there?" She's standing and flapping her hands and for a moment I see a head shape bobbing in the waves. She's standing in the water, I, on the boulder. The tide is low, and a round, black, headsized rock has just risen from the waves. She returns, her sari end dripping and ruined and her face is a twisted remnant of hope, the way mine was a hundred hours ago, still laughing but inwardly knowing that nothing but the ultimate tragedy could bring two women together at six o'clock on a Sunday morning. I watch her face sag into blankness.

"That water felt warm, Shaila," she says at length.

"You can't," I say. "We have to wait for our turn to come."

I haven't eaten in four days, haven't brushed my teeth.

45   "I know," she says. "I tell myself I have no right to grieve. They are in a better place than we are. My swami says I should be thrilled for them. My swami says depression is a sign of our selfishness."

Maybe I'm selfish. Selfishly I break away from Kusum and run, sandals slapping against stones, to the water's edge. What if my boys aren't lying pinned under the debris? What if they aren't stuck a mile below that innocent blue chop? What if, given the strong currents. . . .

Now I've ruined my sari, one of my best. Kusum has joined me, knee-deep in water that feels to me like a swimming pool. I could settle in the water, and my husband would take my hand and the boys would slap water in my face just to see me scream.

"Do you remember what good swimmers my boys were, Kusum?"

"I saw the medals," she says.

50   One of the widowers, Dr. Ranganathan from Montreal, walks out to us, carrying his shoes in one hand. He's an electrical engineer. Someone at the hotel mentioned his work is famous around the world, something about the place where physics and electricity come together. He has lost a huge family, something indescribable. "With some luck," Dr. Ranganathan suggests to me, " a good swimmer could make it safely to some island. It is quite possible that

there may be many, many microscopic islets scattered around."

"You're not just saying that?" I tell Dr. Ranganathan about Vinod, my elder son. Last year he took diving as well.

"It's a parent's duty to hope," he says. "It is foolish to rule out possibilities that have not been tested. I myself have not surrendered hope."

Kusum is sobbing once again. "Dear lady," he says, laying his free hand on her arm, and she calms down.

"Vinod is how old?" he asks me. He's very careful, as we all are. *Is*, not was.

"Fourteen. Yesterday he was fourteen. His father and uncle were going to   55
take him down to the Taj and give him a big birthday party. I couldn't go with them because I couldn't get two weeks off from my stupid job in June." I process bills for a travel agent. June is a big travel month.

Dr. Ranganathan whips the pockets of his suit jacket inside out. Squashed roses, in darkening shades of pink, float on the water. He tore the roses off creepers in somebody's garden. He didn't ask anyone if he could pluck the roses, but now there's been an article about it in the local papers. When you see an Indian person, it says, please give him or her flowers.

"A strong youth of fourteen," he says, "can very likely pull to safety a younger one."

My sons, though four years apart, were very close. Vinod wouldn't let Mithun drown. *Electrical engineering*, I think, foolishly perhaps: this man knows important secrets of the universe, things closed to me. Relief spins me lightheaded. No wonder my boys' photographs haven't turned up in the gallery of photos of the recovered dead. "Such pretty roses," I say.

"My wife loved pink roses. Every Friday I had to bring a bunch home. I used to say, why? After twenty-odd years of marriage you're still needing proof positive of my love?" He has identified his wife and three of his children. Then others from Montreal, the lucky ones, intact families with no survivors. He chuckles as he wades back to shore. Then he swings around to ask me a question. "Mrs. Bhave, you are wanting to throw in some roses for your loved ones? I have two big ones left."

But I have other things to float: Vinod's pocket calculator; a half-painted   60
model B-52 for my Mithun. They'd want them on their island. And for my husband? For him I let fall into the calm, glassy waters a poem I wrote in the hospital yesterday. Finally he'll know my feelings for him.

"Don't tumble, the rocks are slippery," Dr. Ranganathan cautions. He holds out a hand for me to grab.

Then it's time to get back on the bus, time to rush back to our waiting posts on hospital benches.

Kusum is one of the lucky ones. The lucky ones flew here, identified in multiplicate their loved ones, then will fly to India with the bodies for proper ceremonies. Satish is one of the few males who surfaced. The photos of faces we saw on the walls in an office at Heathrow and here in the hospital are mostly of women. Women have more body fat, a nun said to me matter-of-factly. They float better.

Today I was stopped by a young sailor on the street. He had loaded bodies, he'd gone into the water when—he checks my face for signs of strength—when the sharks were first spotted. I don't blush, and he breaks down. "It's all right," I say. "Thank you." I had heard about the sharks from Dr. Ranganathan. In his orderly mind, science brings understanding, it holds no terror. It is the shark's duty. For every deer there is a hunter, for every fish a fisherman.

65 The Irish are not shy; they rush to me and give me hugs and some are crying. I cannot imagine reactions like that on the streets of Toronto. Just strangers, and I am touched. Some carry flowers with them and give them to any Indian they see.

After lunch, a policeman I have gotten to know quite well catches hold of me. He says he thinks he has a match for Vinod. I explain what a good swimmer Vinod is.

"You want me with you when you look at photos?" Dr. Ranganathan walks ahead of me into the picture gallery. In these matters, he is a scientist, and I am grateful. It is a new perspective. "They have performed miracles," he says. "We are indebted to them."

The first day or two the policemen showed us relatives only one picture at a time; now they're in a hurry, they're eager to lay out the possibles, and even the probables.

The face on the photo is of a boy much like Vinod; the same intelligent eyes, the same thick brows dipping into a V. But this boy's features, even his cheeks, are puffier, wider, mushier.

70 "No." My gaze is pulled by other pictures. There are five other boys who look like Vinod.

The nun assigned to console me rubs the first picture with a fingertip. "When they've been in the water for a while, love, they look a little heavier." The bones under the skin are broken, they said on the first day—try to adjust your memories. It's important.

"It's not him. I'm his mother. I'd know."

"I know this one!" Dr. Ranganathan cries out suddenly from the back of the gallery. "And this one!" I think he senses that I don't want to find my boys. "They are the Kutty brothers. They were also from Montreal." I don't mean to be crying. On the contrary, I am ecstatic. My suitcase in the hotel is packed heavy with dry clothes for my boys.

The policeman starts to cry. "I am so sorry, I am so sorry, ma'am. I really thought we had a match."

75 With the nun ahead of us and the policeman behind, we, the unlucky ones without our children's bodies, file out of the makeshift gallery.

From Ireland most of us go on to India. Kusum and I take the same direct flight to Bombay, so I can help her clear customs quickly. But we have to argue with a man in uniform. He has large boils on his face. The boils swell and glow with sweat as we argue with him. He wants Kusum to wait in line and he refuses to take authority because his boss is on a tea break. But Kusum won't let her coffins out of sight, and I shan't desert her though I know that my parents, elderly and diabetic, must be waiting in a stuffy car in a scorching lot.

"You bastard!" I scream at the man with the popping boils. Other passengers press closer. "You think we're smuggling contraband in those coffins!"

Once upon a time we were well brought up women; we were dutiful wives who kept our heads veiled, our voices shy and sweet.

In India, I become, once again, an only child of rich, ailing parents. Old friends of the family come to pay their respects. Some are Sikh, and inwardly, involuntarily, I cringe. My parents are progressive people; they do not blame communities for a few individuals.

In Canada it is a different story now.   80

"Stay longer," my mother pleads. "Canada is a cold place. Why would you want to be all by yourself?" I stay.

Three months pass. Then another.

"Vikram wouldn't have wanted you to give up things!" they protest. They call my husband by the name he was born with. In Toronto he'd changed to Vik so the men he worked with at his office would find his name as easy as Rod or Chris. "You know, the dead aren't cut off from us!"

My grandmother, the spoiled daughter of a rich *zamindar*[4], shaved her head with rusty razor blades when she was widowed at sixteen. My grandfather died of childhood diabetes when he was nineteen, and she saw herself as the harbinger of bad luck. My mother grew up without parents, raised indifferently by an uncle, while her true mother slept in a hut behind the main estate house and took her food with the servants. She grew up a rationalist. My parents abhor mindless mortification.

The zamindar's daughter kept stubborn faith in Vedic rituals; my parents   85
rebelled. I am trapped between two modes of knowledge. At thirty-six, I am too old to start over and too young to give up. Like my husband's spirit, I flutter between worlds.

Courting aphasia, we travel. We travel with our phalanx of servants and poor relatives. To hill stations and to beach resorts. We play contract bridge in dusty gymkhana clubs. We ride stubby ponies up crumbly mountain trails. At tea dances, we let ourselves be twirled twice round the ballroom. We hit the holy spots we hadn't made time for before. In Varanasi, Kalighat, Rishikesh, Hardwar, astrologers and palmists seek me out and for a fee offer me cosmic consolations.

Already the widowers among us are being shown new bride candidates. They cannot resist the call of custom, the authority of their parents and older brothers. They must marry; it is the duty of a man to look after a wife. The new wives will be young widows with children, destitute but of good family. They will make loving wives, but the men will shun them. I've had calls from the men over crackling Indian telephone lines. "Save me," they say, these substantial, edu-

---

4. Landowner.

cated, successful men of forty. "My parents are arranging a marriage for me." In a month they will have buried one family and returned to Canada with a new bride and partial family.

I am comparatively lucky. No one here thinks of arranging a husband for an unlucky widow.

Then, on the third day of the sixth month into this odyssey, in an abandoned temple in a tiny Himalayan village, as I make my offering of flowers and sweetmeats to the god of a tribe of animists, my husband descends to me. He is squatting next to a scrawny *sadhu* in moth-eaten robes. Vikram wears the vanilla suit he wore the last time I hugged him. The *sadhu* tosses petals on a butter-fed flame, reciting Sanskrit mantras and sweeps his face of flies. My husband takes my hands in his.

90   *You're beautiful,* he starts. Then, *What are you doing here?*

Shall I stay? I ask. He only smiles, but already the image is fading. *You must finish alone what we started together.* No seaweed wreathes his mouth. He speaks too fast just as he used to when we were an envied family in our pink split-level. He is gone.

In the windowless altar room, smoky with joss sticks and clarified butter lamps, a sweaty hand gropes for my blouse. I do not shriek. The *sadhu* arranges his robe. The lamps hiss and sputter out.

When we come out of the temple, my mother says, "Did you feel something weird in there?"

My mother has no patience with ghosts, prophetic dreams, holy men, and cults.

95   "No," I lie. "Nothing."

But she knows that she's lost me. She knows that in days I shall be leaving.

Kusum's put her house up for sale. She wants to live in an ashram in Hardwar. Moving to Hardwar was her swami's idea. Her swami runs two ashrams, the one in Hardwar and another here in Toronto.

"Don't run away," I tell her.

"I'm not running away," she says. "I'm pursuing inner peace. You think you or that Ranganathan fellow are better off?"

100   Pam's left for California. She wants to do some modelling, she says. She says when she comes into her share of the insurance money she'll open a yoga-cum-aerobics studio in Hollywood. She sends me postcards so naughty I daren't leave them on the coffee table. Her mother has withdrawn from her and the world.

The rest of us don't lose touch, that's the point. Talk is all we have, says Dr. Ranganathan, who has also resisted his relatives and returned to Montreal and to his job, alone. He says, whom better to talk with than other relatives? We've been melted down and recast as a new tribe.

He calls me twice a week from Montreal. Every Wednesday night and every Saturday afternoon. He is changing jobs, going to Ottawa. But Ottawa is over a hundred miles away, and he is forced to drive two hundred and twenty miles a day. He can't bring himself to sell his house. The house is a temple, he says; the king-sized bed in the master bedroom is a shrine. He sleeps on a folding cot. A devotee.

There are still some hysterical relatives. Judith Templeton's list of those needing help and those who've "accepted" is in nearly perfect balance. Acceptance means you speak of your family in the past tense and you make active plans for moving ahead with your life. There are courses at Seneca and Ryerson[5] we could be taking. Her gleaming leather briefcase is full of college catalogues and lists of cultural societies that need our help. She has done impressive work, I tell her.

"In the textbooks on grief management," she replies—I am her confidante, I realize, one of the few whose grief has not sprung bizarre obsessions—"there are stages to pass through: rejection, depression, acceptance, reconstruction." She has compiled a chart and finds that six months after the tragedy, none of us still reject reality, but only a handful are reconstructing. "Depressed Acceptance" is the plateau we've reached. Remarriage is a major step in reconstruction (though she's a little surprised, even shocked, over *how* quickly some of the men have taken on new families). Selling one's house and changing jobs and cities is healthy.

How do I tell Judith Templeton that my family surrounds me, and that like creatures in epics, they've changed shapes? She sees me as calm and accepting but worries that I have no job, no career. My closest friends are worse off than I. I cannot tell her my days, even my nights, are thrilling.

She asks me to help with families she can't reach at all. An elderly couple in Agincourt whose sons were killed just weeks after they had brought their parents over from a village in Punjab. From their names, I know they are Sikh. Judith Templeton and a translator have visited them twice with offers of money for air fare to Ireland, with bank forms, power-of-attorney forms, but they have refused to sign, or to leave their tiny apartment. Their sons' money is frozen in the bank. Their sons' investment apartments have been trashed by tenants, the furnishings sold off. The parents fear that anything they sign or any money they receive will end the company's or the country's obligations to them. They fear they are selling their sons for two airline tickets to a place they've never seen.

The high-rise apartment is a tower of Indians and West Indians, with a sprinkling of Orientals. The nearest bus stop kiosk is lined with women in saris. Boys practice cricket in the parking lot. Inside the building, even I wince a bit from the ferocity of onion fumes, the distinctive and immediate Indianness of frying *ghee*, but Judith Templeton maintains a steady flow of information. These poor old people are in imminent danger of losing their place and all their services.

I say to her, "They are Sikh. They will not open up to a Hindu woman." And what I want to add is, as much as I try not to, I stiffen now at the sight of

5. Seneca College of Applied Arts and Technology, in Willowdale; Ryerson Polytechnical Institute, Toronto.

beards and turbans. I remember a time when we all trusted each other in this new country, it was only the new country we worried about.

The two rooms are dark and stuffy. The lights are off, and an oil lamp sputters on the coffee table. The bent old lady has let us in, and her husband is wrapping a white turban over his oiled, hip-length hair. She immediately goes to the kitchen, and I hear the most familiar sound of an Indian home, tap water hitting and filling a teapot.

110   They have not paid their utility bills, out of fear and the inability to write a check. The telephone is gone; electricity and gas and water are soon to follow. They have told Judith their sons will provide. They are good boys, and they have always earned and looked after their parents.

We converse a bit in Hindi. They do not ask about the crash and I wonder if I should bring it up. If they think I am here merely as a translator, then they may feel insulted. There are thousands of Punjabi-speakers, Sikhs, in Toronto to do a better job. And so I say to the old lady, "I too have lost my sons, and my husband, in the crash."

Her eyes immediately fill with tears. The man mutters a few words which sound like a blessing. "God provides and God takes away," he says.

I want to say, but only men destroy and give back nothing. "My boys and my husband are not coming back," I say. "We have to understand that."

Now the old woman responds. "But who is to say? Man alone does not decide these things." To this her husband adds his agreement.

115   Judith asks about the bank papers, the release forms. With a stroke of the pen, they will have a provincial trustee to pay their bills, invest their money, send them a monthly pension.

"Do you know this woman?" I ask them.

The man raises his hand from the table, turns it over and seems to regard each finger separately before he answers. "This young lady is always coming here, we make tea for her and she leaves papers for us to sign." His eyes scan a pile of papers in the corner of the room. "Soon we will be out of tea, then will she go away?"

The old lady adds, "I have asked my neighbors and no one else gets *angrezi*[6] visitors. What have we done?"

"It's her job," I try to explain. "The government is worried. Soon you will have no place to stay, no lights, no gas, no water."

120   "Government will get its money. Tell her not to worry, we are honorable people."

I try to explain the government wishes to give money, not take. He raises his hand. "Let them take," he says. "We are accustomed to that. That is no problem."

"We are strong people," says the wife. "Tell her that."

"Who needs all this machinery?" demands the husband. "It is unhealthy, the bright lights, the cold air on a hot day, the cold food, the four gas rings. God will provide, not government."

6. English, Anglo.

"When our boys return," the mother says. Her husband sucks his teeth. "Enough talk," he says.

Judith breaks in. "Have you convinced them?" The snaps on her cordovan briefcase go off like firecrackers in that quiet apartment. She lays the sheaf of legal papers on the coffee table. "If they can't write their names, an X will do— I've told them that." 125

Now the old lady has shuffled to the kitchen and soon emerges with a pot of tea and two cups. "I think my bladder will go first on a job like this," Judith says to me, smiling. "If only there was some way of reaching them. Please thank her for the tea. Tell her she's very kind."

I nod in Judith's direction and tell them in Hindi, "She thanks you for the tea. She thinks you are being very hospitable but she doesn't have the slightest idea what it means."

I want to say, humor her. I want to say, my boys and my husband are with me too, more than ever. I look in the old man's eyes and I can read his stubborn, peasant's message: *I have protected this woman as best I can. She is the only person I have left. Give to me or take from me what you will, but I will not sign for it. I will not pretend that I accept.*

In the car, Judith says, "You see what I'm up against? I'm sure they're lovely people, but their stubbornness and ignorance are driving me crazy. They think signing a paper is signing their sons' death warrants, don't they?"

I am looking out the window. I want to say, *In our culture, it is a parent's duty to hope.* 130

"Now Shaila, this next woman is a real mess. She cries day and night, and she refuses all medical help. We may have to—"

"—Let me out at the subway," I say.

"I beg your pardon?" I can feel those blue eyes staring at me.

It would not be like her to disobey. She merely disapproves, and slows at a corner to let me out. Her voice is plaintive. "Is there anything I said? Anything I did?"

I could answer her suddenly in a dozen ways, but I choose not to. "Shaila? Let's talk about it," I hear, then slam the door. 135

A wife and mother begins her new life in a new country, and that life is cut short. Yet her husband tells her: Complete what we have started. We, who stayed out of politics and came halfway around the world to avoid religious and political feuding have been the first in the New World to die from it. I no longer know what we started, nor how to complete it. I write letters to the editors of local papers and to members of Parliament. Now at least they admit it was a bomb. One MP answers back, with sympathy, but with a challenge. You want to make a difference? Work on a campaign. Work on mine. Politicize the Indian voter.

My husband's old lawyer helps me set up a trust. Vikram was a saver and a careful investor. He had saved the boys' boarding school and college fees. I sell the pink house at four times what we paid for it and take a small apartment downtown. I am looking for a charity to support.

We are deep in the Toronto winter, gray skies, icy pavements. I stay indoors, watching television. I have tried to assess my situation, how best to live my life, to complete what we began so many years ago. Kusum has written me from Hardwar that her life is now serene. She has seen Satish and has heard her daughter sing again. Kusum was on a pilgrimage, passing through a village when she heard a young girl's voice, singing one of her daughter's favorite *bhajans*. She followed the music through the squalor of a Himalayan village, to a hut where a young girl, an exact replica of her daughter, was fanning coals under the kitchen fire. When she appeared, the girl cried out, "Ma!" and ran away. What did I think of that?

I think I can only envy her.

140   Pam didn't make it to California, but writes me from Vancouver. She works in a department store, giving make-up hints to Indian and Oriental girls. Dr. Ranganathan has given up his commute, given up his house and job, and accepted an academic position in Texas where no one knows his story and he has vowed not to tell it. He calls me now once a week.

I wait, I listen, and I pray, but Vikram has not returned to me. The voices and the shapes and the nights filled with visions ended abruptly several weeks ago.

I take it as a sign.

One rare, beautiful, sunny day last week, returning from a small errand on Yonge Street, I was walking through the park from the subway to my apartment. I live equidistant from the Ontario Houses of Parliament and the University of Toronto. The day was not cold, but something in the bare trees caught my attention. I looked up from the gravel, into the branches and the clear blue sky beyond. I thought I heard the rustling of larger forms, and I waited a moment for voices. Nothing.

"What?" I asked.

145   Then as I stood in the path looking north to Queen's Park and west to the university, I heard the voices of my family one last time. *Your time has come,* they said. *Go, be brave.*

I do not know where this voyage I have begun will end. I do not know which direction I will take. I dropped the package on a park bench and started walking.

1988

Let us begin a reader-oriented discussion of this story, by thinking of ourselves first as a general reader reading the opening of this story for the first time:

> A woman I don't know is boiling tea the Indian way in my kitchen. There are a lot of women I don't know in my kitchen, whispering, and moving tactfully. They open doors, rummage through the pantry, and try not to ask me where things are

kept. They remind me of when my sons were small, on Mother's Day or when Vikram and I were tired, and they would make big, sloppy omelets. I would lie in bed pretending I didn't hear them.

We are plunged immediately into the mind of an "I" whose identity we do not know, in a setting specified only as in or near a kitchen, and in a situation about which we know nothing. There is no exposition, no explanation. The more familiar past tense of most stories is absent; we are thrust into a narrative present without known precedent or purpose. The uncertainty makes us look at every word and detail for clues: "my kitchen" and "my sons . . . on Mother's Day" soon identifies the narrator as a mature female.

At this point, whether we find this indirection and uncertainty annoying or engaging (for making us work to figure out what is going on), we may ask a question or two not about the story but about ourselves. The first two stories in this chapter were not only written by men but were almost entirely about men. (No women appear in "The Most Dangerous Game" and the mother, aunt, and daughter in "Barn Burning" are peripheral.) "The Management of Grief" is not only written by a woman but tells the story through the consciousness of a woman, a strong and intelligent woman. On the other hand, this woman is a mother, somewhat older than most college students. The boy in "Barn Burning," though younger than you, is living through a part of life you have already lived through and so know something about first-hand. How much does the age of the central character have to do not just with your understanding, but with your feelings, your affective response to what you are reading?

The name "Vikram" in the first paragraph for many of us suggests little except foreignness, but "Dr. Sharma, the treasurer of the Indo-Canada Society" (par. 2), tells us enough about the cultural setting for the moment. In the ensuing conversation we learn the name of the narrator—Shaila Bhave—and learn that there has been an accident, perhaps a terrorist bombing, which may explain what seems to be the confusion of the opening scene.

The bomb, the next sentence tells us, may have been a Sikh bomb, and in the eighth paragraph we learn that it was a passenger plane that was, or might have been, bombed. What is a Sikh? Why would a Sikh bomb a plane full of people? Does the average American read this story with the same attitudes and emotions as the average Canadian? Indian? Sikh?

This is not to say that an eighteen-year-old male of Polish descent living in Cleveland cannot read this story with strong emotions and with deep sympathy for and understanding of Shaila Bhave and her tragedy. But would his responses be the same in nature and intensity as those of a middle-aged Indian woman living in Toronto or Vancouver?

For Indians, Sikhs, and some Canadians, this incident (which seems to be based on an actual disaster) is also likely to be controversial, even though the story itself does not concentrate on assessing blame or the political tensions or causes involved. Whether or not a story takes sides, touching on an issue that readers recognize as controversial inevitably affects how those readers evaluate the story. This does not necessarily mean that all Sikhs or all Indians hold one view. People often disagree with their own government's or community's actions—as many Americans did during the Vietnam war. The point is not that controversial stories are bad or that considering the politics or ideology of a work in evaluating it is bad. But we need to recognize the ideological or political factor in our assessment, to acknowledge who and where we are, where we are coming from, when we say, "This story is good" or "That story is lousy."

Evaluating a story, then, means reading carefully (and widely), learning as much as we can about the elements of fiction and of narrative strategies, and articulating our analyses; being honest about our own responses and feeling responsible for articulating them as clearly and convincingly as possible; taking our opinions seriously but listening with attention and an open mind to the judgments and reasoning of other readers. It requires as well some examination and knowledge of ourselves, of what in ourselves conditions our responses to fiction, and a willingness to look at what underlies our judgments and how we might learn and grow. Assessing the value of a story is difficult and a firm evaluation elusive in part because it means examining more than words on a page, it means examining so many ideas, beliefs, and feelings we take for granted. It means examining and, to a degree, evaluating our outer world and inner selves.

∨　∨　∨

Reading More Fiction

HENRY JAMES

The Real Thing

I

When the porter's wife, who used to answer the house-bell, announced "A gentleman and a lady, sir" I had, as I often had in those days—the wish being father to the thought—an immediate vision of sitters. Sitters my visitors in this case proved to be; but not in the sense I should have preferred. There was nothing at first however to indicate that they mightn't have come for a portrait. The gentleman, a man of fifty, very high and very straight, with a moustache slightly grizzled and a dark grey walking-coat admirably fitted, both of which I noted professionally—I don't mean as a barber or yet as a tailor—would have struck me as a celebrity if celebrities often were striking. It was a truth of which I had for some time been conscious that a figure with a good deal of frontage was, as one might say, almost never a public institution. A glance at the lady helped to remind me of this paradoxical law: she also looked too distinguished to be a "personality." Moreover one would scarcely come across two variations together.

Neither of the pair immediately spoke—they only prolonged the preliminary gaze suggesting that each wished to give the other a chance. They were visibly shy; they stood there letting me take them in—which, as I afterwards perceived, was the most practical thing they could have done. In this way their embarrassment served their cause. I had seen people painfully reluctant to mention that they desired anything so gross as to be represented on canvas; but the scruples of my new friends appeared almost insurmountable. Yet the gentleman might have said "I should like a portrait of my wife," and the lady might have said "I should like a portrait of my husband." Perhaps they weren't husband and wife—this naturally would make the matter more delicate. Perhaps they wished

623

to be done together—in which case they ought to have brought a third person to break the news.

"We come from Mr. Rivet," the lady finally said with a dim smile that had the effect of a moist sponge passed over a "sunk"[1] piece of painting, as well as of a vague allusion to vanished beauty. She was as tall and straight, in her degree, as her companion, and with ten years less to carry. She looked as sad as a woman could look whose face was not charged with expression; that is her tinted oval mask showed waste as an exposed surface shows friction. The hand of time had played over her freely, but to an effect of elimination. She was slim and stiff, and so well-dressed, in dark blue cloth, with lappets and pockets and buttons, that it was clear she employed the same tailor as her husband. The couple had an indefinable air of prosperous thrift—they evidently got a good deal of luxury for their money. If I was to be one of their luxuries it would behove me to consider my terms.

"Ah, Claude Rivet recommended me?" I echoed; and I added that it was very kind of him, though I could reflect that, as he only painted landscape, this wasn't a sacrifice.

5   The lady looked very hard at the gentleman, and the gentleman looked round the room. Then staring at the floor a moment and stroking his moustache, he rested his pleasant eyes on me with the remark: "He said you were the right one."

"I try to be, when people want to sit."

"Yes, we should like to," said the lady anxiously.

"Do you mean together?"

My visitors exchanged a glance. "If you could do anything with *me* I suppose it would be double," the gentleman stammered.

10   "Oh yes, there's naturally a higher charge for two figures than for one."

"We should like to make it pay," the husband confessed.

"That's very good of you," I returned, appreciating so unwonted a sympathy—for I supposed he meant pay the artist.

A sense of strangeness seemed to draw on the lady.

"We mean for the illustrations—Mr. Rivet said you might put one in."

15   "Put in—an illustration?" I was equally confused.

"Sketch her off, you know," said the gentleman, colouring.

It was only then that I understood the service Claude Rivet had rendered me; he had told them how I worked in black-and-white, for magazines, for story-books, for sketches of contemporary life, and consequently had copious employ-ment for models. These things were true, but it was not less true—I may confess it now; whether because the aspiration was to lead to everything or to nothing I leave the reader to guess—that I couldn't get the honours, to say nothing of the emoluments, of a great painter of portraits out of my head. My "illustrations" were my pot-boilers; I looked to a different branch of art—far and away the most interesting it had always seemed to me—to perpetuate my fame. There was no

1. When colors lose their brilliance after they have dried on the canvas, they have "sunk in."

shame in looking to it also to make my fortune; but that fortune was by so much further from being made from the moment my visitors wished to be "done" for nothing. I was disappointed; for in the pictorial sense I had immediately *seen* them. I had seized their type—I had already settled what I would do with it. Something that wouldn't absolutely have pleased them, I afterwards reflected.

"Ah you're—you're—a—?" I began as soon as I had mastered my surprise. I couldn't bring out the dingy word "models": it seemed so little to fit the case.

"We haven't had much practice," said the lady.

"We've got to *do* something, and we've thought that an artist in your line might perhaps make something of us," her husband threw off. He further mentioned that they didn't know many artists and that they had gone first, on the off-chance—he painted views of course, but sometimes put in figures; perhaps I remembered—to Mr. Rivet, whom they had met a few years before at a place in Norfolk where he was sketching.

"We used to sketch a little ourselves," the lady hinted.

"It's very awkward, but we absolutely *must* do something," her husband went on.

"Of course we're not so *very* young," she admitted with a wan smile.

With the remark that I might as well know something more about them the husband had handed me a card extracted from a neat new pocket-book—their appurtenances were all of the freshest—and inscribed with the words "Major Monarch." Impressive as these words were they didn't carry my knowledge much further; but my visitor presently added: "I've left the army and we've had the misfortune to lose our money. In fact our means are dreadfully small."

"It's awfully trying—a regular strain," said Mrs. Monarch.

They evidently wished to be discreet—to take care not to swagger because they were gentlefolk. I felt them willing to recognise this as something of a drawback, at the same time that I guessed at an underlying sense—their consolation in adversity—that they *had* their points. They certainly had; but these advantages struck me as preponderantly social; such for instance as would help to make a drawing-room look well. However, a drawing-room was always, or ought to be, a picture.

In consequence of his wife's allusion to their age Major Monarch observed: "Naturally it's more for the figure that we thought of going in. We can still hold ourselves up." On the instant I saw that the figure was indeed their strong point. His "naturally" didn't sound vain, but it lighted up the question. "*She* has the best one," he continued, nodding at his wife with a pleasant after-dinner absence of circumlocution. I could only reply, as if we were in fact sitting over our wine, that this didn't prevent his own from being very good; which led him in turn to make answer: "We thought that if you ever have to do people like us we might be something like it. *She* particularly—for a lady in a book, you know."

I was so amused by them that, to get more of it, I did my best to take their point of view; and though it was an embarrassment to find myself appraising physically, as if they were animals on hire or useful blacks, a pair whom I should have expected to meet only in one of the relations in which criticism is tacit, I looked at Mrs. Monarch judicially enough to be able to exclaim after a moment with conviction: "Oh yes, a lady in a book!" She was singularly like a bad illustration.

"We'll stand up, if you like," said the Major; and he raised himself before me with a really grand air.

I could take his measure at a glance—he was six feet two and a perfect gentleman. It would have paid any club in process of formation and in want of a stamp to engage him at a salary to stand in the principal window. What struck me at once was that in coming to me they had rather missed their vocation; they could surely have been turned to better account for advertising purposes. I couldn't of course see the thing in detail, but I could see them make somebody's fortune—I don't mean their own. There was something in them for a waistcoat-maker, an hotel-keeper or a soap-vendor. I could imagine "We always use it" pinned on their bosoms with the greatest effect; I had a vision of the brilliancy with which they would launch a table d'hôte.

Mrs. Monarch sat still, not from pride but from shyness, and presently her husband said to her; "Get up, my dear, and show how smart you are." She obeyed, but she had no need to get up to show it. She walked to the end of the studio and then came back blushing, her fluttered eyes on the partner of her appeal. I was reminded of an incident I had accidentally had a glimpse of in Paris being with a friend there, a dramatist about to produce a play, when an actress came to him to ask to be entrusted with a part. She went through her paces before him, walked up and down as Mrs. Monarch was doing. Mrs. Monarch did it quite as well, but I abstained from applauding. It was very odd to see such people apply for such poor pay. She looked as if she had ten thousand a year. Her husband had used the word that described her: she was in the London current jargon essentially and typically "smart." Her figure was, in the same order of ideas, conspicuously and irreproachably "good." For a woman of her age her waist was surprisingly small; her elbow moreover had the orthodox crook. She held her head at the conventional angle, but why did she come to *me*? She ought to have tried on jackets at a big shop. I feared my visitors were not only destitute but "artistic"—which would be a great complication. When she sat down again I thanked her, observing that what a draughtsman most valued in his model was the faculty of keeping quiet.

"Oh *she* can keep quiet," said Major Monarch. Then he added jocosely: "I've always kept her quiet."

"I'm not a nasty fidget, am I?" It was going to wring tears from me, I felt, the way she hid her head, ostrich-like, in the other's broad bosom.

The owner of this expanse addressed his answer to me. "Perhaps it isn't out of place to mention—because we ought to be quite business-like, oughtn't we?—that when I married her she was known as the Beautiful Statue."

"Oh dear!" said Mrs. Monarch ruefully.

"Of course I should want a certain amount of expression," I rejoined.

"Of *course*!"—and I had never heard such unanimity.

"And then I suppose you know that you'll get awfully tired."

"Oh we *never* get tired!" they eagerly cried.

"Have you had any kind of practice?"   40

They hesitated—they looked at each other. "We've been photographed—*immensely*," said Mrs. Monarch.

"She means the fellows have asked us themselves," added the Major.

"I see—because you're so good-looking."

"I don't know what they thought, but they were always after us."

"We always got our photographs for nothing," smiled Mrs. Monarch.   45

"We might have brought some, my dear," her husband remarked.

"I'm not sure we have any left. We've given quantities away," she explained to me.

"With our autographs and that sort of thing," said the Major.

"Are they to be got in the shops?" I enquired as a harmless pleasantry.

"Oh yes, *hers*—they used to be."   50

"Not now," said Mrs. Monarch with her eyes on the floor.

II

I could fancy the "sort of thing" they put on the presentation copies of their photographs, and I was sure they wrote a beautiful hand. It was odd how quickly I was sure of everything that concerned them. If they were now so poor as to have to earn shillings and pence they could never have had much of a margin. Their good looks had been their capital, and they had good-humouredly made the most of the career that this resource marked out for them. It was in their faces, the blankness, the deep intellectual repose of the twenty years of country-house visiting that had given them pleasant intonations. I could see the sunny drawing-rooms, sprinkled with periodicals she didn't read, in which Mrs. Monarch had continuously sat; I could see the wet shrubberies in which she had walked, equipped to admiration for either exercise. I could see the rich covers[2] the Major had helped to shoot and the wonderful garments in which, late at night, he repaired to the smoking-room to talk about them. I could imagine their leggings and waterproofs, their knowing tweeds and rugs, their rolls of sticks and cases of tackle and neat umbrellas; and I could evoke the exact appearance of their servants and the compact variety of their luggage on the platforms of country stations.

They gave small tips, but they were liked; they didn't do anything themselves, but they were welcome. They looked so well everywhere; they gratified the general relish for stature, complexion and "form." They knew it without fatuity or vulgarity, and they respected themselves in consequence. They weren't superficial; they were thorough and kept themselves up—it had been their line. People with such a taste for activity had to have some line. I could feel how even in a dull house they could have been counted on for the joy of life. At present something had happened—it didn't matter what, their little income had grown less, it had grown least—and they had to do something for pocket-money. Their friends could like them, I made out, without liking to support them. There was

2. Flocks of game birds.

something about them that represented credit—their clothes, their manners, their type; but if credit is a large empty pocket in which an occasional chink reverberates, the chink at least must be audible. What they wanted of me was to help to make it so. Fortunately they had no children—I soon divined that. They would also perhaps wish our relations to be kept secret: this was why it was "for the figure"— the reproduction of the face would betray them.

I liked them—I felt, quite as their friends must have done—they were so simple; and I had no objection to them if they would suit. But somehow with all their perfections I didn't easily believe in them. After all they were amateurs, and the ruling passion of my life was the detestation of the amateur. Combined with this was another perversity—an innate preference for the represented subject over the real one: the defect of the real one was so apt to be a lack of representation. I liked things that appeared; then one was sure. Whether they *were* or not was a subordinate and almost always a profitless question. There were other considerations, the first of which was that I already had two or three recruits in use, notably a young person with big feet, in alpaca, from Kilburn, who for a couple of years had come to me regularly for my illustrations and with whom I was still—perhaps ignobly—satisfied. I frankly explained to my visitors how the case stood, but they had taken more precautions than I supposed. They had reasoned out their opportunity, for Claude Rivet had told them of the projected *édition de luxe* of one of the writers of our day—the rarest of the novelists—who, long neglected by the multitudinous vulgar and dearly prized by the attentive (need I mention Philip Vincent?) had had the happy fortune of seeing, late in life, the dawn and then the full light of a higher criticism; an estimate in which on the part of the public there was something really of expiation. The edition preparing, planned by a publisher of taste, was practically an act of high reparation; the wood-cuts with which it was to be enriched were the homage of English art to one of the most independent representatives of English letters. Major and Mrs. Monarch confessed to me they had hoped I might be able to work *them* into my branch of the enterprise. They knew I was to do the first of the books, "Rutland Ramsay," but I had to make clear to them that my participation in the rest of the affair—this first book was to be a test—must depend on the satisfaction I should give. If this should be limited my employers would drop me with scarce common forms. It was therefore a crisis for me, and naturally I was making special preparations, looking about for new people, should they be necessary, and securing the best types. I admitted however that I should like to settle down to two or three good models who would do for everything.

55   "Should we have often to—a—put on special clothes?" Mrs. Monarch timidly demanded.

"Dear yes—that's half the business."

"And should we be expected to supply our own costumes?"

"Oh no; I've got a lot of things. A painter's models put on—or put off— anything he likes."

"And you mean—a—the same?"

60   "The same?"

Mrs. Monarch looked at her husband again.

"Oh she was just wondering," he explained, "if the costumes are in *general* use." I had to confess that they were, and I mentioned further that some of them—I had a lot of genuine greasy last-century things—had served their time, a hundred years ago, on living world-stained men and women; on figures not perhaps so far removed, in that vanished world, from *their* type, the Monarchs', *quoi!*[3] of a breeched and bewigged age. "We'll put on anything that *fits*," said the Major.

"Oh I arrange that—they fit in the pictures."

"I'm afraid I should do better for the modern books. I'd come as you like," said Mrs. Monarch.

"She has got a lot of clothes at home: they might do for contemporary life," her husband continued.   65

"Oh I can fancy scenes in which you'd be quite natural." And indeed I could see the slipshod rearrangements of stale properties—the stories I tried to produce pictures for without the exasperation of reading them—whose sandy tracts the good lady might help to people. But I had to return to the fact that for this sort of work—the daily mechanical grind—I was already equipped: the people I was working with were fully adequate.

"We only thought we might be more like *some* characters," said Mrs. Monarch mildly, getting up.

Her husband also rose; he stood looking at me with a dim wistfulness that was touching in so fine a man.

"Wouldn't it be rather a pull sometimes to have—a—to have—?" He hung fire; he wanted me to help him by phrasing what he meant. But I couldn't—I didn't know. So he brought it out awkwardly: "The *real* thing; a gentleman, you know, or a lady." I was quite ready to give a general assent—I admitted that there was a great deal in that. This encouraged Major Monarch to say, following up his appeal with an unacted gulp: "It's awfully hard—we've tried everything." The gulp was communicative; it proved too much for his wife. Before I knew it Mrs. Monarch had dropped again upon a divan and burst into tears. Her husband sat down beside her, holding one of her hands; whereupon she quickly dried her eyes with the other, while I felt embarrassed as she looked up at me. "There isn't a confounded job I haven't applied for—waited for—prayed for. You can fancy we'd be pretty bad first. Secretaryships and that sort of thing? You might as well ask for a peerage. I'd be *anything*—I'm strong; a messenger or a coalheaver. I'd put on a gold-laced cap and open carriage-doors in front of the haberdasher's; I'd hang about a station to carry portmanteaux; I'd be a postman. But they won't *look* at you; there are thousands as good as yourself already on the ground. *Gentlemen*, poor beggars, who've drunk their wine, who've kept their hunters!"

I was as reassuring as I knew how to be, and my visitors were presently on their feet again while, for the experiment, we agreed on an hour. We were discussing it when the door opened and Miss Churm came in with a wet umbrella. Miss Churm had to take the omnibus to Maida Vale and then walk   70

3. Whatever.

half a mile. She looked a trifle blowsy and slightly splashed. I scarcely ever saw her come in without thinking fresh how odd it was that, being so little in herself, she should yet be so much in others. She was a meagre little Miss Churm, but was such an ample heroine of romance. She was only a freckled cockney, but she could represent everything, from a fine lady to a shepherdess; she had the faculty as she might have had a fine voice or long hair. She couldn't spell and she loved beer, but she had two or three "points," and practice, and a knack, and mother-wit, and a whimsical sensibility, and a love of the theatre, and seven sisters, and not an ounce of respect, especially for the *h*.[4] The first thing my visitors saw was that her umbrella was wet, and in their spotless perfection they visibly winced at it. The rain had come on since their arrival.

"I'm all in a soak; there *was* a mess of people in the 'bus. I wish you lived near a stytion," said Miss Churm. I requested her to get ready as quickly as possible, and she passed into the room in which she always changed her dress. But before going out she asked me what she was to get into this time.

"It's the Russian princess, don't you know?" I answered; "the one with the 'golden eyes,' in black velvet, for the long thing in the *Cheapside*."

"Golden eyes? I *say!*" cried Miss Churm, while my companions watched her with intensity as she withdrew. She always arranged herself, when she was late, before I could turn around; and I kept my visitors a little on purpose, so that they might get an idea, from seeing her, what would be expected of themselves. I mentioned that she was quite my notion of an excellent model—she was really very clever.

"Do you think she looks like a Russian princess?" Major Monarch asked with lurking alarm.

75 "When I make her, yes."

"Oh if you have to *make* her—!" he reasoned, not without point.

"That's the most you can ask. There are so many who are not makeable."

"Well now, *here's* a lady"—and with a persuasive smile he passed his arm into his wife's—"who's already made!"

"Oh I'm not a Russian princess," Mrs. Monarch protested a little coldly. I could see she had known some and didn't like them. There at once was a complication of a kind I never had to fear with Miss Churm.

80 This young lady came back in black velvet—the gown was rather rusty and very low on her lean shoulders—and with a Japanese fan in her red hands. I reminded her that in the scene I was doing she had to look over some one's head. "I forget whose it is; but it doesn't matter. Just look over a head."

"I'd rather look over a stove," said Miss Churm; and she took her station near the fire. She fell into position, settled herself into a tall attitude, gave a certain backward inclination to her head and a certain forward droop to her fan, and looked, at least to my prejudiced sense, distinguished and charming, foreign and dangerous. We left her looking so while I went downstairs with Major and Mrs. Monarch.

"I believe I could come about as near it as that," said Mrs. Monarch.

4. Working-class Londoners, especially in the East End (cockneys), drop *h*'s 'orribly.

"Oh, you think she's shabby, but you must allow for the alchemy of art."

However, they went off with an evident increase of comfort founded on their demonstrable advantage in being the real thing. I could fancy them shuddering over Miss Churm. She was very droll about them when I went back, for I told her what they wanted.

"Well, if *she* can sit I'll tyke to bookkeeping," said my model.   85

"She's very ladylike," I replied as an innocent form of aggravation.

"So much the worse for *you*. That means she can't turn round."

"She'll do for the fashionable novels."

"Oh yes, she'll *do* for them!" my model humorously declared. "Ain't they bad enough without her?" I had often sociably denounced them to Miss Churm.

III

It was for the elucidation of a mystery in one of these works that I first tried   90
Mrs. Monarch. Her husband came with her, to be useful if necessary—it was sufficiently clear that as a general thing he would prefer to come with her. At first I wondered if this were for "propriety's" sake—if he were going to be jealous and meddling. The idea was too tiresome, and if it had been confirmed it would speedily have brought our acquaintance to a close. But I soon saw there was nothing in it and that if he accompanied Mrs. Monarch it was—in addition to the chance of being wanted—simply because he had nothing else to do. When they were separate his occupation was gone and they never *had* been separate. I judged rightly that in their awkward situation their close union was their main comfort and that this union had no weak spot. It was a real marriage, an encouragement to the hesitating, a nut for pessimists to crack. Their address was humble—I remember afterwards thinking it had been the only thing about them that was really professional—and I could fancy the lamentable lodgings in which the Major would have been left alone. He could sit there more or less grimly with his wife—he couldn't sit there anyhow without her.

He had too much tact to try and make himself agreeable when he couldn't be useful; so when I was too absorbed in my work to talk he simply sat and waited. But I liked to hear him talk—it made my work, when not interrupting it, less mechanical, less special. To listen to him was to combine the excitement of going out with the economy of staying at home. There was only one hindrance—that I seemed not to know any of the people this brilliant couple had known. I think he wondered extremely, during the term of our intercourse, whom the deuce I *did* know. He hadn't a stray sixpence of an idea to fumble for, so we didn't spin it very fine; we confined ourselves to questions of leather and even of liquor—saddlers and breeches-makers and how to get excellent claret cheap—and matters like "good trains" and the habits of small game. His lore on these last subjects was astonishing—he managed to interweave the station-master with the ornithologist. When he couldn't talk about greater things he could talk cheerfully about smaller, and since I couldn't accompany him into reminiscences of the fashionable world he could lower the conversation without a visible effort to my level.

So earnest a desire to please was touching in a man who could so easily have knocked one down. He looked after the fire and had an opinion on the draught of the stove without my asking him, and I could see that he thought many of my arrangements not half knowing. I remember telling him that if I were only rich I'd offer him a salary to come and teach me how to live. Sometimes he gave a random sigh of which the essence might have been: "Give me even such a bare old barrack as *this*, and I'd do something with it!" When I wanted to use him he came alone; which was an illustration of the superior courage of women. His wife could bear her solitary second floor, and she was in general more discreet; showing by various small reserves that she was alive to the propriety of keeping our relations markedly professional—not letting them slide into sociability. She wished it to remain clear that she and the Major were employed, not cultivated, and if she approved of me as a superior, who could be kept in his place, she never thought me quite good enough for an equal.

She sat with great intensity, giving the whole of her mind to it, and was capable of remaining for an hour almost as motionless as before a photographer's lens. I could see she had been photographed often, but somehow the very habit that made her good for that purpose unfitted her for mine. At first I was extremely pleased with her ladylike air, and it was a satisfaction, on coming to follow her lines, to see how good they were and how far they could lead the pencil. But after a little skirmishing I began to find her too insurmountably stiff; do what I would with it my drawing looked like a photograph or a copy of a photograph. Her figure had no variety of expression—she herself had no sense of variety. You may say that this was my business and was only a question of placing her. Yet I placed her in every conceivable position and she managed to obliterate their differences. She was always a lady certainly, and into the bargain was always the same lady. She was the real thing, but always the same thing. There were moments when I rather writhed under the serenity of her confidence that she *was* the real thing. All her dealings with me and all her husband's were an implication that this was lucky for *me*. Meanwhile I found myself trying to invent types that approached her own, instead of making her own transform itself—in the clever way that was not impossible for instance to poor Miss Churm. Arrange as I would and take the precautions I would, she always came out, in my pictures, too tall—landing me in the dilemma of having represented a fascinating woman as seven feet high, which (out of respect perhaps to my own very much scantier inches) was far from my idea of such personage.

The case was worse with the Major—nothing I could do would keep *him* down, so that he became useful only for representation of brawny giants. I adored variety and range, I cherished human accidents, the illustrative note; I wanted to characterise closely, and the thing in the world I most hated was the danger of being ridden by a type. I had quarrelled with some of my friends about it; I had parted company with them for maintaining that one *had* to be, and that if the type was beautiful—witness Raphael and Leonardo[5]—the servitude was

---

5. Raffaello Sanzio (1483–1520), Leonardo da Vinci (1452–1519), famous Italian Renaissance painters. Leonardo, of course, was also an inventor, military engineer, architect, sculptor, anatomist, etc.

only a gain. I was neither Leonardo nor Raphael—I might only be a presumptuous young modern searcher; but I held that everything was to be sacrificed sooner than character. When they claimed that the obsessional form could easily *be* character I retorted, perhaps superficially, "Whose?" It couldn't be everybody's—it might end in being nobody's.

After I had drawn Mrs. Monarch a dozen times I felt surer even than before   95
that the value of such a model as Miss Churm resided precisely in the fact that she had no positive stamp, combined of course with the other fact that what she did have was a curious and inexplicable talent for imitation. Her usual appearance was like a curtain which she could draw up at request for a capital performance. This performance was simply suggestive; but it was a word to the wise— it was vivid and pretty. Sometimes even I thought it, though she was plain herself, too insipidly pretty; I made it a reproach to her that the figures drawn from her were monotonously (*bêtement*,[6] as we used to say) graceful. Nothing made her more angry: it was so much of her pride to feel she could sit for characters that had nothing in common with each other. She would accuse me at such moments of taking away her "reputytion."

It suffered a certain shrinkage, this queer quantity, from the repeated visits of my new friends. Miss Churm was greatly in demand, never in want of employment, so I had no scruple in putting her off occasionally, to try them more at my ease. It was certainly amusing at first to do the real thing—it was amusing to do Major Monarch's trousers. They *were* the real thing, even if he did come out colossal. It was amusing to do his wife's back hair—it was so mathematically neat—and the particular "smart" tension of her tight stays. She lent herself especially to positions in which the face was somewhat averted or blurred; she abounded in ladylike back views and *profils perdus*.[7] When she stood erect she took naturally one of the attitudes in which court-painters represent queens and princesses; so that I found myself wondering whether, to draw out this accomplishment, I couldn't get the editor of the *Cheapside* to publish a really royal romance, "A Tale of Buckingham Palace." Sometimes however the real thing and the make-believe came into contact; by which I mean that Miss Churm, keeping an appointment or coming to make one on days when I had much work in hand, encountered her invidious rivals. The encounter was not on their part, for they noticed her no more than if she had been the housemaid; not from intentional loftiness, but simply because as yet, professionally, they didn't know how to fraternise, as I could imagine they would have liked—or at least that the Major would. They couldn't talk about the omnibus—they always walked; and they didn't know what else to try—she wasn't interested in good trains or cheap claret. Besides, they must have felt—in the air—that she was amused at them, secretly derisive of their ever knowing how. She wasn't a person to conceal the limits of her faith if she had had a chance to show them. On the other hand Mrs. Monarch didn't think her tidy; for why else did she take pains to say to me—it was going out of the way, for Mrs. Monarch—that she didn't like dirty women?

6. Foolishly.   7. Incomplete profile, showing more of the back of the head and less of the face.

One day when my young lady happened to be present with my other sitters—she even dropped in, when it was convenient, for a chat—I asked her to be so good as to lend a hand in getting tea, a service with which she was familiar and which was one of a class that, living as I did in a small way, with slender domestic resources, I often appealed to my models to render. They liked to lay hands on my property, to break the sitting, and sometimes the china—it made them feel Bohemian. The next time I saw Miss Churm after this incident she surprised me greatly by making a scene about it—she accused me of having wished to humiliate her. She hadn't resented the outrage at the time, but had seemed obliging and amused, enjoying the comedy of asking Mrs. Monarch, who sat vague and silent, whether she would have cream and sugar, and putting an exaggerated simper into the question. She had tried intonations—as if she too wished to pass for the real thing—till I was afraid my other visitors would take offence.

Oh they were determined not to do this, and their touching patience was the measure of their great need. They would sit by the hour, uncomplaining, till I was ready to use them; they would come back on the chance of being wanted and would walk away cheerfully if it failed. I used to go to the door with them to see in what magnificent order they retreated. I tried to find other employment for them—I introduced them to several artists. But they didn't "take," for reasons I could appreciate, and I became rather anxiously aware that after such disappointments they fell back upon me with a heavier weight. They did me the honor to think me most *their* form. They weren't romantic enough for the painters, and in those days there were few serious workers in black-and-white. Besides, they had an eye to the great job I had mentioned to them—they had secretly set their hearts on supplying the right essence for my pictorial vindication of our fine novelist. They knew that for this undertaking I should want no costume-effects, none of the frippery of past ages—that it was a case in which everything would be contemporary and satirical and presumably genteel. If I could work them into it their future would be assured, for the labour would of course be long and the occupation steady.

One day Mrs. Monarch came without her husband—she explained his absence by his having had to go to the City.[8] While she sat there in her usual relaxed majesty there came at the door a knock which I immediately recognised as the subdued appeal of a model out of work. It was followed by the entrance of a young man whom I at once saw to be a foreigner and who proved in fact an Italian acquainted with no English word but my name, which he uttered in a way that made it seem to include all others. I hadn't then visited his country, nor was I proficient in his tongue; but as he was not so meanly constituted—what Italian is?—as to depend only on that member for expression he conveyed to me, in familiar but graceful mimicry, that he was in search of exactly the employment in which the lady before me was engaged. I was not struck with him at first, and while I continued to draw I dropped few signs of interest or encouragement. He stood his ground however—not importunately, but with a

8. Financial and legal center of London.

dumb dog-like fidelity in his eyes that amounted to innocent impudence, the manner of a devoted servant—he might have been in the house for years—unjustly suspected. Suddenly it struck me that this very attitude and expression made a picture; whereupon I told him to sit down and wait till I should be free. There was another picture in the way he obeyed me, and I observed as I worked that there were others still in the way he looked wonderingly, with his head thrown back, about the high studio. He might have been crossing himself in Saint Peter's. Before I finished I said to myself "The fellow's a bankrupt orange-monger, but a treasure."

When Mrs. Monarch withdrew he passed across the room like a flash to open the door for her, standing there with the rapt pure gaze of the young Dante spellbound by the young Beatrice.[9] As I never insisted, in such situations, on the blankness of the British domestic, I reflected that he had the making of a servant—and I needed one, but couldn't pay him to be only that—as well as of a model; in short I resolved to adopt my bright adventurer if he would agree to officiate in the double capacity. He jumped at my offer, and in the event my rashness—for I had really known nothing about him—wasn't brought home to me. He proved a sympathetic though a desultory ministrant, and had in a won-derful degree the *sentiment de la pose*.[1] It was uncultivated, instinctive, a part of the happy instinct that had guided him to my door and helped him to spell out my name on the card nailed to it. He had had no other introduction to me than a guess, from the shape of my high north window, seen outside, that my place was a studio and that as a studio it would contain an artist. He had wandered to England in search of fortune, like other itinerants, and had embarked, with a partner and a small green hand-cart, on the sale of penny ices. The ices had melted away and the partner had dissolved in their train. My young man wore tight yellow trousers with reddish stripes and his name was Oronte. He was sallow but fair, and when I put him into some old clothes of my own he looked like an Englishman. He was as good as Miss Churm, who could look, when requested, like an Italian.

100

IV

I thought Mrs. Monarch's face slightly convulsed when, on her coming back with her husband, she found Oronte installed. It was strange to have to recognise in a scrap of a lazzarone[2] a competitor to her magnificent Major. It was she who scented danger first, for the Major was anecdotically unconscious. But Oronte gave us tea, with a hundred eager confusions—he had never been concerned in so queer a process—and I think she thought better of me for having at last an "establishment." They saw a couple of drawings that I had made of the establish-ment, and Mrs. Monarch hinted that it never would have struck her he had sat for them. "Now the drawings you make from *us*, they look exactly like us," she

---

9. Dante Alighieri (1265–1321), Italian poet, author of *The Divine Comedy*, was inspired for life poetically and spiritually by Beatrice Portinari, whom he first saw when they were children and saw only infrequently thereafter.   1. Instinct for striking poses.   2. Street-person.

reminded me, smiling in triumph; and I recognized that this was indeed just their defect. When I drew the Monarchs I couldn't anyhow get away from them—get into the character I wanted to represent; and I hadn't the least desire my model should be discoverable in my picture. Miss Churm never was, and Mrs. Monarch thought I hid her, very properly, because she was vulgar; whereas if she was lost it was only as the dead who go to heaven are lost—in the gain of an angel the more.

By this time I had got a certain start with "Rutland Ramsay," the first novel in the great projected series; that is I had produced a dozen drawings, several with the help of the Major and his wife, and I had sent them in for approval. My understanding with the publishers, as I have already hinted, had been that I was to be left to do my work, in this particular case, as I liked, with the whole book committed to me; but my connexion with the rest of the series was only contingent. There were moments when, frankly, it *was* a comfort to have the real thing under one's hand; for there were characters in "Rutland Ramsay" that were very much like it. There were people presumably as erect as the Major and women of as good a fashion as Mrs. Monarch. There was a great deal of country-house life—treated, it is true, in a fine fanciful ironical generalised way—and there was a considerable implication of knickerbockers and kilts. There were certain things I had to settle at the outset; such things for instance as the exact appearance of the hero and the particular bloom and figure of the heroine. The author of course gave me a lead, but there was a margin for interpretation. I took the Monarchs into my confidence, I told them frankly what I was about, I mentioned my embarrassments and alternatives. "Oh take *him!*" Mrs. Monarch murmured sweetly, looking at her husband; and "What could you want better than my wife?" the Major enquired with the comfortable candour that now prevailed between us.

I wasn't obliged to answer these remarks—I was only obliged to place my sitters. I wasn't easy in mind, and I postponed a little timidly perhaps the solving of my question. The book was a large canvas, the other figures were numerous, and I worked off at first some of the episodes in which the hero and the heroine were not concerned. When once I had set *them* up I should have to stick to them—I couldn't make my young man seven feet high in one place and five feet nine in another. I inclined on the whole to the latter measurement, though the Major more than once reminded me that *he* looked about as young as any one. It was indeed quite possible to arrange him, for the figure, so that it would have been difficult to detect his age. After the spontaneous Oronte had been with me a month, and after I had given him to understand several times over that his native exuberance would presently constitute an insurmountable barrier to our further intercourse, I waked to a sense of his heroic capacity. He was only five feet seven, but the remaining inches were latent. I tried him almost secretly at first, for I was really rather afraid of the judgment my other models would pass on such a choice. If they regarded Miss Churm as little better than a snare what would they think of the representation by a person so little the real thing as an Italian street-vendor of a protagonist formed by a public school?

If I went a little in fear of them it wasn't because they bullied me, because they had got an oppressive foothold, but because in their really pathetic decorum and mysteriously permanent newness they counted on me so intensely. I was therefore very glad when Jack Hawley came home: he was always of such good counsel. He painted badly himself, but there was no one like him for putting his finger on the place. He had been absent from England for a year; he had been somewhere—I don't remember where—to get a fresh eye. I was in a good deal of dread of any such organ, but we were old friends; he had been away for months and a sense of emptiness was creeping into my life. I hadn't dodged a missile for a year.

He came back with a fresh eye, but with the same old black velvet blouse, and the first evening he spent in my studio we smoked cigarettes till the small hours. He had done no work himself, he had only got the eye; so the field was clear for the production of my little things. He wanted to see what I had produced for the *Cheapside*, but he was disappointed in the exhibition. That at least seemed the meaning of two or three comprehensive groans which, as he lounged on my big divan, his leg folded under him, looking at my latest drawings, issued from his lips with the smoke of the cigarette.

"What's the matter with you?" I asked.

"What's the matter with *you?*"

"Nothing save that I'm mystified."

"You are indeed. You're quite off the hinge. What's the meaning of this new fad?" And he tossed me, with visible irreverence, a drawing in which I happened to have depicted both my elegant models. I asked if he didn't think it good, and he replied that it struck him as execrable, given the sort of thing I had always represented myself to him as wishing to arrive at; but I let that pass—I was so anxious to see exactly what he meant. The two figures in the picture looked colossal, but I supposed this was *not* what he meant, inasmuch as, for aught he knew the contrary, I might have been trying for some such effect. I maintained that I was working exactly in the same way as when he last had done me the honour to tell me I might do something some day. "Well, there's a screw loose somewhere," he answered; "wait a bit and I'll discover it." I depended upon him to do so: where else was the fresh eye? But he produced at last nothing more luminous than "I don't know—I don't like your types." This was lame for a critic who had never consented to discuss with me anything but the question of execution, the direction of strokes and the mystery of values.

"In the drawings you've been looking at I think my types are very handsome."

"Oh they won't do!"

"I've been working with new models."

"I see you have. *They* won't do."

"Are you very sure of that?"

"Absolutely—they're stupid."

"You mean I am—for I ought to get round that."

"You *can't*—with such people. Who are they?"

105

110

115

I told him, so far as was necessary, and he concluded heartlessly: "Ce sont des gens qu'il faut mettre à la porte."[3]

"You've never seen them; they're awfully good"—I flew to their defence.

120

"Not seen them? Why all this recent work of yours drops to pieces with them. It's all I want to see of them."

"No one else has said anything against it—the *Cheapside* people are pleased."

"Everyone else is an ass, and the *Cheapside* people the biggest asses of all. Come, don't pretend at this time of day to have pretty illusions about the public, especially about publishers and editors. It's not for *such* animals you work—it's for those who know, *coloro che sanno;*[4] so keep straight for *me* if you can't keep straight for yourself. There was a certain sort of thing you used to try for—and a very good thing it was. But this twaddle isn't *in* it." When I talked with Hawley later about "Rutland Ramsay" and its possible successors he declared that I must get back into my boat again or I should go to the bottom. His voice in short was the voice of warning.

I noted the warning, but I didn't turn my friends out of doors. They bored me a good deal; but the very fact that they bored me admonished me not to sacrifice them—if there was anything to be done with them—simply to irritation. As I look back at this phase they seem to me to have pervaded my life not a little. I have a vision of them as most of the time in my studio, seated against the wall on an old velvet bench to be out of the way, and resembling the while a pair of patient courtiers in a royal ante-chamber. I'm convinced that during the coldest weeks of the winter they held their ground because it saved them fire. Their newness was losing its gloss, and it was impossible not to feel them objects of charity. Whenever Miss Churm arrived they went away, and after I was fairly launched in "Rutland Ramsay" Miss Churm arrived pretty often. They managed to express to me tacitly that they supposed I wanted her for the low life of the book, and I let them suppose it, since they had attempted to study the work—it was lying about the studio—without discovering that it dealt only with the highest circles. They had dipped into the most brilliant of our novelists without deciphering many passages. I still took an hour from them, now and again, in spite of Jack Hawley's warning: it would be time enough to dismiss them, if dismissal should be necessary, when the rigour of the season was over. Hawley had made their acquaintance—he had met them at my fireside—and thought them a ridiculous pair. Learning that he was a painter they tried to approach him, to show him too that they were the real thing; but he looked at them, across the big room, as if they were miles away: they were a compendium of everything he most objected to in the social system of his country. Such people as that, all convention and patent-leather, with ejaculations that stopped conversation, had no business in a studio. A studio was a place to learn to see, and how could you see through a pair of feather-beds?

---

3. "That kind of person should be shown the door."   4. Dante, *The Divine Comedy*, "The Inferno," 4:131: actually, *color che sanno*—"those who know."

The main inconvenience I suffered at their hands was that at first I was shy of letting it break upon them that my artful little servant had begun to sit to me for "Rutland Ramsay." They knew I had been odd enough—they were prepared by this time to allow oddity to artists—to pick a foreign vagabond out of the streets when I might have had a person with whiskers and credentials, but it was some time before they learned how high I rated his accomplishments. They found him in an attitude more than once, but they never doubted I was doing him as an organ-grinder. There were several things they never guessed, and one of them was that for a striking scene in the novel, in which a footman briefly figured, it occurred to me to make use of Major Monarch as the menial. I kept putting this off, I didn't like to ask him to don the livery—besides the difficulty of finding a livery to fit him. At last, one day late in the winter, when I was at work on the despised Oronte, who caught one's idea on the wing, and was in the glow of feeling myself go very straight, they came in, the Major and his wife, with their society laugh about nothing (there was less and less to laugh at); came on like country-callers—they always reminded me of that—who have walked across the park after church and are presently persuaded to stay to luncheon. Luncheon was over, but they could stay to tea—I knew they wanted it. The fit was on me, however, and I couldn't let my ardour cool and my work wait, with the fading daylight, while my model prepared it. So I asked Mrs. Monarch if she would mind laying it out—a request which for an instant brought all the blood to her face. Her eyes were on her husband's for a second, and some mute telegraphy passed between them. Their folly was over the next instant; his cheerful shrewdness put an end to it. So far from pitying their wounded pride, I must add, I was moved to give it as complete a lesson as I could. They bustled about together and got out the cups and saucers and made the kettle boil. I know they felt as if they were waiting on my servant, and when the tea was prepared I said: "He'll have a cup, please—he's tired." Mrs. Monarch brought him one where he stood, and he took it from her, as if he had been a gentleman at a party squeezing a crush-hat with an elbow.

Then it came over me that she had made a great effort for me—made it with a kind of nobleness—and that I owed her a compensation. Each time I saw her after this I wondered what the compensation could be. I couldn't go on doing the wrong thing to oblige them. Oh it *was* the wrong thing, the stamp of the work for which they sat—Hawley was not the only person to say it now. I sent in a large number of the drawings I had made for "Rutland Ramsay," and I received a warning that was more to the point than Hawley's. The artistic adviser of the house for which I was working was of opinion that many of my illustrations were not what had been looked for. Most of these illustrations were the subjects in which the Monarchs had figured. Without going into the question of what *had* been looked for, I had to face the fact that at this rate I shouldn't get the other books to do. I hurled myself in despair on Miss Churm—I put her through all her paces. I not only adopted Oronte publicly as my hero, but one morning when the Major looked in to see if I didn't require him to finish a *Cheapside* figure for which he had begun to sit the week before, I told him I

125

had changed my mind—I'd do the drawing from my man. At this my visitor turned pale and stood looking at me. "Is *he* your idea of an English gentleman?" he asked.

I was disappointed, I was nervous, I wanted to get on with my work; so I replied with irritation: "Oh my dear Major—I can't be ruined for *you!*" . . .

It was a horrid speech, but he stood another moment—after which, without a word, he quitted the studio. I drew a long breath, for I said to myself that I shouldn't see him again. I hadn't told him definitely that I was in danger of having my work rejected, but I was vexed at his not having felt the catastrophe in the air, read with me the moral of our fruitless collaboration, the lesson that in the deceptive atmosphere of art even the highest respectability may fail of being plastic.

I didn't owe my friends money, but I did see them again. They reappeared together three days later, and, given all the other facts, there was something tragic in that one. It was a clear proof they could find nothing else in life to do. They had threshed the matter out in a dismal conference—they had digested the bad news that they were not in for the series. If they weren't useful to me even for the *Cheapside* their function seemed difficult to determine, and I could only judge at first that they had come, forgivingly, decorously, to take a last leave. This made me rejoice in secret that I had little leisure for a scene; for I had placed both my other models in position together and I was pegging away at a drawing from which I hoped to derive glory. It had been suggested by the passage in which Rutland Ramsay, drawing up a chair to Artemisia's piano-stool, says extraordinary things to her while she ostensibly fingers out a difficult piece of music. I had done Miss Churm at the piano before—it was an attitude in which she knew how to take on an absolutely poetic grace. I wished the two figures to "compose" together with intensity, and my little Italian had entered perfectly into my conception. The pair were vividly before me, the piano had been pulled out; it was a charming show of blended youth and murmured love, which I had only to catch and keep. My visitors stood and looked at it, and I was friendly to them over my shoulder.

They made no response, but I was used to silent company and went on with my work, only a little disconcerted—even though exhilarated by the sense that *this* was at least the ideal thing—at not having got rid of them after all. Presently I heard Mrs. Monarch's sweet voice beside or rather above me: "I wish her hair were a little better done." I looked up and she was staring with a strange fixedness at Miss Churm, whose back was turned to her. "Do you mind my just touching it?" she went on—a question which made me spring up for an instant as with the instinctive fear that she might do the young lady a harm. But she quieted me with a glance I shall never forget—I confess I should like to have been able to paint *that*—and went for a moment to my model. She spoke to her softly, laying a hand on her shoulder and bending over her; and as the girl, understanding, gratefully assented, she disposed her rough curls, with a few quick passes, in such a way as to make Miss Churm's head twice as charming. It was one of the most heroic personal services I've ever seen rendered. Then Mrs. Monarch turned away with a low sigh and, looking about her as if for something to do, stooped to the floor with a noble humility and picked up a dirty rag that had dropped out of my paint-box.

The Major meanwhile had also been looking for something to do, and, wandering to the other end of the studio, saw before him my breakfast-things neglected, unremoved. "I say, can't I be useful *here?*" he called out to me with an irrepressible quaver. I assented with a laugh that I fear was awkward, and for the next ten minutes, while I worked, I heard the light clatter of china and the tinkle of spoons and glass. Mrs. Monarch assisted her husband—they washed up my crockery, they put it away. They wandered off into my little scullery, and I afterwards found that they had cleaned my knives and that my slender stock of plate had an unprecedented surface. When it came over me, the latent eloquence of what they were doing, I confess that my drawing was blurred for a moment—the picture swam. They had accepted their failure, but they couldn't accept their fate. They had bowed their heads in bewilderment to the perverse and cruel law in virtue of which the real thing could be so much less precious than the unreal; but they didn't want to starve. If my servants were my models; then my models might be my servants. They would reverse the parts—the others would sit for the ladies and gentlemen and *they* would do the work. They would still be in the studio—it was an intense dumb appeal to me not to turn them out. "Take us on," they wanted to say—"we'll do *anything.*"

My pencil dropped from my hand; my sitting was spoiled and I got rid of my sitters, who were also evidently rather mystified and awestruck. Then, alone with the Major and his wife I had a most uncomfortable moment. He put their prayer into a single sentence: "I say, you know—just let *us* do for you, can't you?" I couldn't—it was dreadful to see them emptying my slops; but I pretended I could, to oblige them, for about a week. Then I gave them a sum of money to go away, and I never saw them again. I obtained the remaining books, but my friend Hawley repeats that Major and Mrs. Monarch did me a permanent harm, got me into false ways. If it be true I'm content to have paid the price—for the memory.

1892, 1909

CHARLOTTE PERKINS GILMAN

The Yellow Wallpaper

It is very seldom that mere ordinary people like John and myself secure ancestral halls for the summer.

A colonial mansion, a hereditary estate, I would say a haunted house, and reach the height of romantic felicity—but that would be asking too much of fate!

Still I will proudly declare that there is something queer about it.

Else, why should it be let so cheaply? And why have stood so long untenanted?

5   John laughs at me, of course, but one expects that in marriage.

John is practical in the extreme. He has no patience with faith, an intense horror of superstition, and he scoffs openly at any talk of things not to be felt and seen and put down in figures.

John is a physician, and *perhaps*—(I would not say it to a living soul, of course, but this is dead paper and a great relief to my mind—) *perhaps* that is one reason I do not get well faster.

You see he does not believe I am sick!

And what can one do?

10   If a physician of high standing, and one's own husband, assures friends and relatives that there is really nothing the matter with one but temporary nervous depression—a slight hysterical tendency—what is one to do?

My brother is also a physician, and also of high standing, and he says the same thing.

So I take phosphates or phosphites—whichever it is, and tonics, and journeys, and air, and exercise, and am absolutely forbidden to "work" until I am well again.

Personally, I disagree with their ideas.

Personally, I believe that congenial work, with excitement and change, would do me good.

15   But what is one to do?

I did write for a while in spite of them; but it *does* exhaust me a good deal—having to be so sly about it, or else meet with heavy opposition.

I sometimes fancy that in my condition if I had less opposition and more society and stimulus—but John says the very worst thing I can do is to think about my condition, and I confess it always makes me feel bad.

So I will let it alone and talk about the house.

The most beautiful place! It is quite alone, standing well back from the road, quite three miles from the village. It makes me think of English places that you read about, for there are hedges and walls and gates that lock, and lots of separate little houses for the gardeners and people.

20   There is a *delicious* garden! I never saw such a garden—large and shady, full of box-bordered paths, and lined with long grape-covered arbors with seats under them.

There were greenhouses, too, but they are all broken now.

There was some legal trouble, I believe, something about the heirs and coheirs; anyhow, the place has been empty for years.

That spoils my ghostliness, I am afraid, but I don't care—there is something strange about the house—I can feel it.

I even said so to John one moonlight evening, but he said what I felt was a *draught*, and shut the window.

25   I get unreasonably angry with John sometimes. I'm sure I never used to be so sensitive. I think it is due to this nervous condition.

But John says if I feel so, I shall neglect proper self-control; so I take pains to control myself—before him, at least, and that makes me very tired.

I don't like our room a bit. I wanted one downstairs that opened on the piazza and had roses all over the window, and such pretty old-fashioned chintz hangings! but John would not hear of it.

He said there was only one window and not room for two beds, and no near room for him if he took another.

He is very careful and loving, and hardly lets me stir without special direction.

I have a schedule prescription for each hour in the day; he takes all care   30
from me, and so I feel basely ungrateful not to value it more.

He said we came here solely on my account, that I was to have perfect rest and all the air I could get. "Your exercise depends on your strength, my dear," said he, "and your food somewhat on your appetite; but air you can absorb all the time." So we took the nursery at the top of the house.

It is a big, airy room, the whole floor nearly, with windows that look all ways, and air and sunshine galore. It was nursery first and then playroom and gymnasium, I should judge; for the windows are barred for little children, and there are rings and things in the walls.

The paint and paper look as if a boys' school had used it. It is stripped off— the paper—in great patches all around the head of my bed, about as far as I can reach, and in a great place on the other side of the room low down. I never saw a worse paper in my life.

One of those sprawling flamboyant patterns committing every artistic sin.

It is dull enough to confuse the eye in following, pronounced enough to   35
constantly irritate and provoke study, and when you follow the lame uncertain curves for a little distance they suddenly commit suicide—plunge off at outrageous angles, destroy themselves in unheard of contradictions.

The color is repellant, almost revolting; a smouldering unclean yellow, strangely faded by the slow-turning sunlight.

It is a dull yet lurid orange in some places, a sickly sulphur tint in others.

No wonder the children hated it! I should hate it myself if I had to live in this room long.

There comes John, and I must put this away,—he hates to have me write a word.

We have been here two weeks, and I haven't felt like writing before, since   40
that first day.

I am sitting by the window now, up in this atrocious nursery, and there is nothing to hinder my writing as much as I please, save lack of strength.

John is away all day, and even some nights when his cases are serious.

I am glad my case is not serious!

But these nervous troubles are dreadfully depressing.

John does not know how much I really suffer. He knows there is no *reason*   45
to suffer, and that satisfies him.

Of course it is only nervousness. It does weigh on me so not to do my duty in any way!

I mean to be such a help to John, such a real rest and comfort, and here I am a comparative burden already!

Nobody would believe what an effort it is to do what little I am able,—to dress and entertain, and order things.

It is fortunate Mary is so good with the baby. Such a dear baby!

And yet I *cannot* be with him, it makes me so nervous.

I suppose John never was nervous in his life. He laughs at me so about this wallpaper!

At first he meant to repaper the room, but afterwards he said that I was letting it get the better of me, and that nothing was worse for a nervous patient than to give way to such fancies.

He said that after the wallpaper was changed it would be the heavy bedstead, and then the barred windows, and then that gate at the head of the stairs, and so on.

"You know the place is doing you good," he said, "and really, dear, I don't care to renovate the house just for a three months' rental."

"Then do let us go downstairs," I said, "there are such pretty rooms there."

Then he took me in his arms and called me a blessed little goose, and said he would go down cellar, if I wished, and have it whitewashed into the bargain.

But he is right enough about the beds and windows and things.

It is an airy and comfortable room as any one need wish, and, of course, I would not be so silly as to make him uncomfortable just for a whim.

I'm really getting quite fond of the big room, all but that horrid paper.

Out of one window I can see the garden, those mysterious deep-shaded arbors, the riotous old-fashioned flowers, and bushes and gnarly trees.

Out of another I get a lovely view of the bay and a little private wharf belonging to the estate. There is a beautiful shaded lane that runs down there from the house. I always fancy I see people walking in these numerous paths and arbors, but John has cautioned me not to give way to fancy in the least. He says that with my imaginative power and habit of story-making, a nervous weakness like mine is sure to lead to all manner of excited fancies, and that I ought to use my will and good sense to check the tendency. So I try.

I think sometimes that if I were only well enough to write a little it would relieve the press of ideas and rest me.

But I find I get pretty tired when I try.

It is so discouraging not to have any advice and companionship about my work. When I get really well, John says we will ask Cousin Henry and Julia down for a long visit; but he says he would as soon put fireworks in my pillowcase as to let me have those stimulating people about now.

I wish I could get well faster.

But I must not think about that. This paper looks to me as if it *knew* what a vicious influence it had!

There is a recurrent spot where the pattern lolls like a broken neck and two bulbous eyes stare at you upside down.

I get positively angry with the impertinence of it and the everlastingness. Up and down and sideways they crawl, and those absurd, unblinking eyes are everywhere. There is one place where two breadths didn't match, and the eyes go all up and down the line, one a little higher than the other.

I never saw so much expression in an inanimate thing before, and we all know how much expression they have! I used to lie awake as a child and get more entertainment and terror out of blank walls and plain furniture than most children could find in a toy-store.

I remember what a kindly wink the knobs of our big, old bureau used to have, and there was one chair that always seemed like a strong friend.

I used to feel that if any of the other things looked too fierce I could always hop into that chair and be safe.

The furniture in this room is no worse than inharmonious, however, for we had to bring it all from downstairs. I suppose when this was used as a playroom they had to take the nursery things out, and no wonder! I never saw such ravages as the children have made here.

The wallpaper, as I said before, is torn off in spots, and it sticketh closer than a brother—they must have had perseverance as well as hatred.

Then the floor is scratched and gouged and splintered, the plaster itself is dug out here and there, and this great heavy bed which is all we found in the room, looks as if it had been through the wars.

But I don't mind it a bit—only the paper.

There comes John's sister. Such a dear girl as she is, and so careful of me! I must not let her find me writing.

She is a perfect and enthusiastic housekeeper, and hopes for no better profession. I verily believe she thinks it is the writing which made me sick!

But I can write when she is out, and see her a long way off from these windows.

There is one that commands the road, a lovely shaded winding road, and one that just looks off over the country. A lovely country, too, full of great elms and velvet meadows.

This wallpaper has a kind of sub-pattern in a different shade, a particularly irritating one, for you can only see it in certain lights, and not clearly then.

But in the places where it isn't faded and where the sun is just so—I can see a strange, provoking, formless sort of figure, that seems to skulk about behind that silly and conspicuous front design.

There's sister on the stairs!

Well, the Fourth of July is over! The people are all gone and I am tired out. John thought it might do me good to see a little company, so we just had mother and Nellie and the children down for a week.

Of course I didn't do a thing. Jennie sees to everything now.

But it tired me all the same.

John says if I don't pick up faster he shall send me to Weir Mitchell[1] in the fall.

But I don't want to go there at all. I had a friend who was in his hands once, and she says he is just like John and my brother, only more so!

---

1. Silas Weir Mitchell (1829–1914), American physician, novelist, and specialist in nerve disorders, popularized the "rest cure."

Besides, it is such an undertaking to go so far.

I don't feel as if it was worth while to turn my hand over for anything, and I'm getting dreadfully fretful and querulous.

90   I cry at nothing, and cry most of the time.

Of course I don't when John is here, or anybody else, but when I am alone.

And I am alone a good deal just now. John is kept in town very often by serious cases, and Jennie is good and lets me alone when I want her to.

So I walk a little in the garden or down that lovely lane, sit on the porch under the roses, and lie down up here a good deal.

I'm getting really fond of the room in spite of the wallpaper. Perhaps *because* of the wallpaper.

95   It dwells in my mind so!

I lie here on this great immovable bed—it is nailed down, I believe—and follow that pattern about by the hour. It is as good as gymnastics, I assure you. I start, we'll say, at the bottom, down in the corner over there where it has not been touched, and I determine for the thousandth time that I *will* follow that pointless pattern to some sort of conclusion.

I know a little of the principle of design, and I know this thing was not arranged on any laws of radiation, or alternation, or repetition, or symmetry, or anything else that I ever heard of.

It is repeated, of course, by the breadths, but not otherwise.

Looked at in one way each breadth stands alone, the bloated curves and flourishes—a kind of "debased Romanesque" with *delirium tremens*—go waddling up and down in isolated columns of fatuity.

100   But, on the other hand, they connect diagonally, and the sprawling outlines run off in great slanting waves of optic horror, like a lot of wallowing seaweeds in full chase.

The whole thing goes horizontally, too, at least it seems so, and I exhaust myself in trying to distinguish the order of its going in that direction.

They have used a horizontal breadth for a frieze, and that adds wonderfully to the confusion.

There is one end of the room where it is almost intact, and there, when the crosslights fade and the low sun shines directly upon it, I can almost fancy radiation after all,—the interminable grotesque seem to form around a common center and rush off in headlong plunges of equal distraction.

It makes me tired to follow it. I will take a nap I guess.

105   I don't know why I should write this.

I don't want to.

I don't feel able.

And I know John would think it absurd. But I *must* say what I feel and think in some way—it is such a relief!

But the effort is getting to be greater than the relief.

110   Half the time now I am awfully lazy, and lie down ever so much.

John says I mustn't lose my strength, and has me take cod liver oil and lots of tonics and things, to say nothing of ale and wine and rare meat.

Dear John! He loves me very dearly, and hates to have me sick. I tried to have a real earnest reasonable talk with him the other day, and tell him how I wish he would let me go and make a visit to Cousin Henry and Julia.

But he said I wasn't able to go, nor able to stand it after I got there; and I did not make out a very good case for myself, for I was crying before I had finished.

It is getting to be a great effort for me to think straight. Just this nervous weakness I suppose.

And dear John gathered me up in his arms, and just carried me upstairs and laid me on the bed, and sat by me and read to me till it tired my head.

He said I was his darling and his comfort and all he had, and that I must take care of myself for his sake, and keep well.

He says no one but myself can help me out of it, that I must use my will and self-control and not let any silly fancies run away with me.

There's one comfort, the baby is well and happy, and does not have to occupy this nursery with the horrid wallpaper.

If we had not used it, that blessed child would have! What a fortunate escape! Why, I wouldn't have a child of mine, an impressionable little thing, live in such a room for worlds.

I never thought of it before, but it is lucky that John kept me here after all, I can stand it so much easier than a baby, you see.

Of course I never mention it to them any more—I am too wise,—but I keep watch of it all the same.

There are things in that paper that nobody knows but me, or ever will.

Behind that outside pattern the dim shapes get clearer every day.

It is always the same shape, only very numerous.

And it is like a woman stooping down and creeping about behind that pattern. I don't like it a bit. I wonder—I begin to think—I wish John would take me away from here!

It is so hard to talk with John about my case, because he is so wise, and because he loves me so.

But I tried it last night.

It was moonlight. The moon shines in all around just as the sun does.

I hate to see it sometimes, it creeps so slowly, and always comes in by one window or another.

John was asleep and I hated to waken him, so I kept still and watched the moonlight on that undulating wallpaper till I felt creepy.

The faint figure behind seemed to shake the pattern, just as if she wanted to get out.

I got up softly and went to feel and see if the paper *did* move, and when I came back John was awake.

"What is it, little girl?" he said. "Don't go walking about like that—you'll get cold."

I thought it was a good time to talk, so I told him that I really was not gaining here, and that I wished he would take me away.

135 "Why, darling!" said he, "our lease will be up in three weeks, and I can't see how to leave before.

"The repairs are not done at home, and I cannot possibly leave town just now. Of course if you were in any danger, I could and would, but you really are better, dear, whether you can see it or not. I am a doctor, dear, and I know. You are gaining flesh and color, your appetite is better, I feel really much easier about you."

"I don't weigh a bit more," said I, "nor as much; and my appetite may be better in the evening when you are here, but it is worse in the morning when you are away!"

"Bless her little heart!" said he with a big hug, "she shall be as sick as she pleases! But now let's improve the shining hours by going to sleep, and talk about it in the morning!"

"And you won't go away?" I asked gloomily.

140 "Why, how can I, dear? It is only three weeks more and then we will take a nice little trip of a few days while Jennie is getting the house ready. Really dear you are better!"

"Better in body perhaps—" I began, and stopped short, for he sat up straight and looked at me with such a stern, reproachful look that I could not say another word.

"My darling," said he, "I beg of you, for my sake and for our child's sake, as well as for your own, that you will never for one instant let that idea enter your mind! There is nothing so dangerous, so fascinating, to a temperament like yours. It is a false and foolish fancy. Can you not trust me as a physician when I tell you so?"

So of course I said no more on that score, and we went to sleep before long. He thought I was asleep first, but I wasn't, and lay there for hours trying to decide whether that front pattern and the back pattern really did move together or separately.

On a pattern like this, by daylight, there is a lack of sequence, a defiance of law, that is a constant irritant to a normal mind.

145 The color is hideous enough, and unreliable enough, and infuriating enough, but the pattern is torturing.

You think you have mastered it, but just as you get well underway in following, it turns a back-somersault and there you are. It slaps you in the face, knocks you down, and tramples upon you. It is like a bad dream.

The outside pattern is a florid arabesque, reminding one of a fungus. If you can imagine a toadstool in joints, an interminable string of toadstools, budding and sprouting in endless convolutions—why, that is something like it.

That is, sometimes!

There is one marked peculiarity about this paper, a thing nobody seems to notice but myself, and that is that it changes as the light changes.

150 When the sun shoots in through the east window—I always watch for that first long, straight ray—it changes so quickly that I never can quite believe it.

That is why I watch it always.

By moonlight—the moon shines in all night when there is a moon—I wouldn't know it was the same paper.

At night in any kind of light, in twilight, candlelight, lamplight, and worst of all by moonlight, it becomes bars! The outside pattern I mean, and the woman behind it is as plain as can be.

I didn't realize for a long time what the thing was that showed behind, that dim sub-pattern, but now I am quite sure it is a woman.

By daylight she is subdued, quiet. I fancy it is the pattern that keeps her so still. It is so puzzling. It keeps me quiet by the hour.

I lie down ever so much now. John says it is good for me, and to sleep all I can.

Indeed he started the habit by making me lie down for an hour after each meal.

It is a very bad habit I am convinced, for you see I don't sleep.

And that cultivates deceit, for I don't tell them I'm awake—O no!

The fact is I am getting a little afraid of John.

He seems very queer sometimes, and even Jennie has an inexplicable look.

It strikes me occasionally, just as a scientific hypothesis,—that perhaps it is the paper!

I have watched John when he did not know I was looking, and come into the room suddenly on the most innocent excuses, and I've caught him several times *looking at the paper!* And Jennie too. I caught Jennie with her hand on it once.

She didn't know I was in the room, and when I asked her in a quiet, a very quiet voice, with the most restrained manner possible, what she was doing with the paper—she turned around as if she had been caught stealing, and looked quite angry—asked me why I should frighten her so!

Then she said that the paper stained everything it touched, that she had found yellow smooches on all my clothes and John's, and she wished we would be more careful!

Did not that sound innocent? But I know she was studying that pattern, and I am determined that nobody shall find it out but myself!

Life is very much more exciting now than it used to be. You see I have something more to expect, to look forward to, to watch. I really do eat better, and am more quiet than I was.

John is so pleased to see me improve! He laughed a little the other day, and said I seemed to be flourishing in spite of my wallpaper.

I turned it off with a laugh. I had no intention of telling him it was *because* of the wallpaper—he would make fun of me. He might even want to take me away.

I don't want to leave now until I have found it out. There is a week more, and I think that will be enough.

I'm feeling ever so much better! I don't sleep much at night, for it is so interesting to watch developments; but I sleep a good deal in the daytime.

In the daytime it is tiresome and perplexing.

There are always new shoots on the fungus, and new shades of yellow all over it. I cannot keep count of them, though I have tried conscientiously.

It is the strangest yellow, that wallpaper! It makes me think of all the yellow things I ever saw—not beautiful ones like buttercups, but old foul, bad yellow things.

175 But there is something else about that paper—the smell! I noticed it the moment we came into the room, but with so much air and sun it was not bad. Now we have had a week of fog and rain, and whether the windows are open or not, the smell is here.

It creeps all over the house.

I find it hovering in the dining-room, skulking in the parlor, hiding in the hall, lying in wait for me on the stairs.

It gets into my hair.

Even when I go to ride, if I turn my head suddenly and surprise it—there is that smell!

180 Such a peculiar odor, too! I have spent hours in trying to analyze it, to find what it smelled like.

It is not bad—at first, and very gentle, but quite the subtlest, most enduring odor I ever met.

In this damp weather it is awful, I wake up in the night and find it hanging over me.

It used to disturb me at first. I thought seriously of burning the house—to reach the smell.

But now I am used to it. The only thing I can think of that it is like is the *color* of the paper! A yellow smell.

185 There is a very funny mark on this wall, low down, near the mopboard. A streak that runs round the room. It goes behind every piece of furniture, except the bed, a long, straight, even *smooch*, as if it had been rubbed over and over.

I wonder how it was done and who did it, and what they did it for. Round and round and round—round and round and round—it makes me dizzy!

I really have discovered something at last.

Through watching so much at night, when it changes so, I have finally found out.

The front pattern *does* move—and no wonder! The woman behind shakes it!

190 Sometimes I think there are a great many women behind, and sometimes only one, and she crawls around fast, and her crawling shakes it all over.

Then in the very bright spots she keeps still, and in the very shady spots she just takes hold of the bars and shakes them hard.

And she is all the time trying to climb through. But nobody could climb through that pattern—it strangles so; I think that is why it has so many heads.

They get through, and then the pattern strangles them off and turns them upside down, and makes their eyes white!

If those heads were covered or taken off it would not be half so bad.

I think that woman gets out in the daytime!   195
And I'll tell you why—privately—I've seen her!

I can see her out of every one of my windows!

It is the same woman, I know, for she is always creeping, and most women do not creep by daylight.

I see her in that long shaded lane, creeping up and down. I see her in those   200
dark grape arbors, creeping all around the garden.

I see her on that long road under the trees, creeping along, and when a carriage comes she hides under the blackberry vines.

I don't blame her a bit. It must be very humiliating to be caught creeping by daylight!

I always lock the door when I creep by daylight. I can't do it at night, for I know John would suspect something at once.

And John is so queer now, that I don't want to irritate him. I wish he would take another room! Besides, I don't want anybody to get that woman out at night but myself.

I often wonder if I could see her out of all the windows at once.

But, turn as fast as I can, I can only see out of one at one time.   205

And though I always see her, she *may* be able to creep faster than I can turn!

I have watched her sometimes away off in the open country, creeping as fast as a cloud shadow in a high wind.

If only that top pattern could be gotten off from the under one! I mean to try it, little by little.

I have found out another funny thing, but I shan't tell it this time! It does not do to trust people too much.

There are only two more days to get this paper off, and I believe John is   210
beginning to notice. I don't like the look in his eyes.

And I heard him ask Jennie a lot of professional questions about me. She had a very good report to give.

She said I slept a good deal in the daytime.

John knows I don't sleep very well at night, for all I'm so quiet!

He asked me all sorts of questions, too, and pretended to be very loving and kind.

As if I couldn't see through him!   215

Still, I don't wonder he acts so, sleeping under this paper for three months.

It only interests me, but I feel sure John and Jennie are secretly affected by it.

Hurrah! This is the last day, but it is enough. John to stay in town over night, and won't be out until this evening.

Jennie wanted to sleep with me—the sly thing! but I told her I should undoubtedly rest better for a night all alone.

That was clever, for really I wasn't alone a bit! As soon as it was moonlight and that poor thing began to crawl and shake the pattern, I got up and ran to help her.

I pulled and she shook, I shook and she pulled, and before morning we had peeled off yards of that paper.

A strip about as high as my head and half around the room.

And then when the sun came and that awful pattern began to laugh at me, I declared I would finish it to-day!

We go away to-morrow, and they are moving all my furniture down again to leave things as they were before.

Jennie looked at the wall in amazement, but I told her merrily that I did it out of pure spite at the vicious thing.

She laughed and said she wouldn't mind doing it herself, but I must not get tired.

How she betrayed herself that time!

But I am here, and no person touches this paper but me,—not *alive!*

She tried to get me out of the room—it was too patent! But I said it was so quiet and empty and clean now that I believed I would lie down again and sleep all I could; and not to wake me even for dinner—I would call when I woke.

So now she is gone, and the servants are gone, and the things are gone, and there is nothing left but that great bedstead nailed down, with the canvas mattress we found on it.

We shall sleep downstairs to-night, and take the boat home to-morrow.

I quite enjoy the room, now it is bare again.

How those children did tear about here!

This bedstead is fairly gnawed!

But I must get to work.

I have locked the door and thrown the key down into the front path.

I don't want to go out, and I don't want to have anybody come in, till John comes.

I want to astonish him.

I've got a rope up here that even Jennie did not find. If that woman does get out, and tries to get away, I can tie her!

But I forgot I could not reach far without anything to stand on!

This bed will *not* move!

I tried to lift and push it until I was lame, and then I got so angry I bit off a little piece at one corner—but it hurt my teeth.

Then I peeled off all the paper I could reach standing on the floor. It sticks horribly and the pattern just enjoys it! All those strangled heads and bulbous eyes and waddling fungus growths just shriek with derision!

I am getting angry enough to do something desperate. To jump out of the window would be admirable exercise, but the bars are too strong even to try.

Besides I wouldn't do it. Of course not. I know well enough that a step like that is improper and might be misconstrued.

I don't like to *look* out of the windows even—there are so many of those creeping women, and they creep so fast.

I wonder if they all come out of that wallpaper as I did?

But I am securely fastened now by my well-hidden rope—you don't get *me* out in the road there!

I suppose I shall have to get back behind the pattern when it comes night, and that is hard!

It is so pleasant to be out in this great room and creep around as I please!

I don't want to go outside. I won't, even if Jennie asks me to.

For outside you have to creep on the ground, and everything is green instead of yellow.

But here I can creep smoothly on the floor, and my shoulder just fits in that long smooch around the wall, so I cannot lose my way.

Why there's John at the door!

It is no use, young man, you can't open it!

How he does call and pound!

Now he's crying for an axe.

It would be a shame to break down that beautiful door!

"John dear!" said I in the gentlest voice, "the key is down by the front steps, under a plantain leaf!"

That silenced him for a few moments.

Then he said—very quietly indeed, "Open the door, my darling!"

"I can't," said I. "The key is down by the front door under a plantain leaf!"

And then I said it again, several times, very gently and slowly, and said it so often that he had to go and see, and he got it of course, and came in. He stopped short by the door.

"What is the matter?" he cried. "For God's sake, what are you doing!"

I kept on creeping just the same, but I looked at him over my shoulder.

"I've got out at last," said I, "in spite of you and Jane? And I've pulled off most of the paper, so you can't put me back!"

Now why should that man have fainted? But he did, and right across my path by the wall, so that I had to creep over him every time!

1892

EDITH WHARTON

The Other Two

I

Waythorn, on the drawing-room hearth, waited for his wife to come down to dinner.

It was their first night under his own roof, and he was surprised at his thrill of boyish agitation. He was not so old, to be sure—his glass gave him little more than the five-and-thirty years to which his wife confessed—but he had fancied himself already in the temperate zone; yet here he was listening for her step with a tender sense of all it symbolised, with some old trail of verse about the garlanded nuptial door-posts floating through his enjoyment of the pleasant room and the good dinner just beyond it.

They had been hastily recalled from their honeymoon by the illness of Lily Haskett, the child of Mrs. Waythorn's first marriage. The little girl, at Waythorn's desire, had been transferred to his house on the day of her mother's wedding, and the doctor, on their arrival, broke the news that she was ill with typhoid, but declared that all the symptoms were favourable. Lily could show twelve years of unblemished health, and the case promised to be a light one. The nurse spoke as reassuringly, and after a moment of alarm Mrs. Waythorn had adjusted herself to the situation. She was very fond of Lily—her affection for the child had perhaps been her decisive charm in Waythorn's eyes—but she had the perfectly balanced nerves which her little girl had inherited, and no woman ever wasted less tissue in unproductive worry. Waythorn was therefore quite prepared to see her come in presently, a little late because of a last look at Lily, but as serene and well-appointed as if her goodnight kiss had been laid on the brow of health. Her composure was restful to him; it acted as ballast to his somewhat unstable sensibilities. As he pictured her bending over the child's bed he thought how soothing her presence must be in illness: her very step would prognosticate recovery.

His own life had been a gray one, from temperament rather than circumstance, and he had been drawn to her by the unperturbed gaiety which kept her fresh and elastic at an age when most woman's activities are growing either slack or febrile. He knew what was said about her; for, popular as she was, there had always been a faint undercurrent of detraction. When she had appeared in New York, nine or ten years earlier, as the pretty Mrs. Haskett whom Gus Varick had unearthed somewhere—was it in Pittsburg or Utica?—society, while promptly accepting her, had reserved the right to cast a doubt on its own indiscrimination. Enquiry, however, established her undoubted connection with a socially reigning family, and explained her recent divorce as the natural result of a runaway match at seventeen; and as nothing was known of Mr. Haskett it was easy to believe the worst of him.

5 Alice Haskett's remarriage with Gus Varick was a passport to the set whose recognition she coveted, and for a few years the Varicks were the most popular couple in town. Unfortunately the alliance was brief and stormy, and this time the husband had his champions. Still, even Varick's stanchest supporters admitted that he was not meant for matrimony, and Mrs. Varick's grievances were of a nature to bear the inspection of the New York courts. A New York divorce is in itself a diploma of virtue, and in the semi-widowhood of this second separation Mrs. Varick took on an air of sanctity, and was allowed to confide her wrongs to some of the most scrupulous ears in town. But when it was known that she was to marry Waythorn there was a momentary reaction. Her best friends would have preferred to see her remain in the rôle of the injured wife,

which was as becoming to her as crape to a rosy complexion. True, a decent time had elapsed, and it was not even suggested that Waythorn had supplanted his predecessor. People shook their heads over him, however, and one grudging friend, to whom he affirmed that he took the step with his eyes open, replied oracularly: "Yes—and with your ears shut."

Waythorn could afford to smile at these innuendoes. In the Wall Street phrase, he had "discounted" them. He knew that society has not yet adapted itself to the consequences of divorce, and that till the adaptation takes place every woman who uses the freedom the law accords her must be her own social justification. Waythorn had an amused confidence in his wife's ability to justify herself. His expectations were fulfilled, and before the wedding took place Alice Varick's group had rallied openly to her support. She took it all imperturbably: she had a way of surmounting obstacles without seeming to be aware of them, and Waythorn looked back with wonder at the trivialities over which he had worn his nerves thin. He had the sense of having found refuge in a richer, warmer nature than his own, and his satisfaction, at the moment, was humourously summed up in the thought that his wife, when she had done all she could for Lily, would not be ashamed to come down and enjoy a good dinner.

The anticipation of such enjoyment was not, however, the sentiment expressed by Mrs. Waythorn's charming face when she presently joined him. Though she had put on her most engaging teagown she had neglected to assume the smile that went with it, and Waythorn thought he had never seen her look so nearly worried.

"What is it?" he asked. "Is anything wrong with Lily?"

"No; I've just been in and she's still sleeping." Mrs. Waythorn hesitated. "But something tiresome has happened."

He had taken her two hands, and now perceived that he was crushing a paper between them.

"This letter?"

"Yes—Mr. Haskett has written—I mean his lawyer has written."

Waythorn felt himself flush uncomfortably. He dropped his wife's hands.

"What about?"

"About seeing Lily. You know the courts—"

"Yes, yes," he interrupted nervously.

Nothing was known about Haskett in New York. He was vaguely supposed to have remained in the outer darkness from which his wife had been rescued, and Waythorn was one of the few who were aware that he had given up his business in Utica and followed her to New York in order to be near his little girl. In the days of his wooing, Waythorn had often met Lily on the doorstep, rosy and smiling, on her way "to see papa."

"I am so sorry," Mrs. Waythorn murmured.

He roused himself. "What does he want?"

"He wants to see her. You know she goes to him once a week."

"Well—he doesn't expect her to go to him now, does he?"

"No—he has heard of her illness; but he expects to come here."

"*Here?*"

Mrs. Waythorn reddened under his gaze. They looked away from each other.

25 "I'm afraid he has the right. . . . You'll see. . . ." She made a proffer of the letter.

Waythorn moved away with a gesture of refusal. He stood staring about the softly lighted room, which a moment before had seemed so full of bridal intimacy.

"I'm so sorry," she repeated. "If Lily could have been moved—"

"That's out of the question," he returned impatiently.

"I suppose so."

30 Her lip was beginning to tremble, and he felt himself a brute.

"He must come, of course," he said. "When is—his day?"

"I'm afraid—to-morrow."

"Very well. Send a note in the morning."

The butler entered to announce dinner.

35 Waythorn turned to his wife. "Come—you must be tired. It's beastly, but try to forget about it," he said, drawing her hand through his arm.

"You're so good, dear. I'll try," she whispered back.

Her face cleared at once, and as she looked at him across the flowers, between the rosy candle-shades, he saw her lips waver back into a smile.

"How pretty everything is!" she sighed luxuriously.

He turned to the butler. "The champagne at once, please. Mrs. Waythorn is tired."

40 In a moment or two their eyes met above the sparkling glasses. Her own were quite clear and untroubled: he saw that she had obeyed his injunction and forgotten.

II

Waythorn, the next morning, went down town earlier than usual. Haskett was not likely to come till the afternoon, but the instinct of flight drove him forth. He meant to stay away all day—he had thoughts of dining at his club. As his door closed behind him he reflected that before he opened it again it would have admitted another man who had as much right to enter it as himself, and the thought filled him with a physical repugnance.

He caught the "elevated" at the employés' hour, and found himself crushed between two layers of pendulous humanity. At Eighth Street the man facing him wriggled out, and another took his place. Waythorn glanced up and saw that it was Gus Varick. The men were so close together that it was impossible to ignore the smile of recognition on Varick's handsome overblown face. And after all—why not? They had always been on good terms, and Varick had been divorced before Waythorn's attentions to his wife began. The two exchanged a word on the perennial grievance of the congested trains, and when a seat at their side was miraculously left empty the instinct of self-preservation made Waythorn slip into it after Varick.

The latter drew the stout man's breath of relief. "Lord—I was beginning to feel like a pressed flower." He leaned back, looking unconcernedly at Waythorn. "Sorry to hear that Sellers is knocked out again."

"Sellers?" echoed Waythorn, starting at his partner's name.

Varick looked surprised. "You didn't know he was laid up with the gout?"   45

"No. I've been away—I only got back last night." Waythorn felt himself reddening in anticipation of the other's smile.

"Ah—yes; to be sure. And Seller's attack came on two days ago. I'm afraid he's pretty bad. Very awkward for me, as it happens, because he was just putting through a rather important thing for me."

"Ah?" Waythorn wondered vaguely since when Varick had been dealing in "important things." Hitherto he had dabbled only in the shallow pools of speculation, with which Waythorn's office did not usually concern itself.

It occurred to him that Varick might be talking at random, to relieve the strain of their propinquity. That strain was becoming momentarily more apparent to Waythorn, and when, at Cortlandt Street, he caught sight of an acquaintance and had a sudden vision of the picture he and Varick must present to an initiated eye, he jumped up with a muttered excuse.

"I hope you'll find Sellers better," said Varick civilly, and he stammered   50
back: "If I can be of any use to you—" and let the departing crowd sweep him to the platform.

At his office he heard that Sellers was in fact ill with the gout, and would probably not be able to leave the house for some weeks.

"I'm sorry it should have happened so, Mr. Waythorn," the senior clerk said with affable significance. "Mr. Sellers was very much upset at the idea of giving you such a lot of extra work just now."

"Oh, that's no matter," said Waythorn hastily. He secretly welcomed the pressure of additional business, and was glad to think that, when the day's work was over, he would have to call at his partner's on the way home.

He was late for luncheon, and turned in at the nearest restaurant instead of going to his club. The place was full, and the waiter hurried him to the back of the room to capture the only vacant table. In the cloud of cigar-smoke Waythorn did not at once distinguish his neighbours: but presently, looking about him, he saw Varick seated a few feet off. This time, luckily, they were too far apart for conversation, and Varick, who faced another way, had probably not even seen him; but there was an irony in their renewed nearness.

Varick was said to be fond of good living, and as Waythorn sat despatching   55
his hurried luncheon he looked across half enviously at the other's leisurely degustation of his meal. When Waythorn first saw him he had been helping himself with critical deliberation to a bit of Camembert at the ideal point of liquefaction, and now, the cheese removed, he was just pouring his *café double* from its little two-storied earthen pot. He poured slowly, his ruddy profile bent above the task, and one beringed white hand steadying the lid of the coffee-pot; then he stretched his other hand to the decanter of cognac at his elbow, filled a liqueur-glass, took a tentative sip, and poured the brandy into his coffee-cup.

Waythorn watched him in a kind of fascination. What was he thinking of—

only of the flavour of the coffee and the liqueur? Had the morning's meeting left no more trace in his thoughts than on his face? Had his wife so completely passed out of his life that even this odd encounter with her present husband, within a week after her remarriage, was no more than an incident in his day? And as Waythorn mused, another idea struck him: had Haskett ever met Varick as Varick and he had just met? The recollection of Haskett perturbed him, and he rose and left the restaurant, taking a circuitous way out to escape the placid irony of Varick's nod.

It was after seven when Waythorn reached home. He thought the footman who opened the door looked at him oddly.

"How is Miss Lily?" he asked in haste.

"Doing very well, sir. A gentleman—"

"Tell Barlow to put off dinner for half an hour," Waythorn cut him off, hurrying upstairs.

He went straight to his room and dressed without seeing his wife. When he reached the drawing-room she was there, fresh and radiant. Lily's day had been good; the doctor was not coming back that evening.

At dinner Waythorn told her of Sellers's illness and of the resulting complications. She listened sympathetically, adjuring him not to let himself be overworked, and asking vague feminine questions about the routine of the office. Then she gave him the chronicle of Lily's day; quoted the nurse and doctor, and told him who had called to inquire. He had never seen her more serene and unruffled. It struck him, with a curious pang, that she was very happy in being with him, so happy that she found a childish pleasure in rehearsing the trivial incidents of her day.

After dinner they went to the library, and the servant put the coffee and liqueurs on a low table before her and left the room. She looked singularly soft and girlish in her rosy pale dress, against the dark leather of one of his bachelor armchairs. A day earlier the contrast would have charmed him.

He turned away now, choosing a cigar with affected deliberation.

"Did Haskett come?" he asked, with his back to her.

"Oh, yes—he came."

"You didn't see him, of course?"

She hesitated a moment. "I let the nurse see him."

That was all. There was nothing more to ask. He swung round toward her, applying a match to his cigar. Well, the thing was over for a week, at any rate. He would try not to think of it. She looked up at him, a trifle rosier than usual, with a smile in her eyes.

"Ready for your coffee, dear?"

He leaned against the mantelpiece, watching her as she lifted the coffee-pot. The lamplight struck a gleam from her bracelets and tipped her soft hair with brightness. How light and slender she was, and how each gesture flowed into the next! She seemed a creature all compact of harmonies. As the thought of Haskett receded, Waythorn felt himself yielding again to the joy of possessorship. They were his, those white hands with their flitting motions, his the light haze of hair, the lips and eyes. . . .

She set down the coffee-pot, and reaching for the decanter of cognac, measured off a liqueur-glass and poured it into his cup.

Waythorn uttered a sudden exclamation.

"What is the matter?" she said, startled.

"Nothing; only—I don't take cognac in my coffee." 75

"Oh, how stupid of me," she cried.

Their eyes met, and she blushed a sudden agonised red.

III

Ten days later, Mr. Sellers, still house-bound, asked Waythorn to call on his way down town.

The senior partner, with his swaddled foot propped up by the fire, greeted his associate with an air of embarrassment.

"I'm sorry, my dear fellow; I've got to ask you to do an awkward thing for 80 me."

Waythorn waited, and the other went on, after a pause apparently given to the arrangement of his phrases: "The fact is, when I was knocked out I had just gone into a rather complicated piece of business for—Gus Varick."

"Well?" said Waythorn, with an attempt to put him at his ease.

"Well—it's this way: Varick came to me the day before my attack. He had evidently had an inside tip from somebody, and had made about a hundred thousand. He came to me for advice, and I suggested his going in with Vanderlyn."

"Oh, the deuce!" Waythorn exclaimed. He saw in a flash what had happened. The investment was an alluring one, but required negotiation. He listened quietly while Sellers put the case before him, and, the statement ended, he said: "You think I ought to see Varick?"

"I'm afraid I can't as yet. The doctor is obdurate. And this thing can't wait. I 85 hate to ask you, but no one else in the office knows the ins and outs of it."

Waythorn stood silent. He did not care a farthing for the success of Varick's venture, but the honour of the office was to be considered, and he could hardly refuse to oblige his partner.

"Very well," he said, "I'll do it."

That afternoon, apprised by telephone, Varick called at the office. Waythorn, waiting in his private room, wondered what the others thought of it. The newspapers, at the time of Mrs. Waythorn's marriage, had acquainted their readers with every detail of her previous matrimonial ventures, and Waythorn could fancy the clerks smiling behind Varick's back as he was ushered in.

Varick bore himself admirably. He was easy without being undignified, and Waythorn was conscious of cutting a much less impressive figure. Varick had no experience of business, and the talk prolonged itself for nearly an hour while Waythorn set forth with scrupulous precision the details of the proposed transaction.

"I'm awfully obliged to you," Varick said as he rose. "The fact is I'm not used 90 to having much money to look after, and I don't want to make an ass of myself—" He smiled, and Waythorn could not help noticing that there was something pleasant about his smile. "It feels uncommonly queer to have enough cash to pay one's bills. I'd have sold my soul for it a few years ago!"

Waythorn winced at the allusion. He had heard it rumoured that a lack of funds had been one of the determining causes of the Varick separation, but it did not occur to him that Varick's words were intentional. It seemed more likely that the desire to keep clear of embarrassing topics had fatally drawn him into one. Waythorn did not wish to be outdone in civility.

"We'll do the best we can for you," he said. "I think this is a good thing you're in."

"Oh, I'm sure it's immense. It's awfully good of you—" Varick broke off, embarrassed. "I suppose the thing's settled now—but if—"

"If anything happens before Sellers is about, I'll see you again," said Waythorn quietly. He was glad, in the end, to appear the more self-possessed of the two.

•   •   •

95 The course of Lily's illness ran smooth, and as the days passed Waythorn grew used to the idea of Haskett's weekly visit. The first time the day came round, he stayed out late, and questioned his wife as to the visit on his return. She replied at once that Haskett had merely seen the nurse downstairs, as the doctor did not wish any one in the child's sick-room till after the crisis.

The following week Waythorn was again conscious of the recurrence of the day, but had forgotten it by the time he came home to dinner. The crisis of the disease came a few days later, with a rapid decline of fever, and the little girl was pronounced out of danger. In the rejoicing which ensued the thought of Haskett passed out of Waythorn's mind, and one afternoon, letting himself into the house with a latch-key, he went straight to his library without noticing a shabby hat and umbrella in the hall.

In the library he found a small effaced-looking man with a thinnish gray beard sitting on the edge of a chair. The stranger might have been a piano-tuner, or one of those mysteriously efficient persons who are summoned in emergencies to adjust some detail of the domestic machinery. He blinked at Waythorn through a pair of gold-rimmed spectacles and said mildly: "Mr. Waythorn, I presume? I am Lily's father."

Waythorn flushed. "Oh—" he stammered uncomfortably. He broke off, disliking to appear rude. Inwardly he was trying to adjust the actual Haskett to the image of him projected by his wife's reminiscences. Waythorn had been allowed to infer that Alice's first husband was a brute.

"I am sorry to intrude," said Haskett, with his over-the-counter politeness.

100 "Don't mention it," returned Waythorn, collecting himself. "I suppose the nurse has been told?"

"I presume so. I can wait," said Haskett. He had a resigned way of speaking, as though life had worn down his natural powers of resistance.

Waythorn stood on the threshold, nervously pulling off his gloves.

"I'm sorry you've been detained. I will send for the nurse," he said; and as he opened the door he added with an effort: "I'm glad we can give you a good report of Lily." He winced as the *we* slipped out, but Haskett seemed not to notice it.

"Thank you, Mr. Waythorn. It's been an anxious time for me."

"Ah, well, that's past. Soon she'll be able to go to you." Waythorn nodded and passed out.

In his own room he flung himself down with a groan. He hated the woman-ish sensibility which made him suffer so acutely from the grotesque chances of life. He had known when he married that his wife's former husbands were both living, and that amid the multiplied contacts of modern existence there were a thousand chances to one that he would run against one or the other, yet he found himself as much disturbed by his brief encounter with Haskett as though the law had not obligingly removed all difficulties in the way of their meeting.

Waythorn sprang up and began to pace the room nervously. He had not suffered half as much from his two meetings with Varick. It was Haskett's pres-ence in his own house that made the situation so intolerable. He stood still, hearing steps in the passage.

"This way, please," he heard the nurse say. Haskett was being taken upstairs, then: not a corner of the house but was open to him. Waythorn dropped into another chair, staring vaguely ahead of him. On his dressing-table stood a photo-graph of Alice, taken when he had first known her. She was Alice Varick then—how fine and exquisite he had thought her! Those were Varick's pearls about her neck. At Waythorn's instance they had been returned before her marriage. Had Haskett ever given her any trinkets—and what had become of them, Way-thorn wondered? He realised suddenly that he knew very little of Haskett's past or present situation; but from the man's appearance and manner of speech he could reconstruct with curious precision the surroundings of Alice's first mar-riage. And it startled him to think that she had, in the background of her life, a phase of existence so different from anything with which he had connected her. Varick, whatever his faults, was a gentleman, in the conventional, traditional sense of the term: the sense which at that moment seemed, oddly enough, to have most meaning to Waythorn. He and Varick had the same social habits, spoke the same language, understood the same allusions. But this other man . . . it was grotesquely uppermost in Waythorn's mind that Haskett had worn a made-up tie attached with an elastic. Why should that ridiculous detail symbolise the whole man? Waythorn was exasperated by his own paltriness, but the fact of the tie expanded, forced itself on him, became as it were the key to Alice's past. He could see her, as Mrs. Haskett, sitting in a "front parlour" furnished in plush, with a pianola, and a copy of "Ben Hur" on the centre-table. He could see her going to the theatre with Haskett—or perhaps even to a "Church Sociable"—she in a "picture hat" and Haskett in a black frock coat, a little creased, with the made-up tie on an elastic. On the way home they would stop and look at the illuminated shop-windows, lingering over the photographs of New York actresses. On Sunday afternoons Haskett would take her for a walk, pushing Lily ahead of them in a white enamelled perambulator, and Waythorn had a vision

105

of the people they would stop and talk to. He could fancy how pretty Alice must have looked, in a dress adroitly constructed from the hints of a New York fashion-paper, and how she must have looked down on the other women, chafing at her life, and secretly feeling that she belonged in a bigger place.

For the moment his foremost thought was one of wonder at the way in which she had shed the phase of existence which her marriage with Haskett implied. It was as if her whole aspect, every gesture, every inflection, every allusion, were a studied negation of that period of her life. If she had denied being married to Haskett she could hardly have stood more convicted of duplicity than in this obliteration of the self which had been his wife.

110   Waythorn started up, checking himself in the analysis of her motives. What right had he to create a fantastic effigy of her and then pass judgment on it? She had spoken vaguely of her first marriage as unhappy, had hinted, with becoming reticence, that Haskett had wrought havoc among her young illusions. . . . It was a pity for Waythorn's peace of mind that Haskett's very inoffensiveness shed a new light on the nature of those illusions. A man would rather think that his wife has been brutalised by her first husband than that the process has been reversed.

IV

"Mr. Waythorn, I don't like that French governess of Lily's."

Haskett, subdued and apologetic, stood before Waythorn in the library, revolving his shabby hat in his hand.

Waythorn, surprised in his armchair over the evening paper, stared back perplexedly at his visitor.

"You'll excuse me asking to see you," Haskett continued. "But this is my last visit, and I thought if I could have a word with you it would be a better way than writing to Mrs. Waythorn's lawyer."

115   Waythorn rose uneasily. He did not like the French governess either; but that was irrelevant.

"I am not so sure of that," he returned stiffly; "but since you wish it I will give your message to—my wife." He always hesitated over the possessive pronoun in addressing Haskett.

The latter sighed. "I don't know as that will help much. She didn't like it when I spoke to her."

Waythorn turned red. "When did you see her?" he asked.

"Not since the first day I came to see Lily—right after she was taken sick. I remarked to her then that I didn't like the governess."

120   Waythorn made no answer. He remembered distinctly that, after the first visit, he had asked his wife if she had seen Haskett. She had lied to him then, but she had respected his wishes since; and the incident cast a curious light on her character. He was sure she would not have seen Haskett the first day if she had divined that Waythorn would object, and the fact that she did not divine it was almost as disagreeable to the latter as the discovery that she had lied to him.

"I don't like the woman," Haskett was repeating with mild persistency. "She ain't straight, Mr. Waythorn—she'll teach the child to be underhand. I've noticed a change in Lily—she's too anxious to please—and she doesn't always tell the truth. She used to be the straightest child, Mr. Waythorn—" He broke off, his voice a little thick. "Not but what I want her to have a stylish education," he ended.

Waythorn was touched. "I'm sorry, Mr. Haskett; but frankly, I don't quite see what I can do."

Haskett hesitated. Then he laid his hat on the table, and advanced to the hearth-rug, on which Waythorn was standing. There was nothing aggressive in his manner, but he had the solemnity of a timid man resolved on a decisive measure.

"There's just one thing you can do, Mr. Waythorn," he said. "You can remind Mrs. Waythorn that, by the decree of the courts, I am entitled to have a voice in Lily's bringing up." He paused, and went on more deprecatingly: "I'm not the kind to talk about enforcing my rights, Mr. Waythorn. I don't know as I think a man is entitled to rights he hasn't known how to hold on to; but this business of the child is different. I've never let go there—and I never mean to."

• • •

The scene left Waythorn deeply shaken. Shamefacedly, in indirect ways, he had been finding out about Haskett; and all that he learned was favourable. The little man, in order to be near his daughter, had sold out his share in a profitable business in Utica, and accepted a modest clerkship in a New York manufacturing house. He boarded in a shabby street and had few acquaintances. His passion for Lily filled his life. Waythorn felt that this exploration of Haskett was like groping about with a dark-lantern in his wife's past; but he saw now that there were recesses his lantern had not explored. He had never enquired into the exact circumstances of his wife's first matrimonial rupture. On the surface all had been fair. It was she who had obtained the divorce, and the court had given her the child. But Waythorn knew how many ambiguities such a verdict might cover. The mere fact that Haskett retained a right over his daughter implied an unsuspected compromise. Waythorn was an idealist. He always refused to recognise unpleasant contingencies till he found himself confronted with them, and then he saw them followed by a spectral train of consequences. His next days were thus haunted, and he determined to try to lay the ghosts by conjuring them up in his wife's presence.

When he repeated Haskett's request a flame of anger passed over her face; but she subdued it instantly and spoke with a slight quiver of outraged motherhood.

"It is very ungentlemanly of him," she said.

The word grated on Waythorn. "That is neither here nor there. It's a bare question of rights."

She murmured: "It's not as if he could ever be a help to Lily—"

Waythorn flushed. This was even less to his taste. "The question is," he repeated, "what authority has he over her?"

125

130

She looked downward, twisting herself a little in her seat. "I am willing to see him—I thought you objected," she faltered.

In a flash he understood that she knew the extent of Haskett's claims. Perhaps it was not the first time she had resisted them.

"My objecting has nothing to do with it," he said coldly; "if Haskett has a right to be consulted you must consult him."

She burst into tears, and he saw that she expected him to regard her as a victim.

135 Haskett did not abuse his rights. Waythorn had felt miserably sure that he would not. But the governess was dismissed, and from time to time the little man demanded an interview with Alice. After the first outburst she accepted the situation with her usual adaptability. Haskett had once reminded Waythorn of the piano-tuner, and Mrs. Waythorn, after a month or two, appeared to class him with that domestic familiar. Waythorn could not but respect the father's tenacity. At first he had tried to cultivate the suspicion that Haskett might be "up to" something, that he had an object in securing a foothold in the house. But in his heart Waythorn was sure of Haskett's single-mindedness; he even guessed in the latter a mild contempt for such advantages as his relation with the Waythorns might offer. Haskett's sincerity of purpose made him invulnerable, and his successor had to accept him as a lien on the property.

•   •   •

Mr. Sellers was sent to Europe to recover from his gout, and Varick's affairs hung on Waythorn's hands. The negotiations were prolonged and complicated; they necessitated frequent conferences between the two men, and the interests of the firm forbade Waythorn's suggesting that his client should transfer his business to another office.

Varick appeared well in the transaction. In moments of relaxation his coarse streak appeared, and Waythorn dreaded his geniality; but in the office he was concise and clear-headed, with a flattering deference to Waythorn's judgment. Their business relations being so affably established, it would have been absurd for the two men to ignore each other in society. The first time they met in a drawing-room, Varick took up their intercourse in the same easy key, and his hostess's grateful glance obliged Waythorn to respond to it. After that they ran across each other frequently, and one evening at a ball Waythorn, wandering through the remoter rooms, came upon Varick seated beside his wife. She coloured a little, and faltered in what she was saying; but Varick nodded to Waythorn without rising, and the latter strolled on.

In the carriage, on the way home, he broke out nervously: "I didn't know you spoke to Varick."

Her voice trembled a little. "It's the first time—he happened to be standing near me; I didn't know what to do. It's so awkward, meeting everywhere—and he said you had been very kind about some business."

140 "That's different," said Waythorn.

She paused a moment. "I'll do just as you wish," she returned pliantly. "I thought it would be less awkward to speak to him when we meet."

Her pliancy was beginning to sicken him. Had she really no will of her own—no theory about her relation to these men? She had accepted Haskett— did she mean to accept Varick? It was "less awkward," as she had said, and her instinct was to evade difficulties or to circumvent them. With sudden vividness Waythorn saw how the instinct had developed. She was "as easy as an old shoe"—a shoe that too many feet had worn. Her elasticity was the result of tension in too many different directions. Alice Haskett—Alice Varick—Alice Waythorn—she had been each in turn, and had left hanging to each name a little of her privacy, a little of her personality, a little of the inmost self where the unknown god abides.

"Yes—it's better to speak to Varick," said Waythorn wearily.

V

The winter wore on, and society took advantage of the Waythorns' acceptance of Varick. Harassed hostesses were grateful to them for bridging over a social difficulty, and Mrs. Waythorn was held up as a miracle of good taste. Some experimental spirits could not resist the diversion of throwing Varick and his former wife together, and there were those who thought he found a zest in the propinquity. But Mrs. Waythorn's conduct remained irreproachable. She nei-ther avoided Varick nor sought him out. Even Waythorn could not but admit that she had discovered the solution of the newest social problem.

He had married her without giving much thought to that problem. He had fancied that a woman can shed her past like a man. But now he saw that Alice was bound to hers both by the circumstances which forced her into continued relation with it, and by the traces it had left on her nature. With grim irony Waythorn compared himself to a member of a syndicate. He held so many shares in his wife's personality and his predecessors were his partners in the business. If there had been any element of passion in the transaction he would have felt less deteriorated by it. The fact that Alice took her change of husbands like a change of weather reduced the situation to mediocrity. He could have forgiven her for blunders, for excesses; for resisting Haskett, for yielding to Var-ick; for anything but her acquiescence and her tact. She reminded him of a juggler tossing knives; but the knives were blunt and she knew they would never cut her.

And then, gradually, habit formed a protecting surface for his sensibilities. If he paid for each day's comfort with the small change of his illusions, he grew daily to value the comfort more and set less store upon the coin. He had drifted into a dulling propinquity with Haskett and Varick and he took refuge in the cheap revenge of satirising the situation. He even began to reckon up the advan-tages which accrued from it, to ask himself if it were not better to own a third of a wife who knew how to make a man happy than a whole one who had lacked opportunity to acquire the art. For it *was* an art, and made up, like all others, of concessions, eliminations and embellishments; of lights judiciously thrown and shadows skilfully softened. His wife knew exactly how to manage the lights, and he knew exactly to what training she owed her skill. He even tried to trace the source of his obligations, to discriminate between the influences which had combined to produce his domestic happiness: he perceived that Haskett's commonness had made Alice worship good breeding, while Varick's liberal construction of the marriage bond had taught her to value the conjugal virtues; so that he was directly indebted to his predecessors for the devotion which made his life easy if not inspiring.

From this phase he passed into that of complete acceptance. He ceased to satirise himself because time dulled the irony of the situation and the joke lost its humour with its sting. Even the sight of Haskett's hat on the hall table had ceased to touch the springs of epigram. The hat was often seen there now, for it had been decided that it was better for Lily's father to visit her than for the little girl to go to his boarding-house. Waythorn, having acquiesced in this arrangement, had been surprised to find how little difference it made. Haskett was never obtrusive, and the few visitors who met him on the stairs were unaware of his identity. Waythorn did not know how often he saw Alice, but with himself Haskett was seldom in contact.

One afternoon, however, he learned on entering that Lily's father was waiting to see him. In the library he found Haskett occupying a chair in his usual provisional way. Waythorn always felt grateful to him for not leaning back.

"I hope you'll excuse me, Mr. Waythorn," he said rising. "I wanted to see Mrs. Waythorn about Lily, and your man asked me to wait here till she came in."

150 "Of course," said Waythorn, remembering that a sudden leak had that morning given over the drawing-room to the plumbers.

He opened his cigar-case and held it out to his visitor, and Haskett's acceptance seemed to mark a fresh stage in their intercourse. The spring evening was chilly, and Waythorn invited his guest to draw up his chair to the fire. He meant to find an excuse to leave Haskett in a moment; but he was tired and cold, and after all the little man no longer jarred on him.

The two were enclosed in the intimacy of their blended cigar smoke when the door opened and Varick walked into the room. Waythorn rose abruptly. It was the first time that Varick had come to the house, and the surprise of seeing him, combined with the singular inopportuneness of his arrival, gave a new edge to Waythorn's blunted sensibilities. He stared at his visitor without speaking.

Varick seemed too preoccupied to notice his host's embarrassment.

"My dear fellow," he exclaimed in his most expansive tone, "I must apologize for tumbling in on you in this way, but I was too late to catch you down town, and so I thought—"

155 He stopped short, catching sight of Haskett, and his sanguine colour deepened to a flush which spread vividly under his scant blond hair. But in a moment he recovered himself and nodded slightly. Haskett returned the bow in silence, and Waythorn was still groping for speech when the footman came in carrying a tea-table.

The intrusion offered a welcome vent to Waythorn's nerves. "What the deuce are you bringing this here for?" he said sharply.

"I beg your pardon, sir, but the plumbers are still in the drawing-room, and

Mrs. Waythorn said she would have tea in the library." The footman's perfectly respectful tone implied a reflection on Waythorn's reasonableness.

"Oh, very well," said the latter resignedly, and the footman proceeded to open the folding tea-table and set out its complicated appointments. While this interminable process continued the three men stood motionless, watching it with a fascinated stare, till Waythorn, to break the silence, said to Varick: "Won't you have a cigar?"

He held out the case he had just tendered to Haskett, and Varick helped himself with a smile. Waythorn looked about for a match, and finding none, proferred a light from his own cigar. Haskett, in the background, held his ground mildly, examining his cigar-tip now and then, and stepping forward at the right moment to knock its ashes into the fire.

The footman at last withdrew, and Varick immediately began: "If I could just say half a word to you about this business—"   160

"Certainly," stammered Waythorn; "in the dining-room—"

But as he placed his hand on the door it opened from without, and his wife appeared on the threshold.

She came in fresh and smiling, in her street dress and hat, shedding a fragrance from the boa which she loosened in advancing.

"Shall we have tea in here, dear?" she began; and then she caught sight of Varick. Her smile deepened, veiling a slight tremor of surprise.

"Why, how do you do?" she said with a distinct note of pleasure.   165

As she shook hands with Varick she saw Haskett standing behind him. Her smile faded for a moment, but she recalled it quickly, with a scarcely perceptible side-glance at Waythorn.

"How do you do, Mr. Haskett?" she said, and shook hands with him a shade less cordially.

The three men stood awkwardly before her, till Varick, always the most self-possessed, dashed into an explanatory phrase.

"We—I had to see Waythorn a moment on business," he stammered, brick-red from chin to nape.

Haskett stepped forward with his air of mild obstinacy. "I am sorry to intrude;   170
but you appointed five o'clock—" he directed his resigned glance to the time-piece on the mantel.

She swept aside their embarrassment with a charming gesture of hospitality.

"I'm so sorry—I'm always late; but the afternoon was so lovely." She stood drawing off her gloves, propitiatory and graceful, diffusing about her a sense of ease and familiarity in which the situation lost its grotesqueness. "But before talking business," she added brightly, "I'm sure every one wants a cup of tea."

She dropped into her low chair by the tea-table, and the two visitors, as if drawn by her smile, advanced to receive the cups she held out.

She glanced about for Waythorn, and he took the third cup with a laugh.

1904

FRANZ KAFKA

A Hunger Artist[1]

During these last decades the interest in professional fasting has markedly diminished. It used to pay very well to stage such great performances under one's own management, but today that is quite impossible. We live in a different world now. At one time the whole town took a lively interest in the hunger artist; from day to day of his fast the excitement mounted; everybody wanted to see him at least once a day; there were people who bought season tickets for the last few days and sat from morning till night in front of his small barred cage; even in the nighttime there were visiting hours, when the whole effect was heightened by torch flares; on fine days the cage was set out in the open air, and then it was the children's special treat to see the hunger artist; for their elders he was often just a joke that happened to be in fashion, but the children stood openmouthed, holding each other's hands for greater security, marveling at him as he sat there pallid in black tights, with his ribs sticking out so prominently, not even on a seat but down among straw on the ground, sometimes giving a courteous nod, answering questions with a constrained smile, or perhaps stretching an arm through the bars so that one might feel how thin it was, and then again withdrawing deep into himself, paying no attention to anyone or anything, not even to the all-important striking of the clock that was the only piece of furniture in his cage, but merely staring into vacancy with half shut eyes, now and then taking a sip from a tiny glass of water to moisten his lips.

Besides casual onlookers there were also relays of permanent watchers selected by the public, usually butchers, strangely enough, and it was their task to watch the hunger artist day and night, three of them at a time, in case he should have some secret recourse to nourishment. This was nothing but a formality, instituted to reassure the masses, for the initiates knew well enough that during his fast the artist would never in any circumstances, not even under forcible compulsion, swallow the smallest morsel of food: the honor of his profession forbade it. Not every watcher, of course, was capable of understanding this, there were often groups of night watchers who were very lax in carrying out their duties and deliberately huddled together in a retired corner to play cards with great absorption, obviously intending to give the hunger artist the chance of a little refreshment, which they supposed he could draw from some private hoard. Nothing annoyed the artist more than such watchers; they made him miserable; they made his fast seem unendurable; sometimes he mastered his feebleness sufficiently to sing during their watch for as long as he could keep going, to show them how unjust their suspicions were. But that was of little use; they only wondered at his cleverness in being able to fill his mouth even while singing. Much more to his taste were the watchers who sat close up to the bars, who were not content with the dim night lighting of the hall but focused him

1. Translated by Edwin and Willa Muir.

in the full glare of the electric pocket torch given them by the impresario. The harsh light did not trouble him at all, in any case he could never sleep properly, and he could always drowse a little, whatever the light, at any hour, even when the hall was thronged with noisy onlookers. He was quite happy at the prospect of spending a sleepless night with such watchers; he was ready to exchange jokes with them, to tell them stories out of his nomadic life, anything at all to keep them awake and demonstrate to them again that he had no eatables in his cage and that he was fasting as not one of them could fast. But his happiest moment was when the morning came and an enormous breakfast was brought them, at his expense, on which they flung themselves with the keen appetite of healthy men after a weary night of wakefulness. Of course there were people who argued that this breakfast was an unfair attempt to bribe the watchers, but that was going rather too far, and when they were invited to take on a night's vigil without a breakfast, merely for the sake of the cause, they made themselves scarce, although they stuck stubbornly to their suspicions.

Such suspicions, anyhow, were a necessary accompaniment to the profession of fasting. No one could possibly watch the hunger artist continuously, day and night, and so no one could produce first-hand evidence that the fast had really been rigorous and continuous; only the artist himself could know that, he was therefore bound to be the sole completely satisfied spectator of his own fast. Yet for other reasons he was never satisfied; it was not perhaps mere fasting that had brought him to such skeleton thinness that many people had regretfully to keep away from his exhibitions, because the sight of him was too much for them, perhaps it was dissatisfaction with himself that had worn him down. For he alone knew, what no other initiate knew, how easy it was to fast. It was the easiest thing in the world. He made no secret of this, yet people did not believe him, at the best they set him down as modest, most of them, however, thought he was out for publicity or else was some kind of cheat who found it easy to fast because he had discovered a way of making it easy, and then had the impudence to admit the fact, more or less. He had to put up with all that, and in the course of time had got used to it, but his inner dissatisfaction always rankled, and never yet, after any term of fasting—this must be granted to his credit—had he left the cage of his own free will. The longest period of fasting was fixed by his impresario at forty days, beyond that term he was not allowed to go, not even in great cities, and there was good reason for it, too. Experience had proved that for about forty days the interest of the public could be stimulated by a steadily increasing pressure of advertisement, but after that the town began to lose interest, sympathetic support began notably to fall off; there were of course local variations as between one town and another or one country and another, but as a general rule forty days marked the limit. So on the fortieth day the flower-bedecked cage was opened, enthusiastic spectators filled the hall, a military band played, two doctors entered the cage to measure the results of the fast, which were announced through a megaphone, and finally two young ladies appeared, blissful at having been selected for the honor, to help the hunger artist down the few steps leading to a small table on which was spread a carefully chosen invalid repast. And at this very moment the artist always turned stubborn.

True, he would entrust his bony arms to the outstretched helping hands of the ladies bending over him, but stand up he would not. Why stop fasting at this particular moment, after forty days of it? He had held out for a long time, an illimitably long time; why stop now, when he was in his best fasting form, or rather, not yet quite in his best fasting form? Why should he be cheated of the fame he would get for fasting longer, for being not only the record hunger artist of all time, which presumably he was already, but for beating his own record by a performance beyond human imagination, since he felt that there were no limits to his capacity for fasting? His public pretended to admire him so much, why should it have so little patience with him; if he could endure fasting longer, why shouldn't the public endure it? Besides, he was tired, he was comfortable sitting in the straw, and now he was supposed to lift himself to his full height and go down to a meal the very thought of which gave him a nausea that only the presence of the ladies kept him from betraying, and even that with an effort. And he looked up into the eyes of the ladies who were apparently so friendly and in reality so cruel, and shook his head, which felt too heavy on its strengthless neck. But then there happened yet again what always happened. The impresario came forward, without a word—for the band made speech impossible—lifted his arms in the air above the artist, as if inviting Heaven to look down upon its creature here in the straw, this suffering martyr, which indeed he was, although in quite another sense; grasped him round the emaciated waist, with exaggerated caution, so that the frail condition he was in might be appreciated; and committed him to the care of the blenching ladies, not without secretly giving him a shaking so that his legs and body tottered and swayed. The artist now submitted completely; his head lolled on his breast as if it had landed there by chance; his body was hollowed out; his legs in a spasm of self-preservation clung close to each other at the knees, yet scraped on the ground as if it were not really solid ground, as if they were only trying to find solid ground; and the whole weight of his body, a feather-weight after all, relapsed onto one of the ladies, who, looking round for help and panting a little—this post of honor was not at all what she had expected it to be—first stretched her neck as far as she could to keep her face at least free from contact with the artist, when finding this impossible, and her more fortunate companion not coming to her aid but merely holding extended on her own trembling hand the little bunch of knucklebones that was the artist's, to the great delight of the spectators burst into tears and had to be replaced by an attendant who had long been stationed in readiness. Then came the food, a little of which the impresario managed to get between the artist's lips, while he sat in a kind of half-fainting trance, to the accompaniment of cheerful patter designed to distract the public's attention from the artist's condition; after that, a toast was drunk to the public, supposedly prompted by a whisper from the artist in the impresario's ear; the band confirmed it with a mighty flourish, the spectators melted away, and no one had any cause to be dissatisfied with the proceedings, no one except the hunger artist himself, he only, as always.

So he lived for many years, with small regular intervals of recuperation, in visible glory, honored by the world, yet in spite of that troubled in spirit, and all the more troubled because no one would take his trouble seriously. What comfort could he possibly need? What more could he possibly wish for? And if some good-natured person, feeling sorry for him, tried to console him by pointing out that his melancholy was probably caused by fasting, it could happen, especially when he had been fasting for some time, that he reacted with an outburst of fury and to the general alarm began to shake the bars of his cage like a wild animal. Yet the impresario had a way of punishing these outbreaks which he rather enjoyed putting into operation. He would apologize publicly for the artist's behavior, which was only to be excused, he admitted, because of the irritability caused by fasting; a condition hardly to be understood by well-fed people; then by natural transition he went on to mention the artist's equally incomprehensible boast that he could fast for much longer than he was doing; he praised the high ambition, the good will, the great self-denial undoubtedly implicit in such a statement; and then quite simply countered it by bringing out photographs, which were also on sale to the public, showing the artist on the fortieth day of a fast lying in bed almost dead from exhaustion. This perversion of the truth, familiar to the artist though it was, always unnerved him afresh and proved too much for him. What was a consequence of the premature ending of his fast was here presented as the cause of it! To fight against this lack of understanding, against a whole world of non-understanding, was impossible. Time and again in good faith he stood by the bars listening to the impresario, but as soon as the photographs appeared he always let go and sank with a groan back on to his straw, and the reassured public could once more come close and gaze at him.

A few years later when the witnesses of such scenes called them to mind, they often failed to understand themselves at all. For meanwhile the aforementioned change in public interest had set in; it seemed to happen almost overnight; there may have been profound causes for it, but who was going to bother about that; at any rate the pampered hunger artist suddenly found himself deserted one fine day by the amusement seekers, who went streaming past him to other more favored attractions. For the last time the impresario hurried him over half Europe to discover whether the old interest might still survive here and there; all in vain; everywhere, as if by secret agreement, a positive revulsion from professional fasting was in evidence. Of course it could not really have sprung up so suddenly as all that, and many premonitory symptoms which had not been sufficiently remarked or suppressed during the rush and glitter of success now came retrospectively to mind, but it was now too late to take any countermeasures. Fasting would surely come into fashion again at some future date, yet that was no comfort for those living in the present. What, then, was the hunger artist to do? He had been applauded by thousands in his time and could hardly come down to showing himself in a street booth at village fairs, and as for adopting another profession, he was not only too old for that but too fanatically devoted to fasting. So he took leave of the impresario, his partner in an unparalleled career, and hired himself to a large circus; in order to spare his own feelings he avoided reading the conditions of his contract.

A large circus with its enormous traffic in replacing and recruiting men, animals and apparatus can always find a use for people at any time, even for a

5

hunger artist, provided of course that he does not ask too much, and in this particular case anyhow it was not only the artist who was taken on but his famous and long-known name as well, indeed considering the peculiar nature of his performance, which was not impaired by advancing age, it could not be objected that here was an artist past his prime, no longer at the height of his professional skill, seeking a refuge in some quiet corner of a circus; on the contrary, the hunger artist averred that he could fast as well as ever, which was entirely credible, he even alleged that if he were allowed to fast as he liked, and this was at once promised him without more ado, he could astound the world by establishing a record never yet achieved, a statement which certainly provoked a smile among the other professionals, since it left out of account the change in public opinion, which the hunger artist in his zeal conveniently forgot.

He had not, however, actually lost his sense of the real situation and took it as a matter of course that he and his cage should be stationed, not in the middle of the ring as a main attraction, but outside, near the animal cages, on a site that was after all easily accessible. Large and gaily painted placards made a frame for the cage and announced what was to be seen inside it. When the public came thronging out in the intervals to see the animals, they could hardly avoid passing the hunger artist's cage and stopping there for a moment, perhaps they might even have stayed longer had not those pressing behind them in the narrow gangway, who did not understand why they should be held up on their way toward the excitements of the menagerie, made it impossible for anyone to stand gazing quietly for any length of time. And that was the reason why the hunger artist, who had of course been looking forward to these visiting hours as the main achievement of his life, began instead to shrink from them. At first he could hardly wait for the intervals; it was exhilarating to watch the crowds come streaming his way, until only too soon—not even the most obstinate self-deception, clung to almost consciously, could hold out against the fact—the conviction was borne in upon him that these people, most of them, to judge from their actions, again and again, without exception, were all on their way to the menagerie. And the first sight of them from the distance remained the best. For when they reached his cage he was at once deafened by the storm of shouting and abuse that arose from the two contending factions, which renewed themselves continuously, of those who wanted to stop and stare at him—he soon began to dislike them more than the others—not out of real interest but only out of obstinate self-assertiveness, and those who wanted to go straight on to the animals. When the first great rush was past, the stragglers came along, and these, whom nothing could have prevented from stopping to look at him as long as they had breath, raced past with long strides, hardly even glancing at him, in their haste to get to the menagerie in time. And all too rarely did it happen that he had a stroke of luck, when some father of a family fetched up before him with his children, pointed a finger at the hunger artist and explained at length what the phenomenon meant, telling stories of earlier years when he himself had watched similar but much more thrilling performances, and the children, still rather uncomprehending, since neither inside nor outside school had they been sufficiently prepared for this lesson—what did they care about fasting?—

yet showed by the brightness of their intent eyes that new and better times might be coming. Perhaps, said the hunger artist to himself many a time, things would be a little better if his cage were set not quite so near the menagerie. That made it too easy for people to make their choice, to say nothing of what he suffered from the stench of the menagerie, the animals' restlessness by night, the carrying past of raw lumps of flesh for the beasts of prey, the roaring at feeding times, which depressed him continually. But he did not dare to lodge a complaint with the management; after all, he had the animals to thank for the troops of people who passed his cage, among whom there might always be one here and there to take an interest in him, and who could tell where they might seclude him if he called attention to his existence and thereby to the fact that, strictly speaking, he was only an impediment on the way to the menagerie.

A small impediment, to be sure, one that grew steadily less. People grew familiar with the strange idea that they could be expected, in times like these, to take an interest in a hunger artist, and with this familiarity the verdict went out against him. He might fast as much as he could, and he did so; but nothing could save him now, people passed him by. Just try to explain to anyone the art of fasting! Anyone who has no feeling for it cannot be made to understand it. The fine placards grew dirty and illegible, they were torn down; the little notice board telling the number of fast days achieved, which at first was changed carefully every day, had long stayed at the same figure, for after the first few weeks even this small task seemed pointless to the staff; and so the artist simply fasted on and on, as he had once dreamed of doing, and it was no trouble to him, just as he had always foretold, but no one counted the days, no one, not even the artist himself, knew what records he was already breaking, and his heart grew heavy. And when once in a time some leisurely passer-by stopped, made merry over the old figure on the board and spoke of swindling, that was in its way the stupidest lie ever invented by indifference and inborn malice, since it was not the hunger artist who was cheating; he was working honestly, but the world was cheating him of his reward.

Many more days went by, however, and that too came to an end. An overseer's eye fell on the cage one day and he asked the attendants why this perfectly good cage should be left standing there unused with dirty straw inside it; nobody knew, until one man, helped out by the notice board, remembered about the hunger artist. They poked into the straw with sticks and found him in it. "Are you still fasting?" asked the overseer. "When on earth do you mean to stop?" "Forgive me, everybody," whispered the hunger artist; only the overseer, who had his ear to the bars, understood him. "Of course," said the overseer, and tapped his forehead with a finger to let the attendants know what state the man was in, "we forgive you." "I always wanted you to admire my fasting," said the hunger artist. "We do admire it," said the overseer, affably. "But you shouldn't admire it," said the hunger artist. "Well, then we don't admire it," said the overseer, "but why shouldn't we admire it?" "Because I have to fast, I can't help it," said the hunger artist. "What a fellow you are," said the overseer, "and why can't you help it?" "Because," said the hunger artist, lifting his head a little and speaking, with his lips pursed, as if for a kiss, right into the overseer's ear, so that no syllable might be lost, "because I couldn't find the food I liked. If I had found it, believe me, I should have made no fuss and stuffed myself like you or anyone else." These were his last words, but in his dimming eyes remained the firm though no longer proud persuasion that he was still continuing to fast.

10   "Well, clear this out now!" said the overseer, and they buried the hunger artist, straw and all. Into the cage they put a young panther. Even the most insensitive felt it refreshing to see this wild creature leaping around the cage that had so long been dreary. The panther was all right. The food he liked was brought him without hesitation by the attendants; he seemed not even to miss his freedom; his noble body, furnished almost to the bursting point with all that it needed, seemed to carry freedom around with it too; somewhere in his jaws it seemed to lurk; and the joy of life streamed with such ardent passion from his throat that for the onlookers it was not easy to stand the shock of it. But they braced themselves, crowded round the cage, and did not want ever to move away.

1924

MORDECAI RICHLER

The Summer My Grandmother Was Supposed to Die

Dr. Katzman discovered the gangrene on one of his monthly visits. "She won't last a month," he said.

He repeated that the second month, the third, and the fourth, and now she lay dying in the heat of the back bedroom.

"If only she'd die," my mother said. "Oh, God, why doesn't she die? God in heaven, what's she holding on for?"

The summer my grandmother was supposed to die we did not chip in with the Breenbaums to take a cottage in the Laurentians.[1] It wouldn't have been practical. The old lady couldn't be moved, the nurse came daily and the doctor twice a week, and so it seemed best to stay in the city and wait for her to die or, as my mother said, pass away. It was a hot summer, her bedroom was just behind the kitchen, and when we sat down to eat we could smell her. The dressings on my grandmother's left leg had to be changed several times a day and, according to Dr. Katzman, her condition was hopeless. "It's in the hands of the Almighty," he said.

5   "It won't be long now," my father said, "and she'll be better off, if you know what I mean."

"Please," my mother said.

A nurse came every day from the Royal Victorian Order. She arrived punctu-

1. Mountains in eastern Canada between Hudson Bay and the St. Lawrence River.

ally at noon and at five to twelve I'd join the rest of the boys under the outside staircase to look up her dress as she climbed to our second-story flat. Miss Monohan favored lacy pink panties and that was better than waiting under the stairs for Cousin Bessie, for instance. She wore enormous cotton bloomers, rain or shine.

I was sent out to play as often as possible, because my mother felt it was not good for me to see somebody dying. Usually I'd just roam the scorched streets shooting the breeze. There was Arty, Gas sometimes, Hershey, Stan, and me. We talked about everything from A to Z.

"Why is it," Arty wanted to know, "that Tarzan never shits?"

"Dick Tracy too."

"Or Wonder Woman."

"She's a dame."

"So?"

"Jees, wouldn't it be something if Superman crapped in the sky? He could just be flying over Waverly Street when, whamo, Mr. Rabinovitch catches it right in the kisser."

Mr. Rabinovitch was our Hebrew teacher.

"But there's Tarzan," Arty insisted, "in the jungle, week in and week out, and never once does he need to go to the toilet. It's not real, that's all."

Arty told me, "Before your grandma dies she's going to roll her eyes and gurgle. That's what they call the death-rattle."

"Aw, you know everything. Big shot."

"I *read* it, you jerk," Arty said, whacking me one, "in Perry Mason."

Home again I'd find my mother weeping.

"She's dying by inches," she said to my father one stifling night, "and none of them even come to see her. Oh, such children! They should only rot in hell."

"They're not behaving right. It's certainly not according to Hoyle," my father said.

"When I think of all the money and effort that went into making a rabbi out of Israel—the way Mother doted on him—and for what? Oh, what's the world coming to? God."

"It's not right."

Dr. Katzman was amazed. "I never believed she'd last this long. Really, it must be will-power alone that keeps her going. And your excellent care."

"I want her to die, Doctor. That's not my mother in the back room. It's an animal. I want her to please please die."

"Hush. You don't mean it. You're tired." And Dr. Katzman gave my father some pills for my mother to take. "A remarkable woman," he said. "A born nurse."

At night in bed my brother Harvey and I used to talk about our grandmother. "After she dies," I said, "her hair will go on growing for another twenty-four hours."

"Sez who?"

"Arty. It's a scientific fact. Do you think Uncle Lou will come from New York for the funeral?"

"Sure."

"Boy, that means another fiver for me. You too."

"You shouldn't say things like that, kiddo, or *her ghost will come back to haunt you.*"

"Well," I said, "I'll be able to go to her funeral, anyway. I'm not too young any more."

35   I was only six years old when my grandfather died, and I wasn't allowed to go to his funeral.

I have only one memory of my grandfather. Once he called me into his study, set me down on his lap, and made a drawing of a horse for me. On the horse he drew a rider. While I watched and giggled he gave the rider a beard and the round fur-trimmed cap of a rabbi.

My grandfather was a Zaddik,[2] one of the Righteous, and I've been told that to study Talmud with him had been a rare pleasure. I wasn't allowed to go to his funeral, but years after I was shown the telegrams of condolence that had come from Eire and Poland and Israel and even Japan. My grandfather had written many books: a translation of the Zohar into modern Hebrew—some twenty years' work—and lots of slender volumes of sermons, chassidic tales, and rabbinical commentaries. His books had been published in Warsaw and later in New York. He had been famous.

"At the funeral," my mother told me, "they had to have six motorcycle policemen to control the crowds. It was such a heat that twelve women fainted— and I'm *not* counting Mrs. Waxman from upstairs. With her, you know, *anything* to fall into a man's arms. Even Pinsky's. And did I tell you that there was even a French-Canadian priest there?"

"No kidding?"

40   "The priest was a real big *knacker.*[3] A bishop maybe. He used to study with the *zeyda.*[4] The *zeyda* was some personality, you know. Spiritual and worldly-wise at the same time. Such personalities they don't make any more. Today, rabbis and peanuts are the same size."

But, according to my father, the *zeyda* (his father-in-law) hadn't been as famous as all that. "There are things I could say," he told me. "There was another side to him."

My grandfather had come from generations and generations of rabbis, his youngest son was a rabbi, but none of his grandchildren would be one. My brother Harvey was going to be a dentist and at the time, 1937, I was interested in flying and my cousin Jerry was already a communist. I once heard Jerry say, "Our grandpappy wasn't all he was cracked up to be." When the men at the kosher bakeries went out on strike he spoke up against them on the streets where they were picketing and in the *shule.*[5] It was of no consequence to him that they were grossly underpaid. His superstitious followers had to have bread. "Grand-pappy," Jerry said, "was a prize reactionary."

A week after my grandfather died my grandmother suffered a stroke. Her right side was completely paralyzed. She couldn't speak. At first, it's true, my

2. "Righteous man" in Hebrew.   **3.** Big shot.   **4.** Grandfather.   **5.** Synagogue.

grandmother could say a few words and move her right hand enough to write her name in Hebrew. Her name was Malka. But her condition soon began to deteriorate.

My grandmother had six children and seven stepchildren, for my grandfather had been married before. His first wife had died in the old country. Two years later he had married my grandmother, the only daughter of the richest man in the village, and their marriage had been a singularly happy one. My grandmother had been a beautiful girl. She had also been a wise, resourceful, and patient wife. Qualities, I fear, indispensable to life with a Zaddik. For the synagogue had paid my grandfather no stipulated salary and much of the money he had picked up here and there he had habitually distributed among rabbinical students, needy immigrants, and widows. A vice, and such it was to his hard-pressed family, which made him as unreliable a provider as a drunkard. And indeed, to carry the analogy further, my grandmother had had to make many hurried trips to the pawnbroker with her jewelry. Not all of it had been redeemed, either. But her children had been looked after. The youngest, her favorite, was a rabbi in Boston, the eldest was the actor-manager of a Yiddish theater in New York, and another was a lawyer. One daughter lived in Toronto, two in Montreal. My mother was the youngest daughter, and when my grandmother had her stroke there was a family meeting and it was decided that my mother would take care of her. This was my father's fault. All the other husbands spoke up—they protested their wives had too much work, they could never manage it—but my father detested quarrels, and he was silent. So my grandmother came to stay with us.

Her bedroom, the back bedroom, had actually been promised to me for my seventh birthday. But all that was forgotten now, and I had to go on sharing a bedroom with my brother Harvey. So naturally I was resentful when each morning before I left for school my mother said, "Go in and kiss the *baba*[6] good-bye."

All the same I'd go into the bedroom and kiss my grandmother hastily. She'd say "Bouyo-bouyo," for that was the only sound she could make. And after school it was, "Go in and tell the *baba* you're home."

"I'm home, *baba*."

"Bouyo-bouyo."

During those first hopeful months—"Twenty years ago who would have thought there'd be a cure for diabetes?" my father asked; "where there's life there's hope, you know"—she'd smile at me and try to speak, her eyes charged with effort. And even later there were times when she pressed my head urgently to her bosom with her surprisingly strong left arm. But as her illness dragged on and on and she became a condition in the house, something beyond hope or reproach, like the leaky icebox, there was less recognition and more ritual in those kisses. I came to dread her room. A clutter of sticky medicine bottles and the cracked toilet chair beside the bed; glazed but imploring eyes and a feeble smile, the wet slap of her lips against my cheeks. I flinched from her touch.

45

6. Grandma.

After two years of it I protested to my mother. "Look what's the use of telling her I'm going or I'm here. She doesn't even recognize me any more."

"Don't be fresh. She's your grandmother."

My uncle who was in the theater in New York sent money regularly to help support my grandmother and, for the first few months, so did the other children. But once the initial and sustaining excitement had passed and it became likely that my grandmother might linger in her invalid condition for two or maybe even three more years, the checks began to drop off, and the children seldom came to our house any more. Anxious weekly visits—"and how is she today, poor lamb?"—quickly dwindled to a dutiful monthly looking in, then a semiannual visit, and these always on the way to somewhere.

"The way they act," my father said, "you'd think that if they stayed long enough to take off their coats we'd make them take the *baba* home with them."

When the children did come to visit, my mother made it difficult for them.

"It's killing me," she said. "I have to lift her onto that chair three times a day maybe. Have you any idea how heavy she is? And what makes you think I always catch her in time? Sometimes I have to change her bed twice a day. That's a job I'd like to see your wife do," she said to my uncle, the rabbi.

"We could sent her to the Old People's Home," the rabbi said.

"Now there's an idea," my father said.

But my mother began to sob. "Not as long as I'm alive," she said. And she gave my father a stony look. "Say something."

"It wouldn't be according to Hoyle."

"You want to be able to complain to everybody in town about all the other children," the rabbi said. "You've got a martyr complex."

"Everybody has a point of view, you know. You know what I mean?" my father said. "So what's the use of fighting?"

Meanwhile, Dr. Katzman came once a month to examine my grandmother. "It's remarkable, astonishing," he'd say each time. "She's as strong as a horse."

"Some life for a person," my father said. "She can't speak—she doesn't recognize anybody—what is there for her?"

The doctor was a cultivated man; he spoke often for women's clubs, sometimes on Yiddish literature and other times, his rubicund face hot with impatience, the voice taking on a doomsday tone, on the cancer threat.

"Who are we to judge?" he asked.

Every evening, during the first months of my grandmother's illness, my mother read her a story by Sholem Aleichem.[7] "Tonight she smiled," my mother would say. "She understood. I can tell." And my father, my brother, and I would not comment. Once a week my mother used to give the old lady a manicure. Sunny afternoons she'd lift her into a wheelchair and put her out in the sun. Somebody always had to stay in the house in case my grandmother called. Often, during the night, she would begin to wail unaccountably, and my mother

---

7. "Peace be with you," pen name of Yiddish author and humorist Shalom Rabinovitz (1859–1916).

would get up and rock the old lady in her arms for hours. But in the fourth year of my grandmother's illness the strain and fatigue began to tell on my mother. Besides looking after my grandmother—"and believe you me," the doctor assured her with a clap on the back, "it would be a full-time job for a professional nurse"—she had to keep house for a husband and two sons. She began to quarrel with my father and she became sharp with Harvey and me. My father started to spend his evenings playing pinochle at Tansky's Cigar & Soda. Weekends he took Harvey and me to visit his brothers and sisters. And everywhere he went people had little bits of advice for him.

"Sam, you might as well be a bachelor. You're just going to have to put your foot down for once."

"Yeah, in your face maybe."

My cousin Libby, who was at McGill,[8] said, "This could have a very damaging effect on the development of your boys. These are their formative years, Uncle Samuel, and the omnipresence of death in the house . . ."

"What you need," my father said, "is a boy friend. *And how.*"

At Tansky's Cigar & Soda it was, "Come clean, Sam. It's no hardship. If I know you, the old lady's got a big insurance policy and when the time comes . . ."   70

My mother lost lots of weight. After dinner she'd fall asleep in her chair in the middle of Lux Radio Theater.[9] One minute she'd be sewing a patch on my breeches or be making a list of girls to call for a bingo party (proceeds for the Talmud Torah[1]), and the next she'd be snoring. Then, one morning, she just couldn't get out of bed, and Dr. Katzman came round a week before his regular visit. "Well, well, this won't do, will it?" He sat in the kitchen with my father and the two men drank apricot brandy out of small glasses.

"Your wife is a remarkable woman," Dr. Katzman said.

"You don't say?"

"She's got a gallstone condition."

My father shrugged. "Have another one for the road," he said.   75

"Thank you, but I have several more calls to make." Dr. Katzman rose, sighing. "There she lies in that back room, poor old woman," he said, "hanging desperately onto life. There's food for thought there."

My grandmother's children met again, and the five of them sat around my mother's bed embarrassed, irritated, and quick to take insult. All except my uncle who was in the theater. He sucked a cigar and drank whisky. He teased my mother, the rabbi, and my aunts, and if not for him I think they would have been at each other's throats. It was decided, over my mother's protests, to send my grandmother to the Old People's Home on Esplanade Street. An ambulance came to take my grandmother away and Dr. Katzman said, "It's for the best." But my father had been in the back bedroom when the old lady had held on tenaciously to the bedpost, not wanting to be moved by the two men in white—

8. University in Montreal.   9. Weekly radio drama sponsored by Lux soap.   1. Orthodox Jewish school for boys.

"Easy does it, granny," the younger one had said—and afterwards he could not go in to see my mother. He went out for a walk.

"She looked at me with such a funny expression," he told my brother. "Is it my fault?"

My mother stayed in bed for another two weeks. My father cooked for us and we hired a woman to do the housework. My mother put on weight quickly, her cheeks regained their normal pinkish hue and, for the first time in months, she actually joked with Harvey and me. She became increasingly curious about our schools and whether or not we shined our shoes regularly. She began to cook again, special dishes for my father, and she resumed old friendships with women on the parochial school board. The change reflected on my father. Not only did his temper improve, but he stopped going to Tansky's every other night, and began to come home early from work. Life at home had never been so rich. But my grandmother's name was never mentioned. The back bedroom remained empty and I continued to share a room with Harvey. I couldn't see the point and so one evening I said, "Look, why don't I move into the back bedroom?"

80   My father glared at me across the table.

"But it's empty like."

My mother left the table. And the next afternoon she put on her best dress and coat and new spring hat.

"Where are you going?" my father asked.

"To see my mother."

85   "Don't go looking for trouble."

"It's been a month. Maybe they're not treating her right."

"They're experts."

"Did you think I was never going to visit her? I'm not inhuman, you know."

"All right, go," he said.

90   But after she'd gone my father went to the window and said, "Son-of-a-bitch."

Harvey and I sat outside on the steps watching the cars go by. My father sat on the balcony above, cracking peanuts. It was six o'clock, maybe later, when the ambulance turned the corner, slowed down, and parked right in front of the house.

"Son-of-a-bitch," my father said. "I knew it."

My mother got out first, her eyes red and swollen, and hurried upstairs to make my grandmother's bed.

"I'm sorry, Sam, I had to do it."

95   "You'll get sick again, that's what."

"You think she doesn't recognize people. From the moment she saw me she cried and cried. Oh, it was terrible."

"They're experts there. They know how to handle her better than you do."

"Experts? Expert murderers you mean. She's got bedsores, Sam. Those dirty little Irish nurses they don't change her linen often enough, they hate her. She must have lost twenty pounds there."

"Another month and you'll be flat on your back again."

100   "Sam, what could I do? Please Sam."

"She'll outlive all of us. Even Muttel.[2] I'm going out for a walk."
She was back and I was to blame.

My father became a regular at Tansky's Cigar & Soda again and every morning I had to go in and kiss my grandmother. She began to look like a man. Little hairs had sprouted on her chin, she had a spiky gray mustache and, of course, she was practically bald. This near-baldness, I guess, sprang from the fact that she had been shaving her head ever since she had married my grandfather the rabbi.[3] My grandmother had four different wigs, but she had not worn one since the first year of her illness. She wore a little pink cap instead. And so, as before, she said, "bouyo-bouyo," to everything.

Once more uncles and aunts sent five-dollar bills, though erratically, to help pay for my grandmother's support. Elderly people, former followers of my grandfather, came to inquire after the old lady's health. They sat in the back bedroom with her for hours, leaning on their canes, talking to themselves, rocking, always rocking to and fro. "The Holy Shakers," my father called them, and Harvey and I avoided them, because they always wanted to pinch our cheeks, give us a dash of snuff and laugh when we sneezed, or offer us a sticky old candy from a little brown bag with innumerable creases in it. When the visit was done the old people would unfailingly sit in the kitchen with my mother for another hour, watching her make lockshen[4] or bake bread. My mother always served them lemon tea and they would talk about my grandfather, recalling his books, his sayings, and his charitable deeds.

And so another two years passed, with no significant change in my grand-   105
mother's condition. But fatigue, bad temper, and even morbidity enveloped my mother again. She fought with her brothers and sisters and once, when I stepped into the living room, I found her sitting with her head in her hands, and she looked up at me with such anguish that I was frightened.

"What did I do now?" I asked.

"If, God forbid, I had a stroke, would you send me to the Old People's Home?"

"Don't be a joke. Of course not."

"I hope that never in my life do I have to count on my children for anything."

The summer my grandmother was supposed to die, the seventh year of her   110
illness, my brother took a job as a shipper and he kept me awake at night with stories about the factory. "What we do, see, is clear out the middle of a huge pile of lengths of material. That makes for a kind of secret cave. A hideout. Well, then you coax one of the *shiksas*[5] inside and hi-diddle-diddle."

One night Harvey waited until I had fallen asleep and then he wrapped himself in a white sheet, crept up to my bed, and shouted, "Bouyo-bouyo."

I hit him. He shouted.

---

2. The narrator's Yiddish name; could be the equivalent of Mordecai.   3. Married Orthodox Jewish women customarily shave their heads or cover their hair.   4. Noodles.   5. Gentile girls.

"Children. Children, please," my mother called. "I must get some rest."

As my grandmother's condition worsened—from day to day we didn't know when she'd die—I was often sent out to eat at my aunt's or at my other grandmother's house. I was hardly ever at home. On Saturday mornings I'd get together with the other guys and we'd walk all the way past the mountain to Eaton's, which was our favorite department store for riding up and down escalators and stealing.

In those days they let boys into the left-field bleachers free during the week and we spent many an afternoon at the ball park. The Montreal Royals, part of the Dodger farm system, was some ball club too. There was Jackie Robinson and Roy Campanella, Honest John Gabbard, Chuck Connors, and Kermit Kitman was our hero. It used to kill us to see that crafty little hebe[6] running around there with all those tall dumb *goyim*.[7] "Hey, Kitman," we'd yell. "Hey, hey, shohead,[8] if your father knew you played ball on *shabus*[9]—" Kitman, unfortunately, was all field and no hit. He never made the majors. "There goes Kermit Kitman," we'd yell, after he'd gone down swinging again, "the first Jewish strikeout king of the International League." This we usually followed up by bellowing some choice imprecations in Yiddish.

It was after one of these games, on a Friday afternoon, that I came home to find a small crowd gathered in front of the house.

"That's the grandson."

"Poor kid."

Old people stood silent and expressionless across the street staring at our front door. A taxi pulled up and my aunt hurried out, hiding her face in her hands.

"After so many years," somebody said.

"And probably next year they'll discover a cure. Isn't that *always* the case?"

I took the stairs two at a time. The flat was full. Uncles and aunts from my father's side of the family, odd old people, Dr. Katzman, Harvey, neighbors, were all standing around and talking in hushed voices in the living room. I found my father in the kitchen, getting out the apricot brandy. "Your grandmother's dead," he said.

"She didn't suffer," somebody said. "She passed away in her sleep."

"A merciful death."

"Where's Maw?"

"In the bedroom with . . . you'd better not go in," my father said.

"I want to see her."

My mother's face was long with grief. She wore a black shawl, and glared down at a knot of handkerchief clutched in a fist that had been cracked by washing soda. "Don't come in here," she said.

Several bearded, round-shouldered men in black shiny coats stood round the bed. I couldn't see my grandmother.

---

6. Hebrew, Jew.   7. Gentiles.   8. Possibly *shorn-head*(?), referring to the short hair or crew cut of an athlete, in contrast to traditional long locks of Orthodox Jews(?).   9. Sabbath.

130   "Your grandmother's dead."

"Daddy told me."

"Go and wash your face and comb your hair. You'll have to get your own supper."

"O.K."

"One minute. The *baba* left some jewelry. The ring is for Harvey's wife and the necklace is for yours."

"Who's getting married?"   135

"Better go and wash your face. And remember behind the ears, Muttel."

Telegrams were sent, long-distance calls were made, and all through the evening relatives and neighbors came and went like swarms of fish when crumbs have been dropped into the water.

"When my father died," my mother said, "they had to have *six* motorcycle policemen to control the crowds. Twelve people fainted, such a heat . . ."

The man from the funeral parlor came.

"There goes the only Jewish businessman in town," my Uncle Harry said,   140
"who wishes all his customers were Germans."

"This is no time for jokes."

"Listen, life goes on."

My cousin Jerry had begun to use a cigarette holder. "Everyone's going to be sickeningly sentimental," he said. "Soon the religious mumbo-jumbo starts. I can hardly wait."

Tomorrow was the Sabbath and so, according to the law, my grandmother couldn't be buried until Sunday. She would have to lie on the floor all night. Two old grizzly women in white came to move and wash the body and a professional mourner arrived to sit up and pray for her.

"I don't trust his face," my mother said. "He'll fall asleep. You watch him,   145
Sam."

"A fat lot of good prayers will do her now."

"Will you just watch him, please."

"I'll watch him, I'll watch him." My father was livid about my Uncle Harry. "The way he's gone after that apricot brandy you'd think that guy never saw a bottle in his life before."

Harvey and I were sent to bed, but we couldn't sleep. My aunt was sobbing over the body in the living room—"That dirty hypocrite," my mother said—there was the old man praying, coughing, and spitting into his handkerchief each time he woke; and hushed voices and whimpering from the kitchen, where my father and mother sat. Harvey was in a good mood, he let me have a few puffs of his cigarette.

"Well, kiddo, this is our last night together. Tomorrow you can take over the   150
back bedroom."

"*Are you crazy?*"

"You always wanted it for yourself."

"She died in there, bud. You think I'm going to sleep in there?"

"Good night. Happy dreams, kiddo."

155 "Hey, let's talk some more."

Harvey told me a ghost story. "Did you know that when they hang a man," he said, "the last thing that happens is that he has an orgasm?"

"A what?"

"Forget it. I forgot you were still in kindergarten."

"I know plenty. Don't worry."

160 "At the funeral they're going to open her coffin to throw dirt in her face. It's supposed to be earth from Eretz.[1] They open it and you're going to have to look." Harvey stood up on his bed, holding his hands over his head like claws. He made a hideous face. "Bouyo-bouyo. Who's that sleeping in my bed? Woo-woo."

My uncle who was in the theater, the rabbi, and my aunt from Toronto, all came to Montreal for the funeral. Dr. Katzman came too.

"As long as she was alive," my mother said, "he couldn't even send five dollars a month. Some son! What a rabbi! I don't want him in my house, Sam. I can't bear the sight of him."

"You don't mean a word of that and you know it," Dr. Katzman said.

"Maybe you'd better give her a sedative," the rabbi said.

165 "Sam. Sam, will you say something, please."

My father stepped up to the rabbi, his face flushed. "I'll tell you this straight to your face, Israel," he said. "You've gone down in my estimation."

"Really," the rabbi said, smiling a little.

My father's face burned a deeper red. "Year by year," he said, "your stock has gone down with me."

And my mother began to weep bitterly, helplessly, without control. She was led unwillingly to bed. While my father tried his best to comfort her, as he said consoling things, Dr. Katzman plunged a needle into her arm. "There we are," he said.

170 I went to sit in the sun on the outside stairs with Arty. "I'm going to the funeral," I said.

"I couldn't go anyway."

Arty was descended from the tribe of high priests and so was not allowed to be in the presence of a dead body. I was descended from the Yisroelis.[2]

"The lowest of the low," Arty said.

"Aw."

175 My uncle, the rabbi, and Dr. Katzman stepped into the sun to light cigarettes.

"It's remarkable that she held out for so long," Dr. Katzman said.

"Remarkable?" my uncle said. "It's written that if a man has been married twice he will spend as much time with his first wife in heaven as he did on earth. My father, may he rest in peace, was married to his first wife for seven years and my mother, may she rest in peace, has managed to keep alive for seven years. Today in heaven she will be able to join my father, may he rest in peace."

1. Eretz Yisrael, the Land of Israel.   2. The lowest of the three categories into which the Jewish people are traditionally divided.

Dr. Katzman shook his head, he pursed his lips. "It's amazing," he said. "The mysteries of the human heart. Astonishing."

My father hurried outside. "Dr. Katzman, please. It's my wife. Maybe the injection wasn't strong enough? She just doesn't stop crying. It's like a tap. Could you come please?"

"Excuse me," Dr. Katzman said to my uncle.   180

"Of course."

My uncle approached Arty and me.

"Well, boys," he said, "what would you like to be when you grow up?"

1961

BOBBIE ANN MASON

Shiloh

Leroy Moffitt's wife, Norma Jean, is working on her pectorals. She lifts three-pound dumbbells to warm up, then progresses to a twenty-pound barbell. Standing with her legs apart, she reminds Leroy of Wonder Woman.

"I'd give anything if I could just get these muscles to where they're real hard," says Norma Jean. "Feel this arm. It's not as hard as the other one."

"That's cause you're right-handed," says Leroy, dodging as she swings the barbell in an arc.

"Do you think so?"

"Sure."   5

Leroy is a truckdriver. He injured his leg in a highway accident four months ago, and his physical therapy, which involves weights and a pulley, prompted Norma Jean to try building herself up. Now she is attending a body-building class. Leroy has been collecting temporary disability since his tractor-trailer jack-knifed in Missouri, badly twisting his left leg in its socket. He has a steel pin in his hip. He will probably not be able to drive his rig again. It sits in the backyard, like a gigantic bird that has flown home to roost. Leroy has been home in Kentucky for three months, and his leg is almost healed, but the accident frightened him and he does not want to drive any more long hauls. He is not sure what to do next. In the meantime, he makes things from craft kits. He started by building a miniature log cabin from notched Popsicle sticks. He varnished it and placed it on the TV set, where it remains. It reminds him of a rustic Nativity scene. Then he tried string art (sailing ships on black velvet), a macramé owl kit, a snap-together B-17 Flying Fortress,[1] and a lamp made out of a model truck, with a light fixture screwed in the top of the cab. At first the kits were diversions, something to kill time, but now he is thinking about building a full-scale log house from a kit. It would be considerably cheaper than building a regular

---

1. World War II bomber.

house, and besides, Leroy has grown to appreciate how things are put together. He has begun to realize that in all the years he was on the road he never took time to examine anything. He was always flying past scenery.

"They won't let you build a log cabin in any of the new subdivisions," Norma Jean tells him.

"They will if I tell them it's for you," he says, teasing her. Ever since they were married, he has promised Norma Jean he would build her a new home one day. They have always rented, and the house they live in is small and nondescript. It does not even feel like a home, Leroy realizes now.

Norma Jean works at the Rexall drugstore, and she has acquired an amazing amount of information about cosmetics. When she explains to Leroy the three stages of complexion care, involving creams, toners, and moisturizers, he thinks happily of other petroleum products—axle grease, diesel fuel. This is a connection between him and Norma Jean. Since he has been home, he has felt unusually tender about his wife and guilty over his long absences. But he can't tell what she feels about him. Norma Jean has never complained about his traveling; she has never made hurt remarks, like calling his truck a "widow-maker." He is reasonably certain she has been faithful to him, but he wishes she would celebrate his permanent homecoming more happily. Norma Jean is often startled to find Leroy at home, and he thinks she seems a little disappointed about it. Perhaps he reminds her too much of the early days of their marriage, before he went on the road. They had a child who died as an infant, years ago. They never speak about their memories of Randy, which have almost faded, but now that Leroy is home all the time, they sometimes feel awkward around each other, and Leroy wonders if one of them should mention the child. He has the feeling that they are waking up out of a dream together—that they must create a new marriage, start afresh. They are lucky they are still married. Leroy has read that for most people losing a child destroys the marriage—or else he heard this on *Donahue*. He can't always remember where he learns things anymore.

10   At Christmas, Leroy bought an electric organ for Norma Jean. She used to play the piano when she was in high school. "It don't leave you," she told him once. "It's like riding a bicycle."

The new instrument had so many keys and buttons that she was bewildered by it at first. She touched the keys tentatively, pushed some buttons, then pecked out "Chopsticks." It came out in an amplified fox-trot rhythm, with marimba sounds.

"It's an orchestra!" she cried.

The organ had a pecan-look finish and eighteen preset chords, with optional flute, violin, trumpet, clarinet, and banjo accompaniments. Norma Jean mastered the organ almost immediately. At first she played Christmas songs. Then she bought *The Sixties Songbook* and learned every tune in it, adding variations to each with the rows of brightly colored buttons.

"I didn't like these old songs back then," she said. "But I have this crazy feeling I missed something."

15   "You didn't miss a thing," said Leroy.

Leroy likes to lie on the couch and smoke a joint and listen to Norma Jean play "Can't Take My Eyes Off You" and "I'll Be Back."[2] He is back again. After fifteen years on the road, he is finally settling down with the woman he loves. She is still pretty. Her skin is flawless. Her frosted curls resemble pencil trimmings.

Now that Leroy has come home to stay, he notices how much the town has changed. Subdivisions are spreading across western Kentucky like an oil slick. The sign at the edge of town says "Pop: 11,500" — only seven hundred more than it said twenty years before. Leroy can't figure out who is living in all the new houses. The farmers who used to gather around the courthouse square on Saturday afternoons to play checkers and spit tobacco juice have gone. It has been years since Leroy has thought about the farmers, and they have disappeared without his noticing.

Leroy meets a kid named Stevie Hamilton in the parking lot at the new shopping center. While they pretend to be strangers meeting over a stalled car, Stevie tosses an ounce of marijuana under the front seat of Leroy's car. Stevie is wearing orange jogging shoes and a T-shirt that says CHATTAHOOCHEE SUPER-RAT. His father is a prominent doctor who lives in one of the expensive subdivisons in a new white-columned brick house that looks like a funeral parlor. In the phone book under his name there is a separate number, with the listing "Teenagers."

"Where do you get this stuff?" asks Leroy. "From your pappy!"

"That's for me to know and you to find out," Stevie says. He is slit-eyed and   20
skinny.

"What else you got?"

"What you interested in?'

"Nothing special. Just wondered."

Leroy used to take speed on the road. Now he has to go slowly. He needs to be mellow. He leans back against the car and says, "I'm aiming to build me a log house, soon as I get time. My wife, though, I don't think she likes the idea."

"Well, let me know when you want me again," Stevie says. He has a cigarette   25
in his cupped palm, as though sheltering it from the wind. He takes a long drag, then stomps it on the asphalt and slouches away.

Stevie's father was two years ahead of Leroy in high school. Leroy is thirty-four. He married Norma Jean when they were both eighteen, and their child Randy was born a few months later, but he died at the age of four months and three days. He would be about Stevie's age now. Norma Jean and Leroy were at the drive-in, watching a double feature (*Dr. Strangelove* and *Lover Come Back*),[3] and the baby was sleeping in the back seat. When the first movie ended, the baby was dead. It was the sudden infant death syndrome. Leroy remembers handing Randy to a nurse at the emergency room, as though he were offering her a large doll as a present. A dead baby feels like a sack of flour. "It just happens sometimes," said the doctor, in what Leroy always recalls as a noncha-

2. 1960s hit songs.   3. A 1963 satire on nuclear war and a 1961 Rock Hudson–Doris Day romantic comedy satirizing the advertising business.

lant tone. Leroy can hardly remember the child anymore, but he still sees vividly a scene from *Dr. Strangelove* in which the President of the United States was talking in a folksy voice on the hot line to the Soviet premier about the bomber accidentally headed toward Russia. He was in the War Room, and the world map was lit up. Leroy remembers Norma Jean catatonically beside him in the hospital and himself thinking: Who is this strange girl? He had forgotten who she was. Now scientists are saying that crib death is caused by a virus. Nobody knows anything, Leroy thinks. The answers are always changing.

When Leroy gets home from the shopping center, Norma Jean's mother, Mabel Beasley, is there. Until this year, Leroy has not realized how much time she spends with Norma Jean. When she visits, she inspects the closets and then the plants, informing Norma Jean when a plant is droopy or yellow. Mabel calls the plants "flowers," although there are never any blooms. She always notices if Norma Jean's laundry is piling up. Mabel is a short, overweight woman whose tight, brown-dyed curls look more like a wig than the actual wig she sometimes wears. Today she has brought Norma Jean an off-white dust ruffle she made for the bed; Mabel works in a custom-upholstery shop.

"This is the tenth one I made this year," Mabel says. "I got started and couldn't stop."

"It's real pretty," says Norma Jean.

30   "Now we can hide things under the bed," says Leroy, who gets along with his mother-in-law primarily by joking with her. Mabel has never really forgiven him for disgracing her by getting Norma Jean pregnant. When the baby died, she said that fate was mocking her.

"What's that thing?" Mabel says to Leroy in a loud voice, pointing to a tangle of yarn on a piece of canvas.

Leroy holds it up for Mabel to see. "It's my needlepoint," he explains. "This is a *Star Trek* pillow cover."

"That's what a woman would do," says Mabel. "Great day in the morning!"

"All the big football players on TV do it," he says.

35   "Why, Leroy, you're always trying to fool me. I don't believe you for one minute. You don't know what to do with yourself—that's the whole trouble. Sewing!"

"I'm aiming to build us a log house," says Leroy. "Soon as my plans come."

"Like *heck* you are," says Norma Jean. She takes Leroy's needlepoint and shoves it into a drawer. "You have to find a job first. Nobody can afford to build now anyway."

Mabel straightens her girdle and says, "I still think before you get tied down y'all ought to take a little run to Shiloh."

"One of these days, Mama," Norma Jean says impatiently.

40   Mabel is talking about Shiloh, Tennessee. For the past few years, she has been urging Leroy and Norma Jean to visit the Civil War battleground there.[4]

---

4. Where, in April 1862, more than 23,000 troops of the North and South, one-quarter of those who fought there, died. This was the first real indication of how bitter and bloody the war was to be. General Ulysses S. Grant, when reinforcements arrived, drove the Confederate forces, which had gained an initial victory by a surprise attack, back to their base in Corinth, Mississippi.

Mabel went there on her honeymoon—the only real trip she ever took. Her husband died of a perforated ulcer when Norma Jean was ten, but Mabel, who was accepted into the United Daughters of the Confederacy in 1975, is still preoccupied with going back to Shiloh.

"I've been to kingdom come and back in that truck out yonder," Leroy says to Mabel, "but we never yet set foot in that battleground. Ain't that something? How did I miss it?"

"It's not even that far," Mabel says.

After Mabel leaves, Norma Jean reads to Leroy from a list she has made. "Thing you could do," she announces. "You could get a job as a guard at Union Carbide, where they'd let you set on a stool. You could get on at the lumberyard. You could do a little carpenter work, if you want to build so bad. You could—"

"I can't do something where I'd have to stand up all day."

"You ought to try standing up all day behind a cosmetics counter. It's amazing that I have strong feet, coming from two parents that never had strong feet at all." At the moment Norma Jean is holding on to the kitchen counter, raising her knees one at a time as she talks. She is wearing two-pound ankle weights.

"Don't worry," says Leroy. "I'll do something."

"You could truck calves to slaughter for somebody. You wouldn't have to drive any big old truck for that."

"I'm going to build you this house," says Leroy. "I want to make you a real home."

"I don't want to live in any log cabin."

"It's not a cabin. It's a house."

"I don't care. It looks like a cabin."

"You and me together could lift those logs. It's just like lifting weights."

Norma Jean doesn't answer. Under her breath, she is counting. Now she is marching through the kitchen. She is doing goose steps.

Before his accident, when Leroy came home he used to stay in the house with Norma Jean, watching TV in bed and playing cards. She would cook fried chicken, picnic ham, chocolate pie—all his favorites. Now he is home alone much of the time. In the mornings, Norma Jean disappears, leaving a cooling place in the bed. She eats a cereal called Body Buddies, and she leaves the bowl on the table, with soggy tan balls floating in a milk puddle. He sees things about Norma Jean that he never realized before. When she chops onions, she stares off into a corner, as if she can't bear to look. She puts on her house slippers almost precisely at nine o'clock every evening and nudges her jogging shoes under the couch. She saves bread heels for the birds. Leroy watches the birds at the feeder. He notices the peculiar way goldfinches fly past the window. They close their wings, then fall, then spread their wings to catch and lift themselves. He wonders if they close their eyes when they fall. Norma Jean closes her eyes when they are in bed. She wants the lights turned out. Even then, he is sure she closes her eyes.

He goes for long drives around town. He tends to drive a car rather carelessly. Power steering and an automatic shift make a car feel so small and inconsequential that his body is hardly involved in the driving process. His injured leg stretches out comfortably. Once or twice he has almost hit something, but even the prospect of an accident seems minor in a car. He cruises the new subdivisions, feeling like a criminal rehearsing for a robbery. Norma Jean is probably right about a log house being inappropriate here in the new subdivisions. All the houses look grand and complicated. They depress him.

One day when Leroy comes home from a drive he finds Norma Jean in tears. She is in the kitchen making a potato and mushroom-soup casserole, with grated-cheese topping. She is crying because her mother caught her smoking.

"I didn't hear her coming. I was standing here puffing away pretty as you please," Norma Jean says, wiping her eyes.

"I knew it would happen sooner or later," says Leroy, putting his arm around her.

"She don't know the meaning of the word 'knock,' " says Norma Jean. "It's a wonder she hadn't caught me years ago."

60 "Think of it this way," Leroy says. "What if she caught me with a joint?"

"You better not let her!" Norma Jean shrieks. "I'm warning you, Leroy Moffitt!"

"I'm just kidding. Here, play me a tune. That'll help you relax."

Norma Jean puts the casserole in the oven and sets the timer. Then she plays a ragtime tune, with horns and banjo, as Leroy lights up a joint and lies on the couch, laughing to himself about Mabel's catching him at it. He thinks of Stevie Hamilton—a doctor's son pushing grass. Everything is funny. The whole town seems crazy and small. He is reminded of Virgil Mathis, a boastful policeman Leroy used to shoot pool with. Virgil recently led a drug bust in a back room at a bowling alley, where he seized ten thousand dollars' worth of marijuana. The newspaper had a picture of him holding up the bags of grass and grinning widely. Right now, Leroy can imagine Virgil breaking down the door and arresting him with a lungful of smoke. Virgil would probably have been alerted to the scene because of all the racket Norma Jean is making. Now she sounds like a hard-rock band. Norma Jean is terrific. When she switches to a latin-rhythm version of "Sunshine Superman," Leroy hums along. Norma Jean's foot goes up and down, up and down.

"Well, what do you think?" Leroy says, when Norma Jean pauses to search through her music.

65 "What do I think about what?"

His mind has gone blank. Then he says, "I'll sell my rig and build us a house." That wasn't what he wanted to say. He wanted to know what she thought—what she *really* thought—about them.

"Don't start in on that again," says Norma Jean. She begins playing "Who'll Be the Next in Line?"

Leroy used to tell hitchhikers his whole life story—about his travels, his hometown, the baby. He would end with a question: "Well, what do you think?" It was just a rhetorical question. In time, he had the feeling that he'd been telling the same story over and over to the same hitchhikers. He quit talking to hitchhikers when he realized how his voice sounded—whining and self-pitying, like some teenage-tragedy song. Now Leroy has the sudden impulse to tell Norma Jean about himself, as if he had just met her. They have known each other so long they have forgotten a lot about each other. They could become reacquainted. But when the oven timer goes off and she runs to the kitchen, he forgets why he wants to do this.

The next day, Mabel drops by. It is Saturday and Norma Jean is cleaning. Leroy is studying the plans of his log house, which have finally come in the mail. He has them spread out on the table—big sheets of stiff blue paper, with diagrams and numbers printed in white. While Norma Jean runs the vacuum, Mabel drinks coffee. She sets her coffee cup on a blueprint.

"I'm just waiting for time to pass," she says to Leroy, drumming her fingers on the table.   70

As soon as Norma Jean switches off the vacuum, Mabel says in a loud voice, "Did you hear about the datsun dog that killed the baby?"

Norma Jean says, "The word is 'dachshund.' "

"They put the dog on trial. It chewed the baby's legs off. The mother was in the next room all the time." She raises her voice. "They thought it was neglect."

Norma Jean is holding her ears. Leroy manages to open the refrigerator and get some Diet Pepsi to offer Mabel. Mabel still has some coffee and she waves away the Pepsi.

"Datsuns are like that," Mabel says. "They're jealous dogs. They'll tear a   75
place to pieces if you don't keep an eye on them."

"You better watch out what you're saying, Mabel," says Leroy.

"Well, facts is facts."

Leroy looks out the window at his rig. It is like a huge piece of furniture gathering dust in the backyard. Pretty soon it will be an antique. He hears the vacuum cleaner. Norma Jean seems to be cleaning the living room rug again.

Later, she says to Leroy, "She just said that about the baby because she caught me smoking. She's trying to pay me back."

"What are you talking about?" Leroy says, nervously shuffling blueprints.   80

"You know good and well," Norma Jean says. She is sitting in a kitchen chair with her feet up and her arms wrapped around her knees. She looks small and helpless. She says, "The very idea, her bringing up a subject like that! Saying it was neglect."

"She didn't mean that," Leroy says.

"She might not have *thought* she meant it. She always says things like that. You don't know how she goes on."

"But she didn't really mean it. She was just talking."

Leroy opens a king-sized bottle of beer and pours it into two glasses, dividing   85
it carefully. He hands a glass to Norma Jean and she takes it from him mechanically. For a long time, they sit by the kitchen window watching the birds at the feeder.

Something is happening. Norma Jean is going to night school. She has graduated from her six-week body-building course and now she is taking an adult-education course in composition at Paducah Community College. She spends her evenings outlining paragraphs.

"First you have a topic sentence," she explains to Leroy. "Then you divide it up. Your secondary topic has to be connected to your primary topic."

To Leroy, this sounds intimidating. "I never was any good in English," he says.

"It makes a lot of sense."

90 "What are you doing this for, anyhow?"

She shrugs. "It's something to do." She stands up and lifts her dumbbells a few times.

"Driving a rig, nobody cared about my English."

"I'm not criticizing your English."

Norma Jean used to say, "If I lose ten minutes' sleep, I just drag all day." Now she stays up late, writing compositions. She got a B on her first paper—a how-to theme on soup-based casseroles. Recently Norma Jean has been cooking unusual foods—tacos, lasagna, Bombay chicken. She doesn't play the organ anymore, though her second paper was called "Why Music Is Important to Me." She sits at the kitchen table, concentrating on her outlines, while Leroy plays with his log house plans, practicing with a set of Lincoln Logs. The thought of getting a truckload of notched, numbered logs scares him, and he wants to be prepared. As he and Norma Jean work together at the kitchen table, Leroy has the hopeful thought that they are sharing something, but he knows he is a fool to think this. Norma Jean is miles away. He knows he is going to lose her. Like Mabel, he is just waiting for time to pass.

95 One day, Mabel is there before Norma Jean gets home from work, and Leroy finds himself confiding in her. Mabel, he realizes, must know Norma Jean better than he does.

"I don't know what's got into that girl," Mabel says. "She used to go to bed with the chickens. Now you say she's up all hours. Plus her a-smoking. I like to died."

"I want to make her this beautiful home," Leroy says, indicating the Lincoln Logs. "I don't think she even wants it. Maybe she was happier with me gone."

"She don't know what to make of you, coming home like this."

"Is that it?"

100 Mabel takes the roof off his Lincoln Log cabin. "You couldn't get *me* in a log cabin," she says. "I was raised in one. It's no picnic, let me tell you."

"They're different now," says Leroy.

"I tell you what," Mabel says, smiling oddly at Leroy.

"What?"

"Take her on down to Shiloh. Y'all need to get out together, stir a little. Her brain's all balled up over them books."

105 Leroy can see traces of Norma Jean's features in her mother's face. Mabel's face has the texture of crinkled cotton, but suddenly she looks pretty. It occurs to Leroy that Mabel has been hinting all along that she wants them to take her with them to Shiloh.

"Let's all go to Shiloh," he says. "You and me and her. Come Sunday."

Mabel throws up her hands in protest. "Oh, no, not me. Young folks want to be by theirselves."

When Norma Jean comes in with groceries, Leroy says excitedly, "Your mama here's been dying to go to Shiloh for thirty-five years. It's about time we went, don't you think?"

"I'm not going to butt in on anybody's second honeymoon," Mabel says.

"Who's going on a honeymoon, for Christ's sake?" Norma Jean says loudly. 110

"I never raised no daughter of mine to talk that-a-way," Mabel says.

"You ain't seen nothing yet," says Norma Jean. She starts putting away boxes and cans, slamming cabinet doors.

"There's a log cabin at Shiloh." Mabel says, "It was there during the battle. There's bullet holes in it."

"When are you going to *shut up* about Shiloh, Mama?" asks Norma Jean.

"I always thought Shiloh was the prettiest place, so full of history," Mabel 115 goes on. "I just hoped y'all could see it once before I die, so you could tell me about it." Later, she whispers to Leroy, "You do what I said. A little change is what she needs."

"Your name means 'the king,' " Norma Jean says to Leroy that evening. He is trying to get her to go to Shiloh, and she is reading a book about another century.

"Well, I reckon I ought to be right proud."

"I guess so."

"Am I still king around here?"

Norma Jean flexes her biceps and feels them for hardness. "I'm not fooling 120 around with anybody, if that's what you mean," she says.

"Would you tell me if you were?"

"I don't know."

"What does *your* name mean?"

"It was Marilyn Monroe's real name."

"No kidding!" 125

"Norma comes from the Normans. They were invaders," she says. She closes her book and looks hard at Leroy. "I'll go to Shiloh with you if you'll stop staring at me."

On Sunday, Norma Jean packs a picnic and they go to Shiloh. To Leroy's relief, Mabel says she does not want to come with them. Norma Jean drives, and Leroy, sitting beside her, feels like some boring hitchhiker she has picked up. He tries some conversation, but she answers him in monosyllables. At Shiloh, she drives aimlessly through the park, past bluffs and trails and steep ravines. Shiloh is an immense place, and Leroy cannot see it as a battleground. It is not what he expected. He thought it would look like a golf course. Monuments are everywhere, showing through the thick clusters of trees. Norma Jean passes the log cabin Mabel mentioned. It is surrounded by tourists looking for bullet holes.

"That's not the kind of log house I've got in mind," says Leroy apologetically.

"I know *that*."

"This is a pretty place. Your mama was right." 130

"It's O.K.," says Norma Jean. "Well, we've seen it. I hope she's satisfied."

They burst out laughing together.

At the park museum, a movie on Shiloh is shown every half hour, but they decide that they don't want to see it. They buy a souvenir Confederate flag for Mabel, and then they find a picnic spot near the cemetery. Norma Jean has brought a picnic cooler, with pimiento sandwiches, soft drinks, and Yodels. Leroy eats a sandwich and then smokes a joint, hiding it behind the picnic cooler. Norma Jean has quit smoking altogether. She is picking cake crumbs from the cellophane wrapper, like a fussy bird.

Leroy says, "So the boys in gray ended up in Corinth. The Union soldiers zapped 'em finally. April 7, 1862."

135 They both know that he doesn't know any history. He is just talking about some of the historical plaques they have read. He feels awkward, like a boy on a date with an older girl. They are still just making conversation.

"Corinth is where Mama eloped to," says Norma Jean.

They sit in silence and stare at the cemetery for the Union dead and, beyond, at a tall cluster of trees. Campers are parked nearby, bumper to bumper, and small children in bright clothing are cavorting and squealing. Norma Jean wads up the cake wrapper and squeezes it tightly in her hand. Without looking at Leroy, she says, "I want to leave you."

Leroy takes a bottle of Coke out of the cooler and flips off the cap. He holds the bottle poised near his mouth but cannot remember to take a drink. Finally he says, "No, you don't."

"Yes, I do."

140 "I won't let you."

"You can't stop me."

"Don't do me that way."

Leroy knows Norma Jean will have her own way. "Didn't I promise to be home from now on?" he says.

"In some ways, a woman prefers a man who wanders," says Norma Jean. "That sounds crazy, I know."

145 "You're not crazy."

Leroy remembers to drink from his Coke. Then he says, "Yes, you *are* crazy. You and me could start all over again. Right back at the beginning."

"We *have* started all over again," says Norma Jean. "And this is how it turned out."

"What did I do wrong?"

"Nothing."

150 "Is this one of those women's lib things?" Leroy asks.

"Don't be funny."

The cemetery, a green slope dotted with white markers, looks like a subdivision site. Leroy is trying to comprehend that his marriage is breaking up, but for some reason he is wondering about white slabs in a graveyard.

"Everything was fine till Mama caught me smoking," says Norma Jean, standing up. "That set something off."

"What are you talking about?"

155 "She won't leave me alone—*you* won't leave me alone." Norma Jean seems to be crying, but she is looking away from him. "I feel eighteen again. I can't

face that all over again." She starts walking away. "No, it *wasn't* fine. I don't know what I'm saying. Forget it."

Leroy takes a lungful of smoke and closes his eyes as Norma Jean's words sink in. He tries to focus on the fact that thirty-five hundred soldiers died on the grounds around him. He can only think of that war as a board game with plastic soldiers. Leroy almost smiles, as he compares the Confederates' daring attack on the Union camps and Virgil Mathis's raid on the bowling alley. General Grant, drunk and furious, shoved the Southerners back to Corinth, where Mabel and Jet Beasley were married years later, when Mabel was still thin and good-look-ing. The next day, Mabel and Jet visited the battleground, and then Norma Jean was born, and then she married Leroy and they had a baby, which they lost, and now Leroy and Norma Jean are here at the same battleground. Leroy knows he is leaving out a lot. He is leaving out the insides of history. History was always just names and dates to him. It occurs to him that building a house out of logs is similarly empty—too simple. And the real inner workings of a marriage, like most of history, have escaped him. Now he sees that building a log house is the dumbest idea he could have had. It was clumsy of him to think Norma Jean would want a log house. It was a crazy idea. He'll have to think of something else, quickly. He will wad the blueprints into tight balls and fling them into the lake. Then he'll get moving again. He opens his eyes. Norma Jean has moved away and is walking through the cemetery, following a serpentine brick path.

Leroy gets up to follow his wife, but his good leg is asleep and his bad leg still hurts him. Norma Jean is far away, walking rapidly toward the bluff by the river, and he tries to hobble toward her. Some children run past him, screaming noisily. Norma Jean has reached the bluff, and she is looking out over the Ten-nessee River. Now she turns toward Leroy and waves her arms. Is she beckoning to him? She seems to be doing an exercise for her chest muscles. The sky is unusually pale—the color of the dust ruffle Mabel made for their bed.

1982

RICHARD FORD

Great Falls

This is not a happy story. I warn you.

My father was a man named Jack Russell, and when I was a young boy in my early teens, we lived with my mother in a house to the east of Great Falls, Montana, near the small town of Highwood and the Highwood Mountains and the Missouri River. It is a flat, treeless benchland there, all of it used for wheat farming, though my father was never a farmer, but was brought up near Tacoma, Washington, in a family that worked for Boeing.

He—my father—had been an Air Force sergeant and had taken his discharge in Great Falls. And instead of going home to Tacoma, where my mother wanted to go, he had taken a civilian's job with the Air Force, working on planes, which was what he liked to do. And he had rented the house out of town from a farmer who did not want it left standing empty.

The house itself is gone now—I have been to the spot. But the double row of Russian olive trees and two of the outbuildings are still standing in the milkweeds. It was a plain, two-story house with a porch on the front and no place for the cars. At the time, I rode the school bus to Great Falls every morning, and my father drove in while my mother stayed home.

My mother was a tall pretty woman, thin, with black hair and slightly sharp features that made her seem to smile when she wasn't smiling. She had grown up in Wallace, Idaho, and gone to college a year in Spokane, then moved out to the coast, which is where she met Jack Russell. She was two years older than he was, and married him, she said to me, because he was young and wonderful looking, and because she thought they could leave the sticks and see the world together—which I suppose they did for a while. That was the life she wanted, even before she knew much about wanting anything else or about the future.

When my father wasn't working on airplanes, he was going hunting or fishing, two things he could do as well as anyone. He had learned to fish, he said, in Iceland, and to hunt ducks up on the DEW line—stations he had visited in the Air Force. And during the time of this—it was 1960—he began to take me with him on what he called his "expeditions." I thought even then, with as little as I knew, that these were opportunities other boys would dream of having but probably never would. And I don't think that I was wrong in that.

It is a true thing that my father did not know limits. In the spring, when we would go east to the Judith River Basin and camp up on the banks, he would catch a hundred fish in a weekend, and sometimes more than that. It was all he did from morning until night, and it was never hard for him. He used yellow corn kernels stacked onto a #4 snelled hook, and he would rattle this rig-up along the bottom of a deep pool below a split-shot sinker, and catch fish. And most of the time, because he knew the Judith River and knew how to feel his bait down deep, he would catch fish of good size.

It was the same with ducks, the other thing he liked. When the northern birds were down, usually by mid-October, he would take me and we would build a cattail and wheatstraw blind on one of the tule ponds or sloughs he knew about down the Missouri, where the water was shallow enough to wade. We would set out his decoys to the leeward side of our blind, and he would sprinkle corn on a hunger-line from the decoys to where we were. In the evenings when he came home from the base, we would go and sit out in the blind until the roosting fights came and put down among the decoys—there was never calling involved. And after a while, sometimes it would be an hour and full dark, the ducks would find the corn, and the whole raft of them—sixty, sometimes—would swim in to us. At the moment he judged they were close enough, my father would say to me, "Shine, Jackie," and I would stand and shine a seal-beam car light out onto the pond, and he would stand up beside me and shoot all the ducks that were there, on the water if he could, but flying and getting up as well. He owned a Model 11 Remington with a long-tube magazine that would hold ten shells, and with that many, and shooting straight over the surface rather than down onto it, he could kill or wound thirty ducks in twenty seconds' time.

I remember distinctly the report of that gun and the flash of it over the water into the dark air, one shot after another, not even so fast, but measured in a way to hit as many as he could.

What my father did with the ducks he killed, and the fish, too, was sell them. It was against the law then to sell wild game, and it is against the law now. And though he kept some for us, most he would take—his fish laid on ice, or his ducks still wet and bagged in the burlap corn sacks—down to the Great Northern Hotel, which was still open then on Second Street in Great Falls, and sell them to the Negro caterer who bought them for his wealthy customers and for the dining car passengers who came through. We would drive in my father's Plymouth to the back of the hotel—always this was after dark—to a concrete loading ramp and lighted door that were close enough to the yards that I could sometimes see passenger trains waiting at the station, their car lights yellow and warm inside, the passengers dressed in suits, all bound for someplace far away from Montana—Milwaukee or Chicago or New York City, unimaginable places to me, a boy fourteen years old, with my father in the cold dark selling illegal game.

The caterer was a tall, stooped-back man in a white jacket, who my father called "Professor Ducks" or "Professor Fish," and the Professor referred to my father as "Sarge." He paid a quarter per pound for trout, a dime for whitefish, a dollar for a mallard duck, two for a speckle or a blue goose, and four dollars for a Canada. I have been with my father when he took away a hundred dollars for fish he'd caught and, in the fall, more than that for ducks and geese. When he had sold game in that way, we would drive out 10th Avenue and stop at a bar called The Mermaid which was by the air base, and he would drink with some friends he knew there, and they would laugh about hunting and fishing while I played pinball and wasted money in the jukebox.

It was on such a night as this that the unhappy things came about. It was in late October. I remember the time because Halloween had not been yet, and in the windows of the houses that I passed every day on the bus to Great Falls, people had put pumpkin lanterns, and set scarecrows in their yards in chairs.

My father and I had been shooting ducks in a slough on the Smith River, upstream from where it enters on the Missouri. He had killed thirty ducks, and we'd driven them down to the Great Northern and sold them there, though my father had kept two back in his corn sack. And when we had driven away, he suddenly said, "Jackie, let's us go back home tonight. Who cares about those hard-dicks at The Mermaid. I'll cook these ducks on the grill. We'll do something different tonight." He smiled at me in an odd way. This was not a thing he usually said, or the way he usually talked. He liked The Mermaid, and my mother—as far as I knew—didn't mind it if he went there.

"That sounds good," I said.

"We'll surprise your mother," he said. "We'll make her happy."

We drove out past the air base on Highway 87, past where there were planes taking off into the night. The darkness was dotted by the green and red beacons, and the tower light swept the sky and trapped planes as they disappeared over the flat landscape toward Canada or Alaska and the Pacific.

"Boy-oh-boy," my father said—just out of the dark. I looked at him and his eyes were narrow, and he seemed to be thinking about something. "You know, Jackie" he said, "your mother said something to me once I've never forgotten. She said, 'Nobody dies of a broken heart.' This was somewhat before you were born. We were living down in Texas and we'd had some big blow-up, and that was the idea she had. I don't know why." He shook his head.

He ran his hand under the seat, found a half-pint bottle of whiskey, and held it up to the lights of the car behind us to see what there was left of it. He unscrewed the cap and took a drink, then held the bottle out to me. "Have a drink, son," he said. "Something oughta be good in life." And I felt that something was wrong. Not because of the whiskey, which I had drunk before and he had reason to know about, but because of some sound in his voice, something I didn't recognize and did not know the importance of, though I was certain it was important.

I took a drink and gave the bottle back to him, holding the whiskey in my mouth until it stopped burning and I could swallow it a little at a time. When we turned out the road to Highwood, the lights of Great Falls sank below the horizon, and I could see the small white lights of farms, burning at wide distances in the dark.

"What do you worry about, Jackie," my father said. "Do you worry about girls? Do you worry about your future sex life? Is that some of it?" He glanced at me, then back at the road.

20   "I don't worry about that," I said.

"Well, what then?" my father said. "What else is there?"

"I worry if you're going to die before I do," I said, though I hated saying that, "or if Mother is. That worries me."

"It'd be a miracle if we didn't," my father said, with the half-pint held in the same hand he held the steering wheel. I had seen him drive that way before. "Things pass too fast in your life, Jackie. Don't worry about that. If I were you, I'd worry we might not." He smiled at me, and it was not the worried, nervous smile from before, but a smile that meant he was pleased. And I don't remember him ever smiling at me that way again.

We drove on out behind the town of Highwood and onto the flat field roads toward our house. I could see, out on the prairie, a moving light where the farmer who rented our house to us was disking his field for winter wheat. "He's waited too late with that business," my father said and took a drink, then threw the bottle right out the window. "He'll lose that," he said, "the cold'll kill it." I did not answer him, but what I thought was that my father knew nothing about farming, and if he was right it would be an accident. He knew about planes and hunting game, and that seemed all to me.

25   "I want to respect your privacy," he said then, for no reason at all that I understood. I am not even certain he said it, only that it is in my memory that way. I don't know what he was thinking of. Just words. But I said to him, I remember well, "It's all right. Thank you."

We did not go straight out the Geraldine Road to our house. Instead my father went down another mile and turned, went a mile and turned back again so that we came home from the other direction."I want to stop and listen now," he said. "The geese should be in the stubble." We stopped and he cut the lights and engine, and we opened the car windows and listened. It was eight o'clock at night and it was getting colder, though it was dry. But I could hear nothing, just the sound of air moving lightly through the cut field, and not a goose sound. Though I could smell the whiskey on my father's breath and on mine, could hear the motor ticking, could hear him breathe, hear the sound we made sitting side by side on the car seat, our clothes, our feet, almost our hearts beating. And I could see out in the night the yellow lights of our house, shining through the olive trees south of us like a ship on the sea. "I hear them, by God," my father said, his head stuck out the window. "But they're high up. They won't stop here now, Jackie. They're high flyers, those boys. Long gone geese."

There was a car parked off the road, down the line of wind-break trees, beside a steel thresher the farmer had left there to rust. You could see moonlight off the taillight chrome. It was a Pontiac, a two-door hard-top. My father said nothing about it and I didn't either, though I think now for different reasons.

The floodlight was on over the side door of our house and lights were on inside, upstairs and down. My mother had a pumpkin on the front porch, and the wind chime she had hung by the door was tinkling. My dog, Major, came out of the quonset shed and stood in the car lights when we drove up.

"Let's see what's happening here," my father said, opening the door and stepping out quickly. He looked at me inside the car, and his eyes were wide and his mouth drawn tight.

We walked in the side door and up the basement steps into the kitchen, and a man was standing there—a man I had never seen before, a young man with blond hair, who might've been twenty or twenty-five. He was tall and was wearing a short-sleeved shirt and beige slacks with pleats. He was on the other side of the breakfast table, his fingertips just touching the wooden tabletop. His blue eyes were on my father, who was dressed in hunting clothes.

"Hello," my father said.

"Hello," the young man said, and nothing else. And for some reason I looked at his arms, which were long and pale. They looked like a young man's arms, like my arms. His short sleeves had each been neatly rolled up, and I could see the bottom of a small green tattoo edging out from underneath. There was a glass of whiskey on the table, but no bottle.

"What's your name?" my father said, standing in the kitchen under the bright ceiling light. He sounded like he might be going to laugh.

"Woody," the young man said and cleared his throat. He looked at me, then he touched the glass of whiskey, just the rim of the glass. He wasn't nervous, I could tell that. He did not seem to be afraid of anything.

"Woody," my father said and looked at the glass of whiskey. He looked at me, then sighed and shook his head. "Where's Mrs. Russell, Woody? I guess you aren't robbing my house, are you?"

Woody smiled. "No," he said. "Upstairs. I think she went upstairs."

"Good," my father said, "that's a good place." And he walked straight out of the room, but came back and stood in the doorway. "Jackie, you and Woody

30

35

step outside and wait on me. Just stay there and I'll come out." He looked at Woody then in a way I would not have liked him to look at me, a look that meant he was studying Woody. "I guess that's your car," he said.

"That Pontiac." Woody nodded.

"Okay. Right," my father said. Then he went out again and up the stairs. At that moment the phone started to ring in the living room, and I heard my mother say, "Who's that?" And my father say, "It's me. It's Jack." And I decided I wouldn't go answer the phone. Woody looked at me, and I understood he wasn't sure what to do. Run, maybe. But he didn't have run in him. Though I thought he would probably do what I said if I would say it.

40   "Let's just go outside," I said.

And he said, "All right."

Woody and I walked outside and stood in the light of the floodlamp above the side door. I had on my wool jacket, but Woody was cold and stood with his hands in him pockets, and his arms bare, moving from foot to foot. Inside, the phone was ringing again. Once I looked up and saw my mother come to the window and look down at Woody and me. Woody didn't look up or see her, but I did. I waved at her, and she waved back at me and smiled. She was wearing a powder-blue dress. In another minute the phone stopped ringing.

Woody took a cigarette out of his shirt pocket and lit it. Smoke shot through his nose into the cold air, and he sniffed, looked around the ground and threw his match on the gravel. His blond hair was combed backwards and neat on the sides, and I could smell his aftershave on him, a sweet, lemon smell. And for the first time I noticed his shoes. They were twotones, black with white tops and black laces. They stuck out below his baggy pants and were long and polished and shiny, as if he had been planning on a big occasion. They looked like shoes some country singer would wear, or a salesman. He was handsome, but only like someone you would see beside you in a dime store and not notice again.

"I like it out here," Woody said, his head down, looking at his shoes. "Nothing to bother you. I bet you'd see Chicago if the world was flat. The Great Plains commence here."

45   "I don't know," I said.

Woody looked up at me, cupping his smoke with one hand. "Do you play football?"

"No," I said. I thought about asking him something about my mother. But I had no idea what it would be.

"I *have* been drinking," Woody said, "but I'm not drunk now."

The wind rose then, and from behind the house I could hear Major bark once from far away, and I could smell the irrigation ditch, hear it hiss in the field. It ran down from Highwood Creek to the Missouri, twenty miles away. It was nothing Woody knew about, nothing he could hear or smell. He knew nothing about anything that was here. I heard my father say the words, "That's a real joke," from inside the house, then the sound of a drawer being opened and shut, and a door closing. Then nothing else.

50   Woody turned and looked into the dark toward where the glow of Great Falls rose on the horizon, and we both could see the flashing lights of a plane low-

ering to land there. "I once passed my brother in the Los Angeles airport and didn't even recognize him," Woody said, staring into the night. "He recognized *me*, though. He said, 'Hey, bro, are you mad at me, or what?' I wasn't mad at him. We both had to laugh."

Woody turned and looked at the house. His hands were still in his pockets, his cigarette clenched between his teeth, his arms taut. They were, I saw, bigger, stronger arms than I had thought. A vein went down the front of each of them. I wondered what Woody knew that I didn't. Not about my mother—I didn't know anything about that and didn't want to—but about a lot of things, about the life out in the dark, about coming out here, about airports, even about me. He and I were not so far apart in age, I knew that. But Woody was one thing, and I was another. And I wondered how I would ever get to be like him, since it didn't necessarily seem so bad a thing to be.

"Did you know your mother was married before?" Woody said.

"Yes," I said. "I knew that."

"It happens to all of them, now," he said. "They can't wait to get divorced."

Woody dropped his cigarette into the gravel and toed it out with his black-and-white shoe. He looked up at me and smiled the way he had inside the house, a smile that said he knew something he wouldn't tell, a smile to make you feel bad because you weren't Woody and never could be. 55

It was then that my father came out of the house. He still had on his plaid hunting coat and his wool cap, but his face was as white as snow, as white as I have ever seen a human being's face to be. It was odd. I had the feeling that he might've fallen inside, because he looked roughed up, as though he had hurt himself somehow.

My mother came out the door behind him and stood in the floodlight at the top of the steps. She was wearing the powder-blue dress I'd seen through the window, a dress I had never seen her wear before, though she was also wearing a car coat and carrying a suitcase. She looked at me and shook her head in a way that only I was supposed to notice, as if it was not a good idea to talk now.

My father had his hands in his pockets, and he walked right up to Woody. He did not even look at me. "What do you do for a living?" he said, and he was very close to Woody. His coat was close enough to touch Woody's shirt.

"I'm in the Air Force," Woody said. He looked at me and then at my father. 60 He could tell my father was excited.

"Is this your day off, then?" my father said. He moved even closer to Woody, his hands still in his pockets. He pushed Woody with his chest, and Woody seemed willing to let my father push him.

"No," he said, shaking his head.

I looked at my mother. She was just standing, watching. It was as if someone had given her an order, and she was obeying it. She did not smile at me, though I thought she was thinking about me, which made me feel strange.

"What's the matter with you?" my father said into Woody's face, right into his face—his voice tight, as if it had gotten hard for him to talk. "Whatever in the world is the matter with you? Don't you understand something?" My father took a revolver pistol out of his coat and put it up under Woody's chin, into the soft pocket behind the bone, so that Woody's whole face rose, but his arms stayed at his sides, his hands open. "I don't know what to do with you," my father said. "I don't have any idea what to do with you. I just don't." Though I thought that what he wanted to do was hold Woody there just like that until something important took place, or until he could simply forget about all this.

65 My father pulled the hammer back on the pistol and raised it tighter under Woody's chin, breathing into Woody's face—my mother in the light with her suitcase, watching them, and me watching them. A half a minute must've gone by.

And then my mother said, "Jack, let's stop now. Let's just stop."

My father stared into Woody's face as if he wanted Woody to consider doing something—moving or turning around or anything on his own to stop this— that my father would then put a stop to. My father's eyes grew narrowed, and his teeth were gritted together, his lips snarling up to resemble a smile. "You're crazy, aren't you?" he said. "You're a goddamned crazy man. Are you in love with her, too? Are you, crazy man? Are you? Do you say you love her? Say you love her! Say you love her so I can blow your fucking brains in the sky."

"All right," Woody said. "No. It's all right."

"He doesn't love me, Jack. For God's sake," my mother said. She seemed so calm. She shook her head at me again. I do not think she thought my father would shoot Woody. And I don't think Woody thought so. Nobody did, I think, except my father himself. But I think he did, and was trying to find out how to.

70 My father turned suddenly and glared at my mother, his eyes shiny and moving, but with the gun still on Woody's skin. I think he was afraid, afraid he was doing this wrong and could mess all of it up and make matters worse without accomplishing anything.

"You're leaving," he yelled at her. "That's why you're packed. Get out. Go on."

"Jackie has to be at school in the morning," my mother said in just her normal voice. And without another word to any one of us, she walked out of the floodlamp light carrying her bag, turned the corner at the front porch steps and disappeared toward the olive trees that ran in rows back into the wheat.

My father looked back at me where I was standing in the gravel, as if he expected to see me go with my mother toward Woody's car. But I hadn't thought about that—though later I would. Later I would think I should have gone with her, and that things between them might've been different. But that isn't how it happened.

"You're sure you're going to get away now, aren't you, mister?" my father said into Woody's face. He was crazy himself, then. Anyone would've been. Everything must have seemed out of hand to him.

75 "I'd like to," Woody said. "I'd like to get away from here."

"And I'd like to think of some way to hurt you," my father said and blinked his eyes. "I feel helpless about it." We all heard the door to Woody's car close in the dark. "Do you think that I'm a fool?" my father said.

"No," Woody said. "I don't think that."

"Do you think you're important?"

"No," Woody said. "I'm not."

My father blinked again. He seemed to be becoming someone else at that moment, someone I didn't know. "Where are you from?"

And Woody closed his eyes. He breathed in, then out, a long sigh. I was as if this was somehow the hardest part, something he hadn't expected to be asked to say.

"Chicago," Woody said. "A suburb of there."

"Are your parents alive?" my father said, all the time with his blue magnum pistol pushed under Woody's chin.

"Yes," Woody said. "Yessir."

"That's too bad," my father said. "Too bad they have to know what you are. I'm sure you stopped meaning anything to them a long time ago. I'm sure they both wish you were dead. You didn't know that. But I know it. I can't help them out, though. Somebody else'll have to kill you. I don't want to have to think about you anymore. I guess that's it."

My father brought the gun down to his side and stood looking at Woody. He did not back away, just stood, waiting for what I don't know to happen. Woody stood a moment, then he cut his eyes at me uncomfortably. And I know that I looked down. That's all I could do. Though I remember wondering if Woody's heart was broken and what any of this meant to him. Not to me, or my mother, or my father. But to him, since he seemed to be the one left out somehow, the one who would be lonely soon, the one who had done something he would someday wish he hadn't and would have no one to tell him that it was all right, that they forgave him, that these things happen in the world.

Woody took a step back, looked at my father and at me again as if he intended to speak, then stepped aside and walked away toward the front of our house, where the wind chime made a noise in the new cold air.

My father looked at me, his big pistol in his hand. "Does this seem stupid to you?" he said. "All this? Yelling and threatening and going nuts? I wouldn't blame you if it did. You shouldn't even see this. I'm sorry. I don't know what to do now."

"It'll be all right," I said. And I walked out to the road. Woody's car started up behind the olive trees. I stood and watched it back out, its red taillights clouded by exhaust. I could see their two heads inside, with the headlights shining behind them. When they got into the road, Woody touched his brakes, and for a moment I could see that they were talking, their heads turned toward each other, nodding. Woody's head and my mother's. They sat that way for a few seconds, then drove slowly off. And I wondered what they had to say to each other, something important enough that they had to stop right at that moment and say it. Did she say, *I love you?* Did she say, *This is not what I expected to happen?* Did she say, *This is what I've wanted all along?* and did he say, *I'm sorry for all this,* or *I'm glad,* or *None of this matters to me?* These are not the kinds of things you can know if you were not there. And I was not there and did not want to be. It did not seem like I should be there. I heard the door slam when my father went inside, and I turned back from the road where I could still see their taillights disappearing, and went back into the house where I was to be alone with my father.

90   Things seldom end in one event. In the morning I went to school on the bus as usual, and my father drove in to the air base in his car. We had not said very much about all that had happened. Harsh words, in a sense, are all alike. You can make them up yourself and be right. I think we both believed that we were in a fog we couldn't see through yet, though in a while, maybe not even a long while, we would see lights and know something.

In my third-period class that day a messenger brought a note for me that said I was excused from school at noon, and I should meet my mother at a motel down 10th Avenue South—a place not so far from my school—and we would eat lunch together.

It was a gray day in Great Falls that day. The leaves were off the trees and the mountains to the east of town were obscured by a low sky. The night before had been cold and clear, but today it seemed as if it would rain. It was the beginning of winter in earnest. In a few days there would be snow everywhere.

The motel where my mother was staying was called the Tropicana, and was beside the city golf course. There was a neon parrot on the sign out front, and the cabins made a U shape behind a little white office building. Only a couple of cars were parked in front of cabins, and no car was in front of my mother's cabin. I wondered if Woody would be here, or if he was at the air base. I wondered if my father would see him there, and what they would say.

I walked back to cabin 9. The door was open, though a DO NOT DISTURB sign was hung on the knob outside. I looked through the screen and saw my mother sitting on the bed alone. The television was on, but she was looking at me. She was wearing the powder-blue dress she had had on the night before. She was smiling at me, and I liked the way she looked at that moment, through the screen, in shadows. Her features did not seem as sharp as they had before. She looked comfortable where she was, and I felt like we were going to get along, no matter what had happened, and that I wasn't mad at her—that I had never been mad at her.

95   She sat forward and turned the television off. "Come in, Jackie," she said, and I opened the screen door and came inside. "It's the height of grandeur in here, isn't it?" My mother looked around the room. Her suitcase was open on the floor by the bathroom door, which I could see through and out the window onto the golf course, where three men were playing under the milky sky. "Privacy can be a burden, sometimes," she said, and reached down and put on her highheeled shoes. "I didn't sleep very well last night, did you?"

"No," I said, though I had slept all night. I wanted to ask her where Woody was, but it occurred to me at that moment that he was gone now and wouldn't be back, that she wasn't thinking in terms of him and didn't care where he was or ever would be.

"I'd like a nice compliment from you," she said. "Do you have one of those to spend?"

"Yes," I said. "I'm glad to see you."

"That's a nice one," she said and nodded. She had both her shoes on now. "Would you like to go have lunch? We can walk across the street to the cafeteria. You can get hot food."

"No" I said. "I'm not really hungry now." 100

"That's okay," she said and smiled at me again. And, as I said before, I liked the way she looked. She looked pretty in a way I didn't remember seeing her, as if something that had had a hold on her had let her go, and she could be different about things. Even about me.

"Sometimes, you know," she said, "I'll think about something I did. Just anything. Years ago in Idaho, or last week, even. And it's as if I'd read it. Like a story. Isn't that strange?"

"Yes," I said. And it did seem strange to me because I was certain then what the difference was between what had happened and what hadn't, and knew I always would be.

"Sometimes," she said, and she folded her hands in her lap and stared out the little side window of her cabin at the parking lot and the curving row of other cabins. "Sometimes I even have a moment when I completely forget what life's like. Just altogether." She smiled. "That's not so bad, finally. Maybe it's a disease I have. Do you think I'm just sick and I'll get well?"

"No. I don't know," I said. "Maybe. I hope so." I looked out the bathroom 105 window and saw the three men walking down the golf course fairway carrying golf clubs.

"I'm not very good at sharing things right now," my mother said. "I'm sorry." She cleared her throat, and then she didn't say anything for almost a minute while I stood there. "I *will* answer anything you'd like me to answer, though. Just ask me anything, and I'll answer it the truth, whether I want to or not. Okay? I will. You don't even have to trust me. That's not a big issue with us. We're both grown-ups now."

And I said, "Were you ever married before?"

My mother looked at me strangely. Her eyes got small, and for a moment she looked the way I was used to seeing her—sharp-faced, her mouth set and taut. "No," she said. "Who told you that? That isn't true. I never was. Did Jack say that to you? Did your father say that? That's an awful thing to say. I haven't been that bad."

"He didn't say that," I said.

"Oh, of course he did," my mother said. "He doesn't know just to let things 110 go when they're bad enough."

"I wanted to know that," I said. "I just thought about it. It doesn't matter."

"No, it doesn't," my mother said. "I could've been married eight times. I'm just sorry he said that to you. He's not generous sometimes."

"He didn't say that," I said. But I'd said it enough, and I didn't care if she believed me or didn't. It was true that trust was not a big issue between us then. And in any event, I know now that the whole truth of anything is an idea that stops existing finally.

"Is that all you want to know, then?" my mother said. She seemed mad, but not at me, I didn't think. Just at things in general. And I sympathized with her. "Your life's your own business, Jackie," she said. "Sometimes it scares you to death it's so much your own business. You just want to run."

"I guess so," I said.

"I'd like a less domestic life, is all." She looked at me, but I didn't say anything. I didn't see what she meant by that, though I knew there was nothing I could say to change the way her life would be from then on. And I kept quiet.

In a while we walked across 10th Avenue and ate lunch in the cafeteria. When she paid for the meal I saw that she had my father's silver-dollar money clip in her purse and that there was money in it. And I understood that he had been to see her already that day, and no one cared if I knew it. We were all of us on our own in this.

When we walked out onto the street, it was colder and the wind was blowing. Car exhausts were invisible and some drivers had their lights on, though it was only two o'clock in the afternoon. My mother had called a taxi, and we stood and waited for it. I didn't know where she was going, but I wasn't going with her.

"Your father won't let me come back," she said, standing on the curb. It was just a fact to her, not that she hoped I would talk to him or stand up for her or take her part. But I did wish then that I had never let her go the night before. Things can be fixed by staying; but to go out into the night and not come back hazards life, and everything can get out of hand.

My mother's taxi came. She kissed me and hugged me very hard, then got inside the cab in her powder-blue dress and high heels and her car coat. I smelled her perfume on my cheeks as I stood watching her. "I used to be afraid of more things than I am now," she said, looking up at me, and smiled. "I've got a knot in my stomach, of all things." And she closed the cab door, waved at me, and rode away.

I walked back toward my school. I thought I could take the bus home if I got there by three. I walked a long way down 10th Avenue to Second Street, beside the Missouri River, then over to town. I walked by the Great Northern Hotel, where my father had sold ducks and geese and fish of all kinds. There were no passenger trains in the yard and the loading dock looked small. Garbage cans were lined along the edge of it, and the door was closed and locked.

As I walked toward school I thought to myself that my life had turned suddenly, and that I might not know exactly how or which way for possibly a long time. Maybe, in fact, I might never know. It was a thing that happened to you—I knew that—and it had happened to me in this way now. And as I walked on up the cold street that afternoon in Great Falls, the questions I asked myself were these: why wouldn't my father let my mother come back? Why would Woody stand in the cold with me outside my house and risk being killed? Why would he say my mother had been married before, if she hadn't been? And my mother herself—why would she do what she did? In five years my father had gone off to Ely, Nevada, to ride out the oil strike there, and been killed by accident. And in the years since then I have seen my mother from time to time—in one place or another, with one man or other—and I can say, at least, that we know each other. But I have never known the answer to these questions, have never asked anyone their answers. Though possibly it—the answer—is simple: it is just low-life, some coldness in us all, some helplessness that causes us to misunderstand life when it is pure and plain, makes our existence seem like a border between two nothings, and makes us no more or less than animals who meet on the road—watchful, unforgiving, without patience or desire.

1987

LYNNA WILLIAMS

Personal Testimony

The last night of church camp, 1963, and I am sitting in the front row of the junior mixed-voice choir looking out on the crowd in the big sanctuary tent. The tent glows, green and white and unexpected, in the Oklahoma night; our choir director, Dr. Bledsoe, has schooled us in the sudden crescendos needed to compete with the sounds cars make when their drivers cut the corner after a night at the bars on Highway 10 and see the tent rising out of the plain for the first time. The tent is new to Faith Camp this year, a gift to God and the Southern Baptist Convention from the owner of a small circus who repented, and then retired, in nearby Oklahoma City. It is widely rumored among the campers that Mr. Talliferro came to Jesus late in life, after having what my mother would call Life Experiences. Now he walks through camp with the unfailing good humor of a man who, after years of begging hardscrabble farmers to forsake their fields for an afternoon of elephants and acrobats, has finally found a real draw: his weekly talks to the senior boys on "Sin and the Circus" incorporate a standing-room-only question-and-answer period, and no one ever leaves early.

Although I know I will never be allowed in the tent to hear one of Mr. Talliferro's talks—I will not be twelve forever, but I will always be a girl—I am encouraged by his late arrival into our Fellowship of Believers. I will take my time, too, I think: first I will go to high school, to college, to bed with a boy, to New York. (I think of those last two items as one since, as little as I know about sex, I do know it is not something I will ever be able to do in the same time zone as my mother.) Then when I'm fifty-two or so and have had, like Mr. Talliferro, sufficient Life Experiences, I'll move back to west Texas and repent.

Normally, thoughts of that touching—and distant—scene of repentance are how I entertain myself during evening worship service. But tonight I am unable to work up any enthusiasm for the vision of myself sweeping into my hometown to Be Forgiven. For once my thoughts are entirely on the worship service ahead.

My place in the choir is in the middle of six other girls from my father's church in Fort Worth; we are dressed alike in white lace-trimmed wash-and-wear blouses from J. C. Penney and modest navy pedal pushers that stop exactly three inches from our white socks and tennis shoes. We are also alike in having mothers who regard travel irons as an essential accessory to Christian Young Womanhood; our matching outfits are, therefore, neatly ironed.

At least their outfits are. I have been coming to this camp in the southwestern equivalent of the Sahara Desert for six years now, and I know that when it is a hundred degrees at sunset, cotton wilts. When I used my iron I did the front of my blouse and the pants, so I wouldn't stand out, and trusted that anyone standing behind me would think I was wrinkled from the heat.

Last summer, or the summer before, when I was still riding the line that separates good girls from bad, this small deception would have bothered me. This year I am twelve and a criminal. Moral niceties are lost on me. I am singing "Just as I Am" with the choir and I have three hundred dollars in my white Bible, folded and taped over John 3:16.

Since camp started three weeks ago, I have operated a business in the arts and crafts cabin in the break between afternoon Bible study and segregated (boys only / girls only) swimming. The senior boys, the same ones who are learning critical new information from Mr. Talliferro every week, are paying me to write the personal testimonies we are all expected to give at evening worship service.

We do not dwell on personal motivation in my family. When my brother, David, and I sin, it is the deed my parents talk about, not mitigating circumstances, and the deed they punish. This careful emphasis on what we do, never on why we do it, has affected David and me differently. He is a good boy, endlessly kind and cheerful and responsible, but his heroes are not the men my father followed into the ministry. David gives God and our father every outward sign of respect, but he worships Clarence Darrow[1] and the law. At fifteen, he has been my defense lawyer for years.

While David wants to defend the world, I am only interested in defending myself. I know exactly why I have started the testimony business: I am doing it to get back at my father. I am doing it because I am adopted.

Even though I assure my customers with every sale that we will not get caught, I never write a testimony without imagining public exposure of my wrongdoing. The scene is so familiar to me that I do not have to close my eyes to see it: the summons to the camp director's office and the door closing behind me; the shocked faces of other campers when the news leaks out; the Baptist Academy girls who comb their hair and go in pairs, bravely, to offer my brother comfort; the automatic rotation of my name to the top of everyone's prayer list. I spend hours imagining the small details of my shame, always leading to the moment when my father, called from Fort Worth to take me home, arrives at camp.

That will be my moment. I have done something so terrible that even my father will not be able to keep it a secret. I am doing this because of my father's secrets.

We had only been home from church for a few minutes; it was my ninth birthday, and when my father called me to come downstairs to his study, I was

1. Clarence Darrow (1857–1938) was the lawyer who defended biology teacher John Scopes in the 1925 "monkey trial" in Dayton, Tennessee.

still wearing the dress my mother had made for the occasion, pink dotted swiss with a white satin sash. David came out of his room to ask me what I had done this time—he likes to be prepared for court—but I told him not to worry, that I was wholly innocent of any crime in the weeks just before my birthday. At the bottom of the stairs I saw my mother walk out of the study and knew I was right not to be concerned: in matters of discipline my mother and father never work alone. At the door it came to me: my father was going to tell me I was old enough to go with him now and then to churches in other cities. David had been to Atlanta and New Orleans and a dozen little Texas towns; my turn had finally come.

My father was standing by the window. At the sound of my patent-leather shoes sliding across the hardwood floor, he turned and motioned for me to sit on the sofa. He cleared his throat; it was a sermon noise I had heard hundreds of times, and I knew that he had prepared whatever he was going to say.

All thoughts of ordering room-service hamburgers in an Atlanta hotel left me—prepared remarks meant we were dealing with life or death or salvation—and I wished for my mother and David. My father said, "This is hard for your mother; she wanted to be here, but it upsets her so, we thought I should talk to you alone." We had left any territory I knew, and I sat up straight to listen, as though I were still in church.

My father, still talking, took my hands in his; after a moment I recognized the weight of his Baylor[2] ring against my skin as something from my old life, the one in which I had woken up that morning a nine-year-old, dressed for church in my birthday dress, and come home.

My father talked and talked and talked; I stopped listening. I had grown up singing about the power of blood. I required no lengthy explanation of what it meant to be adopted. It meant I was not my father's child. It meant I was a secret, even from myself.

In the three years since that day in my father's study, I have realized, of course, that I am not my mother's child, either. But I have never believed that she was responsible for the lie about my birth. It is my father I blame. I am not allowed to talk about my adoption outside my family ("It would only hurt your mother," my father says. "Do you want to hurt your mother?"). Although I am universally regarded by the women of our church as a Child Who Wouldn't Know a Rule If One Reached Up and Bit Her in the Face, I do keep this one. My stomach hurts when I even think about telling anyone, but it hurts, too, when I think about having another mother and father somewhere. When the pain is enough to make me cry, I try to talk to my parents about it, but my mother's face changes even before I can get the first question out, and my father always follows her out of the room. "You're our child," he says when he returns. "We love you, and you're ours."

I let him hug me, but I am thinking that I have never heard my father tell a lie before. I am not his child. Not in the way David is, not in the way I believed

15

---

2. Baylor University, located in Waco, Texas.

I was. Later I remember that lie and decide that all the secrecy is for my father's benefit, that he is ashamed to tell the world that I am not his child because he is ashamed of me. I think about the Ford my father bought in Dallas three years ago; it has never run right, but he will not take it back. I think about that when I am sitting in my bunk with a flashlight, writing testimonies to the power of God's love.

My father is one reason I am handcrafting Christian testimonies while my bunkmates are making place mats from Popsicle sticks. There is another reason: I'm good at it.

Nothing else has changed. I remain Right Fielder for Life in the daily softball games. The sincerity of my belief in Jesus is perennially suspect among the most pious, and most popular, campers. And I am still the only girl who, in six years of regular attendance, has failed to advance even one step in Girls' Auxiliary. (Other, younger girls have made it all the way to Queen Regent with Scepter, while I remain a perpetual Lady-in-Waiting.) Until this year, only the strength of my family connections has kept me from sinking as low in the camp hierarchy as Cassie Mosley, who lisps and wears colorful native costumes that her missionary parents send from Africa.

20   I arrived at camp this summer as I do every year, resigned and braced to endure but buoyed by a fantasy life that I believe is unrivaled among twelve-year-old Baptist girls. But on our second night here, the promise of fish sticks and carrot salad hanging in the air, Bobby Dunn came and stood behind me in the cafeteria line.

Bobby Dunn, blond, ambitious, and in love with Jesus, is Faith Camp's standard for male perfection. He is David's friend, but he has spoken to me only once, on the baseball field last year, when he suggested that my unhealthy fear of the ball was really a failure to trust God's plan for my life. Since that day I have taken some comfort in noticing that Bobby Dunn follows the Scripture reading by moving his finger along the text.

Feeling him next to me, I took a breath, wondering if Bobby, like other campers in other years, had decided to attempt to bring me to a better understanding of what it means to serve Jesus. But he was already talking, congratulating me on my testimony at evening worship service the night before. (I speak publicly at camp twice every summer, the exact number required by some mysterious formula that allows me to be left alone the rest of the time.)

"You put it just right," he said. "Now me, I know what I want to say, but it comes out all wrong. I've prayed about it, and it seems to be God wants me to do better."

He looked at me hard, and I realized it was my turn to say something. Nothing came to me, though, since I agreed with him completely. He does suffer from what my saintly brother, after one particularly gruesome revival meeting, took to calling Jesus Jaw, a malady that makes it impossible for the devoted to say what they mean and sit down. Finally I said what my mother says to the ladies seeking comfort in the Dorcas Bible class: "Can I help?" Before I could take it back, Bobby Dunn had me by the hand and was pulling me across the cafeteria to a table in the far corner.

The idea of my writing testimonies for other campers—a sort of ghostwriting service for Jesus, as Bobby Dunn saw it—was Bobby's, but before we got up from the table, I had refined it and made it mine. The next afternoon in the arts and crafts cabin I made my first sale: five dollars for a two-minute testimony detailing how God gave Michael Bush the strength to stop swearing. Bobby was shocked when the money changed hands—I could see him thinking, Temple. Money-lenders. Jee-sus!—but Michael Bush is the son of an Austin car dealer, and he quoted his earthly father's scripture: "You get what you pay for." 25

Michael, who made me a professional writer with money he earned polishing used station wagons, is a sweet, slow-talking athlete from Bishop Military School. He'd been dateless for months and was convinced it was because the Baptist Academy girls had heard that he has a tendency to take the Lord's name in vain on difficult fourth downs. After his testimony that night, Michael left the tent with Patsy Lewis, but he waved good night to me.

For an underground business, I have as much word-of-mouth trade from the senior boys as I can handle. I estimate that my volume is second only to that of the snack stand that sells snow cones. Like the snow-cone stand, I have high prices and limited hours of operation. I arrive at the arts and crafts cabin every day at 2:00 P.M., carrying half-finished pot holders from the day before, and senior boys drift in and out for the next twenty minutes. I talk to each customer, take notes, and deliver the finished product by 5:00 P.M. the next day. My prices start at five dollars for words only and go up to twenty dollars for words and concept.

Bobby Dunn has appointed himself my sales force; he recruits customers who he thinks need my services and gives each one a talk about the need for secrecy. Bobby will not accept money from me as payment—he reminds me hourly that he is doing this for Jesus—but he is glad to be thanked in testimonies.

By the beginning of the second week of camp, our director, Reverend Stewart, and the camp counselors were openly rejoicing about the power of the Spirit at work, as reflected in the moving personal testimonies being given night after night. Bobby Dunn has been testifying every other night and smiling at me at breakfast every morning. Patsy Lewis has taught me how to set my hair on big rollers, and I let it dry while I sit up writing testimonies. I have a perfect pageboy, a white Bible bulging with five-dollar bills, and I am popular. There are times when I forget my father.

On this last night of camp I am still at large. But although I have not been caught, I have decided I am not cut out to be a small business. There is the question of good help, for one thing. Bobby Dunn is no good for detail work—clearly, the less he knows about how my mind works, the better—and so I have turned to Missy Tucker. Missy loves Jesus and her father and disapproves of everything about me. I love her because she truly believes I can be saved and, 30 until that happens, is willing to get into almost any trouble I can think of, provided I do not try to stop her from quoting the appropriate Scripture. Even so, she resisted being drawn into the testimony business for more than a week, giving in only after I sank low enough to introduce her to Bobby Dunn and point out that she would be able to apply her cut to the high cost of braces.

The truth is, the business needs Missy. I am no better a disciple of the Palmer Handwriting Method than I am of Christ or of my mother's standards of behavior. No one can read my writing. Missy has won the penmanship medal at E. M. Morrow Elementary School so many times there is talk that it will be retired when we go off to junior high in the fall. When she's done writing, my testimonies look like poems.

The value of Missy's cursive writing skills, however, is offset by the ways in which she manifests herself as a True Believer. I can tolerate the Scripture quoting, but her fears are something else. I am afraid of snakes and of not being asked to pledge my mother's sorority at Baylor, both standard fears in Cabin A. Missy is terrified of Eastern religions.

Her father, a religion professor at a small Baptist college, has two passions: world religions and big-game hunting. In our neighborhood, where not rotating the tires on the family Ford on a schedule is considered eccentric, Dr. Tucker wears a safari jacket to class and greets everyone the same way: "Hi, wallaby." Missy is not allowed to be afraid of the dead animals in her father's den, but a pronounced sensitivity to Oriental mysticism is thought to be acceptable in a young girl.

Unless I watch her, Missy cannot be trusted to resist inserting a paragraph into every testimony in which the speaker thanks the Lord Jesus for not having allowed him or her to be born a Buddhist. I tell Missy repeatedly that if every member of the camp baseball team suddenly begins to compare and contrast Zen and the tenets of Southern Baptist fundamentalism in his three-minute testimony, someone—even in this trusting place—is going to start to wonder.

35

She says she sees my point but keeps arguing for more "spiritual" content in the testimonies, a position in which she is enthusiastically supported by Bobby Dunn. Missy and Bobby have fallen in love; Bobby asked her to wear his friendship ring two nights ago, using his own words. What is art to me is faith—and now love—to Missy, and we are not as close as we were three weeks ago.

I am a success, but a lonely one, since there is no one I can talk to about either my success or my feelings. My brother, David, who normally can be counted on to protect me from myself and others, has only vague, Christian concern for me these days. He has fallen in love with Denise Meeker, universally regarded as the most spiritually developed girl in camp history, and he is talking about following my father into the ministry. I believe that when Denise goes home to Corpus Christi, David will remember law school, but in the meantime he is no comfort to me.

Now, from my place in the front row of the choir, I know that I will not have to worry about a going-out-of-business sale. What I have secretly wished for all summer is about to happen. I am going to get caught.

Ten minutes ago, during Reverend Stewart's introduction of visitors from the pulpit, I looked out at the crowd in the tent and saw my father walking down the center aisle. As I watched, he stopped every few rows to shake hands and say hello, as casual and full of good humor as if this were his church on a Sunday morning. He is a handsome man, and when he stopped at the pew near the front where David is sitting, I was struck by how much my father and brother look alike, their dark heads together as they smiled and hugged. I think of David as belonging to me, not to my father, but there was an unmistakable sameness in their movements that caught me by surprise, and my eyes filled with tears. Suddenly David pointed toward the choir, at me, and my father nodded his head and continued walking toward the front of the tent. I knew he had seen me, and I concentrated on looking straight ahead as he mounted the stairs to the stage and took a seat to the left of the altar. Reverend Stewart introduced him as the special guest preacher for the last night of camp, and for an instant I let myself believe that was the only reason he had come. He would preach and we would go home together tomorrow. Everything would be all right.

I hear a choked-off sound from my left and know without turning to look that it is Missy, about to cry. She has seen my father, too, and I touch her hand to remind her that no one will believe she was at fault. Because of me, teachers have been patiently writing "easily led" and "cries often" on Missy's report cards for years, and she is still considered a good girl. She won't get braces this year, I think, but she will be all right.

In the next moment two things happen at once. Missy starts to cry, really cry, and my father turns in his seat, looks at me, and then away. It is then that I realize that Missy has decided, without telling me, that straight teeth are not worth eternal damnation. She and Bobby Dunn have confessed, and my father has been called. Now, as he sits with his Bible in his hands and his head bowed, his profile shows none of the cheer of a moment before, and none of the success-ful-Baptist-preacher expressions I can identify. He does not look spiritual or joy-ful or weighted down by the burden of God's expectations. He looks furious.

There are more announcements than I ever remember hearing on the last night of camp: prayer lists, final volleyball standings, bus departure times, a Lottie Moon Stewardship Award for Denise Meeker. After each item, I forget I have no reason to expect Jesus to help me and I pray for one more; I know that as soon as the last announcement is read, Reverend Stewart will call for a time of personal testimonies before my father's sermon.

Even with my head down I can see Bobby Dunn sinking lower into a center pew and, next to him, Tim Bailey leaning forward, wanting to be first at the microphone. Tim is another of the Bishop School jocks, and he has combed his hair and put on Sunday clothes. In his left hand he is holding my masterwork, reproduced on three-by-five cards. He paid me twenty-five dollars for it—the most I have ever charged—and it is the best piece of my career. The script calls for Tim to talk movingly about meeting God in a car-truck accident near Galveston, when he was ten. In a dramatic touch of which I am especially proud, he seems to imply that God was driving the truck.

40

Tim, I know, is doing this to impress a Baptist Academy girl who has told him she will go to her cotillion alone before she goes with a boy who doesn't know Jesus as his personal Lord and Savior. He is gripping the notecards as if they were Didi Thornton, and for the first time in a lifetime full of Bible verses, I see an application to my daily living. I truly am about to reap what I have sown.

The announcements end, and Reverend Stewart calls for testimonies. As Tim Bailey rises, so does my father. As he straightens up, he turns again to look at me, and this time he makes a gesture toward the pulpit. It is a mock-gallant motion, the kind I have seen him make to let my mother go first at miniature golf. For an instant that simple reminder that I am not an evil mutant—I have a family that plays miniature golf—makes me think again that everything will be all right. Then I realize what my father is telling me. Tim Bailey will never get to the pulpit to give my testimony. My father will get there first, will tell the worshipers in the packed tent his sorrow and regret over the misdeeds of his little girl. *His little girl.* He is going to do what I have never imagined in all my fantasies about this moment. He is going to forgive me.

45   Without knowing exactly how it has happened, I am standing up, half running from the choir seats to the pulpit. I get there first, before either my father or Tim, and before Reverend Stewart can even say my name, I give my personal testimony.

I begin by admitting what I have been doing for the past three weeks. I talk about being gripped by hate, unable to appreciate the love of my wonderful parents or of Jesus. I talk about making money from other campers who, in their honest desire to honor the Lord, became trapped in my web of wrongdoing.

Bobby Dunn is crying. To his left I can see Mr. Talliferro; something in his face, intent and unsmiling, makes me relax: I am a Draw. Everyone is with me now. I can hear Missy behind me, still sobbing into her hymnal, and to prove I can make it work, I talk about realizing how blessed I am to have been born within easy reach of God's healing love. I could have been born a Buddhist, I say, and the gratifying gasps from the audience make me certain I can say anything I want now.

For an instant I lose control and begin quoting poetry instead of Scripture. There is a shaky moment when all I can remember is bits of "Stopping by Woods on a Snowy Evening,"[3] but I manage to tie the verses back to a point about Christian choices. The puzzled looks on some faces give way to shouts of "Amen!" and as I look out at the rows of people in the green-and-white-striped tent I know I have won. I have written the best testimony anyone at camp has ever given.

I feel, rather than see, my father come to stand beside me, but I do not stop. As I have heard him do hundreds of times, I ask the choir to sing an invitational hymn and begin singing with them, "Softly and tenderly, Jesus is calling, calling to you and to me. Come home, come home. Ye who are weary, come home."

3. A poem by the American poet Robert Frost (1874–1963).

My father never does give a sermon.

While the hymn is still being sung, Bobby Dunn moves from his pew to the stage, and others follow. They hug me; they say they understand; they say they forgive me. As each one moves on to my father, I can hear him thanking them for their concern and saying, yes, he knows they will be praying for the family.

By ten o'clock, the last knot of worshipers has left the tent, and my father and I are alone on the stage. He is looking at me without speaking; there is no expression on his face that I have seen before. "Daddy," I surprise myself by saying. Daddy is a baby name that I have not used since my ninth birthday. My father raises his left hand and slaps me, hard, on my right cheek. He catches me as I start to fall, and we sit down together on the steps leading from the altar. He uses his handkerchief to clean blood from underneath my eye, where his Baylor ring has opened the skin. As he works the white square of cloth carefully around my face, I hear a sound I have never heard before, and I realize my father is crying. I am crying, too, and the mixture of tears and blood on my face makes it impossible to see him clearly. I reach for him anyway and am only a little surprised when he is there.

1992

REGINALD McKNIGHT

Into Night

At two-thirty in the afternoon last Tuesday, just like every day, Sandman got to be as restless as a ghost. Didn't he nor I nor his mama know why he got this way. It mighta had something to do with two-thirty being the time that *Cartoon Tyme* went off the air. That meant to Sandman they wasn't nothing on the box till six in the evening, when *Gimme a Break* come on. Sandman liked that show a whole bunch 'cause it have this big ol' fat woman on it who look like my daughter Erlene and who holler like everybody she talking to a mile away. From two-thirty on, wasn't nothing on but news, game shows, and soaps, programs a five-year-old cain't stand. But I know that didn't have all that much to do with why my grandchild got as fidgety as he did most every day. Most likely it had to do with the fact that his big sister, Tanika, was fend[1] to arrive home from school before long. And little Tanika had what I call a unnatural ability for knowing if Sandman done been in her room, messing with her things, which he did most every day.

Don't know what it was about that boy. Seem like he just couldn't break hisself away from going up to her room. Been doing that since Pauline, my daughter, and her husband, Ricardo, moved me in with them last winter. Didn't know what it was. The child has plenty of his own toys and things. He like to drive his mama and his sister and his daddy insane every day with his constant

---

1. About.

going up to her room and messing with her things. Even though things have changed since Tuesday last, I still think they should put the boy in preschool, like they done Tanika, but they won't. Pauline say, "Mama, they ain't nothing they can teach him at that school that I cain't teach him at home." Course she say it a whole lot prettier and fancier than that, 'cause of all the education she's had, but that's basically what she said. I know she get irritated with me sometimes, and I hates to interfere and get in the way, but I see what I see, and I know what I know. The boy don't mean no harm. When they first brung me here last winter, after Paul passed, I thought they wanted me to help with the chi'ren, and this big ol' house, but it seem like granmas is better seen and not heard. Seem like all they want me to do is sit around the house and crochet and look thankful I got family. Lord, I coulda did that back in Shreveport. Didn't need to come up here.

Now, the "crime of crimes," as far as Tanika was concerned, was "even breathing" on her model aero-planes. Ricardo fond of saying that Tanika is "uncanny" at remembering exactly where she set each and every model she had displayed round her room. But Sandman loves the models as much as his sister do, and he show his love for 'em by playing with 'em. But sometimes he break 'em, too. After a while, though, he got used to Tanika's temper, I suppose, even though the girl can explode like a bone-dry radiator when she want to, and even though she take forever to cool back down. He got used to, too, with her always screaming 'bout how her models is not toys and how "ab-so-loot-ly nooo-body" under nine years old is allowed in her room. That girl can screech and squeak, shake that one itty-bitty fist in his face, threaten the boy with "fis' soup and knuckle samwiches" till she near 'bout blue in the face. But Sandman steady[2] been in her room and steady play with her models. And ol' Sandman'll stand up in fronta Tanika like a deacon stand up before the altar to receive holy reprimand. He stand tall as he can in front of her and try not to look too bored or too sassy. The boy'll stay cool as ice cream, little as he is, nodding every now and then, but not saying a word. Now, before Tuesday, however, when Tanika'd be in a 'specially nasty mood she'd smack Sandman upside his head. And just like any sinner ought to fear one of the Lord's crackly lightning bolts, Sandman was afred of his sister's hurricane swings and lightning knuckles. But things been pretty calm since Tuesday last, like I said.

Well, the light from the T.V. shrunk down to a tiny dot and faded away. I was sitting up in the living room with him, at the time, and I looked up from my crocheting and watched him watch hisself get up from his Cap'n Starheart Official Star Command T.V. cushion, and glide on out the living room. Looked to me, at first, he was going down to the basement where his mama's studio at, but I said, "Uh-uh, baby, Mama's busy. Whyn't you stay up here with Granmama. You hungry?" He said he wasn't hungry.

5   "Well," I said, "I think you ought to go out'n play in the back, or you can take a nap, then."

He didn't say nothing for about a minute, just stood there, standing on the

2. Loosely, "always."

side of his shoes like he always do, so I said, "Baby, don't stand that way, you'll ruin your shoes. You wanna go out?" But he said he didn't wanna go out, said he wanted to take a nap. Well, I knew something was up. Ain't seen many five-year-old boys ask for a nap, but I said, "All right. You want me to go up with you and pat your back?" and he shook his head no, and went on up the stairs. I knew what he was gonna do. He was gonna go right straight up them stairs and go right on into Tanika's room. Don't know who he thought he was fooling. This an old house, and when it's quiet here, you can hear every creak and croak them steps and them floorboards make. Once somebody up on the landing, ain't but a half dozen or so sounds you gonna hear: If it's Sandman's room you gonna hear, "Grunt-grunt"—that's to the right. If it's Tanika's room it's gon' be, "Grunt-grunt-o-gruncha?" The bathroom say, "Grunt-grunt-o-pop," or "Grunt-grunt-o-squeak-pop," depending on whether you step on the doorsill or not. The rooms on the left, mine's and the master bedroom, have their own way, too. Didn't even have to get out my chair to know Sandman went up them twelve steps, and instead of going to his room: "Grunt-grunt," I heard, "Grunt" . . . and a long pause, and then . . . "grunt," and then a long, long, long pause, and then—he was sneaking, see—"o-gruncha?" I just had to laugh. And then right when I was thinking 'bout going up after him, Pauline hollered from downstairs, "Mama? Where Sandman at?" See, only a mama could have that kind of feeling that her child ain't up to no good. "Oh, he upstairs," I yelled back. "Napping."

She was quiet for a little bit, then she said, "Would you check on him for me, please?"

"All right, honey," I said. And I tiptoed up them dozen steps, thinking I'd peep at him in his sister's room for a bit before picking his narrow behind up and putting him in his own room. He just love Tanika's room and Tanika's things, but I myself can't stand it. Don't like the smell. Smells like model glue, strawberry talcum powder, and doll plastic. Child must have a thousand dolls in that room, and every one of 'em different. Different colors, different doll tricks, different sizes and shapes. But I'll tell you one thing: ain't never seen the girl play with a one. Most every one a them dolls was sent to her by her and Sandman's granmama who live in Tennessee. That woman just cain't stand the idea a my grandbaby being interested in model planes. Ricardo's mother got a little . . . money, see, and she like everybody to know it, so every chance she get she send Tanika some kinda doll. Don't matter what occasion it is, Christmas, Easter, Tanika's birthday, Sandman's birthday, good report card, bad report card, no report card, or "just for being a sweet thing," don't make no never mind. Woman like to make me spit up. The child got an army a dolls, a legion a dolls that cry, belch, sing, snore, pee, drink, get diaper rash, walk, blink, crawl. But Tanika, bless her heart, won't touch 'em.

If you's to walk into her room on any day, you wouldn't see a one of these dolls. But you can smell 'em. They crammed into her closet, stacked under her bed. Ain't but two or three of 'em ever even been removed from they boxes. Ricardo call Tanika's bedroom "the bone yard," and even joked about buying a plastic wreath to hang on her door. But Pauline didn't find that funny at all. Said Ricardo's sense of humor is morbid. Her and her fancy words—but I agree with her. Talk like that will only give the babies bad dreams.

Well, I opened up Tanika's door just a tee-nine-chee bit and peeked in, and Lord, what did I see. Lord, it made me put my hand to my chest, and made my eyes bug out, and made my breathing like to stop. I seen Sandman standing in the middle of Tanika's room spinning round slow like somebody dancing by hisself, and flying round and round was one of Tanika's aero-planes going round and round the room. I didn't mean to speak so loud, but I hollered, "Sandman!" and the boy jecked his head my way and the plane went zing and smacked right into the door. I jumped back. Well, before I could collect myself and open the door, I heard Pauline's footsteps on the stairs and she saying in her shrieky-high voice, "What's going on up there? What's that boy doing?" I opened up the door just as Pauline got up the stairs. "Paul," I was fend to say, but Pauline said, "Maxwell Sanders Harris! Boy, what'd I tell you about playing in your sister's room?" Pauline very light skinned like her daddy, and when she get upset like she was then, she get this maroon blush on her face, look just like a butterfly. Her daddy, Paul, used to color up the very same way, and so do Tanika. I'll tell you what, when they get to wearing that maroon butterfly, you better look out. "Huh, boy?" Pauline said. "What'd I say?"

"Not to," Sandman said.

"Then why'd you do it, huh?"

Sandman didn't say nothing, and I felt just turrible for the child. He stood there, as he always do on the side of his feet, with his hands behind his back, and his forehead creased, his eyes looking all worried. Like to make me cry. Had on his little suspenders, his little blue jeans a size or two too big. Big head, little scrawny neck. I just felt turrible, looking at that boy, and I said, "Paul, now you got work to do, honey. Let me talk to him."

"Mama, I been talking to this child enough to make my head spin. I'm damn sick and tired of him defying me. Damn sick and tired of it."

"Ain't no reason to cuss me, girl," I said. "I'm your—"

"Mind your bidness—boy, get to your room."

Sandman is usually a well-behaved child, but for some reason he didn't budge. Instead, he looked at my feet and he said, "Mama, that plane flew by itself." Then quick as you could blink, *whap!* Pauline slapped his face. "Oww!" he said, real slow and long. He opened his mouth wide and his eyes got big, and tears filled up his eyes. He put his hand on his face where Pauline'd hit and tears was just rolling, but he didn't make no crying sounds at all. Then again he said, "Oww."

"What'd I tell you about lying?" Pauline said.

"Pauline!" I said.

"Get to your room, boy!"

Whap! She hit him again.

"Pauline!"

And Sandman hunched over and he looked like he couldn't believe what his mama was doing. He opened his mouth wide and saliva was dripping in a long string from his mouth and there was that silent crying for a long, long time. You know how chi'ren be when they gots to rear up they breath before they starts to really let loose. That's just what Sandman did. And Lord-a-mighty he did let loose. Loud. Then he walked past us and went to his room, still all hunched over, still with his hand on his face, just wailing and wailing and wailing. "Shut up that crying," Pauline said. Then she turned to me and the butterfly was like to fly off her face, it was so hot and red. "What you got to say, Mama. Huh? What you got to say?"

And I looked at the boy walk into his room, then I looked at the aero-plane on the floor of Tanika's room, and I seen the fishing line tied to it, and I understood why it looked like the plane'd been flying. See, some of Tanika's models is on chrome stands, and some of 'em hangs from fishing lines from the ceiling. Ricardo give her the line, you understand. Apparently, what happened was the boy'd found something long to smack the plane with and make it fly in a circle like it did. But it was going so fast, I told myself, I couldn't see the line at first. But there it was, just as plain as day, tied onto the aero-plane, and at the other end of the line was the thumbtack that had held the line in the ceiling. I felt foolish, 'cause I was fend to tell Pauline that the plane did too fly. Seen it with my very own eyes, I was gonna say. But looked like I was wrong, so I didn't know what to say about that. The sound a Sandman's crying made me hurt in my chest and in my throat. Don't know why it upset me so. Ain't like I've never heard chi'ren cry before. And I really didn't wanna interfere with how my grown daughter raise her chi'ren. I might be her mama, but I'm a guest in this house. I got to respects what they say and do. Pauline is a good and strong woman, and I'm so proud of what she's done and what she's got. The child's got statues standing, and pictures hanging, in museums in Detroit and California and New York City, and here in Pittsburgh. Sometimes she take me down into her studio in the basement and show me what she working on. The stuff she do is so pretty, all them loud African colors, like a store full of jaw-breakers. Like to make your mouth water. I got to admit I don't care for everything she do, and I think she ought to put some more clothes on some of those women she paint and draw, and not make their faces look so cross, but I guess she know what she doing, and I guess I don't. But the one she working on now, the one she shown me a day or two ago, she call *The Vanishing Blue*,[3] which she tell me is about that Middle Passing,[4] I believe it is, when the white folks took our people from Africa. Well, it's all done in blue dots, like a million tiny blue dots, this one picture, see. Blues so light they nearly white, to blues so dark, they nearly black. And its animals and birds and trees, and it all look like you seeing down from way, way up in the air. Like you done passed from this life, and you looking down on everything. That one I like, and I understand it. But even if I don't understand or don't like something, I don't say anything. No, sir, I don't. She grown, and it's her life. Besides, she got them two fine chi'ren and a good husband who she tell me is the best optometrist in town. They got a nice house. They got two nice cars. And they been so good to me.

---

3. Refers to the disappearing horizon as seen from the stern of a ship.   4. Middle Passage is the term used to describe the transporting of Africans by ship to the Americas for the purpose of selling them into slavery.

20   But I had to say something. I mean, she was standing there in front of me, huffing and puffing with her hands on her hips, and her butterfly a-burning. She looked so tired, had beeswax under her fingernails, and what looked like charcoal on her cheek, a rope a that dreadful Rooster, Rasta, Roster hair, or whatever you calls it, hanging down over one eye. One wrong word might make things worse, I was thinking, and like I say, I didn't want to interfere, but when you looks at it the way a five-year-old do, that plane was flying. So I said, "It's my fault, baby. I was supposed to be watching him, and I wasn't. Don't be too hard on him."

"Mama," she said, and then she pointed her finger at me, which she know I don't like, "I have told him and told him and told him—"

"I know—"

"—to stay out of his sister's room. And I'm sick of it. And you know good and well you raised me to despise lying. Now, you got anything else to say?"

"No."

25   "Good." And she spun around and went. Sounded like a herd a buffalo going down them steps. Then I heard her holler up the stairs, "And, Mama, please leave that mess he made right where it is, till Ricardo and Tani get home. And Maxwell, boy, don't you let me hear you fooling around up there. You get your butt into that bed and stay quiet."

Well I did leave the "mess" where it was. I didn't feel like doing anything no how. Sandman was still in his room, gasping and whooping like his room didn't have no air in it. I shut his door, then went on into my own room and closed my door, too. I could still hear him a little bit. I wanted to go into his room and hold him a spell, but that was for his mama to do. If she'd come back upstairs for some reason, and seen me doing that, why, I think she'd a got upset all over again. Didn't know what to do with myself, so I just kicked off my shoes, pulled off my glasses, untucked my blouse, unfastened the top button of my pants, and laid down on my bed.

Just before my eyes got heavy, I heard a sound that said, "Doomp, d-doom doomp. Doomp, d-doom doomp," kinda like the way that Sergeant Joe Friday[5] music go. I knew it was Sandman fiddling around with something, and I got up and out my room in my stocking feet, stood outside the door to his room, and listened. He was talking to hisself, real quiet like. And the sound said, "Doomp, d-doom doomp." Got down on my knees and looked through the keyhole. Sandman was sitting on his toy box, his chin resting in his hands, bouncing his heels off the side of the toy box. "Doomp, d-doom doomp." Then he hopped down off the box, th'ew it open, and started digging through it. After a good deal of digging and searching and looking, he took out this little rubber super-hero doll—didn't know what its name was, only ones I know is Superman, Batman, and that Starheart fella he so crazy about, but this one I didn't know; besides, I couldn't see it all that well no how, since I didn't have my glasses on.

5. Sergeant Joe Friday, played by Jack Webb, was the head detective on *Dragnet*, the popular 1950s television series. The theme music that accompanied the capture and conviction of the criminal was always the ominous single notes: "Doomp, de-doom doomp. Doomp, de-doom doomp, doo!"

Well now, he closed the lid on the box, and stood the doll up on its feets, and backed up a few steps from the box. I could just barely see the doll's head poking up over Sandman's shoulder. What is he doing? I asked myself. Then he pointed his finger at the doll, and said in the loudest whisper he could, "Fly, Spiderman!" Well, I be dogged, I was thinking. Maybe he can too, make things fly. "Fly, Spiderman!" he said again. Almost made me laugh out loud. Then the boy said, "Shazzam!" and then when that didn't work, he said, "Eeeeagle Power!" then, "By the Power of Greeey-skuuull," "Up, up, and awaaaay," and "Spaaaace Ghooost!"[6] and his voice kept getting louder and louder, till I knew I better go on in there and tell him to hesh up before his mama come up and peel his behind. I stood up, and Lord did my knees argue with me. Used to be only on cloudy days when my arthur-itis trouble me, but since I come up here, it seem like just about a daily thing.

Well, I took ahold of the doorknob, and just as I twisted it, I heard Sandman holler, "Tired-ass punk," and I heard him th'ow the doll against the wall. It tickled me; I just had to laugh. But soon's I opened the door, I heard Pauline running back up the stairs. Reckon she wasn't in her studio at all, but in the kitchen, and since Sandman's room is right smack over the kitchen, she musta heard every sound he was making.

Well, she pushed right on past me without so much as a how do, and slammed the door shut, and I heard *whap! whap!* and it started up all over again. Lord-a-mighty it was a ugly sound. I just couldn't bear to hear it. I couldn't stand there two seconds. I went to my room and closed the door, laid on my bed, pressed the heels of my hands over my ears, but I could hear every sound. I heard the boy crying, and I heard Pauline barking just like a dog. "You little bastard, what'd I tell you? Huh? Huh?" Heard the sound of hangers sliding back and forth on the rod in Sandman's closet. Knew she was looking for a belt. She found one, too, 'cause I heard every one of them strokes. Every single one. And every now and then I heard that boy say things like, "Mama? Mama? I love you. I love you," and I heard hard things hitting the floor and I knew they was heels or elbows or knees or noggin. I knew the boy was burning up, scared, in a devil wind of hurt. I knew Pauline was hurting, too, blind, sick, dizzy, excited, and hurting her ownself. But I knew, also, that she didn't know it. I heard, "What I say?" and "black bastard" and "skin you alive" and "don't you dare raise your hand to me." I heard "please" and "sorry" and "didn't mean to" and "forgot to" and "love you, Mama, love you." But I knew Mama couldn't hear a thing but that hissing sound you hear, and blood and heat and ice and nightmares and howling, and the fire on her very own skin—heard it, *heard* it, not seen it— heard the flame tips of memory, and right behind it I heard the hurt of every single one a my babies, Erlene and Justine, Peter, Paul, Mark, and Juline, Pearline and John, Samuel and Pauline. Pauline. I heard my hands on Pauline, my leather on Pauline, switch, cord, ruler, hanger, towel, wet and heavy. And I

30

6. "Fly Spiderman!", "Shazzam!", "Eagle Power!", "By the Power of Greyskull," "Up, up, and away," and "Space Ghost" are powerful utterances employed by the cartoon superheroes Spiderman, Captain Marvel, Masters of the Universe, Superman, and Space Ghost.

heard me, too, my own screams, and my brothers and sisters, my mama, papa, aunts, and uncles and on back, and on back. All that sickening hissing fire. Heard it quivering in my belly, and balling up in my throat . . . and on back and on back. I put my pillow over my head and heard my tears soak into it. Generations and generations of slaves and slavekeepers I heard. I couldn't escape that sound, and I couldn't understand why it was only now I was hearing just how turrible it is. I heard burning crosses and natureless men, women split open like pigs' knuckles, heard the pain of vanishing blue jungles and dry red soil, black long-tooth cats that creep in the night, white long-neck birds that could fill up a blue blue sky. All vanishing into endless ocean and ships full of stink and death. I heard the weight of a thousand leagues of water on my back, heard the howl of a million lost spirits black and white, and black and red, and black and blue. Then just black, so black I couldn't hear nothing no more, nor see, nor breathe, nor move. I wisht I coulda helped that boy, but I couldn't move.

Well, let me see can I go on. Let me get my mind right.

Naturally, Tanika had a hissy fit. Her voice poked me outta my sleep like Paul's skinny elbow used to. Didn't leave my room just then, but I knew her caramelly skin was lit up with the butterfly, them wingtips touching her temple to temple. "But Daddy," I heard her say, "that was my favorite plane."

They were in her bedroom. I could tell.

35   "Seem like to me," said her father, "that whichever model your brother break is your favorite." He talk kinda pretty, too, when he ain't too upset, so I cain't say it exactly the way he did. "You ever notice that?" he said.

"Well, I guess . . . I like 'em all the same. They all my favorites. That's why I builds 'em."

Then Ricardo said back, "Uh-huh." Then his voice changed a notch. "Maybe we *ought* to put a lock on her door till ol' Sandman old enough to do like he ast."

"But Daddy, he is old enough. He five. He be in school next year."

"No," said Pauline. "I will not abide locks on these chi'ren's doors. Naw-aw. No."

40   "Awright, Pauline, calm down." And Ricardo's voice changed back. "I know he five, babygirl, but that's still young. You just got to learn patience. Let's just be patient for now. Now, it might make you happy if I tear his little seater-end up—"

"Yes it would!"

"Don't you backtalk your father, girl."

"—but since your mother already done that, I don't see no reason to. We all done seen enough of that around this house."

"You the one to talk, man."

45   "Hey, I didn't say I'm some kinda saint. I said 'we.' 'We.' "

They was all of 'em quiet for a spell. Then Ricardo said, "Patience, babygirl. You got to learn patience. And it's only one way to learn patience." And then he was quiet for a real long time. "How?" said Tanika. Then I heard Ricardo carry his big self down the stairs. He was chuckling. "How?" Tanika said, and Ricardo laughed a little harder. "How?" Tanika said. "Daddy, how?" Ricardo just laughed, and I heard Tanika following him, and it sound like she smacked him on the behind. "Dad-dy!" she said. I had to smile.

I heard Pauline close Tanika's door and open up Sandman's. Heard her switch on the light and close the door. The only thing I could hear her say was, "You hungry, baby?" and I knew she'd be sitting him on her lap, and wrapping her arms around him. Knew she be rocking him and cooing to him. And her voice be like a warm wind full of spices. She might look him over careful, thinking 'bout, "Maybe I ought to put some Mercurochrome right there, and a little bit back here, too, maybe." She cain't believe what she done, you see. Cain't even remember all of it, really. I knew Sandman be trembling inside, just like a day-old puppy tremble when it find itself too far from its mama's belly and teats. Then it be like he feel the sun rising in his stomach, and maybe he cry a little bit, and say he sorry, and Mama will feel her heart ease into twos and fours and eights, breaking real slow and silent, and she'll cry some too. Try to make him smile, she will, by saying things like, "You knows you a little hellion, boy. But you know Mama love her little rascal." And when she see him smile, her heart'll ease itself from eights to fours to twos and she'll thank Jesus that cain't nobody forgive and forget like a child. She'll get down on her knees and thank Jesus.

But I was sitting there asking myself, What if, after all that holding, after they done eaten and talked and everybody in bed, and Sandman laying there in the dark, what things'll be going through his head when it look like everything back to normal? For my daughter may believe that chi'ren forget, but I know better now. What'll he be thinking? Did I make that plane fly? Was it magic? Is Tanika a witch? Is that why I ain't never allowed to touch them planes? Maybe the whole family is witches—Tanika, Mama, Daddy, Granmama. Maybe late at night they all shrink down to the size of crickets, get inside them planes, and fly to China and New York and Disneyland. Why don't they take me? Maybe they hate me. Maybe they kill if I keep messing with them planes. 'Cause Mama say, "I'ma kill you, boy. I swear I'ma kill you, you don't do as I say." Did I make it fly? Or was it Daddy's fishing line made it fly?

Well, I guess that plane musta flew, all right, 'cause that night, last Tuesday night, we all seen something I don't think we'll ever forget. This is what happened:

I passed on dinner that evening. Just couldn't see sitting down with 'em and getting in their way. Wanted 'em to be just they own family that night. I went to bed, but I couldn't sleep. I tossed and turned in that bed, and it squeaked and squawked, and just about drove me outta my mind. It was a warm night and clear for a night in Pittsburgh, and I went to the window, got down on my knees to pray. I felt like I had to pray against all them sounds I'd heard in my sleep that afternoon, all that pain that been burned into my skin and found its way out my very own hands. Generations and generations. But I couldn't find no words. I looked out that window, and I watched that empty night sky. Never had noticed how big the sky is before, even though I'm in my seventy-seventh year,

50

and seen maybe ten, twenty, thirty thousand such skies. Never noticed how deep it was neither. The very idea of a endless sky made me dizzy, I tell you the truth. I cletched on to the windowsill like I was afred I might fall up and up and up, and keep on falling. I set there a long time on my knees like that, till my arthur-itis started fussing, till the sky turned from dark blue like one of Sandman's cleary marbles to black as a skillet. The clouds was almost invisible. Sky got deeper. Stars began to bleed out from the darkness. It was a glory to behold. "Thank you, Lord," I said. "Thank you." I don't know why I said that.

Next thing I heard was Tanika's elbow voice, poking me outta my sleep once more. "What you doing in my room, boy?" I heard her say. I pulled myself off the cool floor, and my knees and ankles couldn't slow me down none. Not really. Mothers is like that when they hear a child's voice in the night. Don't nothing slow 'em, not arthur-itis, or flu, or migraine, or dropsy. I heard heels and toes hit the floor, robes being pulled on, lights snapped on, doors open. Then Tanika said, "What? You want what?" And just as I was stepping into her room Sandman said, "Granmama, Tani won't teach me to fly her planes." He had a plane in his hand, and it looked like Tanika didn't know it till I did, 'cause her sleepish eyes got big and she screamed, "My Thunderbolt!" Just then Pauline stepped up behind me and her voice cut acrost the room. She said, "What the hell is going on here?" and just about this time Tanika was duking up a storm. Her lips was pushed up into her mouth, nostrils flaring. She chopped at Sandman, and chopped again, had the blind look in her eyes, and knew she heard the hiss. I could hear it. I could hear in that child's head like they was vipers from down below. Pauline was fend to push me out the way, but all in a second I'd grabbed her by her sleeve and hollered, "Tanika, put your hand down, girl! Put it down right this second!"

"Mama, just—"

But I said, "No." I heard that turrible, turrible hissing I know so well and I thought it was me who was gonna start chopping with my hands or with a belt or a shoe or anything else in reach, but it didn't feel like it should have. Didn't burn and build up, like it should have, yet I knew I heard that hissing. I know I did. Then we all turned back to the landing when we heard Ricardo say, "Lookit Sandman!" And when we looked from Ricardo to his son we seen that aero-plane in his hand, and the propeller on that thing was spinning like I don't know what, was just hissing, louder and louder, till you couldn't no longer call it a hiss no more, but a buzz. And wasn't too long before we seen that every aero-plane in that room was buzzing. And the spirit was in me, and I moved across the room on the balls of my feet, like I was Tanika's age. "It's a blessing, chi'ren," I said. "We being blessed." The planes on they chrome stands was buzzing. The planes on the ceiling was buzzing, going round and round on them fishing lines. I went to the window and seen the sky was back to being dark blue again. Didn't have no idea I was asleep that long. Anyway, I opened up the window, pulled up the screen, and put my hand out to Sandman. "Go ahead, Sandman. Go on ahead. It's a blessing. We being blessed." So my grandson walked up to me, and I rested my hand on his head, moved him closer to the window. "Go on, baby," I said. "It's a blessing." Then I turned back to look at the others. Ricardo had his hands in his robe pockets and was looking half crossy-eyed with sleep, half joyful in the presence of the Power, like he didn't know up from down. But Tanika and Pauline, well, they looked like twins to each other, all small and grayish. They eyes was big, but they didn't seem to be looking at anything in particular, and didn't look cross or scared or nothing, and they didn't have no butterflies on 'em neither. Just stood there, the tall twin behind the short one, a big right hand hooking fingers betwixt the fingers of a little right hand. I looked back down at my grandson, and I said, "Go on, baby."

Well Sandman just opened his hand and let that plane go and it floated off just like I knew it would, and I closed my eyes and listened to them tiny engines. I felt everybody move on up behind me. I felt Pauline's arm slip round my shoulder. Lord, Lord, all them little planes just fanning up tiny breezes all around us. A body'd have to carry a *pe*can for a heart not to be moved by all that. I do believe he would. So me and Sandman, Tanika and Ricardo, and my baby Pauline, well, one by one, we let them things fly into the night. They looked like little dots, little ink dots, in that blue sky. And they sounded like a million honeybees.

They sounded just like a million honeybees.

1992

HA JIN

In Broad Daylight

While I was eating corn cake and jellyfish at lunch, our gate was thrown open and Bare Hips hopped in. His large wooden pistol was stuck partly inside the waist of his blue shorts. "White Cat," he called me by my nickname, "hurry, let's go. They caught Old Whore at her home. They're going to take her through the streets this afternoon."

"Really?" I put down my bowl, which was almost empty, and rushed to the inner room for my undershirt and sandals. "I'll be back in a second."

"Bare Hips, did you say they'll parade Mu Ying today?" I heard Grandma ask in her husky voice.

"Yes, all the kids on our street have left for her house. I came to tell White Cat." He paused. "Hey, White Cat, hurry up!"

"Coming," I cried out, still looking for my sandals.

"Good, good!" Grandma said to Bare Hips, while flapping at flies with her large palm-leaf fan. "They should burn the bitch on Heaven Lamp like they did in the old days."

"Come, let's go," Bare Hips said to me the moment I was back. He turned to the door; I picked up my wooden scimitar and followed him.

"Put on your shoes, dear." Grandma stretched out her fan to stop me.

"No time for that, Grandma. I've got to be quick, or I'll miss something and won't be able to tell you the whole story when I get back."

We dashed into the street while Grandma was shouting behind us. "Come back. Take the rubber shoes with you."

5

10

55

We charged toward Mu Ying's home on Eternal Way, waving our weapons above our heads. Grandma was crippled and never came out of our small yard. That was why I had to tell her about what was going on outside. But she knew Mu Ying well, just as all the old women in our town knew Mu well and hated her. Whenever they heard that she had a man in her home again, these women would say, "This time they ought to burn Old Whore on Heaven Lamp."

What they referred to was the old way of punishing an adulteress. Though they had lived in New China for almost two decades, some ancient notions still stuck in their heads. Grandma told me about many of the executions in the old days that she had seen with her own eyes. Officials used to have the criminals of adultery executed in two different ways. They beheaded the man. He was tied to a stake on the platform at the marketplace. At the first blare of horns, a masked headsman ascended the platform holding a broad ax before his chest; at the second blare of horns, the headsman approached the criminal and raised the ax over his head; at the third blare of horns, the head was lopped off and fell to the ground. If the man's family members were waiting beneath the platform, his head would be picked up to be buried together with his body; if no family member was nearby, dogs would carry the head away and chase each other around until they ate up the flesh and returned for the body.

Unlike the man, the woman involved was executed on Heaven Lamp. She was hung naked upside down above a wood fire whose flames could barely touch her scalp. And two men flogged her away with whips made of bulls' penises. Meanwhile she screamed for help and the whole town could hear her. Since the fire merely scorched her head, it took at least half a day for her to stop shrieking and a day and a night to die completely. People used to believe that the way of punishment was justified by Heaven, so the fire was called Heaven Lamp. But that was an old custom; nobody believed they would burn Mu Ying in that way.

Mu's home, a small granite house with cement tiles built a year before, was next to East Wind Inn on the northern side of Eternal Way. When we entered that street, Bare Hips and I couldn't help looking around tremulously, because that area was the territory of the children living there. Two of the fiercest boys, who would kill without having second thoughts, ruled that part of our town. Whenever a boy from another street wandered into Eternal Way, they'd capture him and beat him up. Of course we did the same thing; if we caught one of them in our territory, we'd at least confiscate whatever he had with him: grass-hopper cages, slingshots, bottle caps, marbles, cartridge cases, and so on. We would also make him call every one of us "Father" or "Grandfather." But today hundreds of children and grown-ups were pouring into Eternal Way; two dozen urchins on that street surely couldn't hold their ground. Besides, they had already adopted a truce, since they were more eager to see the Red Guards[1] drag Mu Ying out of her den.

---

1. A national student organization sponsored by Mao Zedong as an instrument to start and develop the Great Proletarian Cultural Revolution (1966–76).

When we arrived, Mu was being brought out through a large crowd at the front gate. Inside her yard there were three rows of colorful washing hung on iron wires, and there was also a grape trellis. Seven or eight children were in there, plucking off grapes and eating them. Two Red Guards held Mu Ying by the arms, and the other Red Guards, about twenty of them, followed behind. They were all from Dalian City and wore home-made army uniforms. God knew how they came to know that there was a bad woman in our town. Though people hated Mu and called her names, no one would rough her up. Those Red Guards were strangers, so they wouldn't mind doing it.

Surprisingly, Mu looked rather calm; she neither protested nor said a word. The two Red Guards let go of her arms, and she followed them quietly into West Street. We all moved with them. Some children ran several paces ahead to look back at her.

Mu wore a sky-blue dress, which made her different from the other women who always wore jackets and pants suitable for honest work. In fact, even we small boys could tell that she was really handsome, perhaps the best looking woman of her age in our town. Though in her fifties, she didn't have a single gray hair; she was a little plump, but because of her long legs and arms she appeared rather queenly. While most of the women had sallow faces, hers looked white and healthy like fresh milk.

Skipping in front of the crowd, Bare Hips turned around and cried out at her, "Shameless Old Whore!"

She glanced at him, her round eyes flashing; the purple wart beside her left nostril grew darker. Grandma had assured me that Mu's wart was not a beauty-wart but a tear-wart. This meant that her life would be soaked in tears.

We knew where we were going, to White Mansion, which was our classroom building, the only two-storied house in the town. As we came to the end of West Street, a short man ran out from a street corner, panting for breath and holding a sickle. He was Meng Su, Mu Ying's husband, who sold bean jelly in summer and sugar-coated haws in winter at the marketplace. He paused in front of the large crowd, as though having forgotten why he had rushed over. He turned his head around to look back; there was nobody behind him. After a short moment he moved close, rather carefully.

"Please let her go," he begged the Red Guards. "Comrade Red Guards, it's all my fault. Please let her go." He put the sickle under his arm and held his hands together before his chest.

"Get out of the way!" commanded a tall young man, who must have been the leader.

"Please don't take her away. It's my fault. I haven't disciplined her well. Please give her a chance to be a new person. I promise, she won't do it again."

The crowd stopped to circle about. "What's your class status?" a square-faced young woman asked in a sharp voice.

"Poor peasant," Meng replied, his small eyes tearful and his cupped ears twitching a little. "Please let her go, sister. Have mercy on us! I'm kneeling down to you if you let her go." Before he was able to fall on his knees, two young men held him back. Tears were rolling down his dark fleshy cheeks, and his gray head began waving about. The sickle was taken away from him.

"Shut up," the tall leader yelled and slapped him across the face. "She's a snake. We traveled a hundred and fifty *li* to come here to wipe out poisonous snakes and worms. If you don't stop interfering, we'll parade you with her together. Do you want to join her?"

Silence. Meng covered his face with his large hands as though feeling dizzy.

A man in the crowd said aloud, "If you can share the bed with her, why can't you share the street?"

Many of the grown-ups laughed. "Take him, take him too!" someone told the Red Guards. Meng looked scared, sobbing quietly.

His wife stared at him without saying a word. Her teeth were clenched; a faint smile passed the corners of her mouth. Meng seemed to wince under her stare. The two Red Guards let his arms go, and he stepped aside, watching his wife and the crowd move toward the school.

Of Meng Su people in our town had different opinions. Some said he was a born cuckold who didn't mind his wife's sleeping with any man as long as she could bring money home. Some believed he was a good-tempered man who had stayed with his wife mainly for their children's sake; they forgot that the three children had grown up long before and were working in big cities far away. Some thought he didn't leave his wife because he had no choice—no woman would marry such a dwarf. Grandma, for some reason, seemed to respect Meng. She told me that Mu Ying had once been raped by a group of Russian soldiers under Northern Bridge and was left on the river bank afterwards. That night her husband sneaked there and carried her back. He looked after her for a whole winter till she recovered. "Old Whore doesn't deserve that good-hearted man," Grandma would say. "She's heartless and knows only how to sell her thighs."

We entered the school's playground where about two hundred people had already gathered. "Hey, White Cat and Bare Hips," Big Shrimp called us, waving his claws. Many boys from our street were there too. We went to join them.

The Red Guards took Mu to the front entrance of the building. Two tables had been placed between the stone lions that crouched on each side of the entrance. On one of the tables stood a tall paper hat with the big black characters on its side: "Down with Old Bitch!"

A young man in glasses raised his bony hand and started to address us, "Folks, we've gathered here today to denounce Mu Ying, who is a demon in this town."

"Down with Bourgeois Demons!" a slim woman Red Guard shouted. We raised our fists and repeated the slogan.

"Down with Old Bitch Mu Ying," a middle-aged man cried out with both hands in the air. He was an active revolutionary in our commune. Again we shouted, in louder voices.

The nearsighted man went on, "First, Mu Ying must confess her crime. We must see her attitude toward her own crime. Then we'll make the punishment fit both her crime and her attitude. All right, folks?"

"Right," some voices replied from the crowd.

"Mu Ying," he turned to the criminal, "you must confess everything. It's up to you now."

She was forced to stand on a bench. Staying below the steps, we had to raise our heads to see her face.

The questioning began. "Why do you seduce men and paralyze their revolutionary will with your bourgeois poison?" the tall leader asked in a solemn voice.

"I've never invited any man to my home, have I?" she said rather calmly. Her husband was standing at the front of the crowd, listening to her without showing any emotion, as though having lost his mind.

"Then why did they go to your house and not to others' houses?"

"They wanted to sleep with me," she replied.

"Shameless!" Several women hissed in the crowd.

"A true whore!"

"Scratch her!"

"Rip apart her filthy mouth!"

"Sisters," she spoke aloud. "All right, it was wrong to sleep with them. But you all know what it feels like when you want a man, don't you? Don't you once in a while have that feeling in your bones?" Contemptuously, she looked at the few withered middle-aged women standing in the front row, then closed her eyes. "Oh, you want that real man to have you in his arms and let him touch every part of your body. For that man alone you want to blossom into a woman, a real woman—"

"Take this, you Fox Spirit!" A stout young fellow struck her on the side with a fist like a sledgehammer. The heavy blow silenced her at once. She held her sides with both hands, gasping for breath.

"You're wrong, Mu Ying," Bare Hips's mother spoke from the front of the crowd, her forefinger pointing upward at Mu. "You have your own man, who doesn't lack an arm or a leg. It's wrong to have others' men and more wrong to pocket their money."

"I have my own man?" Mu glanced at her husband and smirked. She straightened up and said, "My man is nothing. He is no good, I mean in bed. He always comes before I feel anything."

All the adults burst out laughing. "What's that? What's so funny?" Big Shrimp asked Bare Hips.

"You didn't get it?" Bare Hips said impatiently. "You don't know anything about what happens between a man and a woman. It means that whenever she doesn't want him to come close to her he comes. Bad timing."

"It doesn't sound like that," I said.

Before we could argue, a large bottle of ink smashed on Mu's head and knocked her off the bench. Prone on the cement terrace, she broke into swearing and blubbering. "Oh, damn your ancestors! Whoever hit me will be childless!" Her left hand was rubbing her head. "Oh Lord of Heaven, they treat their grandma like this!"

"Serves you right!"

"A cheap weasel."

"Even a knife on her throat can't stop her."

"A pig is born to eat slop!"

When they put her back up on the bench, she became another person—her shoulders covered with black stains, and a red line trickling down her left temple. The scorching sun was blazing down on her as though all the black parts on her body were about to burn up. Still moaning, she turned her eyes to the spot where her husband had been standing a few minutes before. But he was no longer there.

"Down with Old Whore!" a farmer shouted in the crowd. We all followed him in one voice. She began trembling slightly.

The tall leader said to us, "In order to get rid of her counterrevolutionary airs, first, we're going to cut her hair." With a wave of his hand, he summoned the Red Guards behind him. Four men moved forward and held her down. The square-faced woman raised a large pair of scissors and thrust them into the mass of the dark hair.

"Don't, don't, please. Help, help! I'll do whatever you want me to—"

65   "Cut!" someone yelled.

"Shave her head bald!"

The woman Red Guard applied the scissors skillfully. After four or five strokes, Mu's head looked like the tail of a molting hen. She started blubbering again, her nose running and her teeth chattering.

A breeze came and swept away the fluffy curls from the terrace and scattered them on the sandy ground. It was so hot that some people took out fans, waving them continuously. The crowd stank of sweat.

Wooooo, wooooo, woo, woo. That was the train coming from Sand County at 3:30. It was a freight train, whose young drivers would toot the steam horn whenever they saw a young woman in a field beneath the track.

70   The questioning continued. "How many men have you slept with these years?" the nearsighted man asked.

"Three."

"She's lying," a woman in the crowd cried out.

"I told the truth, sister." She wiped off the tears from her cheeks with the back of her hand.

"Who are they?" the young man asked again. "Tell us more about them."

75   "An officer from the Little Dragon Mountain, and—"

"How many times did he come to your house?"

"I can't remember. Probably twenty."

"What's his name?"

"I don't know. He told me he was a big officer."

80   "Did you take money from him?"

"Yes."

"How much for each time?"

"Twenty *yuan*."

"How much altogether?"

85   "Probably five hundred."

"Comrades and Revolutionary Masses," the young man turned to us, "how shall we handle this parasite that sucked blood out of a revolutionary officer?"

"Quarter her with four horses!" an old woman yelled.

"Burn her on Heaven Lamp!"

"Poop on her face!" a small fat girl shouted, her hand raised like a tiny pistol with the thumb cocked up and the forefinger aimed at Mu. Some grown-ups snickered.

Then a pair of old cloth-shoes, a symbol for a promiscuous woman, were passed to the front. The slim young woman took the shoes and tied them together with the laces. She climbed on a table and was about to hang the shoes around Mu's neck. Mu elbowed the woman aside and knocked the shoes to the ground. The stout young fellow picked up the shoes, and jumped twice to slap her on the cheeks with the soles. "You're so stubborn. Do you want to change yourself or not?" he asked.

"Yes, I do," she replied meekly and dared not stir a bit. Meanwhile the shoes were being hung around her neck.

"Now she looks like a real whore," a woman commented.

"Sing us a tune, Sis," a farmer demanded.

"Comrades," the man in glasses resumed, "let us continue the denunciation." He turned to Mu and asked, "Who are the other men?"

"A farmer from Apple Village."

"How many times with him?"

"Once."

"Liar!"

"She's lying!"

"Give her one on the mouth!"

The young man raised his hands to calm the crowd down and questioned her again, "How much did you take from him?"

"Eighty *yuan*."

"One night?"

"Yes."

"Tell us more about it. How can you make us believe you?"

"That old fellow came to town to sell piglets. He sold a whole litter for eighty, and I got the money."

"Why did you charge him more than the officer?"

"No, I didn't. He did it four times in one night."

Some people were smiling and whispering to each other. A woman said that old man must have been a widower or never married.

"What's his name?" the young man went on.

"No idea."

"Was he rich or poor?"

"Poor."

"Comrades," the young man addressed us, "here we have a poor peasant who worked with his sow for a whole year and got only a litter of piglets. That money is the salt and oil money for his family, but this snake swallowed the money with one gulp. What shall we do with her?"

"Kill her!"

"Break her skull!"

"Beat the piss out of her!"

A few farmers began to move forward to the steps, waving their fists or rubbing their hands.

"Hold," a woman Red Guard with a huge Chairman Mao badge on her chest spoke in a commanding voice. "The Great Leader has instructed us: 'For our struggle we need words but not force.' Comrades, we can easily wipe her out with words. Force doesn't solve ideological problems." What she said restrained those enraged farmers, who remained in the crowd.

120   *Wooo, woo, wooo, wooooooooooo,* an engine screamed in the south. It was strange, because the drivers of the four o'clock train were a bunch of old men who seldom blew the horn.

"Who is the third man?" the nearsighted man continued to question Mu.

"A Red Guard."

The crowd broke into laughter. Some women asked the Red Guards to give her another bottle of ink. "Mu Ying, you're responsible for your own words," the young man said in a serious voice.

"I told you the truth."

125   "What's his name?"

"I don't know. He led the propaganda team that passed here last month."

"How many times did you sleep with him?"

"Once."

"How much did you make out of him?"

130   "None. That stingy dog wouldn't pay a cent. He said he was the worker who should be paid."

"So you were outsmarted by him?"

Some men in the crowd guffawed. Mu wiped her nose with her thumb, and at once she wore a thick mustache. "I taught him a lesson, though," she said.

"How?"

"I tweaked his ears, gave him a bleeding nose, and kicked him out. I told him never come back."

135   People began talking to each other. Some said that she was a strong woman who knew what was hers. Some said the Red Guard was no good; if you got something you had to pay for it. A few women declared that the rascal deserved such a treatment.

"Dear Revolutionary Masses," the tall leader started to speak. "We all have heard the crime Mu Ying committed. She lured one of our officers and one of our poor peasants into the evil water, and she beat a Red Guard black and blue. Shall we let her go home without punishment or shall we teach her an unforgettable lesson so that she won't do it again?"

"Teach her a lesson!" some voices cried out in unison.

"Then we're going to parade her through the streets."

Two Red Guards pulled Mu off the bench, and another picked up the tall hat. "Brothers and sisters," she begged, "please let me off just for once. Don't, don't! I promise I'll correct my fault. I'll be a new person. Help! Oh, help!"

140   It was no use resisting; within seconds the huge hat was firmly planted on

her head. They also hung a big placard between the cloth-shoes lying against her chest. The words on the placard read:

I am a Broken Shoe
My Crime Deserves Death

They put a gong in her hands and ordered her to strike it when she announced the words written on the inner side of the gong.

My pals and I followed the crowd, feeling rather tired. Boys from East Street were wilder; they threw stones at Mu's back. One stone struck the back of her head and blood dropped on her neck. But they were stopped immediately by the Red Guards, because a stone missed Mu and hit a man on the shoulder. Old people, who couldn't follow us, were standing on chairs and windowsills with pipes and towels in their hands. We were going to parade her through every street. It would take several hours to finish the whole thing, as the procession would stop for a short while at every street corner.

Bong, Mu struck the gong and declared, "I am an evil monster."

"Louder!"

Dong, bong—"I have stolen men. I stink for a thousand years." 145

When we were coming out of the marketplace, Cross Eyes emerged from a narrow lane. He grasped my wrist and Bare Hips's arm and said, "Someone is dead at the train station. Come, let's go there and have a look." The word "dead" at once roused us. We, half a dozen boys, set out running to the train station.

The dead man was Meng Su. A crowd had gathered at the railroad a hundred meters east of the station house. A few men were examining the rail that was stained with blood and studded with bits of flesh. One man paced along the darker part of the rail and announced that the train had dragged Meng at least twenty meters.

Beneath the track, Meng's headless body lay in a ditch. One of his feet was missing, and the whitish shinbone stuck out several inches long. There were so many openings on his body that he looked like a large piece of fresh meat on the counter in the butcher's. Beyond him, ten paces away, a big straw hat remained on the ground. We were told that his head was under the hat.

Bare Hips and I went down the slope to have a glimpse at the head. Other boys dared not take a peep. We two looked at each other, asking with our eyes who should raise the straw hat. I held out my wooden scimitar and lifted the rim of the hat a little with the sword. A swarm of bluebottles charged out, droning like provoked wasps. We bent over to peek at the head. Two long teeth pierced through the upper lip. An eyeball was missing. The gray hair was no longer perceivable, as it was covered with mud and dirt. The open mouth filled with purplish mucus. A tiny lizard skipped, sliding away into the grass.

"Oh!" Bare Hips began vomiting. Sorghum gruel mixed with bits of string 150 beans splashed on a yellowish boulder. "Leave it alone, White Cat."

We lingered at the station, listening to different versions of the accident. Some people said that Meng had gotten drunk and dropped asleep on the track. Some said he hadn't slept at all but laughed hysterically walking in the middle of the track toward the coming train. Some said he had not drunk a drop, as he had spoken with tears in his eyes to a few persons he had run into on his way to the station. In any case, he was dead, torn to pieces.

That evening when I was coming home, I heard Mu Ying groaning in the smoky twilight. "Take me home. Oh, help me. Who can help me? Where are you? Why don't you come and carry me home?"

She was lying at the bus stop, alone.

1993

∨ ∨ ∨

WRITING
ABOUT
FICTION

INTRODUCTION

Writing about literature ought to be easier than writing about any-thing else. When you write about painting, for example, you have to translate shapes and colors and textures into words. When you write about music, you have to translate various aspects and combinations of sounds into words. When you write about that complex, mysterious, fleeting thing called "reality" or "life," you have an even more difficult task. Worst of all, perhaps, is trying to put into words all that is going on at any given moment inside your particular and unique self. So you ought to be relieved to know that you are going to write about literature—that is, use words to write about words.

But writing about fiction will not be easy if you haven't learned to *read* fic-tion, for in order to write about anything you have to know that something rather well. Helping you to learn to read fiction is what the earlier chapters of this book is about; this chapter is about the writing. (But, as you will see, you cannot fully separate the writing from the reading.)

Another thing keeps writing about fiction from being easy: writing itself is not easy. Writing well requires a variety of language skills—a good working vocabulary, for example—and a sense of how to order your ideas, of how to link one idea or statement to another, of what to put in and what to leave out. Worse, writing is not a finite or definite skill or art; you never really "know how to write," you just learn how to write a little better about a little more. These very words you are reading have been written and revised several times, even though your editor has had a good many years of practice.

REPRESENTING THE LITERARY TEXT

Copying

I f writing about literature is using words about words, what words should you use? Since most writers work very hard to get each word exactly right and in exactly the right order, there are no better words to use in discussing what the literature is about than those of the literary work itself. Faced with writing about a story, then, you could just write the story over again, word for word:

> Once upon a time there was a Siamese cat who pretended to be a lion and spoke inappropriate Zebraic. . .

and so on until the end. **Copying** texts was useful in medieval monasteries, but in our electronic age, with printing, word processors, and Fax machines available to us, it would not seem to be very useful. Besides, if you try to copy a text, you will probably find that spelling or punctuation errors, reversed word order, and missing or added or just different words seem mysteriously to appear. Still, it's a good exercise for teaching yourself accuracy and attention to detail, and you will probably discover things about the text you are copying that you would be unlikely to notice otherwise. Early in a fiction course, particularly, copying can be a useful step in learning how to read and write about fiction; later, being able to copy a passage accurately will help when you want to quote a passage to illustrate or prove a point you are making. But copying is not, in itself, writing *about* fiction.

Reading aloud, a variation of copying, may be a more original and interpretive exercise than copying itself, since by tone, emphasis, and pace you are clarifying the text or indicating the way you understand the text. But it, too, is not *writing* about fiction, and you will not long be satisfied with merely repeating someone else's words. You will have perceptions, responses, and ideas that you will want to express for yourself about what you are reading. And having something to say and wanting to say or write it is the first and most significant step in learning to write about fiction.

Paraphrase

If you look away from the text for a while and then write the same material but in your own words, you are writing a **paraphrase.**

For example, let's try to paraphrase the first sentence of Jane Austen's *Pride and Prejudice:* "It is a truth universally acknowledged that a single man in possession of a good fortune, must be in want of a wife." We can start by making "It is a truth" a little less formal: *It's true that,* perhaps. Now "universally acknowledged": *everybody acknowledges,* or, a little more loosely, *everybody agrees.* Now we may choose to drop the whole first clause and begin, *Everybody agrees that* "a single man"—*a bachelor*—"in possession of a good fortune"—*rich*—"must be in want of a wife"—*wants a wife.* Or is it *needs a wife?* Okay, *Everybody agrees that a rich bachelor needs* (or *wants*) *a wife.* You can see that the process of paraphrase is something like that of translation. We are translating Austen's nineteenth-century formal English prose into twentieth-century informal American prose.

But what good is that? First of all, it enables us to test whether we really understand what we are reading. Second, certain elements of the text become clearer: we may see now that Austen's sentence is meant to be ironic or humorous, and we now understand the two possible meanings of "in want of." Third, we can check our paraphrase with those of others, our classmates' versions, for example, to compare our understanding of the passage with theirs. Finally, we have learned how dependent literature is upon words. A paraphrase, no matter how precise, can render only an approximate equivalent of the meaning of a text—how *good* Austen's sentence is, how *flat* our paraphrase.

Paraphrasing, like copying, is not in itself an entirely satisfactory way of writing about fiction, but, like copying, it can be a useful tool when you write about fiction in other ways. In trying to explain or clarify a literary text for someone, to illustrate a point you are making about that text, or to remind your readers of or to acquaint them with a text or passage, you will at times want to paraphrase. Unlike an exact copy, a paraphrase, being in your own words, adds something of yours to the text or passage—your emphasis, your perspective, your understanding.

Summary

Paraphrase follows faithfully the outlines of the text. But if you stand back far enough from the text so as not to see its specific words or smaller details and put down briefly in your own words what you believe the work is about, you will have a **summary**. How briefly? Well, you could summarize the story of *Hamlet* in a single sentence: "A young man, seeking to avenge the murder of his father by his uncle, kills his uncle, but he himself and others die in the process." Has *too* much been left out? What do you feel it essential to add? Let's try again: "In Denmark, many centuries ago, a young prince avenged the murder of his father, the king, by his uncle, who had usurped the throne, but the prince himself was killed as were others, and a well-led foreign army had no trouble successfully invading the decayed and troubled state." A classmate may have written this summary: "From the ghost of his murdered father a young prince learns that his uncle, who has married the prince's mother, much to the young man's shame and disgust, is the father's murderer, and he plots revenge, feigning madness, acting erratically—even to insulting the woman he loves— and, though gaining his revenge, causes the suicide of his beloved and the deaths of others and, finally, of himself."

The last two, though accurate enough, sound like two different plays, don't they? To summarize means to select and emphasize and so to interpret: that is, not to replicate the text in miniature, as a reduced photograph might replicate the original, but while reducing it to change the angle of vision and even the filter, to represent the essentials as the reader or summarizer sees them. When you write a summary you should try to be as objective as possible; nevertheless, your summary will reflect not only the literary text but also your own understanding and attitudes. There's nothing wrong with your fingerprints or "mindprints" appearing on the summary, so long as you recognize that in summarizing you are doing more than copying, paraphrasing, or merely reflecting the literary text. You might learn something about both literature and yourself by comparing your summaries of, say, three or four short stories with summaries of the same works by several of your classmates. As you read their summaries, try to understand how each viewed the text differently from you. You might then write a composite summary that would include all that any one reader felt important. You might try the same exercise again on different texts. Has the practice made you more careful? More inclusive? Is there a greater degree of uniformity or inclusiveness in your summaries?

A good summary can be a form of literary criticism. Though you will seldom be called upon merely to summarize a work, a good deal of writing about fiction requires that at some point or other you do summarize—a whole work, a particular incident or aspect, chapter, or scene. But beware: a mere summary, no matter how accurate, will seldom fulfill an assignment for a critical essay.

REPLYING TO THE TEXT

Imitation and Parody

While paraphrase is something like translation—a faithful following of the original text but in different words—and summary is the faithful, but inevitably interpretive, reduction of the text, there is another kind of writing about fiction that faithfully follows the manner or matter or both of a literary text, but that does so for different ends. It's called **imitation.**

For many generations, students were taught to write by "writing from models"—imitating good writing. Many serious works are, in one way or another, imitations: *The Aeneid*, for example, may be said to be an imitation of *The Odyssey*, and, in a very different way, so might James Joyce's *Ulysses*. You too may be able to learn a good deal about writing—and reading—by trying your hand at an imitation.

To write an imitation, first analyze the original—that is, break it down into its characteristics or qualities—and decide just what you want to preserve in your version. Sometimes you can poke fun at a work by imitating it but at the same time exaggerating its style or prominent characteristics, or placing it in an inappropriate context; that kind of imitation, a kind that is still popular, is called a **parody.** The list of qualities and the model might be much the same for a serious imitation and for a parody, only in a parody you can exaggerate a little—or a lot. To parody the style of Henry James, around the time of "The Real Thing," you could imitate or, if possible, exaggerate his long, halting, rather roundabout and somewhat obscure sentences, full of phrases interrupting other phrases or clauses, of understatement, reticence, and indirection. You might also parody this subtle, probing style and its air of questioning and mystery by applying it to a ludicrously trivial, unsuitable subject. In Max Beerbohm's "The Mote in the Middle Distance" two Jamesian children awaken on Christmas morning and are tempted to look in their Christmas stocking; Beerbohm begins:

> It was with the sense of a, for him, very memorable something that he peered now into the immediate future, and tried, not without compunction, to take that period

up where he had, prospectively left it. But just where the deuce *had* he left it? The consciousness of dubiety was, for our friend, not, this morning, quite yet clean-cut enough to outline the figures on what she had called his "horizion," between which and himself the twilight was indeed of a quality somewhat intimidating.

You will have noticed that in order to write a good imitation or parody you must read and reread the original very carefully, examine it, and identify just those elements and qualities that make it a unique and recognizable text. Since you admire works you wish to imitate, such close study should be a pleasure. You may or may not greatly admire a work you wish to parody, but parody itself is fun to do and fun to read. In either case, you are having fun while gaining a deeper, more intimate knowledge of the nature and details of a work of literature. Moreover, such close attention to how a professional piece of writing is put together and how its parts function together along with your effort to reproduce the effects in your own imitation or parody are sure to help you understand the process of writing and so help you improve your own ability to write about literature knowledgeably.

Re-creation and Reply

Sometimes a story will seem so partial, biased, or unrealistic that it will stimulate a response. Such a response may involve a shift in perspective: it may tell the same story as the original but from a different angle, not only giving a different view of the same events and people but also adding details that the original focus ignored or could not perceive. In *Jane Eyre*, for example, Bertha Mason Rochester is the hero's bestial, mad wife, whom he has locked away upstairs and whose existence, when it comes to light, prevents for a time our heroine, our Jane, from marrying her heart's desire; Bertha is, in effect, the villainess. In *Wide Sargasso Sea*, Jean Rhys not only gives Bertha's side of Charlotte Brontë's story but tells us more details about Bertha's earlier life: poor Bertha was more sinned against than sinning, it turns out.

We may respond to a work whose view seems partial or distorted by shifting the perspective in time as well as in space. Are Francis Weed's marital and other problems solved by his recognition, at the end of "The Country Husband," that life in the suburbs can be, in its own way, as adventurous as more romantic kinds of existence? What will happen to him next spring? On his fortieth birthday? As he lies dying?

You may have noticed that while retorts can often be witty, they are also serious. Usually they say not merely, "That's not how the story went," but "That's not what life is really like." Try to read literature initially with the aim of understanding it and taking it at its highest value (rather than reducing it and quibbling). Try to "hear" what it is saying; avoid imposing your own notions of reality prematurely upon a work. Open your mind to learning from the work and let it broaden your views. Finally, read it critically as well, asking, "Is this the way things *really* are?" or, more generously, "If I were standing over there, where the story (author, character) is, would things really look that way?"

Perhaps the most familiar kind of literary re-creation or reply is the **adaptation,** especially that of fiction into film. (Among the stories in this anthology that have been made into feature-length films are "The Most Dangerous Game," "An Occurrence at Owl Creek Bridge," "The Lady with the Dog," "Blow-Up" and "The Rocking-Horse Winner.") In adaptation, the rather contradictory demands of faithfulness to the original and appropriateness to the new medium can teach us a great deal about both the content and the medium of the original. It is unlikely you will have the opportunity in this course to make a film based on a story but you can still try your hand at adapting a work or piece of a work to a new medium. You might want to turn "The Cask of Amontillado" into verse (probably as a dramatic monologue) or write a one-act play called "Young Goodman Brown." It is quite likely that you will learn not only about the nature of the original work but also something of the nature of the medium in which you are trying to work.

EXPLAINING THE TEXT

Description

To give an account of the form of a work or passage rather than merely a brief version of its content or plot you may wish to write a **description.** Summaries tend to concentrate on subject and plot, whereas descriptions may concentrate on the narrative structure, point of view, or imagery, though descriptions of stories almost inevitably involve content.

In addition to describing the narrative structure or focus and voice of a short story, you might also describe the diction (word choice), the sentence structure, the amount of description of the characters or landscape, and so on.

Analysis

Like copying, paraphrase, and summary, a description of a work or passage rarely stands alone as a piece of writing about fiction. It is, instead, a tool, a means of supporting a point or opinion. Even the description we have given above borders on **analysis.** To analyze is to break something down into its parts to discover what they are, and, usually, how they function in and relate to the whole. Even a lengthy description of each of the scenes in "The Country Husband" would not in itself constitute an analysis, for you would also have to indicate how each contributes to our understanding of the story as a whole. You might ask yourself what the connection might be between the airplane incident and Francis's crush on Anne Murchison, and from that question you might go on to ask how all the other scenes relate to each other. Perhaps the last sentence of your description—about Francis's state of mind—might be a clue. But, back to the airplane incident. How about a paper called:

To Begin at the Beginning . . ."

In John Cheever's story "The Country Husband,"
Francis Weed, a married man with three children,

744

falls in love with the young girl who baby-sits his children. His marriage almost breaks up, he goes to a psychiatrist, takes up woodworking, and, at the end, is happy in his conventional, suburban life.

This sort of story, that of a middle-aged married man becoming infatuated with a young girl, is not unusual. What is unusual here is the embedding of this story amid other scenes and details that seem to have no obvious connection with the "love affair." For example, the story begins not with man-meets-girl but with the protagonist's being on a plane that nearly crashes. That incident is introduced with the words, "To begin at the beginning, the airplane from Minneapolis . . ." Why is this the beginning?

If a beginning is something that generates the events that follow, this does not seem the true beginning, for it does not seem to cause what follows. Indeed, what follows is that no one wants to listen when Francis tries to tell them about his "brush with death." His friend and fellow-commuter Trace Bearden does not respond and just picks up his newspaper as usual. When Francis gets home his first sentence about the flight is interrupted by a fight among the kids, and the squabble continues all through dinner.

That's the last we hear of the airplane incident, which is supposed to be the beginning of this whole story. The next night Francis and his wife go out to dinner and he recognizes the new French maid as a woman he saw being punished in Normandy just after the war—she had collaborated with the Nazis. This not only has nothing much to do with the plane incident, it does not seem to have much to do with what follows: he takes the young baby sitter home. She cries on his shoulder, he comforts her, and then, "At the steps, she freed her hand and then turned and kissed him swiftly (par. 29)." Shouldn't the story begin where it really begins, when he comes home, "Expecting to see Mrs. Heninlein, the old lady who usually stayed with the children . . . [and] was surprised when a young [beautiful] girl opened the door . . ." (par. 15)?

Why not omit the first two episodes? Let us look at what they have in common, and then see if we can connect them to the central episodes of the story.

The first is a brush with death—not something that happens every day to someone living in the American suburbs. The second seems to have a little to do with death, since it is about World War II and its consequences, but it is not exactly death that connects the two. What is it? The extraordinary, the significant, the newsworthy, the unusual, perhaps even the adventurous. These events clash with the routine, the dullness of Francis's everyday life.

> Between the first two episodes he goes into
> the garden, where all the usual things were going
> on in the neighborhood, but Francis's (and thus
> the reader's) attention is focused on the
> neighbor's dog Jupiter who "was an anomaly . . .
> his high spirits were out of place in Shady Hill
> (par. 10)." High spirits, adventure, even
> mischief, the break with routine and orderliness.
> Francis is prepared for his adventure, his
> mischief.
>
> The story centers on the conflict between the
> domestic and orderly—and dull—and the
> adventurous, romantic—and foolish. The beginning
> is the first event that shakes Francis out of
> his routine . . .

And the paper could go on, connecting the scenes, especially those not directly related to the "romance," bringing in the setting (to enhance the other side of the coin, the suburban routine), and even the focus, balancing analytical statements with textual evidence and evidence with generalizing, analytical statements.

Interpretation

Principles and Procedures

If you have been reading carefully, you may have noticed what looks like a catch: to turn description into analysis, you must relate what you are describing to the theme, the overall effect, and meaning of the work of fiction. But how do you know what the theme is? If analysis relates the part to the whole, how can you know the "whole" before you have analyzed each part? But then, how can you analyze each part—relating it to the whole—if you don't know what that whole is?

Interpretation, or the expression of your understanding of a literary work and its meaning, involves an initial general impression that is then supported and, often, modified by analysis of the particulars. It involves looking at the whole, the part, the whole, the part, the whole, the part, in a series of approximations and adjustments. (Note, in particular, the need to keep your mind open for modifications or changes rather than forcing your analysis to confirm your first impressions.)

This procedure should in turn suggest something of the nature and even the form of the critical essay, or essay of interpretation. The essay should present the overall theme and support that generalization with close analyses of the major elements of the text (or, in some essays, an analysis of one significant element)—showing how one or more of such elements as rhyme or speaker, plot or setting reinforce, define, or modify the theme of the story. Often the conclusion of such an essay will be a fuller, more refined statement of the theme.

Both the definition of and the procedures for interpreting a work suggest that a literary text is unified, probably around a theme, a meaning, and an effect. In interpreting, you therefore keep asking of each element or detail, "How does it fit? How does it contribute to *the* theme or whole?" In most instances, especially when you are writing on shorter works, if you dig hard and deep enough, you will find a satisfactory interpretation or central theme. Even after you have done your best, however, you must hold your "reading" or interpretation as a hypothesis rather than a final truth. Your experience of reading criticism has probably already shown you that more than one reading of a literary work is possible and that no reading exhausts the meaning and totality of a work. Nonetheless, you will want to begin reading a literary text as if it were going to make a central statement and create a single effect, no matter how complex. Try as conscientiously as you can to make sense of the work, to analyze it, show how its elements work together. In analyzing elements, you kept your initial sense of the whole as hypothesis and did not try to force evidence to fit your first impression. Here, too, you will want to hold your interpretation as a hypothesis even in its final stages, even at the end. It is, you must be sure, the fullest and best "reading" of the text you are capable of at this time, with the evidence and knowledge you have at this moment; but only that. In other words, an interpretation is "only an opinion." But just as your political and other opinions are not lightly held but are what you really feel and believe based on all you know and have experienced and all you have thought and felt, so your opinion or interpretation of a literary work should be as responsible as you can make it. Your opinions are a measure of your knowledge, intelligence, and sensibility. They should not be lightly changed but neither should they be obstinately and inflexibly held.

Reading and Theme Making

Because you need a sense of the whole text before you can analyze it, analysis and interpretation would seem to be possible only after repeated readings. Though obvious, logical, and partially true, this may not be *entirely* true. In reading, we actually anticipate theme or meaning much as we anticipate what will happen next. Often this anticipation or expectation of theme or effect begins with reading the first words of a story—or even before, in reading the title.

Such anticipation of theme and effect, projecting and modifying understanding and response, continues as you read. When you read the first four words of "The Zebra Storyteller"—"Once upon a time . . ."—the strange title is to some extent explained and the kind of story you are about to read and its relation to everyday reality have been established. The title and the first short section of "The Most Dangerous Game" arouse expectations of the supernatural, the frightening, the adventurous, creating suspense: "What will happen next?" we ask as we read the first few paragraphs. The brief conversation about hunting, toward the end of that section, not only educates our expectations but also generates a moral and thematic question: "Are there really two animal classes—the hunters and the hunted—and does being lucky enough to be among the hunters justify insensitivity toward the feelings of the hunted?" While the question may recede from the foreground of our attention for a while, it has nonetheless been raised. It is, in addition, reinforced by the break on the page, which forces us to pause and, even if but momentarily, reflect. It comes forward again when General Zaroff introduces the subject of hunting. At these two points, at least, a thematic hypothesis based on hunters and hunted begins forming, however faintly, in our minds. That is enough to give us grounds—even as we read the story for the first time—for an analysis of elements and their relationship to our very tentatively formulated theme, and perhaps for beginning to modify or modulate our articulation of that theme. Many details in the story indicate that there is a political coloring to the theme: Zaroff is a Cossack—a people noted for fierceness—and is, or was, a Czarist general; he keeps a giant Cossack servant who was an official flogger under the Czar; he refers to the Revolution of 1917 in Russia as a "debacle"; he is clearly a racist. We may want to alter "hunter" and "hunted" in our first version of the anticipated theme to something broader—"strong" and "weak," perhaps, or "privileged" and "underprivileged," or we may need fuller definitions of the implications of the terms "hunter" and "hunted."

Just as we have more than one expectation of what may happen next as we read a story, so we may have more than one expectation of what it is going to be "about" in the more general sense: as we read along we have expectations or hypotheses of meaning, and so we consciously or unconsciously try to fit together the pieces of elements of what we are reading into a pattern of significance. By the end of our first reading we should have a fairly well-defined sense of what the story is "about," what it means, even how some of the elements have worked together to produce that meaning and effect. Indeed, isn't this the way we read when we are not reading for a class or performance? Don't most people read most stories only once? And don't we usually think we have understood what we have read? Shouldn't we be able to read a very short story in class just once and immediately write an interpretive paper based on that first reading?

This is not to say that we cannot understand more about a work by repeated readings, or that there is some virtue or purity of response in the naive first reading that is lost in closer study. Our first "reading"—"reading" in the sense of both "casting our eye over" and "interpretation"—is almost certain to be modified or refined by rereading: if nothing else, we know from the beginning what will happen next—what the most dangerous game is, and that the blow-up refers to a photograph. The theme or meaning is likely to be modulated by later readings, the way the elements function in defining or embodying meaning is likely to be clearer; the effect of the second reading is certain to be different from that of the first. It may be instructive to reread several times the short work we interpreted in class after a single reading, write a new interpretive essay, and see how our understanding has been changed and enriched by subsequent readings.

Opinions, Right and Wrong

Just as each of our separate readings is different, so naturally one reader's fullest and "final" reading, interpretation, or opinion will differ somewhat from another's. Seldom will readers agree entirely with any full statement of the theme of a literary text. Nor is one of these interpretations entirely "right" and all the others necessarily "wrong." For no thematic summary, no analysis or interpretation, no matter how full, can exhaust the affective or intellectual significance of a major literary text. There are various approximate readings of varying degrees of acceptability, various competent or "good" readings, not just one single "right" reading.

Anyone who has heard two accomplished musicians faithfully perform the same work, playing all the "same" notes; or anyone who has seen two performances of *Hamlet*, will recognize how "interpretations" can be both correct and different. You might try to get hold of several recordings of one or more of Hamlet's soliloquies—by John Barrymore, Sir John Gielgud, Richard Burton, Sir Laurence Olivier, or Mel Gibson, for example—and notice how each of these actors lends to identical passages his own emphasis, pacing, tone, color, his own effect, and so, ultimately, his own meaning. These actors reading the identical words are, in effect, "copying." They are not paraphrasing or putting Shakespeare's Elizabethan poetry into modern American prose, not "interpreting" as we have defined it, or putting his play into their own words. If merely performing or reading the words aloud generates significant differences in interpretation, it is no wonder that when you write an interpretive essay about literature, when you give your conception of the meaning and effect of the literary text in your own words, your interpretation will differ from other interpretations, even when each of the different interpretations is competent and "correct."

Any communication, even a work of literature, is refracted—that is, interpreted and modified—by the recipient. In one sense, it is not complete until it is received, just as, in a sense, a musical score is not "music" until it is played. Philip Roth reported, not too long ago, how perturbed he was by what the critics and other readers said of his first novel—that was not at all what he intended, what the novel really was, he thought at first. But then he realized that once he had had his say in the novel, it was "out there," and each reader had to understand it within the limits and range of his or her own perspectives and literary and life experiences. His novel, once in print, was no longer merely "his," and rightly so.

That quite different interpretations may be "correct" is not to say, with Alice's Humpty-Dumpty, that a word or a work "means just what I choose it to mean." Though there may not be one "right" reading, some readings are more appropriate and convincing than others and some readings are demonstrably wrong.

What would you say about this reading of *Hamlet*?

> The play is about the hero's sexual love for his mother. He sees his father's "ghost" because he feels guilty, somehow responsible for his father's death, more than likely

because he had often wished his father dead. To free himself from this feeling of guilt, he imagines that he sees his father's ghost and that the ghost tells him that his uncle murdered his father. He focuses upon his uncle because he is fiercely jealous that it is his uncle, not himself, who has replaced his father in his mother's bed. He so resents his mother's choice of so unworthy a mate, he attributes it not to love but to mere lust, clearly a projection of his own lust for his mother, which he calls love. His mother's lust so disgusts him that he hates all women now, even Ophelia. When his father was alive he could be fond of Ophelia, for his sexual feeling for his mother was deflected by his father-the-king's powerful presence. Now, however, he must alienate Ophelia not only because of his new hatred of women but because he has a chance of winning his mother, especially if he can get rid of Claudius, his uncle.

Such a reading explains more or less convincingly certain details in the play, but it wrenches some out of context and it leaves a good deal out and a good deal unexplained: why, for example, do others see the ghost of Hamlet's father if it is just a figment of his imagination? What are Horatio and Fortinbras and the political elements doing in the play? *If* you accept certain Freudian premises about human psychology and see life in Freudian terms; *if* you see literary texts as the *author's* psychic fantasy stimulating your own psychic fantasies and believe that interpretation of *Hamlet* is not merely a reading of the play itself but an analysis of Shakespeare's psyche, you may find this reading somewhat convincing. You will perhaps explain away some of the details of the play that do not seem to fit your Freudian reading as a cover-up, an attempt by Shakespeare to disguise the true but hidden meaning of his dramatic fantasy from others—and from himself. Such a reading is probably neither right nor wrong but only a way of interpreting *Hamlet* based on certain assumptions about psychology and about the way literature *means* and so it could seem "right" or acceptable to those who share those assumptions.

Suppose one of your ingenious classmates were to argue that the real subject of *Hamlet* is that the hero has tuberculosis. This would explain, your classmate would say, the hero's moodiness, his pretended madness that sometimes seems real, his rejection of Ophelia (he wouldn't want their children to suffer from the disease), his father's ghost (he, too, died of consumption), his anger at his uncle (who carries the disease, of course) for marrying Hamlet's mother, and so on. Your classmate might even argue that the text of the play is flawed, that it was just copied down during a performance by someone in the audience or was printed from an actor's imperfect copy. Therefore, "O that this too too *solid flesh*" should read "*sullied flesh*," as many scholars have argued (and might not "sullied flesh" suggest tuberculosis?). And, therefore, isn't it quite possible that the most famous soliloquy in the play really began or was meant to begin, "TB or not TB"? "No way!" we'd say. We would be reasonably sure that this is not just "not proved" but just plain *wrong*. It might be interesting and illuminating to rebut that reading in a paper of your own and to notice what kinds of evidence you bring to bear on an interpretive argument.

Reader and Text

If it is difficult to say exactly what a piece of literature *says*, it is usually not because it is vague or meaning*less* but because it is too specific and meaning-*ful* to paraphrase satisfactorily in any language other than its own. Since no two human beings are identical and no two people can inhabit the same space at the same time, no two people can see exactly the same reality from the same angle and vantage point. Most of us get around this awkward truth by saying that we see what we are "supposed" to see, a generalized, common-sense approximation of reality. We are all, in effect, like Polonius in the third act of *Hamlet*, who sees in a cloud, a camel, a weasel, a whale—whatever Hamlet tells him he sees.

Some individuals struggle to see things as fully and clearly as possible from their own unique vantage point and to communicate to others their particu-lar—even peculiar—vision. But here too we are individuated, for though we speak of our "common language," we each speak a unique language, made up of "dialects" that are not only regional and ethnic but also conditioned by our age group, our profession, our education, travel, reading—all our experiences. Yet if we want to express our unique vision to others who have different visions and different "languages," we have to find some medium that is both true to ourselves and understandable to others.

There is for these individuals—these writers of literature—a constant tug-of-war between the uniqueness of their individual visions and the generalizing nature of language. The battle does not always result in sheer loss, however. Often, in the very struggle to get their own perceptions into language, writers sharpen those perceptions or discover what they themselves did not know when they began to write. You have probably made similar discoveries in the process of writing a letter or an assigned paper. But writers also find that what they have written does not perfectly embody what they meant it to, just as you perhaps have found that your finished papers have been not quite so brilliant as your original idea.

"Understanding" is not a passive reception of a text but an active reaching out from our own experiences toward the text. At least at first we need to do so by meeting the author on the ground of a common or general language and set of conventions—things that everybody "knows." The first task of the reader, therefore, is to get not to the author's intention, but to the general statement that the work itself makes—that is, its theme or thesis. After a few readings we can usually make a stab at articulating the theme of a text. What a work says in the way of a general theme, however, is not necessarily its full or ultimate meaning; otherwise we would read theme summaries and not stories. The theme is the meaning accessible to all through close reading of the text and common to all, but a literary text is not all statement. There are often cloudy areas in the text where we cannot be sure what is **implication,** the suggestion of the text, and what is our **inference,** or interpretation, of the text. Why does Doris Lessing's Judith prefer having a tomcat put to death to having him neutered but does not suggest that the female kitten who has been ruined for procreation be put death? Does this suggest that males, including human males, exist only to fertilize eggs, but that females have other functions as well? Or, at least, that this is what Judith believes? Does this give us more insight into Judith's life, her singleness, her refusal to marry the Greek professor, her ultimate flight from Luigi? The story does not *say* this, but many readers will find this inference convincing. If accepted, this changes the meaning of the story to some degree. Still, it need not be accepted; the story does not, will never say. The meaning of the story for the reader who is convinced will differ from the meaning for the reader who is not convinced.

The full meaning of a work for you is not only in its stated theme, one that everyone can agree on, but in the meaning you derive by bringing together that generalized theme, the precise language of the text, and your own response and experiences—including reading experience—and imagination. That "meaning" is not the total meaning of the work, not what the author originally perceived and "meant to say"; it is the vision of the author as embodied in the work *and re-viewed from your own angle of vision.*

Your role in producing a meaning from the text does not free you from paying very close attention to the precise language of the text, the words and their meanings, their order, the syntax of the sentences, and even such mundane details as punctuation. You cannot impose a meaning on the text, no matter how sincerely and intensely you feel it, in defiance of the rules of grammar and the nature of the language.

Still, the reader has to be an artist too, trying to experience the reality of the work as the author experienced reality, and with the same reverence and sense of responsibility for the original. To write about fiction you need to embody your reading experience—or interpretation—of the work in language.

Alas, writing about fiction, using words about words, is not as easy as it sounds at first. But it is more exciting, giving you a chance to see with anoth-er's eyes, to explore another's perceptions or experiences, and to explore and more fully understand your own in the process, thus expanding the horizon of your experience, perception, consciousness.

When some rich works of literature, like *Hamlet*, seem to have more than one meaning or no entirely satisfactory meaning or universally agreed upon sin-gle theme, it is not that they are not saying something, and saying something very specific, but that what they are saying is too specific, and complex, and profound (and true, perhaps) to be generalized or paraphrased in a few dozen words. The literary work is meaning*ful*—that is, full of meaning or meanings; but it is the reader who produces each particular meaning from the work, using the work itself, the language of the community and of the work, and his or her own language, experience, and imagination.

As a reader trying to understand the unique perception and language of the author, you should try to translate the text as best you can into terms you can understand. Do your best to approach the text with an open, receptive mind.

An interpretation, then, is not a clarification of what the writer "was trying to say"; it is a process that itself says, in effect, "The way I am trying to under-stand this story is . . . ."

It might help to keep in mind that a story is somewhat like a musical score and that you, the reader, are the performer. The "notes," the words of the story, are always the same, but no two "performances" are identical: you may choose to "play" faster or slower, emphasize this or that. And in a story there are always the equivalent of "grace notes," what some critics call "gaps," where the reader not only can but must fill in what the story leaves out. Sometimes it is difficult to tell what is *in* the story and what you as a reader add, extract, or interpret. The most obvious example of this is **implication,** something that is suggested, or, to put it more strongly and accurately, something that though it is not said (explicit) must be understood or filled in by the reader. That which is implied, then, is not in the story but must be put in. Surely you have to put the indentation on the second pillow together with the color of the hair in order to understand the final paragraph of "A Rose for Emily":

> Then we noticed that in the second pillow was the indentation of a head. One
> of us lifted something from it, and leaning forward, that faint and invisible dust dry
> and acrid in the nostrils, we saw a long strand of iron-gray hair.

Some would say that implication is just a brief or single instance of interpreta-tion, that there is a single meaning in or implied in a story and that if you put it all together, fill in all the gaps "correctly," the "real" meaning will emerge. Others argue, however, that this assumes that there is a single meaning, that stories are just vehicles to carry that meaning, and that this is to undervalue the richness and complexity of literature and to make rational, paraphrasable statements more important than the literary incarnation of experience and vision.

CRITICAL APPROACHES

The way you read and talk about a literary text depends on your assumptions, usually unconscious or unarticulated, about what a work of literature is, what is it supposed to do, and what makes it good. Literary critics, however, often define their assumptions about literature and the proper way to go about reading it and writing about it. The results are critical theories or critical approaches. Looking at a few of these, you may recognize some of your own assumptions, see new and exciting ways of looking at literature, or, at the very least, become aware of your own critical premises and prejudices.

Objectivism

We might begin by asking just what, quite literally, a work of literature *is*. There are critics who think of it as a fixed and freestanding object made up of words on a page. It is "freestanding" in that it has no connection on the one hand with the author or his or her intention or life, or, on the other hand, with the historical or cultural context of the author or the reader. These we might call **objectivist** critics; they believe that a text is an independent object, free from the subjectivity of author and reader.

Formalism

Among the objectivist critics are the **formalists.** One common formalist conception is that a work is **autotelic,** that is, complete in itself, written for its own sake, and unified by its form—that which makes it a work of art. Content is less important than form. Literature involves a special kind of language that sets it apart from merely utilitarian writing; the formal strategies that organize and animate that language elevate literature and give it a special, almost religious character.

NEW CRITICISM   One group of formalists, the **New Critics,** dominated literary criticism in the middle of the twentieth century, and New Criticism remains an important influence today. Their critical practice is to demonstrate formal unity by showing how every part of a work—every word, every image, every element—contributes to a central unifying theme. Because the details of the work relate to a theme or idea, they are generally treated as *symbolic*, as figurative or allegorical, representations of that central, unifying idea. The kind of unity thus demonstrated, in which every part is related to the whole and the whole is reflected in each part, is called **organic unity.** The New Critics differentiate organic unity from (and much prefer it to) **mechanical unity,** the external, pre-conceived structure or rules that do not arise from the individuality of the work but from the type or genre. New Critical analysis, or **explication of the text,** is especially effective in the critical reading of lyric poetry. It has become so uni-versally accepted as *at least the first step* in the understanding of literature that it is almost everywhere the critical approach taught in introductory literature courses, even in those that do not share its fundamental autotelic assumption. It is, indeed, the basic approach of the "Understanding the Text" sections in *The Norton Introduction to Fiction.*

The New Critics' focus on theme or meaning as well as form signifies that for them literature is **referential:** it points to something outside itself, things in the real, external world or in human experience—a tree, a sound wave, love. The New Critics, in general, do not question the reality of the phenomenal world or the ability of language to represent it.

Structuralism

For many formalists, however, literature is not referential. The words in a story, poem, or play no longer point outward to the things, people, or world they are supposed to denote, as they might do in ordinary, "nonliterary" discourse, but point inward to each other and to the formal system they create. The critic still focuses on interrelatedness but is less concerned with "meaning"; words are treated not as referential symbols but as natural numbers; poetry is likened to mathematics or music.

Structuralism focuses on the text as an independent aesthetic object and also tends to detach literature from history and social and political implica-tions, but (much more than New Criticism) structuralism emphasizes system-atic analysis, aspiring to make literary criticism a branch of scientific inquiry. It sees every literary work as a separate "system" and seeks to discover the princi-ples or general laws that govern the interaction of parts within the system. Structuralism has its roots in modern linguistic theory; it looks especially to the work of Ferdinand de Saussure (1857–1913), who founded structural linguistics early in the twentieth century. Structuralism in criticism did not, however, flourish internationally until the early 1960s, when a combination of space-age preoccupation with science and cold-war fear of implication led to a view of literature as intellectually challenging yet socially and politically noncontroversial.

Although based on linguistic theory, structuralism tries to extend newly discovered principles about language to other aspects of literature. Drawing on the **semiotic** principle that a vast and intricate system of signs enables human beings to communicate through language, structuralism asks readers to consider the way that other kinds of sign systems within a work—structures all—combine to produce meaning. Language and its characteristic habits are important to structuralists, but it is not enough to consider any single part of a work or any single kind of sign—linguistic or otherwise—within it. Structuralism aspires to elucidate the meaning of a work of literature by seeing the way all of its parts work relationally toward some wholeness of structure and meaning. Like formalism, it shows little interest in the creative process as such and has virtually no interest in authors, their intentions, or the circumstances or contexts of creation. It takes texts to represent interactions of words and ideas apart from individual human identities or sociopolitical commitments, and concentrates its analytical attention on what can be said about how different elements or processes in a text operate in relation to one another. Structuralists are less likely than formalists to concentrate their attention on some single all-explaining characteristic of literature (such as Cleanth Brooks's "tension" or William Empson's "ambiguity") and its practitioners are less likely to privilege a particular text for its revelation or authority. Structuralism may be seen as a sort of secular equivalent of formalism; it is less mysterious and authoritarian, and it has both the advantage and disadvantage of seeming to be less arbitrary and more "objectively" reliable. But in some ways it seems to promise too much for method and "objectivity," and by the 1970s its insights into the ways of language were already beginning to be used against it to attack the certitudes it appeared to promise and to emphasize instead the uncertainties and indeterminateness of texts.

Post-Structuralism

Post-Structuralism is the broad term used to designate the several directions of literary criticism that, while depending crucially on the insights of science-based theory, attack the very idea that any kind of certitude can exist about the meaning, understandability, or sharability of texts. Post-structuralists, disturbed at the optimism of positivist philosophy in suggesting that the world is knowable and explainable, ultimately doubt the possibility of certainties of any kind, and they see language as especially elusive and unfaithful. Much of post-structuralism involves undoing; the best-known variety of post-structuralism, **deconstruction,** suggests as much in its very name.

DECONSTRUCTION   Deconstruction takes the observations of structuralism to their logical conclusion, arguing that the elaborate web of semiotic differentiations created by the principle of difference in language means that no text can ultimately have any stable, definite, or discoverable meaning.

For the deconstructionist, language consists just in black marks on a page that repeat or differ from each other and the reader is the only author, one who can find whatever can be found in, or be made to appear in, those detached, isolated marks. The deconstructionist conception of literature is thus very broad—almost any writing will do. While this may seem "subjective," in that the critical reader has great freedom, it is the object—the black marks on the blank page—that is the sole subject/object of intention/attention.

As practiced by its most famous proponent, the French philosopher Jacques Derrida (b. 1930), deconstruction endeavors to trace the way texts challenge or cancel their explicit meanings and wrestle themselves into stasis or neutrality. Many deconstructionists have strong radical political commitments (it is possible to argue that the radical counterculture of the 1960s and especially the political events in Paris of 1968 are the crucial context for understanding the origins of deconstructionism), but the retreat from meaning and denial of clear signification that characterizes deconstruction also has affinities with formalism and structuralism, particularly as deconstruction is practiced by American critics. Rather than emphasizing form over content, however, deconstruction tries to deny the possibility of content and places value instead on verbal play as a characteristic outlet of a fertile, adroit, and supple human mind. Like structuralism, it lives almost completely in a self-referential verbal world rather than a world in which texts represent some larger or other reality, but unlike structuralism it denies that the verbal world adds up to anything coherent, consistent, or meaningful in itself. Deconstruction also influences other varieties of post-structuralism with different kinds of interests in history and ideology. Michel Foucault (1926–1984), Julia Kristeva (b. 1941), and Jacques Lacan (1901–1981), though their disciplinary interests are in social history, feminist philosophy, and psychoanalysis, respectively, all come out of deconstructionist assumptions and carry the indeterminacies of post-structuralism (and of post-modernism more generally) into kinds of literary criticism with interests fundamentally different from those of structuralism.

Subjectivism

Opposed to objectivism is what might be called **subjectivism.** This loose term can be used to embrace many forms of psychological and self-, subject-, or reader-centered criticism.

Psychological Criticism

The assumption is that literature is the expression of the author's psyche, often his or her unconscious, and, like dreams, needs to be interpreted.

FREUDIAN CRITICISM   The dominant school is the **Freudian,** based on the work of Sigmund Freud (1856–1939). Many of its practitioners assert that the meaning of a literary work does not lie on its surface but in the psyche (some would even claim, in the neuroses) of the author. The value of the work, then, lies in how powerfully and convincingly it expresses the author's unconscious and how universal the psychological elements are. A well-known Freudian reading of *Hamlet*, for example, insists that Hamlet is upset because he is jealous of his uncle, for he, *like all male children*, unconsciously wants to go to bed with his mother. The ghost may then be a manifestation of Hamlet's unconscious desire; his madness is not just acting but is the result of this frustrated desire; his cruelly gross mistreatment of Ophelia is a deflection of his disgust at his mother's being "lecherous," "unfaithful" in her love for him. A Freudian critic may assume then that Hamlet is suffering from an Oedipus complex, a Freudian term for the desire of the son for his mother, its name derived from the Greek myth that is the basis of Sophocles' play *Oedipus the King*.

    Some Freudian critics stress the author's psyche and find *Hamlet* the expression of Shakespeare's own Oedipus complex. Others stress the effect on the reader, the work having a purgative or cleansing effect by expressing in socially and morally acceptable ways unconscious desires that would be unacceptable if expressed directly.

LACANIAN CRITICISM   As it absorbs the indeterminacies of post-structuralism under the influence of thinkers such as Jacques Lacan, psychological criticism has become increasingly complex. Accepting the Oedipal paradigm and the unconscious as the realm of repressed desire, Lacanian psychology (and the critical theory that comes from that psychology) conflates these concepts with the deconstructionist emphasis on language as expressing absence—you use a word to represent an absent object but you cannot make it present. The word, then, like the unconscious desire, is something that cannot be fulfilled. Language, reaching out with one word after the other, striving for but never reaching its object, is the arena of desire.

JUNGIAN CRITICISM   Just as a Freudian assumes that human psyches have similar histories and structures, the **Jungian** critic assumes that we all share a universal or **collective unconscious** (as well as having a racial and individual unconscious). According to Carl Gustav Jung (1875–1961) and his followers, in the collective and in our individual unconscious are universal images, patterns, and forms of human experiences or **archetypes.** These archetypes can never be known directly, but they surface in art in an imperfect, shadowy way, taking the form of **archetypal images**—the snake with its tail in its mouth, rebirth, mother, the double, the descent into Hell. To get a sense of the archetype beneath the archetypal images or shadows in the characters, plot, language, and images of a work, to bring these together in an archetypal interpretation, is the function of the Jungian critic. He is guided by his belief that there is a central myth common to all literature. Just as, for the Freudian literary critic, the "family romance," out of which the Oedipus story comes, is central, so the Jungian assumes there is a **monomyth** that underlies the archetypal images and gives a clue as to how they can be related to suggest the archetypes themselves. The myth is that of the quest. In that all-encompassing myth the hero struggles to free himself (the gender of the pronoun is specific and significant) from the Great Mother, to become a separate, self-sufficient being who is then rewarded by union with his ideal other, the feminine *anima.*

Phenomenological Criticism

Another kind of subjectivist criticism is **phenomenology,** especially as it is practiced by **critics of consciousness.** They consider all the writings of an author—shopping lists and letters as well as lyrics—as the expression of his or her mindset or way of looking at reality. Such a critic looks for repeated or obsessive use of certain key words, incidents, patterns, and angles of vision, and, using these, maps out thereby the inner world of the writer.

Reader-Response Criticism

The formalists focus on the text. Though the psychological critics focus most frequently on the author, their assumptions about the similarity or universality of the human mind make them consider as well the role of the reader. There is another approach that, though not psychological in the usual sense of the word, also focuses on the reception of the text, on **reader response.** The conventional notion of reading is that a writer or speaker has an "idea," **encodes** it—that is, turns it into words—and the reader or listener **decodes** it, deriving, when successful, the writer/speaker's "idea." What the reader-response critic assumes, however, is that such equivalency between sender and receiver is impossible. The literary **work** therefore does *not* exist on the page; that is only the **text.** The text becomes a work only when it is read, just as a score becomes music only when it is played. And just as every musical performance, even of exactly the same notes, is somewhat different, a different "interpretation," so no two readers read or perform exactly the same work from identical texts. Besides the individual differences of readers, space is made for different readings or interpretations by **gaps** in a text itself. Some of these are temporary—such as the withholding of the name of the murderer until the end—and are closed by the text sooner or later, though each reader will in the meantime fill them differently. But others are permanent, and can never be filled with certainty; the result is a degree of uncertainty or **indeterminacy** in the text.

The reader-response critic's focus on the reading process is especially useful in the study of long works such as novels. The critic follows the text sequentially, observing what **expectations** are being aroused, how they are being satisfied or modified, how the reader recapitulates "evidence" from the portion of the text he has read to project forward a **configuration,** a tentative assumption of what the work as a whole will be and mean once it is done. The expectations are in part built by the text and in part by the repertoire of the reader, i.e., the reader's reading experience plus his or her social and cultural knowledge.

Historical Criticism

Dialogism

Another critical approach that gives a significant role to the reader and is particularly useful for long fiction is **dialogism,** largely identified with the work of Mikhail Bakhtin (1895–1975). The dialogic critic bases the study of language and literature on the individual utterance, taking into account the specific time, the place, the speaker, and the listener or reader. Such critics thus see language as a continuous dialogue, each utterance being a reply to what has gone before. Even thought, which they define as inner speech, is a dialogue between utterances that you have taken in. Even your own language (and thus thought) is itself dialogic, for it is made up of the dialogue in which you are engaged, that which you have heard from parents and peers, teachers and television, all kinds of social and professional discourse and reading. Indeed, you speak many "languages"—those of your ethnic, social, economic, national, professional, gender, and other identities. Your individual language consists in the combination of those languages. The literary form in which the dialogic is most interesting, complex, and significant is the novel, for there you have the languages not only of the characters (as you do in drama), but also that of a mediator or narrator and passages of description or analysis or information that seem to come from other voices—newspapers, whaling manuals, legal cases, and so on. Because the world is growing more interrelated and we have multiple voices rather than one dominant voice or language, the novel has become the most appropriate form for the representation of that world.

Because the dialogic sees utterances, including literary utterances or works, as specific to a time and place, one of its dimensions, unlike formalist, structuralist, or psychological criticism, is *historical*. Nineteenth-century **historical criticism** took the obvious fact that a work is created in a specific historical and cultural context and that the author is a part of that context in order to treat literature as a product of the culture. Formalists and others emphasizing the **aesthetic** value of literature saw this as reducing the literary work to the status of a mere historical document and the abandonment of literary study to history. The dialogic critic sees the work in relation to its host context, a part of the dialogue of the culture. The work in turn helps to create the context for other utterances, literary and otherwise. Some consider dialogic criticism a form of sociological criticism.

SOCIOLOGICAL CRITICISM   More recently, as scientists from psychology to physics recognized the role of the perceiver in perception, historians realized that they were not only discovering and looking at facts but were finding what they were looking for, selecting facts to fit preconceived views or interpretations. Literary historians or historical critics began to see literature not as a mere passive product of "history" but a contributor and even creator of history. An early form of this kind of historicism was **sociological criticism,** in which literature is seen as one aspect of the larger processes of history, especially those processes involving people acting in social groups or as members of social institutions or movements. Much sociological criticism uses literary texts to illustrate social attitudes and tendencies—and therefore has been strongly resisted by formalists, structuralists, and other "objectivist" critics as not being properly literary—but sociological criticism also attempts to relate what happens in texts to social events and patterns and is as concerned about the effects of texts on human events as about the effects of historical events on texts. Sociological criticism assumes that the most significant aspects of human beings are social and that the most important functions of literature thus involve the way that literature both portrays and influences human interactions. Much sociological criticism centers its attention on contemporary life and texts, seeking to affect both societal directions and literary ones in the present, but some sociological criticism is historical, concerned with differences in different times and places and anxious to interpret directions of literature in terms of historical emphases and patterns.

MARXIST CRITICISM The most insistent and vigorous historicism through most of the twentieth century has been **Marxism,** based on the work of Karl Marx (1818–1883). Marxist criticism, like other historical critical methods in the nineteenth century, treated literature as a passive product of the culture, specifically of the economic aspect, and therefore of class warfare. Economics, the underlying cause of history, was thus the *base*, and culture, including literature and the other arts, the *superstructure*. Viewed from the Marxist perspective, the literary works of a period would, then, reveal the state of the struggle between classes in the historical place and moment.

Marxist critics, however, early on recognized the role of perception. They insisted that all use of language, including literary and critical language, is **ideological,** that is, that it derives from and expresses preconceived ideas, particularly economic or class values. Criticism is thus not just the product of the culture but part of the discourse or "conversation" that we call history. Formalism and even the extreme apolitical position of **aestheticism,** "art for art's sake," by placing art in a realm above the grubbiness of everyday life—above such mundane things as politics and money—removes art from having any importance in that life. According to Marxists, this "bourgeois mystification of art" tends to support the class in power. Marxism has traditionally been sensitive to and articulate about power politics in both life and literature, and both its social and literary analyses have often been based on an explicit or implicit political agenda, though many Marxist critics are motivated more by theoretical than practical aims. In recent years, especially in the wake of post-structuralism and the psychoanalytical criticism of the 1970s and 1980s, Marxist criticism has become increasingly theoretical and less doctrinaire politically. Critics such as Raymond Williams, Fredric Jameson, Terry Eagleton, Pierre

Macherey, Walter Benjamin, and Louis Althusser have gained wide audiences among readers with a variety of political and literary commitments. Over the course of the century, it has been Marxism that has most often and most consistently raised referential and historical issues about literature, and those readers who have been interested in the interactive relationship between literature and life have most often turned for their guidance on such issues to Marxist analysts, whether or not they share their philosophical or political assumptions. In the past decade, however, two other critical schools with strong commitments to historical and cultural issues have become very powerful intellectually and have attracted many practitioners and adherents. These two, feminism and new historicism, have (along with Marxism and, in its way, dialogism) turned critical attention powerfully toward historical and representational issues, and since the mid-1980s they have set the dominant directions in literary criticism.

FEMINIST CRITICISM   Like Marxist criticism, feminist criticism derives from firm political and ideological commitments and insists that literature both reflects and influences human behavior in the larger world. Feminist criticism often, too, has practical and political aims. Strongly conscious that most of recorded history has given grossly disproportionate attention to the interests, thoughts, and actions of men, feminist thought endeavors both to extend contemporary attention to distinctively female concerns, ideas, and accomplishments and to recover the largely unrecorded and unknown history of women in earlier times. Not all directions of feminist criticism are historical; feminism has, in fact, taken many different directions and forms in recent years, and it has many different concerns. French feminist criticism, for example, has been deeply influenced by psychoanalysis, especially Lacanian psychoanalysis, and by French post-structuralist emphasis on language. Beyond their common aim of explicating and furthering specifically female interests, feminist critics may differ substantially in their assumptions and emphases. Like Marxism, feminism draws creatively on various other approaches and theories for its several methodologies. The most common historical directions of American feminism in particular involve the recovery of neglected or forgotten texts written by women in earlier times, the redrawing of literary values to include forms of writing (letters and autobiography, for example) that women were able to create when more public and accepted forms were denied to them, the discovery of the roles (positive and negative) that reading played in the lives and consciousnesses of women when they were unable to pursue more "active" and "public" courses, and the sorting out of cultural values implicit in the way women are represented in the texts of particular times and places.

New Historicism

New historicism has less obvious ideological commitments than Marxism or feminism, but it shares their interest in the investigation of how power is distributed and used in different cultures. Drawing on the insights of modern anthropology (and especially on the work of Clifford Geertz), new historicism wishes to isolate the fundamental values in texts and cultures, and it regards texts both as evidence of basic cultural patterns and as forces in cultural and social change. Many of the most influential practitioners of the new historicism come out of the ranks of Marxism and feminism, and new historicists are usually knowledgeable about most varieties of literary theory. Like Marxists and feminists, they are anxious to uncover the ideological commitments in texts, and they care deeply about historical and cultural difference and the way texts represent it. But personal commitments and specific political agendas usually are less important—at least explicitly—to new historicists, and one of the main contentions between feminists and new historicists—or between Marxists and new historicists—involves disagreement about the role that one's own politics should play in the practice of criticism. Many observers regard new historicism as politically to the left in its analysis of traditional cultural values, but critics on the left are suspicious of new historicism, especially of its reluctance to state its premises openly, and they generally regard its assumptions as conservative. Whatever its fundamental political commitments, however (or whether its commitments can be fairly described as having a consistent and specifiable bias), new historicism is far more interested than any other literary approach in social groups generally ignored by literary historians, and it refuses to privilege "literature" over other printed, oral, or material texts. "Popular literature" often gets major attention in the work of new historicists, who see all texts in a culture as somehow expressive of its values and directions and thus as equally useful in determining the larger intellectual, epistemological, and ethical system of which any text is a part. Texts here are thus seen as less specifically individual and distinctive than in most objectivist criticisms, and although new historicists are sometimes interested in the psychology of authors or readers their main concern is with the prevailing tendencies shared across a culture and thus shared across all kinds of texts, whatever their class status, literary value, or political aim.

Pluralism

These classifications are not pigeonholes, and you will notice that many of the approaches overlap: many feminists, especially French feminist critics, are Lacanian or post-structuralist as well, while British feminists often lean toward sociological, especially Marxist, criticism; dialogic critics accept many of the starting points and methods of reader-response and sociological critics, and so on. These crossovers or combinations are generally enriching; they cause problems only when the critic seems to be operating out of contradictory assumptions.

There is a lively debate among critics and theorists at present involving the question of whether readers should bring together the insights and methods of different schools (practitioners of the mixing of methods are usually called **pluralists**) or whether they should commit themselves wholeheartedly to a single system. Pluralists contend that they make use of promising insights or methods wherever they find them and argue that putting together the values of different approaches leads to a more fair and balanced view of texts and their uses. Opponents—those who insist on a consistency of ideological commitment— argue that pluralists are simply unwilling to state or admit their real commitments, and that any mixing of methods leads to confusion, uncertainty, and inconsistency rather than fairness. Readers, conscious or not of their assumptions and their methods, make this basic choice—to follow one lead or many—and the kind of reading they do and the conclusions they come to depend not only on this basic choice but many others suggested by the dominant strands of recent criticism that have been described here. Not all critics are aware of their assumptions, methodologies, or values, and some would even deny that they begin with any particular assumptions or biases, but is is often useful, especially to readers newly learning to practice literary criticism, to sort out their own beliefs carefully and see exactly what kind of difference it makes in the way they read literature and ask questions of it.

Further Reading on Critical Approaches

For good introductions to the issues discussed here, see the following books from which we have drawn in our discussion and definitions:

Robert Alter, *The Pleasures of Reading in an Ideological Age*, New York, 1989

Jonathan Culler, *The Pursuit of Signs*, London, 1981

Jonathan Culler, *On Deconstruction*, London, 1983

Robert Con Davis and Ronald Schleifer, *Contemporary Literary Criticism*, 2d ed., New York, 1989

Mary Eagleton (ed.), *Feminist Literary Theory: A Reader*, Oxford, 1986

Terry Eagleton, *Literary Theory: An Introduction*, Minneapolis, 1983

Nannerl Keohane, Michelle Z. Rosaldo, and Barbara C. Gelpi (eds.), *Feminist Theory: A Critique of Ideology*, Chicago, 1982

Dominick LaCapra, *History and Criticism*, Ithaca, N.Y., 1985

Frank Lentricchia, *After the New Criticism*, Chicago, 1980

Frank Lentricchia and Thomas McLaughlin (eds.), *Critical Terms for Literary Study*, Chicago, 1990

Richard Macksey and Eugenio Donato (eds.), *The Structuralist Controversy: The Languages of Criticism and the Sciences of Man*, Baltimore, 1972

Toril Moi, *Sexual-Textual Politics*, New York, 1985

Jean Piaget (translated by Chanihan Maschler), *Structuralism*, New York, 1970

Tzvetan Todorov, *Mikhail Bakhtin: The Dialogic Principle*, Minneapolis, 1984

DECIDING WHAT TO
WRITE ABOUT

Having Something to Say

Deciding what to write about—what approach to use, which questions to ask—seems like the first step in the process of writing a paper about a work of fiction. It isn't. Before that, you have to have confidence that you have something to say. If you are a beginner at this kind of writing, you are likely to have deep doubts about that. Developing confidence is not, at first, easy. You may feel as if you can *never* begin and want to put off the paper forever, or you may want to plunge in fast and get it over with. Either of these approaches, though common and tempting, is a mistake: the best way is to begin preparing for the paper as soon as possible—the moment you know you have one to write—but not to hurry into the writing itself.

The first step is to get close enough to the work to feel comfortable with it. Before you can tell anyone else about what you have read—and writing about fiction is just another form of talking about fiction, although a more formal and organized one—you need to "know" the work, to have a sure sense of what the work itself is like, how its parts function, what ideas it expresses, how it creates particular effects, and what your responses are. And the only way you will get to know the work is to spend time with it, reading it carefully and thoughtfully and turning it over in your mind. There is no substitute for reading, several times and with care, the work you are going to write about *before* you pick up a pen and prepare to write. And let your reading be of the *work itself*, not of something *about* that work, at least at first; later, your instructor may steer you to background materials or to critical readings about the work, but at first you should encounter the work alone and become aware of your own private responses to it.

Begin, then, by reading, several times, the work you are going to write about. The first time, read it straight through at one sitting: read slowly, pausing at its natural divisions—between paragraphs, or sections, or chapters, or at the ends of scenes—to consider how you are responding to the work. Later, when your knowledge of the work is more nearly complete and when you have the "feel" of the whole, you can compare your early responses with your more considered thoughts, in effect "correcting" your first impressions in whatever way seems necessary on the basis of new and better knowledge. But if you are noncommittal at first, refusing to notice what you think and feel, you will have nothing to correct, and you may cut yourself off from the most direct routes of response. Feelings are not always reliable—about literature any more than about people—but they are always the first point of contact with a literary work: you feel before you think. Try to start with your mind open, as if it were a blank sheet of paper ready to receive an impression from what you read.

When you have finished a first reading, think about your first impressions. Think about how the work began, how it gained your interest, how it generated expectations, how its conflicts and issues were resolved, how it ended, how it made you feel from beginning to end. Write down any phrases or events that you remember especially vividly, anything you are afraid you might forget. Look back at any parts that puzzled you at first. Write down in one sentence what you think the story, poem, or play is about. Then read it again, this time much more slowly, making notes as you go on any passages that seem especially significant and pausing over any features or passages that puzzle you. Then write a longer statement—three or four sentences—summarizing the work and suggesting more fully what it seems to be about. Try to write the kind of summary described above on pages 739–40. If you get stuck, try brainstorming all of your ideas about the work for fifteen minutes, and then write the summary.

Stop. Do something else for a while, something as different as possible— see a movie, do math problems, ride a bicycle, listen to music, have a meal, take a nap, mow the lawn, build a loft. Do NOT do some other reading you have been meaning to do. When you go back to the work and finish reading it for the third time—rapidly and straight through—write down in a sentence the most important thing you would want to tell someone else who was about to read it for the first time: not just whether you liked it or not, but what exactly you liked, how the whole thing seems to have worked.

Now you are ready to choose a topic.

Choosing a Topic

Once you are ready to choose a topic, the chances are that you have already— quietly and unconsciously—chosen one. The clue is in the last statement you wrote. The desire to tell someone about a work of literature is a wonderful place to begin. Good papers almost always grow out of a desire to communicate. Desire is not enough, of course—the substance (and most of the work, sentence by sentence) is still ahead of you; but desire will get you started. Chances are that what you wrote down as the one thing you most wanted to say is close to the heart of the central issue in the work you are going to write about. Your statement will become, perhaps, in somewhat revised form, your thesis.

The next step is to convert your personal feelings and desire to communicate into a sentence or two that states your purpose—into an "objective" statement about the work, a statement that will mean something to someone else. This will be your thesis. Again, you may already be further along than you realize. Look at the "summary" you wrote after your second reading. The summary will probably sound factual, objective, and general about the work; the personal statement you wrote after the third reading will be more emotional, subjective, and particular about some aspect of the work. In combining the two successfully lies the key to a good paper: what you need to do is to write persuasively an elaboration and explanation of the last statement so that your reader comes to share the "objective" view of the whole work that your summary expresses. The summary you have written will, in short, be implicit in the whole essay; your total essay will suggest to your reader the wholeness of the work you are writing about, but it will do so by focusing its attention on some particular aspect of the work—on a part that leads to, or suggests, or represents the whole. What you want to do is build an essay on the basis of your first statement, taking a firm hold on the handle you have found. The summary is your limit and guide: it reminds you of where you will come out. Any good topic ultimately leads back to the crucial perceptions involved in a summary. Ultimately, any good writing about literature leads to a full and resonant sense of the central thrust of the work, but the most effective way to find that center is by discovering a pathway that particularly interests you. The best writing about fiction presents a clear—and well-argued—thesis about a work or works and presents it from the perspective of personal, individual perception. But the thesis should clarify the central thrust of the work, helping it to open itself up to readers more completely and more satisfyingly.

Topics often suggest themselves after a second or third reading, simply because one feature or problem stands out so prominently that it almost demands to be talked about. What is real in "The Real Thing"? Will the love between Gurov and the lady with the dog last? Sometimes you may be lucky: your instructor may *assign* a topic instead of asking you to choose your own. At

first glance, that may not seem like a good break: it often feels confining to follow specific directions or to have to operate within limits and rules prescribed
by someone else. The advantage is that it may save a lot of time and prevent
floundering around. If your instructor assigns a topic, it is almost certain to be
one that will work, one that has a payoff if you approach it creatively and without too much resentment at being directed so closely and precisely. It is time-
consuming, even when you have tentatively picked a topic, to think through its
implications and be sure it works. And an instructor's directions, especially if
they are detailed and call attention to particular questions or passages, may aid
greatly in helping you focus on particular issues or in leading you to evidence
crucial to the topic.

Or one of these questions and titles might suit or might suggest a similar
topic of interest to you:

1. A Plotless Story about Plot: Grace Paley's "A Converstion with My
   Father"?
2. The Selection and Ordering of the Scenes in "The Country Husband"
3. What does the voice in "Love Medicine" contribute to the story's structure, tone, and effect?
4. Who Am I? The Nature of the Narrator in "Our Friend Judith"
5. The Self-Characterization of Montresor in "The Cask of Amontillado"
6. Sonny's Brother's Character
7. Symbolic Cats and Symbolic Hats? "Our Friend Judith" and "Everything that Rises Must Converge"
8. The Image and Import of the Sea in "The Lady with the Dog"
9. "Only a Girl": The Theme of "Boys and Girls"
10. What is the theme of "The Rocking-Horse Winner," and how does it
    relate to the title of the story?

If your instructor does *not* give you a topic and if no topic suggests itself to
you after you have read a particular work three or four times, you may sometimes have to settle for the kind of topic that will—more or less—be safe for
any literary work. Some topics are almost all-purpose. You can always analyze
devices of characterization in a story, showing how descriptive detail, dialogue,
and the reactions of other people in the story combine to present a particular
character and evoke the reader's response to him or her, for example. Such
"fall-back" topics are, however, best used only as last resorts, when your
instincts have failed you in a particular instance. When choice is free, a more
lively and committed paper is likely to begin from a particular insight or question, something that grabs you and makes you want to say something, or solve

a problem, or formulate a thesis. The best papers are usually very personal in origin; even when a topic is set by the assignment, the best papers come from a sense of having personally found an answer to a significant question. To turn a promising idea into a good paper, however, personal responses usually need to be supported by a considerable mass of evidence; the process often resembles the testing of "evidence" in a laboratory or the formulation of hypotheses and arguments in a law case. You may need to narrow your topic so that your thesis is focused and can be supported by examples from throughout the text. If your topic is too broad, your paper will likely become long, unwieldy, and overly general.

Considering Your Audience

Thinking of your paper as an argument or an explanation will also help with one of the most sensitive issues in writing about literature. The issue: To whom are you writing? Who is your audience? The obvious answer is, your instructor, but in an important sense, that is the wrong answer. It is wrong because, although it could literally be true that your instructor will be the only person (besides you) who will ever read your paper, your object in writing about literature is to learn to write for an audience of peers, people a lot like yourself who are sensible, pretty well educated, and need to have something (in this case a literary work) explained to them so that they will be able to understand it more fully. Picture your ideal reader as someone about your own age and with about the same educational background. Assume that the person is intelligent and has some idea of what literature is like and how it works, but that he or she has just read this particular literary work for the first time and has not yet had a chance to think about it carefully. Don't be insulting and explain the obvious, but don't assume either that your reader has noticed and considered every detail. The object is to inform and convince your reader, not to try to impress.

Should you, then, altogether ignore the obvious fact that it is an instructor—probably with a master's degree or Ph.D. in literature—who is your actual reader? Not altogether: you don't want to get so carried away with speaking to people of your own age and interests that you slip into slang, or feel the need to explain what a stanza is, or leave an allusion to a rock star unexplained, and you do want to learn from the kind of advice your instructor has given in class or from comments he or she may have made on other papers you have written.

But don't become preoccupied with the idea that you are writing for someone in "authority" or someone you need to please. Most of all, don't think of yourself as writing for a captive audience, for a reader who *has* to read what you write. It is not always easy to know exactly who your audience is or how interested your readers may be, so you have to make the most of every single word. It is your job to get the reader's attention. And you will have to do it subtly, making conscious assumptions about what your reader already knows and what he or she can readily understand. The tone of your paper should be serious and straightforward and its attitude respectful toward the reader, as well as toward the literary work. But its approach and vocabulary, while formal enough for academic writing, should be readily understandable by someone with your own background and reading experience. And it should be lively enough to interest someone like you. Try to imagine, as your ideal reader, the person in your class whom you most respect. Write to get, and hold, that person's serious attention. Try to communicate, try to teach.

FROM TOPIC TO ROUGH DRAFT

Writing about literature is very much like talking about literature. But there is one important difference. When we talk, we organize as we go—trying to get a handle, experimenting, working toward an understanding. And the early stages of preparing a paper—the notetaking, the outlining, the rough drafts—are much like that. A "finished" paper, however, has the uncertainties and tentativeness worked out and presents an argument that moves carefully and compellingly toward a conclusion. How does one get from here to there?

Once you have decided on a topic, the process of planning is fairly straightforward, but it can be time consuming and (often) frustrating. There are three basic steps in the planning process: first you gather the evidence, then you sort it into order, and (finally) you develop it into a convincing argument. The easiest way is to take these steps one by one.

Gathering Evidence

The first step involves accumulating evidence that supports the statement you have decided to make about your topic (that is, your thesis), and that takes you back to the text. But before you read the text again, look over the notes you have already made in the margin of that text or on separate pieces of paper. Which of them have something to do with the topic you have now defined? Which of them say something about your main point? Which ones can you now set aside as irrelevant to your topic?

Reading over the notes you have already made is a good preparation for re-reading the work again, for this time as you read it you will be looking at it in a new and quite specific way, looking for all the things in it that relate to the topic you have decided on. This time you will, in effect, be flagging everything—words, phrases, structural devices, changes of tone, anything—that bears upon your topic. As you read—very slowly and single-mindedly, with your topic always in mind—keep your pen constantly poised to mark useful points. Be ready to say something about the points as you come upon them; it's a good idea to write down, immediately, any sentences that occur to you as you reread this time. Some of these sentences will turn out to be useful when you actually begin to write your paper. Some will be incorporated in your paper; but some will not: you will find that a lot of the notes you take, like a lot of the footage shot in making a film, will end up on the cutting room floor.

No one can tell you exactly how to take notes but there are some general guidelines that may be useful. The notes you will need to take and how you take them will depend on the particulars of the paper you are about to write. Here are five hints toward successful notetaking.

1. Keep your topic and your thesis about your topic constantly in mind as you reread and take notes. Mark all passages in the text that bear on your topic, and for each one write on a note card a single sentence that describes how the passage relates to your topic and thesis. Add a "key" word that identifies the note at the top of the card to help you to organize the cards into clusters later in the process. Then indicate, for each passage, the specific location in the text by page or paragraph number. If you are taking notes on a computer, put page breaks between each one, so that when you print them out, there will be one note per page.

2. Keep rereading and taking notes until one of five things happens:
   a. You get too tired and lose your concentration. (If that happens, stop and then start again later, preferably the next day.)
   b. You stop finding relevant passages or perceive a noticeable drying up of your ideas. (Again, time to pause; give the work at least one more reading later when your mind is fresh and see whether the juices start anew. If they don't, you may be ready to outline and write.)
   c. You begin to find yourself annotating every single sentence or line, and the evidence all begins to run together into a single blob. (If this happens, your thesis is probably too broad. Try simplifying and narrowing it so that you don't try to include everything. Then go back to your notetaking and discriminate more carefully between what actually is important to your thesis and what only relates at some distance.)
   d. You become impatient with your notetaking and can't wait to get started writing. (Start writing. Use scrap paper, and be prepared to go back to systematic notetaking if your ideas or your energy fades. The chances are that the prose passages you write this way will find a place in your paper, but they may not belong exactly where you think they do when you first write them down.)

e. You find that there is insufficient evidence for your thesis, that the evidence points in another direction, or that the evidence contradicts your thesis. (Revise your topic to reflect the evidence, and begin rereading once more.)

3. When you think you have finished your notetaking, read all your note cards over slowly, one by one, and jot down any further ideas as they occur to you, each one on a separate note card. Computer users can either read the file on screen and add notes as they wish, or print out all of the notes and read through them on paper. (Sometimes it will seem as if note cards beget note cards. Too much is better than too little at the notetaking stage: you can always discard them before the final draft. Don't worry if you seem to have too many notes and too much material. But later, when you boil down to essentials, you will have to be ruthless and omit some of your favorite ideas.)

4. Transfer all of your notes to pieces of paper—or note cards—that are all the same size, one note on each. It is easier to sort them this way when you get ready to organize and outline. If you like to write notes in the margin of your text (or on the backs of envelopes, or on dinner napkins, or shirtsleeves), systematically transfer every note to uniform sheets of paper or cards before you begin to outline. Having everything easily recorded on sortable cards that can be moved from one pile to another makes organizing easier later, especially when you change your mind (as you will) and decide to move a point from one part of your paper to another. Index cards—either 3 × 5, if you write small and make economical notes, or 4 × 6, if you need more space—are ideal for notetaking and sorting.

5. When you think you are done taking notes (because you are out of ideas, or out of time, or getting beyond a manageable number of pieces of evidence), read through the whole pile one more time, again letting any new ideas—or ideas that take on a fresh look because you combine them in a new way—spawn new sentences for new note cards.

How many times should you read a story before you stop taking notes? There is no right answer. If you have read the work three times before settling on a topic, two more readings may do. But it could take several more. Common sense, endurance, and deadlines will all have an effect on how many rereadings you do. Let your conscience, your judgment, and your clock be your guides.

Organizing Your Notes

The notes you have taken will become, in the next few hours, almost the whole content of your paper. The task remaining is to give that content the form and shape that will make it appealing and persuasive. But it is not an easy task: the best content in the world isn't worth much if it isn't effectively presented. The key to the task is getting all your ideas into the right order, that is, into a sequence that will allow them to argue your thesis most persuasively.

In order to put your notes into a proper order, you will need (ironically) to get a little distance from your notes. (The key to good planning and writing—and to many other pursuits—is in knowing when to back away and get some perspective.) Set your notes aside, but not too far away. On a fresh sheet of paper, write down all the major points you want to be sure to make. Write them down randomly, as they occur to you. Now read quickly through your pack of note cards and add to your list any important points you have left out. Then decide which ideas should go first, which should go second, and so on.

Putting your points in order is something of a guess at this point. You may well want to reorder them before you begin to write—or later when you are writing a first (or even later) draft. But make your best guess. The easiest way to try out an order is to take your random list and put a **1** in front of the point you will probably begin with, a **2** before the probable second point, and so on. Then copy the list, in numerical order, onto a clean sheet of paper, revising (if you need to) as you go. Do not be surprised if later you have to revise your list further. Your next task is to match up your note cards (and the examples they contain) with the points on your outline. If you've added "key" words to the top of each card, you can make a "rough cut" according to these words.

Putting things in a particular order is a spatial problem, and by having your notes on cards or pieces of paper of a uniform size you can do much of your organizing physically. Do your sorting on a large table or sit in the middle of the floor. Prepare a title card for each point in your outline, writing on it the point and its probable place in your paper, then line them up on the table or floor in order before you begin writing. If you're using your computer, you can use the search function to find each instance of a key word, phrase, or name, and arrange your electronic "cards" under the headings on your list by blocking and moving your "cards" to new parts of the document.

Two-thirds of this exercise is quite easy: most examples and ideas you have written down will match quite easily with a particular point. But some cards will resist classification. Some cards will seem to belong in two or more places;

others will not seem to belong at all. If a card seems to belong to more than one point, put it in the pile with the lowest number (but write on it the number or numbers of other possible locations). If, for example, a card might belong in point 2 but could also belong in point 6 or 9, put it in the pile of 2's and write "maybe 6 or 9" on the card; if you don't use it in writing about point 2 move it to pile 6; if you don't use it in 6, move it to 9. Remember that you will work your way through the piles in numerical order, so that you have a safety system for notes that don't seem to belong where you first thought but that still belong somewhere in your paper. Move them to a possible later point, or put them in a special file (marked "?" or "use in revised draft") and, once you have completed a first draft on your paper, go through this file, carefully looking for places in your paper where these ideas may belong. Almost never will everything fit neatly into your first draft. If everything does seem to fit exactly as you had originally planned, you have either done an incredible job of planning and guessing about the organization of your paper, or you are forcing things into inappropriate places.

Don't be surprised if you have a large number of leftover note cards, that is, cards whose ideas you haven't yet used, after you have written your first draft. You will probably find places for many of these ideas later, but some just won't fit and won't be needed for the paper you ultimately write, no matter how good the ideas are. No paper will do everything it could do. Writing a paper is a *human* project; it has limits.

Before you actually start writing, you may want to develop a more elaborate outline, incorporating your examples and including topic sentences for each paragraph, or you may wish to work from your sketchy outline and the accompanying packs of cards. Do the more detailed outline if it seems right to you, but don't delay the writing too long. You are probably ready right now, and any exercises you invent to delay writing are probably just excuses.

Developing an Argument

Once you have decided on your major points and assembled your evidence, you have to decide how you are going to present your argument and how you are going to present *yourself*. What you say is, of course, more important than how you say it, but your manner of presentation can make a world of difference. Putting your evidence together effectively—in a coherent and logical order so that your readers' curiosities and questions are answered systematically and fully—is half the task in developing a persuasive argument. The other half involves your choice of a voice and tone that will make readers want to read on—and make them favorably disposed toward what you say.

The tone of your paper is the basis of your relationship with your reader. "I will be just *me*," you may say, "and write naturally." But writing is not a "natural" act, any more than swinging a tennis racket, carrying a football, or dancing a pirouette. The "me" you choose to present is only one of several possible me's; you will project a certain mood, a certain attitude toward your subject, a certain confidence. How do you want your readers to feel about you and your argument? Being too positive can make your readers fell stupid and inadequate and can turn them into defensive, resistant readers who will rebel at your every point. Friendship with your reader is better than an adversary relationship. Sounding like a nice person who is talking reasonably and sensibly is not enough if in fact you don't make sense or have nothing to say, but the purpose of the tone you choose is to make your reader receptive to your content, not hostile. The rest of the job depends on the argument itself.

It has been said that all good papers should be organized in the same way:

1. Tell 'em what you're going to tell 'em.
2. Tell 'em.
3. Tell 'em what you told 'em.

That description fits—in pretty general terms—the most common kind of organization, which includes an introduction, a body of argument, and a conclusion, but if it is followed too simplistically it can lead to a paper that sounds simple-minded. The beginning does need to introduce the subject, sort out the essential issues, and suggest what your perspective will be, and the conclusion does need to sum up what you have said in the main part of your paper, but the first paragraph shouldn't give *everything* away, nor should the final one simply repeat what is already clear. Lead into your subject clearly but with a little subtlety; arrange your main points in the most effective manner you can think of, building a logical argument and supporting your general points with clear textual evidence, concisely phrased and presented, and at the end *show how* your argument has added up—don't just *say* that it did.

There are, of course, other ways to organize than the basic Tell-3 method, but the imagination and originality that can be exercised in a straightforward Tell-3 paper are practically unlimited.

Writing the First Draft

It is now time to set pen to paper or fingers to keyboard. No one can help you much now for a while. The main thing is to get started right, with a clear first sentence that expresses your sense of direction and arrests the attention of your readers. (If you can't think of a good first sentence, don't pause over it too long. Write down a paraphrase of what you want it to say—something like the statement you wrote down after your third reading—and go on to start writing about your main points. Your "first" sentence may sometimes be the last one you will write.) And then you inch along, word by word and sentence by sentence, as you follow your outline from one paragraph to another. Keep at it. Struggle. Stare into space. Bite your pen when you feel like it. Get up and stride about the room. Scratch your head. Sharpen a pencil. Run your fingers through your hair. Groan. Snap your fingers. But keep writing.

It is often frustrating as you search for the right word or struggle to decide how the next sentence begins, but it is satisfying when you get it right. If you get stuck, try working out your ideas on a separate piece of paper or free writing for a while inside your computer document. Sometimes, working out an idea away from your draft can be helpful. Stay with your draft until you're reasonably satisfied with it. Write "The End" at the bottom and set it aside. Breathe a sigh of relief and put it away until tomorrow.

FROM ROUGH DRAFT TO
COMPLETED PAPER

Revising

This final stage of the process is the most important of all, and it is the easiest one to mismanage. There is a world of difference between a bunch of ideas that present a decent interpretation of a work of literature and a cogent, coherent, persuasive essay that will stir your readers to a nod of agreement and shared pleasure in a moment of insight. If you haven't done good literary analysis and sorted out your insights earlier, nothing you do at this stage will help much, but if what you have done so far is satisfactory, this is the stage that can turn your paper into something special.

The important thing is not to allow yourself to be too easily satisfied. If you have struggled with earlier stages, it may be tempting to think you are finished when you have put a period to the last sentence in your first draft. It will often feel as if you are done: you may feel drained, tired of the subject, anxious to get on to other things, such as sleep or food or friends or another project. And it *is* a good idea to take a break once you've finished a draft and let what you have done settle for a few hours, preferably overnight. (The Roman poet and critic Horace suggested putting a draft aside for nine years, but most instructors won't wait that long.) Rereading it "cold" may be discouraging, though: all those sentences that felt so good when you wrote them often seem flat and stale, or even worthless, when a little time has elapsed. The biggest struggle in moving from a first draft to a second one is to keep from throwing what you have written into a wastebasket. You've spent a lot of time on this already, and with some more work, you'll have a paper you can be proud of.

It may take *several* more drafts to produce your best work. Often it is tempting to cut corners—to smooth out a troublesome paragraph by obscuring the issue or by omitting the difficult point altogether instead of confronting it, or to ask a roommate or friend for help in figuring out what is wrong with a particular passage. But you will learn more in the long run—and probably do better in the short run as well—if you make yourself struggle a bit. When a particular word or phrase you have used turns out to be imprecise, or misleading, or ambiguous, search until you find the *right* word or phrase. (At the least put a big X in the margin so that you will come back and fix it later.) If a paragraph is incomplete or poorly organized, fill it out or reorganize it. If a transition from one point to another does not work, look again at your outline and see if another way of ordering your points would help. *Never* decide that the problem can best be solved by hoping that your reader will not notice. The satisfaction of finally solving the problem will build your confidence and sooner or later make your writing easier and better.

Reviewing Your Work and Revising Again

Precisely how you move from one draft to another is up to you and will depend on the ways you work best; the key is to find all the things that bother you (and that *should* bother you) and then gradually correct them, moving toward a better paper with each succeeding draft. Here are some things to watch for.

Thesis and central thrust: Is it clear what your main point is? Do you state it clearly, effectively, and early? Do you make clear what the work is about? Are you fair to the spirit and emphasis of the work? Do you make clear the relationship between your thesis and the central thrust of the work? Do you explain *how* the work creates its effect rather than just asserting it?

Organization: Does your paper move logically from beginning to end? Does your first paragraph set up the main issue you are going to discuss and suggest the direction of your discussion? Do your paragraphs follow each other in a coherent and logical order? Does the first sentence of each paragraph accurately suggest what that paragraph will contain? Does your final paragraph draw a conclusion that follows from the body of your paper? Do you resolve the issues you say you resolve?

Use of evidence: Do you use enough examples? Too many? Does each example prove what you say it does? Do you explain each example fully enough? Are the examples sufficiently varied? Are any of them labored, or overexplained, or made to bear more weight than they can stand? Have you left out any examples useful to your thesis? Do you include any gratuitous ones just because you like them? Have you achieved a good balance between examples and generalizations?

Tone: How does your voice sound in the paper? Confident? Does it show off too much? Is it too timid or self-effacing? Do you ever sound smug? Too tentative? Too dogmatic? Would a neutral reader be put off by any of your assertions? By your way of arguing? By your choice of examples? By the language you use?

Sentences: Does each sentence read clearly and crisply? Have you rethought and rewritten any sentences you can't explain? Is the first sentence of your paper a strong, clear one likely to gain the interest of a neutral reader? Is the first sentence of each paragraph an especially vigorous one? Are your sentences varied enough? Do you avoid the passive voice and "there is/there are" sentences?

Word Choice: Have you used any words whose meaning you are not sure of? In any cases in which you were not sure of what word to use, did you stay with the problem until you found the exact word? Do your metaphors and figures of speech make literal sense? Are all the idioms used correctly? Is your terminology correct? Are your key words always used to mean *exactly* the same thing? Have you avoided sounding repetitive by varying your sentences rather than using several different terms to mean precisely the same thing?

Conciseness: Have you eliminated all the padding you put in when you didn't think your paper would be long enough? Have you gone through your paper, sentence by sentence, to eliminate all the unnecessary words and phrases? Have you looked for sentences (or even paragraphs) that essentially repeat what you have already said—and eliminated all repetition? Have you checked for multiple examples and pared down to the best and most vivid ones? Have you got rid of all inflated phrasing calculated to impress readers? Have you eliminated all roundabout phrases and rewritten long, complicated, or confusing sentences into shorter, clearer ones? Are you convinced that you have trimmed every possible bit of excess and that you cannot say what you have to say any more economically?

Punctuation and mechanics: Have you checked the syntax in each *separate* sentence? Have you checked the spelling of any words that you are not sure of or that look funny? Have you examined each sentence separately for punctuation? Have you checked every quotation word by word against the original? Have you given proper credit for all material—written or oral—that you have borrowed from others? Have you followed the directions your instructor gave you for citations, footnotes, and form?

As you begin to revise it's a good idea to look first at the larger issues (your thesis, organization, and supporting evidence) to make sure you find and solve any major problems early on. Then, you're in a better position to work on your tone, sentences, choice of words, and punctuation and mechanics. In the final stages, the most effective way to revise is to read through your paper looking for one problem at a time, that is, to go through it once looking at paragraphing, another time looking at individual sentences, still another for word choice or problems of grammar. It is almost impossible to check too many things too often—although you can get so absorbed with little things that you overlook larger matters. With practice, you will learn to watch carefully for the kinds of mistakes you are most prone to. Everyone has individual weaknesses and flaws. Here are some of the most common stumbling blocks for beginning writers:

1. Haste. (Don't start too late, or finish too soon after you begin.)
2. Pretentiousness. (Don't use words you don't understand, tackle problems that are too big for you, or write sentences you can't explain; it is more important to make sense than to make a big, empty impression.)
3. Boredom. (The quickest way to bore others is to be bored yourself. If you think your paper will be a drag, you are probably right. It is hard to fake interest in something you can't get excited about; keep at it until you find a spark.)
4. Randomness. (Don't try to string together half a dozen unrelated ideas or insights and con yourself into thinking that you have written a paper.)
5. Imprecision. (Don't settle for approximation, either in words or ideas; something that is 50 percent right is also 50 percent wrong.)
6. Universalism. (Don't try to be a philosopher and make grand statements about life; stick to what is in the work you are writing about.)
7. Vagueness. (Don't settle for a general "sense" of the work you are talking about; get it detailed, get it right.)
8. Wandering. (Don't lose track of your subject or the work that you are talking about.)
9. Sloppiness. (Don't sabotage all your hard work on analysis and writing by failing to notice misspelled words, grammatical mistakes, misquotations, incorrect citations or references, or typographical errors. Little oversights make readers suspicious.)
10. Impatience. (Don't be too anxious to get done. Enjoy the experience; savor the process. Have fun watching yourself learn.)

Being flexible—being willing to rethink your ideas and reorder your argument as you go—is crucial to success in writing, especially in writing about fiction. You will find different (and better) ways to express your ideas and feelings as you struggle with revisions, and you will also find that—in the course of analyzing the work, preparing to write, writing, and rewriting—your response to the work itself will have grown and shifted somewhat. Part of the reason is that you will have become more knowledgeable as a result of the time and effort you have spent, and you will have a more subtle understanding of the work. But part of the reason will also be that the work itself will not be exactly the same. Just as a work is a little different for every reader, it is also a little different with every successive reading by the *same* reader, and what you will be capturing in your words is some of the subtlety of the work, its capacity to produce effects that are alive and that are therefore always changing just slightly. You need not, therefore, feel that you must say the final word about the work you are writing about—but you do want to say whatever word you have to say in the best possible way.

You can turn all this into a full-time job, of course, but you needn't. It is hard work, and at first the learning seems slow and the payoff questionable. A basketball novice watching the magic of Michael Jordan may find it hard to see the point of practicing lay-ups, but even creative geniuses have to go through those awful moments of sitting down and putting pen to paper (and then crossing out and rewriting again and again). But that's the way you learn to make it seem easy. Art is mostly craft, and craft means methodical work.

It *will* come more easily with practice. But you needn't aspire to professional writing to take pleasure in what you accomplish. Learning to write well about fiction will help you with all sorts of tasks, some of them having little to do with writing. Writing trains the mind, creates habits, teaches you procedures that will have all kinds of long-range effects that you may not immediately recognize or be able to predict. And ultimately it is very satisfying, even if it is not easy, to be able to stand back and say, "That is mine. Those are my words. I know what I'm talking about. I understand, and I can make someone else understand."

One final bit of advice: do not follow, too rigidly or too closely, anyone's advice, including ours. We have suggested some general strategies and listed some common pitfalls. But writing is a very personal experience, and you will have talents (and faults) that are a little different from anyone else's. Learn to play to your own strengths and avoid the weaknesses that you are especially prone to. Pay attention to your instructor's comments; learn from your own mistakes.

A SUMMARY OF THE PROCESS

Here, briefly, is a summary, step by step, of the stages we have suggested you move through in preparing a paper about fiction.

Stage One: Deciding what to write about

- Read the work straight through, thoughtfully. Make notes at the end on any points that caught your special attention.
- Read the work again more slowly, pausing to think through all the parts you don't understand. When you finish, write a three- or four-sentence summary.
- Read the work again, carefully but quite quickly. Decide what you feel most strongly about in the work, and write down the one thing you would most want to explain to a friend about how the story works, or (if the work still puzzles you) the one question you would most like to be able to answer.
- Decide how the statement you made at the end of your third reading relates to the summary you wrote down after the second reading.
- Write a one-paragraph "promise" of what your paper is going to argue.

Stage Two: Planning and drafting your paper

- Read the work at least twice more and make notes on anything that relates to your thesis.
- Read through all your notes so far, and for each write a sentence articulating how it relates to your thesis.
- Transfer all your notes to note cards of uniform size.
- Read through all your notes again and record any new observations or ideas on additional note cards.
- Set aside your note cards for the moment, and make a brief outline of the major points you intend to make.
- Sort the note cards into piles corresponding to the major points in your outline. Sort the cards in each separate pile into the most likely order of their use in the paper.
- Make a more detailed outline (including the most significant examples) from your pile of note cards on each point.

- Reconsider your order of presentation and make any necessary adjustments.
- Write a first draft.

Stage Three: Rewriting

- Go over your writing, word by word, sentence by sentence, and paragraph by paragraph, in draft after draft until your paper expresses your ideas clearly and concisely.

Stage Four: Final preparation

- If you have not been working on a computer, type or word-process your paper.
- Proofread carefully for errors of all kinds—spelling, typing, etc.
- Proofread again. Find your mistakes before someone else does.
- Congratulate yourself on a job well done.

BIOGRAPHICAL SKETCHES[1]

RUDOLFO ANAYA (b. 1937)

Born in Pastura, New Mexico, Anaya studied at the University of New Mexico, where he now directs the creative writing program. He also serves as the editor for the *Blue Mesa Review*. Anaya is the recipient of many literary awards, including an NEA Fellowship and the prestigious Premio Quinto Sol in 1972 for his novel *Bless Me Ultima*. His many publications include *Heart of Aztlan* (1976), *Tortuga* (1979), *A Chicano in China* (1986), *Lord of Dawn* (1987), and *Albuquerque* (1992).

MARGARET ATWOOD (b. 1939)

Atwood spent her first eleven years in sparsely populated areas of northern Ontario and Quebec, where her father worked as an entomologist. After her education at the University of Toronto and Harvard, she held various jobs in Canada, America, England, and Italy. Atwood published her first poem when she was just nineteen, and she has won numerous prizes for her poetry as well as her fiction, which has become increasingly political over the years. Her novels include *The Edible Woman* (1969), *Surfacing* (1972), *Lady Oracle* (1976), *Life Before Man* (1979), *Bodily Harm* (1982), *The Handmaid's Tale* (1985), *Cat's Eye* (1988), and *Robber Bride* (1993). Many of her stories have been collected in *Dancing Girls and Other Stories* (1978), *Murder in the Dark* (1983), *Bluebeard's Egg* (1983), and *Wilderness Tips* (1991).

JAMES BALDWIN (1924–1987)

Baldwin was for some time a leading literary spokesman for black Americans. Born in Harlem, long a resident of France, he first attracted critical attention with two extraordinary novels, *Go Tell It on the Mountain* (1953) and *Giovanni's Room* (1956), which dealt, somewhat autobiographically, with religious awakening (Baldwin was a minister at fourteen but later left his church) and the anguish of being black and homosexual in a white and heterosexual society. Baldwin was also a dramatist and an outstanding essayist, his best-known nonfiction prose being *Notes of a Native Son* (1955), *Nobody Knows My Name* (1961), and *The Fire Next Time* (1963), aimed at unraveling the repressive myths of white society and at healing the disastrous estrangement he found in the lives of black people in America. His stories are collected in *Going to Meet the Man* (1965), from which "Sonny's Blues" is taken.

TONI CADE BAMBARA (b. 1939)

Born in New York City, Bambara grew up in Harlem and Bedford-Stuyvesant, two of its poorest neighborhoods. She began writing while still a child. After graduating from Queens College, she worked at various jobs while studying for her M.A. at the City College of New York, writing fiction all the while in "the predawn in-betweens." Bambara began to publish her stories in 1962. She has also been a dancer, teacher, editor, and critic, and has worked in psychiatric and drug therapy, youth organizing, and settlement houses. Her work includes two anthologies, *The Black Woman* (1970) and *Stories for Black Folks* (1971), and two collections of stories, *Gorilla My Love* (1972) and *The Sea*

Birds Are Still Alive (1977). She has also written two novels, *The Salt Eaters* (1980) and *If Blessing Comes* (1987).

CHARLES BAXTER (b. 1947)

Baxter was born in Minneapolis and teaches at the University of Michigan in Ann Arbor. His short story collections include *Harmony of the World* (1984) and *A Relative Stranger* (1990), and his novels are *First Light* (1987) and *Shadow Play* (1993).

ANN BEATTIE (b. 1947)

Beattie grew up in the Washington suburb of Chevy Chase, Maryland. She received a B.A. from American University and went on to the University of Connecticut as a graduate student in English literature. Beattie's first published story, "A Rose for Judy Garland's Casket," appeared in 1972, and after many rejections she began publishing in the *New Yorker* shortly thereafter. Beattie's stories have made her a spokesperson for a generation that came of age in the 1960s as they adapt to or are baffled and worn out by the oncoming years. Many of them have been collected in *Distortions* (1976), *Secrets and Surprises* (1979), *Jacklighting* (1981), *The Burning House* (1982), *Where You'll Find Me* (1986), and *What Was Mine: Stories* (1990). Her novels are *Chilly Scenes of Winter* (1976), *Falling In Place* (1980), *Love Always* (1985), and *Picturing Will* (1990).

AMBROSE BIERCE (1842–1914?)

The tenth child of a poor Ohio family, Bierce rose during the Civil War to the rank of major, was twice wounded and cited fifteen times for bravery. He stayed in the army for a time after the war, then was a journalist in California and London, where his boisterous western mannerisms and savage wit made him a celebrity and earned him the name "Bitter Bierce." He published *Tales of Soldiers and Civilians* (later called *In the Midst of Life*) (1891) and another volume of short stories, *Can Such Things Be?* (1893). the death of his two sons in 1889 and 1901, along with his divorce in 1891, might well have led him to Mexico, where he reportedly rode with Pancho Villa's revolutionaries. He disappeared and is presumed to have died there. Bierce is well known as the author of *The Cynic's Wordbook* (later called *The Devil's Dictionary*) (1906), but his short stories are his finest achievement.

ANGELA CARTER (1940–1992)

Born in Eastbourne, Sussex, England, Carter chose to take a job in journalism rather than attend Oxford University, though she later enrolled at the University of Bristol and studied medieval literature. Her early novels were *Honeybuzzard* (1967), *The Magic Toyshop* (1967), and *Several Perceptions* (1968), which won the Somerset Maugham Award in 1969. Her later novels included *The Infernal Desire Machines of Dr. Hoffman* (1972), *The Passion of New Eve* (1977), and *Wise Children* (1991). "A Souvenir of Japan" is from her 1974 short story volume, *Fireworks*. Carter's writing gained widespread popularity after the release of the film *The Company of Wolves* (1984), which was based on a story from *The Bloody Chamber* (1979), a collection of macabre and erotic retellings of fairy tales. Her chief nonfiction work was *The Sadeian Woman: An Exercise in Cultural History* (1979).

DENISE CHÁVEZ (b. 1948)

Actor, playwright, and novelist, Chávez was born in Las Cruces, New Mexico, and educated at the University of New Mexico. She served as writer-in-residence at many colleges until she was appointed professor of drama at the University of Houston. Chávez has written many plays as well as two books of fiction, *The Last of the Menu Girls* (1986) and *Face of an Angel* (1993).

JOHN CHEEVER (1912–1982)

Cheever was born in Quincy, Massachusetts. His formal education ended when he was expelled from Thayer Academy at the age of seventeen; thereafter he devoted himself completely to fiction writing, except for brief interludes of teaching at Barnard College and the University of Iowa, and script-writing for television. Cheever published his first story when he was sixteen, and until his first novel, *The Wapshot Chronicle*, won the National Book Award in 1958, he was known primarily as a superb and prolific writer of short stories. Built around a strong moral core and tinged with melancholy nostalgia for the past, they form a running commentary on the tensions, manners, and crippled aspirations of urban and suburban life. Many have won awards, including the O. Henry Award in 1956 for "The Country Husband." *The Stories of John Cheever* (1978) won the Pulitzer Prize.

ANTON CHEKHOV (1860–1904)

Chekhov was born in Taganrog, a small town in southern Russia. After attending medical school at Moscow University, he began practicing medicine in 1884, while writing short stories, jokes, and plays to support his family. His writing was well-received, and he left medicine to write full time. Stanislavsky was the first to direct Chekhov's *The Seagull* (1896) and *The Cherry Orchard* (1903), which he adapted as a tragedy though Chekhov considered it a comedy. Along with these plays, he wrote a number of other realistic dramas dealing with turn of the century Russian life, including *The Three Sisters* (1901).

KATE CHOPIN (1851–1904)

Born Katherine O'Flaherty in St. Louis, Missouri, Chopin moved to Louisiana when she married Oscar Chopin in 1870. She did not begin writing until after her husband's death, but produced many short stories, collected in *Bayou Folk* (1894) and *A Night in Acadie* (1897), and the now-classic novel *The Awakening* (1899).

RICHARD CONNELL (1893–1949)

Connell, like Ernest Hemingway, began his writing career as a journalist. At the age of sixteen, he was city editor of his native *Poughkeepsie News-Press*; later he was editor of both the *Crimson* and the *Lampoon* at Harvard, from which he graduated in 1915. After World War I, he left his New York job as an advertising editor to become a freelance writer, traveling to Paris and London and finally settling in Beverly Hills, California. His works include volumes of short stories—*Apes and Angels* (1924), *The Sin of Monsieur Pettipon* (1925), *Variety* (1925), and *Ironies* (1930)—and novels: *Mad Lover* (1927), *Murder at Sea* (1929), *Playboy* (1936), and *What Ho!* (1937).

JOSEPH CONRAD (1857–1924)

Jozeph Teodor Konrad Nalecz Korzeniowski was born in Berdyczew, Polish Ukraine. At five he accompanied his parents into exile in northern Russia and later near Kiev; he was left an orphan at eleven. Before he was seventeen he was off to Marseilles, making several trips to the West Indies as an apprentice seaman. After some veiled troubles in France, involving gambling debts and an apparent suicide attempt, he sailed on a British ship, landed in England in 1878, and spent the next sixteen years in the British merchant service, rising to master in 1886, the year he became a British subject. In 1890, he worked on a boat that sailed up the Congo, the inspiration for *Heart of Darkness* (1899). He began writing in 1889 but did not publish his first novel, *Almayer's Folly*, until 1896. Though a successful writer, he was not truly popular or financially independent until the publication of *Chance* in 1912–13. Among his major novels are *The Nigger of the "Narcissus"* (1897), *Lord Jim* (1900), *Nostromo* (1904), *Under Western Eyes* (1910), and *Victory* (1915). His short-story collections include *Tales of Unrest* (1898), *Typhoon and Other Stories* (1903), *'Twixt Land and Sea* (1912), from which "The Secret Sharer" is taken, and *Within the Tides: Tales* (1915).

JULIO CORTÁZAR (1914–1984)

Born in Brussels to Argentinian parents, Cortázar was raised in Argentina and moved to Paris in 1952. A poet, translator, and amateur musician, as well as a fiction writer, Cortázar's publications include *The Winners, Hopscotch, Blow-Up and Other Stories, 62: A Model Kit, All Fires the Fire and Other Stories, A Manual for Manuel, A Change of Light, We Love Glenda So Much,* and *A Certain Lucas.*

RICHARD DOKEY

A native of Stockton, California, and a graduate of the University of California, Berkeley, Dokey has worked as a laborer on a railroad, in a shipyard, for a soft drink bottling company, and for an ink factory, but he now teaches philosophy at San Joachin Delta Community College in Stockton, California. His works include *August Heat* (1982), *Funeral: A Play* (1982), and *Sánchez and Other Stories* (1981). His novel, *The Adidas Kid,* was published in 1993.

LOUISE ERDRICH (b. 1954)

Born in Little Falls, Minnesota, of German-American and Chippewa descent, Erdrich grew up in Wahpeton, North Dakota, as a member of the Turtle Mountain Band of Chippewa, and attended Dartmouth College. After graduation, she returned to teach in North Dakota's Poetry in the Schools Program. She received an M.A. in creative writing from Johns Hopkins University in 1979. In the same year, *Jacklight,* a collection of poetry, was published. Her first novel, *Love Medicine* (1984), has been praised as a landmark work in its depiction of the lives of contemporary Native Americans, and was the winner of the National Book Critics' Circle Award for Fiction. An expanded version was published in 1993. Erdrich has also published another collection of poetry, *Baptism of Desire* (1989), several novels in the North American series that includes *Love Medicine, The Beet Queen* (1986), *Tracks* (1988), and *The Bingo Palace* (1993), and jointly authored *The Crown of Columbus* (1991) with her husband Michael Dorris.

WILLIAM FAULKNER (1897–1962)

Faulkner spent almost his entire life in his native state of Mississippi. He left high school without graduating, joined the Royal Canadian Air Force in 1918, and in the mid-1920s lived briefly in New Orleans, where he was encouraged by Sherwood Anderson. He then spent a few miserable months as a clerk in a New York bookstore, published a collection of poems, *The Marble Faun,* in 1924, and took a long walking tour of Europe in 1925. In later years he made several visits to Hollywood, writing a screenplay for *The Big Sleep,* among others, and spent his last years in Charlottesville, Virginia. With the publication of *Sartoris* in 1929, Faulkner began a cycle of works interrelated by his fictional Yoknapatawpha County and the reappearance of characters or families from work to work. These include *As I Lay Dying* (1930), *Light in August* (1932), *Absalom, Absalom!* (1936), *The Unvanquished* (1939), *The Hamlet* (1940), and *Go Down, Moses* (1942). His short fiction can be found in *The Collected Stories of William Faulkner* (1950). He received the Nobel Prize for Literature in 1950.

RICHARD FORD (b. 1944)

Ford was born in Jackson, Mississippi, attended Michigan State University, and received an M.F.A. in creative writing from the University of California. Since that time he has been awarded a Guggenheim Foundation Fellowship and lived in western Montana, New York, Mississippi, and currently New Orleans. His first novel, *A Piece of My Heart*, was published in 1976. He has published three more novels, *The Ultimate Good Luck* (1981), *The Sportswriter* (1986), and *Wildlife* (1990), and a volume of short stories, *Rock Springs* (1987). His most recent novel is *Independence Day* (1995).

GABRIEL GARCÍA MÁRQUEZ (b. 1928)

Born in Aracataca, a remote town in Magdalena province near the Caribbean coast of Colombia, García Márquez studied law at the University of Bogotá and then worked as a journalist in Latin America, Europe, and the United States. In 1967 he took up permanent residence in Barcelona, Spain. His first published book, *Leaf Storm* (1955, translated 1972), in which "A Very Old Man with Enormous Wings" appears, is set in the fictional small town of Macondo, based on the myths and legends of his childhood home. His most famous novel, *One Hundred Years of Solitude* (1967, translated 1970) presents six generations of one family in Macondo, fusing magic, reality, fable, and fantasy in a way that also allows the town to serve as a microcosm of many of the social, political, and economic problems of Latin America. Among his works are *The Autumn of the Patriarch* (1975, translated 1976), *Innocent Eréndira and Other Stories* (1972, translated 1978), *Chronicle of a Death Foretold* (1981, translated 1982), and *Love in the Time of Cholera* (1987, translated 1988). García Márquez won the Nobel Prize for Literature in 1982.

CHARLOTTE PERKINS GILMAN (1860–1935)

Charlotte Anna Perkins was born in Hartford, Connecticut. After a painful, lonely childhood and several years supporting herself as a governess, art teacher, and designer of greeting cards, Charlotte Perkins married the artist Charles Stetson. Following several extended periods of depression, she was put by her husband into the hands of Dr. S. Weir Mitchell, who "sent me home with the solemn advice to 'live as domestic a life as . . . possible,' to 'have but two hours' intellectual life a day,' and 'never to touch pen, brush, or pencil again' as long as I lived." Three months of this, ending "near the borderline of utter mortal ruin," became the inspiration for "The Yellow Wallpaper." In 1900 she married George Houghton Gilman, having divorced Stetson in 1892. Her nonfiction works, which placed her at the center of the early women's movement, include *Women and Economics* (1898) and *Man-Made World* (1911). She also wrote several utopian novels, including *Moving the Mountain* (1911) and *Herland* (1915).

NATHANIEL HAWTHORNE (1804–1864)

Hawthorne was born in Salem, Massachusetts, a descendant of Puritan immigrants; one ancestor had been a judge in the Salem witchcraft trials. Educated at Bowdoin College, he was agonizingly slow in winning acclaim for his work, and supported himself from time to time in government service—working in the custom houses of Boston and Salem and serving as the United States consul in Liverpool. His early collections of stories, *Twice-Told Tales* (1837) and *Mosses from an Old Manse* (1846), in which "Young Good-man Brown" appears, did not sell well, and it was not until the publication in 1850 of his most famous novel, *The Scarlet Letter*, that his fame spread beyond a discerning few. His other novels include *The House of the Seven Gables* (1851) and *The Blithedale Romance* (1852).

ERNEST HEMINGWAY (1899–1961)

Born in Oak Park, Illinois, Hemingway was first a reporter, then an ambulance-service volunteer in France and infantryman in Italy in 1918, when he was wounded and decor-ated for valor. After the war and more reporting, he settled for a time in Paris, where he knew Gertrude Stein and Ezra Pound, among others. From 1925 to 1935 he published two volumes of stories, *In Our Time* (1925) and *Death in the Afternoon* (1932), and two major novels, *The Sun Also Rises* (1926) and *A Farewell to Arms* (1929), which established his international reputation. Hemingway helped the Loyalists in the Spanish Civil War, the subject of *For Whom the Bell Tolls* (1940), served as a war correspondent in the Second World War, and from 1950 to 1962 lived in Cuba. *The Old Man and the Sea* was published in 1952, winning a Pulitzer Prize. Hemingway was awarded the Nobel Prize for Literature in 1954. He committed suicide in 1961.

SPENCER HOLST (b. 1926)

Well known in the literary underground, Holst has published his short stories and poetry in numerous periodicals such as *Mademoiselle* and *Oui*. He has translated the work of German poet Vera Lachmann and published several volumes of his own writing, includ-ing two volumes of short stories, *The Language of Cats and Other Stories* (1971) and *Spencer Holst Stories* (1976), a collection of imaginative and humorous fables that play with reality and fantasy.

HENRY JAMES (1843–1916)

Son of a writer and religious philosopher, brother of the philosopher William James, Henry James was born in New York and entered Harvard Law School in 1862, after private study, art school, and study and residence abroad. Thereafter his American home was in Cambridge, Massachusetts, but he lived in England from 1876 until his death forty years later, having become a British subject in 1915. James's fiction often centers on the confrontation of Americans with Europe or Europeans; he treats the two as moral or value systems as much as geographical entities. His practice and theory of fiction, set forth mainly in the prefaces to his novels, dominated fiction criticism for generations. Among his works are *The American* (1877), *Daisy Miller* (1879), *Portrait of a Lady* (1881), *The Turn of the Screw* (1898), *The Wings of the Dove* (1902), *The Ambassadors* (1903), and *The Golden Bowl* (1904).

HA JIN (b. 1956)

Ha Jin grew up in mainland China. From the age of fourteen to eighteen he served in the People's Army; he then worked in a railroad company for three years. He has degrees from Heilongjiang and Shandong universities in China and a doctorate from Brandeis. After the Tiananmen massacre, he decided to emigrate and write in English. He has published a book of poems, *Between Silences* (1990) and two books of short fiction, *Ocean of Worlds: Army Stories* and *Man to Be: Country Stories* from which "In Broad Daylight" is taken. He teaches creative writing at Emory University.

JAMES JOYCE (1882–1941)

In 1902, after graduating from University College, Dublin, Joyce left his native city for Paris, only to return in April 1903 to teach school. In the spring of 1904 he lived at the Martello Tower, Sandycove, a site made famous by his great novel, *Ulysses* (1921). In October 1904 he eloped with Nora Barnacle and left Ireland again, this time for Trieste, where he taught English for the Berlitz school. Though he lived abroad the rest of his life, that first abortive trip proved symbolic: in his fiction the expatriate could never leave Dublin. Joyce had more than his share of difficulties with publication and censorship. His volume of short stories, *Dubliners* (in which "Araby" appears), completed in 1905, was not published until 1914. His *Portrait of the Artist as a Young Man*, dated "Dublin 1904, Trieste 1914," appeared first in America, in 1916. *Ulysses* was banned for a dozen years in the United States and as long or longer elsewhere. Though he published a play, *Exiles*, and poetry, the three works mentioned and the monumental, experimental, and puzzling *Finnegans Wake* (1939) are the basis of his reputation.

FRANZ KAFKA (1883–1924)

Born in Prague of a middle-class Jewish family, Kafka earned a doctorate in law from the German University in that city and held an inconspicuous position in the civil service for many years. Emotionally and physically ill for the last seven or eight years of his short life, he died of tuberculosis in Vienna, never having married (though he was twice engaged to the same woman and lived with an actress in Berlin for some time before he died) and not having published his three major novels, *The Trial* (1925), *The Castle* (1926), and *Amerika* (1927). Indeed, he ordered his friend Max Brod to destroy them and other works he had left in manuscript. Fortunately, Brod did not, and not long after his death, Kafka's work was world famous and widely influential. His stories in English translation can be found in *The Great Wall of China* (1933), *The Penal Colony* (1948), and *The Complete Stories* (1976).

YASUNARI KAWABATA (1899–1972)

Born in Osaka, Japan, Kawabata graduated from Tokyo Imperial University in 1924 and made his literary debut with the semiautobiographical *The Izu Dancer* (1926). He was a cofounder of what was called the Neosensualist group, which shared much in common with the European literary movements of Dadaism, Expressionism, and Cubism. His best-known novels include *Snow Country* (1948), *Thousand Cranes*, and *The Sound of the Mountain* (1954). "The Grasshopper and the Cricket" is from his collection *Palm-of-the-Hand Stories*, translated in 1988. Kawabata was awarded the Nobel Prize for Literature in 1968.

JAMAICA KINCAID (b. 1949)

Born in St. John's, Antigua (an island in the West Indies north of Guadeloupe), Kincaid now lives in New York, where she is a staff writer for the *New Yorker*. She is the author of a volume of short stories, *At the Bottom of the River* (1984), and two novels, *Annie John* (1985) and *Lucy* (1990). Although Kincaid left her native island as a teenager, a deeply felt—and richly evocative—sense of place pervades her work.

MARGARET LAURENCE (1926–1987)

Laurence was born in Neepwa, Manitoba, which reappeared as the fictional town of Manawaka in many of her novels and short stories, including *The Stone Angel* (1964), *A Jest of God* (1966), and the collection *A Bird in the House* (1970). *This Side of Jordan*

(1960), her first novel, was set in Africa during the 1950s rather than in her native Canada, but reflected a similar concern with the oppression of native peoples that characterizes her later work.

D. H. LAWRENCE (1885–1930)

Son of a coal miner and a middle-class schoolteacher, Lawrence won a scholarship to Nottingham High School at thirteen but had to leave a few years later when his elder brother died. He worked for a surgical appliance manufacturer, attended Nottingham College, and taught school in Croydon, near London. In 1911, when his first novel, *The White Peacock*, was published, he left teaching to devote his time to writing, though it was not until the publication of *Sons and Lovers* (1913) that he was established as a major literary figure. In 1912 he eloped to the Continent with Frieda von Richthofen, and in 1914, after her divorce, they were married. During World War I, both his novels and the fact that his wife was German gave him trouble: *The Rainbow* was published in September 1915 and suppressed in November. In November 1919 the Lawrences left England and their years of wandering began: first Italy, then Ceylon and Australia, Mexico and New Mexico, then back to England and Italy. *Women in Love* was published in New York in 1920, and *Lady Chatterley's Lover*, his most sexually explicit and controversial novel, eight years later. Through it all he suffered from tuberculosis, the disease from which he finally died, in France. Lawrence's stories are available in a three-volume edition, first published in 1961.

DORIS LESSING (b. 1919)

Born in Persia, Lessing lived for twenty-five years in Southern Rhodesia (now Zimbabwe) before moving to England, where soon thereafter her first novel, *The Grass Is Singing* (1950), was published. She has since published voluminously. Her books include *The Golden Notebook* (1962), the five Martha Quest novels, *Children of Violence*, published between 1952 and 1969, *Briefing for a Descent into Hell* (1971), *The Summer Before the Dark* (1973), and *The Good Terrorist* (1985). She has also published eight volumes of short fiction, including *A Man and Two Women* (1963) and *The Memoirs of a Survivor* (1975), and has written plays, television plays, poetry, and essays. Her work is known for its range and variety, some of it set in Africa, a significant portion of it political (she was once a Communist), much of it examining inner lives of women in modern society, and some of it lately reflecting her interest in extrasensory perception. Lessing published a five-volume science fiction collection under the collective title *Caopus in Argos: Archives* between 1979 and 1983, and tried her hand at satire with *The Good Terrorist* (1985). *Particularly Cats . . . and Rufus* (1991) is a reflection on various pets in Lessing's life, and *African Lands* (1992) is based on her recent visit to Zimbabwe.

REGINALD MCKNIGHT (b. 1956)

McKnight teaches writing at Carnegie-Mellon University in Pittsburgh and has earned such prizes for his writing as the O. Henry Award for Short Stories and the Kenyon Review New Fiction Prize. McKnight has published two collections of short stories, *Moustapha's Eclipse* (1988) and *The Kind of Light That Shines on Texas* (1992), and a novel, *I Get on the Bus* (1990).

KATHERINE MANSFIELD (1888–1923)

Born in New Zealand, Mansfield studied music at Queen's College, London, and was an accomplished cellist. She published three major volumes of short stories during her short life: *Bliss* (1920), which established her reputation, *The Garden-Party* (1922), and *The Dove's Nest* (1923). With John Middleton Murry and D. H. Lawrence she founded an influential literary review, *The Signature*. She died of tuberculosis in France, and a final volume of stories, *Something Childish* (1924), appeared shortly after her death. Her *Collected Stories* were published in 1945.

BOBBIE ANN MASON (b. 1940)

Mason, who grew up on a farm near Mayfield, Kentucky, has written for *Movie Stars*, *Movie Life*, and *T.V. Star Parade*. The *New Yorker* published her first story in 1980. Since then, she has been awarded a Guggenheim Foundation Fellowship, has had stories in *Best American Short Stories* in 1981 and 1983, and won the Pushcart Prize for Fiction in 1983. *Shiloh and Other Stories* (1982), her first collection, won the Ernest Hemingway Foundation Award. She has also written two novels, *In Country* (1985) and *Feather Crowns* (1993), a short novel, *Spence and Lila* (1988), and a second collection of stories, *Love Life* (1989). "The people I write about," she says "either want to get away from home, get away from town, see the world, or they want to stay home, and they're afraid to leave, so they accommodate. . . . I'm interested in that tension between longing to stay and longing to go."

GUY DE MAUPASSANT (1850–1893)

Born Henri René Albert in Normandy, France, at sixteen Maupassant was expelled from a Rouen seminary and finished his education in a public high school. After serving in the Franco-Prussian War, he was for ten years a government clerk in Paris. A protégé of Flaubert, during the 1880s he published some three hundred stories, a half-dozen novels, and plays. The short stories, which appeared regularly in popular periodicals, sampled military and peasant life, the decadent world of politics and journalism, prostitution, the supernatural, and the hypocrisies of solid citizens. With Chekhov, he may be said to have created the modern short story; his reliance on plot, plot twists, and sometimes heavy irony became facile in the hands of his followers and has somewhat diminished his own reputation the past quarter-century and more. His life ended somewhat like one of his own stories: he died in an asylum, of syphilis. His novels include *Une Vie* (*A Life*, 1883), *Bel Ami* (*Handsome Friend*, 1885), and *Pierre et Jean* (1888). His stories are most readily available in his *Collected Works*.

BHARATI MUKHERJEE (b. 1940)

Brought up in an upper-class Bengali family of the Brahmin caste, Mukherjee attended private schools in India, London, and Switzerland before a business disaster wiped out the family fortune. She won a scholarship in 1961 to the University of Iowa Writer's Workshop, and has since lived with her husband (also a writer) and two children in Canada, India, and the United States, supporting herself through teaching and other jobs, and writing in the small hours of the morning. In 1971 her critically acclaimed first novel, *The Tiger's Daughter*, appeared; her other novels are *Wife* (1975) and *Jasmine* (1989). Mukherjee's short fiction collections are *Darkness* (1985), stories of South Asian immigrants, and *The Middleman* (1988), which includes characters and voices from various countries and social strata: "Mine is not minimalism, which strips away, but compression, which reflects many layers of meaning."

ALICE MUNRO (b. 1931)

Munro grew up on a farm near Lake Huron in Ontario and attended the University of Western Ontario, where she began publishing short stories. Much of her fiction grows out of her childhood memories of rural family life: "I write about places where your roots are and most people don't live that kind of life anymore at all." Her first book, a collection of stories entitled *Dance of the Happy Shades* (1968) in which "Boys and Girls" appears, won a Governor General's Award. Munro has written a novel, *Lives of Girls and Women* (1971), and six other short-story collections, *Something I've Been Meaning to Tell You* (1974), *Who Do You Think You Are?* (1978, published in the United States as *The Beggar Maid* in 1979), *The Moons of Jupiter* (1983), *The Progress of Love* (1986), *Friend of My Youth* (1990), and *Open Secrets* (1994).

FLANNERY O'CONNOR (1925–1964)

O'Connor was born in Savannah, Georgia, studied at the Georgia State College for Women, and won a fellowship to the Writer's Workshop of the University of Iowa, where she received an M.F.A. degree. Her first novel, *Wise Blood*, was published in 1952, and her first collection of stories, *A Good Man Is Hard to Find*, in 1955. She was able to complete only one more novel, *The Violent Bear It Away* (1960), and a second collection of stories, *Everything That Rises Must Converge* (1965), before dying of an incurable illness in Milledgeville, Georgia. Her reputation has grown steadily since her untimely death. A collection of letters, edited by Sally Fitzgerald under the title *The Habit of Being*, appeared in 1979.

GRACE PALEY (b. 1922)

Born to Russian immigrants in New York, Paley never finished college because she was too busy reading and writing. Her short stories are collected in *The Little Disturbances of Man: Stories of Men and Women at Love* (1959), *Enormous Changes at the Last Minute* (1974), and *Later the Same Day* (1985). Her poetry has been published in *New and Collected Poems* (1992). Paley has been conferred an honorary doctorate and most recently has taught at Dartmouth University.

EDGAR ALLAN POE (1809–1849)

Poe's actor father deserted his wife and son when Edgar was less than a year old. His mother died before he was three, and he and his younger sister were separated and taken into different families. The Allans (who gave Poe his middle name) moved, in 1815, to England, where Edgar had his early schooling. He studied briefly at the University of Virginia and in 1827 paid to have a volume of poems published in Boston (his birthplace); a second volume appeared in 1829 in Baltimore (where he was to die twenty years later). Having served for two years in the army, he was appointed to West Point in 1830 but apparently managed to have himself expelled within the year for cutting classes. Living in Baltimore with his grandmother, aunt, and cousin Virginia (whom he married in 1835 when she was thirteen), Poe began to attract critical attention but made very little money. For the twelve years of his bizarre marriage, he wrote, worked as journalist and editor, and drank. Not long after his wife died in 1847 he seemed to be straightening himself out when, on election day—October 3—he was found semiconscious near a polling place and died four days later without fully regaining consciousness. It is testimony to the continuing fame of his works that they need not be named here.

MORDECAI RICHLER (b. 1931)

Richler was born in Montreal, the son of working-class Jewish parents; *The Street* (1975) is a loosely autobiographical depiction of his childhood. Richler attended Sir George Williams University for two years and worked as a freelance writer in Paris and London from 1952, returning to live in his native Quebec only in 1980. His writing is varied and includes short stories, essays, screenplays, and novels. His *Cocksure* (1968) and *St. Urbain's Horseman* (1971) won the Governor General's Award, and his own screen adaptation of his novel *The Apprenticeship of Duddy Kravitz* (1959) was nominated for an Academy Award in 1974. His novels include *Joshua Then and Now* (1980) and *Solomon Gursky Was Here* (1990).

ELIZABETH TALLENT (b. 1954)

Tallent studied anthropology at the University of Illinois before turning to writing. Best known for her stories, she has won the Pushcart Prize and has had work published in the *New Yorker*, the *Paris Review*, *Esquire*, and *Grand Street*. Tallent makes her home in both Little River and Davis, California, where she teaches at the University of California. Her published books include the story collections *In Constant Flight* (1983), *Time with Children* (1987), and *Honey: Stories* (1993), as well as the novel *Museum Pieces* (1985).

AMY TAN (b. 1952)

Tan was born in Oakland, California, just two and a half years after her parents immigrated there from China. She has worked as a consultant to programs for disabled children and as a freelance writer. In 1987 she visited China for the first time—"As soon as my feet touched China, I became Chinese"—and returned to write her first book, *The Joy Luck Club* (1989). Tan has since published a second book, *The Kitchen God's Wife* (1991), and co-authored the screenplay for the film adaptation of *The Joy Luck Club*.

LEO TOLSTOY (1828–1910)

Tolstoy's life would have made a fitting subject for one of his novels. Born into a noble Russian family, orphaned before he was ten, he studied Oriental languages, then law, then settled on the family estate where he tried to improve the lot of his serfs though they treated him with suspicion. He served in the army, returned home to found a school, married, and wrote two monumental novels, his masterpieces *War and Peace* (1863–69) and *Anna Karenina* (1873–76). But he wasn't satisfied; he found his life, in his own words, "absurd . . . a stupid and spiteful joke," and was converted, first to his national religion, then to a kind of "primitive" Christianity. He opposed the military, capital punishment, persecution of the Jews; he gave up alcohol, meat, and as much of his property as his family would allow. In the end he fled from home—where his wife was trying to have him declared incompetent—intending to enter a monastery, but died in a railway station en route. His works, after his conversion, include *The Death of Iván Ilyich* (1886), "How Much Land Does a Man Need?" and many other stories, parables, and novels.

GUY VANDERHAEGHE (b. 1951)

A native of Saskatchewan, Canada, Vanderhaeghe worked as an archivist and teacher until the early 1980s. He has published collections of short stories, including *Man Descending* (1982), which won the Governor General's Award for Fiction, *The Trouble with Heroes* (1983), and *Things As They Are* (1992), as well as two novels, *My Present Age* (1984) and *Homesick* (1989).

EUDORA WELTY (b. 1909)

Welty, a prolific and highly acclaimed southern writer, was born in Jackson, Mississippi, attended Mississippi State College for Women, and earned a B.A. from the University of

Wisconsin. She has earned two Guggenheim Fellowships, three O. Henry Awards, a Pulitzer Prize, the National Medal for Literature, and the Presidential Medal of Freedom. Although Welty has authored many novels, including *The Robber Bridegroom* (1942), *The Optimist's Daughter* (1972), and the autobiographical *One Writer's Beginnings* (1984), she is best known for her short stories, many of which have been published in *The Collected Stories of Eudora Welty* (1980).

EDITH WHARTON (1862–1937)

Though she spent her later life among literary expatriates in Europe, Edith Newbold Jones was born and raised a New York City aristocrat. At twenty-three she married Edward (Teddy) Wharton of Boston, but the marriage was an unhappy one and they finally divorced in 1913. A writer of poetry and romantic novellas as an adolescent, Wharton began publishing short stories in magazines in the 1890s. She achieved her first major success in 1905 with *The House of Mirth* and went on to produce over fifty volumes in her lifetime. Other titles include *Ethan Frome* (1911), *The Custom of the Country* (1913), *Summer* (1917), and *The Age of Innocence* (1920), for which she became the first woman to win a Pulitzer Prize. In 1930 she was awarded a gold medal of the National Institute of Arts and Letters, the first woman to receive that honor as well.

LYNNA WILLIAMS (b. 1951)

Born in Waco, Texas, Williams attended the University of Missouri School of Journalism and earned a Master's in Fine Arts at George Mason University. She currently teaches creative writing at Emory University in Atlanta. Her short fiction has been published in *Atlantic Monthly* and *Lear's*, and has earned Williams the Dobie-Pisano Fellowship from the Texas Institute of Letters and a nomination for the Townsend Prize. A collection of short stories, *Things Not Seen and Other Stories*, was published in 1992, and Williams is currently at work on her first novel, which follows the protagonist of "Personal Testimony" into adulthood.

RUDOLFO ANAYA: "The Water People," Chapter 11 from *Bless Me Ultima* by Rudolfo Anaya. Copyright © 1972 by Rudolfo Anaya. Reprinted by permission of the author.

MARGARET ATWOOD: "Happy Endings" by Margaret Atwood. Originally published in *Murder in the Dark* (Coach House Press). Reprinted by permission of the author.

JAMES BALDWIN: "Sonny's Blues" from *Going to Meet the Man*. Copyright © 1948, 1951, 1957, 1958, 1960, 1965 by James Baldwin. Reprinted by Doubleday, a division of Bantam, Doubleday, Dell Publishing Group, Inc.

TONI CADE BAMBARA: "Gorilla, My Love" from *Gorilla, My Love* by Toni Cade Bambara. Copyright © 1972 by Toni Cade Bambara. Reprinted by permission of Random House, Inc.

CHARLES BAXTER: "Fenstad's Mother" reprinted from *A Relative Stranger, Stories* by Charles Baxter, by permission of W. W. Norton & Company, Inc. Copyright © 1990 by Charles Baxter.

ANN BEATTIE: "Janus" from *Where You'll Find Me*. Copyright © 1986 by Irony & Pity. Reprinted with permission of Simon & Schuster, Inc.

ANGELA CARTER: "A Souvenir from Japan" from *Fireworks*. Copyright © 1974 by Angela Carter. Reprinted by permission of HarperCollins Publishers, Inc., and Rogers, Coleridge & White, Ltd.

DENISE CHÁVEZ: "The Last of the Menu Girls" from *The Last of the Menu Girls* by Denise Chávez. Copyright © 1987 by Denise Chávez. Reprinted by permission from Arte Publico Press, University of Houston.

JOHN CHEEVER: "The Country Husband" from *The Stories of John Cheever* by John Cheever. Copyright 1954 by John Cheever. Reprinted by permission of Alfred A. Knopf, Inc.

ANTON CHEKHOV: "The Lady with the Dog" reprinted from *The Russian Master and Other Stories* by Anton Chekhov, translated by Ronald Hingley (Worlds Classics, 1984), from *The Oxford Chekhov, Vol. 9* (1975) by permission of Oxford University Press.

RICHARD CONNELL: "The Most Dangerous Game" by Richard Connell. Copyright © 1924 by Richard Connell. Copyright renewed © 1965 by Louise Fox Connell. Reprinted by permission of Brandt & Brandt.

JULIO CORTÁZAR: "Blow-Up" from *End of the Game and Other Stories* by Julio Cortázar, translated by Paul Blackburn. Copyright © 1967 by Random House, Inc. Reprinted by permission of Pantheon Books, a Division of Random House, Inc.

RICHARD DOKEY: "Sánchez," by Richard Dokey. Copyright © 1967. This story first appeared in *Southwest Review*. Reprinted by permission of the author.

LOUISE ERDRICH: "Love Medicine" from *Love Medicine* by Louise Erdrich. Copyright © 1984, 1993 Louise Erdrich. Reprinted by permission of Henry Holt and Co., Inc. Revised and expanded edition.

WILLIAM FAULKNER: "Barn Burning" and "A Rose for Emily" from *The Collected Stories of William Faulkner*. Copyright 1939 and renewed 1967 by Estelle Faulkner and Jill Faulkner Summers. Copyright 1930 and renewed 1958 by William Faulkner.

RICHARD FORD: "Great Falls" from *Rock Springs*. Copyright © 1987 by Richard Ford. Used by permission of Grove/Atlantic, Inc.

HA JIN: "In Broad Daylight." First published in *The Kenyon Review*—New Series, Summer 1993, vol. XV, no. 3, Copyright © 1993 by Kenyon College. Reprinted with permission by *The Kenyon Review*.

ERNEST HEMINGWAY: "A Very Short Story" from *In Our Time* by Ernest Hemingway. Copyright 1925 by Charles Scribner's Sons. Copyright renewed 1953 by Ernest Hemingway. Reprinted with permission of Scribner's, an imprint of Simon & Schuster, Inc.

SPENCER HOLST: "The Zebra Storyteller" © 1971. Reprinted with permission of the author. *The Zebra Storyteller: Collected Stories of Spencer Holst/93*. Station Hill Press, Barrytown, New York 12507.

FRANZ KAFKA: "A Hunger Artist" from *Franz Kafka: The Complete Stories* by Franz Kafka, edited by Nahum N. Glatzer. Copyright 1946, 1947, 1948, 1954, 1958, 1971 by Schoken Books, Inc. Reprinted by permission of Schoken Books, published by Pantheon Books, a Division of Random House, Inc.

YASUNARI KAWABATA: "The Grasshopper and the Bell Cricket" from *Palm-of-the-Hand Stories* by Yasunari Kawabata. Copyright by Yasunari Kawabata. Reprinted with permission from Farrar, Straus & Giroux, Inc.

EUDORA WELTY: "Why I Live at the P.O." from *A Curtain of Green and Other Stories*, copyright © 1941 and renewed 1969 by Eudora Welty, reprinted by permission of Harcourt Brace and Company.

LYNNA WILLIAMS: "Personal Testimony" from *Things Not Seen and Other Stories* by Lynna Williams. Copyright © 1992 by Lynna Williams. Reprinted by permission of Little, Brown & Company.

INDEX OF AUTHORS

INDEX OF TITLES

INDEX OF LITERARY TERMS